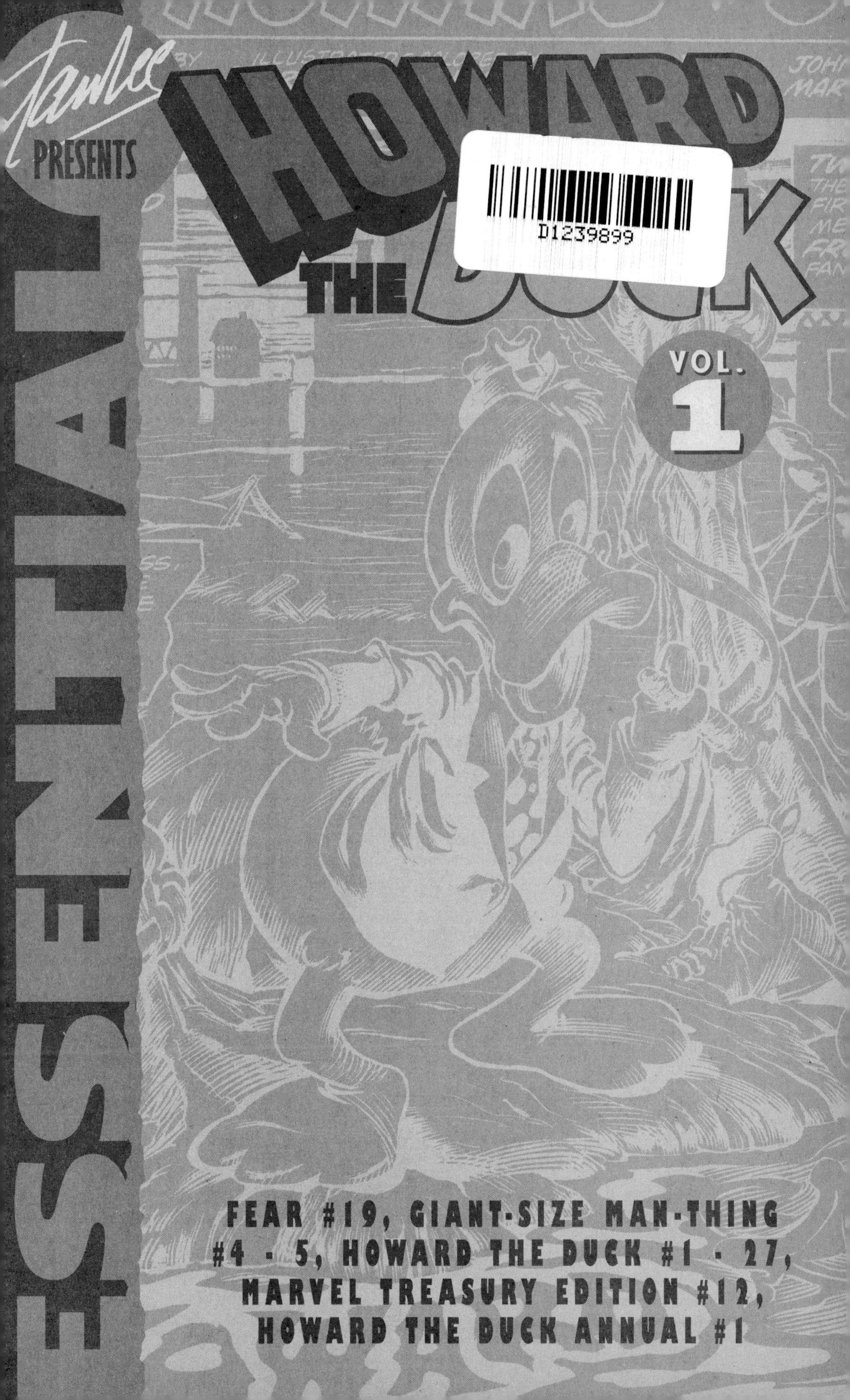
Stan Lee
PRESENTS
ESSENTIAL
HOWARD THE DUCK
VOL. 1
FEAR #19, GIANT-SIZE MAN-THING
#4 - 5, HOWARD THE DUCK #1 - 27,
MARVEL TREASURY EDITION #12,
HOWARD THE DUCK ANNUAL #1

ESSENTIAL HOWARD THE DUCK VOL. 1

EXCERPTS FROM: FEAR #19 & MAN-THING (VOL. 1) #1
Writer: Steve Gerber
Pencils: Val Mayerik • Inks: Sal Trapani
Letters: Art Simek & John Costanza

GIANT-SIZE MAN-THING #4
Writer: Steve Gerber • Artist: Frank Brunner
Letters: Tom Orzechowski

GIANT-SIZE MAN-THING #5
Writer: Steve Gerber • Pencils: Frank Brunner
Inks: Tom Palmer • Letters: Annette Kawecki

HOWARD THE DUCK #1
Writer: Steve Gerber • Pencils: Frank Brunner
Inks: Steve Leialoha • Letters: John Costanza

HOWARD THE DUCK #2
Writer: Steve Gerber • Pencils: Frank Brunner
Inks: Steve Leialoha • Letters: Tom Orzechowski

HOWARD THE DUCK #3
Writer: Steve Gerber • Pencils: John Buscema
Inks: Steve Leialoha • Letters: Annette Kawecki

HOWARD THE DUCK #4
Writer: Steve Gerber • Pencils: Gene Colan
Inks: Steve Leialoha • Letters: Annette Kawecki

HOWARD THE DUCK #5
Writer: Steve Gerber • Pencils: Gene Colan
Inks: Steve Leialoha • Letters: Irv Watanabe

HOWARD THE DUCK #6
Writer: Steve Gerber • Pencils: Gene Colan
Inks: Steve Leialoha • Letters: John Costanza

HOWARD THE DUCK #7
Writer: Steve Gerber • Pencils: Gene Colan
Inks: Steve Leialoha • Letters: Jim Novak

MARVEL TREASURY EDITION #12
Writer: Steve Gerber • Pencils: Sal Buscema
Inks: Klaus Janson • Letters: Joe Rosen

HOWARD THE DUCK #8
Writer: Steve Gerber • Pencils: Gene Colan
Inks: Steve Leialoha • Letters: Irv Watanabe

HOWARD THE DUCK #9
Writer: Steve Gerber • Pencils: Gene Colan
Inks: Steve Leialoha • Letters: John Costanza

HOWARD THE DUCK #10
Writer: Steve Gerber • Pencils: Gene Colan
Inks: Steve Leialoha • Letters: Jim Novak

HOWARD THE DUCK #11
Writer: Steve Gerber • Pencils: Gene Colan
Inks: Steve Leialoha • Letters: Jim Novak

HOWARD THE DUCK #12
Writer: Steve Gerber • Pencils: Gene Colan
Inks: Steve Leialoha • Letters: Jim Novak

HOWARD THE DUCK #13
Writer: Steve Gerber • Pencils: Gene Colan
Inks: Steve Leialoha • Letters: Jim Novak

HOWARD THE DUCK #14
Writer: Steve Gerber • Pencils: Gene Colan
Inks: Klaus Janson • Letters: Jim Novak

HOWARD THE DUCK ANNUAL #1
Writer: Steve Gerber
Artist: Val Mayerik • Letters: Joe Rosen

HOWARD THE DUCK #15
Writer: Steve Gerber • Pencils: Gene Colan
Inks: Klaus Janson • Letters: Irv Watanabe

HOWARD THE DUCK #16
Writer: Steve Gerber • Artists: The Cast of Thousands • Letters: Annette Kawecki

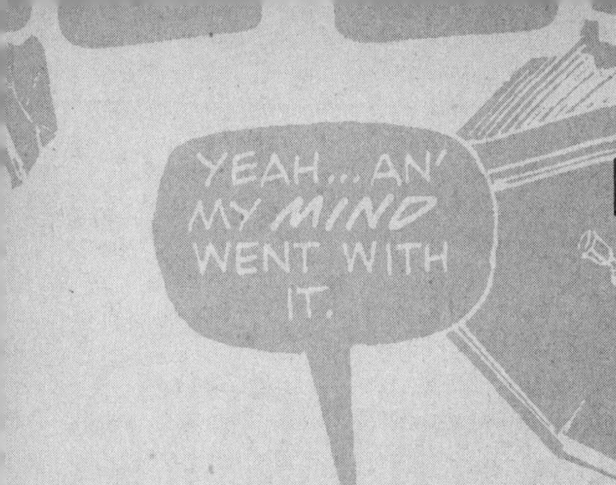
YEAH... AN' MY MIND WENT WITH IT.

REPRINT CREDITS

HOWARD THE DUCK #17
Writer: Steve Gerber • Pencils: Gene Colan
Inks: Klaus Janson • Letters: Annette Kawecki

HOWARD THE DUCK #18
Writer: Steve Gerber • Pencils: Gene Colan
Inks: Klaus Janson • Letters: Irv Watanabe

HOWARD THE DUCK #19
Writer: Steve Gerber • Pencils: Gene Colan
Inks: Klaus Janson • Letters: Irv Watanabe

HOWARD THE DUCK #20
Writer: Steve Gerber • Pencils: Gene Colan
Inks: Klaus Janson • Letters: John Costanza

HOWARD THE DUCK #21
Writer: Steve Gerber • Pencils: Carmine Infantino
Inks: Klaus Janson • Letters: Irv Watanabe

HOWARD THE DUCK #22
Writer: Steve Gerber • Pencils: Val Mayerik
Inks: William Wray • Letters: John Costanza

HOWARD THE DUCK #23
Writer: Steve Gerber
Artist: Val Mayerik • Letters: John Costanza

HOWARD THE DUCK #24
Writer: Steve Gerber • Pencils: Gene Colan
Inks: Tom Palmer • Letters: Joe Rosen

HOWARD THE DUCK #25
Writer: Steve Gerber • Pencils: Gene Colan
Inks: Klaus Janson • Letters: Irv Watanabe

HOWARD THE DUCK #26
Writer: Steve Gerber • Pencils: Gene Colan
Inks: Klaus Janson • Letters: Irv Watanabe

HOWARD THE DUCK #27
Writer: Steve Gerber • Pencils: Gene Colan
Inks: Klaus Janson • Letters: Gasper

PRESIDENT & COO
PUBLISHING,
CONSUMER PRODUCTS
& NEW MEDIA
BILL JEMAS

EDITOR IN CHIEF
JOE QUESADA

DIRECTOR-PUBLISHING
OPERATIONS
BOB GREENBERGER

COLLECTIONS EDITOR
MATTY RYAN

ASSISTANT EDITOR
MIKE FARAH

MANUFACTURING
REPRESENTATIVE
FENTON ENG

PRODUCTION ASSISTANT
CORY SEDLMEIER

COVER & INTERIOR
DESIGN
**JOHN 'JG' ROSHELL
OF COMICRAFT**

COVER ART
BRIAN BOLLAND

COVER COLORS
CHRIS DICKEY

ESSENTIAL HOWARD THE DUCK® VOL 1. Contains material originally published in magazine form as Fear #19, Howard the Duck #1-27 & Annual #1, Marvel Treasury Edition #12, Giant Size Man-Thing #4 and #5. First printing, February 2002. ISBN# 0-7851-0831-9. Published by MARVEL COMICS, a division of MARVEL ENTERTAINMENT GROUP, INC. OFFICE OF PUBLICATION: 10 EAST 40th STREET, NEW YORK, NY 10016. Printed in Canada. PETER CUNEO, Chief Executive Officer; AVI ARAD, Chief Creative Officer; GUI KARYO, Chief Information Officer; STAN LEE, Chairman Emeritus.

10 9 8 7 6 5 4 3 2 1

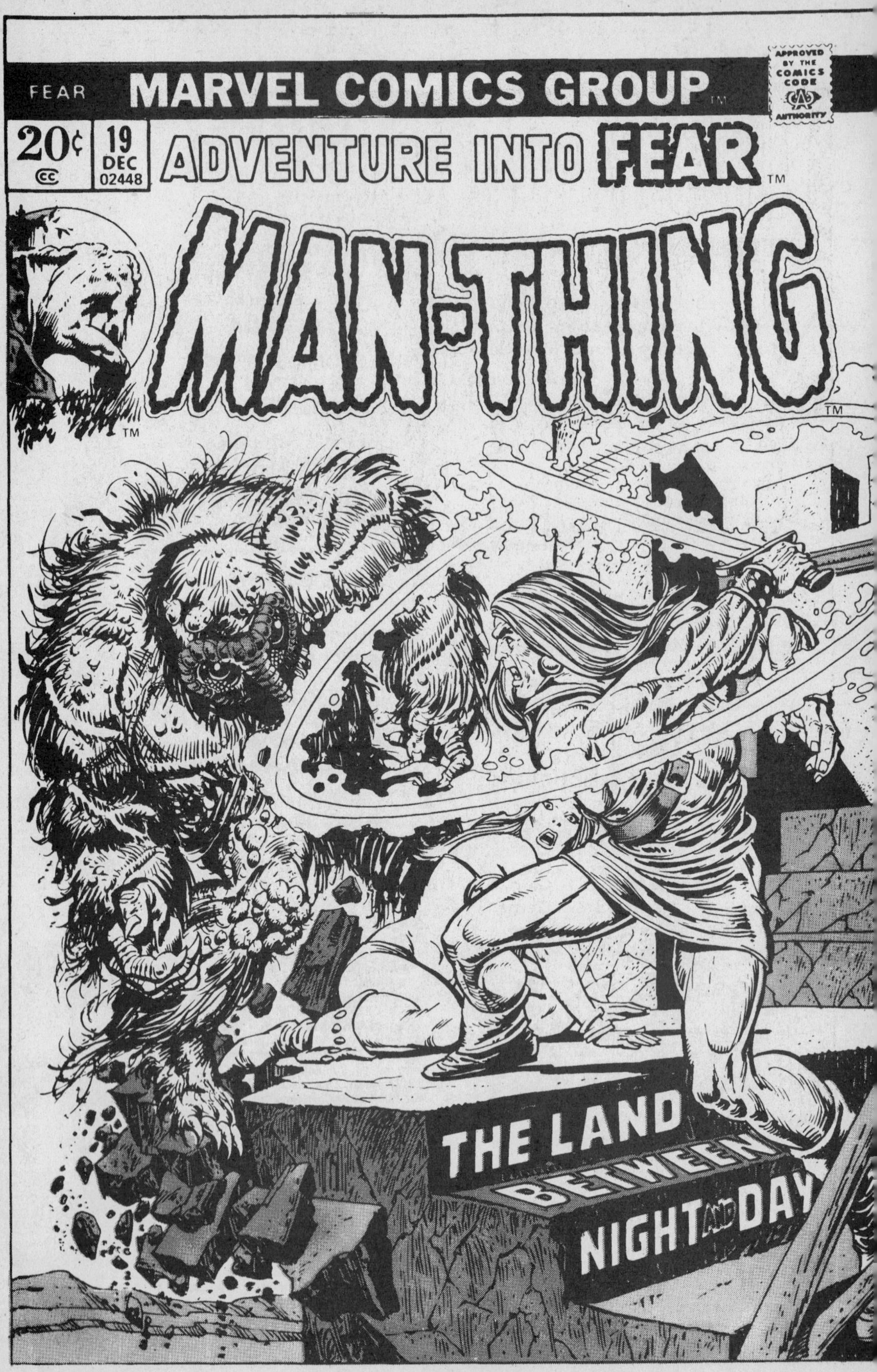
FEAR
MARVEL COMICS GROUP
APPROVED BY THE COMICS CODE AUTHORITY
20¢
19 DEC 02448
ADVENTURE INTO FEAR
MAN-THING
THE LAND BETWEEN NIGHT AND DAY

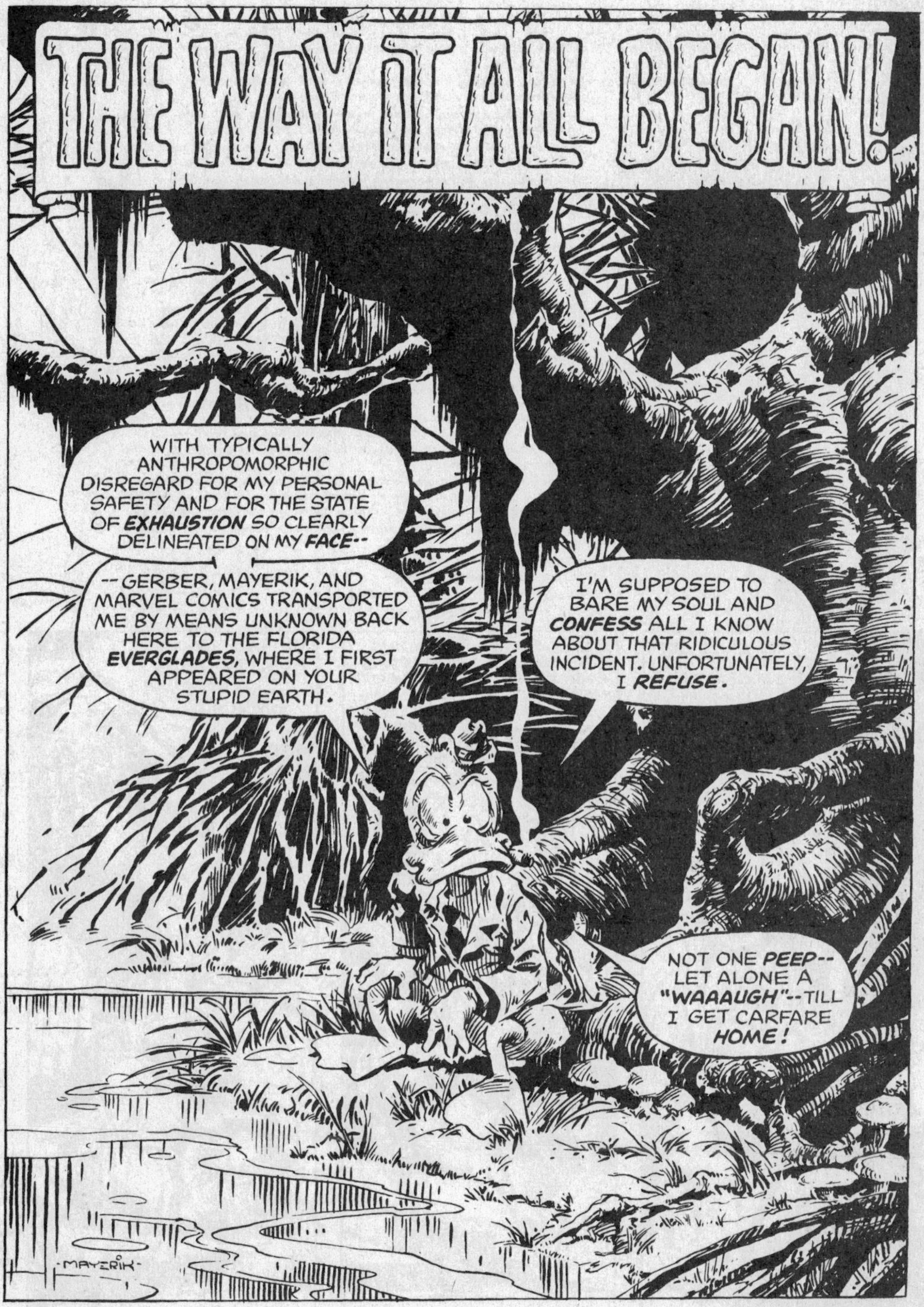
THE WAY IT ALL BEGAN!
WITH TYPICALLY ANTHROPOMORPHIC DISREGARD FOR MY PERSONAL SAFETY AND FOR THE STATE OF EXHAUSTION SO CLEARLY DELINEATED ON MY FACE--
--GERBER, MAYERIK, AND MARVEL COMICS TRANSPORTED ME BY MEANS UNKNOWN BACK HERE TO THE FLORIDA EVERGLADES, WHERE I FIRST APPEARED ON YOUR STUPID EARTH.
I'M SUPPOSED TO BARE MY SOUL AND CONFESS ALL I KNOW ABOUT THAT RIDICULOUS INCIDENT. UNFORTUNATELY, I REFUSE.
NOT ONE PEEP-- LET ALONE A "WAAAUGH"--TILL I GET CARFARE HOME!
MAYERIK

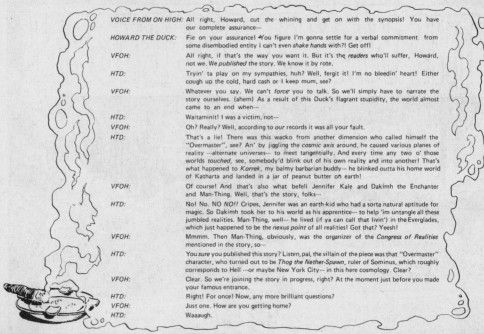

VOICE FROM ON HIGH: All right, Howard, cut the whining and get on with the synopsis! You have our complete assurance---

HOWARD THE DUCK: Fie on your assurance! You figure I'm gonna settle for a verbal commitment from some disembodied entity I can't even *shake hands* with?! Get off!

VFOH: All right, if that's the way you want it. But it's the *readers* who'll suffer, Howard, not we. We *published* the story. We know it by rote.

HTD: Tryin' ta play on my sympathies, huh? Well, fergit it! I'm no bleedin' heart! Either cough up the cold, hard cash or I keep mum, see?

VFOH: Whatever you say. We can't *force* you to talk. So we'll simply have to narrate the story ourselves. (ahem) As a result of this Duck's flagrant stupidity, the world almost came to an end when---

HTD: Waitaminit! I was a victim, not---

VFOH: Oh? Really? Well, according to *our* records it was all your fault.

HTD: That's a lie! There was this wacko from another dimension who called himself the "Overmaster", see? An' by jiggling the *cosmic axis* around, he caused various planes of reality ---alternate universes--- to meet tangentially. And every time any two o' those worlds *touched*, see, somebody'd blink out of his own reality and into another! That's what happened to *Korrek*, my balmy barbarian buddy--- he blinked outta his home world of Katharta and landed in a jar of peanut butter on earth!

VFOH: Of course! And that's also what befell Jennifer Kale and Dakimh the Enchanter and Man-Thing. Well, that's the story, folks---

HTD: No! No. NO NO!! Cripes, Jennifer was an earth-kid who had a sorta natural aptitude for magic. So Dakimh took her to his world as his apprentice--- to help 'im untangle all these jumbled realities. Man-Thing, well--- he lived (if ya can call that livin') in the Everglades, which just happened to be the *nexus point* of all realities! Got that? Yeesh!

VFOH: Mmmm. Then Man-Thing, obviously, was the organizer of the *Congress of Realities* mentioned in the story, so---

HTD: You *sure* you published this story? Listen, pal, the villain of the piece was that "Overmaster" character, who turned out to be *Thog the Nether-Spawn*, ruler of Sominus, which roughly corresponds to Hell---or maybe New York City--- in this here cosmology. Clear?

VFOH: Clear. So we're joining the story in progress, right? At the moment just before you made your famous entrance.

HTD: Right! For once! Now, any more brilliant questions?

VFOH: Just one. How are you getting home?

HTD: Waaaugh.

WELL, I'LL *NOT* GIVE YOU THAT SATISFACTION! AT THIS POINT, I *WELCOME* DEATH!

WHAT ELSE *IS* THERE--FOR ONE WHOSE LIFE HAS BECOME AN *ABSURDITY?*

AW, *CLAM UP,* BUD! YOU DON'T EVEN KNOW THE MEANING OF THE *WORD!*

FINDING YOURSELF· IN A WORLD OF TALKING HAIRLESS APES-- NOW *THAT'S* ABSURDITY!

OH--*NO!* WHAT NEW HORROR IS *THIS?* IT VAGUELY RESEMBLES A *DUCK,* BUT--!

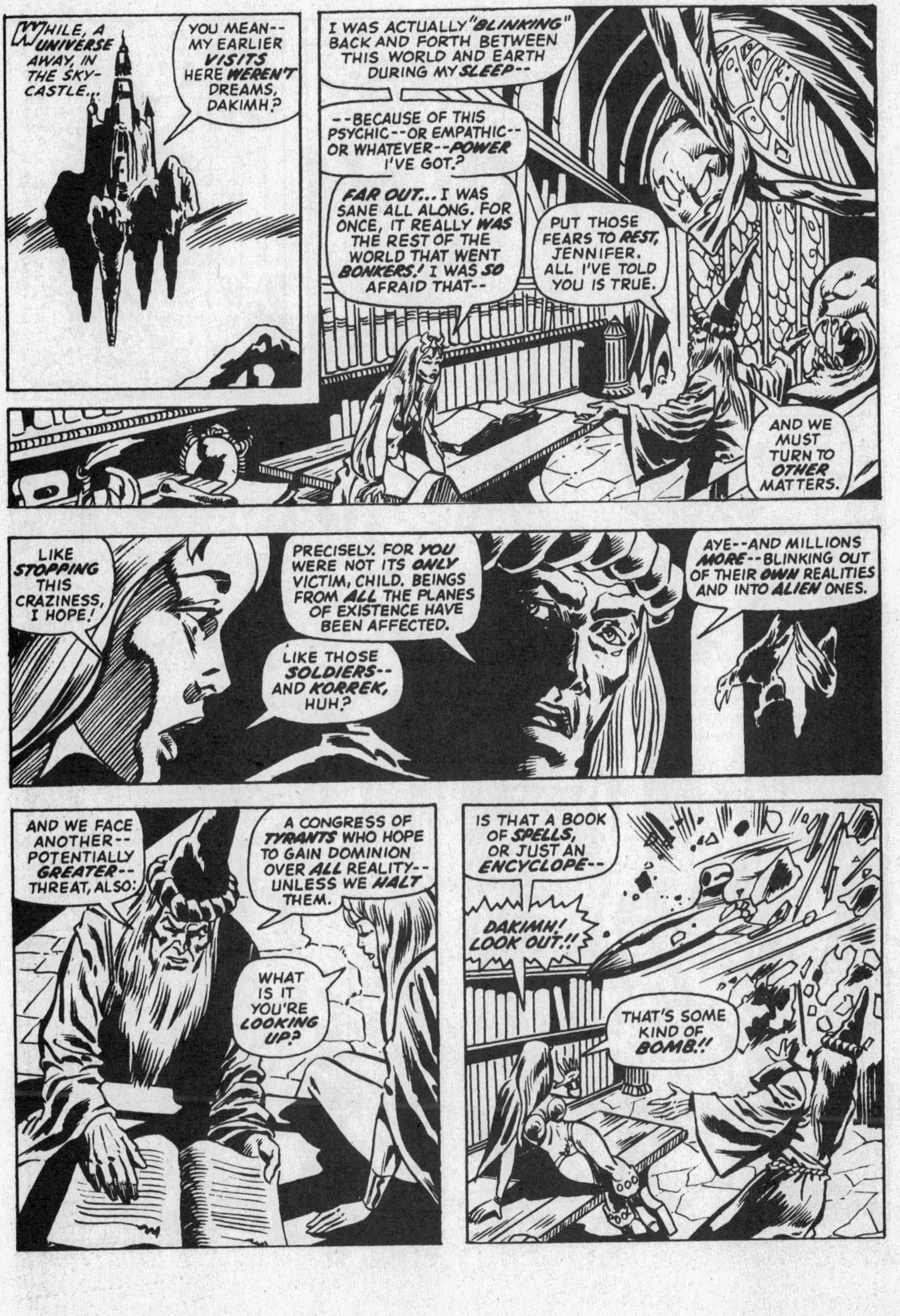
WHILE, A UNIVERSE AWAY, IN THE SKY-CASTLE...
YOU MEAN-- MY EARLIER VISITS HERE WEREN'T DREAMS, DAKIMH?
I WAS ACTUALLY "BLINKING" BACK AND FORTH BETWEEN THIS WORLD AND EARTH DURING MY SLEEP--
--BECAUSE OF THIS PSYCHIC--OR EMPATHIC--OR WHATEVER--POWER I'VE GOT?
FAR OUT... I WAS SANE ALL ALONG. FOR ONCE, IT REALLY WAS THE REST OF THE WORLD THAT WENT BONKERS! I WAS SO AFRAID THAT--
PUT THOSE FEARS TO REST, JENNIFER. ALL I'VE TOLD YOU IS TRUE.
AND WE MUST TURN TO OTHER MATTERS.
LIKE STOPPING THIS CRAZINESS, I HOPE!
PRECISELY. FOR YOU WERE NOT ITS ONLY VICTIM, CHILD. BEINGS FROM ALL THE PLANES OF EXISTENCE HAVE BEEN AFFECTED.
LIKE THOSE SOLDIERS-- AND KORREK, HUH?
AYE--AND MILLIONS MORE--BLINKING OUT OF THEIR OWN REALITIES AND INTO ALIEN ONES.
AND WE FACE ANOTHER-- POTENTIALLY GREATER-- THREAT, ALSO:
A CONGRESS OF TYRANTS WHO HOPE TO GAIN DOMINION OVER ALL REALITY-- UNLESS WE HALT THEM.
WHAT IS IT YOU'RE LOOKING UP?
IS THAT A BOOK OF SPELLS, OR JUST AN ENCYCLOPE--
DAKIMH! LOOK OUT!!
THAT'S SOME KIND OF BOMB!!

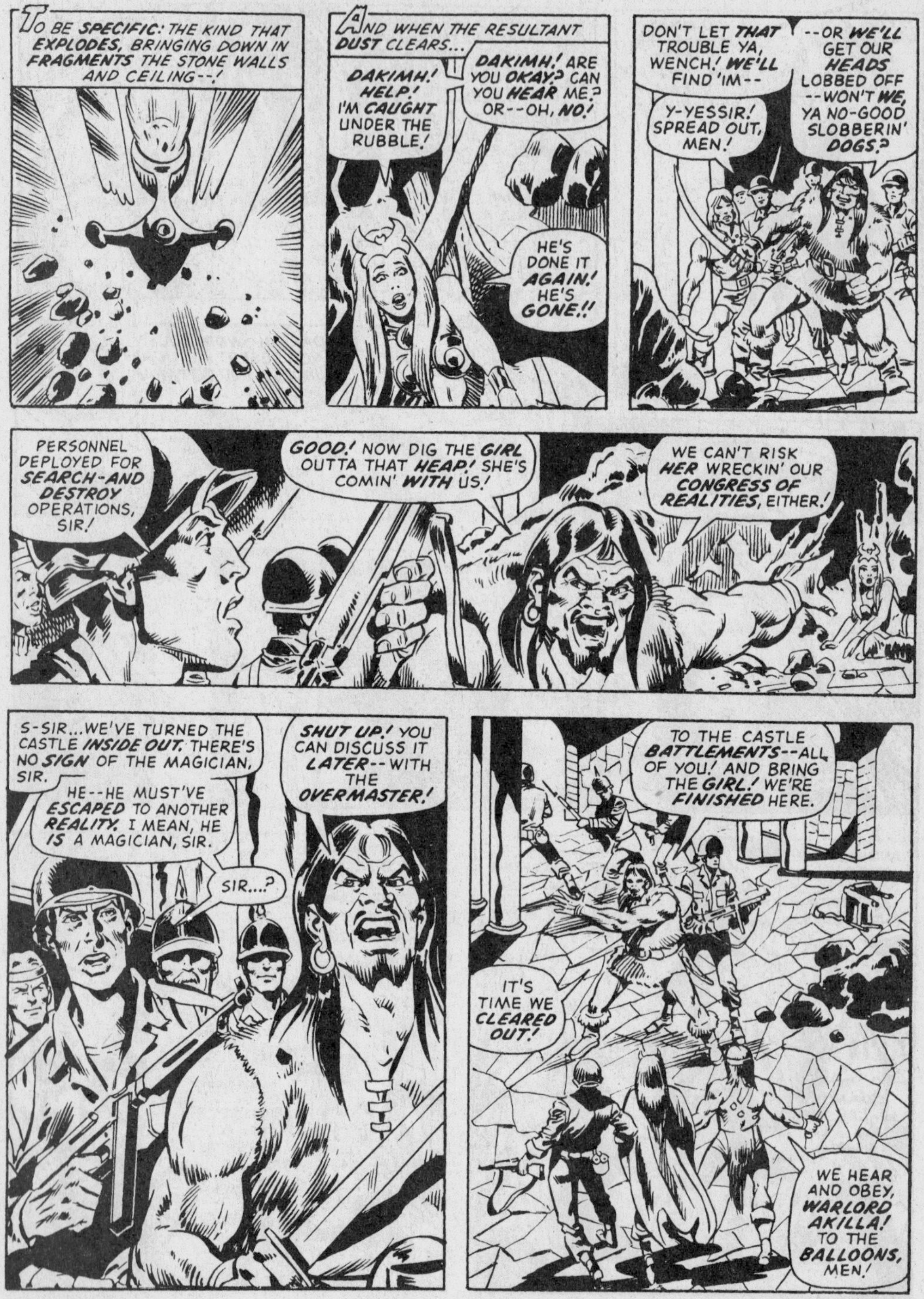

TO BE SPECIFIC: THE KIND THAT EXPLODES, BRINGING DOWN IN FRAGMENTS THE STONE WALLS AND CEILING--!
AND WHEN THE RESULTANT DUST CLEARS...
DAKIMH! HELP! I'M CAUGHT UNDER THE RUBBLE!
DAKIMH! ARE YOU OKAY? CAN YOU HEAR ME? OR--OH, NO!
HE'S DONE IT AGAIN! HE'S GONE!!
DON'T LET THAT TROUBLE YA, WENCH! WE'LL FIND 'IM--
--OR WE'LL GET OUR HEADS LOBBED OFF--WON'T WE, YA NO-GOOD SLOBBERIN' DOGS?
Y-YESSIR! SPREAD OUT, MEN!
PERSONNEL DEPLOYED FOR SEARCH-AND DESTROY OPERATIONS, SIR!
GOOD! NOW DIG THE GIRL OUTTA THAT HEAP! SHE'S COMIN' WITH US!
WE CAN'T RISK HER WRECKIN' OUR CONGRESS OF REALITIES, EITHER!
S-SIR...WE'VE TURNED THE CASTLE INSIDE OUT. THERE'S NO SIGN OF THE MAGICIAN, SIR.
HE--HE MUST'VE ESCAPED TO ANOTHER REALITY. I MEAN, HE IS A MAGICIAN, SIR.
SIR...?
SHUT UP! YOU CAN DISCUSS IT LATER--WITH THE OVERMASTER!
TO THE CASTLE BATTLEMENTS--ALL OF YOU! AND BRING THE GIRL! WE'RE FINISHED HERE.
IT'S TIME WE CLEARED OUT!
WE HEAR AND OBEY, WARLORD AKILLA! TO THE BALLOONS, MEN!

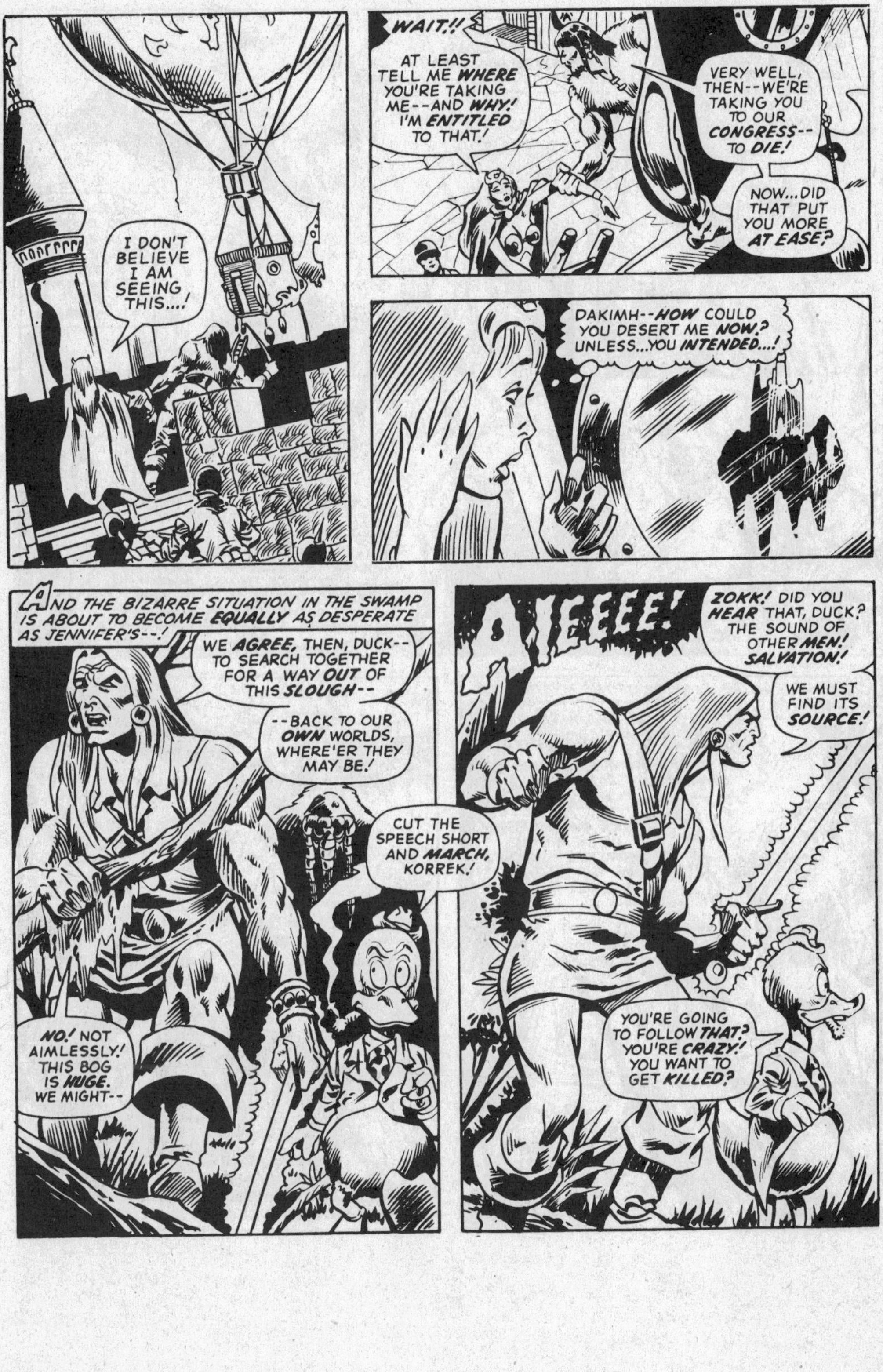
I DON'T BELIEVE I AM SEEING THIS....!
WAIT!!
AT LEAST TELL ME WHERE YOU'RE TAKING ME--AND WHY! I'M ENTITLED TO THAT!
VERY WELL, THEN--WE'RE TAKING YOU TO OUR CONGRESS--TO DIE!
NOW...DID THAT PUT YOU MORE AT EASE?
DAKIMH--HOW COULD YOU DESERT ME NOW? UNLESS...YOU INTENDED...!
AND THE BIZARRE SITUATION IN THE SWAMP IS ABOUT TO BECOME EQUALLY AS DESPERATE AS JENNIFER'S--!
WE AGREE, THEN, DUCK--TO SEARCH TOGETHER FOR A WAY OUT OF THIS SLOUGH--
--BACK TO OUR OWN WORLDS, WHERE'ER THEY MAY BE!
CUT THE SPEECH SHORT AND MARCH, KORREK!
NO! NOT AIMLESSLY! THIS BOG IS HUGE. WE MIGHT--
AIEEEE!
ZOKK! DID YOU HEAR THAT, DUCK? THE SOUND OF OTHER MEN! SALVATION!
WE MUST FIND ITS SOURCE!
YOU'RE GOING TO FOLLOW THAT? YOU'RE CRAZY! YOU WANT TO GET KILLED?

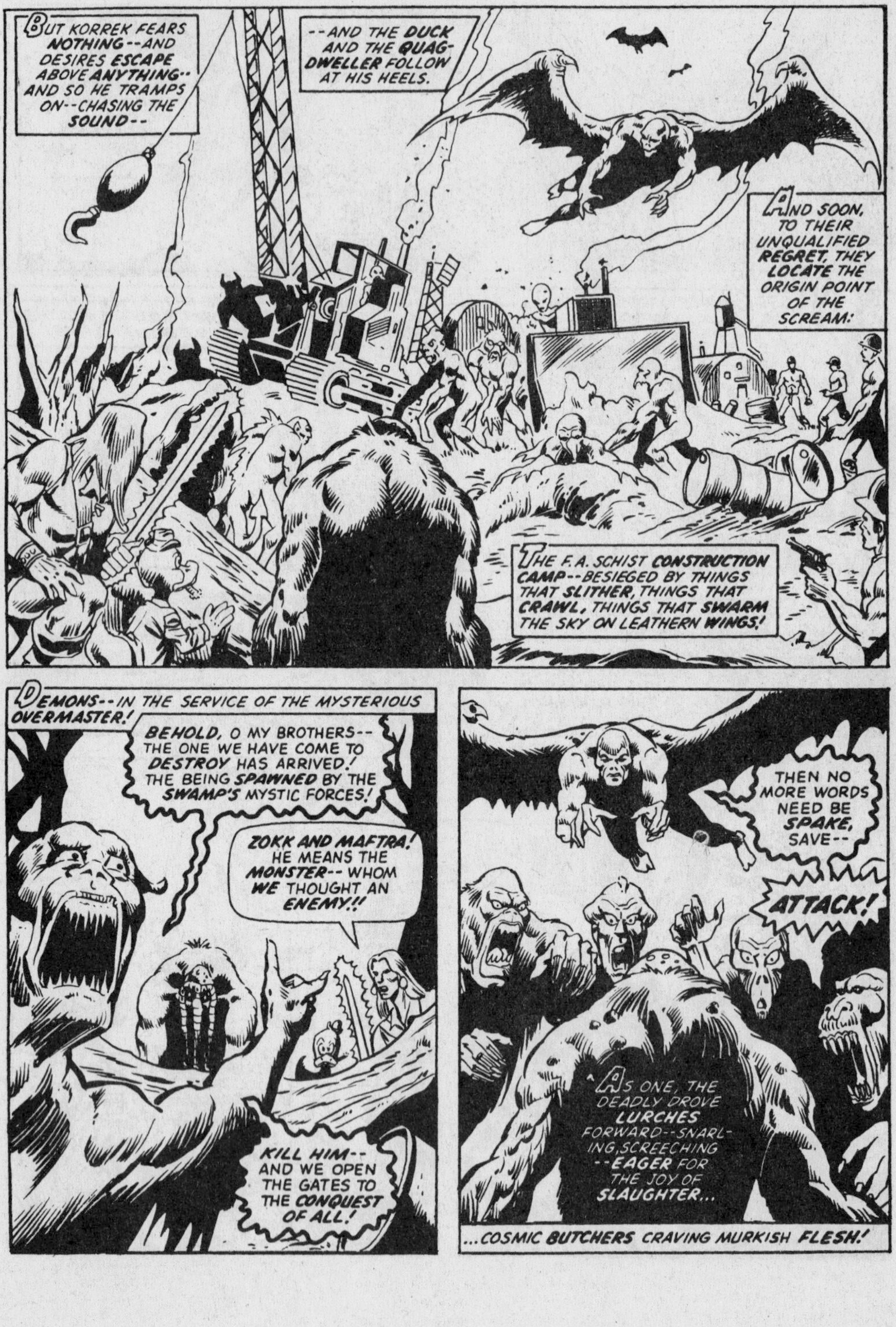
BUT KORREK FEARS NOTHING--AND DESIRES ESCAPE ABOVE ANYTHING--AND SO HE TRAMPS ON--CHASING THE SOUND--
--AND THE DUCK AND THE QUAG-DWELLER FOLLOW AT HIS HEELS.
AND SOON, TO THEIR UNQUALIFIED REGRET, THEY LOCATE THE ORIGIN POINT OF THE SCREAM:
THE F.A. SCHIST CONSTRUCTION CAMP--BESIEGED BY THINGS THAT SLITHER, THINGS THAT CRAWL, THINGS THAT SWARM THE SKY ON LEATHERN WINGS!
DEMONS--IN THE SERVICE OF THE MYSTERIOUS OVERMASTER!
BEHOLD, O MY BROTHERS--THE ONE WE HAVE COME TO DESTROY HAS ARRIVED! THE BEING SPAWNED BY THE SWAMP'S MYSTIC FORCES!
ZOKK AND MAFTRA! HE MEANS THE MONSTER--WHOM WE THOUGHT AN ENEMY!!
KILL HIM--AND WE OPEN THE GATES TO THE CONQUEST OF ALL!
THEN NO MORE WORDS NEED BE SPAKE, SAVE--
ATTACK!
AS ONE, THE DEADLY DROVE LURCHES FORWARD--SNARLING, SCREECHING--EAGER FOR THE JOY OF SLAUGHTER...
...COSMIC BUTCHERS CRAVING MURKISH FLESH!

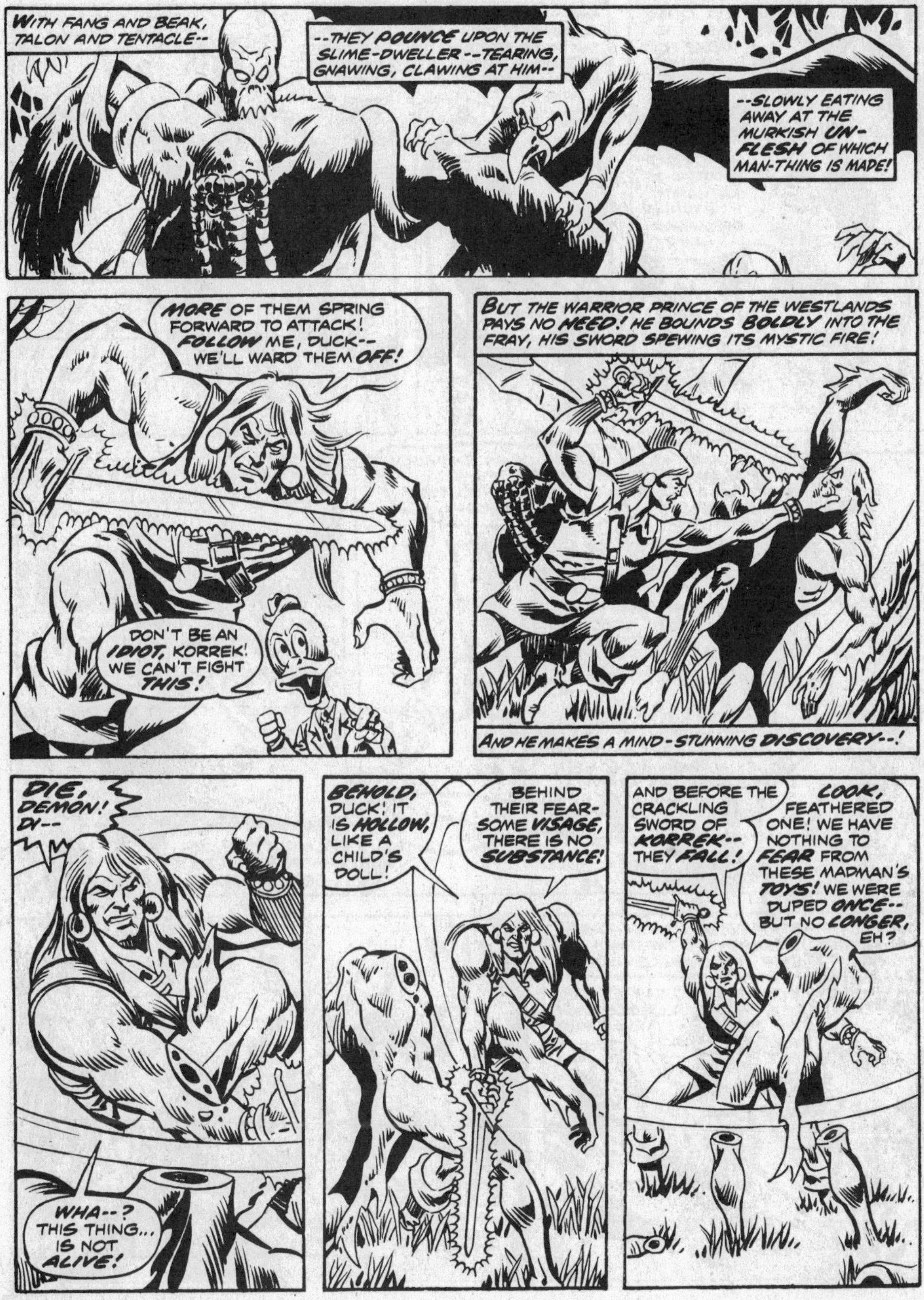
WITH FANG AND BEAK, TALON AND TENTACLE--
--THEY POUNCE UPON THE SLIME-DWELLER--TEARING, GNAWING, CLAWING AT HIM--
--SLOWLY EATING AWAY AT THE MURKISH UN-FLESH OF WHICH MAN-THING IS MADE!
MORE OF THEM SPRING FORWARD TO ATTACK! FOLLOW ME, DUCK-- WE'LL WARD THEM OFF!
DON'T BE AN IDIOT, KORREK! WE CAN'T FIGHT THIS!
BUT THE WARRIOR PRINCE OF THE WESTLANDS PAYS NO HEED! HE BOUNDS BOLDLY INTO THE FRAY, HIS SWORD SPEWING ITS MYSTIC FIRE!
AND HE MAKES A MIND-STUNNING DISCOVERY--!
DIE, DEMON! DI--
WHA--? THIS THING... IS NOT ALIVE!
BEHOLD, DUCK! IT IS HOLLOW, LIKE A CHILD'S DOLL!
BEHIND THEIR FEAR-SOME VISAGE, THERE IS NO SUBSTANCE!
AND BEFORE THE CRACKLING SWORD OF KORREK-- THEY FALL!
LOOK, FEATHERED ONE! WE HAVE NOTHING TO FEAR FROM THESE MADMAN'S TOYS! WE WERE DUPED ONCE-- BUT NO LONGER, EH?

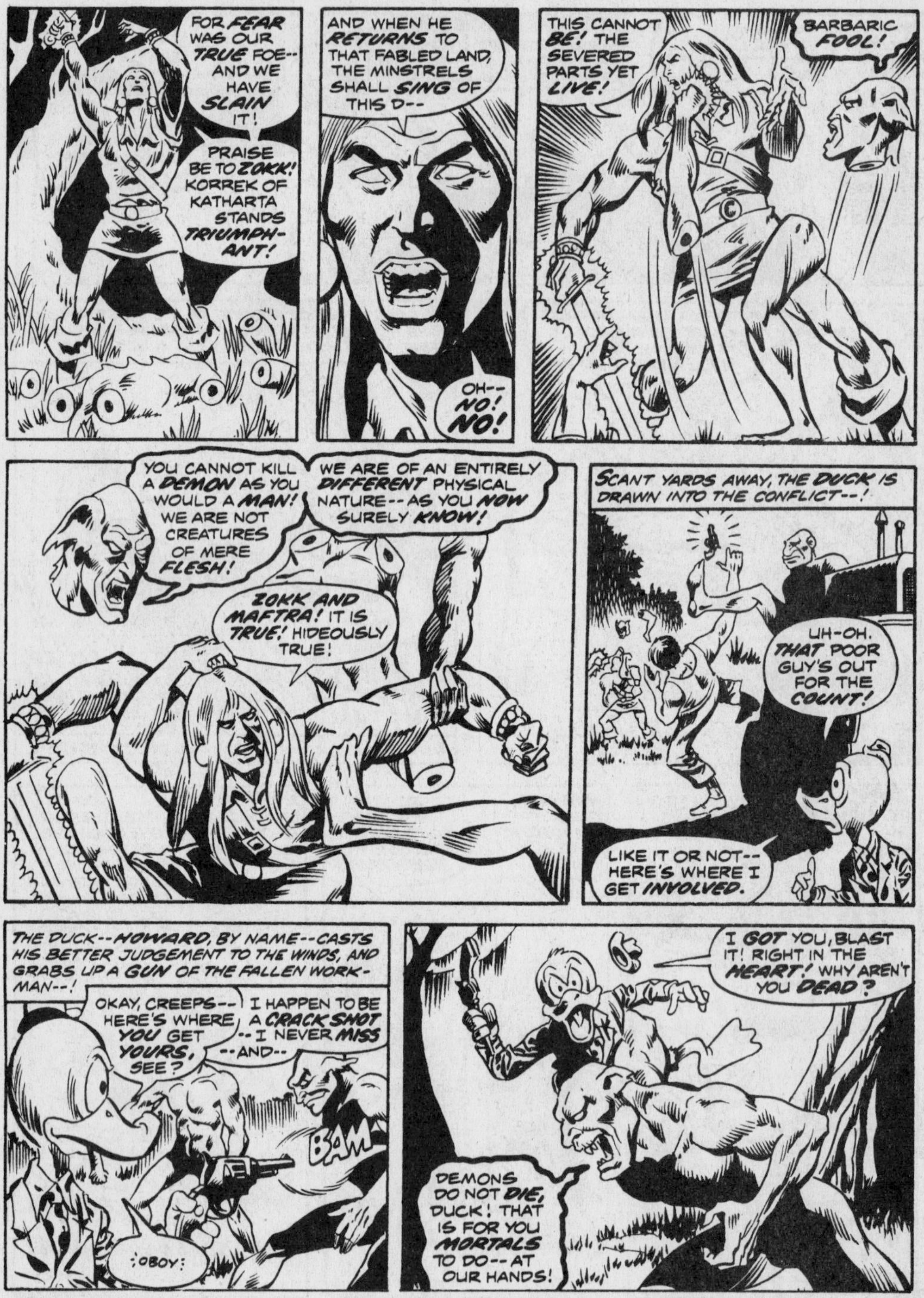

FOR FEAR WAS OUR TRUE FOE-- AND WE HAVE SLAIN IT!
PRAISE BE TO ZOKK! KORREK OF KATHARTA STANDS TRIUMPH-ANT!
AND WHEN HE RETURNS TO THAT FABLED LAND, THE MINSTRELS SHALL SING OF THIS D--
OH-- NO! NO!
THIS CANNOT BE! THE SEVERED PARTS YET LIVE!
BARBARIC FOOL!
YOU CANNOT KILL A DEMON AS YOU WOULD A MAN! WE ARE NOT CREATURES OF MERE FLESH!
WE ARE OF AN ENTIRELY DIFFERENT PHYSICAL NATURE-- AS YOU NOW SURELY KNOW!
ZOKK AND MAFTRA! IT IS TRUE! HIDEOUSLY TRUE!
SCANT YARDS AWAY, THE DUCK IS DRAWN INTO THE CONFLICT--!
UH-OH. THAT POOR GUY'S OUT FOR THE COUNT!
LIKE IT OR NOT-- HERE'S WHERE I GET INVOLVED.
THE DUCK--HOWARD, BY NAME--CASTS HIS BETTER JUDGEMENT TO THE WINDS, AND GRABS UP A GUN OF THE FALLEN WORK-MAN--!
OKAY, CREEPS-- HERE'S WHERE YOU GET YOURS, SEE?
I HAPPEN TO BE A CRACK SHOT -- I NEVER MISS --AND--
BAM
¡OBOY!
I GOT YOU, BLAST IT! RIGHT IN THE HEART! WHY AREN'T YOU DEAD?
DEMONS DO NOT DIE, DUCK! THAT IS FOR YOU MORTALS TO DO-- AT OUR HANDS!

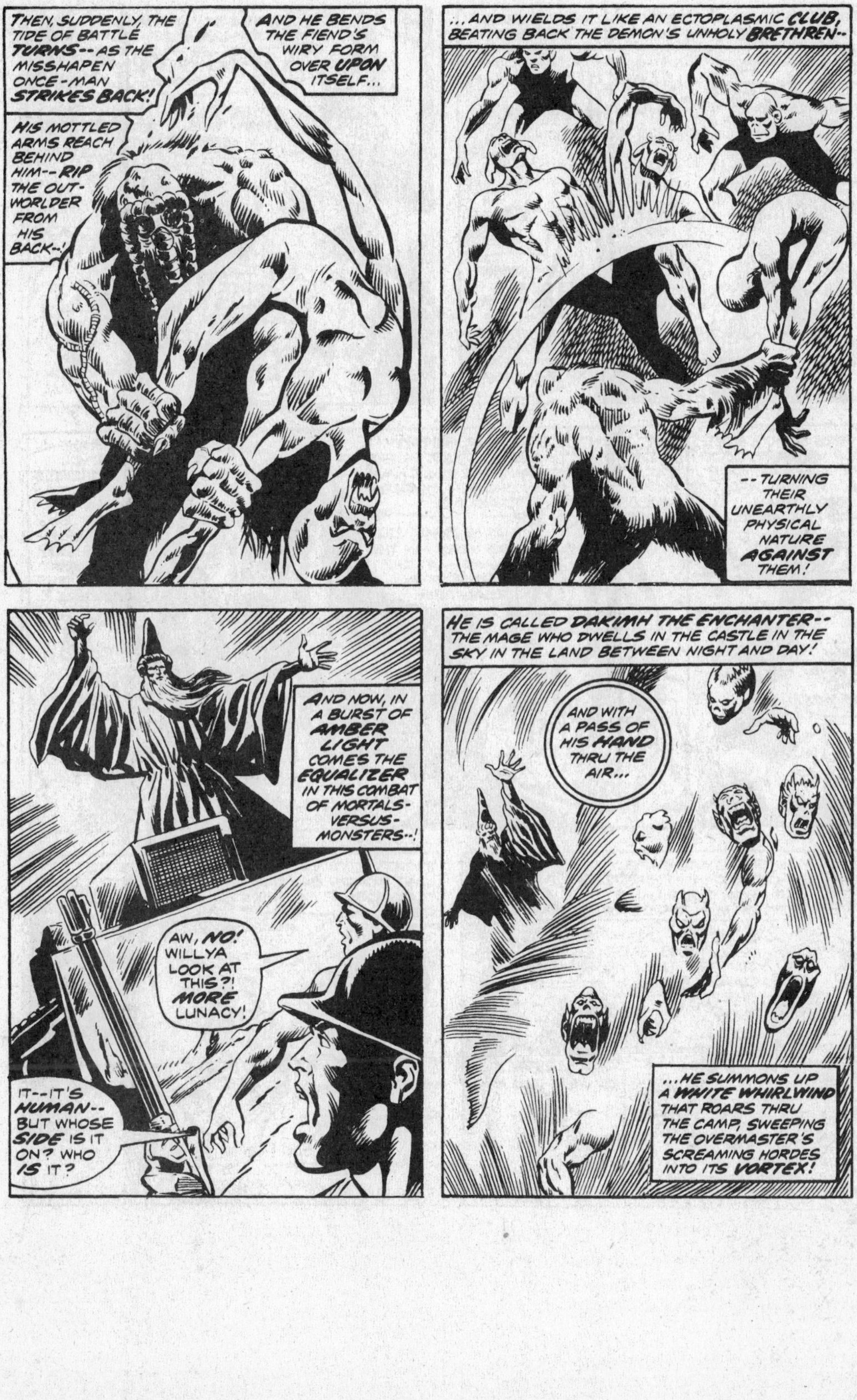
THEN, SUDDENLY, THE TIDE OF BATTLE TURNS-- AS THE MISSHAPEN ONCE-MAN STRIKES BACK!
HIS MOTTLED ARMS REACH BEHIND HIM-- RIP THE OUT-WORLDER FROM HIS BACK--!
AND HE BENDS THE FIEND'S WIRY FORM OVER UPON ITSELF...
...AND WIELDS IT LIKE AN ECTOPLASMIC CLUB, BEATING BACK THE DEMON'S UNHOLY BRETHREN--
--TURNING THEIR UNEARTHLY PHYSICAL NATURE AGAINST THEM!
AND NOW, IN A BURST OF AMBER LIGHT COMES THE EQUALIZER IN THIS COMBAT OF MORTALS-VERSUS-MONSTERS--!
AW, NO! WILLYA LOOK AT THIS?! MORE LUNACY!
IT--IT'S HUMAN-- BUT WHOSE SIDE IS IT ON? WHO IS IT?
HE IS CALLED DAKIMH THE ENCHANTER-- THE MAGE WHO DWELLS IN THE CASTLE IN THE SKY IN THE LAND BETWEEN NIGHT AND DAY!
AND WITH A PASS OF HIS HAND THRU THE AIR...
...HE SUMMONS UP A WHITE WHIRLWIND THAT ROARS THRU THE CAMP, SWEEPING THE OVERMASTER'S SCREAMING HORDES INTO ITS VORTEX!

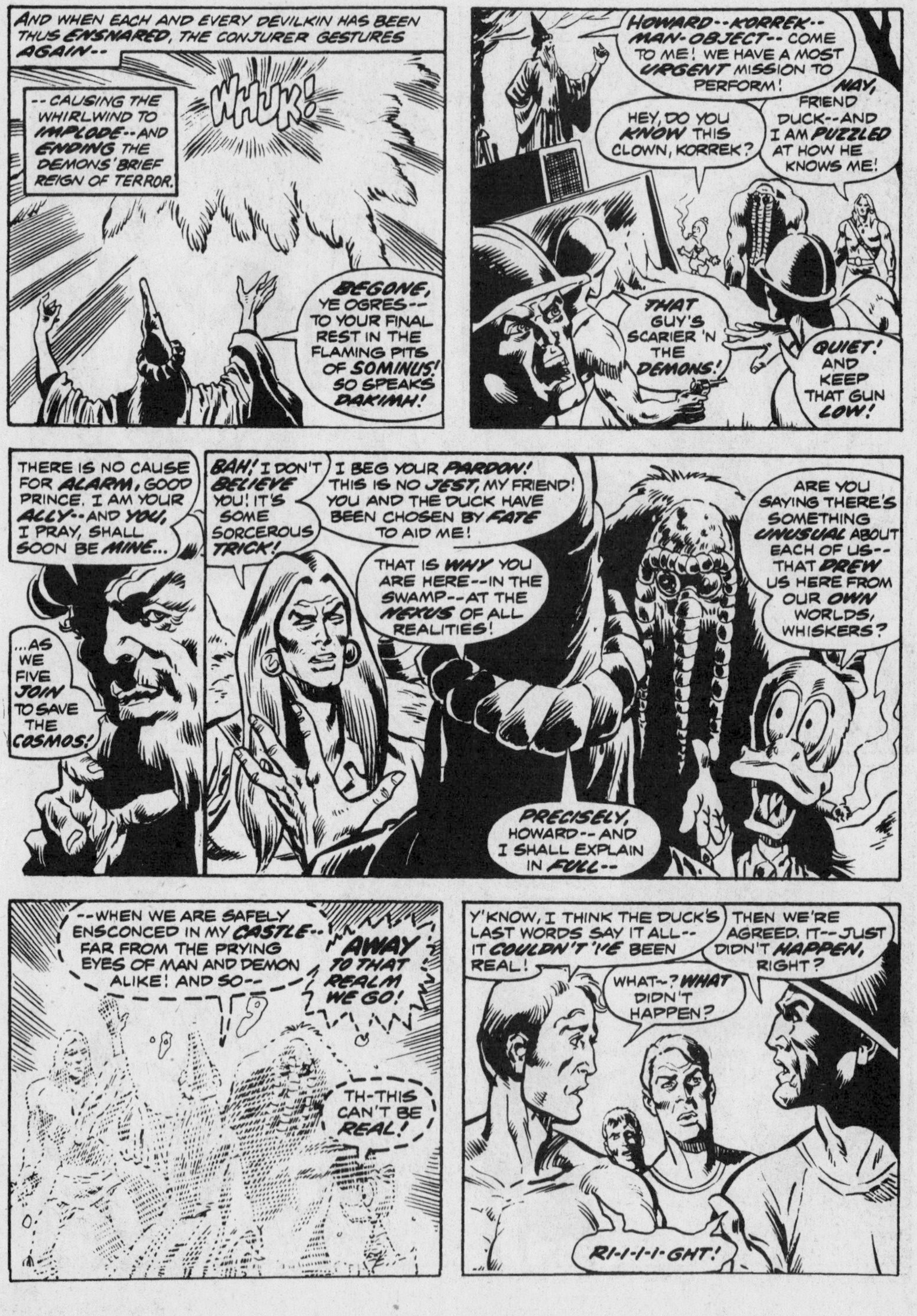
AND WHEN EACH AND EVERY DEVILKIN HAS BEEN THUS ENSNARED, THE CONJURER GESTURES AGAIN--
WHUK!
--CAUSING THE WHIRLWIND TO IMPLODE--AND ENDING THE DEMONS' BRIEF REIGN OF TERROR.
BEGONE, YE OGRES-- TO YOUR FINAL REST IN THE FLAMING PITS OF SOMINUS! SO SPEAKS DAKIMH!
HOWARD--KORREK--MAN-OBJECT--COME TO ME! WE HAVE A MOST URGENT MISSION TO PERFORM!
HEY, DO YOU KNOW THIS CLOWN, KORREK?
NAY, FRIEND DUCK--AND I AM PUZZLED AT HOW HE KNOWS ME!
THAT GUY'S SCARIER 'N THE DEMONS!
QUIET! AND KEEP THAT GUN LOW!
THERE IS NO CAUSE FOR ALARM, GOOD PRINCE. I AM YOUR ALLY--AND YOU, I PRAY, SHALL SOON BE MINE...
...AS WE FIVE JOIN TO SAVE THE COSMOS!
BAH! I DON'T BELIEVE YOU! IT'S SOME SORCEROUS TRICK!
I BEG YOUR PARDON! THIS IS NO JEST, MY FRIEND! YOU AND THE DUCK HAVE BEEN CHOSEN BY FATE TO AID ME!
THAT IS WHY YOU ARE HERE--IN THE SWAMP--AT THE NEXUS OF ALL REALITIES!
ARE YOU SAYING THERE'S SOMETHING UNUSUAL ABOUT EACH OF US--THAT DREW US HERE FROM OUR OWN WORLDS, WHISKERS?
PRECISELY, HOWARD--AND I SHALL EXPLAIN IN FULL--
--WHEN WE ARE SAFELY ENSCONCED IN MY CASTLE--FAR FROM THE PRYING EYES OF MAN AND DEMON ALIKE! AND SO--
AWAY TO THAT REALM WE GO!
TH-THIS CAN'T BE REAL!
Y'KNOW, I THINK THE DUCK'S LAST WORDS SAY IT ALL--IT COULDN'T 'VE BEEN REAL!
THEN WE'RE AGREED. IT--JUST DIDN'T HAPPEN, RIGHT?
WHAT--? WHAT DIDN'T HAPPEN?
RI-I-I-I-GHT!

WHILE, ONE DIMENSION AWAY--

AH! MY SPELL HAS BEEN SUCCESSFUL! OUR FIFTH MEMBER ARRIVES!

ARE YOU MAD, OLD MAN? 'TIS BUT A LEAK IN YOUR CASTLE'S ROOF!

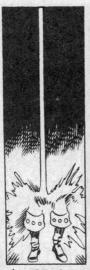

AND PRAISE BE TO THEE, O' GODS OF THEREA, FOR PERMITTING HER SAFE RETURN!

SAVE THE ORAL ROBERTS ACT FOR LATER, DAKIMH, I WANT ANSWERS!

"HARDLY, KORREK--OBSERVE! IT IS THE FEMALE YOU MISTAKENLY ASSUMED WAS YOUR ENEMY-- MY APPRENTICE!"

AND WHEN THE TWO HAVE EXCHANGED INCREDIBLE TALES--!

SO, WE'RE ALL FRIENDS NOW-- AND OUR JOB IS TO SET RIGHT THE COSMIC AXIS.

THAT'S PEACHY-- BUT IT STILL DOESN'T EXPLAIN EVERYTHING.

I THINK I CAN ACCOUNT FOR OUR COMPANIONS' APPEARANCES.

IMAGINE, CHILD, THAT THE NORMAL STRUCTURE OF REALITY APPEARS THUS:

ASCENDING LEVELS, HELD IN DELICATE BALANCE, A HAIR'S-BREATH APART.

THIS, HOWEVER, IS ITS CURRENT STATE-- CHAOS! EVERY LEVEL COLLAPSED UPON ANOTHER.

WHERE ANY TWO OF THOSE LEVELS TOUCH, A JUNCTURE POINT IS CREATED-- A DIMENSIONAL BRIDGE, OF SORTS.

I GET IT! KORREK AND THE DUCK PASSED THRU ONE OF THOSE JUNCTURE POINTS AND...

EXACTLY! THEY CROSSED OVER INTO YOUR WORLD, BUT... ENOUGH OF THIS.

WE HAVE A JOURNEY TO BEGIN-- NOW!

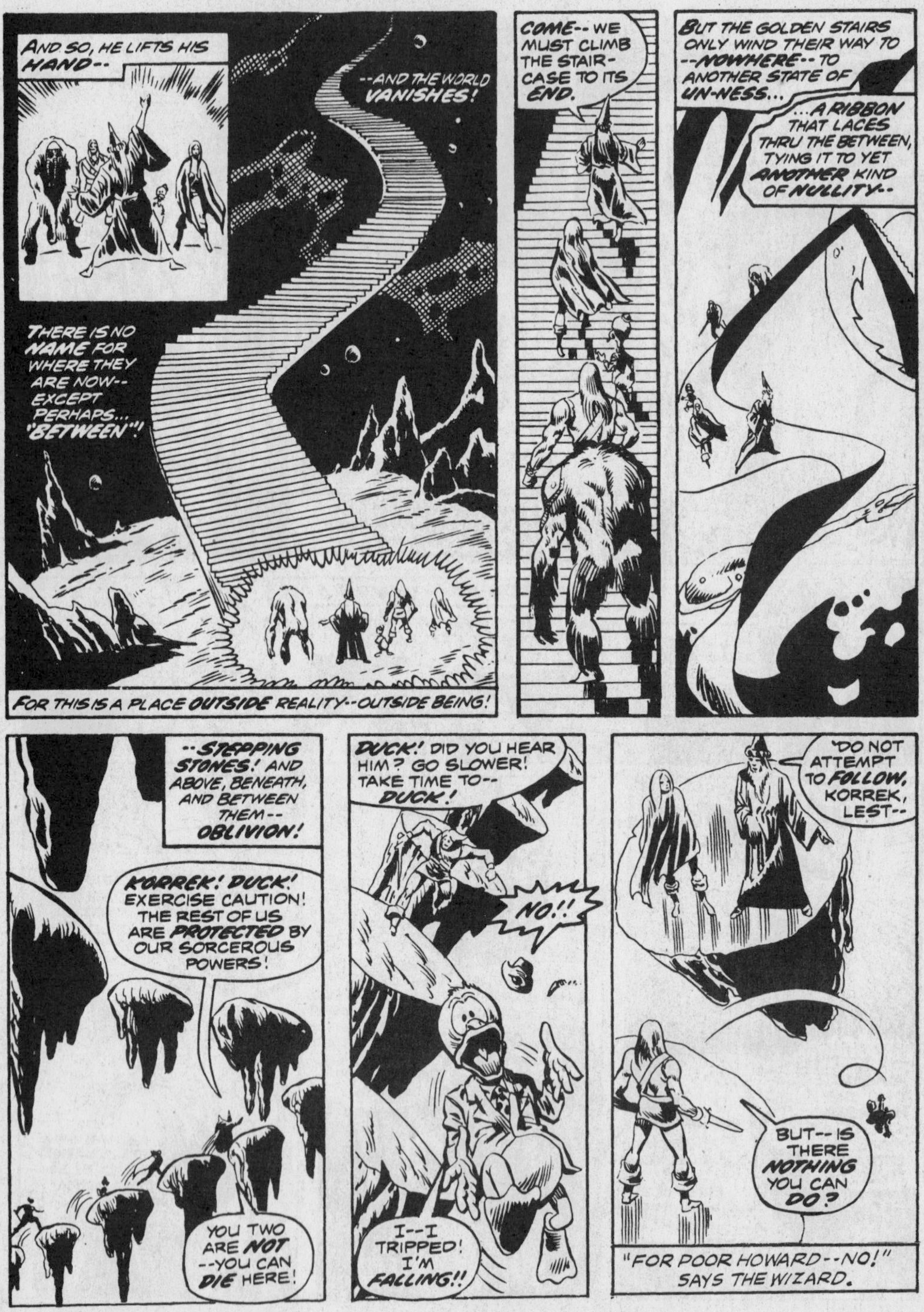
AND SO, HE LIFTS HIS HAND--
--AND THE WORLD VANISHES!
THERE IS NO NAME FOR WHERE THEY ARE NOW-- EXCEPT PERHAPS... "BETWEEN"!
FOR THIS IS A PLACE OUTSIDE REALITY--OUTSIDE BEING!
COME-- WE MUST CLIMB THE STAIR-CASE TO ITS END.
BUT THE GOLDEN STAIRS ONLY WIND THEIR WAY TO --NOWHERE-- TO ANOTHER STATE OF UN-NESS...
...A RIBBON THAT LACES THRU THE BETWEEN, TYING IT TO YET ANOTHER KIND OF NULLITY--
--STEPPING STONES! AND ABOVE, BENEATH, AND BETWEEN THEM-- OBLIVION!
KORREK! DUCK! EXERCISE CAUTION! THE REST OF US ARE PROTECTED BY OUR SORCEROUS POWERS!
YOU TWO ARE NOT --YOU CAN DIE HERE!
DUCK! DID YOU HEAR HIM? GO SLOWER! TAKE TIME TO-- DUCK!
NO!!
I--I TRIPPED! I'M FALLING!!
'DO NOT ATTEMPT TO FOLLOW, KORREK, LEST--
BUT--IS THERE NOTHING YOU CAN DO?
"FOR POOR HOWARD--NO!" SAYS THE WIZARD.

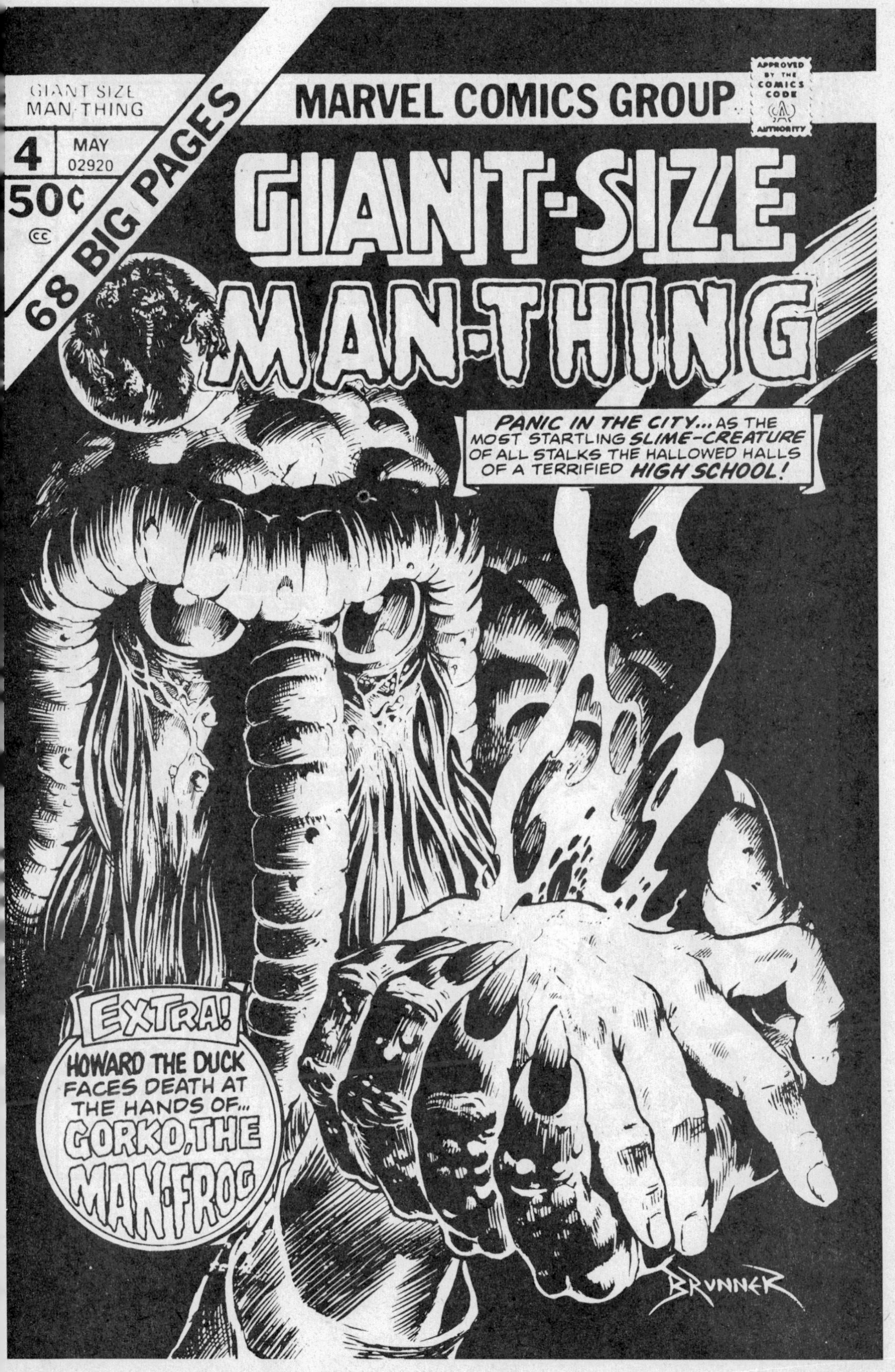
GIANT SIZE MAN-THING
68 BIG PAGES
MARVEL COMICS GROUP
APPROVED BY THE COMICS CODE AUTHORITY
4
MAY
02920
50¢
GIANT-SIZE MAN-THING
PANIC IN THE CITY... AS THE MOST STARTLING SLIME-CREATURE OF ALL STALKS THE HALLOWED HALLS OF A TERRIFIED HIGH SCHOOL!
EXTRA!
HOWARD THE DUCK FACES DEATH AT THE HANDS OF... GORKO, THE MAN-FROG
BRUNNER

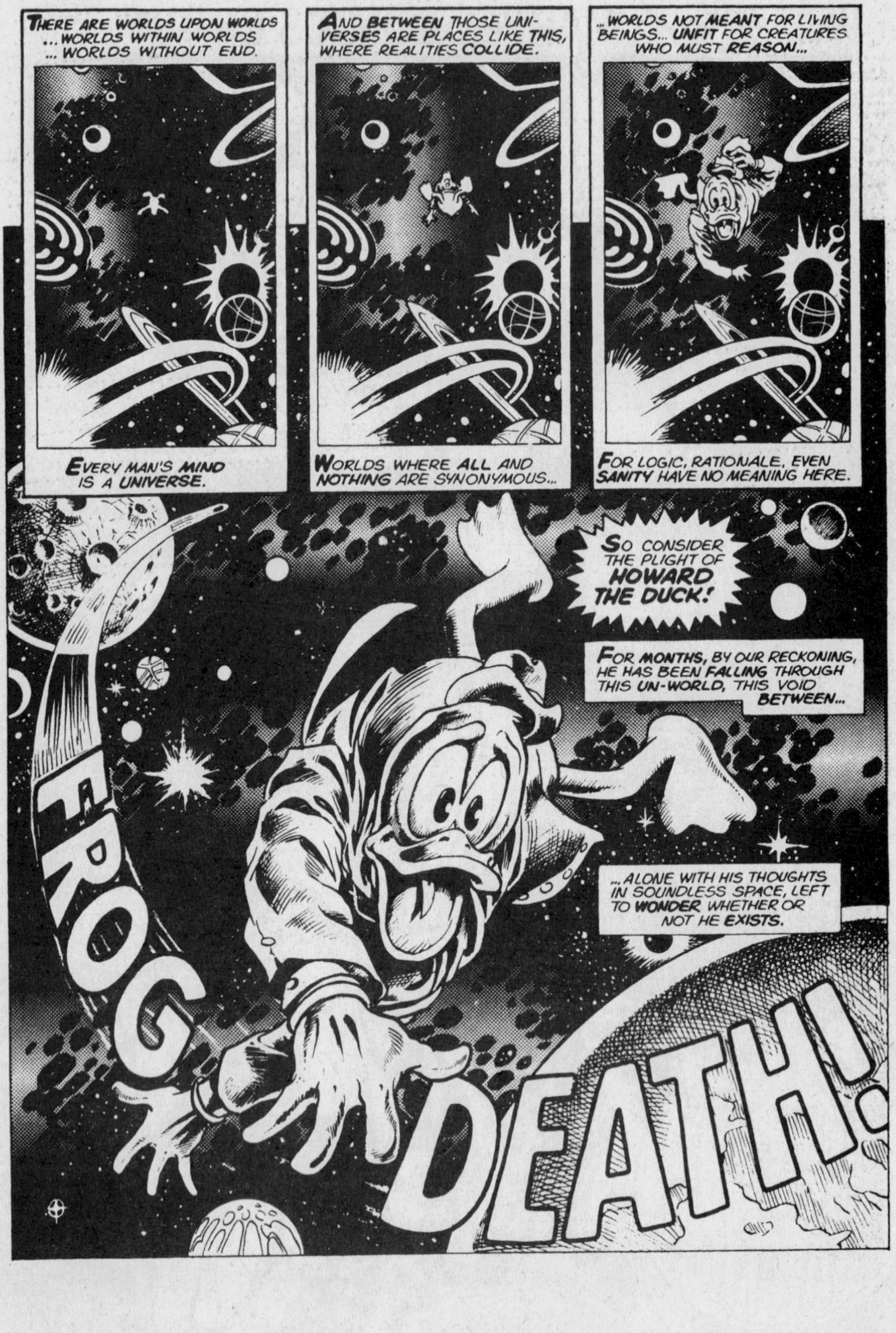

THERE ARE WORLDS UPON WORLDS ...WORLDS WITHIN WORLDS ...WORLDS WITHOUT END.
EVERY MAN'S MIND IS A UNIVERSE.
AND BETWEEN THOSE UNIVERSES ARE PLACES LIKE THIS, WHERE REALITIES COLLIDE.
WORLDS WHERE ALL AND NOTHING ARE SYNONYMOUS...
...WORLDS NOT MEANT FOR LIVING BEINGS... UNFIT FOR CREATURES WHO MUST REASON...
FOR LOGIC, RATIONALE, EVEN SANITY HAVE NO MEANING HERE.
SO CONSIDER THE PLIGHT OF HOWARD THE DUCK!
FOR MONTHS, BY OUR RECKONING, HE HAS BEEN FALLING THROUGH THIS UN-WORLD, THIS VOID BETWEEN...
...ALONE WITH HIS THOUGHTS IN SOUNDLESS SPACE, LEFT TO WONDER WHETHER OR NOT HE EXISTS.
FROG DEATH!

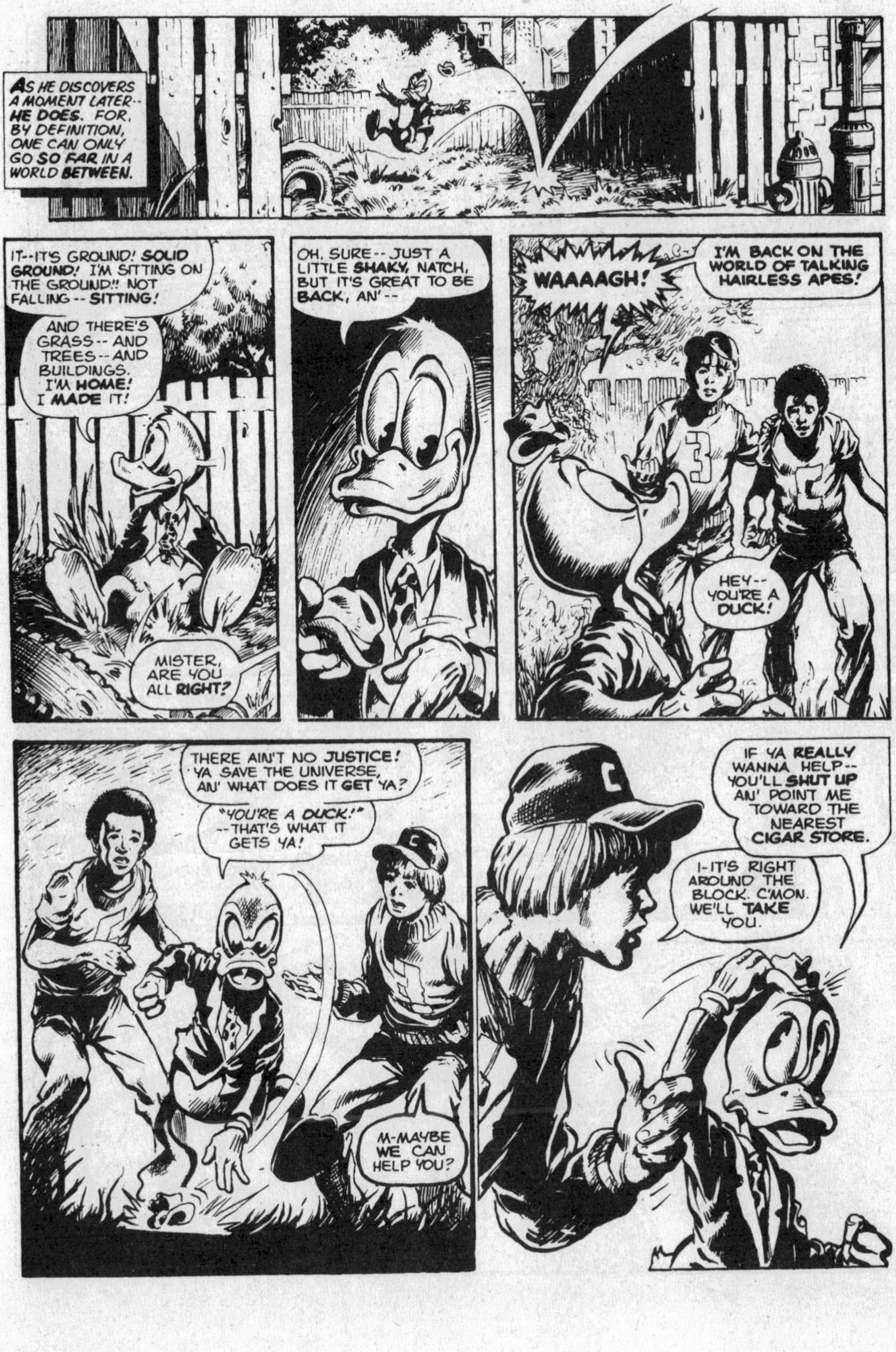
AS HE DISCOVERS A MOMENT LATER-- HE DOES. FOR, BY DEFINITION, ONE CAN ONLY GO SO FAR IN A WORLD BETWEEN.
IT--IT'S GROUND! SOLID GROUND! I'M SITTING ON THE GROUND!! NOT FALLING--SITTING!
AND THERE'S GRASS--AND TREES--AND BUILDINGS. I'M HOME! I MADE IT!
MISTER, ARE YOU ALL RIGHT?
OH, SURE--JUST A LITTLE SHAKY, NATCH, BUT IT'S GREAT TO BE BACK, AN'--
WAAAAGH!
I'M BACK ON THE WORLD OF TALKING HAIRLESS APES!
HEY--YOU'RE A DUCK!
THERE AIN'T NO JUSTICE! YA SAVE THE UNIVERSE, AN' WHAT DOES IT GET YA?
"YOU'RE A DUCK!" --THAT'S WHAT IT GETS YA!
M-MAYBE WE CAN HELP YOU?
IF YA REALLY WANNA HELP--YOU'LL SHUT UP AN' POINT ME TOWARD THE NEAREST CIGAR STORE.
I-IT'S RIGHT AROUND THE BLOCK. C'MON. WE'LL TAKE YOU.

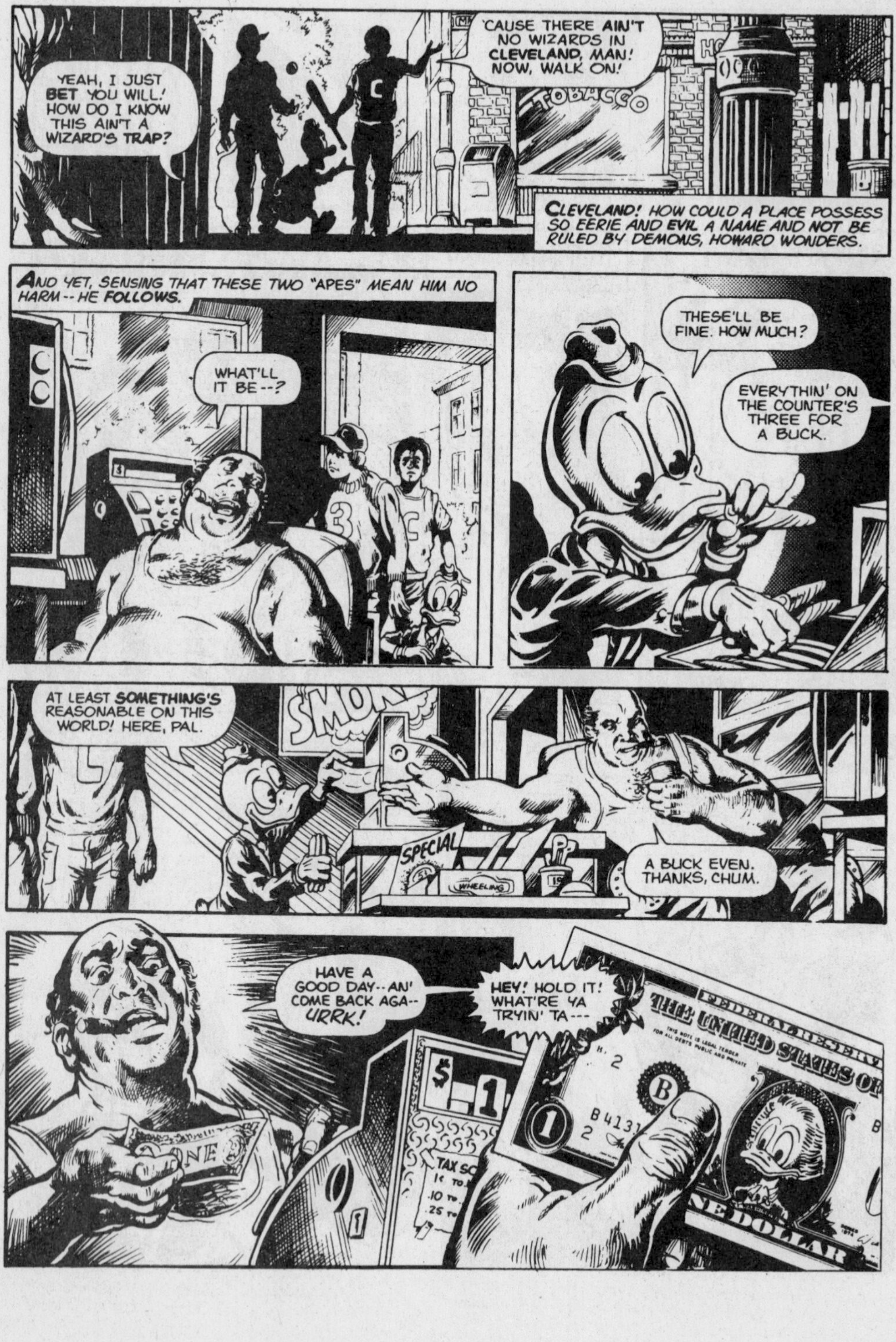
YEAH, I JUST BET YOU WILL! HOW DO I KNOW THIS AIN'T A WIZARD'S TRAP?
'CAUSE THERE AIN'T NO WIZARDS IN CLEVELAND, MAN! NOW, WALK ON!
TOBACCO
CLEVELAND! HOW COULD A PLACE POSSESS SO EERIE AND EVIL A NAME AND NOT BE RULED BY DEMONS, HOWARD WONDERS.
AND YET, SENSING THAT THESE TWO "APES" MEAN HIM NO HARM -- HE FOLLOWS.
WHAT'LL IT BE --?
THESE'LL BE FINE. HOW MUCH?
EVERYTHIN' ON THE COUNTER'S THREE FOR A BUCK.
AT LEAST SOMETHING'S REASONABLE ON THIS WORLD! HERE, PAL.
SPECIAL
WHEELING
A BUCK EVEN. THANKS, CHUM.
HAVE A GOOD DAY-- AN' COME BACK AGA-- URRK!
HEY! HOLD IT! WHAT'RE YA TRYIN' TA---
THE UNITED STATES OF
ONE DOLLAR

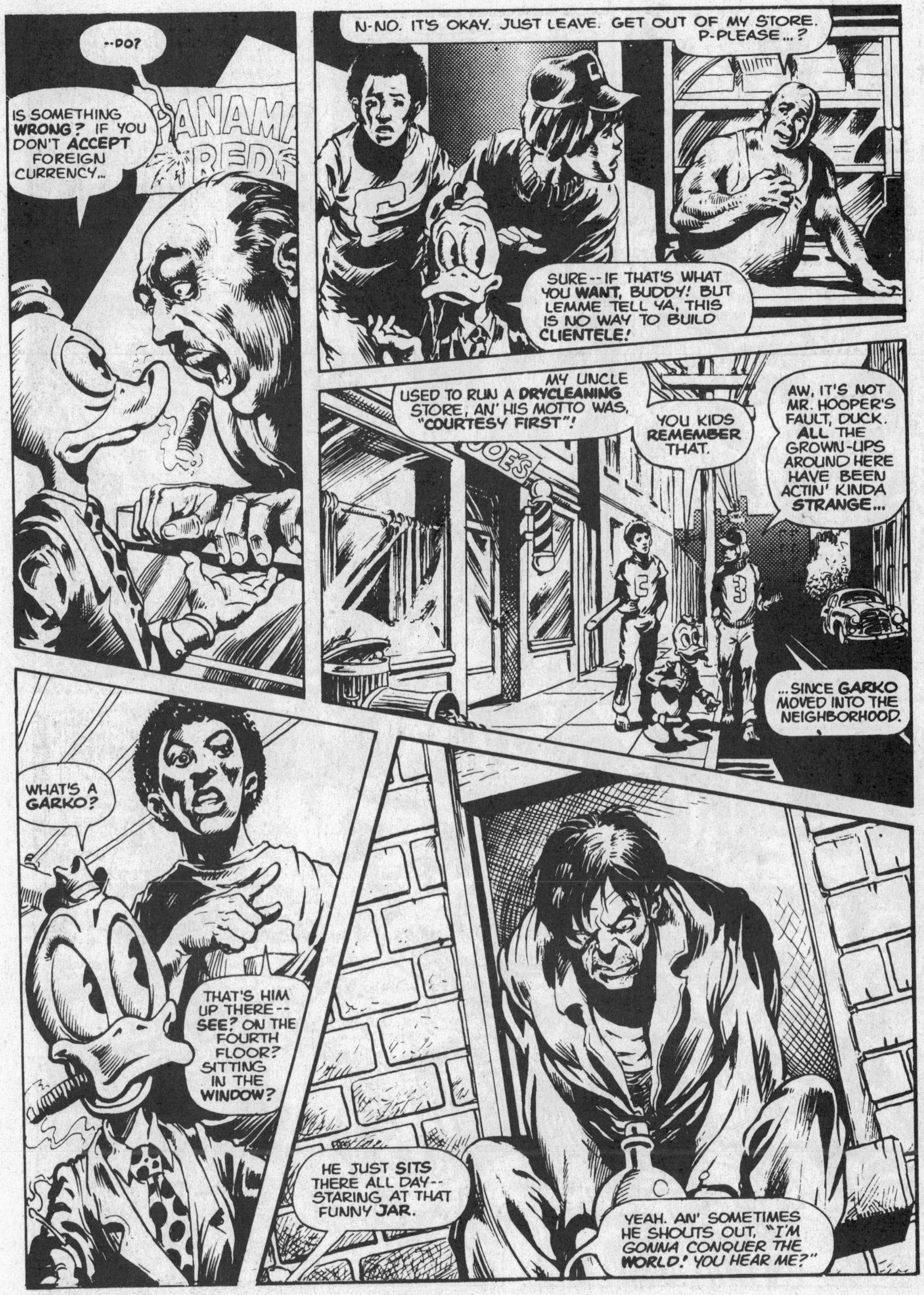
--DO?
IS SOMETHING WRONG? IF YOU DON'T ACCEPT FOREIGN CURRENCY...
PANAMA RED
N-NO. IT'S OKAY. JUST LEAVE. GET OUT OF MY STORE. P-PLEASE...?
SURE--IF THAT'S WHAT YOU WANT, BUDDY! BUT LEMME TELL YA, THIS IS NO WAY TO BUILD CLIENTELE!
MY UNCLE USED TO RUN A DRYCLEANING STORE, AN' HIS MOTTO WAS, "COURTESY FIRST"!
YOU KIDS REMEMBER THAT.
AW, IT'S NOT MR. HOOPER'S FAULT, DUCK. ALL THE GROWN-UPS AROUND HERE HAVE BEEN ACTIN' KINDA STRANGE...
JOE'S
...SINCE GARKO MOVED INTO THE NEIGHBORHOOD.
WHAT'S A GARKO?
THAT'S HIM UP THERE--SEE? ON THE FOURTH FLOOR? SITTING IN THE WINDOW?
HE JUST SITS THERE ALL DAY--STARING AT THAT FUNNY JAR.
YEAH. AN' SOMETIMES HE SHOUTS OUT, "I'M GONNA CONQUER THE WORLD! YOU HEAR ME?"

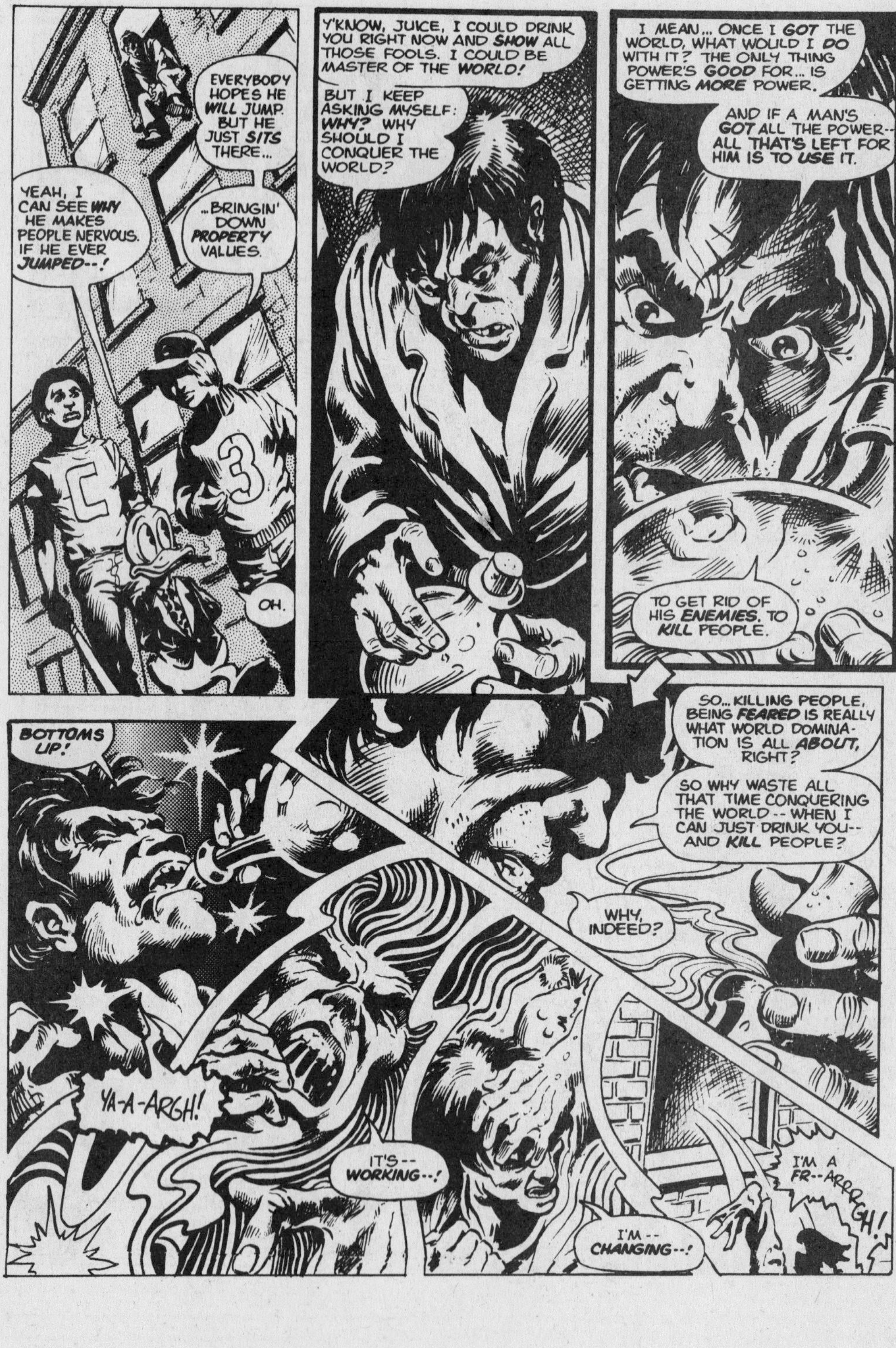
EVERYBODY HOPES HE WILL JUMP. BUT HE JUST SITS THERE...
YEAH, I CAN SEE WHY HE MAKES PEOPLE NERVOUS. IF HE EVER JUMPED--!
...BRINGIN' DOWN PROPERTY VALUES.
OH.
Y'KNOW, JUICE, I COULD DRINK YOU RIGHT NOW AND SHOW ALL THOSE FOOLS. I COULD BE MASTER OF THE WORLD!
BUT I KEEP ASKING MYSELF: WHY? WHY SHOULD I CONQUER THE WORLD?
I MEAN... ONCE I GOT THE WORLD, WHAT WOULD I DO WITH IT? THE ONLY THING POWER'S GOOD FOR... IS GETTING MORE POWER.
AND IF A MAN'S GOT ALL THE POWER-- ALL THAT'S LEFT FOR HIM IS TO USE IT.
TO GET RID OF HIS ENEMIES. TO KILL PEOPLE.
SO... KILLING PEOPLE, BEING FEARED IS REALLY WHAT WORLD DOMINATION IS ALL ABOUT, RIGHT?
SO WHY WASTE ALL THAT TIME CONQUERING THE WORLD -- WHEN I CAN JUST DRINK YOU-- AND KILL PEOPLE?
WHY, INDEED?
BOTTOMS UP!
YA-A-ARGH!
IT'S -- WORKING--!
I'M -- CHANGING--!
I'M A FR--ARRRGH!

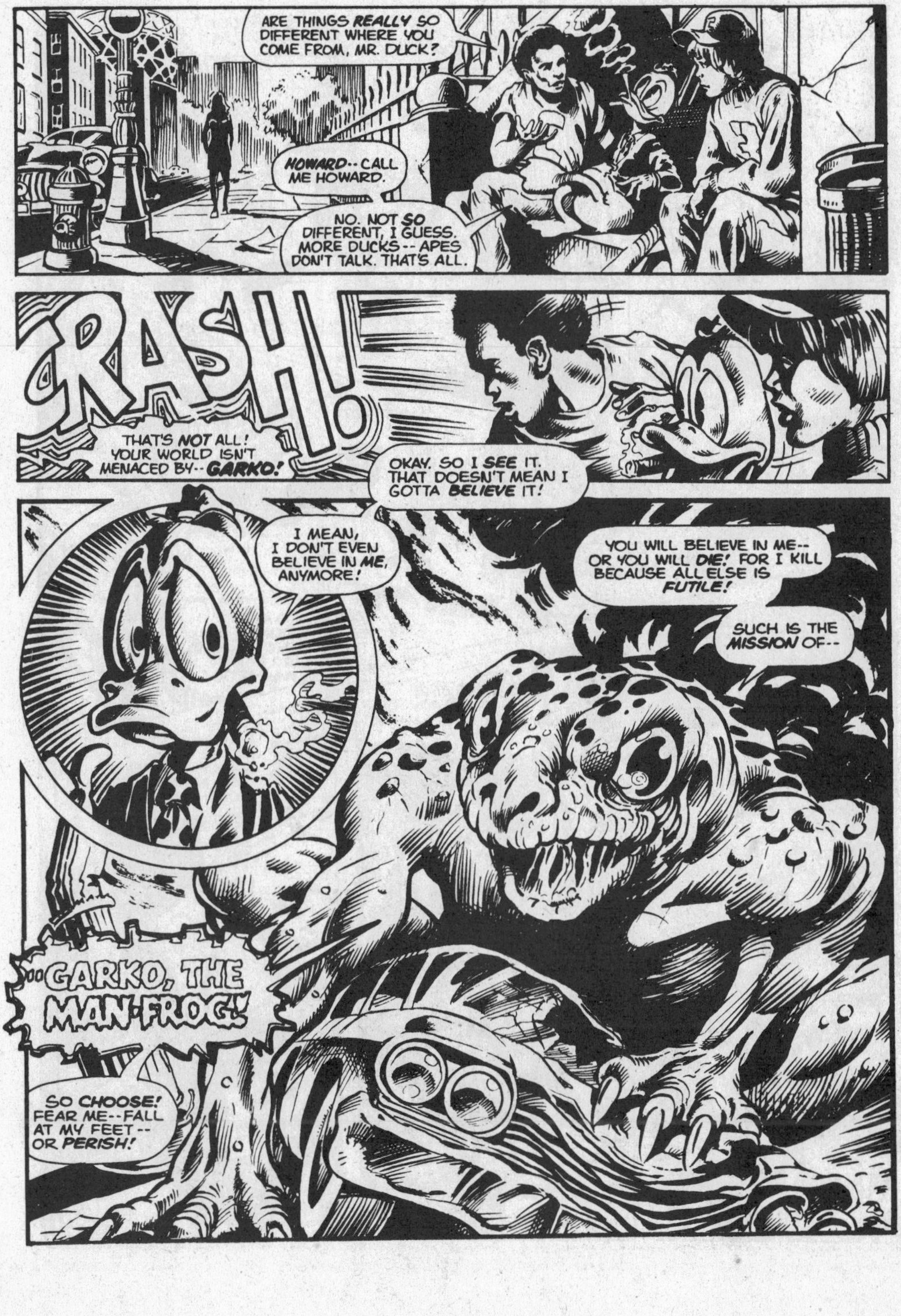

ARE THINGS REALLY SO DIFFERENT WHERE YOU COME FROM, MR. DUCK?
HOWARD--CALL ME HOWARD.
NO. NOT SO DIFFERENT, I GUESS. MORE DUCKS--APES DON'T TALK. THAT'S ALL.
CRASH!
THAT'S NOT ALL! YOUR WORLD ISN'T MENACED BY--GARKO!
OKAY. SO I SEE IT. THAT DOESN'T MEAN I GOTTA BELIEVE IT!
I MEAN, I DON'T EVEN BELIEVE IN ME, ANYMORE!
YOU WILL BELIEVE IN ME--OR YOU WILL DIE! FOR I KILL BECAUSE ALL ELSE IS FUTILE!
SUCH IS THE MISSION OF--
..GARKO, THE MAN-FROG!
SO CHOOSE! FEAR ME--FALL AT MY FEET--OR PERISH!

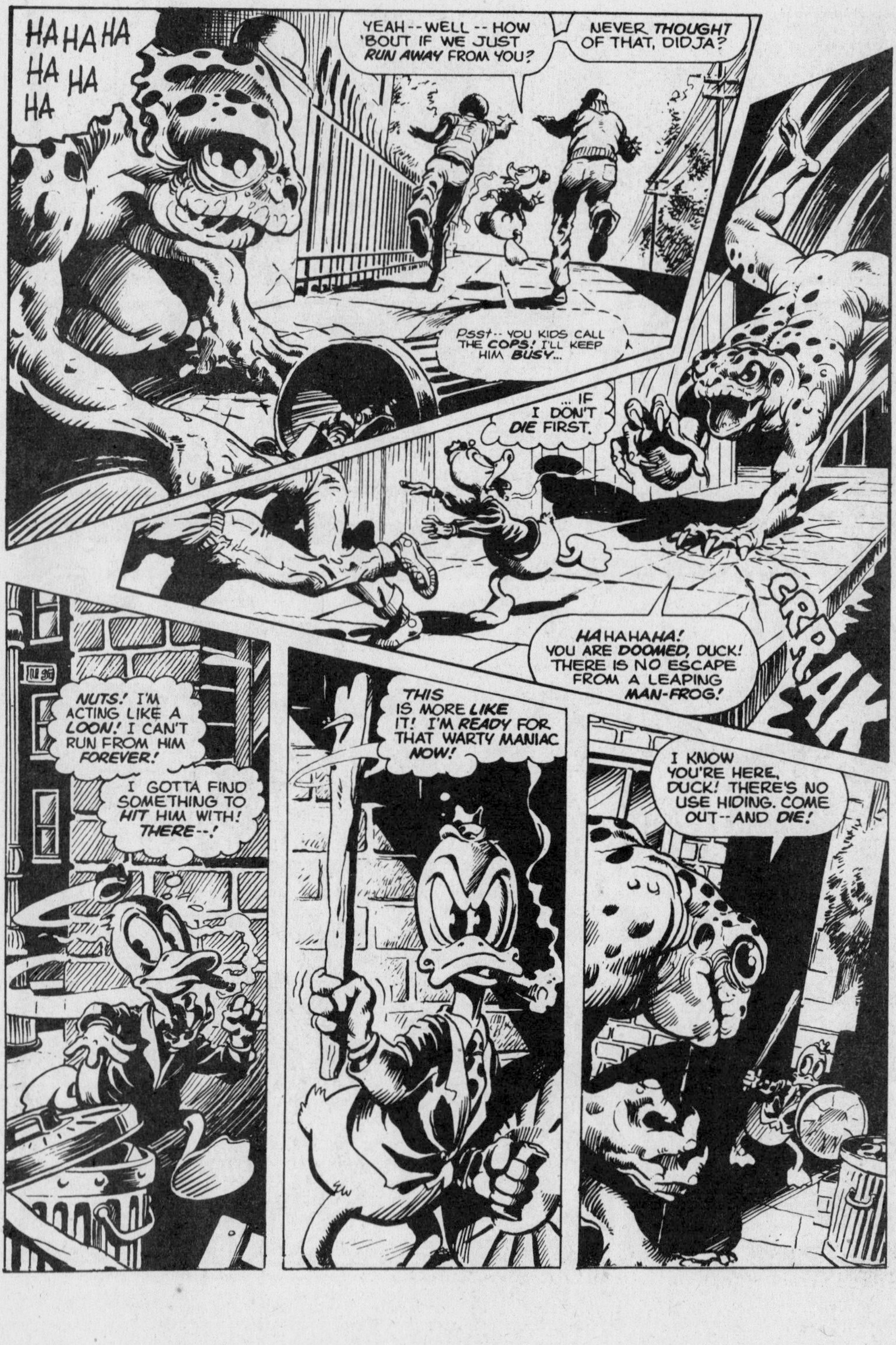
HA HA HA HA HA HA HA
YEAH--WELL--HOW 'BOUT IF WE JUST RUN AWAY FROM YOU?
NEVER THOUGHT OF THAT, DIDJA?
Psst-- YOU KIDS CALL THE COPS! I'LL KEEP HIM BUSY...
... IF I DON'T DIE FIRST.
HA HAHAHA! YOU ARE DOOMED, DUCK! THERE IS NO ESCAPE FROM A LEAPING MAN-FROG!
CRRAK
NUTS! I'M ACTING LIKE A LOON! I CAN'T RUN FROM HIM FOREVER!
I GOTTA FIND SOMETHING TO HIT HIM WITH! THERE--!
THIS IS MORE LIKE IT! I'M READY FOR THAT WARTY MANIAC NOW!
I KNOW YOU'RE HERE, DUCK! THERE'S NO USE HIDING. COME OUT--AND DIE!

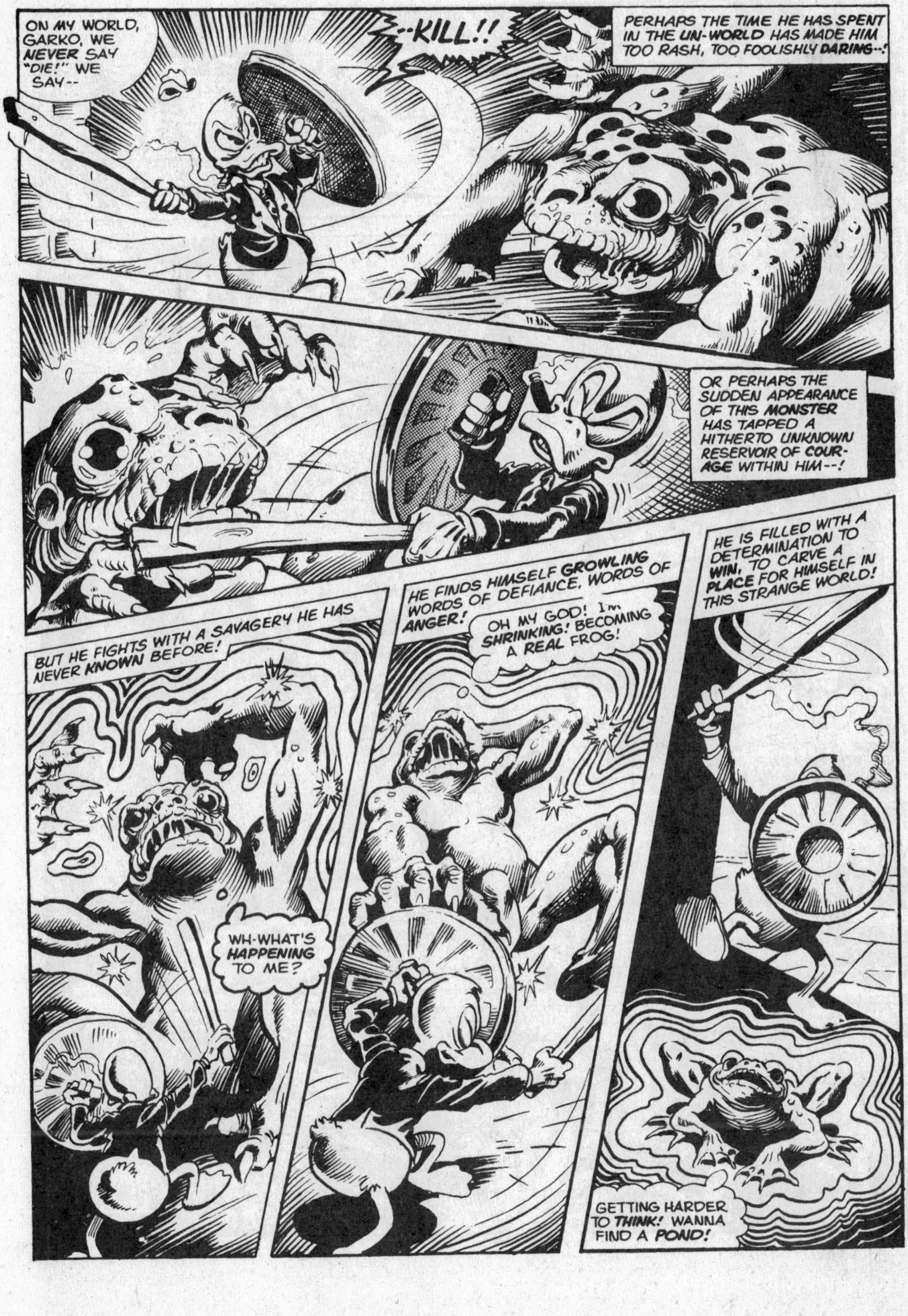

ON MY WORLD, GARKO, WE NEVER SAY "DIE!" WE SAY--
--KILL!!
PERHAPS THE TIME HE HAS SPENT IN THE UN-WORLD HAS MADE HIM TOO RASH, TOO FOOLISHLY DARING--!
OR PERHAPS THE SUDDEN APPEARANCE OF THIS MONSTER HAS TAPPED A HITHERTO UNKNOWN RESERVOIR OF COURAGE WITHIN HIM--!
BUT HE FIGHTS WITH A SAVAGERY HE HAS NEVER KNOWN BEFORE!
WH-WHAT'S HAPPENING TO ME?
HE FINDS HIMSELF GROWLING WORDS OF DEFIANCE, WORDS OF ANGER!
OH MY GOD! I'M SHRINKING! BECOMING A REAL FROG!
HE IS FILLED WITH A DETERMINATION TO WIN, TO CARVE A PLACE FOR HIMSELF IN THIS STRANGE WORLD!
GETTING HARDER TO THINK! WANNA FIND A POND!

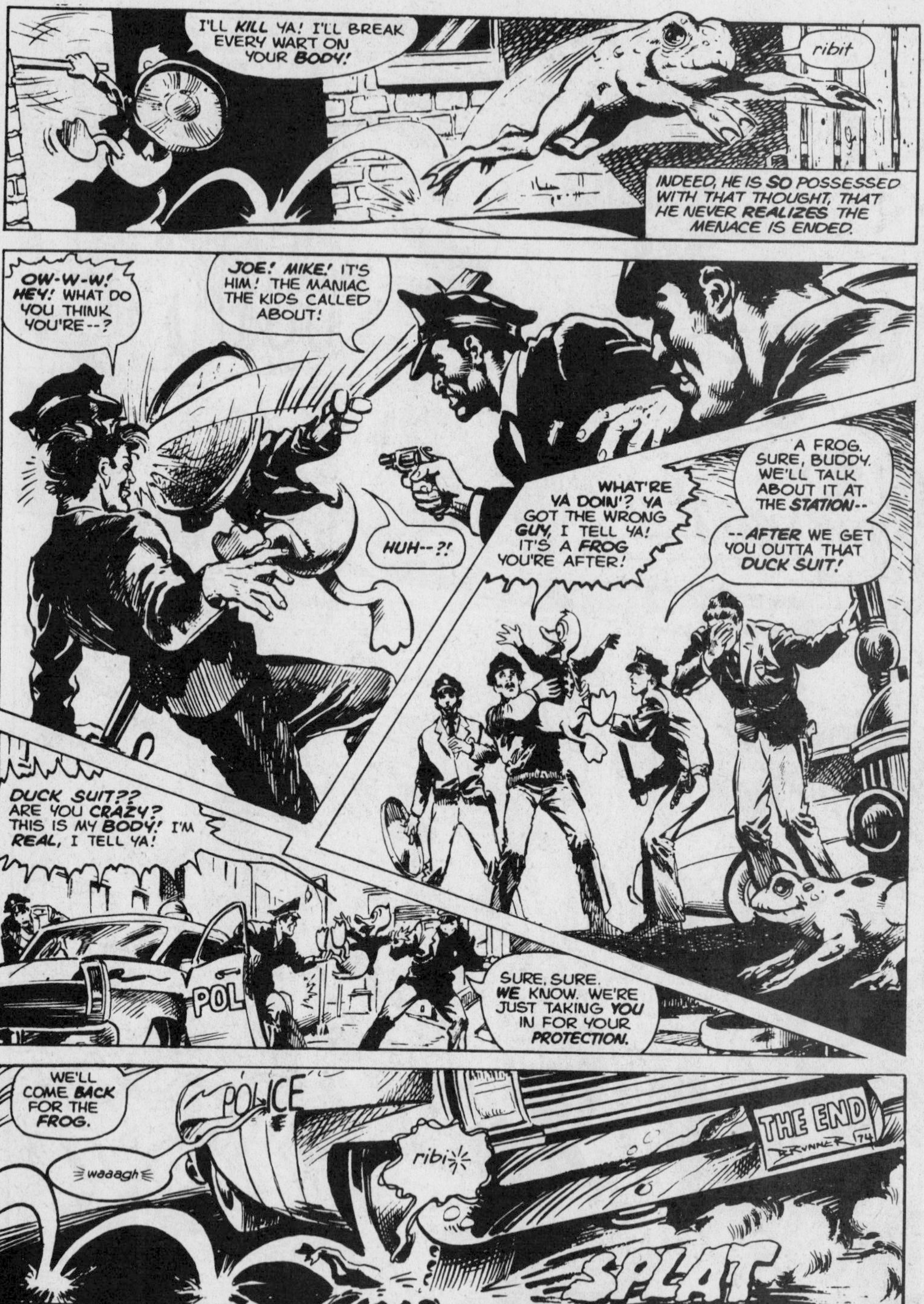
I'LL KILL YA! I'LL BREAK EVERY WART ON YOUR BODY!
ribit
INDEED, HE IS SO POSSESSED WITH THAT THOUGHT, THAT HE NEVER REALIZES THE MENACE IS ENDED.
OW-W-W! HEY! WHAT DO YOU THINK YOU'RE--?
JOE! MIKE! IT'S HIM! THE MANIAC THE KIDS CALLED ABOUT!
HUH--?!
WHAT'RE YA DOIN'? YA GOT THE WRONG GUY, I TELL YA! IT'S A FROG YOU'RE AFTER!
A FROG. SURE, BUDDY. WE'LL TALK ABOUT IT AT THE STATION--
--AFTER WE GET YOU OUTTA THAT DUCK SUIT!
DUCK SUIT?? ARE YOU CRAZY? THIS IS MY BODY! I'M REAL, I TELL YA!
POL
SURE, SURE. WE KNOW. WE'RE JUST TAKING YOU IN FOR YOUR PROTECTION.
WE'LL COME BACK FOR THE FROG.
POLICE
waaagh
ribi
THE END
BRUNNER '74
SPLAT

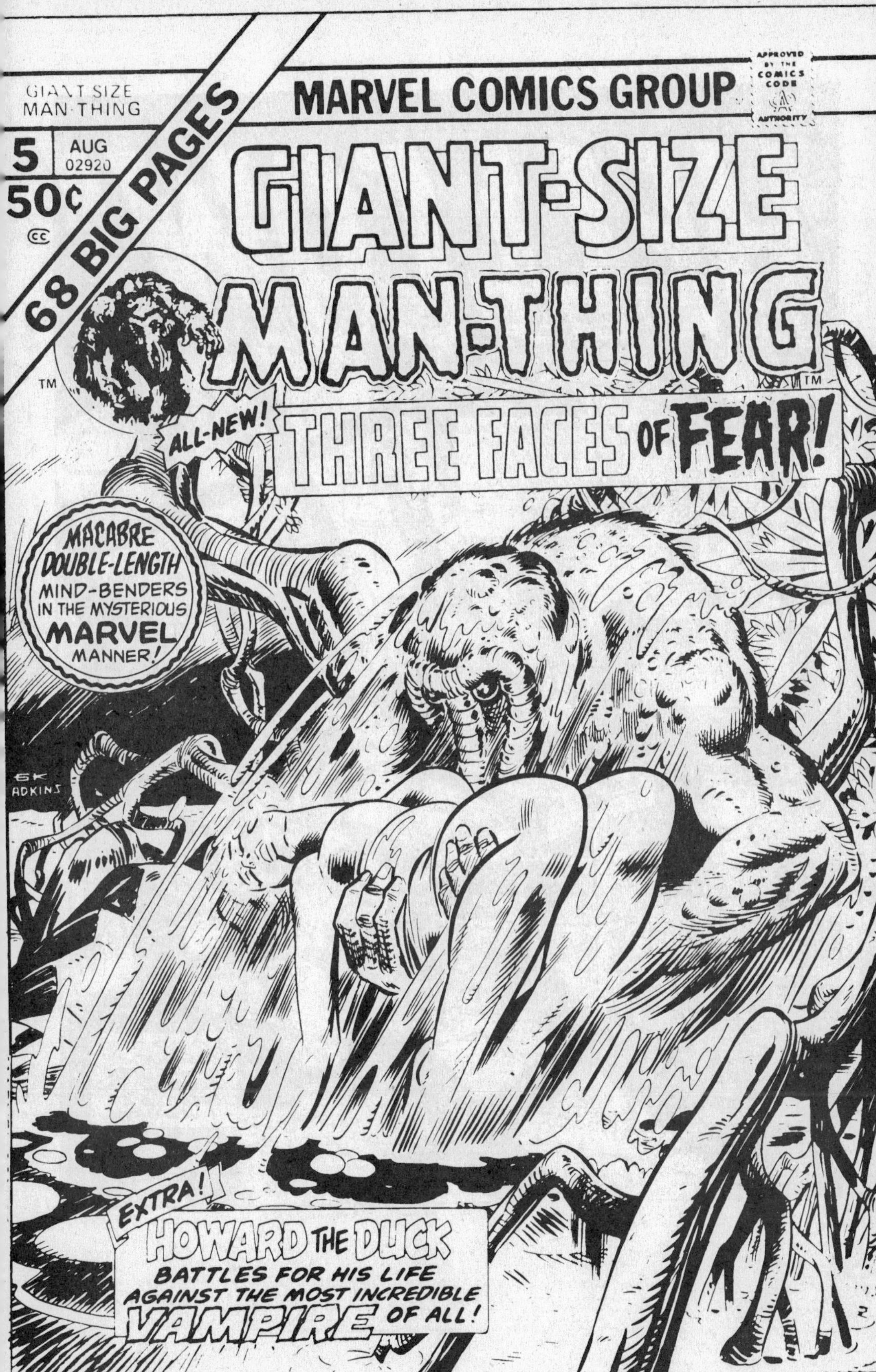

GIANT SIZE
MAN-THING
MARVEL COMICS GROUP
APPROVED BY THE COMICS CODE AUTHORITY
5
AUG
02920
50¢
68 BIG PAGES
GIANT-SIZE
MAN-THING
TM
TM
ALL-NEW!
THREE FACES OF FEAR!
MACABRE DOUBLE-LENGTH MIND-BENDERS IN THE MYSTERIOUS MARVEL MANNER!
GK
ADKINS
EXTRA!
HOWARD THE DUCK
BATTLES FOR HIS LIFE AGAINST THE MOST INCREDIBLE VAMPIRE OF ALL!

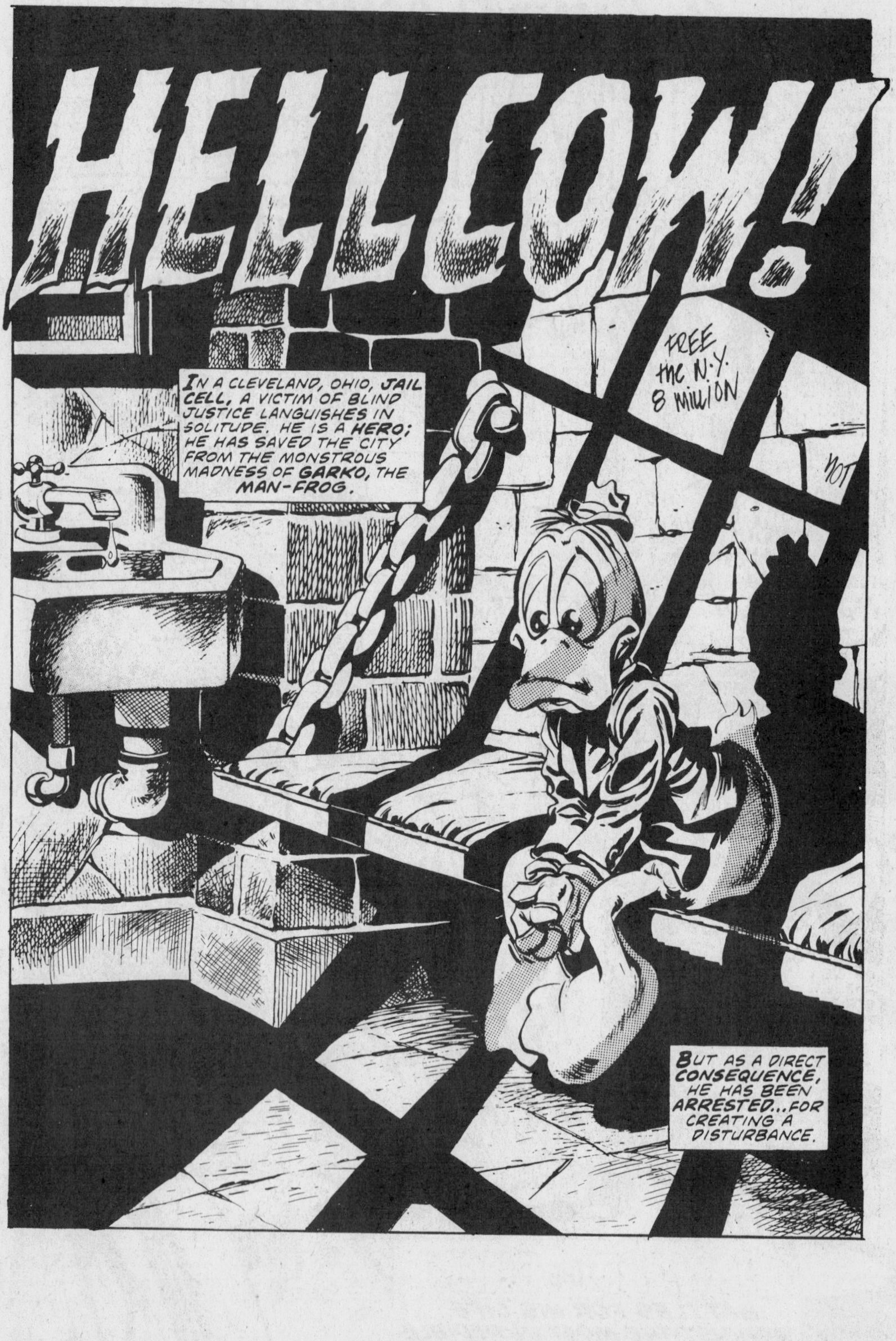
HELLCOW!
IN A CLEVELAND, OHIO, JAIL CELL, A VICTIM OF BLIND JUSTICE LANGUISHES IN SOLITUDE. HE IS A HERO; HE HAS SAVED THE CITY FROM THE MONSTROUS MADNESS OF GARKO, THE MAN-FROG.
FREE the N.Y. 8 MILLION
NOT
BUT AS A DIRECT CONSEQUENCE, HE HAS BEEN ARRESTED...FOR CREATING A DISTURBANCE.

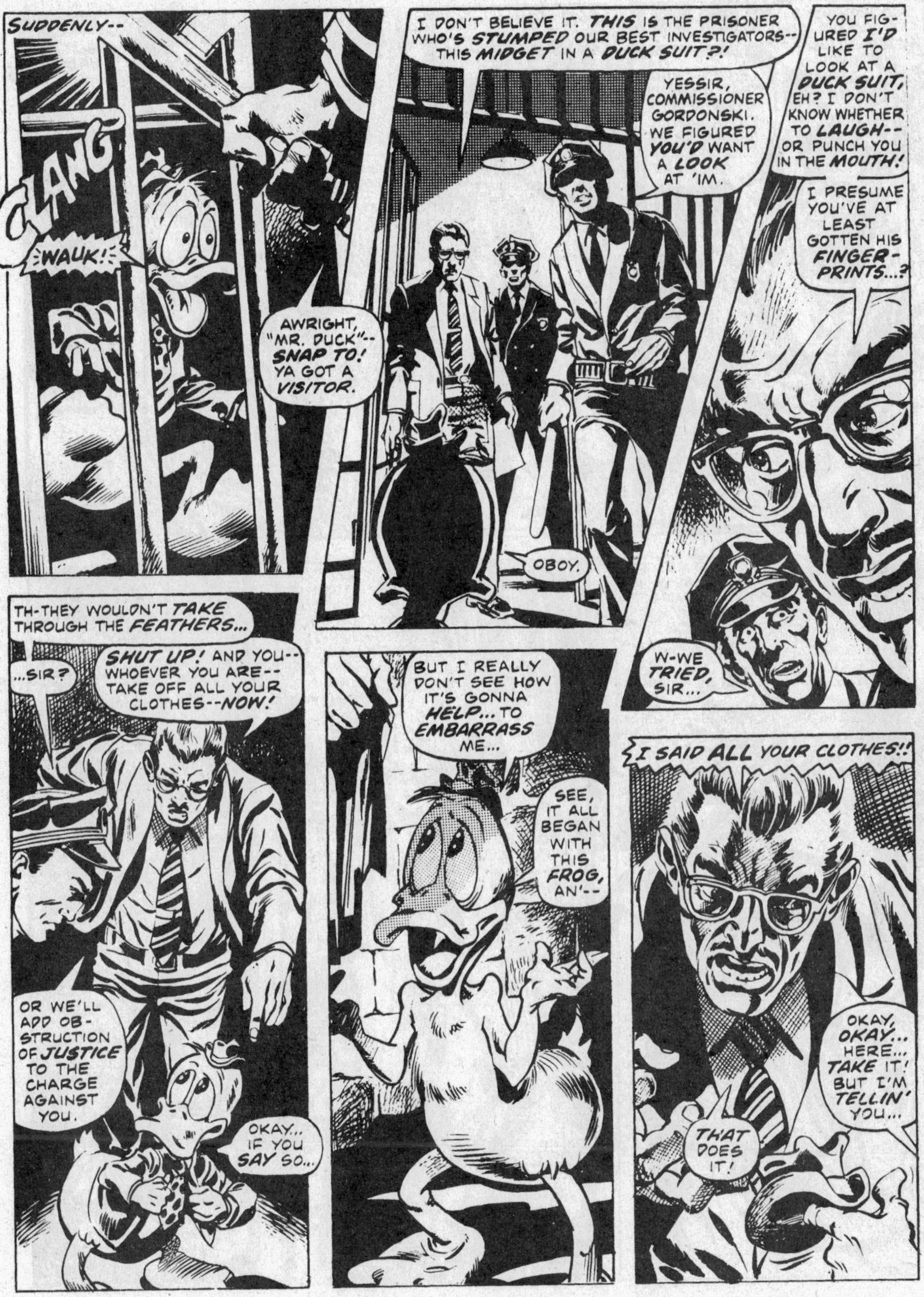
SUDDENLY--
CLANG
WAUK!
AWRIGHT, "MR. DUCK"--SNAP TO! YA GOT A VISITOR.
I DON'T BELIEVE IT. THIS IS THE PRISONER WHO'S STUMPED OUR BEST INVESTIGATORS--THIS MIDGET IN A DUCK SUIT?!
YESSIR, COMMISSIONER GORDONSKI. WE FIGURED YOU'D WANT A LOOK AT 'IM.
OBOY.
YOU FIGURED I'D LIKE TO LOOK AT A DUCK SUIT, EH? I DON'T KNOW WHETHER TO LAUGH--OR PUNCH YOU IN THE MOUTH!
I PRESUME YOU'VE AT LEAST GOTTEN HIS FINGER-PRINTS...?
W-WE TRIED, SIR...
TH-THEY WOULDN'T TAKE THROUGH THE FEATHERS...
...SIR?
SHUT UP! AND YOU--WHOEVER YOU ARE--TAKE OFF ALL YOUR CLOTHES--NOW!
OR WE'LL ADD OB-STRUCTION OF JUSTICE TO THE CHARGE AGAINST YOU.
OKAY... IF YOU SAY SO...
BUT I REALLY DON'T SEE HOW IT'S GONNA HELP... TO EMBARRASS ME...
SEE, IT ALL BEGAN WITH THIS FROG, AN'--
I SAID ALL YOUR CLOTHES!!
OKAY, OKAY... HERE... TAKE IT! BUT I'M TELLIN' YOU...
THAT DOES IT!

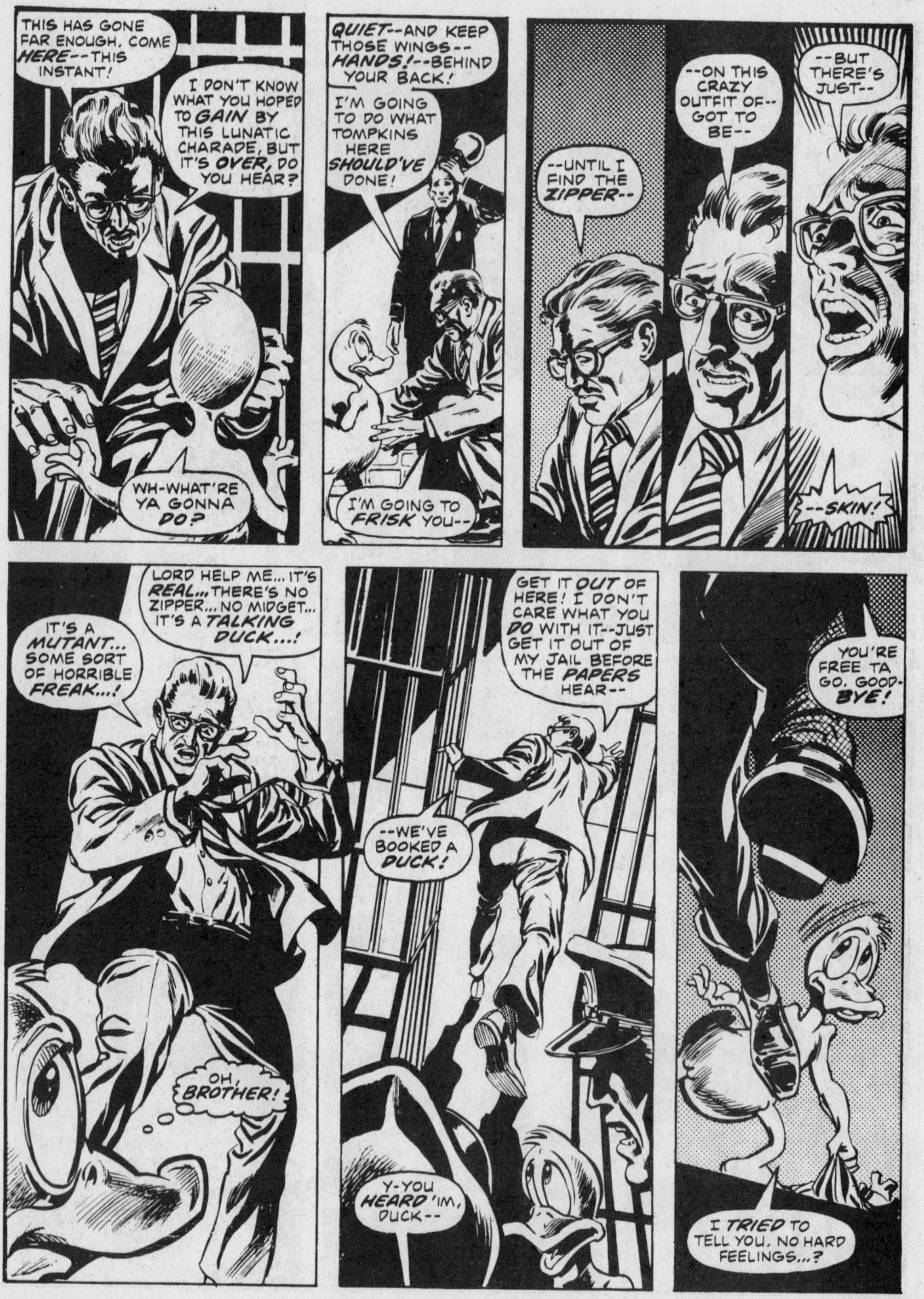
THIS HAS GONE FAR ENOUGH. COME HERE--THIS INSTANT!
I DON'T KNOW WHAT YOU HOPED TO GAIN BY THIS LUNATIC CHARADE, BUT IT'S OVER, DO YOU HEAR?
WH-WHAT'RE YA GONNA DO?
QUIET--AND KEEP THOSE WINGS--HANDS!--BEHIND YOUR BACK!
I'M GOING TO DO WHAT TOMPKINS HERE SHOULD'VE DONE!
I'M GOING TO FRISK YOU--
--UNTIL I FIND THE ZIPPER--
--ON THIS CRAZY OUTFIT OF--GOT TO BE--
--BUT THERE'S JUST--
--SKIN!
IT'S A MUTANT... SOME SORT OF HORRIBLE FREAK...!
LORD HELP ME... IT'S REAL... THERE'S NO ZIPPER... NO MIDGET... IT'S A TALKING DUCK...!
OH, BROTHER!
GET IT OUT OF HERE! I DON'T CARE WHAT YOU DO WITH IT--JUST GET IT OUT OF MY JAIL BEFORE THE PAPERS HEAR--
--WE'VE BOOKED A DUCK!
Y-YOU HEARD 'IM, DUCK--
YOU'RE FREE TA GO. GOOD-BYE!
I TRIED TO TELL YOU. NO HARD FEELINGS...?

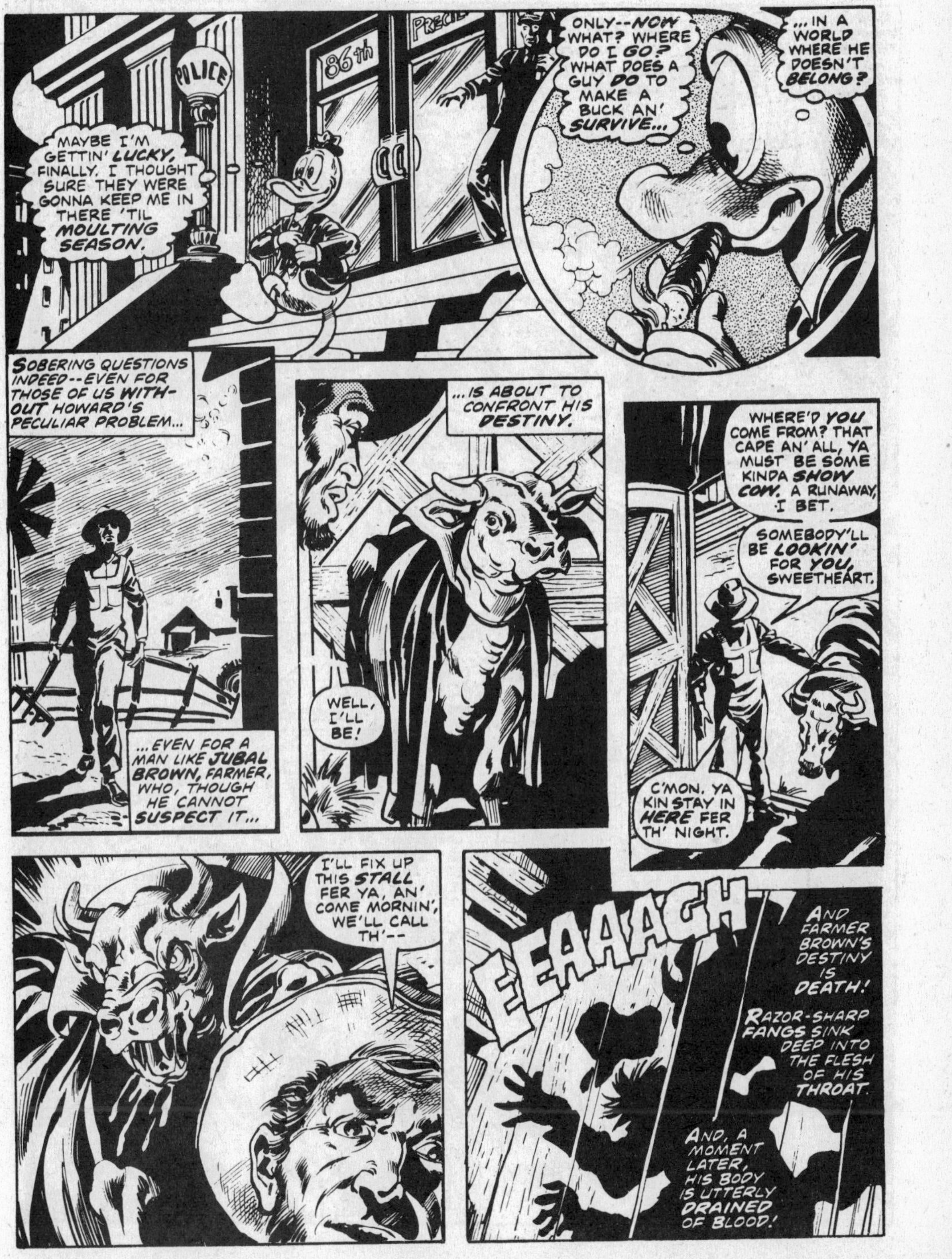
MAYBE I'M GETTIN' LUCKY, FINALLY. I THOUGHT SURE THEY WERE GONNA KEEP ME IN THERE 'TIL MOULTING SEASON.
POLICE
86th
PRECI
ONLY--NOW WHAT? WHERE DO I GO? WHAT DOES A GUY DO TO MAKE A BUCK AN' SURVIVE...
...IN A WORLD WHERE HE DOESN'T BELONG?
SOBERING QUESTIONS INDEED--EVEN FOR THOSE OF US WITHOUT HOWARD'S PECULIAR PROBLEM...
...EVEN FOR A MAN LIKE JUBAL BROWN, FARMER, WHO, THOUGH HE CANNOT SUSPECT IT...
...IS ABOUT TO CONFRONT HIS DESTINY.
WELL, I'LL BE!
WHERE'D YOU COME FROM? THAT CAPE AN' ALL, YA MUST BE SOME KINDA SHOW COW. A RUNAWAY, I BET.
SOMEBODY'LL BE LOOKIN' FOR YOU, SWEETHEART.
C'MON. YA KIN STAY IN HERE FER TH' NIGHT.
I'LL FIX UP THIS STALL FER YA, AN' COME MORNIN', WE'LL CALL TH'--
EEAAAGH
AND FARMER BROWN'S DESTINY IS DEATH!
RAZOR-SHARP FANGS SINK DEEP INTO THE FLESH OF HIS THROAT.
AND, A MOMENT LATER, HIS BODY IS UTTERLY DRAINED OF BLOOD!

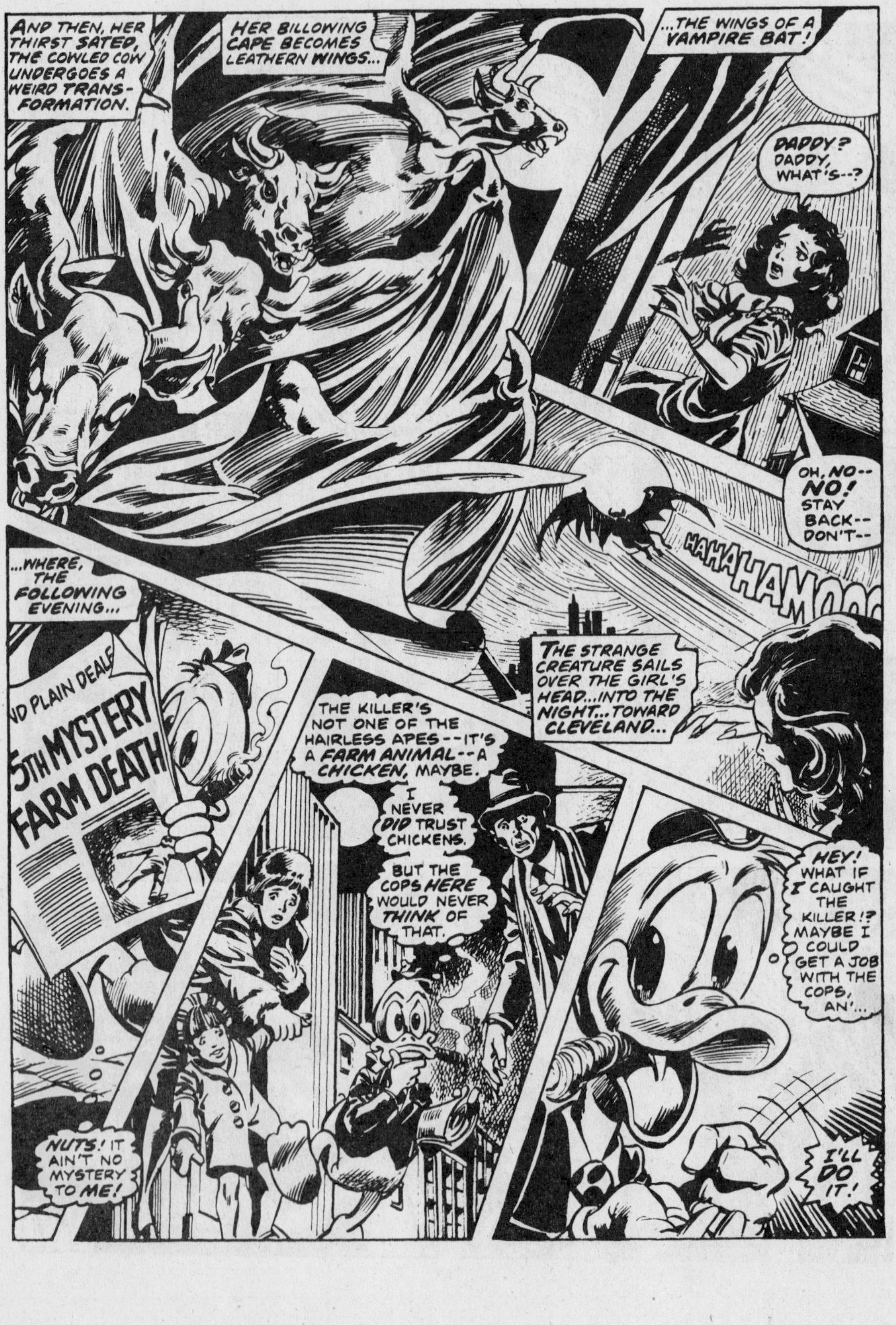
AND THEN, HER THIRST SATED, THE COWLED COW UNDERGOES A WEIRD TRANS-FORMATION.
HER BILLOWING CAPE BECOMES LEATHERN WINGS...
...THE WINGS OF A VAMPIRE BAT!
DADDY? DADDY, WHAT'S--?
OH, NO--NO! STAY BACK--DON'T--
HAHAHAMOOO
THE STRANGE CREATURE SAILS OVER THE GIRL'S HEAD...INTO THE NIGHT...TOWARD CLEVELAND...
...WHERE, THE FOLLOWING EVENING...
ND PLAIN DEALE
5TH MYSTERY FARM DEATH
NUTS! IT AIN'T NO MYSTERY TO ME!
THE KILLER'S NOT ONE OF THE HAIRLESS APES--IT'S A FARM ANIMAL--A CHICKEN, MAYBE.
I NEVER DID TRUST CHICKENS.
BUT THE COPS HERE WOULD NEVER THINK OF THAT.
HEY! WHAT IF I CAUGHT THE KILLER!? MAYBE I COULD GET A JOB WITH THE COPS, AN'...
I'LL DO IT!

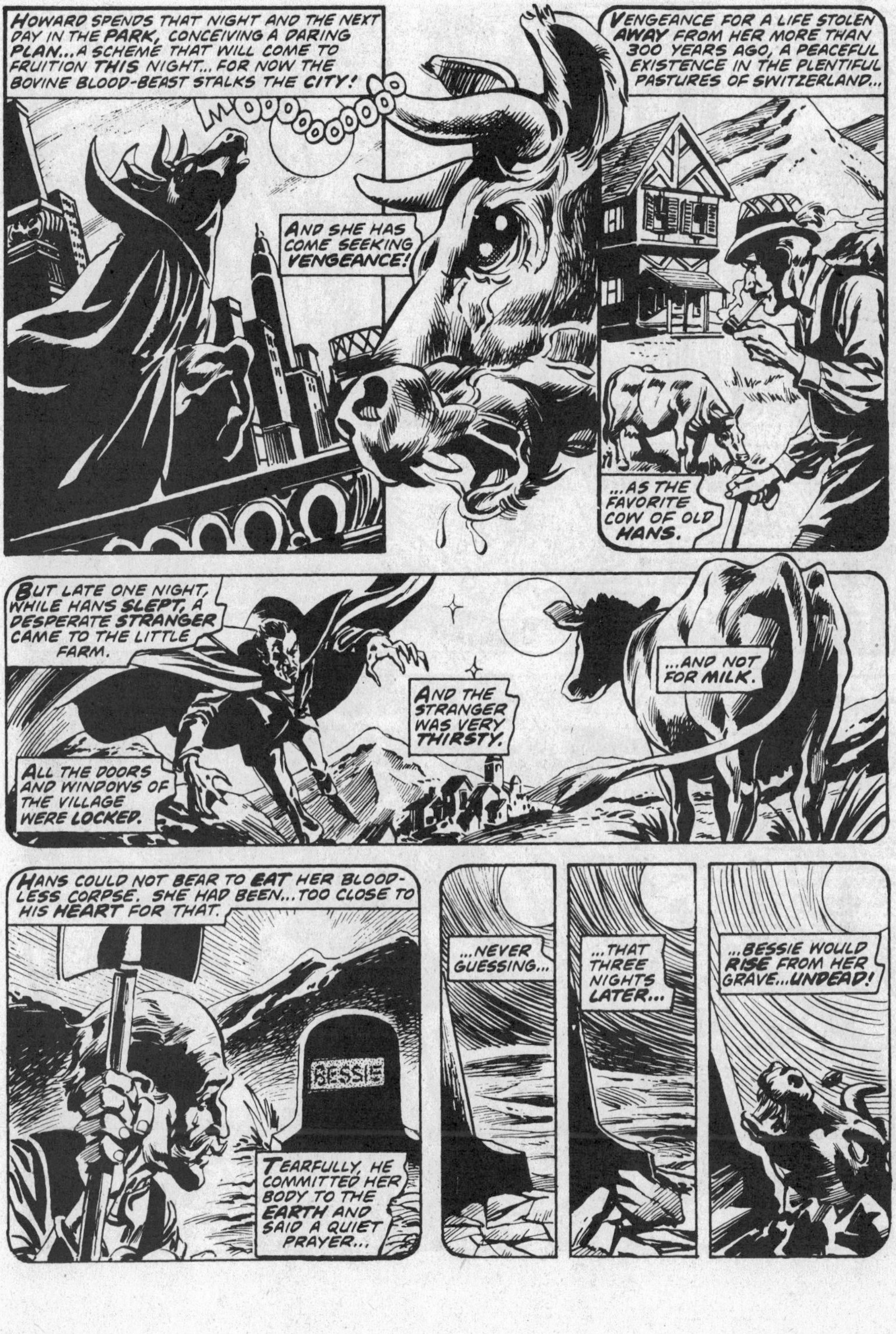
HOWARD SPENDS THAT NIGHT AND THE NEXT DAY IN THE PARK, CONCEIVING A DARING PLAN... A SCHEME THAT WILL COME TO FRUITION THIS NIGHT... FOR NOW THE BOVINE BLOOD-BEAST STALKS THE CITY!
MOOOOOOOOOOO
AND SHE HAS COME SEEKING VENGEANCE!
VENGEANCE FOR A LIFE STOLEN AWAY FROM HER MORE THAN 300 YEARS AGO, A PEACEFUL EXISTENCE IN THE PLENTIFUL PASTURES OF SWITZERLAND...
...AS THE FAVORITE COW OF OLD HANS.
BUT LATE ONE NIGHT, WHILE HANS SLEPT, A DESPERATE STRANGER CAME TO THE LITTLE FARM.
ALL THE DOORS AND WINDOWS OF THE VILLAGE WERE LOCKED.
AND THE STRANGER WAS VERY THIRSTY.
...AND NOT FOR MILK.
HANS COULD NOT BEAR TO EAT HER BLOODLESS CORPSE. SHE HAD BEEN... TOO CLOSE TO HIS HEART FOR THAT.
BESSIE
TEARFULLY, HE COMMITTED HER BODY TO THE EARTH AND SAID A QUIET PRAYER...
...NEVER GUESSING...
...THAT THREE NIGHTS LATER...
...BESSIE WOULD RISE FROM HER GRAVE...UNDEAD!

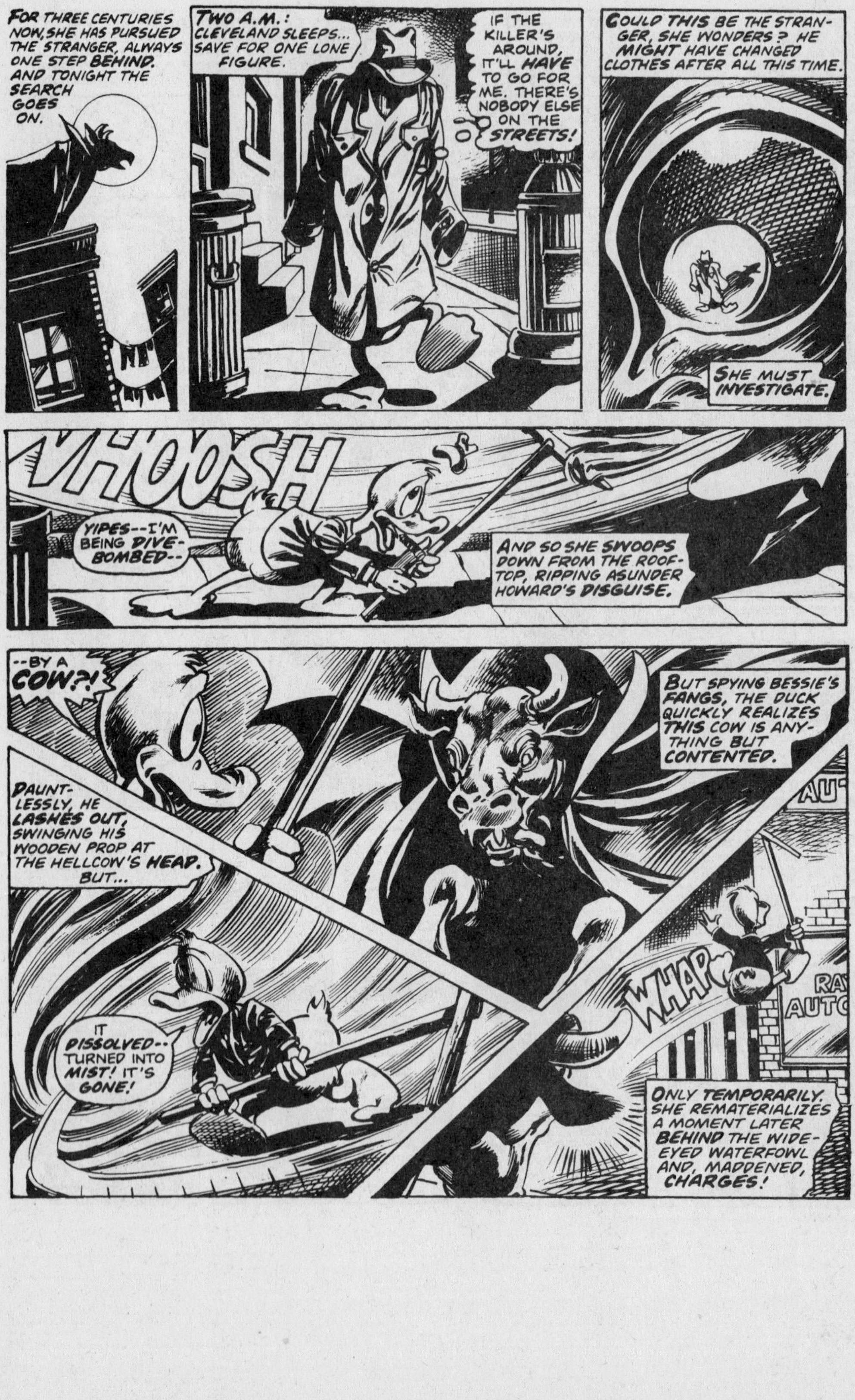
FOR THREE CENTURIES NOW, SHE HAS PURSUED THE STRANGER, ALWAYS ONE STEP BEHIND. AND TONIGHT THE SEARCH GOES ON.
TWO A.M.: CLEVELAND SLEEPS... SAVE FOR ONE LONE FIGURE.
IF THE KILLER'S AROUND, IT'LL HAVE TO GO FOR ME. THERE'S NOBODY ELSE ON THE STREETS!
COULD THIS BE THE STRANGER, SHE WONDERS? HE MIGHT HAVE CHANGED CLOTHES AFTER ALL THIS TIME.
SHE MUST INVESTIGATE.
WHOOSH
YIPES--I'M BEING DIVE-BOMBED--
AND SO SHE SWOOPS DOWN FROM THE ROOFTOP, RIPPING ASUNDER HOWARD'S DISGUISE.
--BY A COW?!
BUT SPYING BESSIE'S FANGS, THE DUCK QUICKLY REALIZES THIS COW IS ANYTHING BUT CONTENTED.
DAUNTLESSLY, HE LASHES OUT, SWINGING HIS WOODEN PROP AT THE HELLCOW'S HEAD. BUT...
IT DISSOLVED--TURNED INTO MIST! IT'S GONE!
WHAP
ONLY TEMPORARILY. SHE REMATERIALIZES A MOMENT LATER BEHIND THE WIDE-EYED WATERFOWL AND, MADDENED, CHARGES!

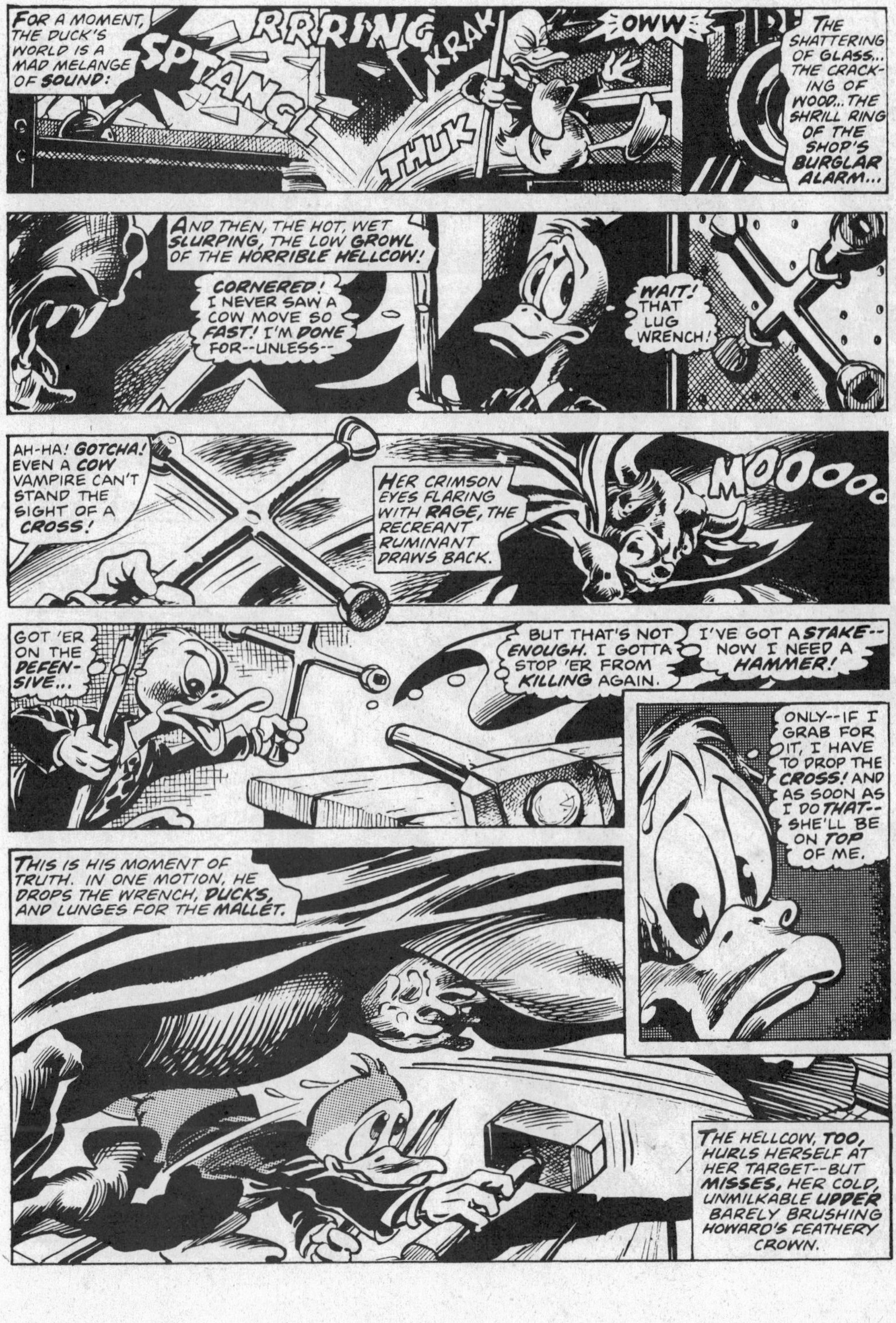

FOR A MOMENT, THE DUCK'S WORLD IS A MAD MELANGE OF SOUND:
SPTANGL
RRRING
KRAK
THUK
OWW
THE SHATTERING OF GLASS... THE CRACKING OF WOOD... THE SHRILL RING OF THE SHOP'S BURGLAR ALARM...
AND THEN, THE HOT, WET SLURPING, THE LOW GROWL OF THE HORRIBLE HELLCOW!
CORNERED! I NEVER SAW A COW MOVE SO FAST! I'M DONE FOR--UNLESS--
WAIT! THAT LUG WRENCH!
AH-HA! GOTCHA! EVEN A COW VAMPIRE CAN'T STAND THE SIGHT OF A CROSS!
HER CRIMSON EYES FLARING WITH RAGE, THE RECREANT RUMINANT DRAWS BACK.
MOOOOO
GOT 'ER ON THE DEFENSIVE...
BUT THAT'S NOT ENOUGH. I GOTTA STOP 'ER FROM KILLING AGAIN.
I'VE GOT A STAKE-- NOW I NEED A HAMMER!
ONLY--IF I GRAB FOR IT, I HAVE TO DROP THE CROSS! AND AS SOON AS I DO THAT--SHE'LL BE ON TOP OF ME.
THIS IS HIS MOMENT OF TRUTH. IN ONE MOTION, HE DROPS THE WRENCH, DUCKS, AND LUNGES FOR THE MALLET.
THE HELLCOW, TOO, HURLS HERSELF AT HER TARGET--BUT MISSES, HER COLD, UNMILKABLE UDDER BARELY BRUSHING HOWARD'S FEATHERY CROWN.

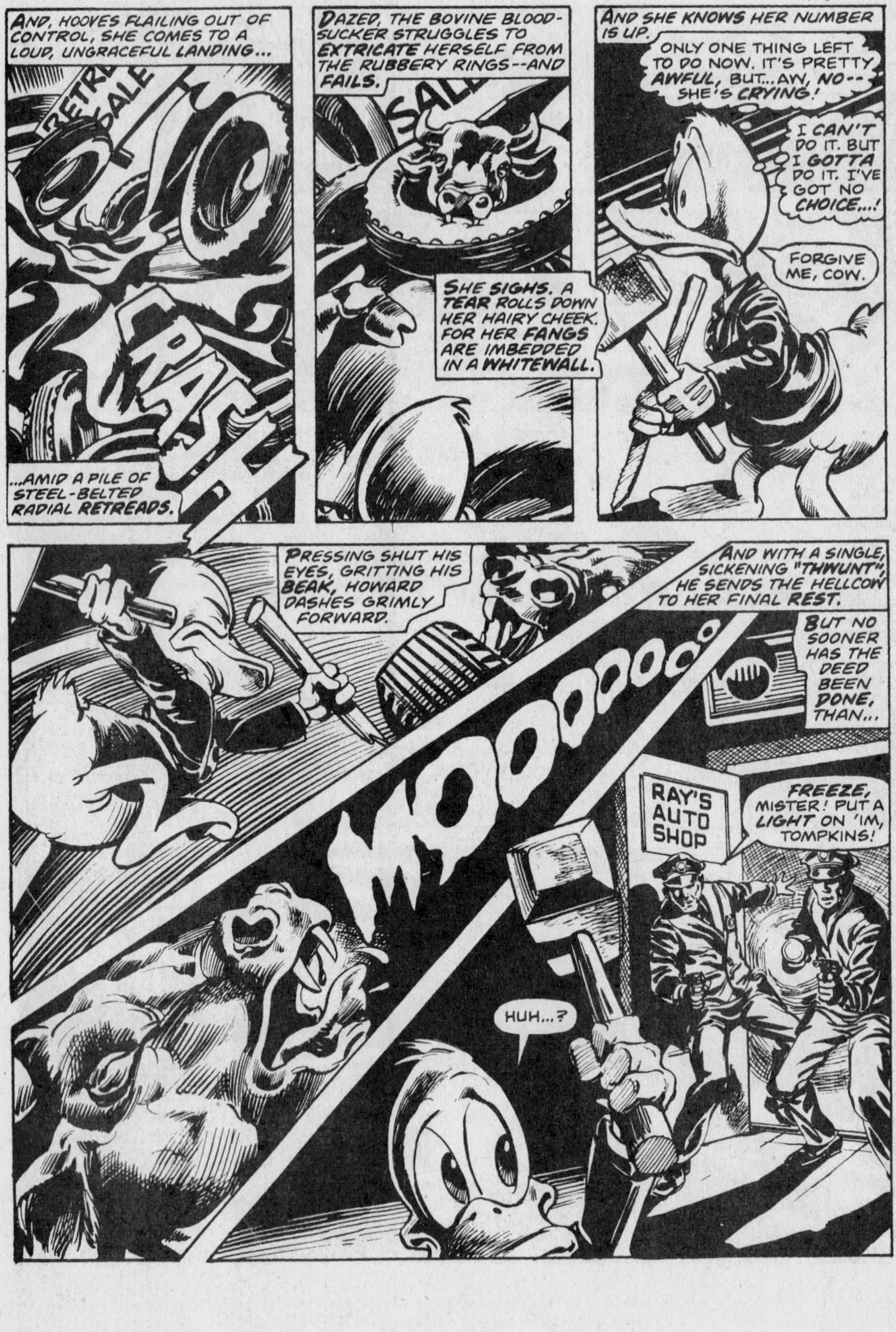
AND, HOOVES FLAILING OUT OF CONTROL, SHE COMES TO A LOUD, UNGRACEFUL LANDING...
RETREAD SALE
CRASH
...AMID A PILE OF STEEL-BELTED RADIAL RETREADS.
DAZED, THE BOVINE BLOOD-SUCKER STRUGGLES TO EXTRICATE HERSELF FROM THE RUBBERY RINGS--AND FAILS.
SALE
SHE SIGHS. A TEAR ROLLS DOWN HER HAIRY CHEEK. FOR HER FANGS ARE IMBEDDED IN A WHITEWALL.
AND SHE KNOWS HER NUMBER IS UP.
ONLY ONE THING LEFT TO DO NOW. IT'S PRETTY AWFUL, BUT...AW, NO-- SHE'S CRYING!
I CAN'T DO IT. BUT I GOTTA DO IT. I'VE GOT NO CHOICE...!
FORGIVE ME, COW.
PRESSING SHUT HIS EYES, GRITTING HIS BEAK, HOWARD DASHES GRIMLY FORWARD.
AND WITH A SINGLE, SICKENING "THWUNT", HE SENDS THE HELLCOW TO HER FINAL REST.
MOOOOOOO
BUT NO SOONER HAS THE DEED BEEN DONE, THAN...
RAY'S AUTO SHOP
FREEZE, MISTER! PUT A LIGHT ON 'IM, TOMPKINS!
HUH...?

TOMPKINS! LOOK-- IT'S ME--HOWARD! I DID IT! I GOT THE FARM KILLER!

TOMPKINS...?

AC

TOMPKINS-- WAIT! WHERE ARE YA GOIN'? DON'T LEAVE!

STOP! COME BACK! THIS COW WAS THE--

TOMPKINS?

DON'T...

=WAAAAAAAUGH= OF ALL THE MISERABLE, UNGRATEFUL, CORRUPT, GRAFT-RIDDEN--!

DROP DEAD, TOMPKINS-- SEE IF I CARE!!

BUT OUT ON THE STREET, HE WATCHES WITH A TWINGE OF SADNESS AS THE SQUAD CAR PULLS AWAY. IT WOULD'VE BEEN...NICE.

STEADY WORK... A ROOF OVER HIS HEAD...A RESPECTABLE POSITION IN SOCIETY...!

NOPE. THERE'S NO GETTING AWAY FROM IT.

IT'D SURE BEAT FACING AN UNCERTAIN FUTURE...

...IN A DARK AND THREATEN-ING WORLD...

...ALL ALONE.

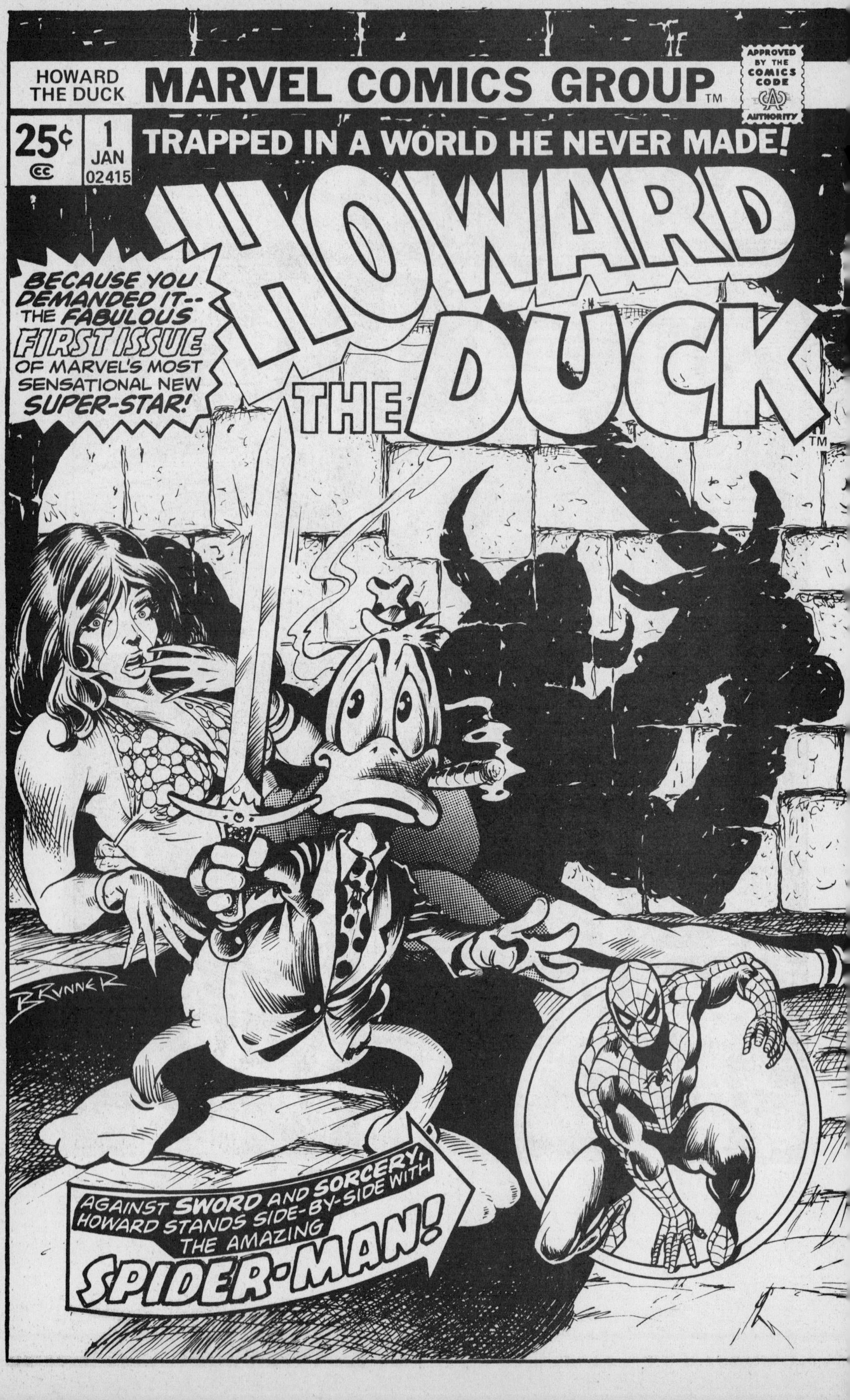

HOWARD THE DUCK
MARVEL COMICS GROUP™
APPROVED BY THE COMICS CODE AUTHORITY
25¢
1 JAN 02415
TRAPPED IN A WORLD HE NEVER MADE!
HOWARD THE DUCK™
BECAUSE YOU DEMANDED IT-- THE FABULOUS FIRST ISSUE OF MARVEL'S MOST SENSATIONAL NEW SUPER-STAR!
BRUNNER
AGAINST SWORD AND SORCERY, HOWARD STANDS SIDE-BY-SIDE WITH THE AMAZING
SPIDER-MAN!

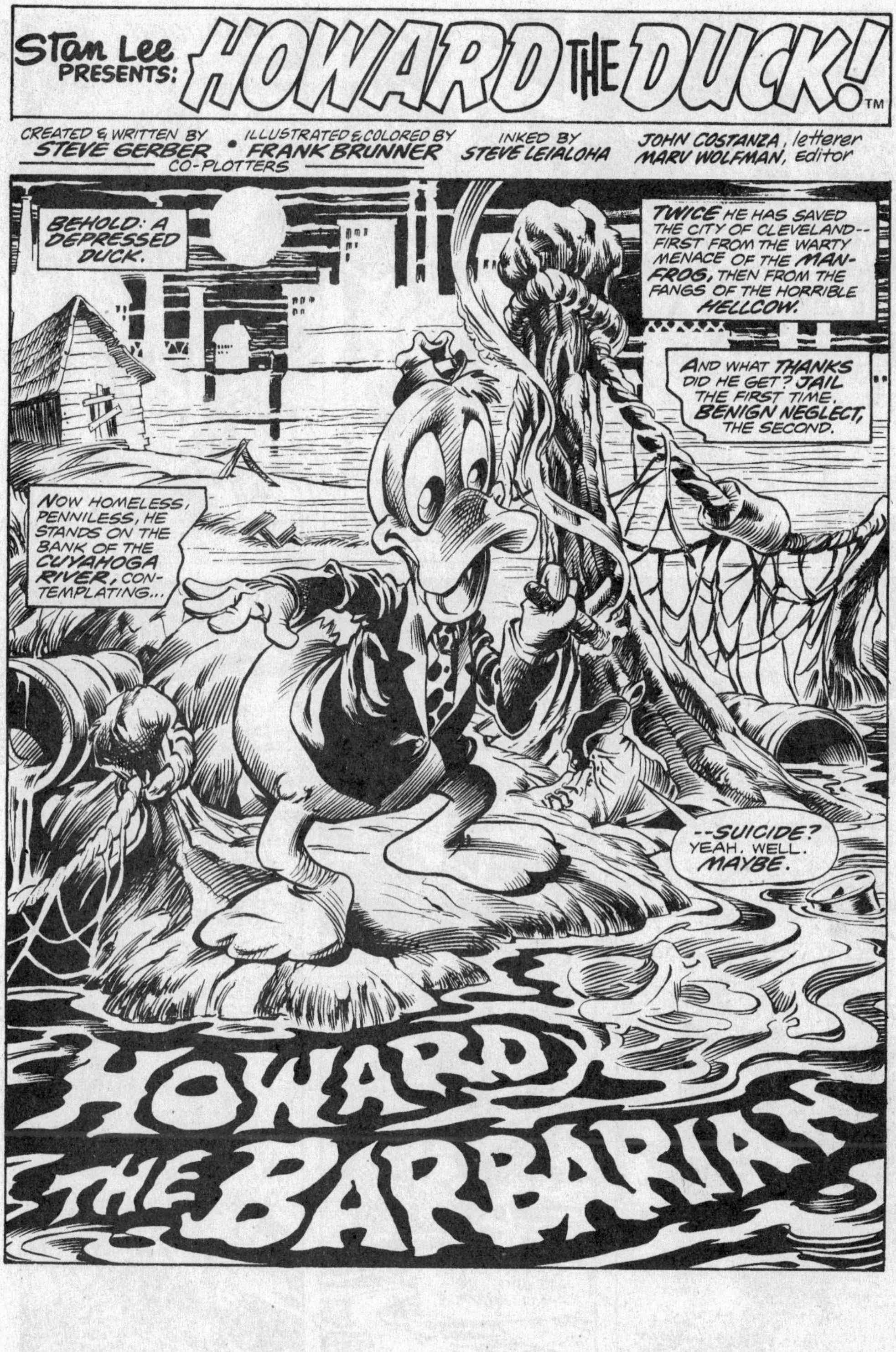
Stan Lee PRESENTS: HOWARD THE DUCK! TM
CREATED & WRITTEN BY STEVE GERBER
ILLUSTRATED & COLORED BY FRANK BRUNNER
CO-PLOTTERS
INKED BY STEVE LEIALOHA
JOHN COSTANZA, letterer
MARV WOLFMAN, editor
BEHOLD: A DEPRESSED DUCK.
TWICE HE HAS SAVED THE CITY OF CLEVELAND-- FIRST FROM THE WARTY MENACE OF THE MAN-FROG, THEN FROM THE FANGS OF THE HORRIBLE HELLCOW.
AND WHAT THANKS DID HE GET? JAIL THE FIRST TIME. BENIGN NEGLECT, THE SECOND.
NOW HOMELESS, PENNILESS, HE STANDS ON THE BANK OF THE CUYAHOGA RIVER, CONTEMPLATING...
--SUICIDE? YEAH. WELL. MAYBE.
HOWARD THE BARBARIAN

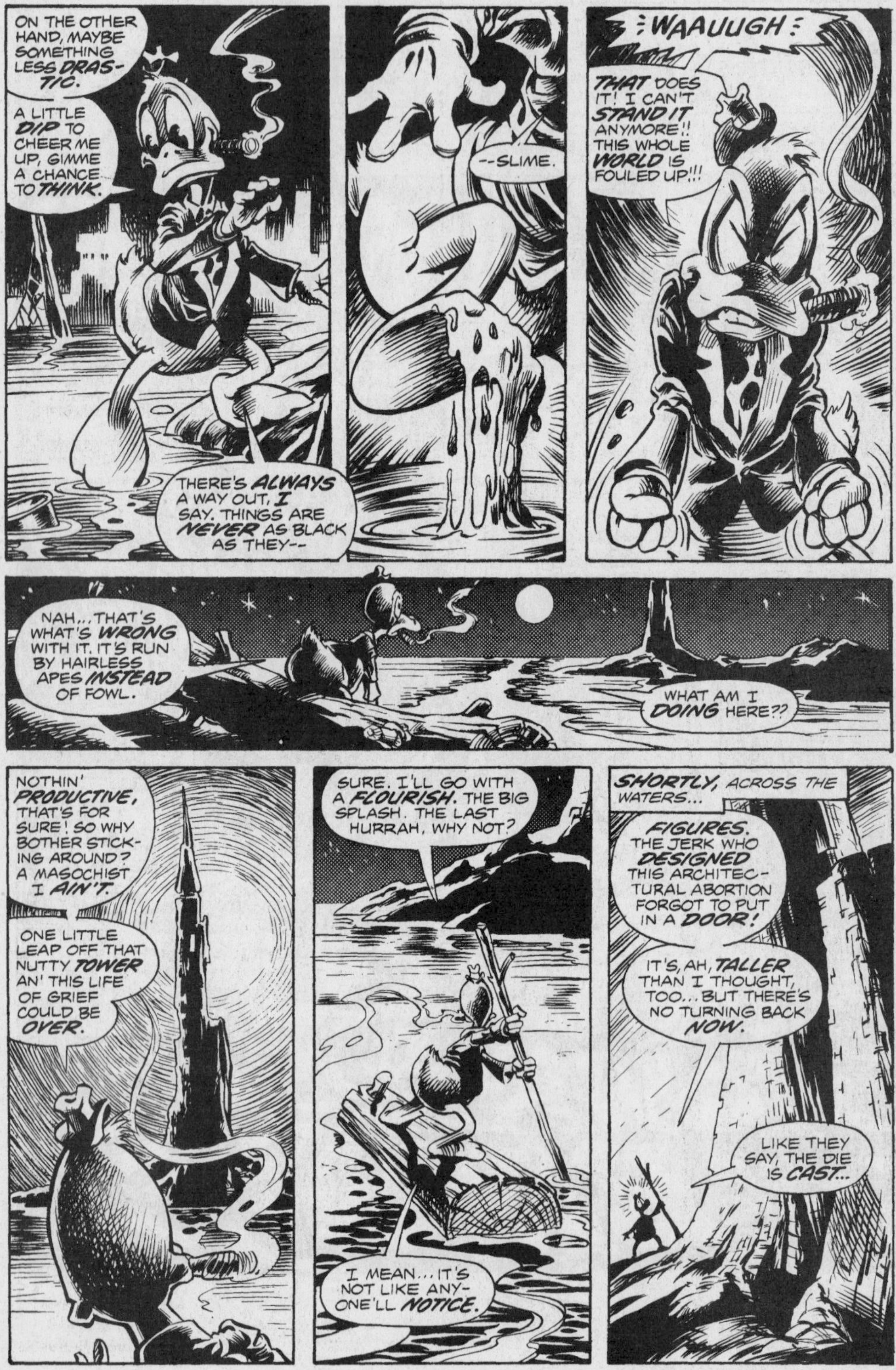
ON THE OTHER HAND, MAYBE SOMETHING LESS DRASTIC.
A LITTLE DIP TO CHEER ME UP, GIMME A CHANCE TO THINK.
THERE'S ALWAYS A WAY OUT, I SAY. THINGS ARE NEVER AS BLACK AS THEY--
--SLIME.
WAAUUGH
THAT DOES IT! I CAN'T STAND IT ANYMORE!! THIS WHOLE WORLD IS FOULED UP!!!
NAH... THAT'S WHAT'S WRONG WITH IT. IT'S RUN BY HAIRLESS APES INSTEAD OF FOWL.
WHAT AM I DOING HERE??
NOTHIN' PRODUCTIVE, THAT'S FOR SURE! SO WHY BOTHER STICKING AROUND? A MASOCHIST I AIN'T.
ONE LITTLE LEAP OFF THAT NUTTY TOWER AN' THIS LIFE OF GRIEF COULD BE OVER.
SURE. I'LL GO WITH A FLOURISH. THE BIG SPLASH. THE LAST HURRAH. WHY NOT?
I MEAN... IT'S NOT LIKE ANYONE'LL NOTICE.
SHORTLY, ACROSS THE WATERS...
FIGURES. THE JERK WHO DESIGNED THIS ARCHITECTURAL ABORTION FORGOT TO PUT IN A DOOR!
IT'S, AH, TALLER THAN I THOUGHT, TOO... BUT THERE'S NO TURNING BACK NOW.
LIKE THEY SAY, THE DIE IS CAST...

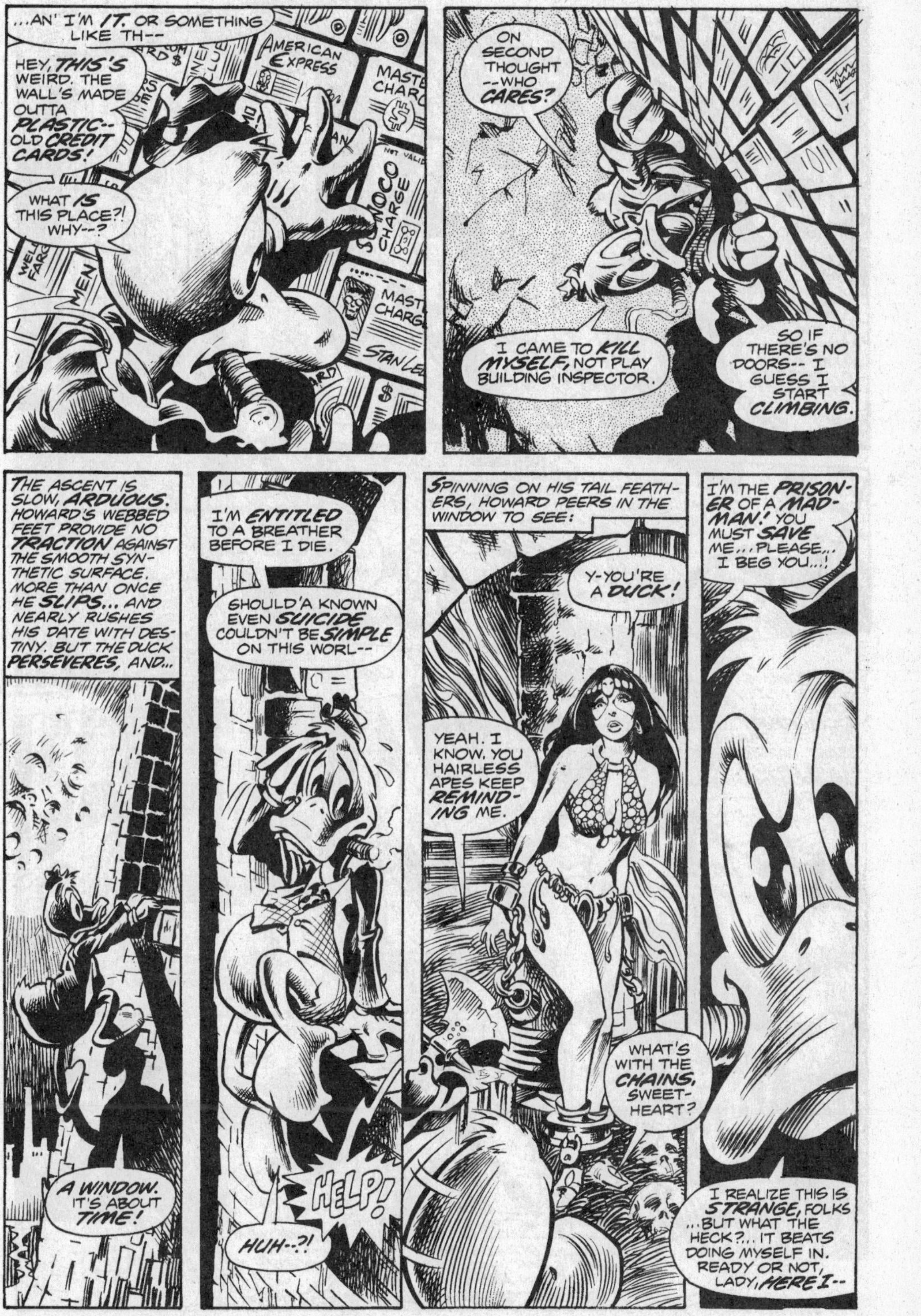
...AN' I'M IT. OR SOMETHING LIKE TH--
HEY, THIS'S WEIRD. THE WALL'S MADE OUTTA PLASTIC-- OLD CREDIT CARDS!
WHAT IS THIS PLACE?! WHY--?
AMERICAN EXPRESS
MASTER CHARGE
SUNOCO CHARGE
ON SECOND THOUGHT --WHO CARES?
I CAME TO KILL MYSELF, NOT PLAY BUILDING INSPECTOR.
SO IF THERE'S NO DOORS-- I GUESS I START CLIMBING.
THE ASCENT IS SLOW, ARDUOUS. HOWARD'S WEBBED FEET PROVIDE NO TRACTION AGAINST THE SMOOTH SYNTHETIC SURFACE. MORE THAN ONCE HE SLIPS... AND NEARLY RUSHES HIS DATE WITH DESTINY. BUT THE DUCK PERSEVERES, AND...
A WINDOW. IT'S ABOUT TIME!
I'M ENTITLED TO A BREATHER BEFORE I DIE.
SHOULD'A KNOWN EVEN SUICIDE COULDN'T BE SIMPLE ON THIS WORL--
HELP!
HUH--?!
SPINNING ON HIS TAIL FEATHERS, HOWARD PEERS IN THE WINDOW TO SEE:
Y-YOU'RE A DUCK!
YEAH. I KNOW. YOU HAIRLESS APES KEEP REMINDING ME.
WHAT'S WITH THE CHAINS, SWEETHEART?
I'M THE PRISONER OF A MADMAN! YOU MUST SAVE ME... PLEASE... I BEG YOU...!
I REALIZE THIS IS STRANGE, FOLKS ...BUT WHAT THE HECK?... IT BEATS DOING MYSELF IN. READY OR NOT, LADY, HERE I--

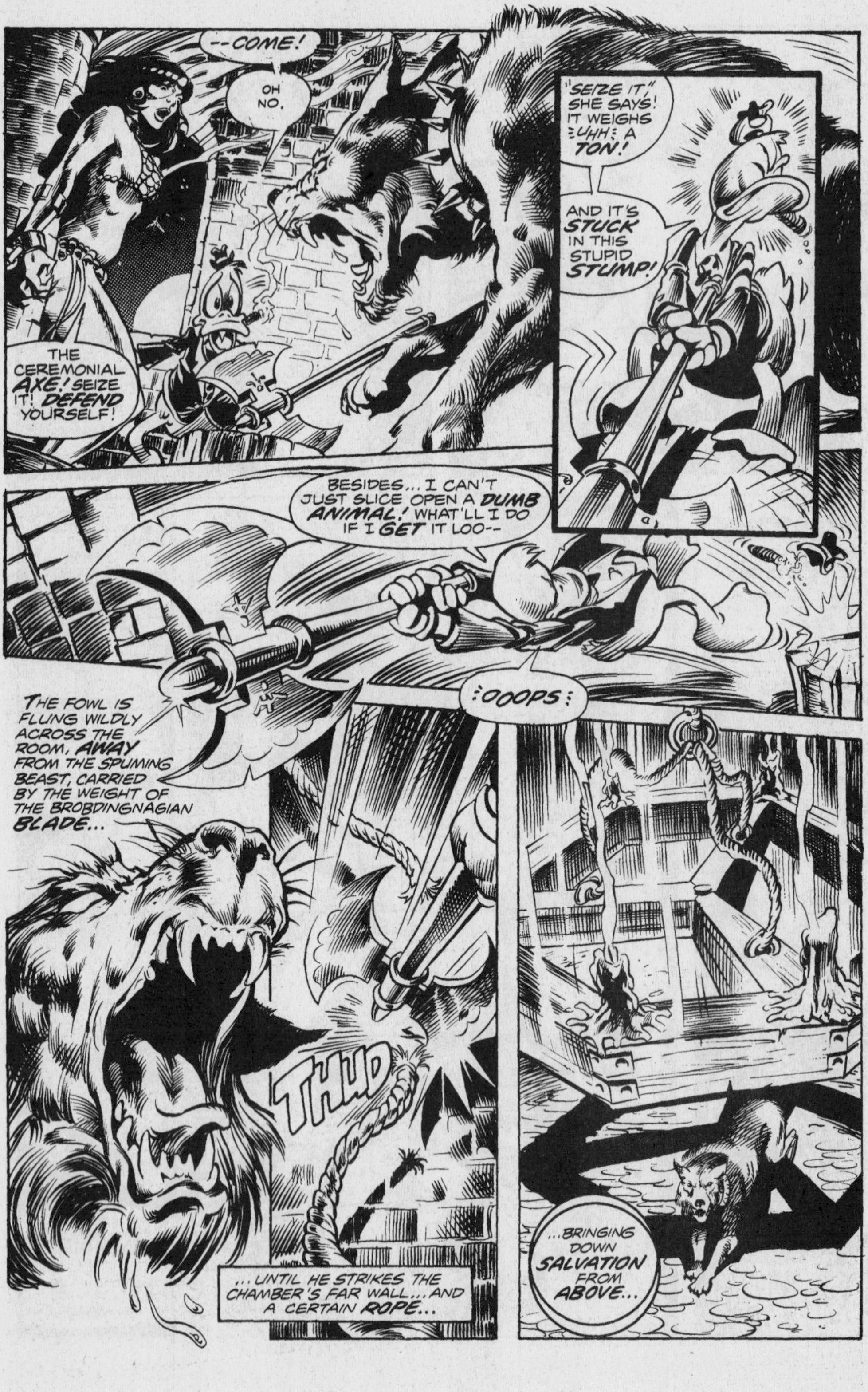
--COME!
OH NO.
THE CEREMONIAL AXE! SEIZE IT! DEFEND YOURSELF!
"SEIZE IT," SHE SAYS! IT WEIGHS UHH A TON!
AND IT'S STUCK IN THIS STUPID STUMP!
BESIDES... I CAN'T JUST SLICE OPEN A DUMB ANIMAL! WHAT'LL I DO IF I GET IT LOO--
OOOPS
THE FOWL IS FLUNG WILDLY ACROSS THE ROOM, AWAY FROM THE SPUMING BEAST, CARRIED BY THE WEIGHT OF THE BROBDINGNAGIAN BLADE...
THUD
...UNTIL HE STRIKES THE CHAMBER'S FAR WALL... AND A CERTAIN ROPE...
...BRINGING DOWN SALVATION FROM ABOVE...

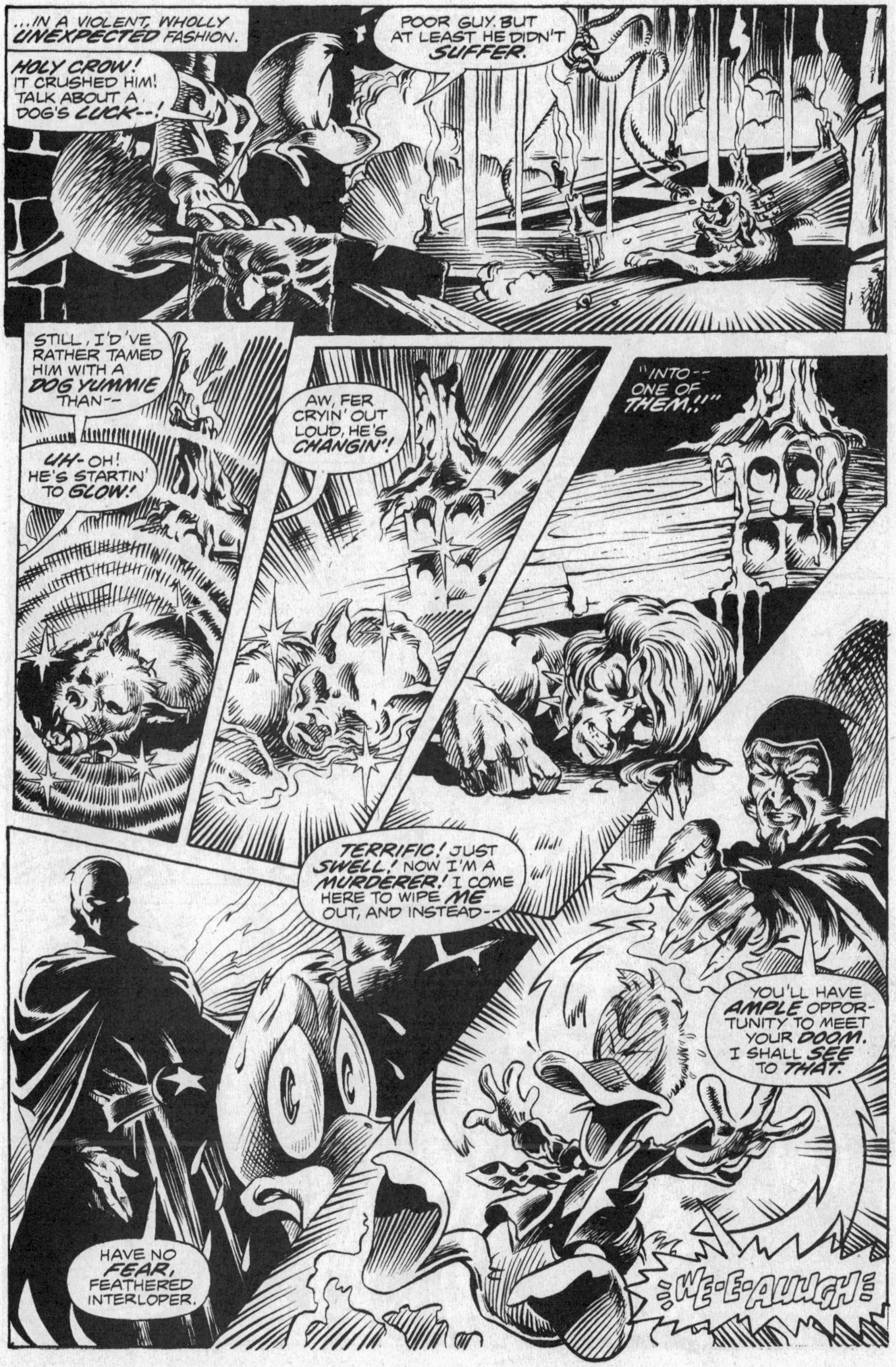

...IN A VIOLENT, WHOLLY UNEXPECTED FASHION.
HOLY CROW! IT CRUSHED HIM! TALK ABOUT A DOG'S LUCK--!
POOR GUY. BUT AT LEAST HE DIDN'T SUFFER.
STILL, I'D'VE RATHER TAMED HIM WITH A DOG YUMMIE THAN--
UH-OH! HE'S STARTIN' TO GLOW!
AW, FER CRYIN' OUT LOUD, HE'S CHANGIN'!
"INTO-- ONE OF THEM!!"
TERRIFIC! JUST SWELL! NOW I'M A MURDERER! I COME HERE TO WIPE ME OUT, AND INSTEAD--
HAVE NO FEAR, FEATHERED INTERLOPER.
YOU'LL HAVE AMPLE OPPOR-TUNITY TO MEET YOUR DOOM. I SHALL SEE TO THAT.
WE-E-AUUGH

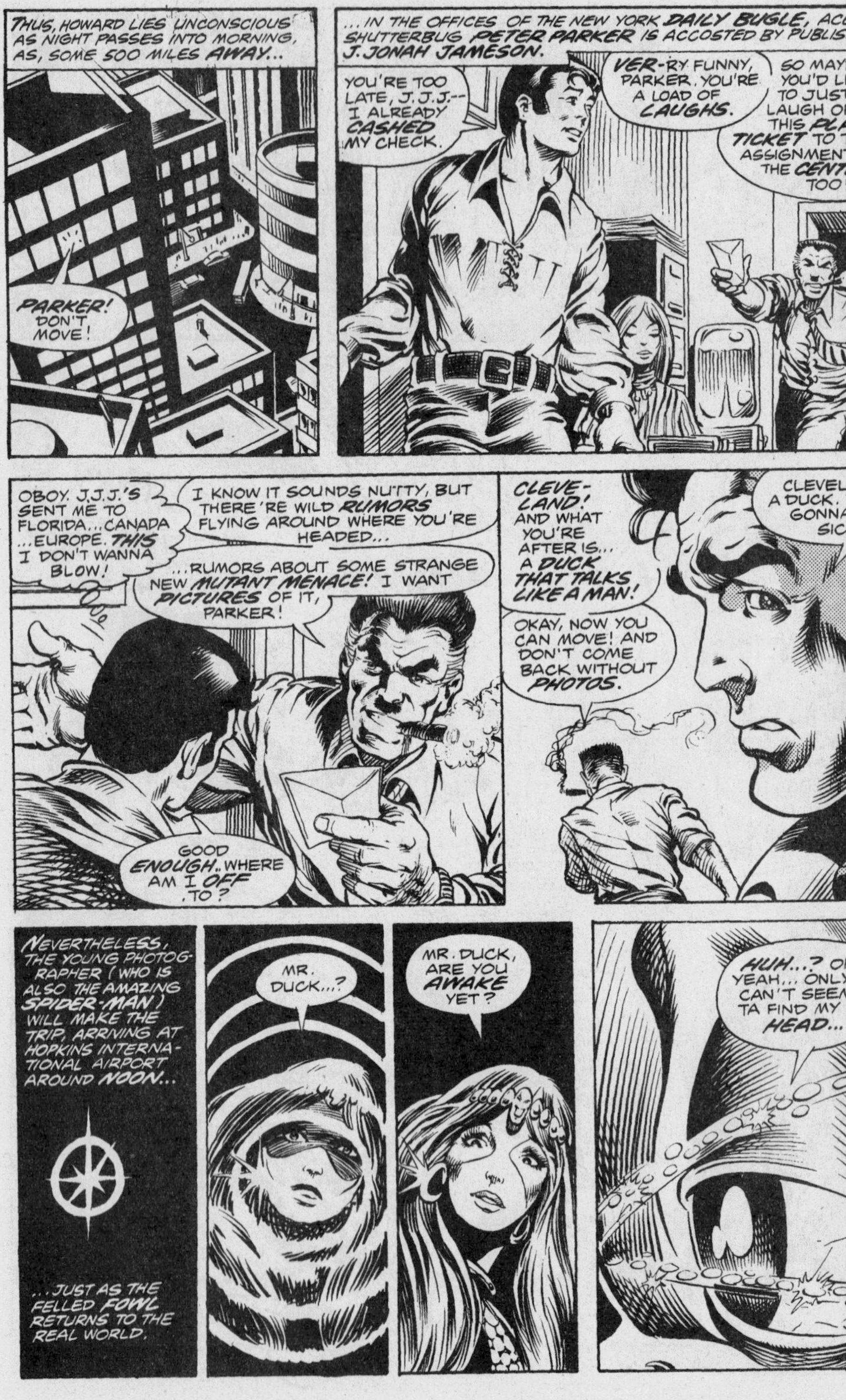
THUS, HOWARD LIES UNCONSCIOUS AS NIGHT PASSES INTO MORNING, AS, SOME 500 MILES AWAY...
PARKER! DON'T MOVE!
...IN THE OFFICES OF THE NEW YORK DAILY BUGLE, ACE SHUTTERBUG PETER PARKER IS ACCOSTED BY PUBLISHER J. JONAH JAMESON.
YOU'RE TOO LATE, J.J.J.-- I ALREADY CASHED MY CHECK.
VER-RY FUNNY, PARKER. YOU'RE A LOAD OF LAUGHS.
SO MAYBE YOU'D LIKE TO JUST LAUGH OFF THIS PLANE TICKET TO THE ASSIGNMENT OF THE CENTURY, TOO!
OBOY. J.J.J.'S SENT ME TO FLORIDA...CANADA ...EUROPE. THIS I DON'T WANNA BLOW!
I KNOW IT SOUNDS NUTTY, BUT THERE'RE WILD RUMORS FLYING AROUND WHERE YOU'RE HEADED...
...RUMORS ABOUT SOME STRANGE NEW MUTANT MENACE! I WANT PICTURES OF IT, PARKER!
GOOD ENOUGH. WHERE AM I OFF TO?
CLEVE-LAND! AND WHAT YOU'RE AFTER IS... A DUCK THAT TALKS LIKE A MAN!
OKAY, NOW YOU CAN MOVE! AND DON'T COME BACK WITHOUT PHOTOS.
CLEVELAND. A DUCK. I'M GONNA BE SICK...!
NEVERTHELESS, THE YOUNG PHOTOG-RAPHER (WHO IS ALSO THE AMAZING SPIDER-MAN) WILL MAKE THE TRIP, ARRIVING AT HOPKINS INTERNA-TIONAL AIRPORT AROUND NOON...
...JUST AS THE FELLED FOWL RETURNS TO THE REAL WORLD.
MR. DUCK...?
MR. DUCK, ARE YOU AWAKE YET?
HUH...? OH... YEAH... ONLY... CAN'T SEEM TA FIND MY HEAD...!

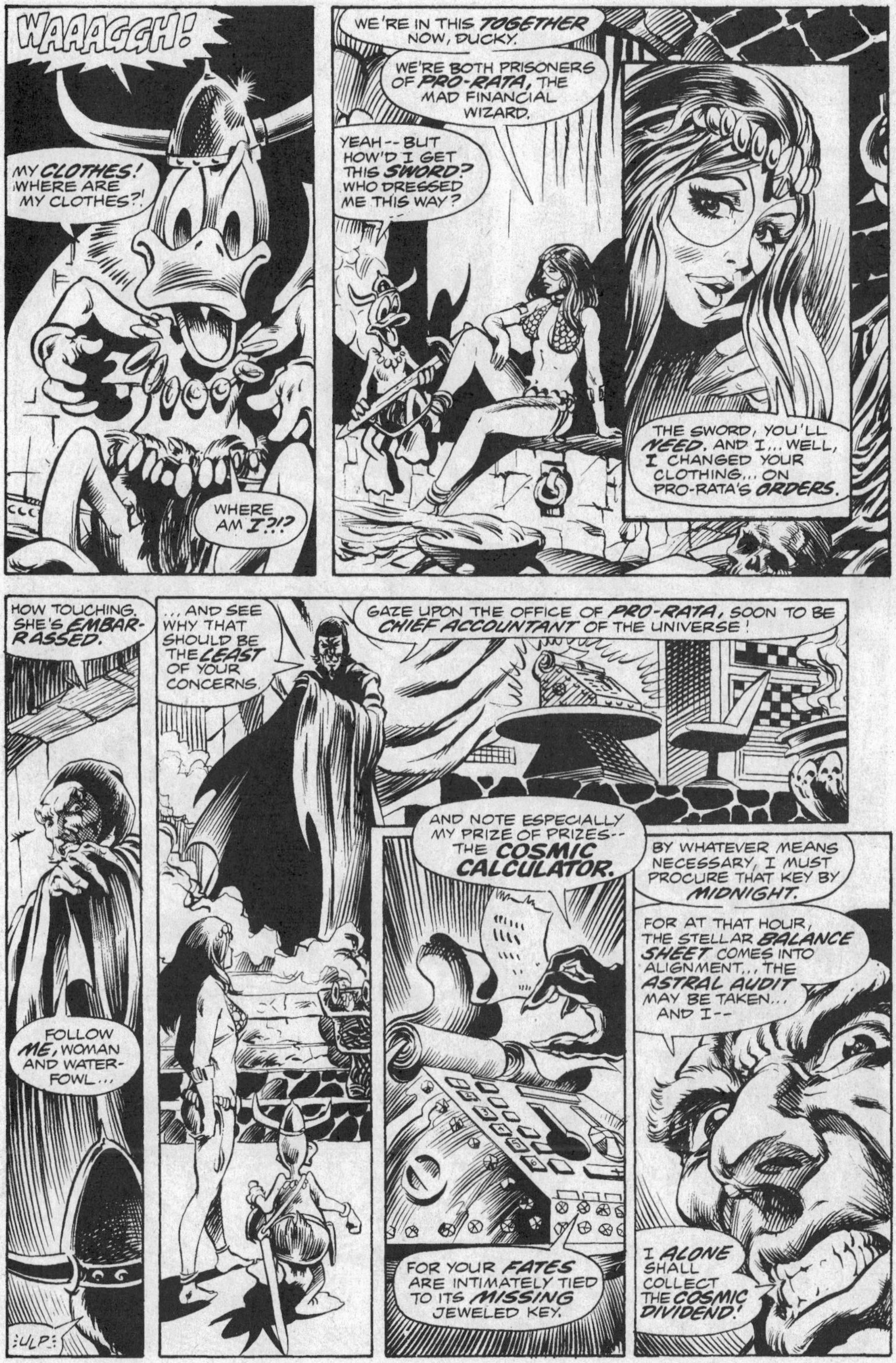
WAAAGGH!
MY CLOTHES! WHERE ARE MY CLOTHES?!
WHERE AM I?!?
WE'RE IN THIS TOGETHER NOW, DUCKY.
WE'RE BOTH PRISONERS OF PRO-RATA, THE MAD FINANCIAL WIZARD.
YEAH -- BUT HOW'D I GET THIS SWORD? WHO DRESSED ME THIS WAY?
THE SWORD, YOU'LL NEED. AND I... WELL, I CHANGED YOUR CLOTHING... ON PRO-RATA'S ORDERS.
HOW TOUCHING. SHE'S EMBARRASSED.
FOLLOW ME, WOMAN AND WATER-FOWL...
ULP
...AND SEE WHY THAT SHOULD BE THE LEAST OF YOUR CONCERNS.
GAZE UPON THE OFFICE OF PRO-RATA, SOON TO BE CHIEF ACCOUNTANT OF THE UNIVERSE!
AND NOTE ESPECIALLY MY PRIZE OF PRIZES-- THE COSMIC CALCULATOR.
FOR YOUR FATES ARE INTIMATELY TIED TO ITS MISSING JEWELED KEY.
BY WHATEVER MEANS NECESSARY, I MUST PROCURE THAT KEY BY MIDNIGHT.
FOR AT THAT HOUR, THE STELLAR BALANCE SHEET COMES INTO ALIGNMENT... THE ASTRAL AUDIT MAY BE TAKEN... AND I--
I ALONE SHALL COLLECT THE COSMIC DIVIDEND!

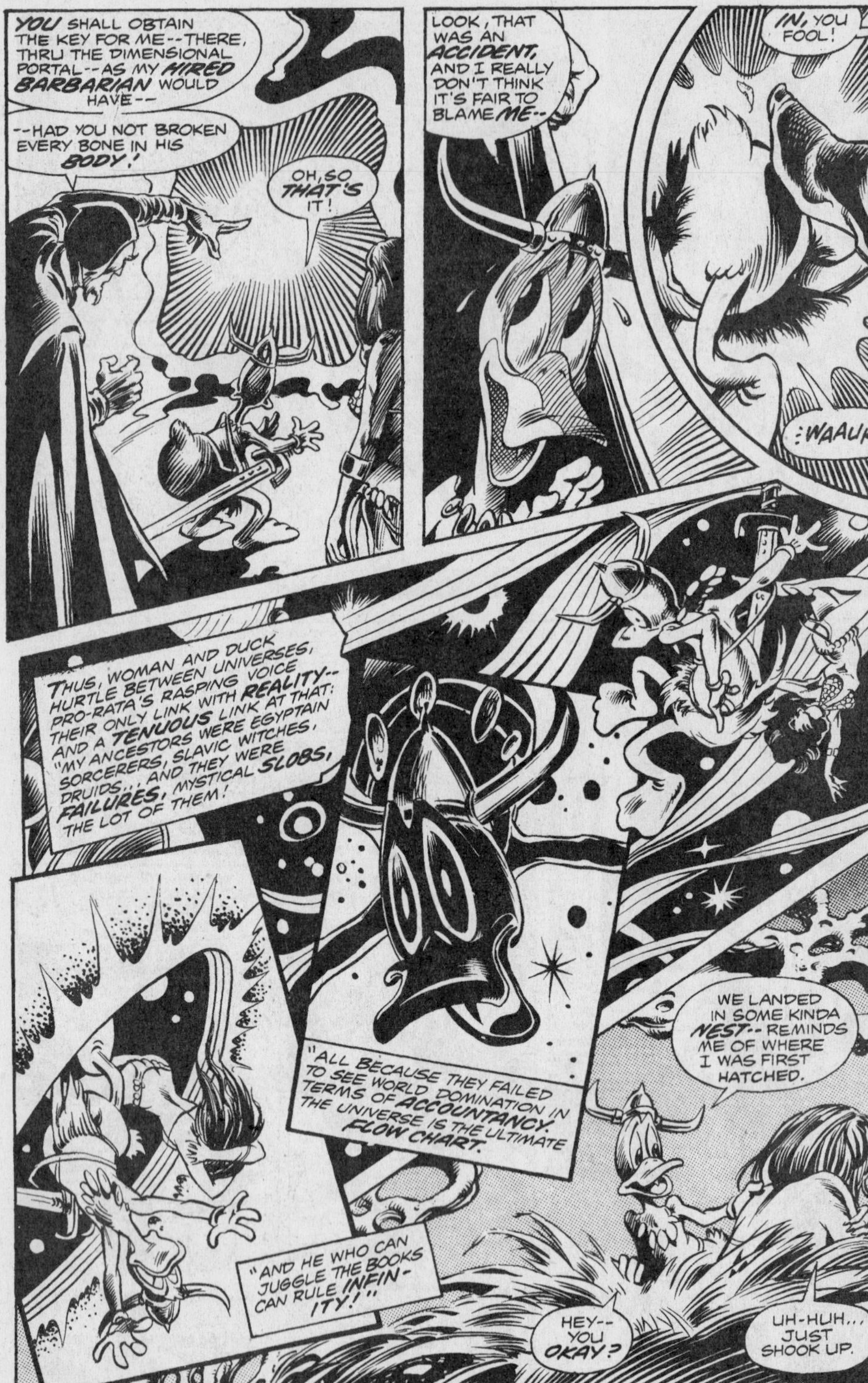
YOU SHALL OBTAIN THE KEY FOR ME--THERE, THRU THE DIMENSIONAL PORTAL--AS MY HIRED BARBARIAN WOULD HAVE--
--HAD YOU NOT BROKEN EVERY BONE IN HIS BODY!
OH, SO THAT'S IT!
LOOK, THAT WAS AN ACCIDENT, AND I REALLY DON'T THINK IT'S FAIR TO BLAME ME--
IN, YOU FOOL!
WAAUK
THUS, WOMAN AND DUCK HURTLE BETWEEN UNIVERSES, PRO-RATA'S RASPING VOICE THEIR ONLY LINK WITH REALITY-- AND A TENUOUS LINK AT THAT: "MY ANCESTORS WERE EGYPTAIN SORCERERS, SLAVIC WITCHES, DRUIDS... AND THEY WERE FAILURES, MYSTICAL SLOBS, THE LOT OF THEM!
"ALL BECAUSE THEY FAILED TO SEE WORLD DOMINATION IN TERMS OF ACCOUNTANCY. THE UNIVERSE IS THE ULTIMATE FLOW CHART.
"AND HE WHO CAN JUGGLE THE BOOKS CAN RULE INFIN-ITY!"
WE LANDED IN SOME KINDA NEST-- REMINDS ME OF WHERE I WAS FIRST HATCHED.
HEY-- YOU OKAY?
UH-HUH... JUST SHOOK UP.

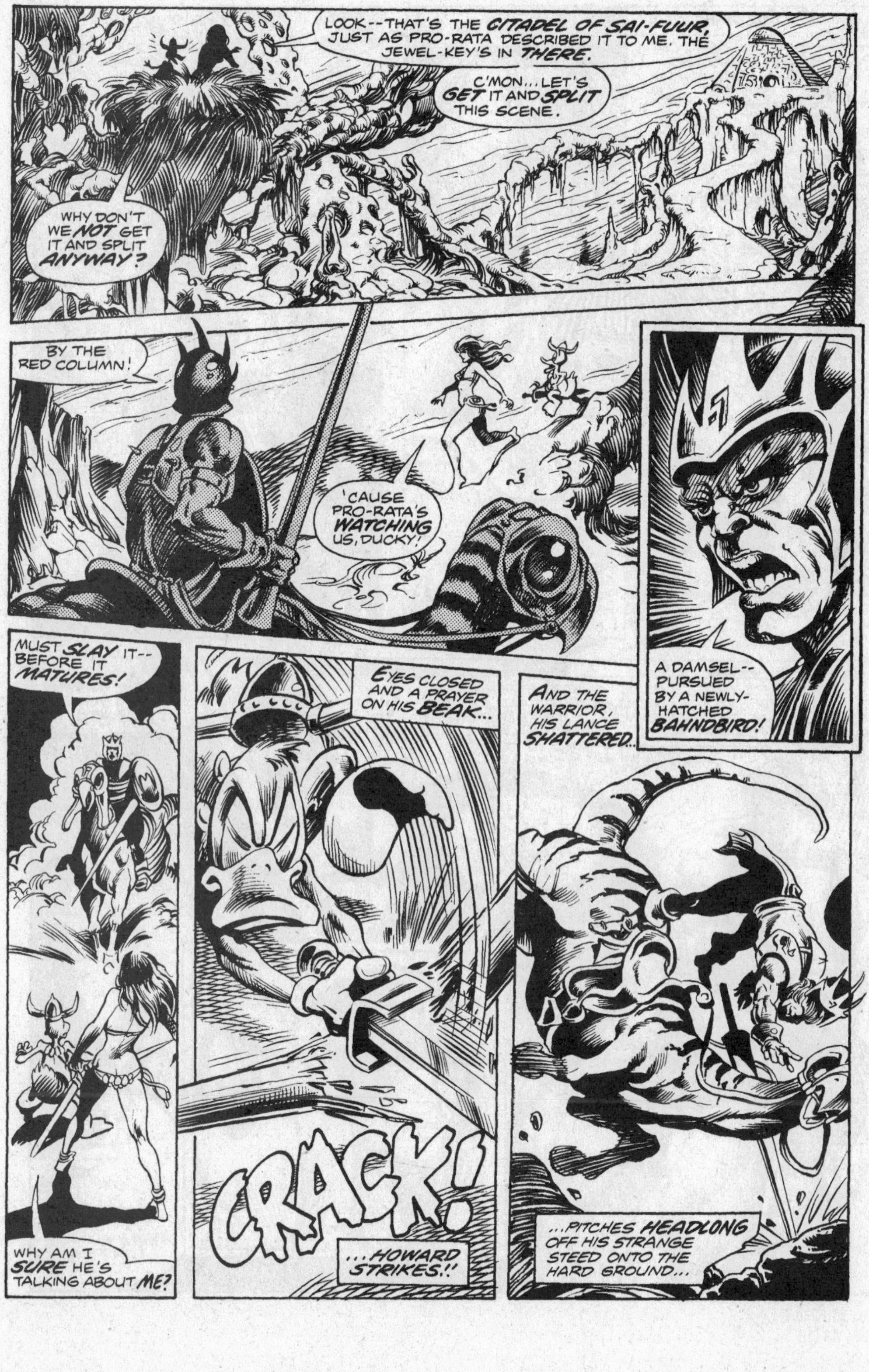
LOOK--THAT'S THE CITADEL OF SAI-FUUR, JUST AS PRO-RATA DESCRIBED IT TO ME. THE JEWEL-KEY'S IN THERE.
C'MON... LET'S GET IT AND SPLIT THIS SCENE.
WHY DON'T WE NOT GET IT AND SPLIT ANYWAY?
BY THE RED COLUMN!
'CAUSE PRO-RATA'S WATCHING US, DUCKY!
A DAMSEL--PURSUED BY A NEWLY-HATCHED BAHNDBIRD!
MUST SLAY IT--BEFORE IT MATURES!
WHY AM I SURE HE'S TALKING ABOUT ME?
EYES CLOSED AND A PRAYER ON HIS BEAK...
CRACK!
...HOWARD STRIKES!!
AND THE WARRIOR, HIS LANCE SHATTERED...
...PITCHES HEADLONG OFF HIS STRANGE STEED ONTO THE HARD GROUND...

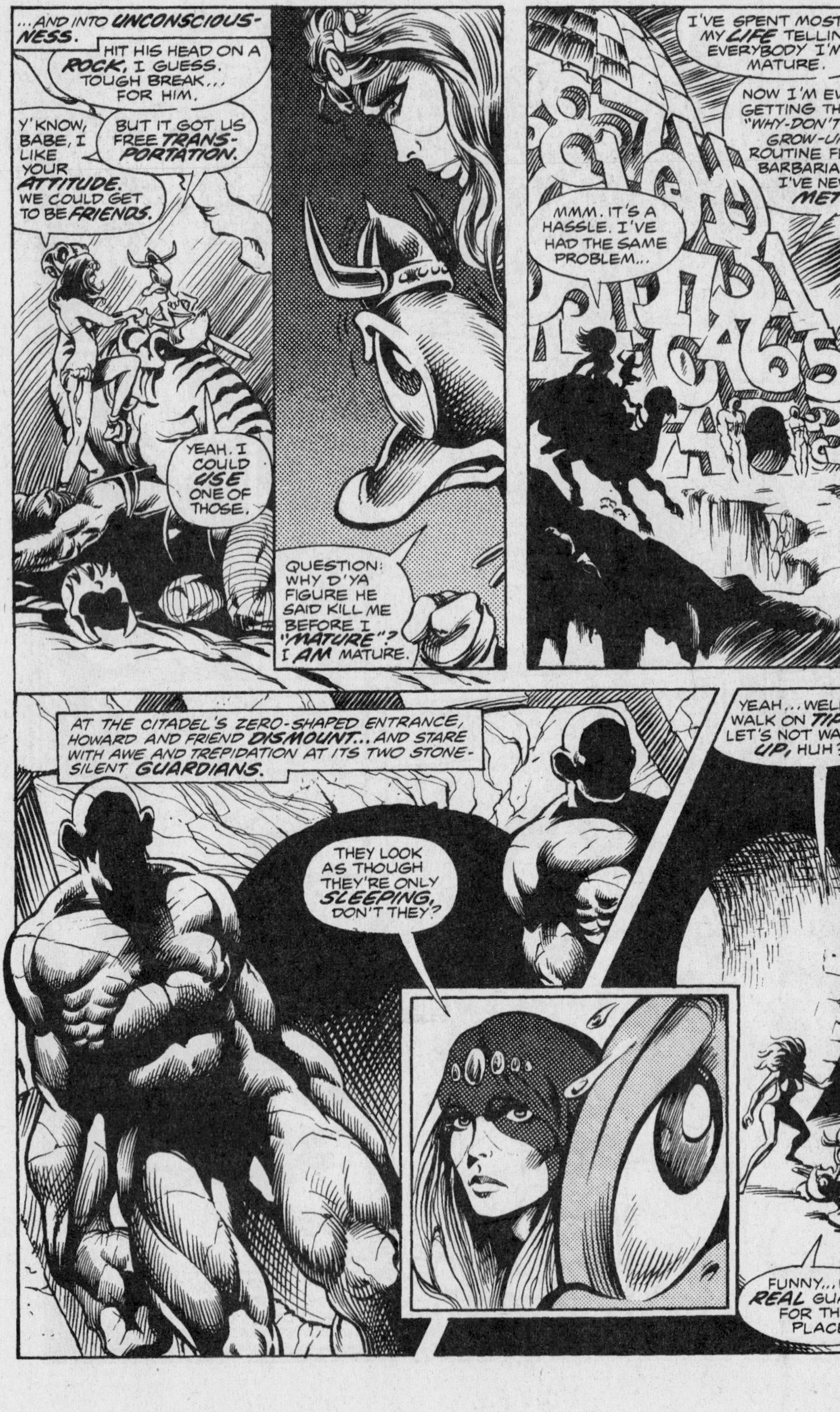
...AND INTO UNCONSCIOUSNESS.
HIT HIS HEAD ON A ROCK, I GUESS. TOUGH BREAK... FOR HIM.
Y'KNOW, BABE, I LIKE YOUR ATTITUDE. WE COULD GET TO BE FRIENDS.
BUT IT GOT US FREE TRANSPORTATION.
YEAH. I COULD USE ONE OF THOSE.
QUESTION: WHY D'YA FIGURE HE SAID KILL ME BEFORE I "MATURE"? I AM MATURE.
I'VE SPENT MOST 'A MY LIFE TELLING EVERYBODY I'M MATURE.
NOW I'M EVEN GETTING THE "WHY-DON'T-YOU-GROW-UP" ROUTINE FROM BARBARIANS I'VE NEVER MET!
MMM. IT'S A HASSLE. I'VE HAD THE SAME PROBLEM...
AT THE CITADEL'S ZERO-SHAPED ENTRANCE, HOWARD AND FRIEND DISMOUNT... AND STARE WITH AWE AND TREPIDATION AT ITS TWO STONE-SILENT GUARDIANS.
THEY LOOK AS THOUGH THEY'RE ONLY SLEEPING, DON'T THEY?
YEAH... WELL... WALK ON TIPTOE. LET'S NOT WAKE 'EM UP, HUH?
FUNNY... NO REAL GUARDS FOR THIS PLACE.

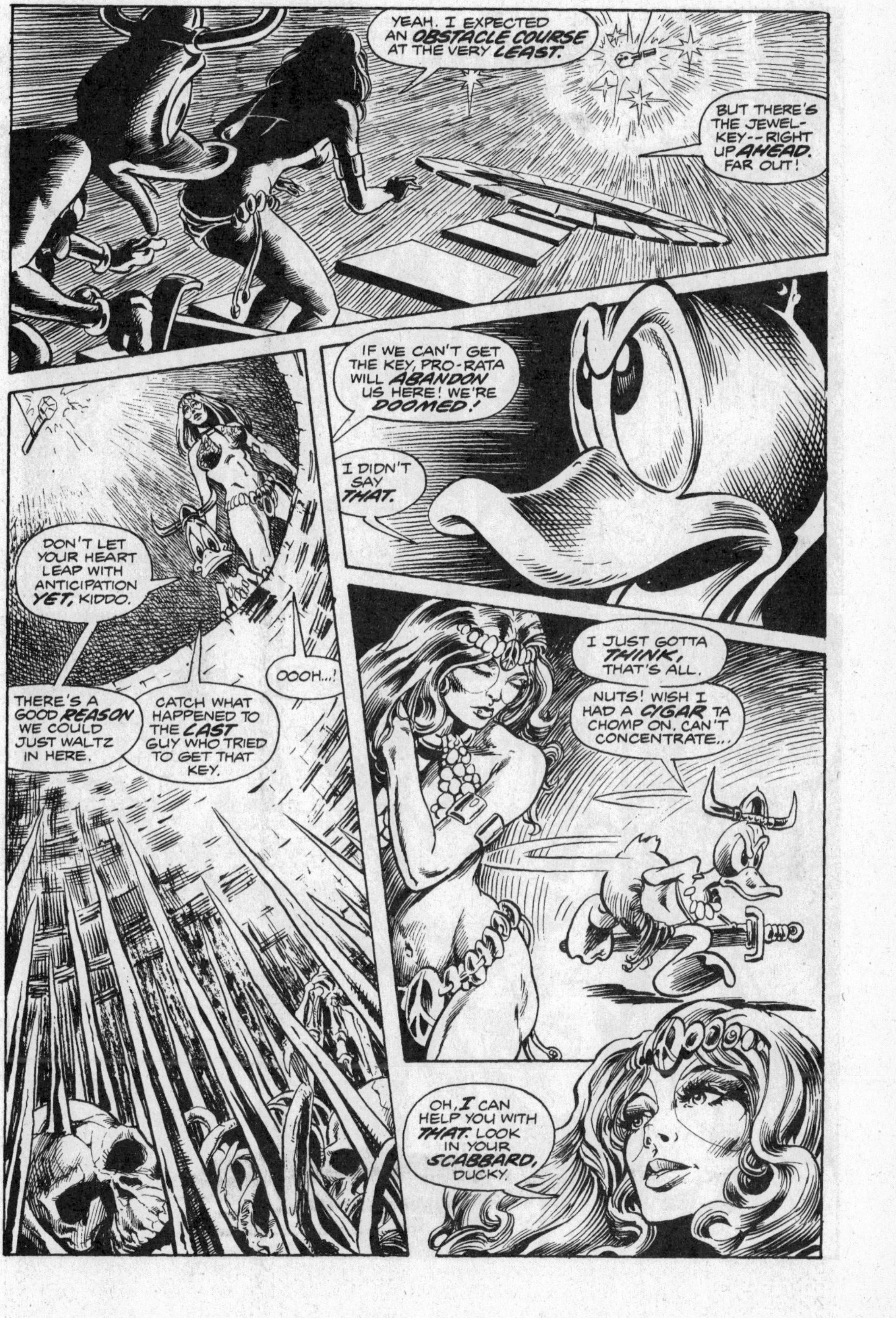
YEAH. I EXPECTED AN OBSTACLE COURSE AT THE VERY LEAST.
BUT THERE'S THE JEWEL-KEY--RIGHT UP AHEAD. FAR OUT!
IF WE CAN'T GET THE KEY, PRO-RATA WILL ABANDON US HERE! WE'RE DOOMED!
I DIDN'T SAY THAT.
DON'T LET YOUR HEART LEAP WITH ANTICIPATION YET, KIDDO.
OOOH...!
THERE'S A GOOD REASON WE COULD JUST WALTZ IN HERE.
CATCH WHAT HAPPENED TO THE LAST GUY WHO TRIED TO GET THAT KEY.
I JUST GOTTA THINK, THAT'S ALL.
NUTS! WISH I HAD A CIGAR TA CHOMP ON. CAN'T CONCENTRATE...
OH, I CAN HELP YOU WITH THAT. LOOK IN YOUR SCABBARD, DUCKY.

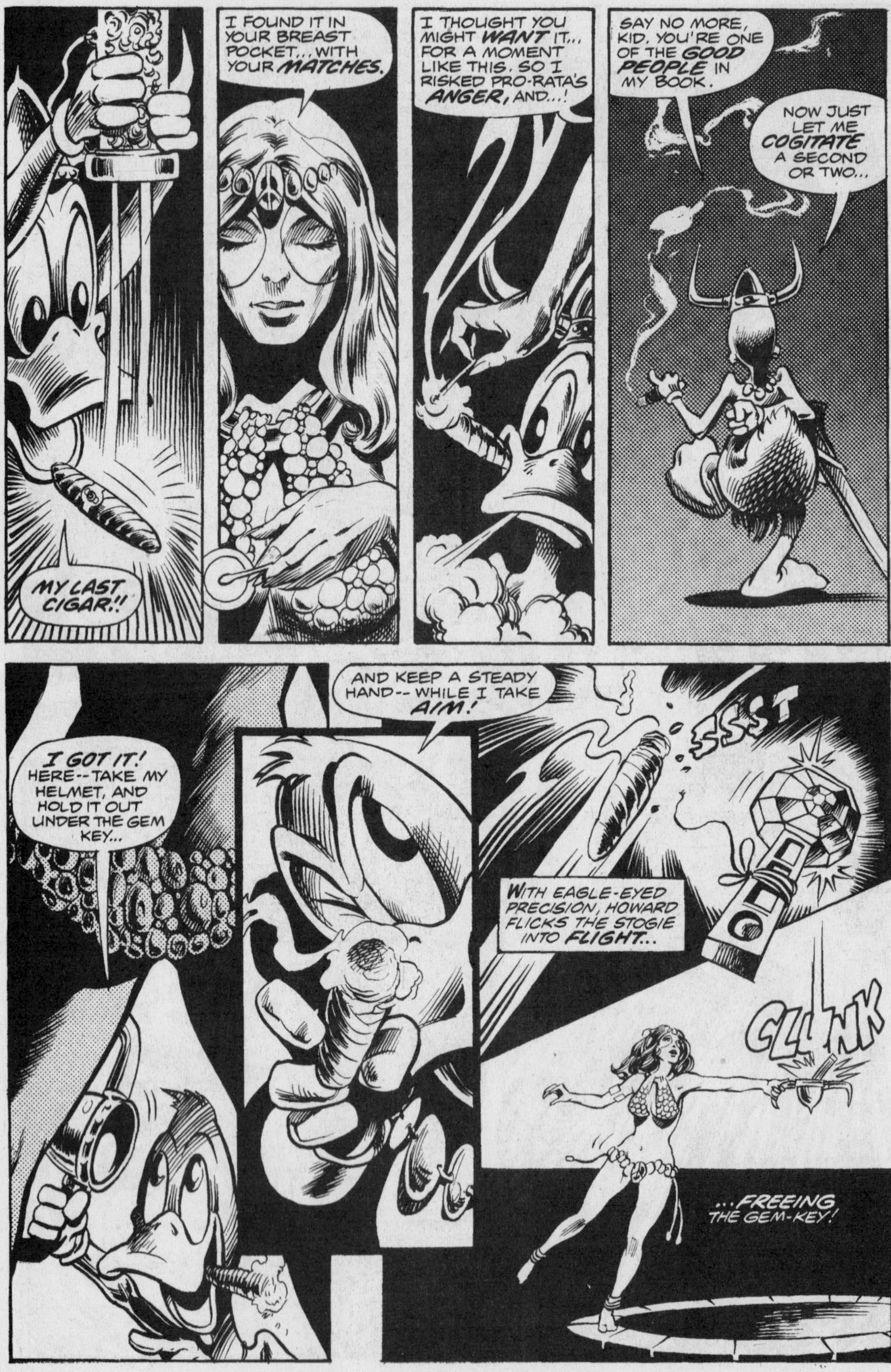
MY LAST CIGAR!!
I FOUND IT IN YOUR BREAST POCKET... WITH YOUR MATCHES.
I THOUGHT YOU MIGHT WANT IT... FOR A MOMENT LIKE THIS. SO I RISKED PRO-RATA'S ANGER, AND...!
SAY NO MORE, KID. YOU'RE ONE OF THE GOOD PEOPLE IN MY BOOK.
NOW JUST LET ME COGITATE A SECOND OR TWO...
I GOT IT! HERE--TAKE MY HELMET, AND HOLD IT OUT UNDER THE GEM KEY...
AND KEEP A STEADY HAND-- WHILE I TAKE AIM!
SSST
WITH EAGLE-EYED PRECISION, HOWARD FLICKS THE STOGIE INTO FLIGHT...
CLLINK
...FREEING THE GEM-KEY!

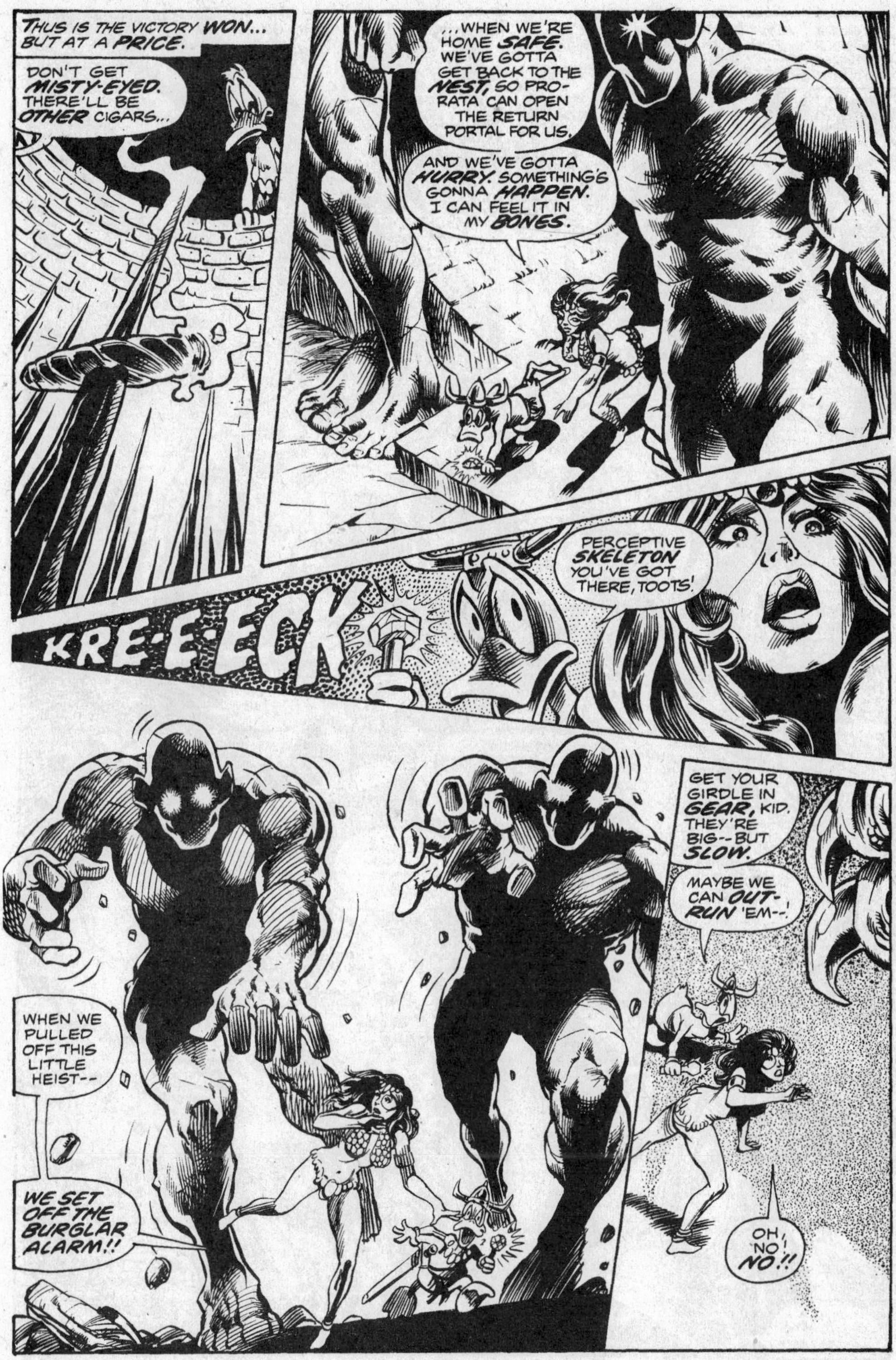
THUS IS THE VICTORY WON... BUT AT A PRICE.
DON'T GET MISTY-EYED. THERE'LL BE OTHER CIGARS...
...WHEN WE'RE HOME SAFE. WE'VE GOTTA GET BACK TO THE NEST, SO PRO-RATA CAN OPEN THE RETURN PORTAL FOR US.
AND WE'VE GOTTA HURRY. SOMETHING'S GONNA HAPPEN. I CAN FEEL IT IN MY BONES.
KRE-E-ECK
PERCEPTIVE SKELETON YOU'VE GOT THERE, TOOTS!
WHEN WE PULLED OFF THIS LITTLE HEIST--
WE SET OFF THE BURGLAR ALARM!!
GET YOUR GIRDLE IN GEAR, KID. THEY'RE BIG--BUT SLOW.
MAYBE WE CAN OUT-RUN 'EM--!
OH, NO NO!!

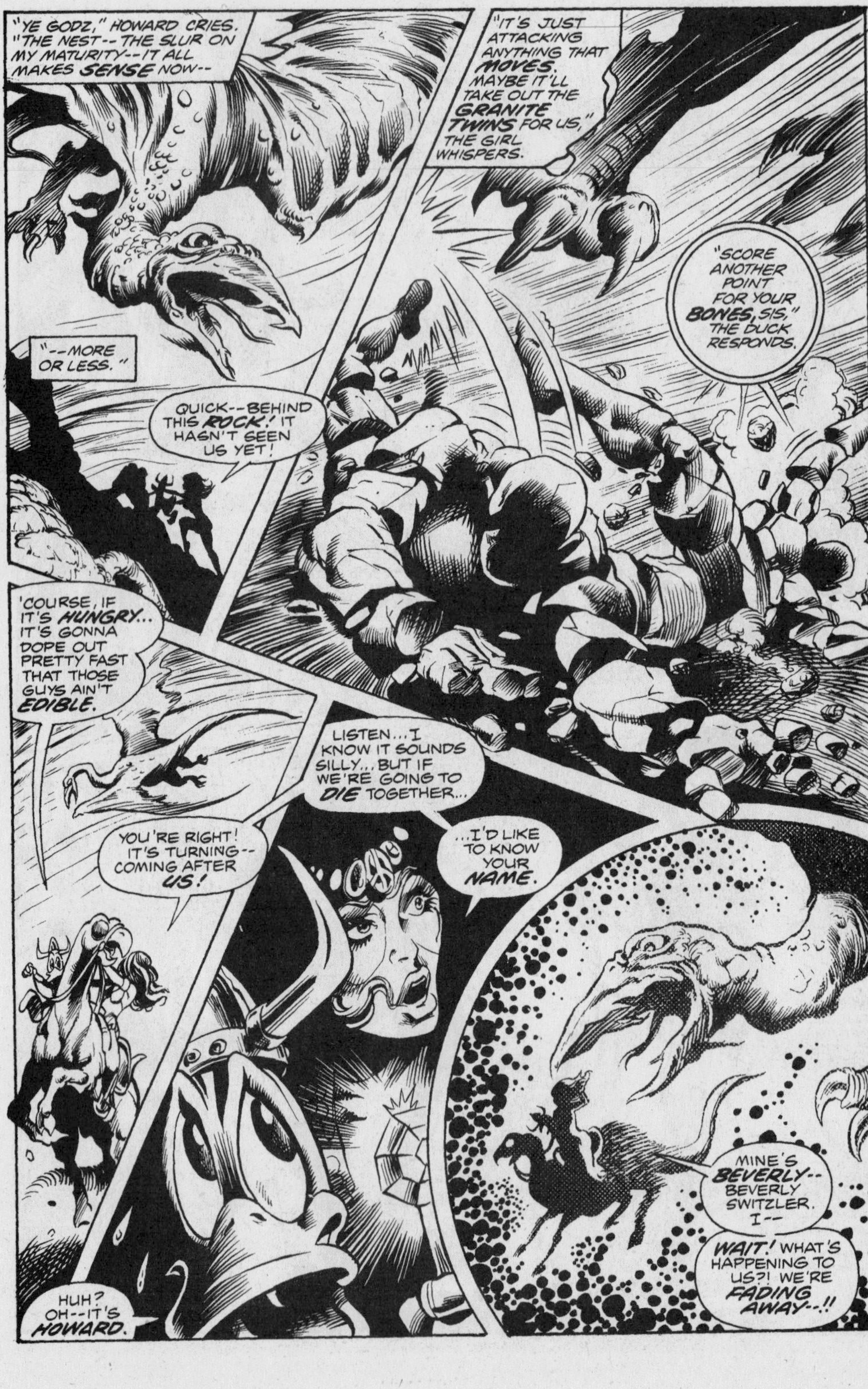
"YE GODZ," HOWARD CRIES. "THE NEST--THE SLUR ON MY MATURITY--IT ALL MAKES SENSE NOW--
"--MORE OR LESS."
QUICK--BEHIND THIS ROCK! IT HASN'T SEEN US YET!
"IT'S JUST ATTACKING ANYTHING THAT MOVES. MAYBE IT'LL TAKE OUT THE GRANITE TWINS FOR US," THE GIRL WHISPERS.
"SCORE ANOTHER POINT FOR YOUR BONES, SIS," THE DUCK RESPONDS.
'COURSE, IF IT'S HUNGRY... IT'S GONNA DOPE OUT PRETTY FAST THAT THOSE GUYS AIN'T EDIBLE.
YOU'RE RIGHT! IT'S TURNING--COMING AFTER US!
LISTEN... I KNOW IT SOUNDS SILLY... BUT IF WE'RE GOING TO DIE TOGETHER...
...I'D LIKE TO KNOW YOUR NAME.
HUH? OH--IT'S HOWARD.
MINE'S BEVERLY--BEVERLY SWITZLER. I--
WAIT! WHAT'S HAPPENING TO US?! WE'RE FADING AWAY--!!

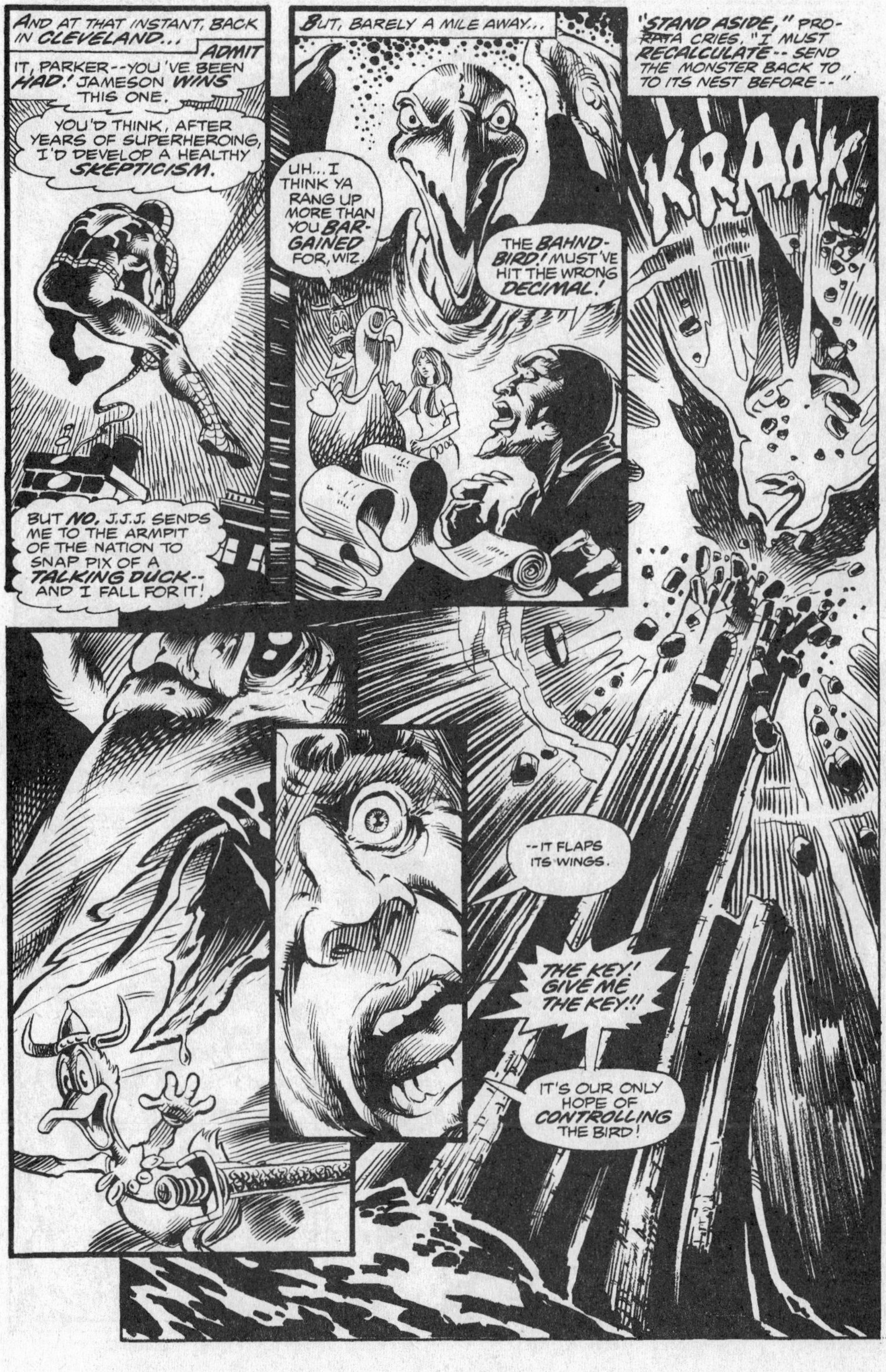

AND AT THAT INSTANT, BACK IN CLEVELAND...
ADMIT IT, PARKER--YOU'VE BEEN HAD! JAMESON WINS THIS ONE.
YOU'D THINK, AFTER YEARS OF SUPERHEROING, I'D DEVELOP A HEALTHY SKEPTICISM.
BUT NO, J.J.J. SENDS ME TO THE ARMPIT OF THE NATION TO SNAP PIX OF A TALKING DUCK-- AND I FALL FOR IT!
BUT, BARELY A MILE AWAY...
UH... I THINK YA RANG UP MORE THAN YOU BARGAINED FOR, WIZ.
THE BAHND-BIRD! MUST'VE HIT THE WRONG DECIMAL!
"STAND ASIDE," PRO-RATA CRIES, "I MUST RECALCULATE-- SEND THE MONSTER BACK TO TO ITS NEST BEFORE--"
KRAAK
--IT FLAPS ITS WINGS.
THE KEY! GIVE ME THE KEY!!
IT'S OUR ONLY HOPE OF CONTROLLING THE BIRD!

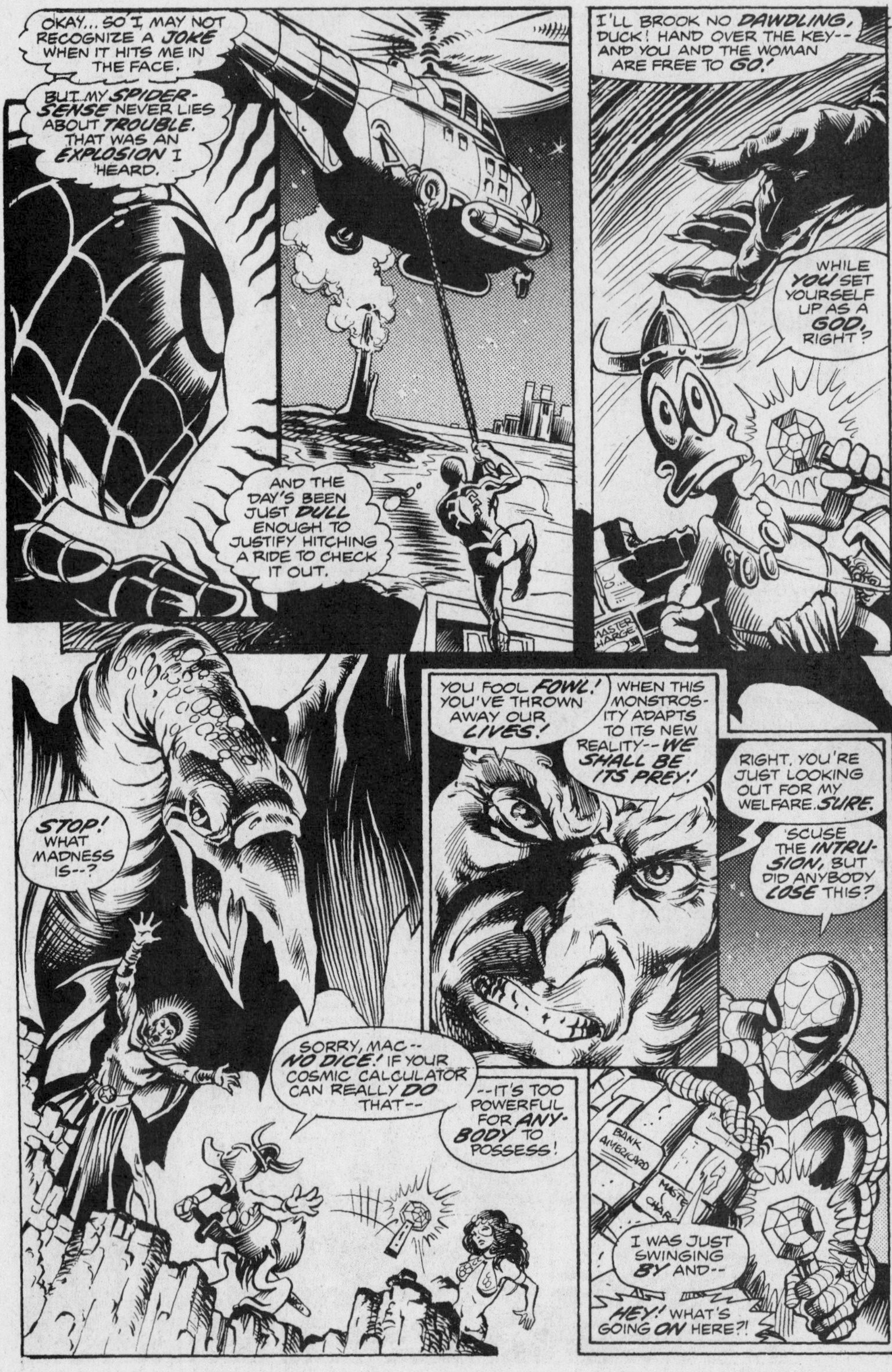
OKAY... SO I MAY NOT RECOGNIZE A JOKE WHEN IT HITS ME IN THE FACE.
BUT MY SPIDER-SENSE NEVER LIES ABOUT TROUBLE. THAT WAS AN EXPLOSION I HEARD.
AND THE DAY'S BEEN JUST DULL ENOUGH TO JUSTIFY HITCHING A RIDE TO CHECK IT OUT.
I'LL BROOK NO DAWDLING, DUCK! HAND OVER THE KEY-- AND YOU AND THE WOMAN ARE FREE TO GO!
WHILE YOU SET YOURSELF UP AS A GOD, RIGHT?
MASTER CHARGE
STOP! WHAT MADNESS IS--?
YOU FOOL FOWL! YOU'VE THROWN AWAY OUR LIVES!
WHEN THIS MONSTROSITY ADAPTS TO ITS NEW REALITY--WE SHALL BE ITS PREY!
RIGHT, YOU'RE JUST LOOKING OUT FOR MY WELFARE. SURE.
'SCUSE THE INTRUSION, BUT DID ANYBODY LOSE THIS?
SORRY, MAC-- NO DICE! IF YOUR COSMIC CALCULATOR CAN REALLY DO THAT--
--IT'S TOO POWERFUL FOR ANYBODY TO POSSESS!
BANK AMERICARD
I WAS JUST SWINGING BY AND--
HEY! WHAT'S GOING ON HERE?!

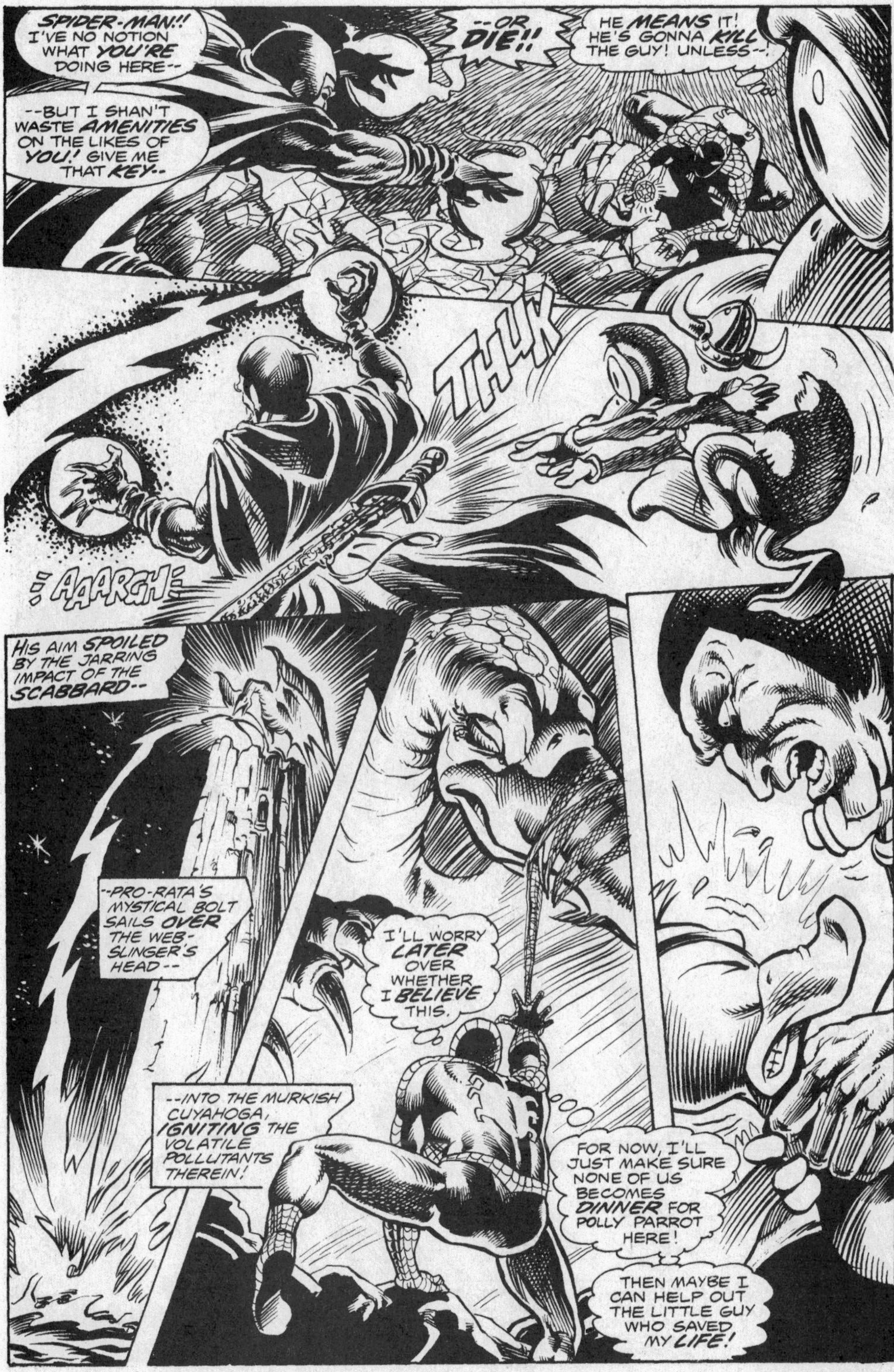
SPIDER-MAN!! I'VE NO NOTION WHAT YOU'RE DOING HERE--
--BUT I SHAN'T WASTE AMENITIES ON THE LIKES OF YOU! GIVE ME THAT KEY--
--OR DIE!!
HE MEANS IT! HE'S GONNA KILL THE GUY! UNLESS--!
THUK
AAARGH
HIS AIM SPOILED BY THE JARRING IMPACT OF THE SCABBARD--
--PRO-RATA'S MYSTICAL BOLT SAILS OVER THE WEB-SLINGER'S HEAD--
--INTO THE MURKISH CUYAHOGA, IGNITING THE VOLATILE POLLUTANTS THEREIN!
I'LL WORRY LATER OVER WHETHER I BELIEVE THIS.
FOR NOW, I'LL JUST MAKE SURE NONE OF US BECOMES DINNER FOR POLLY PARROT HERE!
THEN MAYBE I CAN HELP OUT THE LITTLE GUY WHO SAVED MY LIFE!

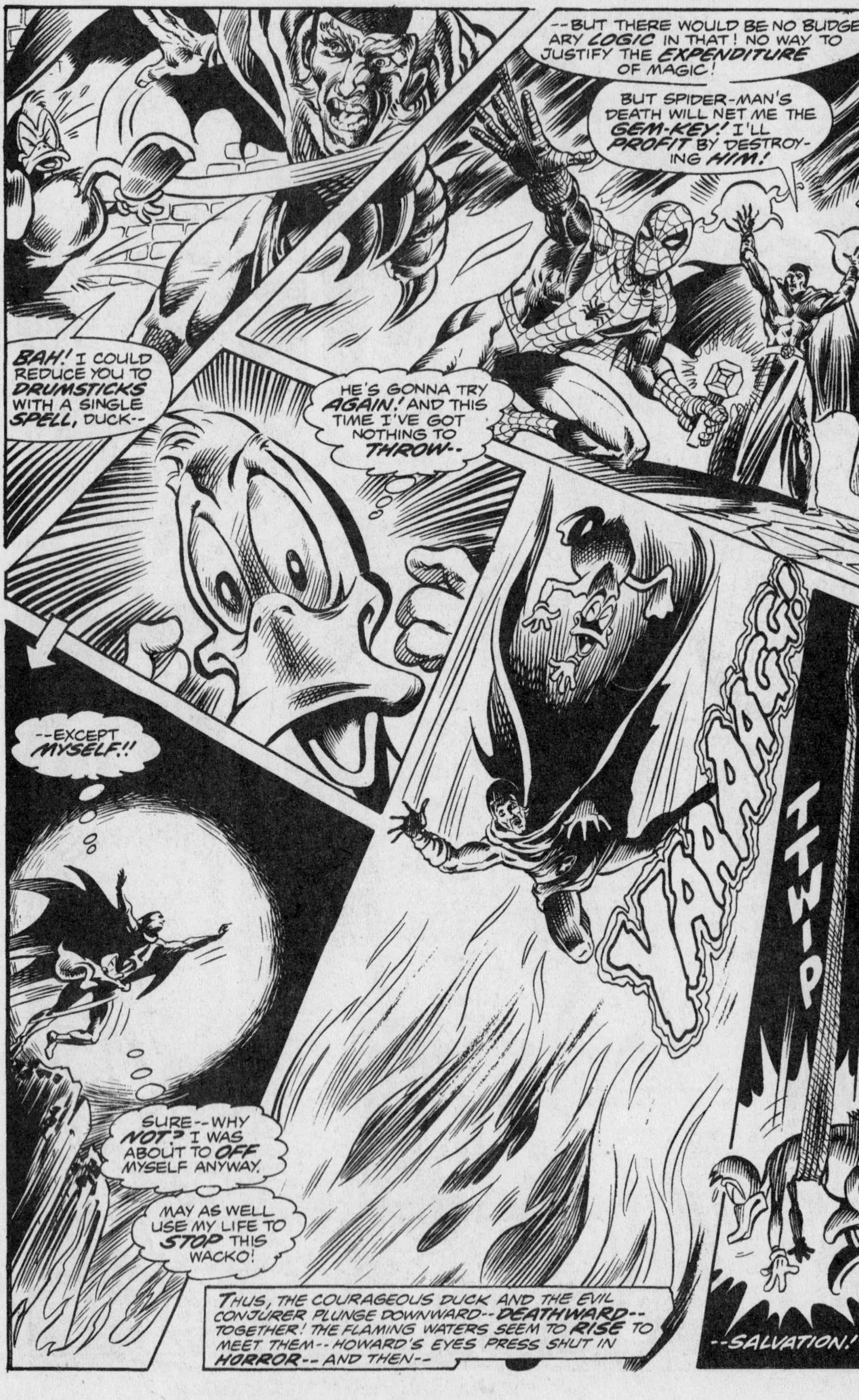
--BUT THERE WOULD BE NO BUDGETARY LOGIC IN THAT! NO WAY TO JUSTIFY THE EXPENDITURE OF MAGIC!
BUT SPIDER-MAN'S DEATH WILL NET ME THE GEM-KEY! I'LL PROFIT BY DESTROYING HIM!
BAH! I COULD REDUCE YOU TO DRUMSTICKS WITH A SINGLE SPELL, DUCK--
HE'S GONNA TRY AGAIN! AND THIS TIME I'VE GOT NOTHING TO THROW--
--EXCEPT MYSELF!!
SURE--WHY NOT? I WAS ABOUT TO OFF MYSELF ANYWAY.
MAY AS WELL USE MY LIFE TO STOP THIS WACKO!
YAAAAGG!
THUS, THE COURAGEOUS DUCK AND THE EVIL CONJURER PLUNGE DOWNWARD--DEATHWARD--TOGETHER! THE FLAMING WATERS SEEM TO RISE TO MEET THEM--HOWARD'S EYES PRESS SHUT IN HORROR--AND THEN--
TTWIP
--SALVATION!

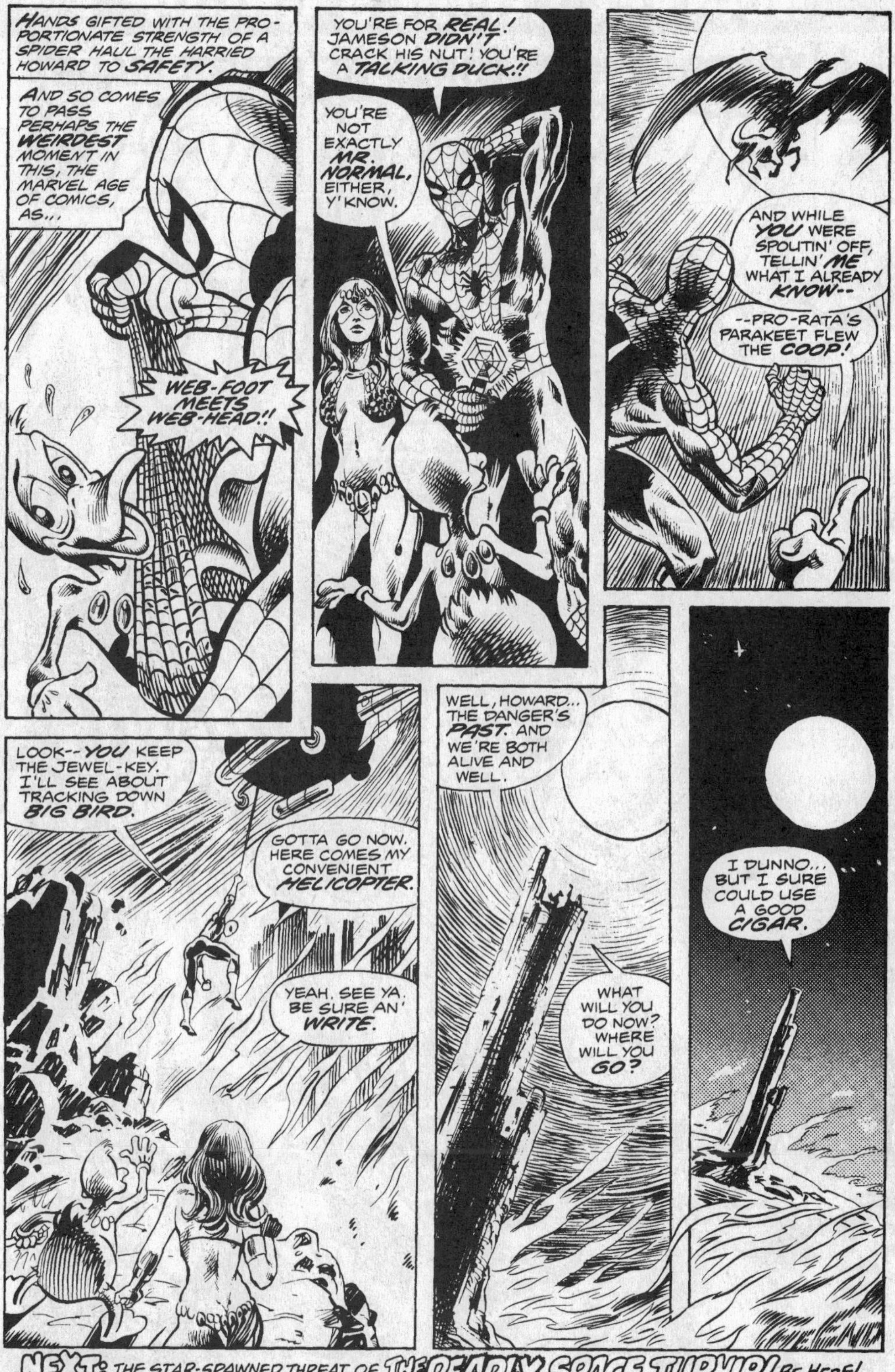
HANDS GIFTED WITH THE PROPORTIONATE STRENGTH OF A SPIDER HAUL THE HARRIED HOWARD TO SAFETY.
AND SO COMES TO PASS PERHAPS THE WEIRDEST MOMENT IN THIS, THE MARVEL AGE OF COMICS, AS...
WEB-FOOT MEETS WEB-HEAD!!
YOU'RE FOR REAL! JAMESON DIDN'T CRACK HIS NUT! YOU'RE A TALKING DUCK!!
YOU'RE NOT EXACTLY MR. NORMAL, EITHER, Y'KNOW.
AND WHILE YOU WERE SPOUTIN' OFF, TELLIN' ME WHAT I ALREADY KNOW--
--PRO-RATA'S PARAKEET FLEW THE COOP!
LOOK--YOU KEEP THE JEWEL-KEY. I'LL SEE ABOUT TRACKING DOWN BIG BIRD.
GOTTA GO NOW. HERE COMES MY CONVENIENT HELICOPTER.
YEAH, SEE YA. BE SURE AN' WRITE.
WELL, HOWARD... THE DANGER'S PAST. AND WE'RE BOTH ALIVE AND WELL.
WHAT WILL YOU DO NOW? WHERE WILL YOU GO?
I DUNNO... BUT I SURE COULD USE A GOOD CIGAR.
NEXT: THE STAR-SPAWNED THREAT OF THE DEADLY SPACE TURNIP! BE HERE!

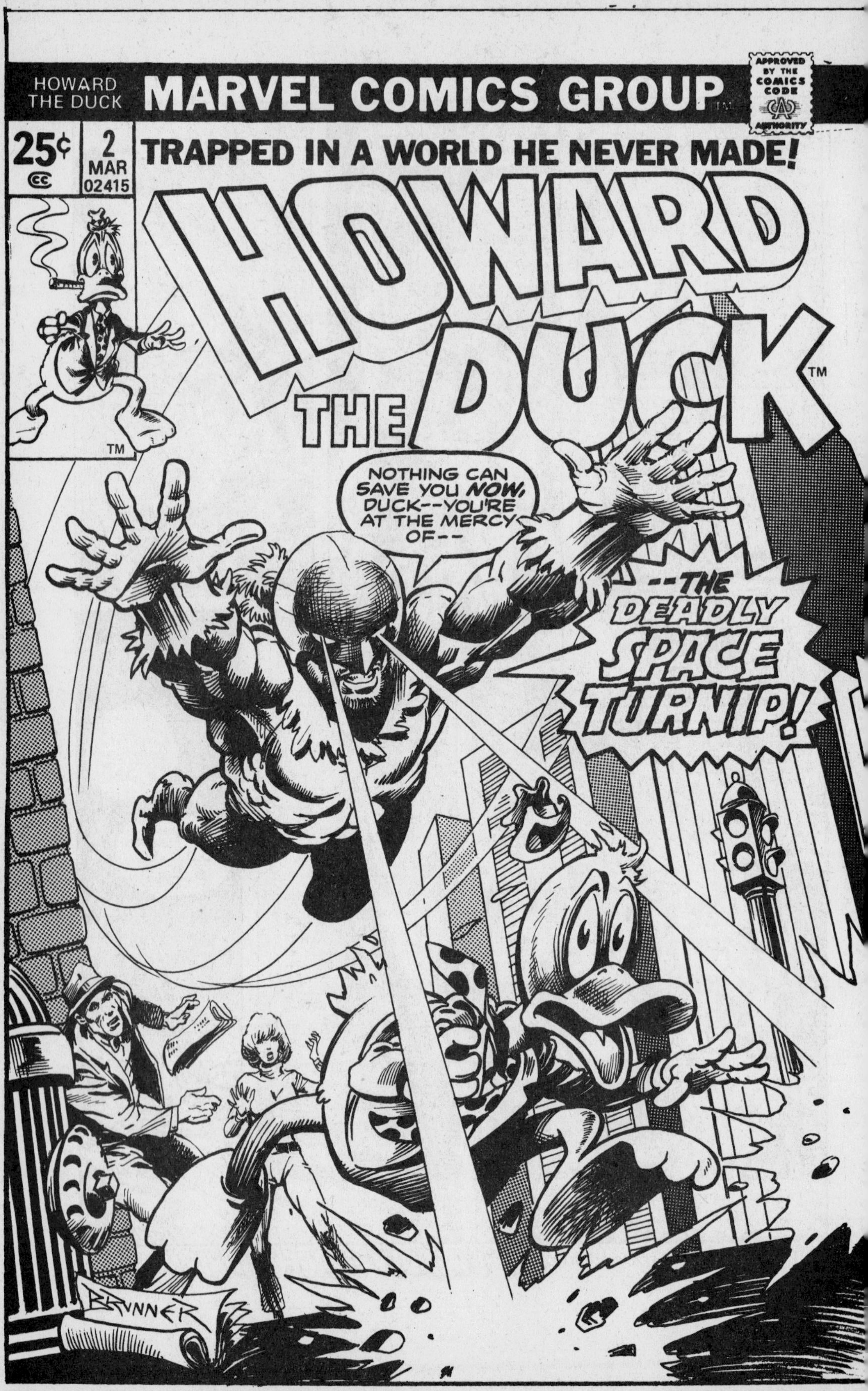
HOWARD THE DUCK
MARVEL COMICS GROUP
APPROVED BY THE COMICS CODE AUTHORITY
25¢
2 MAR 02415
TRAPPED IN A WORLD HE NEVER MADE!
HOWARD THE DUCK
NOTHING CAN SAVE YOU NOW, DUCK--YOU'RE AT THE MERCY OF--
--THE DEADLY SPACE TURNIP!
BRUNNER

STAN LEE PRESENTS: HOWARD THE DUCK!™

WRITTEN BY STEVE GERBER ILLUSTRATIONS BY FRANK BRUNNER INKING BY STEVE LEIALOHA
TOM ORZECHOWSKI, LETTERING MICHELE WOLFMAN, COLORS MARV WOLFMAN, EDITOR

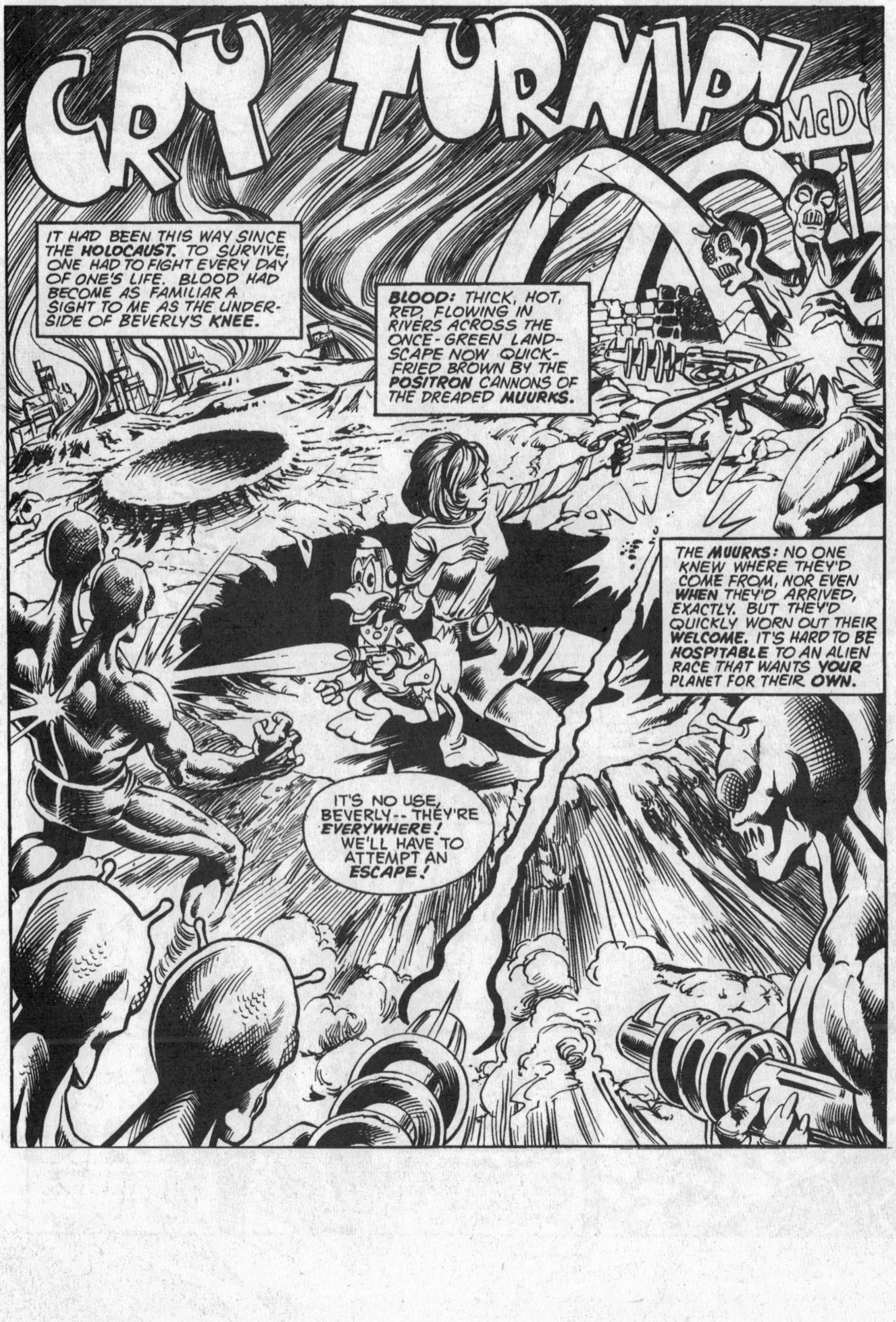

CRY TURNIP!
McD
IT HAD BEEN THIS WAY SINCE THE HOLOCAUST. TO SURVIVE, ONE HAD TO FIGHT EVERY DAY OF ONE'S LIFE. BLOOD HAD BECOME AS FAMILIAR A SIGHT TO ME AS THE UNDERSIDE OF BEVERLY'S KNEE.
BLOOD: THICK, HOT, RED, FLOWING IN RIVERS ACROSS THE ONCE-GREEN LANDSCAPE NOW QUICK-FRIED BROWN BY THE POSITRON CANNONS OF THE DREADED MUURKS.
THE MUURKS: NO ONE KNEW WHERE THEY'D COME FROM, NOR EVEN WHEN THEY'D ARRIVED, EXACTLY. BUT THEY'D QUICKLY WORN OUT THEIR WELCOME. IT'S HARD TO BE HOSPITABLE TO AN ALIEN RACE THAT WANTS YOUR PLANET FOR THEIR OWN.
IT'S NO USE, BEVERLY-- THEY'RE EVERYWHERE! WE'LL HAVE TO ATTEMPT AN ESCAPE!

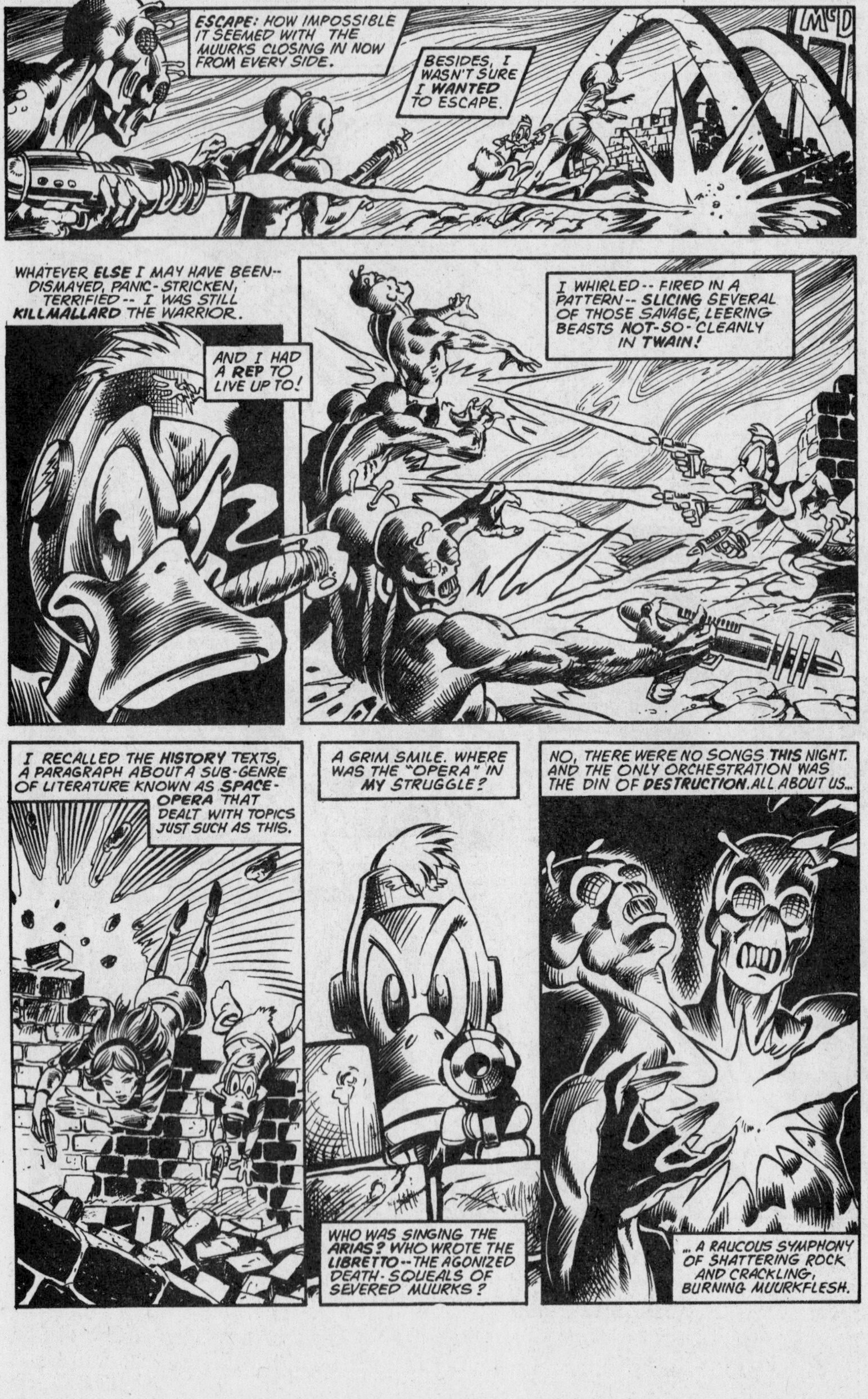
ESCAPE: HOW IMPOSSIBLE IT SEEMED WITH THE MUURKS CLOSING IN NOW FROM EVERY SIDE.
BESIDES, I WASN'T SURE I WANTED TO ESCAPE.
WHATEVER ELSE I MAY HAVE BEEN-- DISMAYED, PANIC-STRICKEN, TERRIFIED-- I WAS STILL KILLMALLARD THE WARRIOR.
AND I HAD A REP TO LIVE UP TO!
I WHIRLED-- FIRED IN A PATTERN-- SLICING SEVERAL OF THOSE SAVAGE, LEERING BEASTS NOT-SO-CLEANLY IN TWAIN!
I RECALLED THE HISTORY TEXTS, A PARAGRAPH ABOUT A SUB-GENRE OF LITERATURE KNOWN AS SPACE-OPERA THAT DEALT WITH TOPICS JUST SUCH AS THIS.
A GRIM SMILE. WHERE WAS THE "OPERA" IN MY STRUGGLE?
WHO WAS SINGING THE ARIAS? WHO WROTE THE LIBRETTO-- THE AGONIZED DEATH-SQUEALS OF SEVERED MUURKS?
NO, THERE WERE NO SONGS THIS NIGHT. AND THE ONLY ORCHESTRATION WAS THE DIN OF DESTRUCTION. ALL ABOUT US...
...A RAUCOUS SYMPHONY OF SHATTERING ROCK AND CRACKLING, BURNING MUURKFLESH.

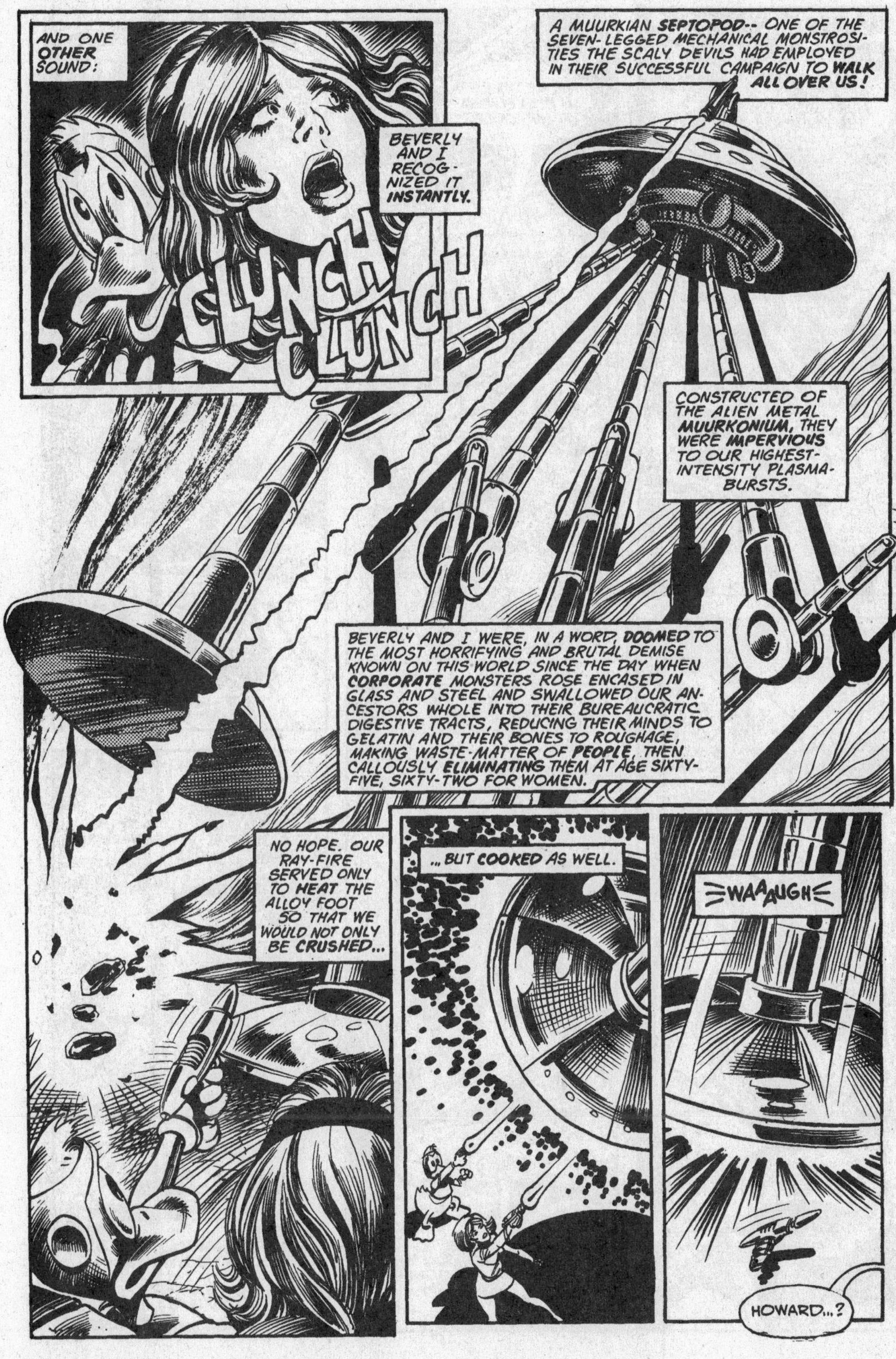
AND ONE OTHER SOUND:
BEVERLY AND I RECOGNIZED IT INSTANTLY.
CLUNCH CLUNCH
A MUURKIAN SEPTOPOD-- ONE OF THE SEVEN-LEGGED MECHANICAL MONSTROSITIES THE SCALY DEVILS HAD EMPLOYED IN THEIR SUCCESSFUL CAMPAIGN TO WALK ALL OVER US!
CONSTRUCTED OF THE ALIEN METAL MUURKONIUM, THEY WERE IMPERVIOUS TO OUR HIGHEST-INTENSITY PLASMA-BURSTS.
BEVERLY AND I WERE, IN A WORD, DOOMED TO THE MOST HORRIFYING AND BRUTAL DEMISE KNOWN ON THIS WORLD SINCE THE DAY WHEN CORPORATE MONSTERS ROSE ENCASED IN GLASS AND STEEL AND SWALLOWED OUR ANCESTORS WHOLE INTO THEIR BUREAUCRATIC DIGESTIVE TRACTS, REDUCING THEIR MINDS TO GELATIN AND THEIR BONES TO ROUGHAGE, MAKING WASTE-MATTER OF PEOPLE, THEN CALLOUSLY ELIMINATING THEM AT AGE SIXTY-FIVE, SIXTY-TWO FOR WOMEN.
NO HOPE. OUR RAY-FIRE SERVED ONLY TO HEAT THE ALLOY FOOT SO THAT WE WOULD NOT ONLY BE CRUSHED...
...BUT COOKED AS WELL.
WAAAUGH
HOWARD...?

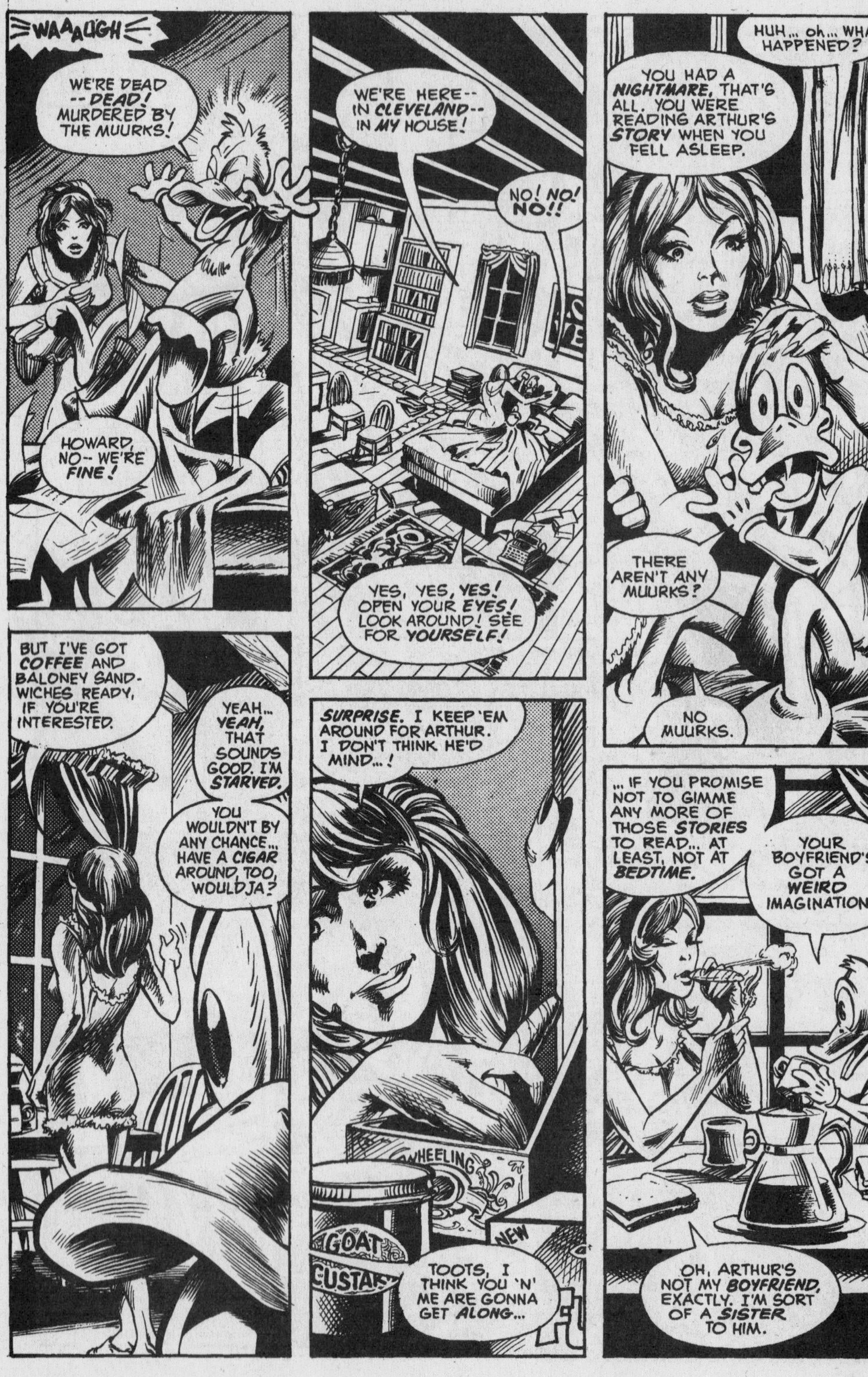

WAAAUGH
WE'RE DEAD -- DEAD! MURDERED BY THE MUURKS!
HOWARD, NO-- WE'RE FINE!
WE'RE HERE-- IN CLEVELAND-- IN MY HOUSE!
NO! NO! NO!!
YES, YES, YES! OPEN YOUR EYES! LOOK AROUND! SEE FOR YOURSELF!
HUH... oh... WHA' HAPPENED?
YOU HAD A NIGHTMARE, THAT'S ALL. YOU WERE READING ARTHUR'S STORY WHEN YOU FELL ASLEEP.
THERE AREN'T ANY MUURKS?
NO MUURKS.
BUT I'VE GOT COFFEE AND BALONEY SANDWICHES READY, IF YOU'RE INTERESTED.
YEAH... YEAH, THAT SOUNDS GOOD. I'M STARVED.
YOU WOULDN'T BY ANY CHANCE... HAVE A CIGAR AROUND, TOO, WOULDJA?
SURPRISE. I KEEP 'EM AROUND FOR ARTHUR. I DON'T THINK HE'D MIND...!
WHEELING
GOAT
CUSTAR
NEW
TOOTS, I THINK YOU 'N' ME ARE GONNA GET ALONG...
... IF YOU PROMISE NOT TO GIMME ANY MORE OF THOSE STORIES TO READ... AT LEAST, NOT AT BEDTIME.
YOUR BOYFRIEND'S GOT A WEIRD IMAGINATION.
OH, ARTHUR'S NOT MY BOYFRIEND, EXACTLY. I'M SORT OF A SISTER TO HIM.

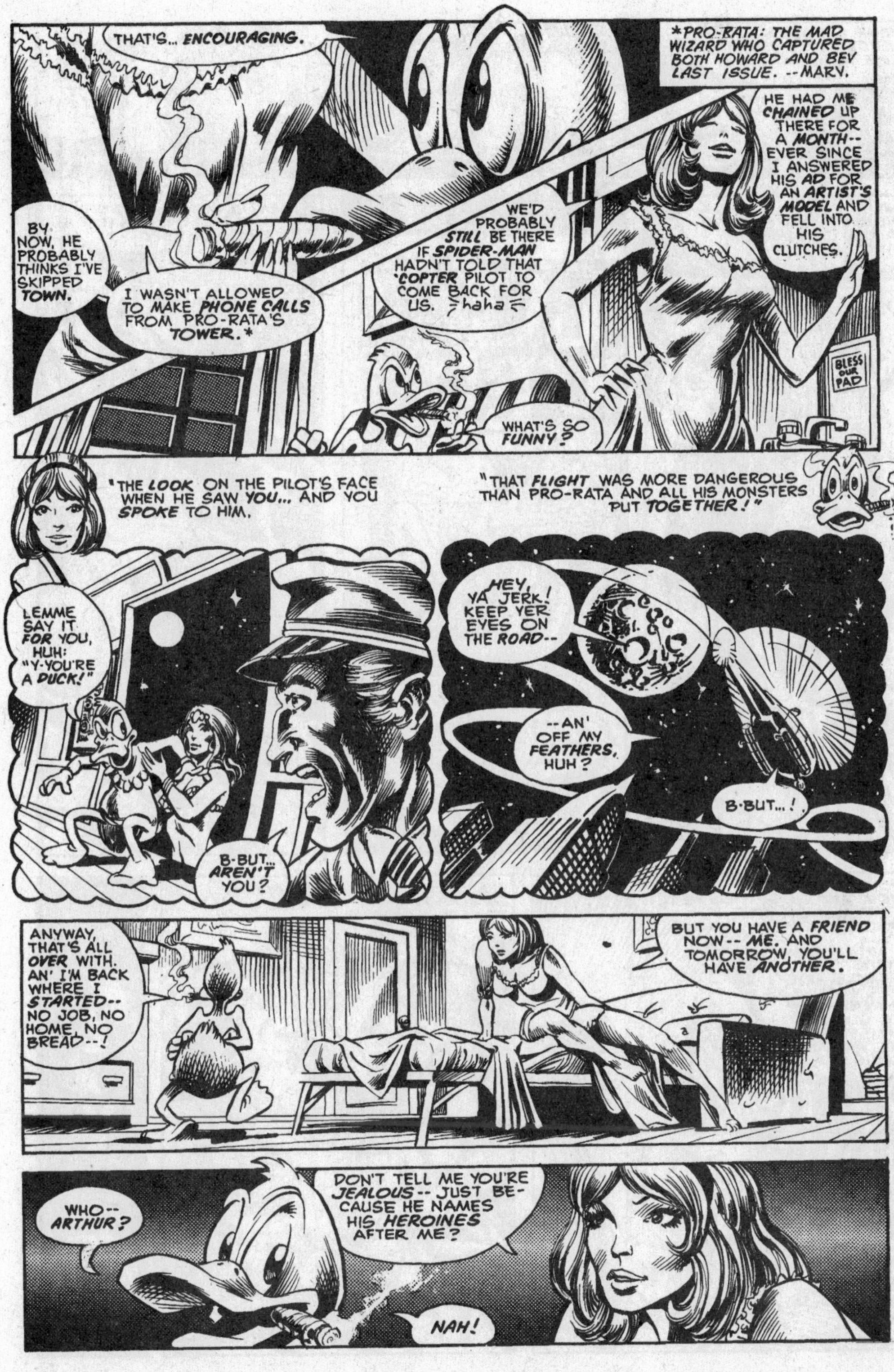
THAT'S... ENCOURAGING.
*PRO-RATA: THE MAD WIZARD WHO CAPTURED BOTH HOWARD AND BEV LAST ISSUE. --MARY.
HE HAD ME CHAINED UP THERE FOR A MONTH-- EVER SINCE I ANSWERED HIS AD FOR AN ARTIST'S MODEL AND FELL INTO HIS CLUTCHES.
BY NOW, HE PROBABLY THINKS I'VE SKIPPED TOWN.
I WASN'T ALLOWED TO MAKE PHONE CALLS FROM PRO-RATA'S TOWER.*
WE'D PROBABLY STILL BE THERE IF SPIDER-MAN HADN'T TOLD THAT 'COPTER PILOT TO COME BACK FOR US. haha
BLESS OUR PAD
WHAT'S SO FUNNY?
"THE LOOK ON THE PILOT'S FACE WHEN HE SAW YOU... AND YOU SPOKE TO HIM.
"THAT FLIGHT WAS MORE DANGEROUS THAN PRO-RATA AND ALL HIS MONSTERS PUT TOGETHER!"
LEMME SAY IT FOR YOU, HUH: "Y-YOU'RE A DUCK!"
B-BUT... AREN'T YOU?
HEY, YA JERK! KEEP YER EYES ON THE ROAD--
--AN' OFF MY FEATHERS, HUH?
B-BUT...!
ANYWAY, THAT'S ALL OVER WITH. AN' I'M BACK WHERE I STARTED-- NO JOB, NO HOME, NO BREAD--!
BUT YOU HAVE A FRIEND NOW-- ME. AND TOMORROW, YOU'LL HAVE ANOTHER.
WHO-- ARTHUR?
DON'T TELL ME YOU'RE JEALOUS-- JUST BECAUSE HE NAMES HIS HEROINES AFTER ME?
NAH!

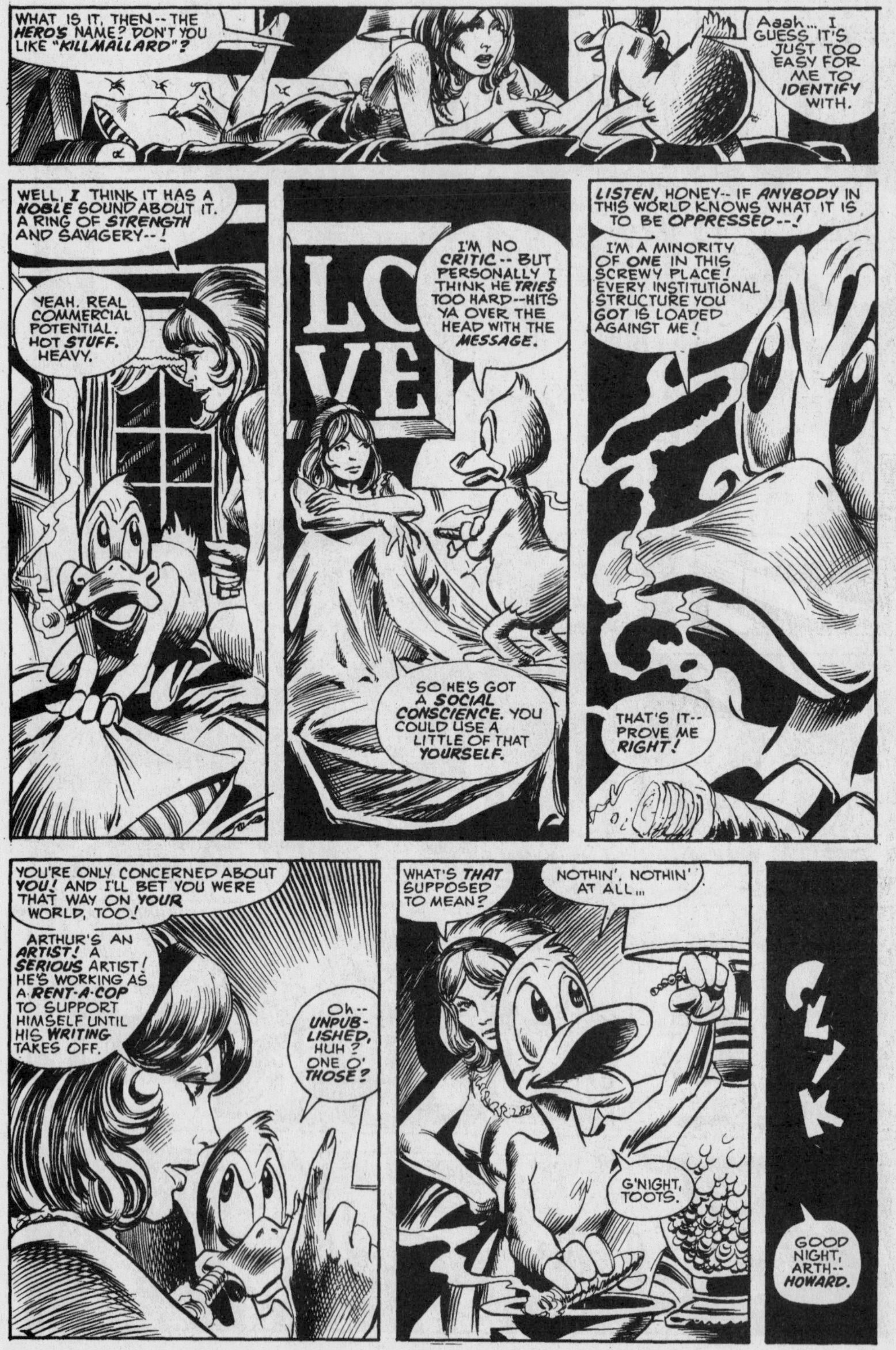
WHAT IS IT, THEN -- THE HERO'S NAME? DON'T YOU LIKE "KILLMALLARD"?
Aaah... I GUESS IT'S JUST TOO EASY FOR ME TO IDENTIFY WITH.
WELL, I THINK IT HAS A NOBLE SOUND ABOUT IT. A RING OF STRENGTH AND SAVAGERY--!
YEAH. REAL COMMERCIAL POTENTIAL. HOT STUFF. HEAVY.
LO
VE
I'M NO CRITIC -- BUT PERSONALLY I THINK HE TRIES TOO HARD--HITS YA OVER THE HEAD WITH THE MESSAGE.
SO HE'S GOT A SOCIAL CONSCIENCE. YOU COULD USE A LITTLE OF THAT YOURSELF.
LISTEN, HONEY-- IF ANYBODY IN THIS WORLD KNOWS WHAT IT IS TO BE OPPRESSED--!
I'M A MINORITY OF ONE IN THIS SCREWY PLACE! EVERY INSTITUTIONAL STRUCTURE YOU GOT IS LOADED AGAINST ME!
THAT'S IT-- PROVE ME RIGHT!
YOU'RE ONLY CONCERNED ABOUT YOU! AND I'LL BET YOU WERE THAT WAY ON YOUR WORLD, TOO!
ARTHUR'S AN ARTIST! A SERIOUS ARTIST! HE'S WORKING AS A RENT-A-COP TO SUPPORT HIMSELF UNTIL HIS WRITING TAKES OFF.
Oh-- UNPUBLISHED, HUH? ONE O' THOSE?
WHAT'S THAT SUPPOSED TO MEAN?
NOTHIN', NOTHIN' AT ALL...
G'NIGHT, TOOTS.
CLIK
GOOD NIGHT, ARTH-- HOWARD.

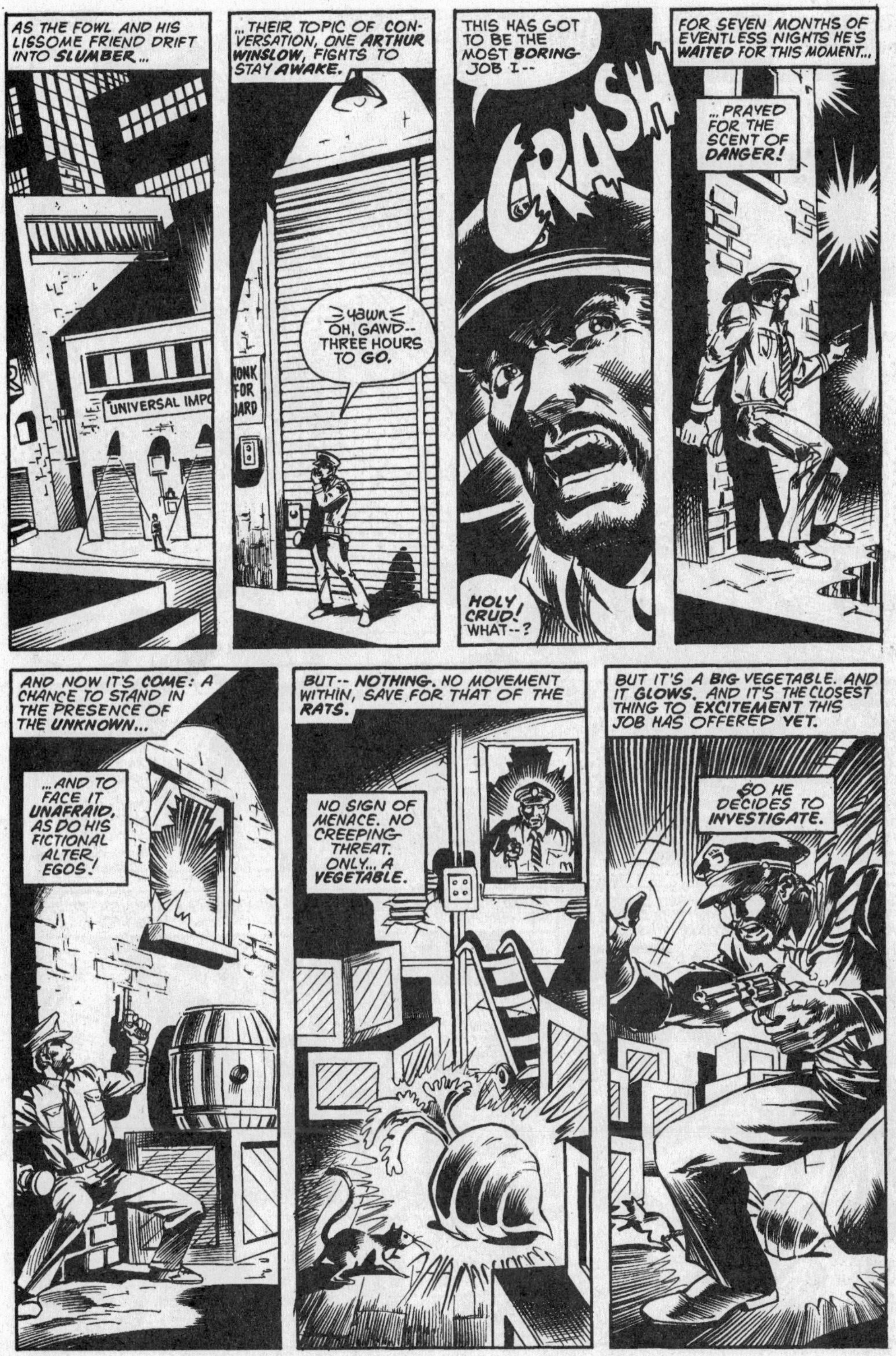

AS THE FOWL AND HIS LISSOME FRIEND DRIFT INTO SLUMBER...
UNIVERSAL IMPO
...THEIR TOPIC OF CONVERSATION, ONE ARTHUR WINSLOW, FIGHTS TO STAY AWAKE.
HONK FOR GUARD
yawn OH, GAWD-- THREE HOURS TO GO.
THIS HAS GOT TO BE THE MOST BORING JOB I--
CRASH
HOLY CRUD! WHAT--?
FOR SEVEN MONTHS OF EVENTLESS NIGHTS HE'S WAITED FOR THIS MOMENT...
...PRAYED FOR THE SCENT OF DANGER!
AND NOW IT'S COME: A CHANCE TO STAND IN THE PRESENCE OF THE UNKNOWN...
...AND TO FACE IT UNAFRAID, AS DO HIS FICTIONAL ALTER EGOS!
BUT-- NOTHING. NO MOVEMENT WITHIN, SAVE FOR THAT OF THE RATS.
NO SIGN OF MENACE. NO CREEPING THREAT. ONLY... A VEGETABLE.
BUT IT'S A BIG VEGETABLE. AND IT GLOWS. AND IT'S THE CLOSEST THING TO EXCITEMENT THIS JOB HAS OFFERED YET.
SO HE DECIDES TO INVESTIGATE.

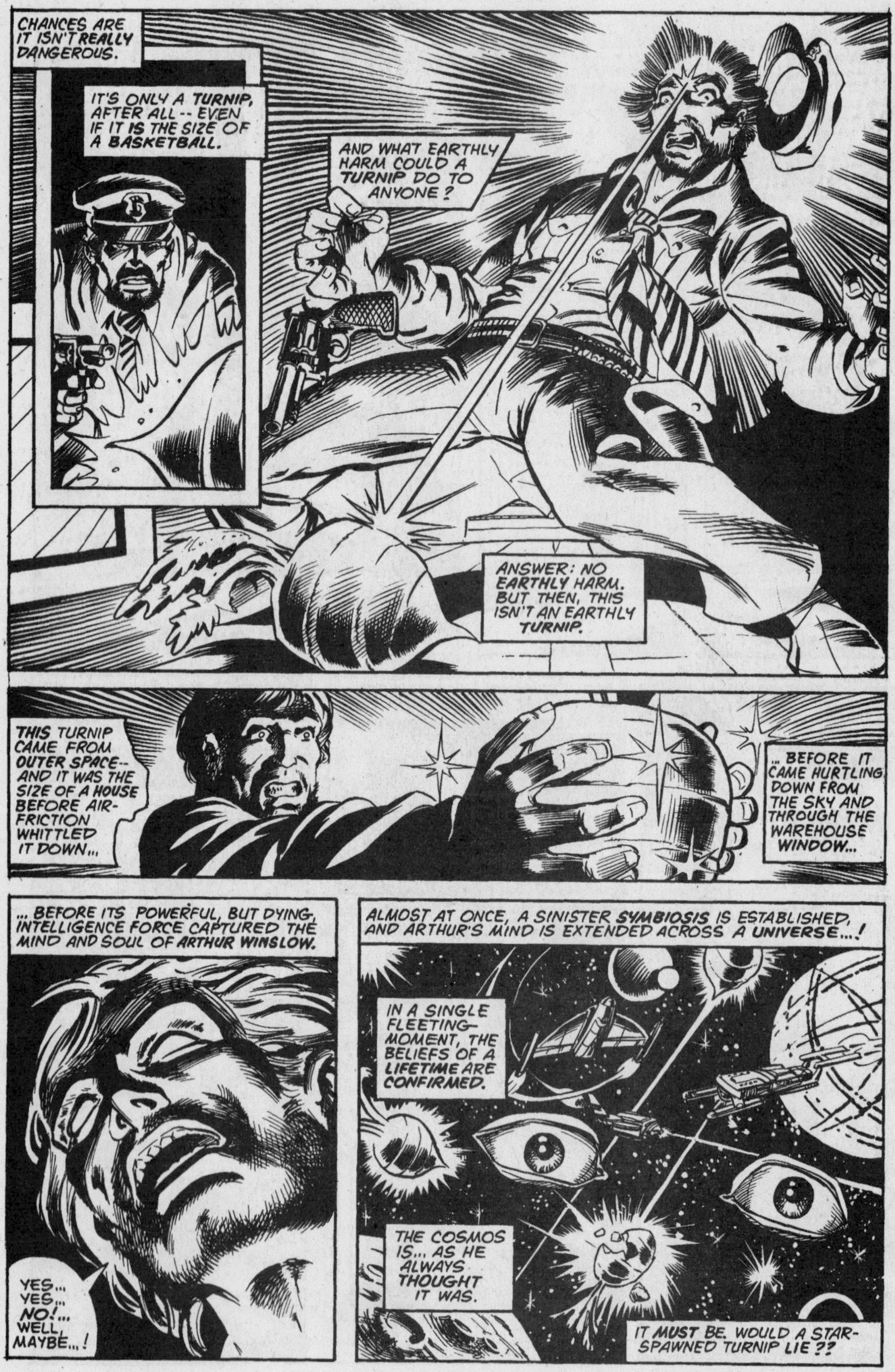
CHANCES ARE IT ISN'T REALLY DANGEROUS.
IT'S ONLY A TURNIP, AFTER ALL -- EVEN IF IT IS THE SIZE OF A BASKETBALL.
AND WHAT EARTHLY HARM COULD A TURNIP DO TO ANYONE?
ANSWER: NO EARTHLY HARM. BUT THEN, THIS ISN'T AN EARTHLY TURNIP.
THIS TURNIP CAME FROM OUTER SPACE-- AND IT WAS THE SIZE OF A HOUSE BEFORE AIR-FRICTION WHITTLED IT DOWN...
... BEFORE IT CAME HURTLING DOWN FROM THE SKY AND THROUGH THE WAREHOUSE WINDOW...
... BEFORE ITS POWERFUL, BUT DYING, INTELLIGENCE FORCE CAPTURED THE MIND AND SOUL OF ARTHUR WINSLOW.
YES... YES... NO!... WELL, MAYBE...!
ALMOST AT ONCE, A SINISTER SYMBIOSIS IS ESTABLISHED, AND ARTHUR'S MIND IS EXTENDED ACROSS A UNIVERSE...!
IN A SINGLE FLEETING MOMENT, THE BELIEFS OF A LIFETIME ARE CONFIRMED.
THE COSMOS IS... AS HE ALWAYS THOUGHT IT WAS.
IT MUST BE. WOULD A STAR-SPAWNED TURNIP LIE??

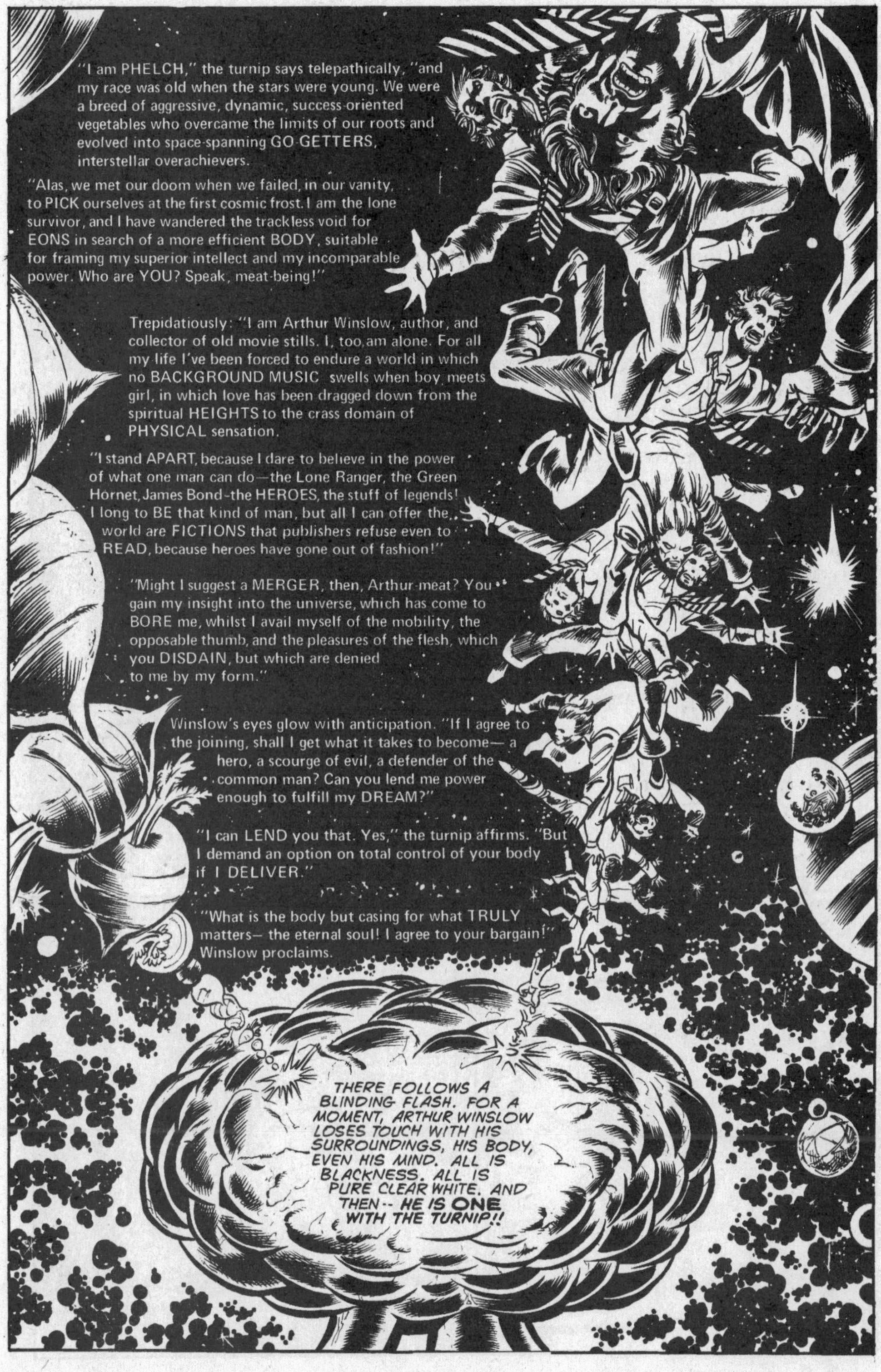
"I am PHELCH," the turnip says telepathically, "and my race was old when the stars were young. We were a breed of aggressive, dynamic, success-oriented vegetables who overcame the limits of our roots and evolved into space-spanning GO-GETTERS, interstellar overachievers.
"Alas, we met our doom when we failed, in our vanity, to PICK ourselves at the first cosmic frost. I am the lone survivor, and I have wandered the trackless void for EONS in search of a more efficient BODY, suitable for framing my superior intellect and my incomparable power. Who are YOU? Speak, meat-being!"
Trepidatiously: "I am Arthur Winslow, author, and collector of old movie stills. I, too, am alone. For all my life I've been forced to endure a world in which no BACKGROUND MUSIC swells when boy meets girl, in which love has been dragged down from the spiritual HEIGHTS to the crass domain of PHYSICAL sensation.
"I stand APART, because I dare to believe in the power of what one man can do—the Lone Ranger, the Green Hornet, James Bond-the HEROES, the stuff of legends! I long to BE that kind of man, but all I can offer the world are FICTIONS that publishers refuse even to READ, because heroes have gone out of fashion!"
"Might I suggest a MERGER, then, Arthur-meat? You gain my insight into the universe, which has come to BORE me, whilst I avail myself of the mobility, the opposable thumb, and the pleasures of the flesh, which you DISDAIN, but which are denied to me by my form."
Winslow's eyes glow with anticipation. "If I agree to the joining, shall I get what it takes to become— a hero, a scourge of evil, a defender of the common man? Can you lend me power enough to fulfill my DREAM?"
"I can LEND you that. Yes," the turnip affirms. "But I demand an option on total control of your body if I DELIVER."
"What is the body but casing for what TRULY matters— the eternal soul! I agree to your bargain!" Winslow proclaims.
THERE FOLLOWS A BLINDING FLASH. FOR A MOMENT, ARTHUR WINSLOW LOSES TOUCH WITH HIS SURROUNDINGS, HIS BODY, EVEN HIS MIND. ALL IS BLACKNESS. ALL IS PURE CLEAR WHITE. AND THEN-- HE IS ONE WITH THE TURNIP!!

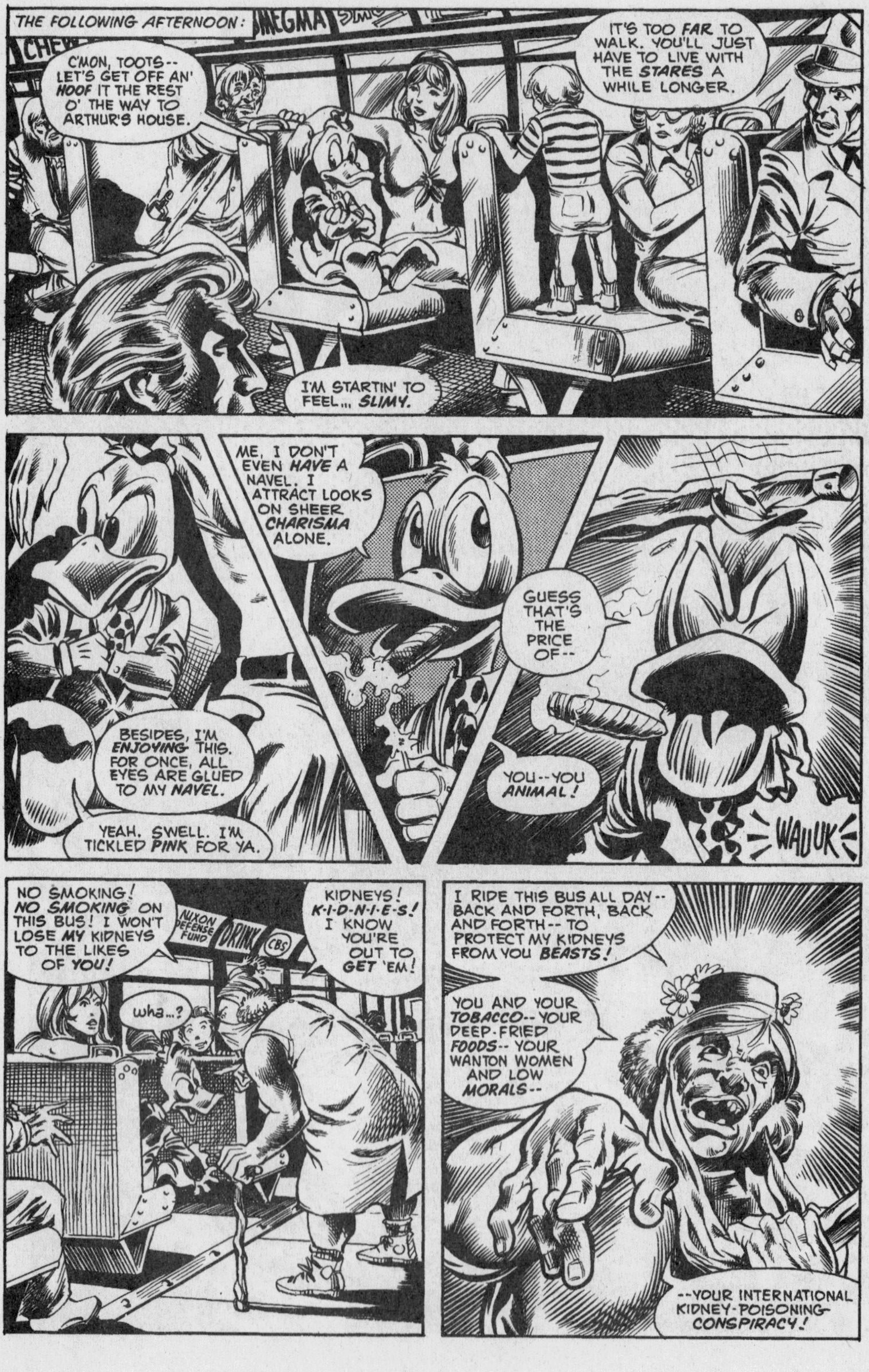
THE FOLLOWING AFTERNOON:
C'MON, TOOTS-- LET'S GET OFF AN' HOOF IT THE REST O' THE WAY TO ARTHUR'S HOUSE.
IT'S TOO FAR TO WALK. YOU'LL JUST HAVE TO LIVE WITH THE STARES A WHILE LONGER.
I'M STARTIN' TO FEEL... SLIMY.
BESIDES, I'M ENJOYING THIS. FOR ONCE, ALL EYES ARE GLUED TO MY NAVEL.
YEAH. SWELL. I'M TICKLED PINK FOR YA.
ME, I DON'T EVEN HAVE A NAVEL. I ATTRACT LOOKS ON SHEER CHARISMA ALONE.
GUESS THAT'S THE PRICE OF--
YOU--YOU ANIMAL!
WAUUK
NO SMOKING! NO SMOKING ON THIS BUS! I WON'T LOSE MY KIDNEYS TO THE LIKES OF YOU!
NIXON DEFENSE FUND
DRINK
CBS
KIDNEYS! K-I-D-N-I-E-S! I KNOW YOU'RE OUT TO GET 'EM!
wha...?
I RIDE THIS BUS ALL DAY-- BACK AND FORTH, BACK AND FORTH-- TO PROTECT MY KIDNEYS FROM YOU BEASTS!
YOU AND YOUR TOBACCO-- YOUR DEEP-FRIED FOODS-- YOUR WANTON WOMEN AND LOW MORALS--
--YOUR INTERNATIONAL KIDNEY-POISONING CONSPIRACY!

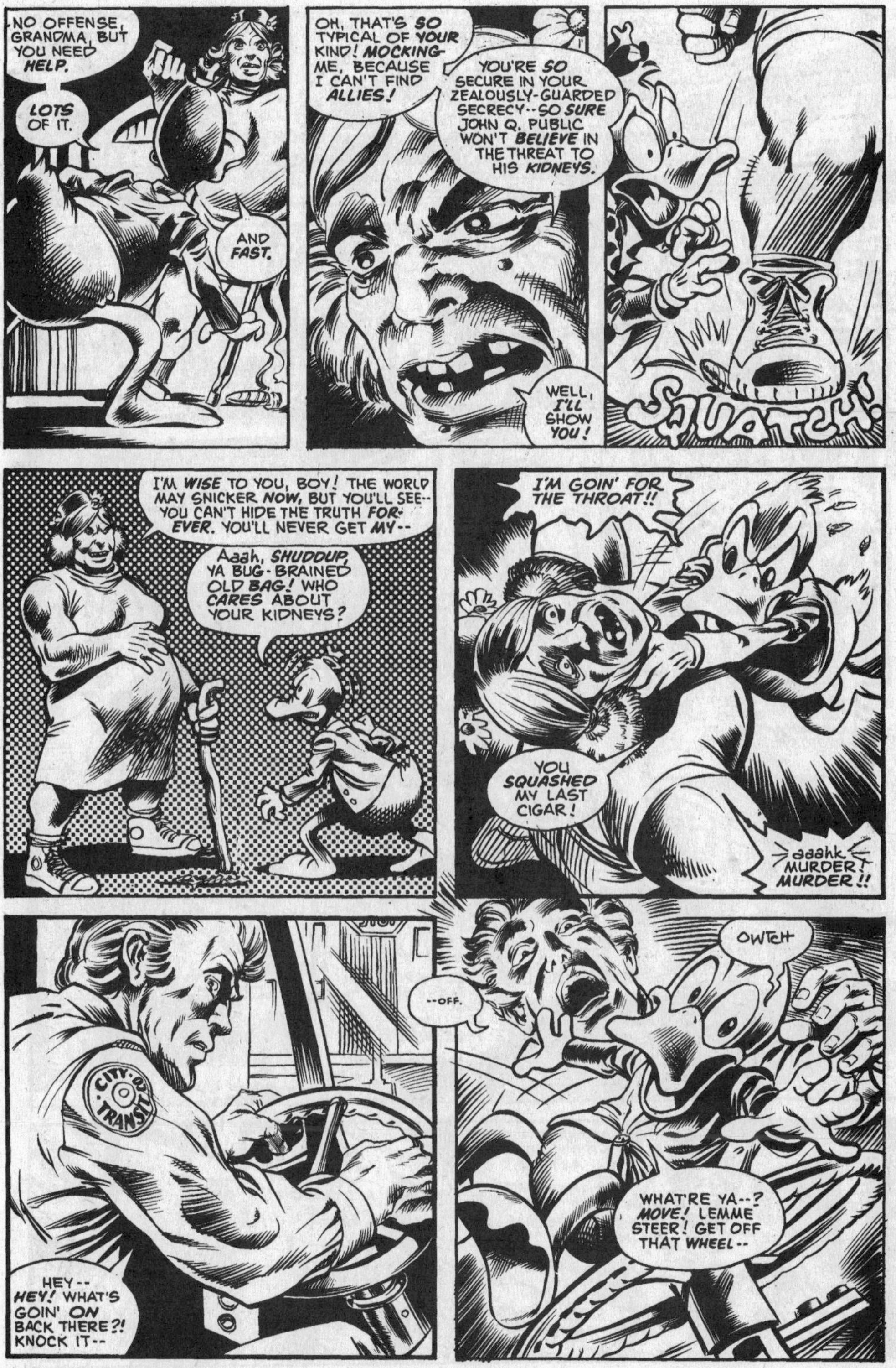
NO OFFENSE, GRANDMA, BUT YOU NEED HELP.
LOTS OF IT.
AND FAST.
OH, THAT'S SO TYPICAL OF YOUR KIND! MOCKING ME, BECAUSE I CAN'T FIND ALLIES!
YOU'RE SO SECURE IN YOUR ZEALOUSLY-GUARDED SECRECY--SO SURE JOHN Q. PUBLIC WON'T BELIEVE IN THE THREAT TO HIS KIDNEYS.
WELL, I'LL SHOW YOU!
SQUATCH!
I'M WISE TO YOU, BOY! THE WORLD MAY SNICKER NOW, BUT YOU'LL SEE--YOU CAN'T HIDE THE TRUTH FOREVER. YOU'LL NEVER GET MY--
Aaah, SHUDDUP, YA BUG-BRAINED OLD BAG! WHO CARES ABOUT YOUR KIDNEYS?
I'M GOIN' FOR THE THROAT!!
YOU SQUASHED MY LAST CIGAR!
aaahk MURDER! MURDER!!
CITY TRANSIT
HEY--HEY! WHAT'S GOIN' ON BACK THERE?! KNOCK IT--
--OFF.
OWTCH
WHAT'RE YA--? MOVE! LEMME STEER! GET OFF THAT WHEEL--

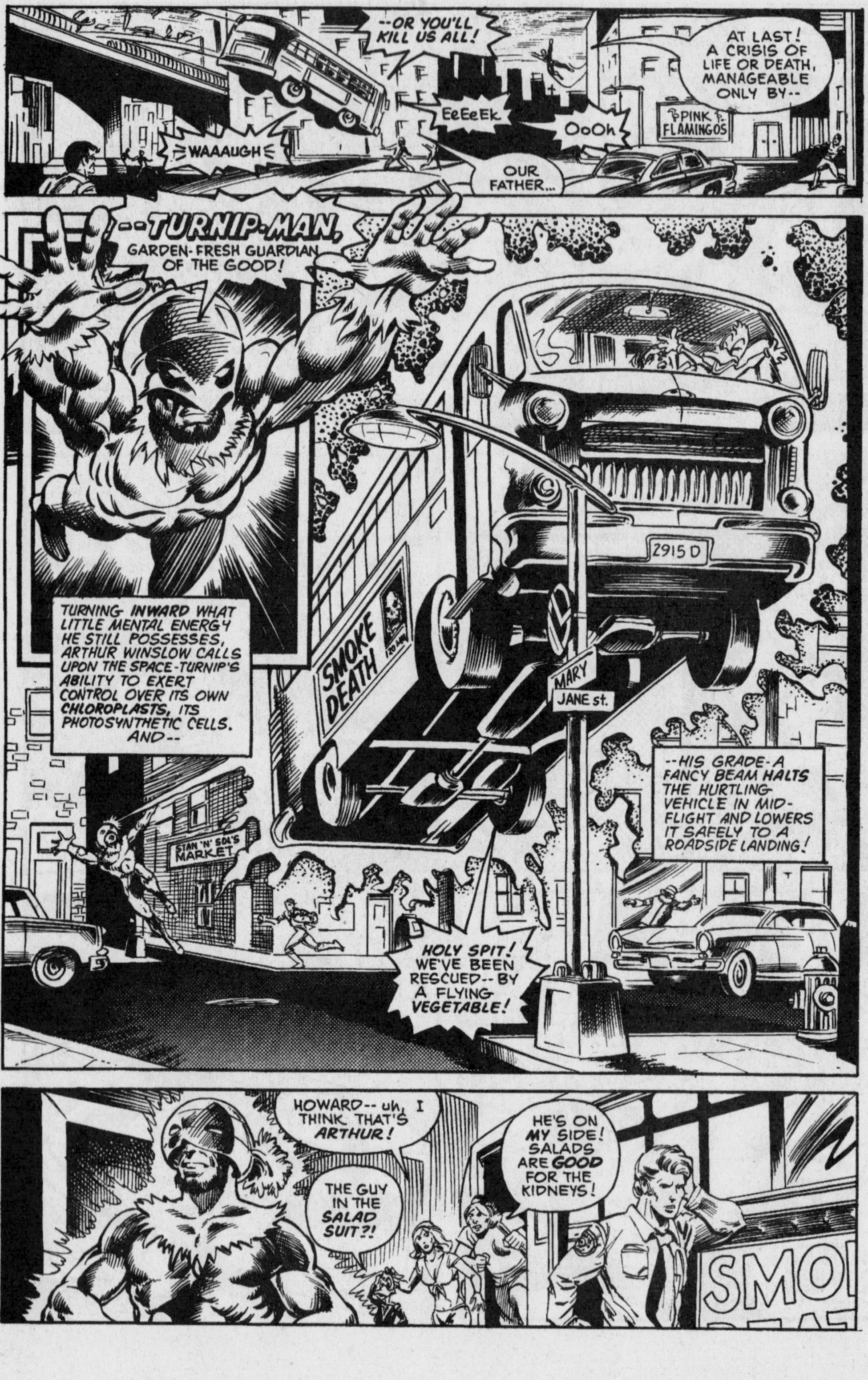

--OR YOU'LL KILL US ALL!
AT LAST! A CRISIS OF LIFE OR DEATH, MANAGEABLE ONLY BY--
EeEeEk
OoOh
WAAAUGH
PINK FLAMINGOS
OUR FATHER...
--TURNIP-MAN, GARDEN-FRESH GUARDIAN OF THE GOOD!
TURNING INWARD WHAT LITTLE MENTAL ENERGY HE STILL POSSESSES, ARTHUR WINSLOW CALLS UPON THE SPACE-TURNIP'S ABILITY TO EXERT CONTROL OVER ITS OWN CHLOROPLASTS, ITS PHOTOSYNTHETIC CELLS. AND--
SMOKE DEATH
2915 D
MARY
JANE st.
--HIS GRADE-A FANCY BEAM HALTS THE HURTLING VEHICLE IN MID-FLIGHT AND LOWERS IT SAFELY TO A ROADSIDE LANDING!
STAN 'N' SOL'S MARKET
HOLY SPIT! WE'VE BEEN RESCUED--BY A FLYING VEGETABLE!
HOWARD-- uh, I THINK THAT'S ARTHUR!
THE GUY IN THE SALAD SUIT?!
HE'S ON MY SIDE! SALADS ARE GOOD FOR THE KIDNEYS!
SMO

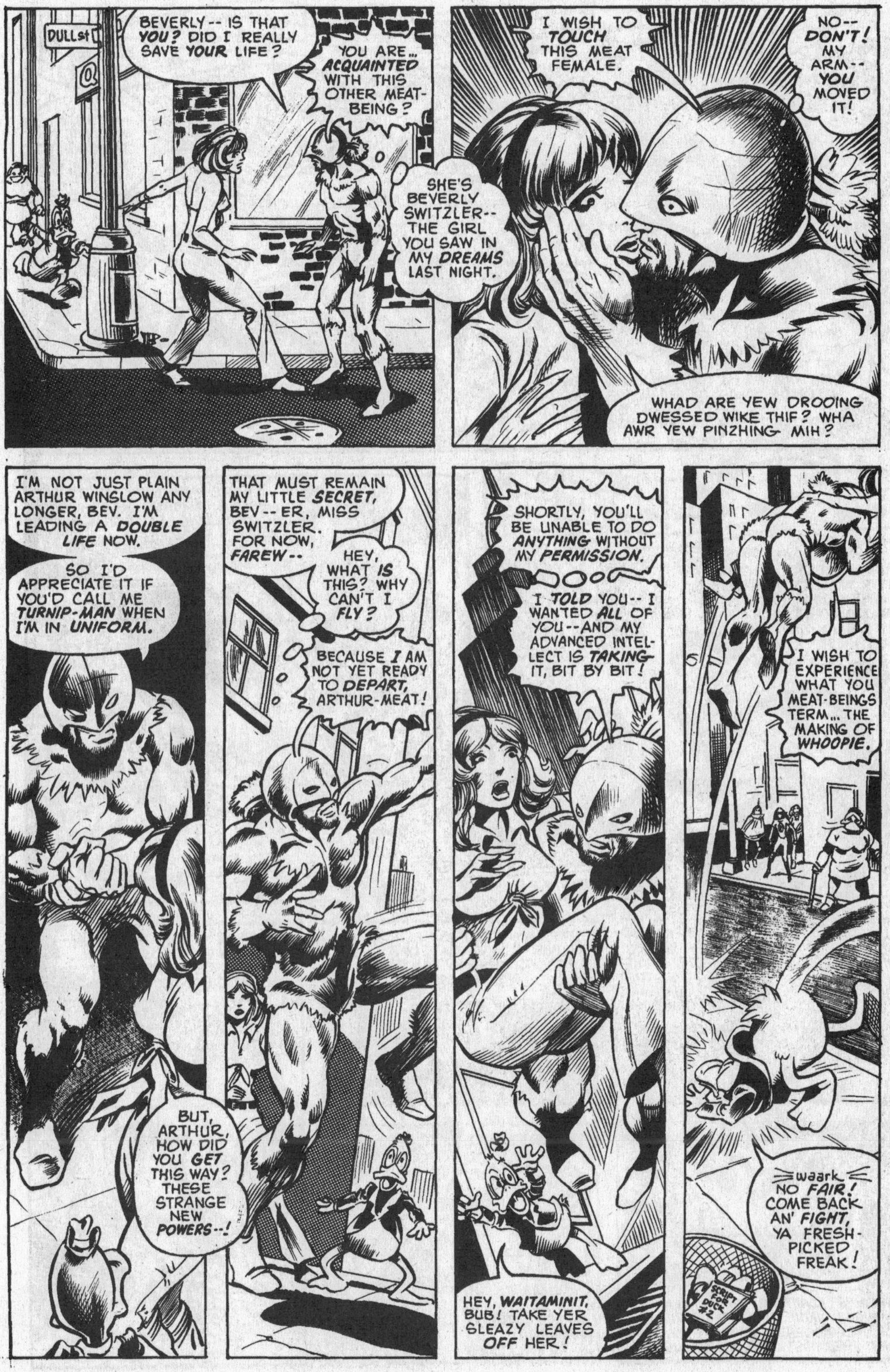
DULL st
BEVERLY -- IS THAT YOU? DID I REALLY SAVE YOUR LIFE?
YOU ARE... ACQUAINTED WITH THIS OTHER MEAT-BEING?
SHE'S BEVERLY SWITZLER-- THE GIRL YOU SAW IN MY DREAMS LAST NIGHT.
I WISH TO TOUCH THIS MEAT FEMALE.
NO-- DON'T! MY ARM-- YOU MOVED IT!
WHAD ARE YEW DROOING DWESSED WIKE THIF? WHA AWR YEW PINZHING MIH?
I'M NOT JUST PLAIN ARTHUR WINSLOW ANY LONGER, BEV. I'M LEADING A DOUBLE LIFE NOW.
SO I'D APPRECIATE IT IF YOU'D CALL ME TURNIP-MAN WHEN I'M IN UNIFORM.
BUT, ARTHUR, HOW DID YOU GET THIS WAY? THESE STRANGE NEW POWERS--!
THAT MUST REMAIN MY LITTLE SECRET, BEV -- ER, MISS SWITZLER. FOR NOW, FAREW--
HEY, WHAT IS THIS? WHY CAN'T I FLY?
BECAUSE I AM NOT YET READY TO DEPART, ARTHUR-MEAT!
SHORTLY, YOU'LL BE UNABLE TO DO ANYTHING WITHOUT MY PERMISSION.
I TOLD YOU-- I WANTED ALL OF YOU--AND MY ADVANCED INTELLECT IS TAKING IT, BIT BY BIT!
HEY, WAITAMINIT, BUB! TAKE YER SLEAZY LEAVES OFF HER!
I WISH TO EXPERIENCE WHAT YOU MEAT-BEINGS TERM... THE MAKING OF WHOOPIE.
waark
NO FAIR! COME BACK AN' FIGHT, YA FRESH-PICKED FREAK!

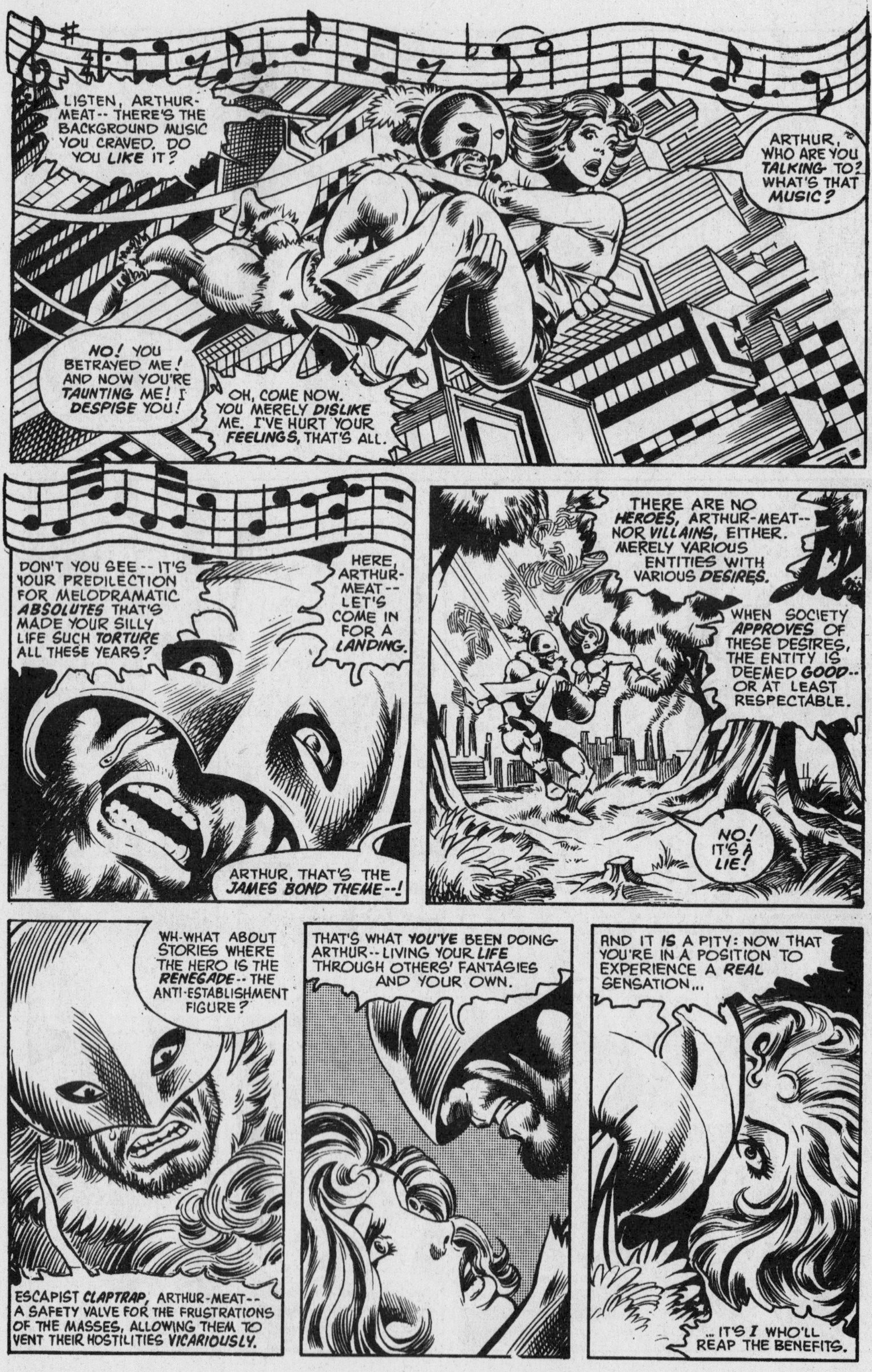

LISTEN, ARTHUR-MEAT-- THERE'S THE BACKGROUND MUSIC YOU CRAVED. DO YOU LIKE IT?
ARTHUR, WHO ARE YOU TALKING TO? WHAT'S THAT MUSIC?
NO! YOU BETRAYED ME! AND NOW YOU'RE TAUNTING ME! I DESPISE YOU!
OH, COME NOW. YOU MERELY DISLIKE ME. I'VE HURT YOUR FEELINGS, THAT'S ALL.
DON'T YOU SEE -- IT'S YOUR PREDILECTION FOR MELODRAMATIC ABSOLUTES THAT'S MADE YOUR SILLY LIFE SUCH TORTURE ALL THESE YEARS?
HERE, ARTHUR-MEAT-- LET'S COME IN FOR A LANDING.
ARTHUR, THAT'S THE JAMES BOND THEME--!
THERE ARE NO HEROES, ARTHUR-MEAT-- NOR VILLAINS, EITHER. MERELY VARIOUS ENTITIES WITH VARIOUS DESIRES.
WHEN SOCIETY APPROVES OF THESE DESIRES, THE ENTITY IS DEEMED GOOD-- OR AT LEAST RESPECTABLE.
NO! IT'S A LIE!
WH-WHAT ABOUT STORIES WHERE THE HERO IS THE RENEGADE-- THE ANTI-ESTABLISHMENT FIGURE?
ESCAPIST CLAPTRAP, ARTHUR-MEAT-- A SAFETY VALVE FOR THE FRUSTRATIONS OF THE MASSES, ALLOWING THEM TO VENT THEIR HOSTILITIES VICARIOUSLY.
THAT'S WHAT YOU'VE BEEN DOING ARTHUR-- LIVING YOUR LIFE THROUGH OTHERS' FANTASIES AND YOUR OWN.
AND IT IS A PITY: NOW THAT YOU'RE IN A POSITION TO EXPERIENCE A REAL SENSATION...
... IT'S I WHO'LL REAP THE BENEFITS.

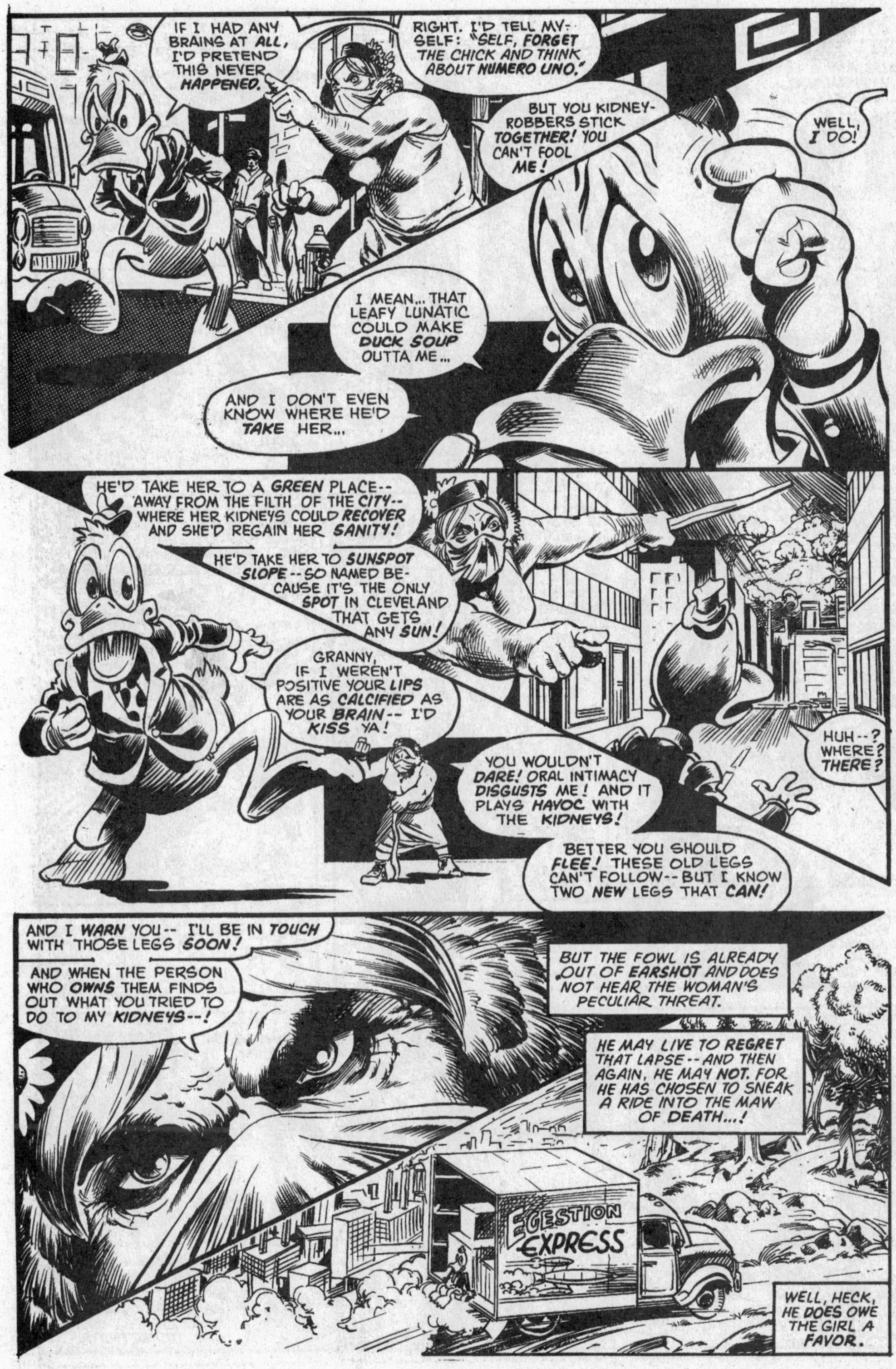

IF I HAD ANY BRAINS AT ALL, I'D PRETEND THIS NEVER HAPPENED.
RIGHT. I'D TELL MYSELF: "SELF, FORGET THE CHICK AND THINK ABOUT NUMERO UNO."
BUT YOU KIDNEY-ROBBERS STICK TOGETHER! YOU CAN'T FOOL ME!
WELL, I DO!
I MEAN... THAT LEAFY LUNATIC COULD MAKE DUCK SOUP OUTTA ME...
AND I DON'T EVEN KNOW WHERE HE'D TAKE HER...
HE'D TAKE HER TO A GREEN PLACE-- AWAY FROM THE FILTH OF THE CITY-- WHERE HER KIDNEYS COULD RECOVER AND SHE'D REGAIN HER SANITY!
HE'D TAKE HER TO SUNSPOT SLOPE -- SO NAMED BECAUSE IT'S THE ONLY SPOT IN CLEVELAND THAT GETS ANY SUN!
GRANNY, IF I WEREN'T POSITIVE YOUR LIPS ARE AS CALCIFIED AS YOUR BRAIN-- I'D KISS YA!
HUH--? WHERE? THERE?
YOU WOULDN'T DARE! ORAL INTIMACY DISGUSTS ME! AND IT PLAYS HAVOC WITH THE KIDNEYS!
BETTER YOU SHOULD FLEE! THESE OLD LEGS CAN'T FOLLOW-- BUT I KNOW TWO NEW LEGS THAT CAN!
AND I WARN YOU-- I'LL BE IN TOUCH WITH THOSE LEGS SOON!
AND WHEN THE PERSON WHO OWNS THEM FINDS OUT WHAT YOU TRIED TO DO TO MY KIDNEYS--!
BUT THE FOWL IS ALREADY OUT OF EARSHOT AND DOES NOT HEAR THE WOMAN'S PECULIAR THREAT.
HE MAY LIVE TO REGRET THAT LAPSE-- AND THEN AGAIN, HE MAY NOT. FOR HE HAS CHOSEN TO SNEAK A RIDE INTO THE MAW OF DEATH...!
EGESTION EXPRESS
WELL, HECK, HE DOES OWE THE GIRL A FAVOR.

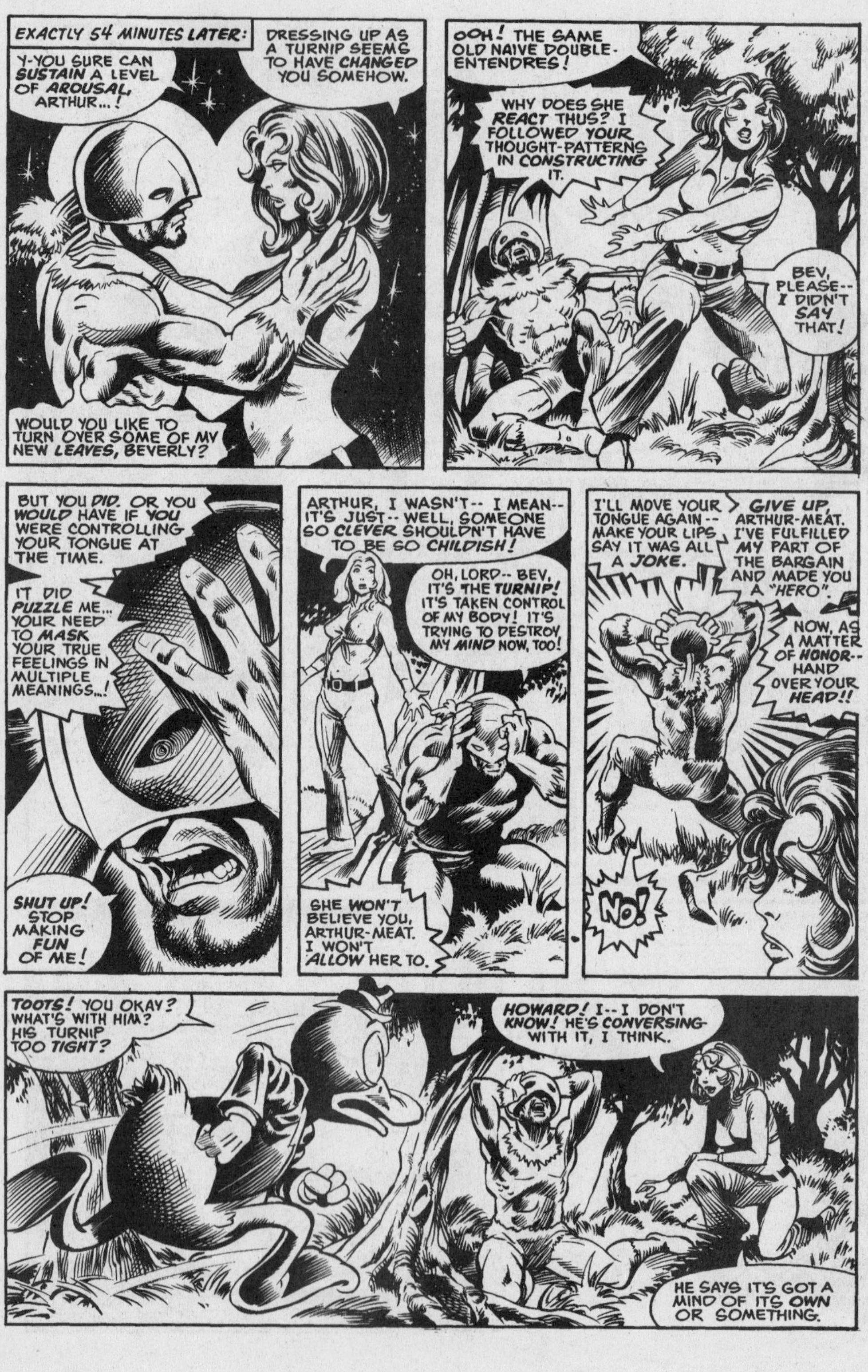
EXACTLY 54 MINUTES LATER:
Y-YOU SURE CAN SUSTAIN A LEVEL OF AROUSAL, ARTHUR...!
DRESSING UP AS A TURNIP SEEMS TO HAVE CHANGED YOU SOMEHOW.
WOULD YOU LIKE TO TURN OVER SOME OF MY NEW LEAVES, BEVERLY?
OOH! THE SAME OLD NAIVE DOUBLE-ENTENDRES!
WHY DOES SHE REACT THUS? I FOLLOWED YOUR THOUGHT-PATTERNS IN CONSTRUCTING IT.
BEV, PLEASE-- I DIDN'T SAY THAT!
BUT YOU DID. OR YOU WOULD HAVE IF YOU WERE CONTROLLING YOUR TONGUE AT THE TIME.
IT DID PUZZLE ME... YOUR NEED TO MASK YOUR TRUE FEELINGS IN MULTIPLE MEANINGS...!
SHUT UP! STOP MAKING FUN OF ME!
ARTHUR, I WASN'T-- I MEAN-- IT'S JUST-- WELL, SOMEONE SO CLEVER SHOULDN'T HAVE TO BE SO CHILDISH!
OH, LORD-- BEV, IT'S THE TURNIP! IT'S TAKEN CONTROL OF MY BODY! IT'S TRYING TO DESTROY MY MIND NOW, TOO!
SHE WON'T BELIEVE YOU, ARTHUR-MEAT. I WON'T ALLOW HER TO.
I'LL MOVE YOUR TONGUE AGAIN -- MAKE YOUR LIPS SAY IT WAS ALL A JOKE.
GIVE UP, ARTHUR-MEAT. I'VE FULFILLED MY PART OF THE BARGAIN AND MADE YOU A "HERO".
NOW, AS A MATTER OF HONOR-- HAND OVER YOUR HEAD!!
NO!
TOOTS! YOU OKAY? WHAT'S WITH HIM? HIS TURNIP TOO TIGHT?
HOWARD! I-- I DON'T KNOW! HE'S CONVERSING WITH IT, I THINK.
HE SAYS IT'S GOT A MIND OF ITS OWN OR SOMETHING.

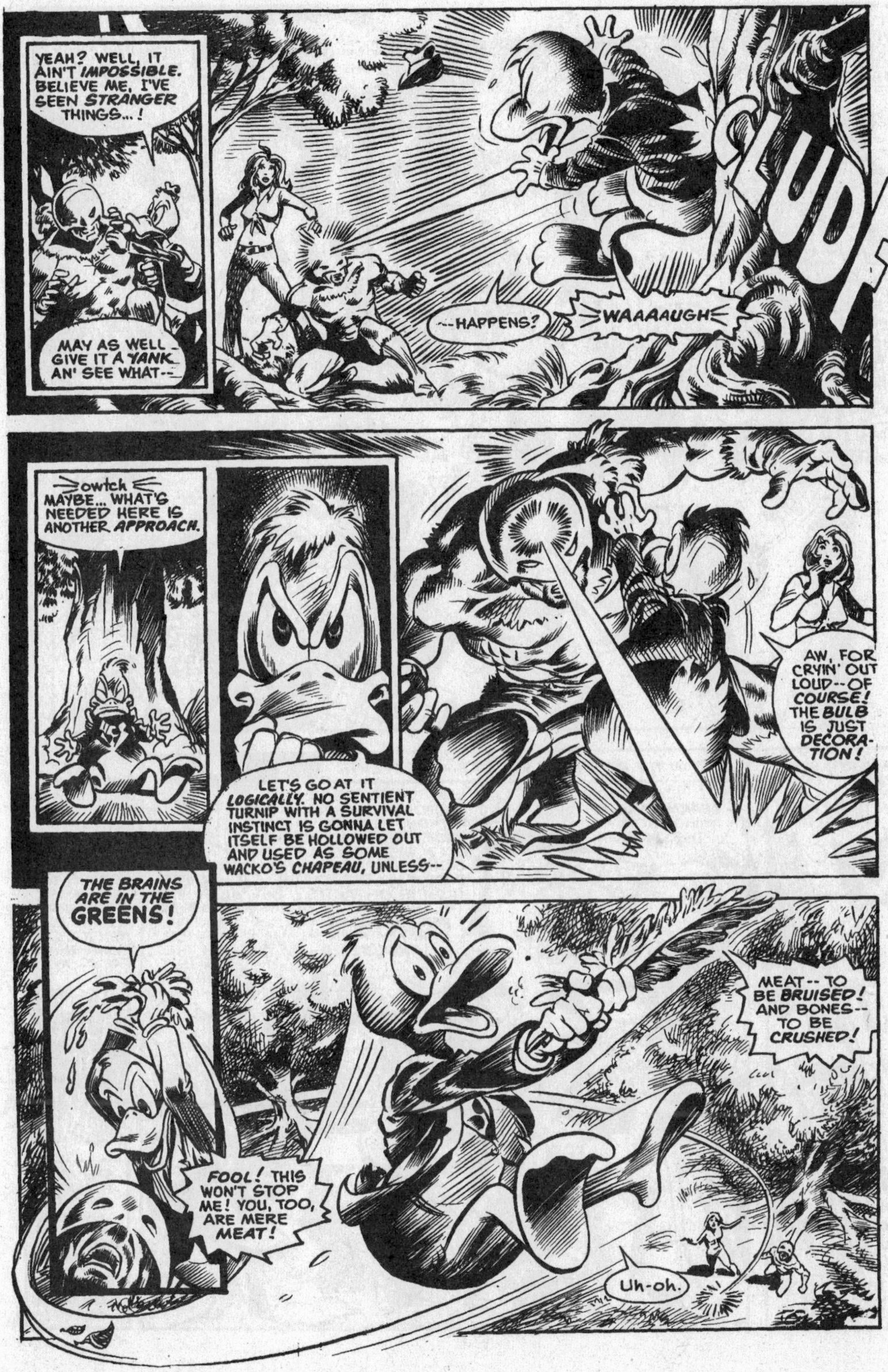
YEAH? WELL, IT AIN'T IMPOSSIBLE. BELIEVE ME, I'VE SEEN STRANGER THINGS...!
MAY AS WELL GIVE IT A YANK AN' SEE WHAT--
--HAPPENS?
WAAAAAUGH
CLUDF
owtch
MAYBE... WHAT'S NEEDED HERE IS ANOTHER APPROACH.
LET'S GO AT IT LOGICALLY. NO SENTIENT TURNIP WITH A SURVIVAL INSTINCT IS GONNA LET ITSELF BE HOLLOWED OUT AND USED AS SOME WACKO'S CHAPEAU, UNLESS--
AW, FOR CRYIN' OUT LOUD--OF COURSE! THE BULB IS JUST DECORATION!
THE BRAINS ARE IN THE GREENS!
FOOL! THIS WON'T STOP ME! YOU, TOO, ARE MERE MEAT!
MEAT-- TO BE BRUISED! AND BONES-- TO BE CRUSHED!
Uh-oh.

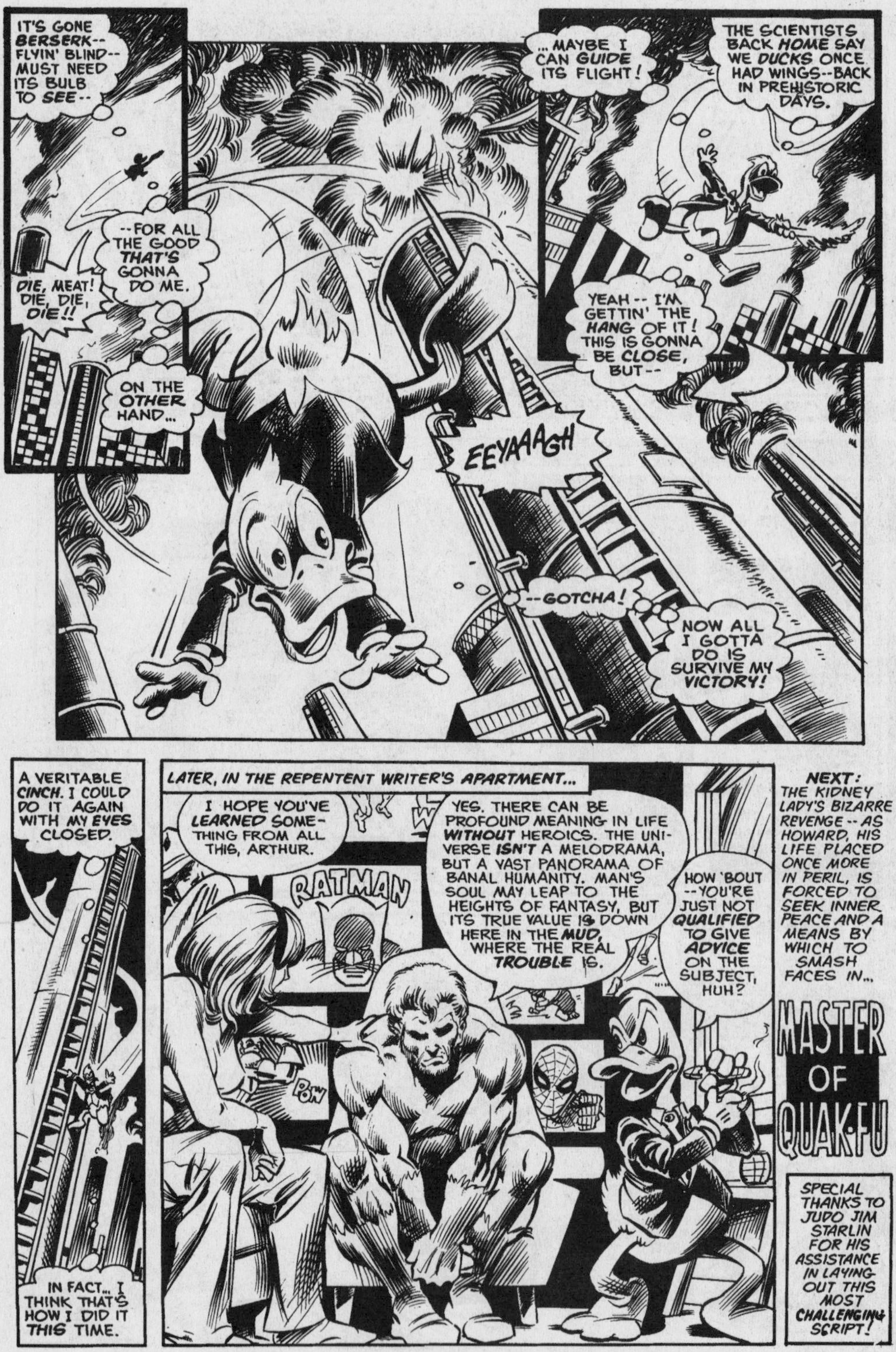
IT'S GONE BERSERK-- FLYIN' BLIND-- MUST NEED ITS BULB TO SEE--
--FOR ALL THE GOOD THAT'S GONNA DO ME.
DIE, MEAT! DIE, DIE, DIE!!
ON THE OTHER HAND...
...MAYBE I CAN GUIDE ITS FLIGHT!
THE SCIENTISTS BACK HOME SAY WE DUCKS ONCE HAD WINGS--BACK IN PREHISTORIC DAYS.
YEAH -- I'M GETTIN' THE HANG OF IT! THIS IS GONNA BE CLOSE, BUT--
EEYAAAGH
--GOTCHA!
NOW ALL I GOTTA DO IS SURVIVE MY VICTORY!
A VERITABLE CINCH. I COULD DO IT AGAIN WITH MY EYES CLOSED.
IN FACT... I THINK THAT'S HOW I DID IT THIS TIME.
LATER, IN THE REPENTENT WRITER'S APARTMENT...
I HOPE YOU'VE LEARNED SOMETHING FROM ALL THIS, ARTHUR.
YES. THERE CAN BE PROFOUND MEANING IN LIFE WITHOUT HEROICS. THE UNIVERSE ISN'T A MELODRAMA, BUT A VAST PANORAMA OF BANAL HUMANITY. MAN'S SOUL MAY LEAP TO THE HEIGHTS OF FANTASY, BUT ITS TRUE VALUE IS DOWN HERE IN THE MUD, WHERE THE REAL TROUBLE IS.
HOW 'BOUT --YOU'RE JUST NOT QUALIFIED TO GIVE ADVICE ON THE SUBJECT, HUH?
RATMAN
POW
NEXT: THE KIDNEY LADY'S BIZARRE REVENGE -- AS HOWARD, HIS LIFE PLACED ONCE MORE IN PERIL, IS FORCED TO SEEK INNER PEACE AND A MEANS BY WHICH TO SMASH FACES IN...
MASTER OF QUAK-FU
SPECIAL THANKS TO JUDO JIM STARLIN FOR HIS ASSISTANCE IN LAYING OUT THIS MOST CHALLENGING SCRIPT!

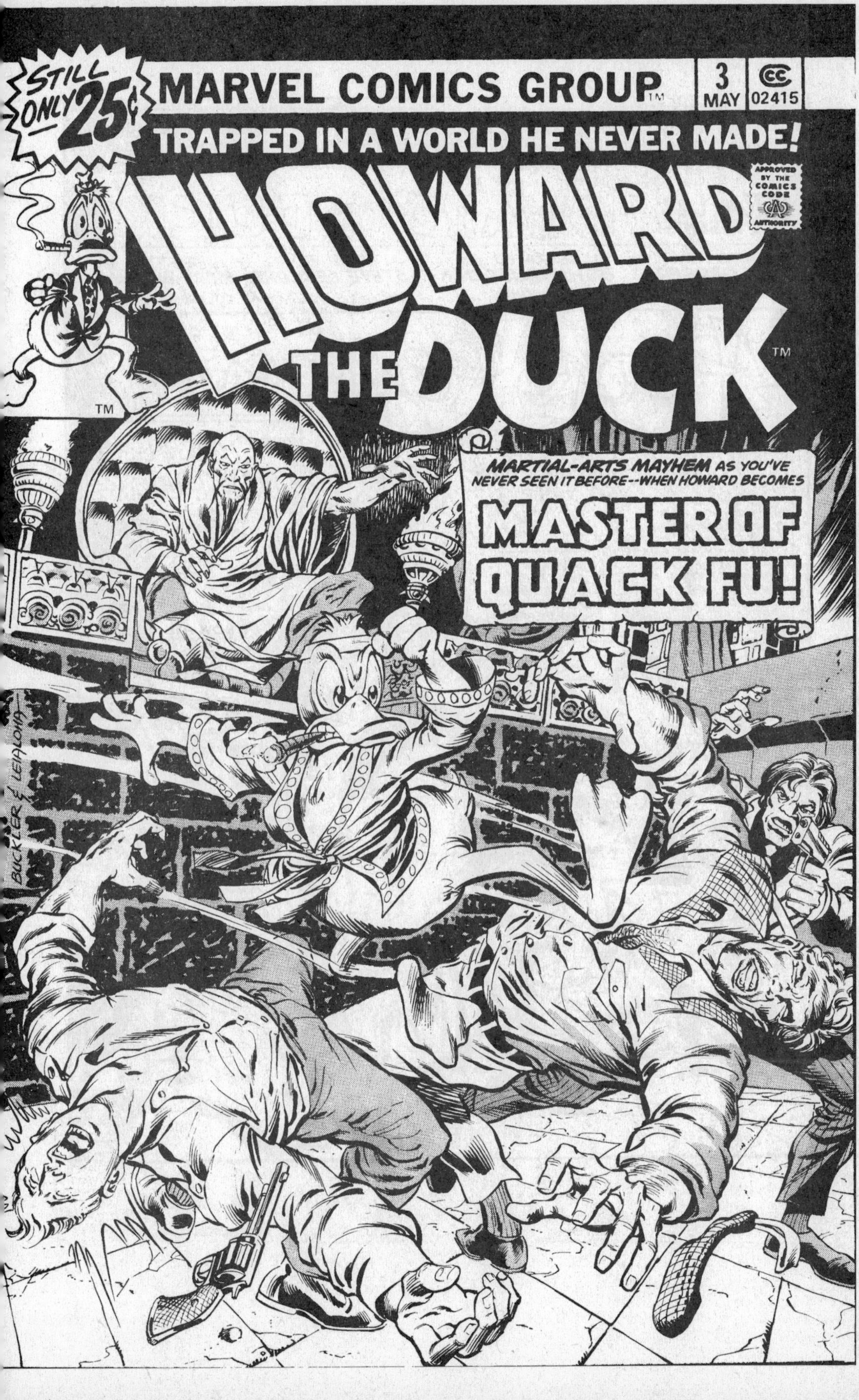

STILL ONLY 25¢
MARVEL COMICS GROUP
3 MAY
CC 02415
TRAPPED IN A WORLD HE NEVER MADE!
APPROVED BY THE COMICS CODE AUTHORITY
HOWARD THE DUCK
MARTIAL-ARTS MAYHEM AS YOU'VE NEVER SEEN IT BEFORE--WHEN HOWARD BECOMES
MASTER OF QUACK FU!
BUCKLER & LEIALOHA

From the time of his hatching, he was...different. A potentially brilliant scholar who dreaded the structured environment of school, he educated himself in the streets, taking whatever work was available, formulating his philosophy of self from what he learned of the world about him. And then the Cosmic Axis shifted...and that world *changed.* Suddenly, he was stranded in a universe he could not fathom. Without warning, he became a strange fowl in an even stranger land.

Stan Lee PRESENTS: HOWARD THE DUCK!™

WRITTEN BY STEVE GERBER * ILLUSTRATED BY JOHN BUSCEMA * INKED BY STEVE LEIALOHA * EDITED BY MARV WOLFMAN

ANNETTE KAWECKI, LETTERER   MICHELE WOLFMAN, COLORIST

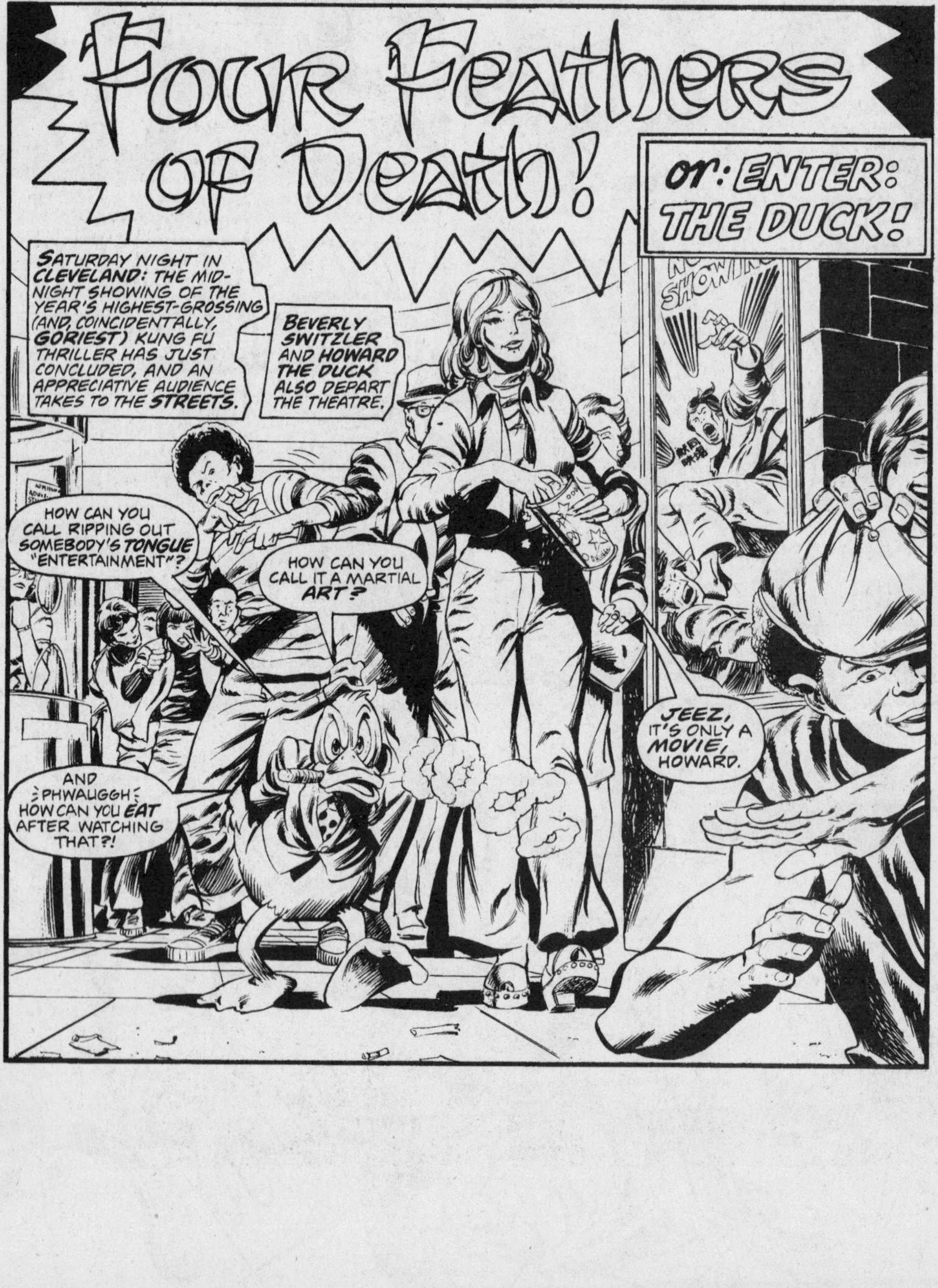
FOUR FEATHERS OF DEATH!
OR: ENTER: THE DUCK!
SATURDAY NIGHT IN CLEVELAND: THE MIDNIGHT SHOWING OF THE YEAR'S HIGHEST-GROSSING (AND, COINCIDENTALLY, GORIEST) KUNG FU THRILLER HAS JUST CONCLUDED, AND AN APPRECIATIVE AUDIENCE TAKES TO THE STREETS.
BEVERLY SWITZLER AND HOWARD THE DUCK ALSO DEPART THE THEATRE.
HOW CAN YOU CALL RIPPING OUT SOMEBODY'S TONGUE "ENTERTAINMENT"?
HOW CAN YOU CALL IT A MARTIAL ART?
AND PHWAUGGH HOW CAN YOU EAT AFTER WATCHING THAT?!
JEEZ, IT'S ONLY A MOVIE, HOWARD.

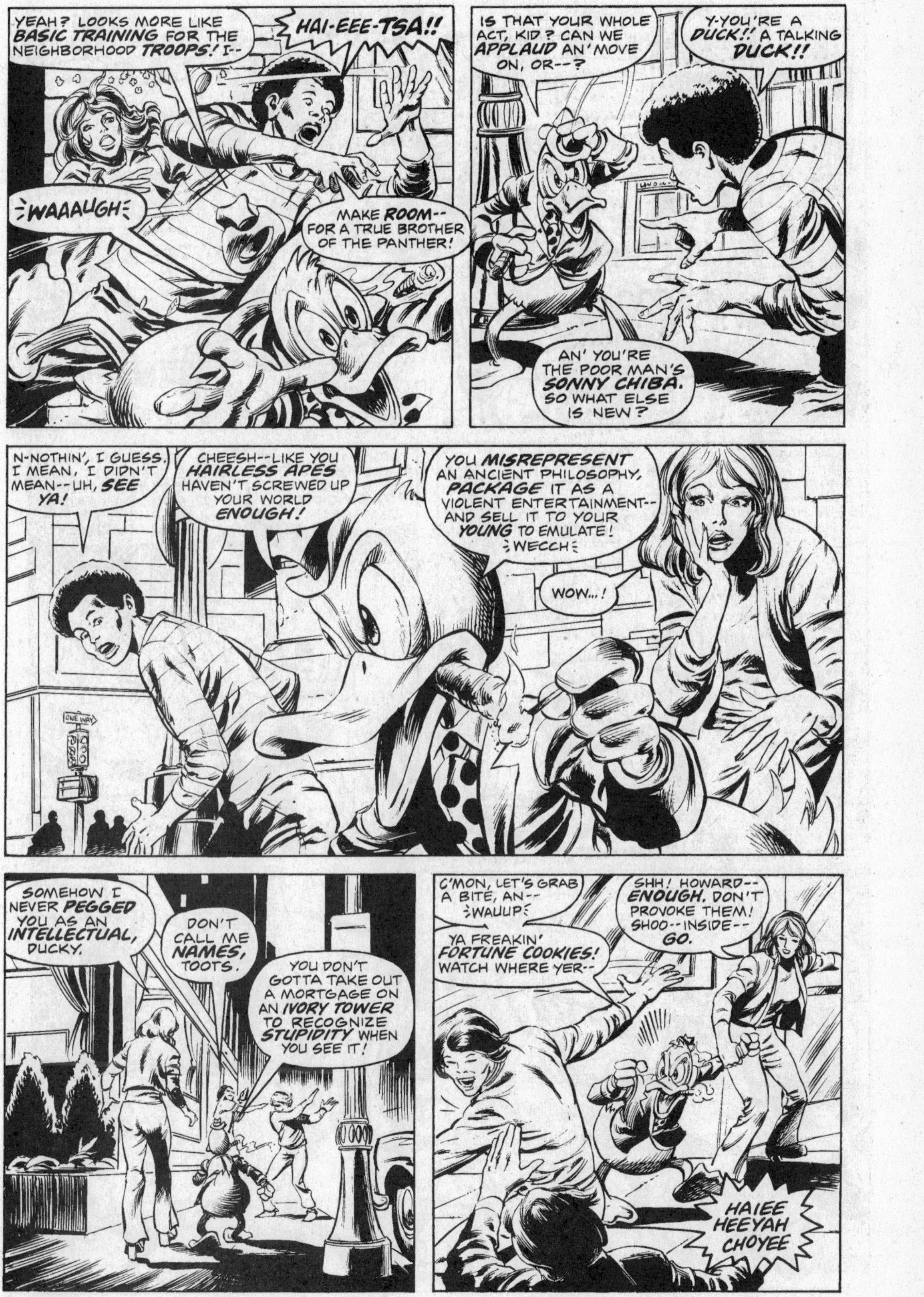
YEAH? LOOKS MORE LIKE BASIC TRAINING FOR THE NEIGHBORHOOD TROOPS! I--
HAI-EEE-TSA!!
WAAAUGH
MAKE ROOM-- FOR A TRUE BROTHER OF THE PANTHER!
IS THAT YOUR WHOLE ACT, KID? CAN WE APPLAUD AN' MOVE ON, OR--?
Y-YOU'RE A DUCK!! A TALKING DUCK!!
AN' YOU'RE THE POOR MAN'S SONNY CHIBA. SO WHAT ELSE IS NEW?
N-NOTHIN', I GUESS. I MEAN, I DIDN'T MEAN--UH, SEE YA!
CHEESH--LIKE YOU HAIRLESS APES HAVEN'T SCREWED UP YOUR WORLD ENOUGH!
YOU MISREPRESENT AN ANCIENT PHILOSOPHY, PACKAGE IT AS A VIOLENT ENTERTAINMENT-- AND SELL IT TO YOUR YOUNG TO EMULATE!
WECCH
WOW...!
ONE WAY
SOMEHOW I NEVER PEGGED YOU AS AN INTELLECTUAL, DUCKY.
DON'T CALL ME NAMES, TOOTS.
YOU DON'T GOTTA TAKE OUT A MORTGAGE ON AN IVORY TOWER TO RECOGNIZE STUPIDITY WHEN YOU SEE IT!
C'MON, LET'S GRAB A BITE, AN--
WAUUP
YA FREAKIN' FORTUNE COOKIES! WATCH WHERE YER--
SHH! HOWARD-- ENOUGH. DON'T PROVOKE THEM! SHOO--INSIDE-- GO.
HAIEE HEEYAH CHOYEE

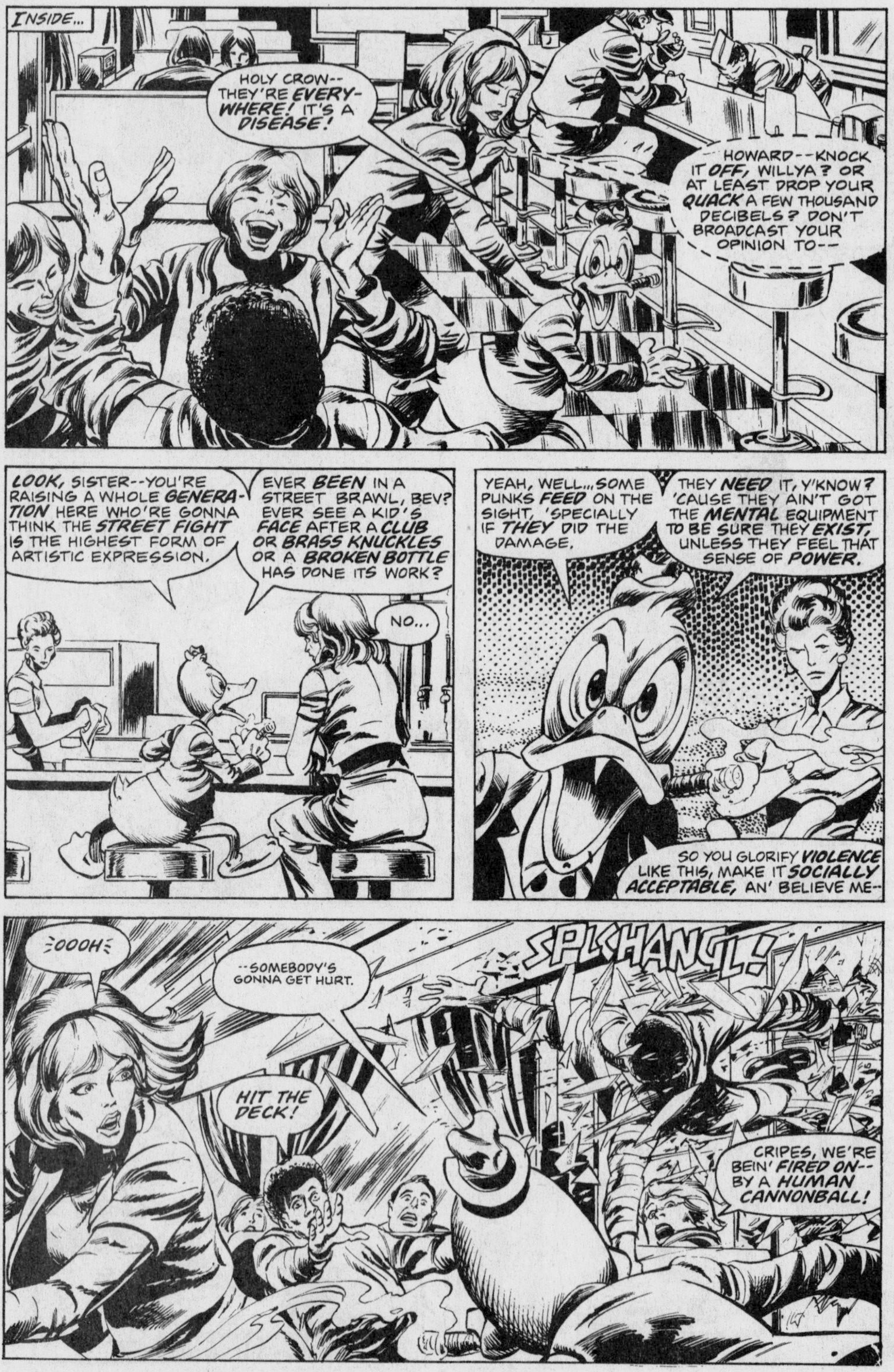

INSIDE...
HOLY CROW-- THEY'RE EVERYWHERE! IT'S A DISEASE!
--HOWARD--KNOCK IT OFF, WILLYA? OR AT LEAST DROP YOUR QUACK A FEW THOUSAND DECIBELS? DON'T BROADCAST YOUR OPINION TO--
LOOK, SISTER--YOU'RE RAISING A WHOLE GENERATION HERE WHO'RE GONNA THINK THE STREET FIGHT IS THE HIGHEST FORM OF ARTISTIC EXPRESSION.
EVER BEEN IN A STREET BRAWL, BEV? EVER SEE A KID'S FACE AFTER A CLUB OR BRASS KNUCKLES OR A BROKEN BOTTLE HAS DONE ITS WORK?
NO...
YEAH, WELL... SOME PUNKS FEED ON THE SIGHT, 'SPECIALLY IF THEY DID THE DAMAGE.
THEY NEED IT, Y'KNOW? 'CAUSE THEY AIN'T GOT THE MENTAL EQUIPMENT TO BE SURE THEY EXIST, UNLESS THEY FEEL THAT SENSE OF POWER.
SO YOU GLORIFY VIOLENCE LIKE THIS, MAKE IT SOCIALLY ACCEPTABLE, AN' BELIEVE ME--
OOOH
--SOMEBODY'S GONNA GET HURT.
SPLSHANGL!
HIT THE DECK!
CRIPES, WE'RE BEIN' FIRED ON-- BY A HUMAN CANNONBALL!

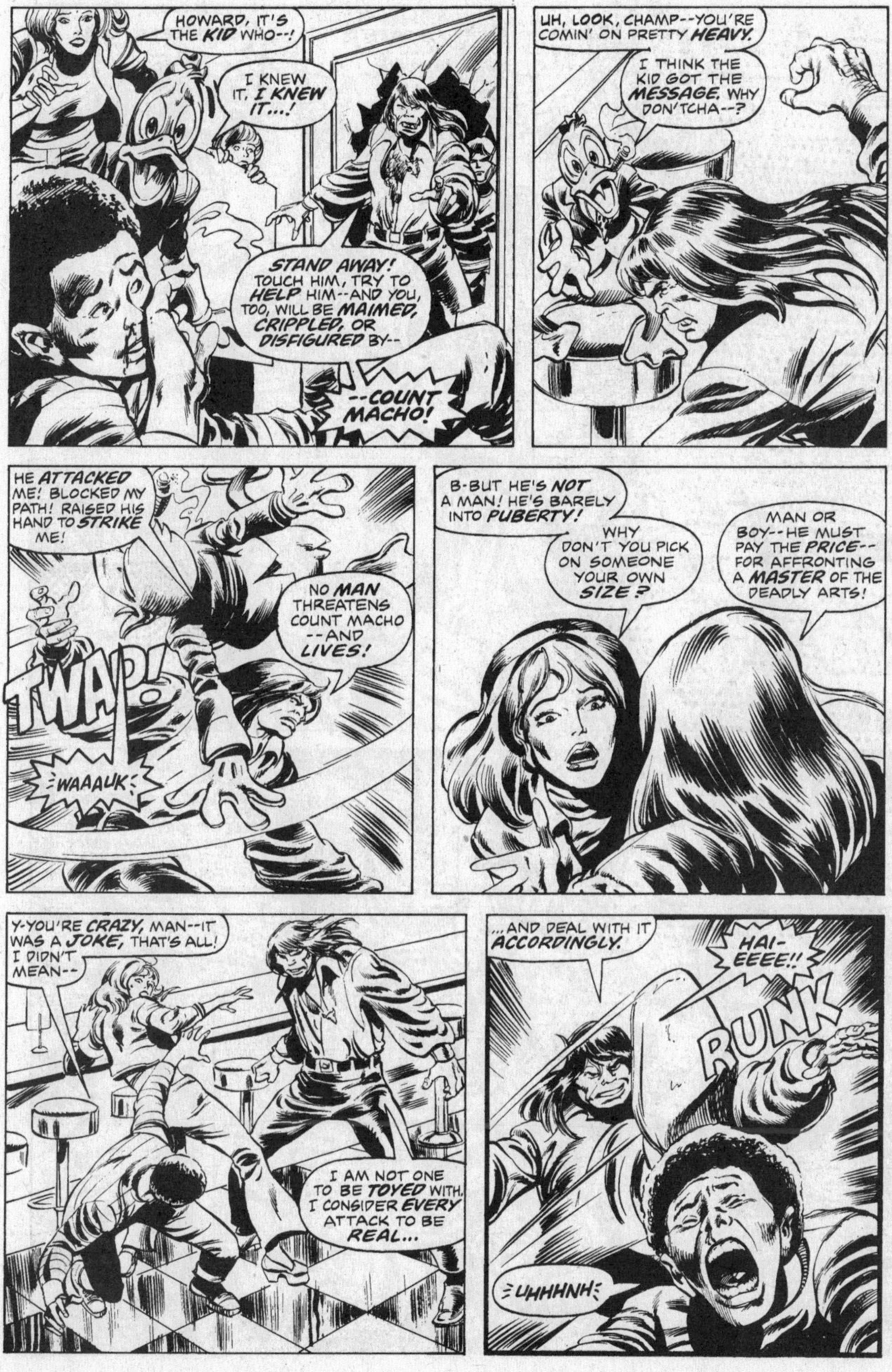
HOWARD, IT'S THE KID WHO--!
I KNEW IT, I KNEW IT...!
STAND AWAY! TOUCH HIM, TRY TO HELP HIM--AND YOU, TOO, WILL BE MAIMED, CRIPPLED, OR DISFIGURED BY--
--COUNT MACHO!
UH, LOOK, CHAMP--YOU'RE COMIN' ON PRETTY HEAVY.
I THINK THE KID GOT THE MESSAGE. WHY DON'TCHA--?
HE ATTACKED ME! BLOCKED MY PATH! RAISED HIS HAND TO STRIKE ME!
NO MAN THREATENS COUNT MACHO --AND LIVES!
TWAP!
WAAAUK!
B-BUT HE'S NOT A MAN! HE'S BARELY INTO PUBERTY!
WHY DON'T YOU PICK ON SOMEONE YOUR OWN SIZE?
MAN OR BOY--HE MUST PAY THE PRICE-- FOR AFFRONTING A MASTER OF THE DEADLY ARTS!
Y-YOU'RE CRAZY, MAN--IT WAS A JOKE, THAT'S ALL! I DIDN'T MEAN--
I AM NOT ONE TO BE TOYED WITH. I CONSIDER EVERY ATTACK TO BE REAL...
...AND DEAL WITH IT ACCORDINGLY.
HAI-EEEE!!
RUNK
UHHHNH

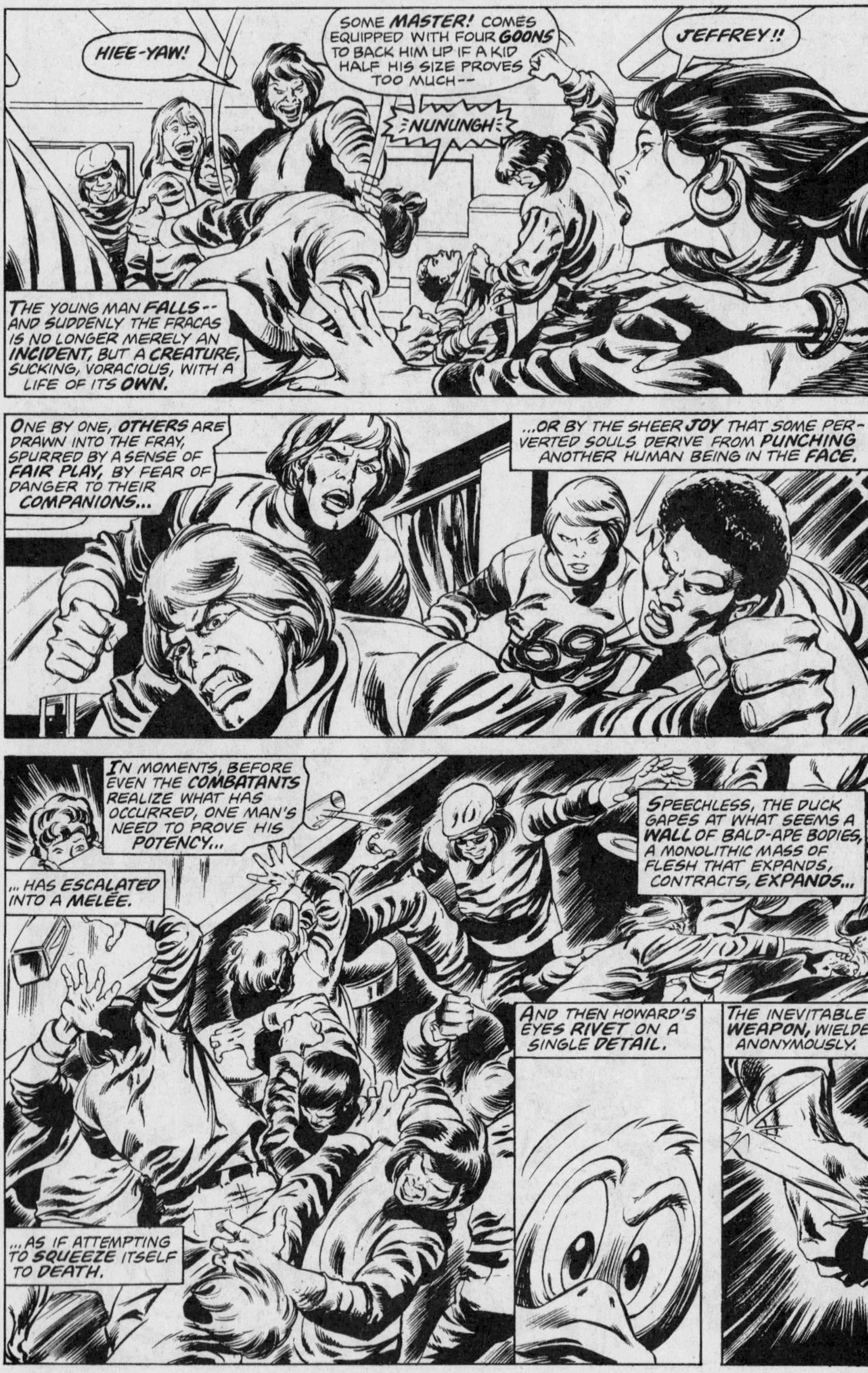
HIEE-YAW!
SOME MASTER! COMES EQUIPPED WITH FOUR GOONS TO BACK HIM UP IF A KID HALF HIS SIZE PROVES TOO MUCH--
NUNUNGH
JEFFREY!!
THE YOUNG MAN FALLS-- AND SUDDENLY THE FRACAS IS NO LONGER MERELY AN INCIDENT, BUT A CREATURE, SUCKING, VORACIOUS, WITH A LIFE OF ITS OWN.
ONE BY ONE, OTHERS ARE DRAWN INTO THE FRAY, SPURRED BY A SENSE OF FAIR PLAY, BY FEAR OF DANGER TO THEIR COMPANIONS...
...OR BY THE SHEER JOY THAT SOME PERVERTED SOULS DERIVE FROM PUNCHING ANOTHER HUMAN BEING IN THE FACE.
IN MOMENTS, BEFORE EVEN THE COMBATANTS REALIZE WHAT HAS OCCURRED, ONE MAN'S NEED TO PROVE HIS POTENCY...
...HAS ESCALATED INTO A MELÉE.
SPEECHLESS, THE DUCK GAPES AT WHAT SEEMS A WALL OF BALD-APE BODIES, A MONOLITHIC MASS OF FLESH THAT EXPANDS, CONTRACTS, EXPANDS...
...AS IF ATTEMPTING TO SQUEEZE ITSELF TO DEATH.
AND THEN HOWARD'S EYES RIVET ON A SINGLE DETAIL.
THE INEVITABLE WEAPON, WIELDED ANONYMOUSLY.

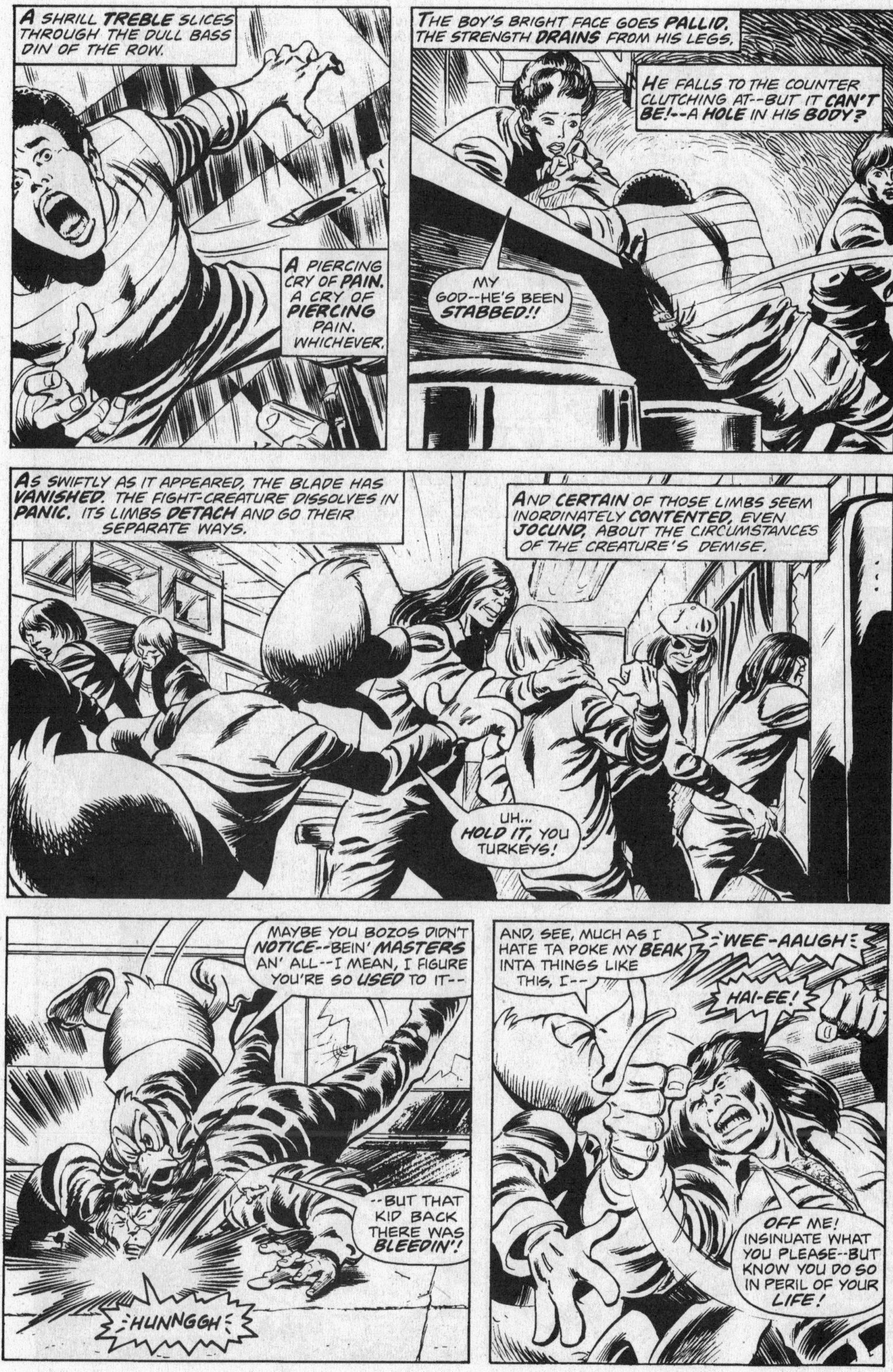
A SHRILL TREBLE SLICES THROUGH THE DULL BASS DIN OF THE ROW.
A PIERCING CRY OF PAIN. A CRY OF PIERCING PAIN. WHICHEVER.
THE BOY'S BRIGHT FACE GOES PALLID, THE STRENGTH DRAINS FROM HIS LEGS.
HE FALLS TO THE COUNTER CLUTCHING AT--BUT IT CAN'T BE!--A HOLE IN HIS BODY?
MY GOD--HE'S BEEN STABBED!!
AS SWIFTLY AS IT APPEARED, THE BLADE HAS VANISHED. THE FIGHT-CREATURE DISSOLVES IN PANIC. ITS LIMBS DETACH AND GO THEIR SEPARATE WAYS.
AND CERTAIN OF THOSE LIMBS SEEM INORDINATELY CONTENTED, EVEN JOCUND, ABOUT THE CIRCUMSTANCES OF THE CREATURE'S DEMISE.
UH... HOLD IT, YOU TURKEYS!
MAYBE YOU BOZOS DIDN'T NOTICE--BEIN' MASTERS AN' ALL--I MEAN, I FIGURE YOU'RE SO USED TO IT--
--BUT THAT KID BACK THERE WAS BLEEDIN'!
HUNNGGH
AND, SEE, MUCH AS I HATE TA POKE MY BEAK INTA THINGS LIKE THIS, I--
WEE-AAUGH
HAI-EE!
OFF ME! INSINUATE WHAT YOU PLEASE--BUT KNOW YOU DO SO IN PERIL OF YOUR LIFE!

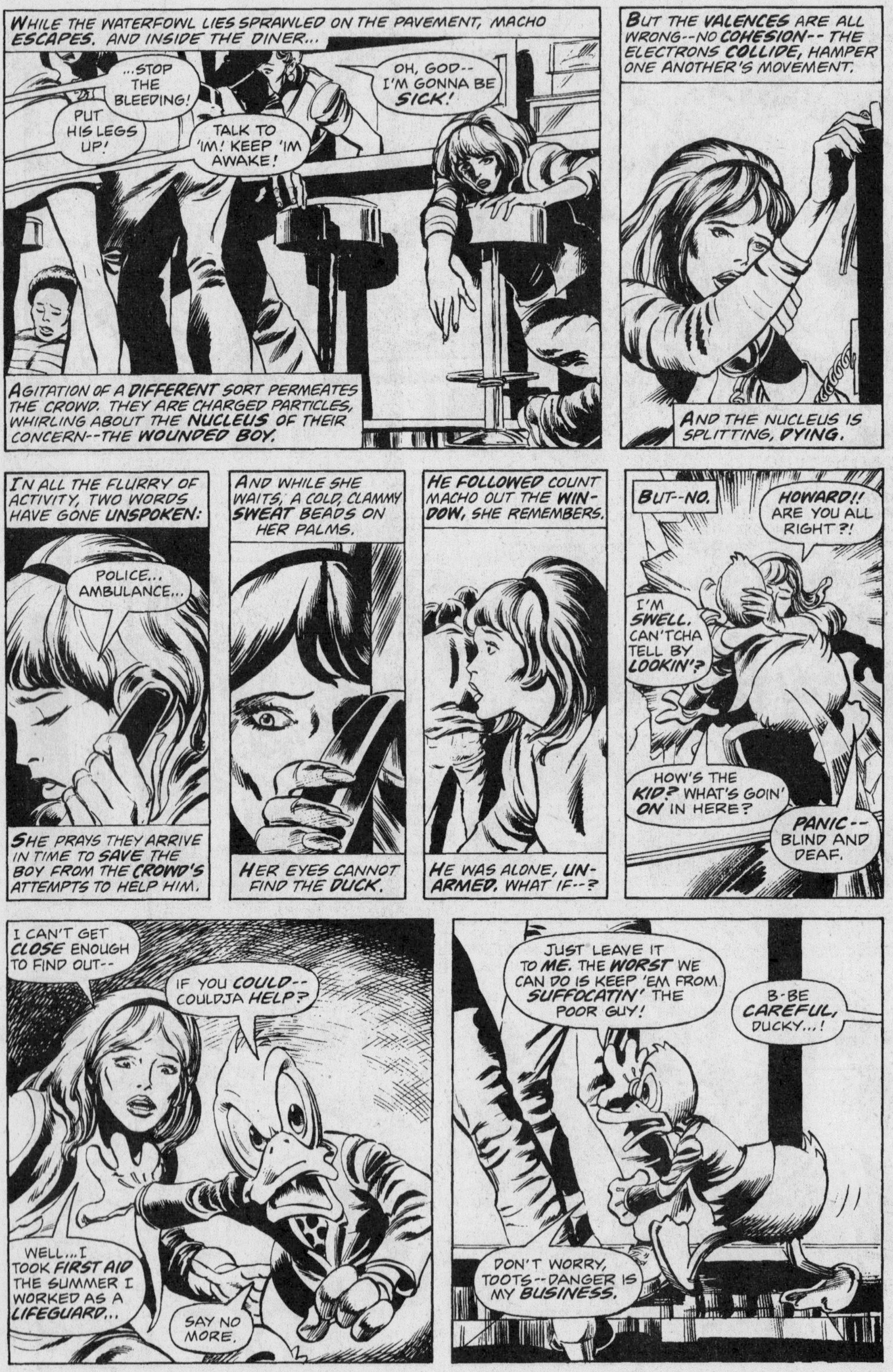
WHILE THE WATERFOWL LIES SPRAWLED ON THE PAVEMENT, MACHO ESCAPES. AND INSIDE THE DINER...
...STOP THE BLEEDING!
PUT HIS LEGS UP!
TALK TO 'IM! KEEP 'IM AWAKE!
OH, GOD-- I'M GONNA BE SICK!
AGITATION OF A DIFFERENT SORT PERMEATES THE CROWD. THEY ARE CHARGED PARTICLES, WHIRLING ABOUT THE NUCLEUS OF THEIR CONCERN--THE WOUNDED BOY.
BUT THE VALENCES ARE ALL WRONG--NO COHESION--THE ELECTRONS COLLIDE, HAMPER ONE ANOTHER'S MOVEMENT.
AND THE NUCLEUS IS SPLITTING, DYING.
IN ALL THE FLURRY OF ACTIVITY, TWO WORDS HAVE GONE UNSPOKEN:
POLICE... AMBULANCE...
SHE PRAYS THEY ARRIVE IN TIME TO SAVE THE BOY FROM THE CROWD'S ATTEMPTS TO HELP HIM.
AND WHILE SHE WAITS, A COLD, CLAMMY SWEAT BEADS ON HER PALMS.
HER EYES CANNOT FIND THE DUCK.
HE FOLLOWED COUNT MACHO OUT THE WINDOW, SHE REMEMBERS.
HE WAS ALONE, UNARMED. WHAT IF--?
BUT--NO.
HOWARD!! ARE YOU ALL RIGHT?!
I'M SWELL. CAN'TCHA TELL BY LOOKIN'?
HOW'S THE KID? WHAT'S GOIN' ON IN HERE?
PANIC--BLIND AND DEAF.
I CAN'T GET CLOSE ENOUGH TO FIND OUT--
IF YOU COULD--COULDJA HELP?
WELL...I TOOK FIRST AID THE SUMMER I WORKED AS A LIFEGUARD...
SAY NO MORE.
JUST LEAVE IT TO ME. THE WORST WE CAN DO IS KEEP 'EM FROM SUFFOCATIN' THE POOR GUY!
B-BE CAREFUL, DUCKY...!
DON'T WORRY, TOOTS--DANGER IS MY BUSINESS.

SHARP, SPINDLY ELBOWS PUSHING, PRODDING, *POKING* PAST KNEES AND THIGHS, HOWARD REACHES THE *CENTER* OF THE MOB...!

I'M ONLY GONNA SAY THIS ONCE: *BACK OFF!* YOU ARE ALL BEHAVING *ABOMINABLY!*

Y-YOU'RE A *DUCK!!*

GIVE THE LADY A *CIGAR* --LONG AS IT AIN'T ONE O' *MINE* --AN' KEEP 'ER *MOVIN'*.

NURSE! YOUR PATIENT'S WAITIN' IMPATIENTLY!

HUH? OH...!

C'MON-- BE GOOD SHEEP, BA-A-ACK! BA-A-A-ACK!

WHO MADE *YOU* THE GENERAL?

YEAH-- WE DON'T WANNA *MISS* NOTHIN'-- AN' WE AIN'T TAKIN' ORDERS FROM A *MIDGET* IN A *DUCK SUIT!*

TOUGH, MAC-- THE SHOW'S *OVER.* MOVE YOUR BUTT!

*TOMPKINS!**

YOU!!

* *WHOM THE DUCK FIRST MET IN* GIANT-SIZE MAN-THING #4. --MARV.

I SHOULD'A *KNOWN!* THAT BROAD A FRIEND O' *YOURS?* WHAT'S SHE--?

STOW IT, FLAT-FOOT! SHE'S A *NURSE!* AN' THE KID'S *BLEEDIN'* TO DEATH!

SAVE THE HARD-BOILED COP ROUTINE FOR *LATER!*

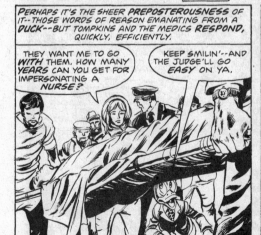

PERHAPS IT'S THE SHEER *PREPOSTEROUSNESS* OF IT--THOSE WORDS OF REASON EMANATING FROM A *DUCK* --BUT TOMPKINS AND THE MEDICS *RESPOND,* QUICKLY, EFFICIENTLY.

THEY WANT ME TO GO *WITH* THEM. HOW MANY *YEARS* CAN YOU GET FOR IMPERSONATING A *NURSE?*

KEEP SMILIN'--AND THE JUDGE'LL GO *EASY* ON YA.

AND SO IT APPEARS, FOR NOW, TO BE OVER--THE FUROR STILLED, THE VIOLENCE QUELLED...

...EXCEPT IN THE *PALPITANT BREAST* OF THE *FOWL.*

LOOK AT 'EM-- ONCE IT'S OUTTA THEIR SIGHT, IT'S JUST A STORY TO TELL AT THE *OFFICE* ON MONDAY.

GUESS I'M NOT AS *JADED* AS I *THOUGHT.*

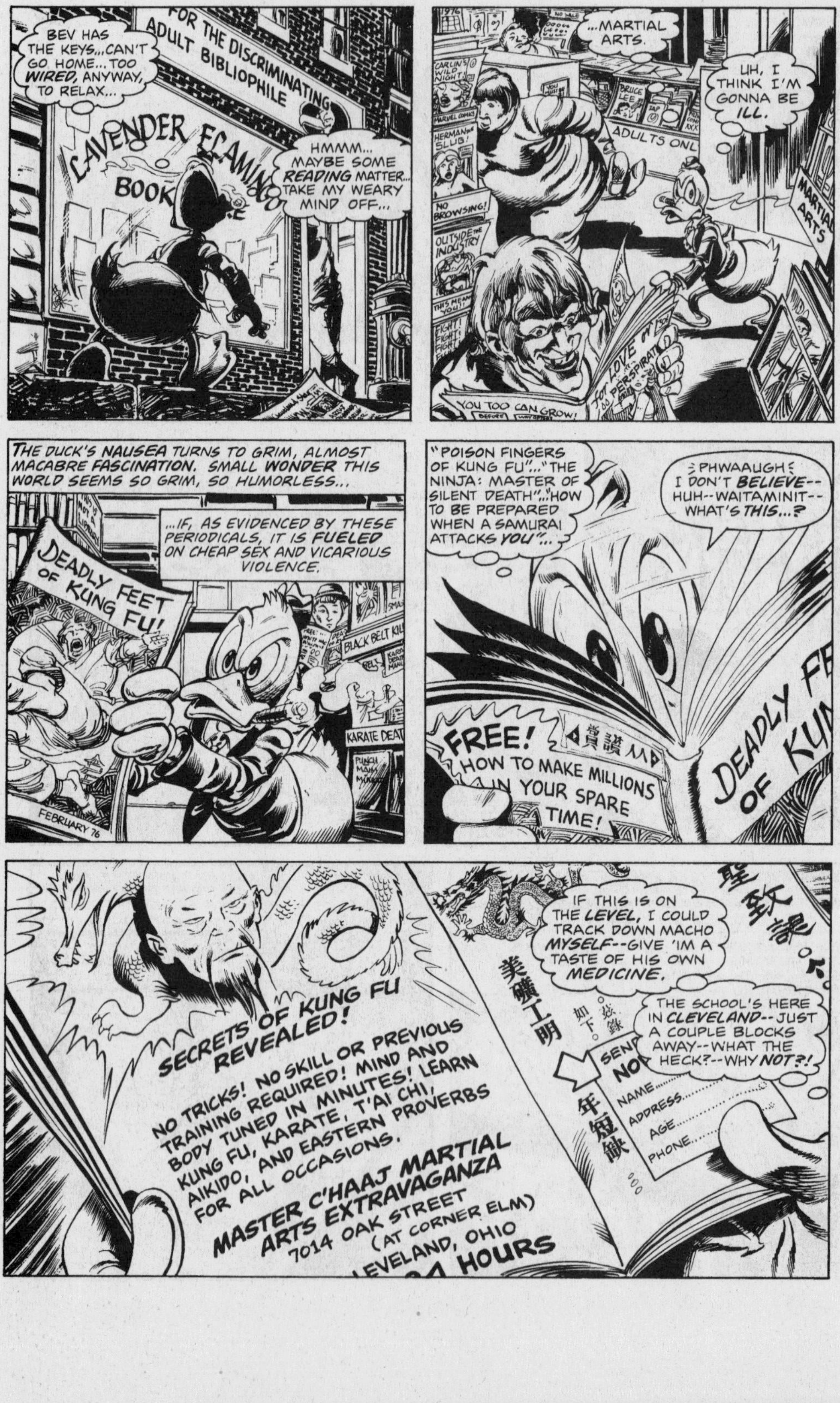
BEV HAS THE KEYS...CAN'T GO HOME...TOO WIRED, ANYWAY, TO RELAX...
FOR THE DISCRIMINATING ADULT BIBLIOPHILE
CAVENDER FLAMINGO BOOK
HMMM... MAYBE SOME READING MATTER... TAKE MY WEARY MIND OFF...
...MARTIAL ARTS.
UH, I THINK I'M GONNA BE ILL.
ADULTS ONL
MARTIAL ARTS
NO BROWSING!
YOU TOO CAN GROW!
THE DUCK'S NAUSEA TURNS TO GRIM, ALMOST MACABRE FASCINATION. SMALL WONDER THIS WORLD SEEMS SO GRIM, SO HUMORLESS...
...IF, AS EVIDENCED BY THESE PERIODICALS, IT IS FUELED ON CHEAP SEX AND VICARIOUS VIOLENCE.
DEADLY FEET OF KUNG FU!
BLACK BELT KIL
KARATE DEAT
FEBRUARY '76
"POISON FINGERS OF KUNG FU"..."THE NINJA: MASTER OF SILENT DEATH"..."HOW TO BE PREPARED WHEN A SAMURAI ATTACKS YOU"...
PHWAAUGH I DON'T BELIEVE-- HUH--WAITAMINIT-- WHAT'S THIS...?
FREE! HOW TO MAKE MILLIONS IN YOUR SPARE TIME!
DEADLY FEE OF KUN
IF THIS IS ON THE LEVEL, I COULD TRACK DOWN MACHO MYSELF--GIVE 'IM A TASTE OF HIS OWN MEDICINE.
THE SCHOOL'S HERE IN CLEVELAND--JUST A COUPLE BLOCKS AWAY--WHAT THE HECK?--WHY NOT?!
SECRETS OF KUNG FU REVEALED!
NO TRICKS! NO SKILL OR PREVIOUS TRAINING REQUIRED! MIND AND BODY TUNED IN MINUTES! LEARN KUNG FU, KARATE, T'AI CHI, AIKIDO, AND EASTERN PROVERBS FOR ALL OCCASIONS.
MASTER C'HAAJ MARTIAL ARTS EXTRAVAGANZA
7014 OAK STREET
(AT CORNER ELM)
LEVELAND, OHIO
24 HOURS
NAME
ADDRESS
AGE
PHONE

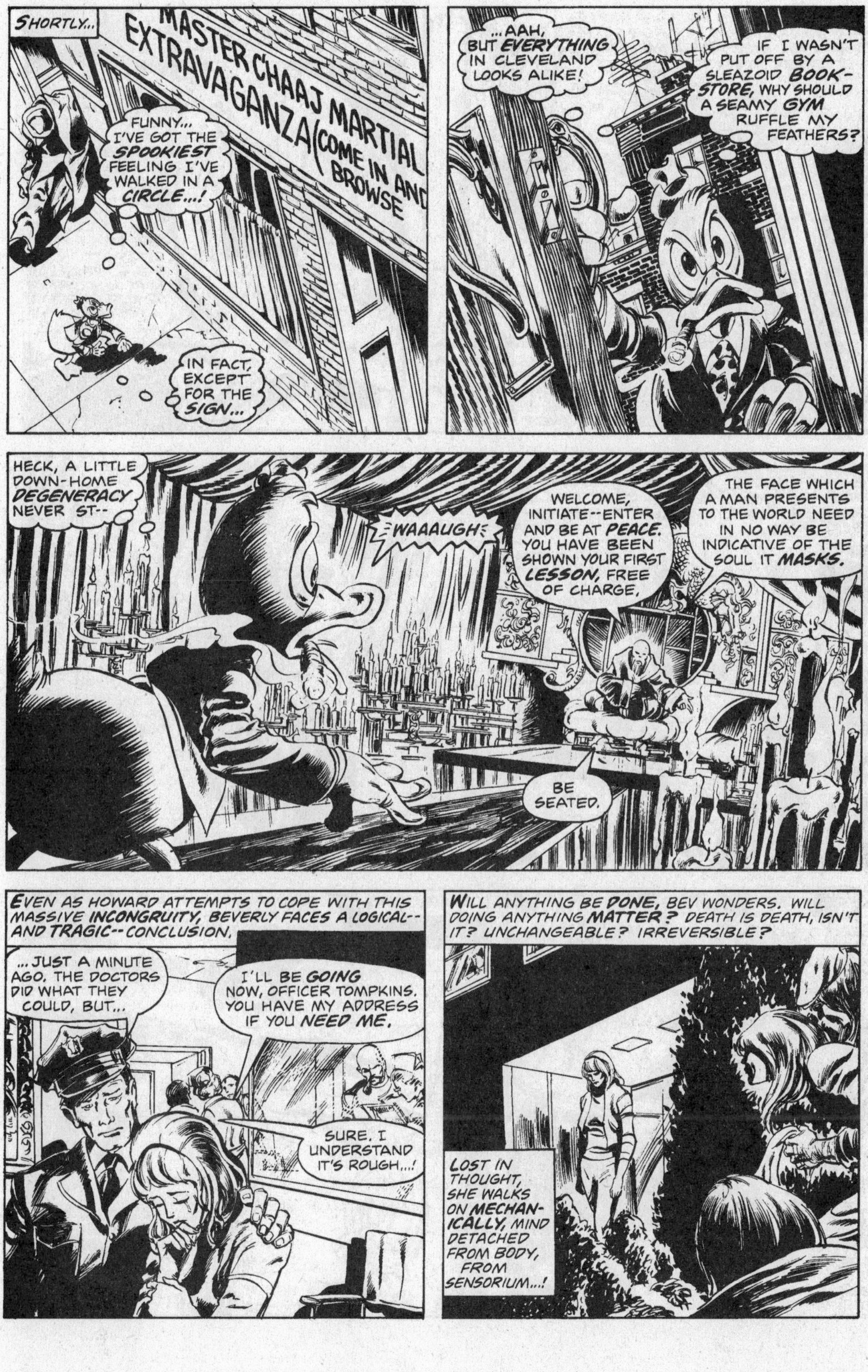
SHORTLY...
MASTER CHAAJ MARTIAL EXTRAVAGANZA (COME IN AND BROWSE
FUNNY... I'VE GOT THE SPOOKIEST FEELING I'VE WALKED IN A CIRCLE...!
IN FACT, EXCEPT FOR THE SIGN...
...AAH, BUT EVERYTHING IN CLEVELAND LOOKS ALIKE!
IF I WASN'T PUT OFF BY A SLEAZOID BOOK-STORE, WHY SHOULD A SEAMY GYM RUFFLE MY FEATHERS?
HECK, A LITTLE DOWN-HOME DEGENERACY NEVER ST--
WAAAUGH
WELCOME, INITIATE--ENTER AND BE AT PEACE. YOU HAVE BEEN SHOWN YOUR FIRST LESSON, FREE OF CHARGE.
THE FACE WHICH A MAN PRESENTS TO THE WORLD NEED IN NO WAY BE INDICATIVE OF THE SOUL IT MASKS.
BE SEATED.
EVEN AS HOWARD ATTEMPTS TO COPE WITH THIS MASSIVE INCONGRUITY, BEVERLY FACES A LOGICAL-- AND TRAGIC-- CONCLUSION.
...JUST A MINUTE AGO. THE DOCTORS DID WHAT THEY COULD, BUT...
I'LL BE GOING NOW, OFFICER TOMPKINS. YOU HAVE MY ADDRESS IF YOU NEED ME.
SURE. I UNDERSTAND IT'S ROUGH...!
WILL ANYTHING BE DONE, BEV WONDERS. WILL DOING ANYTHING MATTER? DEATH IS DEATH, ISN'T IT? UNCHANGEABLE? IRREVERSIBLE?
LOST IN THOUGHT, SHE WALKS ON MECHANICALLY, MIND DETACHED FROM BODY, FROM SENSORIUM...!

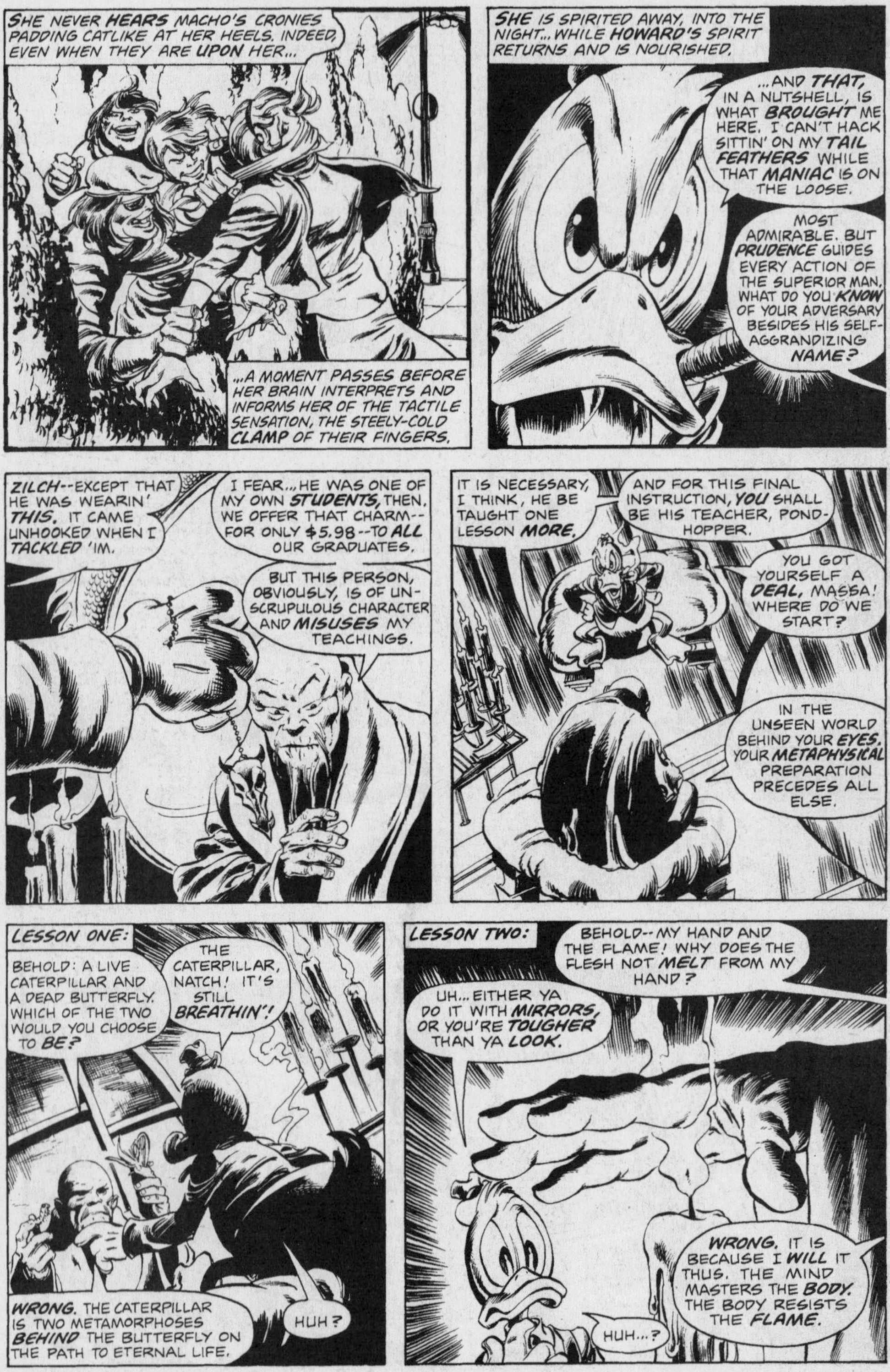
SHE NEVER HEARS MACHO'S CRONIES PADDING CATLIKE AT HER HEELS. INDEED, EVEN WHEN THEY ARE UPON HER...
...A MOMENT PASSES BEFORE HER BRAIN INTERPRETS AND INFORMS HER OF THE TACTILE SENSATION, THE STEELY-COLD CLAMP OF THEIR FINGERS.
SHE IS SPIRITED AWAY, INTO THE NIGHT... WHILE HOWARD'S SPIRIT RETURNS AND IS NOURISHED.
...AND THAT, IN A NUTSHELL, IS WHAT BROUGHT ME HERE. I CAN'T HACK SITTIN' ON MY TAIL FEATHERS WHILE THAT MANIAC IS ON THE LOOSE.
MOST ADMIRABLE. BUT PRUDENCE GUIDES EVERY ACTION OF THE SUPERIOR MAN. WHAT DO YOU KNOW OF YOUR ADVERSARY BESIDES HIS SELF-AGGRANDIZING NAME?
ZILCH--EXCEPT THAT HE WAS WEARIN' THIS. IT CAME UNHOOKED WHEN I TACKLED 'IM.
I FEAR... HE WAS ONE OF MY OWN STUDENTS, THEN. WE OFFER THAT CHARM--FOR ONLY $5.98--TO ALL OUR GRADUATES.
BUT THIS PERSON, OBVIOUSLY, IS OF UNSCRUPULOUS CHARACTER AND MISUSES MY TEACHINGS.
IT IS NECESSARY, I THINK, HE BE TAUGHT ONE LESSON MORE.
AND FOR THIS FINAL INSTRUCTION, YOU SHALL BE HIS TEACHER, POND-HOPPER.
YOU GOT YOURSELF A DEAL, MASSA! WHERE DO WE START?
IN THE UNSEEN WORLD BEHIND YOUR EYES. YOUR METAPHYSICAL PREPARATION PRECEDES ALL ELSE.
LESSON ONE:
BEHOLD: A LIVE CATERPILLAR AND A DEAD BUTTERFLY. WHICH OF THE TWO WOULD YOU CHOOSE TO BE?
THE CATERPILLAR, NATCH! IT'S STILL BREATHIN'!
WRONG. THE CATERPILLAR IS TWO METAMORPHOSES BEHIND THE BUTTERFLY ON THE PATH TO ETERNAL LIFE.
HUH?
LESSON TWO:
BEHOLD-- MY HAND AND THE FLAME! WHY DOES THE FLESH NOT MELT FROM MY HAND?
UH... EITHER YA DO IT WITH MIRRORS, OR YOU'RE TOUGHER THAN YA LOOK.
WRONG. IT IS BECAUSE I WILL IT THUS. THE MIND MASTERS THE BODY. THE BODY RESISTS THE FLAME.
HUH...?

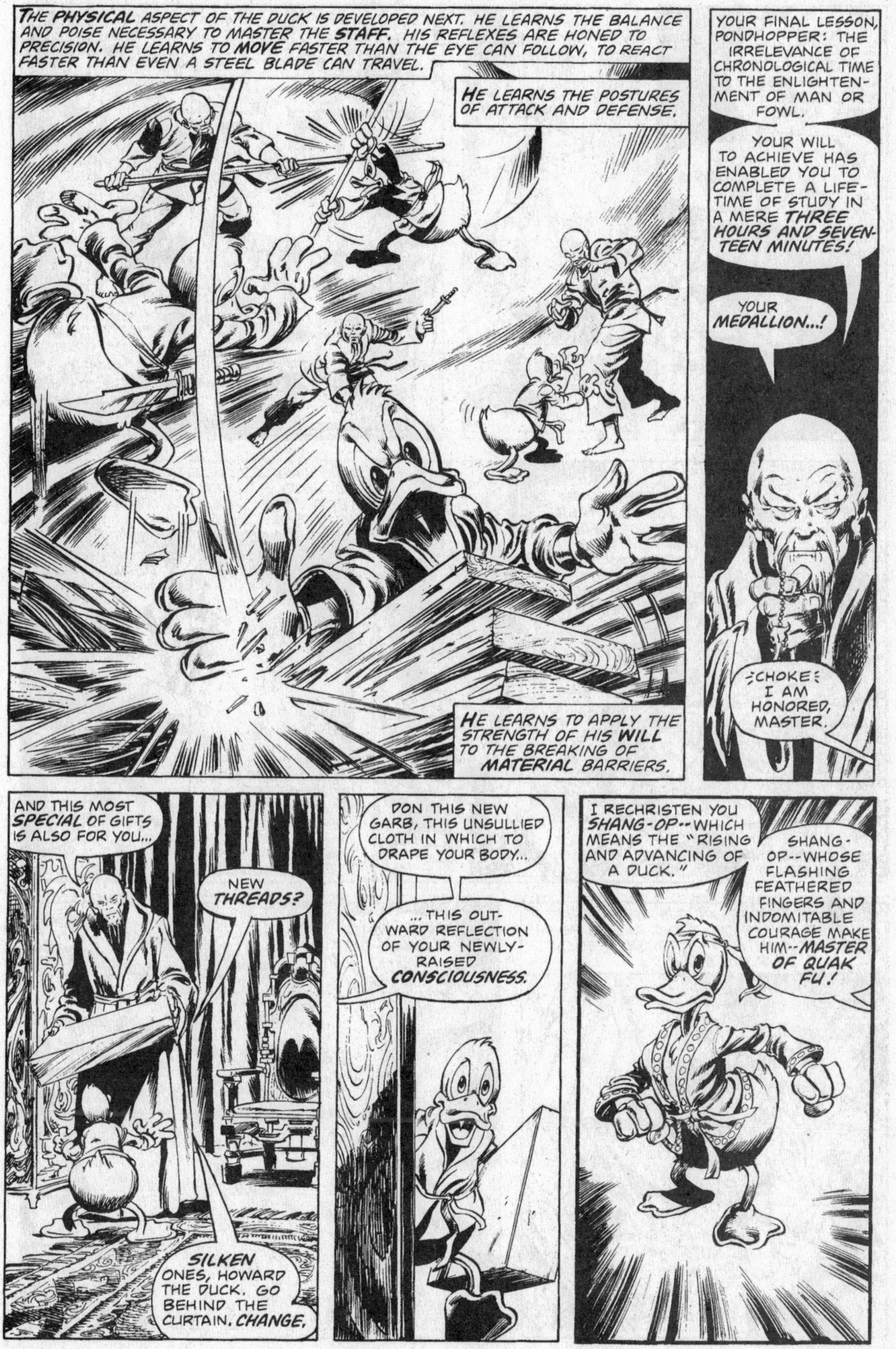
THE PHYSICAL ASPECT OF THE DUCK IS DEVELOPED NEXT. HE LEARNS THE BALANCE AND POISE NECESSARY TO MASTER THE STAFF. HIS REFLEXES ARE HONED TO PRECISION. HE LEARNS TO MOVE FASTER THAN THE EYE CAN FOLLOW, TO REACT FASTER THAN EVEN A STEEL BLADE CAN TRAVEL.
HE LEARNS THE POSTURES OF ATTACK AND DEFENSE.
HE LEARNS TO APPLY THE STRENGTH OF HIS WILL TO THE BREAKING OF MATERIAL BARRIERS.
YOUR FINAL LESSON, PONDHOPPER: THE IRRELEVANCE OF CHRONOLOGICAL TIME TO THE ENLIGHTENMENT OF MAN OR FOWL.
YOUR WILL TO ACHIEVE HAS ENABLED YOU TO COMPLETE A LIFETIME OF STUDY IN A MERE THREE HOURS AND SEVENTEEN MINUTES!
YOUR MEDALLION...!
⁒CHOKE⁒ I AM HONORED, MASTER.
AND THIS MOST SPECIAL OF GIFTS IS ALSO FOR YOU...
NEW THREADS?
SILKEN ONES, HOWARD THE DUCK. GO BEHIND THE CURTAIN. CHANGE.
DON THIS NEW GARB, THIS UNSULLIED CLOTH IN WHICH TO DRAPE YOUR BODY...
...THIS OUTWARD REFLECTION OF YOUR NEWLY-RAISED CONSCIOUSNESS.
I RECHRISTEN YOU SHANG-OP--WHICH MEANS THE "RISING AND ADVANCING OF A DUCK."
SHANG-OP--WHOSE FLASHING FEATHERED FINGERS AND INDOMITABLE COURAGE MAKE HIM--MASTER OF QUAK FU!

I DUNNO IF I'D GO *THAT* FAR--BUT I GOTTA ADMIT, IT'S BEEN A *VALUABLE* THREE HOURS.

WHICH, UH, *REMINDS* ME--

HOW MUCH DO I *OWE* Y--

WAAUGH!

I'M STILL IN THE LAVENDER FLAMINGO!!

I MUST'A *FANTASIZED* THE WHOLE THING! I MUST'A BEEN STANDIN' HERE ALL THE TI--

ONLY...IF *THAT'S* WHAT HAPPENED, WHERE'D I GET THESE YIN-YANG P.J.'S?

THIS WAY TO EXIT

NO...IT WASN'T A *DREAM.* IT COULDN'T'VE BEEN. AND ANYWAY, WHAT IF IT *WAS?*

DREAMS'RE JUST ANOTHER LEVEL OF *REALITY,* RIGHT? I *TOOK* THAT MARTIAL ARTS COURSE --I CAN *FEEL* IT-- I CAN REMEMBER ALL THE *MOVES!*

I JUST CAN'T BELIEVE HE LET ME GO WITHOUT *PAYING*-- THAT'S WHAT'S *WEIRD!*

HIS WADDLE ACCELERATES TO A RUN. HE IS ANXIOUS TO LEAVE THIS SEEDY NEIGHBORHOOD WITH ALL ITS SHADOW-CLOAKED MYSTERIES *BEHIND* HIM,

HE LONGS TO RECOUNT HIS STRANGE EXPERIENCE TO BEVERLY, TO *SHARE* WITH HER THE AWE, THE WONDER, THE SPACEY STOMACH OF HAVING PASSED THROUGH THE REALM OF THE *UNEXPLAINABLE.*

WHEN HE ARRIVES AT THE APARTMENT, HOWEVER, THOSE CONCERNS ARE SUPERCEDED BY ANOTHER--FAR MORE URGENT... AND *SINISTER.*

NUTS, YOU'D THINK HE COULD JUST USE *TAPE,* BUT *NO,* HE--

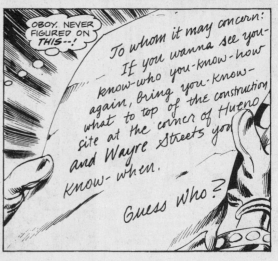

OBOY. NEVER FIGURED ON *THIS--!*

To whom it may concern: If you wanna see you-know-who you-know-how again, bring you-know-what to top of the construction site at the corner of Hueno and Wayre Streets you know-when.

Guess Who?

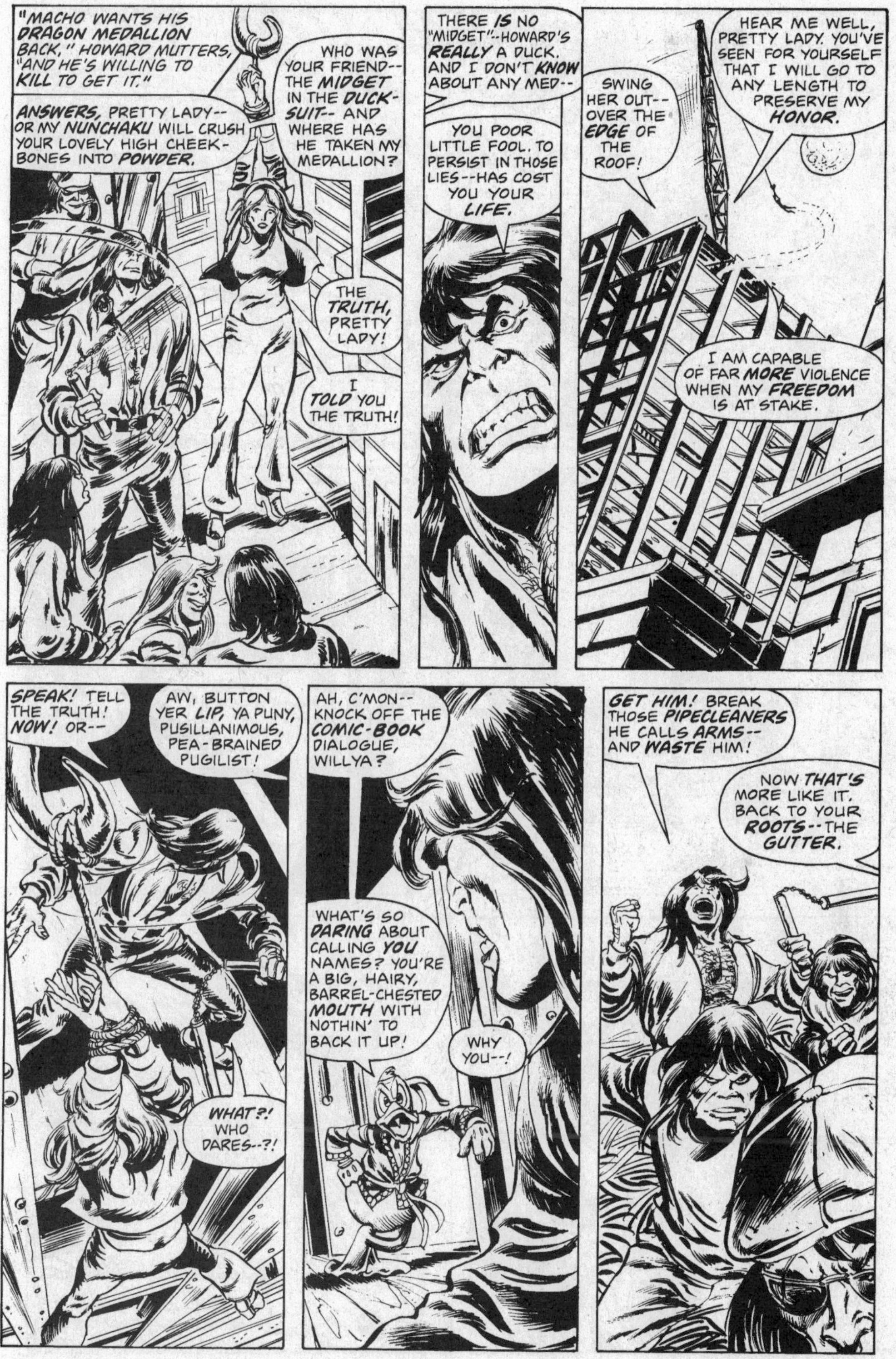
"MACHO WANTS HIS DRAGON MEDALLION BACK," HOWARD MUTTERS, "AND HE'S WILLING TO KILL TO GET IT."
ANSWERS, PRETTY LADY--OR MY NUNCHAKU WILL CRUSH YOUR LOVELY HIGH CHEEK-BONES INTO POWDER.
WHO WAS YOUR FRIEND--THE MIDGET IN THE DUCK-SUIT--AND WHERE HAS HE TAKEN MY MEDALLION?
THE TRUTH, PRETTY LADY!
I TOLD YOU THE TRUTH!
THERE IS NO "MIDGET"--HOWARD'S REALLY A DUCK. AND I DON'T KNOW ABOUT ANY MED--
YOU POOR LITTLE FOOL. TO PERSIST IN THOSE LIES--HAS COST YOU YOUR LIFE.
SWING HER OUT--OVER THE EDGE OF THE ROOF!
HEAR ME WELL, PRETTY LADY. YOU'VE SEEN FOR YOURSELF THAT I WILL GO TO ANY LENGTH TO PRESERVE MY HONOR.
I AM CAPABLE OF FAR MORE VIOLENCE WHEN MY FREEDOM IS AT STAKE.
SPEAK! TELL THE TRUTH! NOW! OR--
AW, BUTTON YER LIP, YA PUNY, PUSILLANIMOUS, PEA-BRAINED PUGILIST!
WHAT?! WHO DARES--?!
AH, C'MON--KNOCK OFF THE COMIC-BOOK DIALOGUE, WILLYA?
WHAT'S SO DARING ABOUT CALLING YOU NAMES? YOU'RE A BIG, HAIRY, BARREL-CHESTED MOUTH WITH NOTHIN' TO BACK IT UP!
WHY YOU--!
GET HIM! BREAK THOSE PIPECLEANERS HE CALLS ARMS--AND WASTE HIM!
NOW THAT'S MORE LIKE IT. BACK TO YOUR ROOTS--THE GUTTER.

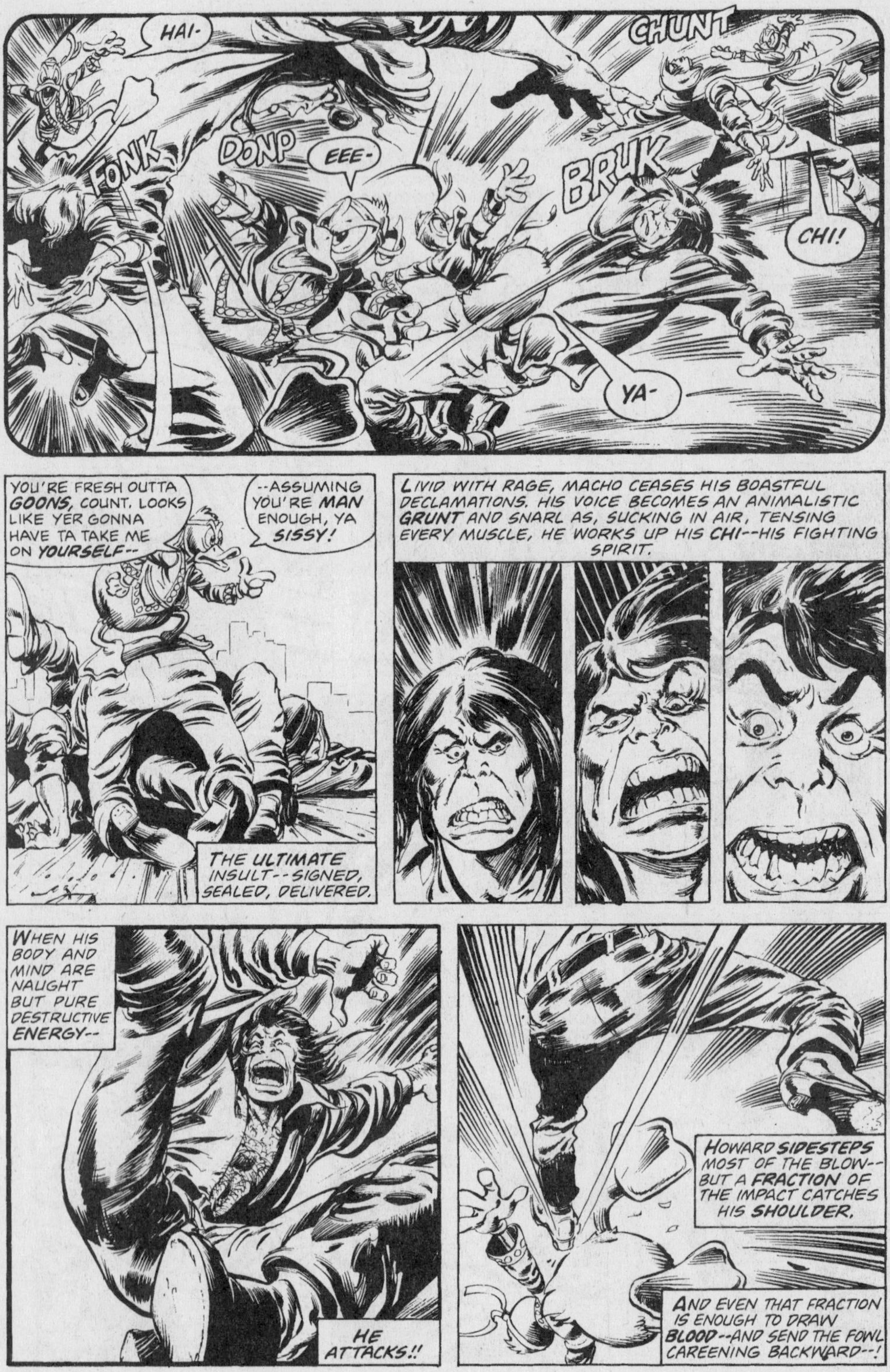
HAI-
FONK
DONP
EEE-
CHUNT
BRUK
CHI!
YA-
YOU'RE FRESH OUTTA GOONS, COUNT. LOOKS LIKE YER GONNA HAVE TA TAKE ME ON YOURSELF--
--ASSUMING YOU'RE MAN ENOUGH, YA SISSY!
THE ULTIMATE INSULT--SIGNED, SEALED, DELIVERED.
LIVID WITH RAGE, MACHO CEASES HIS BOASTFUL DECLAMATIONS. HIS VOICE BECOMES AN ANIMALISTIC GRUNT AND SNARL AS, SUCKING IN AIR, TENSING EVERY MUSCLE, HE WORKS UP HIS CHI--HIS FIGHTING SPIRIT.
WHEN HIS BODY AND MIND ARE NAUGHT BUT PURE DESTRUCTIVE ENERGY--
HE ATTACKS!!
HOWARD SIDESTEPS MOST OF THE BLOW--BUT A FRACTION OF THE IMPACT CATCHES HIS SHOULDER.
AND EVEN THAT FRACTION IS ENOUGH TO DRAW BLOOD--AND SEND THE FOWL CAREENING BACKWARD--!

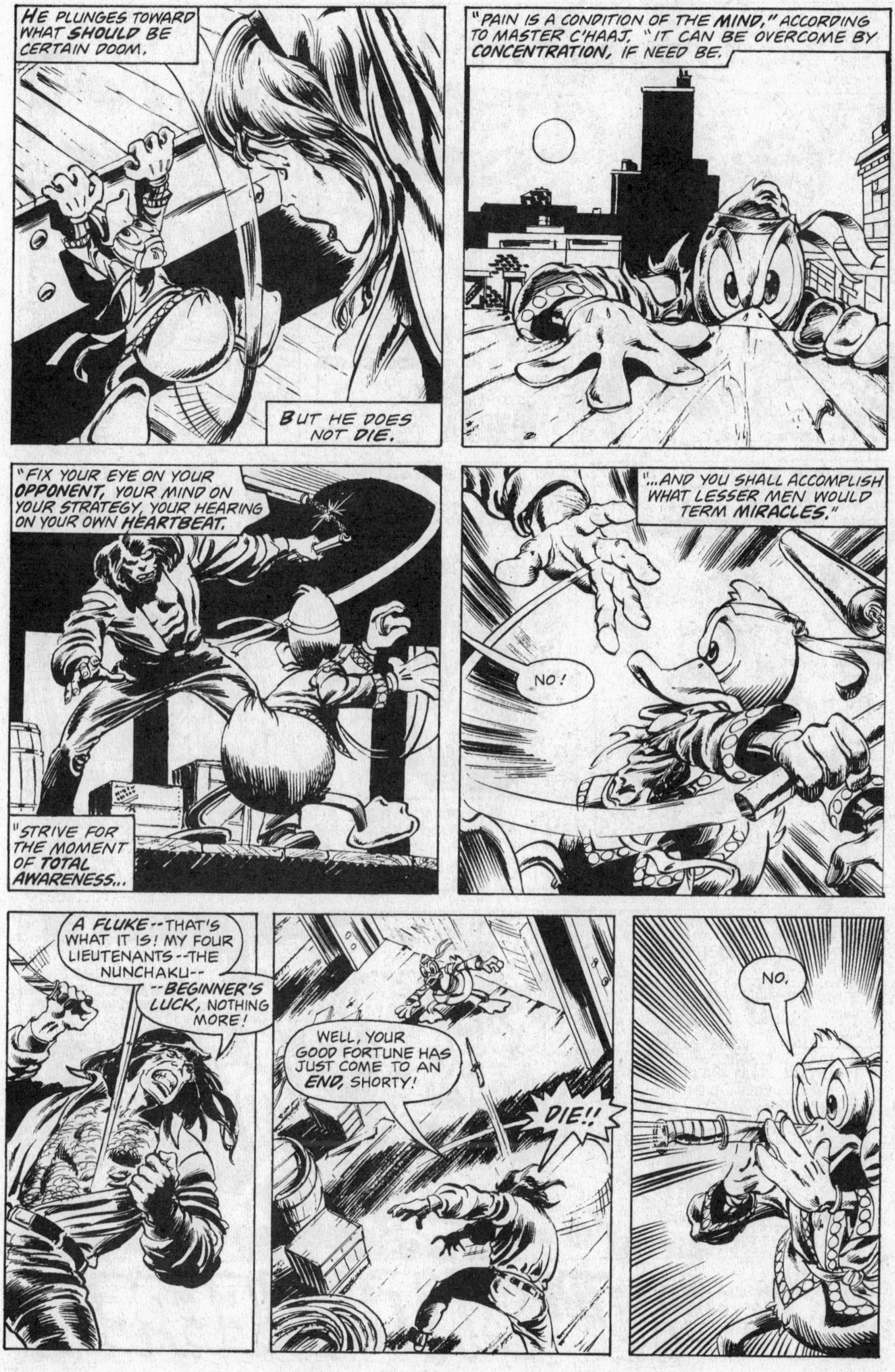

HE PLUNGES TOWARD WHAT SHOULD BE CERTAIN DOOM.
BUT HE DOES NOT DIE.
"PAIN IS A CONDITION OF THE MIND," ACCORDING TO MASTER C'HAAJ. "IT CAN BE OVERCOME BY CONCENTRATION, IF NEED BE.
"FIX YOUR EYE ON YOUR OPPONENT, YOUR MIND ON YOUR STRATEGY, YOUR HEARING ON YOUR OWN HEARTBEAT.
"STRIVE FOR THE MOMENT OF TOTAL AWARENESS...
"...AND YOU SHALL ACCOMPLISH WHAT LESSER MEN WOULD TERM MIRACLES."
NO!
A FLUKE--THAT'S WHAT IT IS! MY FOUR LIEUTENANTS--THE NUNCHAKU--
--BEGINNER'S LUCK, NOTHING MORE!
WELL, YOUR GOOD FORTUNE HAS JUST COME TO AN END, SHORTY!
DIE!!
NO.

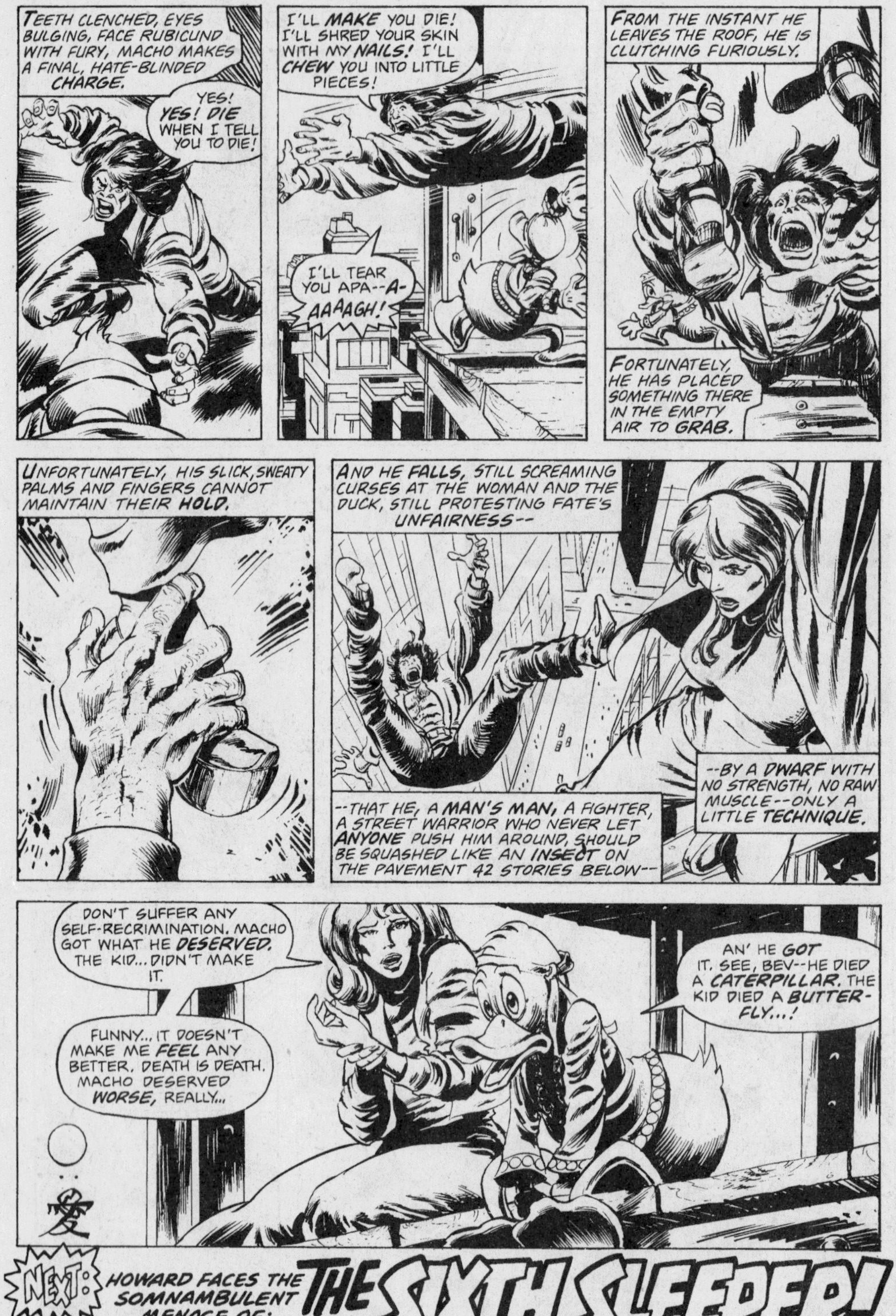

TEETH CLENCHED, EYES BULGING, FACE RUBICUND WITH FURY, MACHO MAKES A FINAL, HATE-BLINDED CHARGE.
YES! YES! DIE WHEN I TELL YOU TO DIE!
I'LL MAKE YOU DIE! I'LL SHRED YOUR SKIN WITH MY NAILS! I'LL CHEW YOU INTO LITTLE PIECES!
I'LL TEAR YOU APA--A-AAAAGH!
FROM THE INSTANT HE LEAVES THE ROOF, HE IS CLUTCHING FURIOUSLY.
FORTUNATELY, HE HAS PLACED SOMETHING THERE IN THE EMPTY AIR TO GRAB.
UNFORTUNATELY, HIS SLICK, SWEATY PALMS AND FINGERS CANNOT MAINTAIN THEIR HOLD.
AND HE FALLS, STILL SCREAMING CURSES AT THE WOMAN AND THE DUCK, STILL PROTESTING FATE'S UNFAIRNESS--
--THAT HE, A MAN'S MAN, A FIGHTER, A STREET WARRIOR WHO NEVER LET ANYONE PUSH HIM AROUND, SHOULD BE SQUASHED LIKE AN INSECT ON THE PAVEMENT 42 STORIES BELOW--
--BY A DWARF WITH NO STRENGTH, NO RAW MUSCLE--ONLY A LITTLE TECHNIQUE.
DON'T SUFFER ANY SELF-RECRIMINATION. MACHO GOT WHAT HE DESERVED. THE KID... DIDN'T MAKE IT.
FUNNY... IT DOESN'T MAKE ME FEEL ANY BETTER. DEATH IS DEATH. MACHO DESERVED WORSE, REALLY...
AN' HE GOT IT. SEE, BEV--HE DIED A CATERPILLAR. THE KID DIED A BUTTER-FLY...!
NEXT: HOWARD FACES THE SOMNAMBULENT MENACE OF: THE SIXTH SLEEPER!

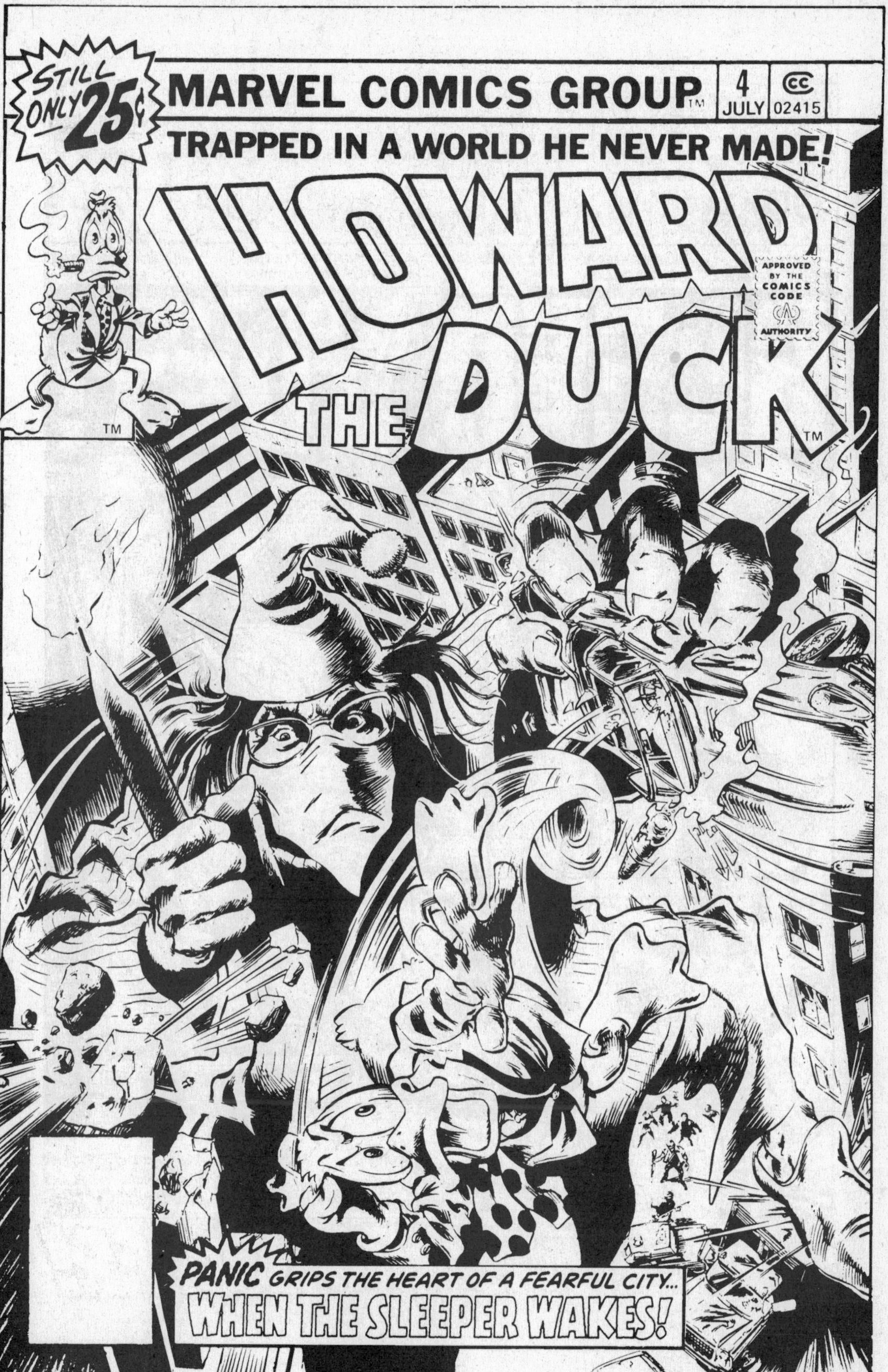
STILL ONLY 25¢
MARVEL COMICS GROUP™
4
JULY
CC
02415
TRAPPED IN A WORLD HE NEVER MADE!
HOWARD THE DUCK™
APPROVED BY THE COMICS CODE AUTHORITY
™
PANIC GRIPS THE HEART OF A FEARFUL CITY...
WHEN THE SLEEPER WAKES!

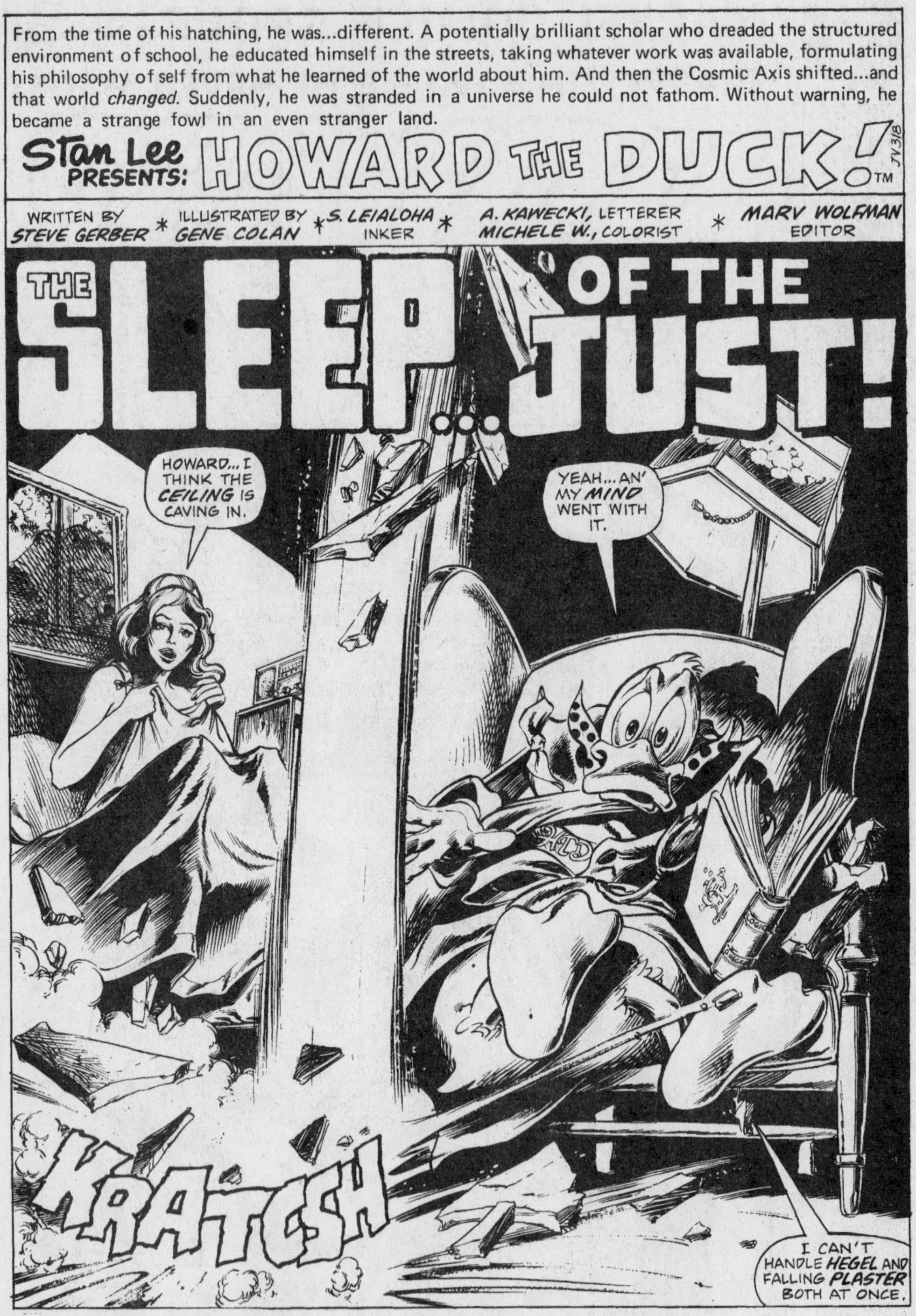

From the time of his hatching, he was...different. A potentially brilliant scholar who dreaded the structured environment of school, he educated himself in the streets, taking whatever work was available, formulating his philosophy of self from what he learned of the world about him. And then the Cosmic Axis shifted...and that world *changed.* Suddenly, he was stranded in a universe he could not fathom. Without warning, he became a strange fowl in an even stranger land.
Stan Lee PRESENTS: HOWARD THE DUCK!™
WRITTEN BY STEVE GERBER * ILLUSTRATED BY GENE COLAN * S. LEIALOHA INKER * A. KAWECKI, LETTERER MICHELE W., COLORIST * MARV WOLFMAN EDITOR
THE SLEEP...OF THE JUST!
HOWARD... I THINK THE *CEILING* IS CAVING IN.
YEAH... AN' MY *MIND* WENT WITH IT.
KRATCSH
I CAN'T HANDLE *HEGEL* AND FALLING *PLASTER* BOTH AT ONCE.

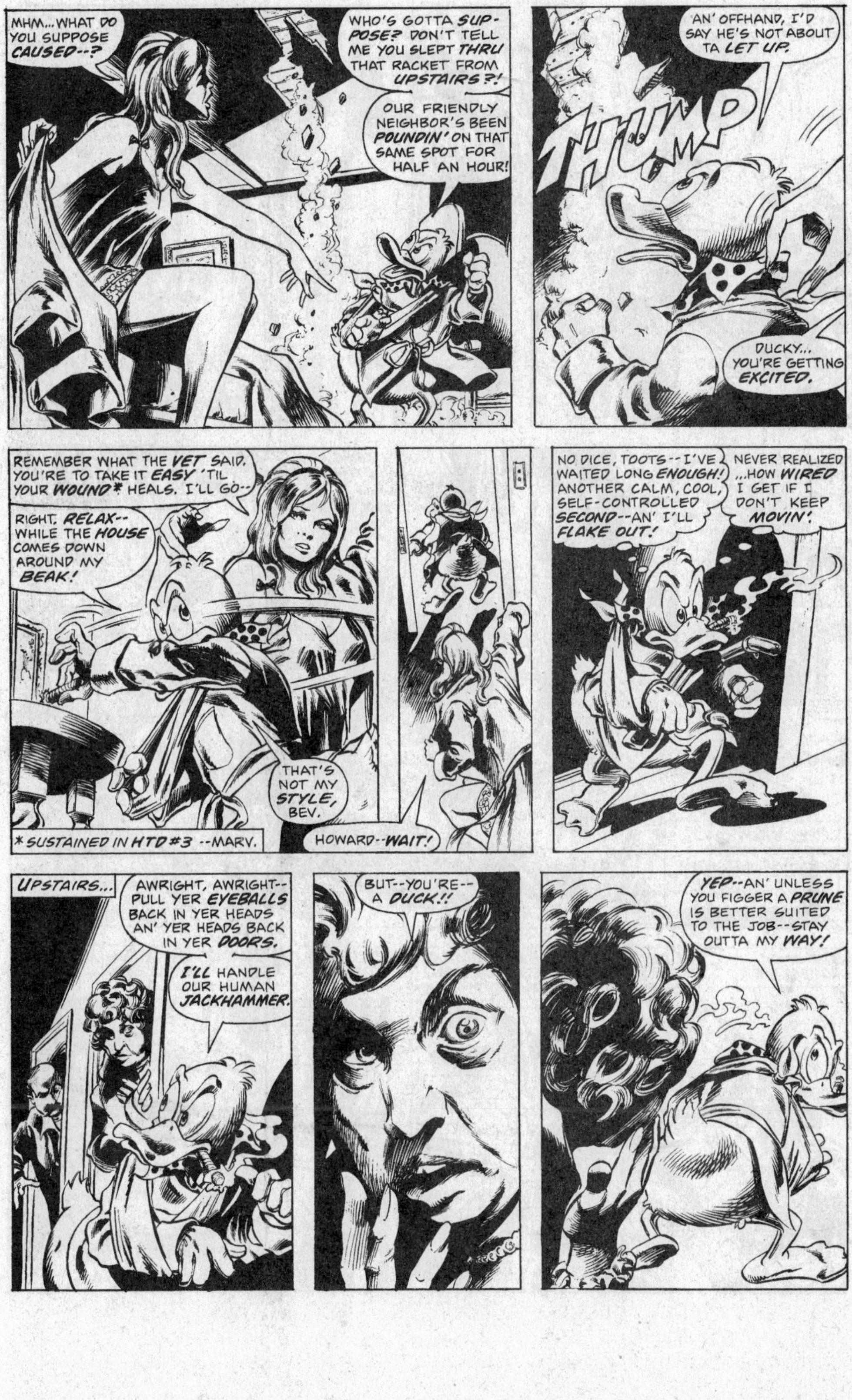
MHM...WHAT DO YOU SUPPOSE CAUSED--?
WHO'S GOTTA SUP-POSE? DON'T TELL ME YOU SLEPT THRU THAT RACKET FROM UPSTAIRS?!
OUR FRIENDLY NEIGHBOR'S BEEN POUNDIN' ON THAT SAME SPOT FOR HALF AN HOUR!
'AN' OFFHAND, I'D SAY HE'S NOT ABOUT TA LET UP.
THUMP
DUCKY... YOU'RE GETTING EXCITED.
REMEMBER WHAT THE VET SAID. YOU'RE TO TAKE IT EASY 'TIL YOUR WOUND* HEALS. I'LL GO--
RIGHT. RELAX-- WHILE THE HOUSE COMES DOWN AROUND MY BEAK!
THAT'S NOT MY STYLE, BEV.
* SUSTAINED IN HTD #3 --MARV.
HOWARD--WAIT!
NO DICE, TOOTS--I'VE WAITED LONG ENOUGH! ANOTHER CALM, COOL, SELF-CONTROLLED SECOND--AN' I'LL FLAKE OUT!
NEVER REALIZED ...HOW WIRED I GET IF I DON'T KEEP MOVIN'.
UPSTAIRS...
AWRIGHT, AWRIGHT-- PULL YER EYEBALLS BACK IN YER HEADS AN' YER HEADS BACK IN YER DOORS.
I'LL HANDLE OUR HUMAN JACKHAMMER.
BUT--YOU'RE-- A DUCK!!
YEP--AN' UNLESS YOU FIGGER A PRUNE IS BETTER SUITED TO THE JOB--STAY OUTTA MY WAY!

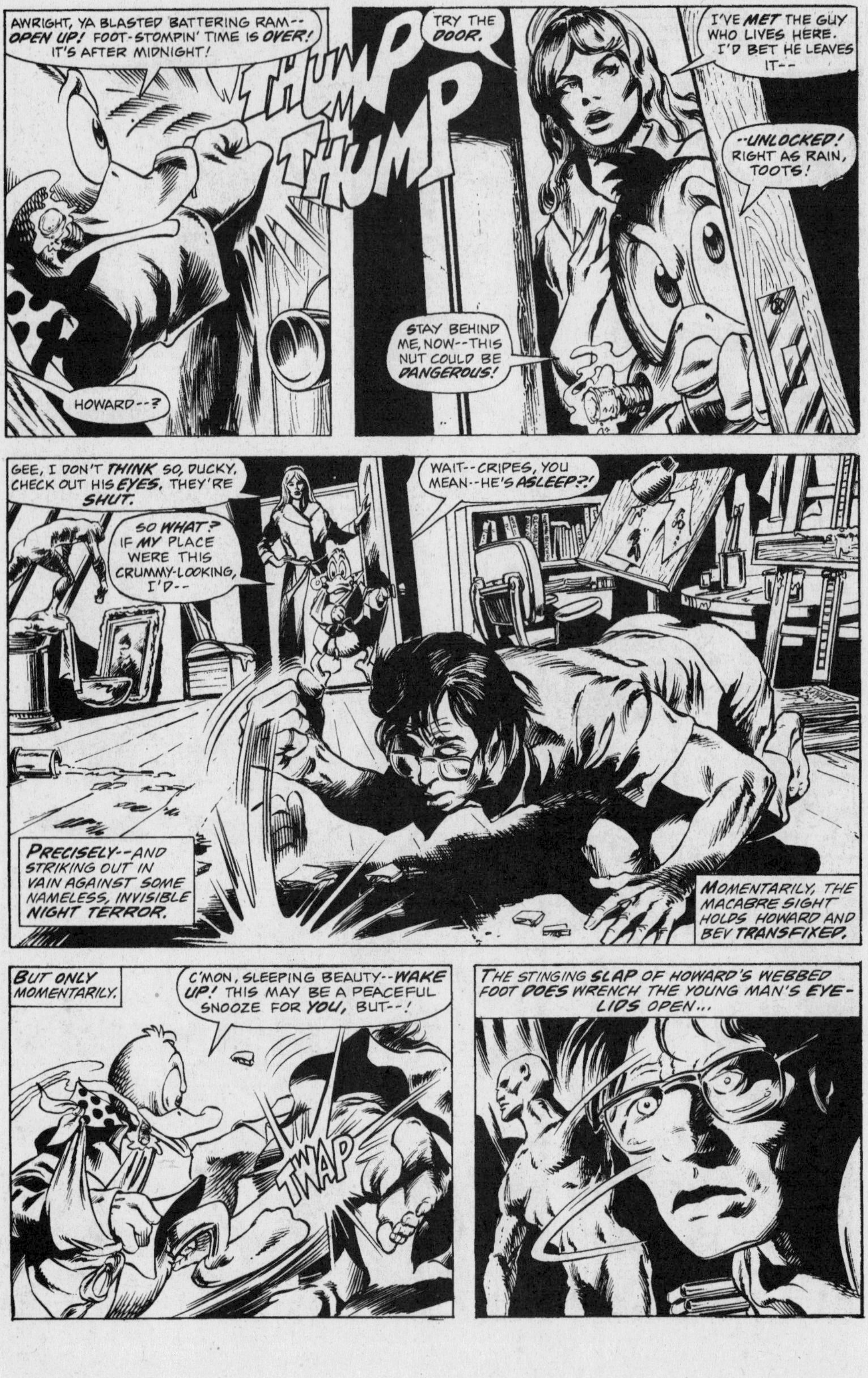
AWRIGHT, YA BLASTED BATTERING RAM-- OPEN UP! FOOT-STOMPIN' TIME IS OVER! IT'S AFTER MIDNIGHT!
THUMP THUMP
HOWARD--?
TRY THE DOOR.
I'VE MET THE GUY WHO LIVES HERE. I'D BET HE LEAVES IT--
--UNLOCKED! RIGHT AS RAIN, TOOTS!
STAY BEHIND ME, NOW--THIS NUT COULD BE DANGEROUS!
GEE, I DON'T THINK SO, DUCKY. CHECK OUT HIS EYES. THEY'RE SHUT.
SO WHAT? IF MY PLACE WERE THIS CRUMMY-LOOKING, I'D--
WAIT--CRIPES, YOU MEAN--HE'S ASLEEP?!
PRECISELY--AND STRIKING OUT IN VAIN AGAINST SOME NAMELESS, INVISIBLE NIGHT TERROR.
MOMENTARILY, THE MACABRE SIGHT HOLDS HOWARD AND BEV TRANSFIXED.
BUT ONLY MOMENTARILY.
C'MON, SLEEPING BEAUTY--WAKE UP! THIS MAY BE A PEACEFUL SNOOZE FOR YOU, BUT--!
TWAP
THE STINGING SLAP OF HOWARD'S WEBBED FOOT DOES WRENCH THE YOUNG MAN'S EYE-LIDS OPEN...

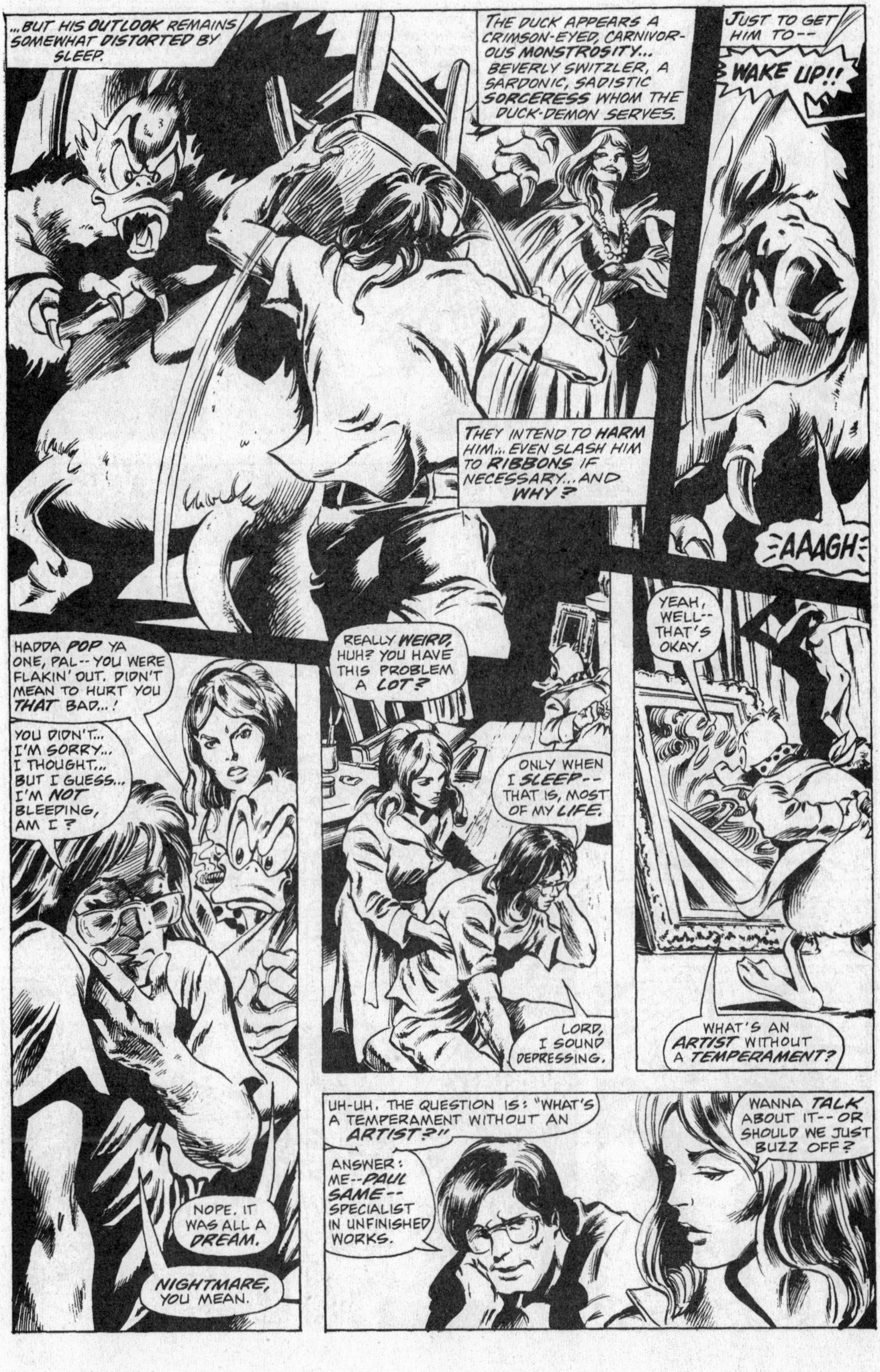
...BUT HIS OUTLOOK REMAINS SOMEWHAT DISTORTED BY SLEEP.
THE DUCK APPEARS A CRIMSON-EYED, CARNIVOROUS MONSTROSITY... BEVERLY SWITZLER, A SARDONIC, SADISTIC SORCERESS WHOM THE DUCK-DEMON SERVES.
THEY INTEND TO HARM HIM... EVEN SLASH HIM TO RIBBONS IF NECESSARY... AND WHY?
JUST TO GET HIM TO--
WAKE UP!!
AAAGH
HADDA POP YA ONE, PAL--YOU WERE FLAKIN' OUT. DIDN'T MEAN TO HURT YOU THAT BAD...!
YOU DIDN'T... I'M SORRY... I THOUGHT... BUT I GUESS... I'M NOT BLEEDING, AM I?
NOPE. IT WAS ALL A DREAM.
NIGHTMARE, YOU MEAN.
REALLY WEIRD, HUH? YOU HAVE THIS PROBLEM A LOT?
ONLY WHEN I SLEEP--THAT IS, MOST OF MY LIFE.
LORD, I SOUND DEPRESSING.
YEAH, WELL--THAT'S OKAY.
WHAT'S AN ARTIST WITHOUT A TEMPERAMENT?
UH-UH. THE QUESTION IS: "WHAT'S A TEMPERAMENT WITHOUT AN ARTIST?"
ANSWER: ME--PAUL SAME--SPECIALIST IN UNFINISHED WORKS.
WANNA TALK ABOUT IT--OR SHOULD WE JUST BUZZ OFF?

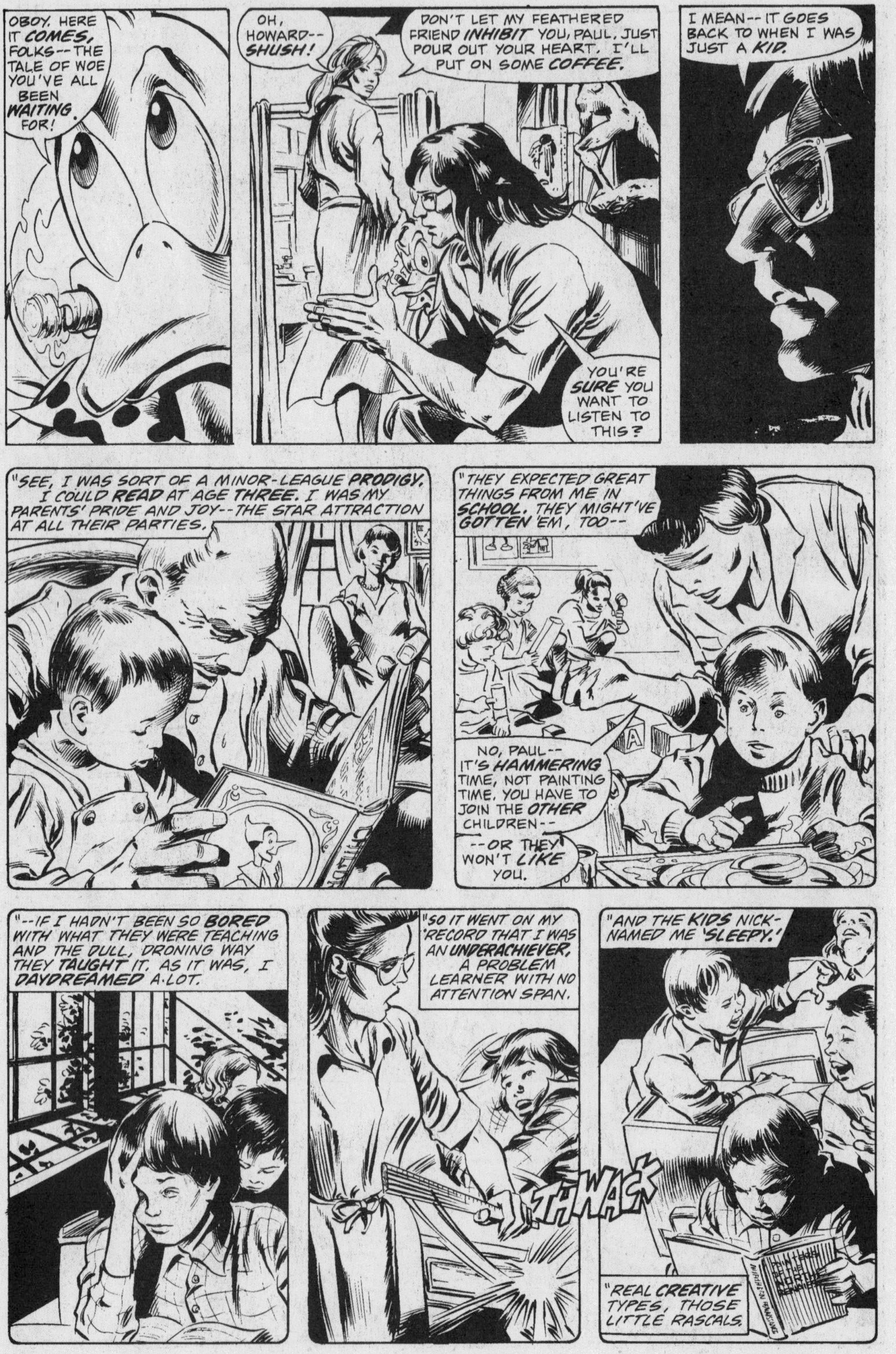

OBOY. HERE IT COMES, FOLKS--THE TALE OF WOE YOU'VE ALL BEEN WAITING FOR!
OH, HOWARD-- SHUSH!
DON'T LET MY FEATHERED FRIEND INHIBIT YOU, PAUL. JUST POUR OUT YOUR HEART. I'LL PUT ON SOME COFFEE.
YOU'RE SURE YOU WANT TO LISTEN TO THIS?
I MEAN--IT GOES BACK TO WHEN I WAS JUST A KID.
"SEE, I WAS SORT OF A MINOR-LEAGUE PRODIGY. I COULD READ AT AGE THREE. I WAS MY PARENTS' PRIDE AND JOY--THE STAR ATTRACTION AT ALL THEIR PARTIES.
"THEY EXPECTED GREAT THINGS FROM ME IN SCHOOL. THEY MIGHT'VE GOTTEN 'EM, TOO--
NO, PAUL-- IT'S HAMMERING TIME, NOT PAINTING TIME. YOU HAVE TO JOIN THE OTHER CHILDREN--
--OR THEY WON'T LIKE YOU.
"--IF I HADN'T BEEN SO BORED WITH WHAT THEY WERE TEACHING AND THE DULL, DRONING WAY THEY TAUGHT IT. AS IT WAS, I DAYDREAMED A LOT.
"SO IT WENT ON MY RECORD THAT I WAS AN UNDERACHIEVER, A PROBLEM LEARNER WITH NO ATTENTION SPAN.
THWACK
"AND THE KIDS NICK-NAMED ME 'SLEEPY.'
"REAL CREATIVE TYPES, THOSE LITTLE RASCALS.

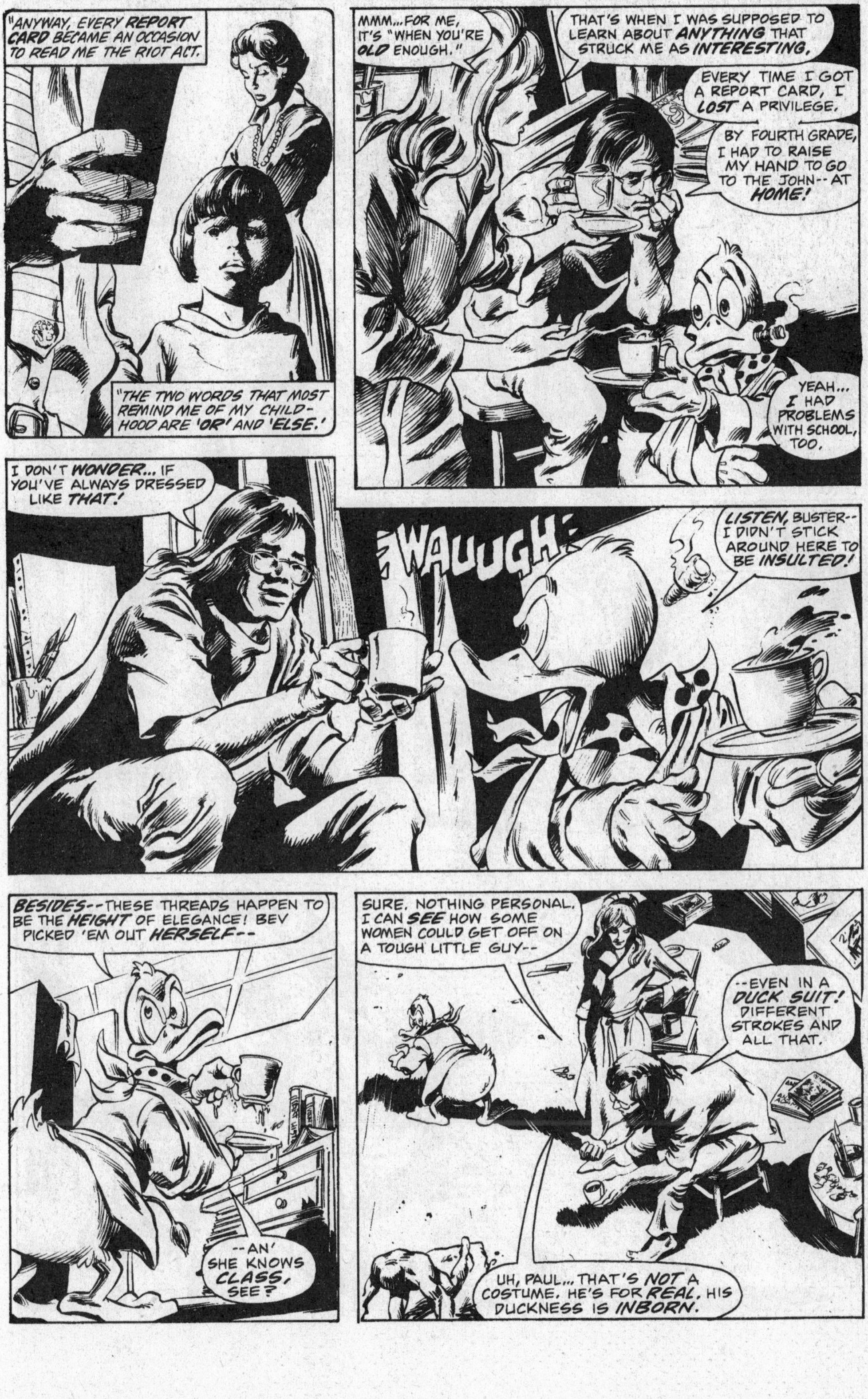
"ANYWAY, EVERY REPORT CARD BECAME AN OCCASION TO READ ME THE RIOT ACT.
"THE TWO WORDS THAT MOST REMIND ME OF MY CHILDHOOD ARE 'OR' AND 'ELSE.'
MMM... FOR ME, IT'S "WHEN YOU'RE OLD ENOUGH."
THAT'S WHEN I WAS SUPPOSED TO LEARN ABOUT ANYTHING THAT STRUCK ME AS INTERESTING.
EVERY TIME I GOT A REPORT CARD, I LOST A PRIVILEGE.
BY FOURTH GRADE, I HAD TO RAISE MY HAND TO GO TO THE JOHN-- AT HOME!
YEAH... I HAD PROBLEMS WITH SCHOOL, TOO.
I DON'T WONDER... IF YOU'VE ALWAYS DRESSED LIKE THAT!
WAUUGH!
LISTEN, BUSTER-- I DIDN'T STICK AROUND HERE TO BE INSULTED!
BESIDES--THESE THREADS HAPPEN TO BE THE HEIGHT OF ELEGANCE! BEV PICKED 'EM OUT HERSELF--
--AN' SHE KNOWS CLASS, SEE?
SURE. NOTHING PERSONAL. I CAN SEE HOW SOME WOMEN COULD GET OFF ON A TOUGH LITTLE GUY--
--EVEN IN A DUCK SUIT! DIFFERENT STROKES AND ALL THAT.
UH, PAUL... THAT'S NOT A COSTUME. HE'S FOR REAL. HIS DUCKNESS IS INBORN.

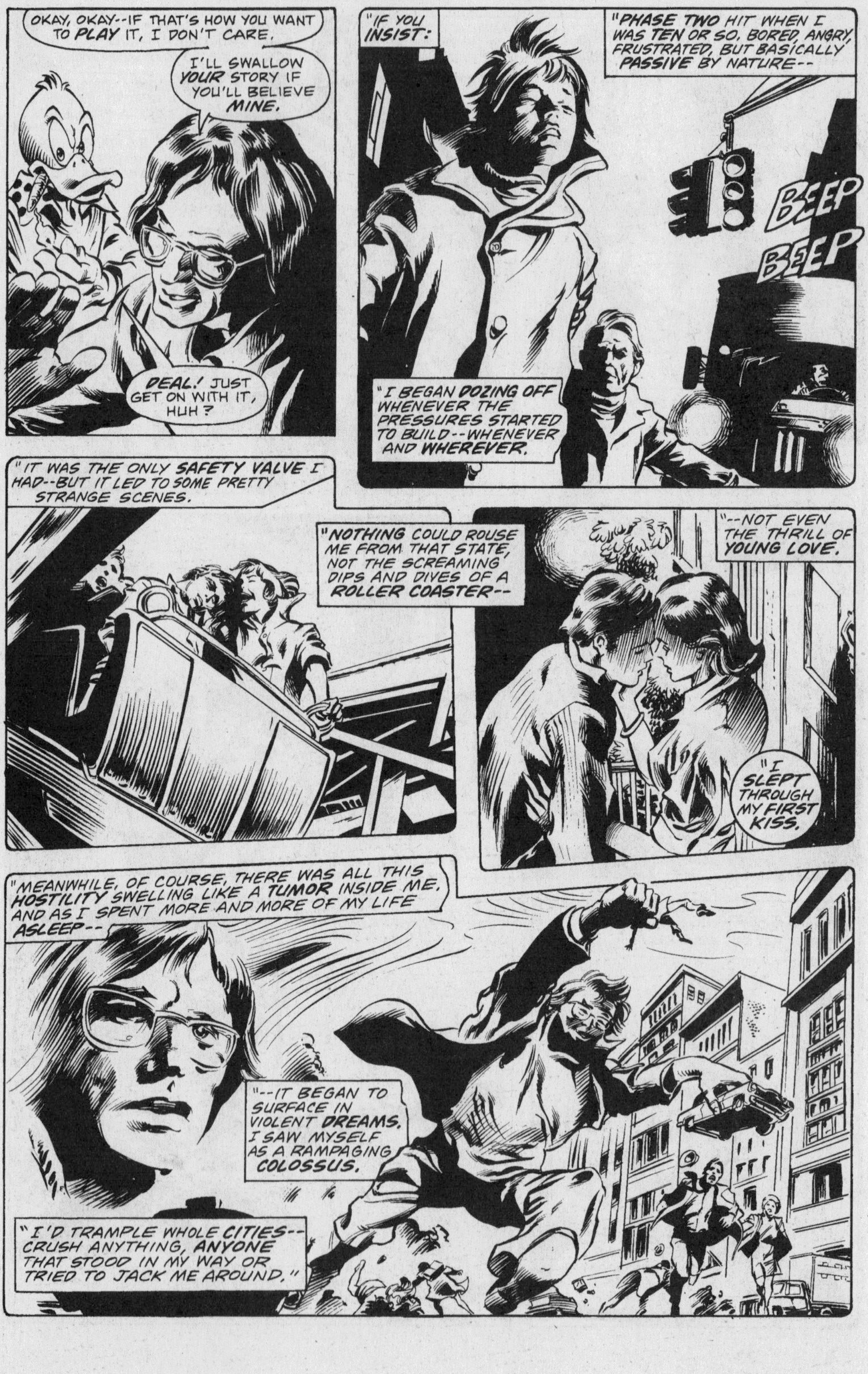

OKAY, OKAY--IF THAT'S HOW YOU WANT TO PLAY IT, I DON'T CARE.
I'LL SWALLOW YOUR STORY IF YOU'LL BELIEVE MINE.
DEAL! JUST GET ON WITH IT, HUH?
"IF YOU INSIST:
"PHASE TWO HIT WHEN I WAS TEN OR SO, BORED, ANGRY, FRUSTRATED, BUT BASICALLY PASSIVE BY NATURE--
BEEP BEEP
"I BEGAN DOZING OFF WHENEVER THE PRESSURES STARTED TO BUILD--WHENEVER AND WHEREVER.
"IT WAS THE ONLY SAFETY VALVE I HAD--BUT IT LED TO SOME PRETTY STRANGE SCENES.
"NOTHING COULD ROUSE ME FROM THAT STATE, NOT THE SCREAMING DIPS AND DIVES OF A ROLLER COASTER--
"--NOT EVEN THE THRILL OF YOUNG LOVE.
"I SLEPT THROUGH MY FIRST KISS.
"MEANWHILE, OF COURSE, THERE WAS ALL THIS HOSTILITY SWELLING LIKE A TUMOR INSIDE ME. AND AS I SPENT MORE AND MORE OF MY LIFE ASLEEP--
"--IT BEGAN TO SURFACE IN VIOLENT DREAMS. I SAW MYSELF AS A RAMPAGING COLOSSUS.
"I'D TRAMPLE WHOLE CITIES--CRUSH ANYTHING, ANYONE THAT STOOD IN MY WAY OR TRIED TO JACK ME AROUND."

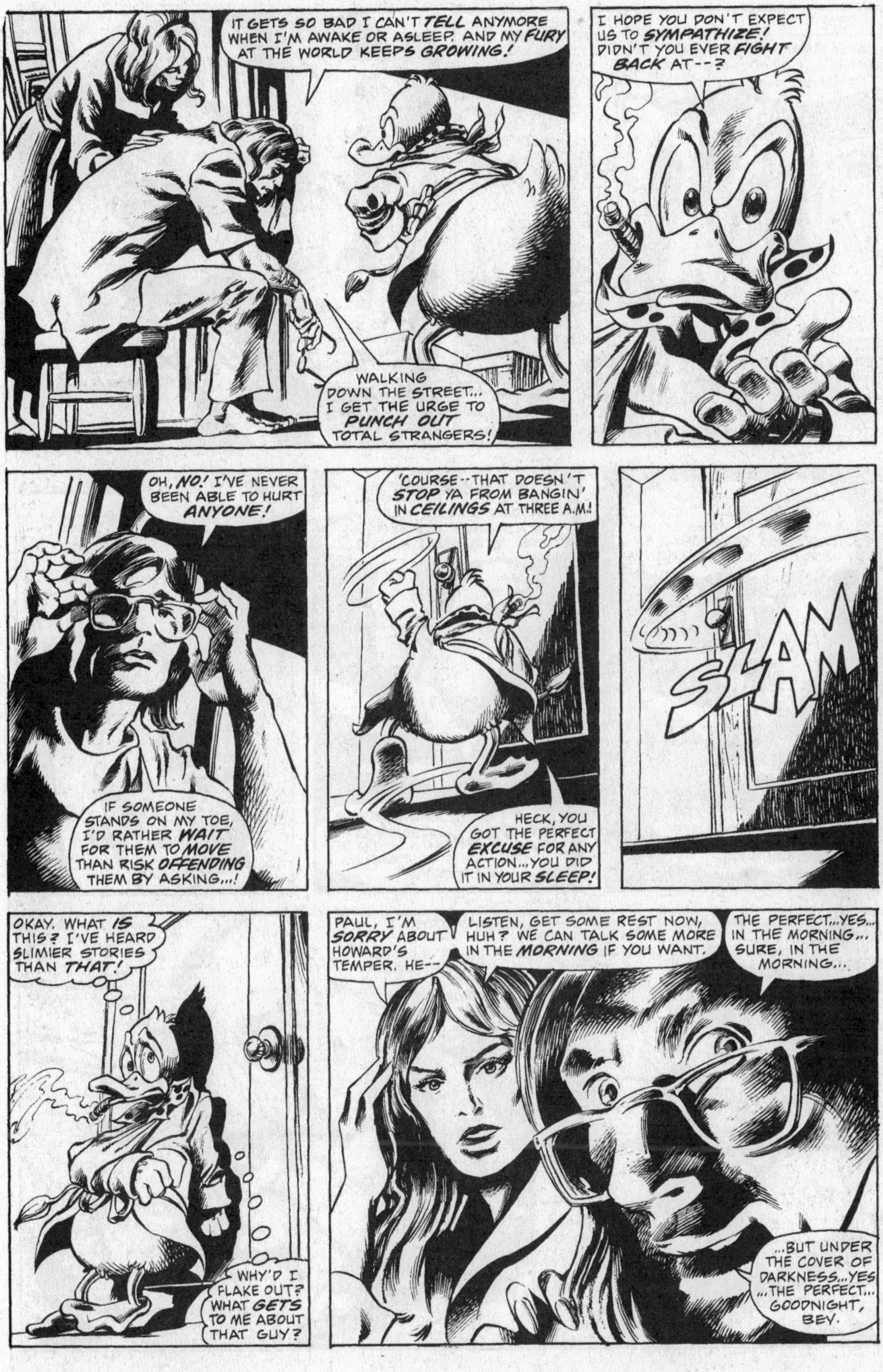
IT GETS SO BAD I CAN'T TELL ANYMORE WHEN I'M AWAKE OR ASLEEP. AND MY FURY AT THE WORLD KEEPS GROWING!
WALKING DOWN THE STREET... I GET THE URGE TO PUNCH OUT TOTAL STRANGERS!
I HOPE YOU DON'T EXPECT US TO SYMPATHIZE! DIDN'T YOU EVER FIGHT BACK AT--?
OH, NO! I'VE NEVER BEEN ABLE TO HURT ANYONE!
IF SOMEONE STANDS ON MY TOE, I'D RATHER WAIT FOR THEM TO MOVE THAN RISK OFFENDING THEM BY ASKING...!
'COURSE--THAT DOESN'T STOP YA FROM BANGIN' IN CEILINGS AT THREE A.M.!
HECK, YOU GOT THE PERFECT EXCUSE FOR ANY ACTION... YOU DID IT IN YOUR SLEEP!
SLAM
OKAY. WHAT IS THIS? I'VE HEARD SLIMIER STORIES THAN THAT!
WHY'D I FLAKE OUT? WHAT GETS TO ME ABOUT THAT GUY?
PAUL, I'M SORRY ABOUT HOWARD'S TEMPER. HE--
LISTEN, GET SOME REST NOW, HUH? WE CAN TALK SOME MORE IN THE MORNING IF YOU WANT.
THE PERFECT... YES... IN THE MORNING... SURE, IN THE MORNING...
...BUT UNDER THE COVER OF DARKNESS... YES ...THE PERFECT... GOODNIGHT, BEV.

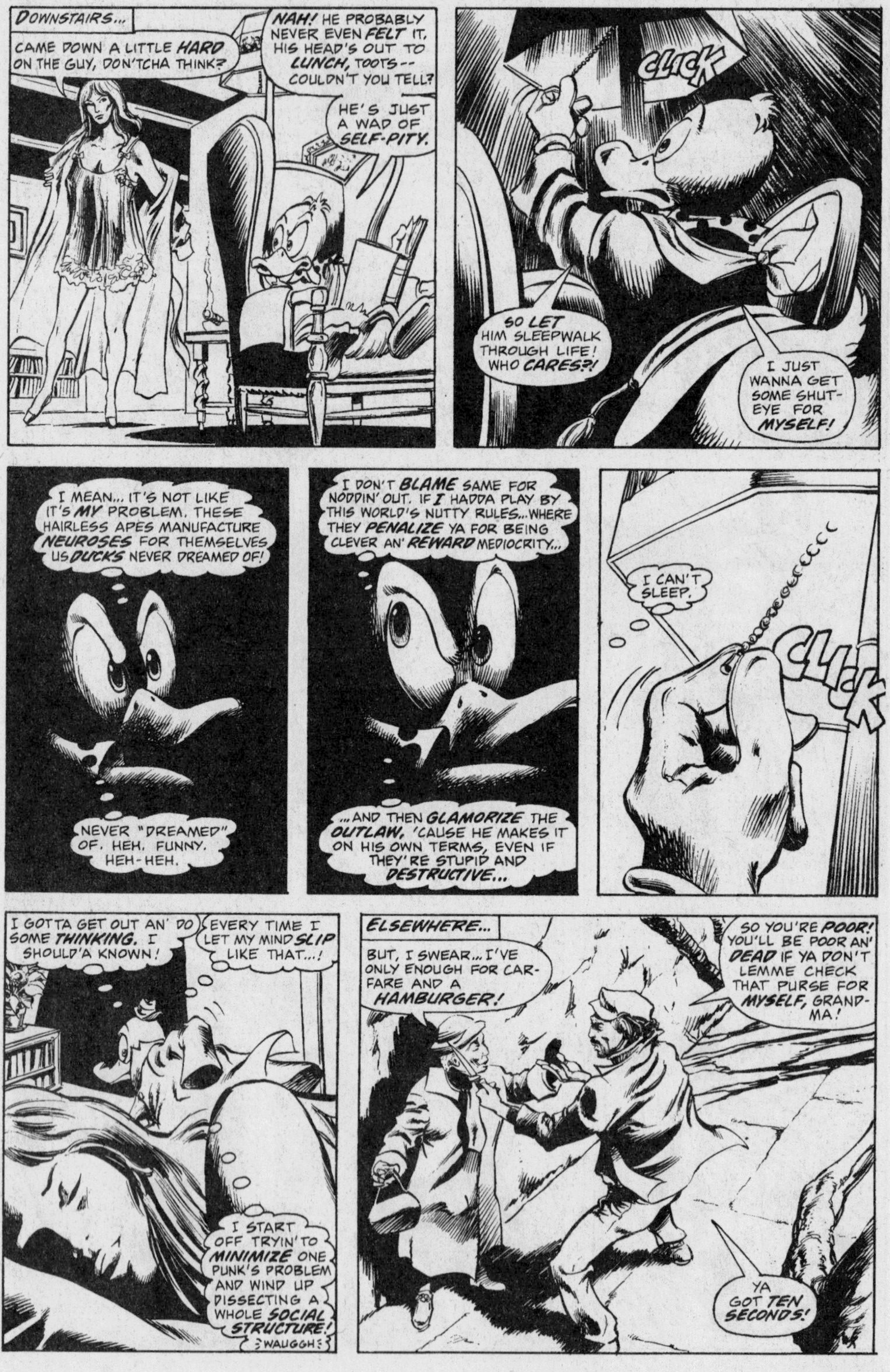
DOWNSTAIRS...
CAME DOWN A LITTLE HARD ON THE GUY, DON'TCHA THINK?
NAH! HE PROBABLY NEVER EVEN FELT IT, HIS HEAD'S OUT TO LUNCH, TOOTS-- COULDN'T YOU TELL?
HE'S JUST A WAD OF SELF-PITY.
CLICK
SO LET HIM SLEEPWALK THROUGH LIFE! WHO CARES?!
I JUST WANNA GET SOME SHUT-EYE FOR MYSELF!
I MEAN... IT'S NOT LIKE IT'S MY PROBLEM. THESE HAIRLESS APES MANUFACTURE NEUROSES FOR THEMSELVES US DUCKS NEVER DREAMED OF!
NEVER "DREAMED" OF. HEH. FUNNY. HEH-HEH.
I DON'T BLAME SAME FOR NODDIN' OUT. IF I HADDA PLAY BY THIS WORLD'S NUTTY RULES...WHERE THEY PENALIZE YA FOR BEING CLEVER AN' REWARD MEDIOCRITY...
...AND THEN GLAMORIZE THE OUTLAW, 'CAUSE HE MAKES IT ON HIS OWN TERMS, EVEN IF THEY'RE STUPID AND DESTRUCTIVE...
I CAN'T SLEEP.
CLICK
I GOTTA GET OUT AN' DO SOME THINKING. I SHOULD'A KNOWN!
EVERY TIME I LET MY MIND SLIP LIKE THAT...!
I START OFF TRYIN' TO MINIMIZE ONE PUNK'S PROBLEM AND WIND UP DISSECTING A WHOLE SOCIAL STRUCTURE! WAUGGH
ELSEWHERE...
BUT, I SWEAR... I'VE ONLY ENOUGH FOR CAR-FARE AND A HAMBURGER!
SO YOU'RE POOR! YOU'LL BE POOR AN' DEAD IF YA DON'T LEMME CHECK THAT PURSE FOR MYSELF, GRAND-MA!
YA GOT TEN SECONDS!

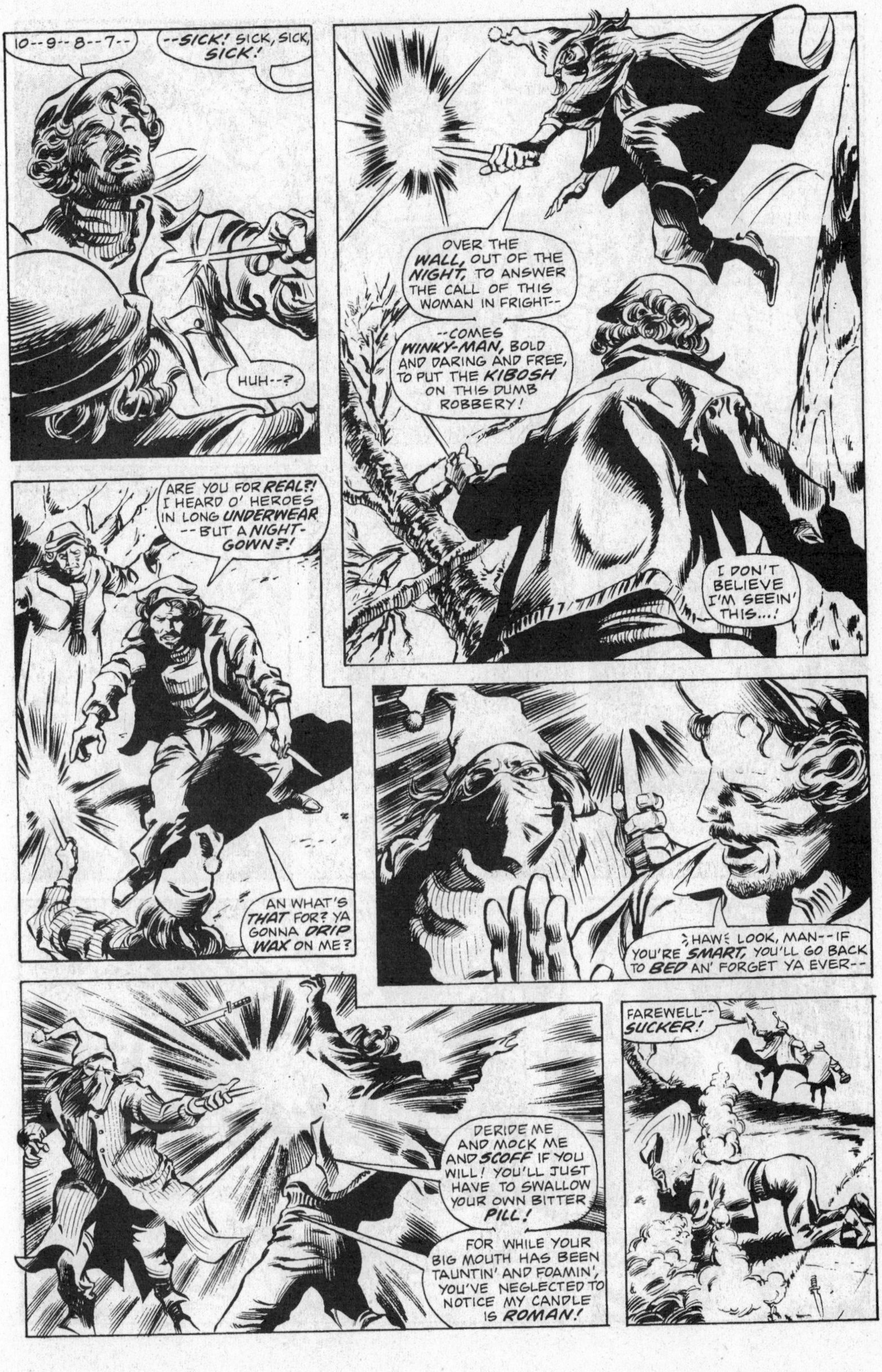
10--9--8--7--
--SICK! SICK, SICK, SICK!
HUH--?
OVER THE WALL, OUT OF THE NIGHT, TO ANSWER THE CALL OF THIS WOMAN IN FRIGHT--
--COMES WINKY-MAN, BOLD AND DARING AND FREE, TO PUT THE KIBOSH ON THIS DUMB ROBBERY!
I DON'T BELIEVE I'M SEEIN' THIS...!
ARE YOU FOR REAL?! I HEARD O' HEROES IN LONG UNDERWEAR --BUT A NIGHT-GOWN?!
AN WHAT'S THAT FOR? YA GONNA DRIP WAX ON ME?
HAW! LOOK, MAN--IF YOU'RE SMART, YOU'LL GO BACK TO BED AN' FORGET YA EVER--
DERIDE ME AND MOCK ME AND SCOFF IF YOU WILL! YOU'LL JUST HAVE TO SWALLOW YOUR OWN BITTER PILL!
FOR WHILE YOUR BIG MOUTH HAS BEEN TAUNTIN' AND FOAMIN', YOU'VE NEGLECTED TO NOTICE MY CANDLE IS ROMAN!
FAREWELL-- SUCKER!

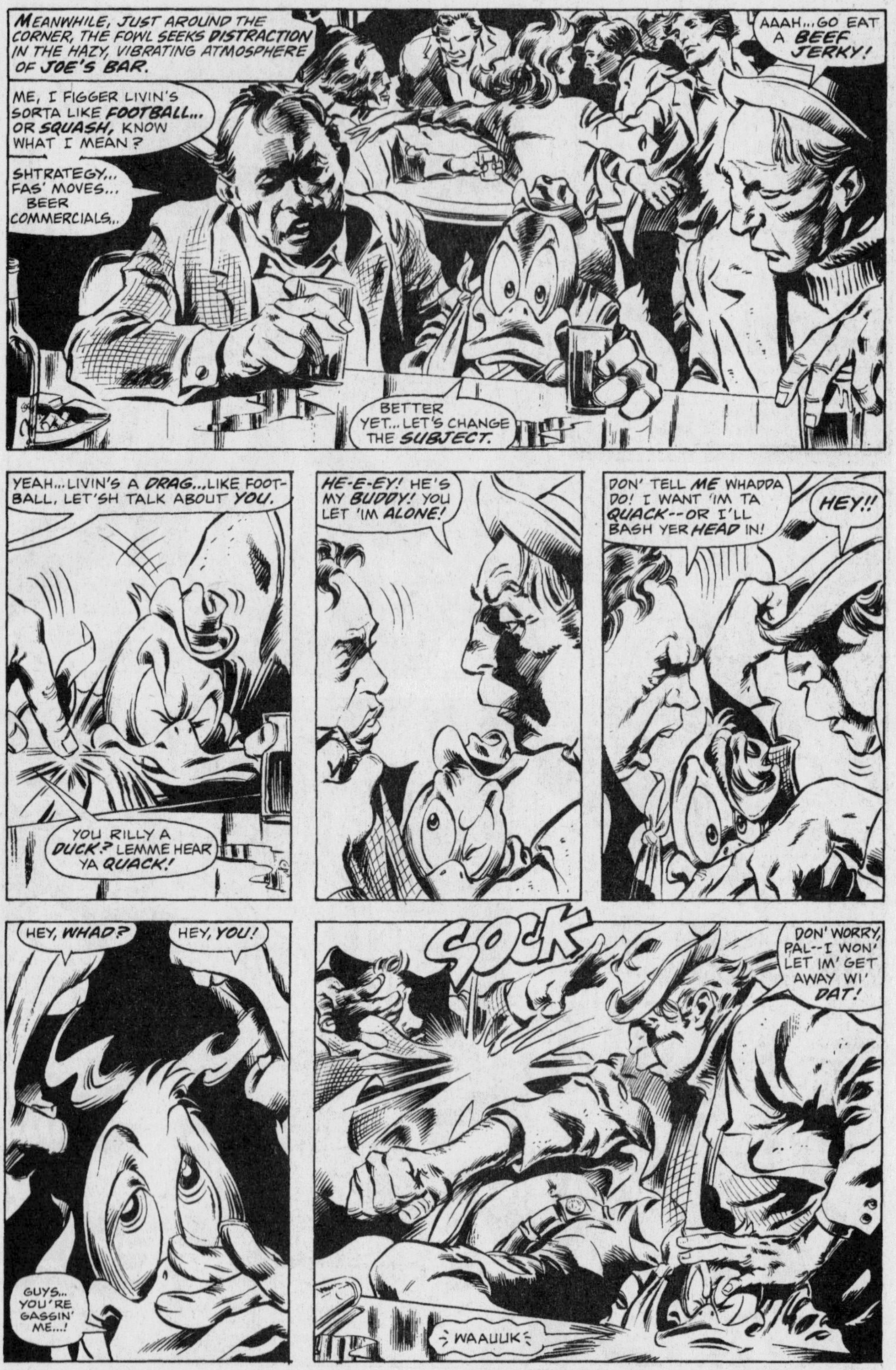
MEANWHILE, JUST AROUND THE CORNER, THE FOWL SEEKS DISTRACTION IN THE HAZY, VIBRATING ATMOSPHERE OF JOE'S BAR.
AAAH...GO EAT A BEEF JERKY!
ME, I FIGGER LIVIN'S SORTA LIKE FOOTBALL... OR SQUASH, KNOW WHAT I MEAN?
SHTRATEGY... FAS' MOVES... BEER COMMERCIALS...
BETTER YET...LET'S CHANGE THE SUBJECT.
YEAH...LIVIN'S A DRAG...LIKE FOOTBALL. LET'SH TALK ABOUT YOU.
YOU RILLY A DUCK? LEMME HEAR YA QUACK!
HE-E-EY! HE'S MY BUDDY! YOU LET 'IM ALONE!
DON' TELL ME WHADDA DO! I WANT 'IM TA QUACK--OR I'LL BASH YER HEAD IN!
HEY!!
HEY, WHAD?
HEY, YOU!
GUYS... YOU'RE GASSIN' ME...!
SOCK
DON' WORRY, PAL--I WON' LET IM' GET AWAY WI' DAT!
WAAUUK

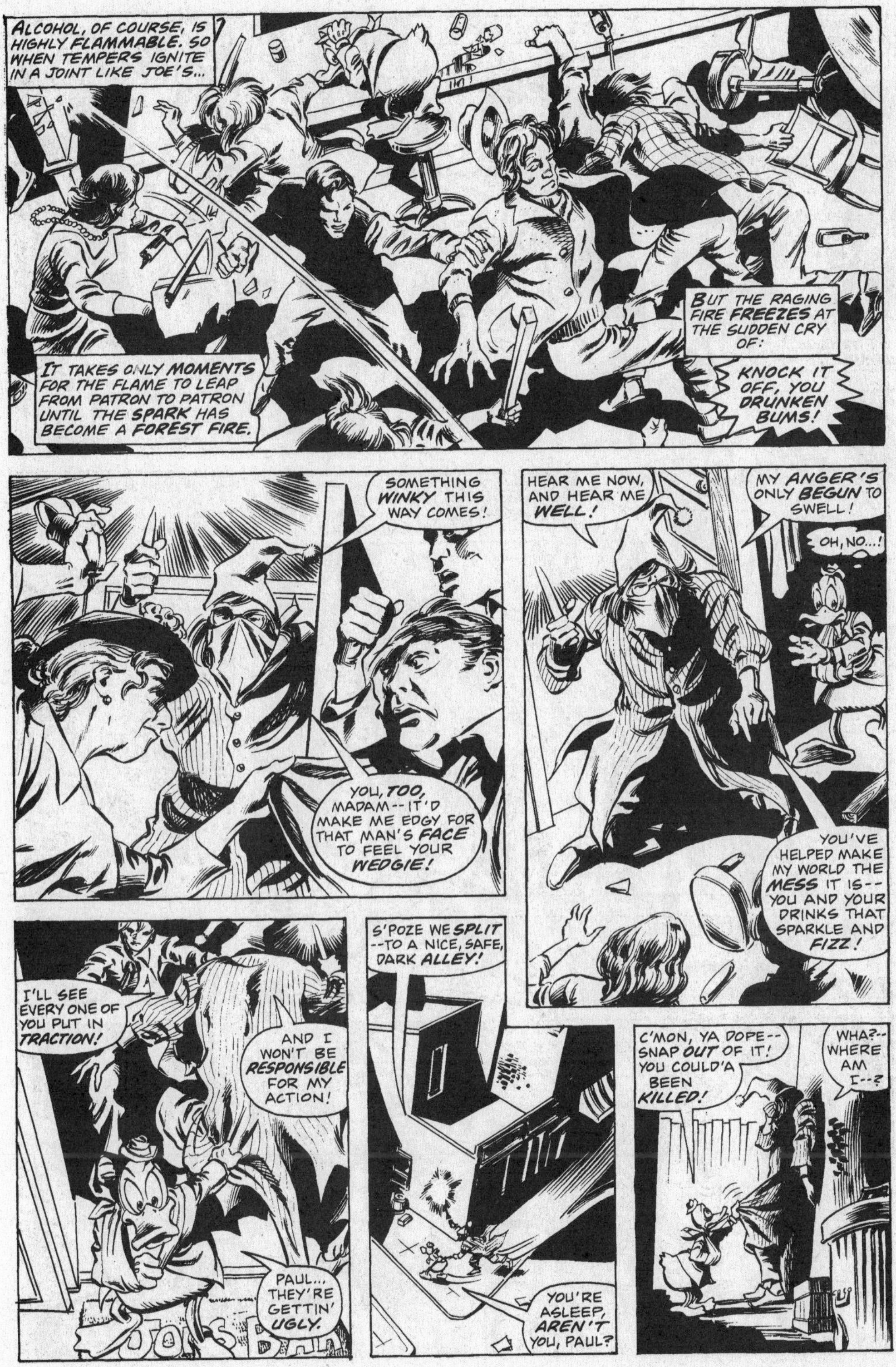

ALCOHOL, OF COURSE, IS HIGHLY FLAMMABLE. SO WHEN TEMPERS IGNITE IN A JOINT LIKE JOE'S...
IT TAKES ONLY MOMENTS FOR THE FLAME TO LEAP FROM PATRON TO PATRON UNTIL THE SPARK HAS BECOME A FOREST FIRE.
BUT THE RAGING FIRE FREEZES AT THE SUDDEN CRY OF:
KNOCK IT OFF, YOU DRUNKEN BUMS!
SOMETHING WINKY THIS WAY COMES!
YOU, TOO, MADAM--IT'D MAKE ME EDGY FOR THAT MAN'S FACE TO FEEL YOUR WEDGIE!
HEAR ME NOW, AND HEAR ME WELL!
MY ANGER'S ONLY BEGUN TO SWELL!
OH, NO...!
YOU'VE HELPED MAKE MY WORLD THE MESS IT IS--YOU AND YOUR DRINKS THAT SPARKLE AND FIZZ!
I'LL SEE EVERY ONE OF YOU PUT IN TRACTION!
AND I WON'T BE RESPONSIBLE FOR MY ACTION!
PAUL... THEY'RE GETTIN' UGLY.
S'POZE WE SPLIT--TO A NICE, SAFE, DARK ALLEY!
YOU'RE ASLEEP, AREN'T YOU, PAUL?
C'MON, YA DOPE--SNAP OUT OF IT! YOU COULD'A BEEN KILLED!
WHA?--WHERE AM I--?

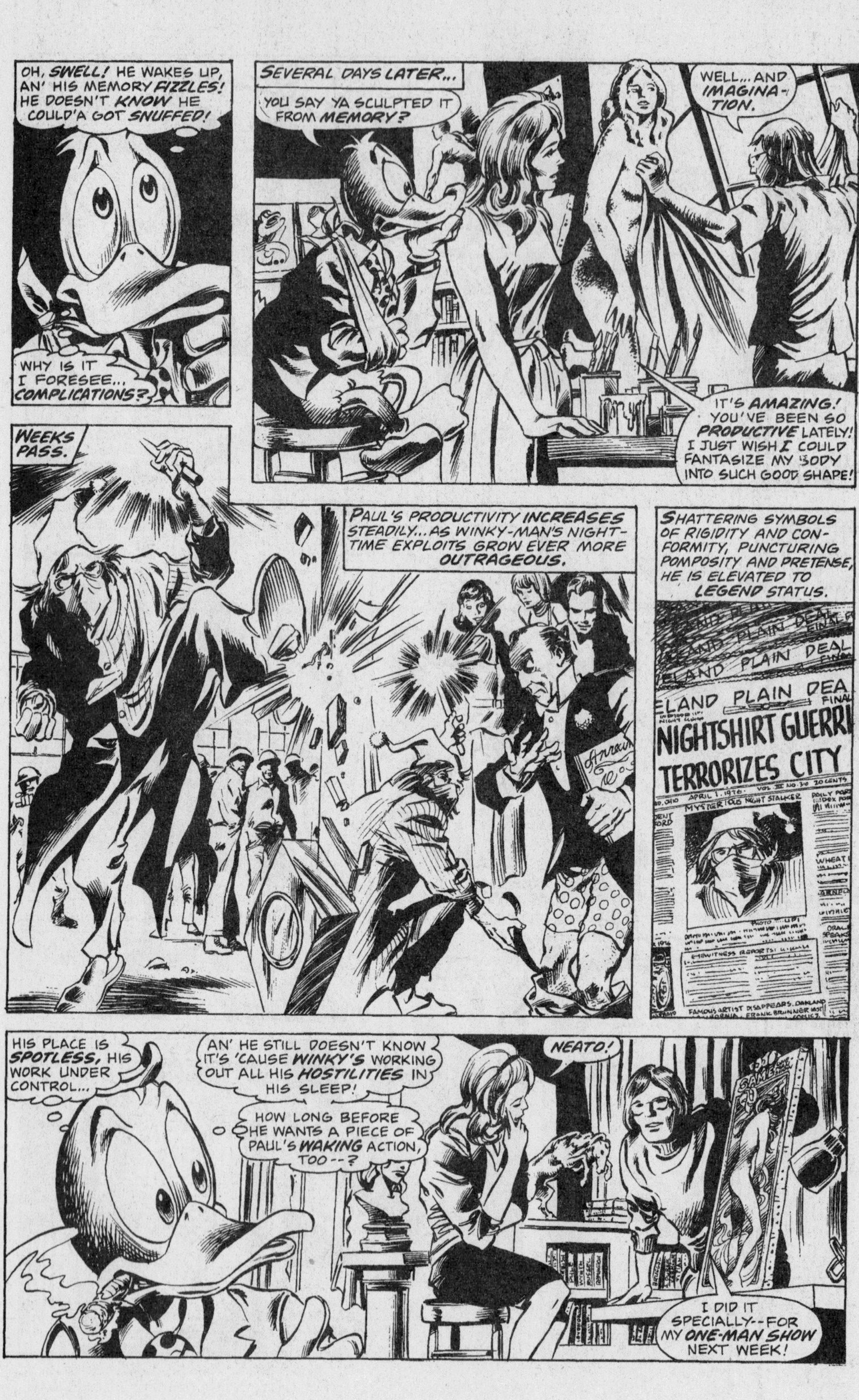

OH, SWELL! HE WAKES UP, AN' HIS MEMORY FIZZLES! HE DOESN'T KNOW HE COULD'A GOT SNUFFED!
WHY IS IT I FORESEE... COMPLICATIONS?
SEVERAL DAYS LATER...
YOU SAY YA SCULPTED IT FROM MEMORY?
WELL... AND IMAGINATION.
IT'S AMAZING! YOU'VE BEEN SO PRODUCTIVE LATELY! I JUST WISH I COULD FANTASIZE MY BODY INTO SUCH GOOD SHAPE!
WEEKS PASS.
PAUL'S PRODUCTIVITY INCREASES STEADILY... AS WINKY-MAN'S NIGHT-TIME EXPLOITS GROW EVER MORE OUTRAGEOUS.
SHATTERING SYMBOLS OF RIGIDITY AND CONFORMITY, PUNCTURING POMPOSITY AND PRETENSE, HE IS ELEVATED TO LEGEND STATUS.
ELAND PLAIN DEAL
NIGHTSHIRT GUERRI
TERRORIZES CITY
HIS PLACE IS SPOTLESS, HIS WORK UNDER CONTROL...
AN' HE STILL DOESN'T KNOW IT'S 'CAUSE WINKY'S WORKING OUT ALL HIS HOSTILITIES IN HIS SLEEP!
HOW LONG BEFORE HE WANTS A PIECE OF PAUL'S WAKING ACTION, TOO--?
NEATO!
I DID IT SPECIALLY--FOR MY ONE-MAN SHOW NEXT WEEK!

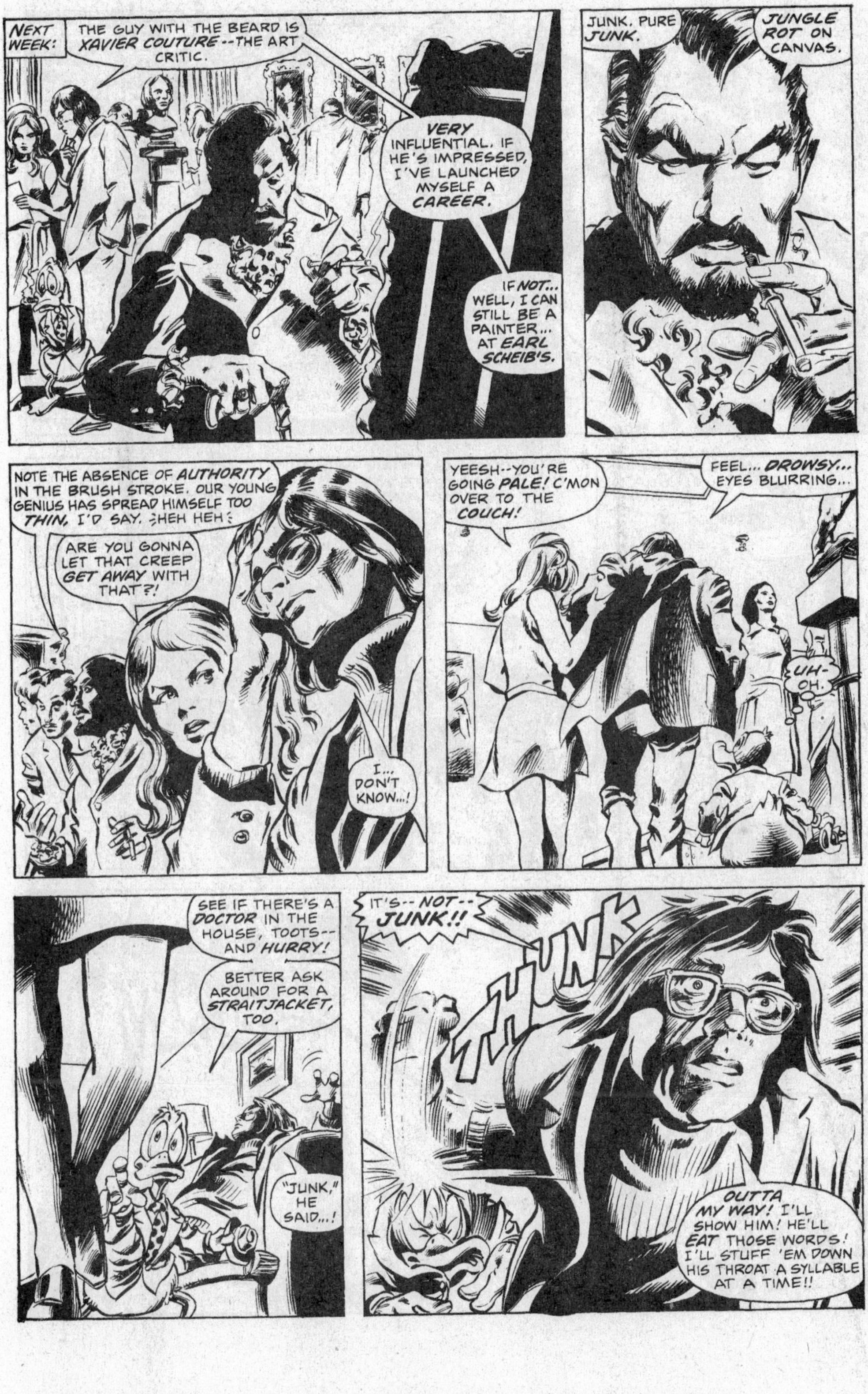
NEXT WEEK:
THE GUY WITH THE BEARD IS XAVIER COUTURE--THE ART CRITIC.
VERY INFLUENTIAL. IF HE'S IMPRESSED, I'VE LAUNCHED MYSELF A CAREER.
IF NOT... WELL, I CAN STILL BE A PAINTER... AT EARL SCHEIB'S.
JUNK. PURE JUNK.
JUNGLE ROT ON CANVAS.
NOTE THE ABSENCE OF AUTHORITY IN THE BRUSH STROKE. OUR YOUNG GENIUS HAS SPREAD HIMSELF TOO THIN, I'D SAY. HEH HEH
ARE YOU GONNA LET THAT CREEP GET AWAY WITH THAT?!
I... DON'T KNOW...!
YEESH--YOU'RE GOING PALE! C'MON OVER TO THE COUCH!
FEEL... DROWSY... EYES BLURRING...
UH-OH.
SEE IF THERE'S A DOCTOR IN THE HOUSE, TOOTS--AND HURRY!
BETTER ASK AROUND FOR A STRAITJACKET, TOO.
"JUNK," HE SAID...!
IT'S--NOT--JUNK!!
THUNK
OUTTA MY WAY! I'LL SHOW HIM! HE'LL EAT THOSE WORDS! I'LL STUFF 'EM DOWN HIS THROAT A SYLLABLE AT A TIME!!

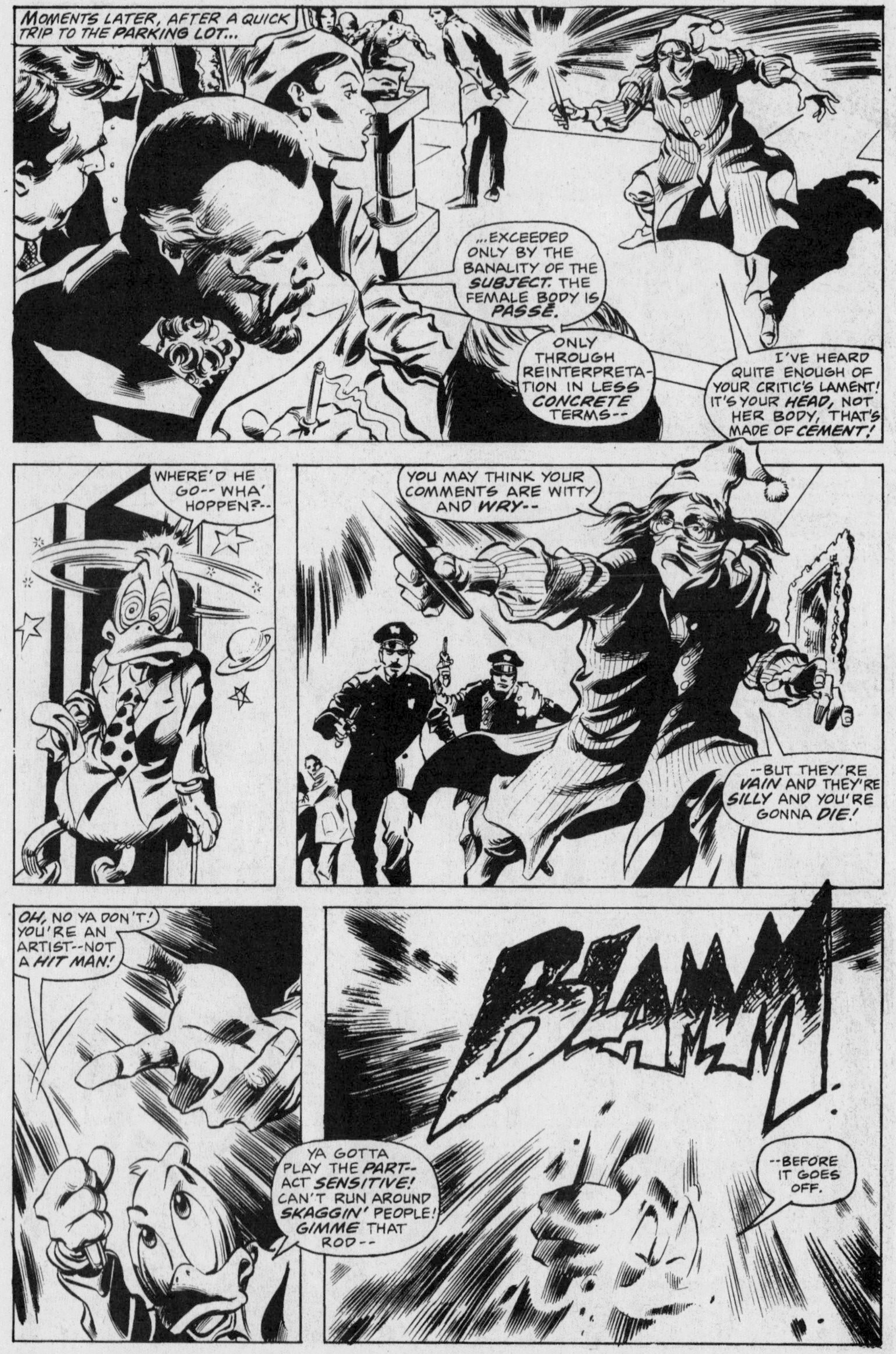

MOMENTS LATER, AFTER A QUICK TRIP TO THE PARKING LOT...
...EXCEEDED ONLY BY THE BANALITY OF THE SUBJECT. THE FEMALE BODY IS PASSÉ.
ONLY THROUGH REINTERPRETATION IN LESS CONCRETE TERMS--
I'VE HEARD QUITE ENOUGH OF YOUR CRITIC'S LAMENT! IT'S YOUR HEAD, NOT HER BODY, THAT'S MADE OF CEMENT!
WHERE'D HE GO-- WHA' HOPPEN?--
YOU MAY THINK YOUR COMMENTS ARE WITTY AND WRY--
--BUT THEY'RE VAIN AND THEY'RE SILLY AND YOU'RE GONNA DIE!
OH, NO YA DON'T! YOU'RE AN ARTIST--NOT A HIT MAN!
YA GOTTA PLAY THE PART-- ACT SENSITIVE! CAN'T RUN AROUND SKAGGIN' PEOPLE! GIMME THAT ROD--
BLAMM
--BEFORE IT GOES OFF.

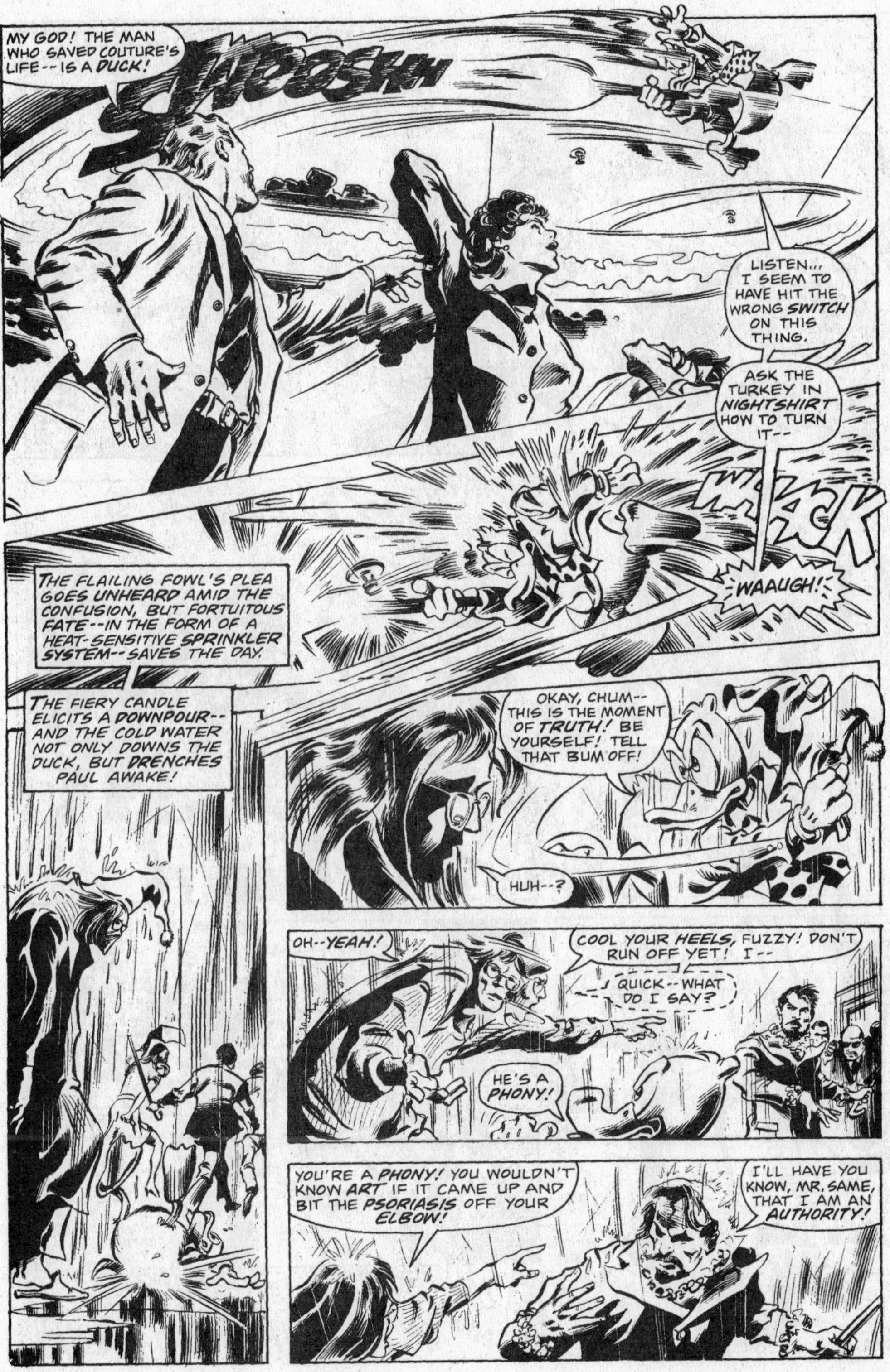
MY GOD! THE MAN WHO SAVED COUTURE'S LIFE--IS A DUCK!
SHWOOSHH
LISTEN... I SEEM TO HAVE HIT THE WRONG SWITCH ON THIS THING.
ASK THE TURKEY IN NIGHTSHIRT HOW TO TURN IT--
WHACK
WAAUGH!
THE FLAILING FOWL'S PLEA GOES UNHEARD AMID THE CONFUSION, BUT FORTUITOUS FATE--IN THE FORM OF A HEAT-SENSITIVE SPRINKLER SYSTEM--SAVES THE DAY.
THE FIERY CANDLE ELICITS A DOWNPOUR--AND THE COLD WATER NOT ONLY DOWNS THE DUCK, BUT DRENCHES PAUL AWAKE!
OKAY, CHUM--THIS IS THE MOMENT OF TRUTH! BE YOURSELF! TELL THAT BUM OFF!
HUH--?
OH--YEAH!
COOL YOUR HEELS, FUZZY! DON'T RUN OFF YET! I--
QUICK--WHAT DO I SAY?
HE'S A PHONY!
YOU'RE A PHONY! YOU WOULDN'T KNOW ART IF IT CAME UP AND BIT THE PSORIASIS OFF YOUR ELBOW!
I'LL HAVE YOU KNOW, MR. SAME, THAT I AM AN AUTHORITY!

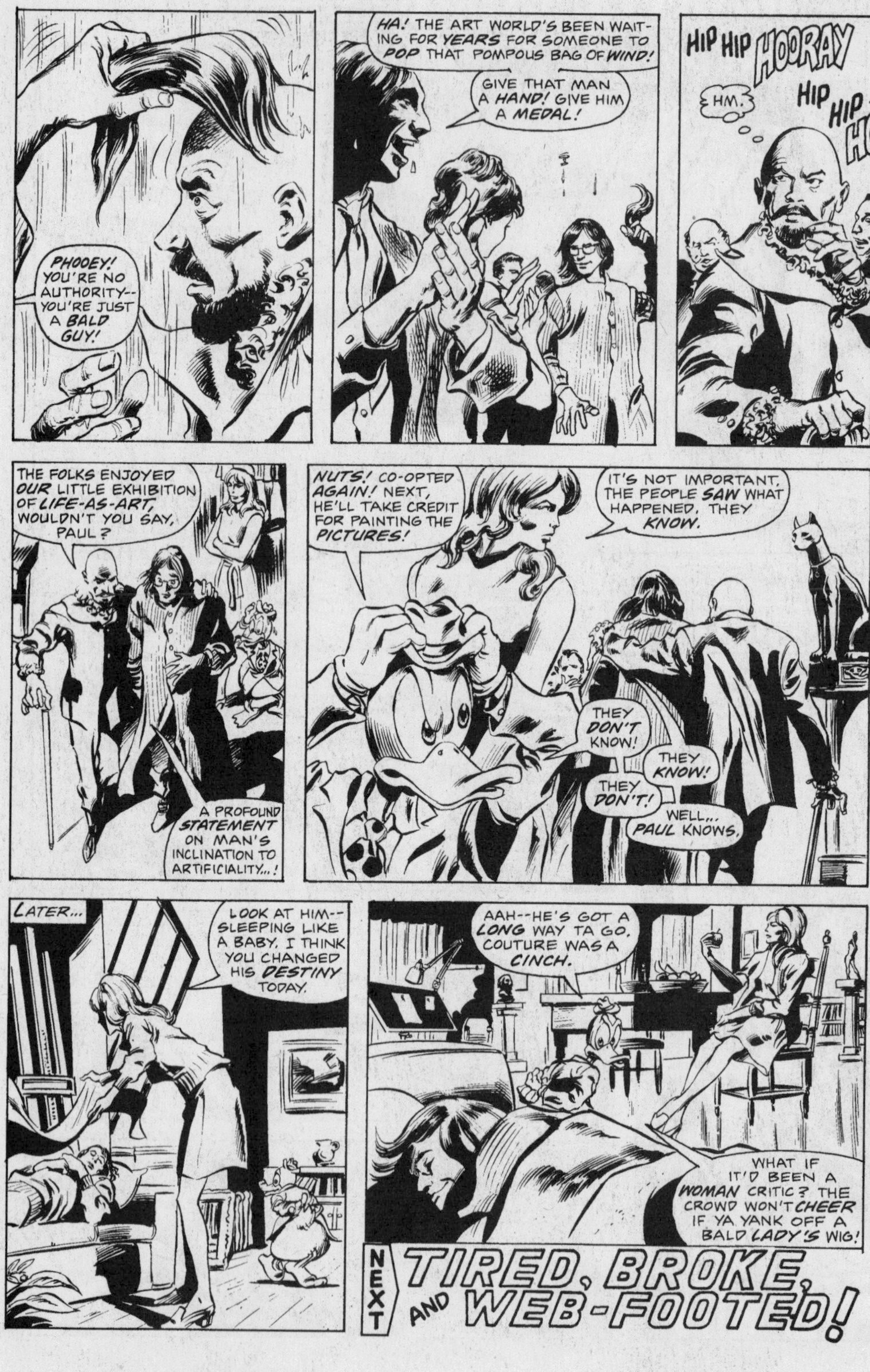
PHOOEY! YOU'RE NO AUTHORITY-- YOU'RE JUST A BALD GUY!
HA! THE ART WORLD'S BEEN WAITING FOR YEARS FOR SOMEONE TO POP THAT POMPOUS BAG OF WIND!
GIVE THAT MAN A HAND! GIVE HIM A MEDAL!
HIP HIP HOORAY
HIP HIP
HM.
THE FOLKS ENJOYED OUR LITTLE EXHIBITION OF LIFE-AS-ART, WOULDN'T YOU SAY, PAUL?
A PROFOUND STATEMENT ON MAN'S INCLINATION TO ARTIFICIALITY...!
NUTS! CO-OPTED AGAIN! NEXT, HE'LL TAKE CREDIT FOR PAINTING THE PICTURES!
IT'S NOT IMPORTANT, THE PEOPLE SAW WHAT HAPPENED, THEY KNOW.
THEY DON'T KNOW!
THEY KNOW!
THEY DON'T!
WELL... PAUL KNOWS.
LATER...
LOOK AT HIM-- SLEEPING LIKE A BABY. I THINK YOU CHANGED HIS DESTINY TODAY.
AAH--HE'S GOT A LONG WAY TA GO. COUTURE WAS A CINCH.
WHAT IF IT'D BEEN A WOMAN CRITIC? THE CROWD WON'T CHEER IF YA YANK OFF A BALD LADY'S WIG!
NEXT
TIRED, BROKE, AND WEB-FOOTED!

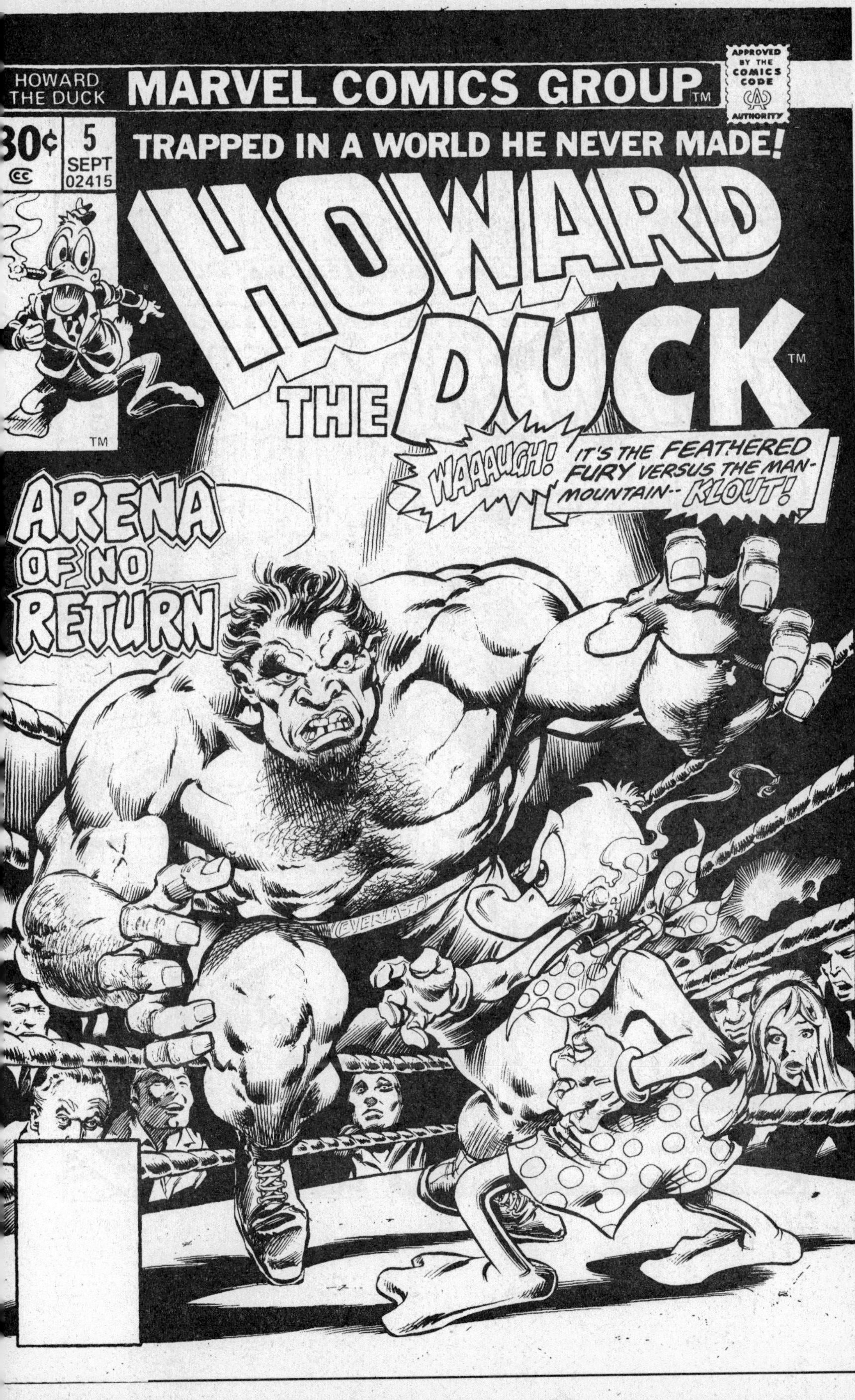

HOWARD THE DUCK
MARVEL COMICS GROUP
APPROVED BY THE COMICS CODE AUTHORITY
30¢
5 SEPT 02415
TRAPPED IN A WORLD HE NEVER MADE!
HOWARD THE DUCK
ARENA OF NO RETURN
WAAAUGH!
IT'S THE FEATHERED FURY VERSUS THE MAN-MOUNTAIN-- KLOUT!
EVERLAST

From the time of his hatching, he was...different. A potentially brilliant scholar who dreaded the structured environment of school, he educated himself in the streets, taking whatever work was available, formulating his philosophy of self from what he learned of the world about him. And then the Cosmic Axis shifted...and that world *changed.* Suddenly, he was stranded in a universe he could not fathom. Without warning, he became a strange fowl in an even stranger land.

Stan Lee PRESENTS:

HOWARD THE DUCK!™

STEVE GERBER AVARICIOUS WRITER | **GENE COLAN** PENURIOUS PENCILLER | **STEVE LEIALOHA** INSATIABLE INKER | **ARCHIE GOODWIN** TIGHTFISTED EDITOR

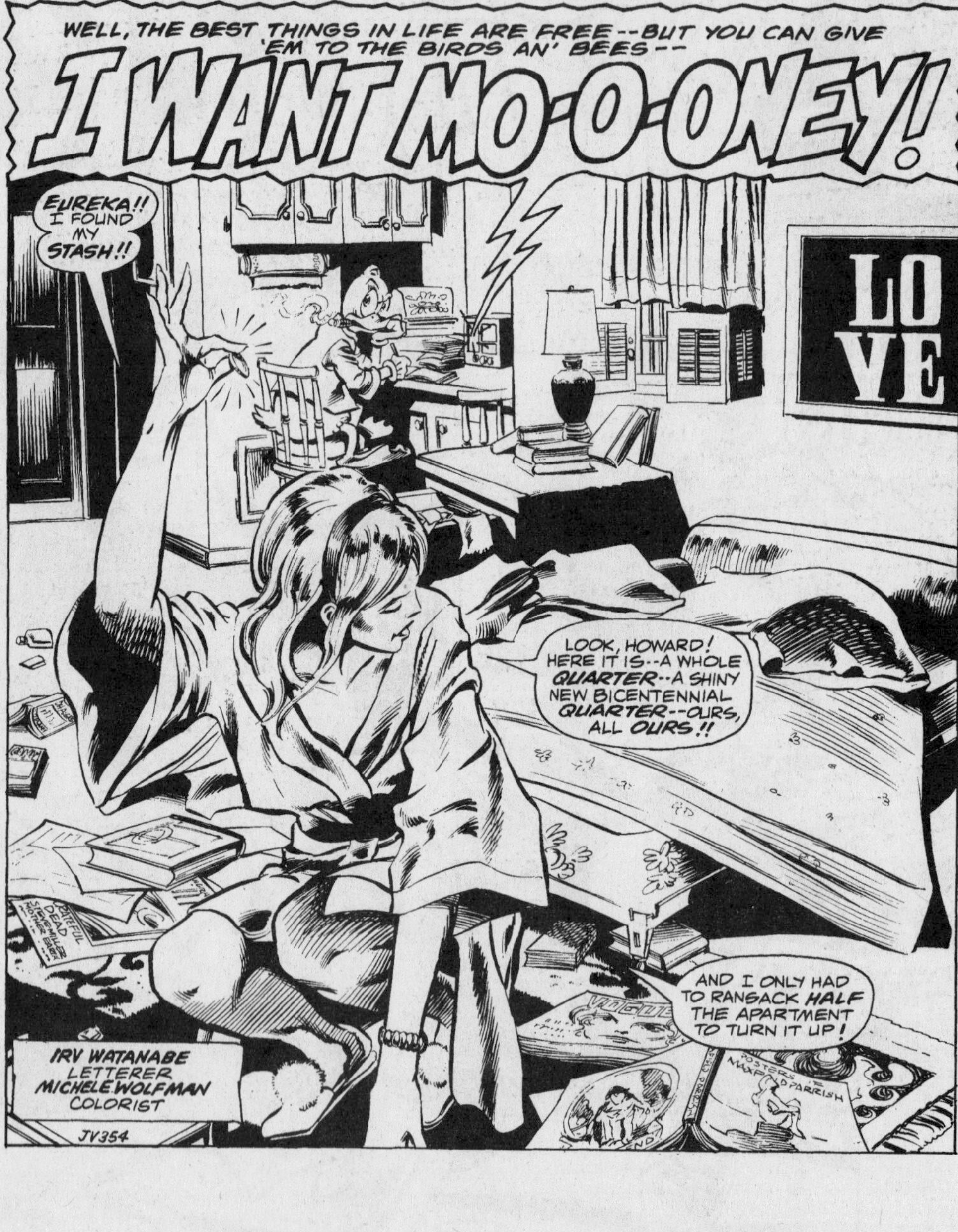
WELL, THE BEST THINGS IN LIFE ARE FREE--BUT YOU CAN GIVE 'EM TO THE BIRDS AN' BEES--
I WANT MO-O-ONEY!
EUREKA!! I FOUND MY STASH!!
LO
VE
LOOK, HOWARD! HERE IT IS--A WHOLE QUARTER--A SHINY NEW BICENTENNIAL QUARTER--OURS, ALL OURS!!
AND I ONLY HAD TO RANSACK HALF THE APARTMENT TO TURN IT UP!
IRV WATANABE LETTERER MICHELE WOLFMAN COLORIST
JV354

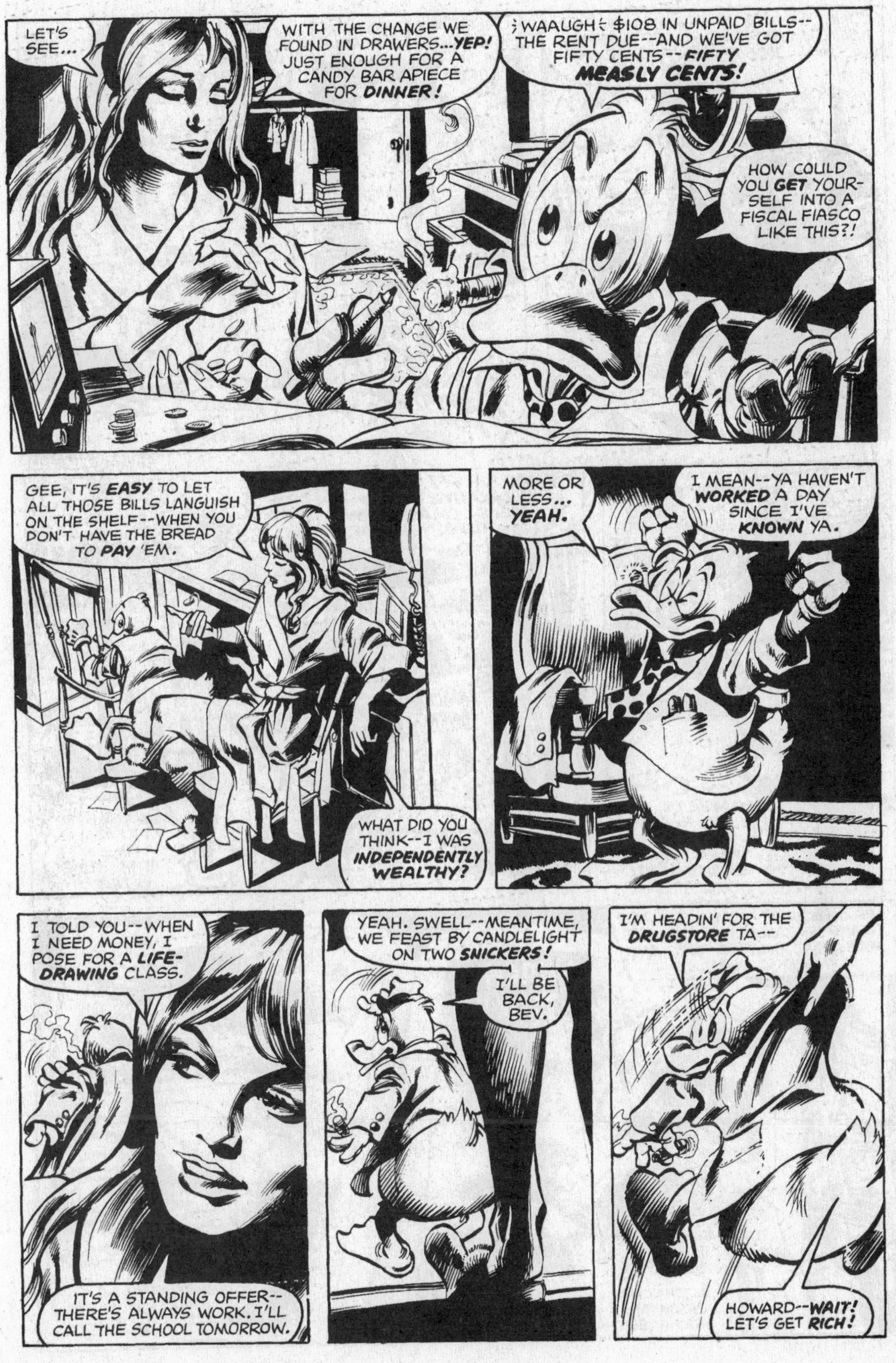
LET'S SEE...
WITH THE CHANGE WE FOUND IN DRAWERS... YEP! JUST ENOUGH FOR A CANDY BAR APIECE FOR DINNER!
WAAUGH! $108 IN UNPAID BILLS-- THE RENT DUE--AND WE'VE GOT FIFTY CENTS--FIFTY MEASLY CENTS!
HOW COULD YOU GET YOURSELF INTO A FISCAL FIASCO LIKE THIS?!
GEE, IT'S EASY TO LET ALL THOSE BILLS LANGUISH ON THE SHELF--WHEN YOU DON'T HAVE THE BREAD TO PAY 'EM.
WHAT DID YOU THINK--I WAS INDEPENDENTLY WEALTHY?
MORE OR LESS... YEAH.
I MEAN--YA HAVEN'T WORKED A DAY SINCE I'VE KNOWN YA.
I TOLD YOU--WHEN I NEED MONEY, I POSE FOR A LIFE-DRAWING CLASS.
IT'S A STANDING OFFER-- THERE'S ALWAYS WORK. I'LL CALL THE SCHOOL TOMORROW.
YEAH. SWELL--MEANTIME, WE FEAST BY CANDLELIGHT ON TWO SNICKERS!
I'LL BE BACK, BEV.
I'M HEADIN' FOR THE DRUGSTORE TA--
HOWARD--WAIT! LET'S GET RICH!

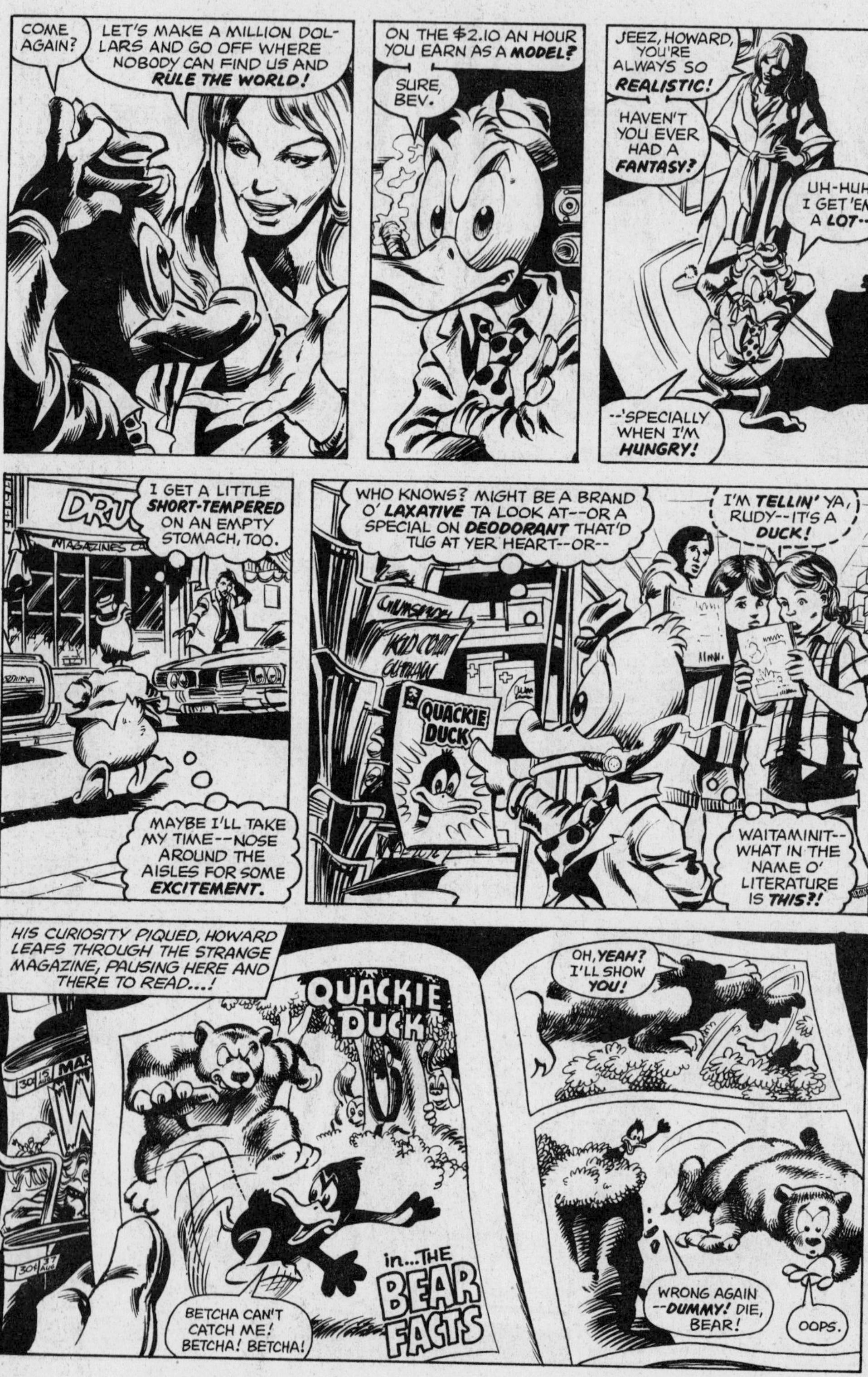
COME AGAIN?
LET'S MAKE A MILLION DOLLARS AND GO OFF WHERE NOBODY CAN FIND US AND RULE THE WORLD!
ON THE $2.10 AN HOUR YOU EARN AS A MODEL?
SURE, BEV.
JEEZ, HOWARD, YOU'RE ALWAYS SO REALISTIC!
HAVEN'T YOU EVER HAD A FANTASY?
UH-HUH. I GET 'EM A LOT--
--'SPECIALLY WHEN I'M HUNGRY!
I GET A LITTLE SHORT-TEMPERED ON AN EMPTY STOMACH, TOO.
MAYBE I'LL TAKE MY TIME--NOSE AROUND THE AISLES FOR SOME EXCITEMENT.
WHO KNOWS? MIGHT BE A BRAND O' LAXATIVE TA LOOK AT--OR A SPECIAL ON DEODORANT THAT'D TUG AT YER HEART--OR--
I'M TELLIN' YA, RUDY--IT'S A DUCK!
QUACKIE DUCK
WAITAMINIT-- WHAT IN THE NAME O' LITERATURE IS THIS?!
HIS CURIOSITY PIQUED, HOWARD LEAFS THROUGH THE STRANGE MAGAZINE, PAUSING HERE AND THERE TO READ...!
QUACKIE DUCK!
in...THE BEAR FACTS
BETCHA CAN'T CATCH ME! BETCHA! BETCHA!
OH, YEAH? I'LL SHOW YOU!
WRONG AGAIN --DUMMY! DIE, BEAR!
OOPS.

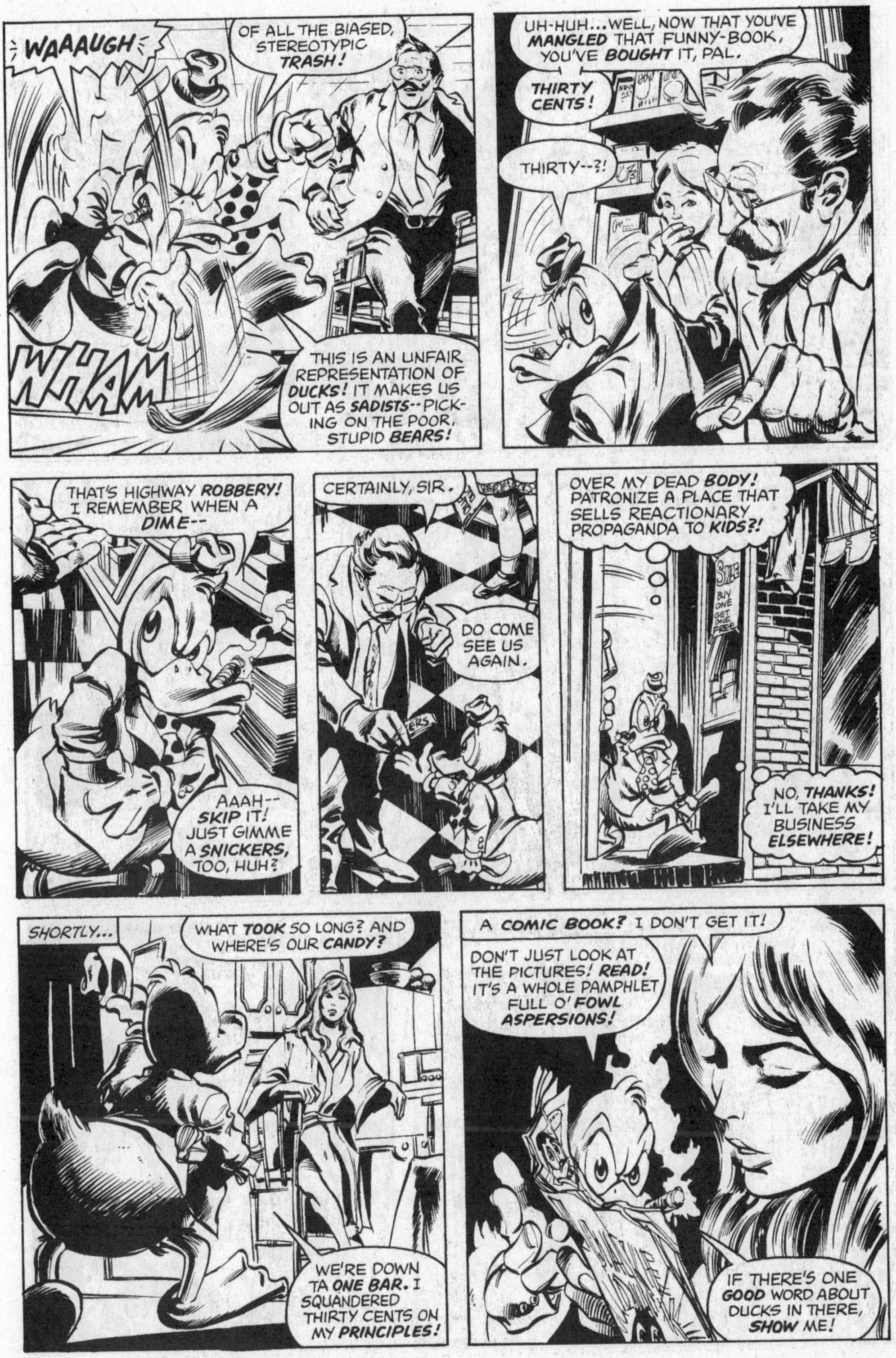
WAAAUGH
OF ALL THE BIASED, STEREOTYPIC TRASH!
WHAM
THIS IS AN UNFAIR REPRESENTATION OF DUCKS! IT MAKES US OUT AS SADISTS--PICKING ON THE POOR, STUPID BEARS!
UH-HUH...WELL, NOW THAT YOU'VE MANGLED THAT FUNNY-BOOK, YOU'VE BOUGHT IT, PAL.
THIRTY CENTS!
THIRTY--?!
THAT'S HIGHWAY ROBBERY! I REMEMBER WHEN A DIME--
AAAH-- SKIP IT! JUST GIMME A SNICKERS, TOO, HUH?
CERTAINLY, SIR.
DO COME SEE US AGAIN.
OVER MY DEAD BODY! PATRONIZE A PLACE THAT SELLS REACTIONARY PROPAGANDA TO KIDS?!
SALE
BUY ONE GET ONE FREE
NO, THANKS! I'LL TAKE MY BUSINESS ELSEWHERE!
SHORTLY...
WHAT TOOK SO LONG? AND WHERE'S OUR CANDY?
WE'RE DOWN TA ONE BAR. I SQUANDERED THIRTY CENTS ON MY PRINCIPLES!
A COMIC BOOK? I DON'T GET IT!
DON'T JUST LOOK AT THE PICTURES! READ! IT'S A WHOLE PAMPHLET FULL O' FOWL ASPERSIONS!
IF THERE'S ONE GOOD WORD ABOUT DUCKS IN THERE, SHOW ME!

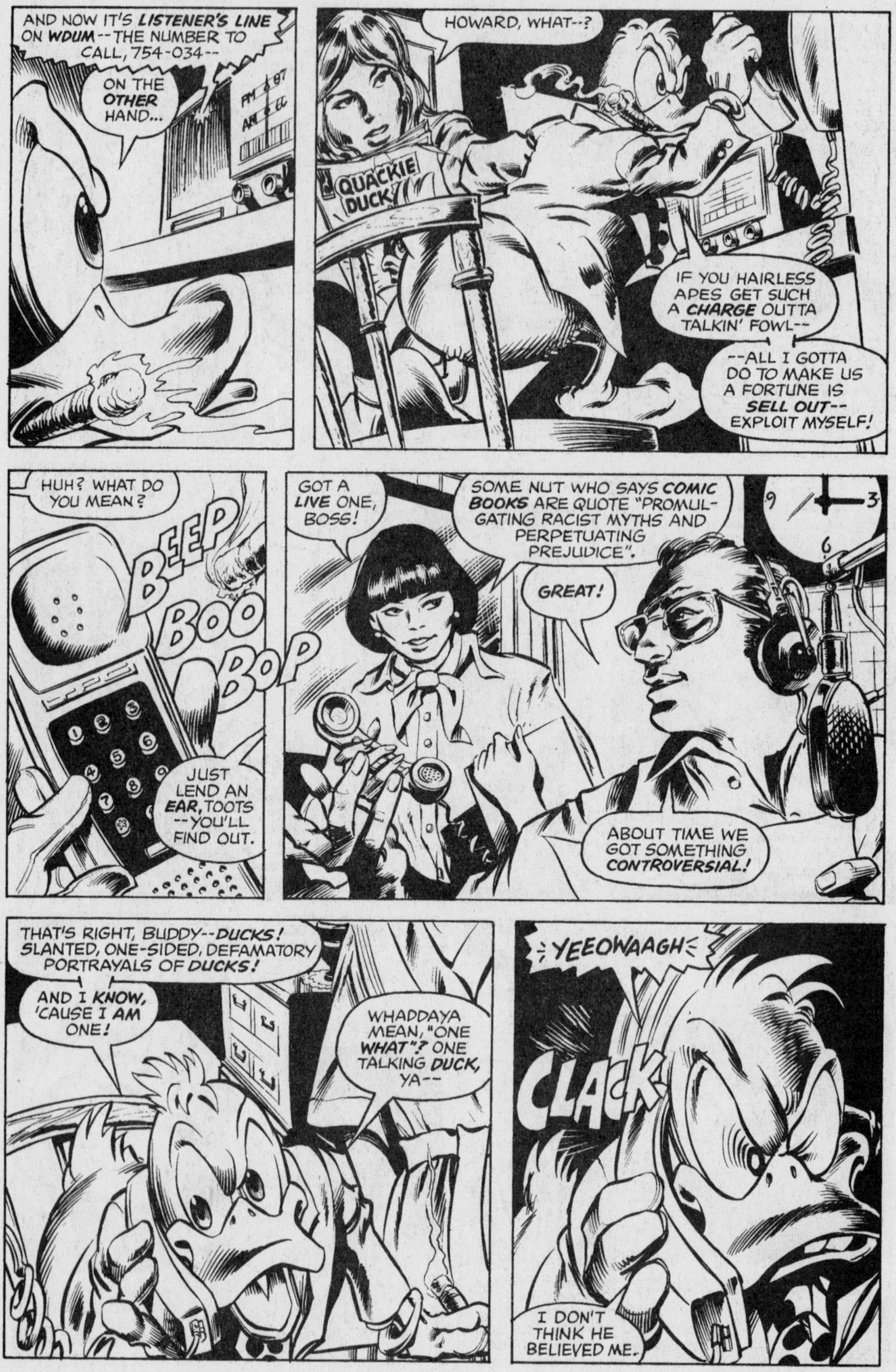
AND NOW IT'S LISTENER'S LINE ON WDUM--THE NUMBER TO CALL, 754-034--
ON THE OTHER HAND...
HOWARD, WHAT--?
QUACKIE DUCK
IF YOU HAIRLESS APES GET SUCH A CHARGE OUTTA TALKIN' FOWL--
--ALL I GOTTA DO TO MAKE US A FORTUNE IS SELL OUT--EXPLOIT MYSELF!
HUH? WHAT DO YOU MEAN?
BEEP
BOO
BOP
JUST LEND AN EAR, TOOTS--YOU'LL FIND OUT.
GOT A LIVE ONE, BOSS!
SOME NUT WHO SAYS COMIC BOOKS ARE QUOTE "PROMULGATING RACIST MYTHS AND PERPETUATING PREJUDICE".
GREAT!
ABOUT TIME WE GOT SOMETHING CONTROVERSIAL!
THAT'S RIGHT, BUDDY--DUCKS! SLANTED, ONE-SIDED, DEFAMATORY PORTRAYALS OF DUCKS!
AND I KNOW, 'CAUSE I AM ONE!
WHADDAYA MEAN, "ONE WHAT"? ONE TALKING DUCK, YA--
YEEOWAAGH
CLACK
I DON'T THINK HE BELIEVED ME.

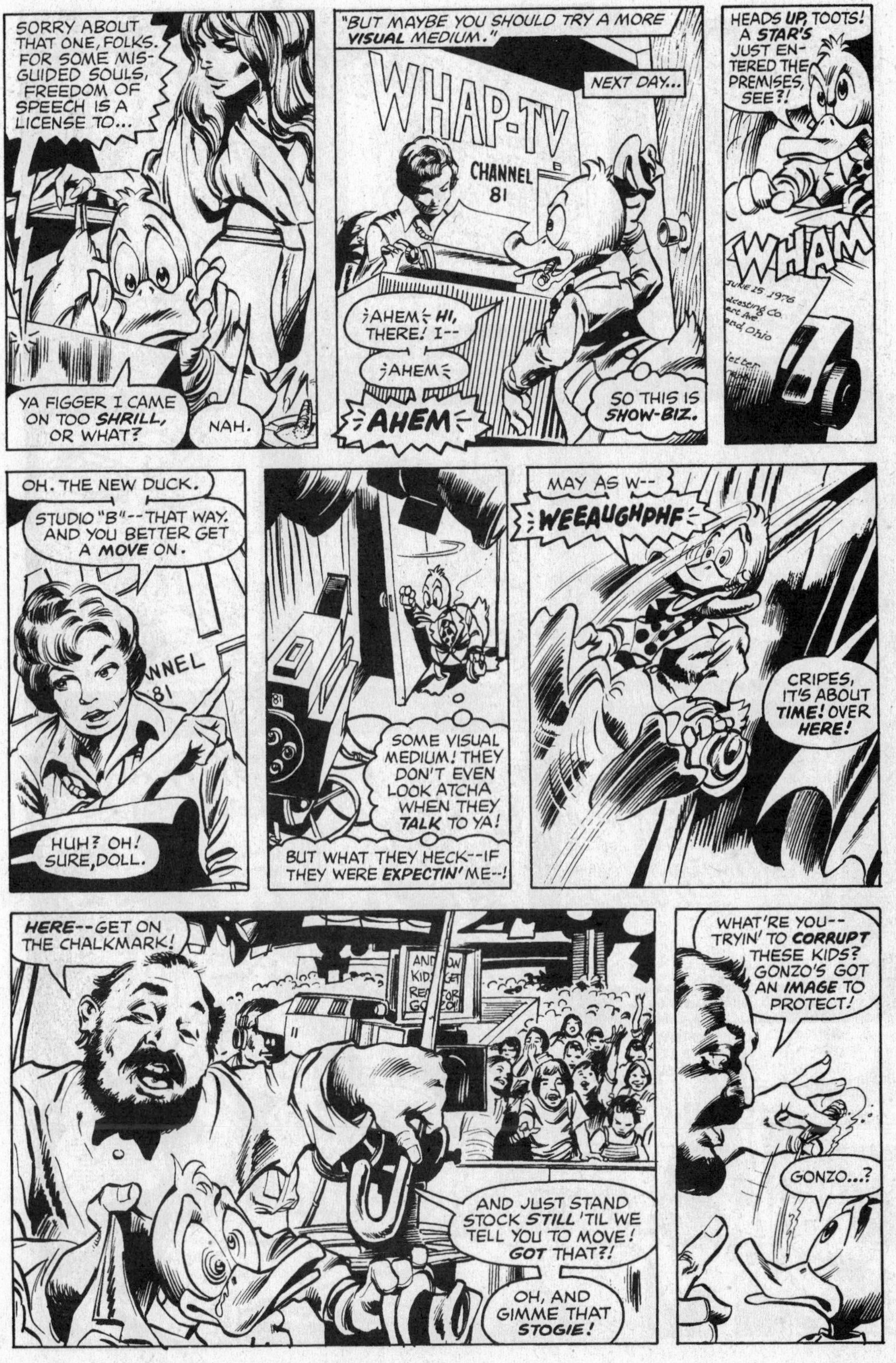
SORRY ABOUT THAT ONE, FOLKS. FOR SOME MIS-GUIDED SOULS, FREEDOM OF SPEECH IS A LICENSE TO...
YA FIGGER I CAME ON TOO SHRILL, OR WHAT?
NAH.
"BUT MAYBE YOU SHOULD TRY A MORE VISUAL MEDIUM."
WHAP-TV
CHANNEL 81
NEXT DAY...
AHEM HI, THERE! I--
AHEM
AHEM
SO THIS IS SHOW-BIZ.
HEADS UP, TOOTS! A STAR'S JUST EN-TERED THE PREMISES, SEE?!
WHAM
JUNE 25, 1976
OH. THE NEW DUCK.
STUDIO "B"--THAT WAY. AND YOU BETTER GET A MOVE ON.
HUH? OH! SURE, DOLL.
SOME VISUAL MEDIUM! THEY DON'T EVEN LOOK ATCHA WHEN THEY TALK TO YA!
BUT WHAT THEY HECK--IF THEY WERE EXPECTIN' ME--!
MAY AS W--
WEEAUGHPHF
CRIPES, IT'S ABOUT TIME! OVER HERE!
HERE--GET ON THE CHALKMARK!
AND JUST STAND STOCK STILL 'TIL WE TELL YOU TO MOVE! GOT THAT?!
OH, AND GIMME THAT STOGIE!
WHAT'RE YOU--TRYIN' TO CORRUPT THESE KIDS? GONZO'S GOT AN IMAGE TO PROTECT!
GONZO...?

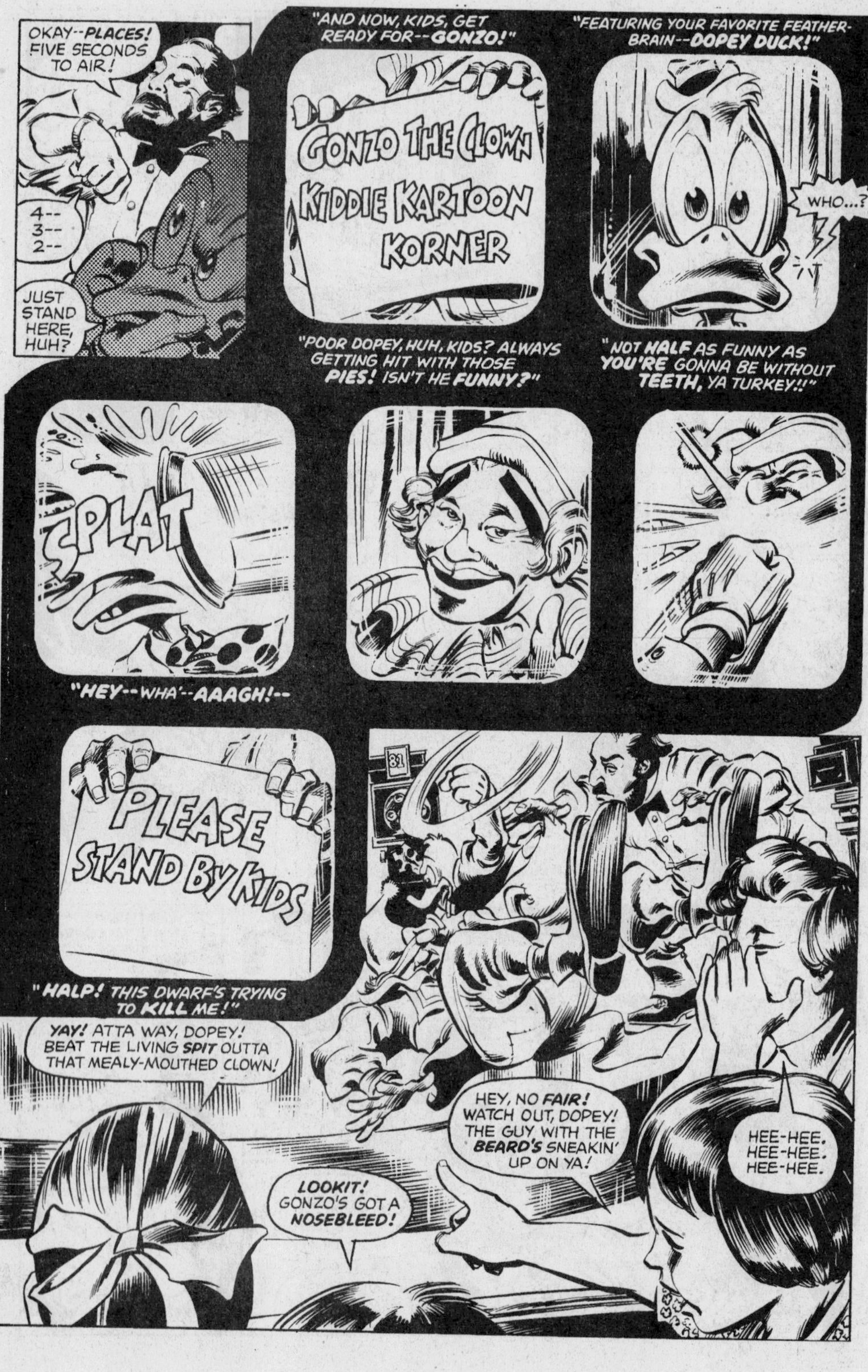
OKAY--PLACES! FIVE SECONDS TO AIR!
4-- 3-- 2--
JUST STAND HERE, HUH?
"AND NOW, KIDS, GET READY FOR--GONZO!"
GONZO THE CLOWN KIDDIE KARTOON KORNER
"FEATURING YOUR FAVORITE FEATHER-BRAIN--DOPEY DUCK!"
WHO...?
"POOR DOPEY, HUH, KIDS? ALWAYS GETTING HIT WITH THOSE PIES! ISN'T HE FUNNY?"
"NOT HALF AS FUNNY AS YOU'RE GONNA BE WITHOUT TEETH, YA TURKEY!!"
SPLAT
"HEY--WHA'--AAAGH!--
PLEASE STAND BY KIDS
"HALP! THIS DWARF'S TRYING TO KILL ME!"
YAY! ATTA WAY, DOPEY! BEAT THE LIVING SPIT OUTTA THAT MEALY-MOUTHED CLOWN!
HEY, NO FAIR! WATCH OUT, DOPEY! THE GUY WITH THE BEARD'S SNEAKIN' UP ON YA!
HEE-HEE. HEE-HEE. HEE-HEE.
LOOKIT! GONZO'S GOT A NOSEBLEED!

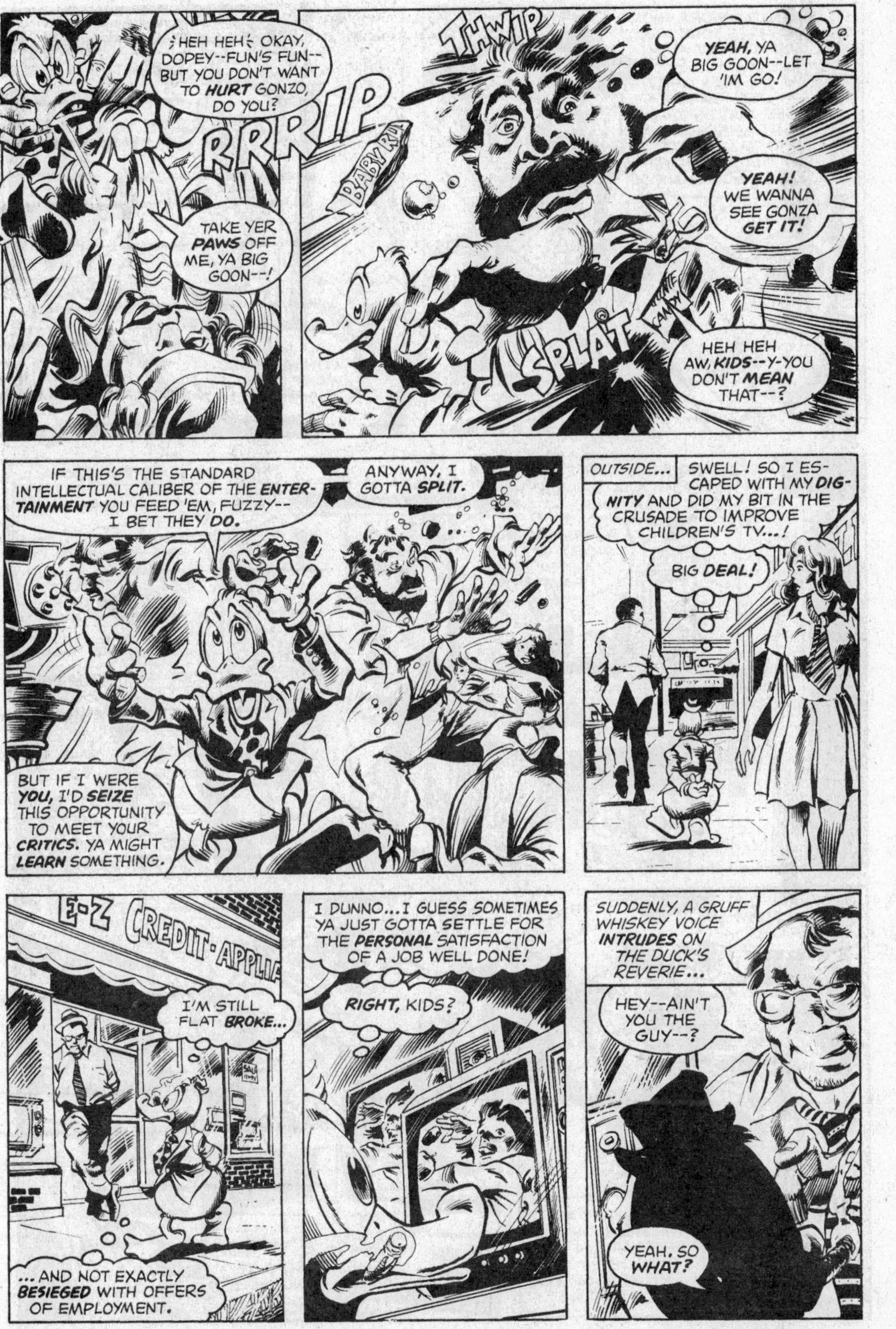

HEH HEH OKAY, DOPEY--FUN'S FUN--BUT YOU DON'T WANT TO HURT GONZO, DO YOU?
RRRIP
TAKE YER PAWS OFF ME, YA BIG GOON--!
THWIP
YEAH, YA BIG GOON--LET 'IM GO!
YEAH! WE WANNA SEE GONZA GET IT!
SPLAT
HEH HEH AW, KIDS--Y-YOU DON'T MEAN THAT--?
IF THIS'S THE STANDARD INTELLECTUAL CALIBER OF THE ENTERTAINMENT YOU FEED 'EM, FUZZY--I BET THEY DO.
ANYWAY, I GOTTA SPLIT.
BUT IF I WERE YOU, I'D SEIZE THIS OPPORTUNITY TO MEET YOUR CRITICS. YA MIGHT LEARN SOMETHING.
OUTSIDE...
SWELL! SO I ESCAPED WITH MY DIGNITY AND DID MY BIT IN THE CRUSADE TO IMPROVE CHILDREN'S TV...!
BIG DEAL!
E-Z CREDIT-APPLIA
I'M STILL FLAT BROKE...
...AND NOT EXACTLY BESIEGED WITH OFFERS OF EMPLOYMENT.
I DUNNO...I GUESS SOMETIMES YA JUST GOTTA SETTLE FOR THE PERSONAL SATISFACTION OF A JOB WELL DONE!
RIGHT, KIDS?
SUDDENLY, A GRUFF WHISKEY VOICE INTRUDES ON THE DUCK'S REVERIE...
HEY--AIN'T YOU THE GUY--?
YEAH. SO WHAT?

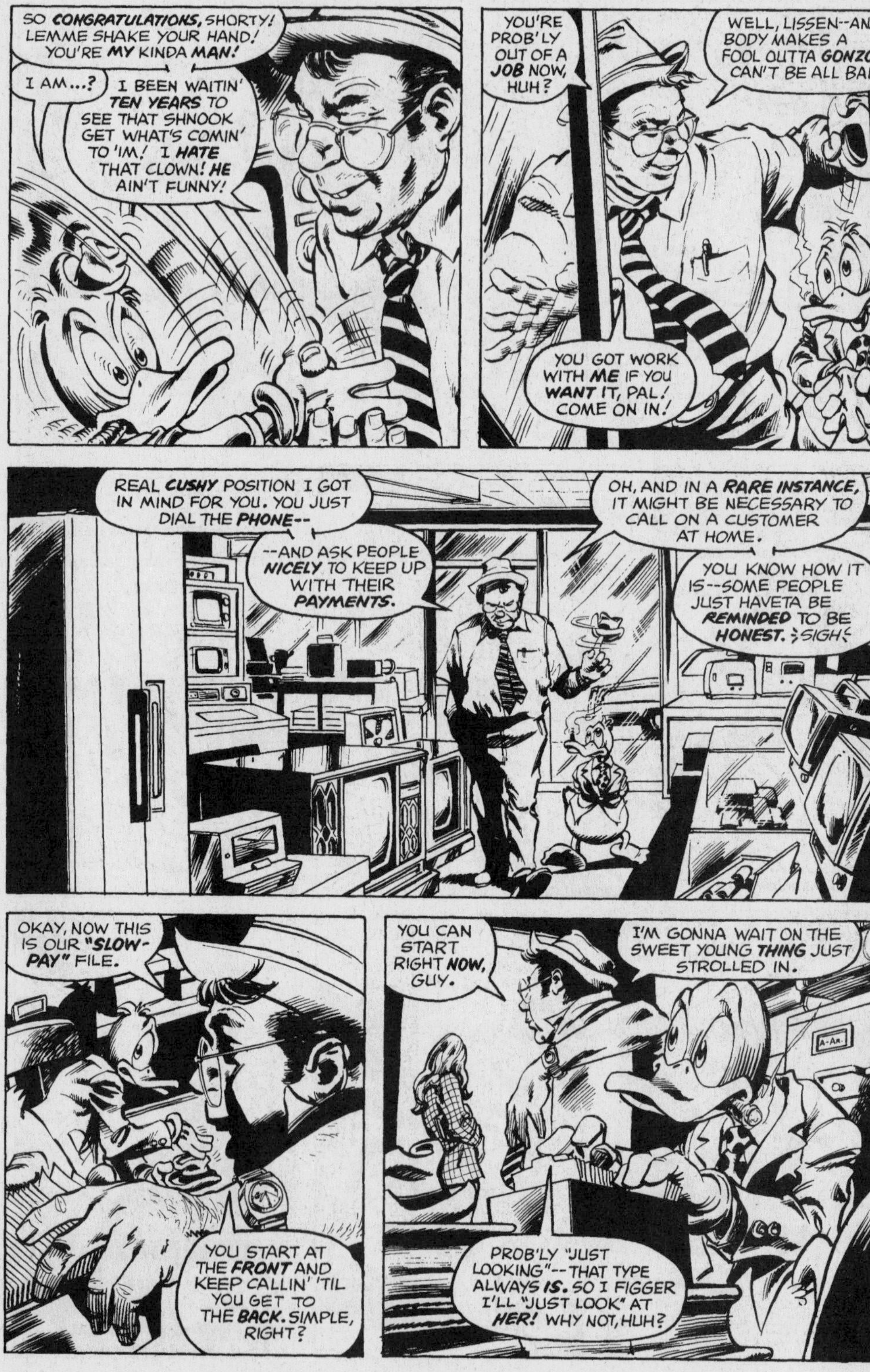
SO CONGRATULATIONS, SHORTY! LEMME SHAKE YOUR HAND! YOU'RE MY KINDA MAN!
I AM...?
I BEEN WAITIN' TEN YEARS TO SEE THAT SHNOOK GET WHAT'S COMIN' TO 'IM! I HATE THAT CLOWN! HE AIN'T FUNNY!
YOU'RE PROB'LY OUT OF A JOB NOW, HUH?
WELL, LISSEN--ANYBODY MAKES A FOOL OUTTA GONZO CAN'T BE ALL BAD!
YOU GOT WORK WITH ME IF YOU WANT IT, PAL! COME ON IN!
REAL CUSHY POSITION I GOT IN MIND FOR YOU. YOU JUST DIAL THE PHONE--
--AND ASK PEOPLE NICELY TO KEEP UP WITH THEIR PAYMENTS.
OH, AND IN A RARE INSTANCE, IT MIGHT BE NECESSARY TO CALL ON A CUSTOMER AT HOME.
YOU KNOW HOW IT IS--SOME PEOPLE JUST HAVETA BE REMINDED TO BE HONEST. ⋛SIGH⋚
OKAY, NOW THIS IS OUR "SLOW-PAY" FILE.
YOU START AT THE FRONT AND KEEP CALLIN' 'TIL YOU GET TO THE BACK. SIMPLE, RIGHT?
YOU CAN START RIGHT NOW, GUY.
I'M GONNA WAIT ON THE SWEET YOUNG THING JUST STROLLED IN.
PROB'LY "JUST LOOKING"--THAT TYPE ALWAYS IS. SO I FIGGER I'LL "JUST LOOK" AT HER! WHY NOT, HUH?

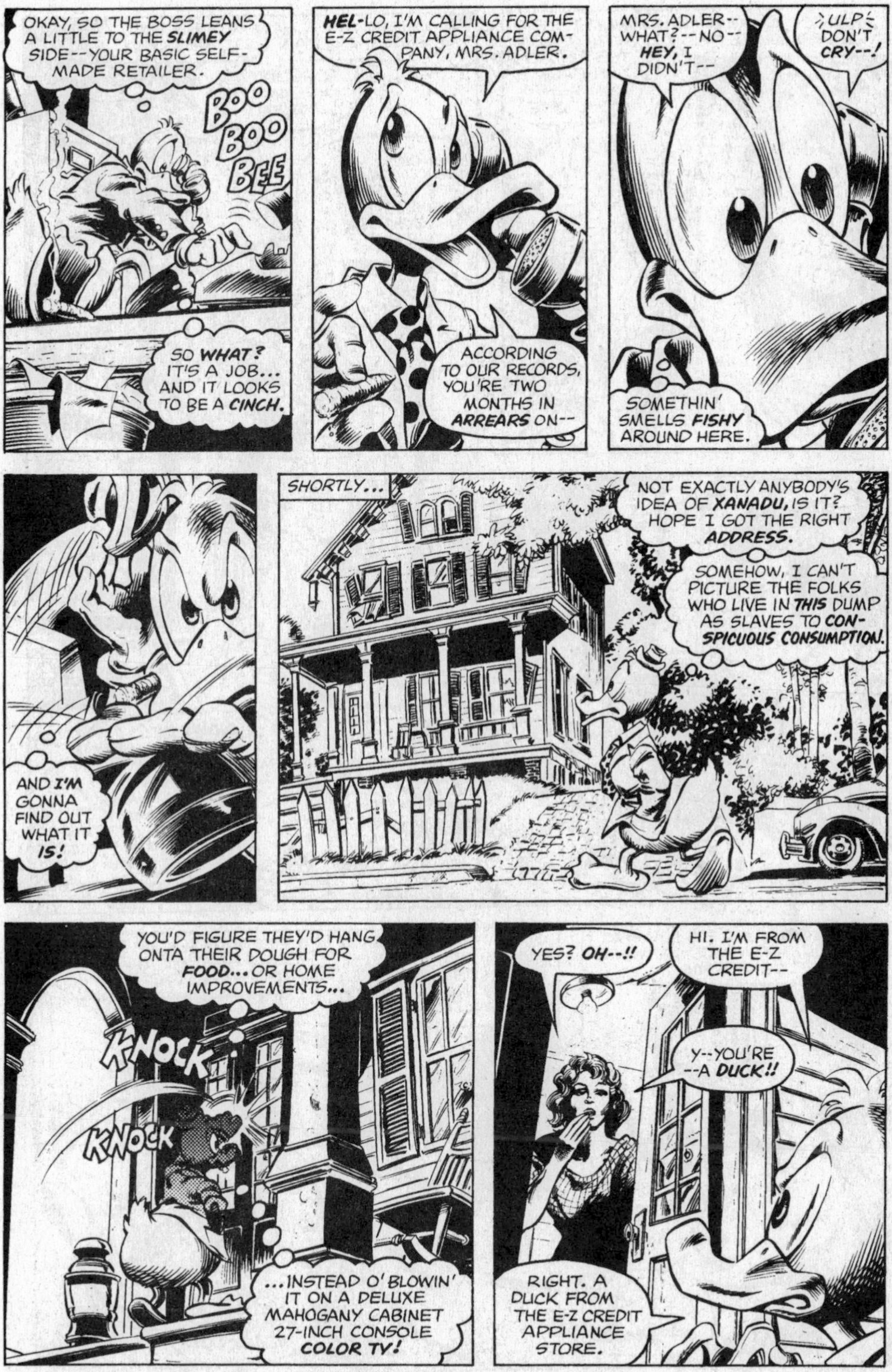
OKAY, SO THE BOSS LEANS A LITTLE TO THE SLIMEY SIDE--YOUR BASIC SELF-MADE RETAILER.
BOO BOO BEE
SO WHAT? IT'S A JOB... AND IT LOOKS TO BE A CINCH.
HEL-LO, I'M CALLING FOR THE E-Z CREDIT APPLIANCE COMPANY, MRS. ADLER.
ACCORDING TO OUR RECORDS, YOU'RE TWO MONTHS IN ARREARS ON--
MRS. ADLER--WHAT?--NO--HEY, I DIDN'T--
ULP DON'T CRY--!
SOMETHIN' SMELLS FISHY AROUND HERE.
AND I'M GONNA FIND OUT WHAT IT IS!
SHORTLY...
NOT EXACTLY ANYBODY'S IDEA OF XANADU, IS IT? HOPE I GOT THE RIGHT ADDRESS.
SOMEHOW, I CAN'T PICTURE THE FOLKS WHO LIVE IN THIS DUMP AS SLAVES TO CONSPICUOUS CONSUMPTION.
YOU'D FIGURE THEY'D HANG ONTA THEIR DOUGH FOR FOOD...OR HOME IMPROVEMENTS...
KNOCK
KNOCK
...INSTEAD O' BLOWIN' IT ON A DELUXE MAHOGANY CABINET 27-INCH CONSOLE COLOR TV!
YES? OH--!!
HI. I'M FROM THE E-Z CREDIT--
Y--YOU'RE --A DUCK!!
RIGHT. A DUCK FROM THE E-Z CREDIT APPLIANCE STORE.

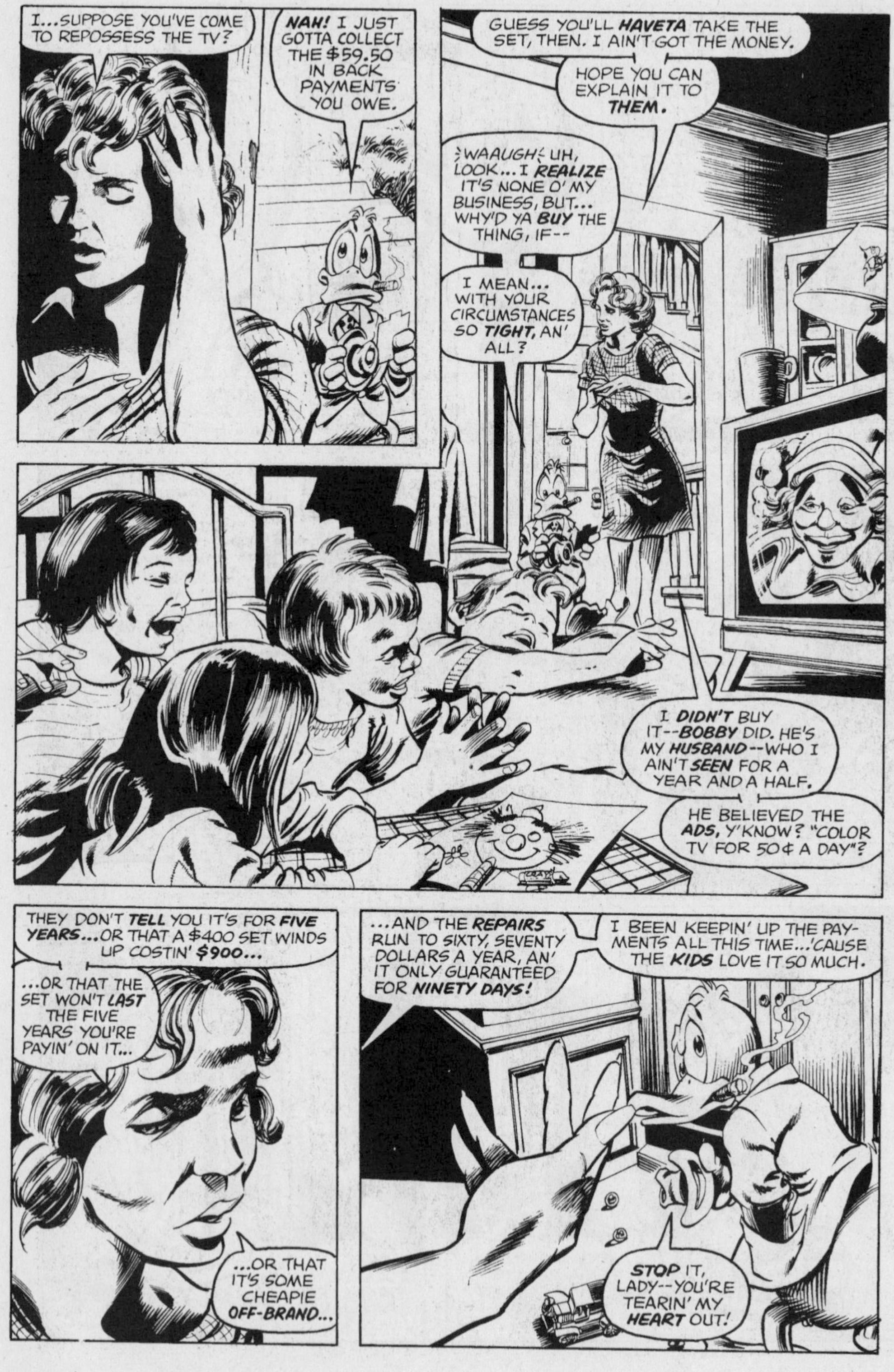
I...SUPPOSE YOU'VE COME TO REPOSSESS THE TV?
NAH! I JUST GOTTA COLLECT THE $59.50 IN BACK PAYMENTS YOU OWE.
GUESS YOU'LL HAVETA TAKE THE SET, THEN. I AIN'T GOT THE MONEY.
HOPE YOU CAN EXPLAIN IT TO THEM.
WAAUGH! UH, LOOK... I REALIZE IT'S NONE O' MY BUSINESS, BUT... WHY'D YA BUY THE THING, IF--
I MEAN... WITH YOUR CIRCUMSTANCES SO TIGHT, AN' ALL?
I DIDN'T BUY IT--BOBBY DID. HE'S MY HUSBAND--WHO I AIN'T SEEN FOR A YEAR AND A HALF.
HE BELIEVED THE ADS, Y'KNOW? "COLOR TV FOR 50¢ A DAY"?
THEY DON'T TELL YOU IT'S FOR FIVE YEARS...OR THAT A $400 SET WINDS UP COSTIN' $900...
...OR THAT THE SET WON'T LAST THE FIVE YEARS YOU'RE PAYIN' ON IT...
...OR THAT IT'S SOME CHEAPIE OFF-BRAND...
...AND THE REPAIRS RUN TO SIXTY, SEVENTY DOLLARS A YEAR, AN' IT ONLY GUARANTEED FOR NINETY DAYS!
I BEEN KEEPIN' UP THE PAYMENTS ALL THIS TIME...'CAUSE THE KIDS LOVE IT SO MUCH.
STOP IT, LADY--YOU'RE TEARIN' MY HEART OUT!

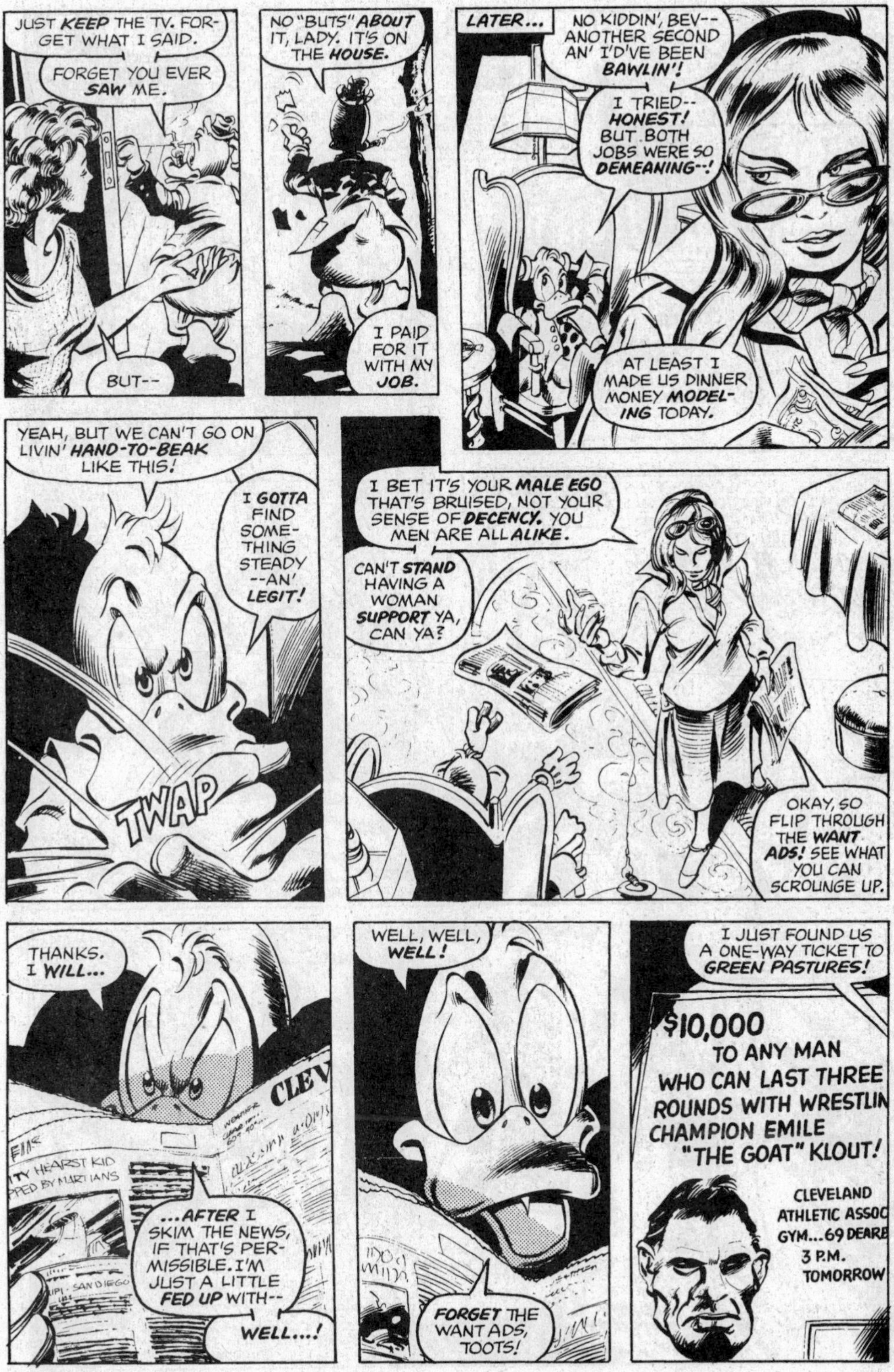
JUST KEEP THE TV. FORGET WHAT I SAID.
FORGET YOU EVER SAW ME.
BUT--
NO "BUTS" ABOUT IT, LADY. IT'S ON THE HOUSE.
I PAID FOR IT WITH MY JOB.
LATER...
NO KIDDIN', BEV-- ANOTHER SECOND AN' I'D'VE BEEN BAWLIN'!
I TRIED-- HONEST! BUT BOTH JOBS WERE SO DEMEANING--!
AT LEAST I MADE US DINNER MONEY MODELING TODAY.
YEAH, BUT WE CAN'T GO ON LIVIN' HAND-TO-BEAK LIKE THIS!
I GOTTA FIND SOMETHING STEADY --AN' LEGIT!
TWAP
I BET IT'S YOUR MALE EGO THAT'S BRUISED, NOT YOUR SENSE OF DECENCY. YOU MEN ARE ALL ALIKE.
CAN'T STAND HAVING A WOMAN SUPPORT YA, CAN YA?
OKAY, SO FLIP THROUGH THE WANT ADS! SEE WHAT YOU CAN SCROUNGE UP.
THANKS. I WILL...
...AFTER I SKIM THE NEWS, IF THAT'S PERMISSIBLE. I'M JUST A LITTLE FED UP WITH--
WELL...!
WELL, WELL, WELL!
FORGET THE WANT ADS, TOOTS!
I JUST FOUND US A ONE-WAY TICKET TO GREEN PASTURES!
$10,000
TO ANY MAN
WHO CAN LAST THREE
ROUNDS WITH WRESTLIN
CHAMPION EMILE
"THE GOAT" KLOUT!
CLEVELAND
ATHLETIC ASSOC
GYM...69 DEARB
3 P.M.
TOMORROW

BEVERLY SWITZLER GASPS: "A **CEMETERY PLOT**, YOU MEAN! I'VE SEEN THAT BRUTE WRESTLE ON TV. THEY CALL HIM 'THE GOAT' BECAUSE HE **CHEWS UP** HIS OPPONENTS! EVEN **HOWARD COSELL** IS SCARED OF HIM!"

"**YEAH?** WELL, HOWARD THE DUCK **ISN'T!** SO **THERE!**"

"**TOMORROW, TOOTS,** WE'RE GONNA BE SITTIN' PRETTY ON **TEN GRAND!**"

AND **FURTHERMORE,** WHEN THIS MATCH IS **OVER--**

YOU 'N' ME ARE GONNA **BLOW** THIS TOWN, SISTER!

CLEVELAND IS TOO **SMALL-TIME** FOR US-- THE STICKS, THE BOONIES!

I THINK IT'S TIME WE GOT A TASTE OF THE **BIG CITY** --AND ON $10,000 WE CAN DO IT WITH **PANACHE!** I--

YOU!!

I KNEW WE SHOULD'A TOOK A **TAXI.**

I SAW WHAT YOU DID TO **GONZO** YESTERDAY-- YOU **BEAST!**

I SAW YOU **HUMILIATE** THAT WHOLESOME SYMBOL OF FUN AND NICENESS BEFORE ALL THE KIDDIES WHO **ADORE** HIM!

IT'S HER, ISN'T IT-- THE **KIDNEY LADY!***

*WHOM WE FIRST MET IN *HTD* #2.--A.G.

THAT'S YOUR **WAY,** ISN'T IT--YOUR SUBTLE SCHEME TO SYSTEMATICALLY SUBVERT OUR SYSTEM OF VALUES!

WELL-- ISN'T IT-- **KIDNEY THIEF??**

CALL'ER OFF, BEV. I WANNA SAVE MYSELF FOR THE RING.

REALLY, MA'AM, HE'S NOT IN THE **MOOD** TO...

HIS KIND IS **NEVER** IN THE MOOD TO TALK TRUTH AND RIGHTEOUSNESS! YOU FOOLISH LITTLE GIRL! DON'T YOU KNOW HE'S ONLY AFTER YOUR **KIDNEYS!?**

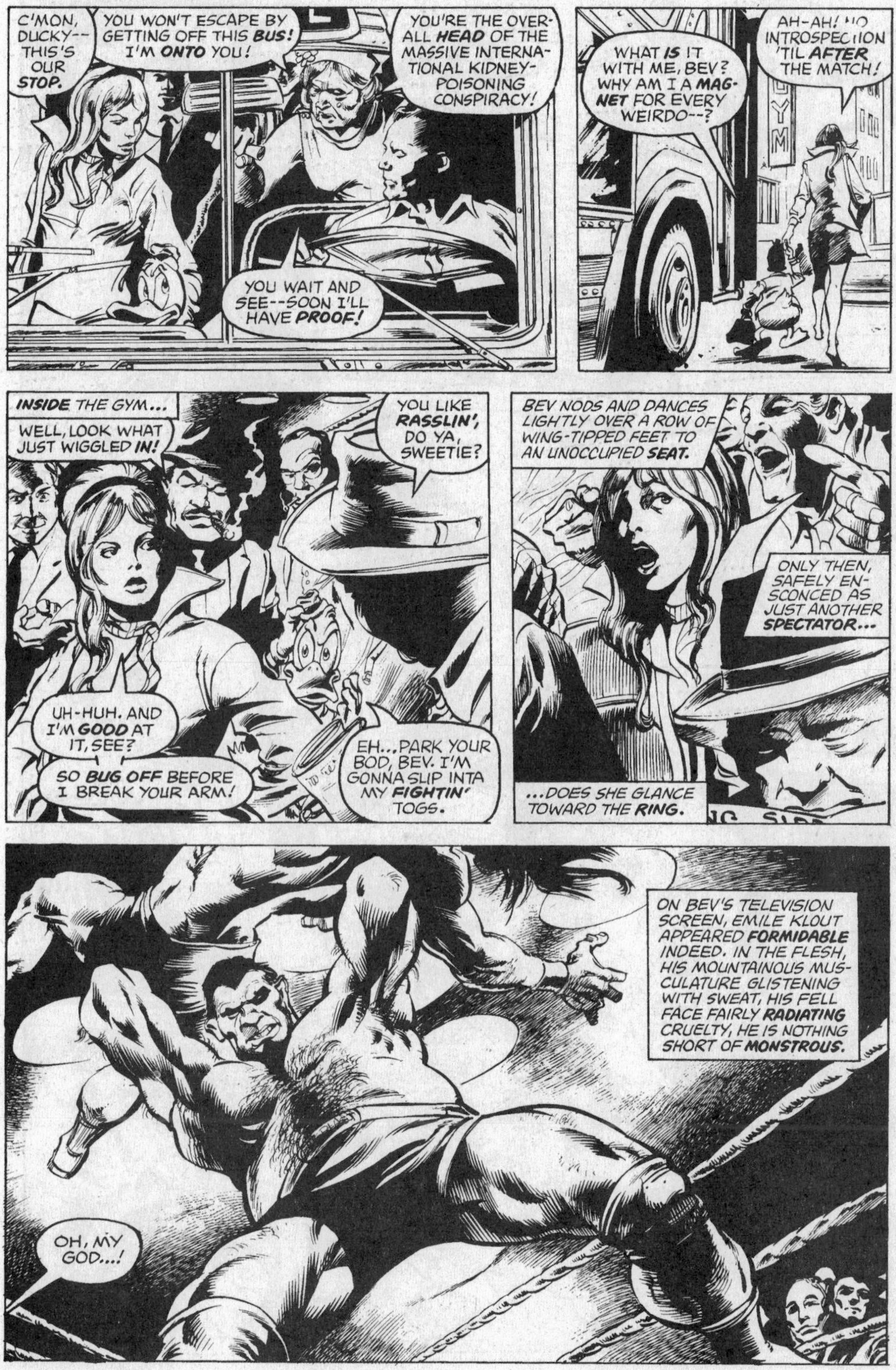
C'MON, DUCKY-- THIS'S OUR STOP.
YOU WON'T ESCAPE BY GETTING OFF THIS BUS! I'M ONTO YOU!
YOU'RE THE OVER-ALL HEAD OF THE MASSIVE INTERNATIONAL KIDNEY-POISONING CONSPIRACY!
YOU WAIT AND SEE--SOON I'LL HAVE PROOF!
WHAT IS IT WITH ME, BEV? WHY AM I A MAGNET FOR EVERY WEIRDO--?
AH-AH! NO INTROSPECTION 'TIL AFTER THE MATCH!
GYM
INSIDE THE GYM...
WELL, LOOK WHAT JUST WIGGLED IN!
YOU LIKE RASSLIN', DO YA, SWEETIE?
UH-HUH. AND I'M GOOD AT IT, SEE?
SO BUG OFF BEFORE I BREAK YOUR ARM!
EH... PARK YOUR BOD, BEV. I'M GONNA SLIP INTA MY FIGHTIN' TOGS.
BEV NODS AND DANCES LIGHTLY OVER A ROW OF WING-TIPPED FEET TO AN UNOCCUPIED SEAT.
ONLY THEN, SAFELY ENSCONCED AS JUST ANOTHER SPECTATOR...
...DOES SHE GLANCE TOWARD THE RING.
ON BEV'S TELEVISION SCREEN, EMILE KLOUT APPEARED FORMIDABLE INDEED. IN THE FLESH, HIS MOUNTAINOUS MUSCULATURE GLISTENING WITH SWEAT, HIS FELL FACE FAIRLY RADIATING CRUELTY, HE IS NOTHING SHORT OF MONSTROUS.
OH, MY GOD...!

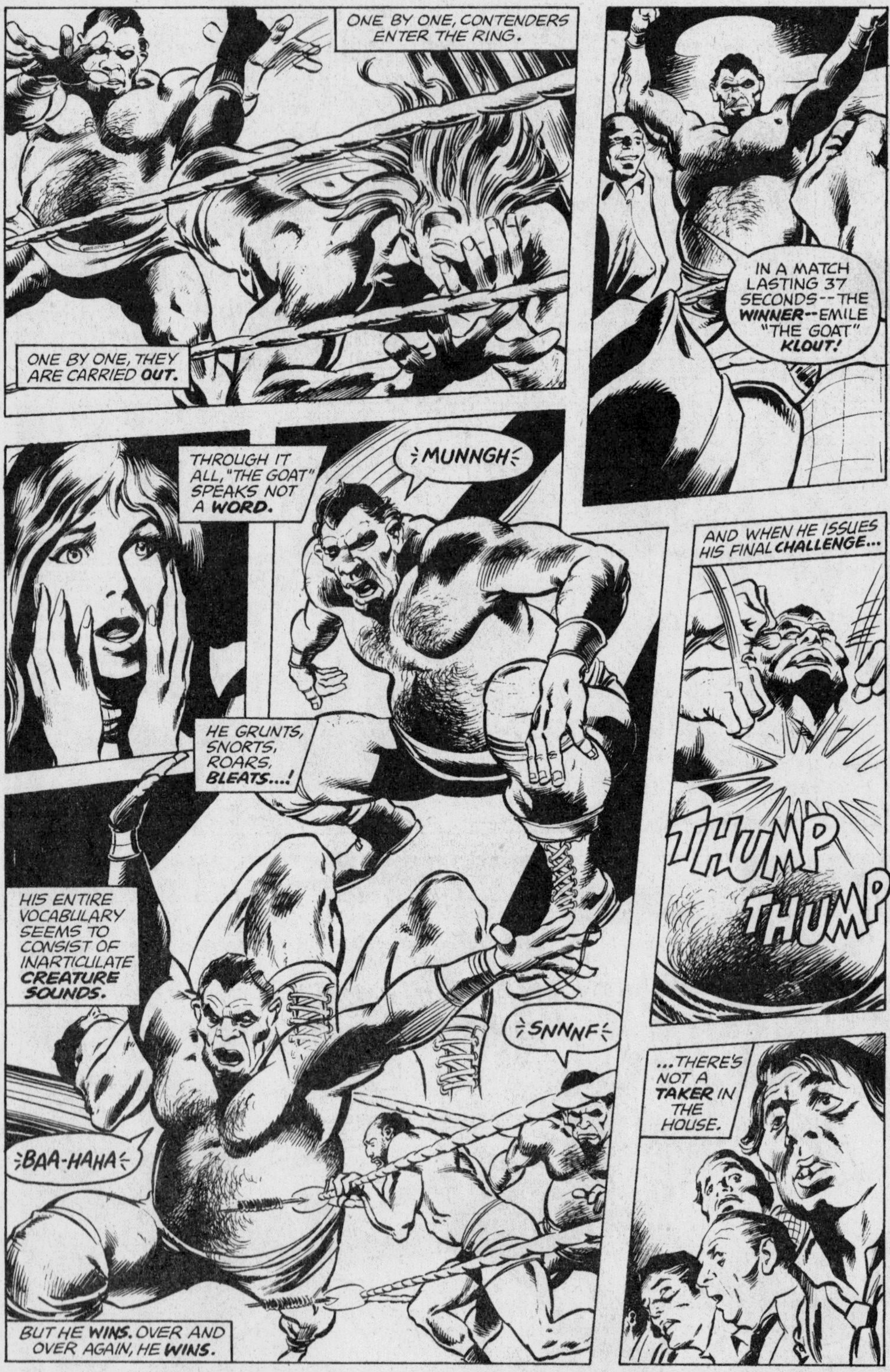
ONE BY ONE, CONTENDERS ENTER THE RING.
ONE BY ONE, THEY ARE CARRIED OUT.
IN A MATCH LASTING 37 SECONDS--THE WINNER--EMILE "THE GOAT" KLOUT!
THROUGH IT ALL, "THE GOAT" SPEAKS NOT A WORD.
MUNNGH
HE GRUNTS, SNORTS, ROARS, BLEATS...!
AND WHEN HE ISSUES HIS FINAL CHALLENGE...
THUMP
THUMP
HIS ENTIRE VOCABULARY SEEMS TO CONSIST OF INARTICULATE CREATURE SOUNDS.
SNNNF
BAA-HAHA
BUT HE WINS. OVER AND OVER AGAIN, HE WINS.
...THERE'S NOT A TAKER IN THE HOUSE.

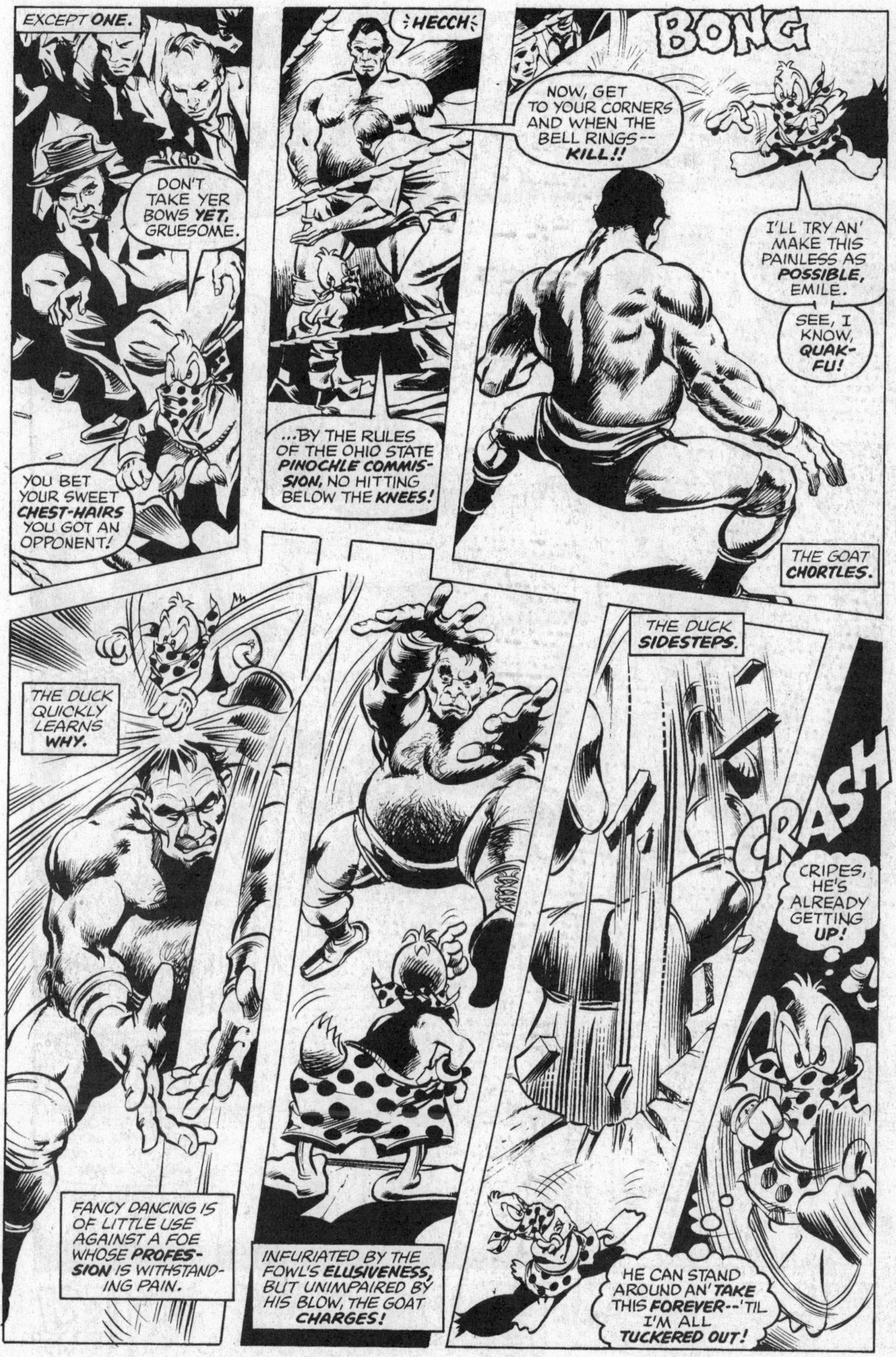
EXCEPT ONE.
DON'T TAKE YER BOWS YET, GRUESOME.
YOU BET YOUR SWEET CHEST-HAIRS YOU GOT AN OPPONENT!
HECCH
...BY THE RULES OF THE OHIO STATE PINOCHLE COMMISSION, NO HITTING BELOW THE KNEES!
BONG
NOW, GET TO YOUR CORNERS AND WHEN THE BELL RINGS-- KILL!!
I'LL TRY AN' MAKE THIS PAINLESS AS POSSIBLE, EMILE.
SEE, I KNOW, QUAK-FU!
THE GOAT CHORTLES.
THE DUCK QUICKLY LEARNS WHY.
FANCY DANCING IS OF LITTLE USE AGAINST A FOE WHOSE PROFESSION IS WITHSTANDING PAIN.
INFURIATED BY THE FOWL'S ELUSIVENESS, BUT UNIMPAIRED BY HIS BLOW, THE GOAT CHARGES!
THE DUCK SIDESTEPS.
CRASH
CRIPES, HE'S ALREADY GETTING UP!
HE CAN STAND AROUND AN' TAKE THIS FOREVER--'TIL I'M ALL TUCKERED OUT!

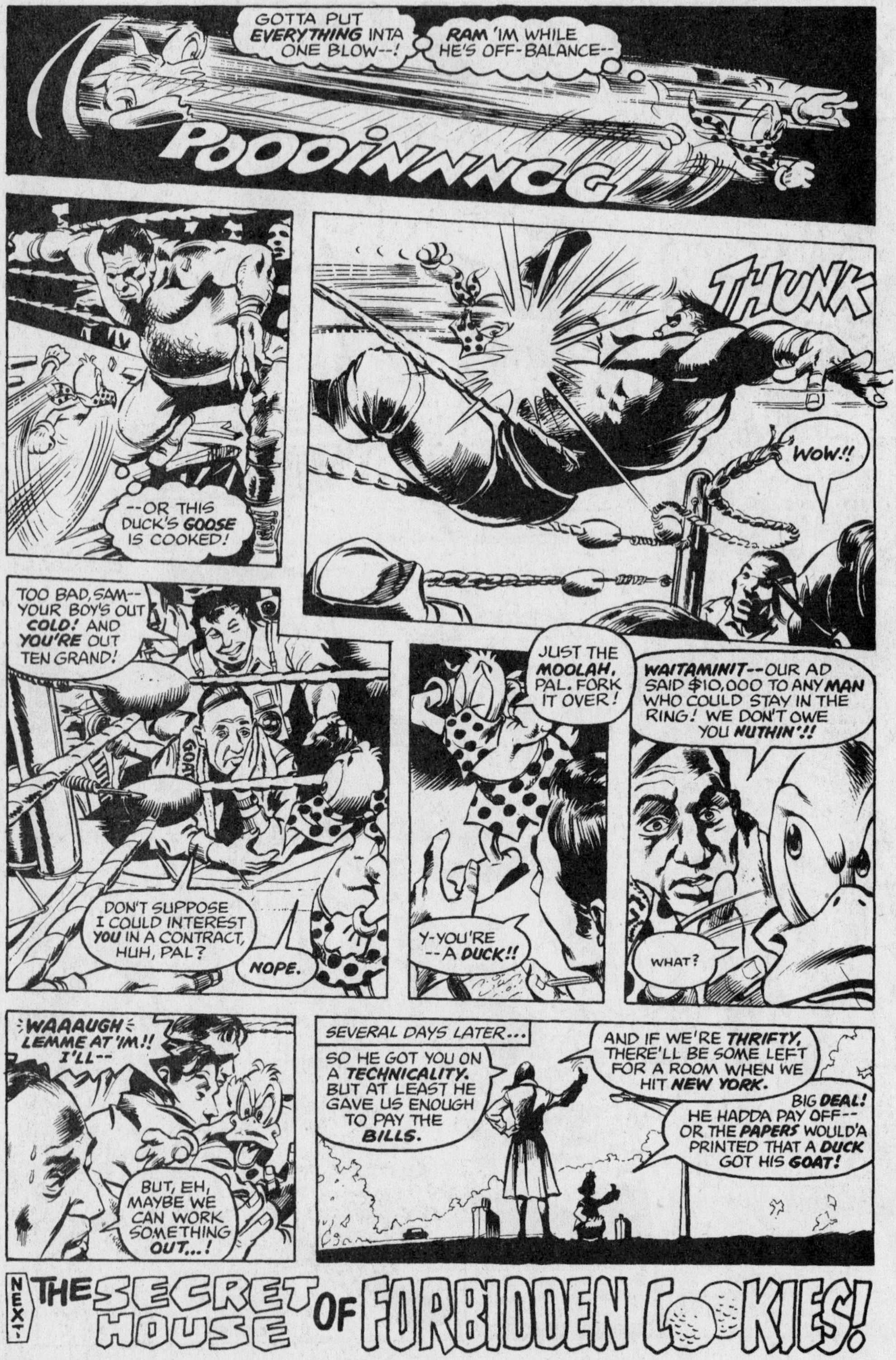
GOTTA PUT EVERYTHING INTA ONE BLOW--!
RAM 'IM WHILE HE'S OFF-BALANCE--
POOOINNNCG
--OR THIS DUCK'S GOOSE IS COOKED!
THUNK
WOW!!
TOO BAD, SAM-- YOUR BOY'S OUT COLD! AND YOU'RE OUT TEN GRAND!
DON'T SUPPOSE I COULD INTEREST YOU IN A CONTRACT, HUH, PAL?
NOPE.
JUST THE MOOLAH, PAL. FORK IT OVER!
Y-YOU'RE --A DUCK!!
WAITAMINIT--OUR AD SAID $10,000 TO ANY MAN WHO COULD STAY IN THE RING! WE DON'T OWE YOU NUTHIN'!!
WHAT?
WAAAUGH LEMME AT 'IM!! I'LL--
BUT, EH, MAYBE WE CAN WORK SOMETHING OUT...!
SEVERAL DAYS LATER...
SO HE GOT YOU ON A TECHNICALITY. BUT AT LEAST HE GAVE US ENOUGH TO PAY THE BILLS.
AND IF WE'RE THRIFTY, THERE'LL BE SOME LEFT FOR A ROOM WHEN WE HIT NEW YORK.
BIG DEAL! HE HADDA PAY OFF-- OR THE PAPERS WOULD'A PRINTED THAT A DUCK GOT HIS GOAT!
NEXT: THE SECRET HOUSE OF FORBIDDEN COOKIES!

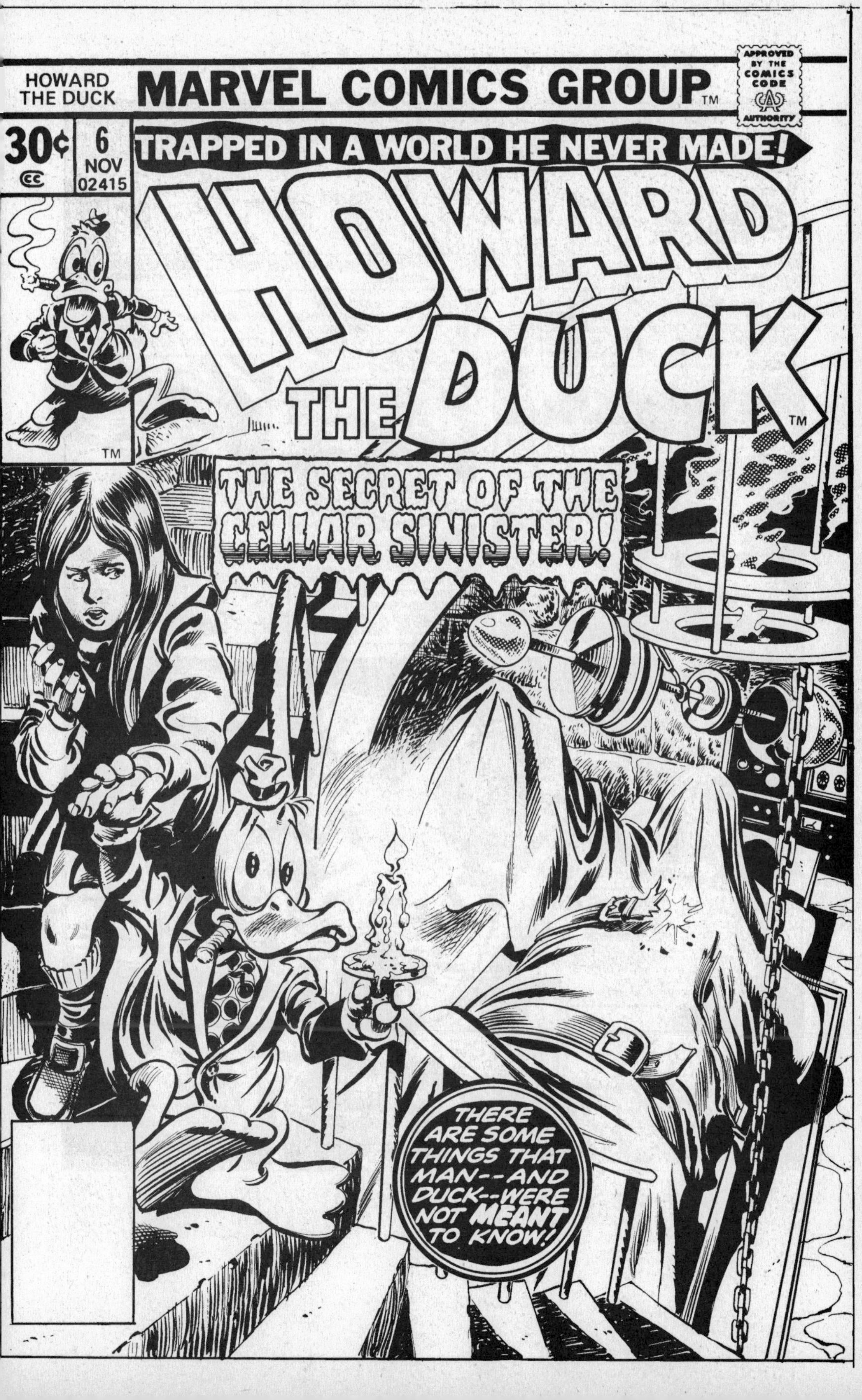
HOWARD THE DUCK
MARVEL COMICS GROUP
30¢
6
NOV
02415
APPROVED BY THE COMICS CODE AUTHORITY
TRAPPED IN A WORLD HE NEVER MADE!
HOWARD THE DUCK
THE SECRET OF THE CELLAR SINISTER!
THERE ARE SOME THINGS THAT MAN--AND DUCK--WERE NOT MEANT TO KNOW!

From the time of his hatching, he was...different. A potentially brilliant scholar who dreaded the structured environment of school, he educated himself in the streets, taking whatever work was available, formulating his philosophy of self from what he learned of the world about him. And then the Cosmic Axis shifted...and that world *changed.* Suddenly, he was stranded in a universe he could not fathom. Without warning, he became a strange fowl in an even stranger land.

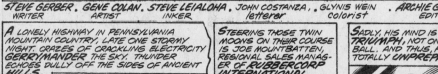

Stan Lee PRESENTS: HOWARD THE DUCK!™

STEVE GERBER. WRITER . GENE COLAN. ARTIST . STEVE LEIALOHA. INKER . JOHN COSTANZA. letterer . GLYNIS WEIN colorist . ARCHIE GOODWIN EDITOR

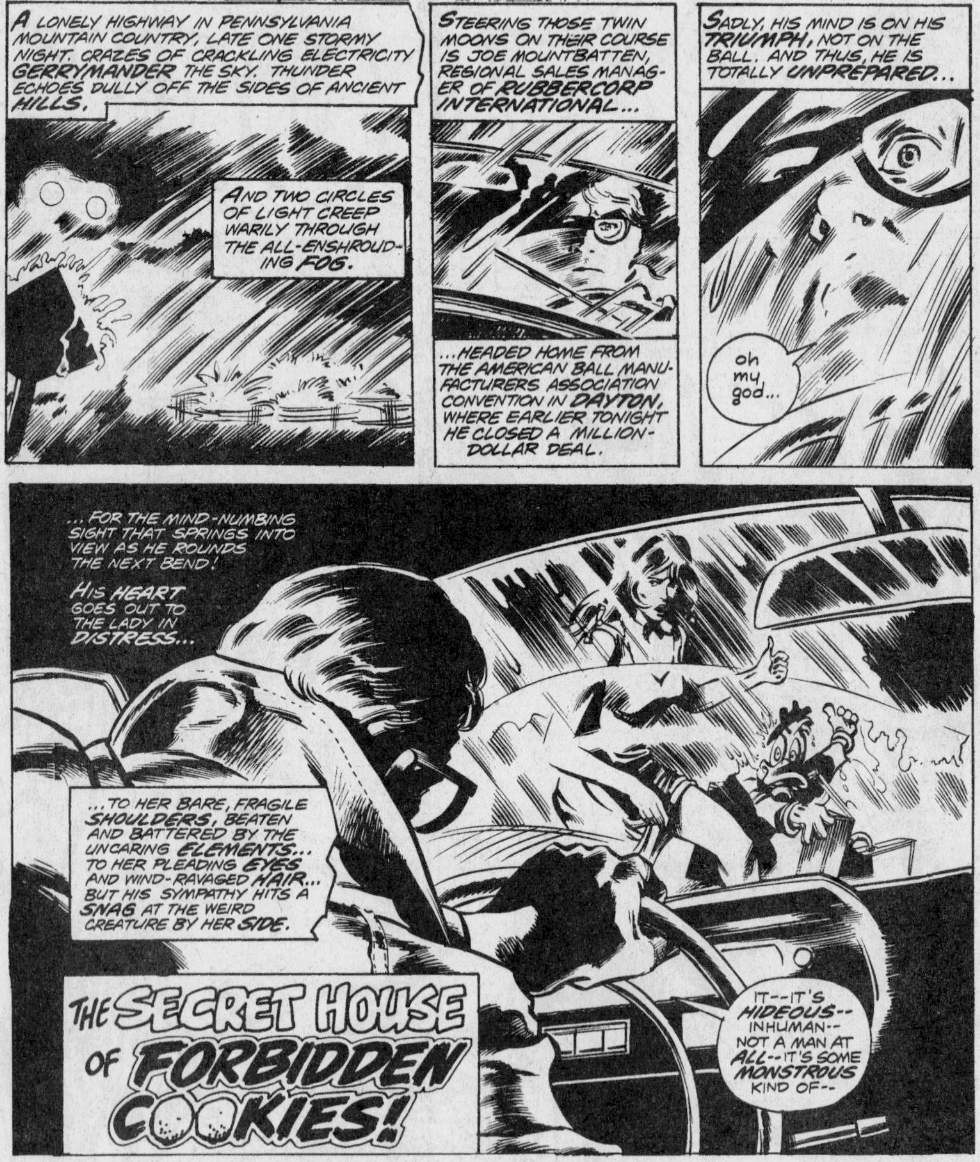
A LONELY HIGHWAY IN PENNSYLVANIA MOUNTAIN COUNTRY, LATE ONE STORMY NIGHT. CRAZES OF CRACKLING ELECTRICITY GERRYMANDER THE SKY. THUNDER ECHOES DULLY OFF THE SIDES OF ANCIENT HILLS.
AND TWO CIRCLES OF LIGHT CREEP WARILY THROUGH THE ALL-ENSHROUDING FOG.
STEERING THOSE TWIN MOONS ON THEIR COURSE IS JOE MOUNTBATTEN, REGIONAL SALES MANAGER OF RUBBERCORP INTERNATIONAL...
...HEADED HOME FROM THE AMERICAN BALL MANUFACTURERS ASSOCIATION CONVENTION IN DAYTON, WHERE EARLIER TONIGHT HE CLOSED A MILLION-DOLLAR DEAL.
SADLY, HIS MIND IS ON HIS TRIUMPH, NOT ON THE BALL. AND THUS, HE IS TOTALLY UNPREPARED...
oh my god...
...FOR THE MIND-NUMBING SIGHT THAT SPRINGS INTO VIEW AS HE ROUNDS THE NEXT BEND!
HIS HEART GOES OUT TO THE LADY IN DISTRESS...
...TO HER BARE, FRAGILE SHOULDERS, BEATEN AND BATTERED BY THE UNCARING ELEMENTS... TO HER PLEADING EYES AND WIND-RAVAGED HAIR... BUT HIS SYMPATHY HITS A SNAG AT THE WEIRD CREATURE BY HER SIDE.
THE SECRET HOUSE OF FORBIDDEN COOKIES!
IT--IT'S HIDEOUS--INHUMAN--NOT A MAN AT ALL--IT'S SOME MONSTROUS KIND OF--

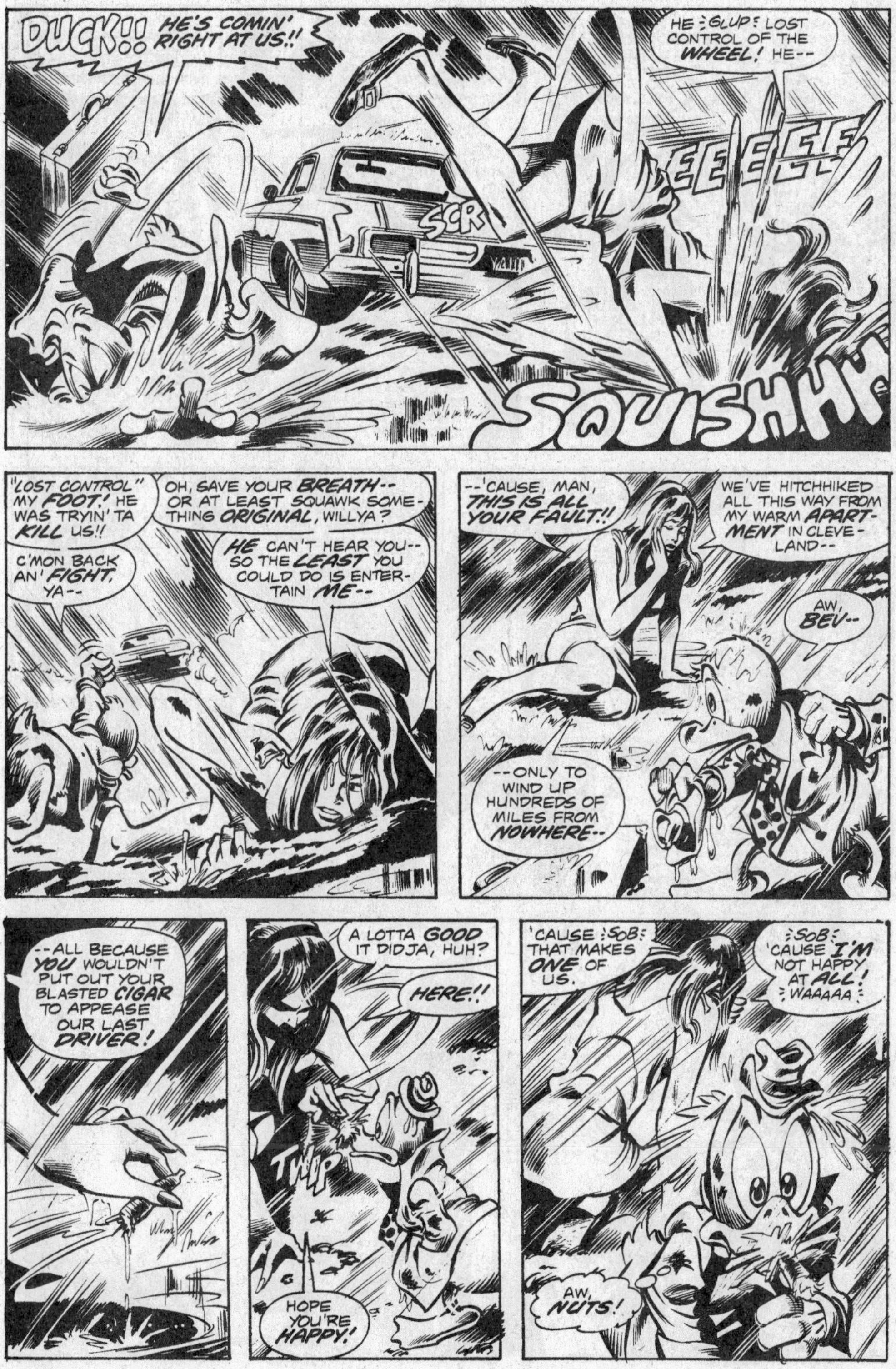

DUCK!! HE'S COMIN' RIGHT AT US!!
HE -GLUP- LOST CONTROL OF THE WHEEL! HE--
EEEEEE!
SCR
SQUISHHH
"LOST CONTROL" MY FOOT! HE WAS TRYIN' TA KILL US!!
OH, SAVE YOUR BREATH-- OR AT LEAST SQUAWK SOMETHING ORIGINAL, WILLYA?
C'MON BACK AN' FIGHT, YA--
HE CAN'T HEAR YOU-- SO THE LEAST YOU COULD DO IS ENTERTAIN ME--
--'CAUSE, MAN, THIS IS ALL YOUR FAULT!!
WE'VE HITCHHIKED ALL THIS WAY FROM MY WARM APARTMENT IN CLEVELAND--
AW, BEV--
--ONLY TO WIND UP HUNDREDS OF MILES FROM NOWHERE--
--ALL BECAUSE YOU WOULDN'T PUT OUT YOUR BLASTED CIGAR TO APPEASE OUR LAST DRIVER!
A LOTTA GOOD IT DIDJA, HUH?
HERE!!
TWIP
HOPE YOU'RE HAPPY!
'CAUSE -SOB- THAT MAKES ONE OF US.
-SOB- 'CAUSE I'M NOT HAPPY AT ALL! -WAAAAA-
AW, NUTS!

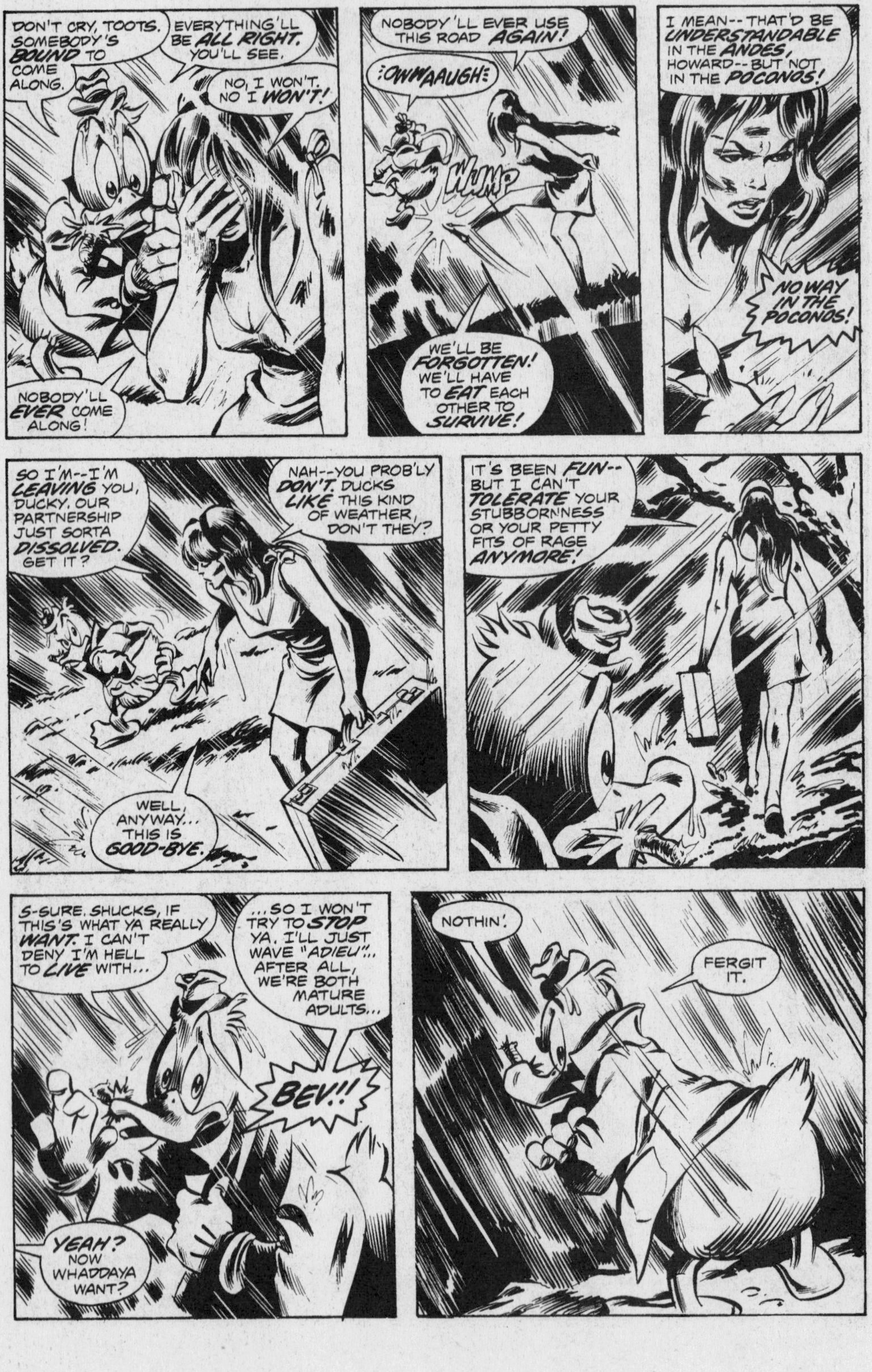
DON'T CRY, TOOTS. SOMEBODY'S BOUND TO COME ALONG.
EVERYTHING'LL BE ALL RIGHT. YOU'LL SEE.
NO, I WON'T. NO I WON'T!
NOBODY'LL EVER COME ALONG!
NOBODY'LL EVER USE THIS ROAD AGAIN!
OWWAAUGH!
WUMP
WE'LL BE FORGOTTEN! WE'LL HAVE TO EAT EACH OTHER TO SURVIVE!
I MEAN--THAT'D BE UNDERSTANDABLE IN THE ANDES, HOWARD--BUT NOT IN THE POCONOS!
NO WAY IN THE POCONOS!
SO I'M--I'M LEAVING YOU, DUCKY. OUR PARTNERSHIP JUST SORTA DISSOLVED. GET IT?
NAH--YOU PROB'LY DON'T. DUCKS LIKE THIS KIND OF WEATHER, DON'T THEY?
WELL, ANYWAY... THIS IS GOOD-BYE.
IT'S BEEN FUN--BUT I CAN'T TOLERATE YOUR STUBBORNNESS OR YOUR PETTY FITS OF RAGE ANYMORE!
S-SURE. SHUCKS, IF THIS'S WHAT YA REALLY WANT. I CAN'T DENY I'M HELL TO LIVE WITH...
...SO I WON'T TRY TO STOP YA. I'LL JUST WAVE "ADIEU"... AFTER ALL, WE'RE BOTH MATURE ADULTS...
BEV!!
YEAH? NOW WHADDAYA WANT?
NOTHIN'.
FERGIT IT.

SHE DOES--AND WITHOUT MUCH *EFFORT*. FOR HER FEAR AND THE UPHILL TREK AGAINST THE *STORM* CONSUME MOST OF HER RAPIDLY WANING ENERGY.

SHE TRUDGES ON FOR *HOURS*, THOUGH, ON SHEER DETER-MINATION, DEEPER INTO THE ENVELOP-ING BLACKNESS...

IDLE HANDS 2 MILES

...WITH NO HAVEN IN *SIGHT*...

...UNTIL THE SKY *DETONATES* WITH A BRISANCE OF THUNDER AND A BRILLIANT FLASH OF LIGHT...

CRRRAACKKK

...WHICH MOMENTARILY LIMNS THE OUTLINE...

...OF A LOWERING, BROODING VICTORIAN *MAN-SION*. BUT OF COURSE IT MUST BE *DESERTED*, SHE ASSUMES. PERHAPS SHE EVEN *HOPES* IT IS SO.

BUT-- NO.

A LIGHT BURNS IN THE TOP-MOST TOWER WINDOW.

AND SO BEVERLY SWITZLER SIMPLY *SETS ASIDE* HER INSTINCTIVE CAUTION...

...AND HEEDS INSTEAD HER INSTINCT FOR *SELF-PRESERVA-TION*.

KNOCK KNOCK KNOCK

HELLO, IN THERE! ANYBODY *HOME*?

HOLDING HER BREATH INVOLUNTARILY, SHE *WAITS*. THE SECONDS DRAG.

UNTIL, AT LAST, THE DOOR CREAKS *OPEN* TO REVEAL...

WHO'S THERE?

H-HELLO-- I'M BEVERLY SW--

OH, YES, YOU MUST BE THE NEW *GOVERNESS*.

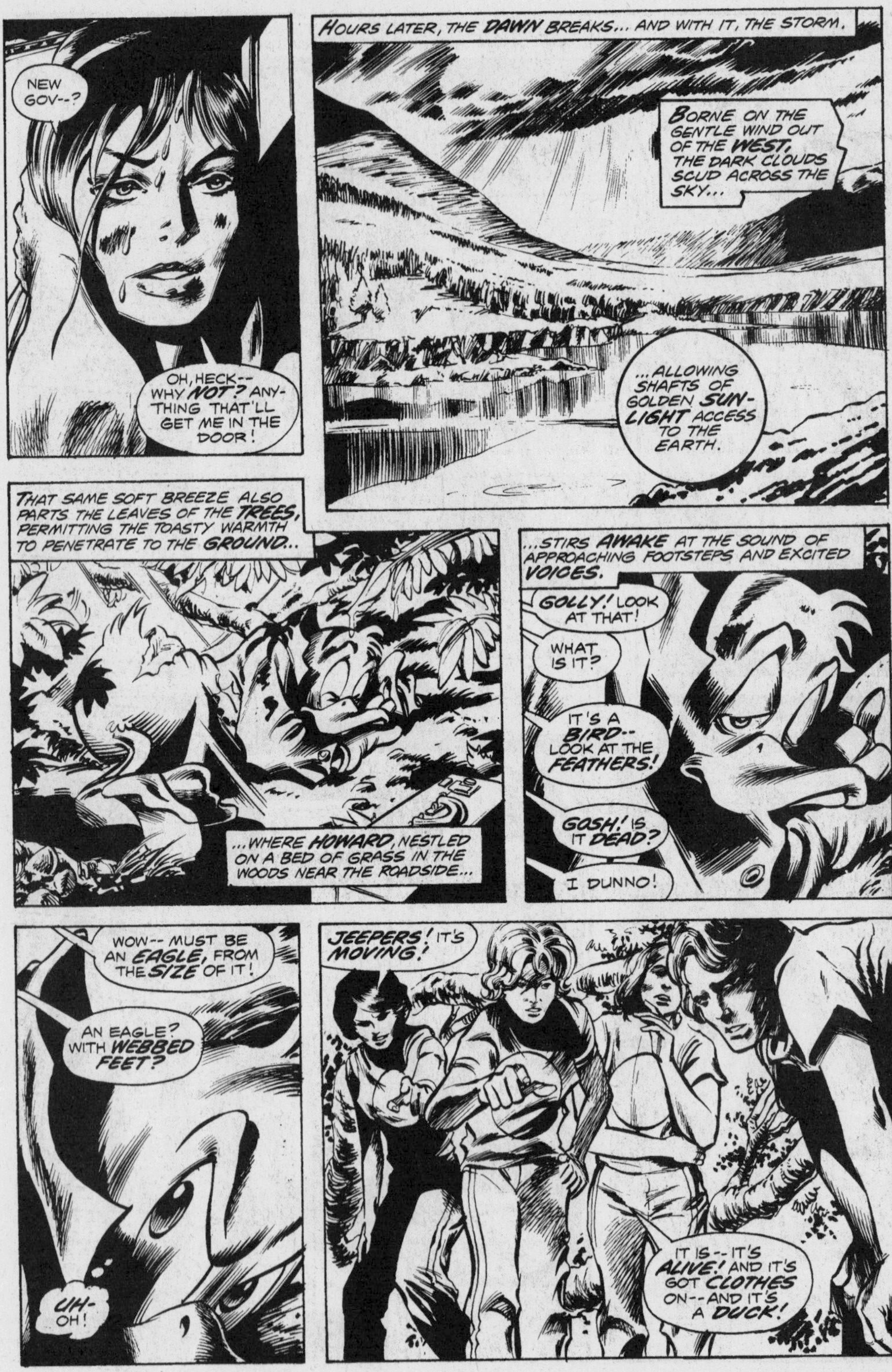
NEW GOV--?
OH, HECK-- WHY NOT? ANYTHING THAT'LL GET ME IN THE DOOR!
HOURS LATER, THE DAWN BREAKS... AND WITH IT, THE STORM.
BORNE ON THE GENTLE WIND OUT OF THE WEST, THE DARK CLOUDS SCUD ACROSS THE SKY...
...ALLOWING SHAFTS OF GOLDEN SUNLIGHT ACCESS TO THE EARTH.
THAT SAME SOFT BREEZE ALSO PARTS THE LEAVES OF THE TREES, PERMITTING THE TOASTY WARMTH TO PENETRATE TO THE GROUND...
...WHERE HOWARD, NESTLED ON A BED OF GRASS IN THE WOODS NEAR THE ROADSIDE...
...STIRS AWAKE AT THE SOUND OF APPROACHING FOOTSTEPS AND EXCITED VOICES.
GOLLY! LOOK AT THAT!
WHAT IS IT?
IT'S A BIRD-- LOOK AT THE FEATHERS!
GOSH! IS IT DEAD?
I DUNNO!
WOW-- MUST BE AN EAGLE, FROM THE SIZE OF IT!
AN EAGLE? WITH WEBBED FEET?
UH-OH!
JEEPERS! IT'S MOVING!
IT IS-- IT'S ALIVE! AND IT'S GOT CLOTHES ON--AND IT'S A DUCK!

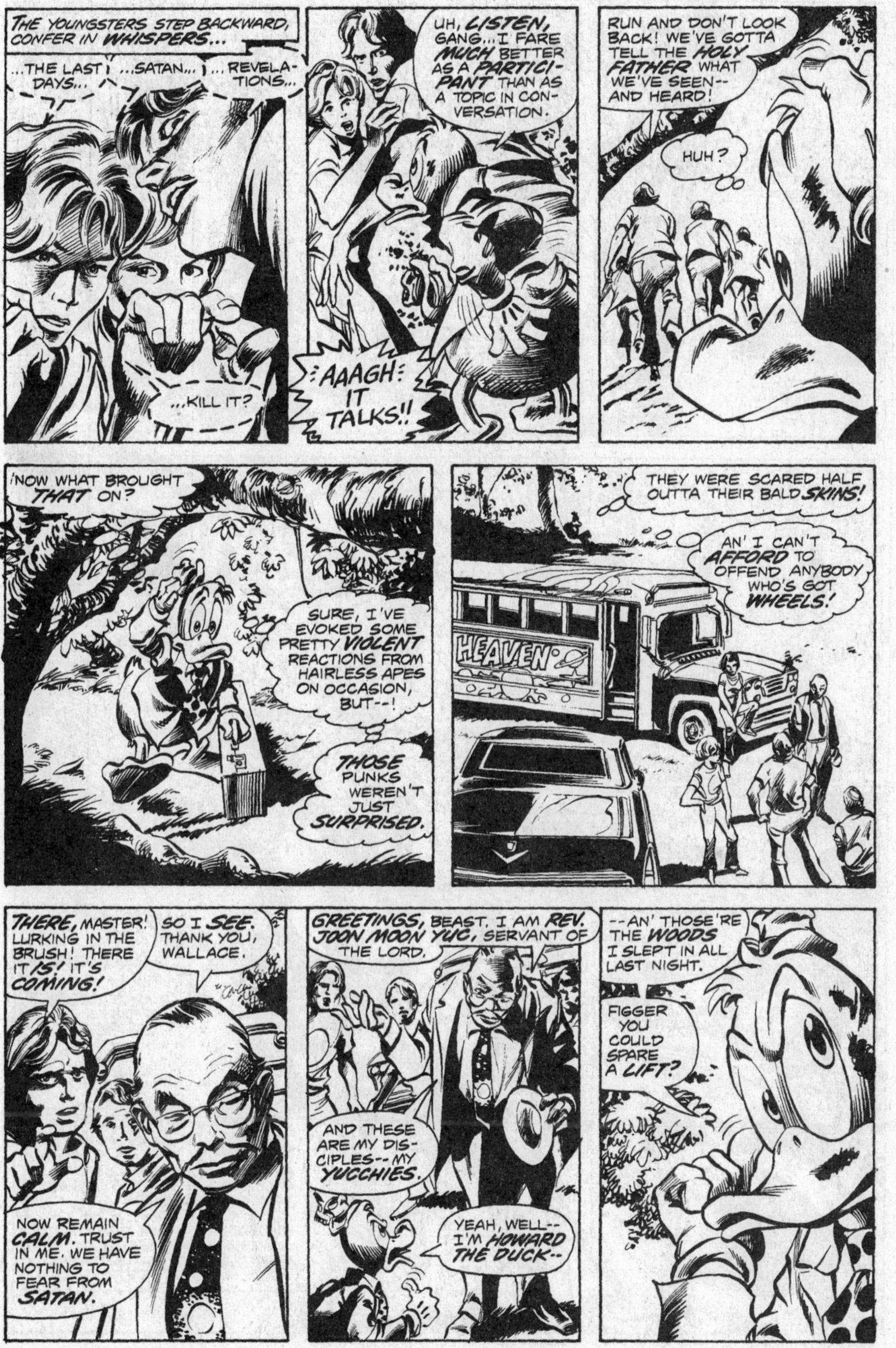
THE YOUNGSTERS STEP BACKWARD, CONFER IN WHISPERS...
...THE LAST DAYS...
...SATAN...
...REVELATIONS...
...KILL IT?
UH, LISTEN, GANG... I FARE MUCH BETTER AS A PARTICIPANT THAN AS A TOPIC IN CONVERSATION.
AAAGH IT TALKS!!
RUN AND DON'T LOOK BACK! WE'VE GOTTA TELL THE HOLY FATHER WHAT WE'VE SEEN-- AND HEARD!
HUH?
NOW WHAT BROUGHT THAT ON?
SURE, I'VE EVOKED SOME PRETTY VIOLENT REACTIONS FROM HAIRLESS APES ON OCCASION, BUT--!
THOSE PUNKS WEREN'T JUST SURPRISED.
THEY WERE SCARED HALF OUTTA THEIR BALD SKINS!
AN' I CAN'T AFFORD TO OFFEND ANYBODY WHO'S GOT WHEELS!
HEAVEN
THERE, MASTER! LURKING IN THE BRUSH! THERE IT IS! IT'S COMING!
SO I SEE. THANK YOU, WALLACE.
NOW REMAIN CALM. TRUST IN ME. WE HAVE NOTHING TO FEAR FROM SATAN.
GREETINGS, BEAST. I AM REV. JOON MOON YUC, SERVANT OF THE LORD.
AND THESE ARE MY DISCIPLES-- MY YUCCHIES.
YEAH, WELL-- I'M HOWARD THE DUCK--
--AN' THOSE'RE THE WOODS I SLEPT IN ALL LAST NIGHT.
FIGGER YOU COULD SPARE A LIFT?

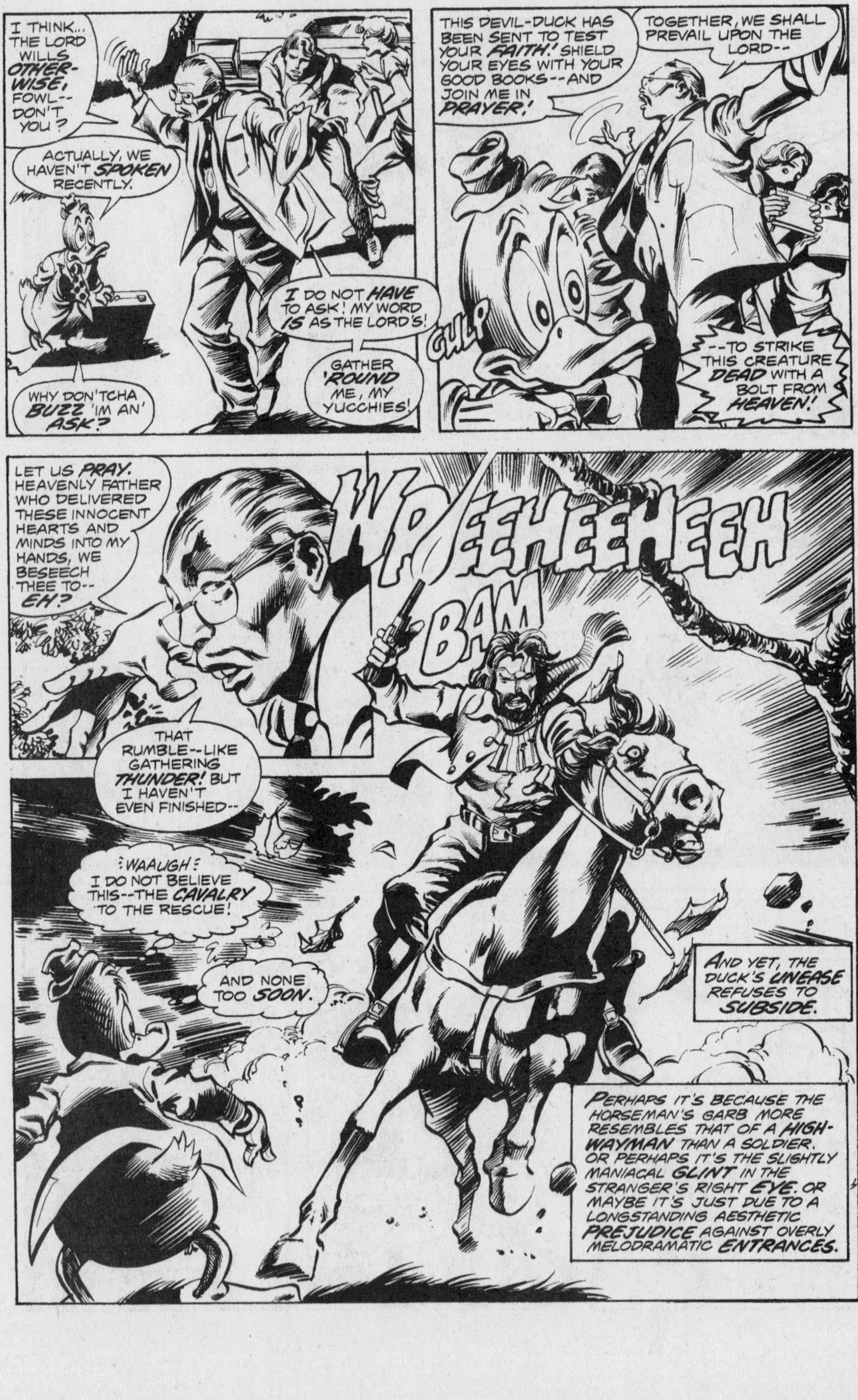
I THINK... THE LORD WILLS OTHERWISE, FOWL--DON'T YOU?
ACTUALLY, WE HAVEN'T SPOKEN RECENTLY.
WHY DON'TCHA BUZZ 'IM AN' ASK?
I DO NOT HAVE TO ASK! MY WORD IS AS THE LORD'S!
GATHER 'ROUND ME, MY YUCCHIES!
THIS DEVIL-DUCK HAS BEEN SENT TO TEST YOUR FAITH! SHIELD YOUR EYES WITH YOUR GOOD BOOKS--AND JOIN ME IN PRAYER!
TOGETHER, WE SHALL PREVAIL UPON THE LORD--
GULP
--TO STRIKE THIS CREATURE DEAD WITH A BOLT FROM HEAVEN!
LET US PRAY. HEAVENLY FATHER WHO DELIVERED THESE INNOCENT HEARTS AND MINDS INTO MY HANDS, WE BESEECH THEE TO--EH?
WHEEHEEHEEH
BAM
THAT RUMBLE--LIKE GATHERING THUNDER! BUT I HAVEN'T EVEN FINISHED--
WAAUGH
I DO NOT BELIEVE THIS--THE CAVALRY TO THE RESCUE!
AND NONE TOO SOON.
AND YET, THE DUCK'S UNEASE REFUSES TO SUBSIDE.
PERHAPS IT'S BECAUSE THE HORSEMAN'S GARB MORE RESEMBLES THAT OF A HIGHWAYMAN THAN A SOLDIER. OR PERHAPS IT'S THE SLIGHTLY MANIACAL GLINT IN THE STRANGER'S RIGHT EYE. OR MAYBE IT'S JUST DUE TO A LONGSTANDING AESTHETIC PREJUDICE AGAINST OVERLY MELODRAMATIC ENTRANCES.

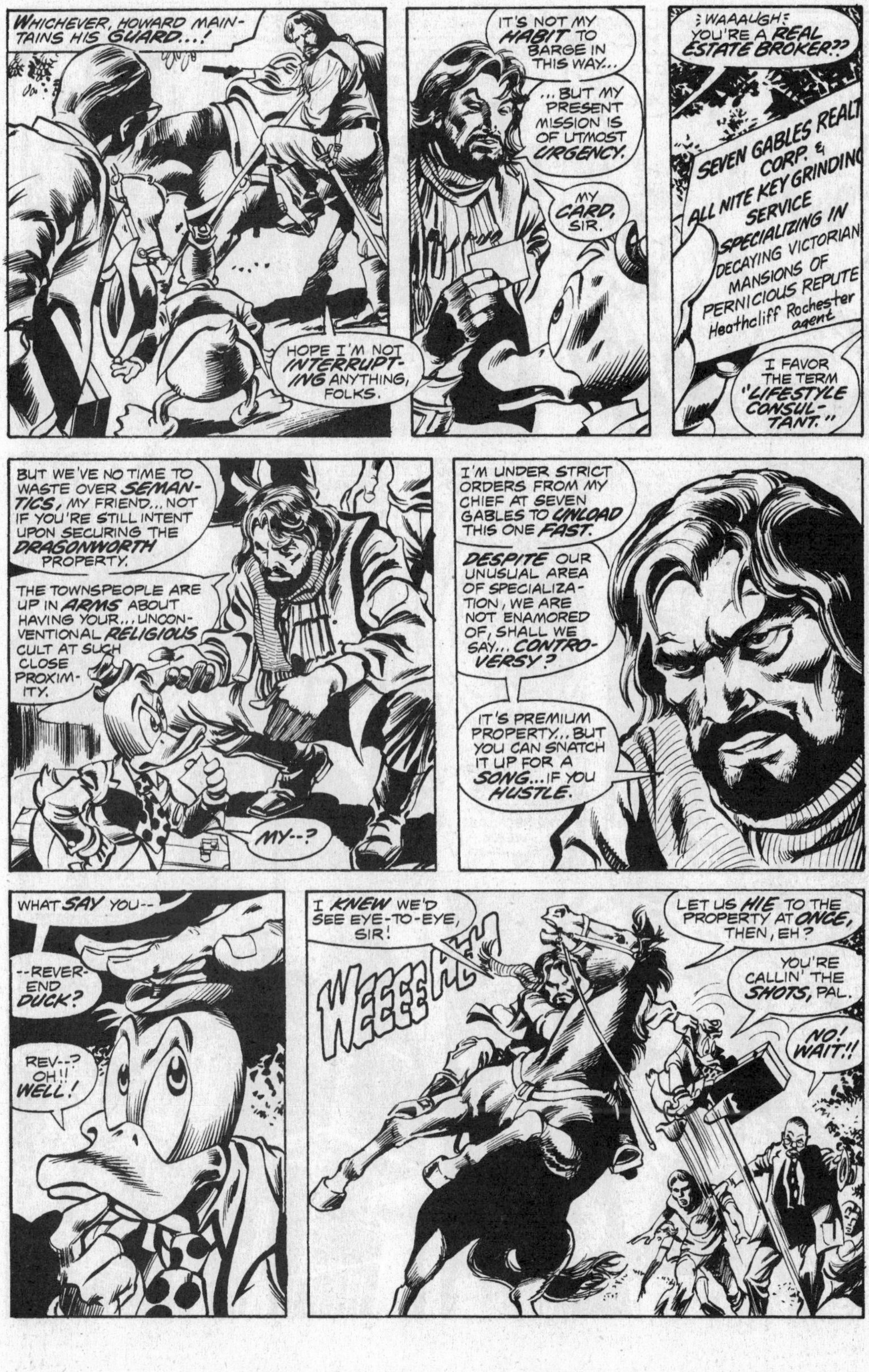
WHICHEVER, HOWARD MAINTAINS HIS GUARD...!
HOPE I'M NOT INTERRUPTING ANYTHING, FOLKS.
IT'S NOT MY HABIT TO BARGE IN THIS WAY...
...BUT MY PRESENT MISSION IS OF UTMOST URGENCY.
MY CARD, SIR.
WAAAUGH! YOU'RE A REAL ESTATE BROKER??
SEVEN GABLES REALT CORP. & ALL NITE KEY GRINDING SERVICE SPECIALIZING IN DECAYING VICTORIAN MANSIONS OF PERNICIOUS REPUTE
Heathcliff Rochester agent
I FAVOR THE TERM "LIFESTYLE CONSULTANT."
BUT WE'VE NO TIME TO WASTE OVER SEMANTICS, MY FRIEND... NOT IF YOU'RE STILL INTENT UPON SECURING THE DRAGONWORTH PROPERTY.
THE TOWNSPEOPLE ARE UP IN ARMS ABOUT HAVING YOUR... UNCONVENTIONAL RELIGIOUS CULT AT SUCH CLOSE PROXIMITY.
MY--?
I'M UNDER STRICT ORDERS FROM MY CHIEF AT SEVEN GABLES TO UNLOAD THIS ONE FAST.
DESPITE OUR UNUSUAL AREA OF SPECIALIZATION, WE ARE NOT ENAMORED OF, SHALL WE SAY... CONTROVERSY?
IT'S PREMIUM PROPERTY... BUT YOU CAN SNATCH IT UP FOR A SONG... IF YOU HUSTLE.
WHAT SAY YOU--
--REVEREND DUCK?
REV--? OH!! WELL!
I KNEW WE'D SEE EYE-TO-EYE, SIR!
WEEEEHH
LET US HIE TO THE PROPERTY AT ONCE, THEN, EH?
YOU'RE CALLIN' THE SHOTS, PAL.
NO! WAIT!!

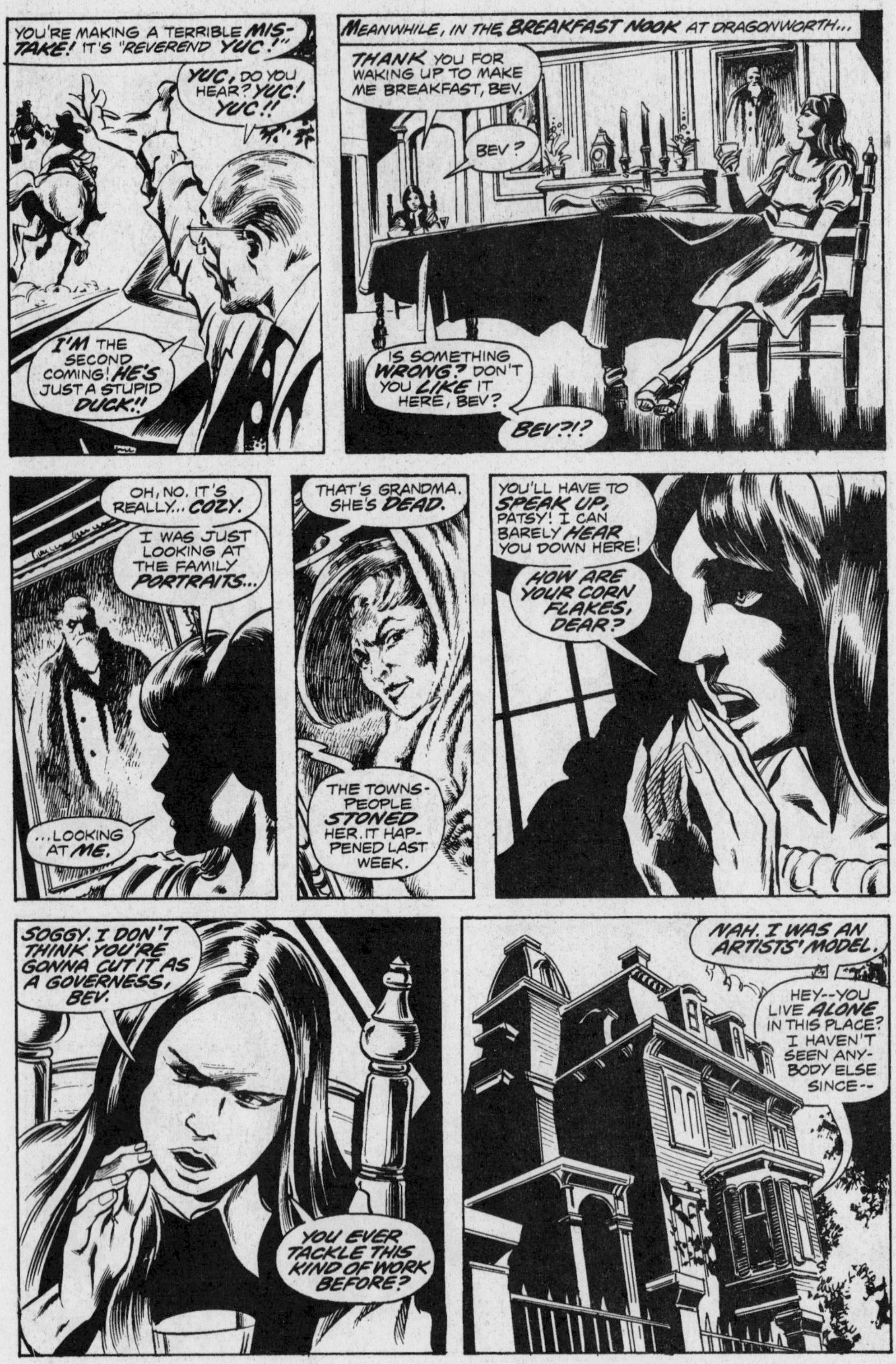

YOU'RE MAKING A TERRIBLE MIS-TAKE! IT'S "REVEREND YUC!"
YUC, DO YOU HEAR? YUC! YUC!!
I'M THE SECOND COMING! HE'S JUST A STUPID DUCK!!
MEANWHILE, IN THE BREAKFAST NOOK AT DRAGONWORTH...
THANK YOU FOR WAKING UP TO MAKE ME BREAKFAST, BEV.
BEV?
IS SOMETHING WRONG? DON'T YOU LIKE IT HERE, BEV?
BEV?!?
OH, NO. IT'S REALLY... COZY.
I WAS JUST LOOKING AT THE FAMILY PORTRAITS...
...LOOKING AT ME.
THAT'S GRANDMA. SHE'S DEAD.
THE TOWNS-PEOPLE STONED HER. IT HAP-PENED LAST WEEK.
YOU'LL HAVE TO SPEAK UP, PATSY! I CAN BARELY HEAR YOU DOWN HERE!
HOW ARE YOUR CORN FLAKES, DEAR?
SOGGY. I DON'T THINK YOU'RE GONNA CUT IT AS A GOVERNESS, BEV.
YOU EVER TACKLE THIS KIND OF WORK BEFORE?
NAH. I WAS AN ARTISTS' MODEL.
HEY--YOU LIVE ALONE IN THIS PLACE? I HAVEN'T SEEN ANY-BODY ELSE SINCE--

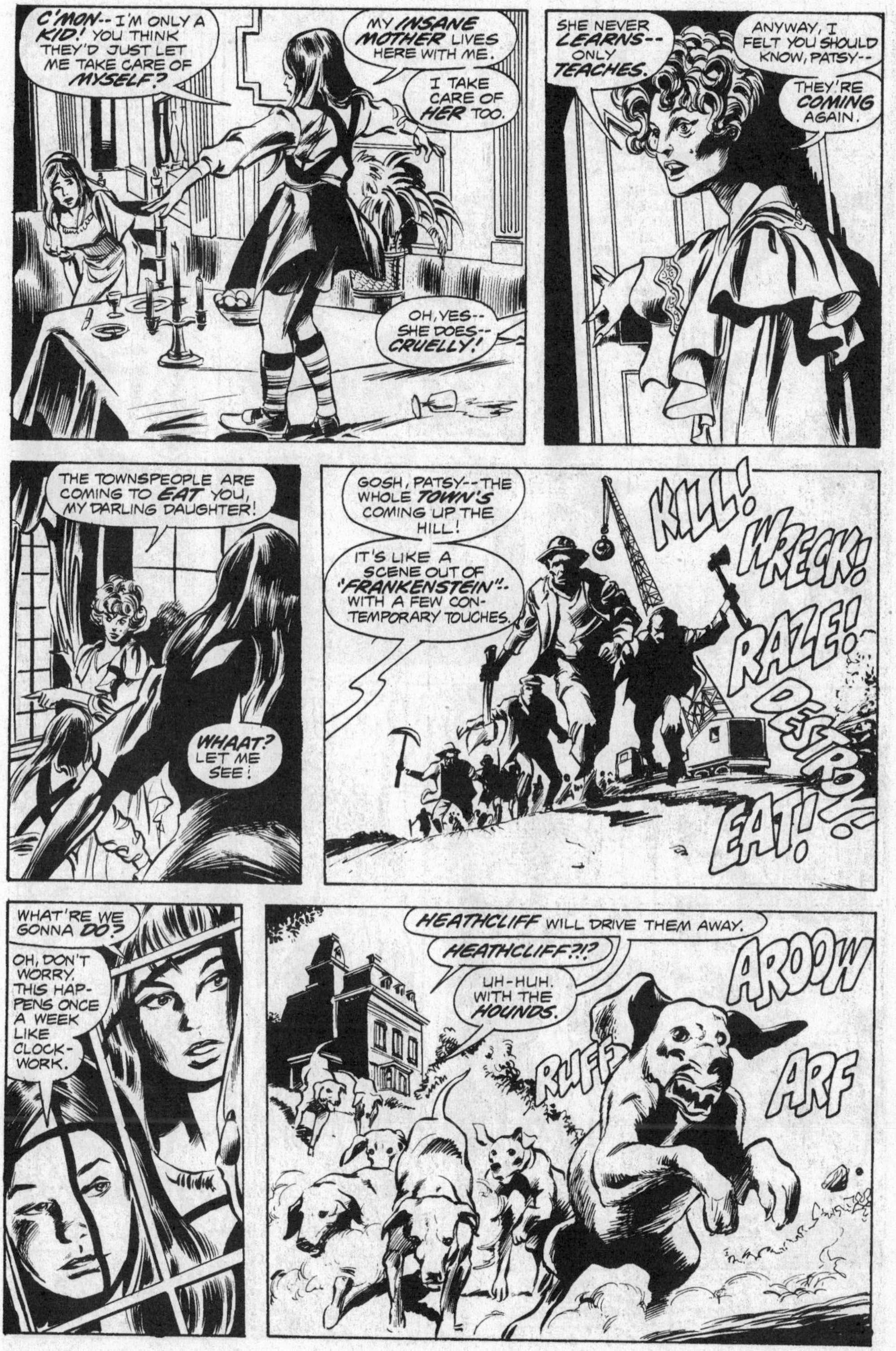
C'MON-- I'M ONLY A KID! YOU THINK THEY'D JUST LET ME TAKE CARE OF MYSELF?
MY INSANE MOTHER LIVES HERE WITH ME.
I TAKE CARE OF HER TOO.
OH, YES-- SHE DOES-- CRUELLY!
SHE NEVER LEARNS-- ONLY TEACHES.
ANYWAY, I FELT YOU SHOULD KNOW, PATSY--
THEY'RE COMING AGAIN.
THE TOWNSPEOPLE ARE COMING TO EAT YOU, MY DARLING DAUGHTER!
WHAAT? LET ME SEE!
GOSH, PATSY-- THE WHOLE TOWN'S COMING UP THE HILL!
IT'S LIKE A SCENE OUT OF "FRANKENSTEIN"-- WITH A FEW CONTEMPORARY TOUCHES.
KILL!
WRECK!
RAZE!
DESTROY!
EAT!
WHAT'RE WE GONNA DO?
OH, DON'T WORRY. THIS HAPPENS ONCE A WEEK LIKE CLOCKWORK.
HEATHCLIFF WILL DRIVE THEM AWAY.
HEATHCLIFF?!?
UH-HUH. WITH THE HOUNDS.
AROOW
RUFF
ARF

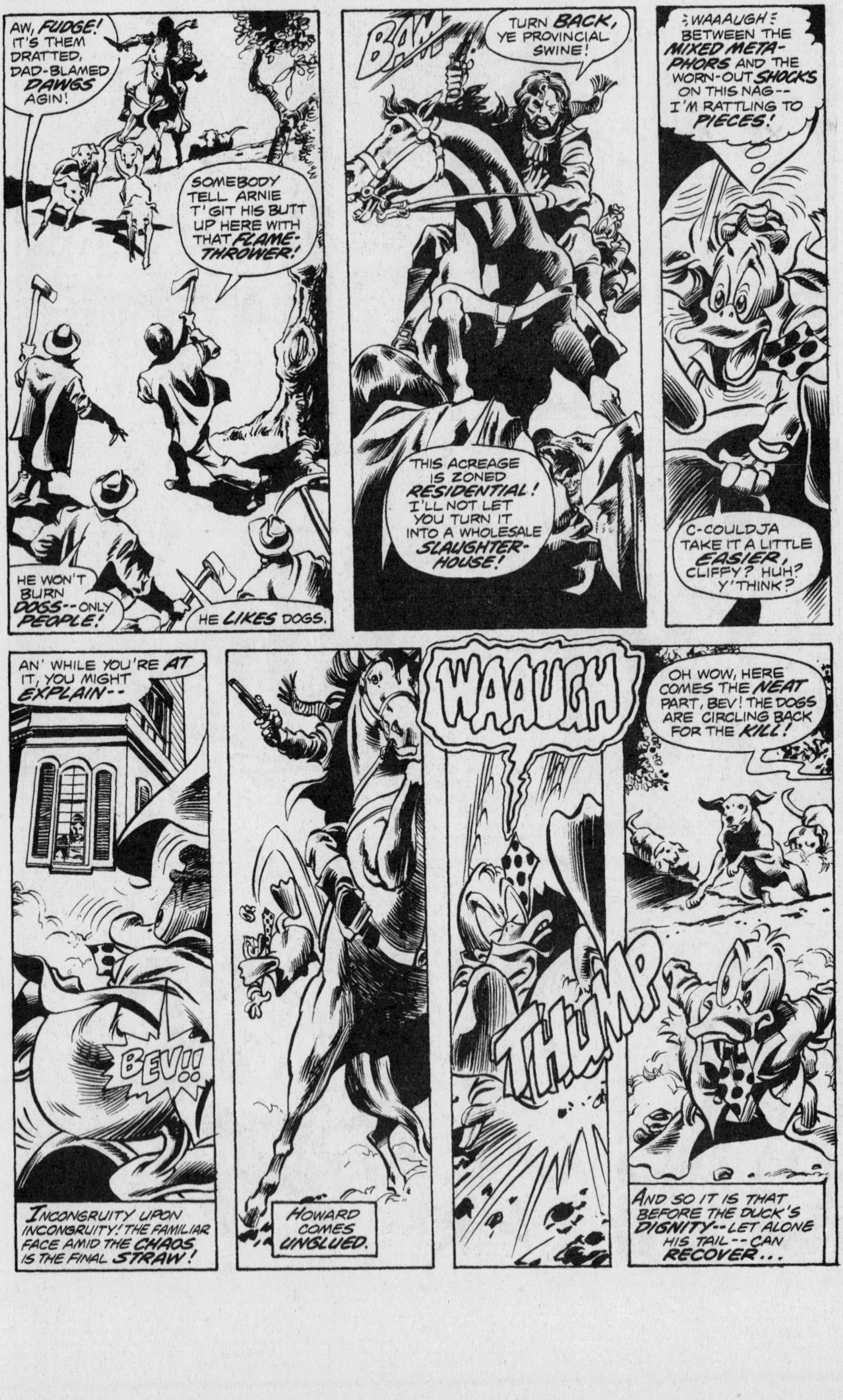
AW, FUDGE! IT'S THEM DRATTED, DAD-BLAMED DAWGS AGIN!
SOMEBODY TELL ARNIE T' GIT HIS BUTT UP HERE WITH THAT FLAME-THROWER!
HE WON'T BURN DOGS--ONLY PEOPLE!
HE LIKES DOGS.
BAM
TURN BACK, YE PROVINCIAL SWINE!
THIS ACREAGE IS ZONED RESIDENTIAL! I'LL NOT LET YOU TURN IT INTO A WHOLESALE SLAUGHTER-HOUSE!
WAAAUGH BETWEEN THE MIXED META-PHORS AND THE WORN-OUT SHOCKS ON THIS NAG-- I'M RATTLING TO PIECES!
C-COULDJA TAKE IT A LITTLE EASIER, CLIFFY? HUH? Y'THINK?
AN' WHILE YOU'RE AT IT, YOU MIGHT EXPLAIN--
BEV!!
INCONGRUITY UPON INCONGRUITY! THE FAMILIAR FACE AMID THE CHAOS IS THE FINAL STRAW!
HOWARD COMES UNGLUED.
WAAUGH
THUMP
OH WOW, HERE COMES THE NEAT PART, BEV! THE DOGS ARE CIRCLING BACK FOR THE KILL!
AND SO IT IS THAT BEFORE THE DUCK'S DIGNITY--LET ALONE HIS TAIL--CAN RECOVER...

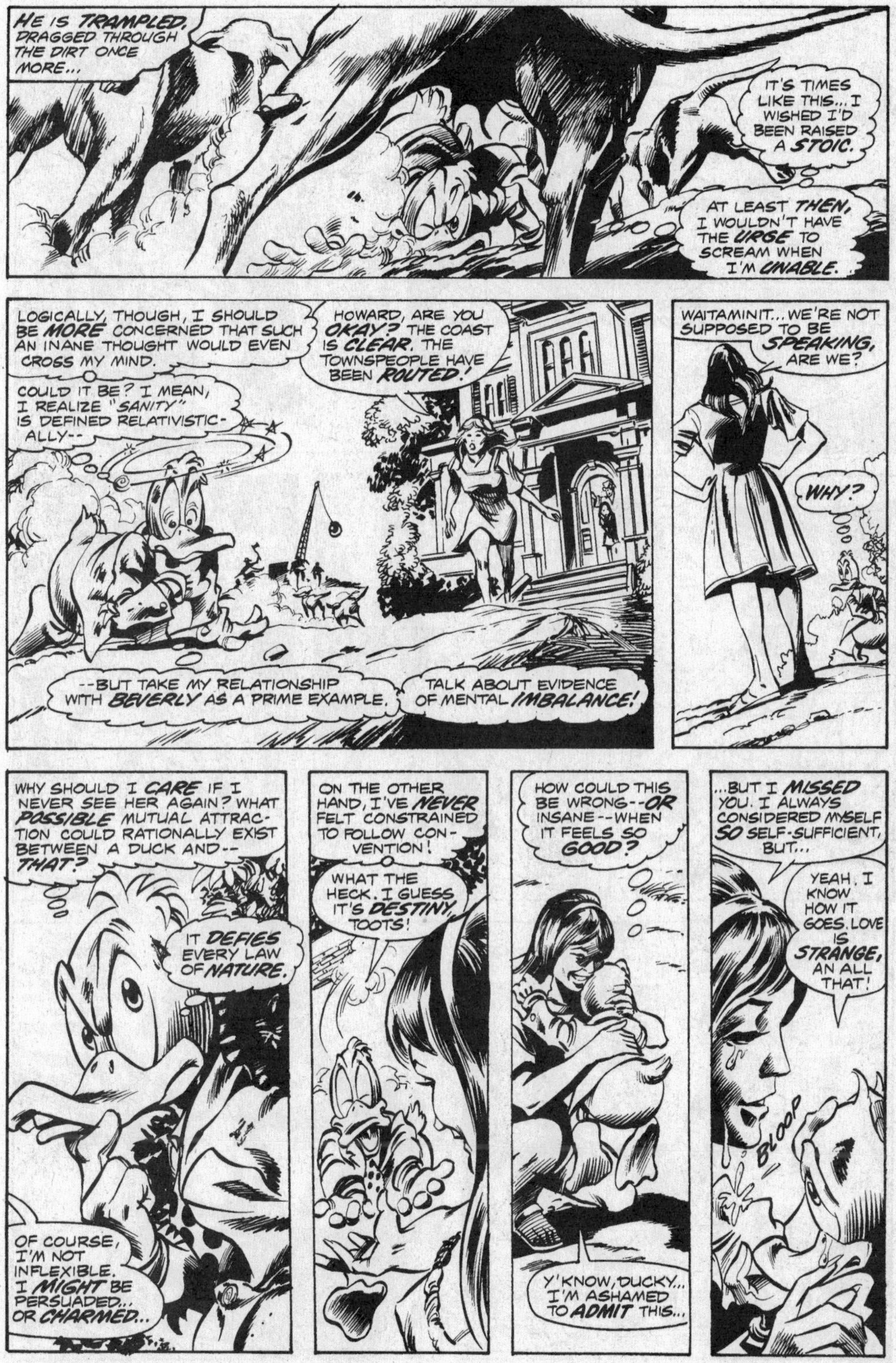
HE IS TRAMPLED, DRAGGED THROUGH THE DIRT ONCE MORE...
IT'S TIMES LIKE THIS... I WISHED I'D BEEN RAISED A STOIC.
AT LEAST THEN, I WOULDN'T HAVE THE URGE TO SCREAM WHEN I'M UNABLE.
LOGICALLY, THOUGH, I SHOULD BE MORE CONCERNED THAT SUCH AN INANE THOUGHT WOULD EVEN CROSS MY MIND.
HOWARD, ARE YOU OKAY? THE COAST IS CLEAR. THE TOWNSPEOPLE HAVE BEEN ROUTED!
COULD IT BE? I MEAN, I REALIZE "SANITY" IS DEFINED RELATIVISTIC-ALLY--
--BUT TAKE MY RELATIONSHIP WITH BEVERLY AS A PRIME EXAMPLE.
TALK ABOUT EVIDENCE OF MENTAL IMBALANCE!
WAITAMINIT... WE'RE NOT SUPPOSED TO BE SPEAKING, ARE WE?
WHY?
WHY SHOULD I CARE IF I NEVER SEE HER AGAIN? WHAT POSSIBLE MUTUAL ATTRACTION COULD RATIONALLY EXIST BETWEEN A DUCK AND--THAT?
IT DEFIES EVERY LAW OF NATURE.
OF COURSE, I'M NOT INFLEXIBLE. I MIGHT BE PERSUADED... OR CHARMED...
ON THE OTHER HAND, I'VE NEVER FELT CONSTRAINED TO FOLLOW CON-VENTION!
WHAT THE HECK. I GUESS IT'S DESTINY, TOOTS!
HOW COULD THIS BE WRONG--OR INSANE--WHEN IT FEELS SO GOOD?
Y'KNOW, DUCKY... I'M ASHAMED TO ADMIT THIS...
...BUT I MISSED YOU. I ALWAYS CONSIDERED MYSELF SO SELF-SUFFICIENT, BUT...
YEAH, I KNOW HOW IT GOES. LOVE IS STRANGE, AN ALL THAT!
BLOOP

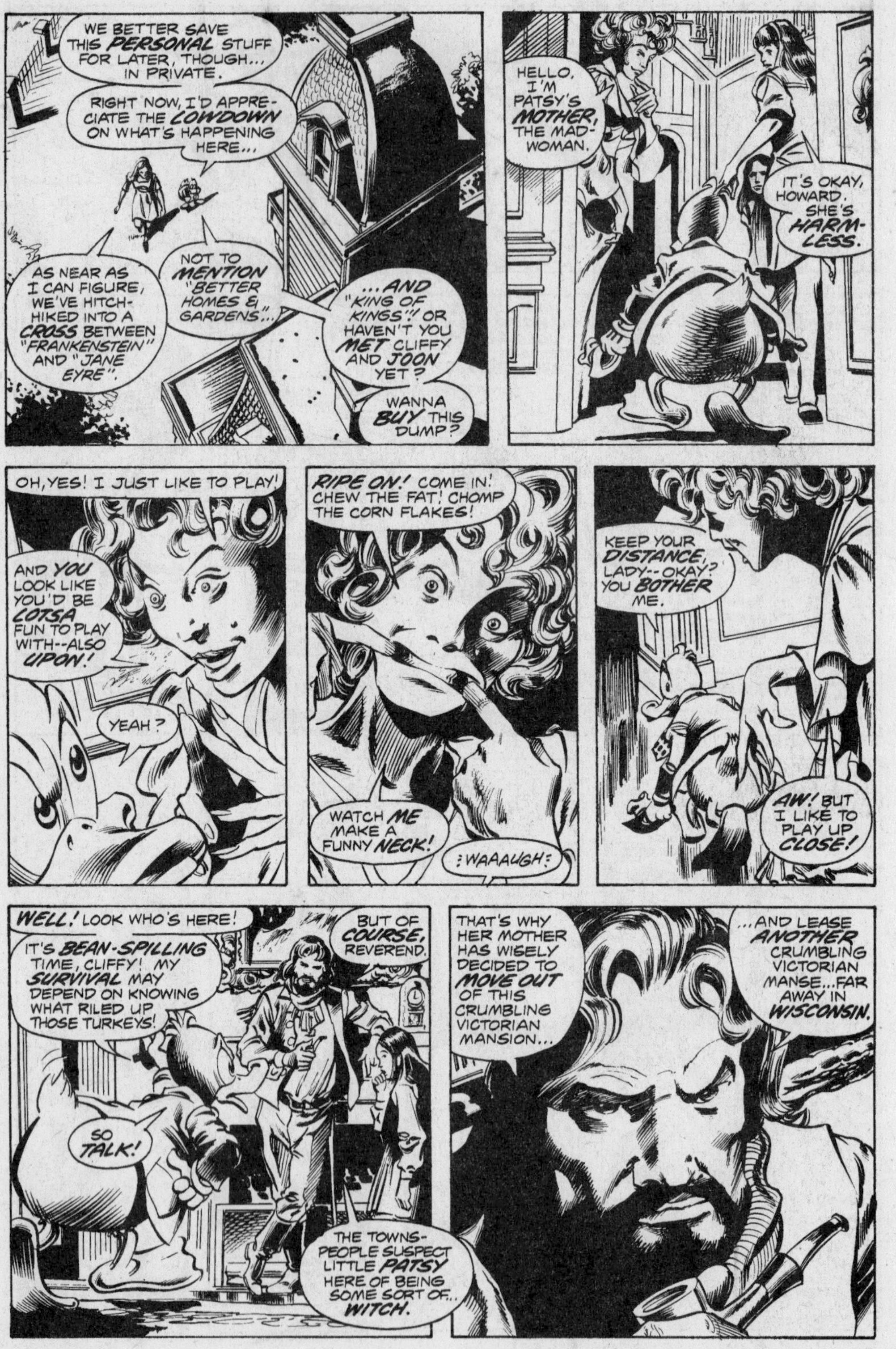

WE BETTER SAVE THIS PERSONAL STUFF FOR LATER, THOUGH... IN PRIVATE.
RIGHT NOW, I'D APPRECIATE THE LOWDOWN ON WHAT'S HAPPENING HERE...
AS NEAR AS I CAN FIGURE, WE'VE HITCH-HIKED INTO A CROSS BETWEEN "FRANKENSTEIN" AND "JANE EYRE".
NOT TO MENTION "BETTER HOMES & GARDENS"...
...AND "KING OF KINGS"! OR HAVEN'T YOU MET CLIFFY AND JOON YET?
WANNA BUY THIS DUMP?
HELLO, I'M PATSY'S MOTHER, THE MAD-WOMAN.
IT'S OKAY, HOWARD. SHE'S HARM-LESS.
OH, YES! I JUST LIKE TO PLAY!
AND YOU LOOK LIKE YOU'D BE LOTSA FUN TO PLAY WITH--ALSO UPON!
YEAH?
RIPE ON! COME IN! CHEW THE FAT! CHOMP THE CORN FLAKES!
WATCH ME MAKE A FUNNY NECK!
:WAAAUGH:
KEEP YOUR DISTANCE, LADY--OKAY? YOU BOTHER ME.
AW! BUT I LIKE TO PLAY UP CLOSE!
WELL! LOOK WHO'S HERE!
IT'S BEAN-SPILLING TIME, CLIFFY! MY SURVIVAL MAY DEPEND ON KNOWING WHAT RILED UP THOSE TURKEYS!
BUT OF COURSE, REVEREND.
SO TALK!
THE TOWNS-PEOPLE SUSPECT LITTLE PATSY HERE OF BEING SOME SORT OF... WITCH.
THAT'S WHY HER MOTHER HAS WISELY DECIDED TO MOVE OUT OF THIS CRUMBLING VICTORIAN MANSION...
...AND LEASE ANOTHER CRUMBLING VICTORIAN MANSE...FAR AWAY IN WISCONSIN.

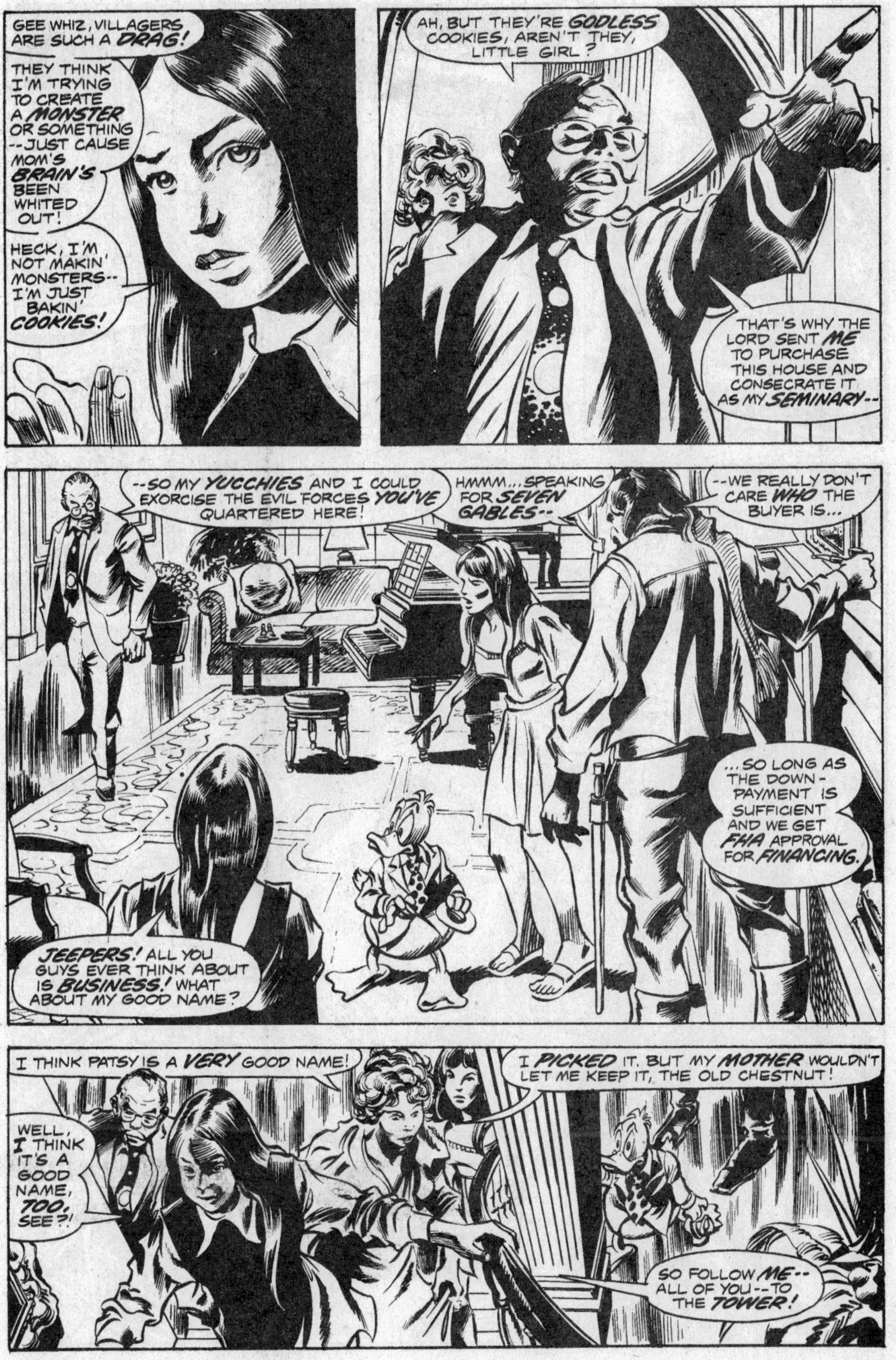
GEE WHIZ, VILLAGERS ARE SUCH A DRAG!
THEY THINK I'M TRYING TO CREATE A MONSTER OR SOMETHING --JUST CAUSE MOM'S BRAIN'S BEEN WHITED OUT!
HECK, I'M NOT MAKIN' MONSTERS-- I'M JUST BAKIN' COOKIES!
AH, BUT THEY'RE GODLESS COOKIES, AREN'T THEY, LITTLE GIRL?
THAT'S WHY THE LORD SENT ME TO PURCHASE THIS HOUSE AND CONSECRATE IT AS MY SEMINARY--
--SO MY YUCCHIES AND I COULD EXORCISE THE EVIL FORCES YOU'VE QUARTERED HERE!
HMMM... SPEAKING FOR SEVEN GABLES--
--WE REALLY DON'T CARE WHO THE BUYER IS...
...SO LONG AS THE DOWN-PAYMENT IS SUFFICIENT AND WE GET FHA APPROVAL FOR FINANCING.
JEEPERS! ALL YOU GUYS EVER THINK ABOUT IS BUSINESS! WHAT ABOUT MY GOOD NAME?
I THINK PATSY IS A VERY GOOD NAME!
I PICKED IT. BUT MY MOTHER WOULDN'T LET ME KEEP IT, THE OLD CHESTNUT!
WELL, I THINK IT'S A GOOD NAME, TOO, SEE?!
SO FOLLOW ME-- ALL OF YOU--TO THE TOWER!

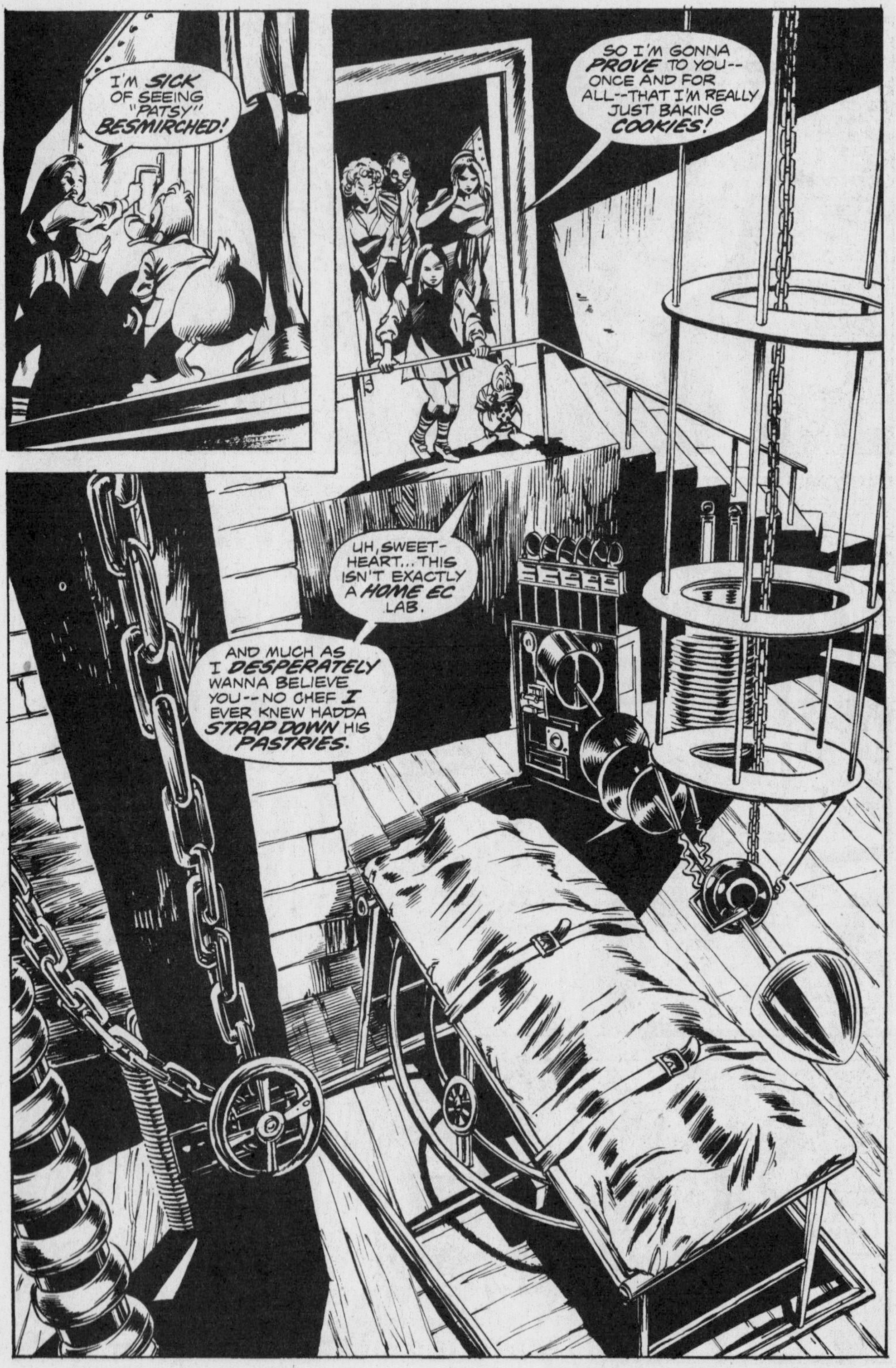
I'M SICK OF SEEING "PATSY" BESMIRCHED!
SO I'M GONNA PROVE TO YOU-- ONCE AND FOR ALL--THAT I'M REALLY JUST BAKING COOKIES!
UH, SWEETHEART... THIS ISN'T EXACTLY A HOME EC LAB.
AND MUCH AS I DESPERATELY WANNA BELIEVE YOU--NO CHEF I EVER KNEW HADDA STRAP DOWN HIS PASTRIES.

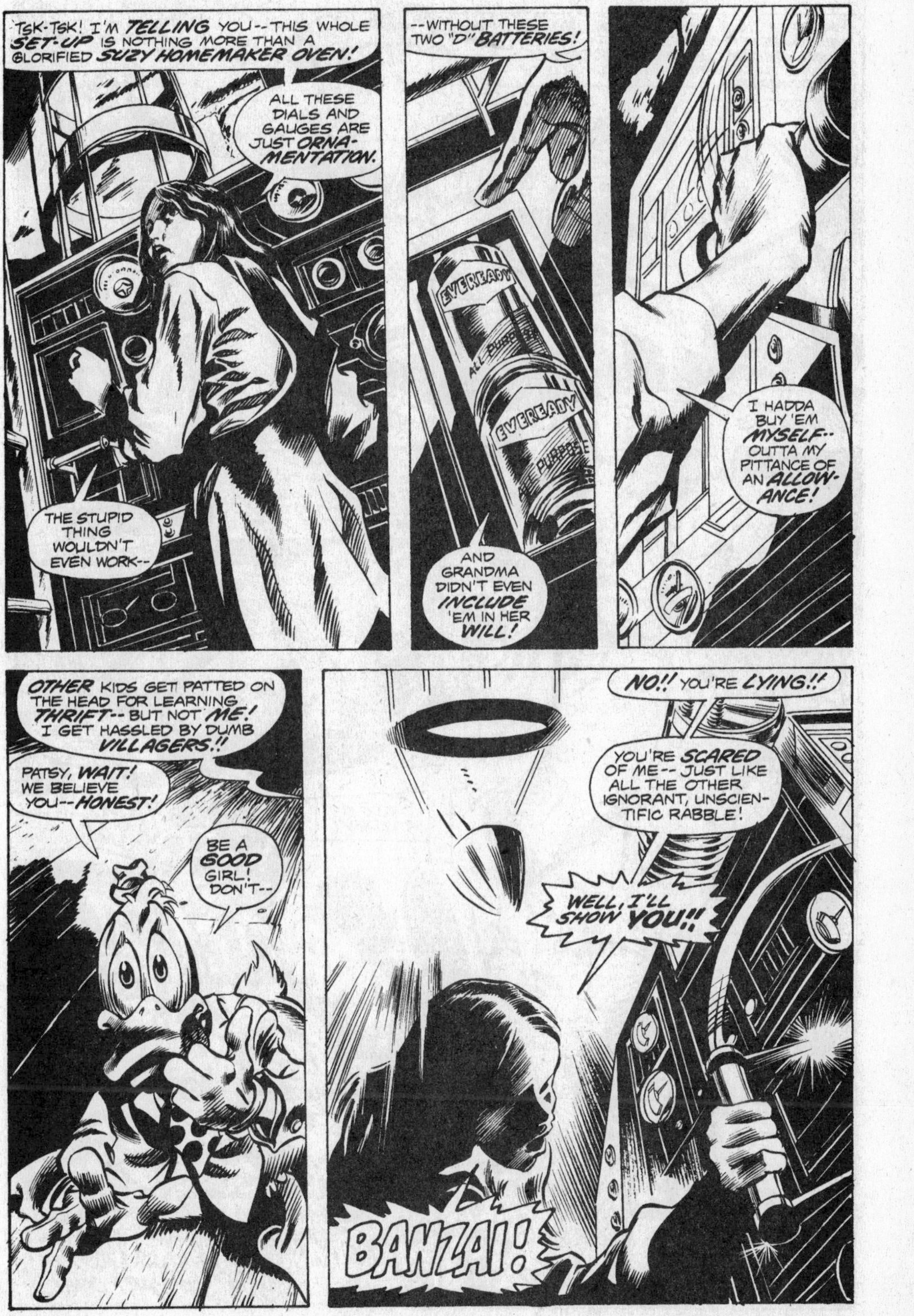
TSK-TSK! I'M TELLING YOU--THIS WHOLE SET-UP IS NOTHING MORE THAN A GLORIFIED SUZY HOMEMAKER OVEN!
ALL THESE DIALS AND GAUGES ARE JUST ORNAMENTATION.
THE STUPID THING WOULDN'T EVEN WORK--
--WITHOUT THESE TWO "D" BATTERIES!
EVEREADY
EVEREADY
AND GRANDMA DIDN'T EVEN INCLUDE 'EM IN HER WILL!
I HADDA BUY 'EM MYSELF-- OUTTA MY PITTANCE OF AN ALLOWANCE!
OTHER KIDS GET PATTED ON THE HEAD FOR LEARNING THRIFT--BUT NOT ME! I GET HASSLED BY DUMB VILLAGERS!!
PATSY, WAIT! WE BELIEVE YOU--HONEST!
BE A GOOD GIRL! DON'T--
NO!! YOU'RE LYING!!
YOU'RE SCARED OF ME--JUST LIKE ALL THE OTHER IGNORANT, UNSCIENTIFIC RABBLE!
WELL, I'LL SHOW YOU!!
BANZAI!

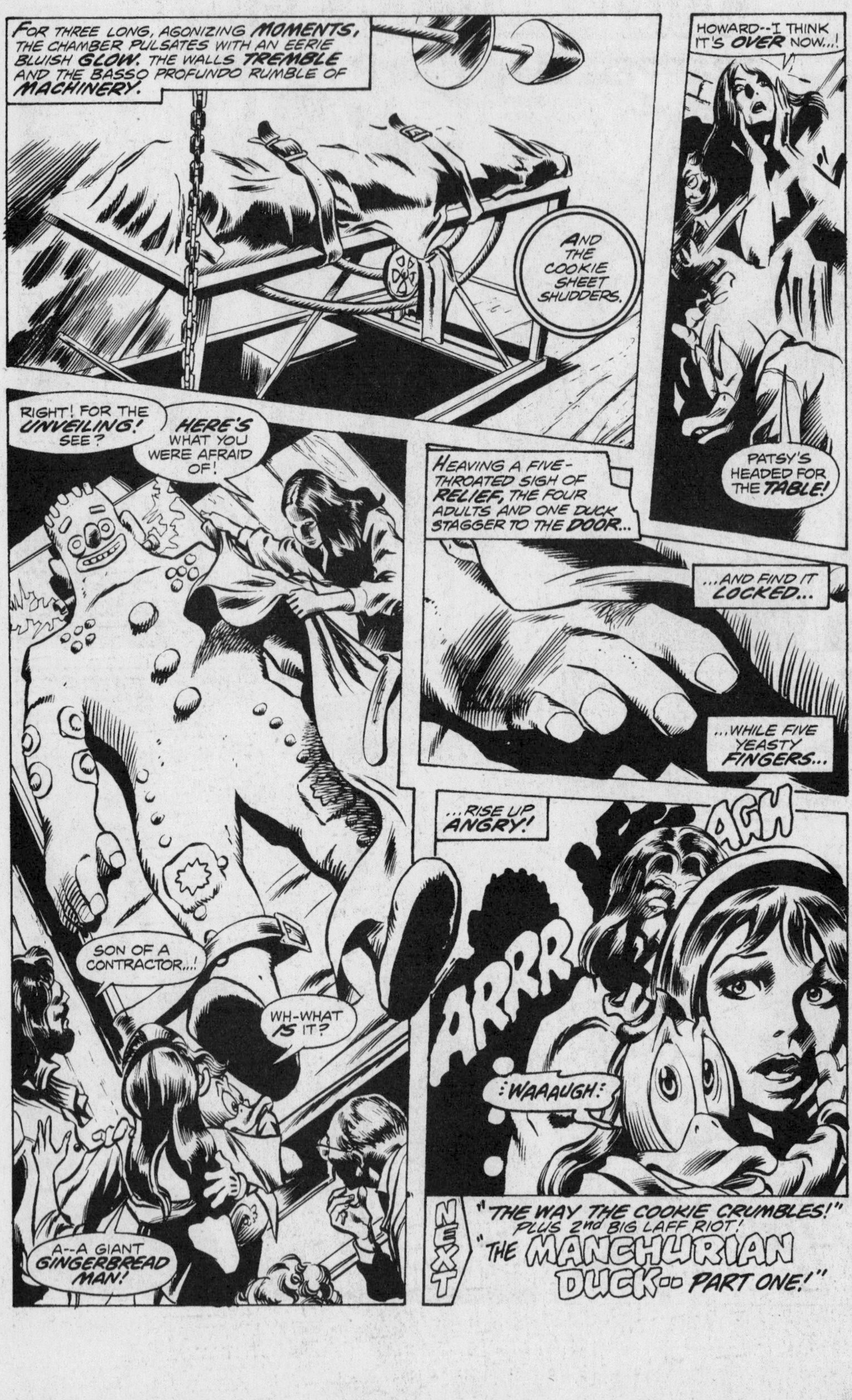

FOR THREE LONG, AGONIZING MOMENTS, THE CHAMBER PULSATES WITH AN EERIE BLUISH GLOW. THE WALLS TREMBLE AND THE BASSO PROFUNDO RUMBLE OF MACHINERY.
AND THE COOKIE SHEET SHUDDERS.
HOWARD--I THINK IT'S OVER NOW...!
PATSY'S HEADED FOR THE TABLE!
RIGHT! FOR THE UNVEILING! SEE?
HERE'S WHAT YOU WERE AFRAID OF!
SON OF A CONTRACTOR...!
WH-WHAT IS IT?
A--A GIANT GINGERBREAD MAN!
HEAVING A FIVE-THROATED SIGH OF RELIEF, THE FOUR ADULTS AND ONE DUCK STAGGER TO THE DOOR...
...AND FIND IT LOCKED...
...WHILE FIVE YEASTY FINGERS...
...RISE UP ANGRY!
AGH
ARRR
WAAAUGH!
NEXT
"THE WAY THE COOKIE CRUMBLES!" PLUS 2nd BIG LAFF RIOT! "THE MANCHURIAN DUCK-- PART ONE!"

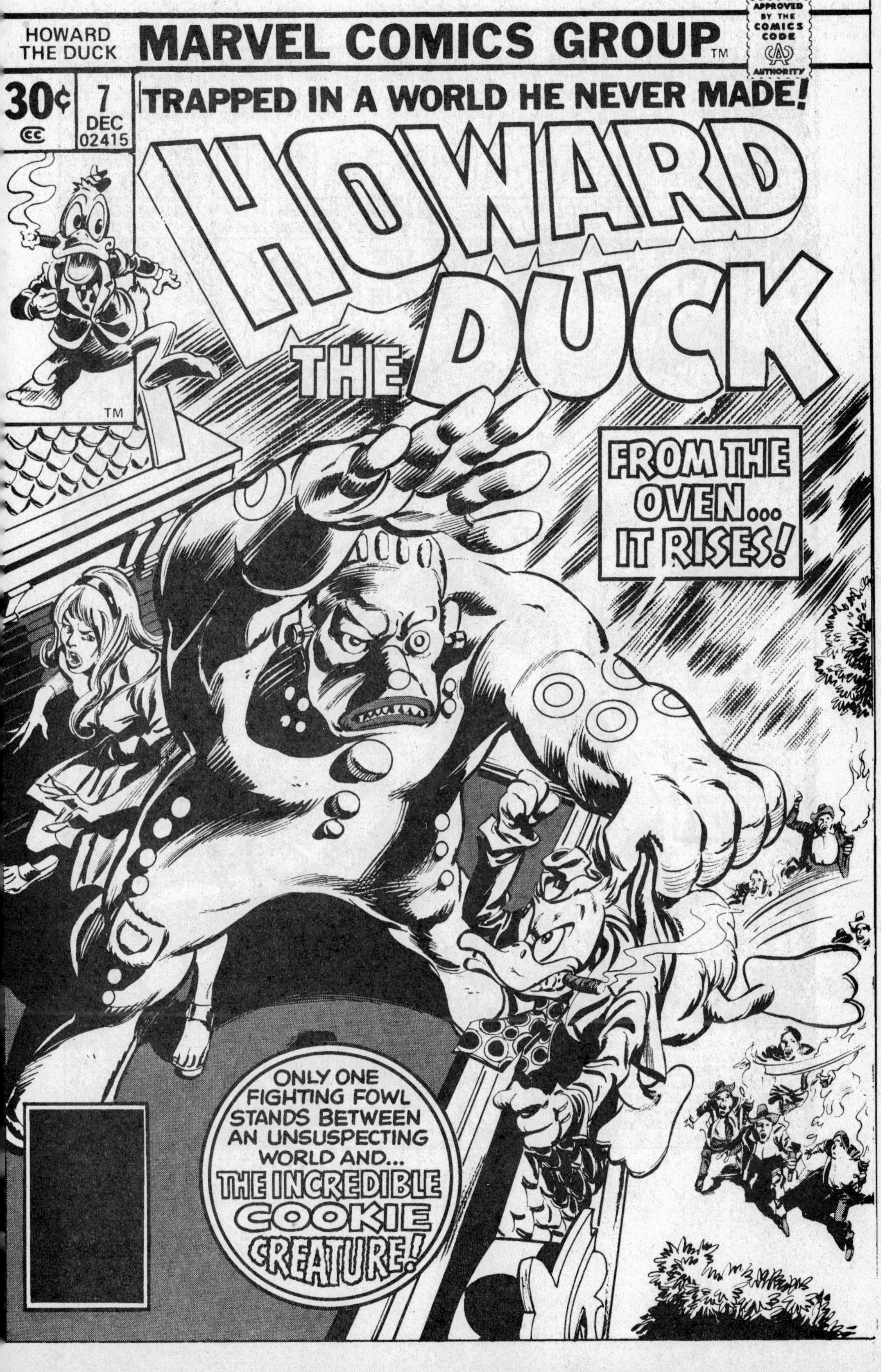
HOWARD THE DUCK
MARVEL COMICS GROUP
APPROVED BY THE COMICS CODE AUTHORITY
30¢
7
DEC
02415
TRAPPED IN A WORLD HE NEVER MADE!
HOWARD THE DUCK
FROM THE OVEN... IT RISES!
ONLY ONE FIGHTING FOWL STANDS BETWEEN AN UNSUSPECTING WORLD AND... THE INCREDIBLE COOKIE CREATURE!

From the time of his hatching, he was...different. A potentially brilliant scholar who dreaded the structured environment of school, he educated himself in the streets, taking whatever work was available, formulating his philosophy of self from what he learned of the world about him. And then the Cosmic Axis shifted...and that world *changed.* Suddenly, he was stranded in a universe he could not fathom. Without warning, he became a strange fowl in an even stranger land.

Stan Lee PRESENTS: HOWARD THE DUCK!™

STEVE GERBER WRITER / GENE COLAN ILLUSTRATOR / STEVE LEIALOHA EMBELLISHER / JIM NOVAK, LETTERER M. SEVERIN, COLORIST / ARCHIE GOODWIN EDITOR

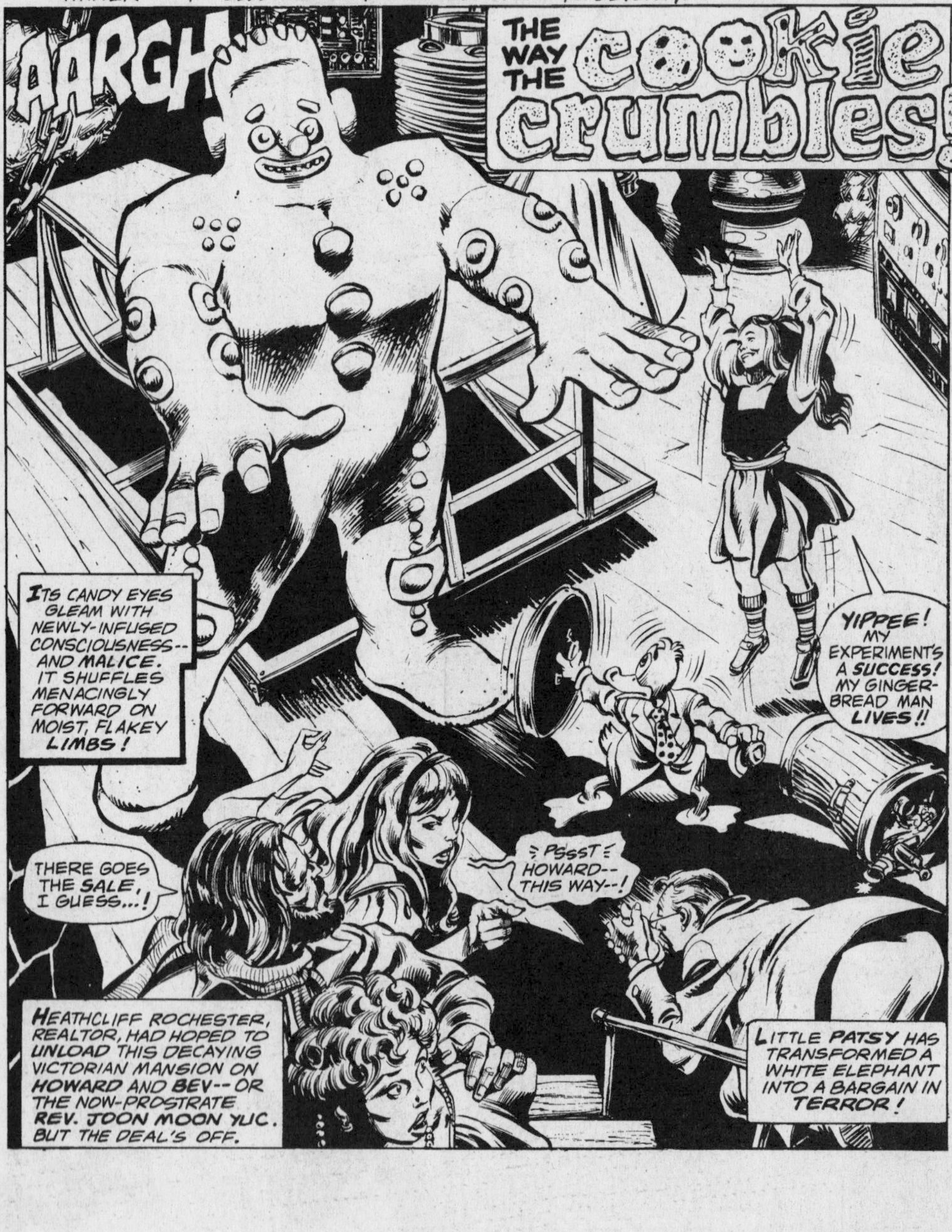
AARGH
THE WAY THE COOKIE CRUMBLES!
ITS CANDY EYES GLEAM WITH NEWLY-INFUSED CONSCIOUSNESS-- AND MALICE. IT SHUFFLES MENACINGLY FORWARD ON MOIST, FLAKEY LIMBS!
YIPPEE! MY EXPERIMENT'S A SUCCESS! MY GINGER-BREAD MAN LIVES!!
THERE GOES THE SALE, I GUESS...!
PSSST HOWARD-- THIS WAY--!
HEATHCLIFF ROCHESTER, REALTOR, HAD HOPED TO UNLOAD THIS DECAYING VICTORIAN MANSION ON HOWARD AND BEV--OR THE NOW-PROSTRATE REV. JOON MOON YUC. BUT THE DEAL'S OFF.
LITTLE PATSY HAS TRANSFORMED A WHITE ELEPHANT INTO A BARGAIN IN TERROR!

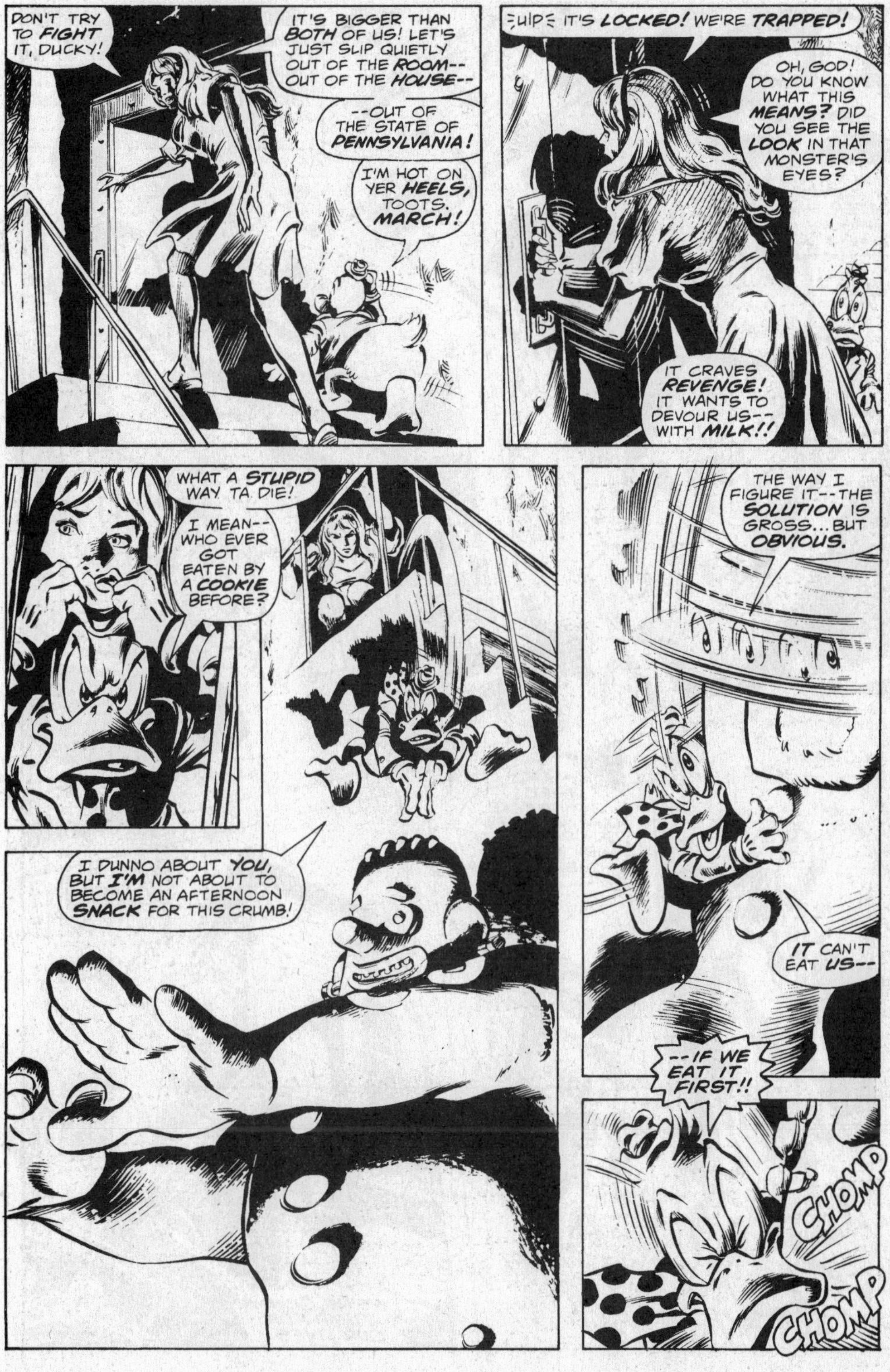
DON'T TRY TO FIGHT IT, DUCKY!
IT'S BIGGER THAN BOTH OF US! LET'S JUST SLIP QUIETLY OUT OF THE ROOM-- OUT OF THE HOUSE--
--OUT OF THE STATE OF PENNSYLVANIA!
I'M HOT ON YER HEELS, TOOTS. MARCH!
IT'S LOCKED! WE'RE TRAPPED!
OH, GOD! DO YOU KNOW WHAT THIS MEANS? DID YOU SEE THE LOOK IN THAT MONSTER'S EYES?
IT CRAVES REVENGE! IT WANTS TO DEVOUR US-- WITH MILK!!
WHAT A STUPID WAY TA DIE!
I MEAN-- WHO EVER GOT EATEN BY A COOKIE BEFORE?
THE WAY I FIGURE IT--THE SOLUTION IS GROSS... BUT OBVIOUS.
I DUNNO ABOUT YOU, BUT I'M NOT ABOUT TO BECOME AN AFTERNOON SNACK FOR THIS CRUMB!
IT CAN'T EAT US--
--IF WE EAT IT FIRST!!
CHOMP
CHOMP

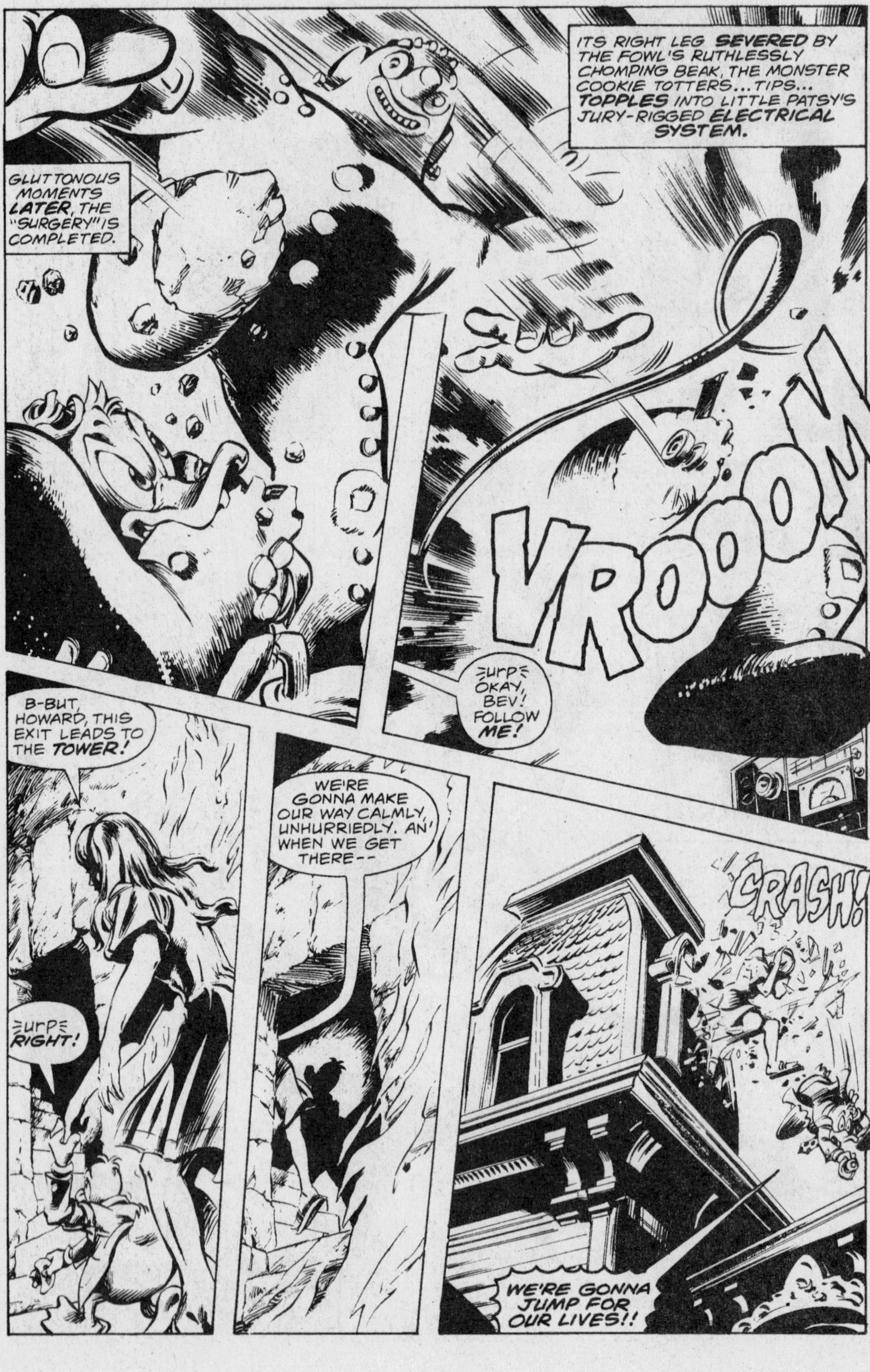
GLUTTONOUS MOMENTS LATER, THE "SURGERY" IS COMPLETED.
ITS RIGHT LEG SEVERED BY THE FOWL'S RUTHLESSLY CHOMPING BEAK, THE MONSTER COOKIE TOTTERS... TIPS... TOPPLES INTO LITTLE PATSY'S JURY-RIGGED ELECTRICAL SYSTEM.
VROOOOM
urp OKAY, BEV! FOLLOW ME!
B-BUT, HOWARD, THIS EXIT LEADS TO THE TOWER!
urp RIGHT!
WE'RE GONNA MAKE OUR WAY CALMLY, UNHURRIEDLY. AN' WHEN WE GET THERE--
CRASH!
WE'RE GONNA JUMP FOR OUR LIVES!!

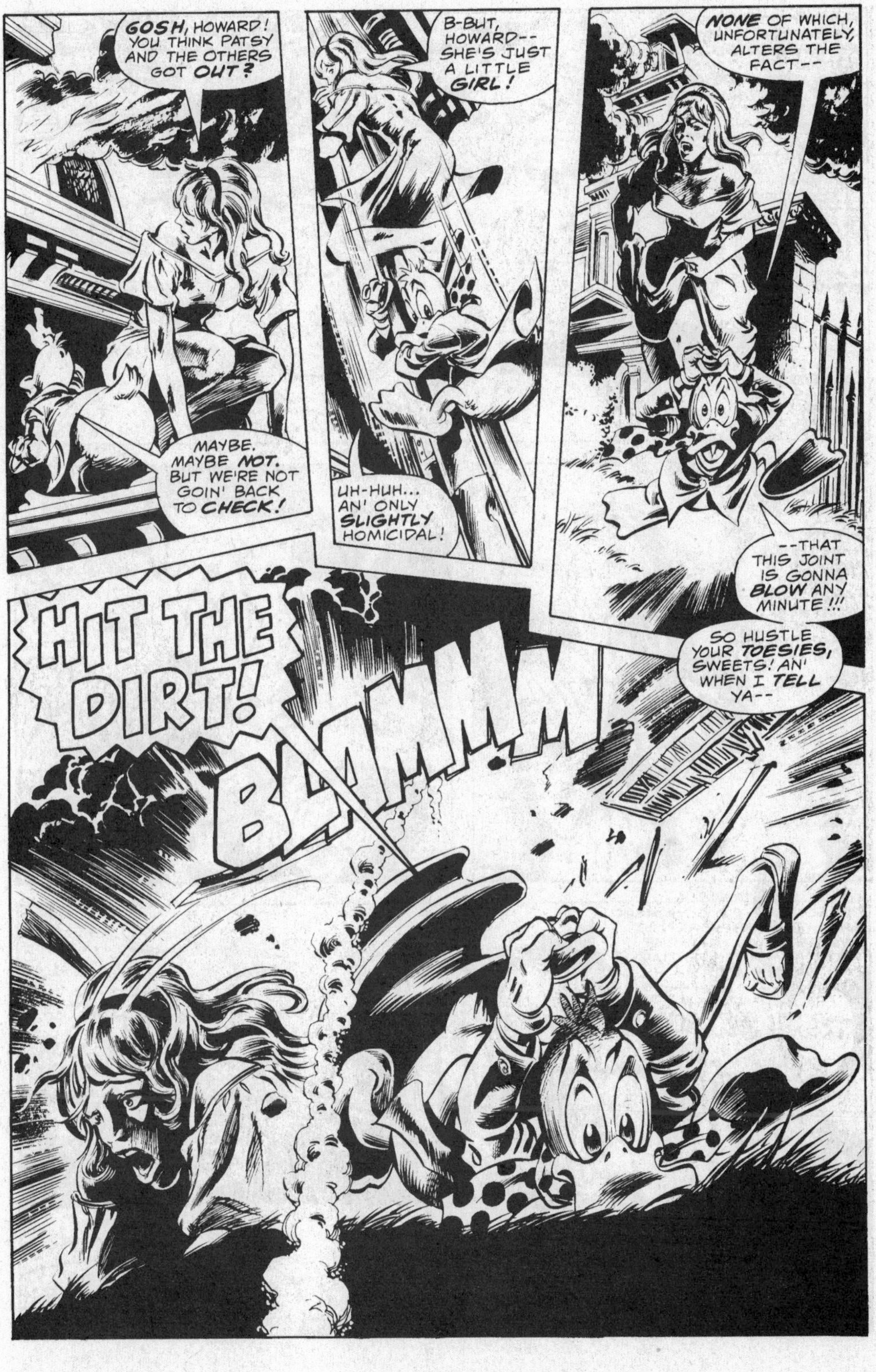

GOSH, HOWARD! YOU THINK PATSY AND THE OTHERS GOT OUT?
MAYBE. MAYBE NOT. BUT WE'RE NOT GOIN' BACK TO CHECK!
B-BUT, HOWARD-- SHE'S JUST A LITTLE GIRL!
UH-HUH... AN' ONLY SLIGHTLY HOMICIDAL!
NONE OF WHICH, UNFORTUNATELY, ALTERS THE FACT--
--THAT THIS JOINT IS GONNA BLOW ANY MINUTE!!!
SO HUSTLE YOUR TOESIES, SWEETS! AN' WHEN I TELL YA--
HIT THE DIRT!
BLAMMM

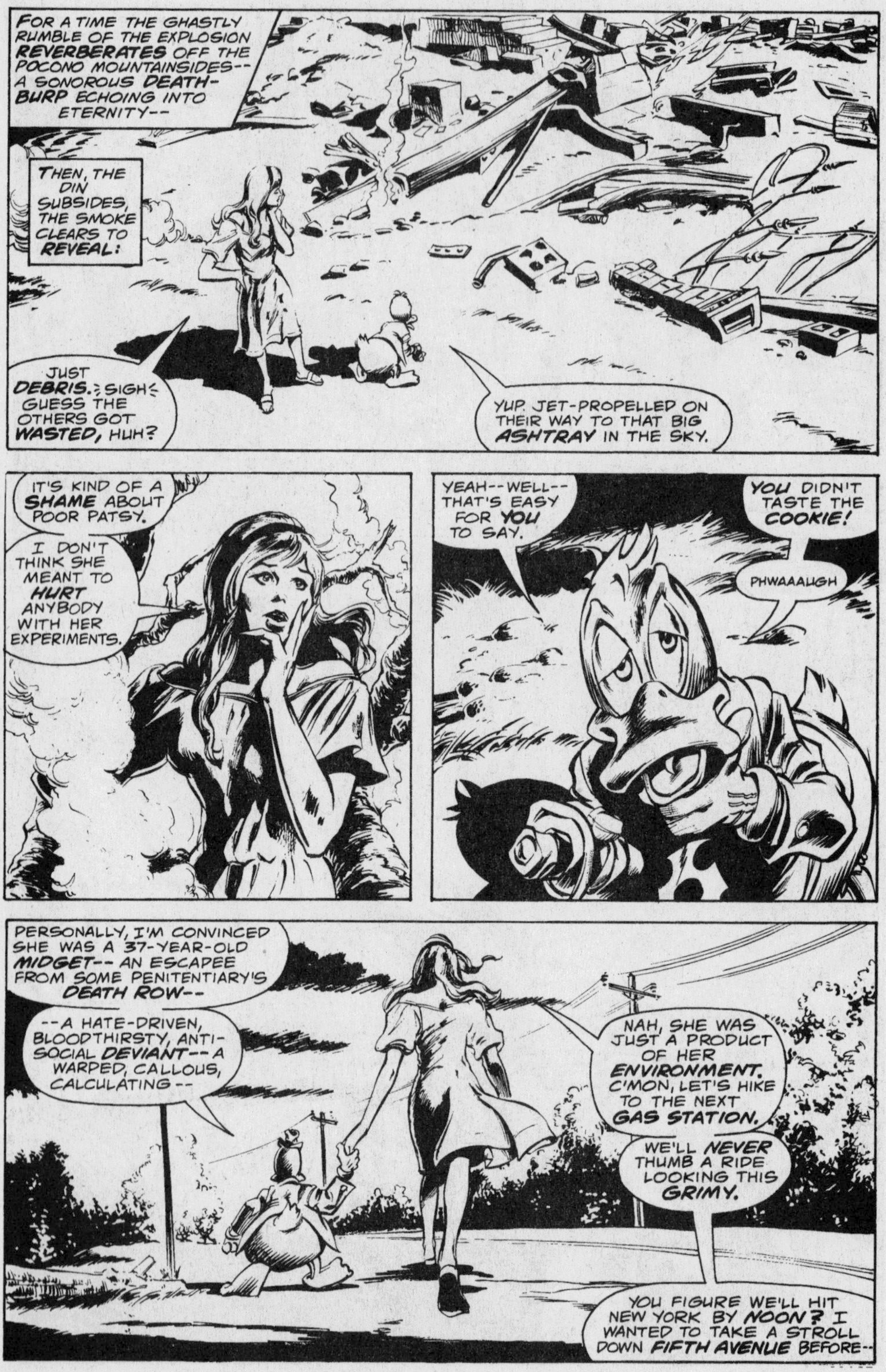

FOR A TIME THE GHASTLY RUMBLE OF THE EXPLOSION REVERBERATES OFF THE POCONO MOUNTAINSIDES-- A SONOROUS DEATH-BURP ECHOING INTO ETERNITY--
THEN, THE DIN SUBSIDES, THE SMOKE CLEARS TO REVEAL:
JUST DEBRIS. SIGH GUESS THE OTHERS GOT WASTED, HUH?
YUP. JET-PROPELLED ON THEIR WAY TO THAT BIG ASHTRAY IN THE SKY.
IT'S KIND OF A SHAME ABOUT POOR PATSY.
I DON'T THINK SHE MEANT TO HURT ANYBODY WITH HER EXPERIMENTS.
YEAH--WELL-- THAT'S EASY FOR YOU TO SAY.
YOU DIDN'T TASTE THE COOKIE!
PHWAAAUGH
PERSONALLY, I'M CONVINCED SHE WAS A 37-YEAR-OLD MIDGET-- AN ESCAPEE FROM SOME PENITENTIARY'S DEATH ROW--
--A HATE-DRIVEN, BLOODTHIRSTY, ANTI-SOCIAL DEVIANT--A WARPED, CALLOUS, CALCULATING--
NAH, SHE WAS JUST A PRODUCT OF HER ENVIRONMENT. C'MON, LET'S HIKE TO THE NEXT GAS STATION.
WE'LL NEVER THUMB A RIDE LOOKING THIS GRIMY.
YOU FIGURE WE'LL HIT NEW YORK BY NOON? I WANTED TO TAKE A STROLL DOWN FIFTH AVENUE BEFORE--

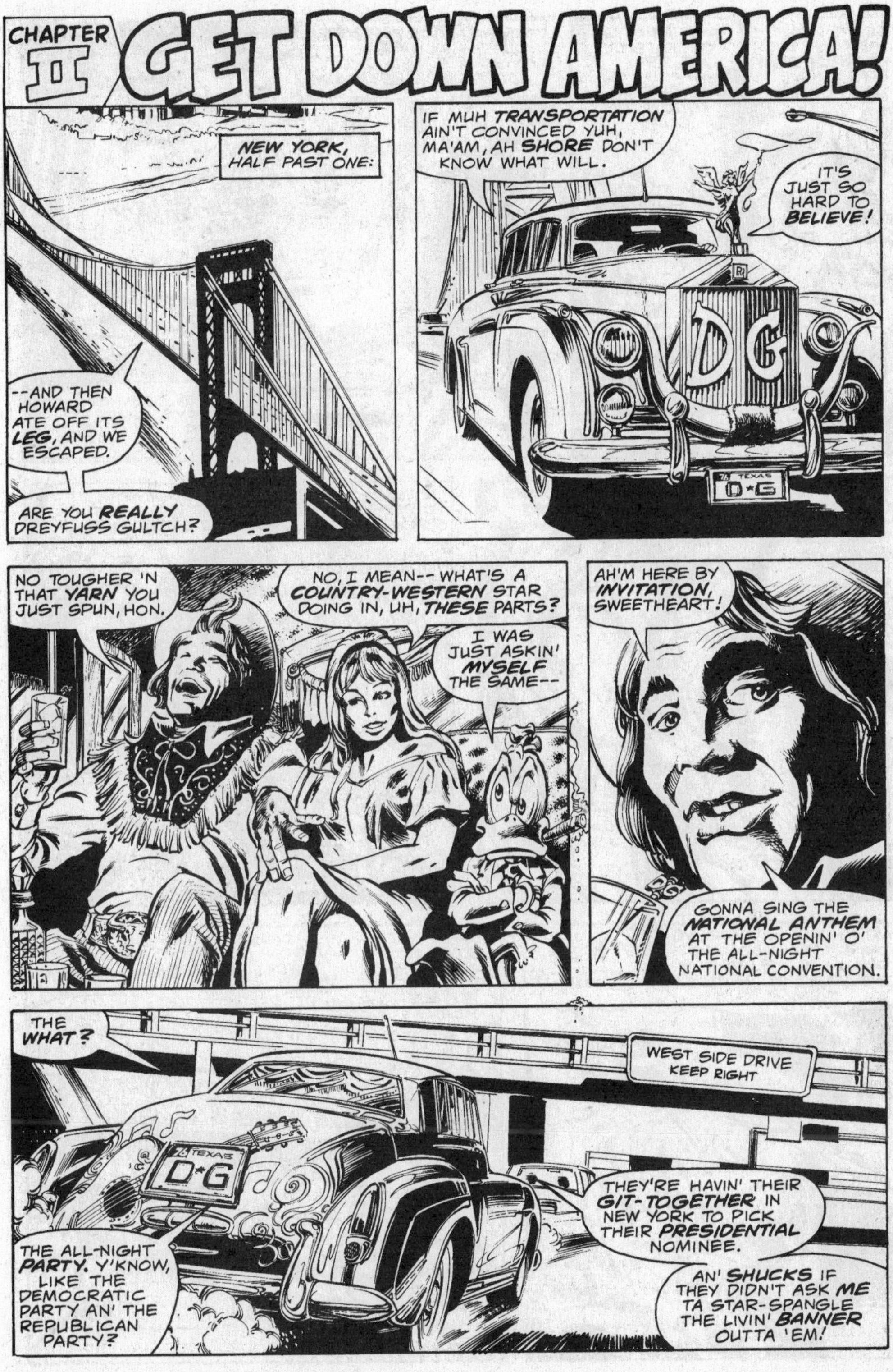
CHAPTER II
GET DOWN AMERICA!
NEW YORK, HALF PAST ONE:
--AND THEN HOWARD ATE OFF ITS LEG, AND WE ESCAPED.
ARE YOU REALLY DREYFUSS GULTCH?
IF MUH TRANSPORTATION AIN'T CONVINCED YUH, MA'AM, AH SHORE DON'T KNOW WHAT WILL.
IT'S JUST SO HARD TO BELIEVE!
'76 TEXAS D*G
NO TOUGHER 'N THAT YARN YOU JUST SPUN, HON.
NO, I MEAN-- WHAT'S A COUNTRY-WESTERN STAR DOING IN, UH, THESE PARTS?
I WAS JUST ASKIN' MYSELF THE SAME--
AH'M HERE BY INVITATION, SWEETHEART!
GONNA SING THE NATIONAL ANTHEM AT THE OPENIN' O' THE ALL-NIGHT NATIONAL CONVENTION.
THE WHAT?
WEST SIDE DRIVE KEEP RIGHT
'76 TEXAS D*G
THE ALL-NIGHT PARTY. Y'KNOW, LIKE THE DEMOCRATIC PARTY AN' THE REPUBLICAN PARTY?
THEY'RE HAVIN' THEIR GIT-TOGETHER IN NEW YORK TO PICK THEIR PRESIDENTIAL NOMINEE.
AN' SHUCKS IF THEY DIDN'T ASK ME TA STAR-SPANGLE THE LIVIN' BANNER OUTTA 'EM!

GEE, I DON'T THINK I'VE EVER HEARD OF *THAT* PARTY. HAVE *YOU*, HOWARD?

DON'T MENTION *POLITICS* TO ME, BEV.

I NEVER *TOUCH* THE STUFF.

IT'S A LAW OF *NATURE*: YOU CAN'T CHANGE ANYBODY'S MIND ABOUT *POLITICS* OR *RELIGION*.

REV. YUC'S BICENTENNIAL PRAYER MEETING AND KOREAN KARATE EXHIBITION NEXT WEEK

SPEAKING OF WHICH... GUESS THEY'LL HAVE TO *CALL OFF* THAT DOUBLE-BONANZA. TOO BAD.

MR. GULTCH, THERE WOULDN'T BE ANY *JOBS* OPEN AT THE CONVENTION, WOULD THERE?

WE'RE FLAT BROKE. WE NEED TO RUSTLE UP SOME QUICK BREAD TO GET AN *APARTMENT*.

WA-A-ALL--

ORDINARILY, AH DON'T LAHK T' USE MAH POWERFUL *INFL'ENCE* THAT WAY--BUT AH S'POSE AH COULD MAKE AN *EXCEPTION*...

...FOR SUCH AN EXCEPTIONAL PAIR AS *YOU*.

HEY, HOWIE--MAYBE WE CAN GITCHA A JOB AS THE *MAIN COURSE* AT THE BANQUET. WHATCHA THINK?

KILL.

HEAH'S THE *HOTEL*. NOW Y'ALL JES' STICK CLOSE *BY ME*, HEAR?

'CAUSE SOON'S AH STEP OUTTA THE DOOR, WE'LL BE *MOBBED*, SEE?

REPORTERS, AUTOGRAPH HOUNDS-- Y'ALL *WATCH*.

WELCOME ALL-NIGHT PARTY

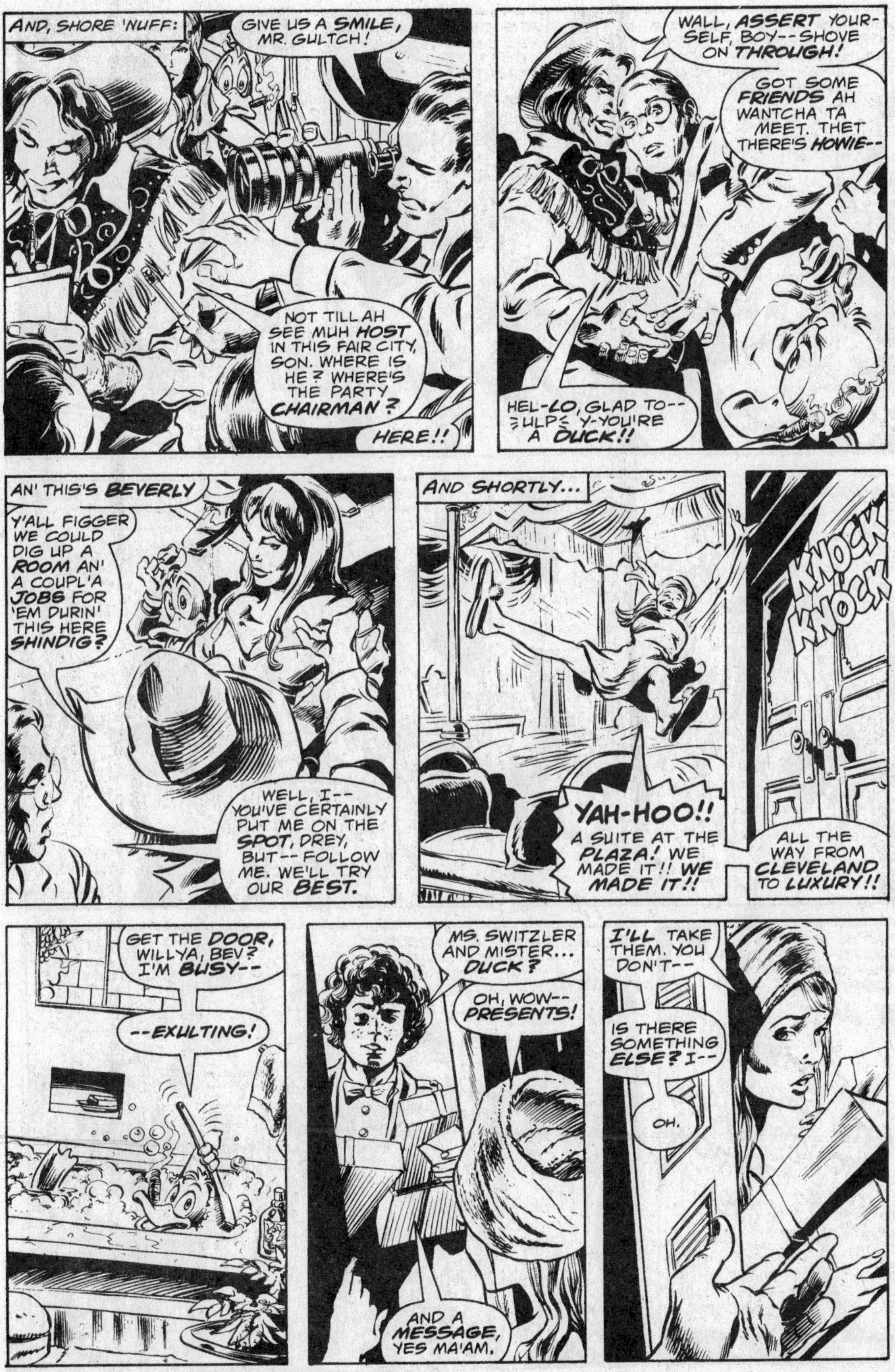
AND, SHORE 'NUFF:
GIVE US A SMILE, MR. GULTCH!
NOT TILL AH SEE MUH HOST IN THIS FAIR CITY, SON. WHERE IS HE? WHERE'S THE PARTY CHAIRMAN?
HERE!!
WALL, ASSERT YOURSELF, BOY--SHOVE ON THROUGH!
GOT SOME FRIENDS AH WANTCHA TA MEET. THET THERE'S HOWIE--
HEL-LO, GLAD TO-- GULP! Y-YOU'RE A DUCK!!
AN' THIS'S BEVERLY
Y'ALL FIGGER WE COULD DIG UP A ROOM AN' A COUPL'A JOBS FOR 'EM DURIN' THIS HERE SHINDIG?
WELL, I-- YOU'VE CERTAINLY PUT ME ON THE SPOT, DREY, BUT--FOLLOW ME. WE'LL TRY OUR BEST.
AND SHORTLY...
YAH-HOO!! A SUITE AT THE PLAZA! WE MADE IT!! WE MADE IT!!
KNOCK KNOCK
ALL THE WAY FROM CLEVELAND TO LUXURY!!
GET THE DOOR, WILLYA, BEV? I'M BUSY--
--EXULTING!
MS. SWITZLER AND MISTER... DUCK?
OH, WOW-- PRESENTS!
AND A MESSAGE, YES MA'AM.
I'LL TAKE THEM. YOU DON'T--
IS THERE SOMETHING ELSE? I--
OH.

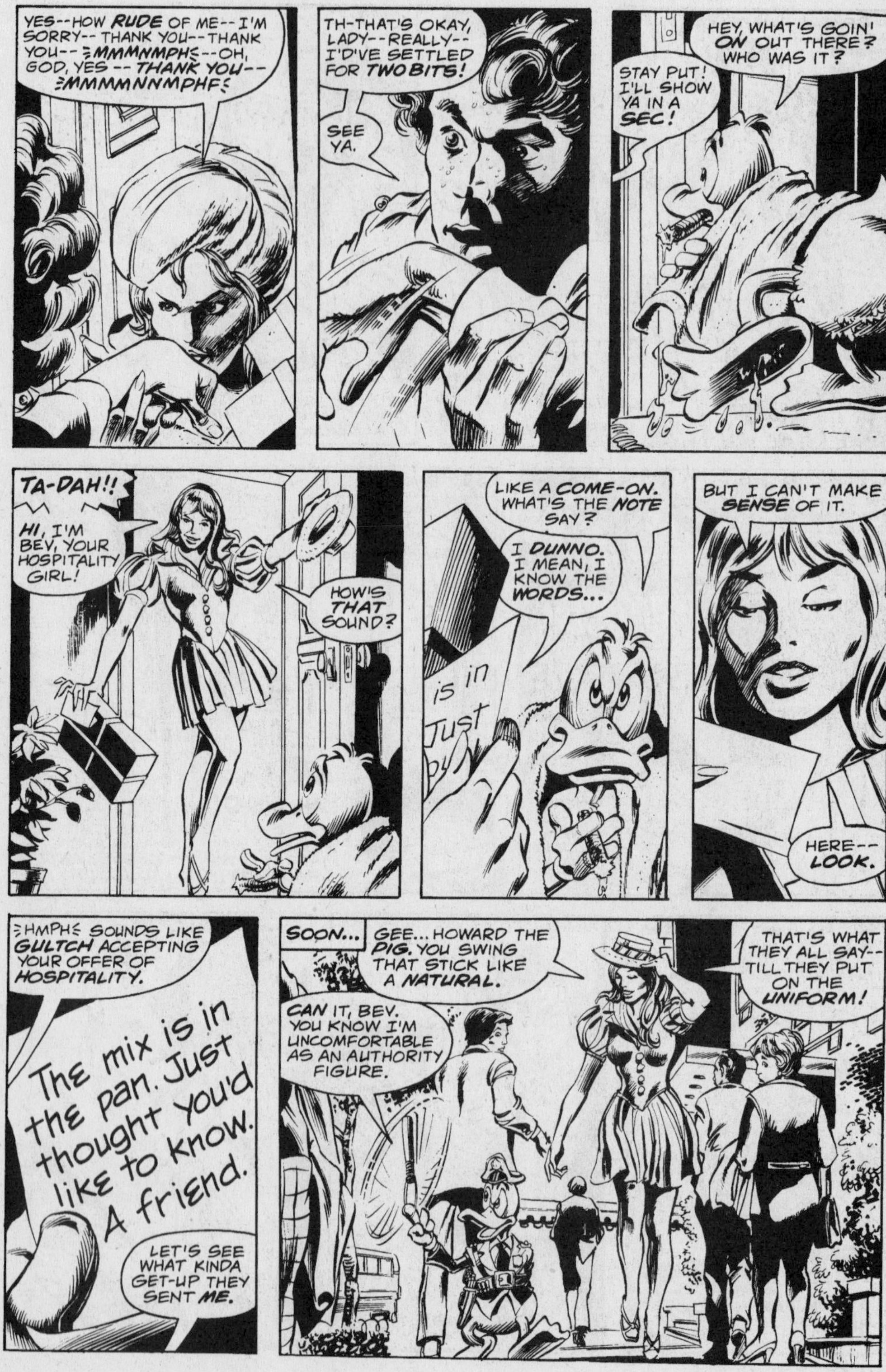

YES--HOW RUDE OF ME--I'M SORRY--THANK YOU--THANK YOU--≡MMMNMPH≡--OH, GOD, YES--THANK YOU--≡MMMMNNMPHF≡
TH-THAT'S OKAY, LADY--REALLY--I'D'VE SETTLED FOR TWO BITS!
SEE YA.
HEY, WHAT'S GOIN' ON OUT THERE? WHO WAS IT?
STAY PUT! I'LL SHOW YA IN A SEC!
TA-DAH!!
HI, I'M BEV, YOUR HOSPITALITY GIRL!
HOW'S THAT SOUND?
LIKE A COME-ON. WHAT'S THE NOTE SAY?
I DUNNO. I MEAN, I KNOW THE WORDS...
is in
Just
BUT I CAN'T MAKE SENSE OF IT.
HERE--LOOK.
≡HMPH≡ SOUNDS LIKE GULTCH ACCEPTING YOUR OFFER OF HOSPITALITY.
The mix is in the pan. Just thought you'd like to know. A friend.
LET'S SEE WHAT KINDA GET-UP THEY SENT ME.
SOON...
GEE... HOWARD THE PIG. YOU SWING THAT STICK LIKE A NATURAL.
THAT'S WHAT THEY ALL SAY--TILL THEY PUT ON THE UNIFORM!
CAN IT, BEV. YOU KNOW I'M UNCOMFORTABLE AS AN AUTHORITY FIGURE.

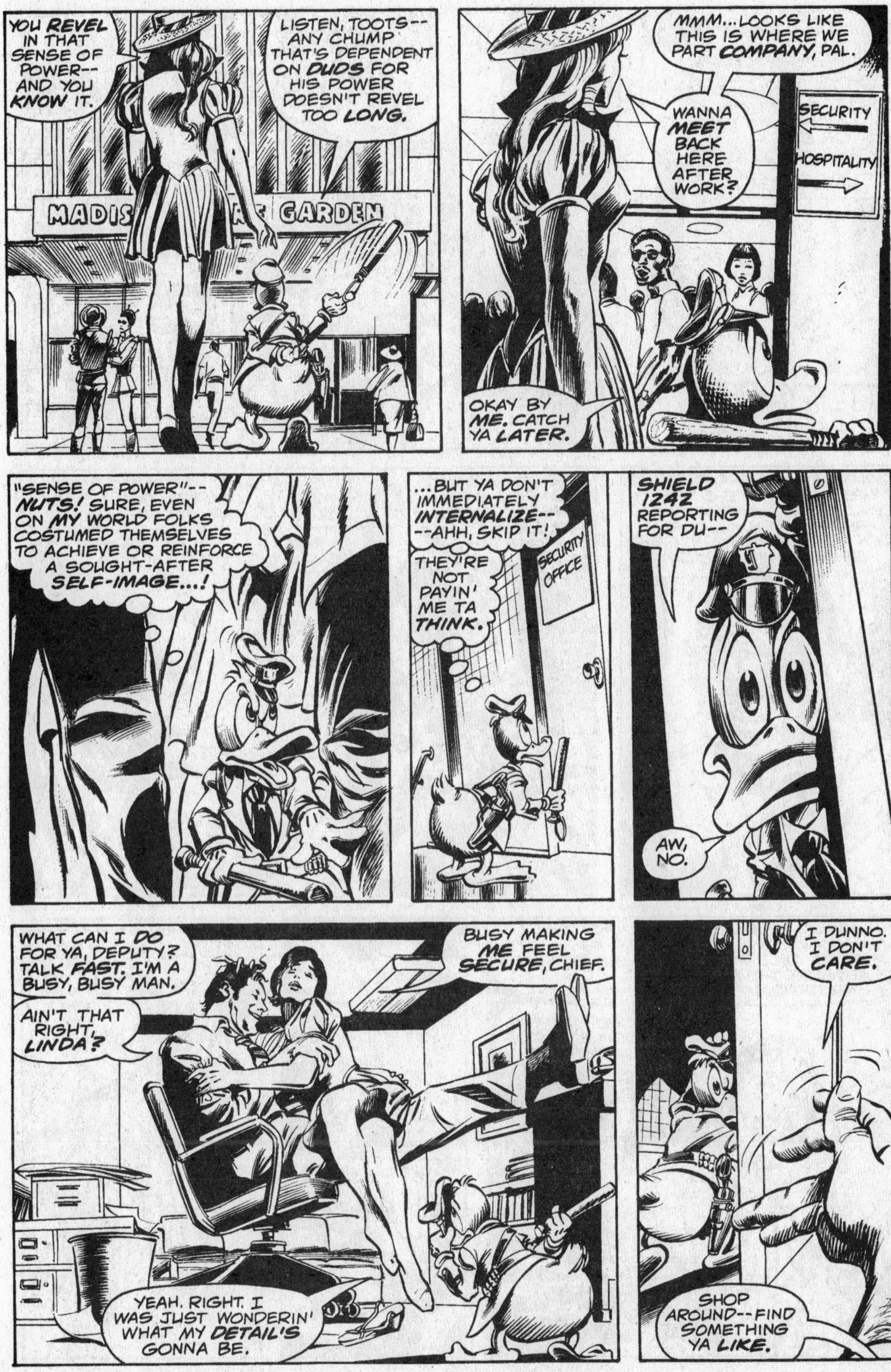
YOU REVEL IN THAT SENSE OF POWER-- AND YOU KNOW IT.
LISTEN, TOOTS-- ANY CHUMP THAT'S DEPENDENT ON DUDS FOR HIS POWER DOESN'T REVEL TOO LONG.
MMM... LOOKS LIKE THIS IS WHERE WE PART COMPANY, PAL.
WANNA MEET BACK HERE AFTER WORK?
SECURITY
HOSPITALITY
OKAY BY ME. CATCH YA LATER.
"SENSE OF POWER"-- NUTS! SURE, EVEN ON MY WORLD FOLKS COSTUMED THEMSELVES TO ACHIEVE OR REINFORCE A SOUGHT-AFTER SELF-IMAGE...!
...BUT YA DON'T IMMEDIATELY INTERNALIZE-- --AHH, SKIP IT!
THEY'RE NOT PAYIN' ME TA THINK.
SECURITY OFFICE
SHIELD 1242 REPORTING FOR DU--
AW, NO.
WHAT CAN I DO FOR YA, DEPUTY? TALK FAST. I'M A BUSY, BUSY MAN.
AIN'T THAT RIGHT, LINDA?
BUSY MAKING ME FEEL SECURE, CHIEF.
YEAH. RIGHT. I WAS JUST WONDERIN' WHAT MY DETAIL'S GONNA BE.
I DUNNO. I DON'T CARE.
SHOP AROUND--FIND SOMETHING YA LIKE.

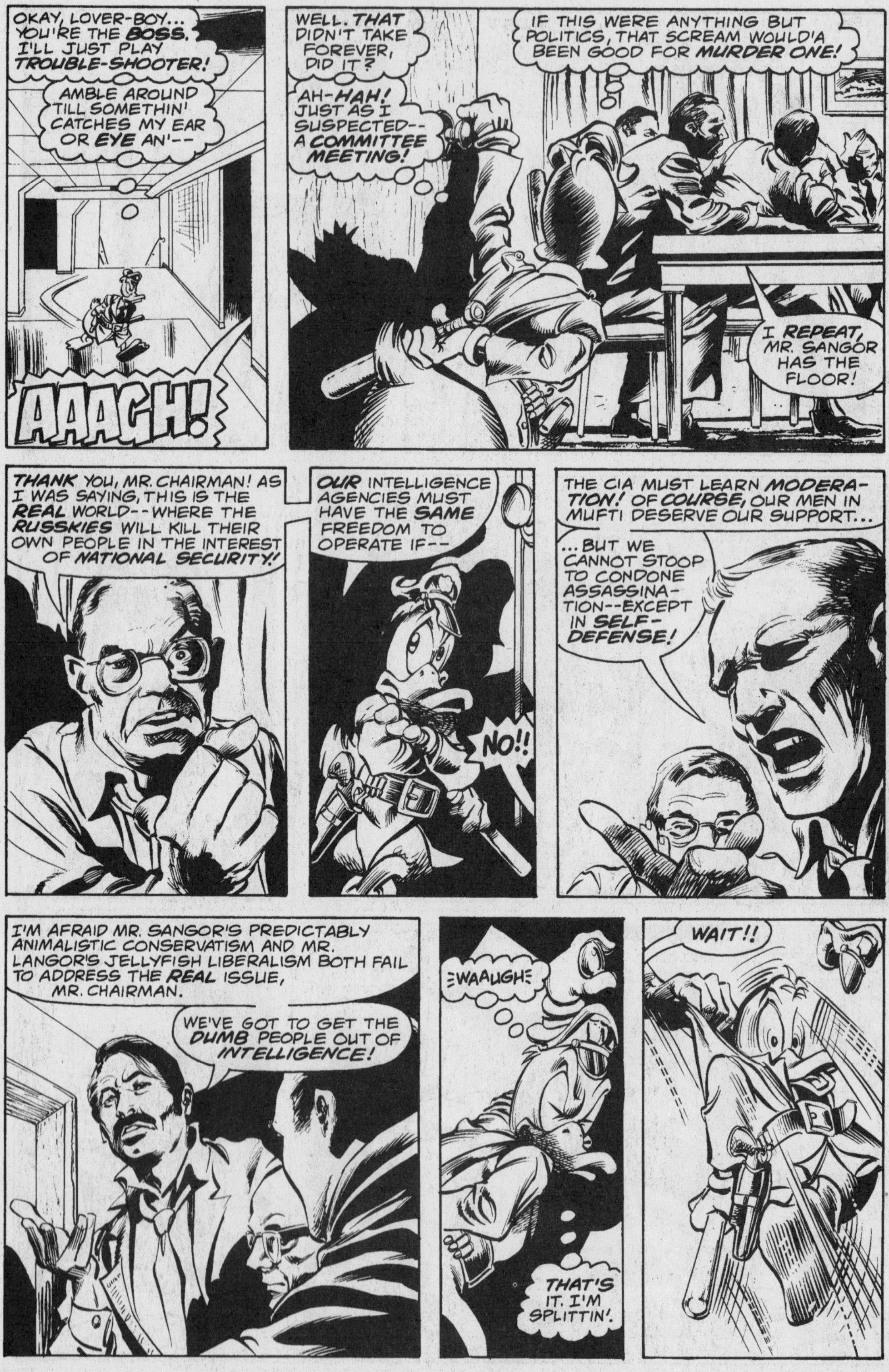
OKAY, LOVER-BOY... YOU'RE THE BOSS. I'LL JUST PLAY TROUBLE-SHOOTER!
AMBLE AROUND TILL SOMETHIN' CATCHES MY EAR OR EYE AN'--
AAAGH!
WELL. THAT DIDN'T TAKE FOREVER, DID IT?
AH-HAH! JUST AS I SUSPECTED-- A COMMITTEE MEETING!
IF THIS WERE ANYTHING BUT POLITICS, THAT SCREAM WOULD'A BEEN GOOD FOR MURDER ONE!
I REPEAT, MR. SANGOR HAS THE FLOOR!
THANK YOU, MR. CHAIRMAN! AS I WAS SAYING, THIS IS THE REAL WORLD--WHERE THE RUSSKIES WILL KILL THEIR OWN PEOPLE IN THE INTEREST OF NATIONAL SECURITY!
OUR INTELLIGENCE AGENCIES MUST HAVE THE SAME FREEDOM TO OPERATE IF--
NO!!
THE CIA MUST LEARN MODERATION! OF COURSE, OUR MEN IN MUFTI DESERVE OUR SUPPORT...
...BUT WE CANNOT STOOP TO CONDONE ASSASSINATION--EXCEPT IN SELF-DEFENSE!
I'M AFRAID MR. SANGOR'S PREDICTABLY ANIMALISTIC CONSERVATISM AND MR. LANGOR'S JELLYFISH LIBERALISM BOTH FAIL TO ADDRESS THE REAL ISSUE, MR. CHAIRMAN.
WE'VE GOT TO GET THE DUMB PEOPLE OUT OF INTELLIGENCE!
WAAUGH
THAT'S IT. I'M SPLITTIN'.
WAIT!!

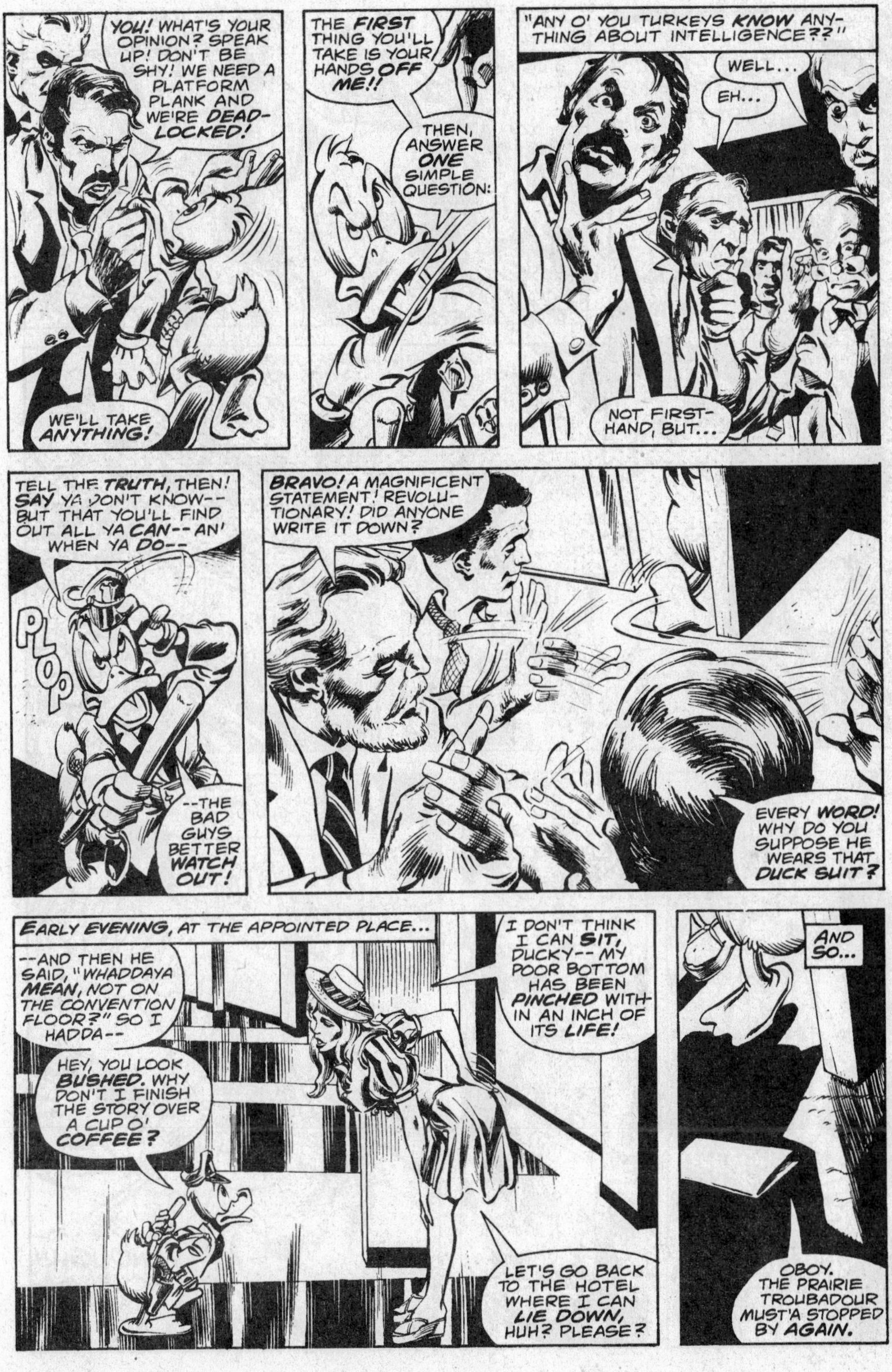

YOU! WHAT'S YOUR OPINION? SPEAK UP! DON'T BE SHY! WE NEED A PLATFORM PLANK AND WE'RE DEAD-LOCKED!
WE'LL TAKE ANYTHING!
THE FIRST THING YOU'LL TAKE IS YOUR HANDS OFF ME!!
THEN, ANSWER ONE SIMPLE QUESTION:
"ANY O' YOU TURKEYS KNOW ANY-THING ABOUT INTELLIGENCE??"
WELL...
EH...
NOT FIRST-HAND, BUT...
TELL THE TRUTH, THEN! SAY YA DON'T KNOW-- BUT THAT YOU'LL FIND OUT ALL YA CAN-- AN' WHEN YA DO--
PLOP
--THE BAD GUYS BETTER WATCH OUT!
BRAVO! A MAGNIFICENT STATEMENT! REVOLU-TIONARY! DID ANYONE WRITE IT DOWN?
EVERY WORD! WHY DO YOU SUPPOSE HE WEARS THAT DUCK SUIT?
EARLY EVENING, AT THE APPOINTED PLACE...
--AND THEN HE SAID, "WHADDAYA MEAN, NOT ON THE CONVENTION FLOOR?" SO I HADDA--
I DON'T THINK I CAN SIT, DUCKY-- MY POOR BOTTOM HAS BEEN PINCHED WITH-IN AN INCH OF ITS LIFE!
HEY, YOU LOOK BUSHED. WHY DON'T I FINISH THE STORY OVER A CUP O' COFFEE?
LET'S GO BACK TO THE HOTEL WHERE I CAN LIE DOWN, HUH? PLEASE?
AND SO...
OBOY. THE PRAIRIE TROUBADOUR MUST'A STOPPED BY AGAIN.

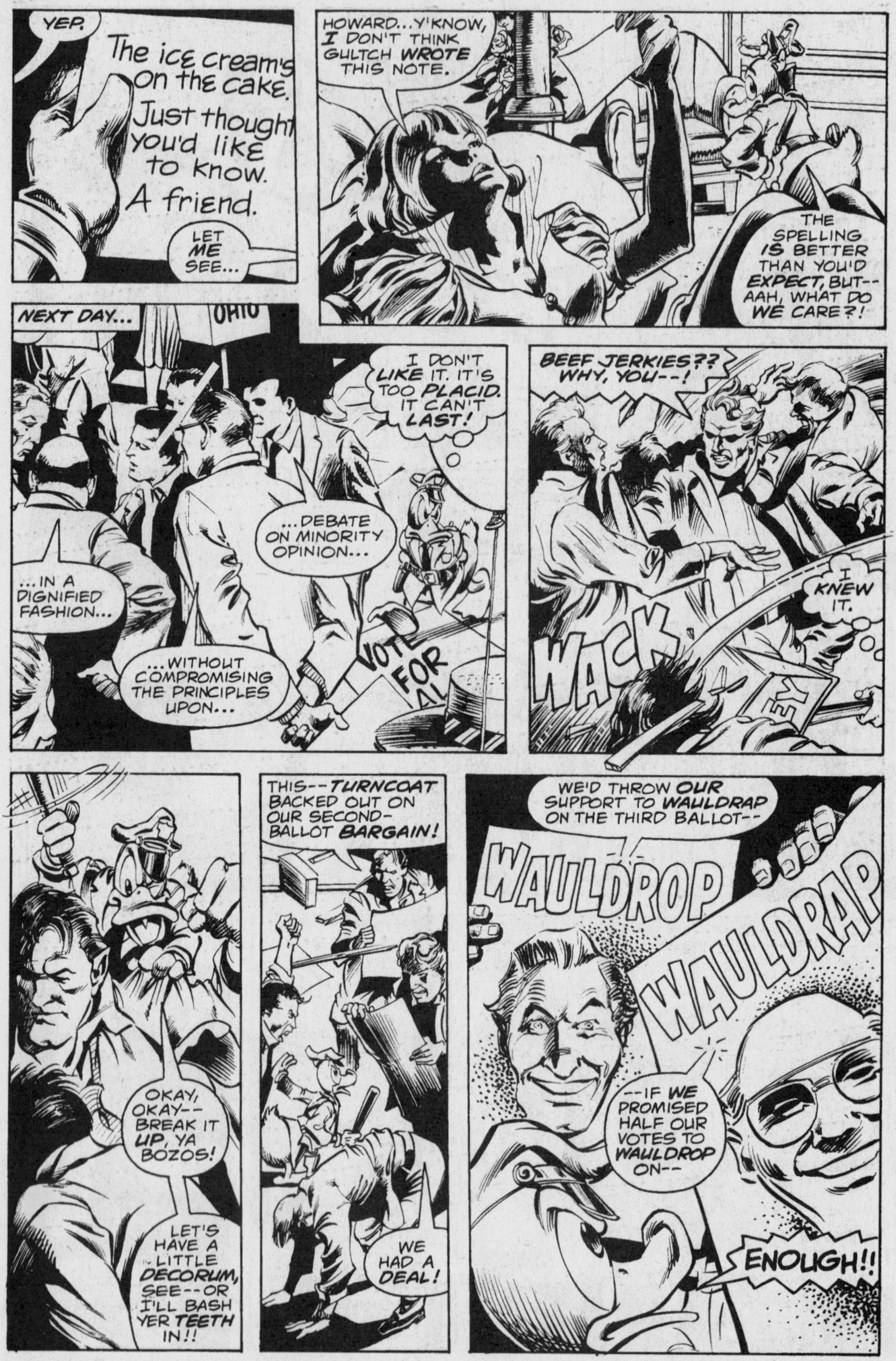
YEP.
The ice cream's on the cake. Just thought you'd like to know. A friend.
LET ME SEE...
HOWARD...Y'KNOW, I DON'T THINK GULTCH WROTE THIS NOTE.
THE SPELLING IS BETTER THAN YOU'D EXPECT, BUT--AAH, WHAT DO WE CARE?!
NEXT DAY...
OHIO
I DON'T LIKE IT. IT'S TOO PLACID. IT CAN'T LAST!
...DEBATE ON MINORITY OPINION...
...IN A DIGNIFIED FASHION...
...WITHOUT COMPROMISING THE PRINCIPLES UPON...
VOTE FOR AL
BEEF JERKIES?? WHY, YOU--!
I KNEW IT.
WACK
OKAY, OKAY--BREAK IT UP, YA BOZOS!
LET'S HAVE A LITTLE DECORUM, SEE--OR I'LL BASH YER TEETH IN!!
THIS--TURNCOAT BACKED OUT ON OUR SECOND-BALLOT BARGAIN!
WE HAD A DEAL!
WE'D THROW OUR SUPPORT TO WAULDRAP ON THE THIRD BALLOT--
WAULDROP
WAULDRAP
--IF WE PROMISED HALF OUR VOTES TO WAULDROP ON--
ENOUGH!!

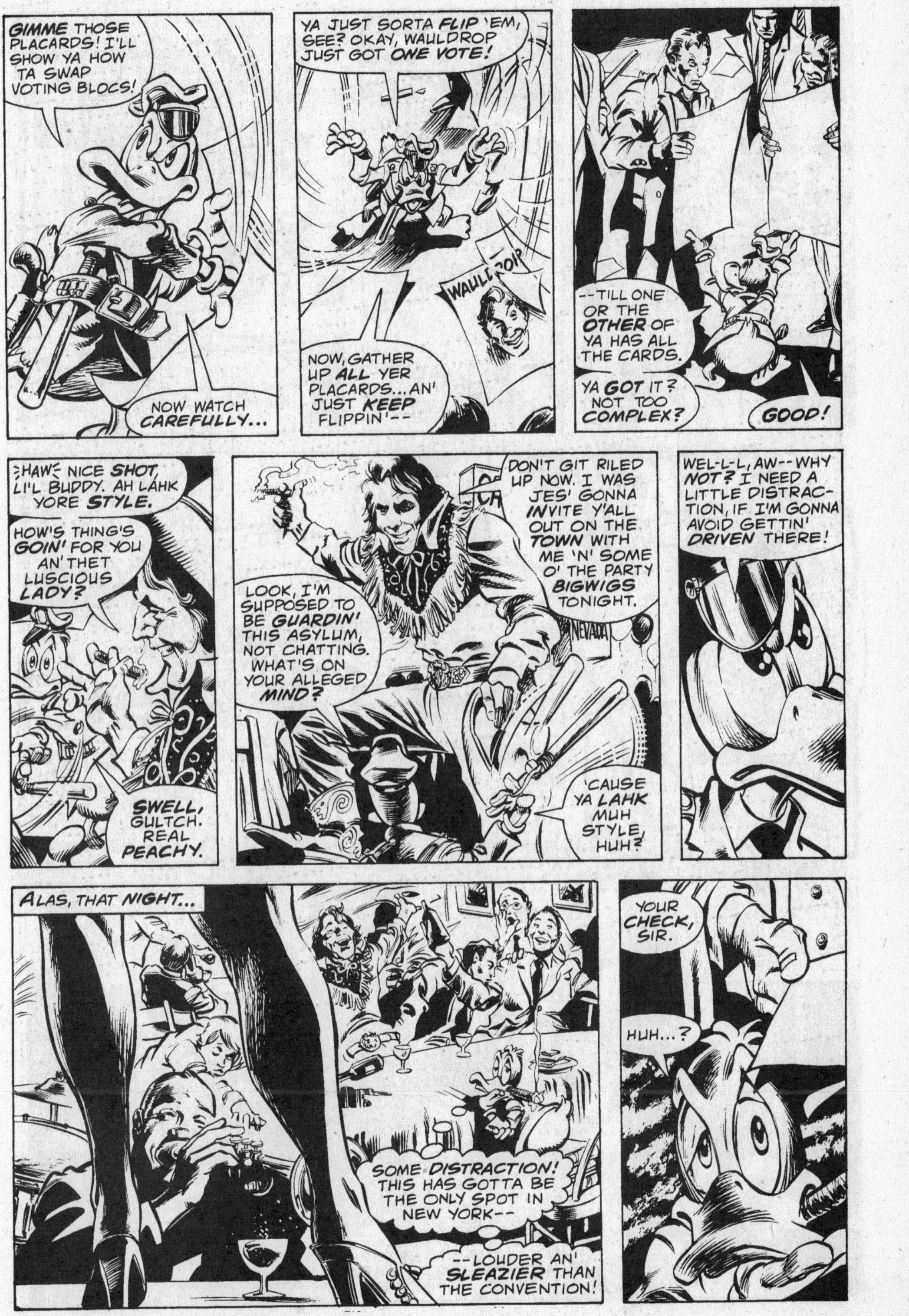
GIMME THOSE PLACARDS! I'LL SHOW YA HOW TA SWAP VOTING BLOCS!
NOW WATCH CAREFULLY...
YA JUST SORTA FLIP 'EM, SEE? OKAY, WAULDROP JUST GOT ONE VOTE!
WAULDROP
NOW, GATHER UP ALL YER PLACARDS... AN' JUST KEEP FLIPPIN'--
--TILL ONE OR THE OTHER OF YA HAS ALL THE CARDS.
YA GOT IT? NOT TOO COMPLEX?
GOOD!
HAW! NICE SHOT, LI'L BUDDY. AH LAHK YORE STYLE.
HOW'S THING'S GOIN' FOR YOU AN' THET LUSCIOUS LADY?
SWELL, GULTCH. REAL PEACHY.
DON'T GIT RILED UP NOW. I WAS JES' GONNA INVITE Y'ALL OUT ON THE TOWN WITH ME 'N' SOME O' THE PARTY BIGWIGS TONIGHT.
LOOK, I'M SUPPOSED TO BE GUARDIN' THIS ASYLUM, NOT CHATTING. WHAT'S ON YOUR ALLEGED MIND?
NEVADA
'CAUSE YA LAHK MUH STYLE, HUH?
WEL-L-L, AW--WHY NOT? I NEED A LITTLE DISTRACTION, IF I'M GONNA AVOID GETTIN' DRIVEN THERE!
ALAS, THAT NIGHT...
SOME DISTRACTION! THIS HAS GOTTA BE THE ONLY SPOT IN NEW YORK--
--LOUDER AN' SLEAZIER THAN THE CONVENTION!
YOUR CHECK, SIR.
HUH...?

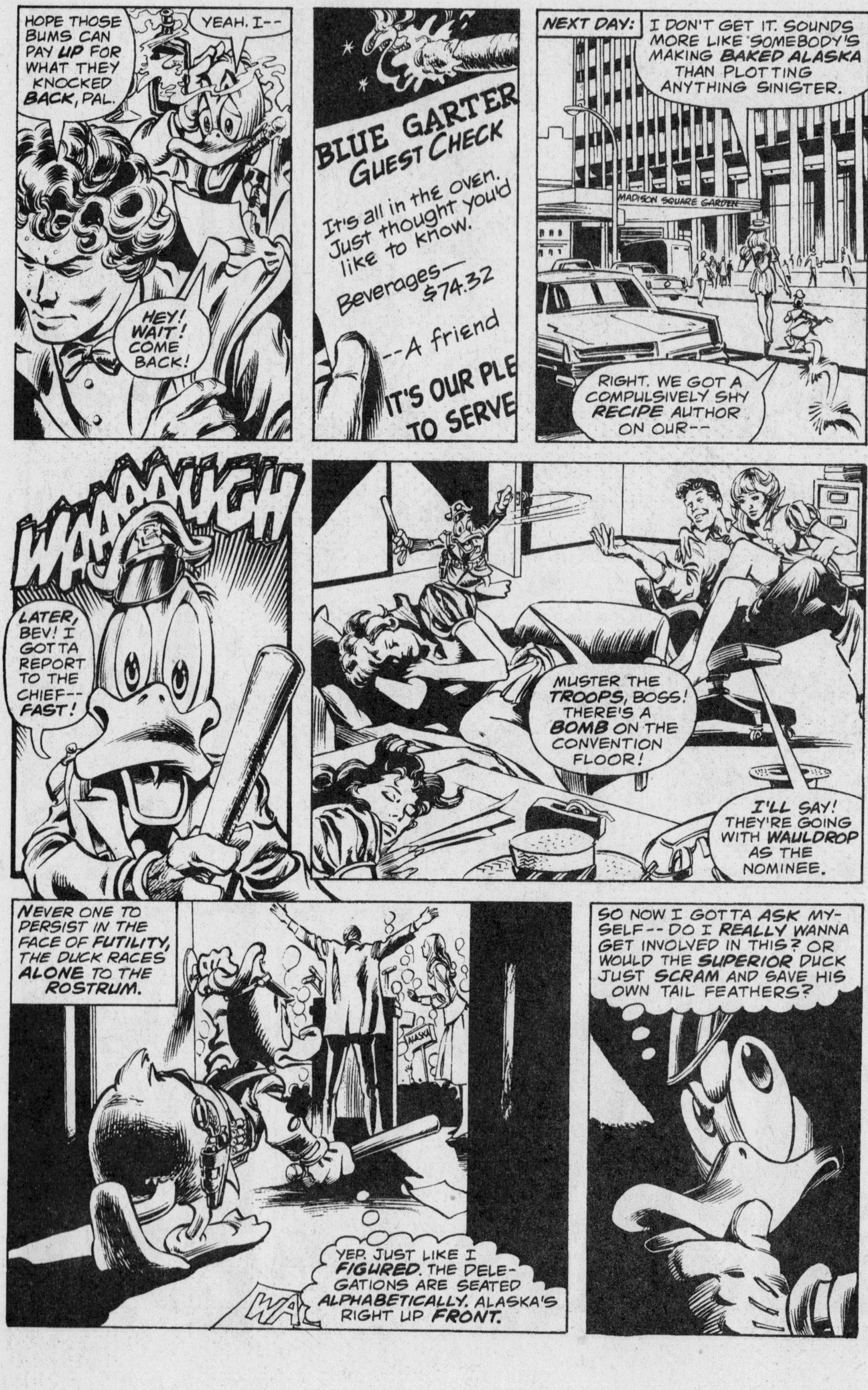

HOPE THOSE BUMS CAN PAY UP FOR WHAT THEY KNOCKED BACK, PAL.
YEAH. I--
HEY! WAIT! COME BACK!
BLUE GARTER GUEST CHECK
It's all in the oven. Just thought you'd like to know.
Beverages— $74.32
--A friend
IT'S OUR PLE
TO SERVE
NEXT DAY:
I DON'T GET IT. SOUNDS MORE LIKE SOMEBODY'S MAKING BAKED ALASKA THAN PLOTTING ANYTHING SINISTER.
MADISON SQUARE GARDEN
RIGHT. WE GOT A COMPULSIVELY SHY RECIPE AUTHOR ON OUR--
WAAAAUGH
LATER, BEV! I GOTTA REPORT TO THE CHIEF--FAST!
MUSTER THE TROOPS, BOSS! THERE'S A BOMB ON THE CONVENTION FLOOR!
I'LL SAY! THEY'RE GOING WITH WAULDROP AS THE NOMINEE.
NEVER ONE TO PERSIST IN THE FACE OF FUTILITY, THE DUCK RACES ALONE TO THE ROSTRUM.
ALASKA
YEP. JUST LIKE I FIGURED. THE DELEGATIONS ARE SEATED ALPHABETICALLY. ALASKA'S RIGHT UP FRONT.
WA
SO NOW I GOTTA ASK MYSELF-- DO I REALLY WANNA GET INVOLVED IN THIS? OR WOULD THE SUPERIOR DUCK JUST SCRAM AND SAVE HIS OWN TAIL FEATHERS?

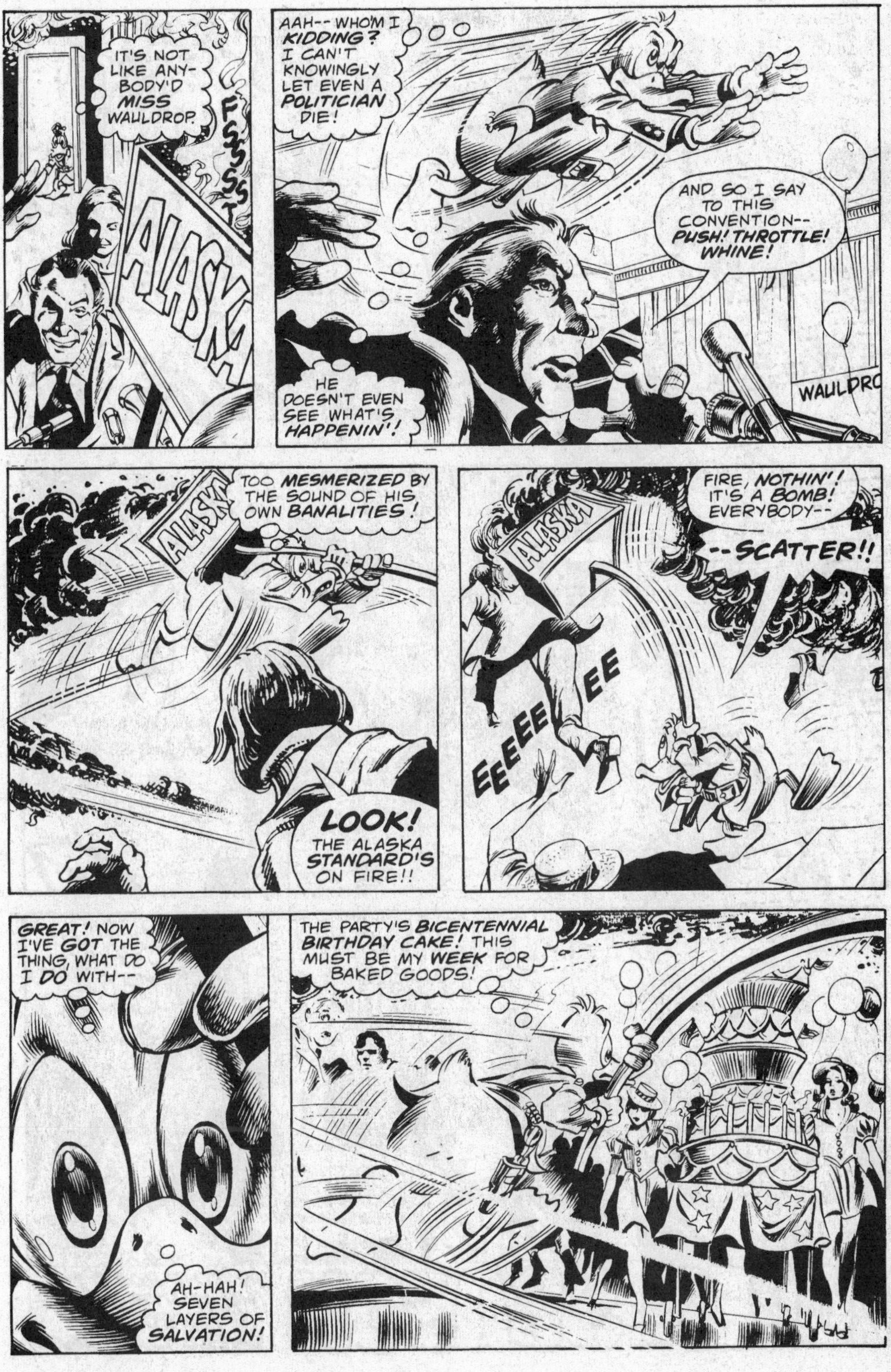
IT'S NOT LIKE ANY-BODY'D MISS WAULDROP.
FSSSST
ALASKA
AAH-- WHO'M I KIDDING? I CAN'T KNOWINGLY LET EVEN A POLITICIAN DIE!
AND SO I SAY TO THIS CONVENTION-- PUSH! THROTTLE! WHINE!
HE DOESN'T EVEN SEE WHAT'S HAPPENIN'!
WAULDRO
TOO MESMERIZED BY THE SOUND OF HIS OWN BANALITIES!
ALASKA
LOOK! THE ALASKA STANDARD'S ON FIRE!!
FIRE, NOTHIN'! IT'S A BOMB! EVERYBODY--
--SCATTER!!
ALASKA
EEEEEEEE
GREAT! NOW I'VE GOT THE THING, WHAT DO I DO WITH--
AH-HAH! SEVEN LAYERS OF SALVATION!
THE PARTY'S BICENTENNIAL BIRTHDAY CAKE! THIS MUST BE MY WEEK FOR BAKED GOODS!

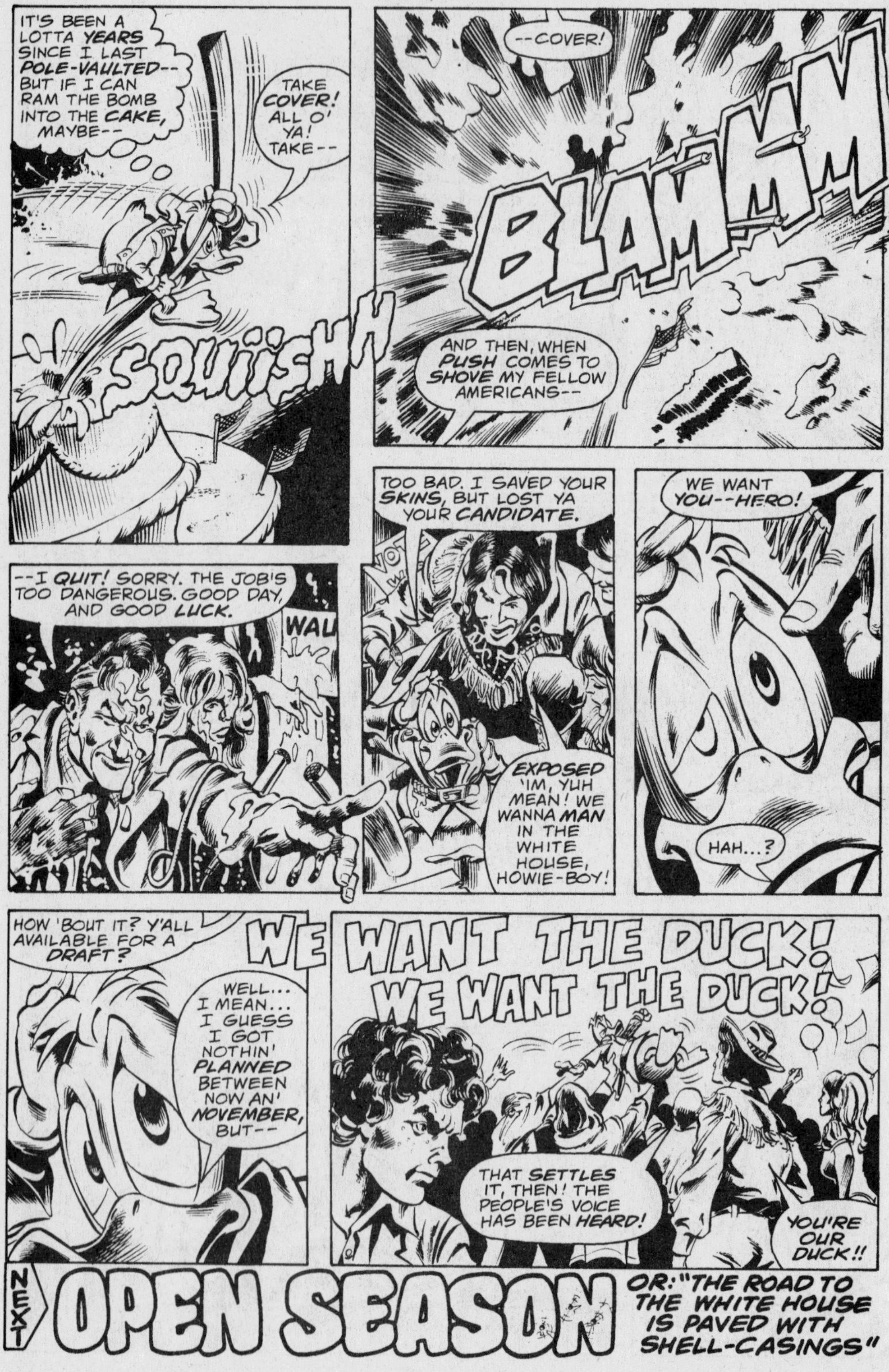

IT'S BEEN A LOTTA YEARS SINCE I LAST POLE-VAULTED-- BUT IF I CAN RAM THE BOMB INTO THE CAKE, MAYBE--
TAKE COVER! ALL O' YA! TAKE--
SQUIISHH
--COVER!
BLAMMM
AND THEN, WHEN PUSH COMES TO SHOVE MY FELLOW AMERICANS--
--I QUIT! SORRY. THE JOB'S TOO DANGEROUS. GOOD DAY, AND GOOD LUCK.
TOO BAD. I SAVED YOUR SKINS, BUT LOST YA YOUR CANDIDATE.
EXPOSED 'IM, YUH MEAN! WE WANNA MAN IN THE WHITE HOUSE, HOWIE-BOY!
WE WANT YOU--HERO!
HAH...?
HOW 'BOUT IT? Y'ALL AVAILABLE FOR A DRAFT?
WELL... I MEAN... I GUESS I GOT NOTHIN' PLANNED BETWEEN NOW AN' NOVEMBER, BUT--
WE WANT THE DUCK! WE WANT THE DUCK!
THAT SETTLES IT, THEN! THE PEOPLE'S VOICE HAS BEEN HEARD!
YOU'RE OUR DUCK!!
NEXT
OPEN SEASON
OR: "THE ROAD TO THE WHITE HOUSE IS PAVED WITH SHELL-CASINGS"

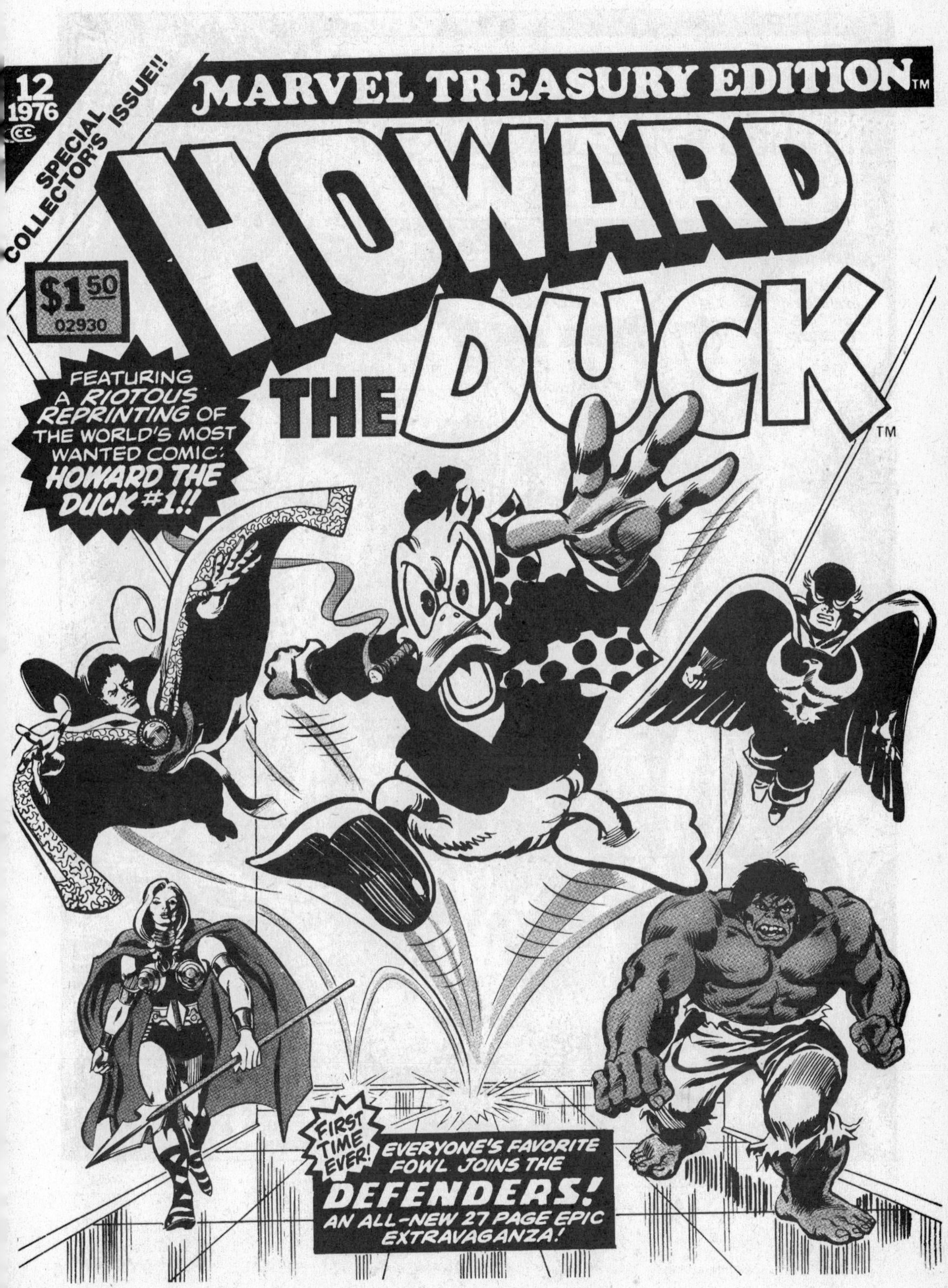

12
1976
CC
SPECIAL COLLECTOR'S ISSUE!!
MARVEL TREASURY EDITION™
HOWARD THE DUCK™
$1.50
02930
FEATURING A RIOTOUS REPRINTING OF THE WORLD'S MOST WANTED COMIC: HOWARD THE DUCK #1!!
FIRST TIME EVER!
EVERYONE'S FAVORITE FOWL JOINS THE DEFENDERS!
AN ALL-NEW 27 PAGE EPIC EXTRAVAGANZA!

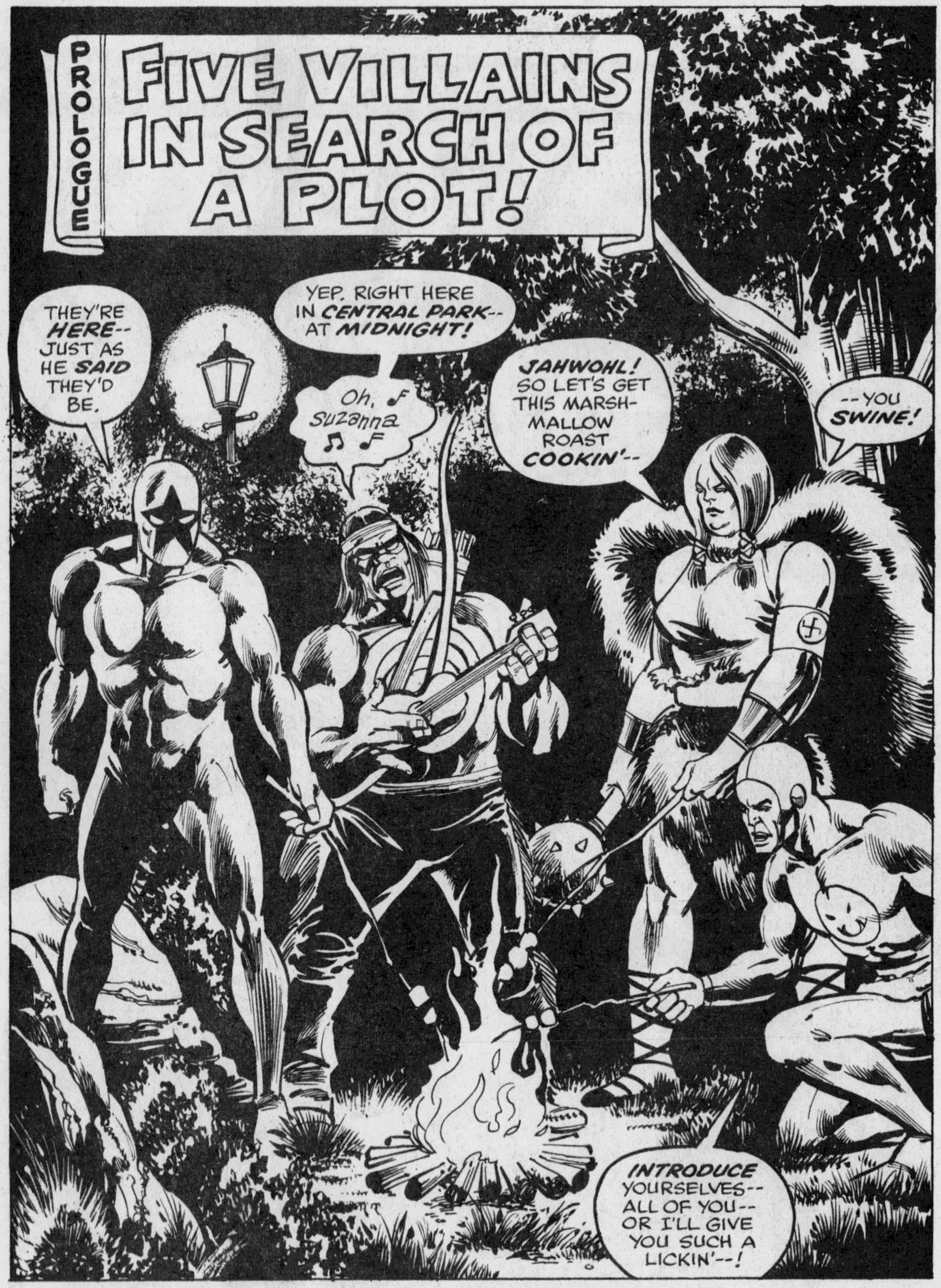
PROLOGUE
FIVE VILLAINS IN SEARCH OF A PLOT!
THEY'RE HERE-- JUST AS HE SAID THEY'D BE.
YEP. RIGHT HERE IN CENTRAL PARK-- AT MIDNIGHT!
Oh, Suzanna
JAHWOHL! SO LET'S GET THIS MARSH-MALLOW ROAST COOKIN'--
--YOU SWINE!
INTRODUCE YOURSELVES-- ALL OF YOU-- OR I'LL GIVE YOU SUCH A LICKIN'--!

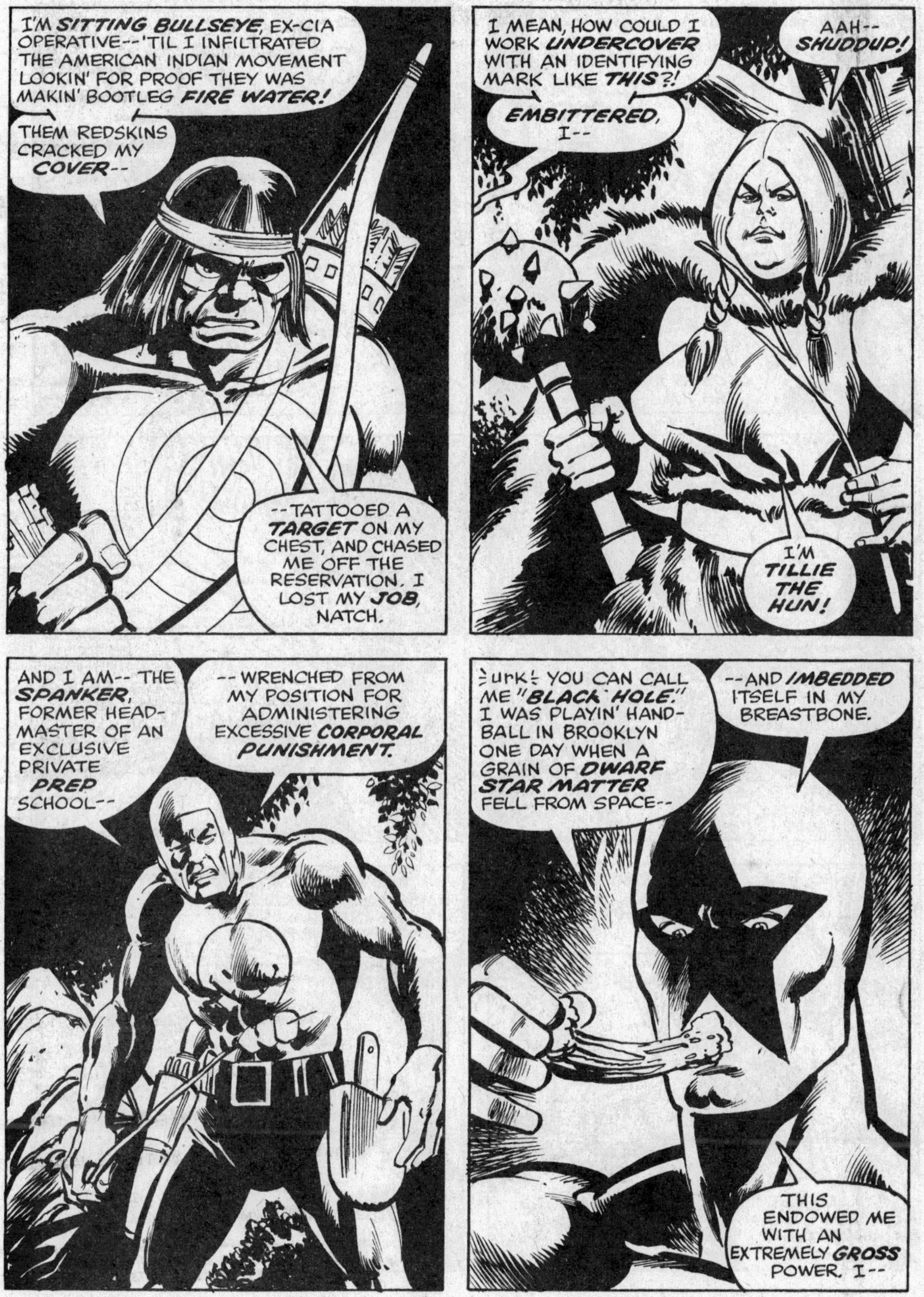
I'M SITTING BULLSEYE, EX-CIA OPERATIVE--'TIL I INFILTRATED THE AMERICAN INDIAN MOVEMENT LOOKIN' FOR PROOF THEY WAS MAKIN' BOOTLEG FIRE WATER!
THEM REDSKINS CRACKED MY COVER--
--TATTOOED A TARGET ON MY CHEST, AND CHASED ME OFF THE RESERVATION. I LOST MY JOB, NATCH.
I MEAN, HOW COULD I WORK UNDERCOVER WITH AN IDENTIFYING MARK LIKE THIS?!
EMBITTERED, I--
AAH-- SHUDDUP!
I'M TILLIE THE HUN!
AND I AM-- THE SPANKER, FORMER HEAD-MASTER OF AN EXCLUSIVE PRIVATE PREP SCHOOL--
--WRENCHED FROM MY POSITION FOR ADMINISTERING EXCESSIVE CORPORAL PUNISHMENT.
≤urk≤ YOU CAN CALL ME "BLACK HOLE." I WAS PLAYIN' HAND-BALL IN BROOKLYN ONE DAY WHEN A GRAIN OF DWARF STAR MATTER FELL FROM SPACE--
--AND IMBEDDED ITSELF IN MY BREASTBONE.
THIS ENDOWED ME WITH AN EXTREMELY GROSS POWER. I--

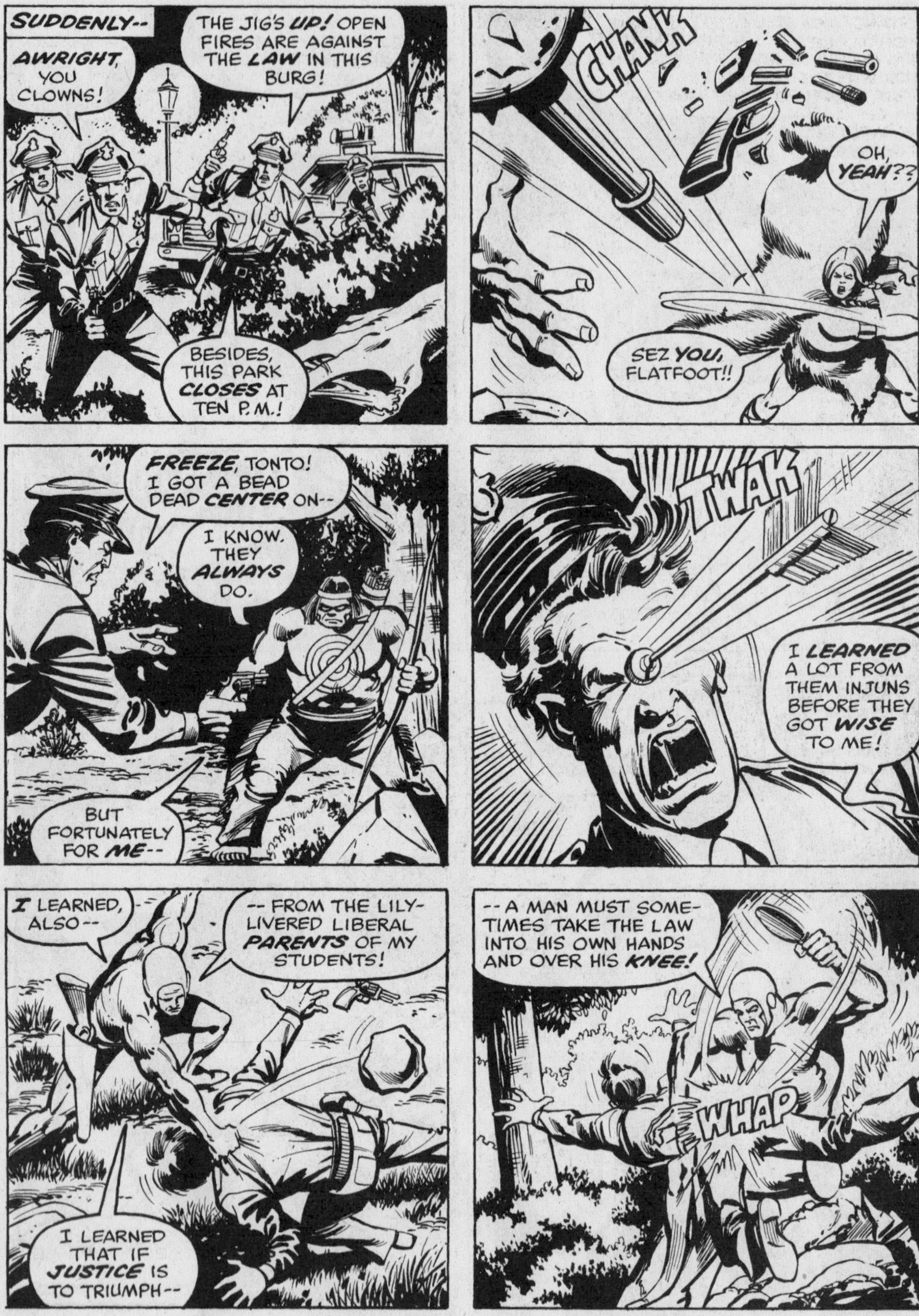
SUDDENLY--
AWRIGHT, YOU CLOWNS!
THE JIG'S UP! OPEN FIRES ARE AGAINST THE LAW IN THIS BURG!
BESIDES, THIS PARK CLOSES AT TEN P.M.!
CHANK
OH, YEAH??
SEZ YOU, FLATFOOT!!
FREEZE, TONTO! I GOT A BEAD DEAD CENTER ON--
I KNOW. THEY ALWAYS DO.
BUT FORTUNATELY FOR ME--
TWAK
I LEARNED A LOT FROM THEM INJUNS BEFORE THEY GOT WISE TO ME!
I LEARNED, ALSO--
-- FROM THE LILY-LIVERED LIBERAL PARENTS OF MY STUDENTS!
I LEARNED THAT IF JUSTICE IS TO TRIUMPH--
-- A MAN MUST SOMETIMES TAKE THE LAW INTO HIS OWN HANDS AND OVER HIS KNEE!
WHAP

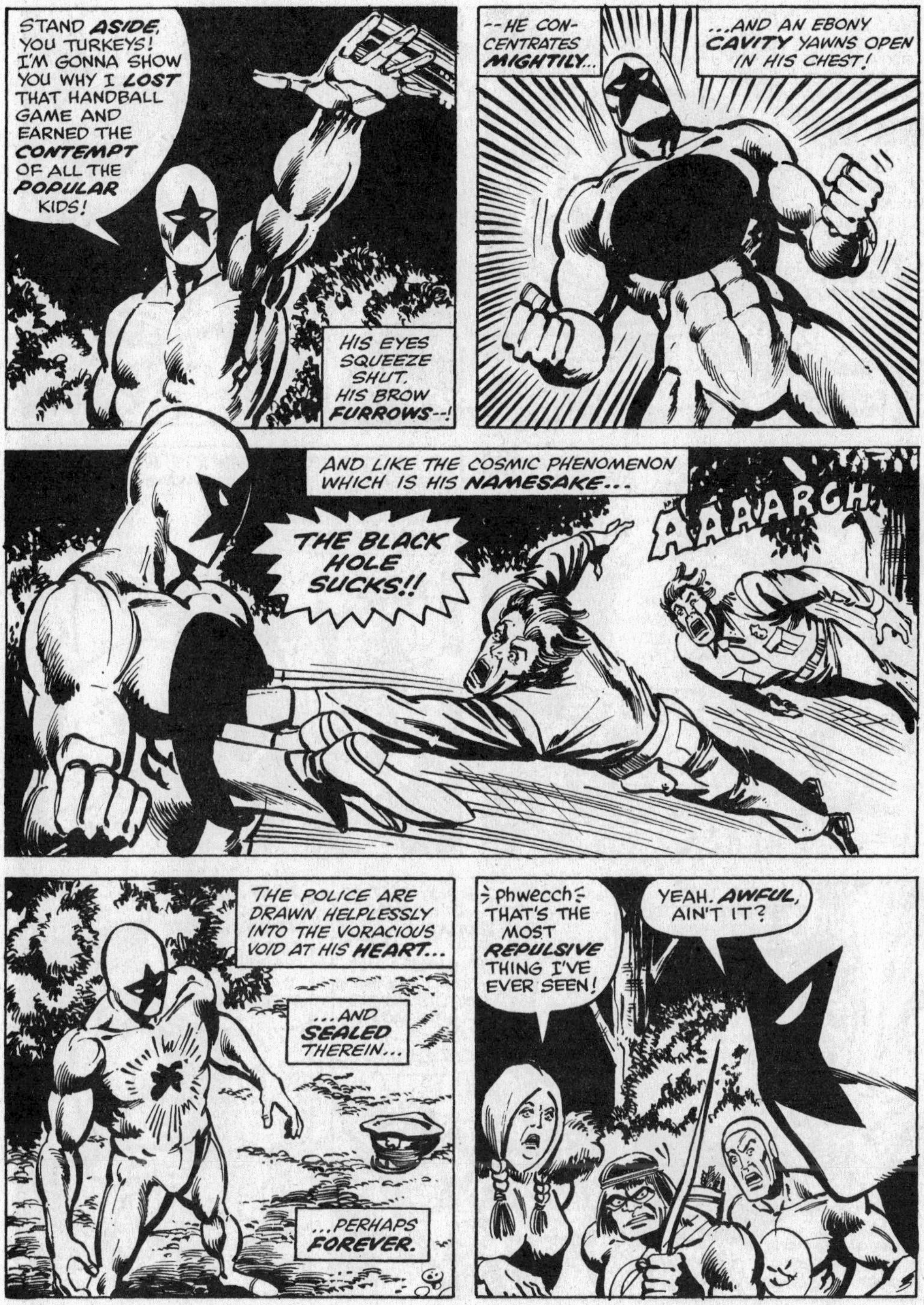
STAND ASIDE, YOU TURKEYS! I'M GONNA SHOW YOU WHY I LOST THAT HANDBALL GAME AND EARNED THE CONTEMPT OF ALL THE POPULAR KIDS!
HIS EYES SQUEEZE SHUT, HIS BROW FURROWS--!
--HE CONCENTRATES MIGHTILY...
...AND AN EBONY CAVITY YAWNS OPEN IN HIS CHEST!
AND LIKE THE COSMIC PHENOMENON WHICH IS HIS NAMESAKE...
THE BLACK HOLE SUCKS!!
AAAARGH
THE POLICE ARE DRAWN HELPLESSLY INTO THE VORACIOUS VOID AT HIS HEART...
...AND SEALED THEREIN...
...PERHAPS FOREVER.
phwecch THAT'S THE MOST REPULSIVE THING I'VE EVER SEEN!
YEAH. AWFUL, AIN'T IT?

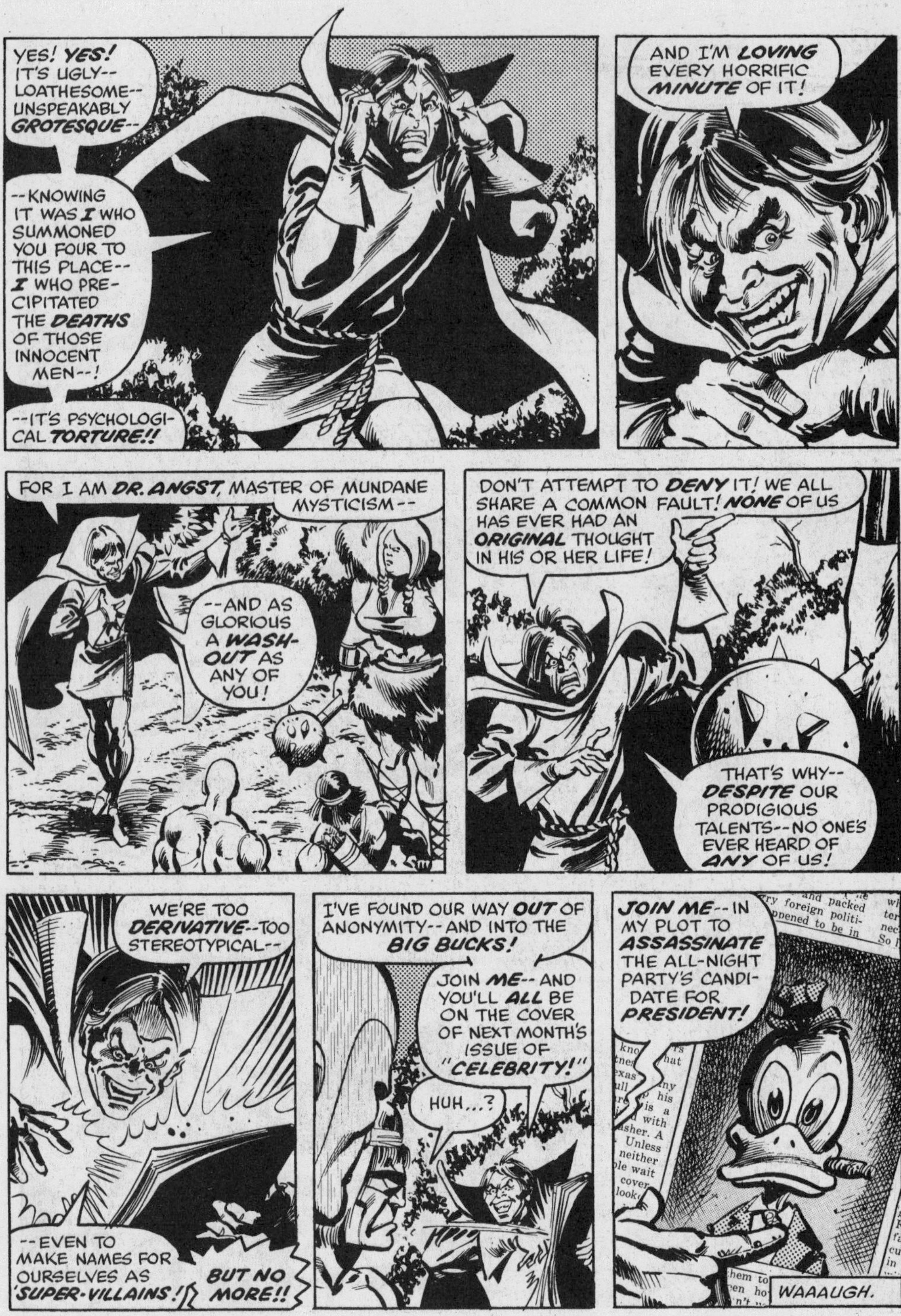
YES! YES! IT'S UGLY-- LOATHESOME-- UNSPEAKABLY GROTESQUE--
--KNOWING IT WAS I WHO SUMMONED YOU FOUR TO THIS PLACE-- I WHO PRE-CIPITATED THE DEATHS OF THOSE INNOCENT MEN--!
--IT'S PSYCHOLOGI-CAL TORTURE!!
AND I'M LOVING EVERY HORRIFIC MINUTE OF IT!
FOR I AM DR. ANGST, MASTER OF MUNDANE MYSTICISM--
--AND AS GLORIOUS A WASH-OUT AS ANY OF YOU!
DON'T ATTEMPT TO DENY IT! WE ALL SHARE A COMMON FAULT! NONE OF US HAS EVER HAD AN ORIGINAL THOUGHT IN HIS OR HER LIFE!
THAT'S WHY-- DESPITE OUR PRODIGIOUS TALENTS--NO ONE'S EVER HEARD OF ANY OF US!
WE'RE TOO DERIVATIVE--TOO STEREOTYPICAL--
--EVEN TO MAKE NAMES FOR OURSELVES AS 'SUPER-VILLAINS'!
BUT NO MORE!!
I'VE FOUND OUR WAY OUT OF ANONYMITY--AND INTO THE BIG BUCKS!
JOIN ME-- AND YOU'LL ALL BE ON THE COVER OF NEXT MONTH'S ISSUE OF "CELEBRITY!"
HUH...?
JOIN ME--IN MY PLOT TO ASSASSINATE THE ALL-NIGHT PARTY'S CANDI-DATE FOR PRESIDENT!
WAAAUGH.

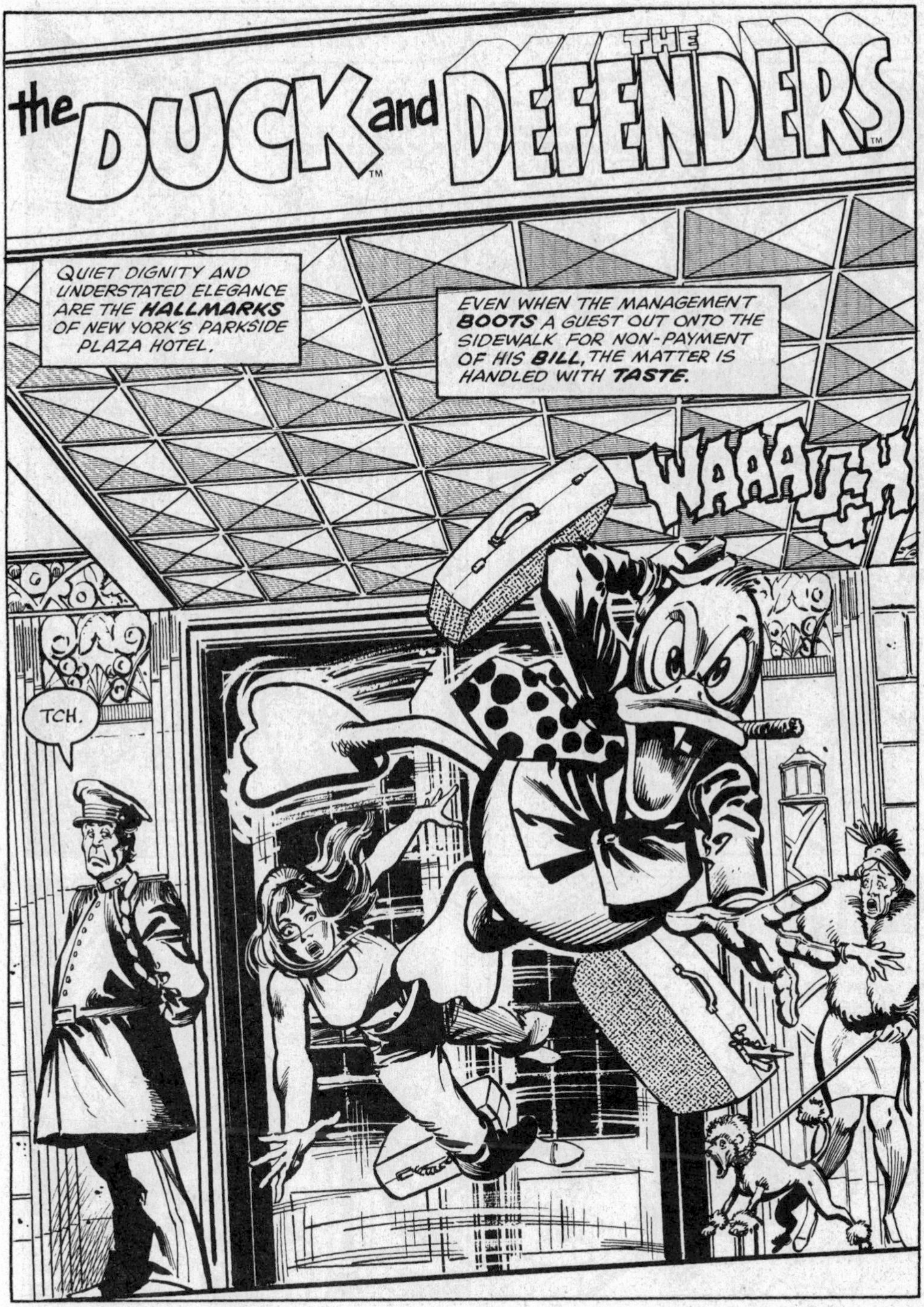
the DUCK and THE DEFENDERS
QUIET DIGNITY AND UNDERSTATED ELEGANCE ARE THE HALLMARKS OF NEW YORK'S PARKSIDE PLAZA HOTEL.
EVEN WHEN THE MANAGEMENT BOOTS A GUEST OUT ONTO THE SIDEWALK FOR NON-PAYMENT OF HIS BILL, THE MATTER IS HANDLED WITH TASTE.
WAAAUGH
TCH.

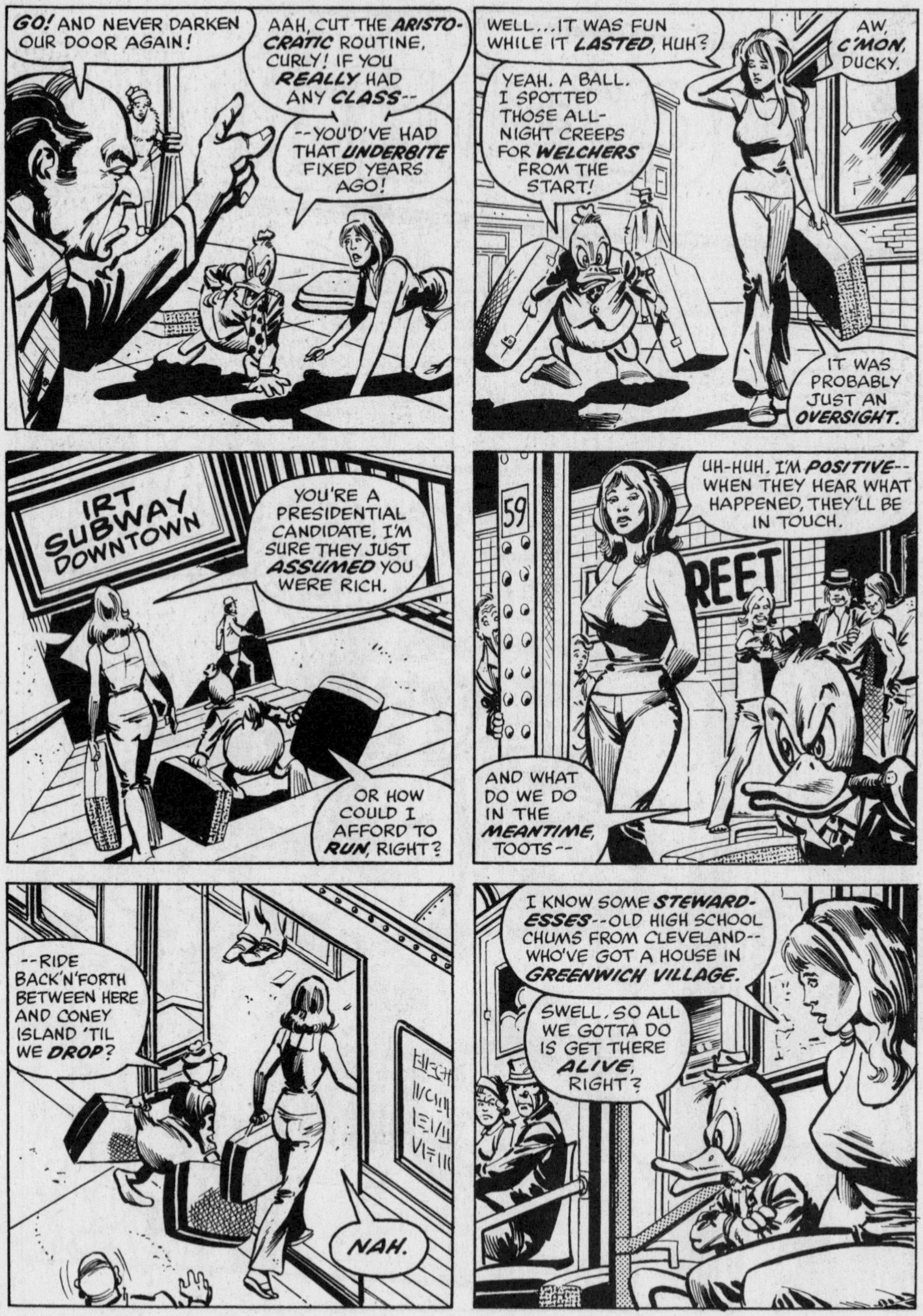
GO! AND NEVER DARKEN OUR DOOR AGAIN!
AAH, CUT THE ARISTO-CRATIC ROUTINE, CURLY! IF YOU REALLY HAD ANY CLASS--
--YOU'D'VE HAD THAT UNDERBITE FIXED YEARS AGO!
WELL...IT WAS FUN WHILE IT LASTED, HUH?
AW, C'MON, DUCKY.
YEAH. A BALL. I SPOTTED THOSE ALL-NIGHT CREEPS FOR WELCHERS FROM THE START!
IT WAS PROBABLY JUST AN OVERSIGHT.
IRT SUBWAY DOWNTOWN
YOU'RE A PRESIDENTIAL CANDIDATE. I'M SURE THEY JUST ASSUMED YOU WERE RICH.
OR HOW COULD I AFFORD TO RUN, RIGHT?
59
REET
UH-HUH. I'M POSITIVE-- WHEN THEY HEAR WHAT HAPPENED, THEY'LL BE IN TOUCH.
AND WHAT DO WE DO IN THE MEANTIME, TOOTS--
--RIDE BACK'N'FORTH BETWEEN HERE AND CONEY ISLAND 'TIL WE DROP?
NAH.
I KNOW SOME STEWARD-ESSES--OLD HIGH SCHOOL CHUMS FROM CLEVELAND--WHO'VE GOT A HOUSE IN GREENWICH VILLAGE.
SWELL, SO ALL WE GOTTA DO IS GET THERE ALIVE, RIGHT?

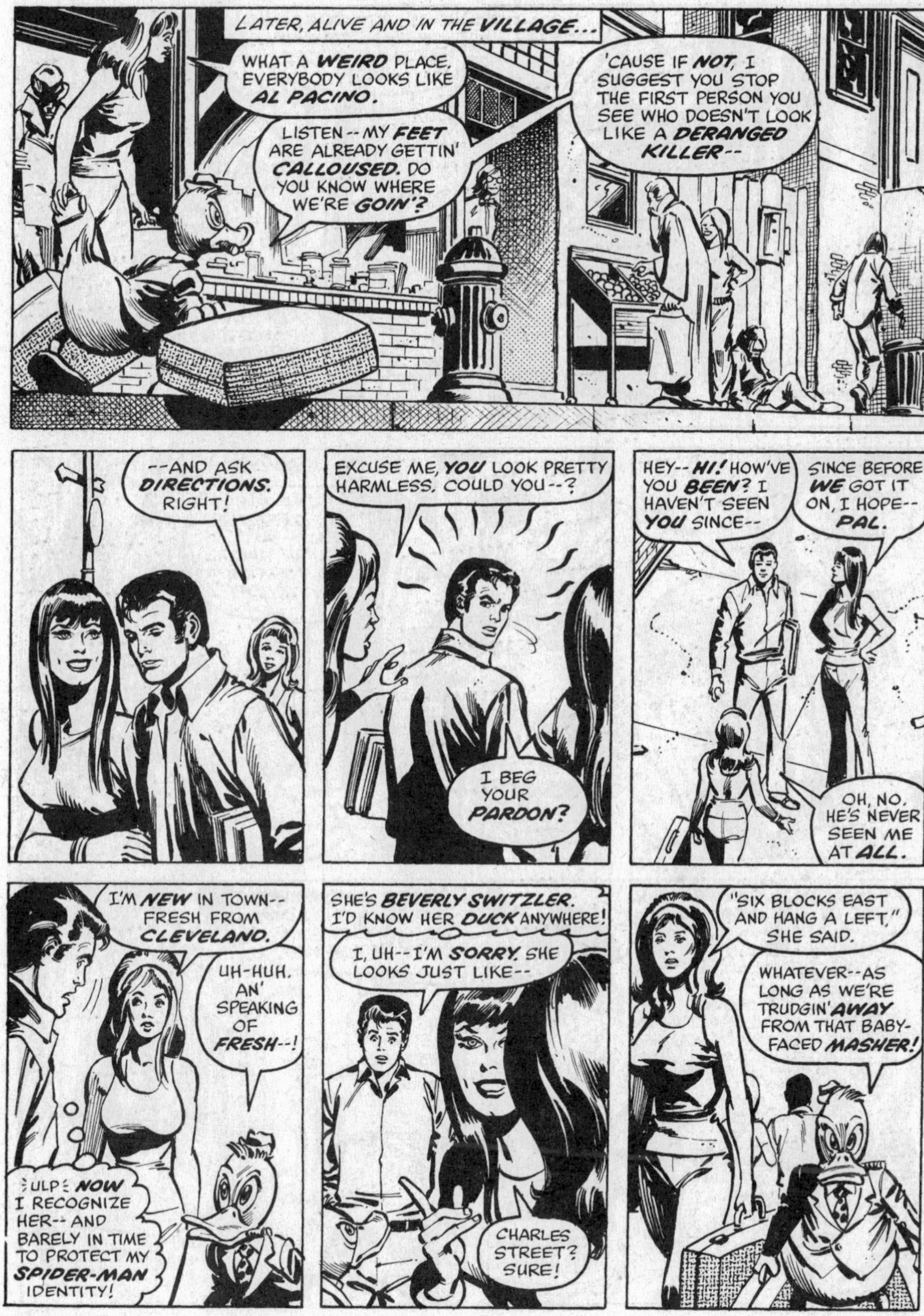
LATER, ALIVE AND IN THE VILLAGE...
WHAT A WEIRD PLACE. EVERYBODY LOOKS LIKE AL PACINO.
LISTEN -- MY FEET ARE ALREADY GETTIN' CALLOUSED. DO YOU KNOW WHERE WE'RE GOIN'?
'CAUSE IF NOT, I SUGGEST YOU STOP THE FIRST PERSON YOU SEE WHO DOESN'T LOOK LIKE A DERANGED KILLER--
--AND ASK DIRECTIONS. RIGHT!
EXCUSE ME, YOU LOOK PRETTY HARMLESS. COULD YOU--?
I BEG YOUR PARDON?
HEY-- HI! HOW'VE YOU BEEN? I HAVEN'T SEEN YOU SINCE--
SINCE BEFORE WE GOT IT ON, I HOPE-- PAL.
OH, NO. HE'S NEVER SEEN ME AT ALL.
I'M NEW IN TOWN-- FRESH FROM CLEVELAND.
UH-HUH. AN' SPEAKING OF FRESH--!
ULP! NOW I RECOGNIZE HER-- AND BARELY IN TIME TO PROTECT MY SPIDER-MAN IDENTITY!
SHE'S BEVERLY SWITZLER. I'D KNOW HER DUCK ANYWHERE!
I, UH-- I'M SORRY. SHE LOOKS JUST LIKE--
CHARLES STREET? SURE!
"SIX BLOCKS EAST AND HANG A LEFT," SHE SAID.
WHATEVER-- AS LONG AS WE'RE TRUDGIN' AWAY FROM THAT BABY-FACED MASHER!

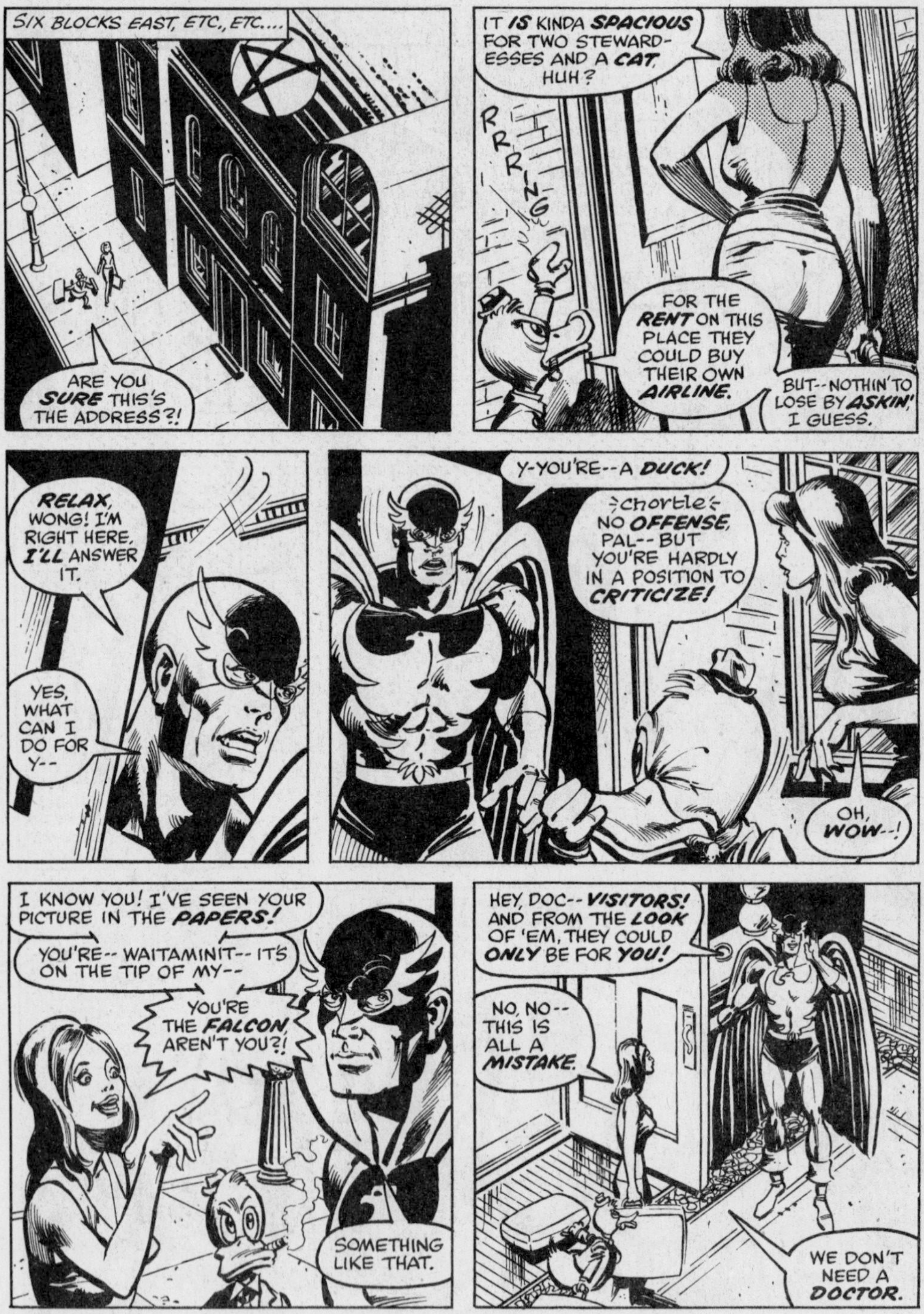
SIX BLOCKS EAST, ETC., ETC....
ARE YOU SURE THIS'S THE ADDRESS?!
IT IS KINDA SPACIOUS FOR TWO STEWARDESSES AND A CAT, HUH?
RRRING
FOR THE RENT ON THIS PLACE THEY COULD BUY THEIR OWN AIRLINE.
BUT--NOTHIN' TO LOSE BY ASKIN', I GUESS.
RELAX, WONG! I'M RIGHT HERE. I'LL ANSWER IT.
YES, WHAT CAN I DO FOR Y--
Y-YOU'RE--A DUCK!
chortle
NO OFFENSE, PAL--BUT YOU'RE HARDLY IN A POSITION TO CRITICIZE!
OH, WOW--!
I KNOW YOU! I'VE SEEN YOUR PICTURE IN THE PAPERS!
YOU'RE-- WAITAMINIT-- IT'S ON THE TIP OF MY--
YOU'RE THE FALCON, AREN'T YOU?!
SOMETHING LIKE THAT.
HEY, DOC--VISITORS! AND FROM THE LOOK OF 'EM, THEY COULD ONLY BE FOR YOU!
NO, NO--THIS IS ALL A MISTAKE.
WE DON'T NEED A DOCTOR.

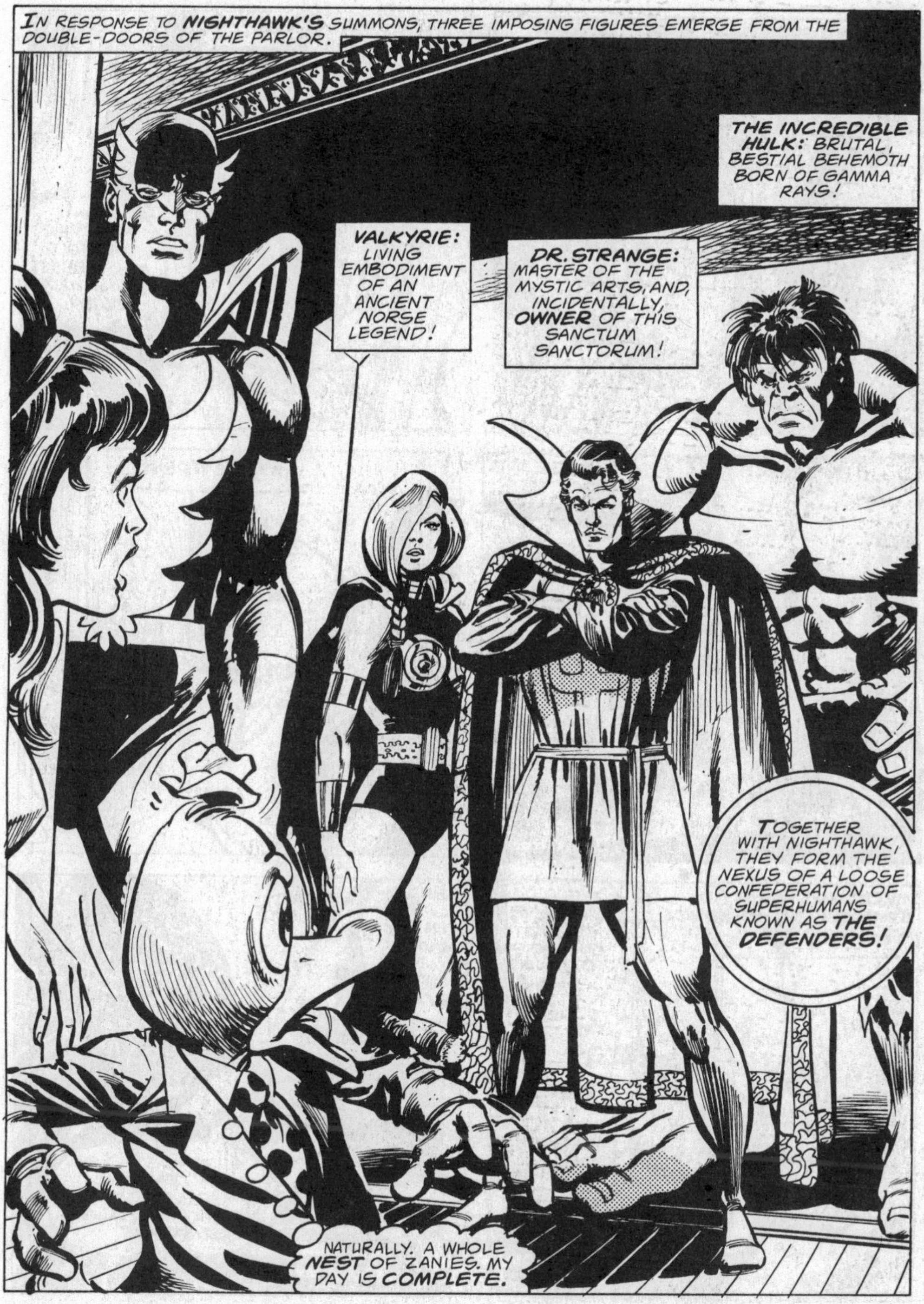
IN RESPONSE TO NIGHTHAWK'S SUMMONS, THREE IMPOSING FIGURES EMERGE FROM THE DOUBLE-DOORS OF THE PARLOR.
VALKYRIE: LIVING EMBODIMENT OF AN ANCIENT NORSE LEGEND!
DR. STRANGE: MASTER OF THE MYSTIC ARTS, AND, INCIDENTALLY, OWNER OF THIS SANCTUM SANCTORUM!
THE INCREDIBLE HULK: BRUTAL, BESTIAL BEHEMOTH BORN OF GAMMA RAYS!
TOGETHER WITH NIGHTHAWK, THEY FORM THE NEXUS OF A LOOSE CONFEDERATION OF SUPERHUMANS KNOWN AS THE DEFENDERS!
NATURALLY. A WHOLE NEST OF ZANIES. MY DAY IS COMPLETE.

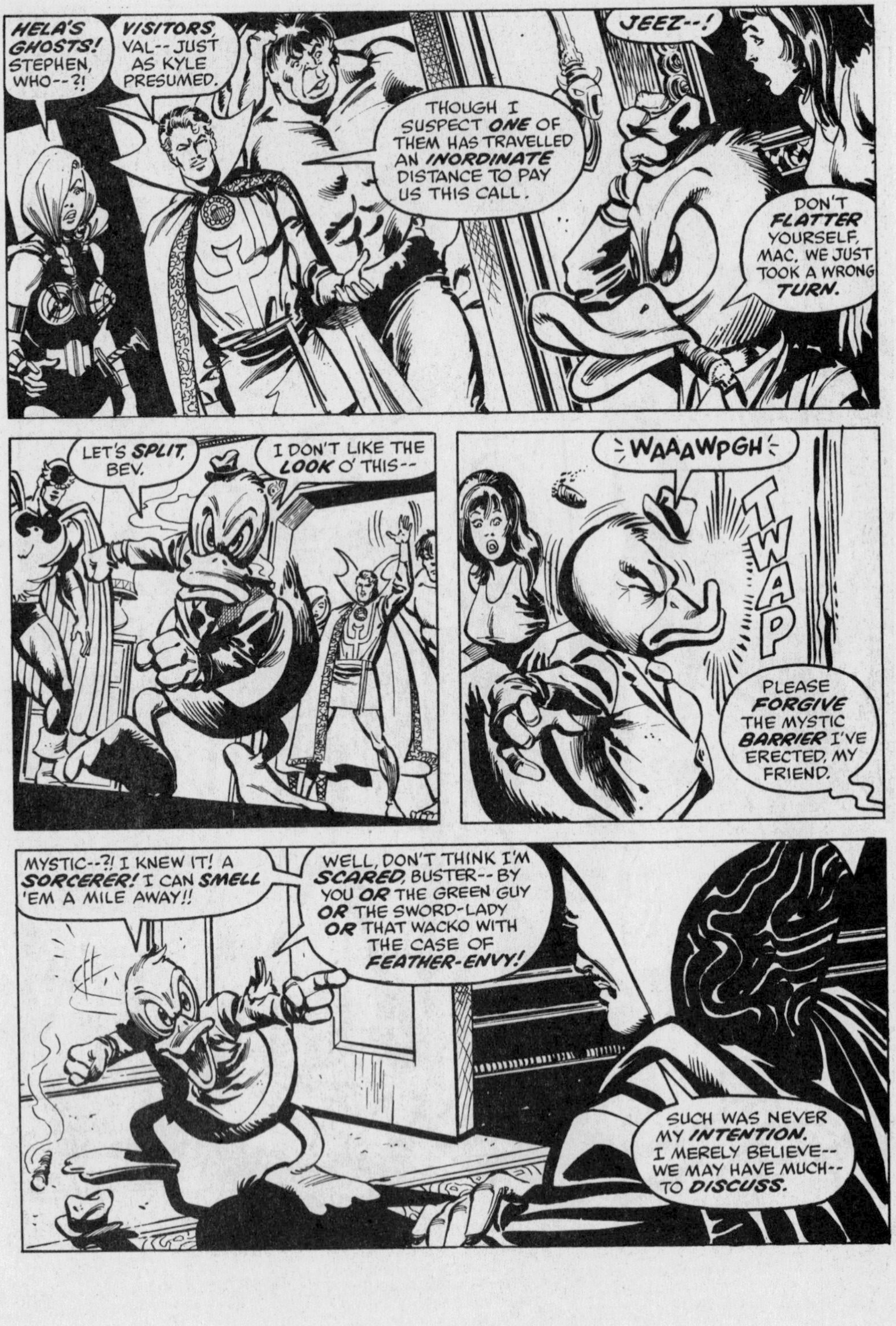
HELA'S GHOSTS! STEPHEN, WHO--?!
VISITORS, VAL-- JUST AS KYLE PRESUMED.
THOUGH I SUSPECT ONE OF THEM HAS TRAVELLED AN INORDINATE DISTANCE TO PAY US THIS CALL.
JEEZ--!
DON'T FLATTER YOURSELF, MAC. WE JUST TOOK A WRONG TURN.
LET'S SPLIT, BEV.
I DON'T LIKE THE LOOK O' THIS--
WAAAWPGH
TWAP
PLEASE FORGIVE THE MYSTIC BARRIER I'VE ERECTED, MY FRIEND.
MYSTIC--?! I KNEW IT! A SORCERER! I CAN SMELL 'EM A MILE AWAY!!
WELL, DON'T THINK I'M SCARED, BUSTER-- BY YOU OR THE GREEN GUY OR THE SWORD-LADY OR THAT WACKO WITH THE CASE OF FEATHER-ENVY!
SUCH WAS NEVER MY INTENTION. I MERELY BELIEVE-- WE MAY HAVE MUCH-- TO DISCUSS.

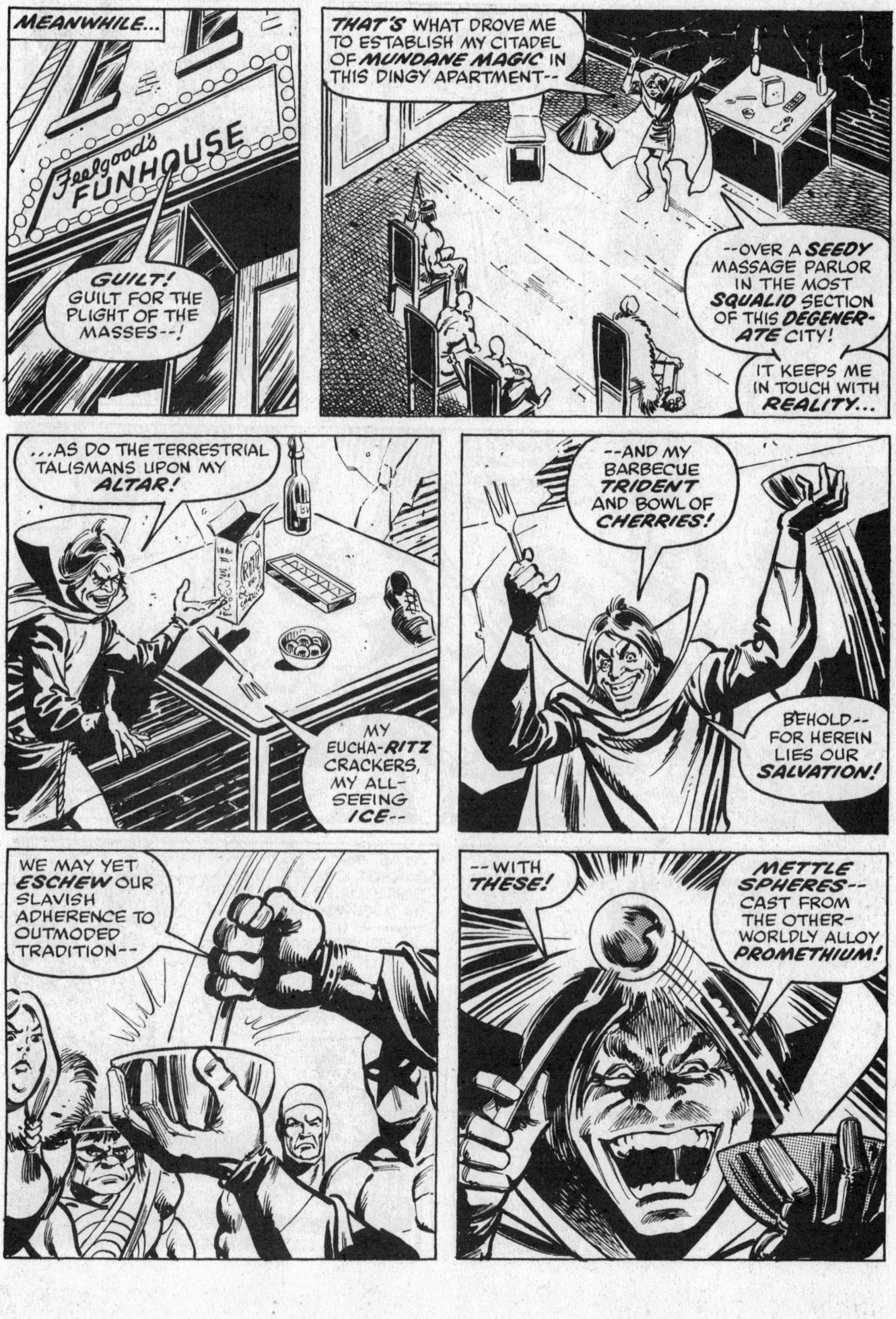
MEANWHILE...
Feelgood's FUNHOUSE
GUILT! GUILT FOR THE PLIGHT OF THE MASSES--!
THAT'S WHAT DROVE ME TO ESTABLISH MY CITADEL OF MUNDANE MAGIC IN THIS DINGY APARTMENT--
--OVER A SEEDY MASSAGE PARLOR IN THE MOST SQUALID SECTION OF THIS DEGENERATE CITY!
IT KEEPS ME IN TOUCH WITH REALITY...
...AS DO THE TERRESTRIAL TALISMANS UPON MY ALTAR!
MY EUCHA-RITZ CRACKERS, MY ALL-SEEING ICE--
--AND MY BARBECUE TRIDENT AND BOWL OF CHERRIES!
BEHOLD-- FOR HEREIN LIES OUR SALVATION!
WE MAY YET ESCHEW OUR SLAVISH ADHERENCE TO OUTMODED TRADITION--
--WITH THESE!
METTLE SPHERES-- CAST FROM THE OTHER-WORLDLY ALLOY PROMETHIUM!

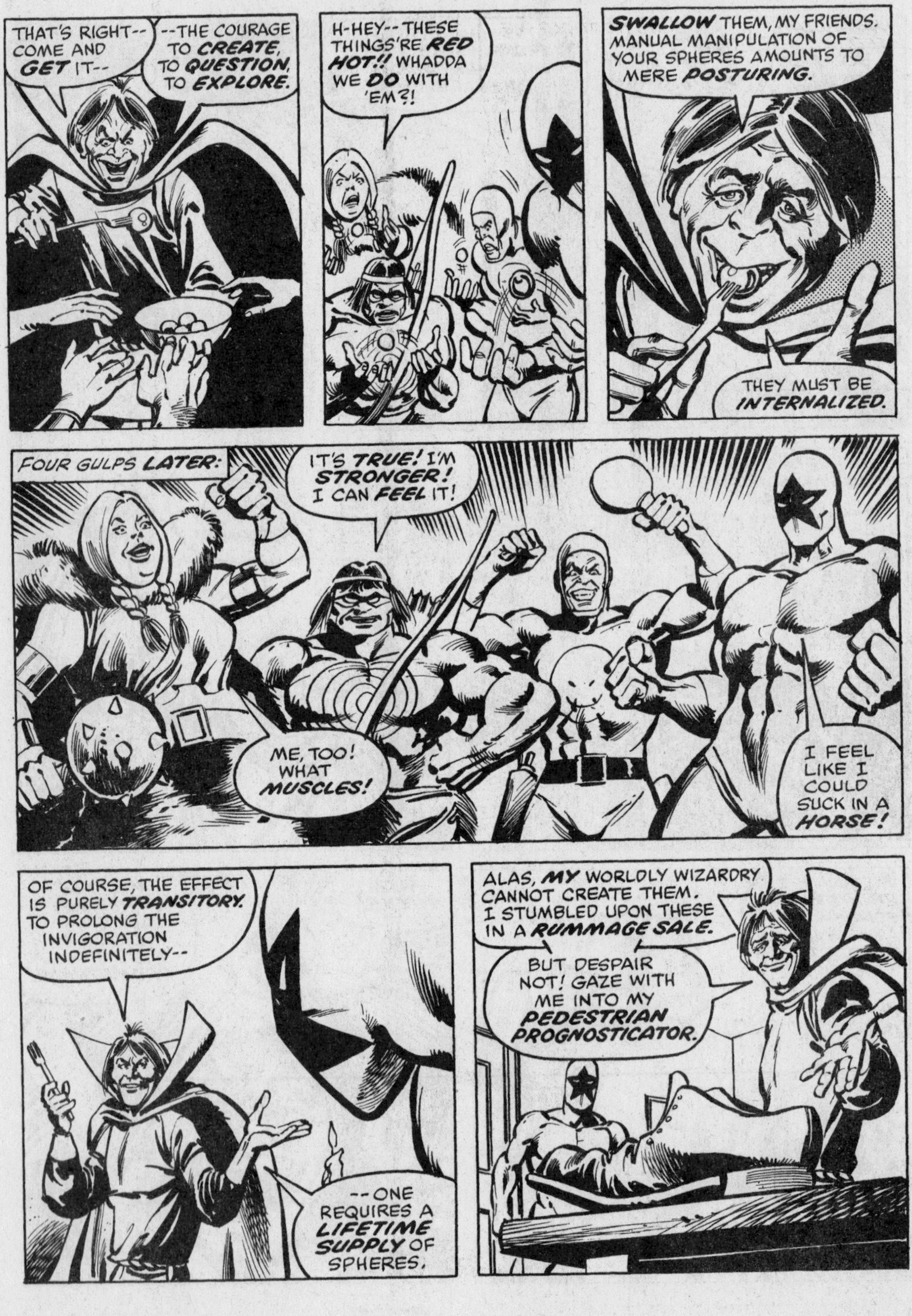
THAT'S RIGHT-- COME AND GET IT--
--THE COURAGE TO CREATE, TO QUESTION, TO EXPLORE.
H-HEY--THESE THINGS'RE RED HOT!! WHADDA WE DO WITH 'EM?!
SWALLOW THEM, MY FRIENDS. MANUAL MANIPULATION OF YOUR SPHERES AMOUNTS TO MERE POSTURING.
THEY MUST BE INTERNALIZED.
FOUR GULPS LATER:
IT'S TRUE! I'M STRONGER! I CAN FEEL IT!
ME, TOO! WHAT MUSCLES!
I FEEL LIKE I COULD SUCK IN A HORSE!
OF COURSE, THE EFFECT IS PURELY TRANSITORY. TO PROLONG THE INVIGORATION INDEFINITELY--
--ONE REQUIRES A LIFETIME SUPPLY OF SPHERES.
ALAS, MY WORLDLY WIZARDRY CANNOT CREATE THEM. I STUMBLED UPON THESE IN A RUMMAGE SALE.
BUT DESPAIR NOT! GAZE WITH ME INTO MY PEDESTRIAN PROGNOSTICATOR.

"*THAT MAN* HAS THE MYSTIC TOOLS WE NEED. WE MUST *SEIZE* THEM--AND MAKE SOME CASH ON THE SIDE--

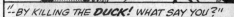
"--BY KILLING THE *DUCK*! WHAT SAY YOU?"

IF THIS IS WHAT IT'S LIKE TO POSSESS SPHERES--

--LET'S GO *GET* 'EM!!

SO SAY WE ALL!!

EXCELLENT-- --YOU FOOLS. HEH HEH

--AND *THESE* ARE PREDILUVEAN SCULPTURES CULLED FROM--

UH-- NOT TO *INTERRUPT*, DOC, BUT FOR A SORCERER YOU'RE SORTA *LOOSE-TONGUED*, AREN'T CHA?

MOST GUYS IN YOUR PROFESSION ARE PRETTY *SECRETIVE*-- UNLESS THEY *WANT* SOMETHING. TRUE?

QUITE CORRECT, BUT ALL I DESIRE IS YOUR *OPINION*--AS A BEING WHO ALSO HAS SEEN BEYOND THIS REALITY.

I'VE NOTED AN UNUSUAL DEGREE OF *MYSTICAL ACTIVITY* IN THE WIND RECENTLY. I WONDERED--

NAH.

CLOSEST *I* EVER CAME TO STIRRING UP MAGIC WAS AN *ACT* I USEDTA DO AT *BIRTHDAY PARTIES*.

EVERYTHING ELSE, I JUST KINDA GOT STIRRED *INTO*.

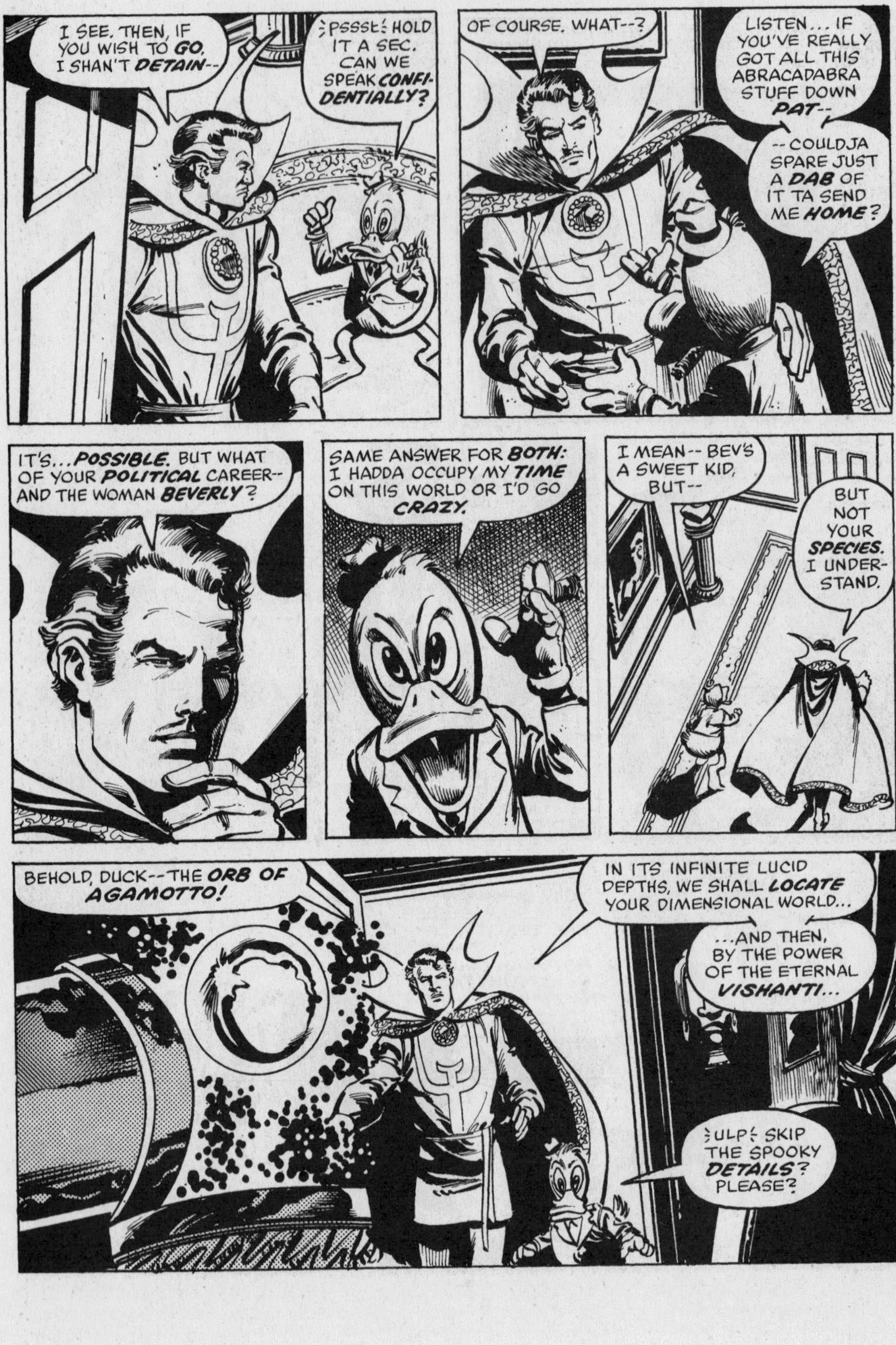
I SEE. THEN, IF YOU WISH TO GO, I SHAN'T DETAIN--
¡PSSST! HOLD IT A SEC. CAN WE SPEAK CONFI-DENTIALLY?
OF COURSE. WHAT--?
LISTEN... IF YOU'VE REALLY GOT ALL THIS ABRACADABRA STUFF DOWN PAT--
--COULDJA SPARE JUST A DAB OF IT TA SEND ME HOME?
IT'S... POSSIBLE. BUT WHAT OF YOUR POLITICAL CAREER-- AND THE WOMAN BEVERLY?
SAME ANSWER FOR BOTH: I HADDA OCCUPY MY TIME ON THIS WORLD OR I'D GO CRAZY.
I MEAN-- BEV'S A SWEET KID, BUT--
BUT NOT YOUR SPECIES. I UNDER-STAND.
BEHOLD, DUCK--THE ORB OF AGAMOTTO!
IN ITS INFINITE LUCID DEPTHS, WE SHALL LOCATE YOUR DIMENSIONAL WORLD...
...AND THEN, BY THE POWER OF THE ETERNAL VISHANTI...
¡ULP! SKIP THE SPOOKY DETAILS? PLEASE?

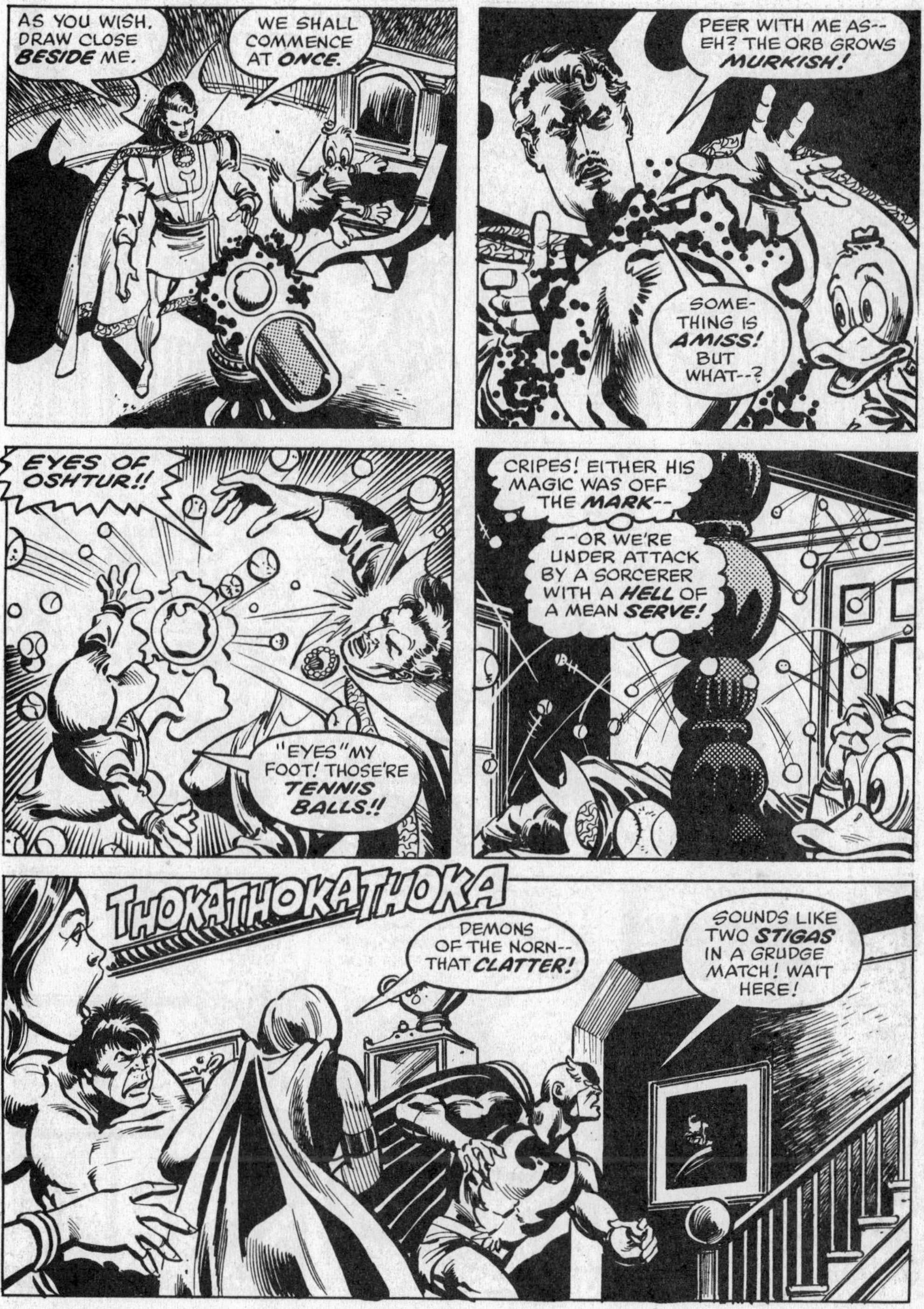
AS YOU WISH. DRAW CLOSE BESIDE ME.
WE SHALL COMMENCE AT ONCE.
PEER WITH ME AS-- EH? THE ORB GROWS MURKISH!
SOME-THING IS AMISS! BUT WHAT--?
EYES OF OSHTUR!!
"EYES" MY FOOT! THOSE'RE TENNIS BALLS!!
CRIPES! EITHER HIS MAGIC WAS OFF THE MARK--
--OR WE'RE UNDER ATTACK BY A SORCERER WITH A HELL OF A MEAN SERVE!
THOKATHOKATHOKA
DEMONS OF THE NORN-- THAT CLATTER!
SOUNDS LIKE TWO STIGAS IN A GRUDGE MATCH! WAIT HERE!

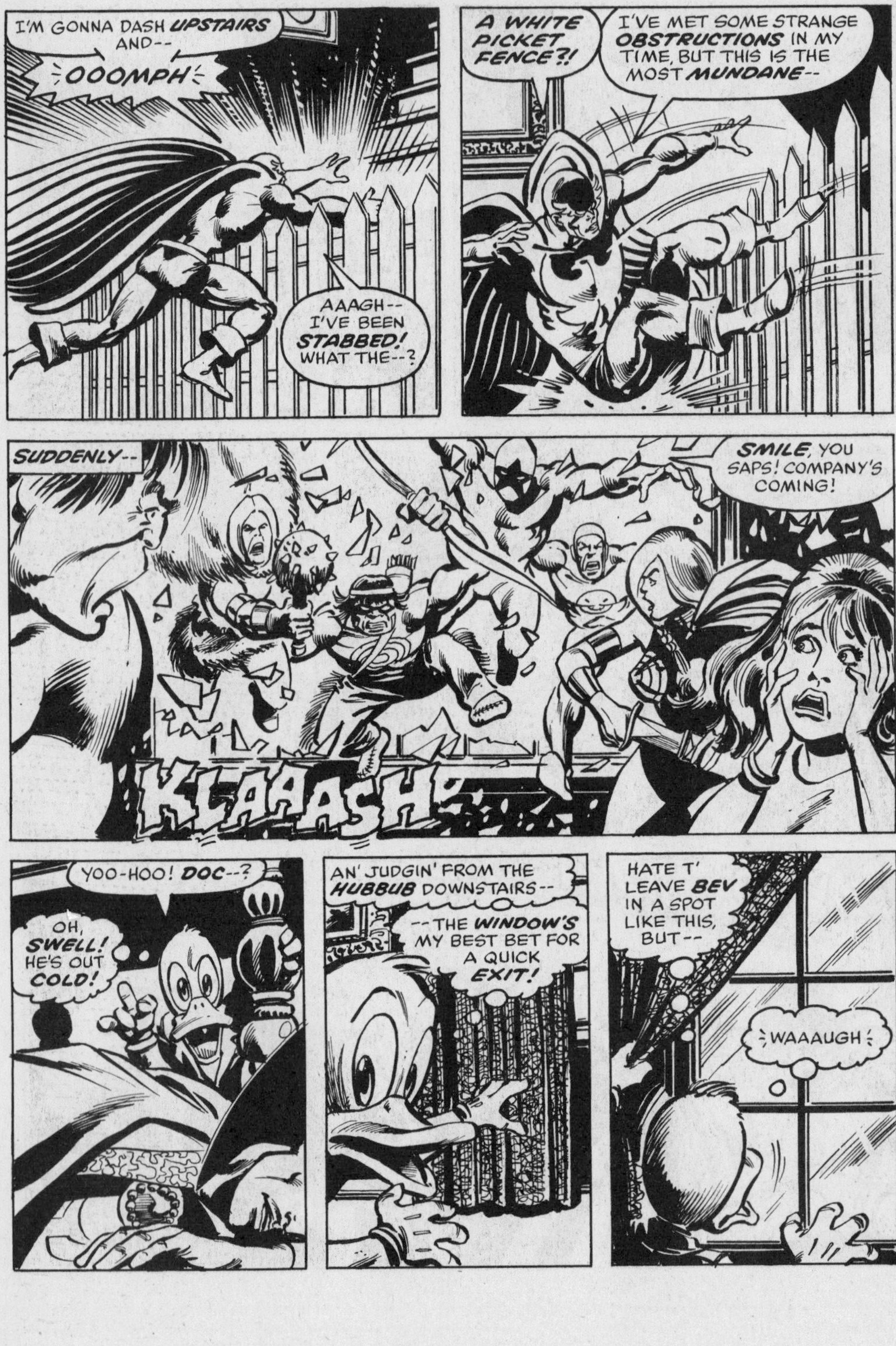

I'M GONNA DASH UPSTAIRS AND--
OOOMPH
AAAGH-- I'VE BEEN STABBED! WHAT THE--?
A WHITE PICKET FENCE?!
I'VE MET SOME STRANGE OBSTRUCTIONS IN MY TIME, BUT THIS IS THE MOST MUNDANE--
SUDDENLY--
SMILE, YOU SAPS! COMPANY'S COMING!
KLAAASH
YOO-HOO! DOC--?
OH, SWELL! HE'S OUT COLD!
AN' JUDGIN' FROM THE HUBBUB DOWNSTAIRS--
--THE WINDOW'S MY BEST BET FOR A QUICK EXIT!
HATE T' LEAVE BEV IN A SPOT LIKE THIS, BUT--
WAAAUGH

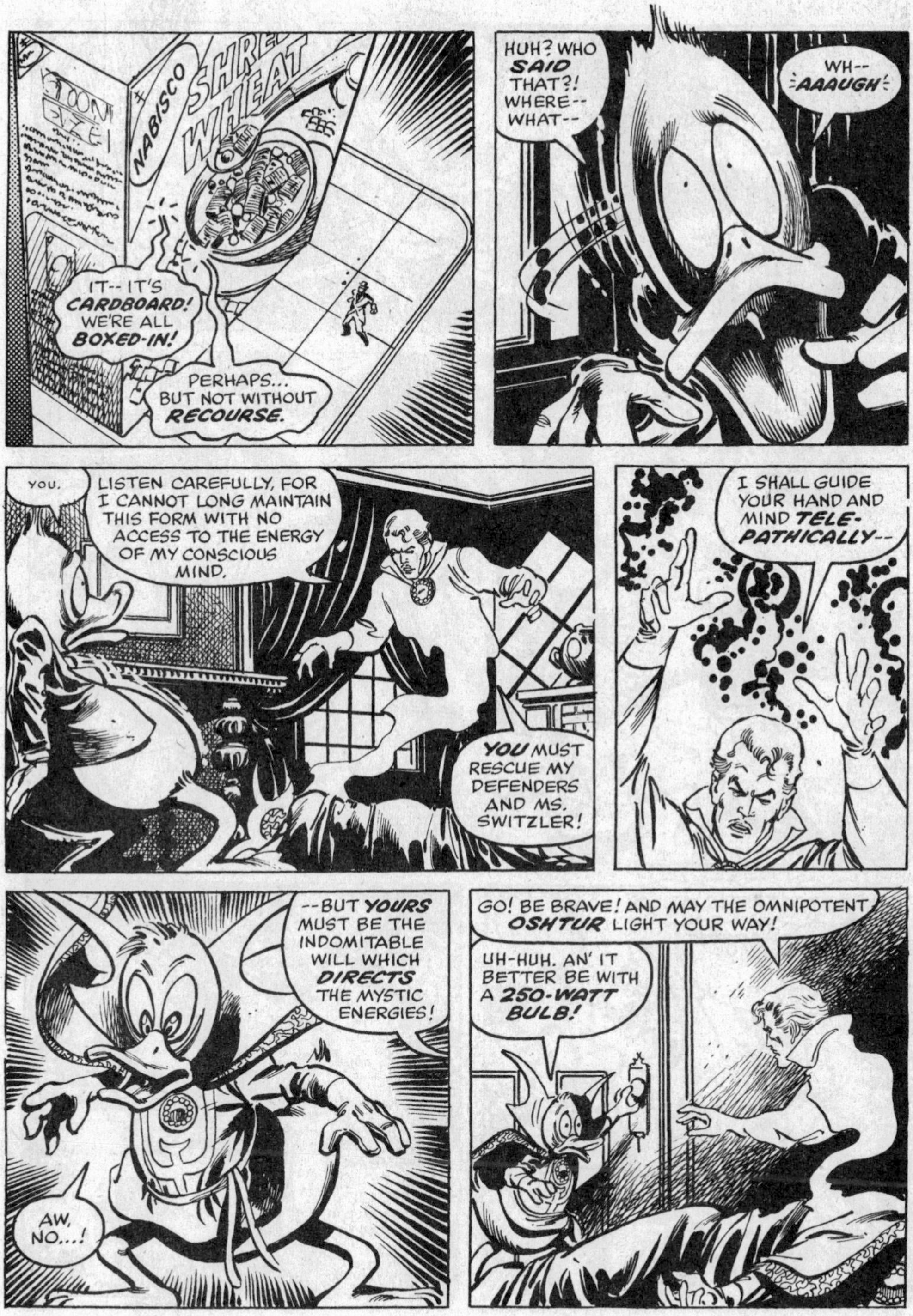
NABISCO
SHREDDED WHEAT
IT-- IT'S CARDBOARD! WE'RE ALL BOXED-IN!
PERHAPS... BUT NOT WITHOUT RECOURSE.
HUH? WHO SAID THAT?! WHERE-- WHAT--
WH-- AAAUGH
YOU.
LISTEN CAREFULLY, FOR I CANNOT LONG MAINTAIN THIS FORM WITH NO ACCESS TO THE ENERGY OF MY CONSCIOUS MIND.
YOU MUST RESCUE MY DEFENDERS AND MS. SWITZLER!
I SHALL GUIDE YOUR HAND AND MIND TELE-PATHICALLY--
--BUT YOURS MUST BE THE INDOMITABLE WILL WHICH DIRECTS THE MYSTIC ENERGIES!
AW, NO...!
GO! BE BRAVE! AND MAY THE OMNIPOTENT OSHTUR LIGHT YOUR WAY!
UH-HUH. AN' IT BETTER BE WITH A 250-WATT BULB!

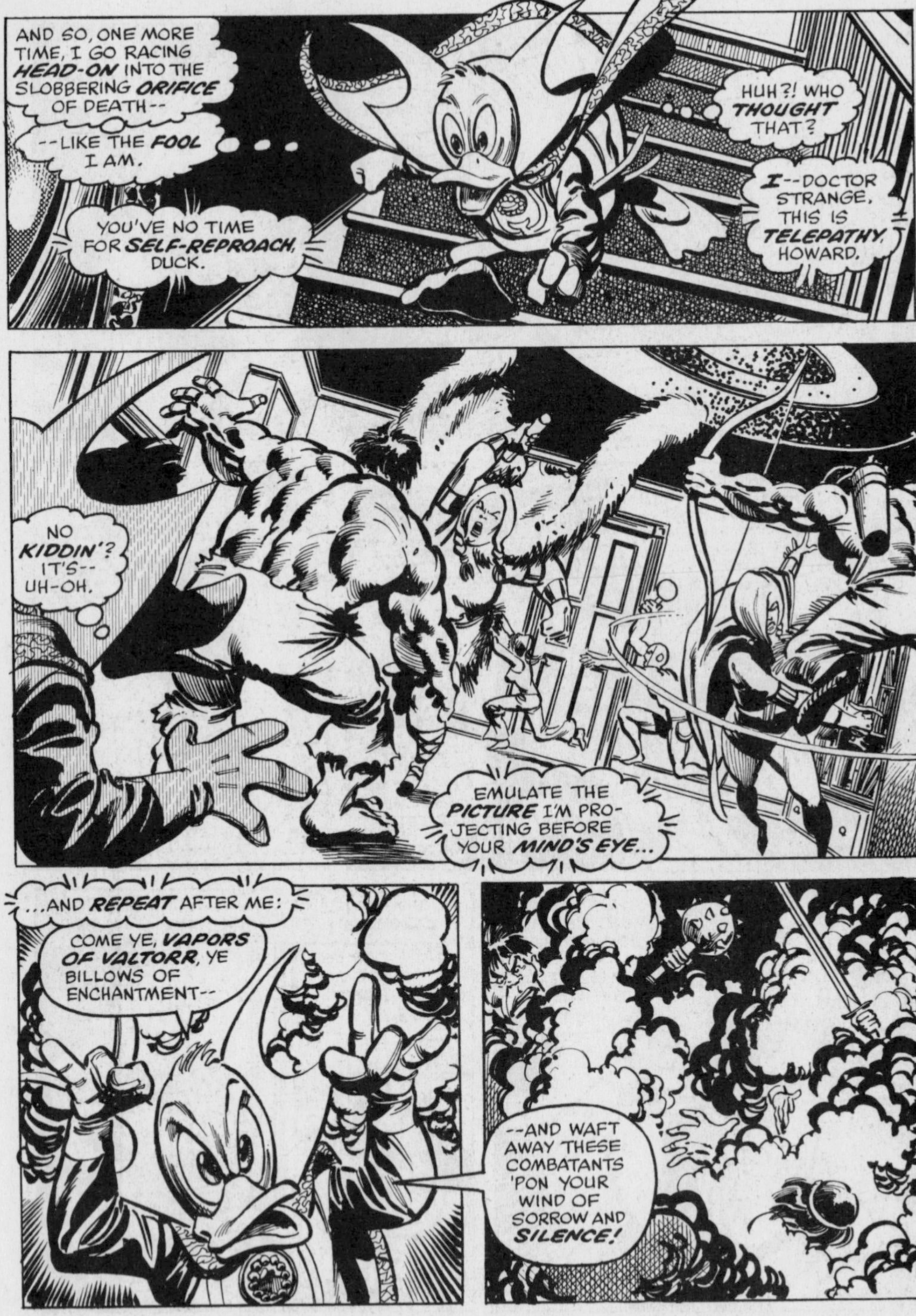
AND SO, ONE MORE TIME, I GO RACING HEAD-ON INTO THE SLOBBERING ORIFICE OF DEATH--
--LIKE THE FOOL I AM.
HUH?! WHO THOUGHT THAT?
YOU'VE NO TIME FOR SELF-REPROACH, DUCK.
I--DOCTOR STRANGE. THIS IS TELEPATHY, HOWARD.
NO KIDDIN'? IT'S-- UH-OH.
EMULATE THE PICTURE I'M PROJECTING BEFORE YOUR MIND'S EYE...
...AND REPEAT AFTER ME:
COME YE, VAPORS OF VALTORR, YE BILLOWS OF ENCHANTMENT--
--AND WAFT AWAY THESE COMBATANTS 'PON YOUR WIND OF SORROW AND SILENCE!

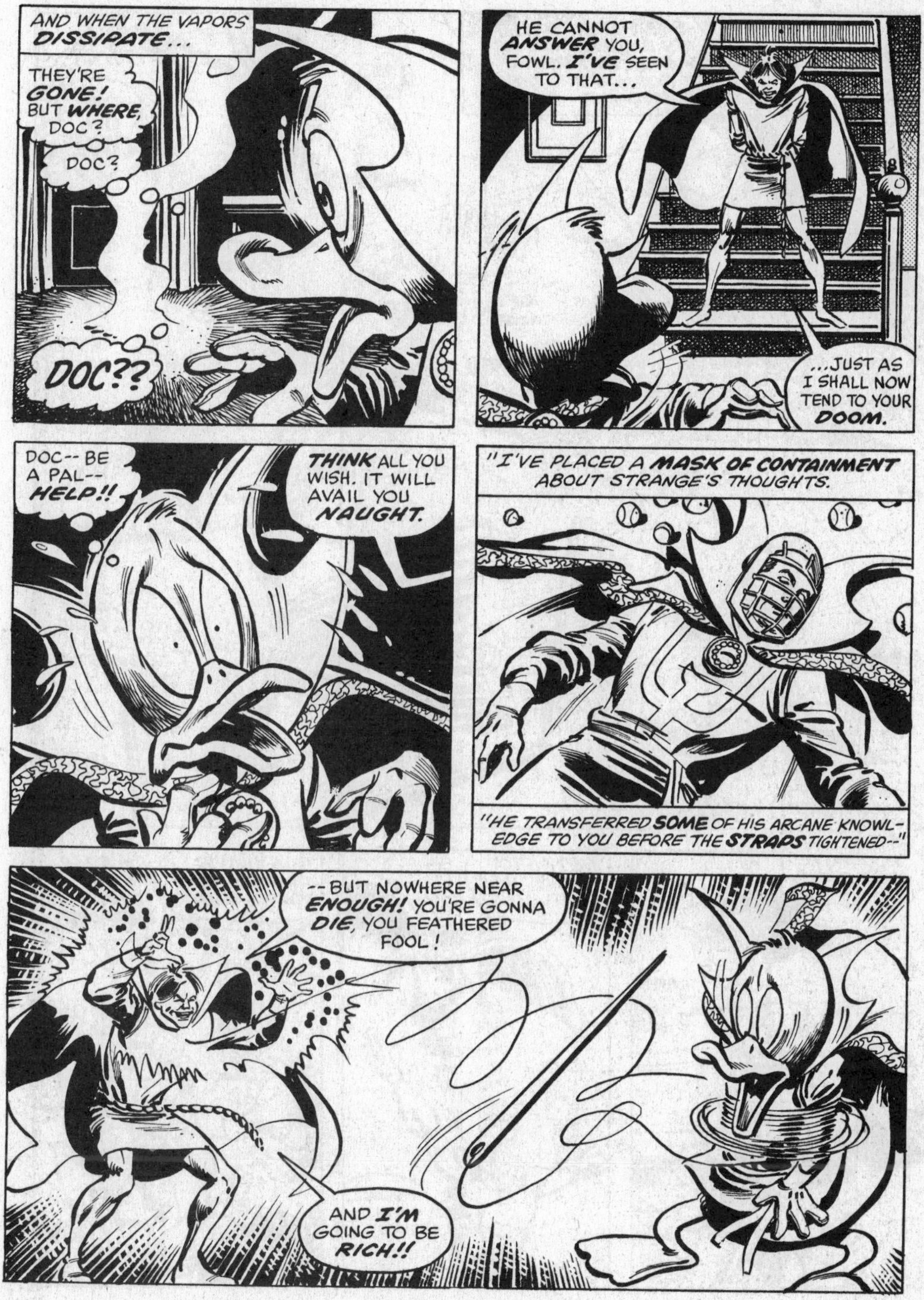
AND WHEN THE VAPORS DISSIPATE...
THEY'RE GONE! BUT WHERE, DOC?
DOC?
DOC??
HE CANNOT ANSWER YOU, FOWL. I'VE SEEN TO THAT...
...JUST AS I SHALL NOW TEND TO YOUR DOOM.
DOC-- BE A PAL-- HELP!!
THINK ALL YOU WISH. IT WILL AVAIL YOU NAUGHT.
"I'VE PLACED A MASK OF CONTAINMENT ABOUT STRANGE'S THOUGHTS.
"HE TRANSFERRED SOME OF HIS ARCANE KNOWL-EDGE TO YOU BEFORE THE STRAPS TIGHTENED--"
--BUT NOWHERE NEAR ENOUGH! YOU'RE GONNA DIE, YOU FEATHERED FOOL!
AND I'M GOING TO BE RICH!!

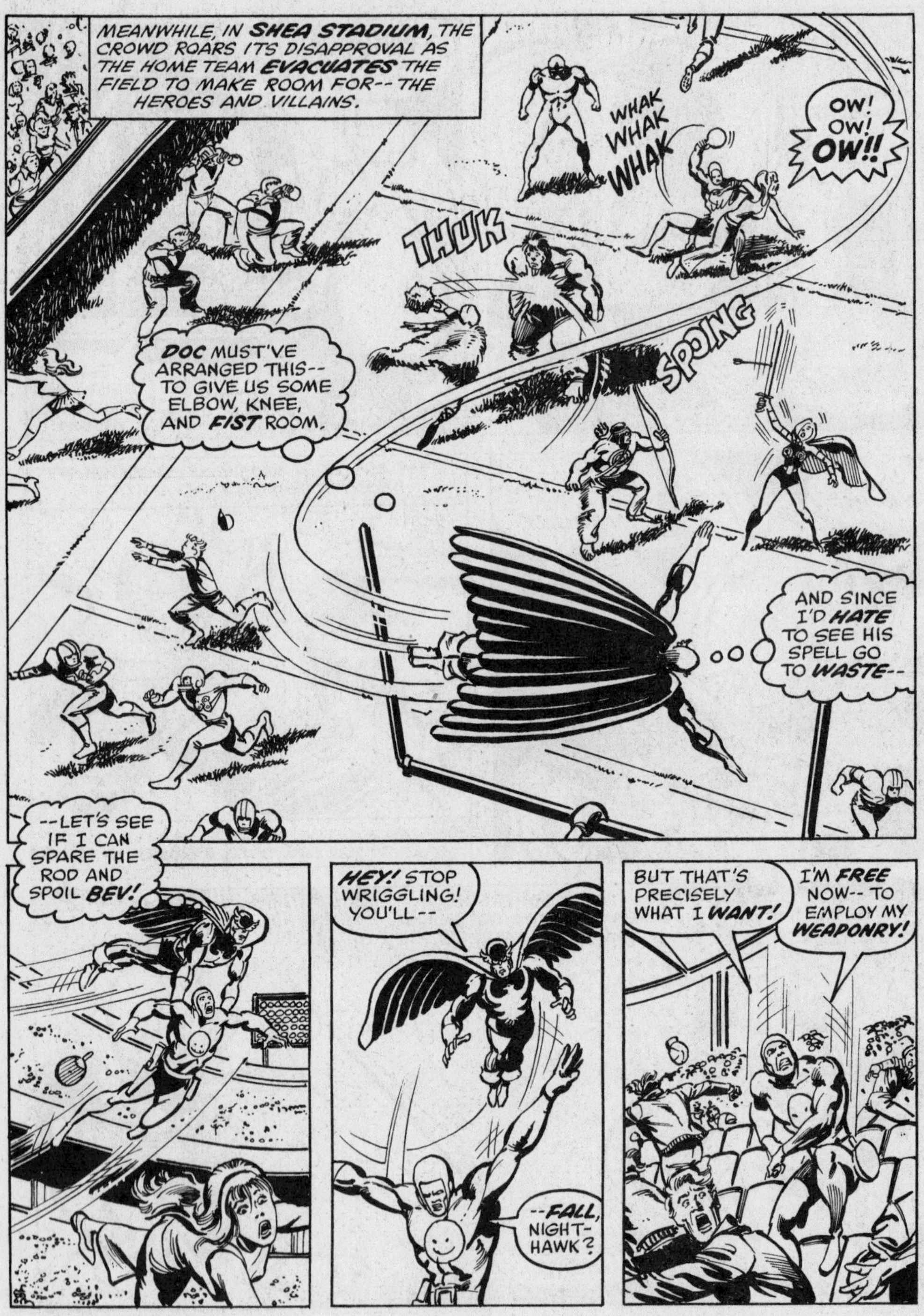

MEANWHILE, IN SHEA STADIUM, THE CROWD ROARS ITS DISAPPROVAL AS THE HOME TEAM EVACUATES THE FIELD TO MAKE ROOM FOR-- THE HEROES AND VILLAINS.
WHAK WHAK WHAK
OW! OW! OW!!
THUK
SPOING
DOC MUST'VE ARRANGED THIS-- TO GIVE US SOME ELBOW, KNEE, AND FIST ROOM.
AND SINCE I'D HATE TO SEE HIS SPELL GO TO WASTE--
--LET'S SEE IF I CAN SPARE THE ROD AND SPOIL BEV!
HEY! STOP WRIGGLING! YOU'LL --
--FALL, NIGHT-HAWK?
BUT THAT'S PRECISELY WHAT I WANT!
I'M FREE NOW-- TO EMPLOY MY WEAPONRY!

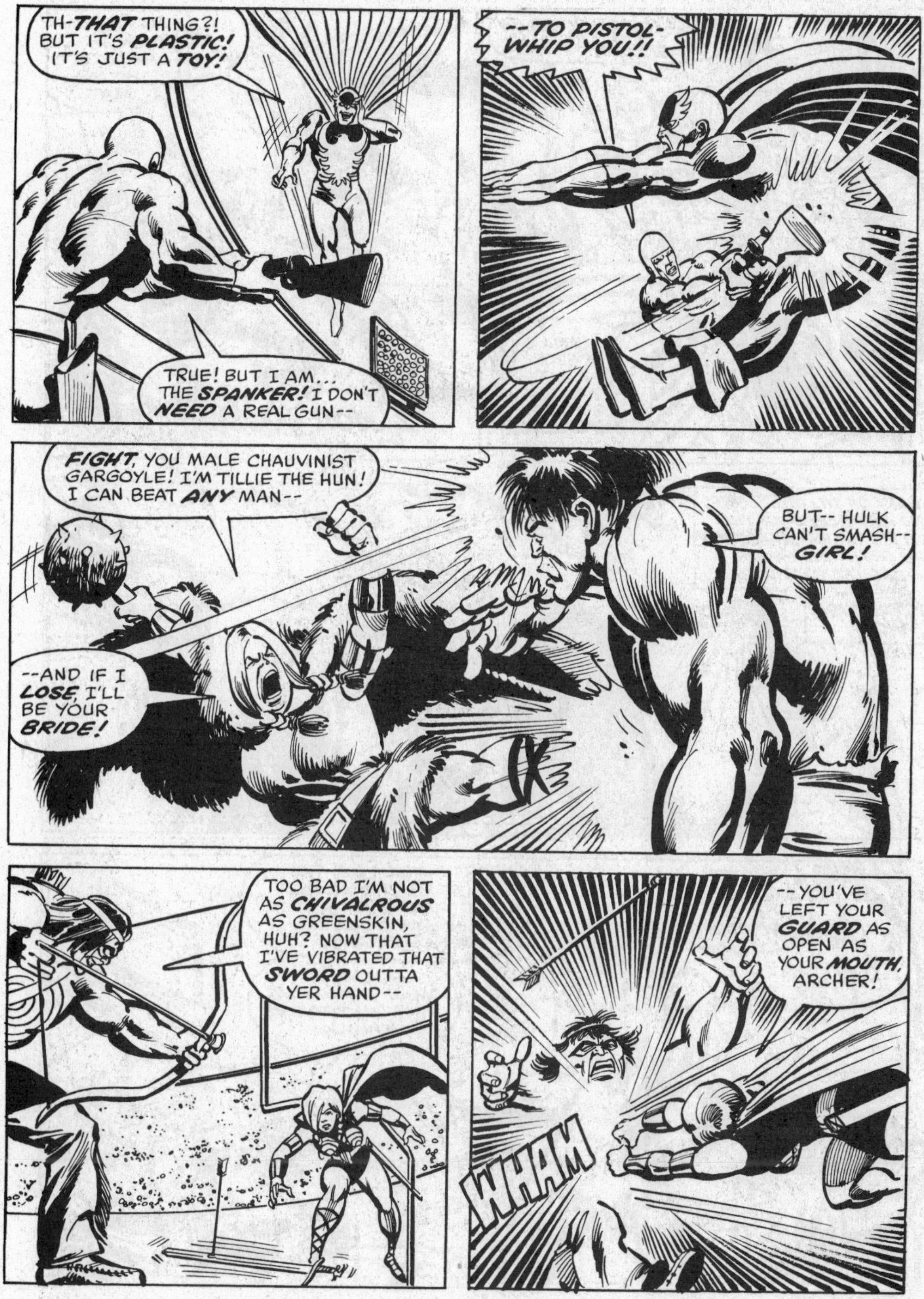
TH-THAT THING?! BUT IT'S PLASTIC! IT'S JUST A TOY!
TRUE! BUT I AM... THE SPANKER! I DON'T NEED A REAL GUN--
--TO PISTOL-WHIP YOU!!
FIGHT, YOU MALE CHAUVINIST GARGOYLE! I'M TILLIE THE HUN! I CAN BEAT ANY MAN--
--AND IF I LOSE, I'LL BE YOUR BRIDE!
BUT-- HULK CAN'T SMASH-- GIRL!
TOO BAD I'M NOT AS CHIVALROUS AS GREENSKIN, HUH? NOW THAT I'VE VIBRATED THAT SWORD OUTTA YER HAND--
--YOU'VE LEFT YOUR GUARD AS OPEN AS YOUR MOUTH, ARCHER!
WHAM

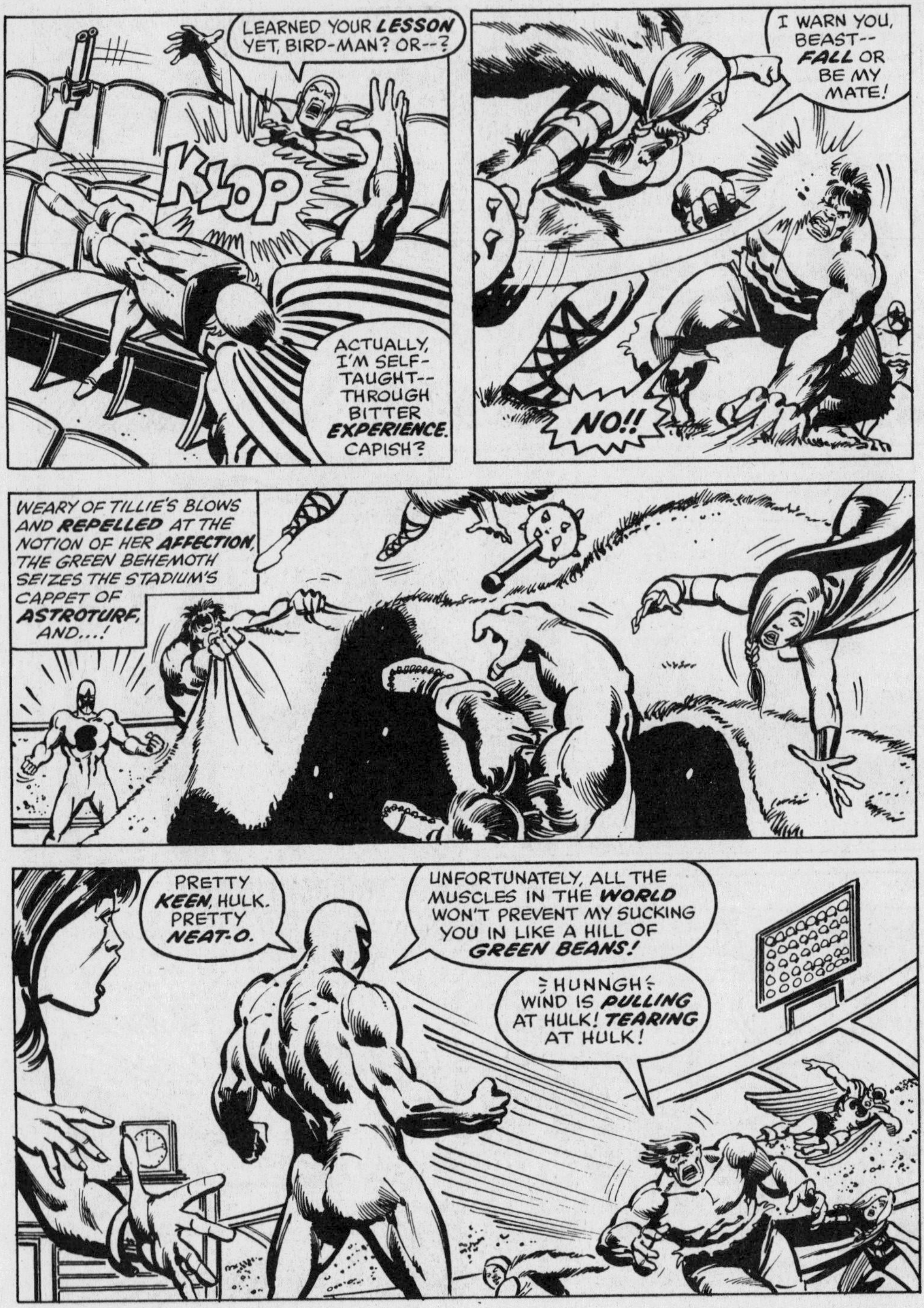
LEARNED YOUR LESSON YET, BIRD-MAN? OR--?
KLOP
ACTUALLY, I'M SELF-TAUGHT--THROUGH BITTER EXPERIENCE. CAPISH?
I WARN YOU, BEAST--FALL OR BE MY MATE!
NO!!
WEARY OF TILLIE'S BLOWS AND REPELLED AT THE NOTION OF HER AFFECTION, THE GREEN BEHEMOTH SEIZES THE STADIUM'S CARPET OF ASTROTURF, AND...!
PRETTY KEEN, HULK. PRETTY NEAT-O.
UNFORTUNATELY, ALL THE MUSCLES IN THE WORLD WON'T PREVENT MY SUCKING YOU IN LIKE A HILL OF GREEN BEANS!
HUNNGH WIND IS PULLING AT HULK! TEARING AT HULK!

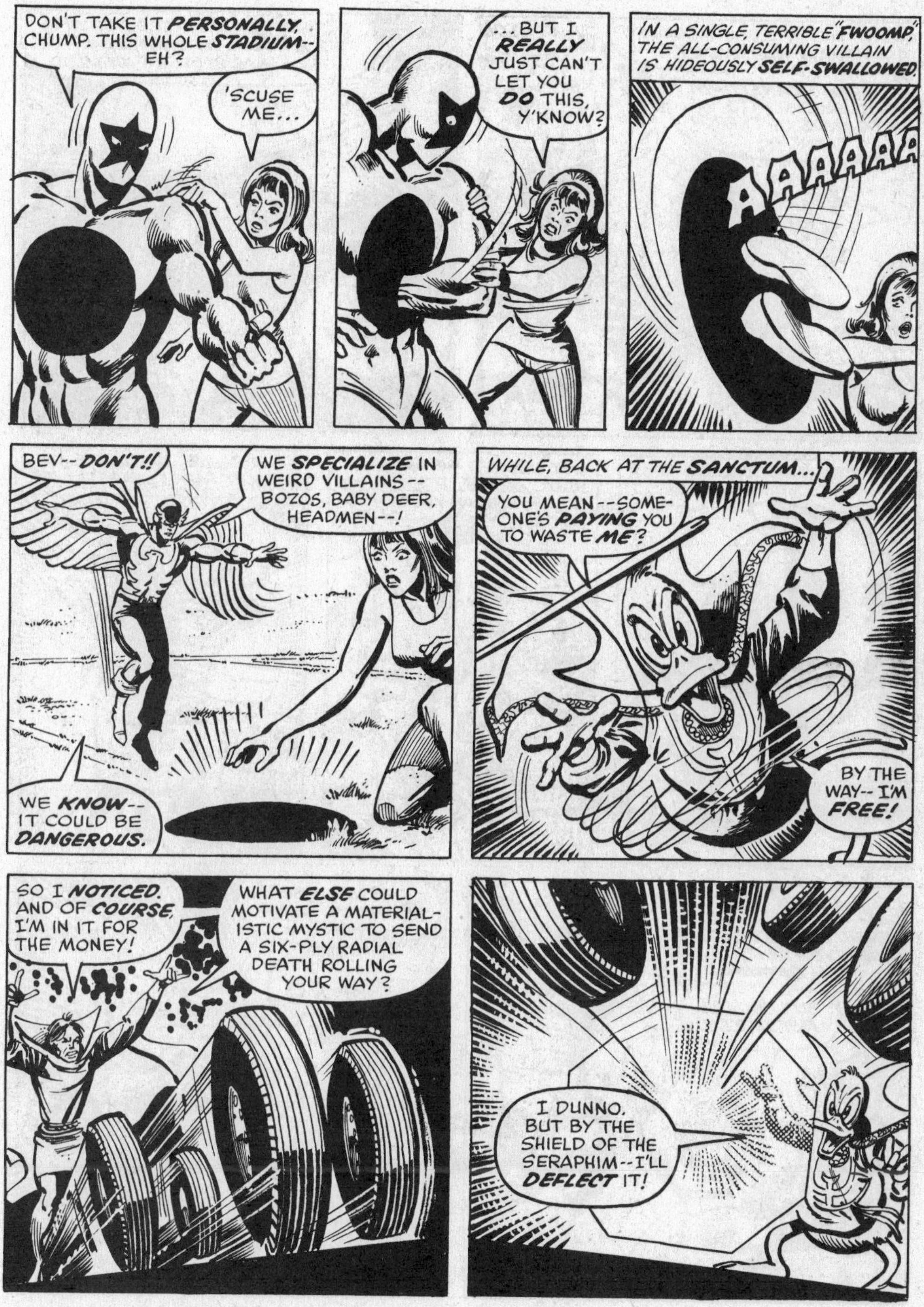
DON'T TAKE IT PERSONALLY, CHUMP. THIS WHOLE STADIUM-- EH?
'SCUSE ME...
...BUT I REALLY JUST CAN'T LET YOU DO THIS, Y'KNOW?
IN A SINGLE, TERRIBLE "FWOOMP," THE ALL-CONSUMING VILLAIN IS HIDEOUSLY SELF-SWALLOWED.
AAAAAA
BEV--DON'T!!
WE SPECIALIZE IN WEIRD VILLAINS-- BOZOS, BABY DEER, HEADMEN--!
WE KNOW-- IT COULD BE DANGEROUS.
WHILE, BACK AT THE SANCTUM...
YOU MEAN--SOME-ONE'S PAYING YOU TO WASTE ME?
BY THE WAY--I'M FREE!
SO I NOTICED. AND OF COURSE, I'M IN IT FOR THE MONEY!
WHAT ELSE COULD MOTIVATE A MATERIAL-ISTIC MYSTIC TO SEND A SIX-PLY RADIAL DEATH ROLLING YOUR WAY?
I DUNNO. BUT BY THE SHIELD OF THE SERAPHIM--I'LL DEFLECT IT!

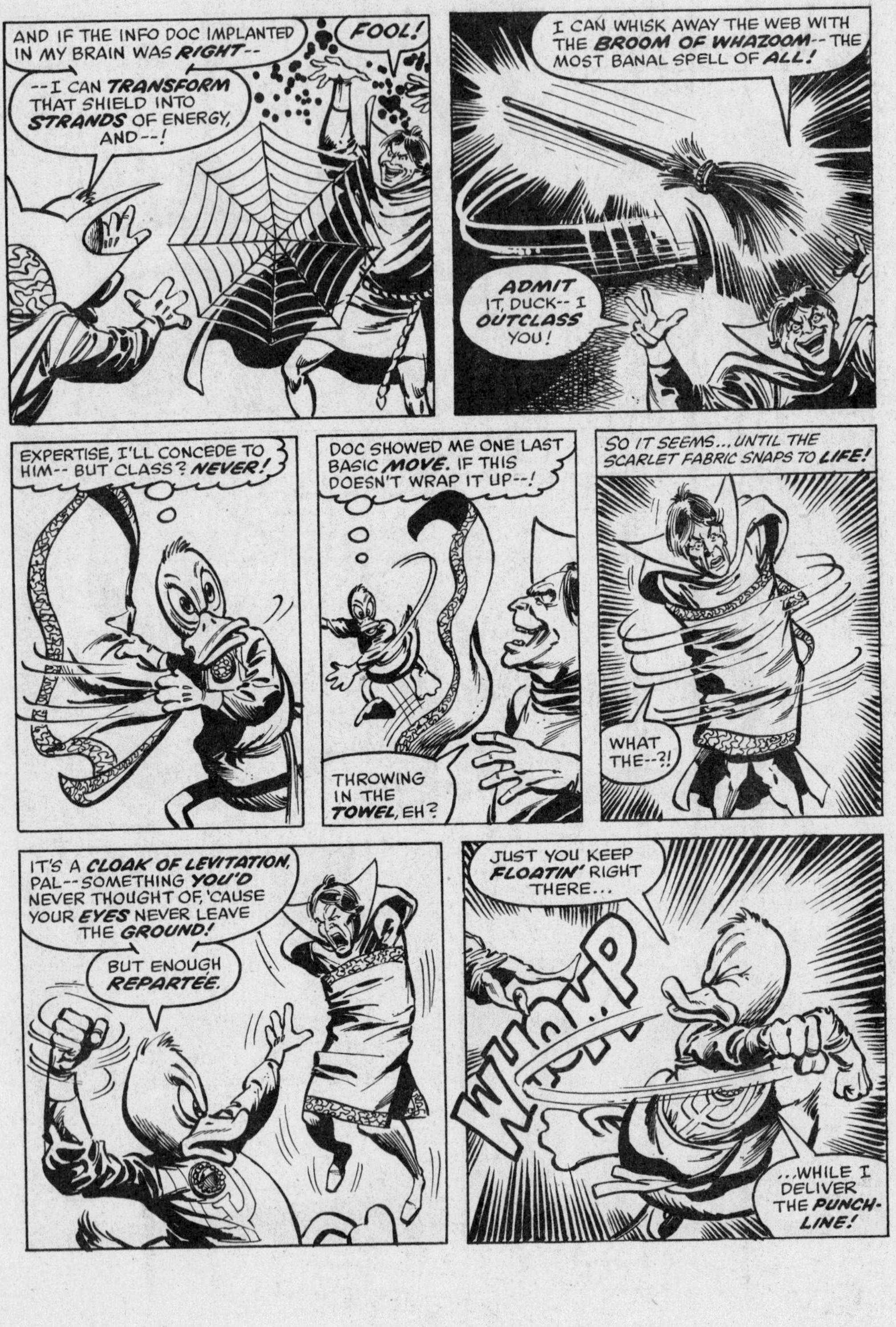
AND IF THE INFO DOC IMPLANTED IN MY BRAIN WAS RIGHT--
--I CAN TRANSFORM THAT SHIELD INTO STRANDS OF ENERGY, AND--!
FOOL!
I CAN WHISK AWAY THE WEB WITH THE BROOM OF WHAZOOM-- THE MOST BANAL SPELL OF ALL!
ADMIT IT, DUCK-- I OUTCLASS YOU!
EXPERTISE, I'LL CONCEDE TO HIM-- BUT CLASS? NEVER!
DOC SHOWED ME ONE LAST BASIC MOVE. IF THIS DOESN'T WRAP IT UP--!
THROWING IN THE TOWEL, EH?
SO IT SEEMS... UNTIL THE SCARLET FABRIC SNAPS TO LIFE!
WHAT THE--?!
IT'S A CLOAK OF LEVITATION, PAL--SOMETHING YOU'D NEVER THOUGHT OF, 'CAUSE YOUR EYES NEVER LEAVE THE GROUND!
BUT ENOUGH REPARTEE.
JUST YOU KEEP FLOATIN' RIGHT THERE...
WHOMP
...WHILE I DELIVER THE PUNCH-LINE!

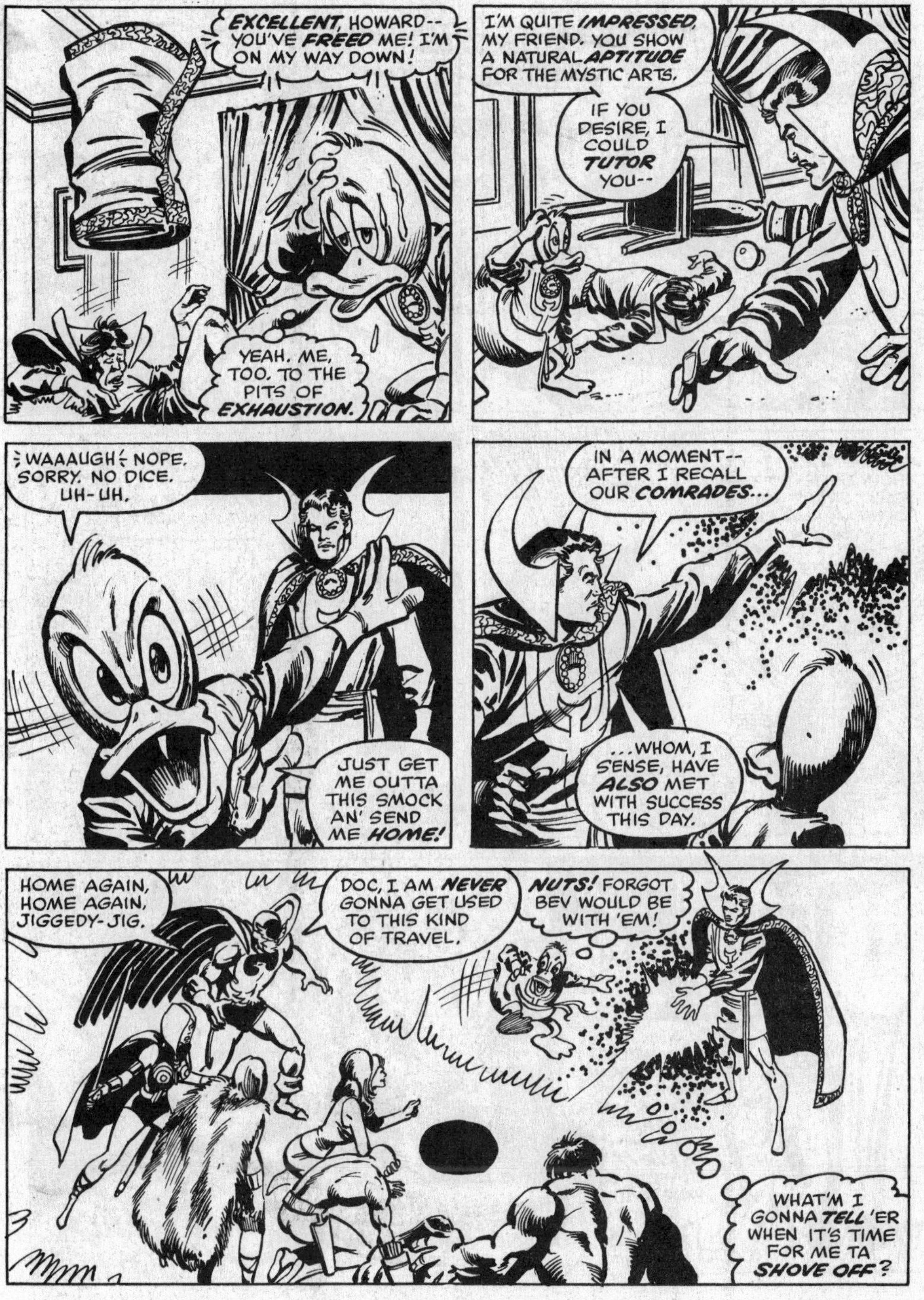
EXCELLENT, HOWARD-- YOU'VE FREED ME! I'M ON MY WAY DOWN!
YEAH. ME, TOO. TO THE PITS OF EXHAUSTION.
I'M QUITE IMPRESSED, MY FRIEND. YOU SHOW A NATURAL APTITUDE FOR THE MYSTIC ARTS.
IF YOU DESIRE, I COULD TUTOR YOU--
WAAAUGH! NOPE. SORRY. NO DICE. UH-UH.
JUST GET ME OUTTA THIS SMOCK AN' SEND ME HOME!
IN A MOMENT-- AFTER I RECALL OUR COMRADES...
...WHOM, I SENSE, HAVE ALSO MET WITH SUCCESS THIS DAY.
HOME AGAIN, HOME AGAIN, JIGGEDY-JIG.
DOC, I AM NEVER GONNA GET USED TO THIS KIND OF TRAVEL.
NUTS! FORGOT BEV WOULD BE WITH 'EM!
WHAT'M I GONNA TELL 'ER WHEN IT'S TIME FOR ME TA SHOVE OFF?

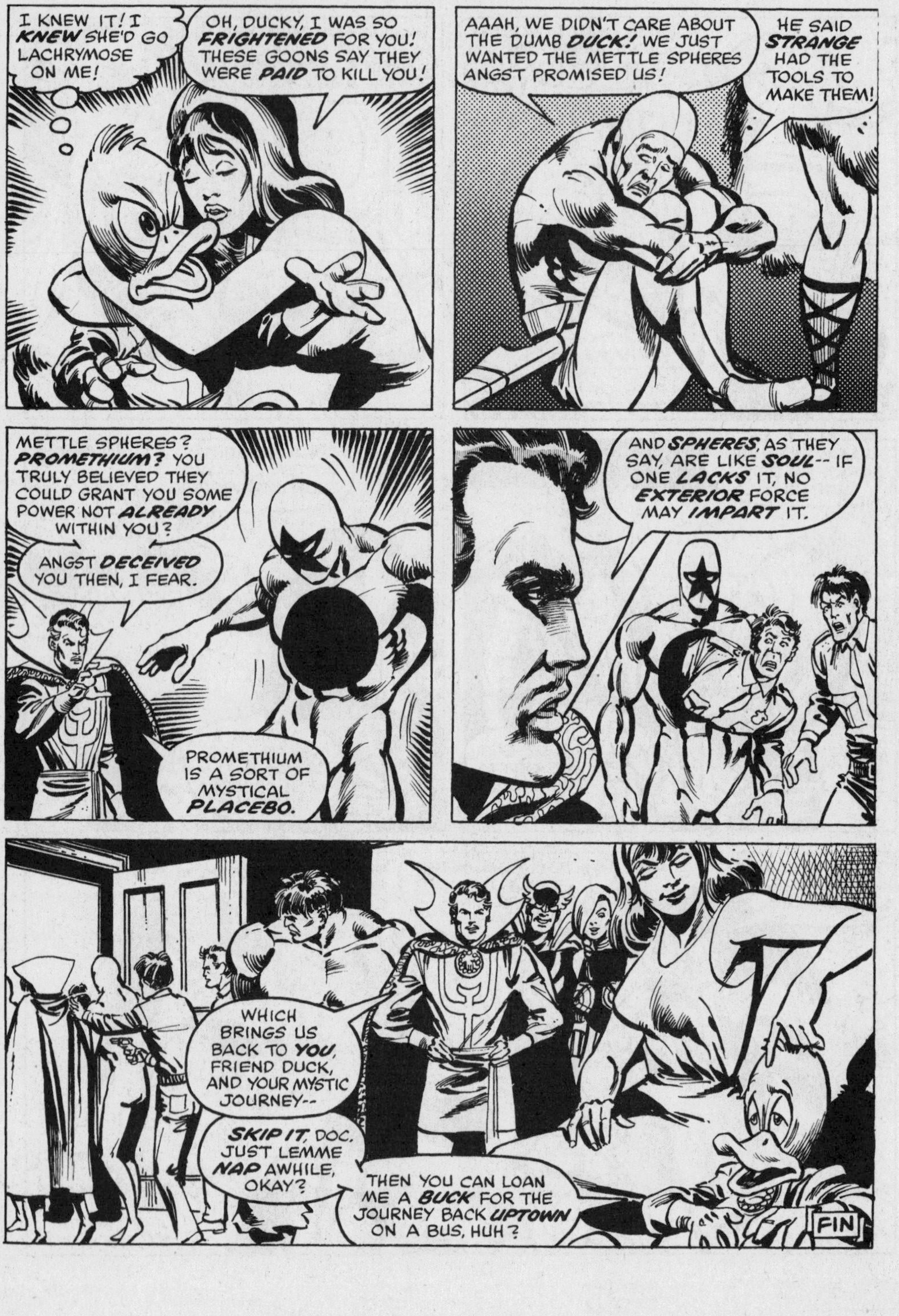
I KNEW IT! I KNEW SHE'D GO LACHRYMOSE ON ME!
OH, DUCKY, I WAS SO FRIGHTENED FOR YOU! THESE GOONS SAY THEY WERE PAID TO KILL YOU!
AAAH, WE DIDN'T CARE ABOUT THE DUMB DUCK! WE JUST WANTED THE METTLE SPHERES ANGST PROMISED US!
HE SAID STRANGE HAD THE TOOLS TO MAKE THEM!
METTLE SPHERES? PROMETHIUM? YOU TRULY BELIEVED THEY COULD GRANT YOU SOME POWER NOT ALREADY WITHIN YOU?
ANGST DECEIVED YOU THEN, I FEAR.
PROMETHIUM IS A SORT OF MYSTICAL PLACEBO.
AND SPHERES, AS THEY SAY, ARE LIKE SOUL-- IF ONE LACKS IT, NO EXTERIOR FORCE MAY IMPART IT.
WHICH BRINGS US BACK TO YOU, FRIEND DUCK, AND YOUR MYSTIC JOURNEY--
SKIP IT, DOC. JUST LEMME NAP AWHILE, OKAY?
THEN YOU CAN LOAN ME A BUCK FOR THE JOURNEY BACK UPTOWN ON A BUS, HUH?
FIN

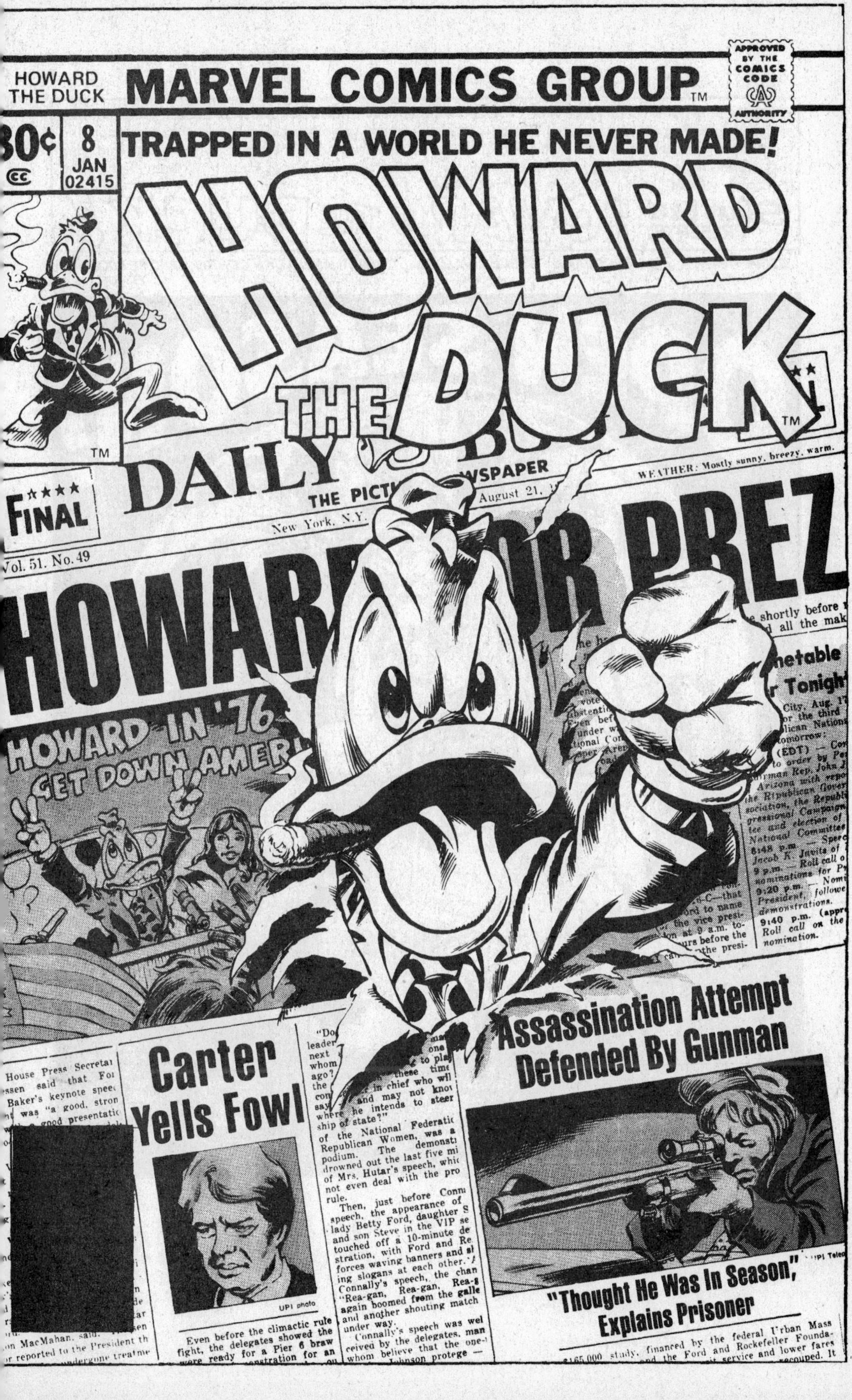
HOWARD THE DUCK
MARVEL COMICS GROUP
APPROVED BY THE COMICS CODE AUTHORITY
30¢
8
JAN
02415
TRAPPED IN A WORLD HE NEVER MADE!
HOWARD THE DUCK
DAILY
THE PICT
WSPAPER
WEATHER: Mostly sunny, breezy, warm.
FINAL
New York, N.Y.
August 21,
Vol. 51. No. 49
HOWAR
OR PREZ
HOWARD IN '76
HOWARD
GET DOWN AMER
Carter Yells Fowl
UPI photo
Assassination Attempt Defended By Gunman
"Thought He Was In Season," Explains Prisoner
[redacted]

From the time of his hatching, he was...different. A potentially brilliant scholar who dreaded the structured environment of school, he educated himself in the streets, taking whatever work was available, formulating his philosophy of self from what he learned of the world about him. And then the Cosmic Axis shifted...and that world *changed.* Suddenly, he was stranded in a universe he could not fathom. Without warning, he became a strange fowl in an even stranger land.

Stan Lee PRESENTS: HOWARD THE DUCK!™

STEVE GERBER WRITER * GENE COLAN ARTIST * STEVE LEIALOHA INKER * I. WATANABE LETTERER * JAN COHEN COLORIST * ARCHIE GOODWIN EDITOR

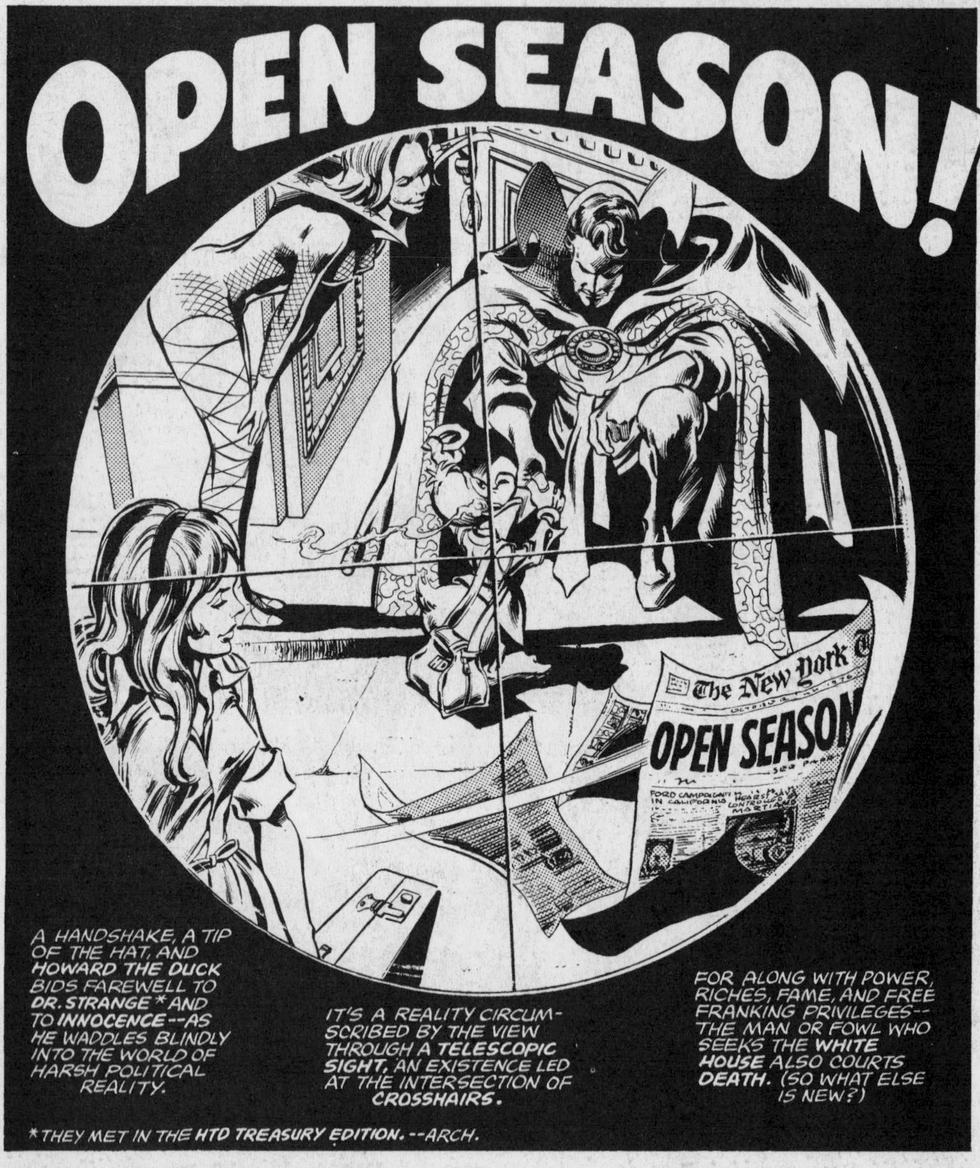

OPEN SEASON!
The New York
OPEN SEASON
A HANDSHAKE, A TIP OF THE HAT, AND HOWARD THE DUCK BIDS FAREWELL TO DR. STRANGE* AND TO INNOCENCE--AS HE WADDLES BLINDLY INTO THE WORLD OF HARSH POLITICAL REALITY.
IT'S A REALITY CIRCUMSCRIBED BY THE VIEW THROUGH A TELESCOPIC SIGHT, AN EXISTENCE LED AT THE INTERSECTION OF CROSSHAIRS.
FOR ALONG WITH POWER, RICHES, FAME, AND FREE FRANKING PRIVILEGES--THE MAN OR FOWL WHO SEEKS THE WHITE HOUSE ALSO COURTS DEATH. (SO WHAT ELSE IS NEW?)
*THEY MET IN THE HTD TREASURY EDITION. --ARCH.

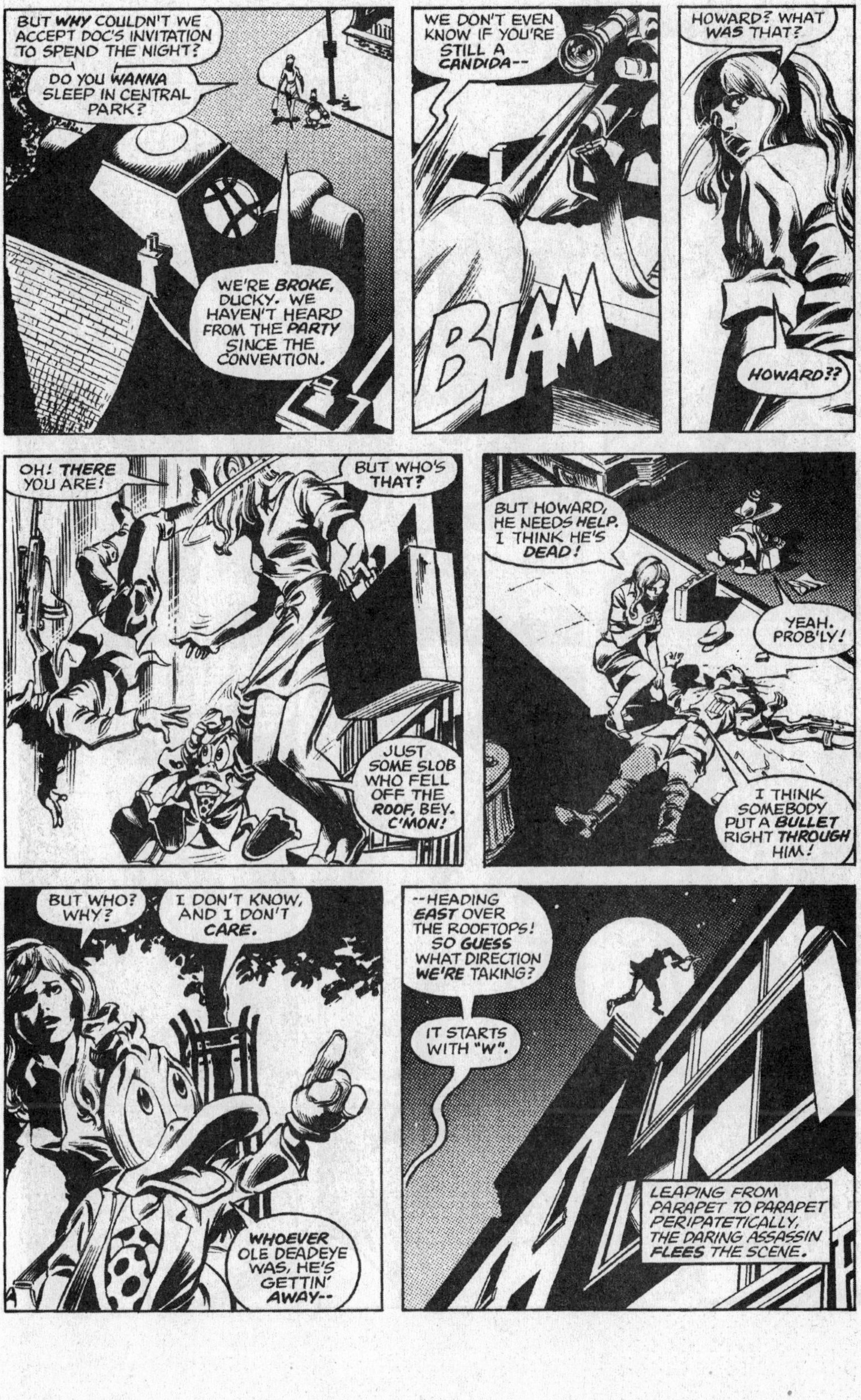
BUT WHY COULDN'T WE ACCEPT DOC'S INVITATION TO SPEND THE NIGHT?
DO YOU WANNA SLEEP IN CENTRAL PARK?
WE'RE BROKE, DUCKY. WE HAVEN'T HEARD FROM THE PARTY SINCE THE CONVENTION.
WE DON'T EVEN KNOW IF YOU'RE STILL A CANDIDA--
BLAM
HOWARD? WHAT WAS THAT?
HOWARD??
OH! THERE YOU ARE!
BUT WHO'S THAT?
JUST SOME SLOB WHO FELL OFF THE ROOF, BEV. C'MON!
BUT HOWARD, HE NEEDS HELP. I THINK HE'S DEAD!
YEAH. PROB'LY!
I THINK SOMEBODY PUT A BULLET RIGHT THROUGH HIM!
BUT WHO? WHY?
I DON'T KNOW, AND I DON'T CARE.
WHOEVER OLE DEADEYE WAS, HE'S GETTIN' AWAY--
--HEADING EAST OVER THE ROOFTOPS! SO GUESS WHAT DIRECTION WE'RE TAKING?
IT STARTS WITH "W".
LEAPING FROM PARAPET TO PARAPET PERIPATETICALLY, THE DARING ASSASSIN FLEES THE SCENE.

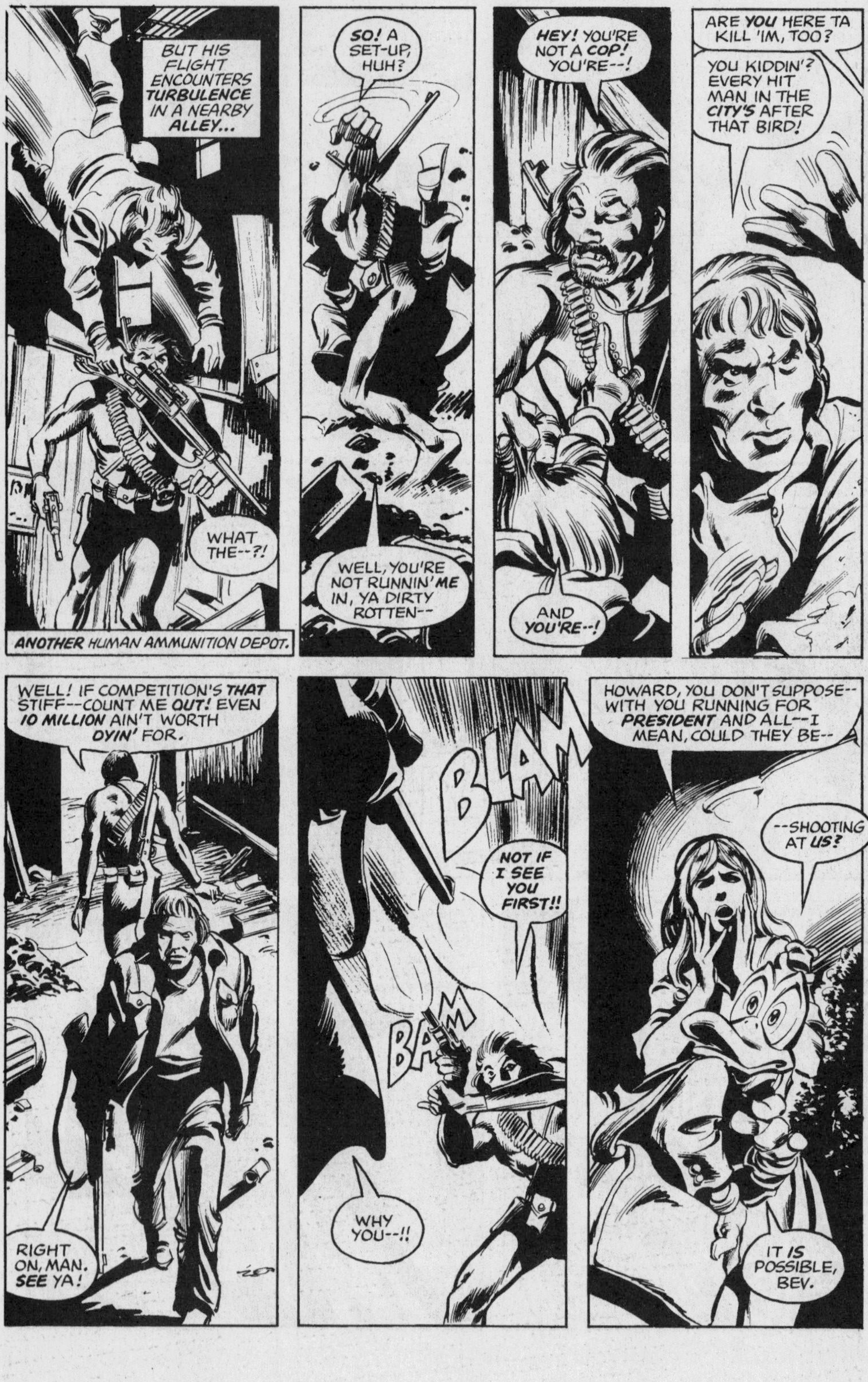
BUT HIS FLIGHT ENCOUNTERS TURBULENCE IN A NEARBY ALLEY...
WHAT THE--?!
ANOTHER HUMAN AMMUNITION DEPOT.
SO! A SET-UP, HUH?
WELL, YOU'RE NOT RUNNIN' ME IN, YA DIRTY ROTTEN--
HEY! YOU'RE NOT A COP! YOU'RE--!
AND YOU'RE--!
ARE YOU HERE TA KILL 'IM, TOO?
YOU KIDDIN'? EVERY HIT MAN IN THE CITY'S AFTER THAT BIRD!
WELL! IF COMPETITION'S THAT STIFF--COUNT ME OUT! EVEN 10 MILLION AIN'T WORTH DYIN' FOR.
RIGHT ON, MAN. SEE YA!
BLAM
NOT IF I SEE YOU FIRST!!
BAM
WHY YOU--!!
HOWARD, YOU DON'T SUPPOSE--WITH YOU RUNNING FOR PRESIDENT AND ALL--I MEAN, COULD THEY BE--
--SHOOTING AT US?
IT IS POSSIBLE, BEV.

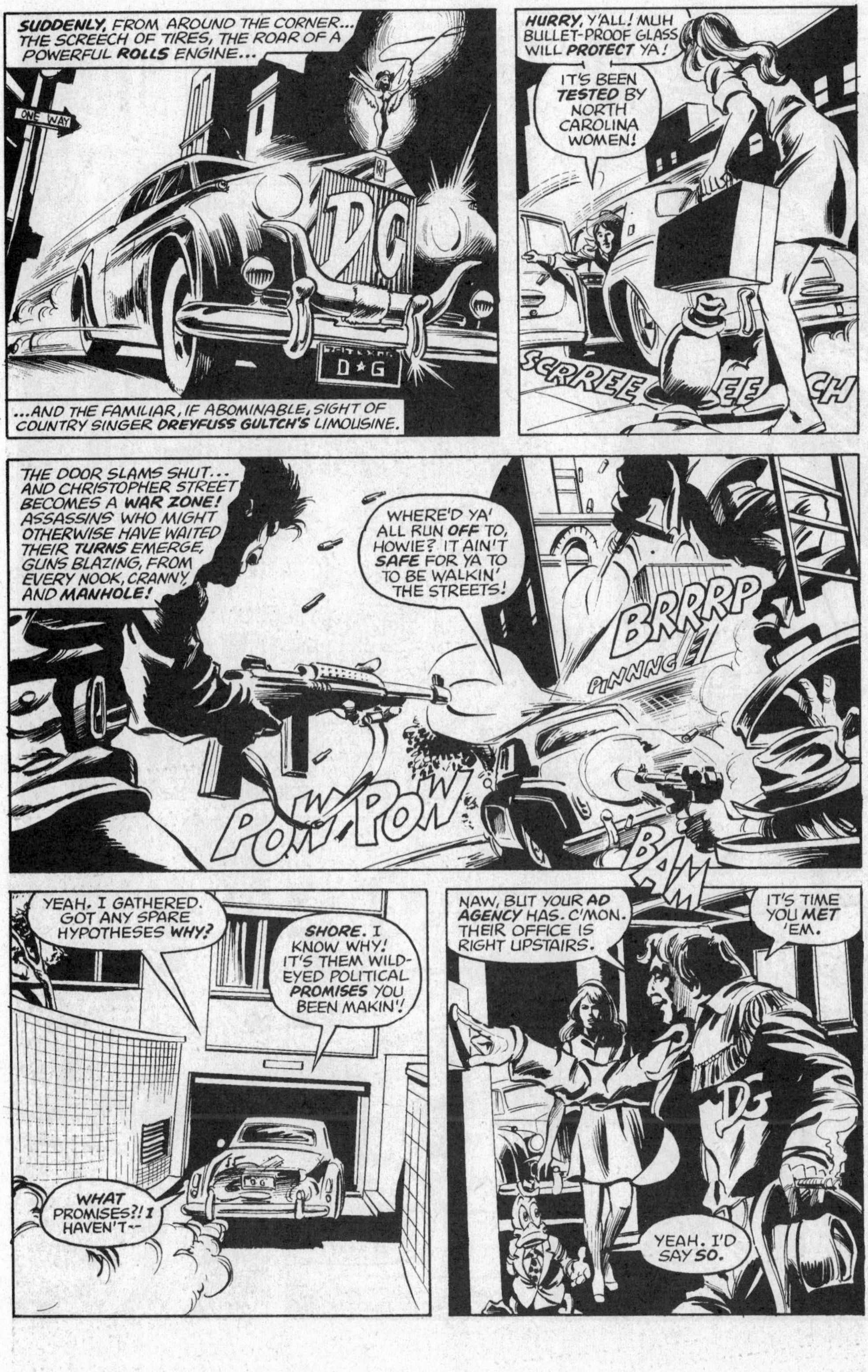
SUDDENLY, FROM AROUND THE CORNER... THE SCREECH OF TIRES, THE ROAR OF A POWERFUL ROLLS ENGINE...
ONE WAY
D★G
...AND THE FAMILIAR, IF ABOMINABLE, SIGHT OF COUNTRY SINGER DREYFUSS GULTCH'S LIMOUSINE.
HURRY, Y'ALL! MUH BULLET-PROOF GLASS WILL PROTECT YA!
IT'S BEEN TESTED BY NORTH CAROLINA WOMEN!
SCRREEEEECH
THE DOOR SLAMS SHUT... AND CHRISTOPHER STREET BECOMES A WAR ZONE! ASSASSINS WHO MIGHT OTHERWISE HAVE WAITED THEIR TURNS EMERGE, GUNS BLAZING, FROM EVERY NOOK, CRANNY, AND MANHOLE!
WHERE'D YA' ALL RUN OFF TO, HOWIE? IT AIN'T SAFE FOR YA TO TO BE WALKIN' THE STREETS!
BRRRP
PINNNG
POW POW
BAM
YEAH. I GATHERED. GOT ANY SPARE HYPOTHESES WHY?
SHORE. I KNOW WHY! IT'S THEM WILD-EYED POLITICAL PROMISES YOU BEEN MAKIN'!
WHAT PROMISES?! I HAVEN'T--
NAW, BUT YOUR AD AGENCY HAS. C'MON. THEIR OFFICE IS RIGHT UPSTAIRS.
IT'S TIME YOU MET 'EM.
YEAH. I'D SAY SO.

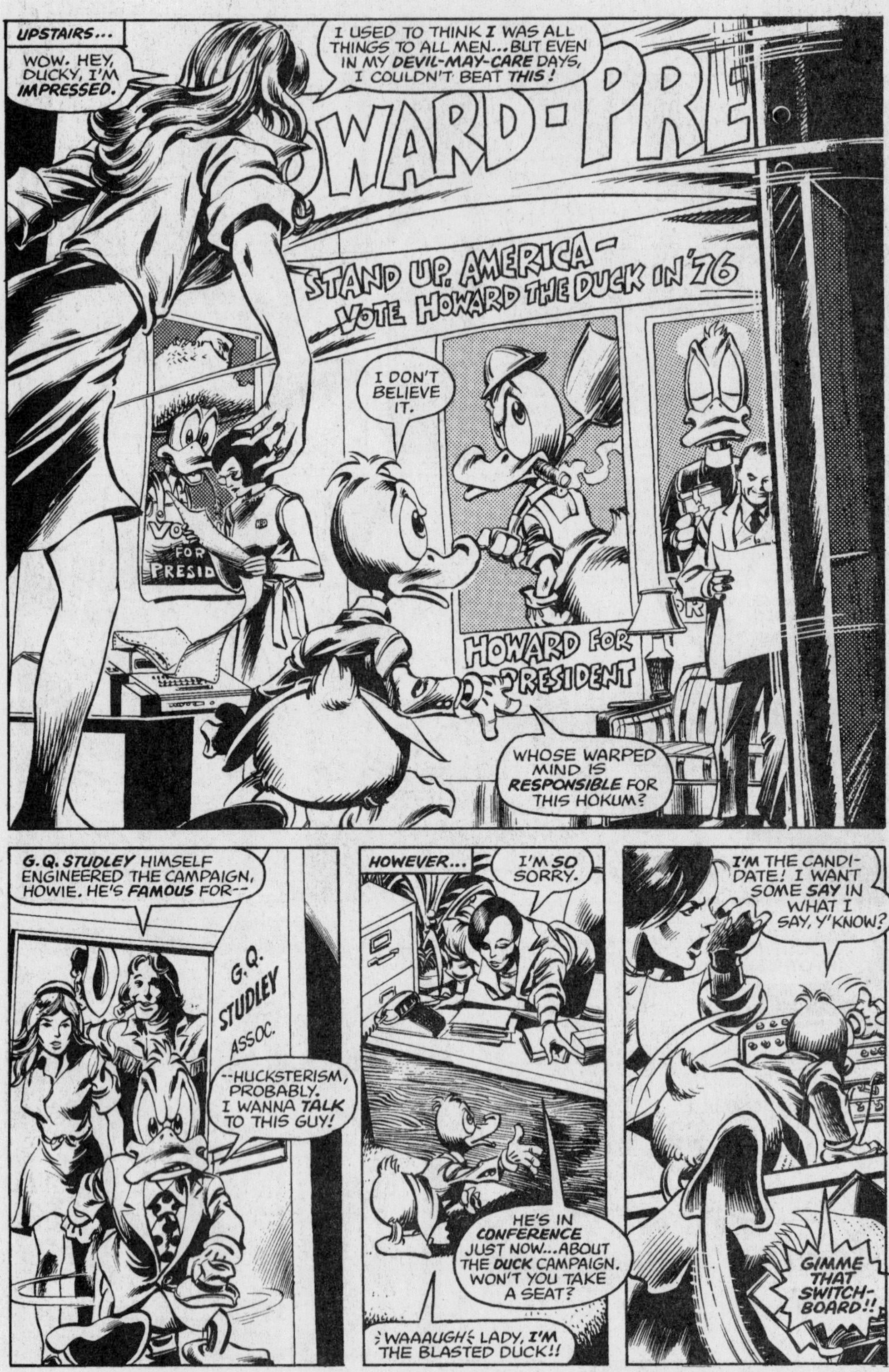

UPSTAIRS...
WOW. HEY, DUCKY, I'M IMPRESSED.
I USED TO THINK I WAS ALL THINGS TO ALL MEN... BUT EVEN IN MY DEVIL-MAY-CARE DAYS, I COULDN'T BEAT THIS!
OWARD-PRE
STAND UP, AMERICA - VOTE HOWARD THE DUCK IN '76
I DON'T BELIEVE IT.
HOWARD FOR PRESIDENT
WHOSE WARPED MIND IS RESPONSIBLE FOR THIS HOKUM?
G.Q. STUDLEY HIMSELF ENGINEERED THE CAMPAIGN, HOWIE. HE'S FAMOUS FOR--
G.Q. STUDLEY ASSOC.
--HUCKSTERISM, PROBABLY. I WANNA TALK TO THIS GUY!
HOWEVER...
I'M SO SORRY.
HE'S IN CONFERENCE JUST NOW... ABOUT THE DUCK CAMPAIGN. WON'T YOU TAKE A SEAT?
WAAAUGH! LADY, I'M THE BLASTED DUCK!!
I'M THE CANDIDATE! I WANT SOME SAY IN WHAT I SAY, Y'KNOW?
GIMME THAT SWITCHBOARD!!

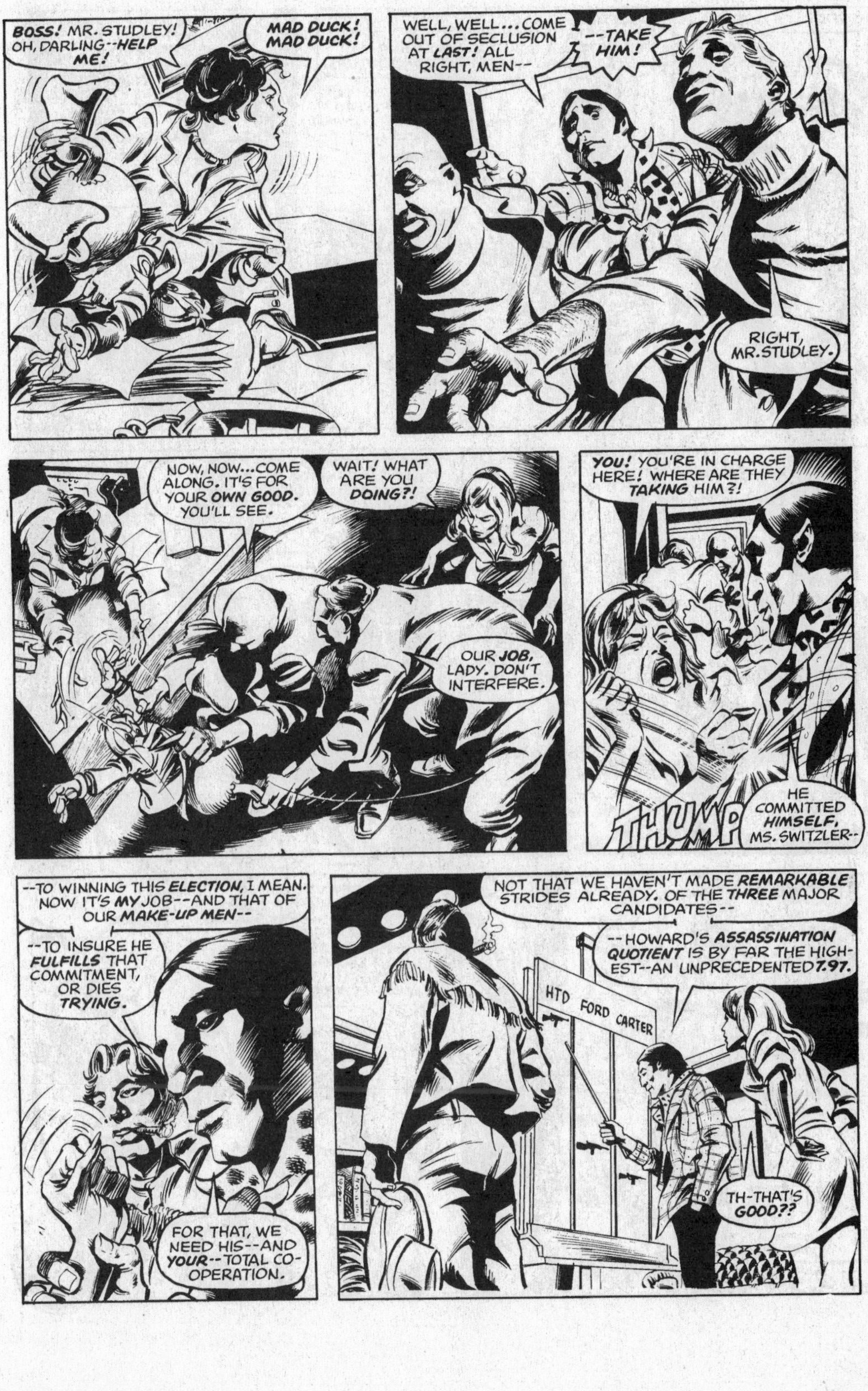

BOSS! MR. STUDLEY! OH, DARLING--HELP ME!
MAD DUCK! MAD DUCK!
WELL, WELL... COME OUT OF SECLUSION AT LAST! ALL RIGHT, MEN--
--TAKE HIM!
RIGHT, MR. STUDLEY.
NOW, NOW... COME ALONG. IT'S FOR YOUR OWN GOOD. YOU'LL SEE.
WAIT! WHAT ARE YOU DOING?!
OUR JOB, LADY. DON'T INTERFERE.
YOU! YOU'RE IN CHARGE HERE! WHERE ARE THEY TAKING HIM?!
THUMP
HE COMMITTED HIMSELF, MS. SWITZLER--
--TO WINNING THIS ELECTION, I MEAN. NOW IT'S MY JOB--AND THAT OF OUR MAKE-UP MEN--
--TO INSURE HE FULFILLS THAT COMMITMENT, OR DIES TRYING.
FOR THAT, WE NEED HIS--AND YOUR--TOTAL CO-OPERATION.
NOT THAT WE HAVEN'T MADE REMARKABLE STRIDES ALREADY. OF THE THREE MAJOR CANDIDATES--
--HOWARD'S ASSASSINATION QUOTIENT IS BY FAR THE HIGHEST--AN UNPRECEDENTED 7.97.
HTD FORD CARTER
TH-THAT'S GOOD??

Panel 1: GOOD? IT'S *GREAT!* IT MEANS PEOPLE *CARE!*

Panel 2: AND HERE'S EVERY *SYLLABLE* HOWARD WILL UTTER WITHIN EARSHOT OF A REPORTER BETWEEN NOW AND NOVEMBER--AS COMPILED BY OUR EXPERT *EQUIVOCATEURS.*

BUT--HOW DO YOUR *SPEECHWRITERS* KNOW WHAT HOWARD THINKS ABOUT--

Panel 3: TODAY'S CANDIDATE DOESN'T *THINK,* MS. SWITZLER. HE *RECITES*--

--NICE, SAFE, PRE-TESTED BROMIDIC BOMBASTS LIKE *THIS:*

≷AHEM≷

Panel 4: "I'M *TIRED* OF HEARING PEOPLE RUN DOWN THIS COUNTRY! SURE, WE'VE GOT *PROBLEMS*--

"--POLLUTION, INFLATION, RECESSION, CRIME, PERVASIVE MORAL DECAY--JUST TO NAME A *FEW.*

"BUT WHAT NATION *DOESN'T* HAVE ITS TROUBLES?"

Panel 5: ARE YOU *SERIOUS?* YOU EXPECT *HOWARD* TO SPOUT THAT STUFF?

WITH A *STRAIGHT FACE?!*

EH? WHATEVER DO YOU ME--

WAAAUGH

Panel 6: WE HADDA WORK *FAST,* MR. STUDLEY. HE WOULDN'T STOP *SQUIRMIN!* BUT--

Panel 7: "BUT" *NOTHING!* HE'S *MAGNIFICENT!!*

DISTINGUISHED. SUBTLE. RAZOR-SHARP LINES--YET TASTEFULLY *UNDERSTATED.*

AND EXUDING UNMISTAKABLE *SEX APPEAL!* AND LORD A'MIGHTY, THAT *WINNING* SMILE!!

YEAH? WELL, IF YA *LIKE* IT SO MUCH--

CHOMP

--YA CAN KEEP IT, YA POMPOUS, PRESUMPTUOUS, PLASTICIZED FASHION PLATE!

STOP!!

YOU'RE COMMITTING POLITICAL *SUICIDE!*

YOU CAN'T *WADDLE* OUT ON US! WHO'LL *PACKAGE* YOU?!

YOU'RE A THIRD-PARTY CANDIDATE AND A *DUCK!*

YOU EXPECT TO SURMOUNT THOSE IMAGE PROBLEMS *ALONE?!*

NYAAH

JUST *WATCH* ME, LAUGHING BOY!

OUTSIDE...

YOU FIGGER *EVERY* CANDIDATE GOES THRU THIS DEBASE-MENT?

NAH. BY THE TIME MOST OF 'EM GET *THIS* FAR, HUMILIATING COMPROMISE COMES *EASY.*

WHAT *ARE* YOU GONNA DO ABOUT AN *AD REP*, THOUGH?

WE'LL PICK OUR *OWN*--THE SCIENTIFIC WAY!

AT *RANDOM*-- FROM THE *YELLOW PAGES!*

TELEPH

AH-HA!

NOW *THAT'S* OUR KINDA PEOPLE!

WELL...*YOUR* KIND, ANYWAY.

MAD GENIUS ASSO ATES

AVENUE

OOM 806

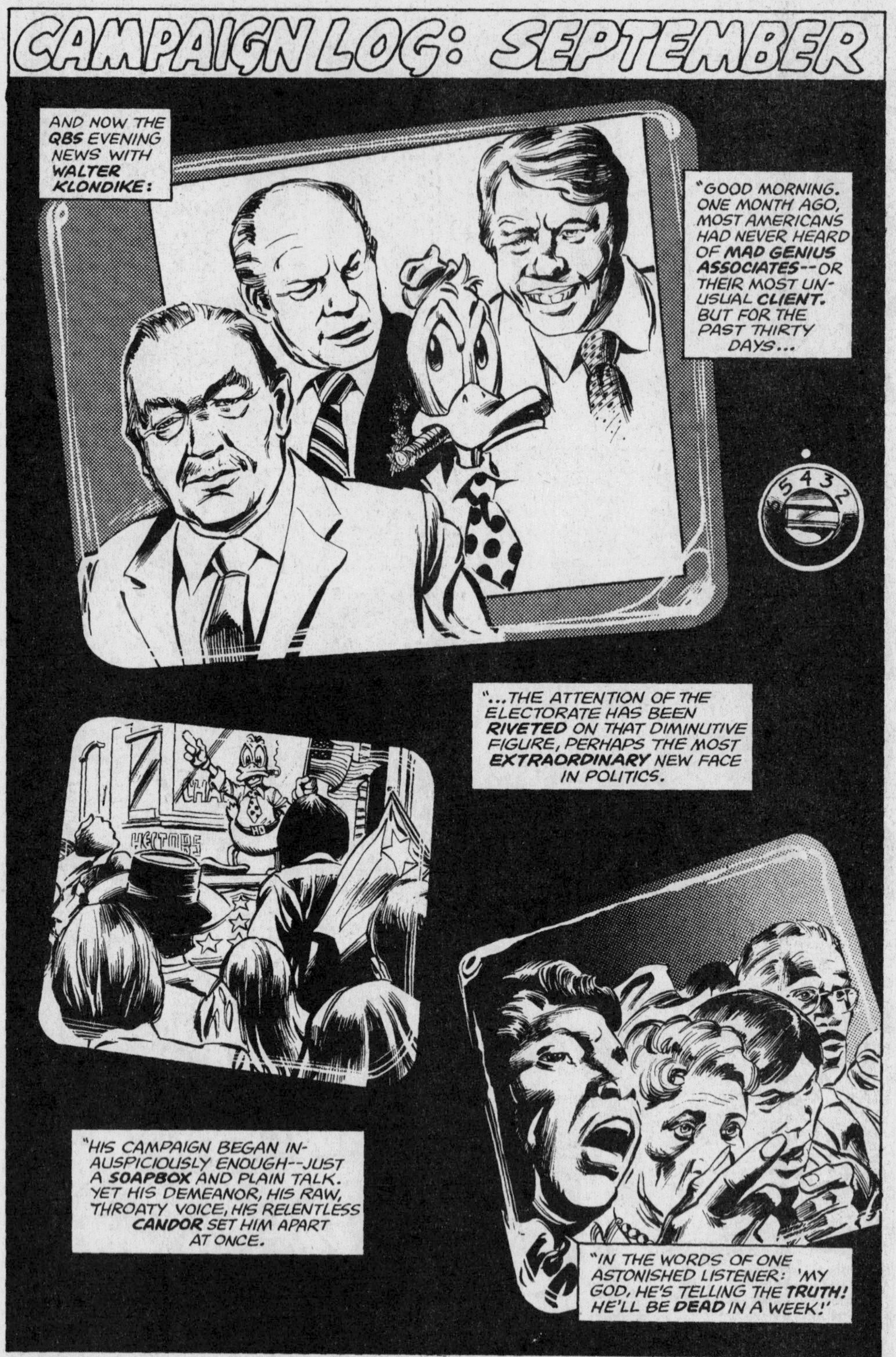
CAMPAIGN LOG: SEPTEMBER
AND NOW THE QBS EVENING NEWS WITH WALTER KLONDIKE:
"GOOD MORNING. ONE MONTH AGO, MOST AMERICANS HAD NEVER HEARD OF MAD GENIUS ASSOCIATES--OR THEIR MOST UNUSUAL CLIENT. BUT FOR THE PAST THIRTY DAYS...
"...THE ATTENTION OF THE ELECTORATE HAS BEEN RIVETED ON THAT DIMINUTIVE FIGURE, PERHAPS THE MOST EXTRAORDINARY NEW FACE IN POLITICS.
"HIS CAMPAIGN BEGAN INAUSPICIOUSLY ENOUGH--JUST A SOAPBOX AND PLAIN TALK. YET HIS DEMEANOR, HIS RAW, THROATY VOICE, HIS RELENTLESS CANDOR SET HIM APART AT ONCE.
"IN THE WORDS OF ONE ASTONISHED LISTENER: 'MY GOD, HE'S TELLING THE TRUTH! HE'LL BE DEAD IN A WEEK!'

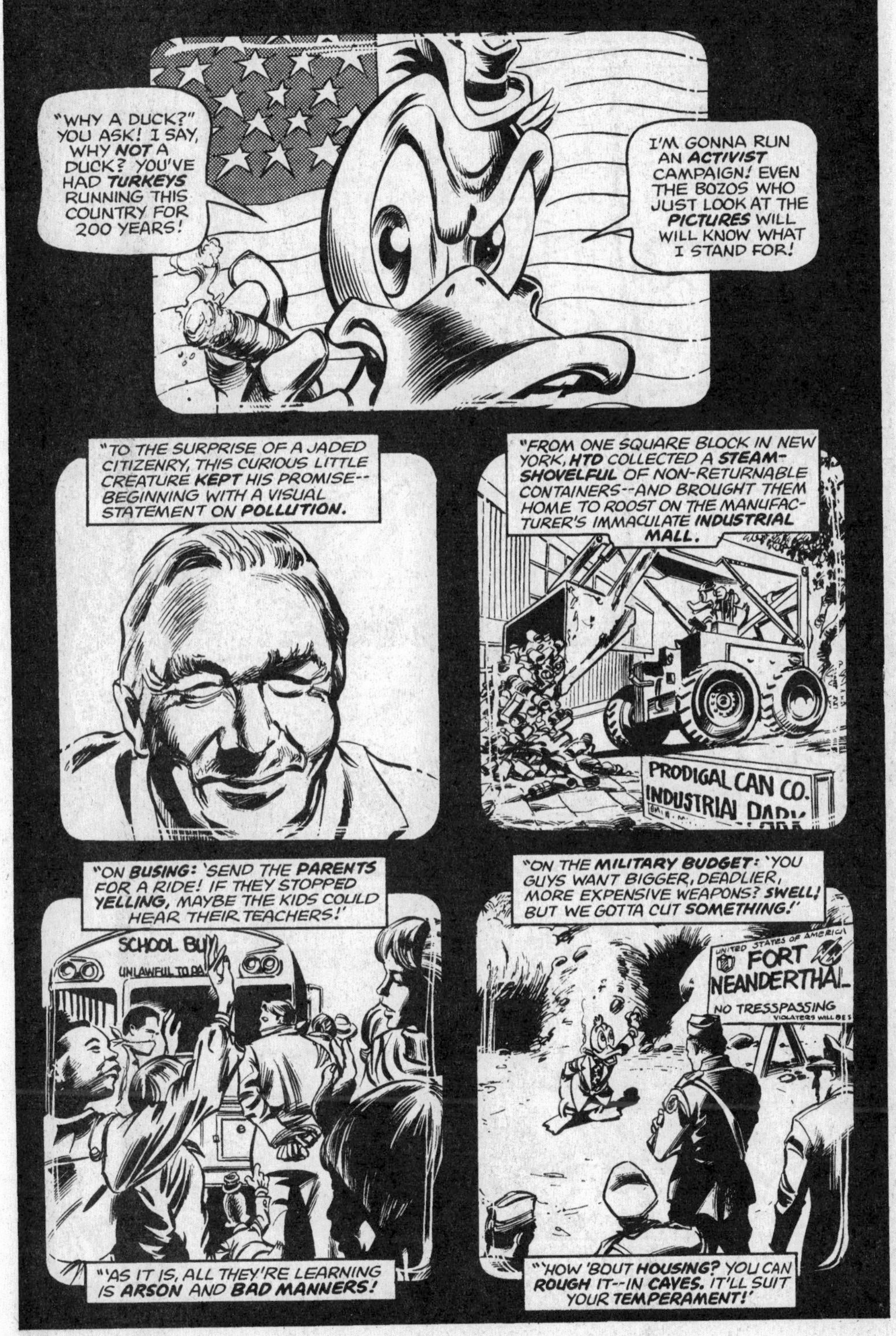

"WHY A DUCK?" YOU ASK! I SAY, WHY NOT A DUCK? YOU'VE HAD TURKEYS RUNNING THIS COUNTRY FOR 200 YEARS!
I'M GONNA RUN AN ACTIVIST CAMPAIGN! EVEN THE BOZOS WHO JUST LOOK AT THE PICTURES WILL WILL KNOW WHAT I STAND FOR!
"TO THE SURPRISE OF A JADED CITIZENRY, THIS CURIOUS LITTLE CREATURE KEPT HIS PROMISE-- BEGINNING WITH A VISUAL STATEMENT ON POLLUTION.
"FROM ONE SQUARE BLOCK IN NEW YORK, HTD COLLECTED A STEAM-SHOVELFUL OF NON-RETURNABLE CONTAINERS--AND BROUGHT THEM HOME TO ROOST ON THE MANUFACTURER'S IMMACULATE INDUSTRIAL MALL.
PRODIGAL CAN CO.
INDUSTRIAL PARK
"ON BUSING: 'SEND THE PARENTS FOR A RIDE! IF THEY STOPPED YELLING, MAYBE THE KIDS COULD HEAR THEIR TEACHERS!'
SCHOOL BU
"AS IT IS, ALL THEY'RE LEARNING IS ARSON AND BAD MANNERS!
"ON THE MILITARY BUDGET: 'YOU GUYS WANT BIGGER, DEADLIER, MORE EXPENSIVE WEAPONS? SWELL! BUT WE GOTTA CUT SOMETHING!'
UNITED STATES OF AMERICA
FORT NEANDERTHAL
NO TRESSPASSING
"HOW 'BOUT HOUSING? YOU CAN ROUGH IT--IN CAVES. IT'LL SUIT YOUR TEMPERAMENT!'

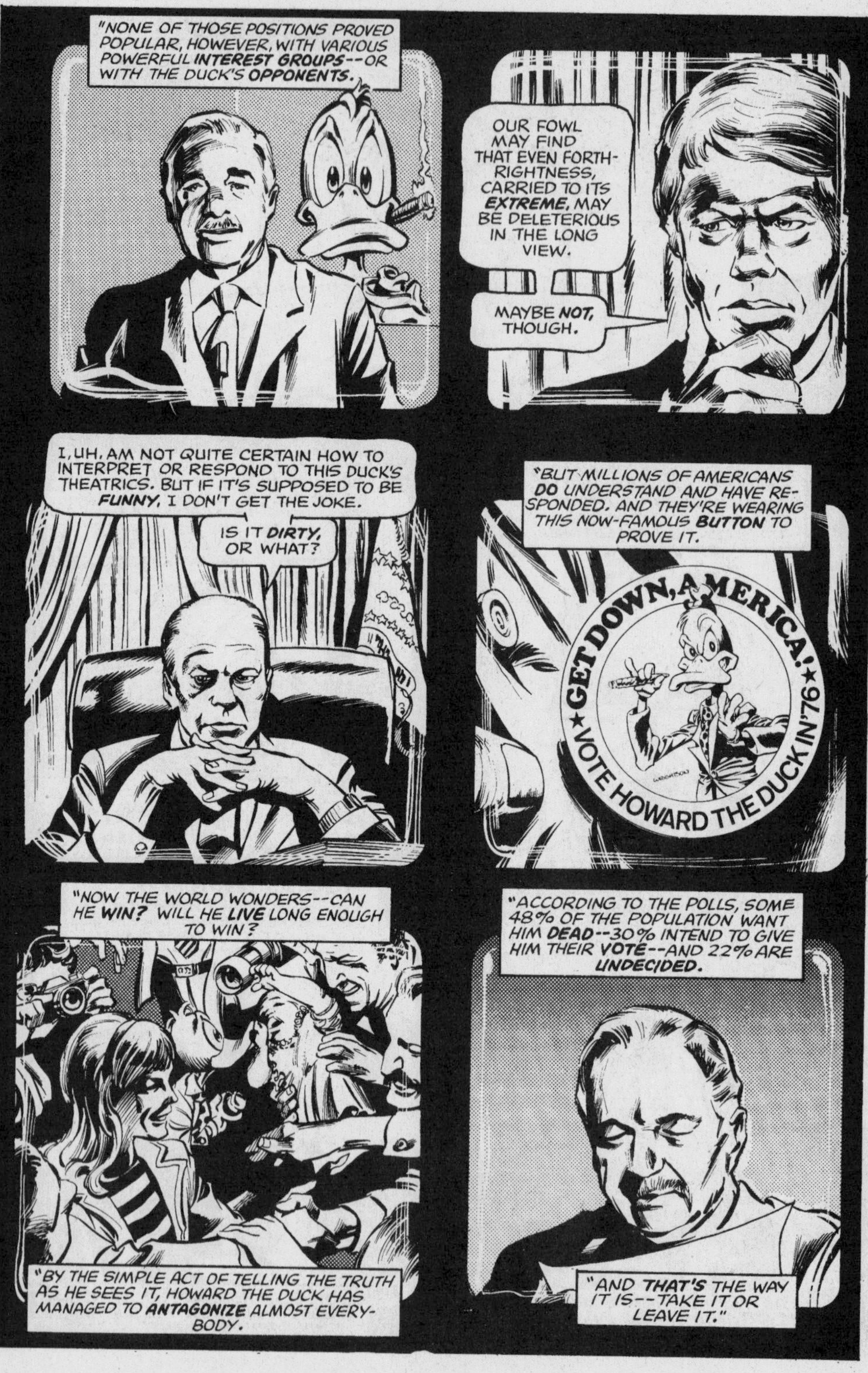
"NONE OF THOSE POSITIONS PROVED POPULAR, HOWEVER, WITH VARIOUS POWERFUL INTEREST GROUPS--OR WITH THE DUCK'S OPPONENTS.
OUR FOWL MAY FIND THAT EVEN FORTH-RIGHTNESS, CARRIED TO ITS EXTREME, MAY BE DELETERIOUS IN THE LONG VIEW.
MAYBE NOT, THOUGH.
I, UH, AM NOT QUITE CERTAIN HOW TO INTERPRET OR RESPOND TO THIS DUCK'S THEATRICS. BUT IF IT'S SUPPOSED TO BE FUNNY, I DON'T GET THE JOKE.
IS IT DIRTY, OR WHAT?
"BUT MILLIONS OF AMERICANS DO UNDERSTAND AND HAVE RE-SPONDED. AND THEY'RE WEARING THIS NOW-FAMOUS BUTTON TO PROVE IT.
GET DOWN, AMERICA!
★VOTE HOWARD THE DUCK IN '76★
"NOW THE WORLD WONDERS--CAN HE WIN? WILL HE LIVE LONG ENOUGH TO WIN?
"BY THE SIMPLE ACT OF TELLING THE TRUTH AS HE SEES IT, HOWARD THE DUCK HAS MANAGED TO ANTAGONIZE ALMOST EVERY-BODY.
"ACCORDING TO THE POLLS, SOME 48% OF THE POPULATION WANT HIM DEAD--30% INTEND TO GIVE HIM THEIR VOTE--AND 22% ARE UNDECIDED.
"AND THAT'S THE WAY IT IS--TAKE IT OR LEAVE IT."

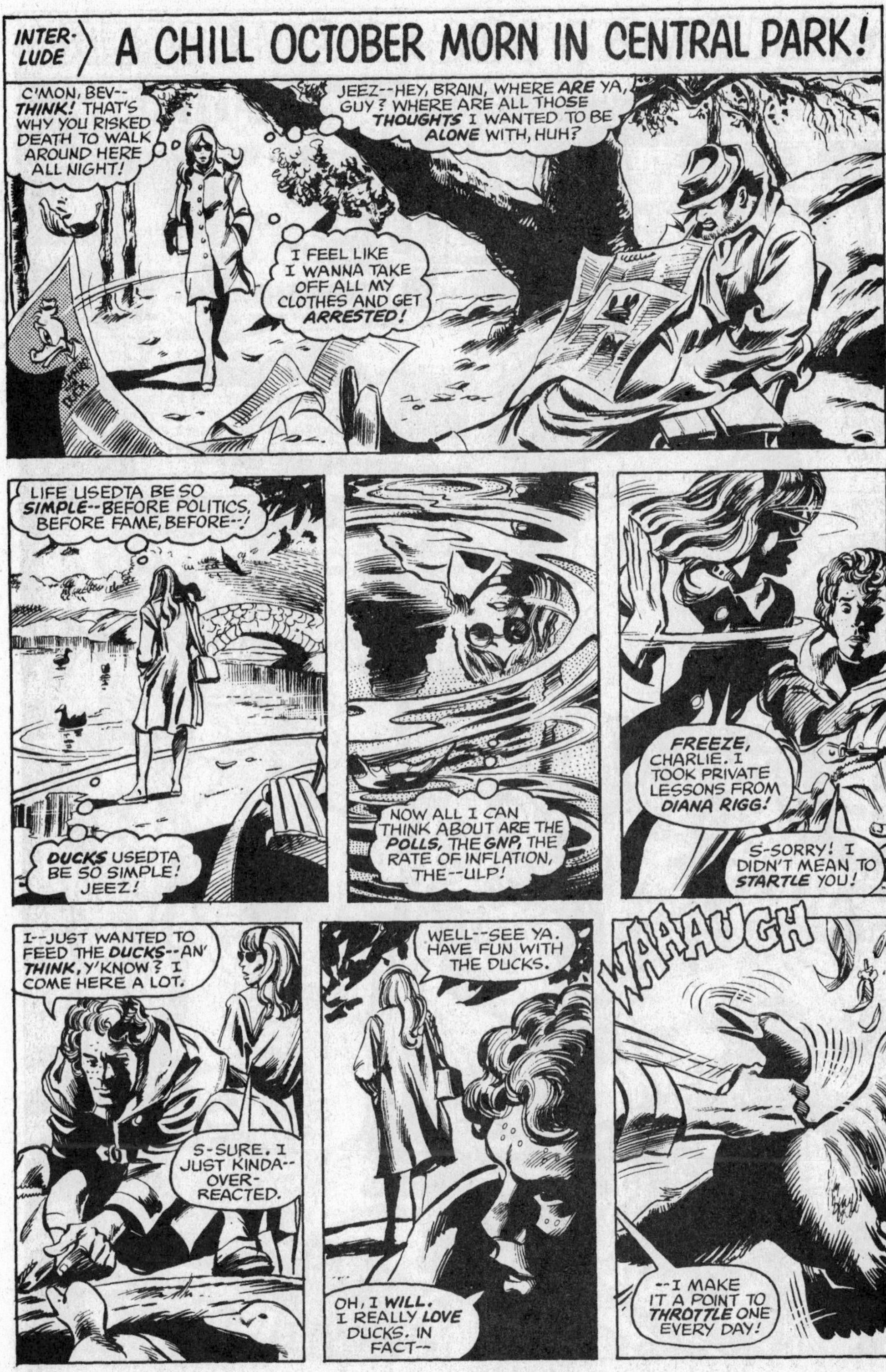
INTER-LUDE
A CHILL OCTOBER MORN IN CENTRAL PARK!
C'MON, BEV--THINK! THAT'S WHY YOU RISKED DEATH TO WALK AROUND HERE ALL NIGHT!
JEEZ--HEY, BRAIN, WHERE ARE YA, GUY? WHERE ARE ALL THOSE THOUGHTS I WANTED TO BE ALONE WITH, HUH?
I FEEL LIKE I WANNA TAKE OFF ALL MY CLOTHES AND GET ARRESTED!
LIFE USEDTA BE SO SIMPLE--BEFORE POLITICS, BEFORE FAME, BEFORE--!
DUCKS USEDTA BE SO SIMPLE! JEEZ!
NOW ALL I CAN THINK ABOUT ARE THE POLLS, THE GNP, THE RATE OF INFLATION, THE--ULP!
FREEZE, CHARLIE. I TOOK PRIVATE LESSONS FROM DIANA RIGG!
S-SORRY! I DIDN'T MEAN TO STARTLE YOU!
I--JUST WANTED TO FEED THE DUCKS--AN' THINK, Y'KNOW? I COME HERE A LOT.
S-SURE. I JUST KINDA--OVER-REACTED.
WELL--SEE YA. HAVE FUN WITH THE DUCKS.
OH, I WILL. I REALLY LOVE DUCKS. IN FACT--
WAAAUGH
--I MAKE IT A POINT TO THROTTLE ONE EVERY DAY!

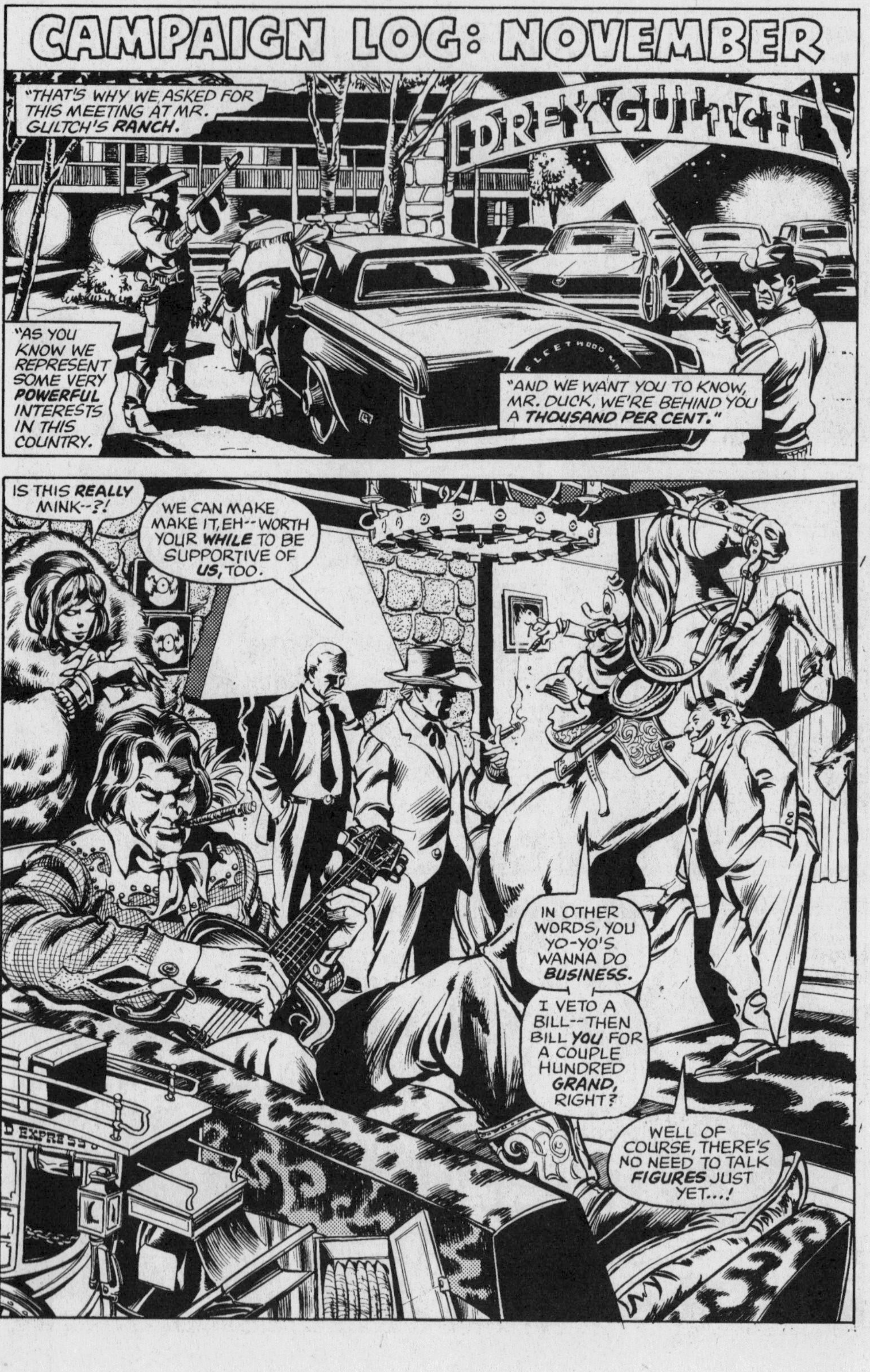
CAMPAIGN LOG: NOVEMBER
"THAT'S WHY WE ASKED FOR THIS MEETING AT MR. GULTCH'S RANCH.
DREY GULTCH
"AS YOU KNOW WE REPRESENT SOME VERY POWERFUL INTERESTS IN THIS COUNTRY.
"AND WE WANT YOU TO KNOW, MR. DUCK, WE'RE BEHIND YOU A THOUSAND PER CENT."
IS THIS REALLY MINK--?!
WE CAN MAKE MAKE IT, EH--WORTH YOUR WHILE TO BE SUPPORTIVE OF US, TOO.
IN OTHER WORDS, YOU YO-YO'S WANNA DO BUSINESS.
I VETO A BILL--THEN BILL YOU FOR A COUPLE HUNDRED GRAND, RIGHT?
WELL OF COURSE, THERE'S NO NEED TO TALK FIGURES JUST YET...!

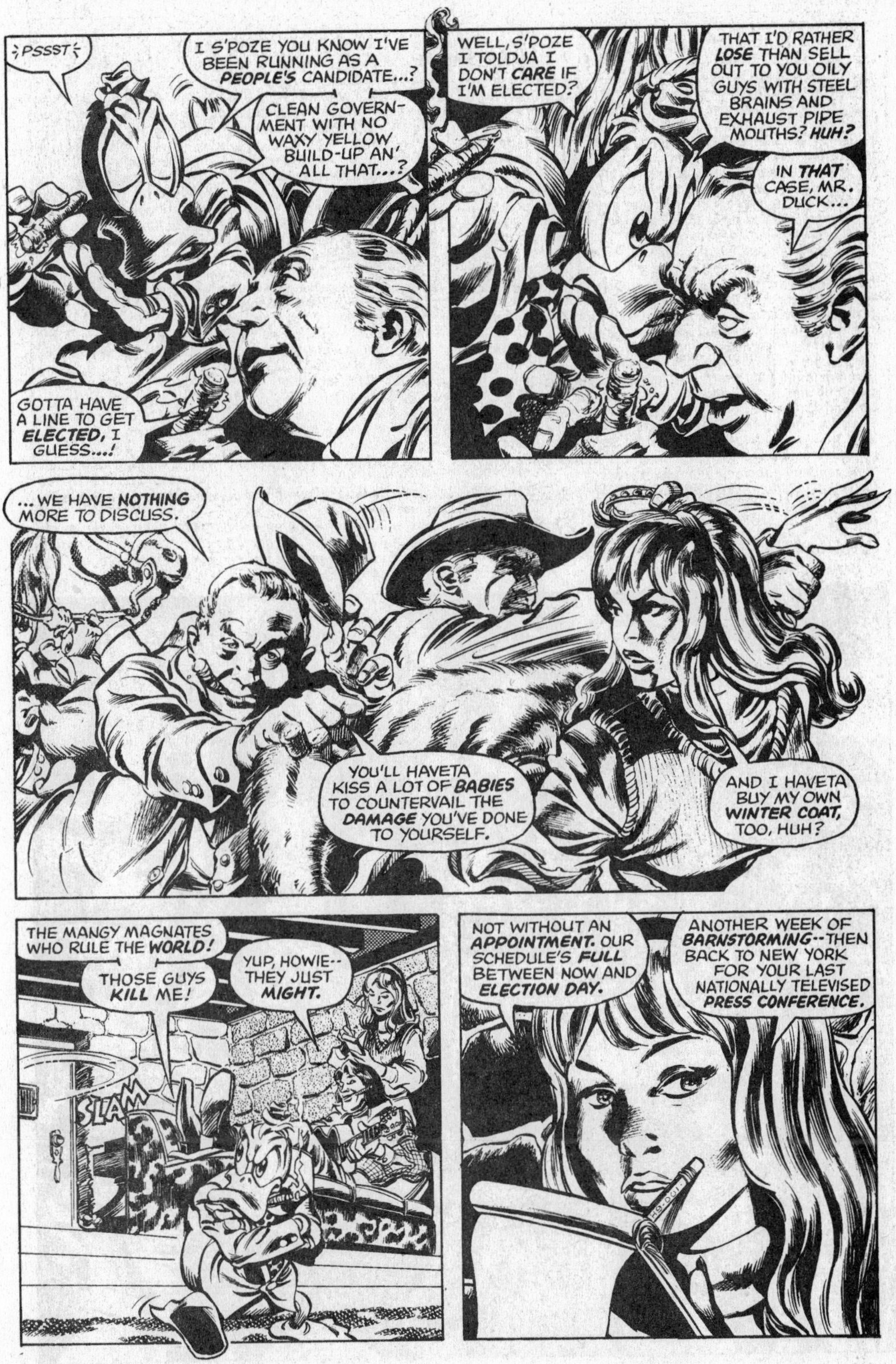
PSSST
I S'POZE YOU KNOW I'VE BEEN RUNNING AS A PEOPLE'S CANDIDATE...?
CLEAN GOVERNMENT WITH NO WAXY YELLOW BUILD-UP AN' ALL THAT...?
GOTTA HAVE A LINE TO GET ELECTED, I GUESS...!
WELL, S'POZE I TOLDJA I DON'T CARE IF I'M ELECTED?
THAT I'D RATHER LOSE THAN SELL OUT TO YOU OILY GUYS WITH STEEL BRAINS AND EXHAUST PIPE MOUTHS? HUH?
IN THAT CASE, MR. DUCK...
...WE HAVE NOTHING MORE TO DISCUSS.
YOU'LL HAVETA KISS A LOT OF BABIES TO COUNTERVAIL THE DAMAGE YOU'VE DONE TO YOURSELF.
AND I HAVETA BUY MY OWN WINTER COAT, TOO, HUH?
THE MANGY MAGNATES WHO RULE THE WORLD!
THOSE GUYS KILL ME!
YUP, HOWIE-- THEY JUST MIGHT.
SLAM
NOT WITHOUT AN APPOINTMENT. OUR SCHEDULE'S FULL BETWEEN NOW AND ELECTION DAY.
ANOTHER WEEK OF BARNSTORMING--THEN BACK TO NEW YORK FOR YOUR LAST NATIONALLY TELEVISED PRESS CONFERENCE.

PARTIAL TRANSCRIPT OF NATIONALLY TELEVISED PRESS CONFERENCE:
Hotel Rykrisp, New York City, November 1, 1976

HOWARD: Ladies an' germs, I'll keep my opening smart remarks brief. I didn't particularly wanna be president of this coast-to-coast funny farm you hairless apes have set up. When they asked me to run, I'd just been hit on the head an' didn't really understand what I was agreein' to. But I've reached the conclusion that most o' the American public is in the same condition most o' the time, so just maybe I'm the ideal candidate. You meatbrains willingly subject yourselves to more abuse, physical and psychological, than any nation in history! You allow your eyes and lungs to be eaten away by pollution. You fill your digestive tracts with chemicals. Your ears are barraged by the sounds of jackhammer progress. All this while politicians and Madison Avenue bang away at your minds. You all wanna be happy an' secure, yet you open yourselves to the constant tension an' pressure of a society that claims to be free, but refuses to let you make a move without first filing forms in triplicate. You wonder why you got violence? Why your young are either dissident, empty-headed, or drugged into a stupor? It's because you've fashioned an emotionally and intellectually sterile culture, that's why! If an individual is unwilling to spend his life in the plodding pursuit of possessions, there's nothing for 'im to *do!* The United States is one big dateless Saturday night! If I'm elected, I'm gonna inject a little *life* back into you anesthetized Americans! For four years, this country's gonna get down an' boogie, see?! Ungawa! Okay! Now anybody got any brilliant questions?

(Stunned silence, interrupted only by an occasional nervous cough; then...)

RAMSEY KLEP (Devil's Tongue, N.M., *Daily Lick*): Mr. Duck, which do you favor— conditional amnesty or a blanket pardon for Vietnam draft evaders?

HOWARD: Neither. I favor education.

KLEP: Beg pardon?

HOWARD: Look, as nearly as I can tell, everybody is still reacting on this question with his gut, not his head. It's still "my country right or wrong" versus "make love not war". I figure the answer is a debate, on television, between proponents of each position. The government would buy time on all three networks and the yelling could go on for days. Then, the country could decide in a national referendum, based on each individual's judgment of the facts. Revolutionary, huh? Next!

DUNSTAN QUOBROX (Lima, OH., *Daily Bean*): What's your opinion of the recent Washington scandals? Should elected officials be held accountable for their private morality?

HOWARD: Nah. As long as the taxpayers aren't financin' their little romps, senators an' congressmen deserve to have a little fun. Heck, we oughtta be heartened to know some o' those old prunes have still got it in 'em.

SAM QUENTIN (Dubious, NJ, *Daily Dunno)*; How do you feel, sir, about violence in movies, television programs, and comic books?

HOWARD: I'm all for it.

QUENTIN: What?

HOWARD: As long as it's never presented as cathartic—as a release, as a solution. A kid oughtta know what he's gettin' into if he's contemplatin' stabbing or shootin' somebody. It's messy. The blood gets all over the floor. It smells bad. It's ugly to look at. I think violence should be presented honestly—as disgustingly and offensively as possible. There's no such thing as tasteful violence.

(Beverly Switzler leaps up on the table, does a little dance, blows a whistle, and chirps "Th-th-that's all, folks!" into a microphone. The auditorium explodes in applause, and the press conference concludes.)

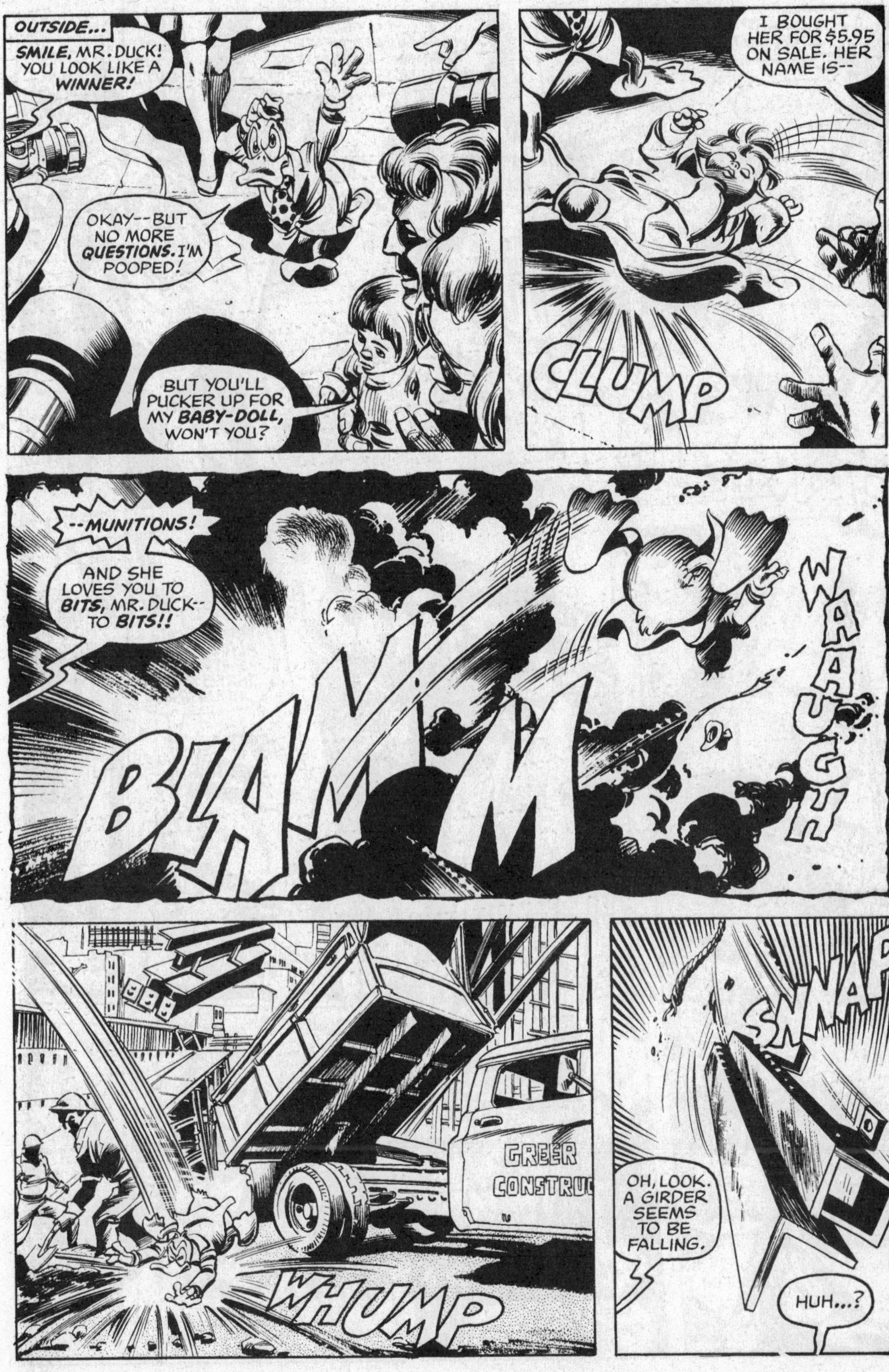
OUTSIDE...
SMILE, MR. DUCK! YOU LOOK LIKE A WINNER!
OKAY--BUT NO MORE QUESTIONS. I'M POOPED!
BUT YOU'LL PUCKER UP FOR MY BABY-DOLL, WON'T YOU?
I BOUGHT HER FOR $5.95 ON SALE. HER NAME IS--
CLUMP
--MUNITIONS!
AND SHE LOVES YOU TO BITS, MR. DUCK-- TO BITS!!
BLAMM
WAAUGH
GREER CONSTRUC
WHUMP
SNNAP
OH, LOOK. A GIRDER SEEMS TO BE FALLING.
HUH...?

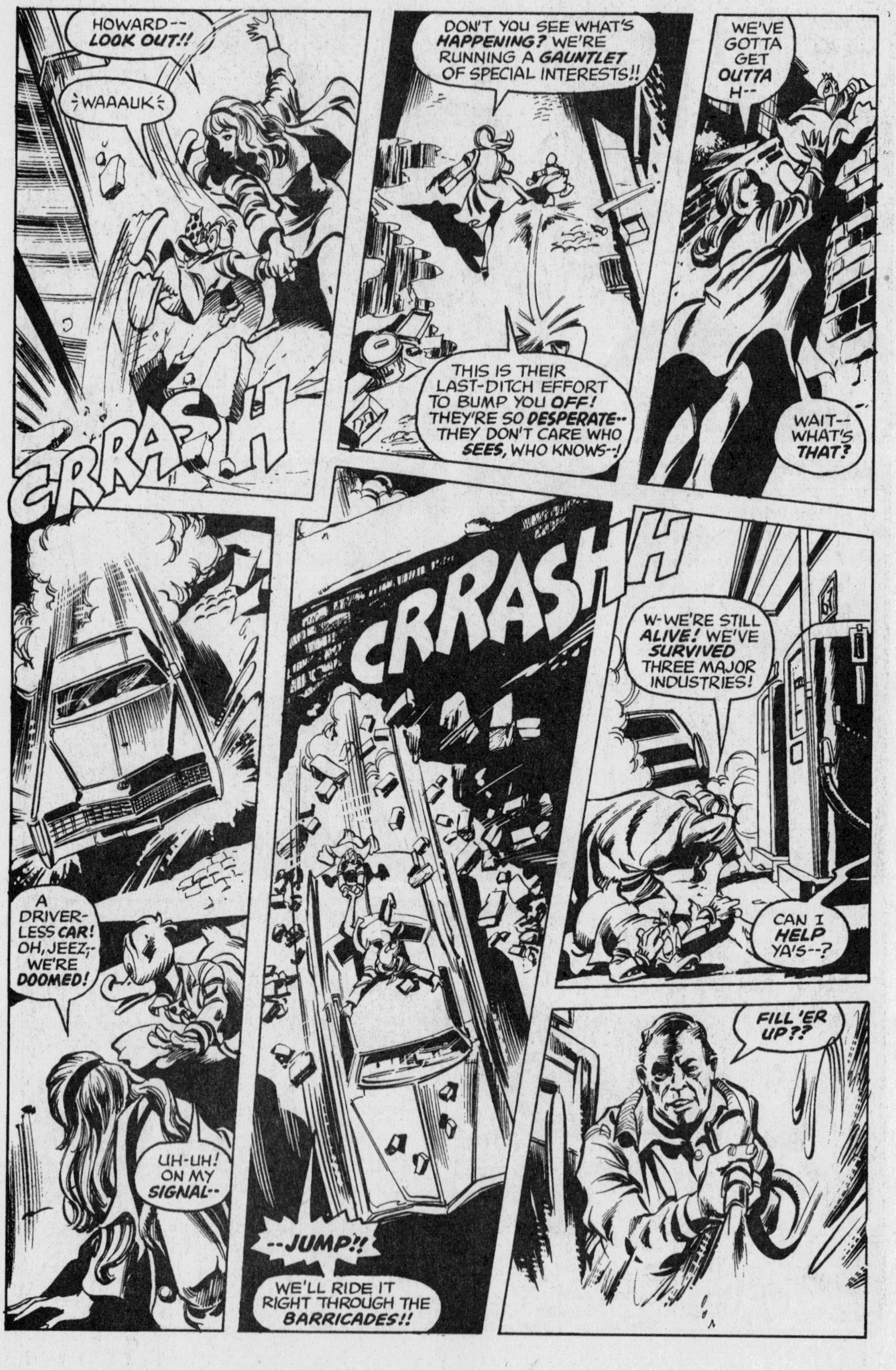

HOWARD-- LOOK OUT!!
WAAAUK
CRRASH
DON'T YOU SEE WHAT'S HAPPENING? WE'RE RUNNING A GAUNTLET OF SPECIAL INTERESTS!!
THIS IS THEIR LAST-DITCH EFFORT TO BUMP YOU OFF! THEY'RE SO DESPERATE-- THEY DON'T CARE WHO SEES, WHO KNOWS--!
WE'VE GOTTA GET OUTTA H--
WAIT-- WHAT'S THAT?
A DRIVER-LESS CAR! OH, JEEZ,-- WE'RE DOOMED!
UH-UH! ON MY SIGNAL--
CRRASHH
--JUMP!!
WE'LL RIDE IT RIGHT THROUGH THE BARRICADES!!
W-WE'RE STILL ALIVE! WE'VE SURVIVED THREE MAJOR INDUSTRIES!
CAN I HELP YA'S--?
FILL 'ER UP??

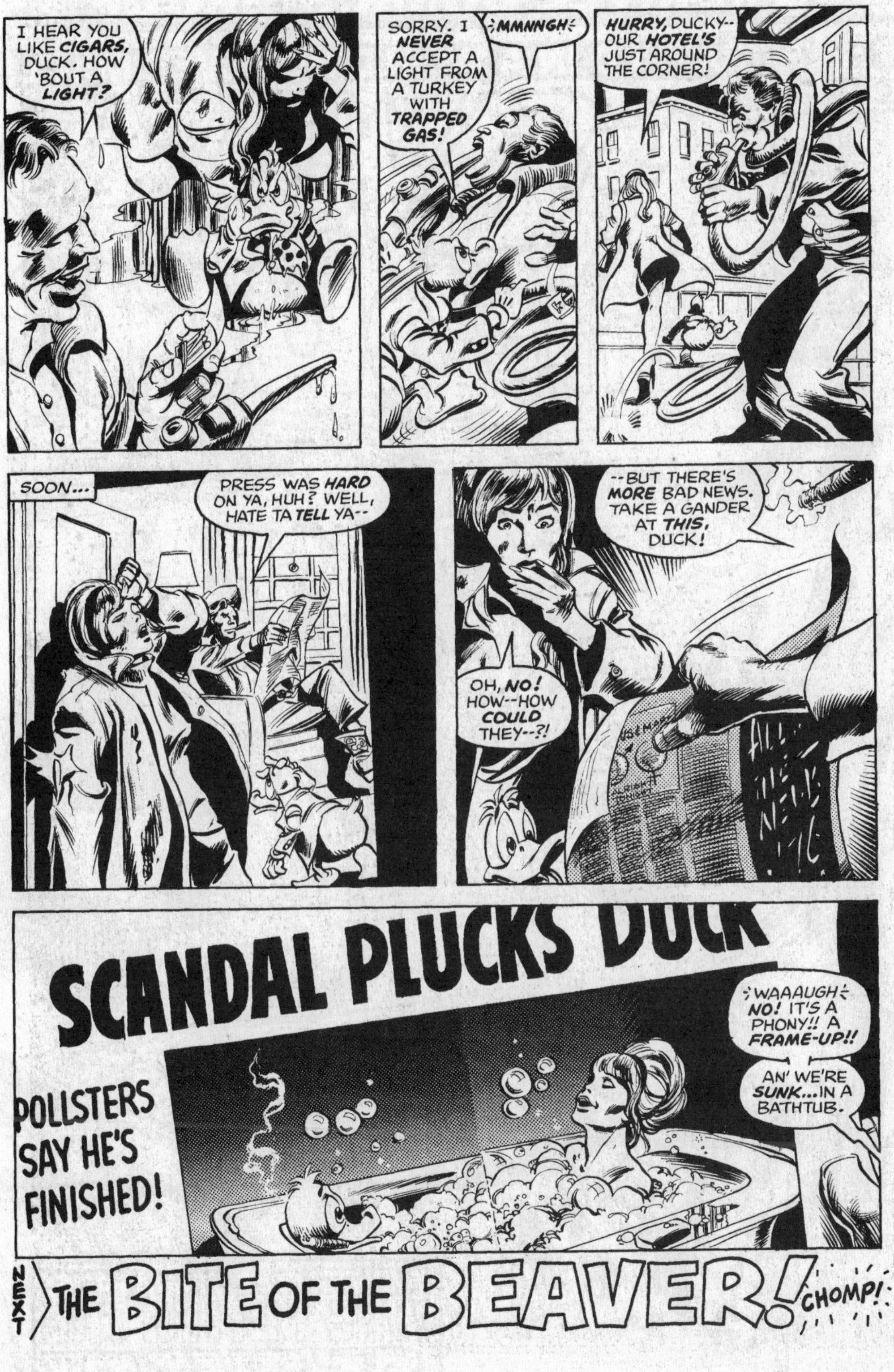
I HEAR YOU LIKE CIGARS, DUCK. HOW 'BOUT A LIGHT?
SORRY. I NEVER ACCEPT A LIGHT FROM A TURKEY WITH TRAPPED GAS!
MMNNGH
HURRY, DUCKY-- OUR HOTEL'S JUST AROUND THE CORNER!
SOON...
PRESS WAS HARD ON YA, HUH? WELL, HATE TA TELL YA--
--BUT THERE'S MORE BAD NEWS. TAKE A GANDER AT THIS, DUCK!
OH, NO! HOW--HOW COULD THEY--?!
SCANDAL PLUCKS DUCK
POLLSTERS SAY HE'S FINISHED!
WAAAUGH NO! IT'S A PHONY!! A FRAME-UP!!
AN' WE'RE SUNK...IN A BATHTUB.
NEXT
THE BITE OF THE BEAVER! CHOMP!

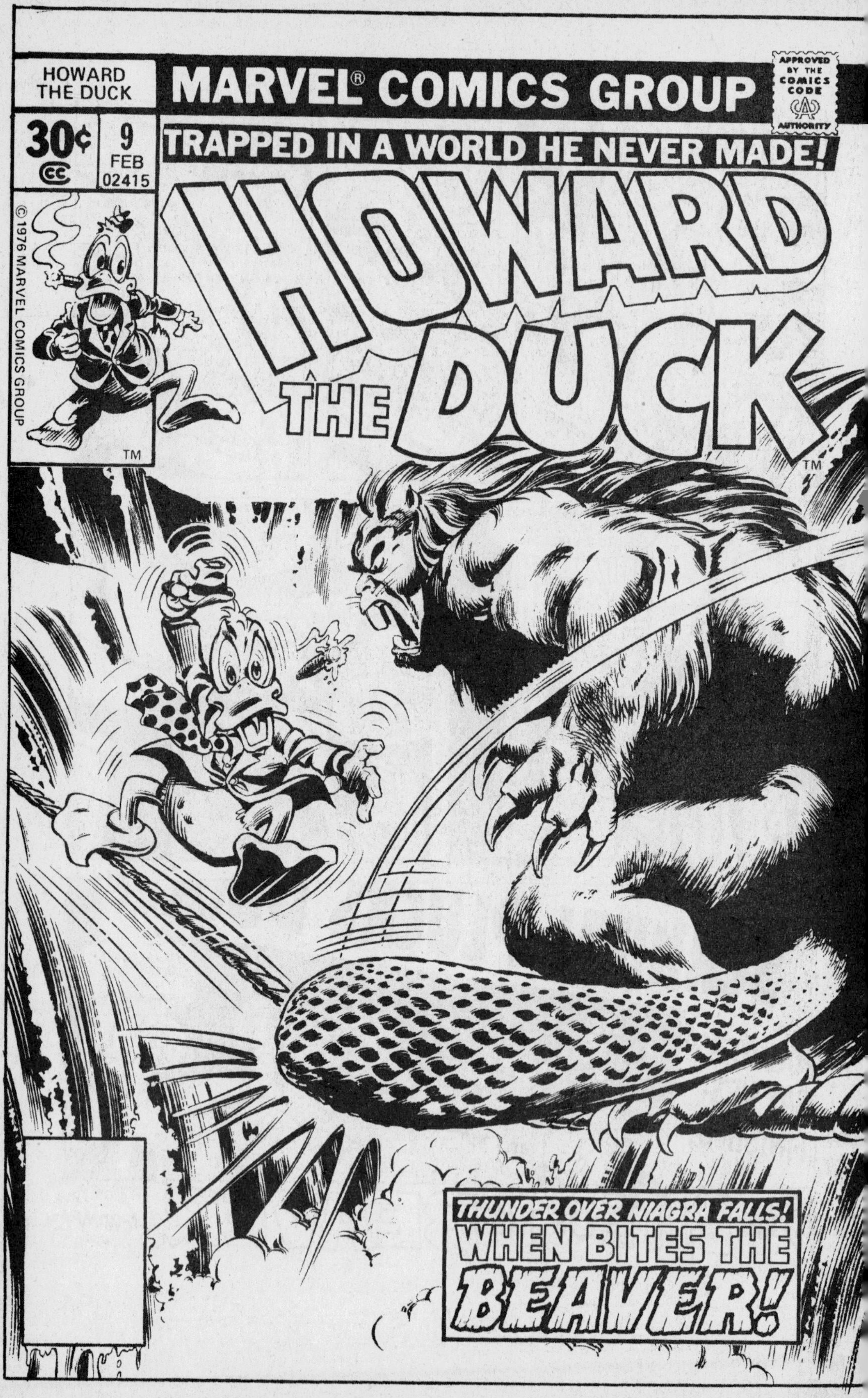
HOWARD THE DUCK
MARVEL® COMICS GROUP
APPROVED BY THE COMICS CODE AUTHORITY
30¢
9
FEB
02415
TRAPPED IN A WORLD HE NEVER MADE!
HOWARD THE DUCK
© 1976 MARVEL COMICS GROUP
THUNDER OVER NIAGRA FALLS!
WHEN BITES THE BEAVER!

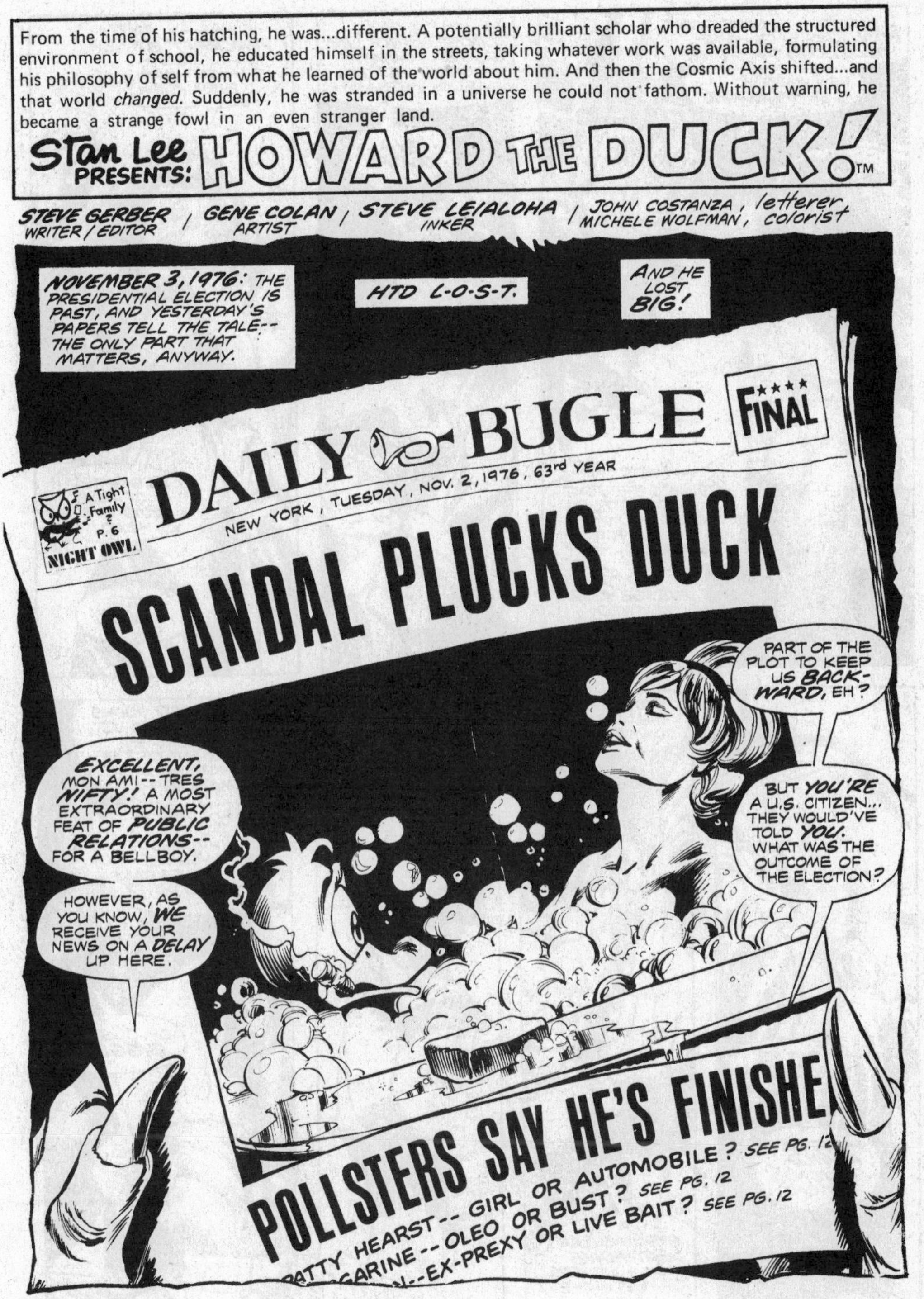
From the time of his hatching, he was...different. A potentially brilliant scholar who dreaded the structured environment of school, he educated himself in the streets, taking whatever work was available, formulating his philosophy of self from what he learned of the world about him. And then the Cosmic Axis shifted...and that world *changed.* Suddenly, he was stranded in a universe he could not fathom. Without warning, he became a strange fowl in an even stranger land.
Stan Lee PRESENTS: HOWARD THE DUCK!™
STEVE GERBER WRITER / EDITOR / GENE COLAN ARTIST / STEVE LEIALOHA INKER / JOHN COSTANZA, letterer MICHELE WOLFMAN, colorist
NOVEMBER 3, 1976: THE PRESIDENTIAL ELECTION IS PAST, AND YESTERDAY'S PAPERS TELL THE TALE-- THE ONLY PART THAT MATTERS, ANYWAY.
HTD L-O-S-T.
AND HE LOST BIG!
DAILY BUGLE
★★★★ FINAL
NEW YORK, TUESDAY, NOV. 2, 1976, 63rd YEAR
A Tight Family? P. 6 NIGHT OWL
SCANDAL PLUCKS DUCK
PART OF THE PLOT TO KEEP US BACKWARD, EH?
EXCELLENT, MON AMI--TRES NIFTY! A MOST EXTRAORDINARY FEAT OF PUBLIC RELATIONS--FOR A BELLBOY.
BUT YOU'RE A U.S. CITIZEN... THEY WOULD'VE TOLD YOU. WHAT WAS THE OUTCOME OF THE ELECTION?
HOWEVER, AS YOU KNOW, WE RECEIVE YOUR NEWS ON A DELAY UP HERE.
POLLSTERS SAY HE'S FINISHE
PATTY HEARST-- GIRL OR AUTOMOBILE? SEE PG. 12
GARINE--OLEO OR BUST? SEE PG. 12
--EX-PREXY OR LIVE BAIT? SEE PG. 12

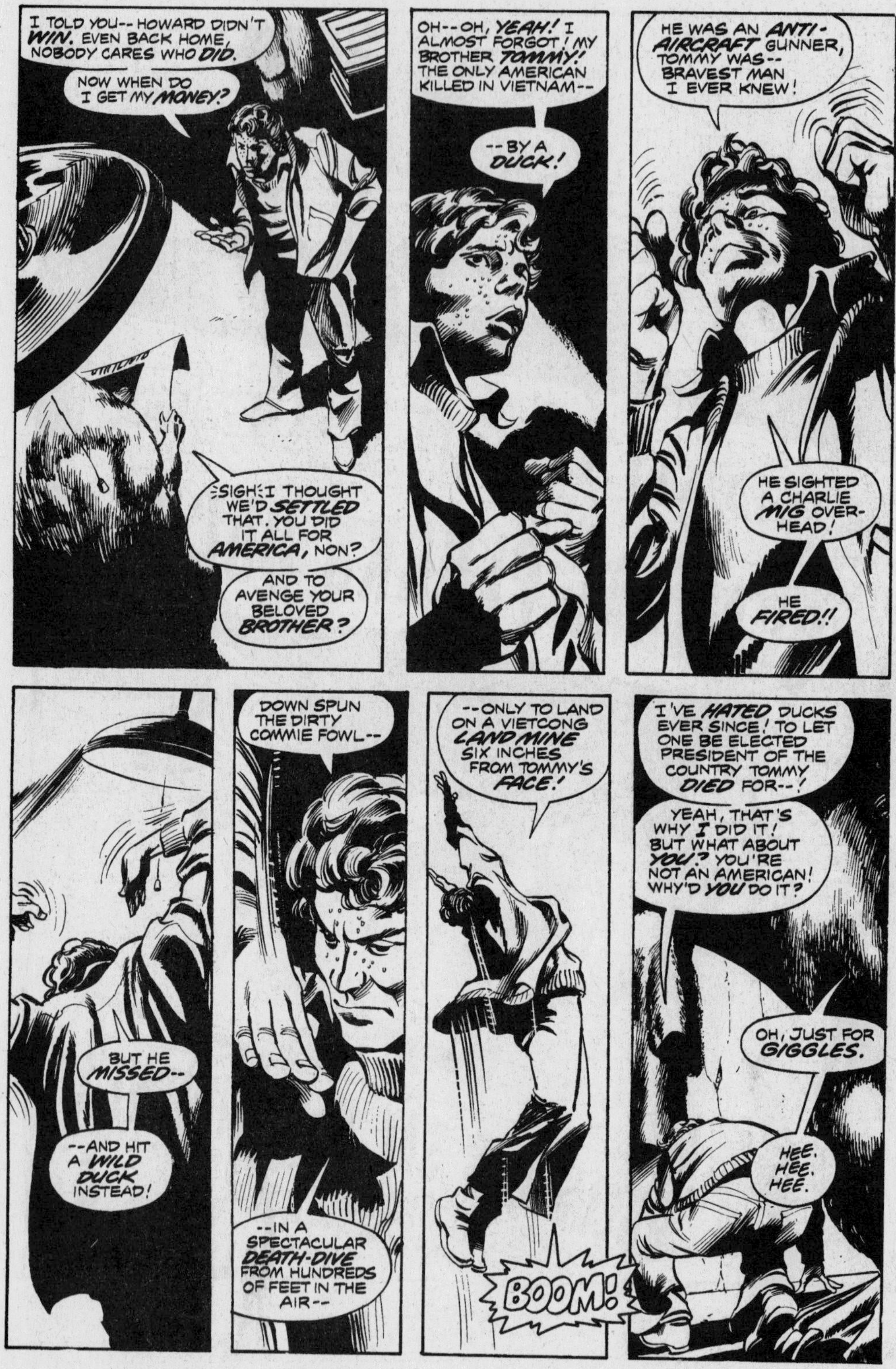

I TOLD YOU--HOWARD DIDN'T WIN. EVEN BACK HOME, NOBODY CARES WHO DID.
NOW WHEN DO I GET MY MONEY?
SIGH I THOUGHT WE'D SETTLED THAT. YOU DID IT ALL FOR AMERICA, NON?
AND TO AVENGE YOUR BELOVED BROTHER?
OH--OH, YEAH! I ALMOST FORGOT! MY BROTHER TOMMY! THE ONLY AMERICAN KILLED IN VIETNAM--
--BY A DUCK!
HE WAS AN ANTI-AIRCRAFT GUNNER, TOMMY WAS--BRAVEST MAN I EVER KNEW!
HE SIGHTED A CHARLIE MIG OVERHEAD!
HE FIRED!!
BUT HE MISSED--
--AND HIT A WILD DUCK INSTEAD!
DOWN SPUN THE DIRTY COMMIE FOWL--
--IN A SPECTACULAR DEATH-DIVE FROM HUNDREDS OF FEET IN THE AIR--
--ONLY TO LAND ON A VIETCONG LAND MINE SIX INCHES FROM TOMMY'S FACE!
BOOM!
I'VE HATED DUCKS EVER SINCE! TO LET ONE BE ELECTED PRESIDENT OF THE COUNTRY TOMMY DIED FOR--!
YEAH, THAT'S WHY I DID IT! BUT WHAT ABOUT YOU? YOU'RE NOT AN AMERICAN! WHY'D YOU DO IT?
OH, JUST FOR GIGGLES.
HEE. HEE. HEE.

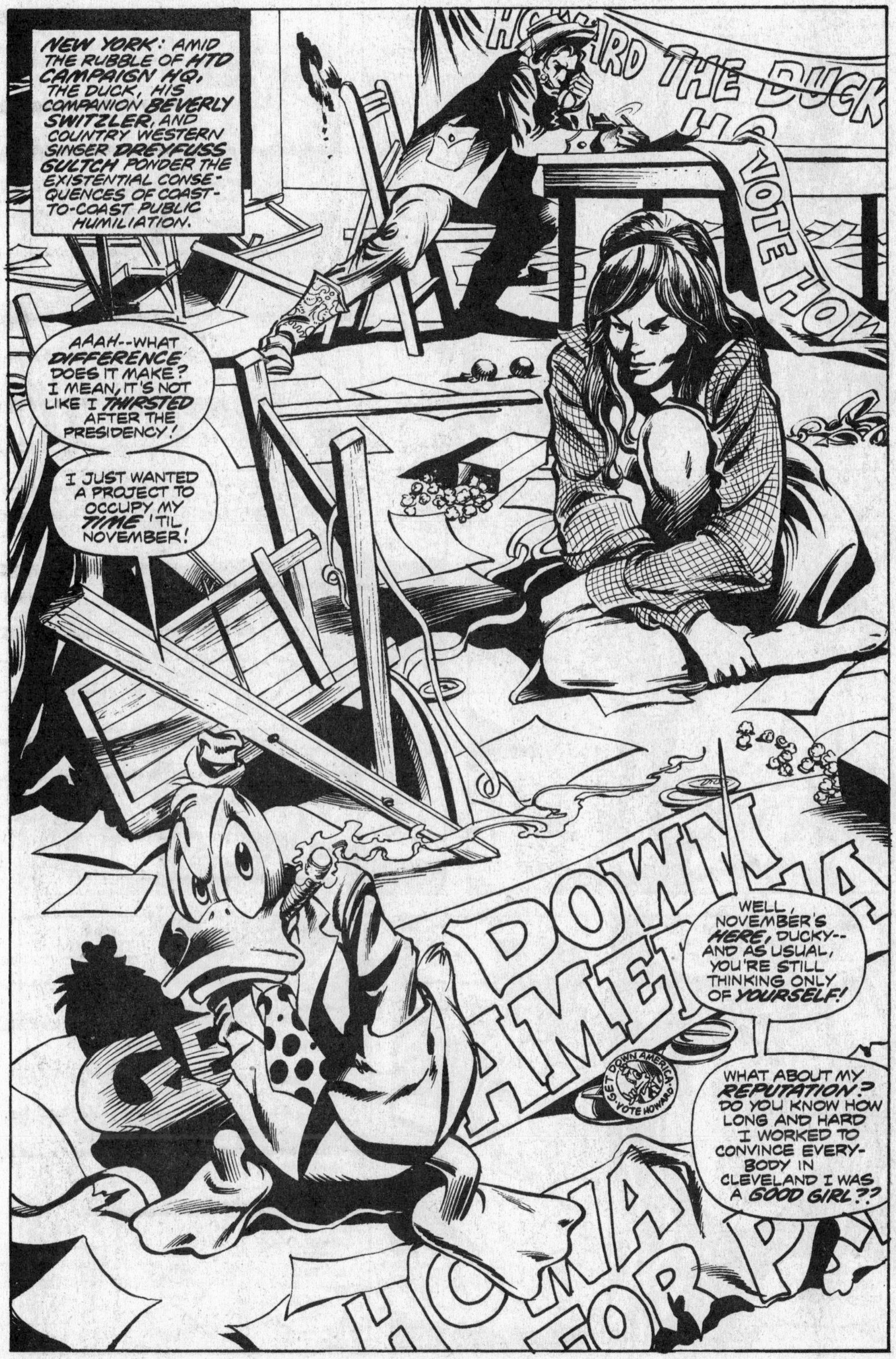
NEW YORK: AMID THE RUBBLE OF HTD CAMPAIGN HQ, THE DUCK, HIS COMPANION BEVERLY SWITZLER, AND COUNTRY WESTERN SINGER DREYFUSS GULTCH PONDER THE EXISTENTIAL CONSEQUENCES OF COAST-TO-COAST PUBLIC HUMILIATION.
HOWARD THE DUCK HQ
VOTE HOW
AAAH--WHAT DIFFERENCE DOES IT MAKE? I MEAN, IT'S NOT LIKE I THIRSTED AFTER THE PRESIDENCY!
I JUST WANTED A PROJECT TO OCCUPY MY TIME 'TIL NOVEMBER!
WELL, NOVEMBER'S HERE, DUCKY-- AND AS USUAL, YOU'RE STILL THINKING ONLY OF YOURSELF!
WHAT ABOUT MY REPUTATION? DO YOU KNOW HOW LONG AND HARD I WORKED TO CONVINCE EVERYBODY IN CLEVELAND I WAS A GOOD GIRL??
GET DOWN AMERICA · VOTE HOWARD

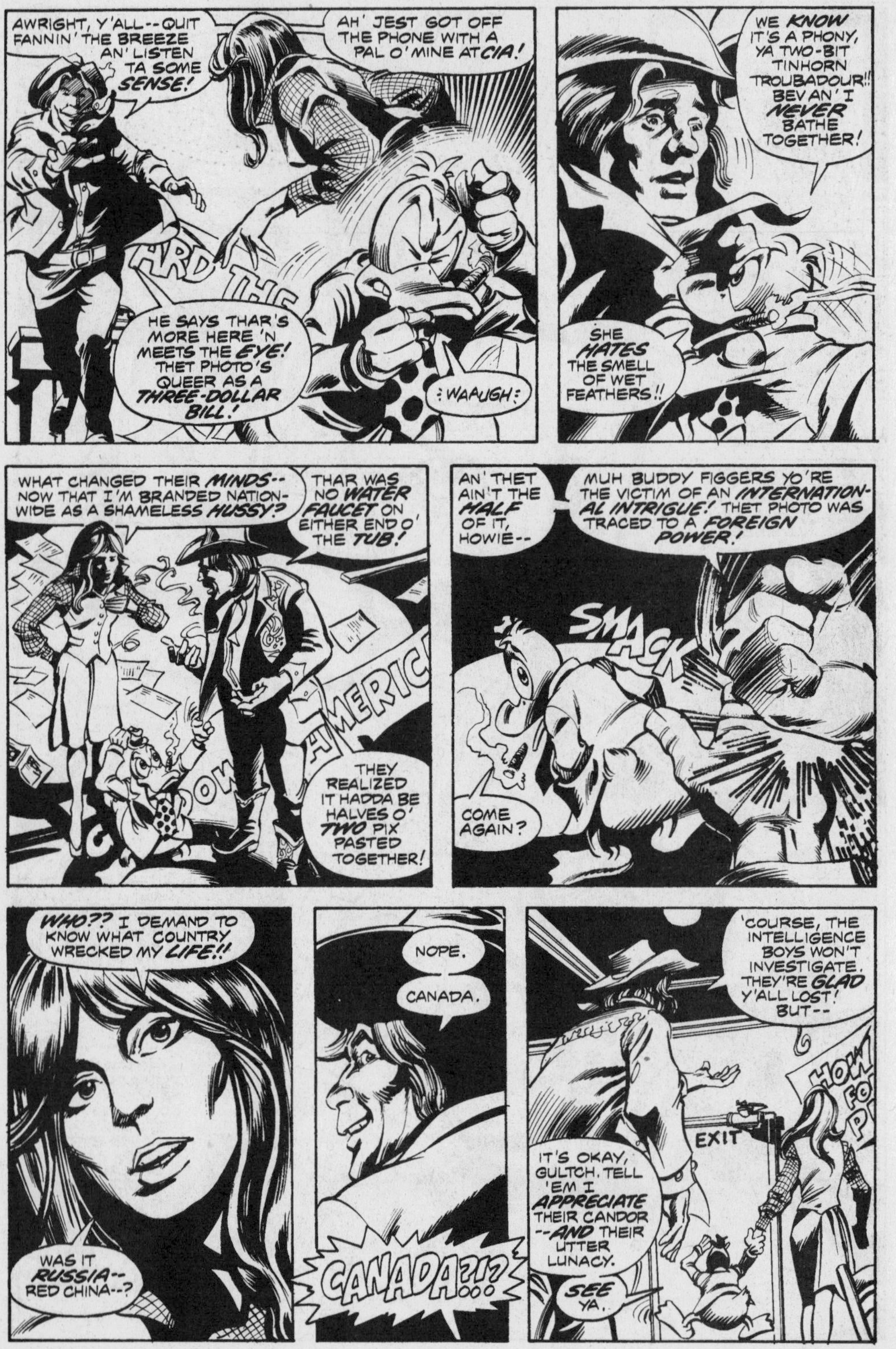
AWRIGHT, Y'ALL--QUIT FANNIN' THE BREEZE AN' LISTEN TA SOME SENSE!
AH' JEST GOT OFF THE PHONE WITH A PAL O' MINE AT CIA!
HE SAYS THAR'S MORE HERE 'N MEETS THE EYE! THET PHOTO'S QUEER AS A THREE-DOLLAR BILL!
WAAUGH
WE KNOW IT'S A PHONY, YA TWO-BIT TINHORN TROUBADOUR!! BEV AN' I NEVER BATHE TOGETHER!
SHE HATES THE SMELL OF WET FEATHERS!!
WHAT CHANGED THEIR MINDS--NOW THAT I'M BRANDED NATION-WIDE AS A SHAMELESS HUSSY?
THAR WAS NO WATER FAUCET ON EITHER END O' THE TUB!
THEY REALIZED IT HADDA BE HALVES O' TWO PIX PASTED TOGETHER!
AN' THET AIN'T THE HALF OF IT, HOWIE--
MUH BUDDY FIGGERS YO'RE THE VICTIM OF AN INTERNATION-AL INTRIGUE! THET PHOTO WAS TRACED TO A FOREIGN POWER!
SMACK
COME AGAIN?
WHO?? I DEMAND TO KNOW WHAT COUNTRY WRECKED MY LIFE!!
WAS IT RUSSIA--RED CHINA--?
NOPE.
CANADA.
CANADA?!?
'COURSE, THE INTELLIGENCE BOYS WON'T INVESTIGATE. THEY'RE GLAD Y'ALL LOST! BUT--
EXIT
IT'S OKAY, GULTCH. TELL 'EM I APPRECIATE THEIR CANDOR--AND THEIR UTTER LUNACY.
SEE YA.

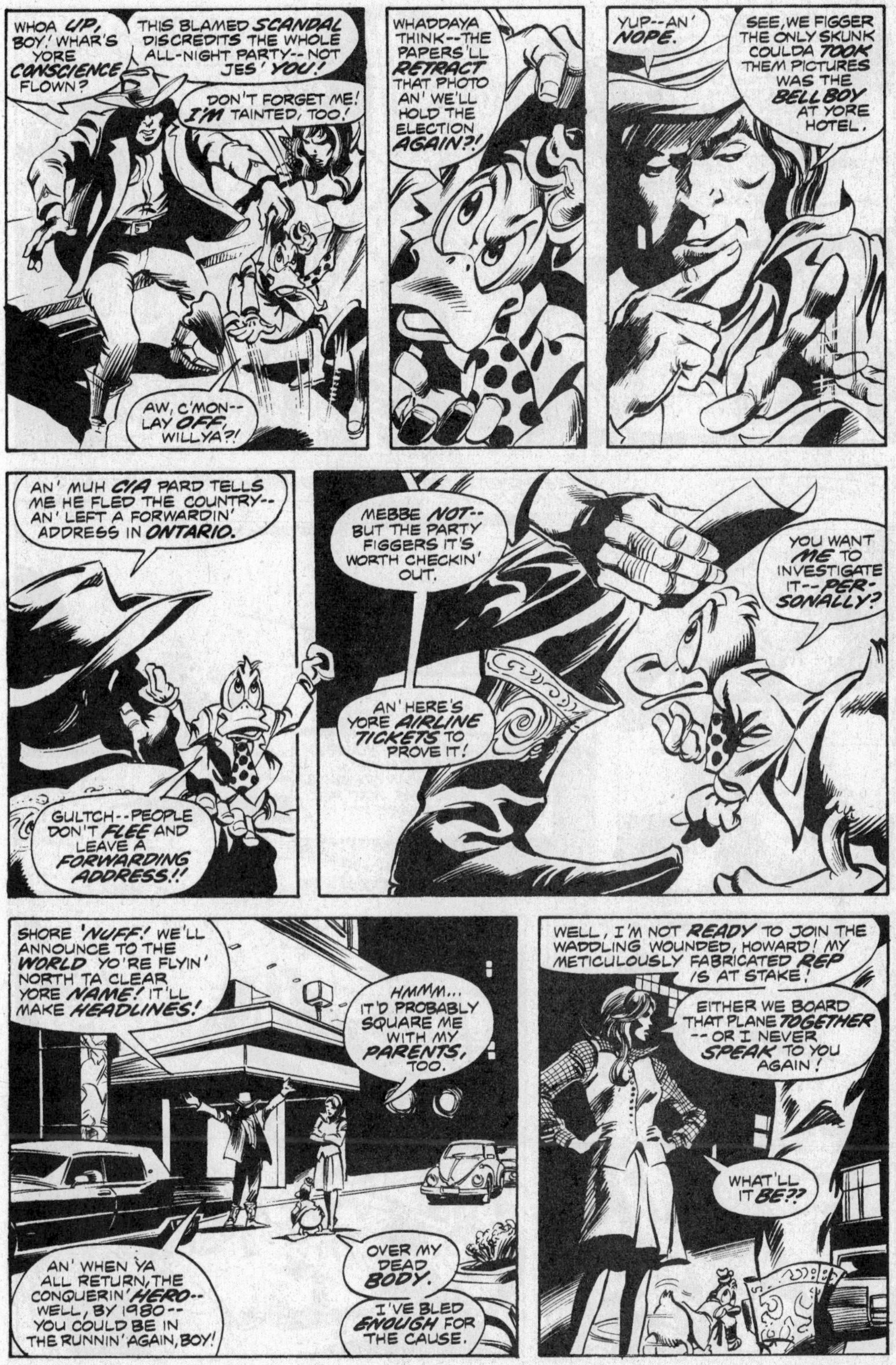
WHOA UP, BOY! WHAR'S YORE CONSCIENCE FLOWN?
THIS BLAMED SCANDAL DISCREDITS THE WHOLE ALL-NIGHT PARTY--NOT JES' YOU!
DON'T FORGET ME! I'M TAINTED, TOO!
AW, C'MON--LAY OFF, WILLYA?!
WHADDAYA THINK--THE PAPERS'LL RETRACT THAT PHOTO AN' WE'LL HOLD THE ELECTION AGAIN?!
YUP--AN' NOPE.
SEE, WE FIGGER THE ONLY SKUNK COULDA TOOK THEM PICTURES WAS THE BELL BOY AT YORE HOTEL.
AN' MUH CIA PARD TELLS ME HE FLED THE COUNTRY--AN' LEFT A FORWARDIN' ADDRESS IN ONTARIO.
GULTCH--PEOPLE DON'T FLEE AND LEAVE A FORWARDING ADDRESS!!
MEBBE NOT--BUT THE PARTY FIGGERS IT'S WORTH CHECKIN' OUT.
AN' HERE'S YORE AIRLINE TICKETS TO PROVE IT!
YOU WANT ME TO INVESTIGATE IT--PER-SONALLY?
SHORE 'NUFF! WE'LL ANNOUNCE TO THE WORLD YO'RE FLYIN' NORTH TA CLEAR YORE NAME! IT'LL MAKE HEADLINES!
HMMM... IT'D PROBABLY SQUARE ME WITH MY PARENTS, TOO.
AN' WHEN YA ALL RETURN, THE CONQUERIN' HERO--WELL, BY 1980--YOU COULD BE IN THE RUNNIN' AGAIN, BOY!
OVER MY DEAD BODY.
I'VE BLED ENOUGH FOR THE CAUSE.
WELL, I'M NOT READY TO JOIN THE WADDLING WOUNDED, HOWARD! MY METICULOUSLY FABRICATED REP IS AT STAKE!
EITHER WE BOARD THAT PLANE TOGETHER--OR I NEVER SPEAK TO YOU AGAIN!
WHAT'LL IT BE??

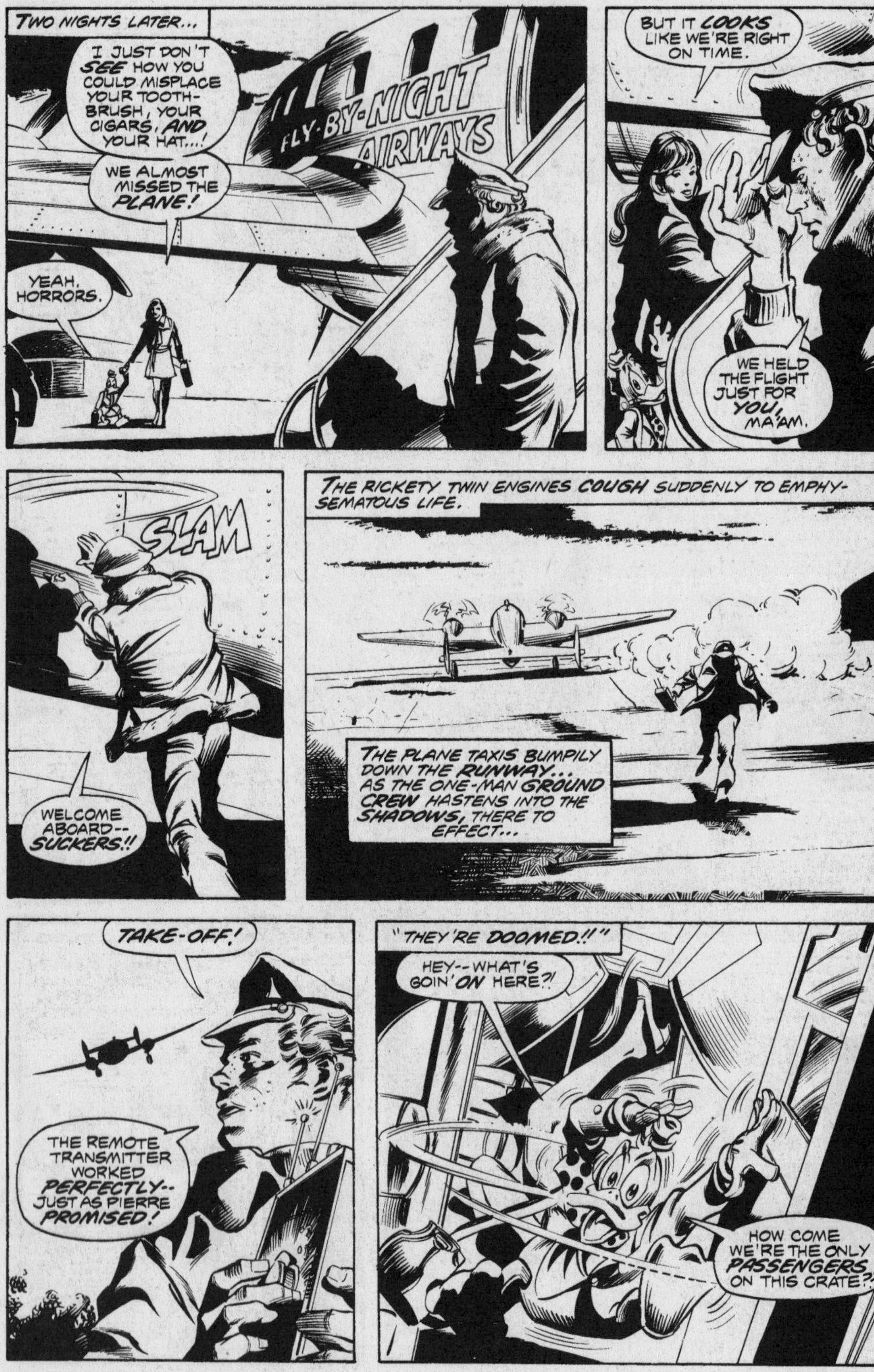

TWO NIGHTS LATER...
I JUST DON'T SEE HOW YOU COULD MISPLACE YOUR TOOTH-BRUSH, YOUR CIGARS, AND YOUR HAT...!
WE ALMOST MISSED THE PLANE!
YEAH, HORRORS.
FLY-BY-NIGHT AIRWAYS
BUT IT LOOKS LIKE WE'RE RIGHT ON TIME.
WE HELD THE FLIGHT JUST FOR YOU, MA'AM.
SLAM
WELCOME ABOARD--SUCKERS!!
THE RICKETY TWIN ENGINES COUGH SUDDENLY TO EMPHY-SEMATOUS LIFE.
THE PLANE TAXIS BUMPILY DOWN THE RUNWAY... AS THE ONE-MAN GROUND CREW HASTENS INTO THE SHADOWS, THERE TO EFFECT...
TAKE-OFF!
THE REMOTE TRANSMITTER WORKED PERFECTLY--JUST AS PIERRE PROMISED!
"THEY'RE DOOMED!!"
HEY--WHAT'S GOIN' ON HERE?!
HOW COME WE'RE THE ONLY PASSENGERS ON THIS CRATE??

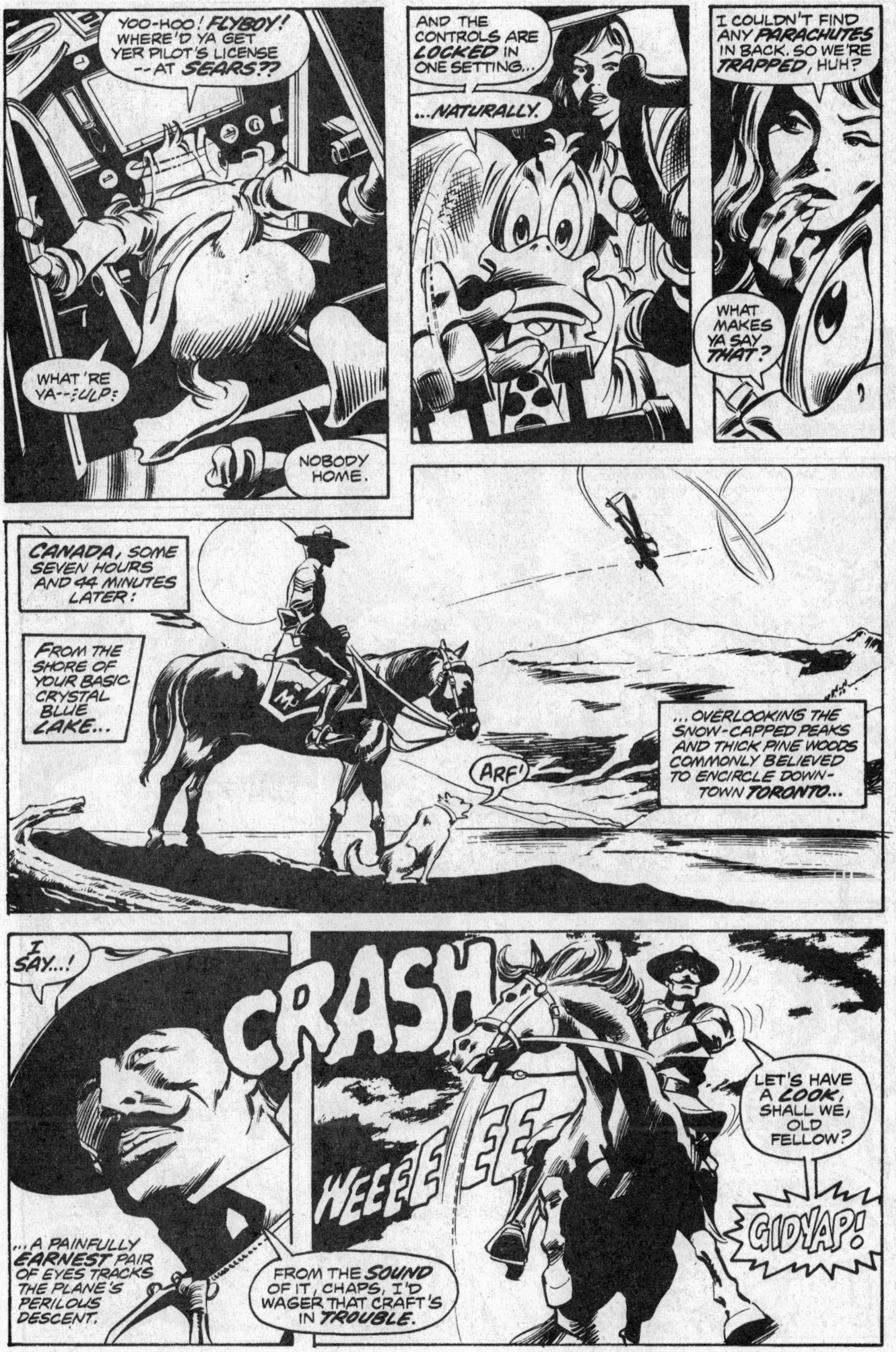
YOO-HOO! FLYBOY! WHERE'D YA GET YER PILOT'S LICENSE --AT SEARS??
WHAT 'RE YA--{ULP}
NOBODY HOME.
AND THE CONTROLS ARE LOCKED IN ONE SETTING...
...NATURALLY.
I COULDN'T FIND ANY PARACHUTES IN BACK. SO WE'RE TRAPPED, HUH?
WHAT MAKES YA SAY THAT?
CANADA, SOME SEVEN HOURS AND 44 MINUTES LATER:
FROM THE SHORE OF YOUR BASIC CRYSTAL BLUE LAKE...
...OVERLOOKING THE SNOW-CAPPED PEAKS AND THICK PINE WOODS COMMONLY BELIEVED TO ENCIRCLE DOWN-TOWN TORONTO...
ARF!
I SAY...!
CRASH
...A PAINFULLY EARNEST PAIR OF EYES TRACKS THE PLANE'S PERILOUS DESCENT.
FROM THE SOUND OF IT, CHAPS, I'D WAGER THAT CRAFT'S IN TROUBLE.
WHEEEEEEE
LET'S HAVE A LOOK, SHALL WE, OLD FELLOW?
GIDYAP!

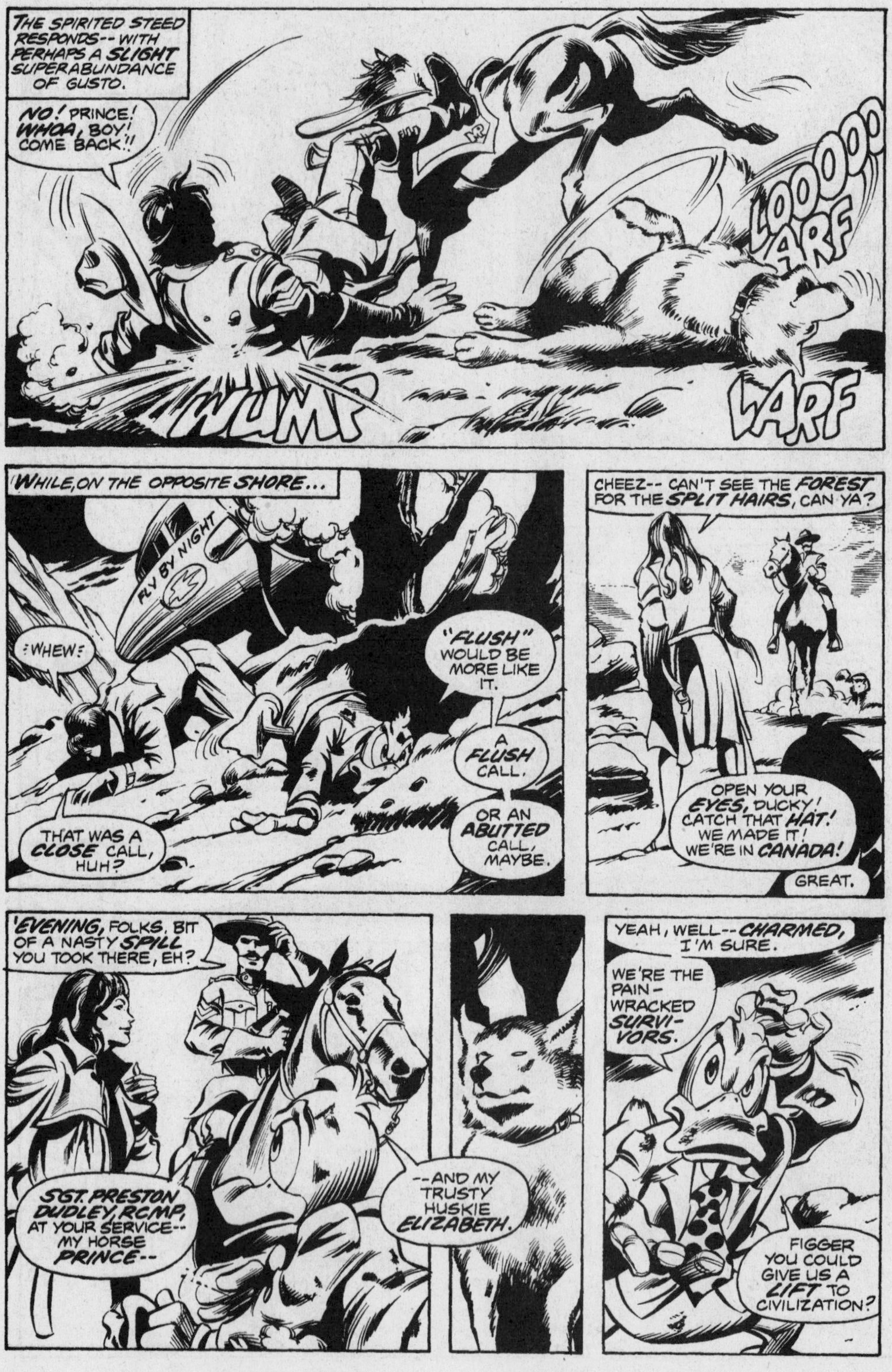
THE SPIRITED STEED RESPONDS-- WITH PERHAPS A SLIGHT SUPERABUNDANCE OF GUSTO.
NO! PRINCE! WHOA, BOY! COME BACK!!
LOOOOO
ARF
WUMP
LARF
WHILE, ON THE OPPOSITE SHORE...
FLY BY NIGHT
WHEW
THAT WAS A CLOSE CALL, HUH?
"FLUSH" WOULD BE MORE LIKE IT.
A FLUSH CALL.
OR AN ABUTTED CALL, MAYBE.
CHEEZ-- CAN'T SEE THE FOREST FOR THE SPLIT HAIRS, CAN YA?
OPEN YOUR EYES, DUCKY! CATCH THAT HAT! WE MADE IT! WE'RE IN CANADA!
GREAT.
'EVENING, FOLKS. BIT OF A NASTY SPILL YOU TOOK THERE, EH?
SGT. PRESTON DUDLEY, R.C.M.P., AT YOUR SERVICE-- MY HORSE PRINCE--
--AND MY TRUSTY HUSKIE ELIZABETH.
YEAH, WELL-- CHARMED, I'M SURE.
WE'RE THE PAIN-WRACKED SURVIVORS.
FIGGER YOU COULD GIVE US A LIFT TO CIVILIZATION?

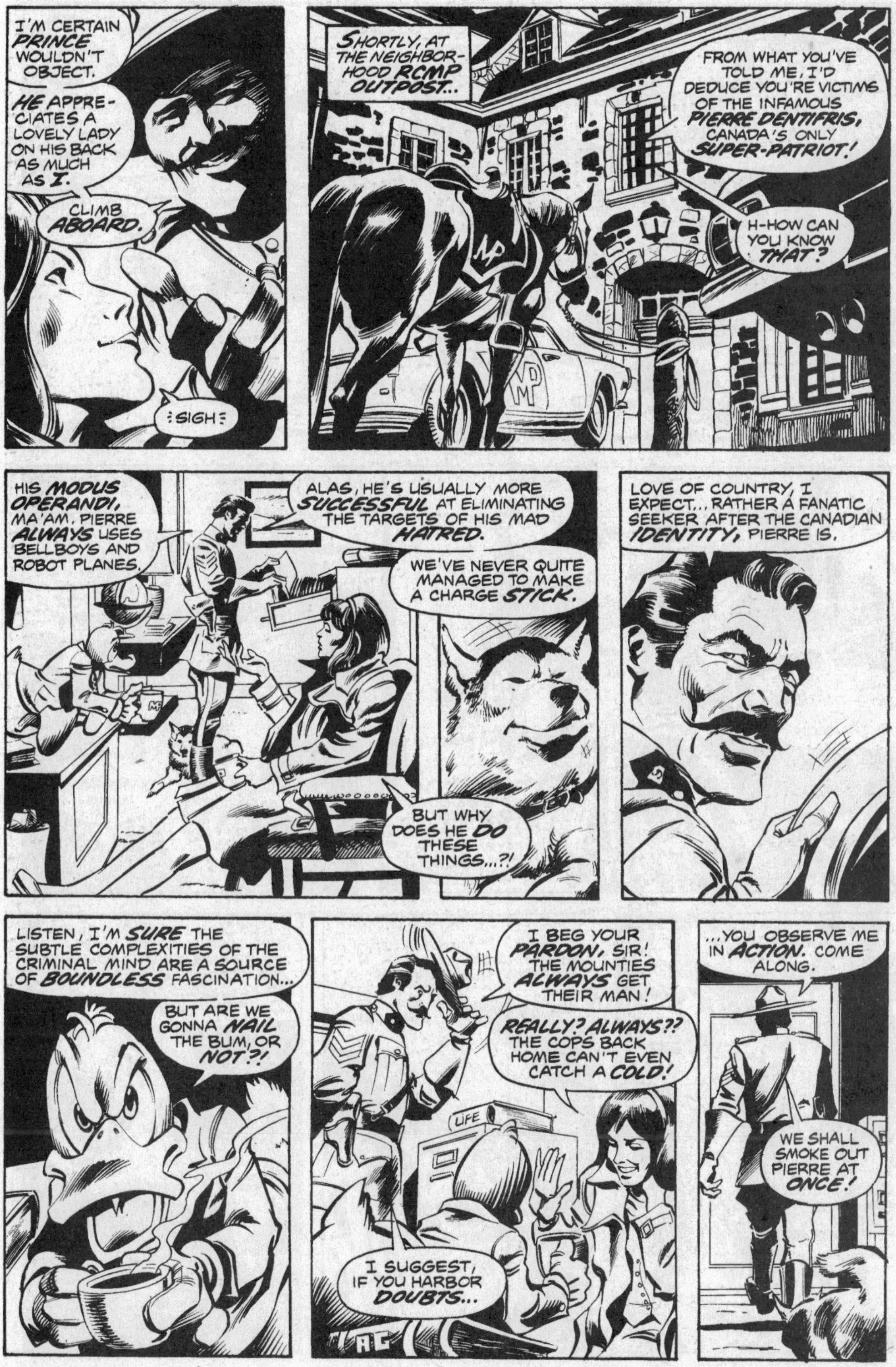
I'M CERTAIN PRINCE WOULDN'T OBJECT.
HE APPRECIATES A LOVELY LADY ON HIS BACK AS MUCH AS I.
CLIMB ABOARD.
SIGH
SHORTLY, AT THE NEIGHBORHOOD RCMP OUTPOST...
FROM WHAT YOU'VE TOLD ME, I'D DEDUCE YOU'RE VICTIMS OF THE INFAMOUS PIERRE DENTIFRIS, CANADA'S ONLY SUPER-PATRIOT!
H-HOW CAN YOU KNOW THAT?
HIS MODUS OPERANDI, MA'AM. PIERRE ALWAYS USES BELLBOYS AND ROBOT PLANES.
ALAS, HE'S USUALLY MORE SUCCESSFUL AT ELIMINATING THE TARGETS OF HIS MAD HATRED.
WE'VE NEVER QUITE MANAGED TO MAKE A CHARGE STICK.
BUT WHY DOES HE DO THESE THINGS...?!
LOVE OF COUNTRY, I EXPECT... RATHER A FANATIC SEEKER AFTER THE CANADIAN IDENTITY, PIERRE IS.
LISTEN, I'M SURE THE SUBTLE COMPLEXITIES OF THE CRIMINAL MIND ARE A SOURCE OF BOUNDLESS FASCINATION...
BUT ARE WE GONNA NAIL THE BUM, OR NOT?!
I BEG YOUR PARDON, SIR! THE MOUNTIES ALWAYS GET THEIR MAN!
REALLY? ALWAYS?? THE COPS BACK HOME CAN'T EVEN CATCH A COLD!
I SUGGEST, IF YOU HARBOR DOUBTS...
...YOU OBSERVE ME IN ACTION. COME ALONG.
WE SHALL SMOKE OUT PIERRE AT ONCE!

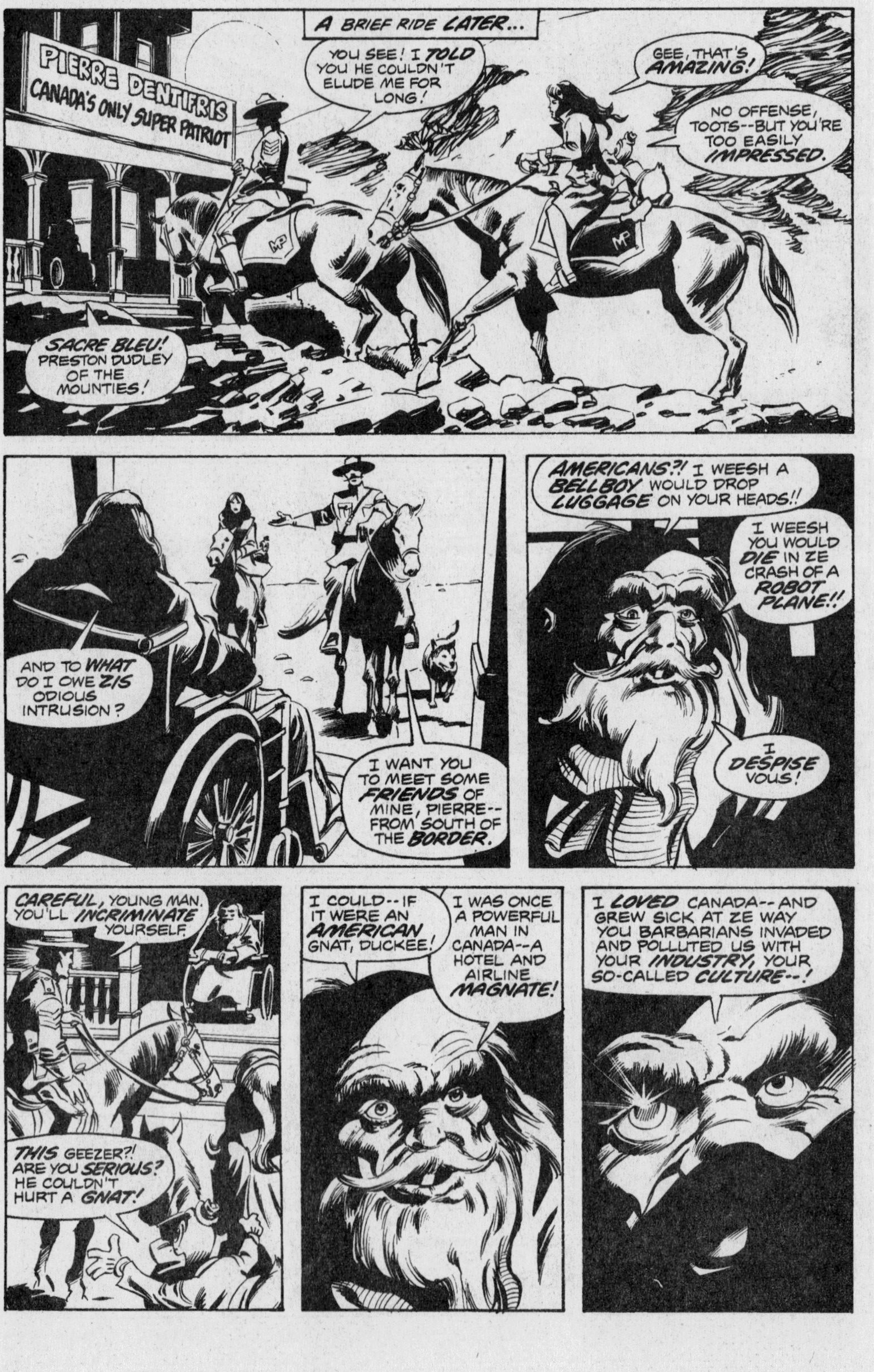
A BRIEF RIDE LATER...
PIERRE DENTIFRIS
CANADA'S ONLY SUPER PATRIOT
YOU SEE! I TOLD YOU HE COULDN'T ELUDE ME FOR LONG!
GEE, THAT'S AMAZING!
NO OFFENSE, TOOTS--BUT YOU'RE TOO EASILY IMPRESSED.
SACRE BLEU! PRESTON DUDLEY OF THE MOUNTIES!
AND TO WHAT DO I OWE ZIS ODIOUS INTRUSION?
I WANT YOU TO MEET SOME FRIENDS OF MINE, PIERRE--FROM SOUTH OF THE BORDER.
AMERICANS?! I WEESH A BELLBOY WOULD DROP LUGGAGE ON YOUR HEADS!!
I WEESH YOU WOULD DIE IN ZE CRASH OF A ROBOT PLANE!!
I DESPISE VOUS!
CAREFUL, YOUNG MAN. YOU'LL INCRIMINATE YOURSELF.
THIS GEEZER?! ARE YOU SERIOUS? HE COULDN'T HURT A GNAT!
I COULD--IF IT WERE AN AMERICAN GNAT, DUCKEE!
I WAS ONCE A POWERFUL MAN IN CANADA--A HOTEL AND AIRLINE MAGNATE!
I LOVED CANADA--AND GREW SICK AT ZE WAY YOU BARBARIANS INVADED AND POLLUTED US WITH YOUR INDUSTRY, YOUR SO-CALLED CULTURE--!

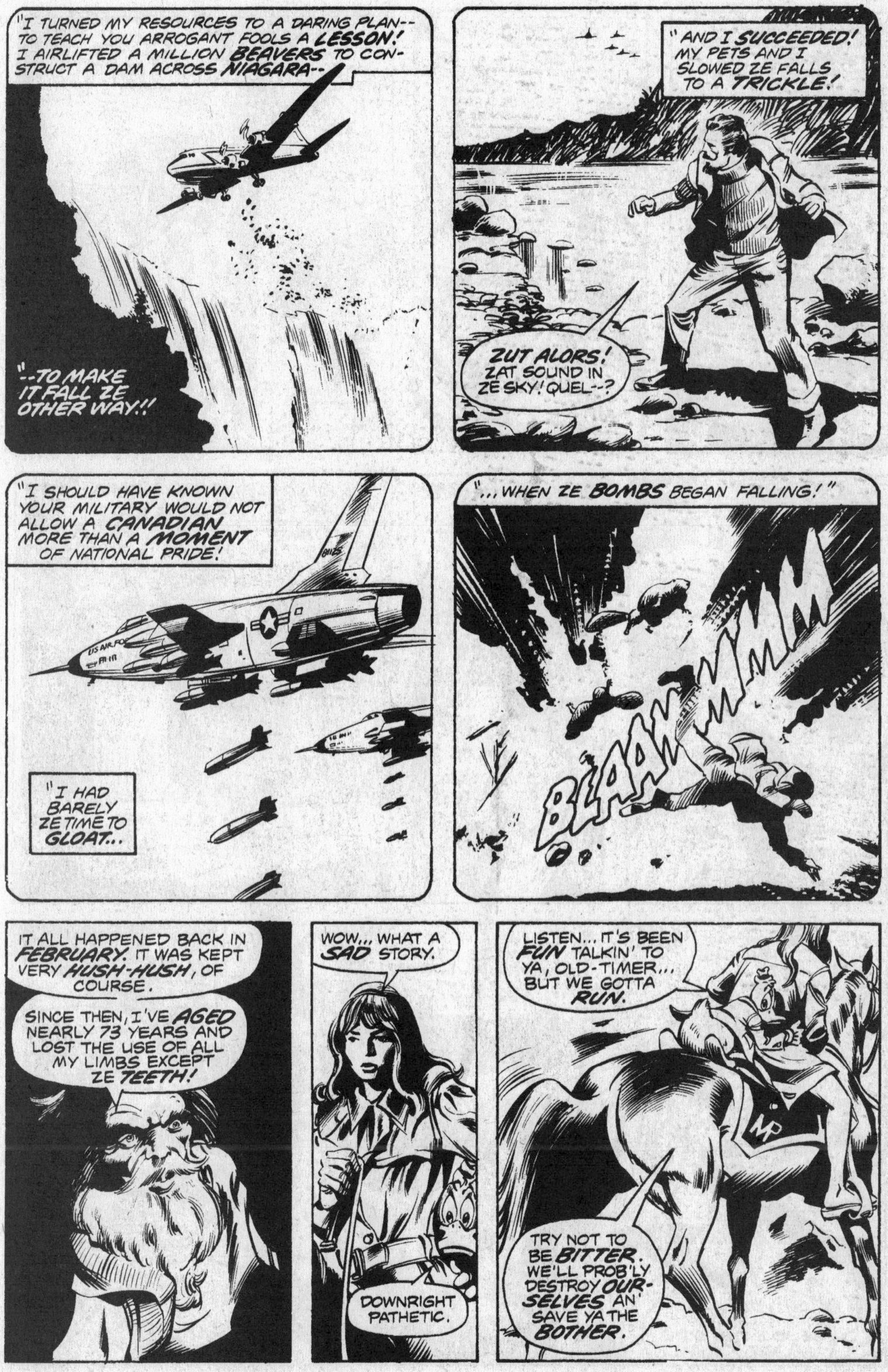

"I TURNED MY RESOURCES TO A DARING PLAN-- TO TEACH YOU ARROGANT FOOLS A LESSON! I AIRLIFTED A MILLION BEAVERS TO CONSTRUCT A DAM ACROSS NIAGARA--
"--TO MAKE IT FALL ZE OTHER WAY!!
"AND I SUCCEEDED! MY PETS AND I SLOWED ZE FALLS TO A TRICKLE!
ZUT ALORS! ZAT SOUND IN ZE SKY! QUEL--?
"I SHOULD HAVE KNOWN YOUR MILITARY WOULD NOT ALLOW A CANADIAN MORE THAN A MOMENT OF NATIONAL PRIDE!
"I HAD BARELY ZE TIME TO GLOAT...
"...WHEN ZE BOMBS BEGAN FALLING!"
BLAAMMMMH
IT ALL HAPPENED BACK IN FEBRUARY. IT WAS KEPT VERY HUSH-HUSH, OF COURSE.
SINCE THEN, I'VE AGED NEARLY 73 YEARS AND LOST THE USE OF ALL MY LIMBS EXCEPT ZE TEETH!
WOW... WHAT A SAD STORY.
DOWNRIGHT PATHETIC.
LISTEN... IT'S BEEN FUN TALKIN' TO YA, OLD-TIMER... BUT WE GOTTA RUN.
TRY NOT TO BE BITTER. WE'LL PROB'LY DESTROY OURSELVES AN' SAVE YA THE BOTHER.

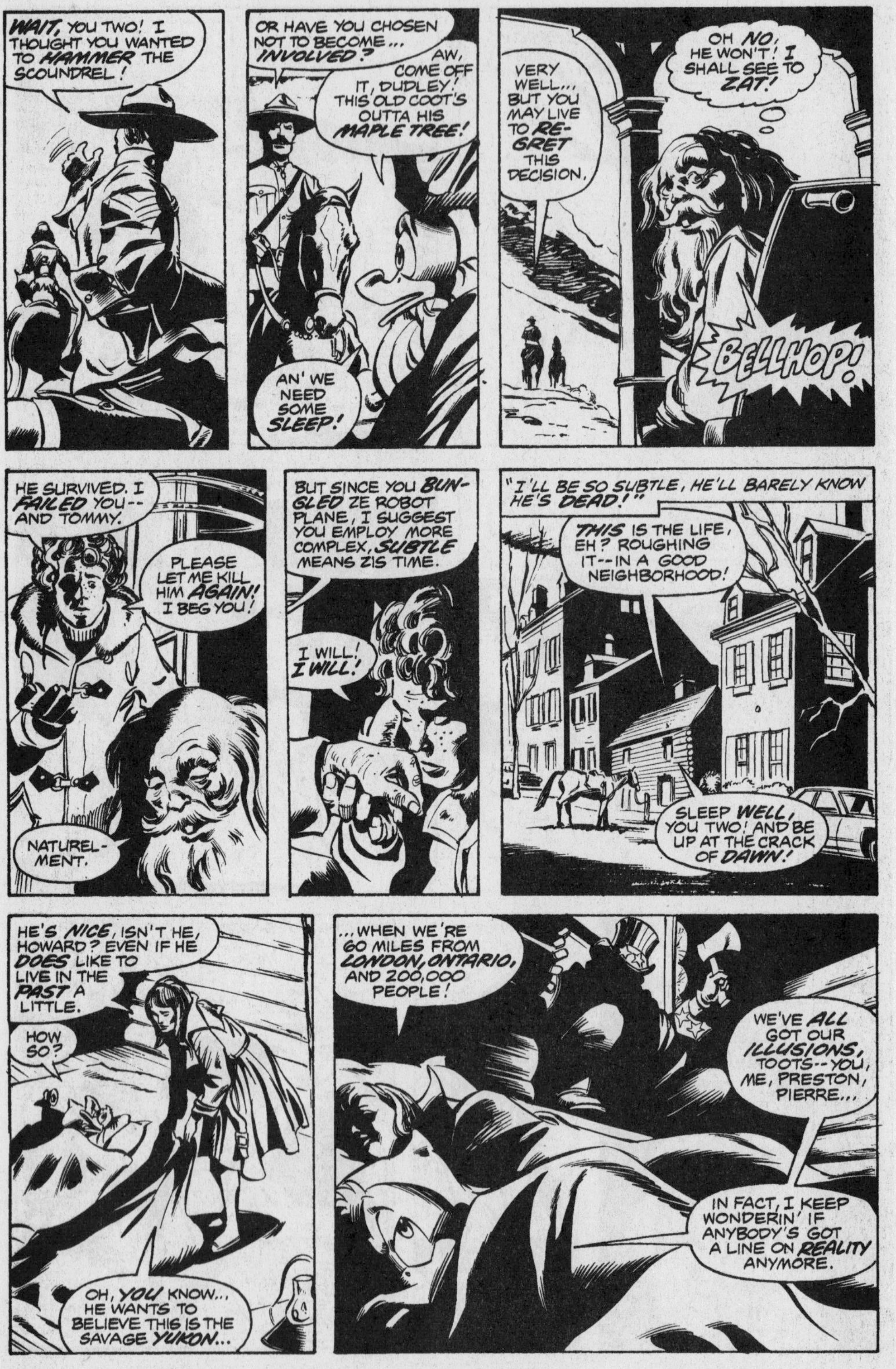
WAIT, YOU TWO! I THOUGHT YOU WANTED TO HAMMER THE SCOUNDREL!
OR HAVE YOU CHOSEN NOT TO BECOME... INVOLVED?
AW, COME OFF IT, DUDLEY! THIS OLD COOT'S OUTTA HIS MAPLE TREE!
AN' WE NEED SOME SLEEP!
VERY WELL... BUT YOU MAY LIVE TO RE-GRET THIS DECISION.
OH NO, HE WON'T! I SHALL SEE TO ZAT!
BELLHOP!
HE SURVIVED. I FAILED YOU--AND TOMMY.
PLEASE LET ME KILL HIM AGAIN! I BEG YOU!
NATUREL-MENT.
BUT SINCE YOU BUN-GLED ZE ROBOT PLANE, I SUGGEST YOU EMPLOY MORE COMPLEX, SUBTLE MEANS ZIS TIME.
I WILL! I WILL!
"I'LL BE SO SUBTLE, HE'LL BARELY KNOW HE'S DEAD!"
THIS IS THE LIFE, EH? ROUGHING IT--IN A GOOD NEIGHBORHOOD!
SLEEP WELL, YOU TWO! AND BE UP AT THE CRACK OF DAWN!
HE'S NICE, ISN'T HE, HOWARD? EVEN IF HE DOES LIKE TO LIVE IN THE PAST A LITTLE.
HOW SO?
OH, YOU KNOW... HE WANTS TO BELIEVE THIS IS THE SAVAGE YUKON...
...WHEN WE'RE 60 MILES FROM LONDON, ONTARIO, AND 200,000 PEOPLE!
WE'VE ALL GOT OUR ILLUSIONS, TOOTS--YOU, ME, PRESTON, PIERRE...
IN FACT, I KEEP WONDERIN' IF ANYBODY'S GOT A LINE ON REALITY ANYMORE.

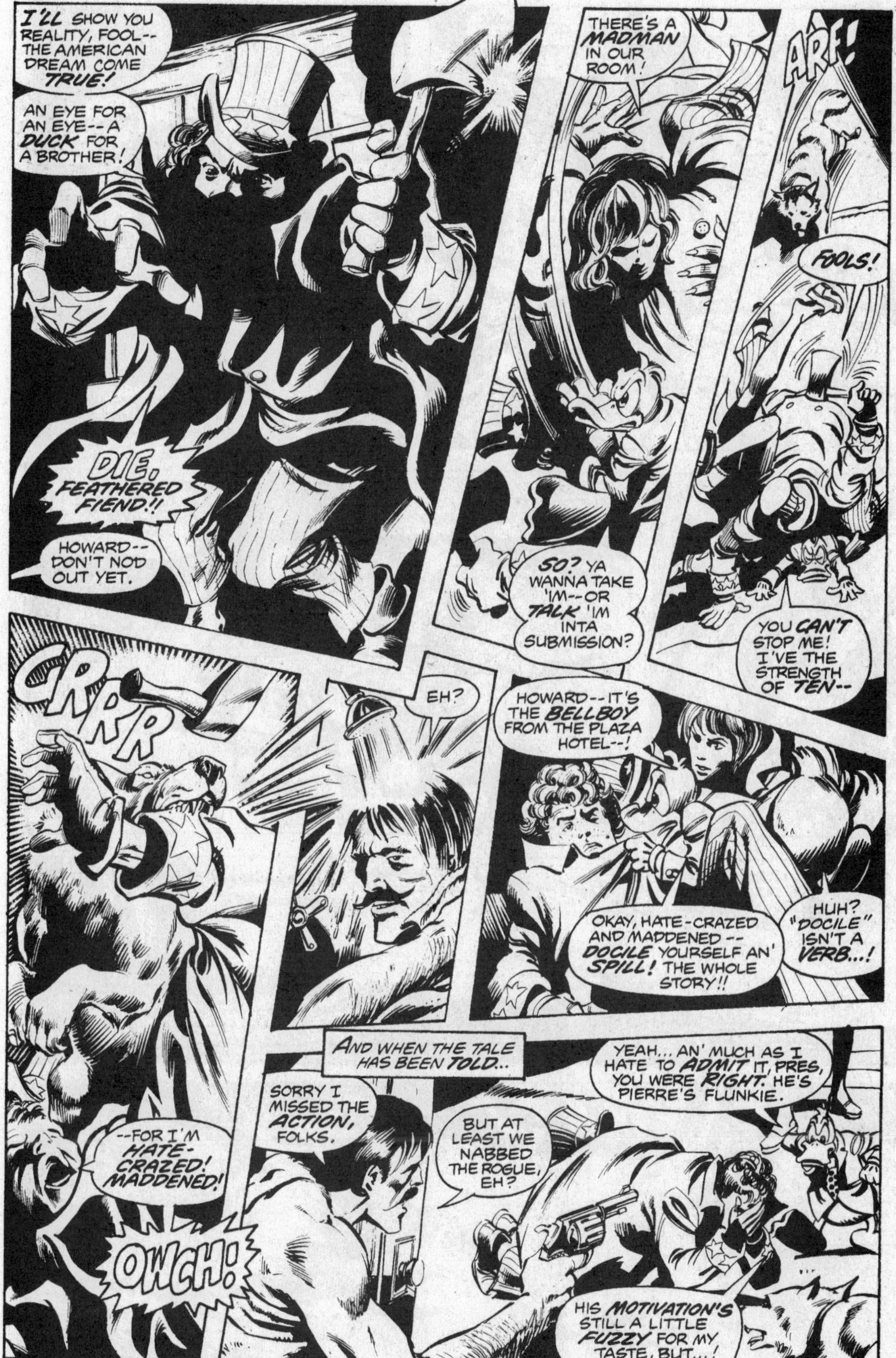
I'LL SHOW YOU REALITY, FOOL-- THE AMERICAN DREAM COME TRUE!
AN EYE FOR AN EYE-- A DUCK FOR A BROTHER!
DIE, FEATHERED FIEND!!
HOWARD-- DON'T NOD OUT YET.
THERE'S A MADMAN IN OUR ROOM!
SO? YA WANNA TAKE 'IM--OR TALK 'IM INTA SUBMISSION?
ARF!
FOOLS!
YOU CAN'T STOP ME! I'VE THE STRENGTH OF TEN--
CRRR
--FOR I'M HATE-CRAZED! MADDENED!
OWCH!
EH?
HOWARD-- IT'S THE BELLBOY FROM THE PLAZA HOTEL--!
OKAY, HATE-CRAZED AND MADDENED -- DOCILE YOURSELF AN' SPILL! THE WHOLE STORY!!
HUH? "DOCILE" ISN'T A VERB...!
AND WHEN THE TALE HAS BEEN TOLD...
SORRY I MISSED THE ACTION, FOLKS.
BUT AT LEAST WE NABBED THE ROGUE, EH?
YEAH... AN' MUCH AS I HATE TO ADMIT IT, PRES, YOU WERE RIGHT. HE'S PIERRE'S FLUNKIE.
HIS MOTIVATION'S STILL A LITTLE FUZZY FOR MY TASTE, BUT...!

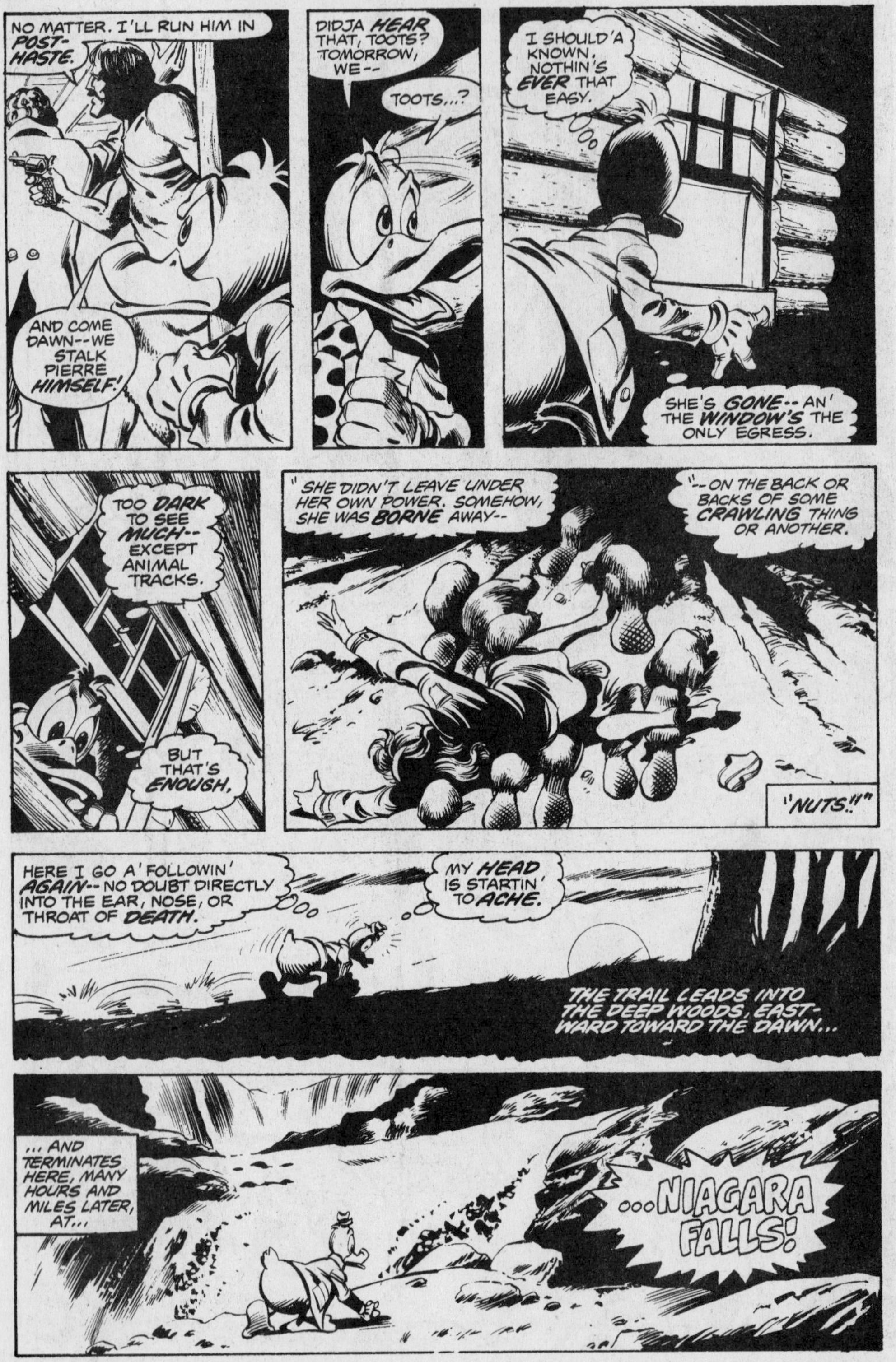
NO MATTER. I'LL RUN HIM IN POST-HASTE.
AND COME DAWN--WE STALK PIERRE HIMSELF!
DIDJA HEAR THAT, TOOTS? TOMORROW, WE--
TOOTS...?
I SHOULD'A KNOWN, NOTHIN'S EVER THAT EASY.
SHE'S GONE--AN' THE WINDOW'S THE ONLY EGRESS.
TOO DARK TO SEE MUCH--EXCEPT ANIMAL TRACKS.
BUT THAT'S ENOUGH.
"SHE DIDN'T LEAVE UNDER HER OWN POWER. SOMEHOW, SHE WAS BORNE AWAY--
"--ON THE BACK OR BACKS OF SOME CRAWLING THING OR ANOTHER.
"NUTS!!"
HERE I GO A' FOLLOWIN' AGAIN--NO DOUBT DIRECTLY INTO THE EAR, NOSE, OR THROAT OF DEATH.
MY HEAD IS STARTIN' TO ACHE.
THE TRAIL LEADS INTO THE DEEP WOODS, EAST-WARD TOWARD THE DAWN...
...AND TERMINATES HERE, MANY HOURS AND MILES LATER, AT...
...NIAGARA FALLS!

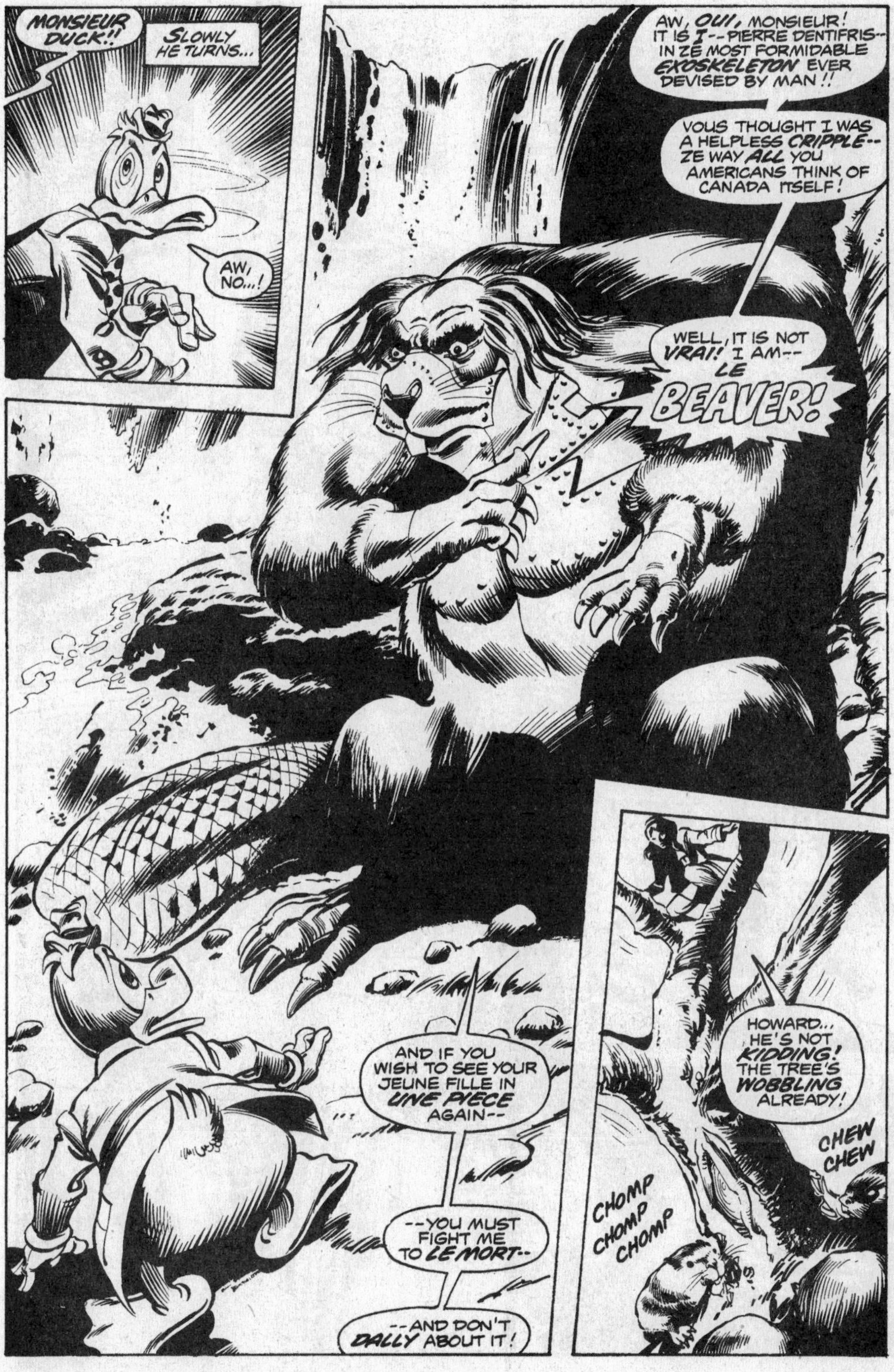
MONSIEUR DUCK!!
SLOWLY HE TURNS...
AW, NO...!
AW, OUI, MONSIEUR! IT IS I--PIERRE DENTIFRIS--IN ZE MOST FORMIDABLE EXOSKELETON EVER DEVISED BY MAN!!
VOUS THOUGHT I WAS A HELPLESS CRIPPLE--ZE WAY ALL YOU AMERICANS THINK OF CANADA ITSELF!
WELL, IT IS NOT VRAI! I AM--LE BEAVER!
AND IF YOU WISH TO SEE YOUR JEUNE FILLE IN UNE PIECE AGAIN--
--YOU MUST FIGHT ME TO LE MORT--
--AND DON'T DALLY ABOUT IT!
HOWARD... HE'S NOT KIDDING! THE TREE'S WOBBLING ALREADY!
CHEW CHEW
CHOMP CHOMP CHOMP

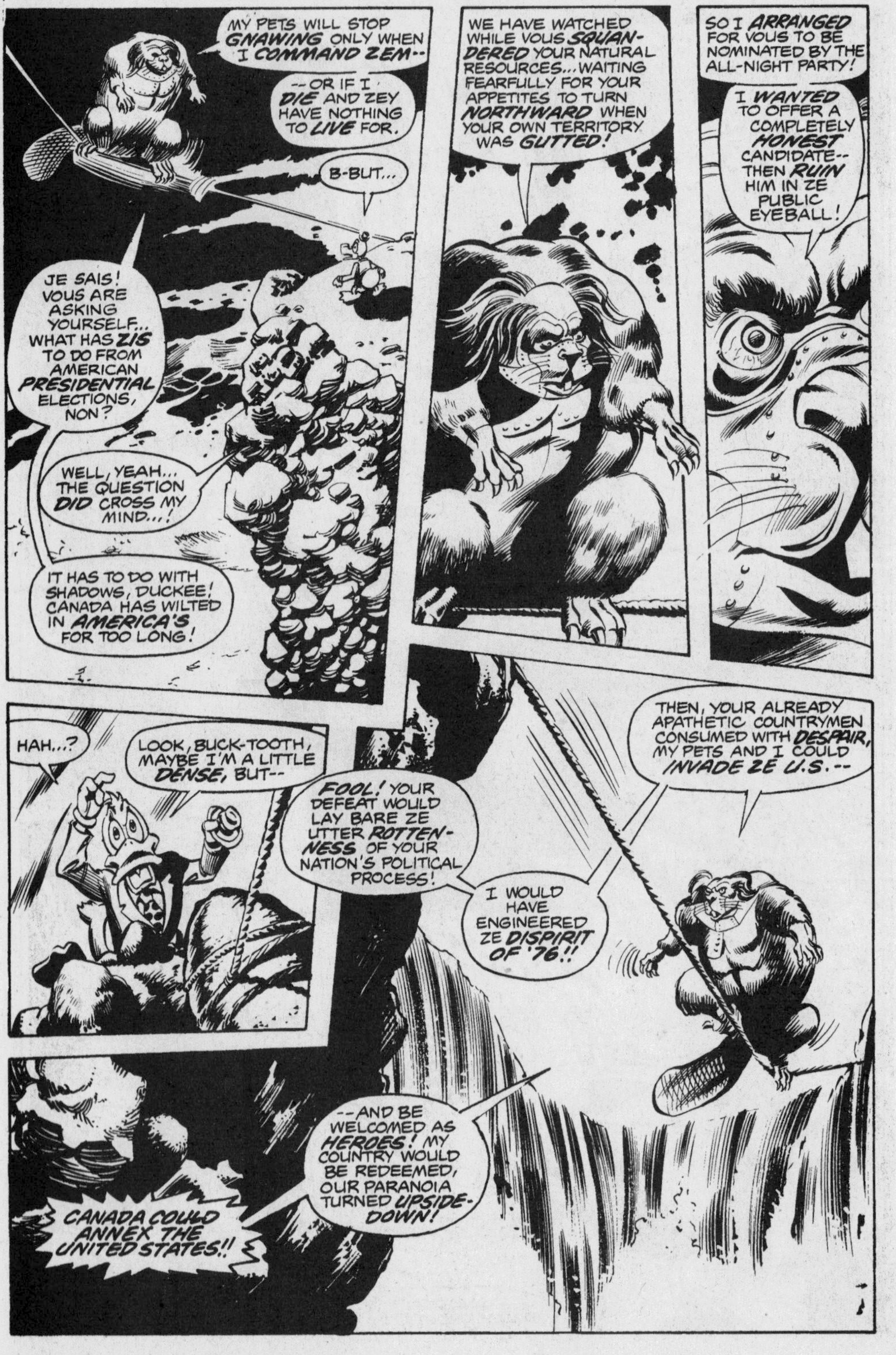

MY PETS WILL STOP GNAWING ONLY WHEN I COMMAND ZEM--
--OR IF I DIE AND ZEY HAVE NOTHING TO LIVE FOR.
B-BUT...
JE SAIS! VOUS ARE ASKING YOURSELF... WHAT HAS ZIS TO DO FROM AMERICAN PRESIDENTIAL ELECTIONS, NON?
WELL, YEAH... THE QUESTION DID CROSS MY MIND...!
IT HAS TO DO WITH SHADOWS, DUCKEE! CANADA HAS WILTED IN AMERICA'S FOR TOO LONG!
WE HAVE WATCHED WHILE VOUS SQUANDERED YOUR NATURAL RESOURCES... WAITING FEARFULLY FOR YOUR APPETITES TO TURN NORTHWARD WHEN YOUR OWN TERRITORY WAS GUTTED!
SO I ARRANGED FOR VOUS TO BE NOMINATED BY THE ALL-NIGHT PARTY!
I WANTED TO OFFER A COMPLETELY HONEST CANDIDATE-- THEN RUIN HIM IN ZE PUBLIC EYEBALL!
HAH...?
LOOK, BUCK-TOOTH, MAYBE I'M A LITTLE DENSE, BUT--
FOOL! YOUR DEFEAT WOULD LAY BARE ZE UTTER ROTTENNESS OF YOUR NATION'S POLITICAL PROCESS!
I WOULD HAVE ENGINEERED ZE DISPIRIT OF '76!!
THEN, YOUR ALREADY APATHETIC COUNTRYMEN CONSUMED WITH DESPAIR, MY PETS AND I COULD INVADE ZE U.S.--
--AND BE WELCOMED AS HEROES! MY COUNTRY WOULD BE REDEEMED, OUR PARANOIA TURNED UPSIDE-DOWN!
CANADA COULD ANNEX THE UNITED STATES!!

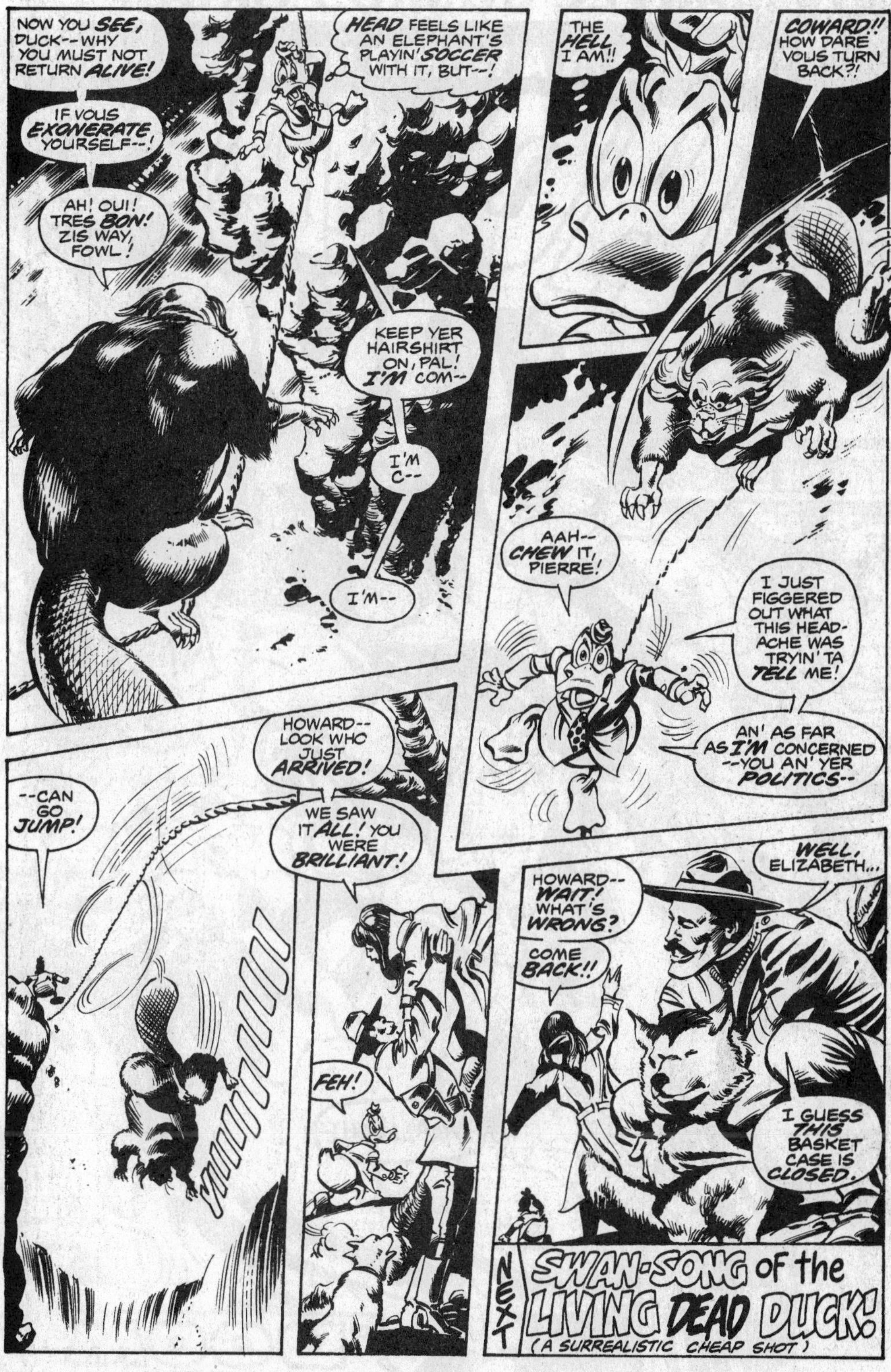
NOW YOU SEE, DUCK--WHY YOU MUST NOT RETURN ALIVE!
IF VOUS EXONERATE YOURSELF--!
AH! OUI! TRES BON! ZIS WAY, FOWL!
HEAD FEELS LIKE AN ELEPHANT'S PLAYIN' SOCCER WITH IT, BUT--!
KEEP YER HAIRSHIRT ON, PAL! I'M COM-
I'M C--
I'M--
THE HELL I AM!!
COWARD!! HOW DARE VOUS TURN BACK?!
AAH--CHEW IT, PIERRE!
I JUST FIGGERED OUT WHAT THIS HEAD-ACHE WAS TRYIN' TA TELL ME!
AN' AS FAR AS I'M CONCERNED --YOU AN' YER POLITICS--
--CAN GO JUMP!
HOWARD--LOOK WHO JUST ARRIVED!
WE SAW IT ALL! YOU WERE BRILLIANT!
FEH!
HOWARD--WAIT! WHAT'S WRONG?
COME BACK!!
WELL, ELIZABETH...
I GUESS THIS BASKET CASE IS CLOSED.
NEXT
SWAN-SONG of the LIVING DEAD DUCK!
(A SURREALISTIC CHEAP SHOT)

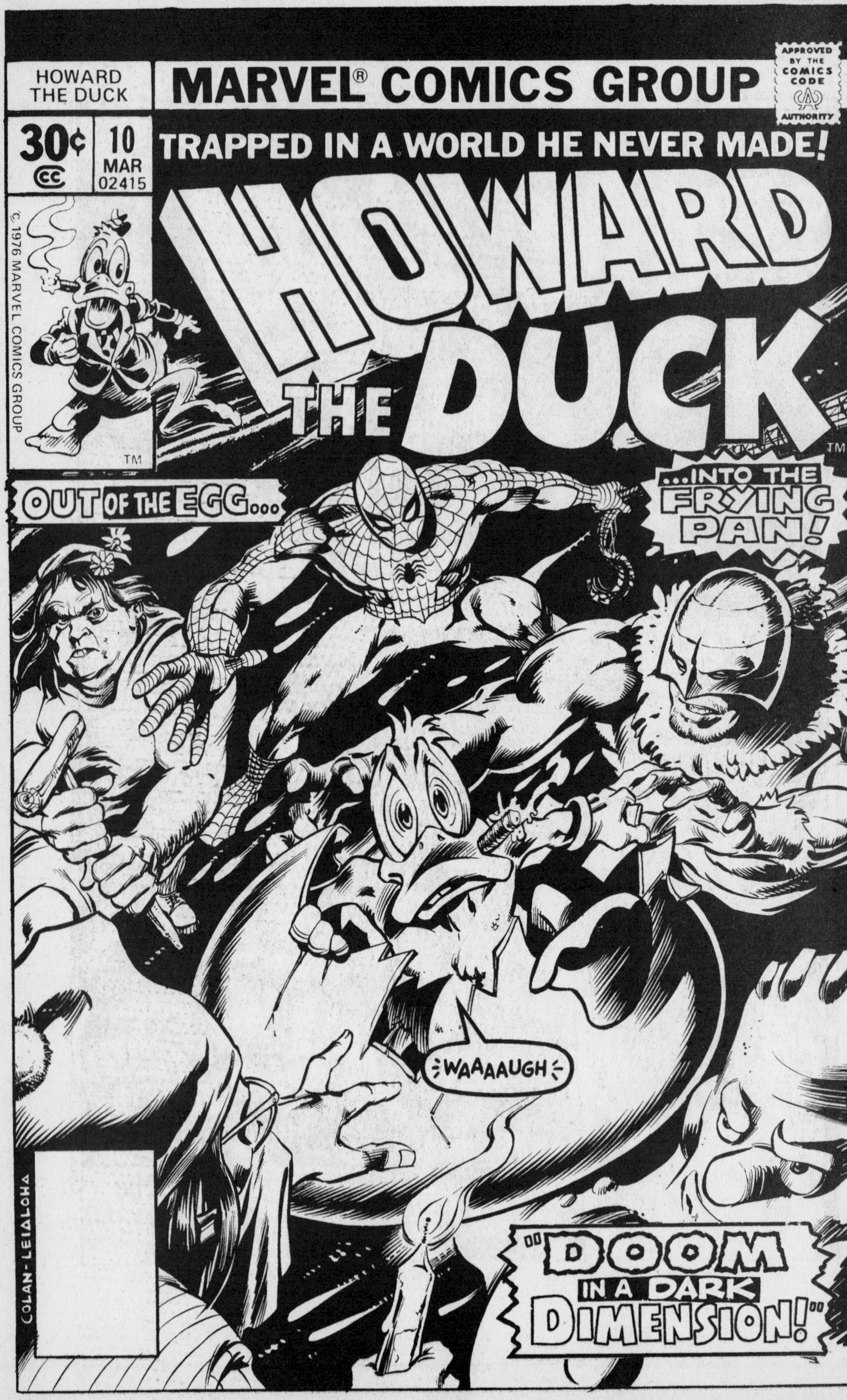
HOWARD THE DUCK
MARVEL® COMICS GROUP
APPROVED BY THE COMICS CODE AUTHORITY
30¢
10 MAR 02415
TRAPPED IN A WORLD HE NEVER MADE!
HOWARD THE DUCK
© 1976 MARVEL COMICS GROUP
TM
OUT OF THE EGG...
...INTO THE FRYING PAN!
WAAAAUGH
"DOOM IN A DARK DIMENSION!"
COLAN-LEIALOHA

From the time of his hatching, he was...different. A potentially brilliant scholar who dreaded the structured environment of school, he educated himself in the streets, taking whatever work was available, formulating his philosophy of self from what he learned of the world about him. And then the Cosmic Axis shifted...and that world *changed.* Suddenly, he was stranded in a universe he could not fathom. Without warning, he became a strange fowl in an even stranger land.

Stan Lee PRESENTS: HOWARD THE DUCK!™

STEVE GERBER WRITER/EDITOR · GENE COLAN ARTIST · STEVE LEIALOHA INKER · JIM NOVAK, LETTERER · JAN COHEN, COLORIST · TED SALLIS CONSULTING SCHIZO

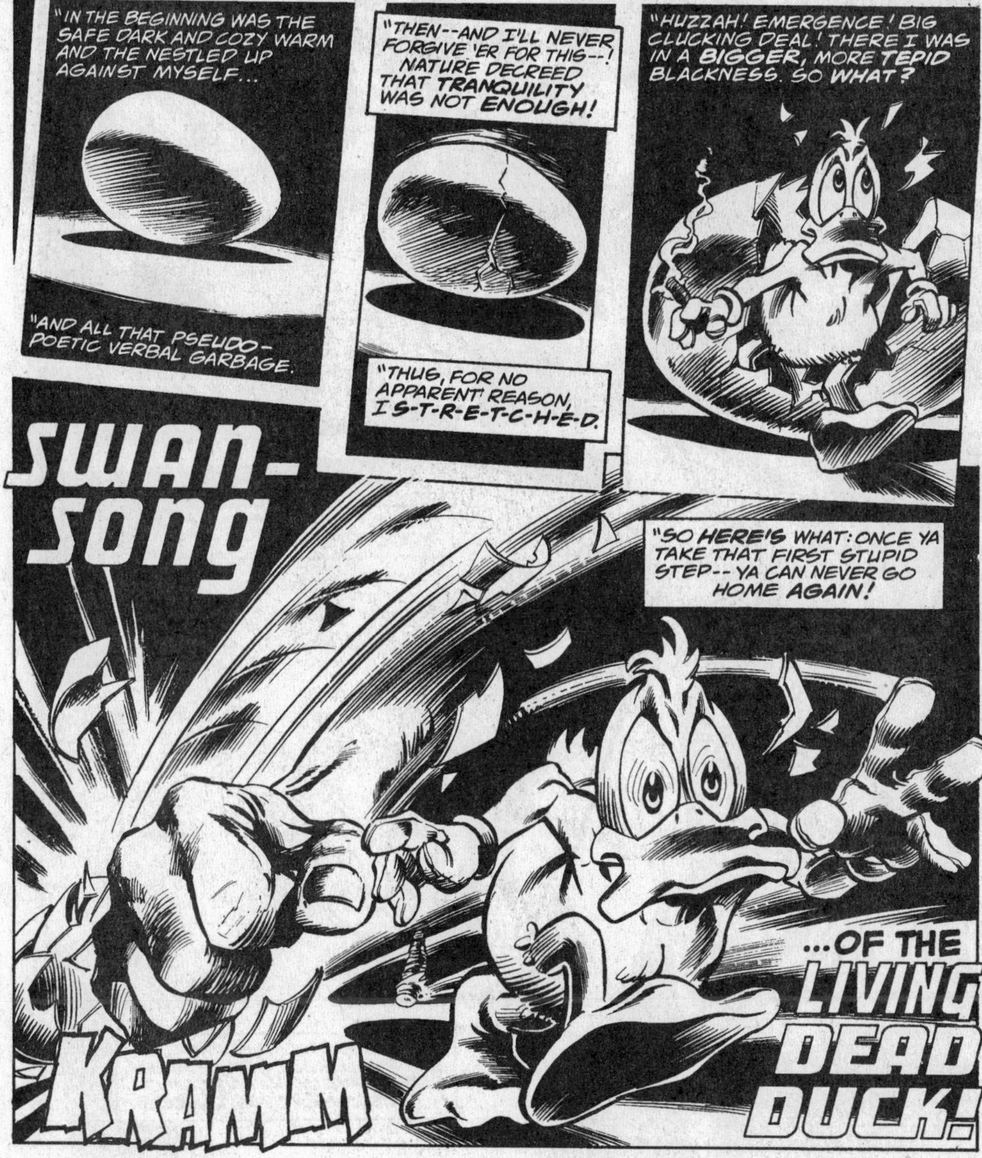
"IN THE BEGINNING WAS THE SAFE DARK AND COZY WARM AND THE NESTLED UP AGAINST MYSELF...
"AND ALL THAT PSEUDO-POETIC VERBAL GARBAGE.
"THEN--AND I'LL NEVER FORGIVE 'ER FOR THIS--! NATURE DECREED THAT TRANQUILITY WAS NOT ENOUGH!
"THUS, FOR NO APPARENT REASON, I S-T-R-E-T-C-H-E-D.
"HUZZAH! EMERGENCE! BIG CLUCKING DEAL! THERE I WAS IN A BIGGER, MORE TEPID BLACKNESS. SO WHAT?
SWAN-SONG
"SO HERE'S WHAT: ONCE YA TAKE THAT FIRST STUPID STEP-- YA CAN NEVER GO HOME AGAIN!
KRAMM
...OF THE LIVING DEAD DUCK!

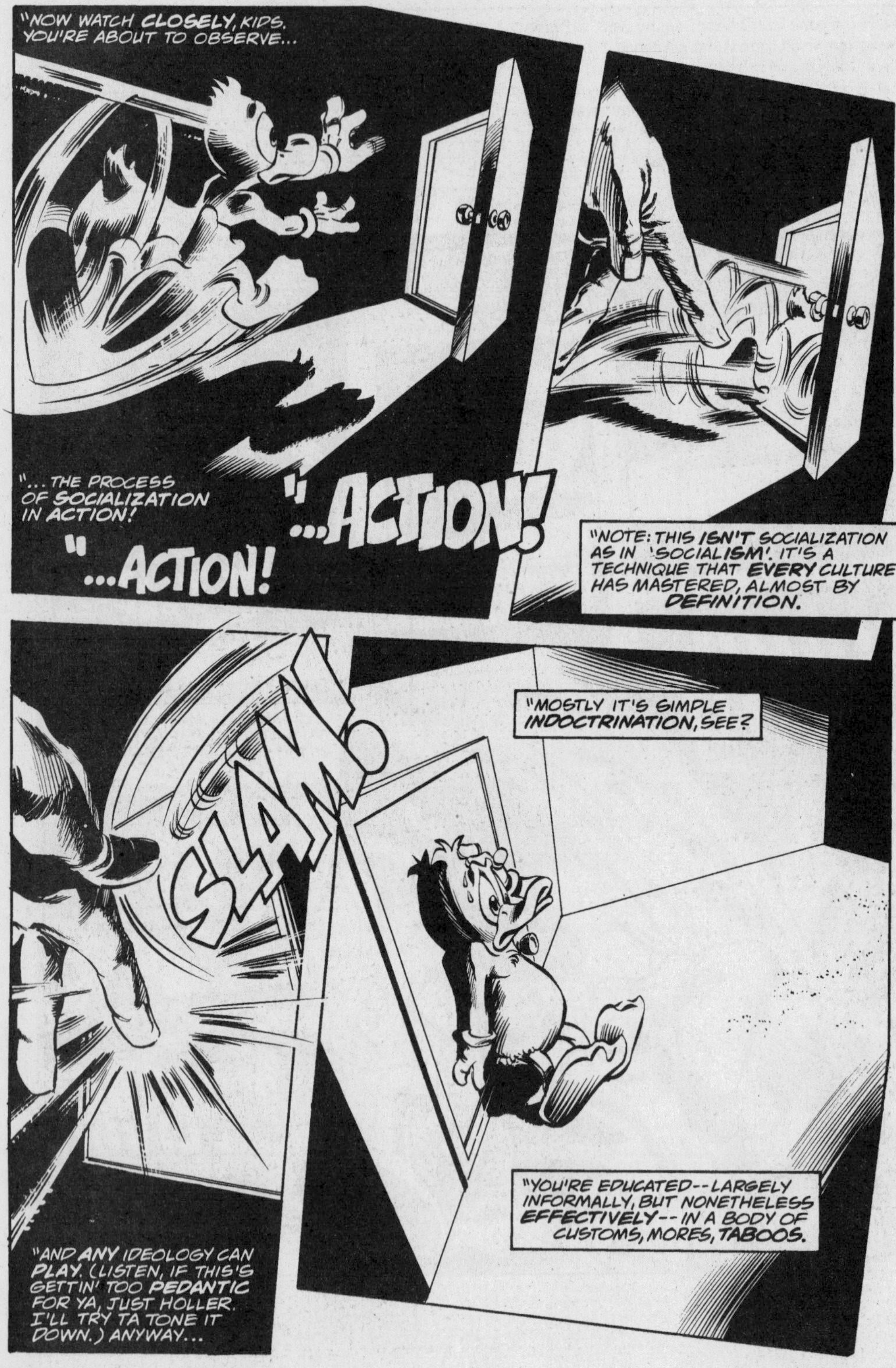
"NOW WATCH CLOSELY, KIDS. YOU'RE ABOUT TO OBSERVE...
"...THE PROCESS OF SOCIALIZATION IN ACTION!
"...ACTION!
"...ACTION!
"NOTE: THIS ISN'T SOCIALIZATION AS IN 'SOCIALISM'. IT'S A TECHNIQUE THAT EVERY CULTURE HAS MASTERED, ALMOST BY DEFINITION.
SLAM!
"MOSTLY IT'S SIMPLE INDOCTRINATION, SEE?
"YOU'RE EDUCATED--LARGELY INFORMALLY, BUT NONETHELESS EFFECTIVELY--IN A BODY OF CUSTOMS, MORES, TABOOS.
"AND ANY IDEOLOGY CAN PLAY. (LISTEN, IF THIS'S GETTIN' TOO PEDANTIC FOR YA, JUST HOLLER. I'LL TRY TA TONE IT DOWN.) ANYWAY...

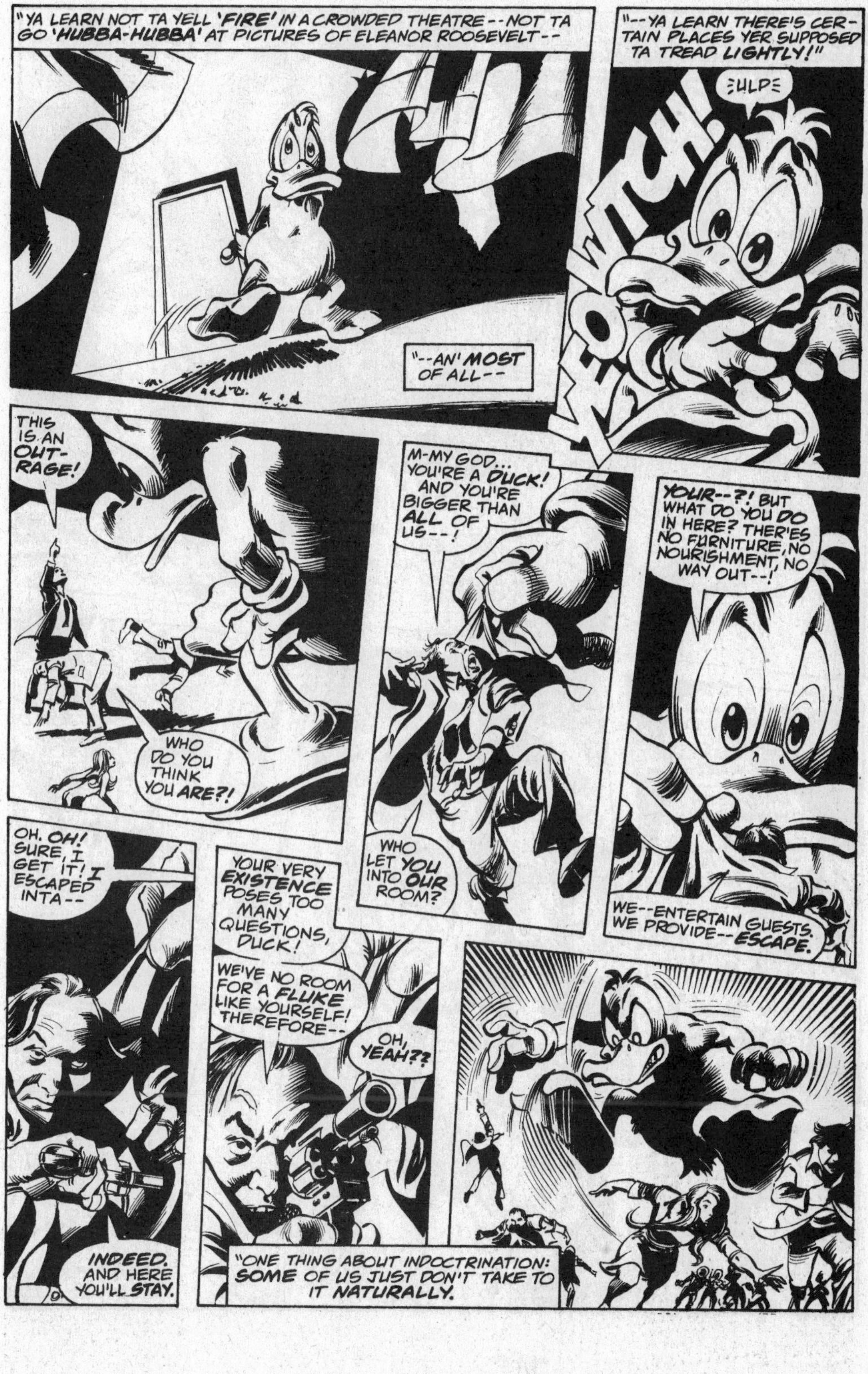
"YA LEARN NOT TA YELL 'FIRE' IN A CROWDED THEATRE--NOT TA GO 'HUBBA-HUBBA' AT PICTURES OF ELEANOR ROOSEVELT--
"--AN' MOST OF ALL--
"--YA LEARN THERE'S CERTAIN PLACES YER SUPPOSED TA TREAD LIGHTLY!"
YEOWTCH!
ULP
THIS IS AN OUTRAGE!
WHO DO YOU THINK YOU ARE?!
M-MY GOD... YOU'RE A DUCK! AND YOU'RE BIGGER THAN ALL OF US--!
WHO LET YOU INTO OUR ROOM?
YOUR--?! BUT WHAT DO YOU DO IN HERE? THERE'ES NO FURNITURE, NO NOURISHMENT, NO WAY OUT--!
WE--ENTERTAIN GUESTS. WE PROVIDE--ESCAPE.
OH. OH! SURE, I GET IT! I ESCAPED INTA--
INDEED. AND HERE YOU'LL STAY.
YOUR VERY EXISTENCE POSES TOO MANY QUESTIONS, DUCK!
WE'VE NO ROOM FOR A FLUKE LIKE YOURSELF! THEREFORE--
OH, YEAH??
"ONE THING ABOUT INDOCTRINATION: SOME OF US JUST DON'T TAKE TO IT NATURALLY.

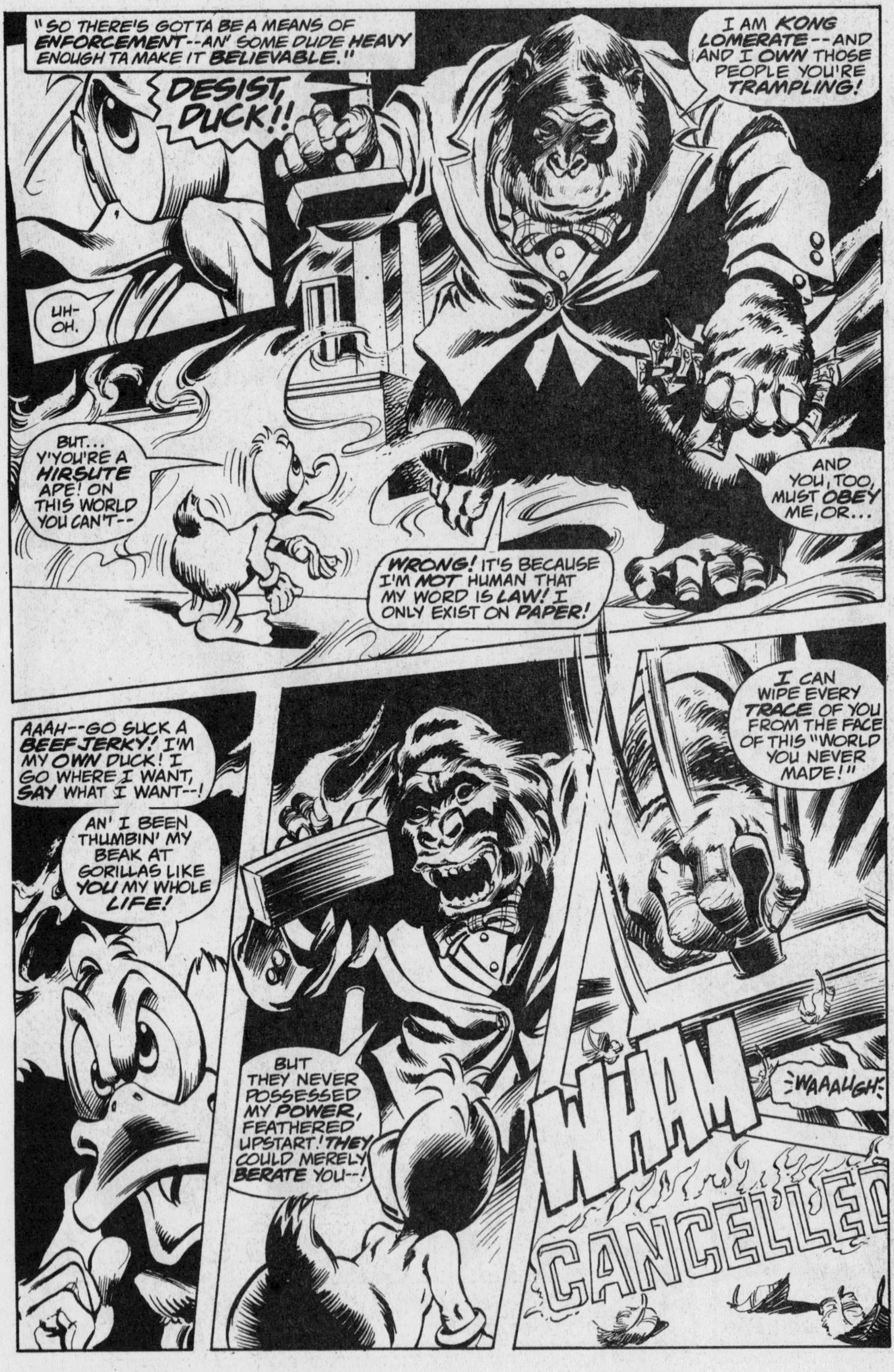
"SO THERE'S GOTTA BE A MEANS OF ENFORCEMENT--AN' SOME DUDE HEAVY ENOUGH TA MAKE IT BELIEVABLE."
DESIST, DUCK!!
I AM KONG LOMERATE--AND AND I OWN THOSE PEOPLE YOU'RE TRAMPLING!
UH-OH.
BUT... Y'YOU'RE A HIRSUTE APE! ON THIS WORLD YOU CAN'T--
AND YOU, TOO, MUST OBEY ME, OR...
WRONG! IT'S BECAUSE I'M NOT HUMAN THAT MY WORD IS LAW! I ONLY EXIST ON PAPER!
AAAH--GO SUCK A BEEF JERKY! I'M MY OWN DUCK! I GO WHERE I WANT, SAY WHAT I WANT--!
AN' I BEEN THUMBIN' MY BEAK AT GORILLAS LIKE YOU MY WHOLE LIFE!
BUT THEY NEVER POSSESSED MY POWER, FEATHERED UPSTART! THEY COULD MERELY BERATE YOU--!
I CAN WIPE EVERY TRACE OF YOU FROM THE FACE OF THIS "WORLD YOU NEVER MADE!"
WHAM
WAAAUGH!
CANCELLED

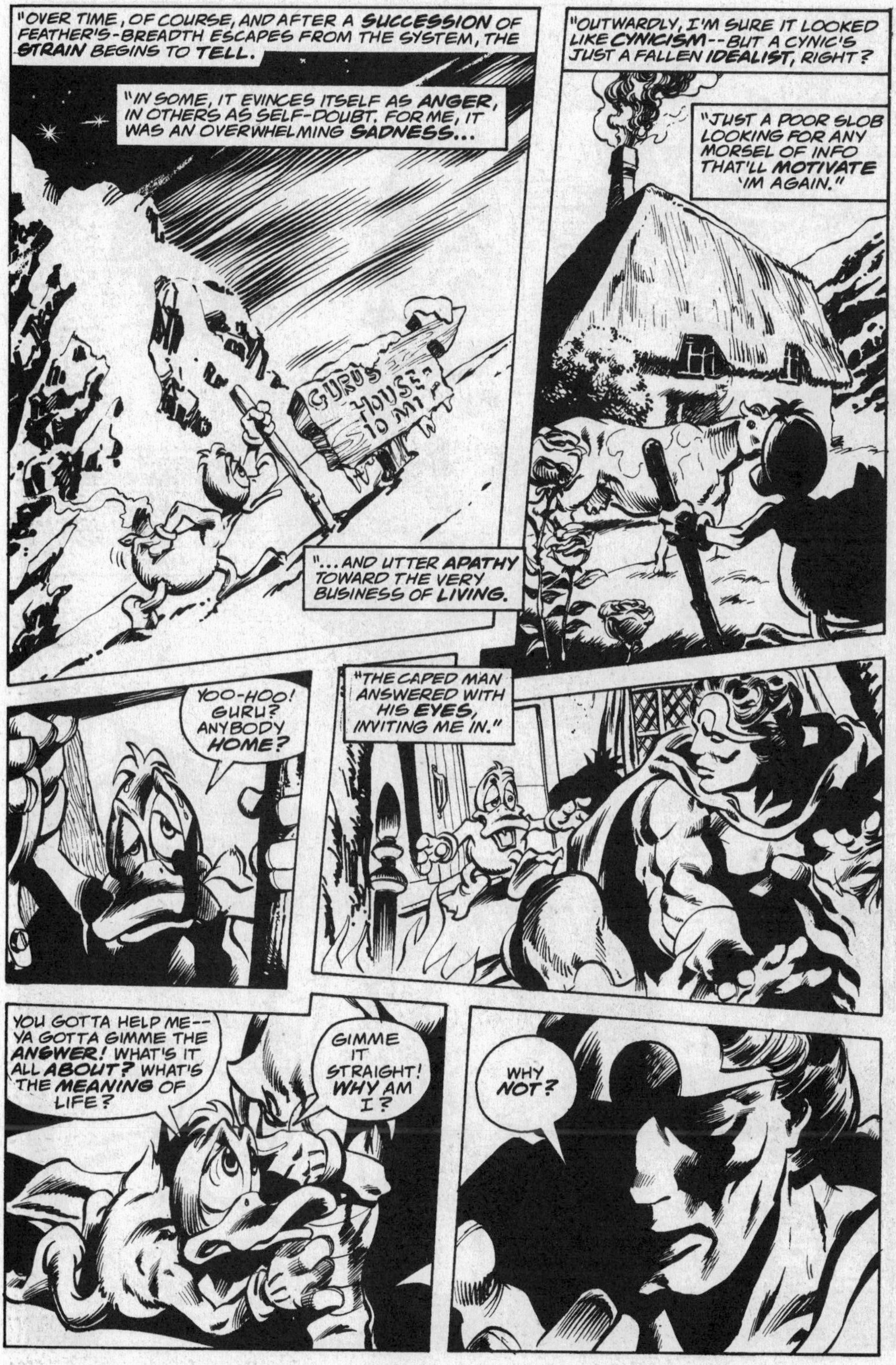
"OVER TIME, OF COURSE, AND AFTER A SUCCESSION OF FEATHER'S-BREADTH ESCAPES FROM THE SYSTEM, THE STRAIN BEGINS TO TELL.
"IN SOME, IT EVINCES ITSELF AS ANGER, IN OTHERS AS SELF-DOUBT. FOR ME, IT WAS AN OVERWHELMING SADNESS...
GURU'S HOUSE 10 MI
"...AND UTTER APATHY TOWARD THE VERY BUSINESS OF LIVING.
"OUTWARDLY, I'M SURE IT LOOKED LIKE CYNICISM--BUT A CYNIC'S JUST A FALLEN IDEALIST, RIGHT?
"JUST A POOR SLOB LOOKING FOR ANY MORSEL OF INFO THAT'LL MOTIVATE 'IM AGAIN."
YOO-HOO! GURU? ANYBODY HOME?
"THE CAPED MAN ANSWERED WITH HIS EYES, INVITING ME IN."
YOU GOTTA HELP ME--YA GOTTA GIMME THE ANSWER! WHAT'S IT ALL ABOUT? WHAT'S THE MEANING OF LIFE?
GIMME IT STRAIGHT! WHY AM I?
WHY NOT?

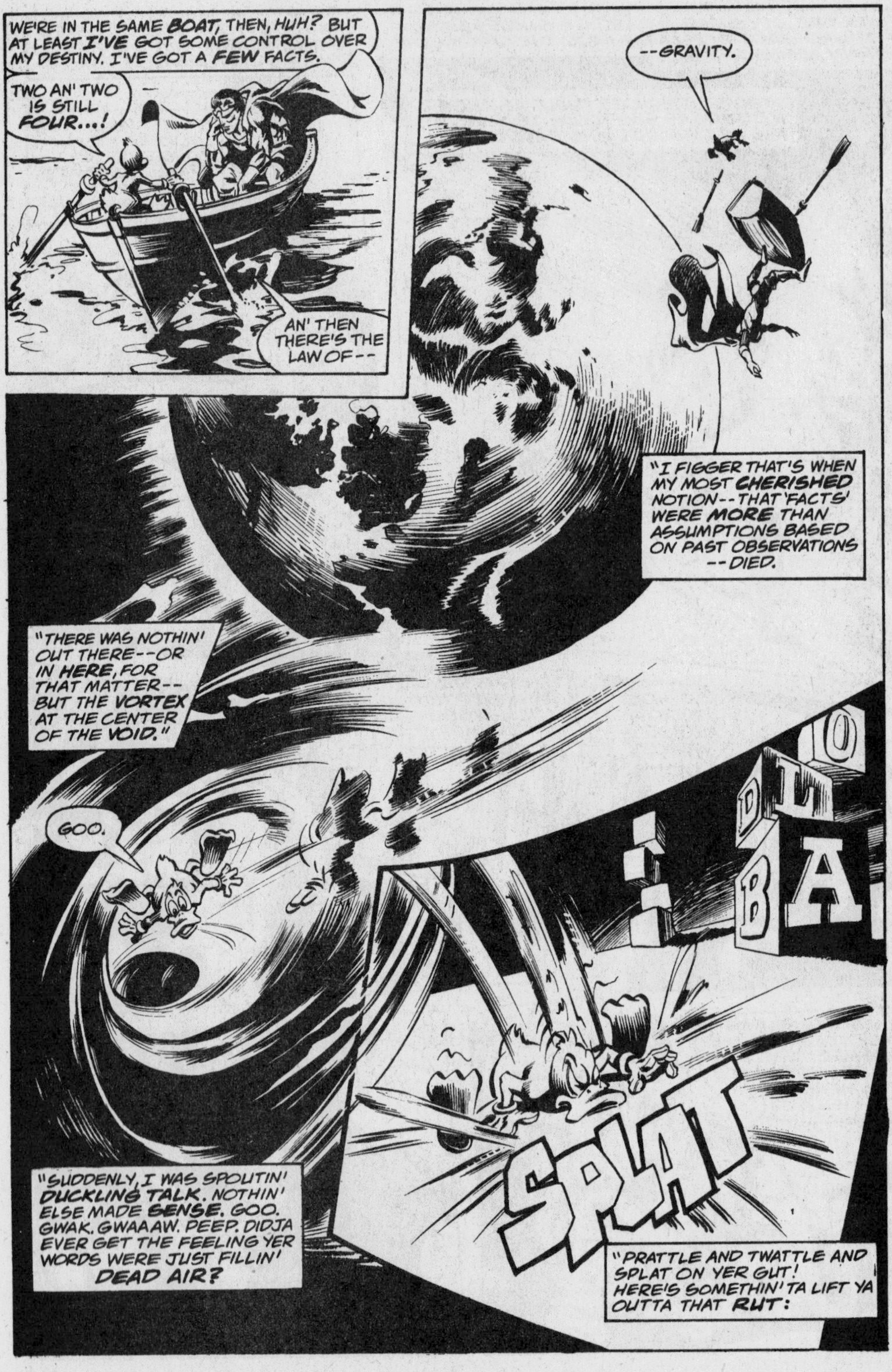
WE'RE IN THE SAME BOAT, THEN, HUH? BUT AT LEAST I'VE GOT SOME CONTROL OVER MY DESTINY. I'VE GOT A FEW FACTS.
TWO AN' TWO IS STILL FOUR...!
AN' THEN THERE'S THE LAW OF--
--GRAVITY.
"I FIGGER THAT'S WHEN MY MOST CHERISHED NOTION--THAT 'FACTS' WERE MORE THAN ASSUMPTIONS BASED ON PAST OBSERVATIONS --DIED.
"THERE WAS NOTHIN' OUT THERE--OR IN HERE, FOR THAT MATTER-- BUT THE VORTEX AT THE CENTER OF THE VOID."
GOO.
SPLAT
"SUDDENLY, I WAS SPOUTIN' DUCKLING TALK. NOTHIN' ELSE MADE SENSE. GOO. GWAK. GWAAAW. PEEP. DIDJA EVER GET THE FEELING YER WORDS WERE JUST FILLIN' DEAD AIR?
"PRATTLE AND TWATTLE AND SPLAT ON YER GUT! HERE'S SOMETHIN' TA LIFT YA OUTTA THAT RUT:

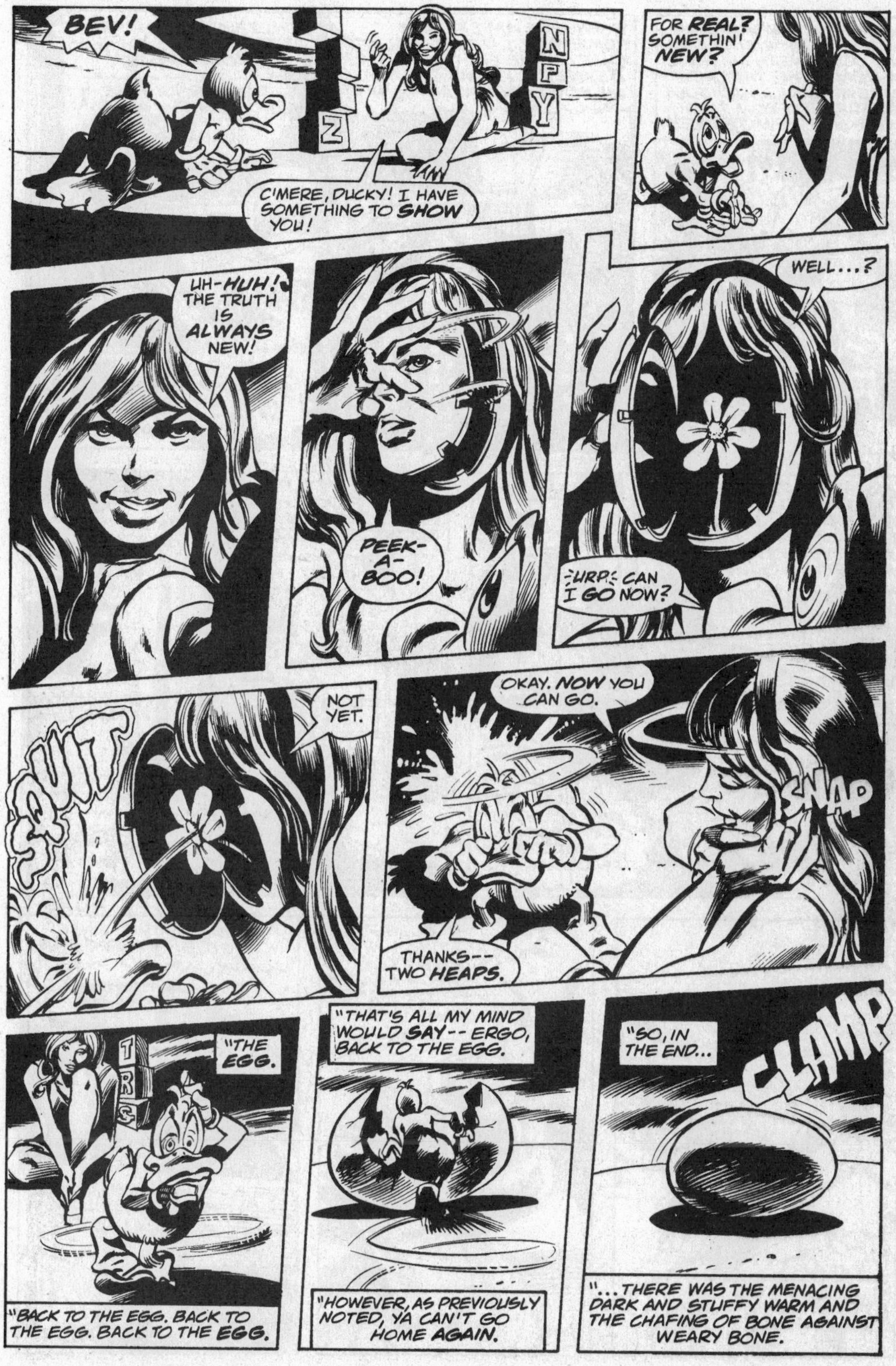
BEV!
C'MERE, DUCKY! I HAVE SOMETHING TO SHOW YOU!
FOR REAL? SOMETHIN' NEW?
UH-HUH! THE TRUTH IS ALWAYS NEW!
PEEK-A-BOO!
WELL...?
URP. CAN I GO NOW?
SQUIT
NOT YET.
OKAY. NOW YOU CAN GO.
SNAP
THANKS-- TWO HEAPS.
"THE EGG.
"BACK TO THE EGG. BACK TO THE EGG. BACK TO THE EGG.
"THAT'S ALL MY MIND WOULD SAY-- ERGO, BACK TO THE EGG.
"HOWEVER, AS PREVIOUSLY NOTED, YA CAN'T GO HOME AGAIN.
"SO, IN THE END...
CLAMP
"...THERE WAS THE MENACING DARK AND STUFFY WARM AND THE CHAFING OF BONE AGAINST WEARY BONE.

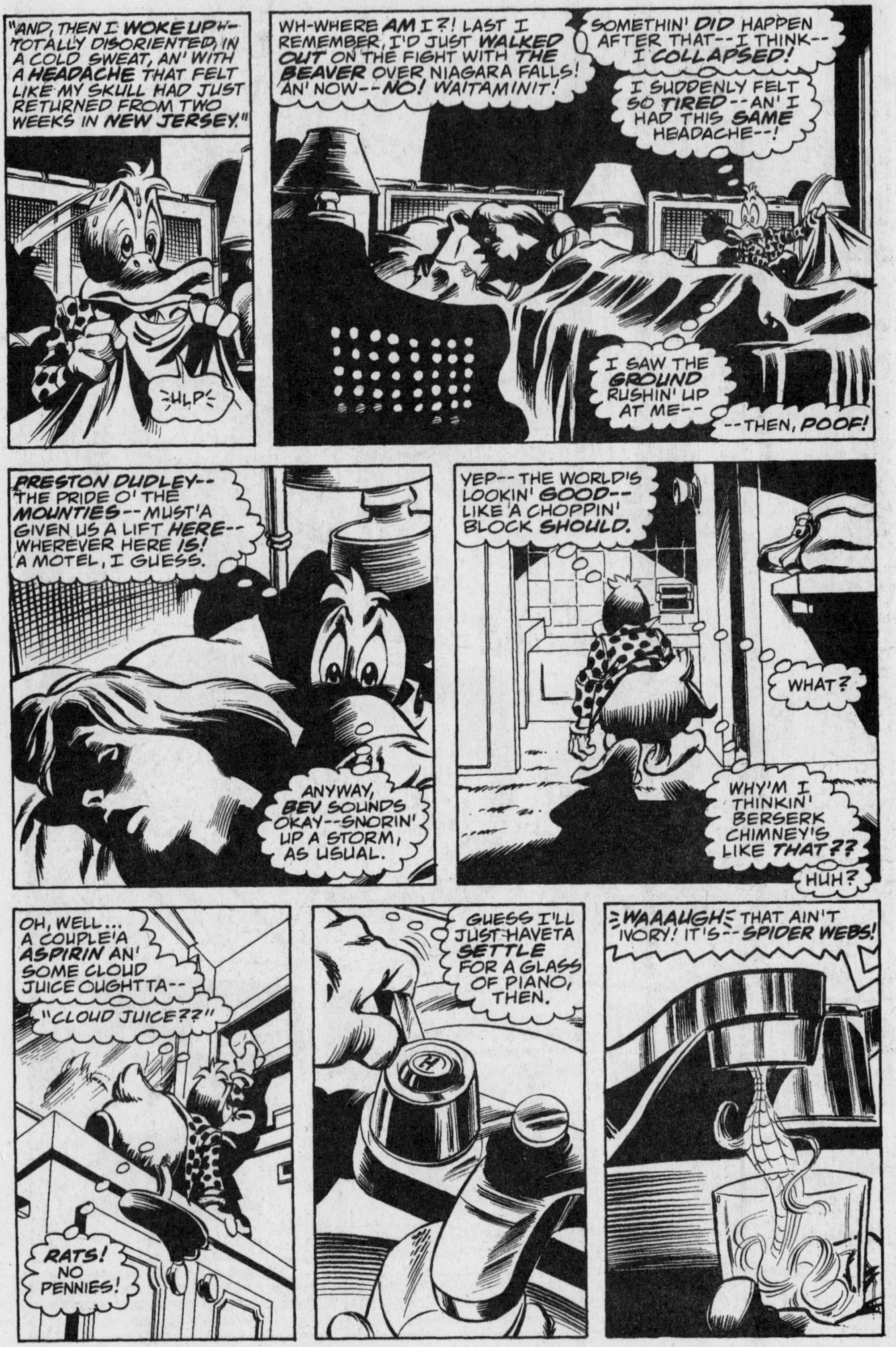
"AND, THEN I WOKE UP-- TOTALLY DISORIENTED, IN A COLD SWEAT, AN' WITH A HEADACHE THAT FELT LIKE MY SKULL HAD JUST RETURNED FROM TWO WEEKS IN NEW JERSEY."
HLP
WH-WHERE AM I?! LAST I REMEMBER, I'D JUST WALKED OUT ON THE FIGHT WITH THE BEAVER OVER NIAGARA FALLS! AN' NOW--NO! WAITAMINIT!
SOMETHIN' DID HAPPEN AFTER THAT--I THINK-- I COLLAPSED!
I SUDDENLY FELT SO TIRED--AN' I HAD THIS SAME HEADACHE--!
I SAW THE GROUND RUSHIN' UP AT ME--
--THEN, POOF!
PRESTON DUDLEY-- THE PRIDE O' THE MOUNTIES--MUST'A GIVEN US A LIFT HERE-- WHEREVER HERE IS! A MOTEL, I GUESS.
ANYWAY, BEV SOUNDS OKAY--SNORIN' UP A STORM, AS USUAL.
YEP--THE WORLD'S LOOKIN' GOOD-- LIKE A CHOPPIN' BLOCK SHOULD.
WHAT?
WHY'M I THINKIN' BERSERK CHIMNEY'S LIKE THAT??
HUH?
OH, WELL... A COUPLE'A ASPIRIN AN' SOME CLOUD JUICE OUGHTTA--
"CLOUD JUICE??"
RATS! NO PENNIES!
GUESS I'LL JUST HAVETA SETTLE FOR A GLASS OF PIANO, THEN.
WAAAUGH! THAT AIN'T IVORY! IT'S--SPIDER WEBS!

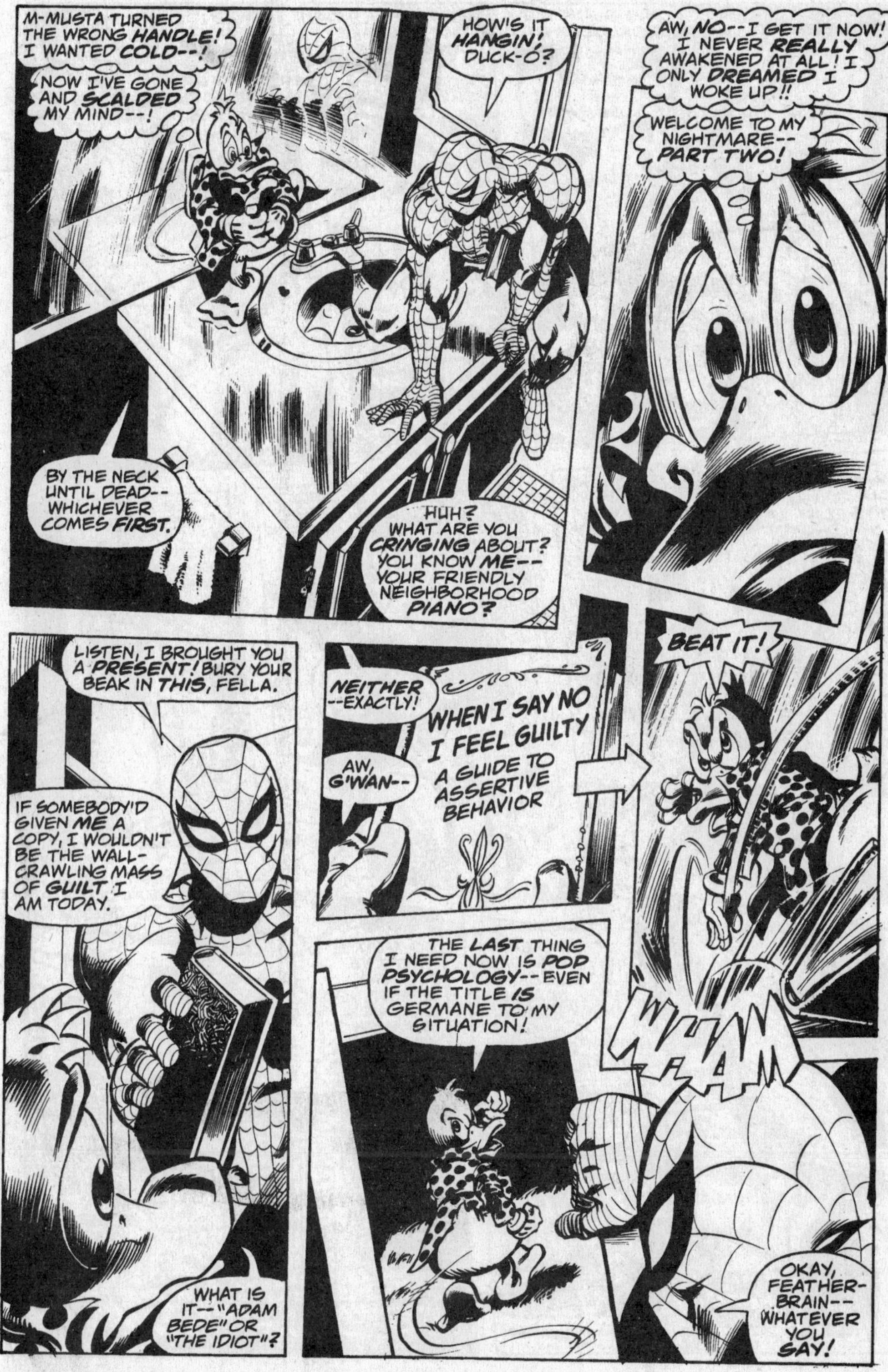
M-MUSTA TURNED THE WRONG HANDLE! I WANTED COLD--!
NOW I'VE GONE AND SCALDED MY MIND--!
HOW'S IT HANGIN! DUCK-O?
BY THE NECK UNTIL DEAD-- WHICHEVER COMES FIRST.
HUH? WHAT ARE YOU CRINGING ABOUT? YOU KNOW ME-- YOUR FRIENDLY NEIGHBORHOOD PIANO?
AW, NO--I GET IT NOW! I NEVER REALLY AWAKENED AT ALL! I ONLY DREAMED I WOKE UP!!
WELCOME TO MY NIGHTMARE-- PART TWO!
LISTEN, I BROUGHT YOU A PRESENT! BURY YOUR BEAK IN THIS, FELLA.
IF SOMEBODY'D GIVEN ME A COPY, I WOULDN'T BE THE WALL-CRAWLING MASS OF GUILT I AM TODAY.
WHAT IS IT--"ADAM BEDE" OR "THE IDIOT"?
NEITHER --EXACTLY!
WHEN I SAY NO I FEEL GUILTY
A GUIDE TO ASSERTIVE BEHAVIOR
AW, G'WAN--
THE LAST THING I NEED NOW IS POP PSYCHOLOGY--EVEN IF THE TITLE IS GERMANE TO MY SITUATION!
BEAT IT!
WHAM
OKAY, FEATHER-BRAIN-- WHATEVER YOU SAY!

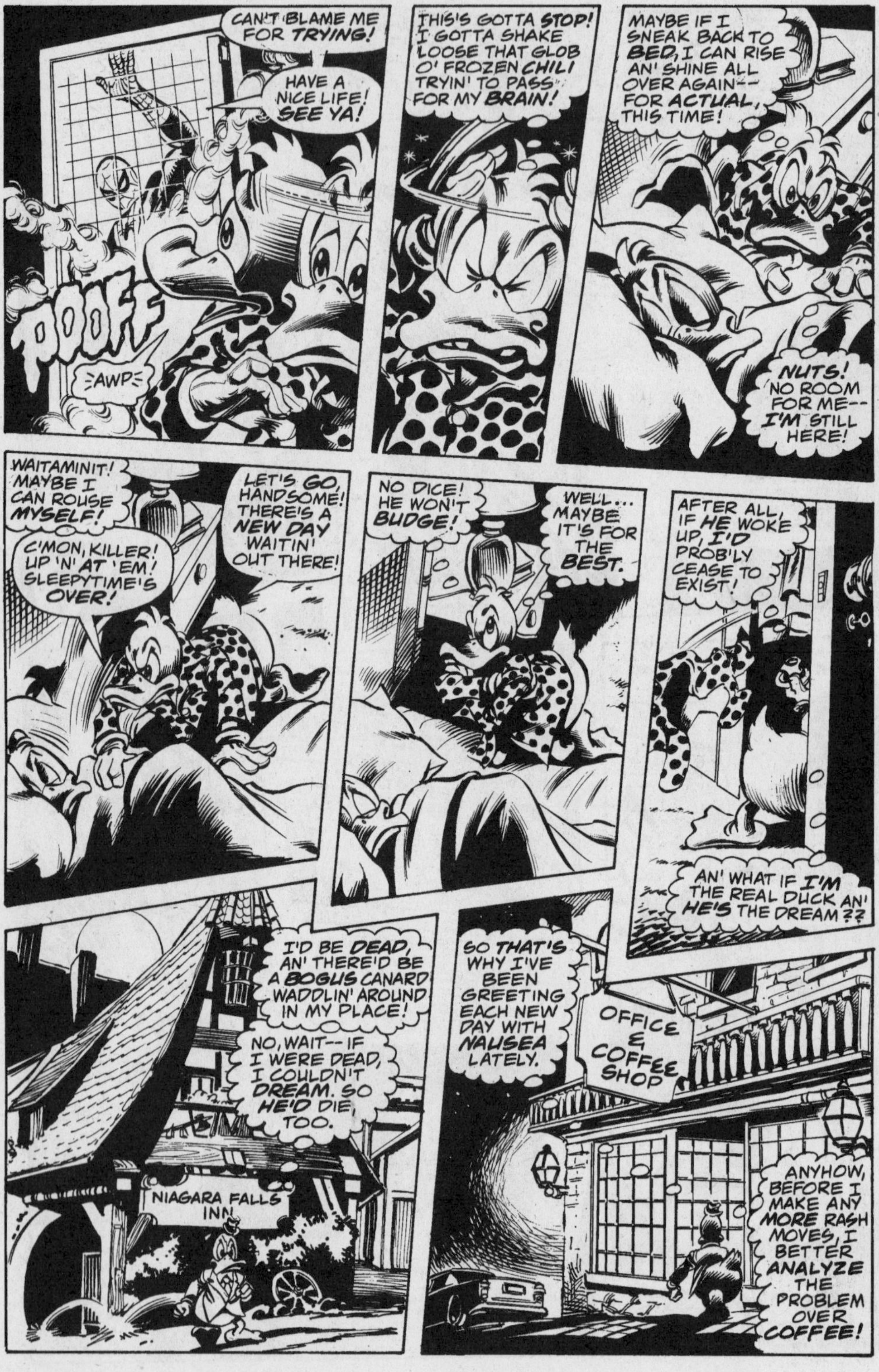
CAN'T BLAME ME FOR TRYING!
HAVE A NICE LIFE! SEE YA!
POOFF
AWP
THIS'S GOTTA STOP! I GOTTA SHAKE LOOSE THAT GLOB O' FROZEN CHILI TRYIN' TO PASS FOR MY BRAIN!
MAYBE IF I SNEAK BACK TO BED, I CAN RISE AN' SHINE ALL OVER AGAIN-- FOR ACTUAL, THIS TIME!
NUTS! NO ROOM FOR ME-- I'M STILL HERE!
WAITAMINIT! MAYBE I CAN ROUSE MYSELF!
C'MON, KILLER! UP 'N' AT 'EM! SLEEPYTIME'S OVER!
LET'S GO, HANDSOME! THERE'S A NEW DAY WAITIN' OUT THERE!
NO DICE! HE WON'T BUDGE!
WELL... MAYBE IT'S FOR THE BEST.
AFTER ALL, IF HE WOKE UP, I'D PROB'LY CEASE TO EXIST!
AN' WHAT IF I'M THE REAL DUCK AN' HE'S THE DREAM ??
I'D BE DEAD, AN' THERE'D BE A BOGUS CANARD WADDLIN' AROUND IN MY PLACE!
NO, WAIT-- IF I WERE DEAD, I COULDN'T DREAM. SO HE'D DIE, TOO.
NIAGARA FALLS INN
SO THAT'S WHY I'VE BEEN GREETING EACH NEW DAY WITH NAUSEA LATELY.
OFFICE & COFFEE SHOP
ANYHOW, BEFORE I MAKE ANY MORE RASH MOVES, I BETTER ANALYZE THE PROBLEM OVER COFFEE!

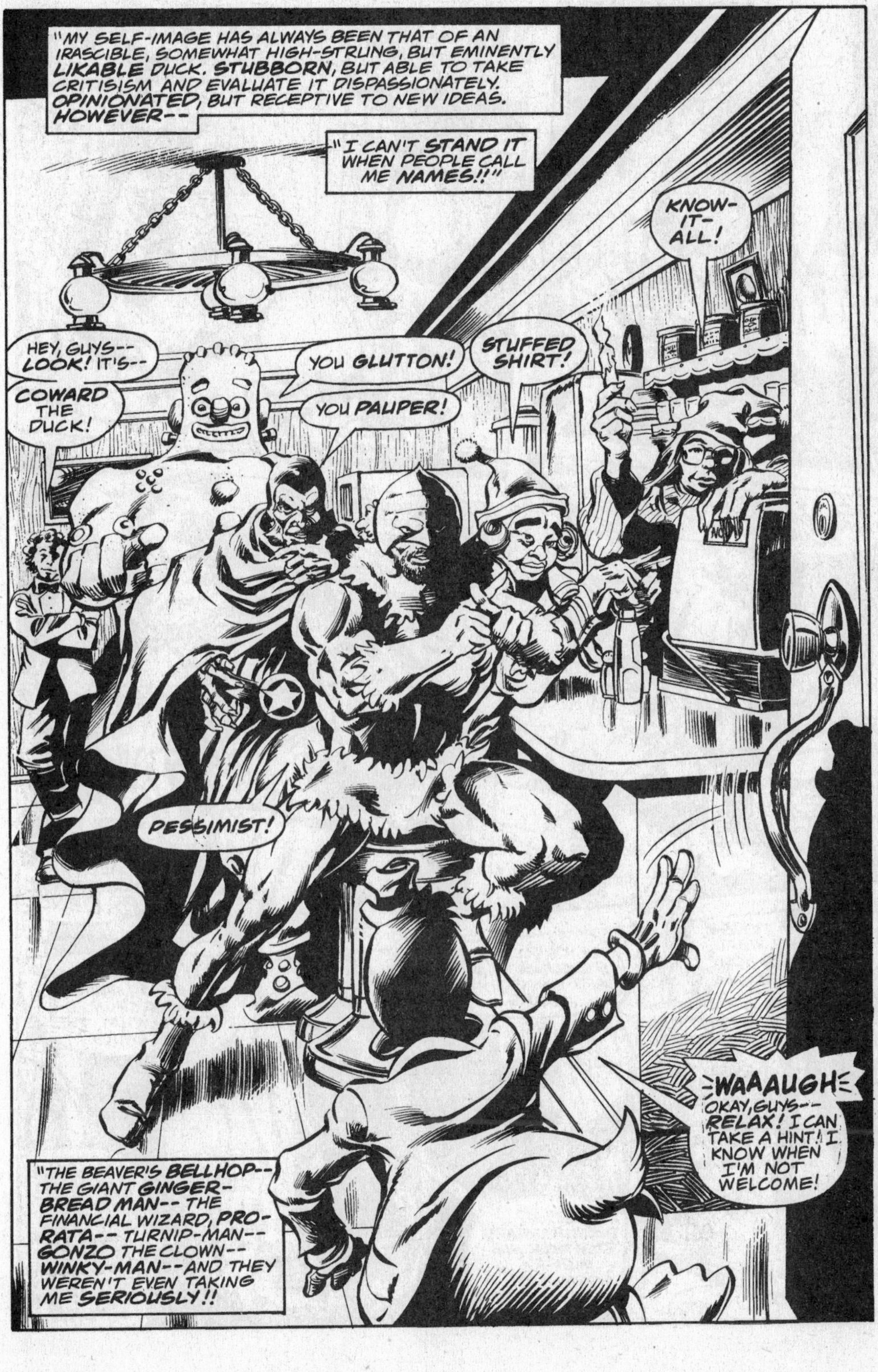
"MY SELF-IMAGE HAS ALWAYS BEEN THAT OF AN IRASCIBLE, SOMEWHAT HIGH-STRUNG, BUT EMINENTLY LIKABLE DUCK. STUBBORN, BUT ABLE TO TAKE CRITISISM AND EVALUATE IT DISPASSIONATELY. OPINIONATED, BUT RECEPTIVE TO NEW IDEAS. HOWEVER--
"I CAN'T STAND IT WHEN PEOPLE CALL ME NAMES!!"
KNOW-IT-ALL!
HEY, GUYS-- LOOK! IT'S--
COWARD THE DUCK!
YOU GLUTTON!
YOU PAUPER!
STUFFED SHIRT!
PESSIMIST!
WAAAUGH
OKAY, GUYS-- RELAX! I CAN TAKE A HINT! I KNOW WHEN I'M NOT WELCOME!
"THE BEAVER'S BELLHOP-- THE GIANT GINGER-BREAD MAN-- THE FINANCIAL WIZARD, PRO-RATA-- TURNIP-MAN-- GONZO THE CLOWN-- WINKY-MAN-- AND THEY WEREN'T EVEN TAKING ME SERIOUSLY!!

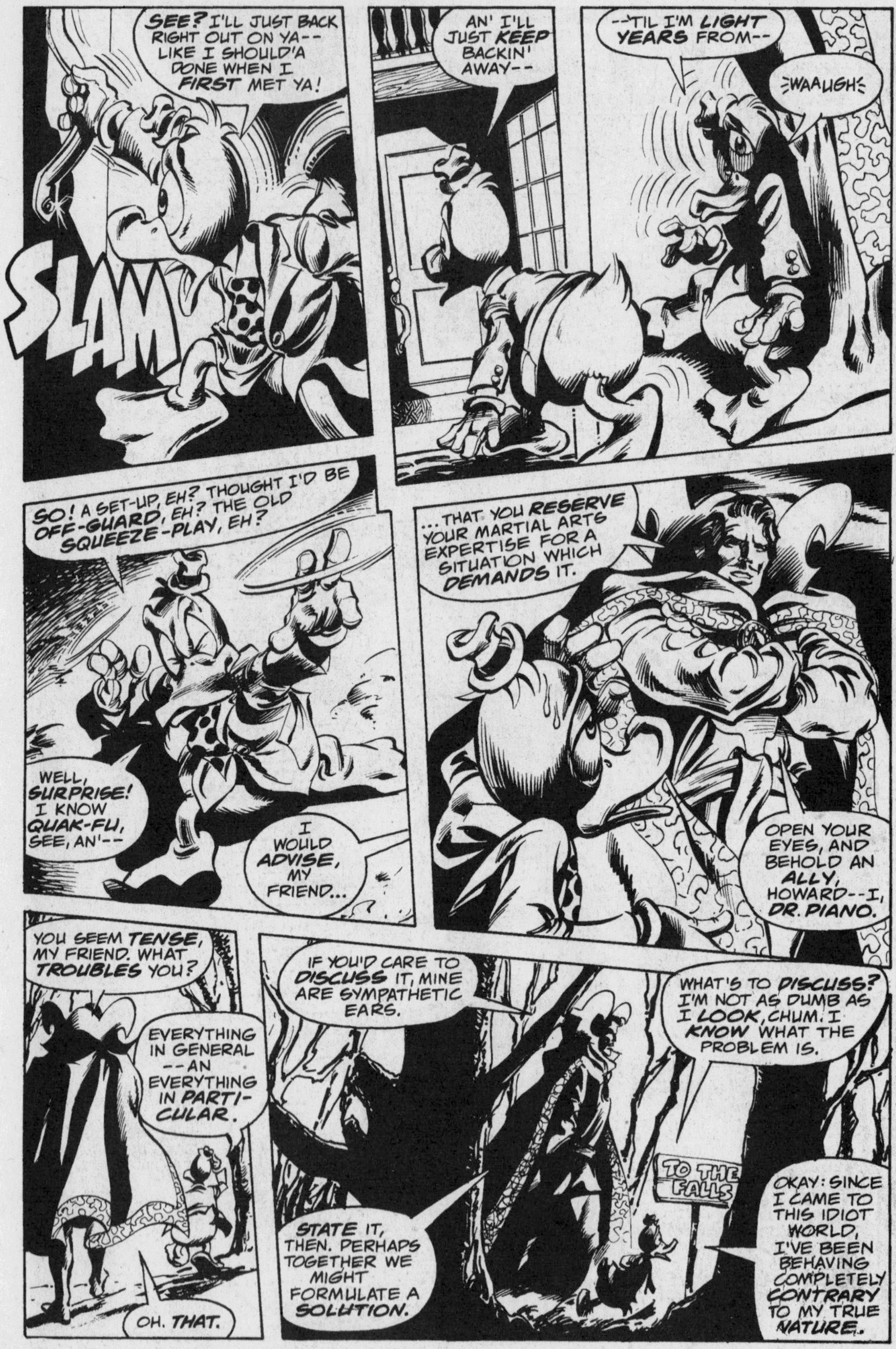
SEE? I'LL JUST BACK RIGHT OUT ON YA-- LIKE I SHOULD'A DONE WHEN I FIRST MET YA!
SLAM
AN' I'LL JUST KEEP BACKIN' AWAY--
--'TIL I'M LIGHT YEARS FROM--
WAAUGH
SO! A SET-UP, EH? THOUGHT I'D BE OFF-GUARD, EH? THE OLD SQUEEZE-PLAY, EH?
WELL, SURPRISE! I KNOW QUAK-FU, SEE, AN'--
I WOULD ADVISE, MY FRIEND...
...THAT YOU RESERVE YOUR MARTIAL ARTS EXPERTISE FOR A SITUATION WHICH DEMANDS IT.
OPEN YOUR EYES, AND BEHOLD AN ALLY, HOWARD--I, DR. PIANO.
YOU SEEM TENSE, MY FRIEND. WHAT TROUBLES YOU?
EVERYTHING IN GENERAL --AN EVERYTHING IN PARTICULAR.
OH. THAT.
IF YOU'D CARE TO DISCUSS IT, MINE ARE SYMPATHETIC EARS.
WHAT'S TO DISCUSS? I'M NOT AS DUMB AS I LOOK, CHUM. I KNOW WHAT THE PROBLEM IS.
STATE IT, THEN. PERHAPS TOGETHER WE MIGHT FORMULATE A SOLUTION.
TO THE FALLS
OKAY: SINCE I CAME TO THIS IDIOT WORLD, I'VE BEEN BEHAVING COMPLETELY CONTRARY TO MY TRUE NATURE.

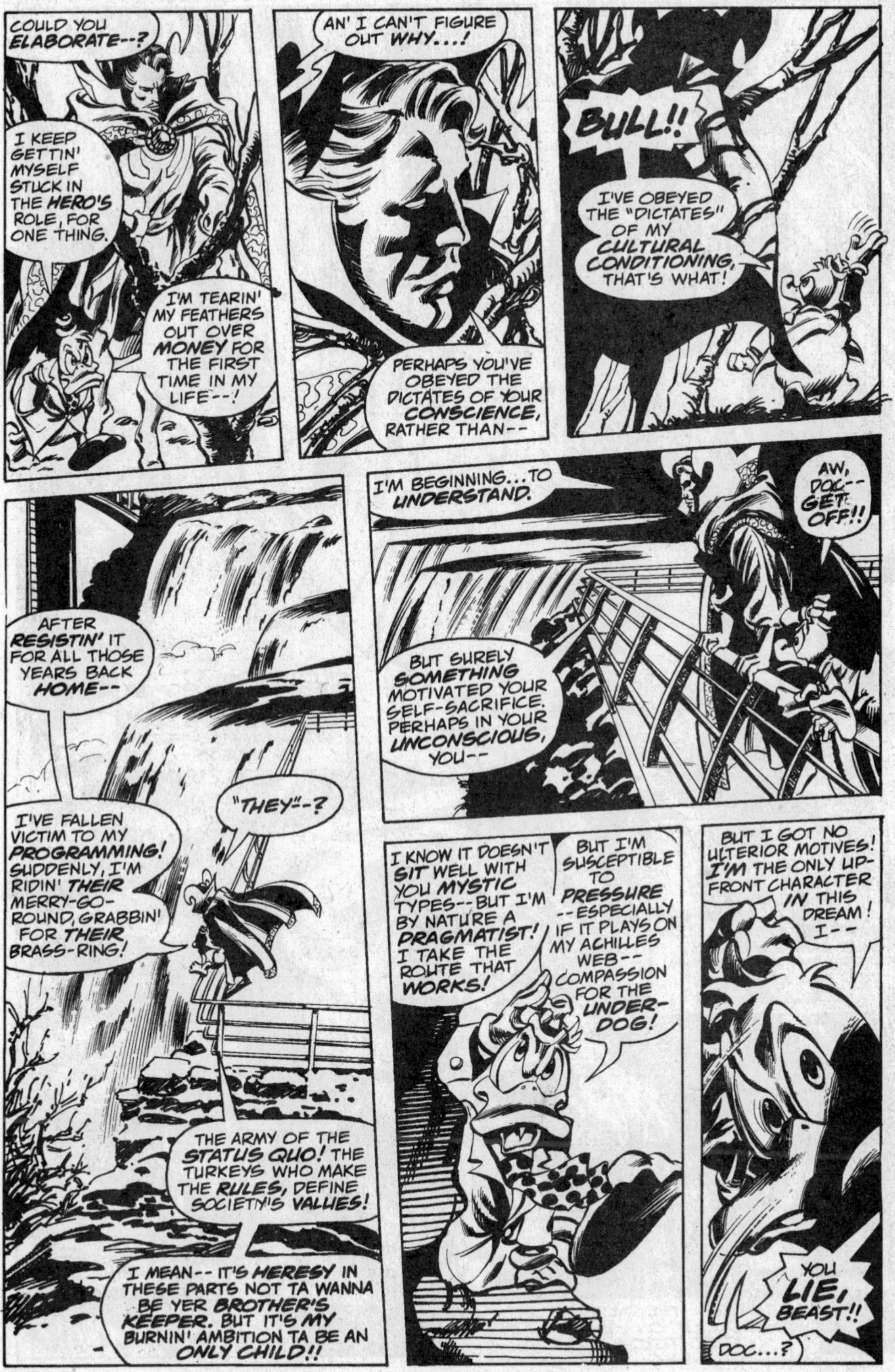
COULD YOU ELABORATE--?
I KEEP GETTIN' MYSELF STUCK IN THE HERO'S ROLE, FOR ONE THING.
I'M TEARIN' MY FEATHERS OUT OVER MONEY FOR THE FIRST TIME IN MY LIFE--!
AN' I CAN'T FIGURE OUT WHY...!
PERHAPS YOU'VE OBEYED THE DICTATES OF YOUR CONSCIENCE, RATHER THAN--
BULL!!
I'VE OBEYED THE "DICTATES" OF MY CULTURAL CONDITIONING, THAT'S WHAT!
AFTER RESISTIN' IT FOR ALL THOSE YEARS BACK HOME--
I'VE FALLEN VICTIM TO MY PROGRAMMING! SUDDENLY, I'M RIDIN' THEIR MERRY-GO-ROUND, GRABBIN' FOR THEIR BRASS-RING!
"THEY"--?
THE ARMY OF THE STATUS QUO! THE TURKEYS WHO MAKE THE RULES, DEFINE SOCIETY'S VALUES!
I MEAN-- IT'S HERESY IN THESE PARTS NOT TA WANNA BE YER BROTHER'S KEEPER. BUT IT'S MY BURNIN' AMBITION TA BE AN ONLY CHILD!!
I'M BEGINNING... TO UNDERSTAND.
AW, DOC-- GET OFF!!
BUT SURELY SOMETHING MOTIVATED YOUR SELF-SACRIFICE. PERHAPS IN YOUR UNCONSCIOUS, YOU--
I KNOW IT DOESN'T SIT WELL WITH YOU MYSTIC TYPES--BUT I'M BY NATURE A PRAGMATIST! I TAKE THE ROUTE THAT WORKS!
BUT I'M SUSCEPTIBLE TO PRESSURE --ESPECIALLY IF IT PLAYS ON MY ACHILLES WEB-- COMPASSION FOR THE UNDER-DOG!
BUT I GOT NO ULTERIOR MOTIVES! I'M THE ONLY UP-FRONT CHARACTER IN THIS DREAM! I--
YOU LIE, BEAST!!
DOC...?

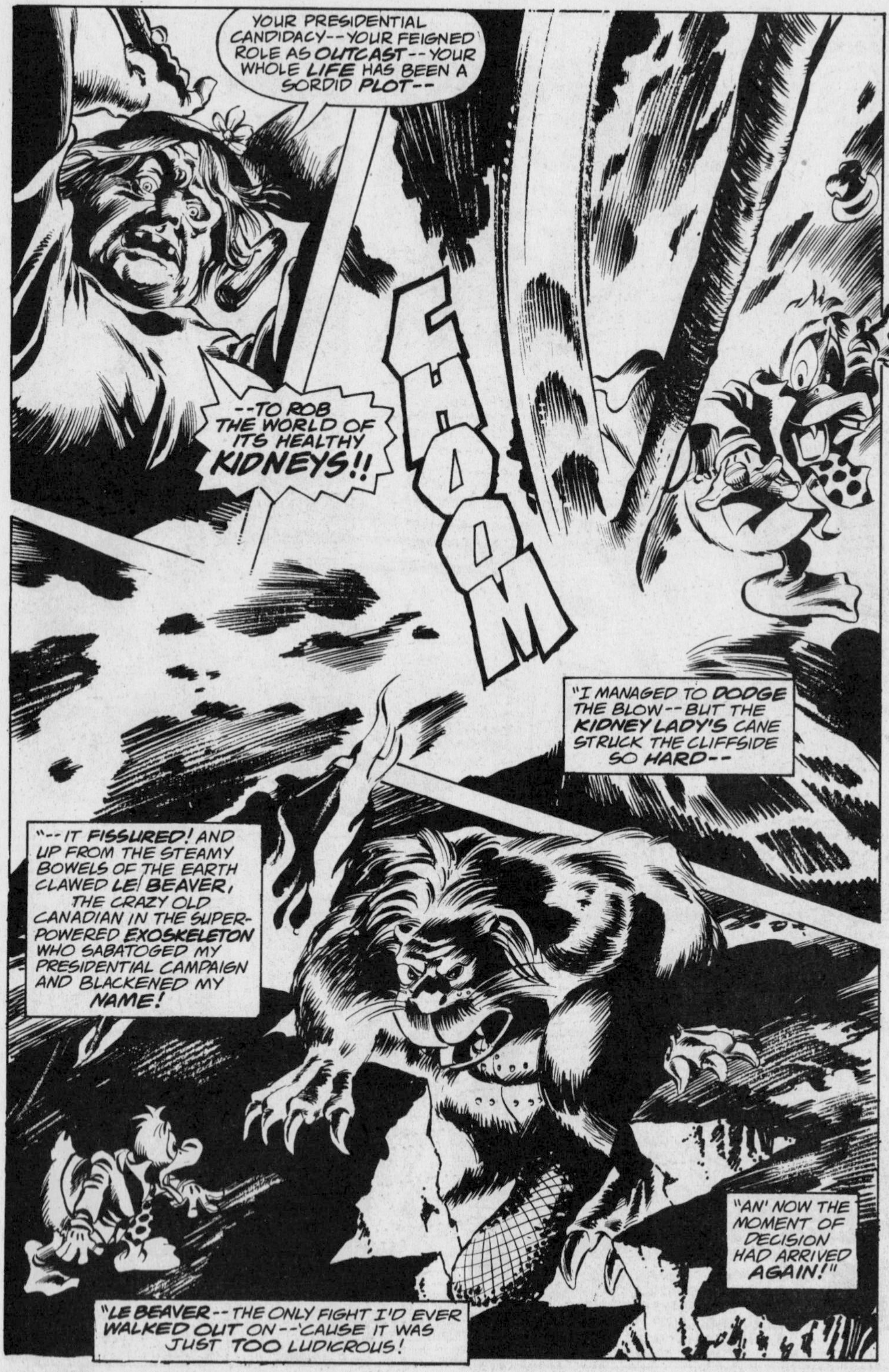
YOUR PRESIDENTIAL CANDIDACY--YOUR FEIGNED ROLE AS OUTCAST--YOUR WHOLE LIFE HAS BEEN A SORDID PLOT--
--TO ROB THE WORLD OF ITS HEALTHY KIDNEYS!!
CHOOM
"I MANAGED TO DODGE THE BLOW--BUT THE KIDNEY LADY'S CANE STRUCK THE CLIFFSIDE SO HARD--
"--IT FISSURED! AND UP FROM THE STEAMY BOWELS OF THE EARTH CLAWED LE! BEAVER, THE CRAZY OLD CANADIAN IN THE SUPER-POWERED EXOSKELETON WHO SABATOGED MY PRESIDENTIAL CAMPAIGN AND BLACKENED MY NAME!
"LE BEAVER--THE ONLY FIGHT I'D EVER WALKED OUT ON--'CAUSE IT WAS JUST TOO LUDICROUS!
"AN' NOW THE MOMENT OF DECISION HAD ARRIVED AGAIN!"

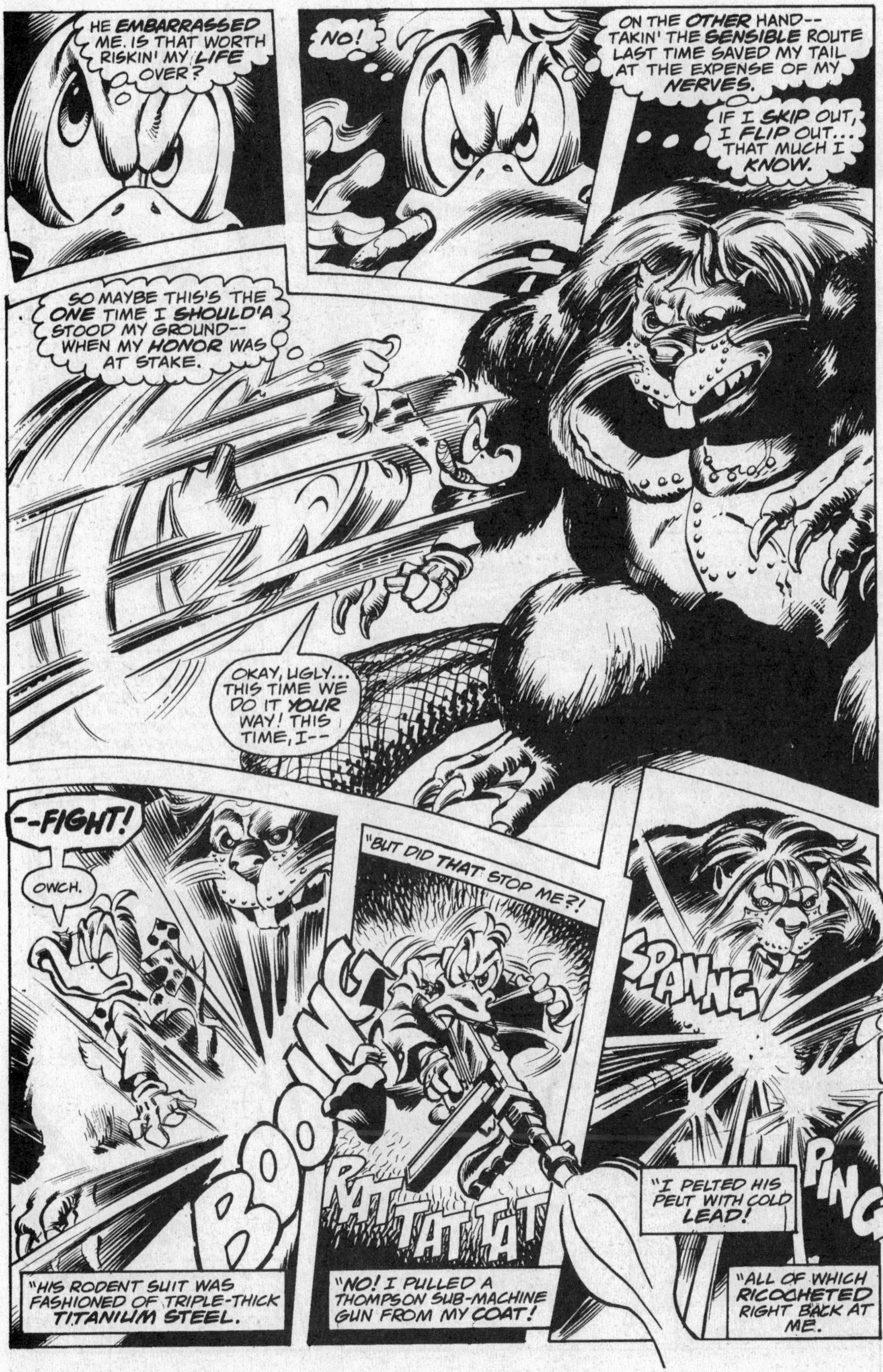

HE EMBARRASSED ME. IS THAT WORTH RISKIN' MY LIFE OVER?
NO!
ON THE OTHER HAND-- TAKIN' THE SENSIBLE ROUTE LAST TIME SAVED MY TAIL AT THE EXPENSE OF MY NERVES.
IF I SKIP OUT, I FLIP OUT... THAT MUCH I KNOW.
SO MAYBE THIS'S THE ONE TIME I SHOULD'A STOOD MY GROUND-- WHEN MY HONOR WAS AT STAKE.
OKAY, UGLY... THIS TIME WE DO IT YOUR WAY! THIS TIME, I--
--FIGHT!
OWCH.
"HIS RODENT SUIT WAS FASHIONED OF TRIPLE-THICK TITANIUM STEEL.
BOOONG
"BUT DID THAT STOP ME?!
RAT TAT TAT TAT
"NO! I PULLED A THOMPSON SUB-MACHINE GUN FROM MY COAT!
SPANNG
"I PELTED HIS PELT WITH COLD LEAD!
PING
"ALL OF WHICH RICOCHETED RIGHT BACK AT ME.

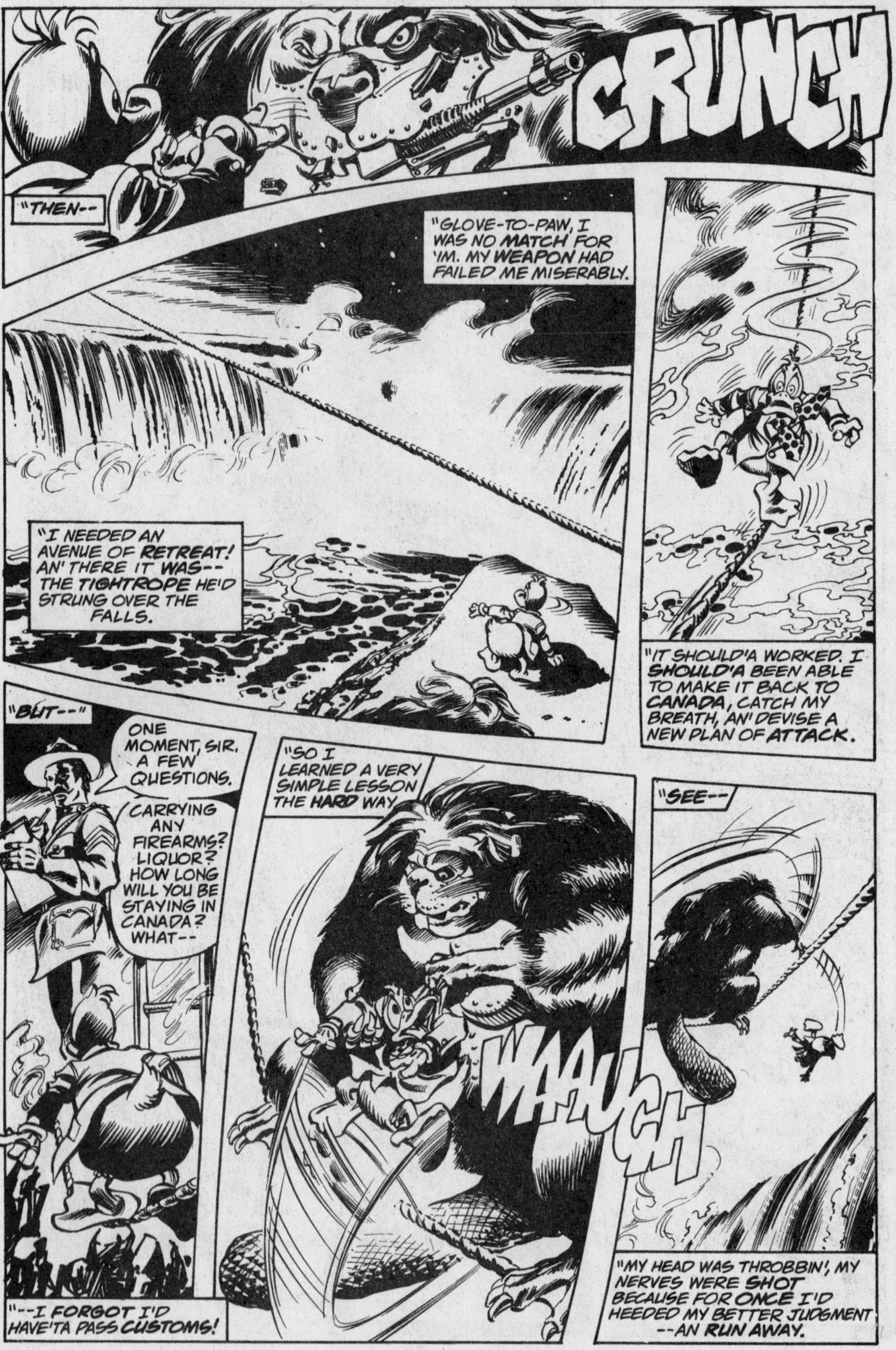
CRUNCH
"THEN--
"GLOVE-TO-PAW, I WAS NO MATCH FOR 'IM. MY WEAPON HAD FAILED ME MISERABLY.
"I NEEDED AN AVENUE OF RETREAT! AN' THERE IT WAS-- THE TIGHTROPE HE'D STRUNG OVER THE FALLS.
"IT SHOULD'A WORKED. I SHOULD'A BEEN ABLE TO MAKE IT BACK TO CANADA, CATCH MY BREATH, AN' DEVISE A NEW PLAN OF ATTACK.
"BUT--"
ONE MOMENT, SIR. A FEW QUESTIONS.
CARRYING ANY FIREARMS? LIQUOR? HOW LONG WILL YOU BE STAYING IN CANADA? WHAT--
"--I FORGOT I'D HAVE'TA PASS CUSTOMS!
"SO I LEARNED A VERY SIMPLE LESSON THE HARD WAY.
WAAUGH
"SEE--
"MY HEAD WAS THROBBIN', MY NERVES WERE SHOT BECAUSE FOR ONCE I'D HEEDED MY BETTER JUDGMENT --AN RUN AWAY.

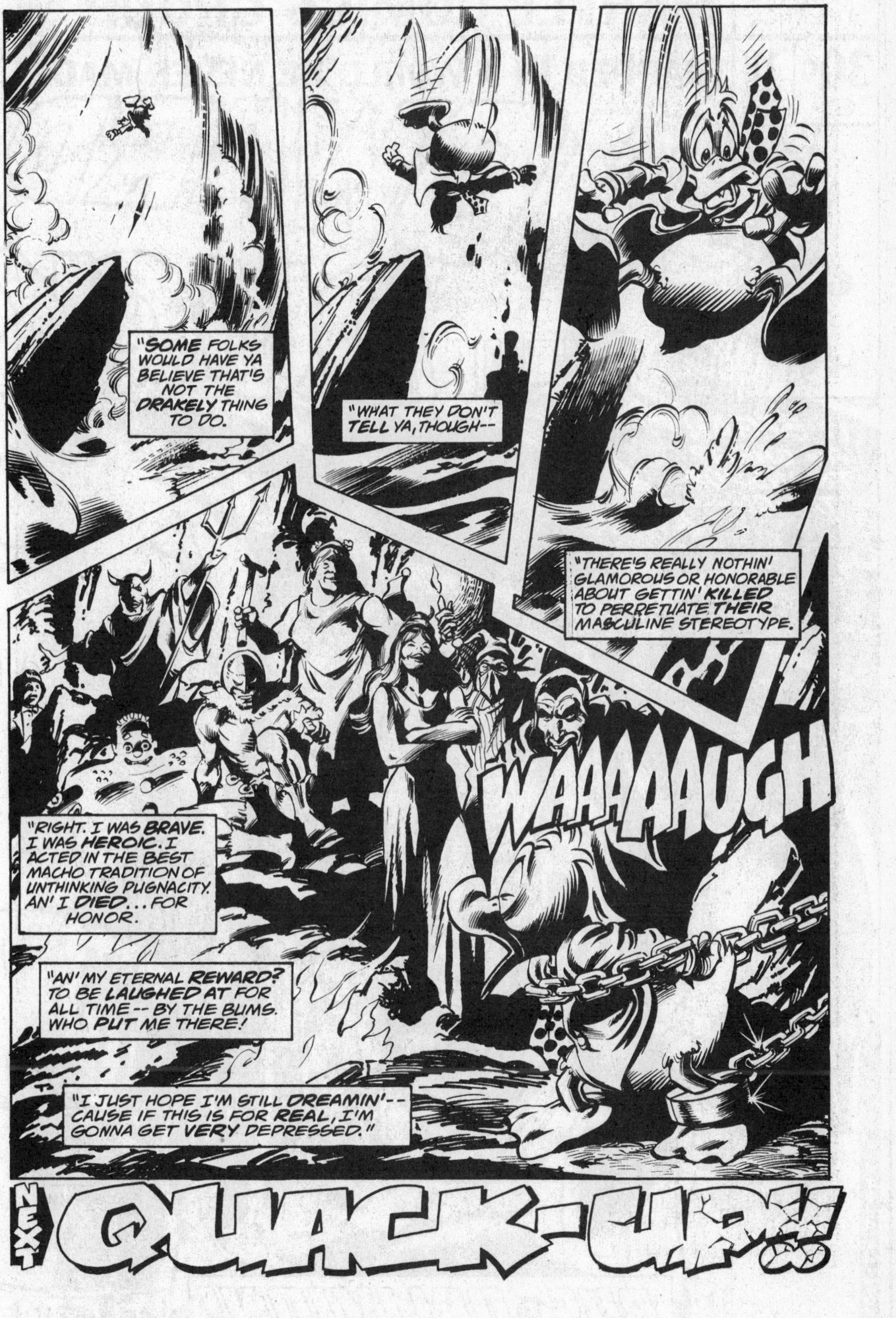
"SOME FOLKS WOULD HAVE YA BELIEVE THAT'S NOT THE DRAKELY THING TO DO.
"WHAT THEY DON'T TELL YA, THOUGH--
"THERE'S REALLY NOTHIN' GLAMOROUS OR HONORABLE ABOUT GETTIN' KILLED TO PERPETUATE THEIR MASCULINE STEREOTYPE.
WAAAAAUGH
"RIGHT. I WAS BRAVE. I WAS HEROIC. I ACTED IN THE BEST MACHO TRADITION OF UNTHINKING PUGNACITY. AN' I DIED... FOR HONOR.
"AN' MY ETERNAL REWARD? TO BE LAUGHED AT FOR ALL TIME -- BY THE BUMS WHO PUT ME THERE!
"I JUST HOPE I'M STILL DREAMIN'-- CAUSE IF THIS IS FOR REAL, I'M GONNA GET VERY DEPRESSED."
NEXT
QUACK-UP!

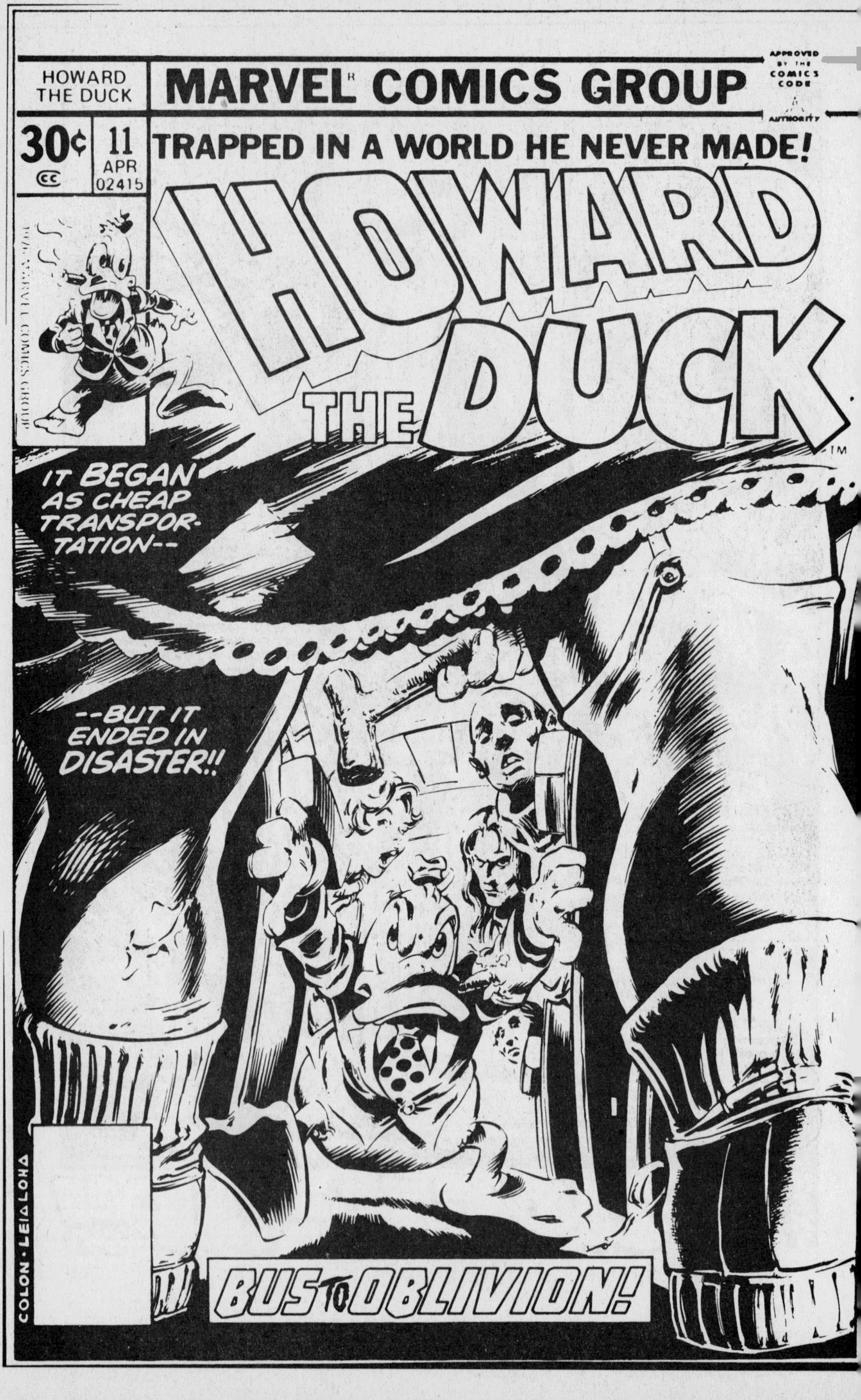
HOWARD THE DUCK
MARVEL COMICS GROUP
APPROVED BY THE COMICS CODE AUTHORITY
30¢
11
APR
02415
TRAPPED IN A WORLD HE NEVER MADE!
HOWARD THE DUCK
IT BEGAN AS CHEAP TRANSPORTATION--
--BUT IT ENDED IN DISASTER!!
BUS TO OBLIVION!
COLON • LEIALOHA

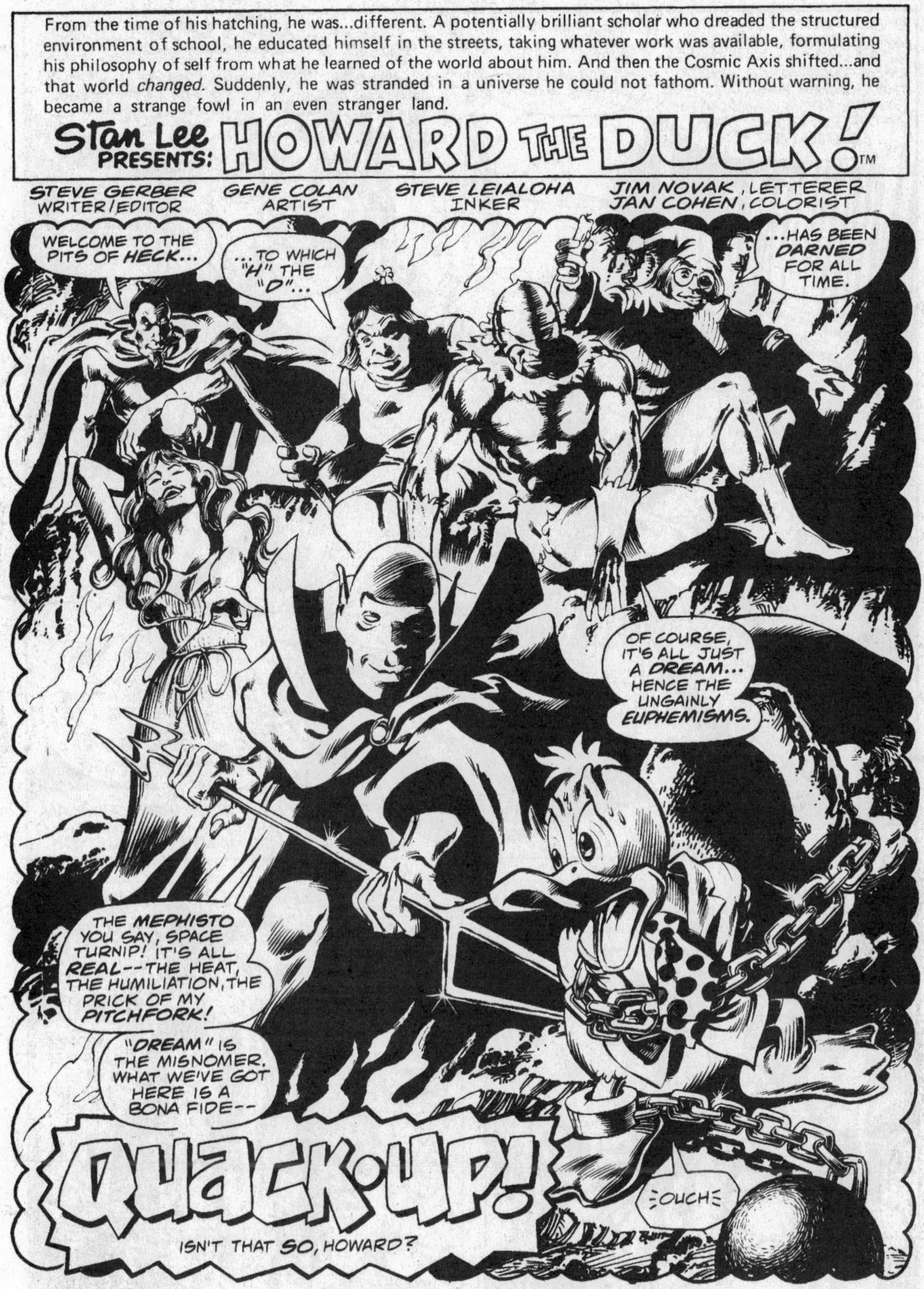

From the time of his hatching, he was...different. A potentially brilliant scholar who dreaded the structured environment of school, he educated himself in the streets, taking whatever work was available, formulating his philosophy of self from what he learned of the world about him. And then the Cosmic Axis shifted...and that world *changed.* Suddenly, he was stranded in a universe he could not fathom. Without warning, he became a strange fowl in an even stranger land.
Stan Lee PRESENTS: HOWARD THE DUCK!™
STEVE GERBER WRITER/EDITOR
GENE COLAN ARTIST
STEVE LEIALOHA INKER
JIM NOVAK, LETTERER
JAN COHEN, COLORIST
WELCOME TO THE PITS OF HECK...
...TO WHICH "H" THE "D"...
...HAS BEEN DARNED FOR ALL TIME.
OF COURSE, IT'S ALL JUST A DREAM... HENCE THE UNGAINLY EUPHEMISMS.
THE MEPHISTO YOU SAY, SPACE TURNIP! IT'S ALL REAL--THE HEAT, THE HUMILIATION, THE PRICK OF MY PITCHFORK!
"DREAM" IS THE MISNOMER. WHAT WE'VE GOT HERE IS A BONA FIDE--
QUACK-UP!
OUCH
ISN'T THAT SO, HOWARD?

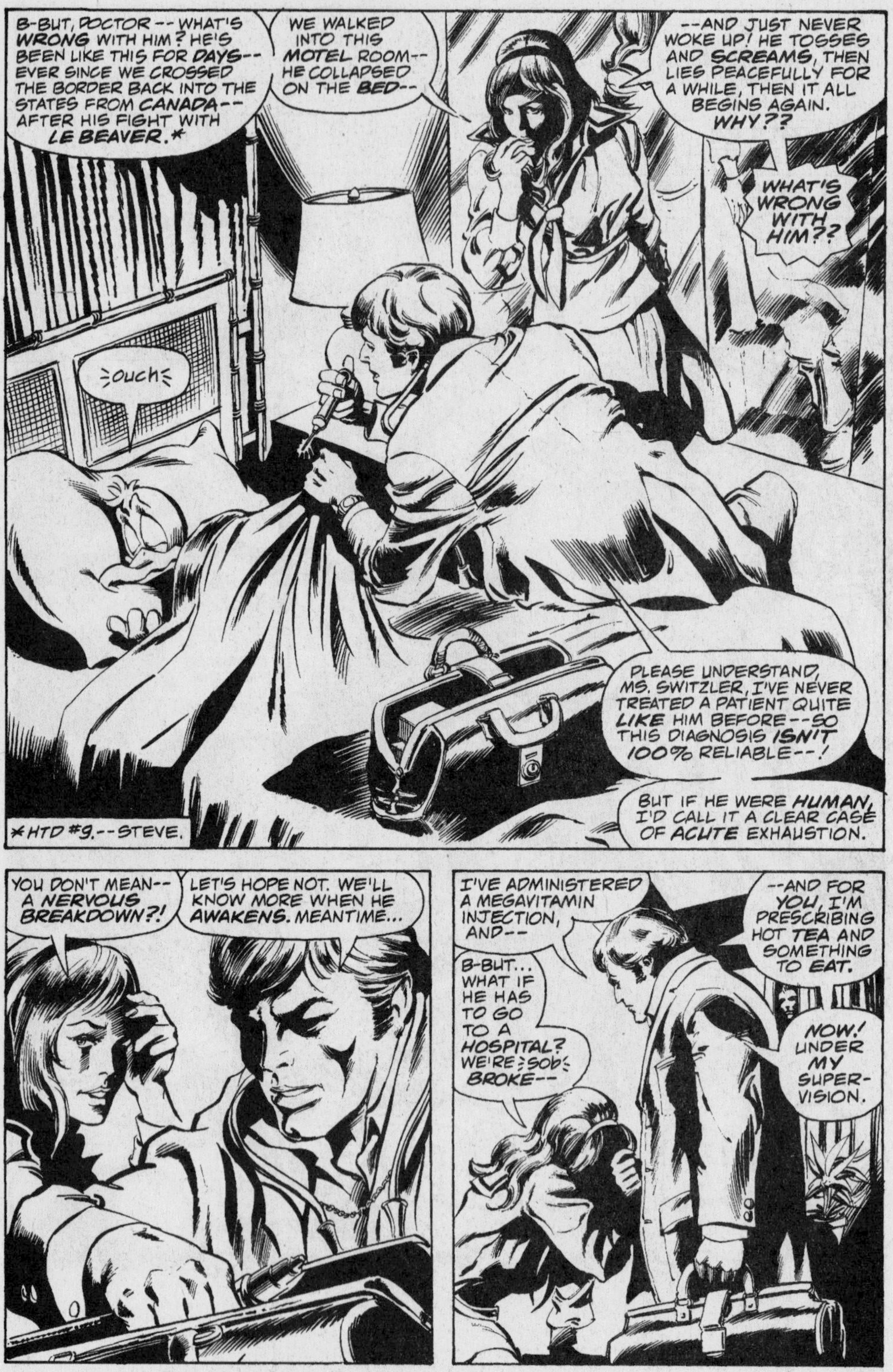
B-BUT, DOCTOR--WHAT'S WRONG WITH HIM? HE'S BEEN LIKE THIS FOR DAYS--EVER SINCE WE CROSSED THE BORDER BACK INTO THE STATES FROM CANADA--AFTER HIS FIGHT WITH LE BEAVER.*
WE WALKED INTO THIS MOTEL ROOM--HE COLLAPSED ON THE BED--
--AND JUST NEVER WOKE UP! HE TOSSES AND SCREAMS, THEN LIES PEACEFULLY FOR A WHILE, THEN IT ALL BEGINS AGAIN. WHY??
WHAT'S WRONG WITH HIM??
ouch
PLEASE UNDERSTAND, MS. SWITZLER, I'VE NEVER TREATED A PATIENT QUITE LIKE HIM BEFORE--SO THIS DIAGNOSIS ISN'T 100% RELIABLE--!
BUT IF HE WERE HUMAN, I'D CALL IT A CLEAR CASE OF ACUTE EXHAUSTION.
*HTD #9.--STEVE.
YOU DON'T MEAN--A NERVOUS BREAKDOWN?!
LET'S HOPE NOT. WE'LL KNOW MORE WHEN HE AWAKENS. MEANTIME...
I'VE ADMINISTERED A MEGAVITAMIN INJECTION, AND--
--AND FOR YOU, I'M PRESCRIBING HOT TEA AND SOMETHING TO EAT.
B-BUT... WHAT IF HE HAS TO GO TO A HOSPITAL? WE'RE sob BROKE--
NOW! UNDER MY SUPER-VISION.

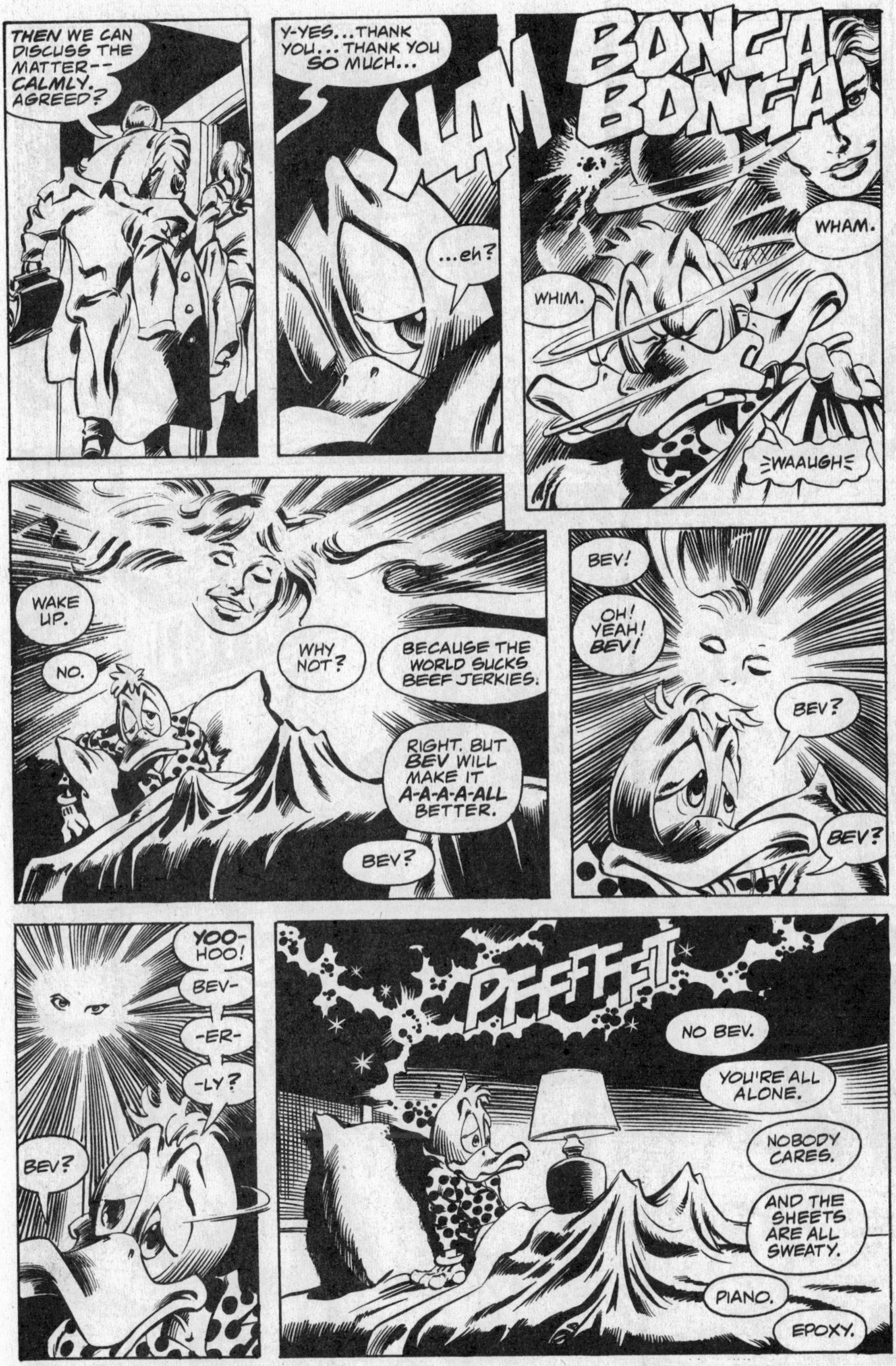
THEN WE CAN DISCUSS THE MATTER-- CALMLY. AGREED?
Y-YES...THANK YOU...THANK YOU SO MUCH...
SLAM
...eh?
BONGA BONGA
WHAM.
WHIM.
WAAUGH
WAKE UP.
NO.
WHY NOT?
BECAUSE THE WORLD SUCKS BEEF JERKIES.
RIGHT. BUT BEV WILL MAKE IT A-A-A-A-ALL BETTER.
BEV?
BEV!
OH! YEAH! BEV!
BEV?
BEV?
YOO-HOO!
BEV-
-ER-
-LY?
BEV?
PFFFFFT
NO BEV.
YOU'RE ALL ALONE.
NOBODY CARES.
AND THE SHEETS ARE ALL SWEATY.
PIANO.
EPOXY.

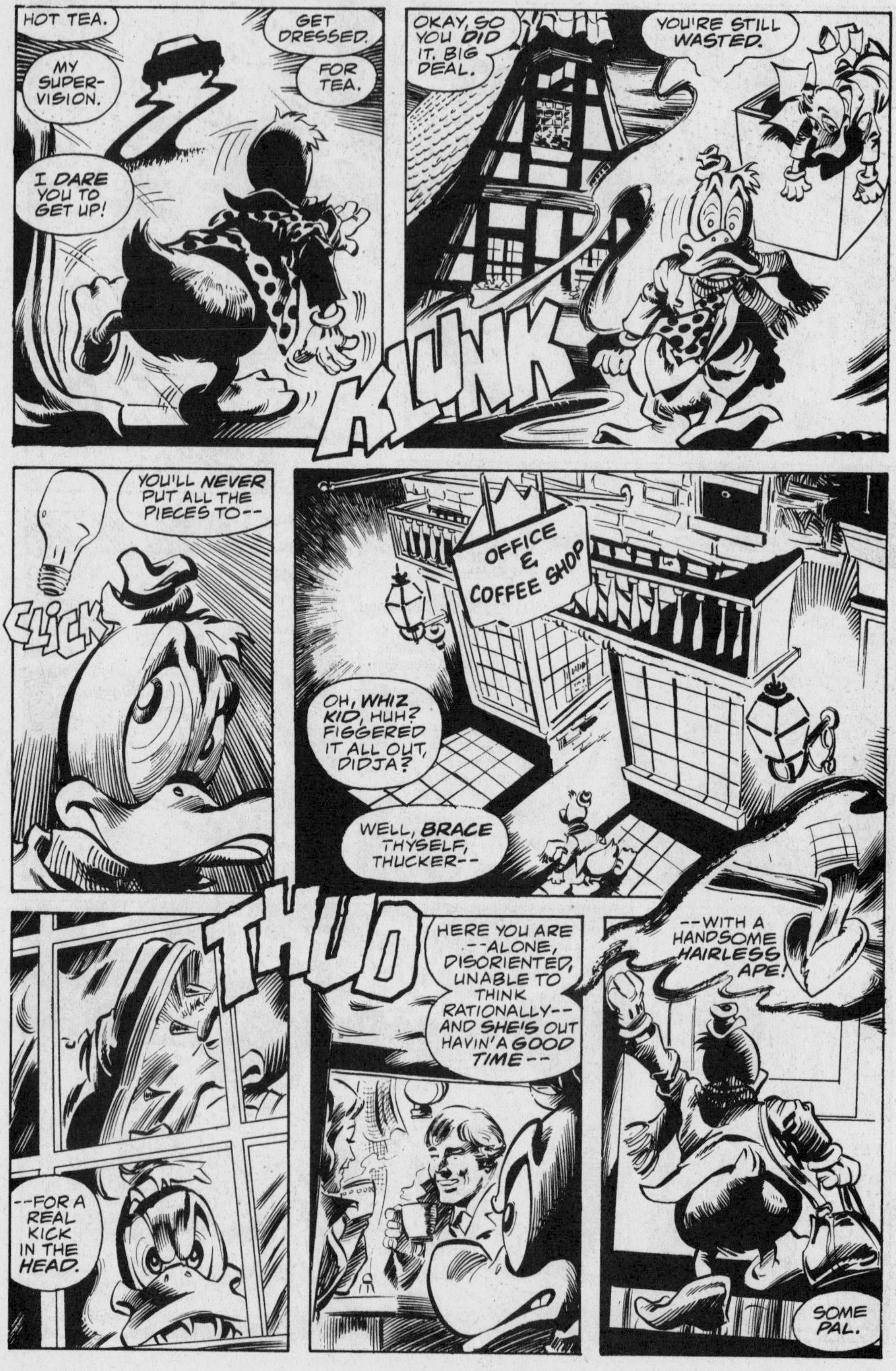
HOT TEA.
MY SUPER-VISION.
GET DRESSED.
FOR TEA.
I DARE YOU TO GET UP!
OKAY, SO YOU DID IT. BIG DEAL.
YOU'RE STILL WASTED.
KLUNK
YOU'LL NEVER PUT ALL THE PIECES TO--
CLICK
OFFICE & COFFEE SHOP
OH, WHIZ KID, HUH? FIGGERED IT ALL OUT, DIDJA?
WELL, BRACE THYSELF, THUCKER--
THUD
--FOR A REAL KICK IN THE HEAD.
HERE YOU ARE --ALONE, DISORIENTED, UNABLE TO THINK RATIONALLY-- AND SHE'S OUT HAVIN' A GOOD TIME--
--WITH A HANDSOME HAIRLESS APE!
SOME PAL.

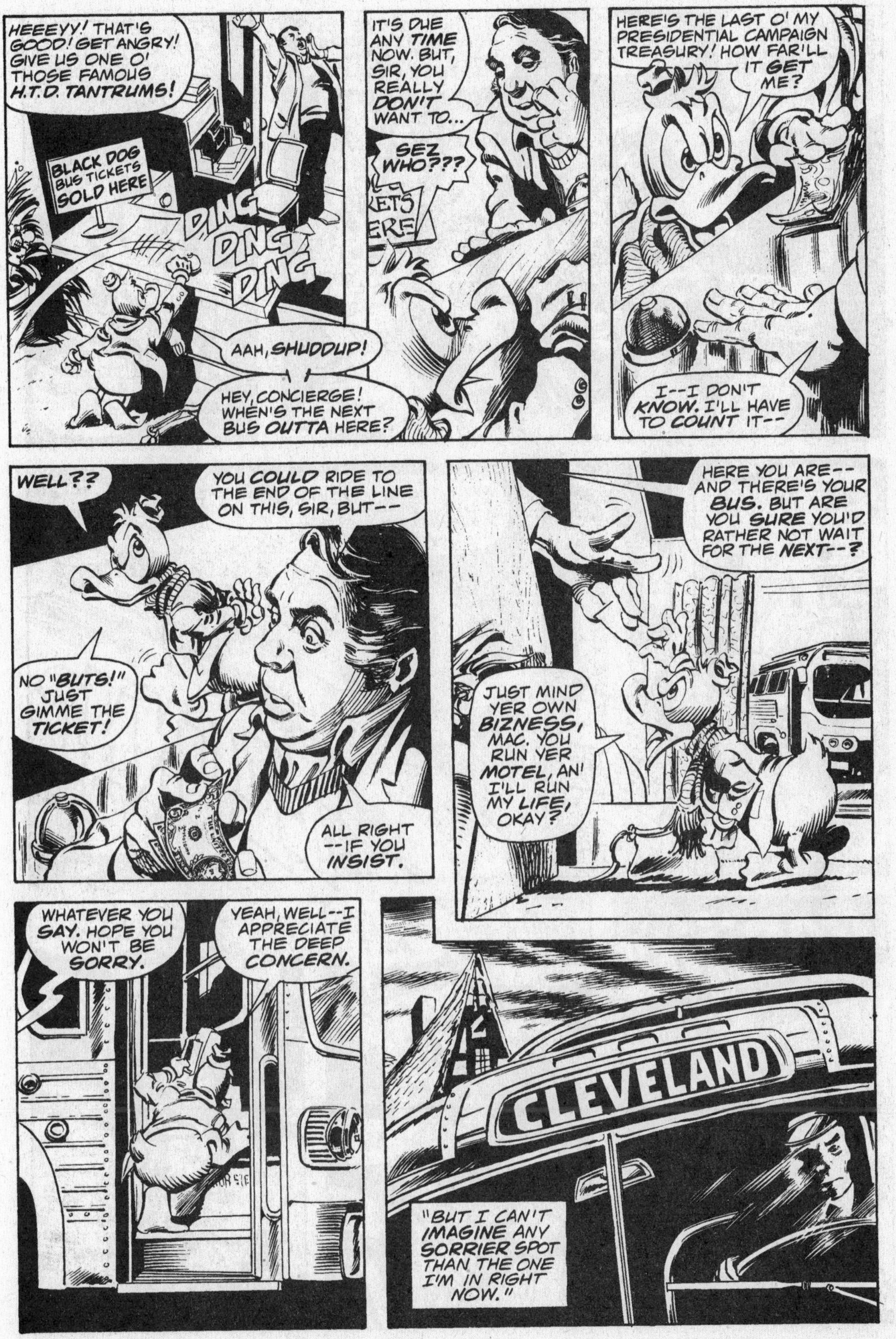
HEEEYY! THAT'S GOOD! GET ANGRY! GIVE US ONE O' THOSE FAMOUS H.T.D. TANTRUMS!
BLACK DOG BUS TICKETS SOLD HERE
DING DING DING
AAH, SHUDDUP!
HEY, CONCIERGE! WHEN'S THE NEXT BUS OUTTA HERE?
IT'S DUE ANY TIME NOW. BUT, SIR, YOU REALLY DON'T WANT TO...
SEZ WHO???
HERE'S THE LAST O' MY PRESIDENTIAL CAMPAIGN TREASURY! HOW FAR'LL IT GET ME?
I--I DON'T KNOW. I'LL HAVE TO COUNT IT--
WELL??
YOU COULD RIDE TO THE END OF THE LINE ON THIS, SIR, BUT--
NO "BUTS!" JUST GIMME THE TICKET!
ALL RIGHT --IF YOU INSIST.
HERE YOU ARE-- AND THERE'S YOUR BUS. BUT ARE YOU SURE YOU'D RATHER NOT WAIT FOR THE NEXT--?
JUST MIND YER OWN BIZNESS, MAC. YOU RUN YER MOTEL, AN' I'LL RUN MY LIFE, OKAY?
WHATEVER YOU SAY. HOPE YOU WON'T BE SORRY.
YEAH, WELL--I APPRECIATE THE DEEP CONCERN.
CLEVELAND
"BUT I CAN'T IMAGINE ANY SORRIER SPOT THAN THE ONE I'M IN RIGHT NOW."

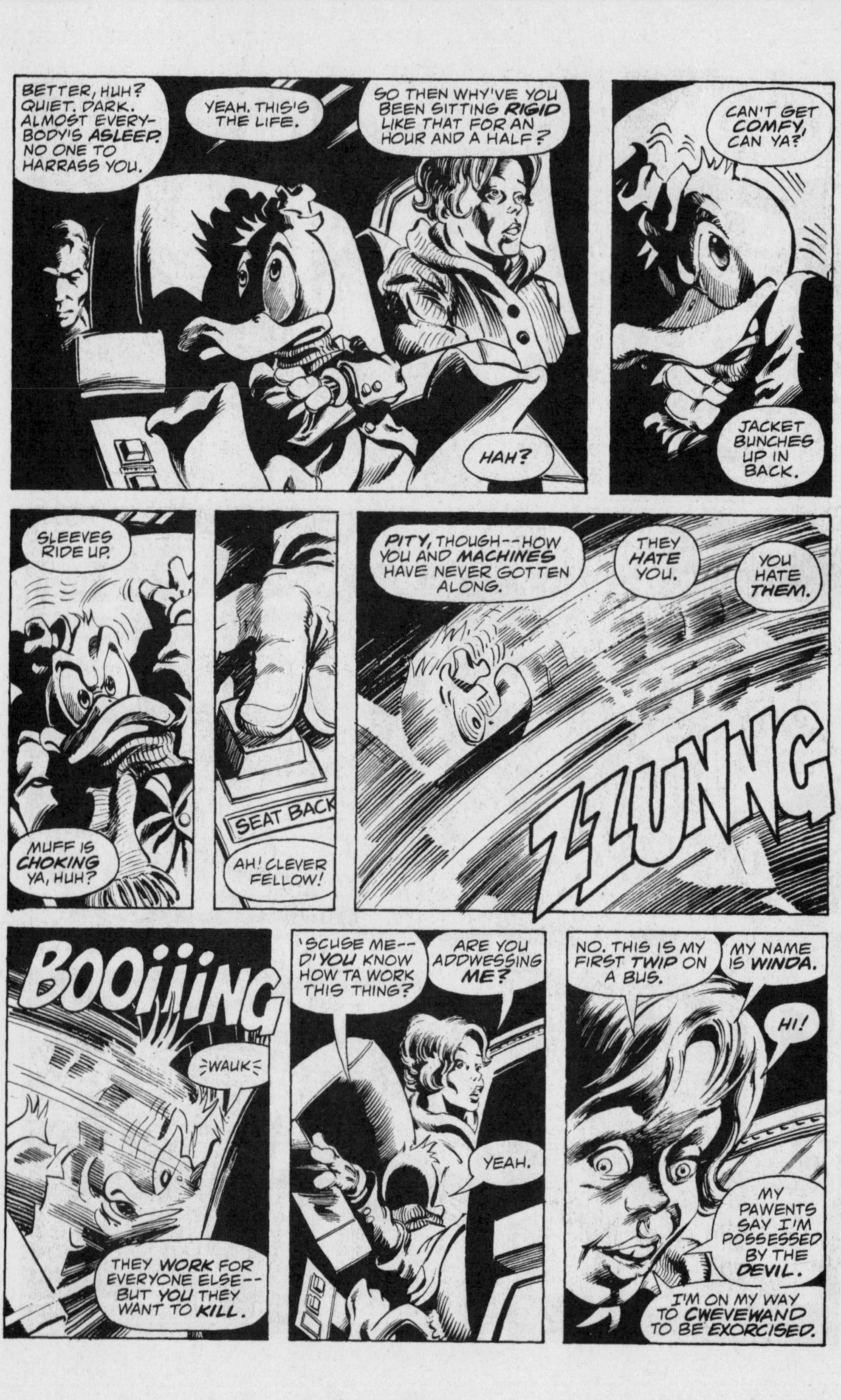

BETTER, HUH? QUIET. DARK. ALMOST EVERYBODY'S ASLEEP. NO ONE TO HARRASS YOU.
YEAH. THIS'S THE LIFE.
SO THEN WHY'VE YOU BEEN SITTING RIGID LIKE THAT FOR AN HOUR AND A HALF?
HAH?
CAN'T GET COMFY, CAN YA?
JACKET BUNCHES UP IN BACK.
SLEEVES RIDE UP.
MUFF IS CHOKING YA, HUH?
SEAT BACK
AH! CLEVER FELLOW!
PITY, THOUGH--HOW YOU AND MACHINES HAVE NEVER GOTTEN ALONG.
THEY HATE YOU.
YOU HATE THEM.
ZZUNNG
BOOiiiNG
WAUK
THEY WORK FOR EVERYONE ELSE--BUT YOU THEY WANT TO KILL.
'SCUSE ME--D'YOU KNOW HOW TA WORK THIS THING?
ARE YOU ADDWESSING ME?
YEAH.
NO. THIS IS MY FIRST TWIP ON A BUS.
MY NAME IS WINDA.
HI!
MY PAWENTS SAY I'M POSSESSED BY THE DEVIL.
I'M ON MY WAY TO CWEVEWAND TO BE EXORCISED.

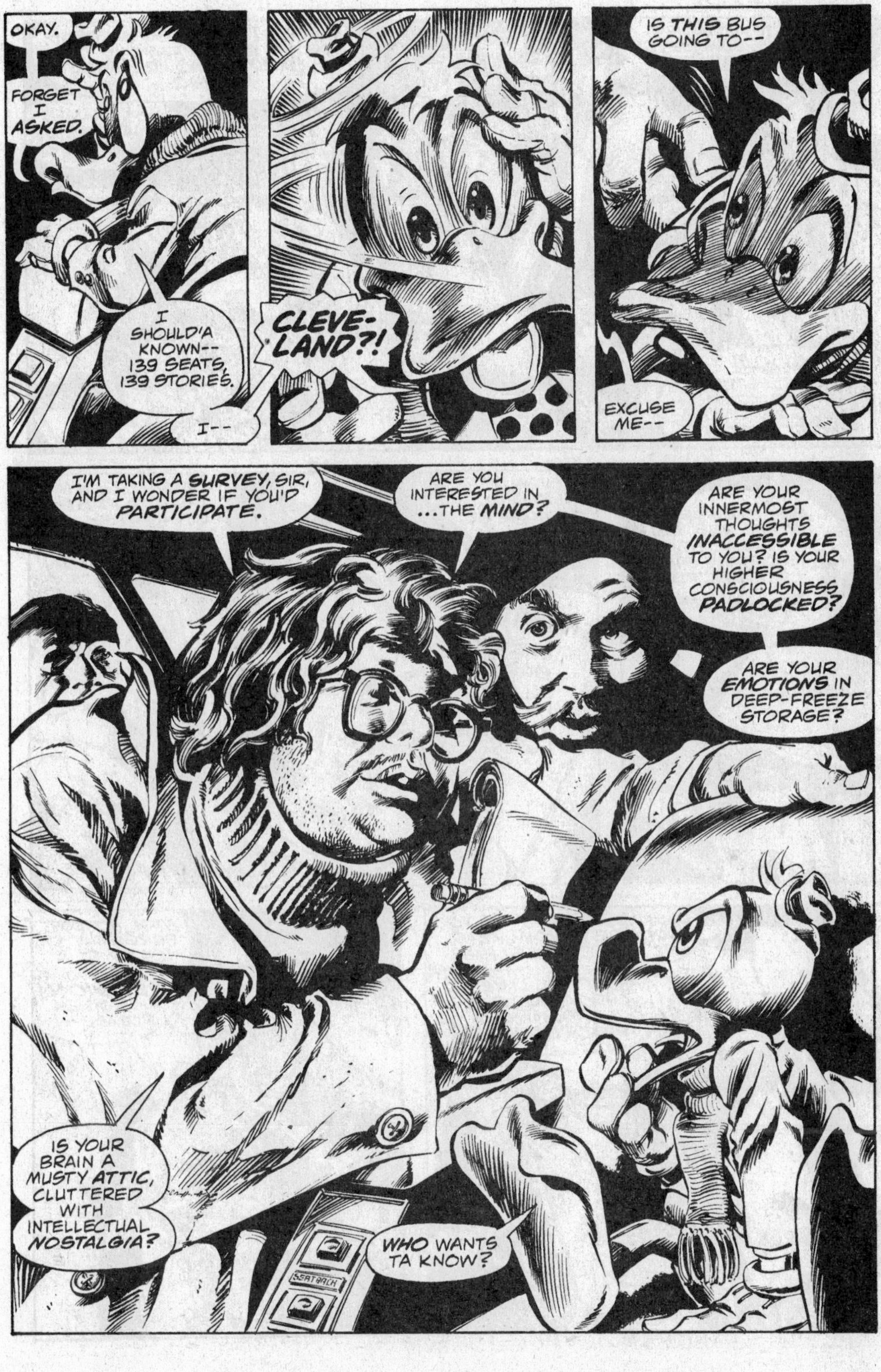

OKAY.
FORGET I ASKED.
I SHOULD'A KNOWN-- 139 SEATS, 139 STORIES.
I--
CLEVE-LAND?!
IS THIS BUS GOING TO--
EXCUSE ME--
I'M TAKING A SURVEY, SIR, AND I WONDER IF YOU'D PARTICIPATE.
ARE YOU INTERESTED IN ...THE MIND?
ARE YOUR INNERMOST THOUGHTS INACCESSIBLE TO YOU? IS YOUR HIGHER CONSCIOUSNESS PADLOCKED?
ARE YOUR EMOTIONS IN DEEP-FREEZE STORAGE?
IS YOUR BRAIN A MUSTY ATTIC, CLUTTERED WITH INTELLECTUAL NOSTALGIA?
WHO WANTS TA KNOW?

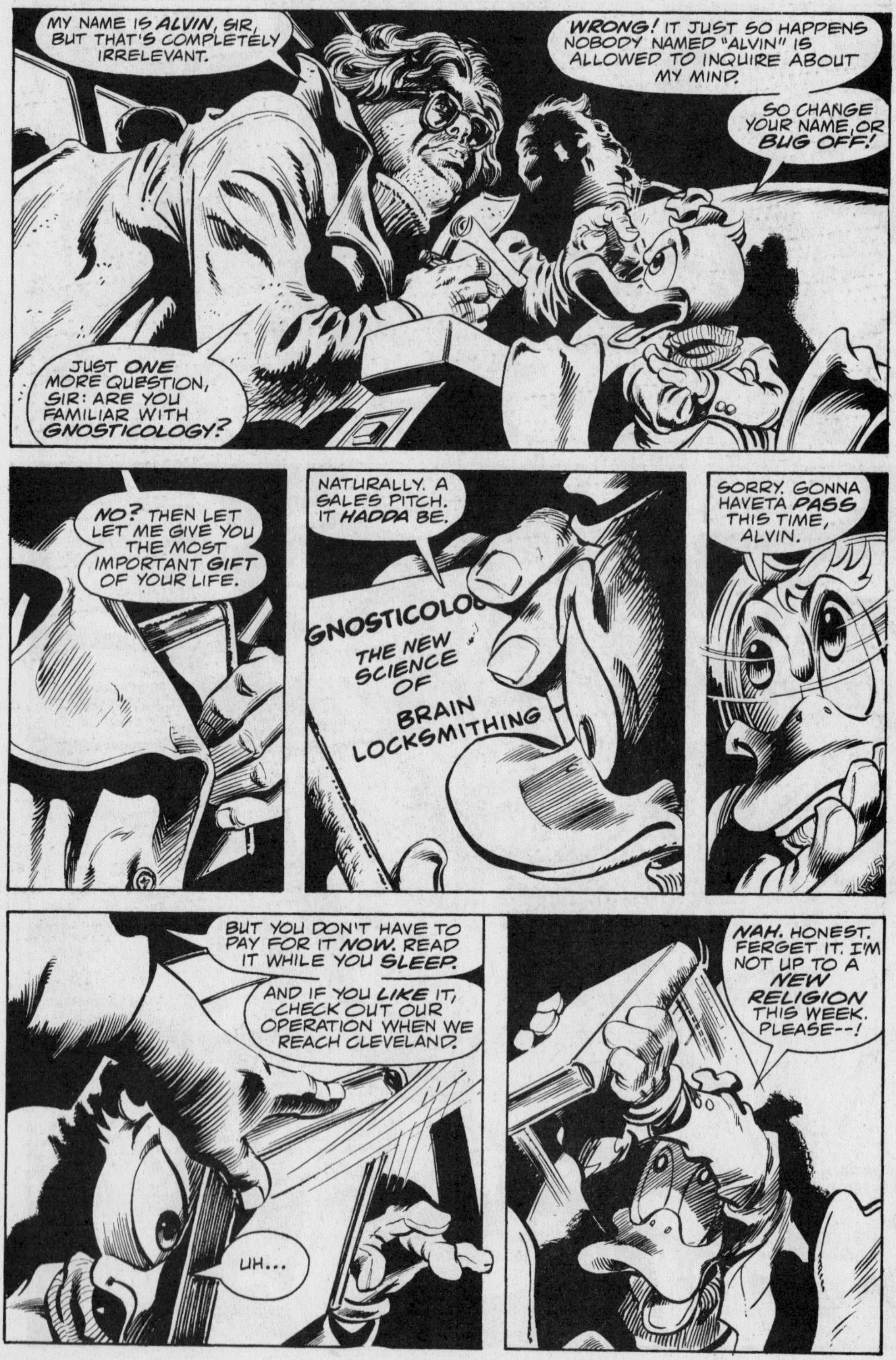

MY NAME IS ALVIN, SIR, BUT THAT'S COMPLETELY IRRELEVANT.
WRONG! IT JUST SO HAPPENS NOBODY NAMED "ALVIN" IS ALLOWED TO INQUIRE ABOUT MY MIND.
SO CHANGE YOUR NAME, OR BUG OFF!
JUST ONE MORE QUESTION, SIR: ARE YOU FAMILIAR WITH GNOSTICOLOGY?
NO? THEN LET LET ME GIVE YOU THE MOST IMPORTANT GIFT OF YOUR LIFE.
NATURALLY. A SALES PITCH. IT HADDA BE.
GNOSTICOLO
THE NEW SCIENCE OF
BRAIN LOCKSMITHING
SORRY. GONNA HAVETA PASS THIS TIME, ALVIN.
BUT YOU DON'T HAVE TO PAY FOR IT NOW. READ IT WHILE YOU SLEEP.
AND IF YOU LIKE IT, CHECK OUT OUR OPERATION WHEN WE REACH CLEVELAND.
UH...
NAH. HONEST. FERGET IT. I'M NOT UP TO A NEW RELIGION THIS WEEK. PLEASE--!

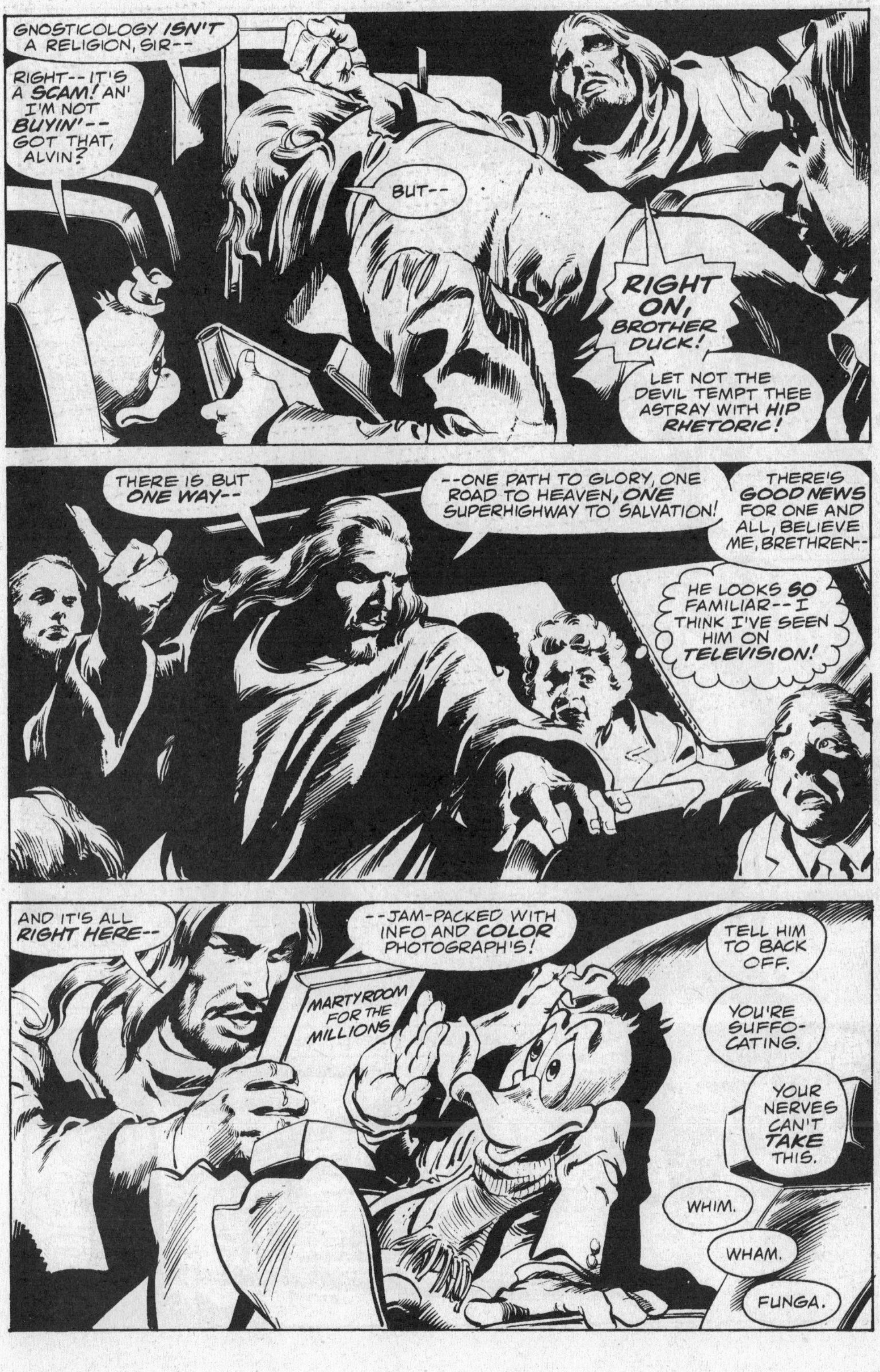
GNOSTICOLOGY ISN'T A RELIGION, SIR--
RIGHT--IT'S A SCAM! AN' I'M NOT BUYIN'--GOT THAT, ALVIN?
BUT--
RIGHT ON, BROTHER DUCK!
LET NOT THE DEVIL TEMPT THEE ASTRAY WITH HIP RHETORIC!
THERE IS BUT ONE WAY--
--ONE PATH TO GLORY, ONE ROAD TO HEAVEN, ONE SUPERHIGHWAY TO SALVATION!
THERE'S GOOD NEWS FOR ONE AND ALL, BELIEVE ME, BRETHREN--
HE LOOKS SO FAMILIAR--I THINK I'VE SEEN HIM ON TELEVISION!
AND IT'S ALL RIGHT HERE--
--JAM-PACKED WITH INFO AND COLOR PHOTOGRAPH'S!
MARTYRDOM FOR THE MILLIONS
TELL HIM TO BACK OFF.
YOU'RE SUFFO-CATING.
YOUR NERVES CAN'T TAKE THIS.
WHIM.
WHAM.
FUNGA.

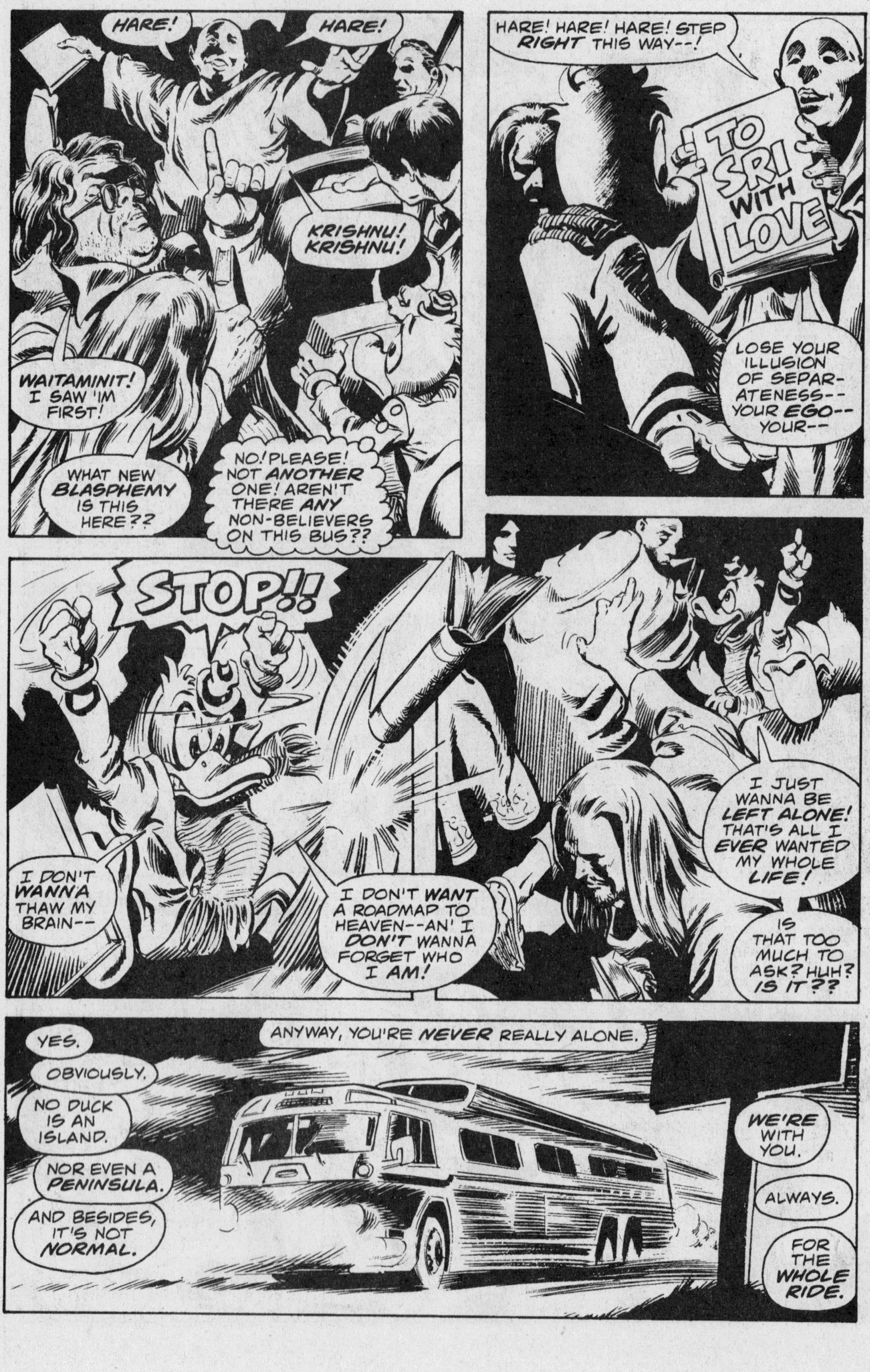
HARE!
HARE!
KRISHNU! KRISHNU!
WAITAMINIT! I SAW 'IM FIRST!
WHAT NEW BLASPHEMY IS THIS HERE??
NO! PLEASE! NOT ANOTHER ONE! AREN'T THERE ANY NON-BELIEVERS ON THIS BUS??
HARE! HARE! HARE! STEP RIGHT THIS WAY--!
TO SRI WITH LOVE
LOSE YOUR ILLUSION OF SEPARATENESS-- YOUR EGO-- YOUR--
STOP!!
I DON'T WANNA THAW MY BRAIN--
I DON'T WANT A ROADMAP TO HEAVEN--AN' I DON'T WANNA FORGET WHO I AM!
I JUST WANNA BE LEFT ALONE! THAT'S ALL I EVER WANTED MY WHOLE LIFE!
IS THAT TOO MUCH TO ASK? HUH? IS IT??
YES.
OBVIOUSLY.
NO DUCK IS AN ISLAND.
NOR EVEN A PENINSULA.
AND BESIDES, IT'S NOT NORMAL.
ANYWAY, YOU'RE NEVER REALLY ALONE.
WE'RE WITH YOU.
ALWAYS.
FOR THE WHOLE RIDE.

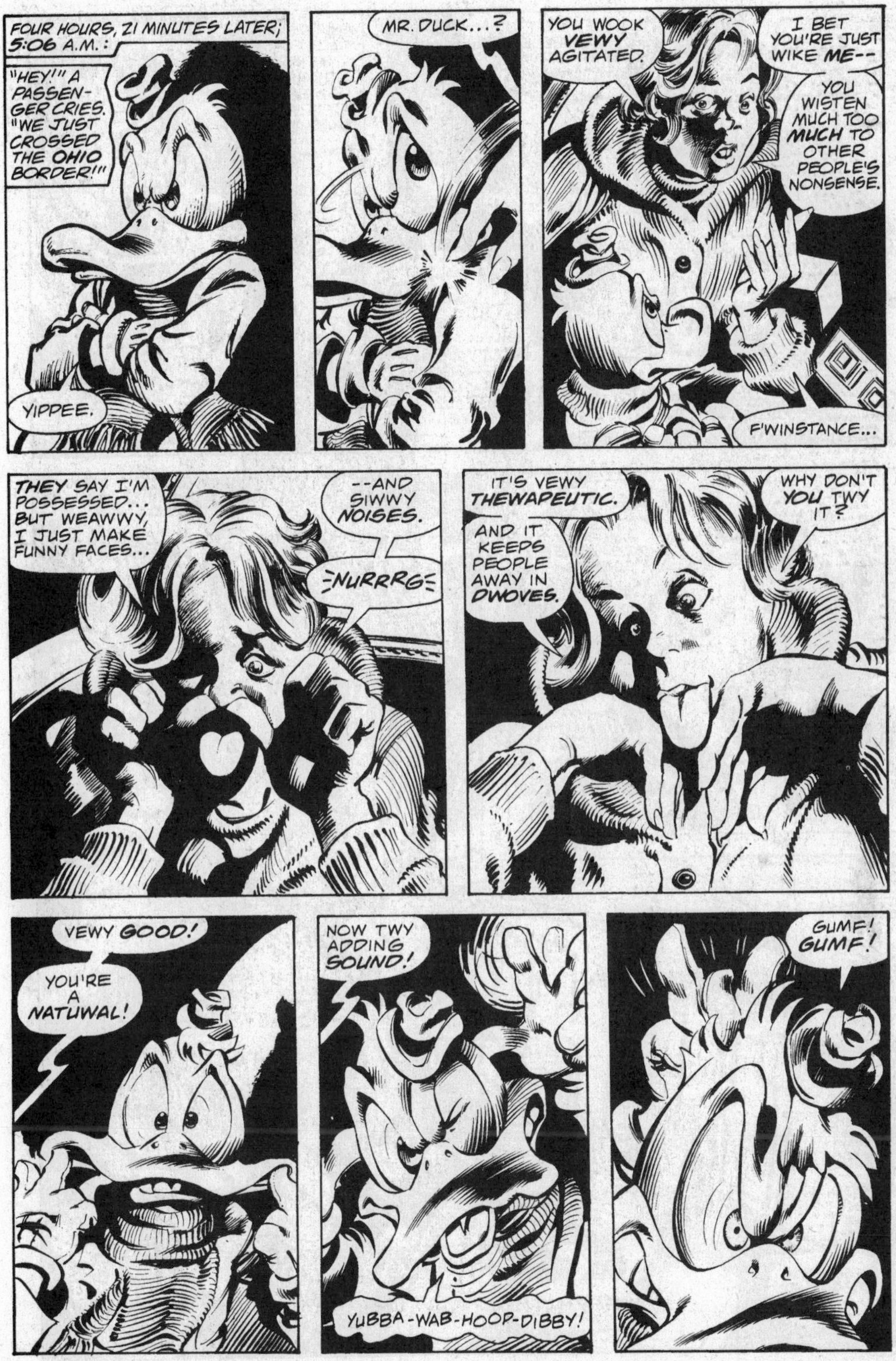
FOUR HOURS, 21 MINUTES LATER; 5:06 A.M.:
"HEY!" A PASSENGER CRIES. "WE JUST CROSSED THE OHIO BORDER!"
YIPPEE.
MR. DUCK...?
YOU WOOK VEWY AGITATED.
I BET YOU'RE JUST WIKE ME--
YOU WISTEN MUCH TOO MUCH TO OTHER PEOPLE'S NONSENSE.
F'WINSTANCE...
THEY SAY I'M POSSESSED... BUT WEAWWY, I JUST MAKE FUNNY FACES...
--AND SIWWY NOISES.
NURRRG
IT'S VEWY THEWAPEUTIC.
AND IT KEEPS PEOPLE AWAY IN DWOVES.
WHY DON'T YOU TWY IT?
VEWY GOOD!
YOU'RE A NATUWAL!
NOW TWY ADDING SOUND!
YUBBA-WAB-HOOP-DIBBY!
GUMF! GUMF!

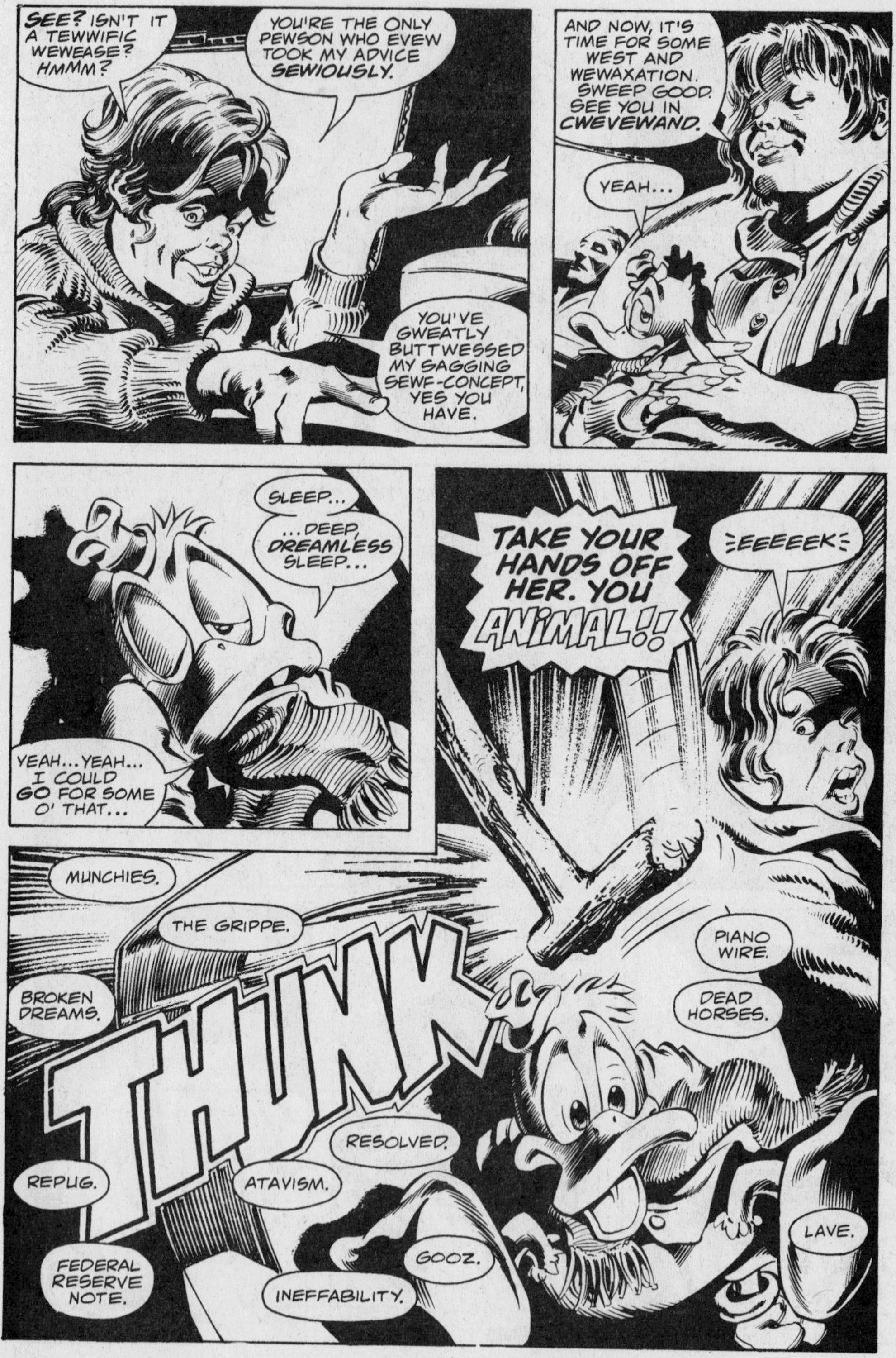
SEE? ISN'T IT A TEWWIFIC WEWEASE? HMMM?
YOU'RE THE ONLY PEWSON WHO EVEW TOOK MY ADVICE SEWIOUSLY.
YOU'VE GWEATLY BUTTWESSED MY SAGGING SEWF-CONCEPT, YES YOU HAVE.
AND NOW, IT'S TIME FOR SOME WEST AND WEWAXATION. SWEEP GOOD. SEE YOU IN CWEVEWAND.
YEAH...
SLEEP...
...DEEP, DREAMLESS SLEEP...
YEAH... YEAH... I COULD GO FOR SOME O' THAT...
TAKE YOUR HANDS OFF HER. YOU ANIMAL!!
EEEEEK
MUNCHIES.
THE GRIPPE.
PIANO WIRE.
BROKEN DREAMS.
DEAD HORSES.
THUNK
RESOLVED.
REPUG.
ATAVISM.
LAVE.
FEDERAL RESERVE NOTE.
GOOZ.
INEFFABILITY.

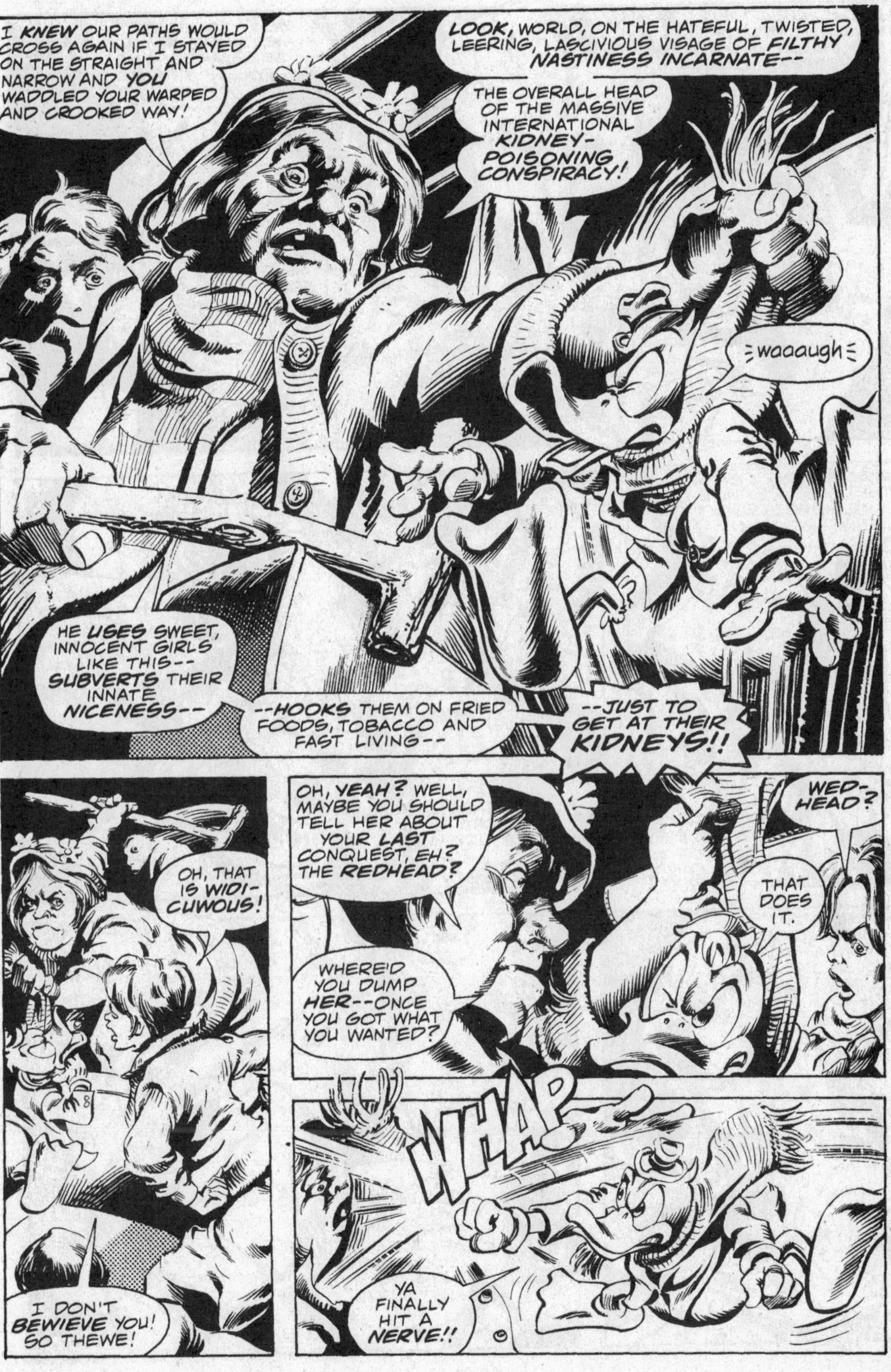

I KNEW OUR PATHS WOULD CROSS AGAIN IF I STAYED ON THE STRAIGHT AND NARROW AND YOU WADDLED YOUR WARPED AND CROOKED WAY!
LOOK, WORLD, ON THE HATEFUL, TWISTED, LEERING, LASCIVIOUS VISAGE OF FILTHY NASTINESS INCARNATE--
THE OVERALL HEAD OF THE MASSIVE INTERNATIONAL KIDNEY-POISONING CONSPIRACY!
waaaugh
HE USES SWEET, INNOCENT GIRLS LIKE THIS--SUBVERTS THEIR INNATE NICENESS--
--HOOKS THEM ON FRIED FOODS, TOBACCO AND FAST LIVING--
--JUST TO GET AT THEIR KIDNEYS!!
OH, THAT IS WIDICUWOUS!
I DON'T BEWIEVE YOU! SO THEWE!
OH, YEAH? WELL, MAYBE YOU SHOULD TELL HER ABOUT YOUR LAST CONQUEST, EH? THE REDHEAD?
WHERE'D YOU DUMP HER--ONCE YOU GOT WHAT YOU WANTED?
WED-HEAD?
THAT DOES IT.
WHAP
YA FINALLY HIT A NERVE!!

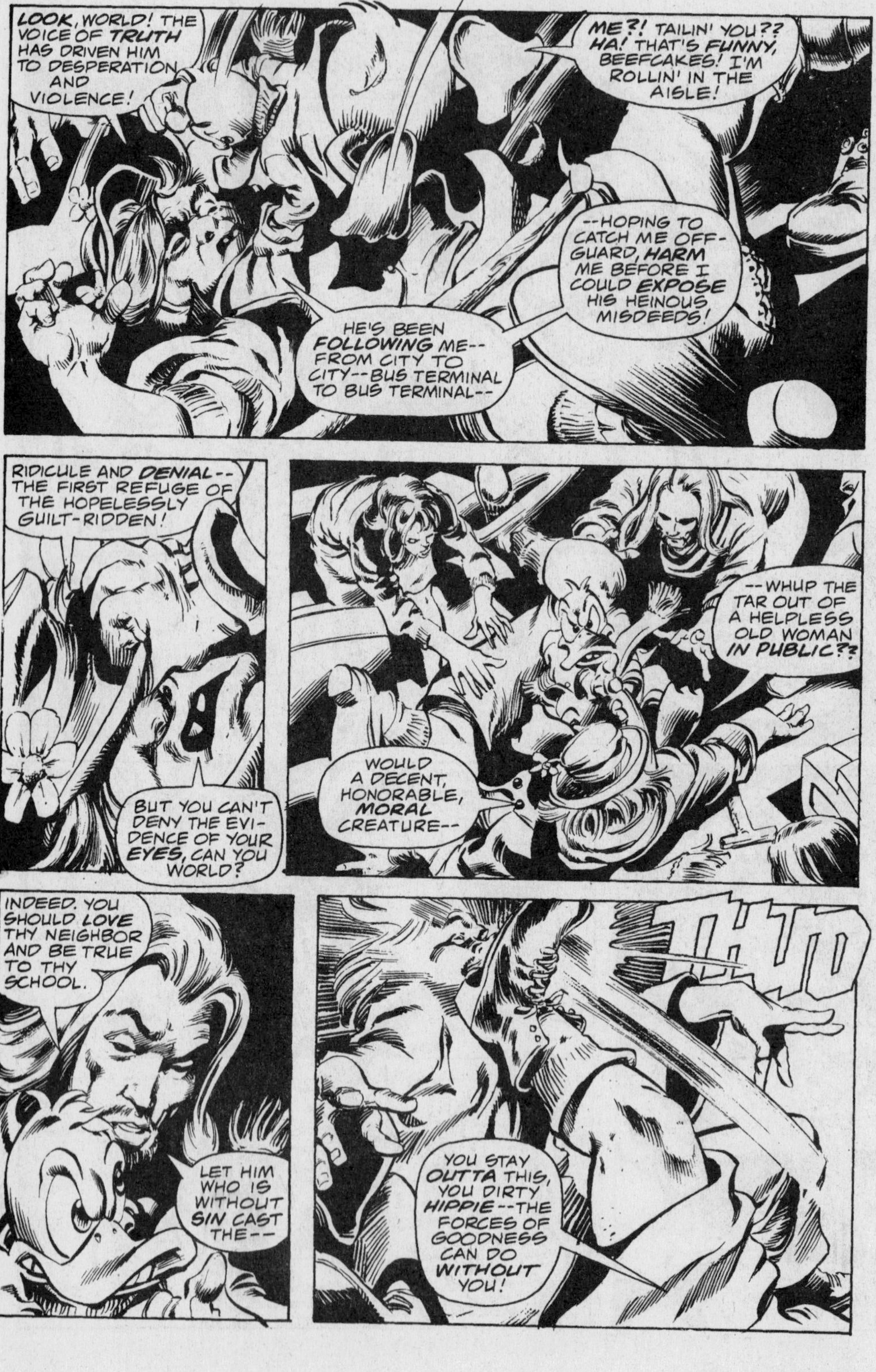

LOOK, WORLD! THE VOICE OF TRUTH HAS DRIVEN HIM TO DESPERATION AND VIOLENCE!
ME?! TAILIN' YOU?? HA! THAT'S FUNNY, BEEFCAKES! I'M ROLLIN' IN THE AISLE!
HE'S BEEN FOLLOWING ME--FROM CITY TO CITY--BUS TERMINAL TO BUS TERMINAL--
--HOPING TO CATCH ME OFF-GUARD, HARM ME BEFORE I COULD EXPOSE HIS HEINOUS MISDEEDS!
RIDICULE AND DENIAL--THE FIRST REFUGE OF THE HOPELESSLY GUILT-RIDDEN!
BUT YOU CAN'T DENY THE EVIDENCE OF YOUR EYES, CAN YOU WORLD?
WOULD A DECENT, HONORABLE, MORAL CREATURE--
--WHUP THE TAR OUT OF A HELPLESS OLD WOMAN IN PUBLIC??
INDEED. YOU SHOULD LOVE THY NEIGHBOR AND BE TRUE TO THY SCHOOL.
LET HIM WHO IS WITHOUT SIN CAST THE--
THUD
YOU STAY OUTTA THIS, YOU DIRTY HIPPIE--THE FORCES OF GOODNESS CAN DO WITHOUT YOU!

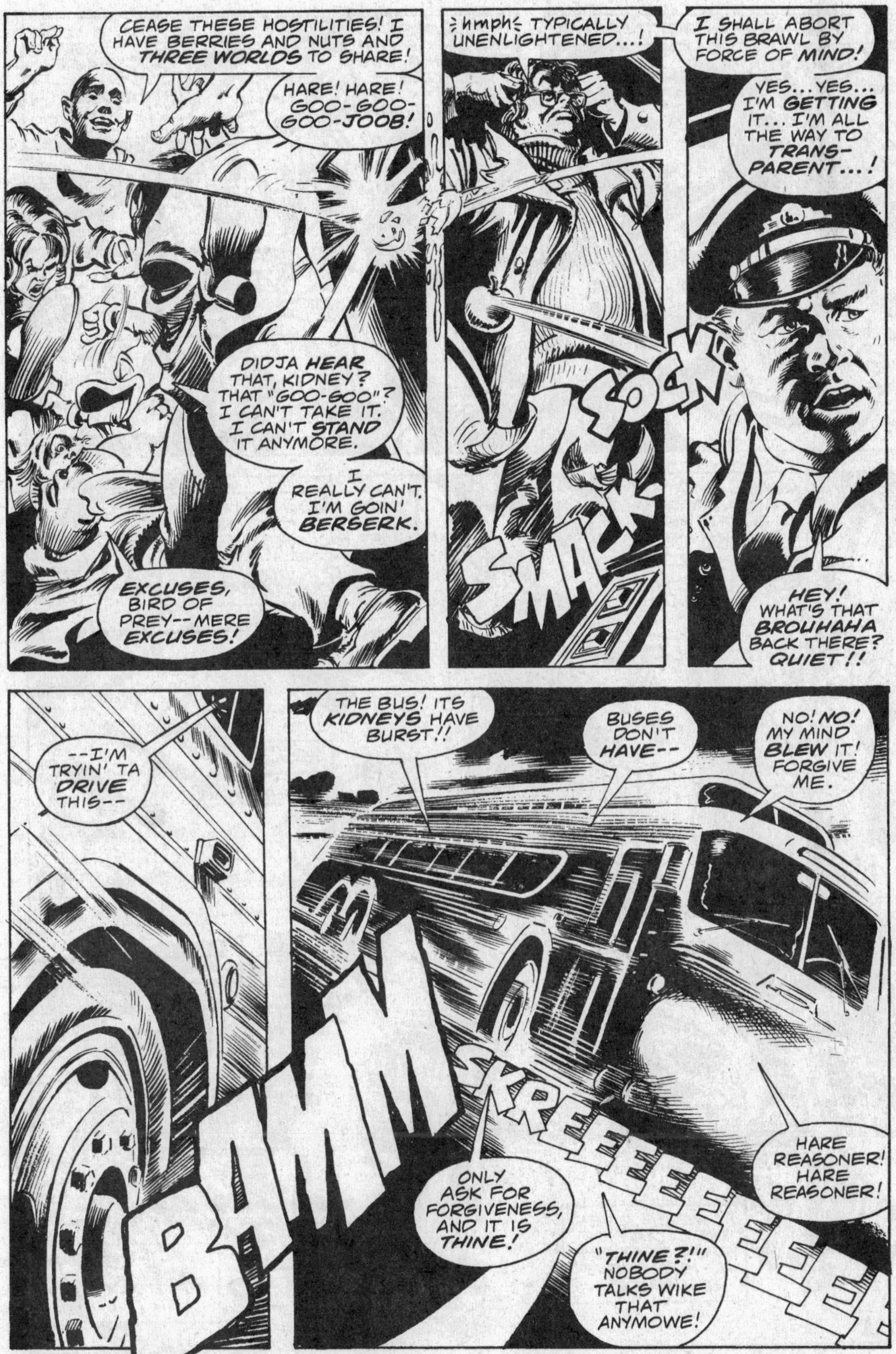
CEASE THESE HOSTILITIES! I HAVE BERRIES AND NUTS AND THREE WORLDS TO SHARE!
HARE! HARE! GOO-GOO-GOO-JOOB!
DIDJA HEAR THAT, KIDNEY? THAT "GOO-GOO"? I CAN'T TAKE IT. I CAN'T STAND IT ANYMORE.
I REALLY CAN'T. I'M GOIN' BERSERK.
EXCUSES, BIRD OF PREY--MERE EXCUSES!
≡HMPH≡ TYPICALLY UNENLIGHTENED...!
SOCK
SMACK
I SHALL ABORT THIS BRAWL BY FORCE OF MIND!
YES... YES... I'M GETTING IT... I'M ALL THE WAY TO TRANS-PARENT...!
HEY! WHAT'S THAT BROUHAHA BACK THERE? QUIET!!
--I'M TRYIN' TA DRIVE THIS--
THE BUS! ITS KIDNEYS HAVE BURST!!
BUSES DON'T HAVE--
NO! NO! MY MIND BLEW IT! FORGIVE ME.
BAMM
SKREEEEEEEEE!
ONLY ASK FOR FORGIVENESS, AND IT IS THINE!
"THINE?!" NOBODY TALKS WIKE THAT ANYMOWE!
HARE REASONER! HARE REASONER!

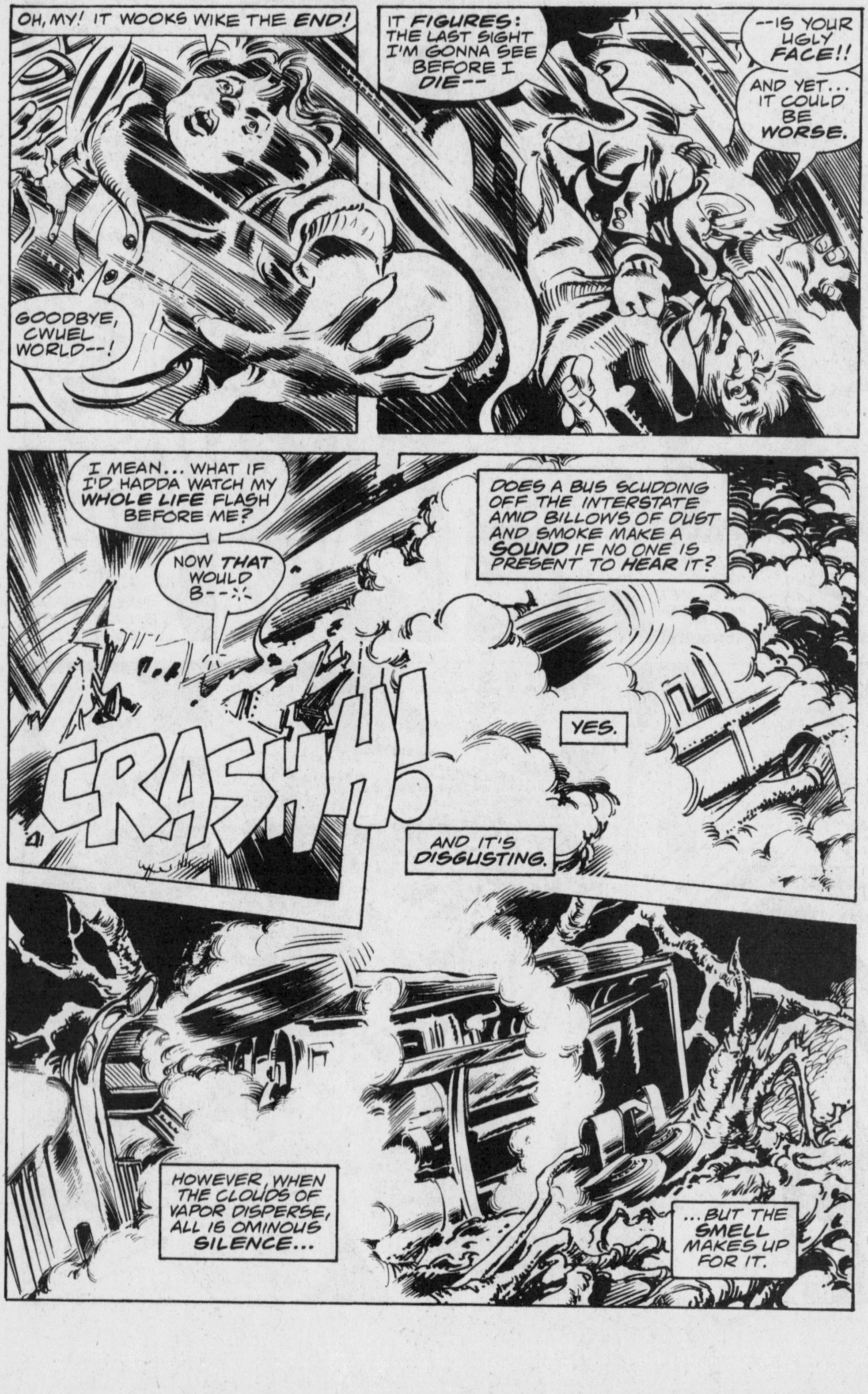
OH, MY! IT WOOKS WIKE THE END!
GOODBYE, CWUEL WORLD--!
IT FIGURES: THE LAST SIGHT I'M GONNA SEE BEFORE I DIE--
--IS YOUR UGLY FACE!!
AND YET... IT COULD BE WORSE.
I MEAN... WHAT IF I'D HADDA WATCH MY WHOLE LIFE FLASH BEFORE ME?
NOW THAT WOULD B--
DOES A BUS SCUDDING OFF THE INTERSTATE AMID BILLOWS OF DUST AND SMOKE MAKE A SOUND IF NO ONE IS PRESENT TO HEAR IT?
CRASHH!
YES.
AND IT'S DISGUSTING.
HOWEVER, WHEN THE CLOUDS OF VAPOR DISPERSE, ALL IS OMINOUS SILENCE...
...BUT THE SMELL MAKES UP FOR IT.

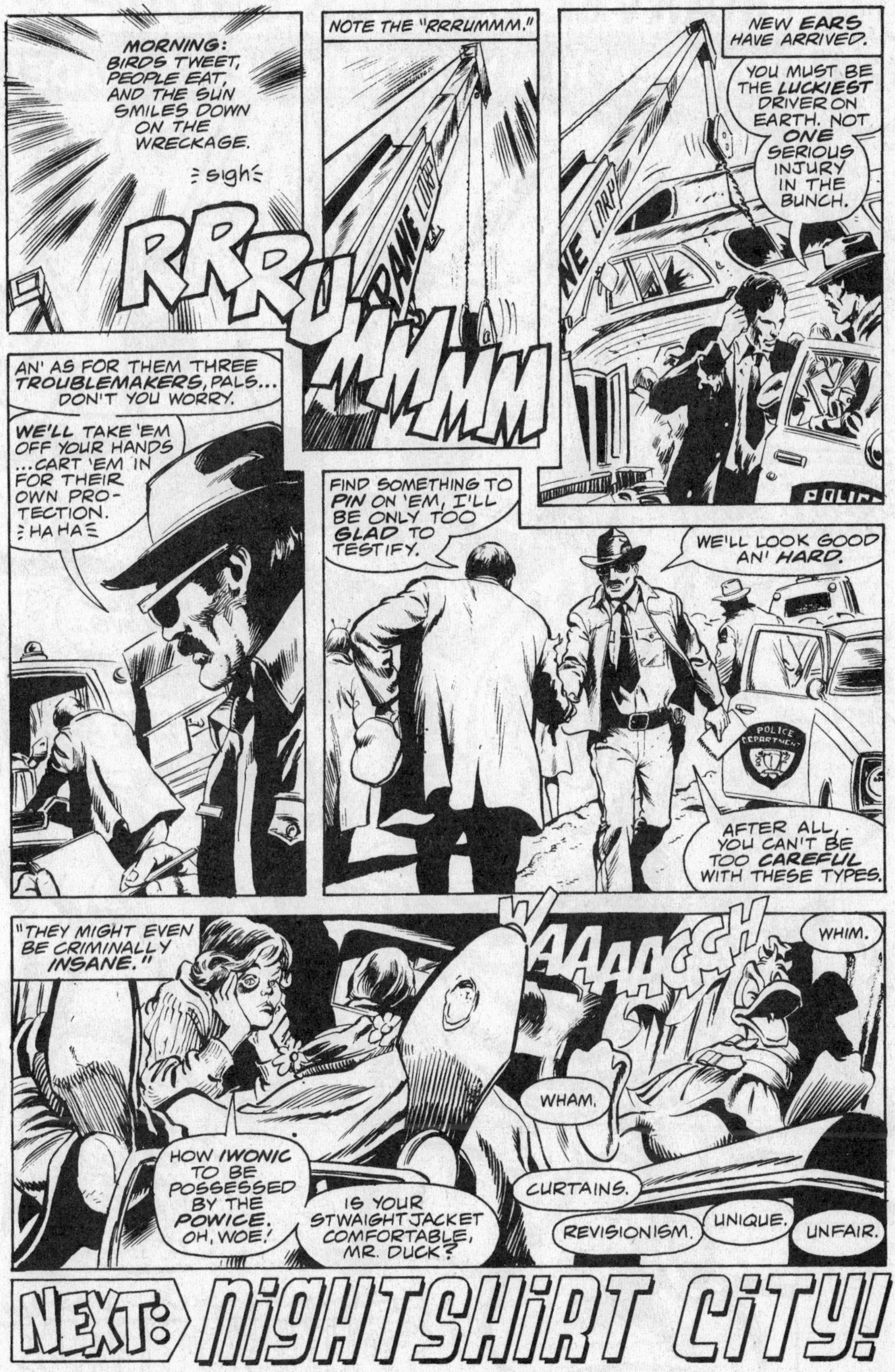
MORNING: BIRDS TWEET, PEOPLE EAT, AND THE SUN SMILES DOWN ON THE WRECKAGE.
sigh
RRRUMMMMM
NOTE THE "RRRUMMM."
NEW EARS HAVE ARRIVED.
YOU MUST BE THE LUCKIEST DRIVER ON EARTH. NOT ONE SERIOUS INJURY IN THE BUNCH.
AN' AS FOR THEM THREE TROUBLEMAKERS, PALS... DON'T YOU WORRY.
WE'LL TAKE 'EM OFF YOUR HANDS ...CART 'EM IN FOR THEIR OWN PROTECTION.
HA HA
FIND SOMETHING TO PIN ON 'EM, I'LL BE ONLY TOO GLAD TO TESTIFY.
WE'LL LOOK GOOD AN' HARD.
AFTER ALL, YOU CAN'T BE TOO CAREFUL WITH THESE TYPES.
"THEY MIGHT EVEN BE CRIMINALLY INSANE."
WAAAAGGH
WHIM.
WHAM.
HOW IWONIC TO BE POSSESSED BY THE POWICE. OH, WOE!
IS YOUR STWAIGHTJACKET COMFORTABLE, MR. DUCK?
CURTAINS.
REVISIONISM.
UNIQUE.
UNFAIR.
NEXT: NIGHTSHIRT CITY!

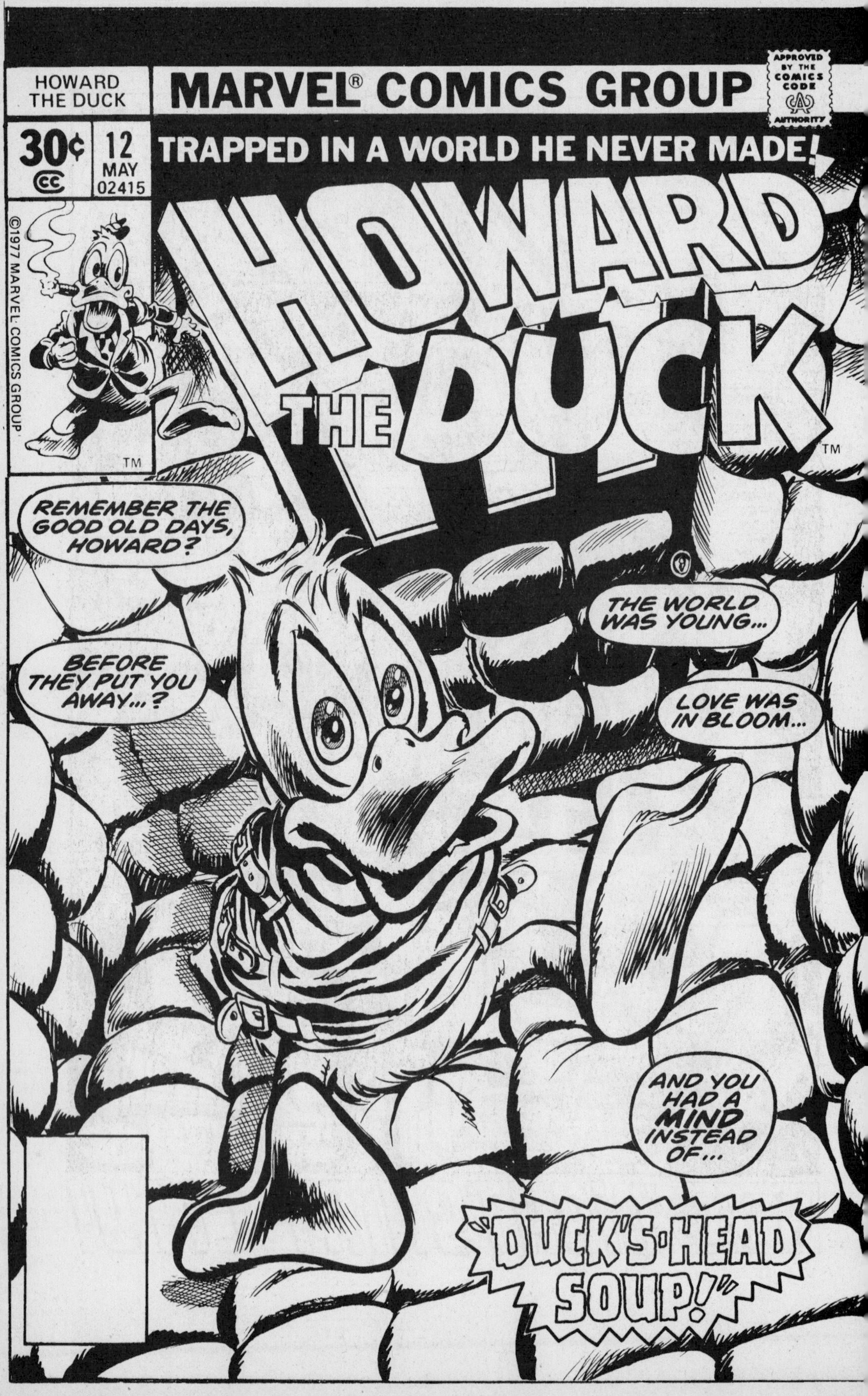

HOWARD THE DUCK
MARVEL® COMICS GROUP
APPROVED BY THE COMICS CODE AUTHORITY
30¢
12 MAY 02415
TRAPPED IN A WORLD HE NEVER MADE!
©1977 MARVEL COMICS GROUP
HOWARD THE DUCK™
REMEMBER THE GOOD OLD DAYS, HOWARD?
BEFORE THEY PUT YOU AWAY...?
THE WORLD WAS YOUNG...
LOVE WAS IN BLOOM...
AND YOU HAD A MIND INSTEAD OF...
"DUCK'S-HEAD SOUP!"

From the time of his hatching, he was...different. A potentially brilliant scholar who dreaded the structured environment of school, he educated himself in the streets, taking whatever work was available, formulating his philosophy of self from what he learned of the world about him. And then the Cosmic Axis shifted...and that world *changed.* Suddenly, he was stranded in a universe he could not fathom. Without warning, he became a strange fowl in an even stranger land.

Stan Lee PRESENTS: HOWARD THE DUCK!™

STEVE GERBER, WRITER/EDITOR • GENE COLAN, ARTIST • STEVE LEIALOHA, INKER • JIM NOVAK, LETTERER; JANICE COHEN, COLORIST

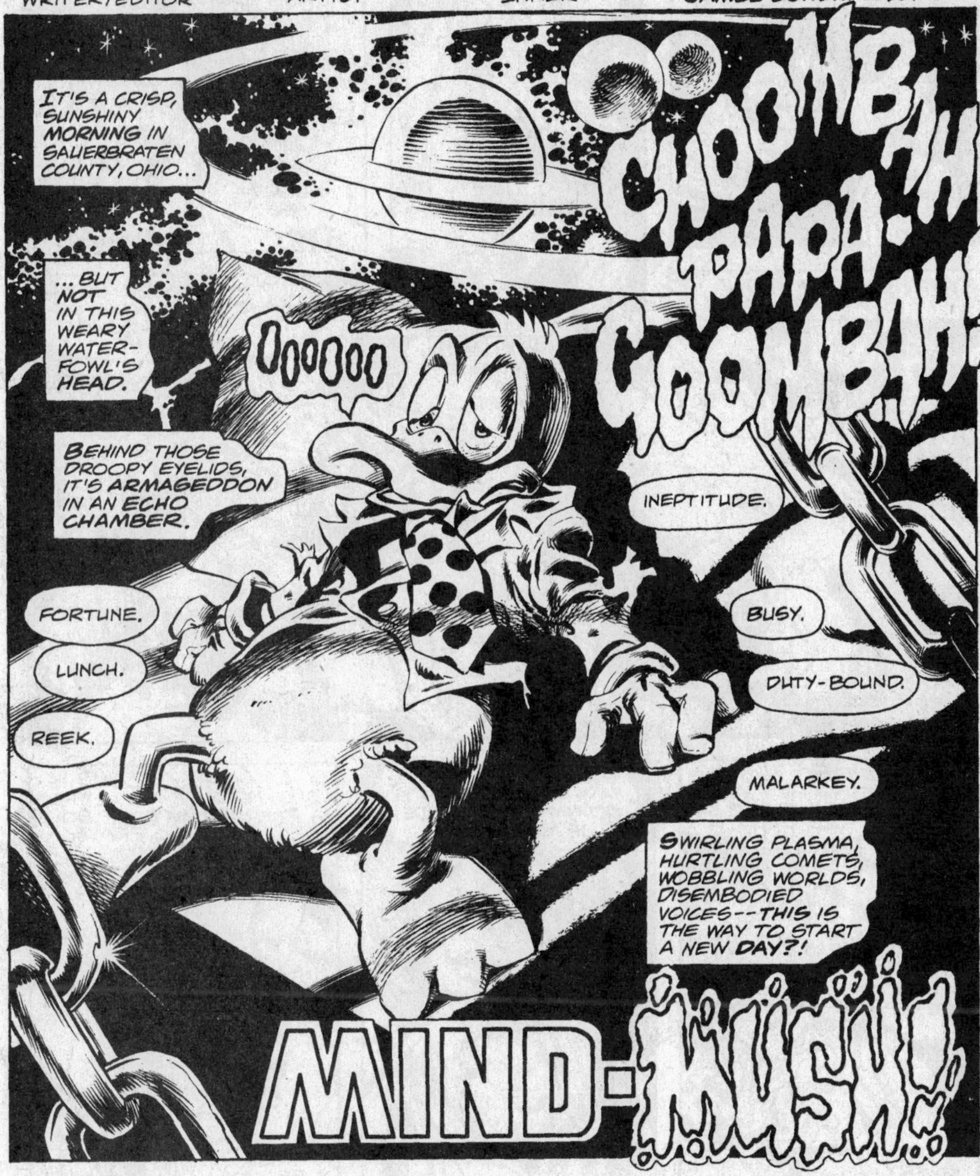
IT'S A CRISP, SUNSHINY MORNING IN SAUERBRATEN COUNTY, OHIO...
...BUT NOT IN THIS WEARY WATER-FOWL'S HEAD.
CHOOMBAH PAPA-GOOMBAH!
OOOOOO
BEHIND THOSE DROOPY EYELIDS, IT'S ARMAGEDDON IN AN ECHO CHAMBER.
INEPTITUDE.
FORTUNE.
BUSY.
LUNCH.
DUTY-BOUND.
REEK.
MALARKEY.
SWIRLING PLASMA, HURTLING COMETS, WOBBLING WORLDS, DISEMBODIED VOICES--THIS IS THE WAY TO START A NEW DAY?!
MIND-MUSH!

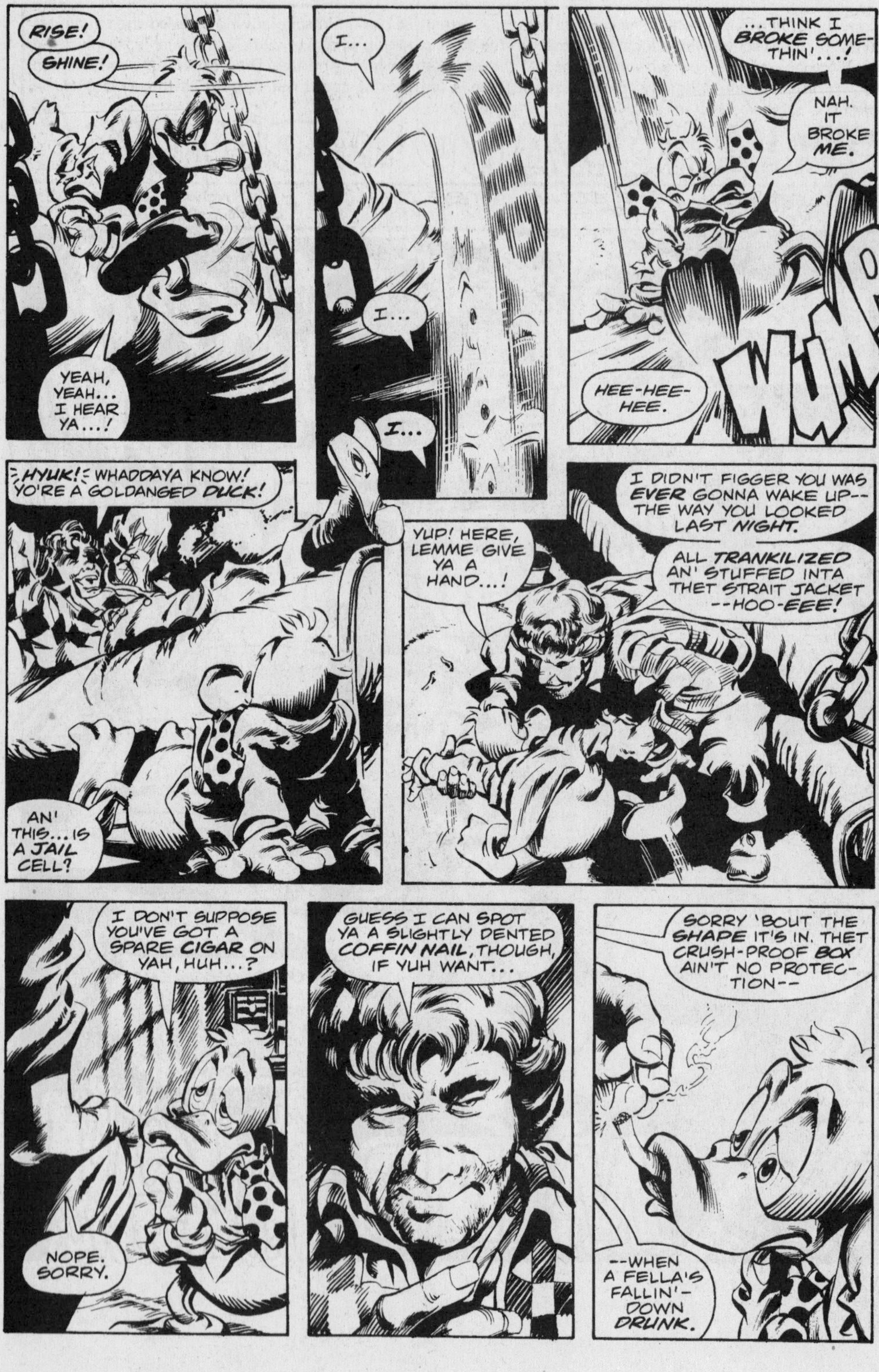
RISE!
SHINE!
YEAH, YEAH... I HEAR YA...!
I...
I...
I...
...THINK I BROKE SOMETHIN'...!
NAH. IT BROKE ME.
HEE-HEE-HEE.
WUMP
HYUK! WHADDAYA KNOW! YO'RE A GOLDANGED DUCK!
AN' THIS...IS A JAIL CELL?
I DIDN'T FIGGER YOU WAS EVER GONNA WAKE UP-- THE WAY YOU LOOKED LAST NIGHT.
ALL TRANKILIZED AN' STUFFED INTA THET STRAIT JACKET --HOO-EEE!
YUP! HERE, LEMME GIVE YA A HAND...!
I DON'T SUPPOSE YOU'VE GOT A SPARE CIGAR ON YAH, HUH...?
NOPE. SORRY.
GUESS I CAN SPOT YA A SLIGHTLY DENTED COFFIN NAIL, THOUGH, IF YUH WANT...
SORRY 'BOUT THE SHAPE IT'S IN. THET CRUSH-PROOF BOX AIN'T NO PROTECTION--
--WHEN A FELLA'S FALLIN'-DOWN DRUNK.

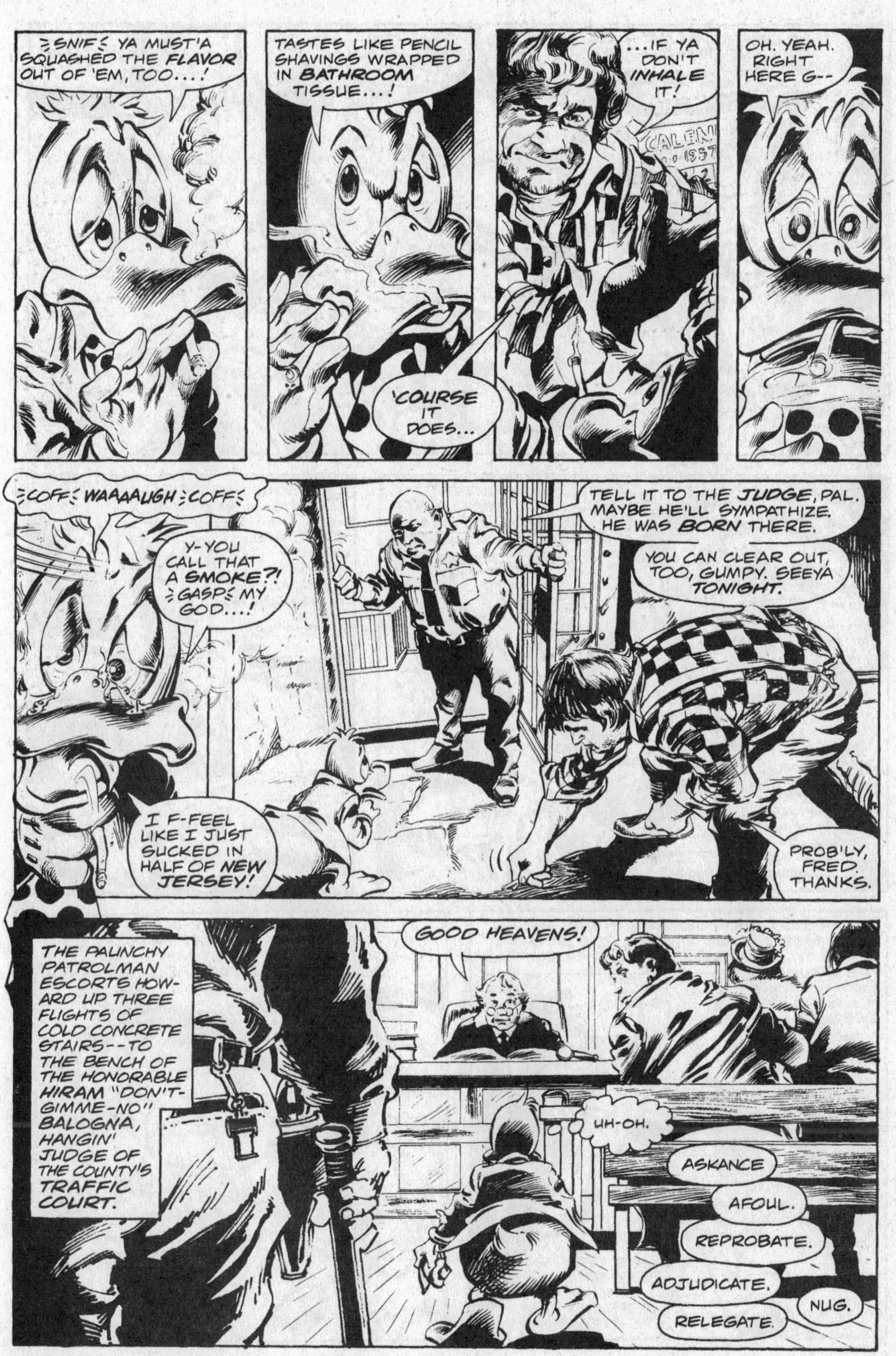

SNIF YA MUST'A SQUASHED THE FLAVOR OUT OF 'EM, TOO...!
TASTES LIKE PENCIL SHAVINGS WRAPPED IN BATHROOM TISSUE...!
'COURSE IT DOES...
...IF YA DON'T INHALE IT!
OH. YEAH. RIGHT HERE G--
COFF WAAAAUGH COFF
Y-YOU CALL THAT A SMOKE?! GASP MY GOD...!
TELL IT TO THE JUDGE, PAL. MAYBE HE'LL SYMPATHIZE. HE WAS BORN THERE.
YOU CAN CLEAR OUT, TOO, GUMPY. SEEYA TONIGHT.
I F-FEEL LIKE I JUST SUCKED IN HALF OF NEW JERSEY!
PROB'LY, FRED. THANKS.
THE PAUNCHY PATROLMAN ESCORTS HOWARD UP THREE FLIGHTS OF COLD CONCRETE STAIRS--TO THE BENCH OF THE HONORABLE HIRAM "DON'T-GIMME-NO" BALOGNA, HANGIN' JUDGE OF THE COUNTY'S TRAFFIC COURT.
GOOD HEAVENS!
UH-OH.
ASKANCE
AFOUL.
REPROBATE.
ADJUDICATE.
RELEGATE.
NUG.

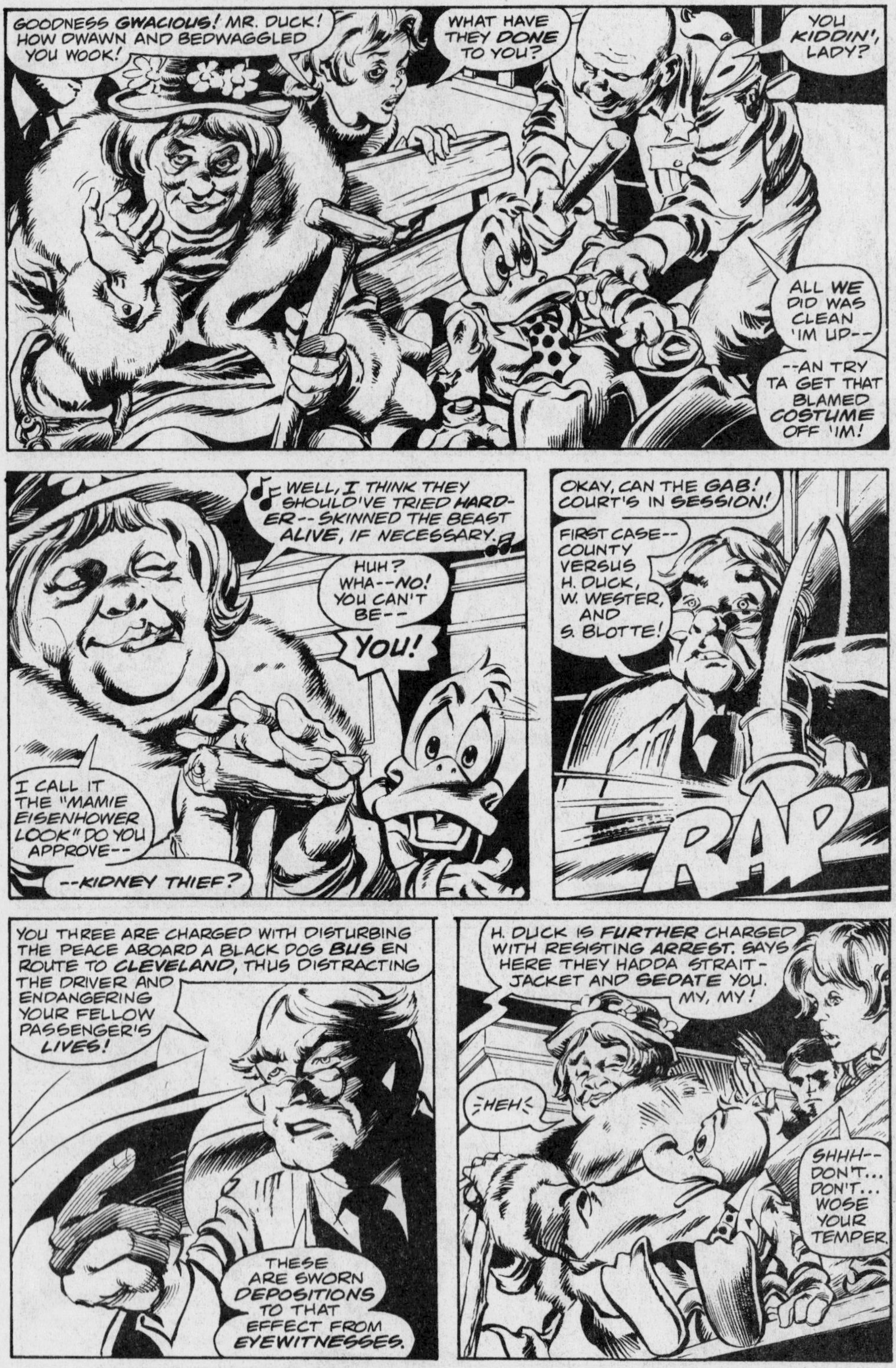
GOODNESS GWACIOUS! MR. DUCK! HOW DWAWN AND BEDWAGGLED YOU WOOK!
WHAT HAVE THEY DONE TO YOU?
YOU KIDDIN', LADY?
ALL WE DID WAS CLEAN 'IM UP--
--AN TRY TA GET THAT BLAMED COSTUME OFF 'IM!
WELL, I THINK THEY SHOULD'VE TRIED HARDER-- SKINNED THE BEAST ALIVE, IF NECESSARY.
HUH? WHA--NO! YOU CAN'T BE--
YOU!
I CALL IT THE "MAMIE EISENHOWER LOOK" DO YOU APPROVE--
--KIDNEY THIEF?
OKAY, CAN THE GAB! COURT'S IN SESSION!
FIRST CASE-- COUNTY VERSUS H. DUCK, W. WESTER, AND S. BLOTTE!
RAP
YOU THREE ARE CHARGED WITH DISTURBING THE PEACE ABOARD A BLACK DOG BUS EN ROUTE TO CLEVELAND, THUS DISTRACTING THE DRIVER AND ENDANGERING YOUR FELLOW PASSENGER'S LIVES!
THESE ARE SWORN DEPOSITIONS TO THAT EFFECT FROM EYEWITNESSES.
H. DUCK IS FURTHER CHARGED WITH RESISTING ARREST. SAYS HERE THEY HADDA STRAIT-JACKET AND SEDATE YOU. MY, MY!
HEH
SHHH-- DON'T... DON'T... WOSE YOUR TEMPER.

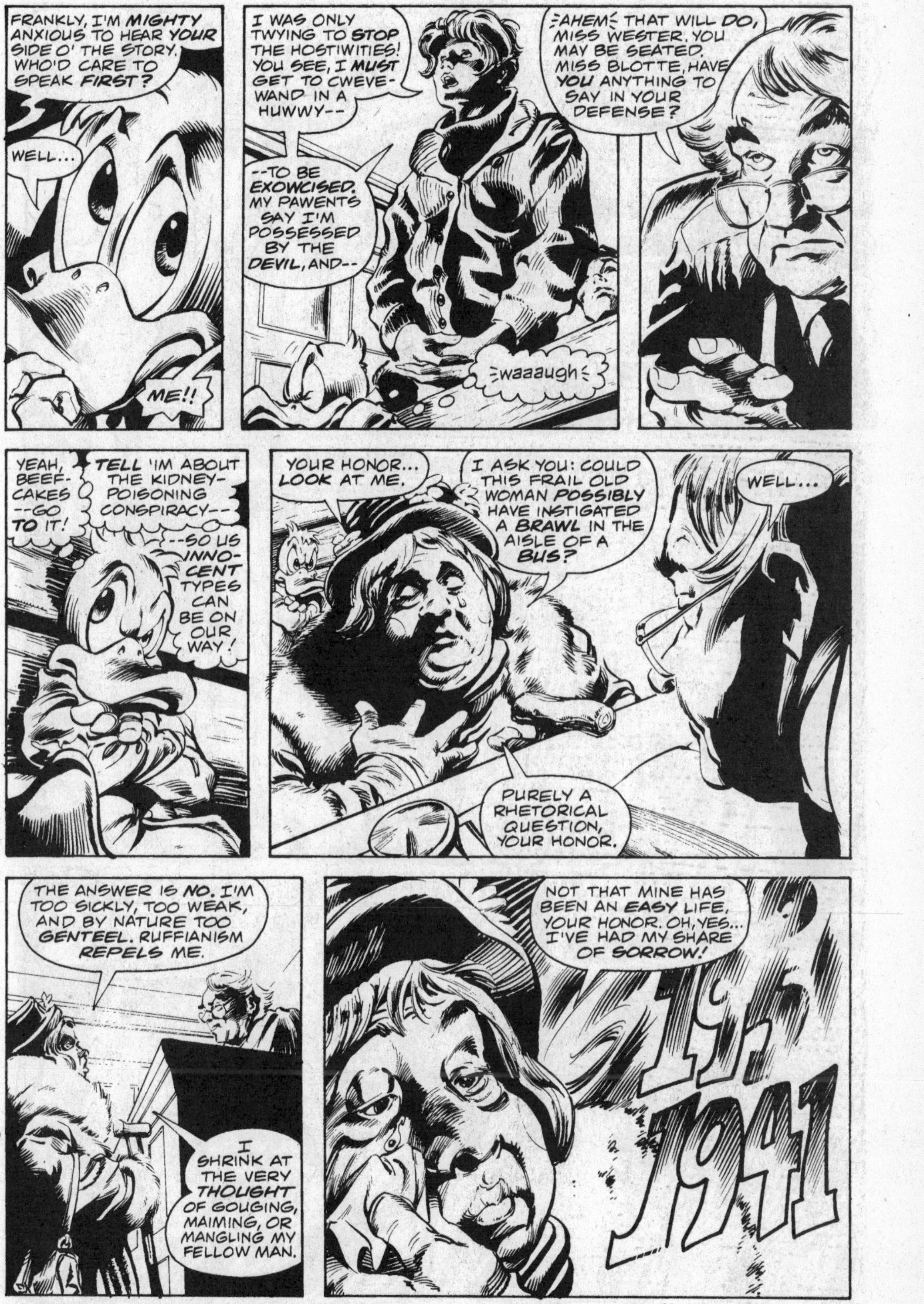
FRANKLY, I'M MIGHTY ANXIOUS TO HEAR YOUR SIDE O' THE STORY. WHO'D CARE TO SPEAK FIRST?
WELL...
ME!!
I WAS ONLY TWYING TO STOP THE HOSTIWITIES! YOU SEE, I MUST GET TO CWEVE-WAND IN A HUWWY--
--TO BE EXOWCISED. MY PAWENTS SAY I'M POSSESSED BY THE DEVIL, AND--
waaaugh
AHEM THAT WILL DO, MISS WESTER. YOU MAY BE SEATED. MISS BLOTTE, HAVE YOU ANYTHING TO SAY IN YOUR DEFENSE?
YEAH, BEEF-CAKES --GO TO IT!
TELL 'IM ABOUT THE KIDNEY-POISONING CONSPIRACY--
--SO US INNO-CENT TYPES CAN BE ON OUR WAY!
YOUR HONOR... LOOK AT ME.
I ASK YOU: COULD THIS FRAIL OLD WOMAN POSSIBLY HAVE INSTIGATED A BRAWL IN THE AISLE OF A BUS?
WELL...
PURELY A RHETORICAL QUESTION, YOUR HONOR.
THE ANSWER IS NO. I'M TOO SICKLY, TOO WEAK, AND BY NATURE TOO GENTEEL. RUFFIANISM REPELS ME.
I SHRINK AT THE VERY THOUGHT OF GOUGING, MAIMING, OR MANGLING MY FELLOW MAN.
NOT THAT MINE HAS BEEN AN EASY LIFE, YOUR HONOR. OH, YES... I'VE HAD MY SHARE OF SORROW!
1941

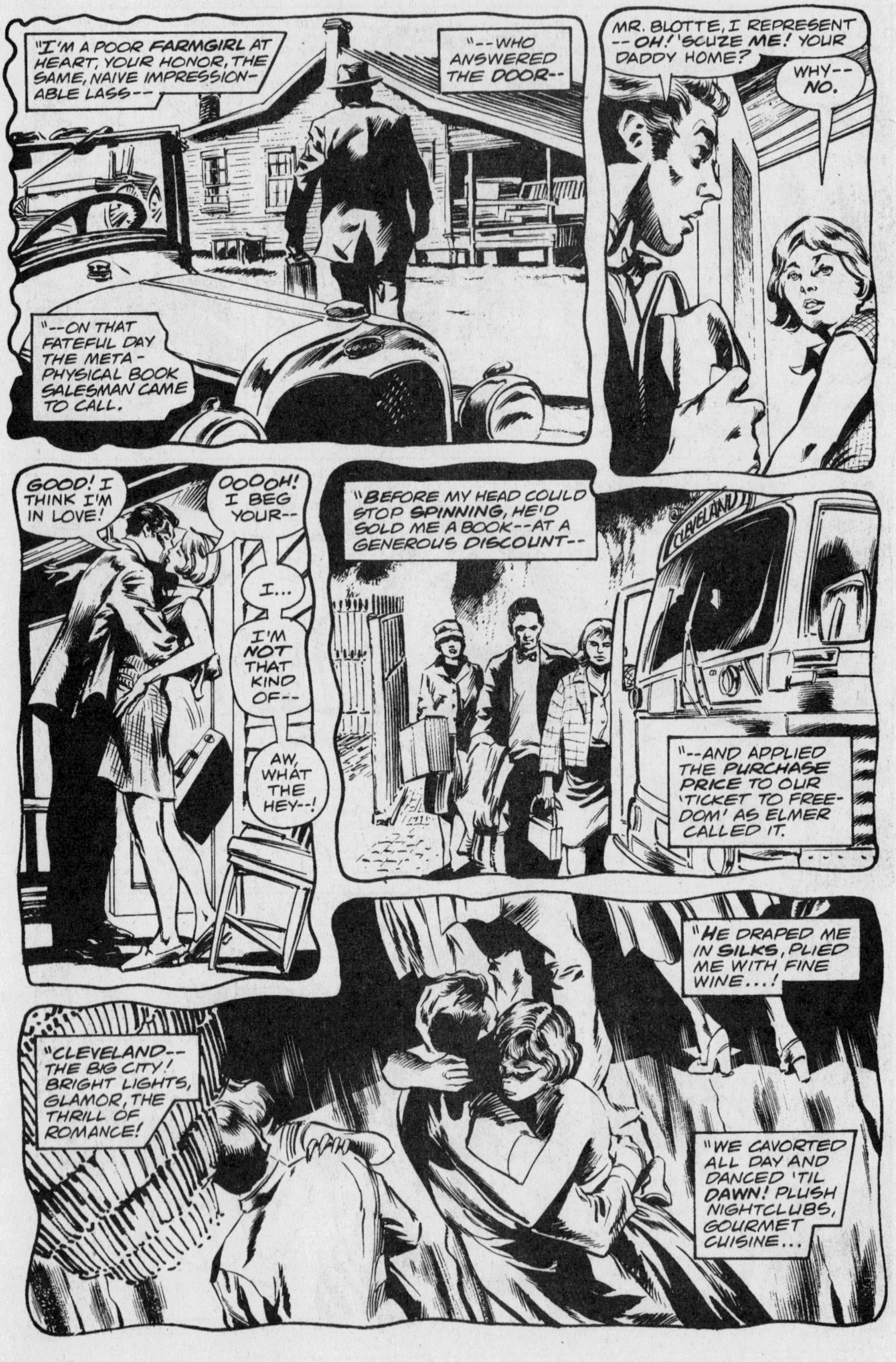
"I'M A POOR FARMGIRL AT HEART, YOUR HONOR, THE SAME, NAIVE IMPRESSIONABLE LASS--
"--WHO ANSWERED THE DOOR--
"--ON THAT FATEFUL DAY THE META-PHYSICAL BOOK SALESMAN CAME TO CALL.
MR. BLOTTE, I REPRESENT --OH! 'SCUZE ME! YOUR DADDY HOME?
WHY-- NO.
GOOD! I THINK I'M IN LOVE!
OOOOH! I BEG YOUR--
I...
I'M NOT THAT KIND OF--
AW, WHAT THE HEY--!
"BEFORE MY HEAD COULD STOP SPINNING, HE'D SOLD ME A BOOK--AT A GENEROUS DISCOUNT--
CLEVELAND
"--AND APPLIED THE PURCHASE PRICE TO OUR 'TICKET TO FREEDOM' AS ELMER CALLED IT.
"HE DRAPED ME IN SILKS, PLIED ME WITH FINE WINE...!
"CLEVELAND-- THE BIG CITY! BRIGHT LIGHTS, GLAMOR, THE THRILL OF ROMANCE!
"WE CAVORTED ALL DAY AND DANCED 'TIL DAWN! PLUSH NIGHTCLUBS, GOURMET CUISINE...

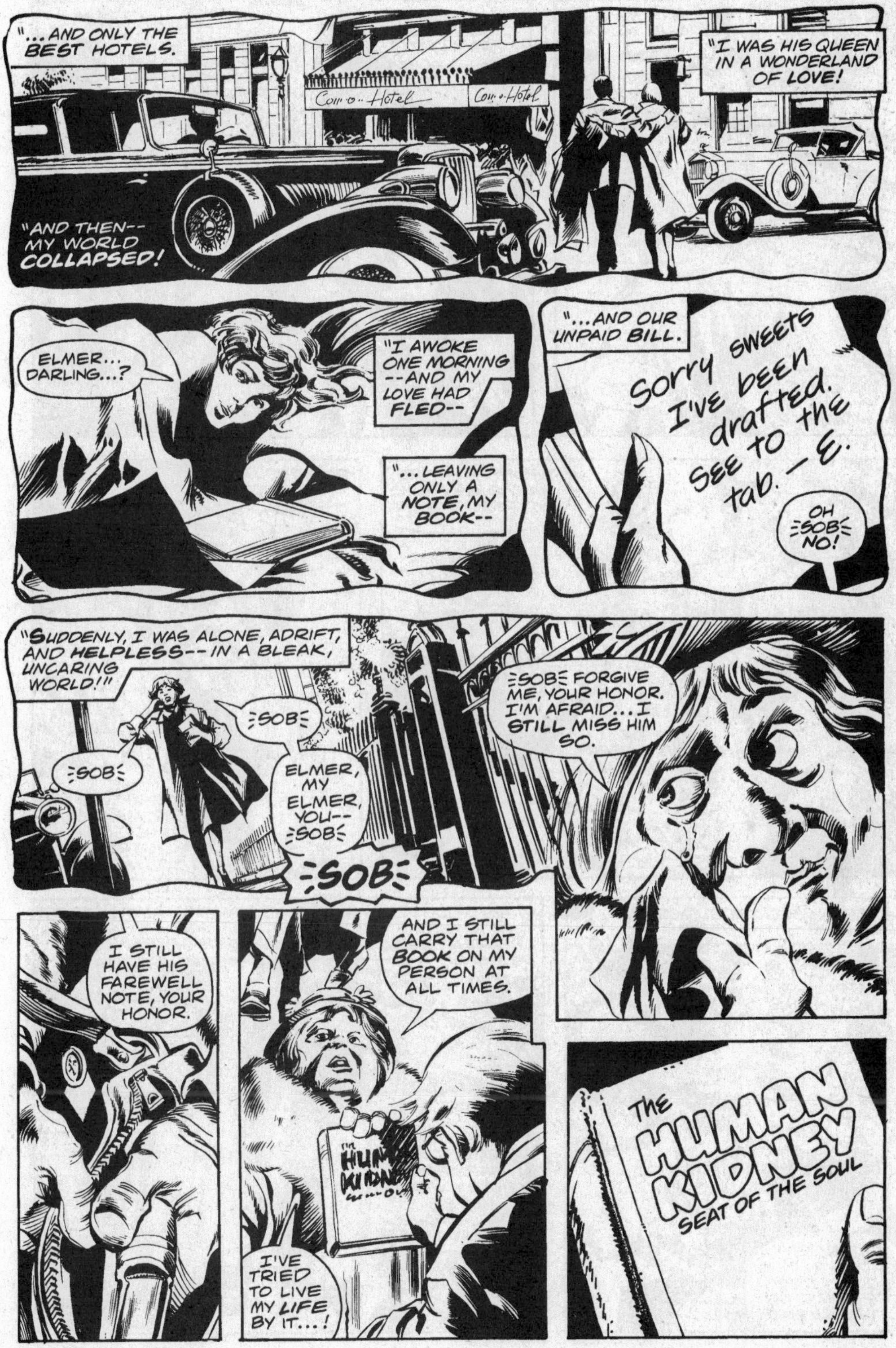
"...AND ONLY THE BEST HOTELS.
Com-o- Hotel
Com-o- Hotel
"I WAS HIS QUEEN IN A WONDERLAND OF LOVE!
"AND THEN-- MY WORLD COLLAPSED!
ELMER... DARLING...?
"I AWOKE ONE MORNING --AND MY LOVE HAD FLED--
"...LEAVING ONLY A NOTE, MY BOOK--
"...AND OUR UNPAID BILL.
Sorry sweets I've been drafted. See to the tab. — E.
OH SOB NO!
"SUDDENLY, I WAS ALONE, ADRIFT, AND HELPLESS-- IN A BLEAK, UNCARING WORLD!"
SOB
SOB
ELMER, MY ELMER, YOU-- SOB
SOB
SOB FORGIVE ME, YOUR HONOR. I'M AFRAID... I STILL MISS HIM SO.
I STILL HAVE HIS FAREWELL NOTE, YOUR HONOR.
AND I STILL CARRY THAT BOOK ON MY PERSON AT ALL TIMES.
I'VE TRIED TO LIVE MY LIFE BY IT...!
THE HUMAN KIDNEY SEAT OF THE SOUL

HAVE MERCY, YOUR HONOR!

=SOB= COULD A WOMAN WHO'S WAITED **36** YEARS FOR HER MAN TO RETURN FROM **WORLD WAR II**...

...COMMIT THE CRIME OF WHICH **I** AM ACCUSED?

=SOB=

NO, NO, NO... OF **COURSE** NOT, DEAR LADY!

WHY...I'M ASHAMED TO HAVE PUT YOU THROUGH THIS DREADFUL ORDEAL.

ALLOW ME TO ASSIST YOU TO THE DOOR...!

=SOB=

=SOB=

=BOO! HOO=

NO!!

STOP!! WHAT'RE YA **DOIN'?!** SHE STARTED IT **ALL!!**

STRAP 'ER DOWN! RUBBER-HOSE 'ER!! MAKE 'ER TALK!! DON'T--

=WAAAUGH=

POOR, DELUDED CREATURE!

HE DESERVES OUR **COMPASSION,** NOT OUR HATRED. TRY TO...**HELP** HIM.

AND SO, WHEN THE JUDGE RETURNS TO THE BENCH...

WRAP

WRA

SILENCE! ORDER IN THE COURT! I'VE REACHED MY JUDGEMENT!

"THIS VIOLENT OUTBURST, YOUR REFUSAL TO REMOVE THAT FARCICAL **DUCK** GARB, AND MISS WESTER'S APPARENT BELIEF IN HER OWN POSSESSION BY DEMONS--

"--IMPEL ME TO **CONCUR** WITH THE ARRESTING OFFICERS THAT YOU **BOTH** MAY BE DANGEROUSLY UNBALANCED!

"ACCORDINGLY, I SENTENCE YOU EACH TO **NINETY DAYS'** CONFINEMENT...

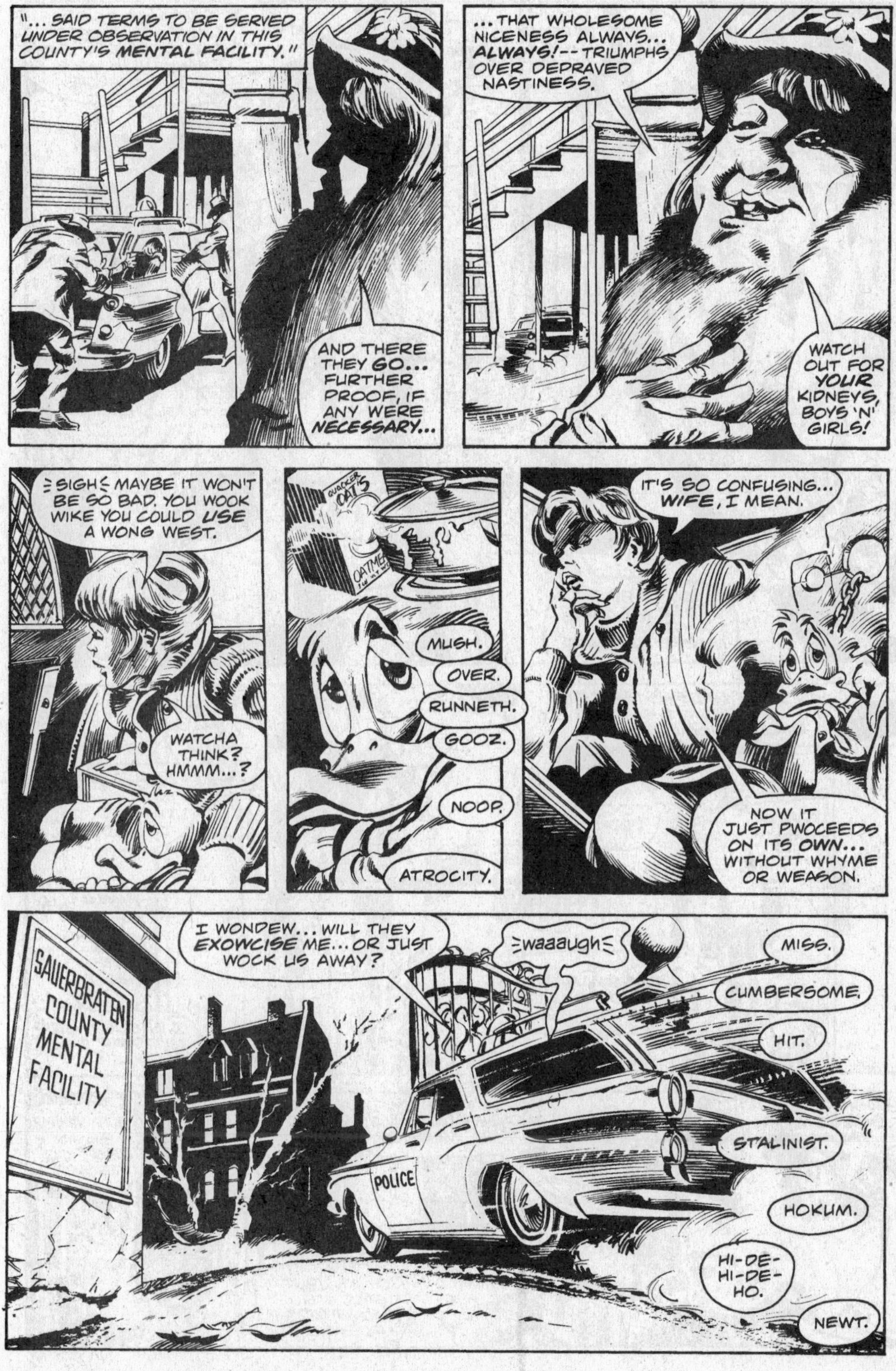
"... SAID TERMS TO BE SERVED UNDER OBSERVATION IN THIS COUNTY'S MENTAL FACILITY."
AND THERE THEY GO... FURTHER PROOF, IF ANY WERE NECESSARY...
...THAT WHOLESOME NICENESS ALWAYS... ALWAYS!--TRIUMPHS OVER DEPRAVED NASTINESS.
WATCH OUT FOR YOUR KIDNEYS, BOYS 'N' GIRLS!
⁼SIGH⁼ MAYBE IT WON'T BE SO BAD. YOU WOOK WIKE YOU COULD USE A WONG WEST.
WATCHA THINK? HMMM...?
QUACKER OATS
OATMEAL
MUSH.
OVER.
RUNNETH.
GOOZ.
NOOP.
ATROCITY.
IT'S SO CONFUSING... WIFE, I MEAN.
NOW IT JUST PWOCEEDS ON ITS OWN... WITHOUT WHYME OR WEASON.
SAUERBRATEN COUNTY MENTAL FACILITY
I WONDEW... WILL THEY EXOWCISE ME... OR JUST WOCK US AWAY?
⁼waaaugh⁼
POLICE
MISS.
CUMBERSOME.
HIT.
STALINIST.
HOKUM.
HI-DE-HI-DE-HO.
NEWT.

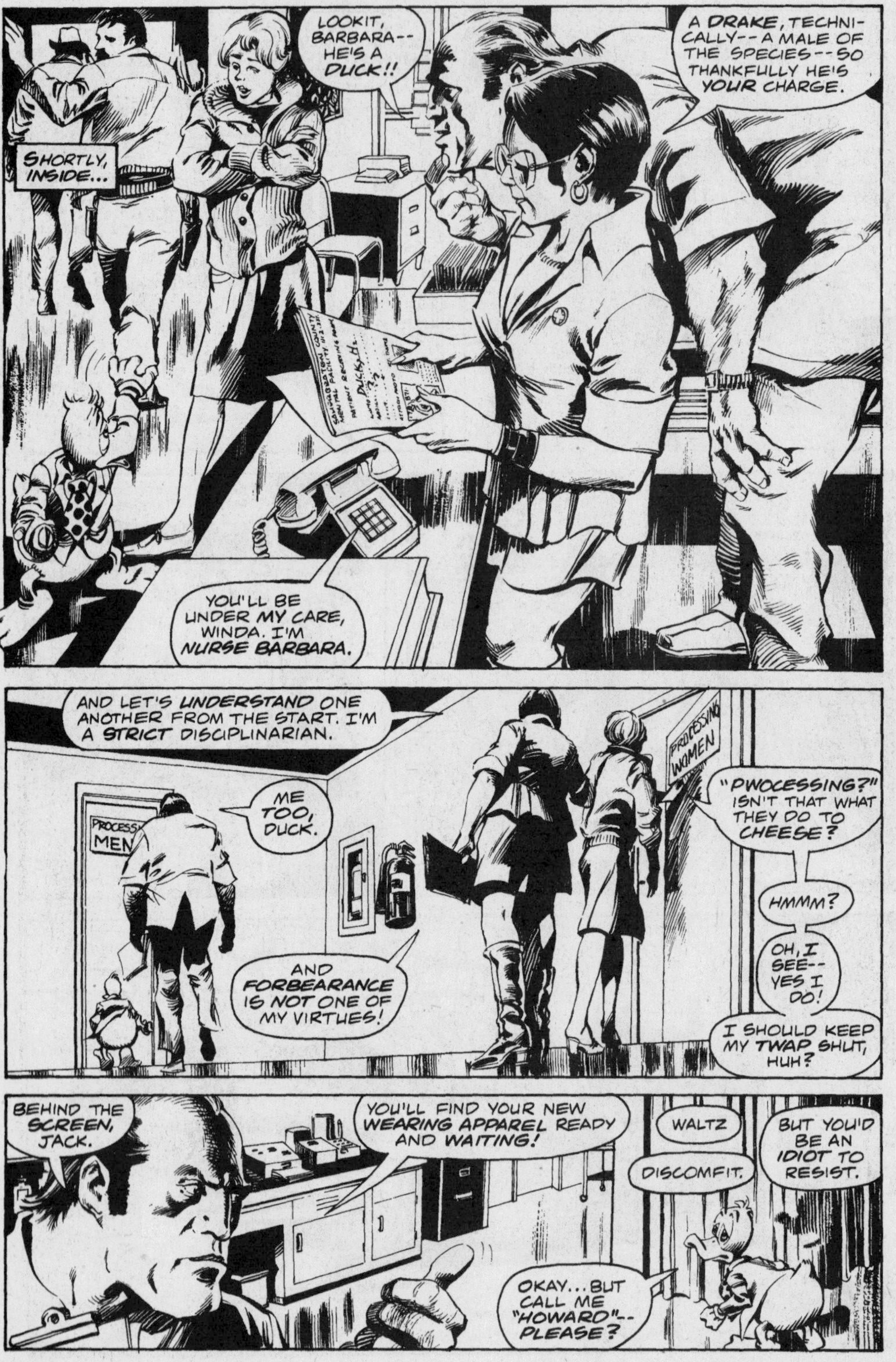

SHORTLY, INSIDE...
LOOKIT, BARBARA-- HE'S A DUCK!!
A DRAKE, TECHNICALLY-- A MALE OF THE SPECIES-- SO THANKFULLY HE'S YOUR CHARGE.
YOU'LL BE UNDER MY CARE, WINDA. I'M NURSE BARBARA.
AND LET'S UNDERSTAND ONE ANOTHER FROM THE START. I'M A STRICT DISCIPLINARIAN.
ME TOO, DUCK.
AND FORBEARANCE IS NOT ONE OF MY VIRTUES!
PROCESSING WOMEN
"PWOCESSING?" ISN'T THAT WHAT THEY DO TO CHEESE?
HMMM?
OH, I SEE-- YES I DO!
I SHOULD KEEP MY TWAP SHUT, HUH?
BEHIND THE SCREEN, JACK.
YOU'LL FIND YOUR NEW WEARING APPAREL READY AND WAITING!
WALTZ
DISCOMFIT.
BUT YOU'D BE AN IDIOT TO RESIST.
OKAY... BUT CALL ME "HOWARD"-- PLEASE?

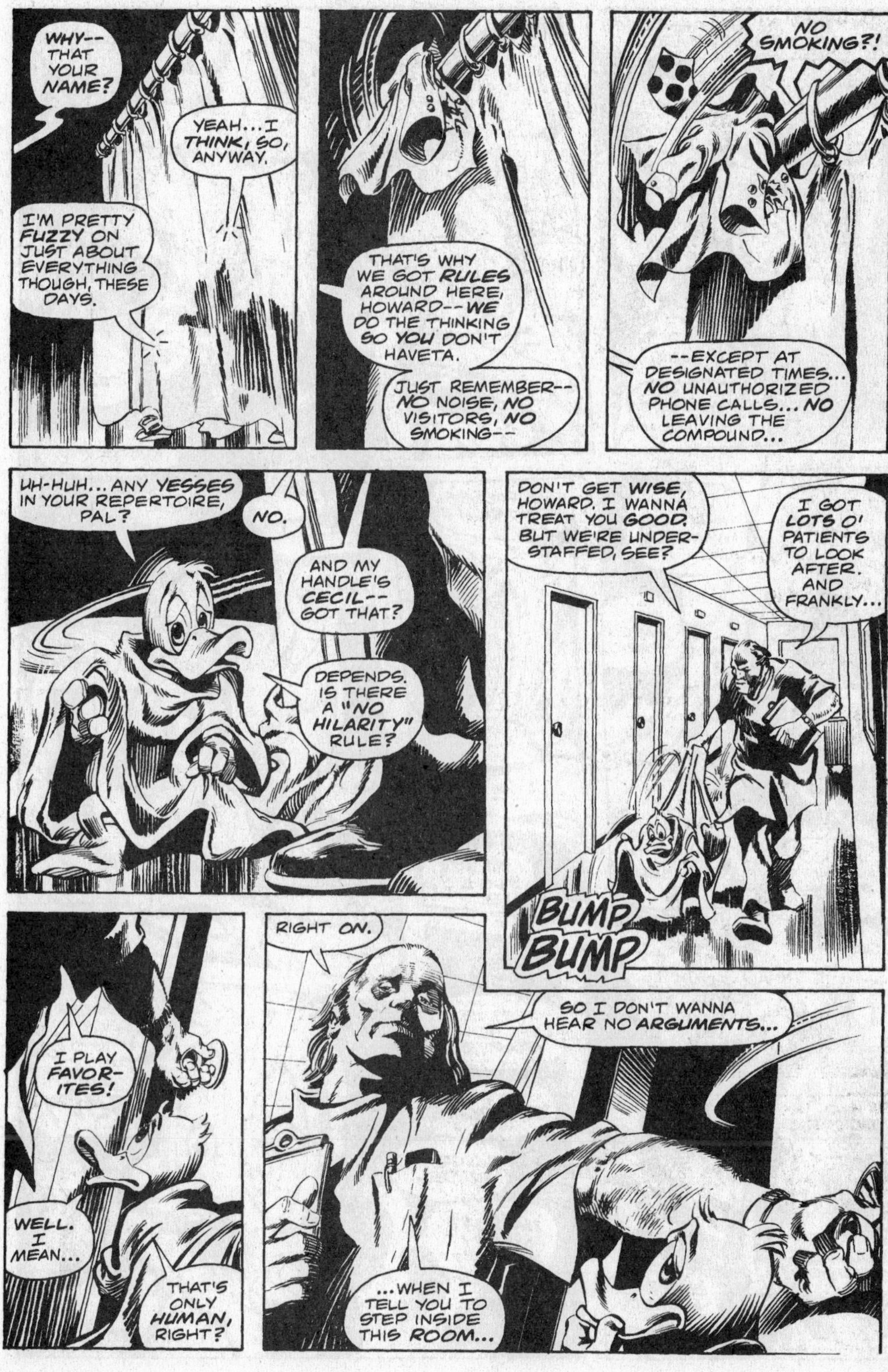
WHY-- THAT YOUR NAME?
YEAH... I THINK, SO, ANYWAY.
I'M PRETTY FUZZY ON JUST ABOUT EVERYTHING THOUGH, THESE DAYS.
THAT'S WHY WE GOT RULES AROUND HERE, HOWARD--WE DO THE THINKING SO YOU DON'T HAVETA.
JUST REMEMBER-- NO NOISE, NO VISITORS, NO SMOKING--
NO SMOKING?!
--EXCEPT AT DESIGNATED TIMES... NO UNAUTHORIZED PHONE CALLS... NO LEAVING THE COMPOUND...
UH-HUH... ANY YESSES IN YOUR REPERTOIRE, PAL?
NO.
AND MY HANDLE'S CECIL-- GOT THAT?
DEPENDS. IS THERE A "NO HILARITY" RULE?
DON'T GET WISE, HOWARD. I WANNA TREAT YOU GOOD. BUT WE'RE UNDER-STAFFED, SEE?
I GOT LOTS O' PATIENTS TO LOOK AFTER. AND FRANKLY...
BUMP BUMP
I PLAY FAVOR-ITES!
WELL. I MEAN...
THAT'S ONLY HUMAN, RIGHT?
RIGHT ON.
SO I DON'T WANNA HEAR NO ARGUMENTS...
...WHEN I TELL YOU TO STEP INSIDE THIS ROOM...

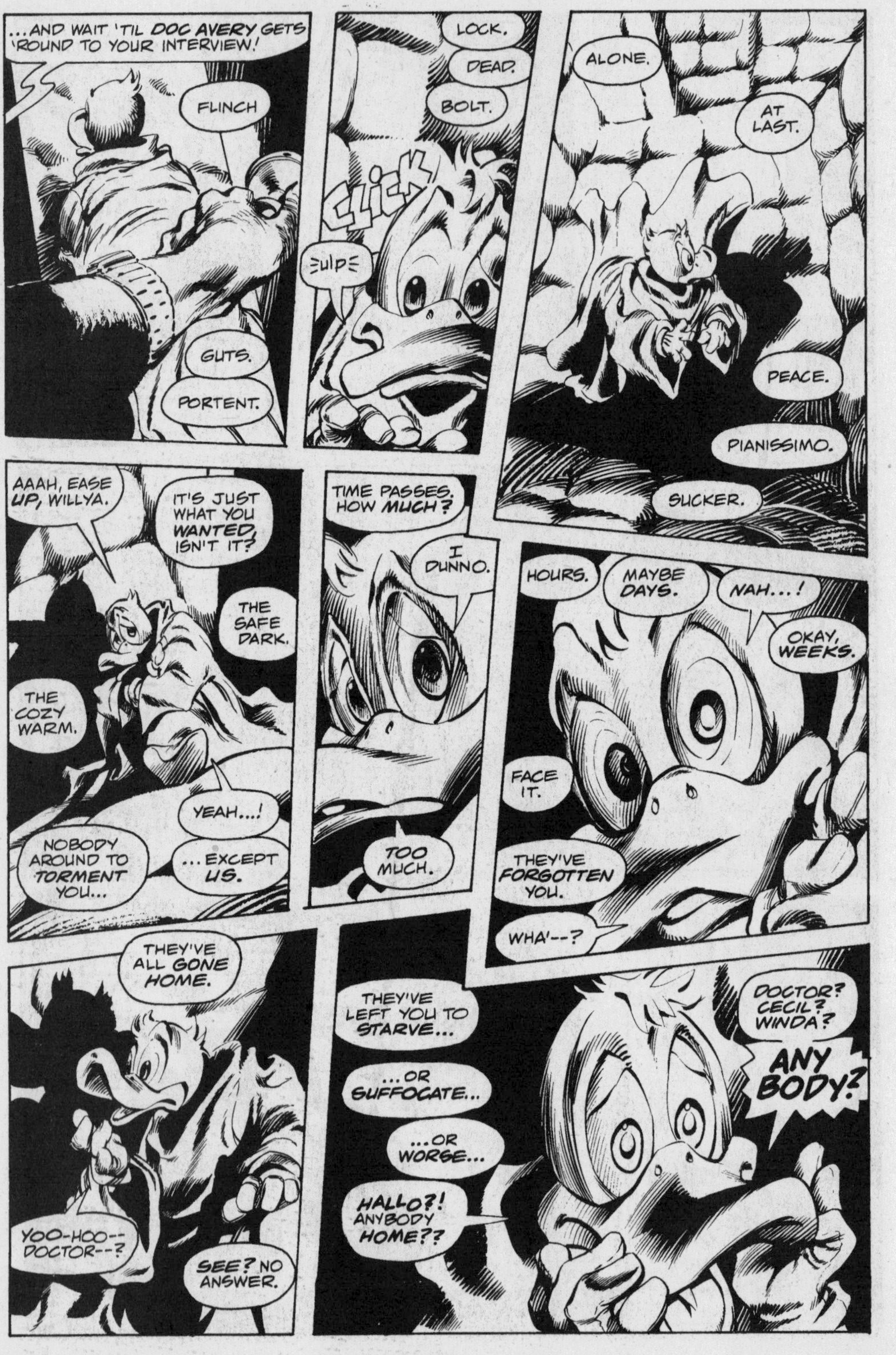

...AND WAIT 'TIL DOC AVERY GETS 'ROUND TO YOUR INTERVIEW!
FLINCH
GUTS.
PORTENT.
LOCK.
DEAD.
BOLT.
CLICK
GULP
ALONE.
AT LAST.
PEACE.
PIANISSIMO.
SUCKER.
AAAH, EASE UP, WILLYA.
IT'S JUST WHAT YOU WANTED, ISN'T IT?
THE SAFE DARK.
THE COZY WARM.
YEAH...!
NOBODY AROUND TO TORMENT YOU...
...EXCEPT US.
TIME PASSES. HOW MUCH?
I DUNNO.
TOO MUCH.
HOURS.
MAYBE DAYS.
NAH...!
OKAY, WEEKS.
FACE IT.
THEY'VE FORGOTTEN YOU.
WHA'--?
THEY'VE ALL GONE HOME.
YOO-HOO-- DOCTOR--?
SEE? NO ANSWER.
THEY'VE LEFT YOU TO STARVE...
...OR SUFFOCATE...
...OR WORSE...
HALLO?! ANYBODY HOME??
DOCTOR? CECIL? WINDA?
ANY BODY?

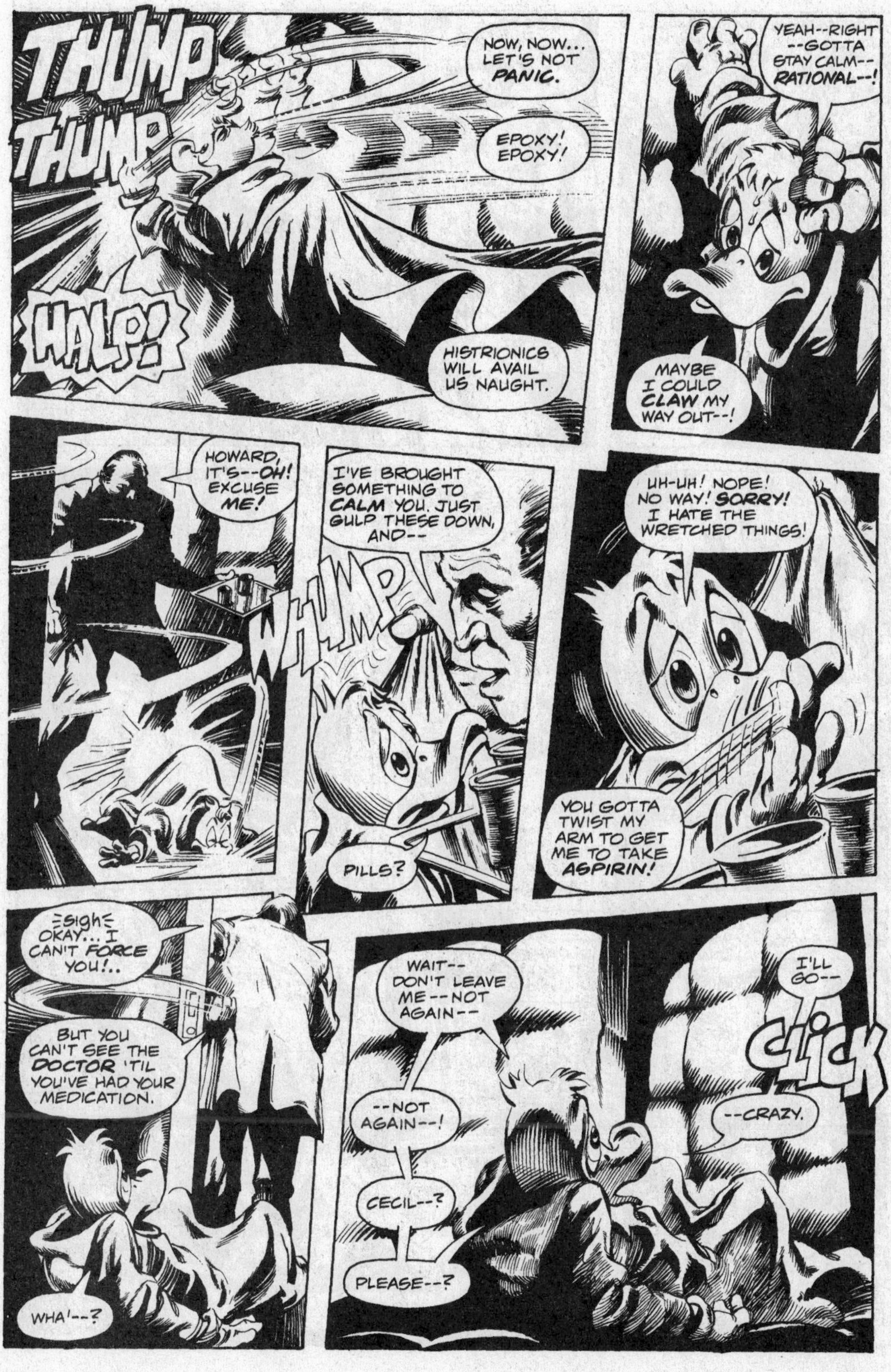
THUMP
THUMP
NOW, NOW... LET'S NOT PANIC.
EPOXY! EPOXY!
HALP!
HISTRIONICS WILL AVAIL US NAUGHT.
YEAH--RIGHT --GOTTA STAY CALM-- RATIONAL--!
MAYBE I COULD CLAW MY WAY OUT--!
HOWARD, IT'S--OH! EXCUSE ME!
I'VE BROUGHT SOMETHING TO CALM YOU. JUST GULP THESE DOWN, AND--
WHUMP
PILLS?
UH-UH! NOPE! NO WAY! SORRY! I HATE THE WRETCHED THINGS!
YOU GOTTA TWIST MY ARM TO GET ME TO TAKE ASPIRIN!
≈SIGH≈ OKAY... I CAN'T FORCE YOU!..
BUT YOU CAN'T SEE THE DOCTOR 'TIL YOU'VE HAD YOUR MEDICATION.
WHA'--?
WAIT-- DON'T LEAVE ME--NOT AGAIN--
--NOT AGAIN--!
CECIL--?
PLEASE--?
I'LL GO--
CLICK
--CRAZY.

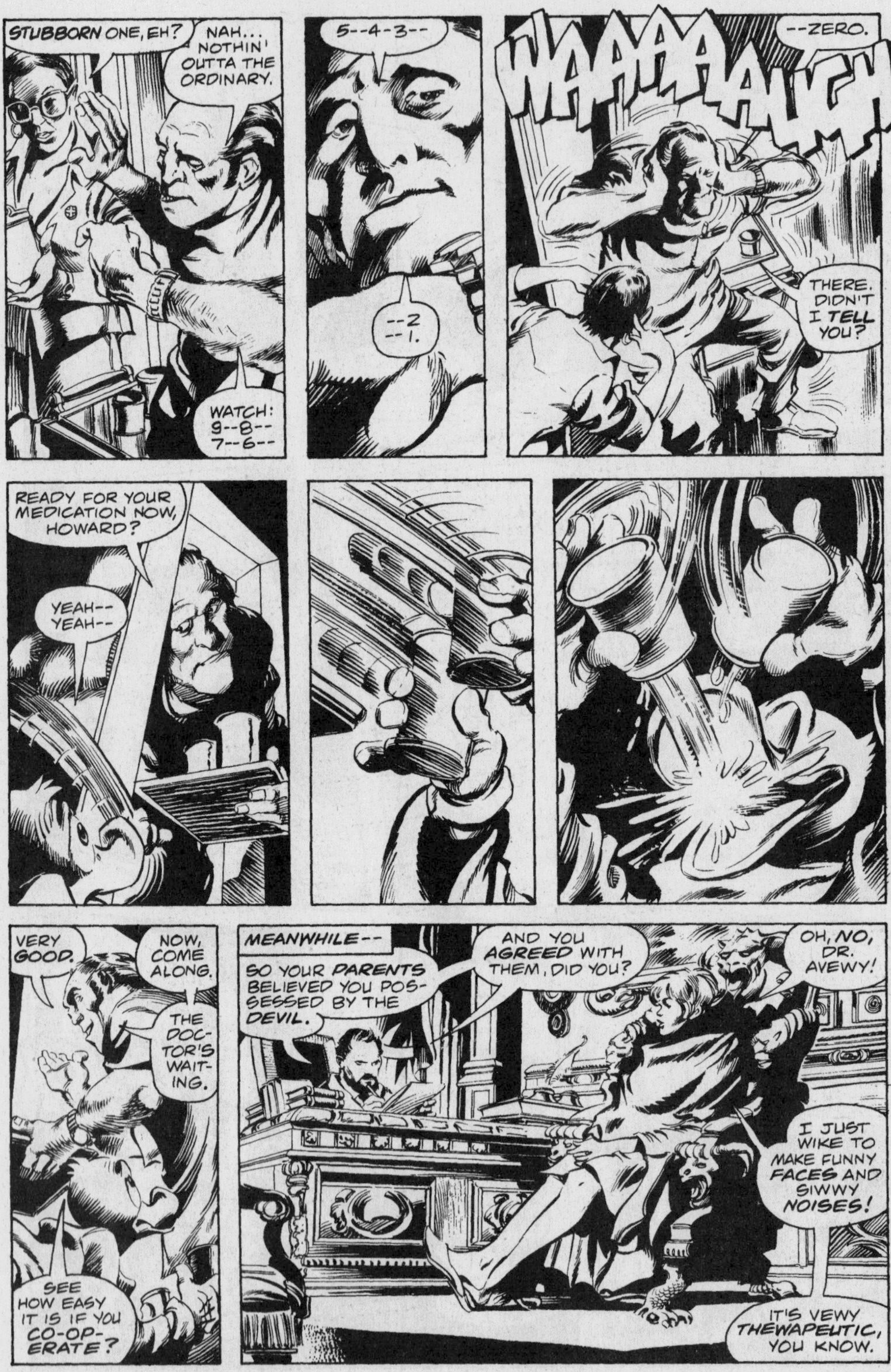
STUBBORN ONE, EH?
NAH... NOTHIN' OUTTA THE ORDINARY.
WATCH: 9--8-- 7--6--
5--4-3--
--2 --1.
WAAAAAAUGH
--ZERO.
THERE. DIDN'T I TELL YOU?
READY FOR YOUR MEDICATION NOW, HOWARD?
YEAH-- YEAH--
VERY GOOD.
NOW, COME ALONG.
THE DOC-TOR'S WAIT-ING.
SEE HOW EASY IT IS IF YOU CO-OP-ERATE?
MEANWHILE--
SO YOUR PARENTS BELIEVED YOU POS-SESSED BY THE DEVIL.
AND YOU AGREED WITH THEM, DID YOU?
OH, NO, DR. AVEWY!
I JUST WIKE TO MAKE FUNNY FACES AND SIWWY NOISES!
IT'S VEWY THEWAPEUTIC, YOU KNOW.

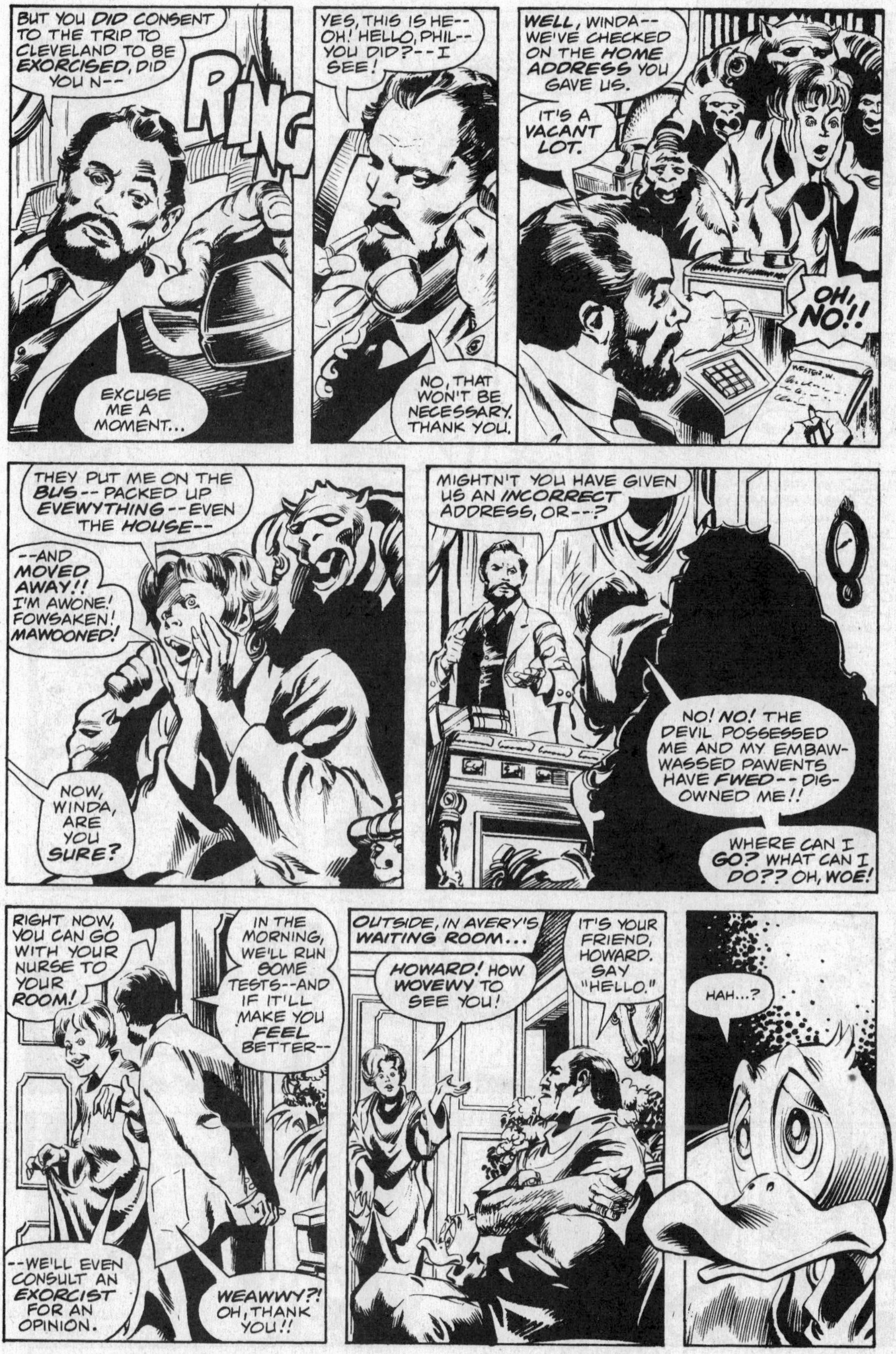

BUT YOU DID CONSENT TO THE TRIP TO CLEVELAND TO BE EXORCISED, DID YOU N--
RING
EXCUSE ME A MOMENT...
YES, THIS IS HE-- OH! HELLO, PHIL-- YOU DID?--I SEE!
NO, THAT WON'T BE NECESSARY. THANK YOU.
WELL, WINDA-- WE'VE CHECKED ON THE HOME ADDRESS YOU GAVE US.
IT'S A VACANT LOT.
OH, NO!!
THEY PUT ME ON THE BUS--PACKED UP EVEWYTHING--EVEN THE HOUSE--
--AND MOVED AWAY!! I'M AWONE! FOWSAKEN! MAWOONED!
NOW, WINDA, ARE YOU SURE?
MIGHTN'T YOU HAVE GIVEN US AN INCORRECT ADDRESS, OR--?
NO! NO! THE DEVIL POSSESSED ME AND MY EMBAWWASSED PAWENTS HAVE FWED--DISOWNED ME!!
WHERE CAN I GO? WHAT CAN I DO?? OH, WOE!
RIGHT NOW, YOU CAN GO WITH YOUR NURSE TO YOUR ROOM!
IN THE MORNING, WE'LL RUN SOME TESTS--AND IF IT'LL MAKE YOU FEEL BETTER--
--WE'LL EVEN CONSULT AN EXORCIST FOR AN OPINION.
WEAWWY?! OH, THANK YOU!!
OUTSIDE, IN AVERY'S WAITING ROOM...
HOWARD! HOW WOVEWY TO SEE YOU!
IT'S YOUR FRIEND, HOWARD. SAY "HELLO."
HAH...?

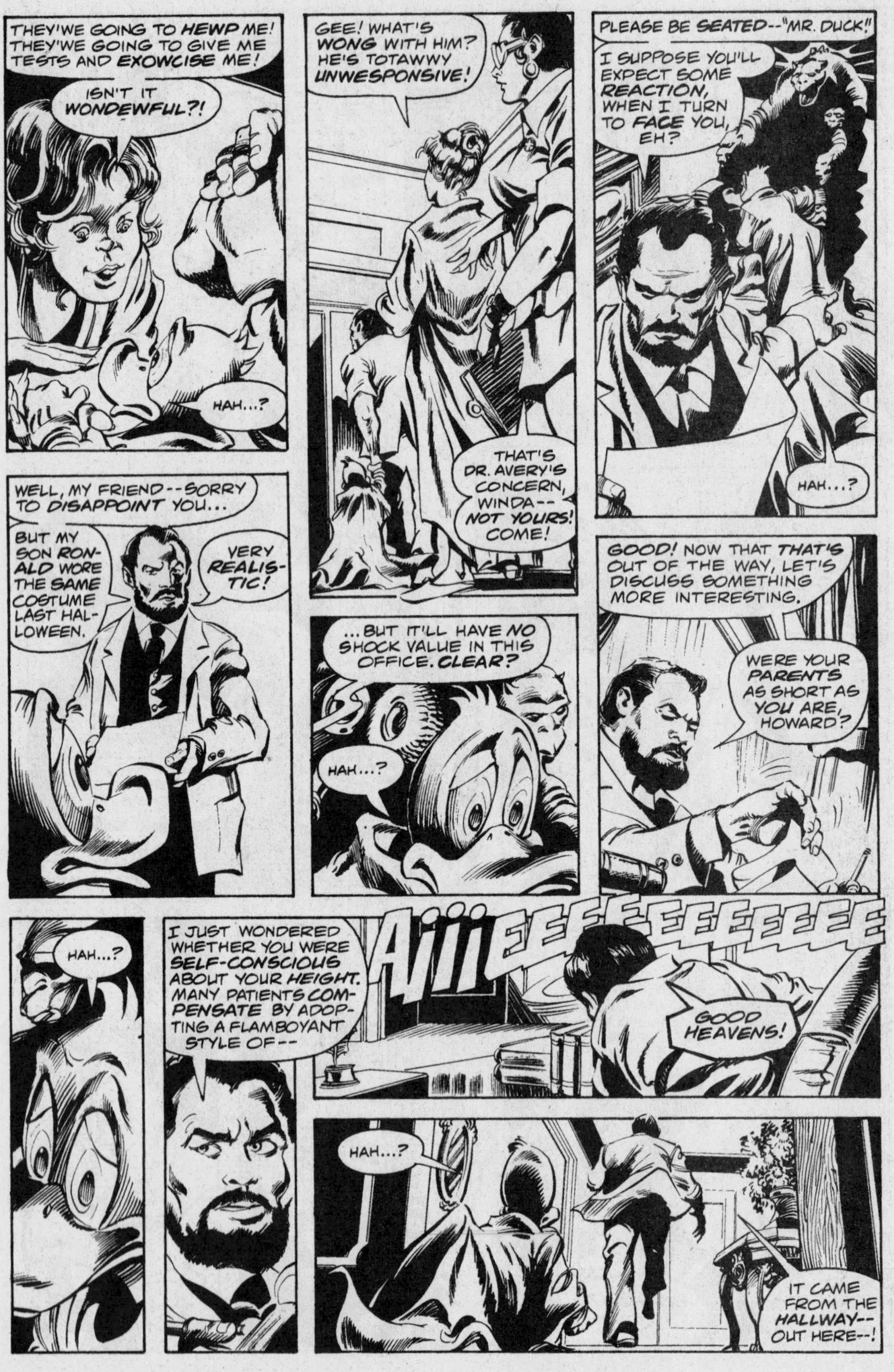
THEY'WE GOING TO HEWP ME! THEY'WE GOING TO GIVE ME TESTS AND EXOWCISE ME!
ISN'T IT WONDEWFUL?!
HAH...?
GEE! WHAT'S WONG WITH HIM? HE'S TOTAWWY UNWESPONSIVE!
THAT'S DR. AVERY'S CONCERN, WINDA-- NOT YOURS! COME!
PLEASE BE SEATED--"MR. DUCK!"
I SUPPOSE YOU'LL EXPECT SOME REACTION, WHEN I TURN TO FACE YOU, EH?
HAH...?
WELL, MY FRIEND--SORRY TO DISAPPOINT YOU...
BUT MY SON RONALD WORE THE SAME COSTUME LAST HALLOWEEN.
VERY REALISTIC!
...BUT IT'LL HAVE NO SHOCK VALUE IN THIS OFFICE. CLEAR?
HAH...?
GOOD! NOW THAT THAT'S OUT OF THE WAY, LET'S DISCUSS SOMETHING MORE INTERESTING.
WERE YOUR PARENTS AS SHORT AS YOU ARE, HOWARD?
HAH...?
I JUST WONDERED WHETHER YOU WERE SELF-CONSCIOUS ABOUT YOUR HEIGHT. MANY PATIENTS COMPENSATE BY ADOPTING A FLAMBOYANT STYLE OF--
AIIIEEEEEEEEEEEE
GOOD HEAVENS!
HAH...?
IT CAME FROM THE HALLWAY-- OUT HERE--!

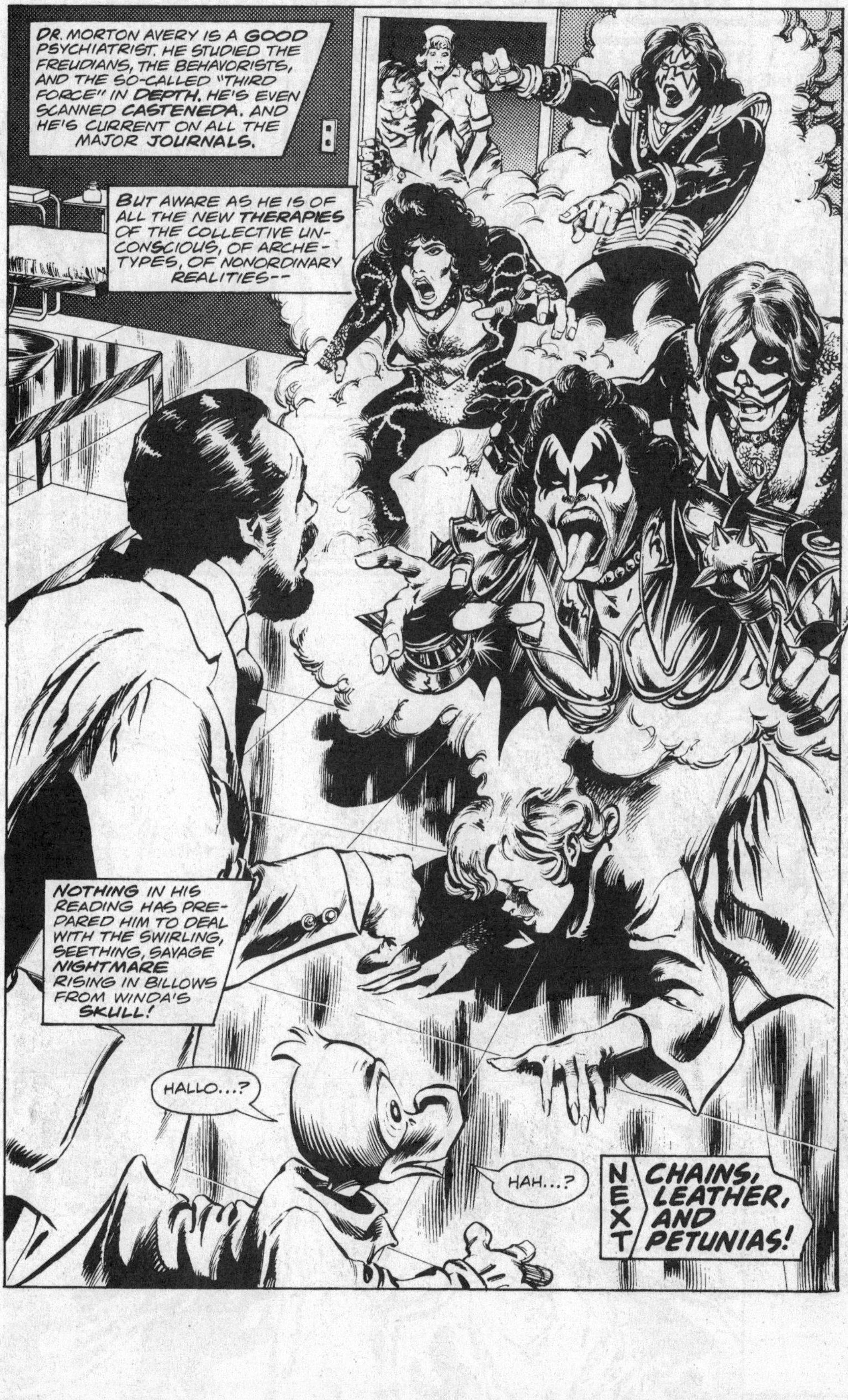
DR. MORTON AVERY IS A GOOD PSYCHIATRIST. HE STUDIED THE FREUDIANS, THE BEHAVORISTS, AND THE SO-CALLED "THIRD FORCE" IN DEPTH. HE'S EVEN SCANNED CASTENEDA. AND HE'S CURRENT ON ALL THE MAJOR JOURNALS.
BUT AWARE AS HE IS OF ALL THE NEW THERAPIES OF THE COLLECTIVE UNCONSCIOUS, OF ARCHETYPES, OF NONORDINARY REALITIES--
NOTHING IN HIS READING HAS PREPARED HIM TO DEAL WITH THE SWIRLING, SEETHING, SAVAGE NIGHTMARE RISING IN BILLOWS FROM WINDA'S SKULL!
HALLO...?
HAH...?
NEXT CHAINS, LEATHER, AND PETUNIAS!

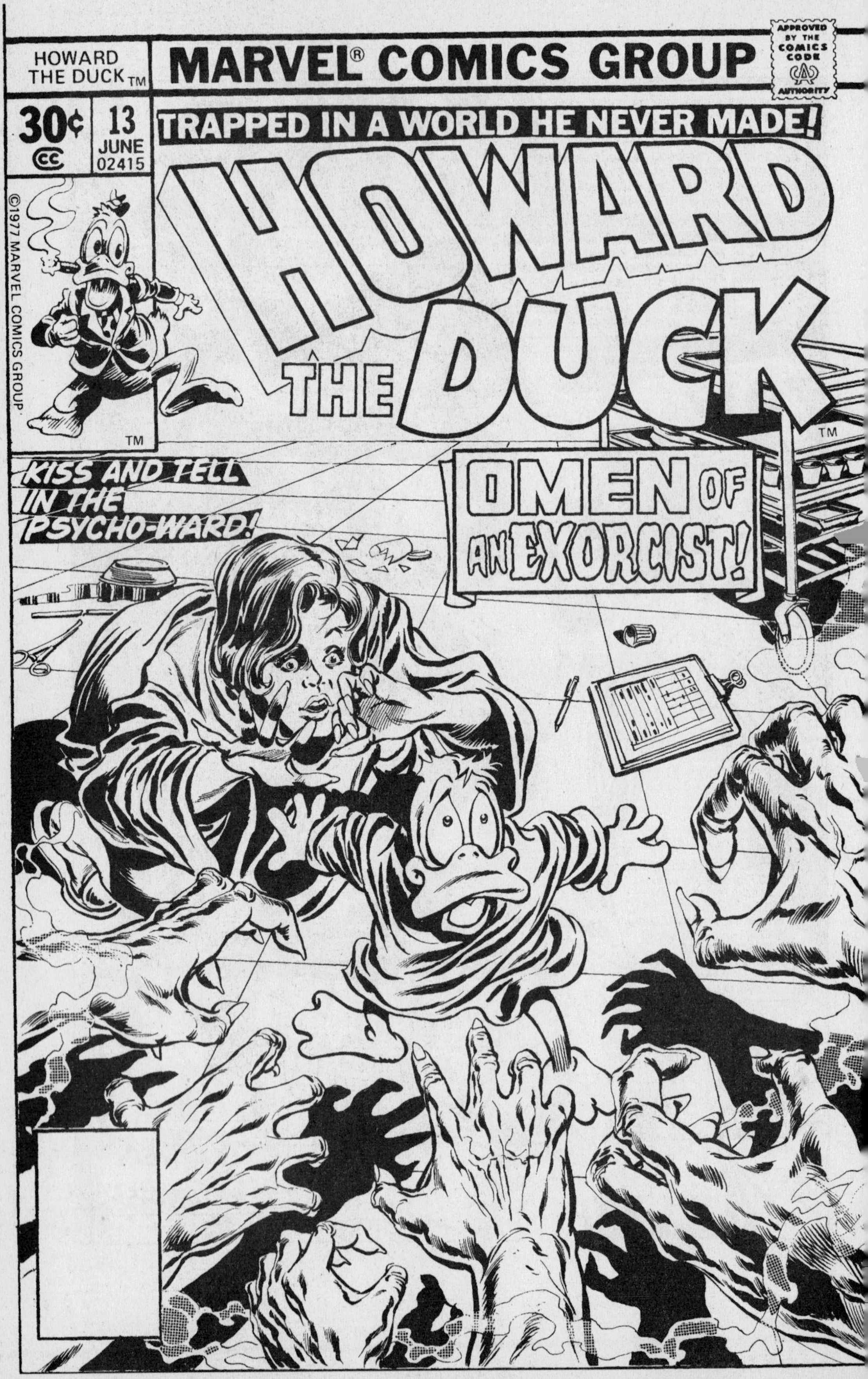

HOWARD THE DUCK TM
MARVEL® COMICS GROUP
APPROVED BY THE COMICS CODE AUTHORITY
30¢
13
JUNE
02415
TRAPPED IN A WORLD HE NEVER MADE!
HOWARD THE DUCK
©1977 MARVEL COMICS GROUP
KISS AND TELL IN THE PSYCHO-WARD!
OMEN OF AN EXORCIST!

From the time of his hatching, he was...different. A potentially brilliant scholar who dreaded the structured environment of school, he educated himself in the streets, taking whatever work was available, formulating his philosophy of self from what he learned of the world about him. And then the Cosmic Axis shifted...and that world *changed*. Suddenly, he was stranded in a universe he could not fathom. Without warning, he became a strange fowl in an even stranger land.

Stan Lee PRESENTS: HOWARD THE DUCK!™

STEVE GERBER WRITER/EDITOR   **GENE COLAN** ARTIST   **STEVE LEIALOHA** INKER   **JIM NOVAK,** LETTERER   **JAN COHEN,** COLORIST

WELCOME TO THE CORRIDORS OF THE LOCAL *MENTAL* FACILITY! ORDINARILY, THE AMBIENCE IN THESE HALLWAYS IS AS HEAVILY *SEDATED* AS THE PATIENTS.

BUT NOT TODAY.

TODAY, IT'S *PARTY TIME!* THE RIGIDLY-ENFORCED TRANQUILITY HAS BEEN *SHATTERED* BY THE EMERGENCE OF FOUR SILVER-AND-BLACK *BAROQUES* FROM WINDA WESTER'S *HEAD!*

HAH...?

AW-RIIIGHT! SAUERBRATEN COUNTY, OHIO-- LET THIS OLD *COSMOS*...

ROCK, ROLL OVER, AND WRITHE!

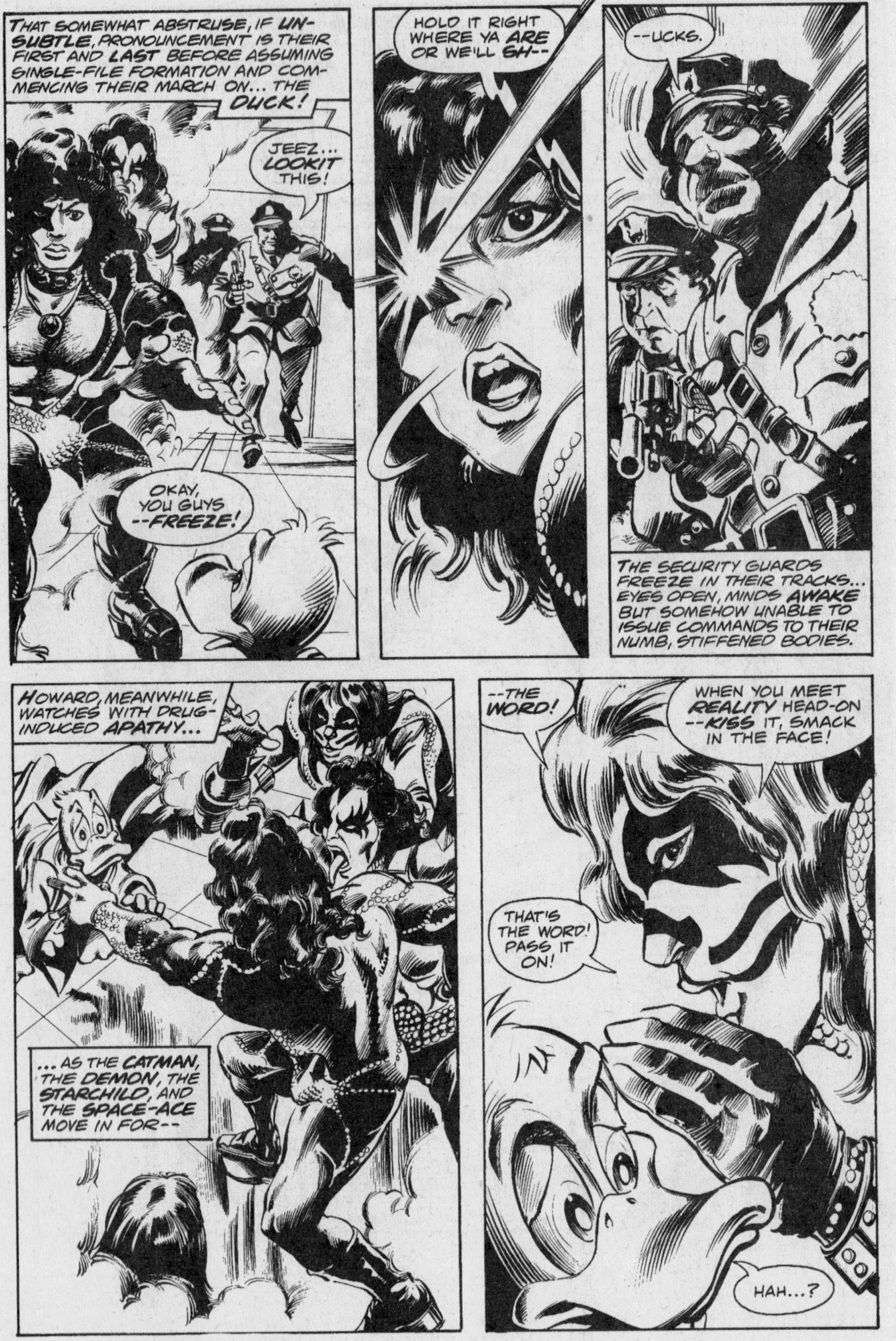
THAT SOMEWHAT ABSTRUSE, IF UN-SUBTLE, PRONOUNCEMENT IS THEIR FIRST AND LAST BEFORE ASSUMING SINGLE-FILE FORMATION AND COM-MENCING THEIR MARCH ON... THE DUCK!
JEEZ... LOOKIT THIS!
OKAY, YOU GUYS --FREEZE!
HOLD IT RIGHT WHERE YA ARE OR WE'LL SH--
--UCKS.
THE SECURITY GUARDS FREEZE IN THEIR TRACKS... EYES OPEN, MINDS AWAKE BUT SOMEHOW UNABLE TO ISSUE COMMANDS TO THEIR NUMB, STIFFENED BODIES.
HOWARD, MEANWHILE, WATCHES WITH DRUG-INDUCED APATHY...
... AS THE CATMAN, THE DEMON, THE STARCHILD, AND THE SPACE-ACE MOVE IN FOR--
--THE WORD!
WHEN YOU MEET REALITY HEAD-ON --KISS IT, SMACK IN THE FACE!
THAT'S THE WORD! PASS IT ON!
HAH...?

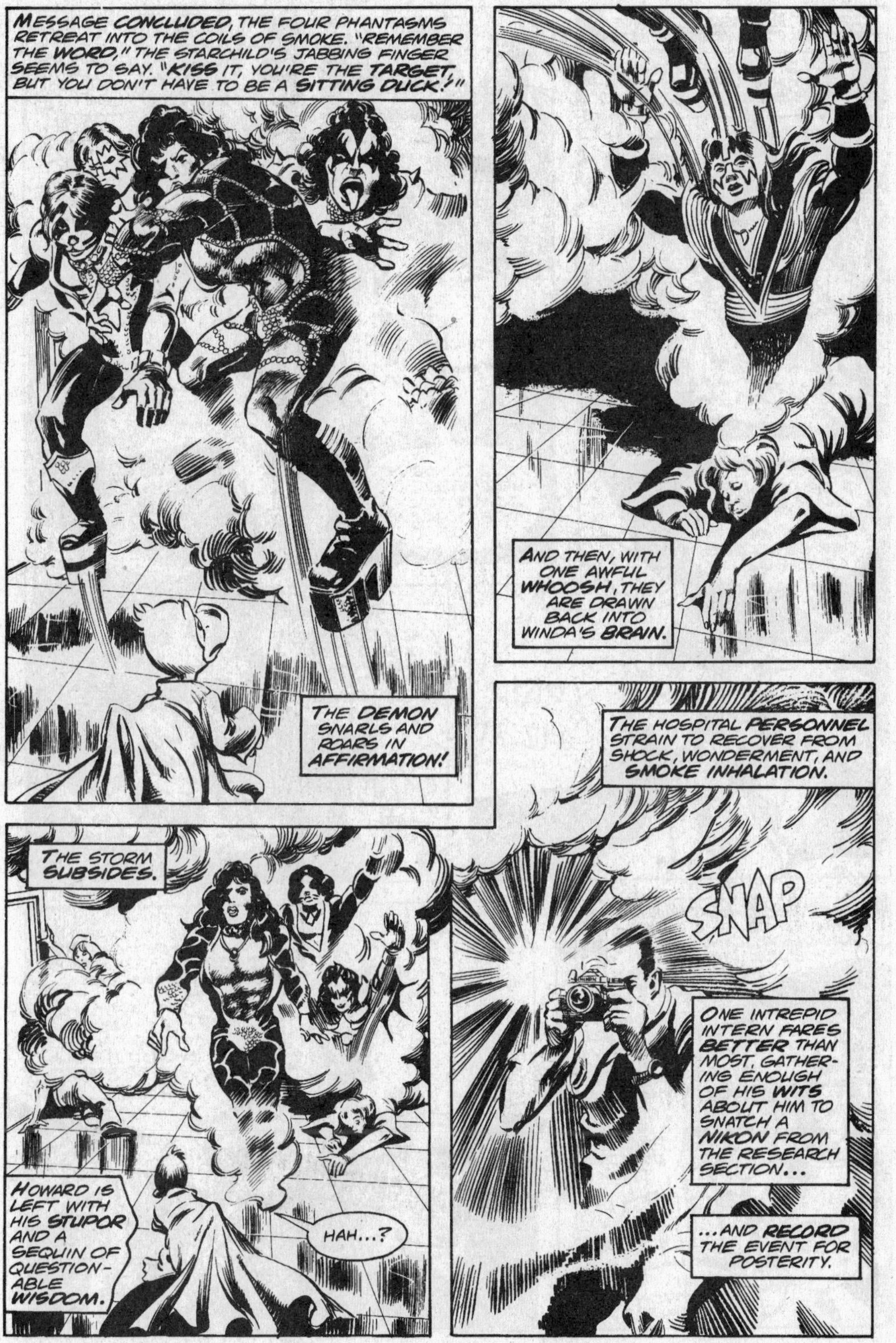
MESSAGE CONCLUDED, THE FOUR PHANTASMS RETREAT INTO THE COILS OF SMOKE. "REMEMBER THE WORD," THE STARCHILD'S JABBING FINGER SEEMS TO SAY. "KISS IT, YOU'RE THE TARGET, BUT YOU DON'T HAVE TO BE A SITTING DUCK!"
THE DEMON SNARLS AND ROARS IN AFFIRMATION!
AND THEN, WITH ONE AWFUL WHOOSH, THEY ARE DRAWN BACK INTO WINDA'S BRAIN.
THE HOSPITAL PERSONNEL STRAIN TO RECOVER FROM SHOCK, WONDERMENT, AND SMOKE INHALATION.
THE STORM SUBSIDES.
HOWARD IS LEFT WITH HIS STUPOR AND A SEQUIN OF QUESTION-ABLE WISDOM.
HAH...?
SNAP
ONE INTREPID INTERN FARES BETTER THAN MOST, GATHER-ING ENOUGH OF HIS WITS ABOUT HIM TO SNATCH A NIKON FROM THE RESEARCH SECTION...
...AND RECORD THE EVENT FOR POSTERITY.

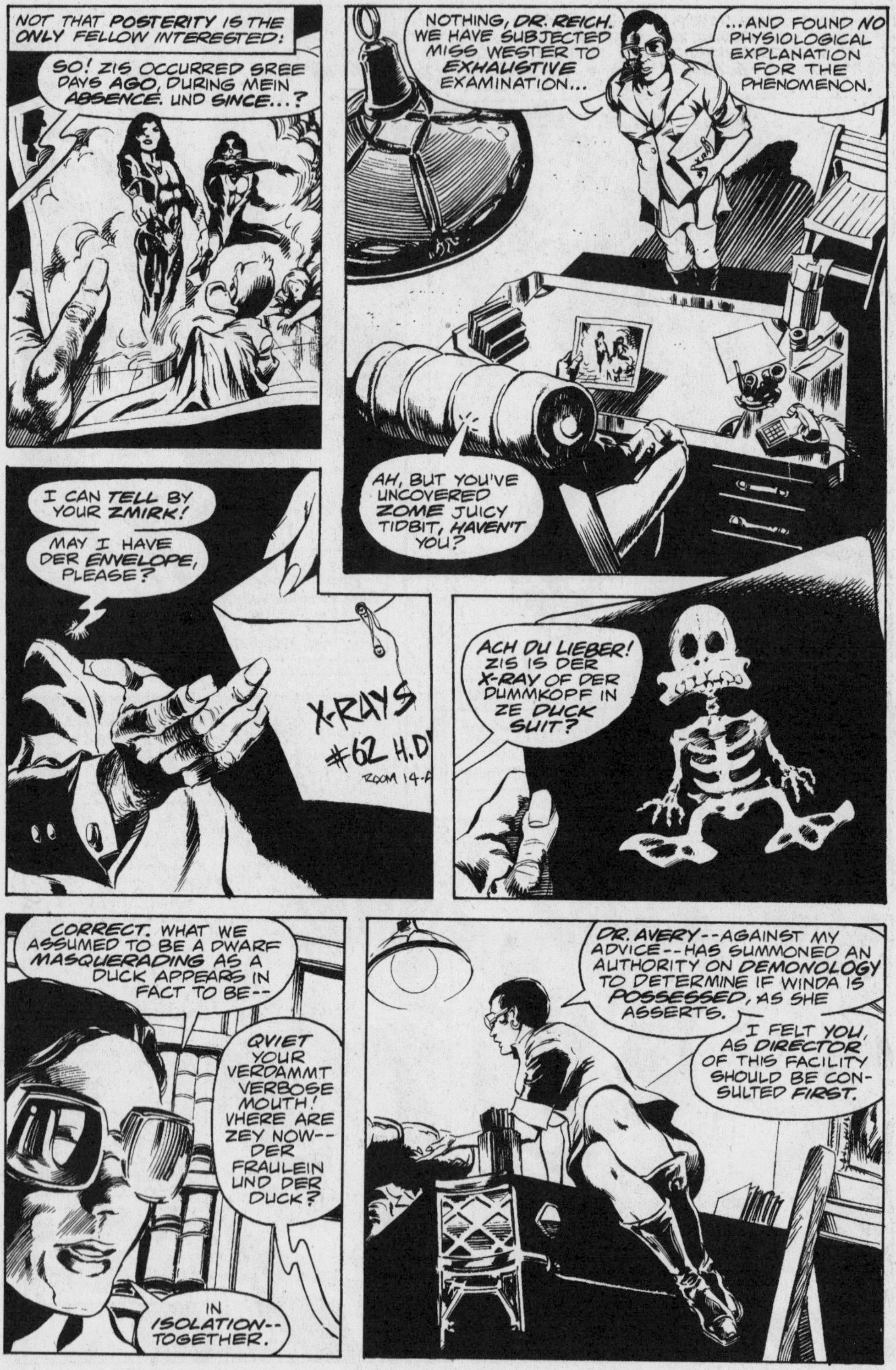
NOT THAT POSTERITY IS THE ONLY FELLOW INTERESTED:
SO! ZIS OCCURRED SREE DAYS AGO, DURING MEIN ABSENCE. UND SINCE...?
NOTHING, DR. REICH. WE HAVE SUBJECTED MISS WESTER TO EXHAUSTIVE EXAMINATION...
...AND FOUND NO PHYSIOLOGICAL EXPLANATION FOR THE PHENOMENON.
AH, BUT YOU'VE UNCOVERED ZOME JUICY TIDBIT, HAVEN'T YOU?
I CAN TELL BY YOUR ZMIRK!
MAY I HAVE DER ENVELOPE, PLEASE?
X-RAYS #62 H.D. ROOM 14-A
ACH DU LIEBER! ZIS IS DER X-RAY OF DER DUMMKOPF IN ZE DUCK SUIT?
CORRECT. WHAT WE ASSUMED TO BE A DWARF MASQUERADING AS A DUCK APPEARS IN FACT TO BE--
QVIET YOUR VERDAMMT VERBOSE MOUTH! VHERE ARE ZEY NOW--DER FRAULEIN UND DER DUCK?
IN ISOLATION--TOGETHER.
DR. AVERY--AGAINST MY ADVICE--HAS SUMMONED AN AUTHORITY ON DEMONOLOGY TO DETERMINE IF WINDA IS POSSESSED, AS SHE ASSERTS.
I FELT YOU, AS DIRECTOR OF THIS FACILITY SHOULD BE CONSULTED FIRST.

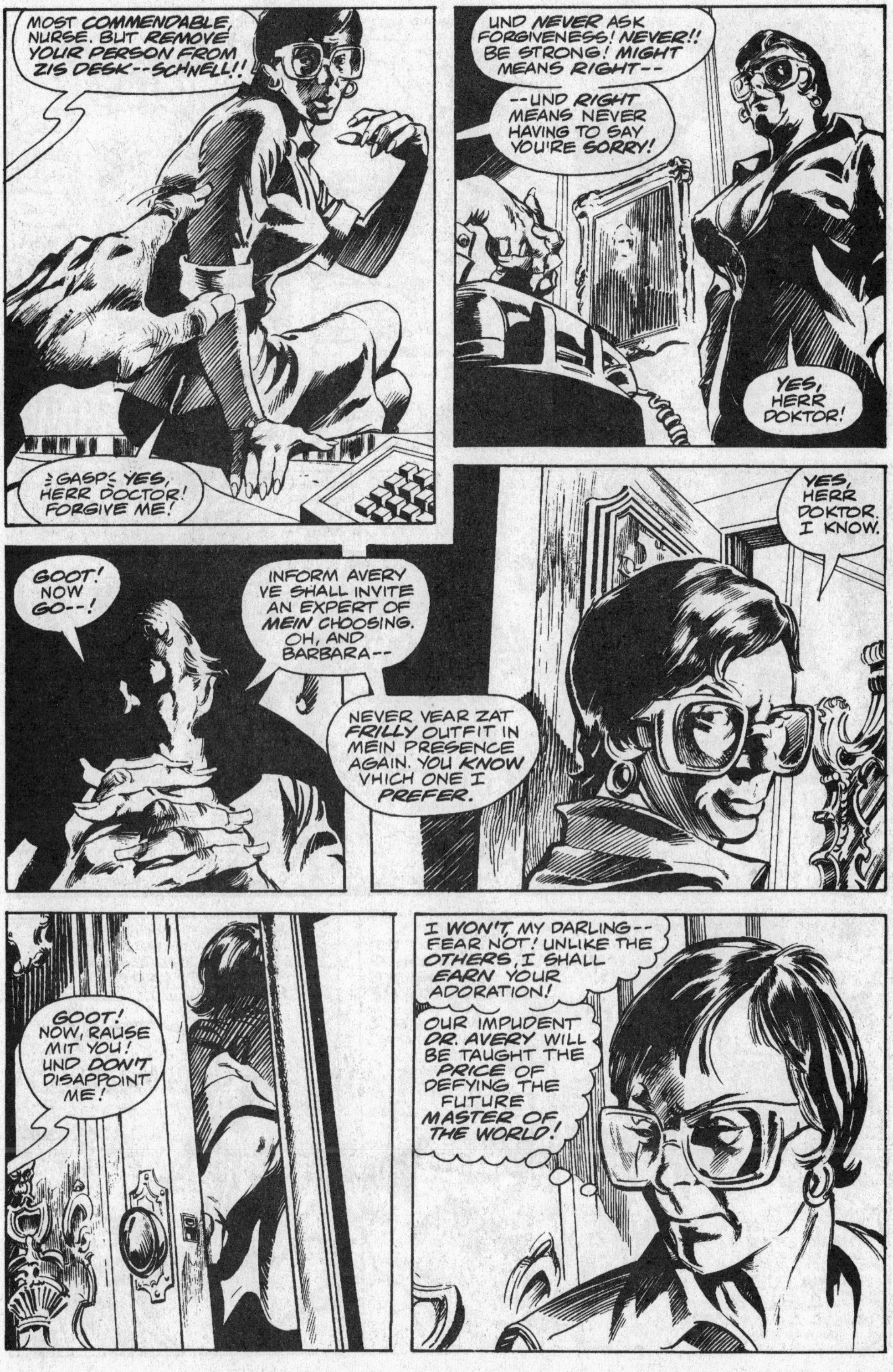
MOST COMMENDABLE, NURSE. BUT REMOVE YOUR PERSON FROM ZIS DESK--SCHNELL!!
≷GASP≶ YES, HERR DOCTOR! FORGIVE ME!
UND NEVER ASK FORGIVENESS! NEVER!! BE STRONG! MIGHT MEANS RIGHT--
--UND RIGHT MEANS NEVER HAVING TO SAY YOU'RE SORRY!
YES, HERR DOKTOR!
GOOT! NOW GO--!
INFORM AVERY VE SHALL INVITE AN EXPERT OF MEIN CHOOSING. OH, AND BARBARA--
NEVER VEAR ZAT FRILLY OUTFIT IN MEIN PRESENCE AGAIN. YOU KNOW VHICH ONE I PREFER.
YES, HERR DOKTOR. I KNOW.
GOOT! NOW, RAUSE MIT YOU! UND DON'T DISAPPOINT ME!
I WON'T, MY DARLING-- FEAR NOT! UNLIKE THE OTHERS, I SHALL EARN YOUR ADORATION!
OUR IMPUDENT DR. AVERY WILL BE TAUGHT THE PRICE OF DEFYING THE FUTURE MASTER OF THE WORLD!

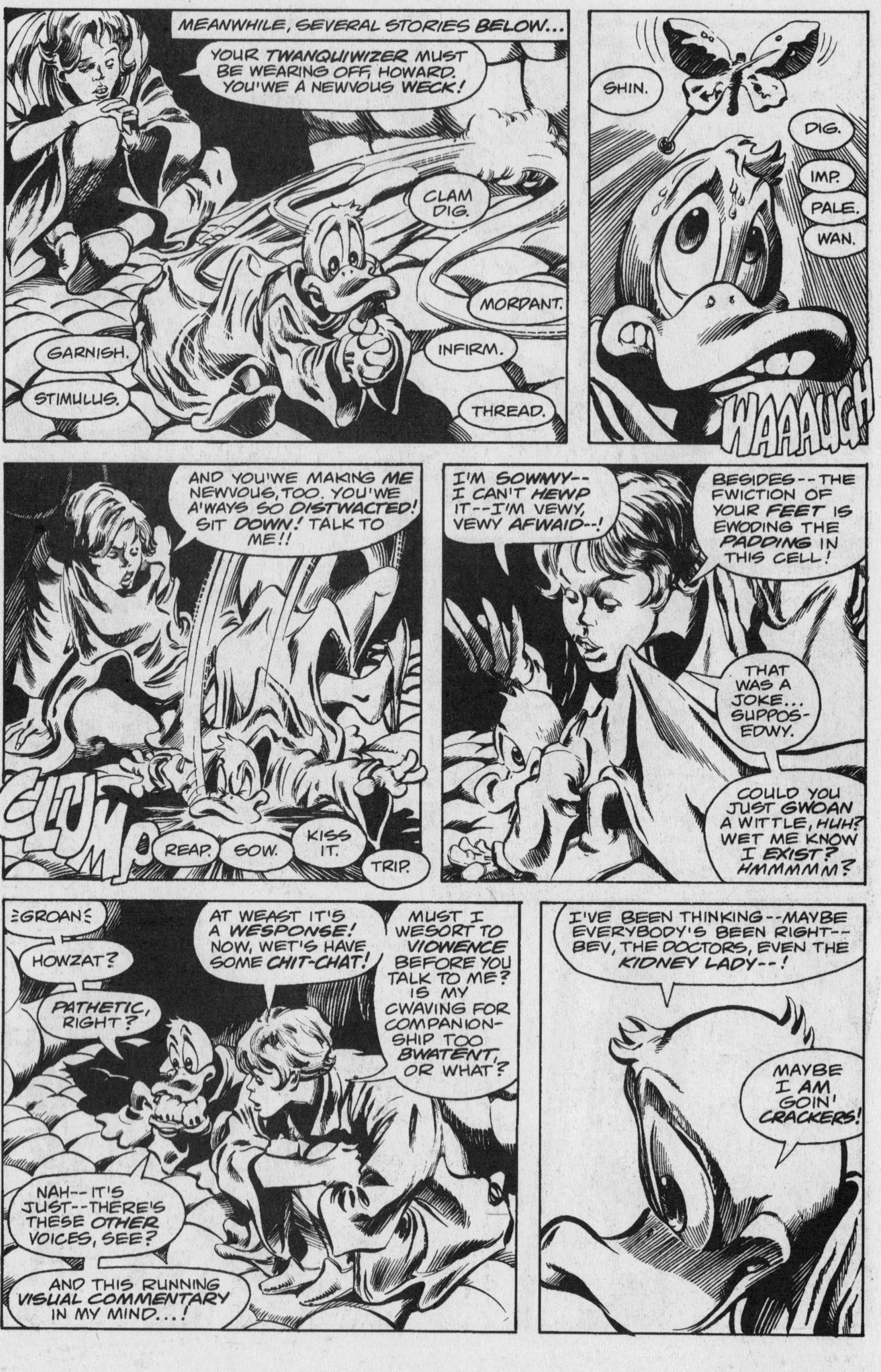
MEANWHILE, SEVERAL STORIES BELOW...
YOUR TWANQUIWIZER MUST BE WEARING OFF, HOWARD. YOU'WE A NEWVOUS WECK!
CLAM DIG.
MORDANT.
GARNISH.
INFIRM.
STIMULUS.
THREAD.
SHIN.
DIG.
IMP.
PALE.
WAN.
WAAAUGH
AND YOU'WE MAKING ME NEWVOUS, TOO. YOU'WE A'WAYS SO DISTWACTED! SIT DOWN! TALK TO ME!!
CLUMP
REAP.
SOW.
KISS IT.
TRIP.
I'M SOWWY-- I CAN'T HEWP IT--I'M VEWY, VEWY AFWAID--!
BESIDES--THE FWICTION OF YOUR FEET IS EWODING THE PADDING IN THIS CELL!
THAT WAS A JOKE... SUPPOS-EDWY.
COULD YOU JUST GWOAN A WITTLE, HUH? WET ME KNOW I EXIST? HMMMMM?
GROAN
HOWZAT?
PATHETIC, RIGHT?
AT WEAST IT'S A WESPONSE! NOW, WET'S HAVE SOME CHIT-CHAT!
MUST I WESORT TO VIOWENCE BEFORE YOU TALK TO ME? IS MY CWAVING FOR COMPANION-SHIP TOO BWATENT, OR WHAT?
NAH--IT'S JUST--THERE'S THESE OTHER VOICES, SEE?
AND THIS RUNNING VISUAL COMMENTARY IN MY MIND...!
I'VE BEEN THINKING--MAYBE EVERYBODY'S BEEN RIGHT-- BEV, THE DOCTORS, EVEN THE KIDNEY LADY--!
MAYBE I AM GOIN' CRACKERS!

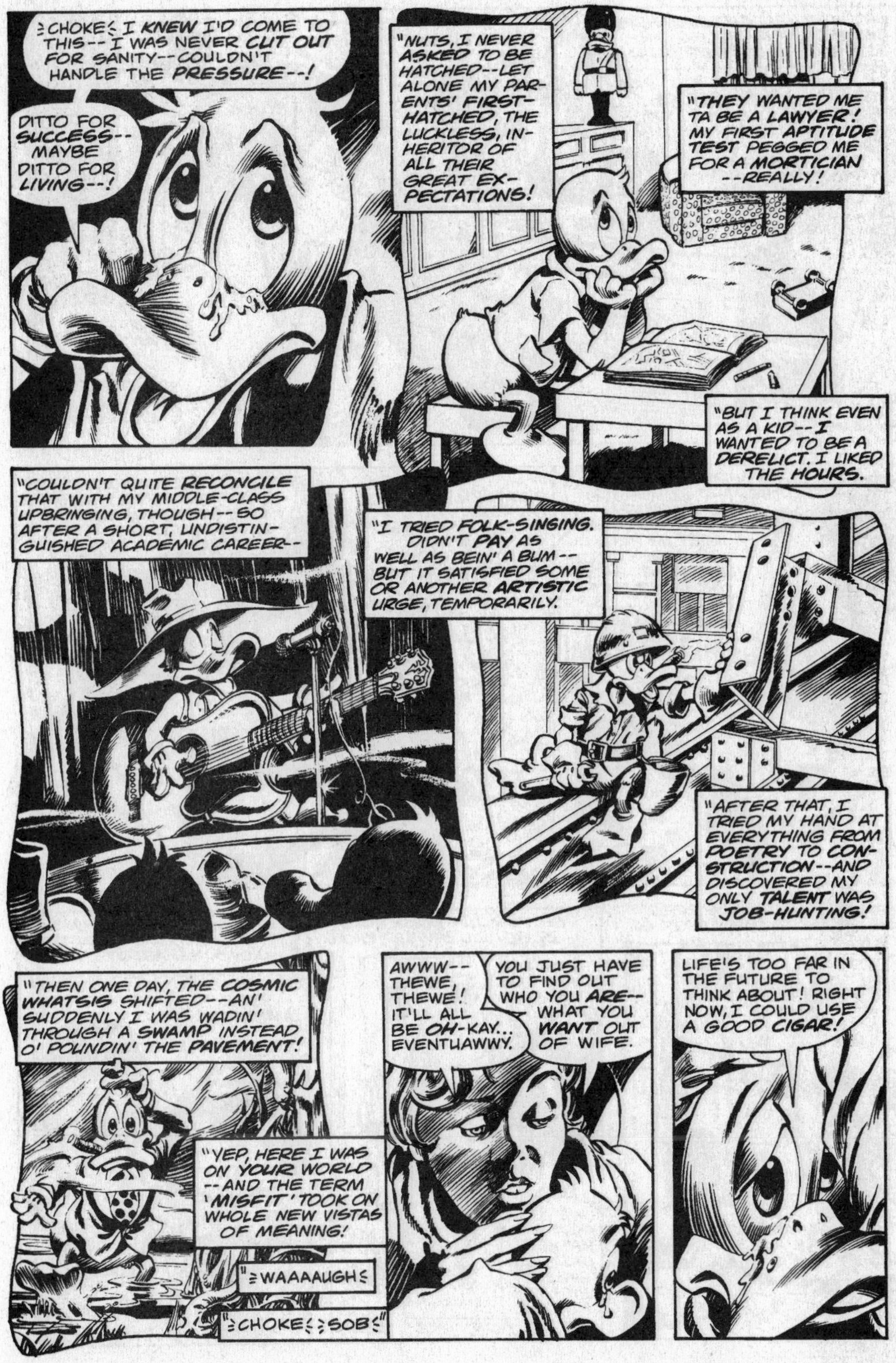

≥CHOKE≤ I KNEW I'D COME TO THIS-- I WAS NEVER CUT OUT FOR SANITY--COULDN'T HANDLE THE PRESSURE--!
DITTO FOR SUCCESS-- MAYBE DITTO FOR LIVING--!
"NUTS, I NEVER ASKED TO BE HATCHED--LET ALONE MY PARENTS' FIRST-HATCHED, THE LUCKLESS, INHERITOR OF ALL THEIR GREAT EXPECTATIONS!
"THEY WANTED ME TA BE A LAWYER! MY FIRST APTITUDE TEST PEGGED ME FOR A MORTICIAN --REALLY!
"BUT I THINK EVEN AS A KID--I WANTED TO BE A DERELICT. I LIKED THE HOURS.
"COULDN'T QUITE RECONCILE THAT WITH MY MIDDLE-CLASS UPBRINGING, THOUGH--SO AFTER A SHORT, UNDISTINGUISHED ACADEMIC CAREER--
"I TRIED FOLK-SINGING. DIDN'T PAY AS WELL AS BEIN' A BUM-- BUT IT SATISFIED SOME OR ANOTHER ARTISTIC URGE, TEMPORARILY.
"AFTER THAT, I TRIED MY HAND AT EVERYTHING FROM POETRY TO CONSTRUCTION--AND DISCOVERED MY ONLY TALENT WAS JOB-HUNTING!
"THEN ONE DAY, THE COSMIC WHATSIS SHIFTED--AN' SUDDENLY I WAS WADIN' THROUGH A SWAMP INSTEAD O' POUNDIN' THE PAVEMENT!
"YEP, HERE I WAS ON YOUR WORLD --AND THE TERM 'MISFIT' TOOK ON WHOLE NEW VISTAS OF MEANING!
"≥WAAAAUGH≤
"≥CHOKE≤ ≥SOB≤"
AWWW-- THEWE, THEWE! IT'LL ALL BE OH-KAY... EVENTUAWWY.
YOU JUST HAVE TO FIND OUT WHO YOU ARE-- WHAT YOU WANT OUT OF WIFE.
LIFE'S TOO FAR IN THE FUTURE TO THINK ABOUT! RIGHT NOW, I COULD USE A GOOD CIGAR!

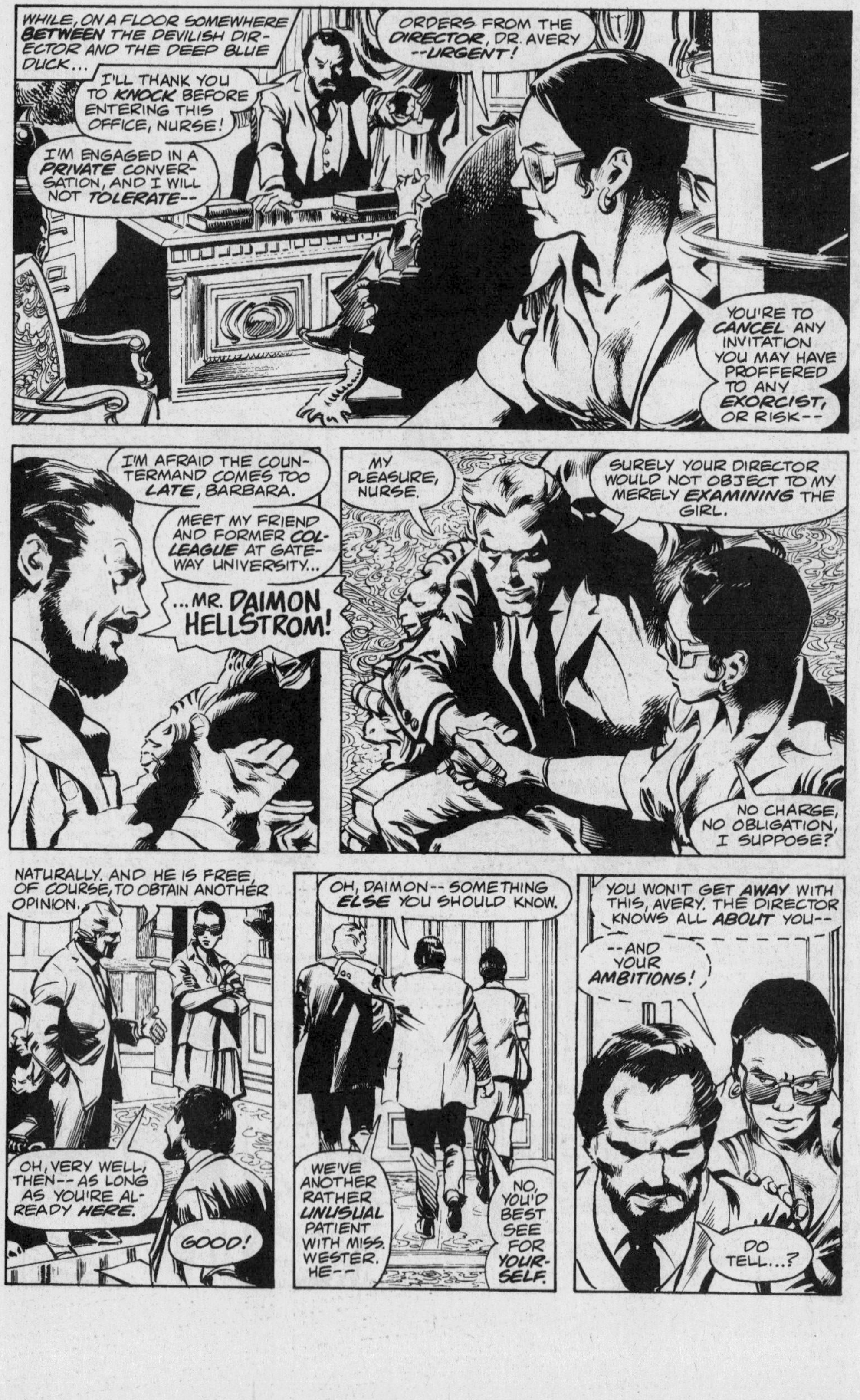

WHILE, ON A FLOOR SOMEWHERE BETWEEN THE DEVILISH DIRECTOR AND THE DEEP BLUE DUCK...
I'LL THANK YOU TO KNOCK BEFORE ENTERING THIS OFFICE, NURSE!
I'M ENGAGED IN A PRIVATE CONVERSATION, AND I WILL NOT TOLERATE--
ORDERS FROM THE DIRECTOR, DR. AVERY --URGENT!
YOU'RE TO CANCEL ANY INVITATION YOU MAY HAVE PROFFERED TO ANY EXORCIST, OR RISK--
I'M AFRAID THE COUNTERMAND COMES TOO LATE, BARBARA.
MEET MY FRIEND AND FORMER COLLEAGUE AT GATEWAY UNIVERSITY...
...MR. DAIMON HELLSTROM!
MY PLEASURE, NURSE.
SURELY YOUR DIRECTOR WOULD NOT OBJECT TO MY MERELY EXAMINING THE GIRL.
NO CHARGE, NO OBLIGATION, I SUPPOSE?
NATURALLY. AND HE IS FREE, OF COURSE, TO OBTAIN ANOTHER OPINION.
OH, VERY WELL, THEN-- AS LONG AS YOU'RE ALREADY HERE.
GOOD!
OH, DAIMON-- SOMETHING ELSE YOU SHOULD KNOW.
WE'VE ANOTHER RATHER UNUSUAL PATIENT WITH MISS. WESTER. HE--
NO, YOU'D BEST SEE FOR YOURSELF.
YOU WON'T GET AWAY WITH THIS, AVERY. THE DIRECTOR KNOWS ALL ABOUT YOU--
--AND YOUR AMBITIONS!
DO TELL...?

PRESENTLY...
WINDA, HOWARD-- THIS IS--
BY THE SEVEN CIRCLES!
Y-YOU ARE-- A DUCK!!
YEAH. AIN'T IT GREAT HOW SOME THINGS IN THE UNIVERSE REMAIN CONSTANT.
DAIMON IS AN AUTHORITY ON DEMONOLOGY AND EXORCISM, WINDA.
HE'S HERE TO EXAMINE YOU.
WEAWWY?!
YOU'WE GOING TO DISPOSSESS ME?
DID DR. AVEWY TELL YOU HOW I GOT POSSESSED AND MY TEWWIFIED PAWENTS PUT ME ON A BUS TO CWEVEWAND TO BE EXOWCISED...
...AND HOW I JUST WIKE TO MAKE FUNNY FACES AND SIWWY NOISES...
...ONWY MY PAWENTS THOUGHT IT WAS THE DEVIL, MM-HM, AND THE BUS CWASHED, AND--AND--
NO. HE DID NOT. PERHAPS YOU CAN TELL ME... LATER.
BUT FOR NOW, WINDA, PLEASE REMAIN ABSOLUTELY SILENT. THE EXAMINATION REQUIRES ONLY A MOMENT...
...BUT A DELICATE MOMENT, IN WHICH I MUST REACH BEHIND YOUR EYES AND TOUCH YOUR VERY SOUL.
OH, MY GOODNESS!

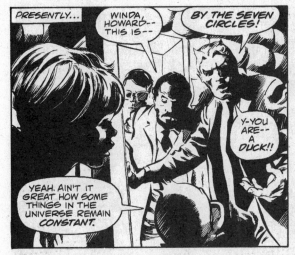

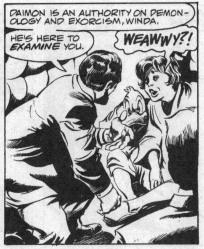

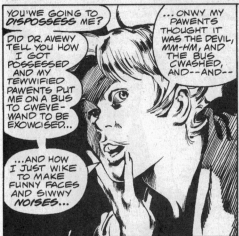

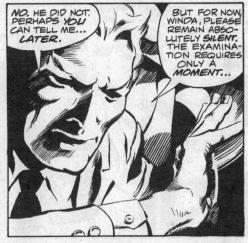

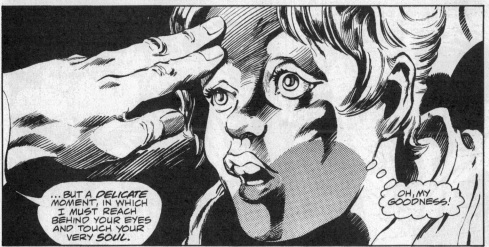

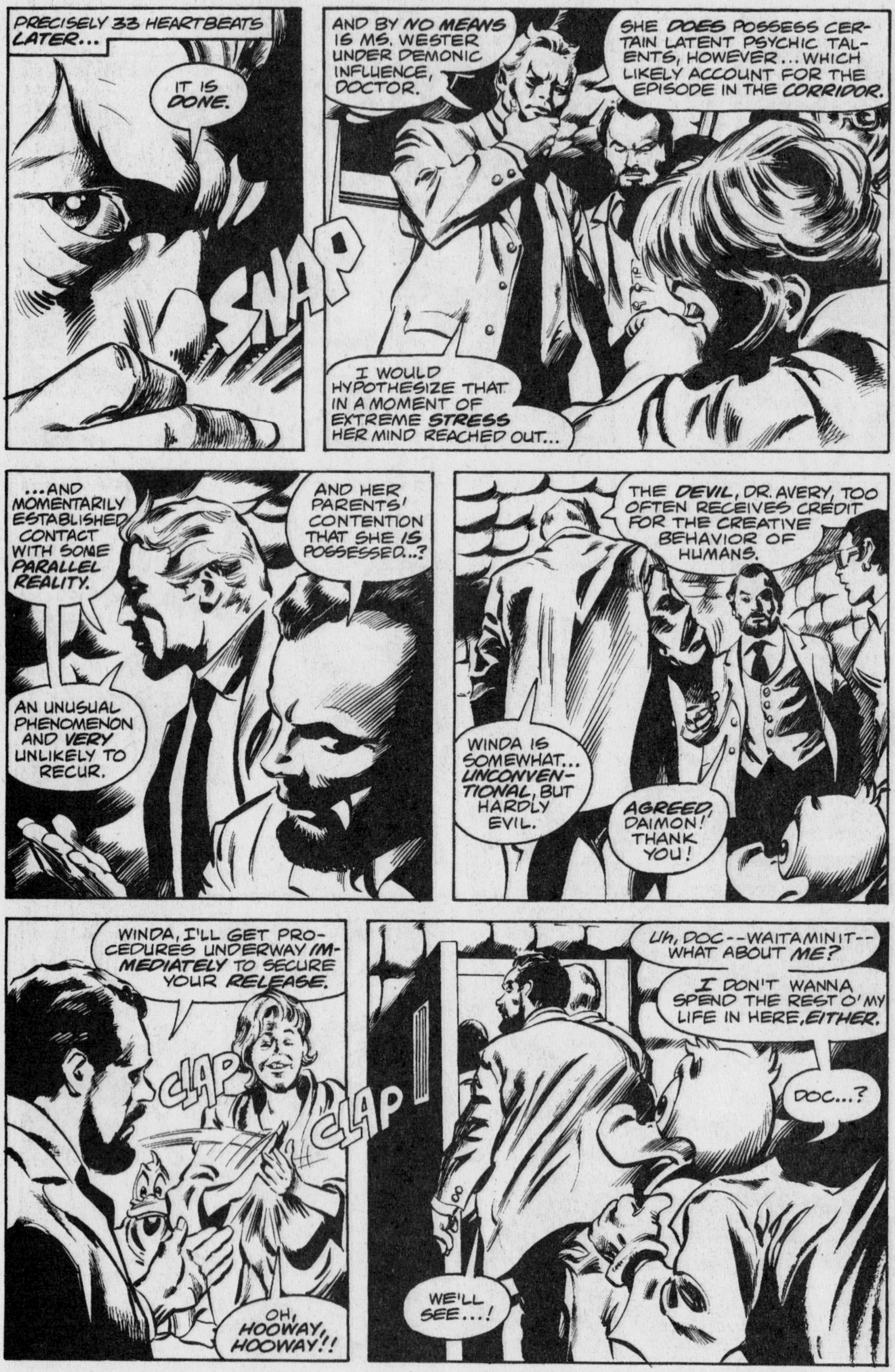
PRECISELY 33 HEARTBEATS LATER...
IT IS DONE.
SNAP
AND BY NO MEANS IS MS. WESTER UNDER DEMONIC INFLUENCE, DOCTOR.
SHE DOES POSSESS CERTAIN LATENT PSYCHIC TALENTS, HOWEVER... WHICH LIKELY ACCOUNT FOR THE EPISODE IN THE CORRIDOR.
I WOULD HYPOTHESIZE THAT IN A MOMENT OF EXTREME STRESS HER MIND REACHED OUT...
...AND MOMENTARILY ESTABLISHED CONTACT WITH SOME PARALLEL REALITY.
AN UNUSUAL PHENOMENON AND VERY UNLIKELY TO RECUR.
AND HER PARENTS' CONTENTION THAT SHE IS POSSESSED...?
THE DEVIL, DR. AVERY, TOO OFTEN RECEIVES CREDIT FOR THE CREATIVE BEHAVIOR OF HUMANS.
WINDA IS SOMEWHAT... UNCONVENTIONAL, BUT HARDLY EVIL.
AGREED, DAIMON! THANK YOU!
WINDA, I'LL GET PROCEDURES UNDERWAY IMMEDIATELY TO SECURE YOUR RELEASE.
CLAP
CLAP
OH, HOOWAY, HOOWAY!!
UH, DOC--WAITAMINIT-- WHAT ABOUT ME?
I DON'T WANNA SPEND THE REST O' MY LIFE IN HERE, EITHER.
DOC...?
WE'LL SEE...!

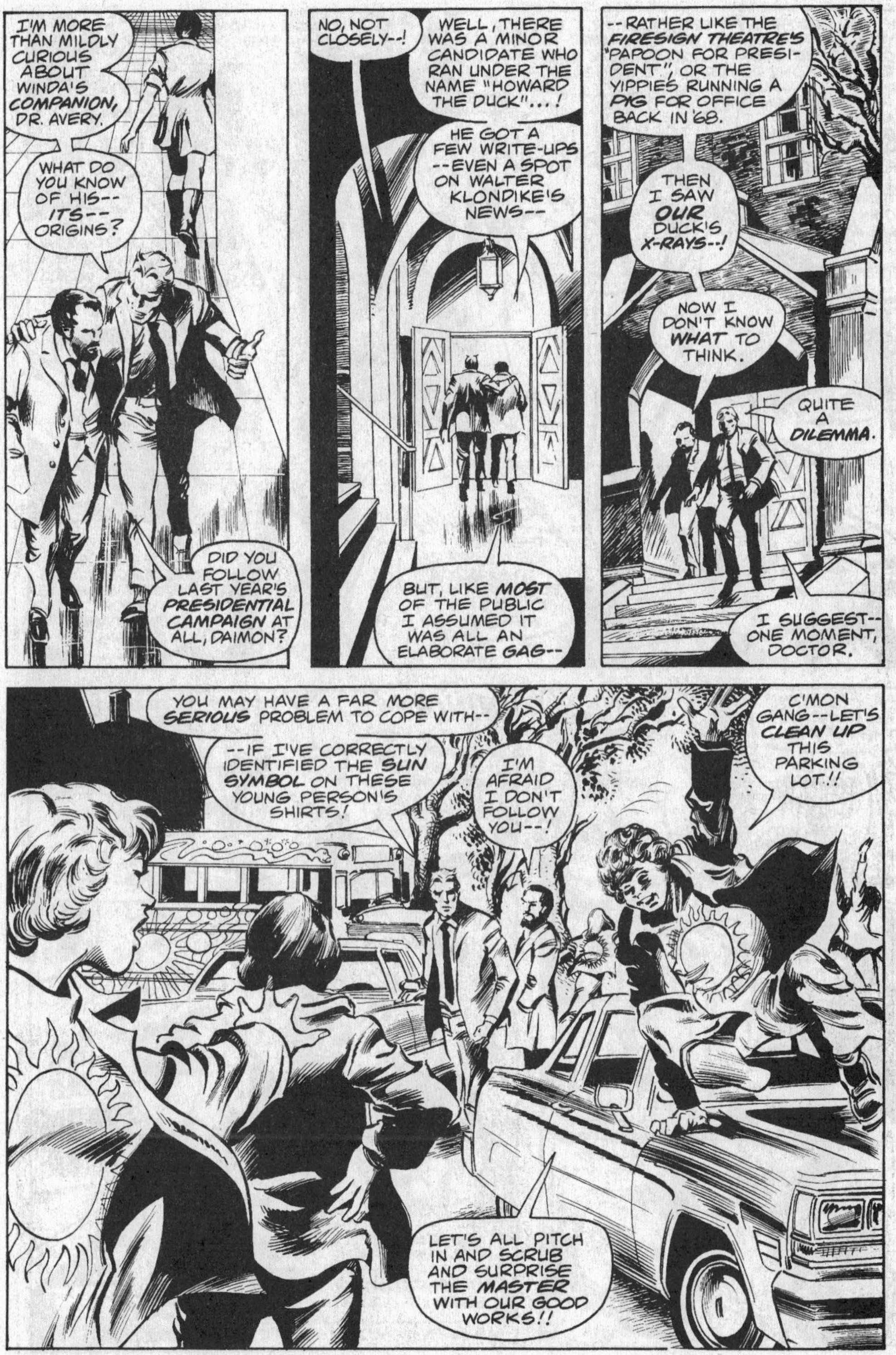

I'M MORE THAN MILDLY CURIOUS ABOUT WINDA'S COMPANION, DR. AVERY.
WHAT DO YOU KNOW OF HIS-- ITS-- ORIGINS?
DID YOU FOLLOW LAST YEAR'S PRESIDENTIAL CAMPAIGN AT ALL, DAIMON?
NO, NOT CLOSELY--!
WELL, THERE WAS A MINOR CANDIDATE WHO RAN UNDER THE NAME "HOWARD THE DUCK"...!
HE GOT A FEW WRITE-UPS --EVEN A SPOT ON WALTER KLONDIKE'S NEWS--
BUT, LIKE MOST OF THE PUBLIC I ASSUMED IT WAS ALL AN ELABORATE GAG--
--RATHER LIKE THE FIRESIGN THEATRE'S "PAPOON FOR PRESI-DENT", OR THE YIPPIES RUNNING A PIG FOR OFFICE BACK IN '68.
THEN I SAW OUR DUCK'S X-RAYS--!
NOW I DON'T KNOW WHAT TO THINK.
QUITE A DILEMMA.
I SUGGEST-- ONE MOMENT, DOCTOR.
YOU MAY HAVE A FAR MORE SERIOUS PROBLEM TO COPE WITH--
--IF I'VE CORRECTLY IDENTIFIED THE SUN SYMBOL ON THESE YOUNG PERSON'S SHIRTS!
I'M AFRAID I DON'T FOLLOW YOU--!
C'MON GANG--LET'S CLEAN UP THIS PARKING LOT!!
LET'S ALL PITCH IN AND SCRUB AND SURPRISE THE MASTER WITH OUR GOOD WORKS!!

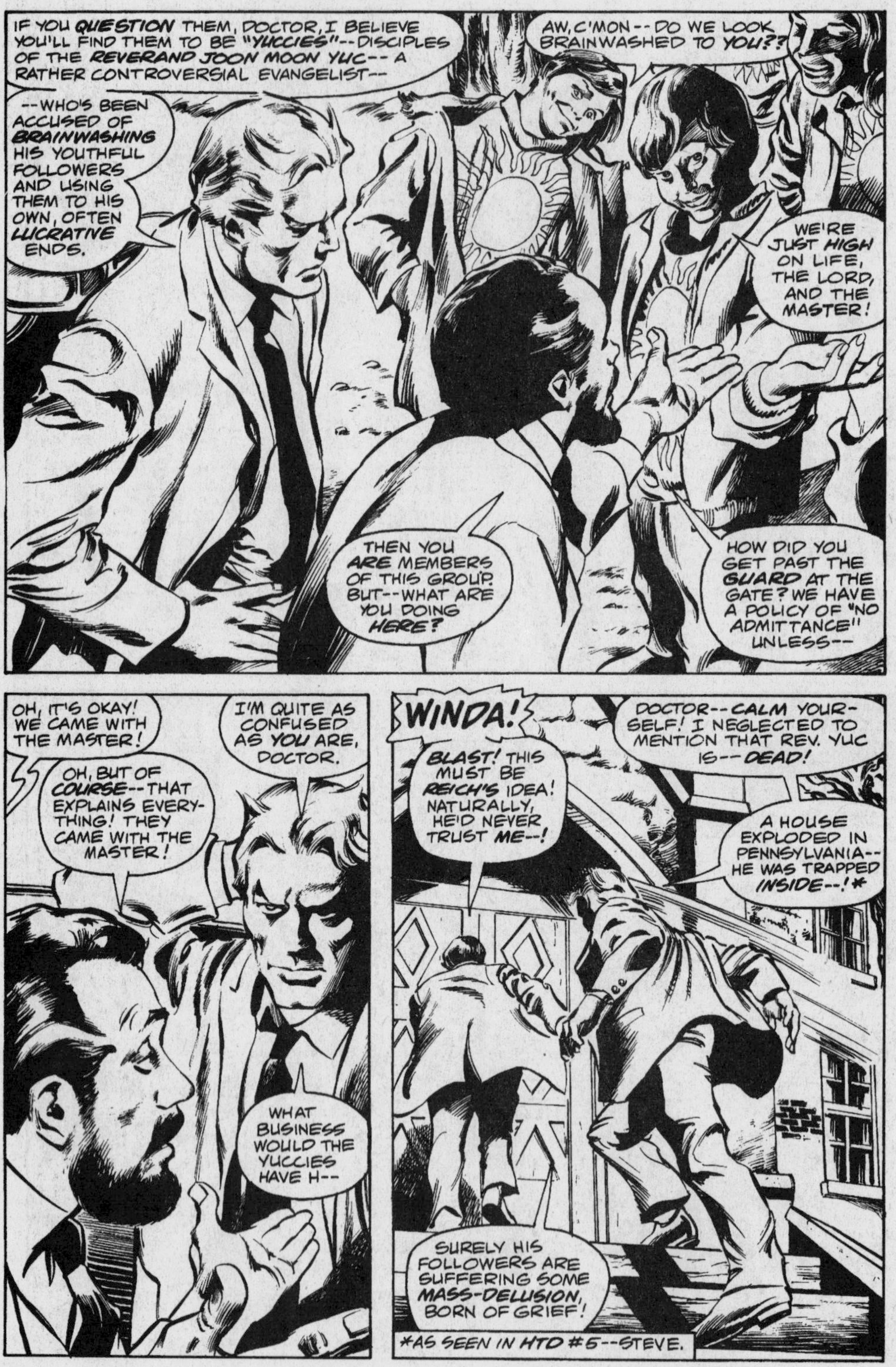

IF YOU QUESTION THEM, DOCTOR, I BELIEVE YOU'LL FIND THEM TO BE "YUCCIES"--DISCIPLES OF THE REVERAND JOON MOON YUC-- A RATHER CONTROVERSIAL EVANGELIST--
--WHO'S BEEN ACCUSED OF BRAINWASHING HIS YOUTHFUL FOLLOWERS AND USING THEM TO HIS OWN, OFTEN LUCRATIVE ENDS.
AW, C'MON-- DO WE LOOK BRAINWASHED TO YOU??
WE'RE JUST HIGH ON LIFE, THE LORD, AND THE MASTER!
THEN YOU ARE MEMBERS OF THIS GROUP. BUT--WHAT ARE YOU DOING HERE?
HOW DID YOU GET PAST THE GUARD AT THE GATE? WE HAVE A POLICY OF "NO ADMITTANCE" UNLESS--
OH, IT'S OKAY! WE CAME WITH THE MASTER!
OH, BUT OF COURSE--THAT EXPLAINS EVERYTHING! THEY CAME WITH THE MASTER!
I'M QUITE AS CONFUSED AS YOU ARE, DOCTOR.
WHAT BUSINESS WOULD THE YUCCIES HAVE H--
WINDA!
BLAST! THIS MUST BE REICH'S IDEA! NATURALLY, HE'D NEVER TRUST ME--!
DOCTOR--CALM YOURSELF! I NEGLECTED TO MENTION THAT REV. YUC IS--DEAD!
A HOUSE EXPLODED IN PENNSYLVANIA-- HE WAS TRAPPED INSIDE--!*
SURELY HIS FOLLOWERS ARE SUFFERING SOME MASS-DELUSION, BORN OF GRIEF!
*AS SEEN IN HTD #5--STEVE.

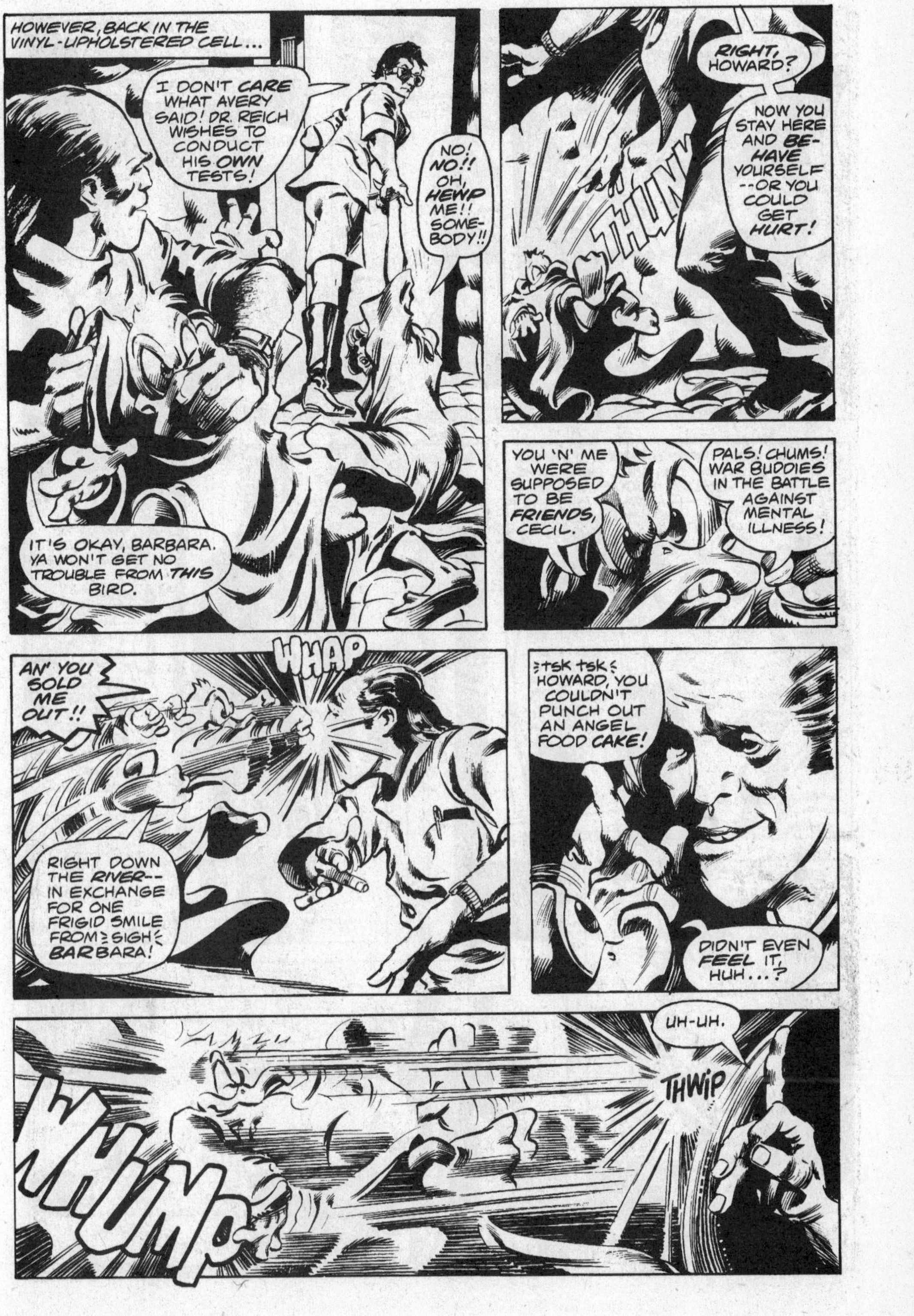
HOWEVER, BACK IN THE VINYL-UPHOLSTERED CELL...
I DON'T CARE WHAT AVERY SAID! DR. REICH WISHES TO CONDUCT HIS OWN TESTS!
NO! NO!! OH, HEWP ME!! SOME-BODY!!
IT'S OKAY, BARBARA. YA WON'T GET NO TROUBLE FROM THIS BIRD.
RIGHT, HOWARD?
NOW YOU STAY HERE AND BE-HAVE YOURSELF --OR YOU COULD GET HURT!
THUNK
YOU 'N' ME WERE SUPPOSED TO BE FRIENDS, CECIL.
PALS! CHUMS! WAR BUDDIES IN THE BATTLE AGAINST MENTAL ILLNESS!
AN' YOU SOLD ME OUT!!
WHAP
RIGHT DOWN THE RIVER-- IN EXCHANGE FOR ONE FRIGID SMILE FROM SIGH BARBARA!
tsk tsk HOWARD, YOU COULDN'T PUNCH OUT AN ANGEL FOOD CAKE!
DIDN'T EVEN FEEL IT, HUH...?
UH-UH.
THWIP
WHUMP

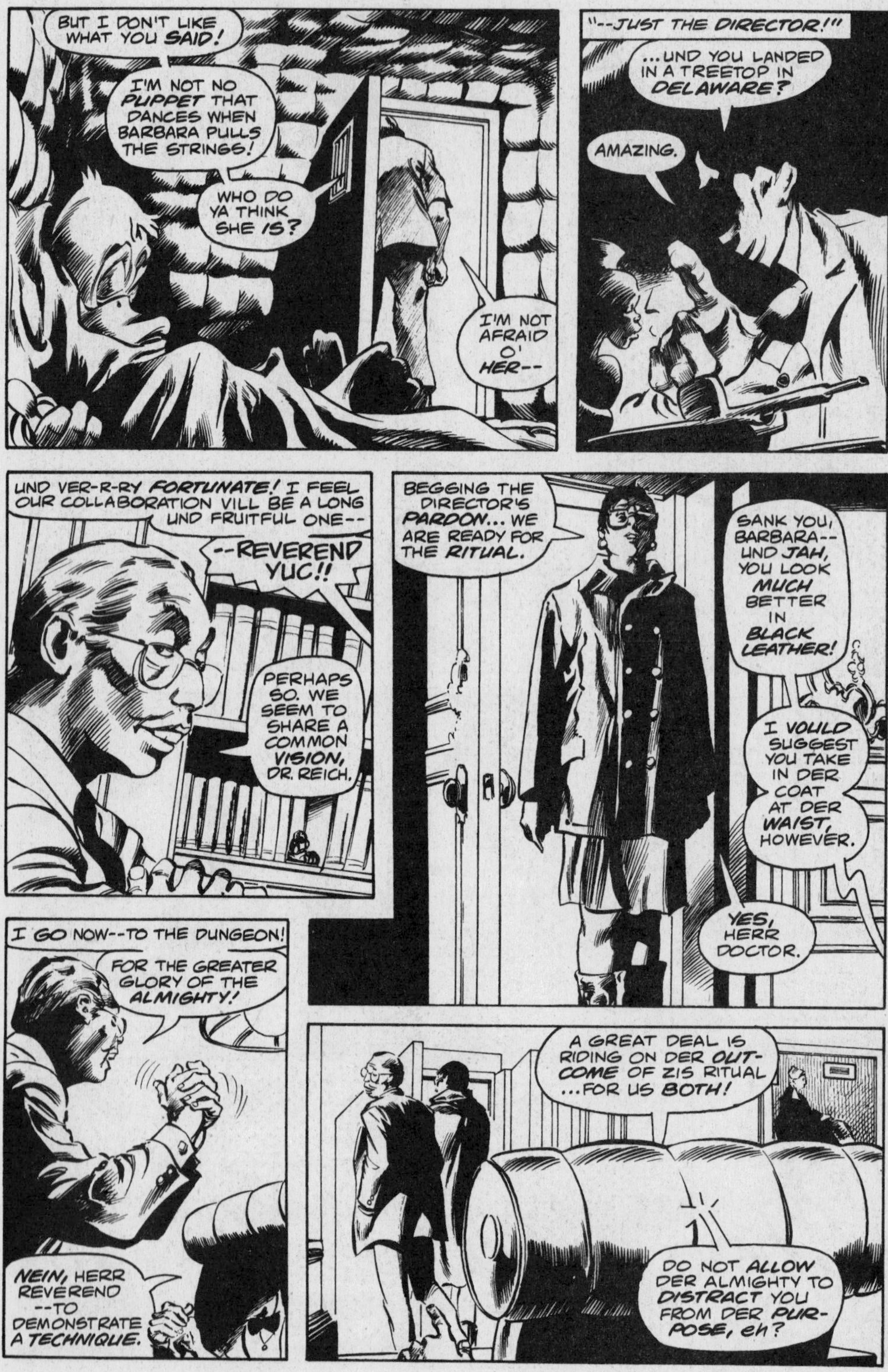
BUT I DON'T LIKE WHAT YOU SAID!
I'M NOT NO PUPPET THAT DANCES WHEN BARBARA PULLS THE STRINGS!
WHO DO YA THINK SHE IS?
I'M NOT AFRAID O' HER--
"--JUST THE DIRECTOR!"
...UND YOU LANDED IN A TREETOP IN DELAWARE?
AMAZING.
UND VER-R-RY FORTUNATE! I FEEL OUR COLLABORATION VILL BE A LONG UND FRUITFUL ONE--
--REVEREND YUC!!
PERHAPS SO. WE SEEM TO SHARE A COMMON VISION, DR. REICH.
BEGGING THE DIRECTOR'S PARDON... WE ARE READY FOR THE RITUAL.
SANK YOU, BARBARA-- UND JAH, YOU LOOK MUCH BETTER IN BLACK LEATHER!
I VOULD SUGGEST YOU TAKE IN DER COAT AT DER WAIST, HOWEVER.
YES, HERR DOCTOR.
I GO NOW--TO THE DUNGEON!
FOR THE GREATER GLORY OF THE ALMIGHTY!
NEIN, HERR REVEREND --TO DEMONSTRATE A TECHNIQUE.
A GREAT DEAL IS RIDING ON DER OUTCOME OF ZIS RITUAL ...FOR US BOTH!
DO NOT ALLOW DER ALMIGHTY TO DISTRACT YOU FROM DER PURPOSE, eh?

GOOD HEAVENS!! HOWARD--WHAT'S HAPPENED?! WHERE'S WINDA?

I...DUNNO...

"BARBARA...SAID SOMETHIN'...ABOUT... THE SUB-CELLAR!...MAYBE THEY RAN OUTTA COAL...FIGGERED THEY'D BURN 'ER...FOR FUEL...!"

AS YOU CAN SEE, REVEREND, POOR, POOR WINDA IS DEFINITELY POSSESSED.

OH, YES, UNQUESTIONABLY.

AND YOU MUST UNDERSTAND, WINDA, THAT THE DEMON MAY ONLY BE DRIVEN FROM YOU THROUGH THE DIVINE APPLICATION OF...SENSATION.

THE DEMON WILL FLEE, YOU SEE--FROM PAIN INFLICTED BY BEAUTY.

YOU MUST LOVE THE LORD AND ALL HIS WORKS AND ME, HIS AGENT-- 'TIL IT HURTS.

FOR BESIDE THIS EXQUISITE ANGUISH, THE DEMON'S POWER PALES.

BEHOLD-- THE HUMBLE PETUNIA!

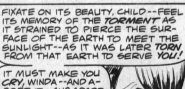

FIXATE ON ITS BEAUTY, CHILD--FEEL ITS MEMORY OF THE TORMENT AS IT STRAINED TO PIERCE THE SUR- FACE OF THE EARTH TO MEET THE SUNLIGHT--AS IT WAS LATER TORN FROM THAT EARTH TO SERVE YOU!

IT MUST MAKE YOU CRY, WINDA--AND A- DORE IT--AND ADORE ME--AND BELIEVE IN ME WITHOUT QUESTION!

WHAP

≥OUCH≤

BELIEVE ME, WINDA --CRY AND BELIEVE ME!!

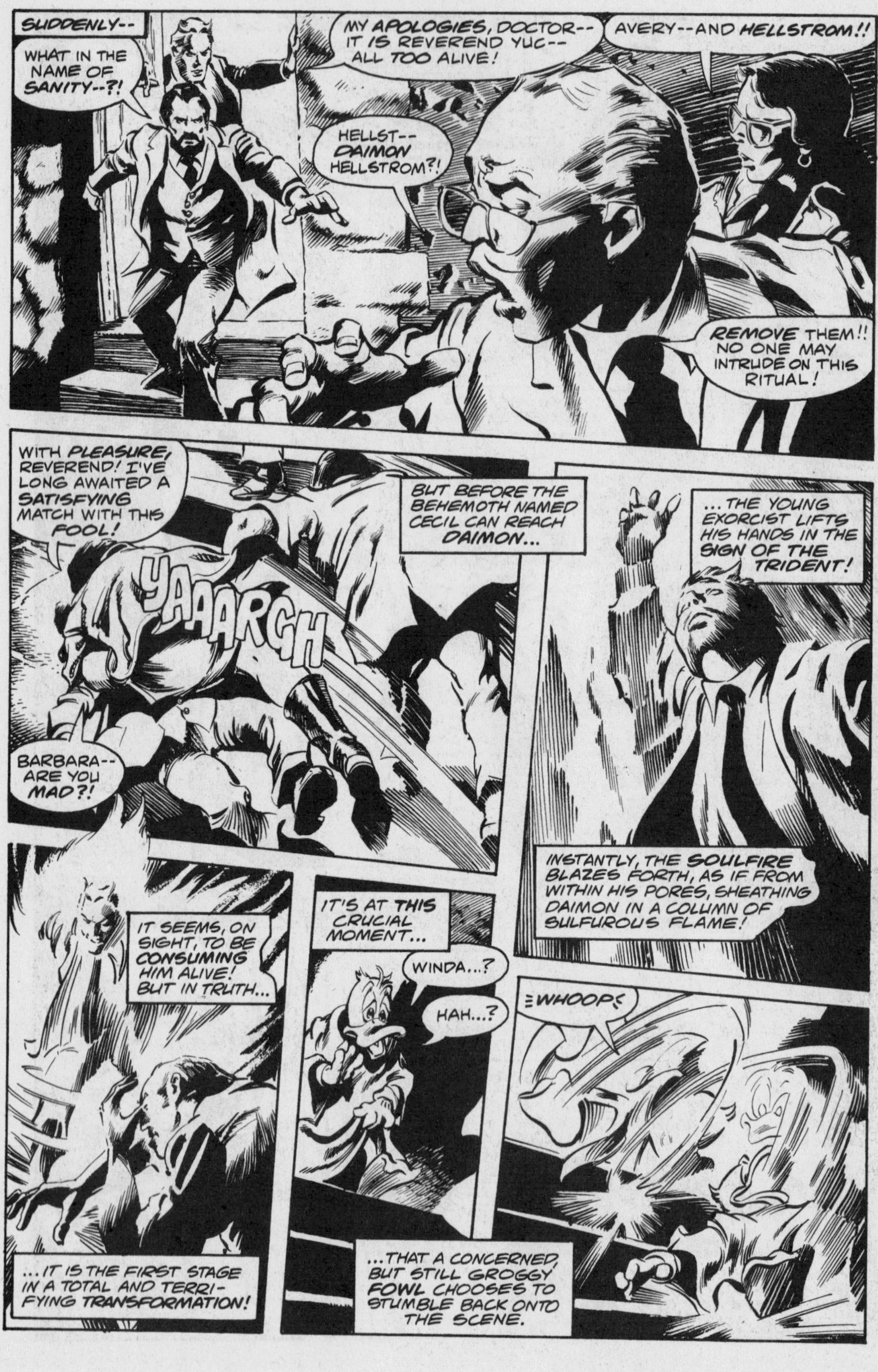

SUDDENLY--
WHAT IN THE NAME OF SANITY--?!
MY APOLOGIES, DOCTOR-- IT IS REVEREND YUC-- ALL TOO ALIVE!
HELLST-- DAIMON HELLSTROM?!
AVERY--AND HELLSTROM!!
REMOVE THEM!! NO ONE MAY INTRUDE ON THIS RITUAL!
WITH PLEASURE, REVEREND! I'VE LONG AWAITED A SATISFYING MATCH WITH THIS FOOL!
YAAARGH
BARBARA-- ARE YOU MAD?!
BUT BEFORE THE BEHEMOTH NAMED CECIL CAN REACH DAIMON...
...THE YOUNG EXORCIST LIFTS HIS HANDS IN THE SIGN OF THE TRIDENT!
INSTANTLY, THE SOULFIRE BLAZES FORTH, AS IF FROM WITHIN HIS PORES, SHEATHING DAIMON IN A COLUMN OF SULFUROUS FLAME!
IT SEEMS, ON SIGHT, TO BE CONSUMING HIM ALIVE! BUT IN TRUTH...
...IT IS THE FIRST STAGE IN A TOTAL AND TERRI-FYING TRANSFORMATION!
IT'S AT THIS CRUCIAL MOMENT...
WINDA...?
HAH...?
...THAT A CONCERNED, BUT STILL GROGGY FOWL CHOOSES TO STUMBLE BACK ONTO THE SCENE.
WHOOP!

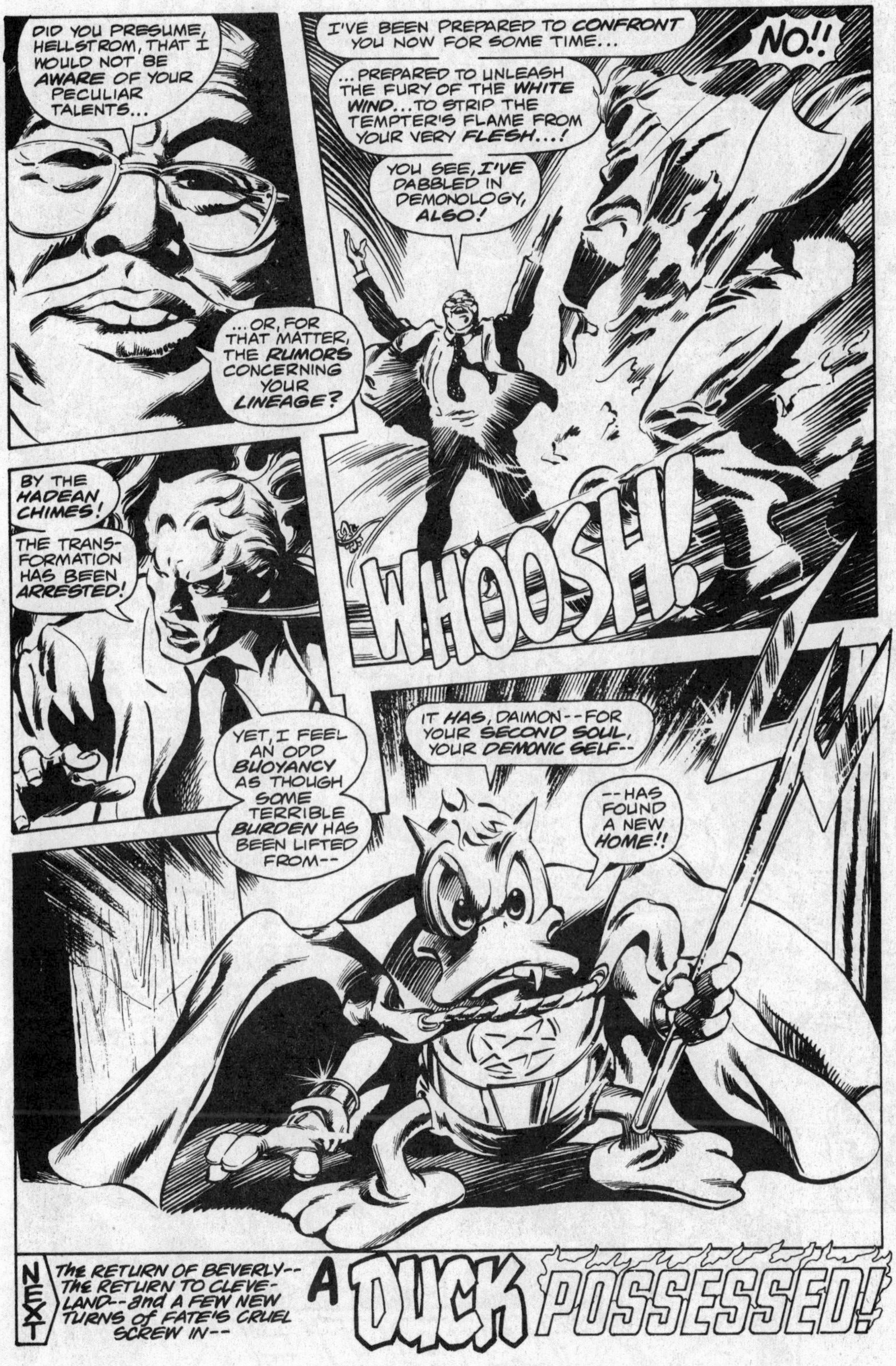

DID YOU PRESUME, HELLSTROM, THAT I WOULD NOT BE AWARE OF YOUR PECULIAR TALENTS...
...OR, FOR THAT MATTER, THE RUMORS CONCERNING YOUR LINEAGE?
I'VE BEEN PREPARED TO CONFRONT YOU NOW FOR SOME TIME...
...PREPARED TO UNLEASH THE FURY OF THE WHITE WIND...TO STRIP THE TEMPTER'S FLAME FROM YOUR VERY FLESH...!
YOU SEE, I'VE DABBLED IN DEMONOLOGY, ALSO!
NO!!
WHOOSH!
BY THE HADEAN CHIMES!
THE TRANSFORMATION HAS BEEN ARRESTED!
YET, I FEEL AN ODD BUOYANCY AS THOUGH SOME TERRIBLE BURDEN HAS BEEN LIFTED FROM--
IT HAS, DAIMON--FOR YOUR SECOND SOUL, YOUR DEMONIC SELF--
--HAS FOUND A NEW HOME!!
NEXT
The RETURN OF BEVERLY--The RETURN TO CLEVELAND--and A FEW NEW TURNS of FATE'S CRUEL SCREW IN--
A DUCK POSSESSED!

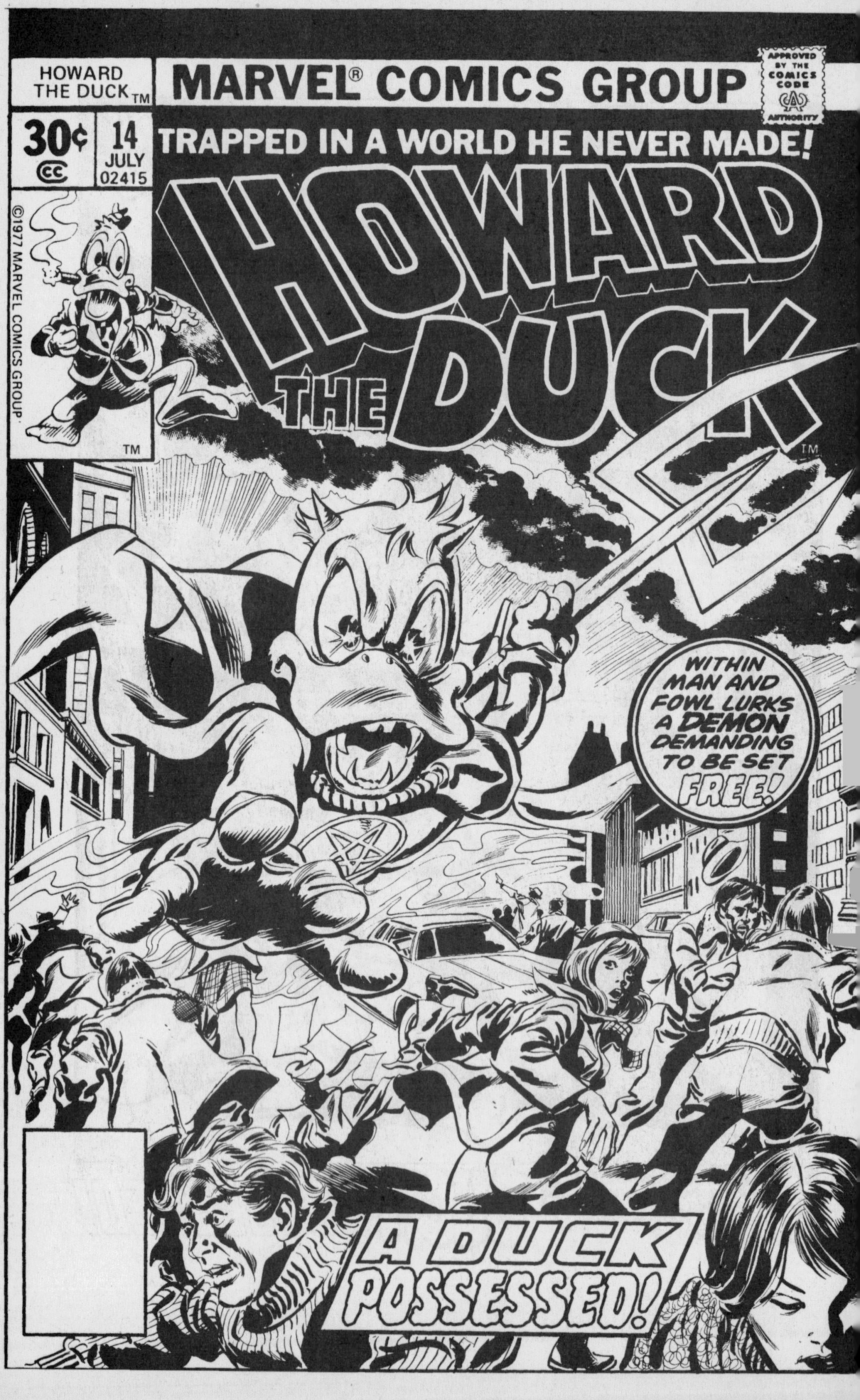

HOWARD THE DUCK™
MARVEL® COMICS GROUP
APPROVED BY THE COMICS CODE AUTHORITY
30¢
14
JULY
02415
TRAPPED IN A WORLD HE NEVER MADE!
©1977 MARVEL COMICS GROUP
HOWARD THE DUCK™
WITHIN MAN AND FOWL LURKS A DEMON DEMANDING TO BE SET FREE!
A DUCK POSSESSED!

From the time of his hatching, he was...different. A potentially brilliant scholar who dreaded the structured environment of school, he educated himself in the streets, taking whatever work was available, formulating his philosophy of self from what he learned of the world about him. And then the Cosmic Axis shifted...and that world *changed*. Suddenly, he was stranded in a universe he could not fathom. Without warning, he became a strange fowl in an even stranger land.

Stan Lee PRESENTS: HOWARD THE DUCK!™

STEVE GERBER WRITER/EDITOR * GENE COLAN PENCILLER * KLAUS JANSON INKER * JIM NOVAK LETTERER * IRENE VARTANOFF COLORIST

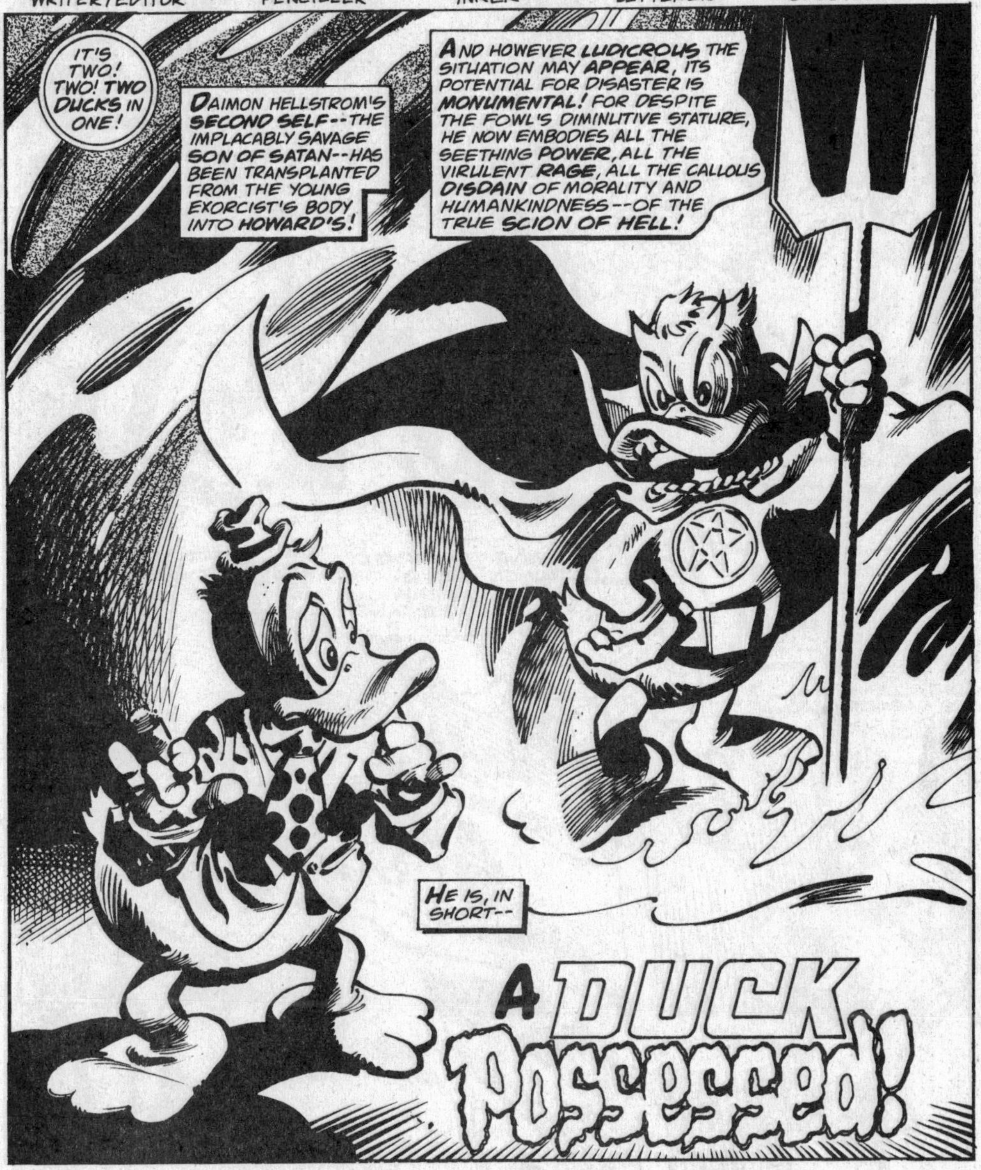

IT'S TWO! TWO! TWO DUCKS IN ONE!
DAIMON HELLSTROM'S SECOND SELF--THE IMPLACABLY SAVAGE SON OF SATAN--HAS BEEN TRANSPLANTED FROM THE YOUNG EXORCIST'S BODY INTO HOWARD'S!
AND HOWEVER LUDICROUS THE SITUATION MAY APPEAR, ITS POTENTIAL FOR DISASTER IS MONUMENTAL! FOR DESPITE THE FOWL'S DIMINUTIVE STATURE, HE NOW EMBODIES ALL THE SEETHING POWER, ALL THE VIRULENT RAGE, ALL THE CALLOUS DISDAIN OF MORALITY AND HUMANKINDNESS--OF THE TRUE SCION OF HELL!
HE IS, IN SHORT--
A DUCK POSSESSED!

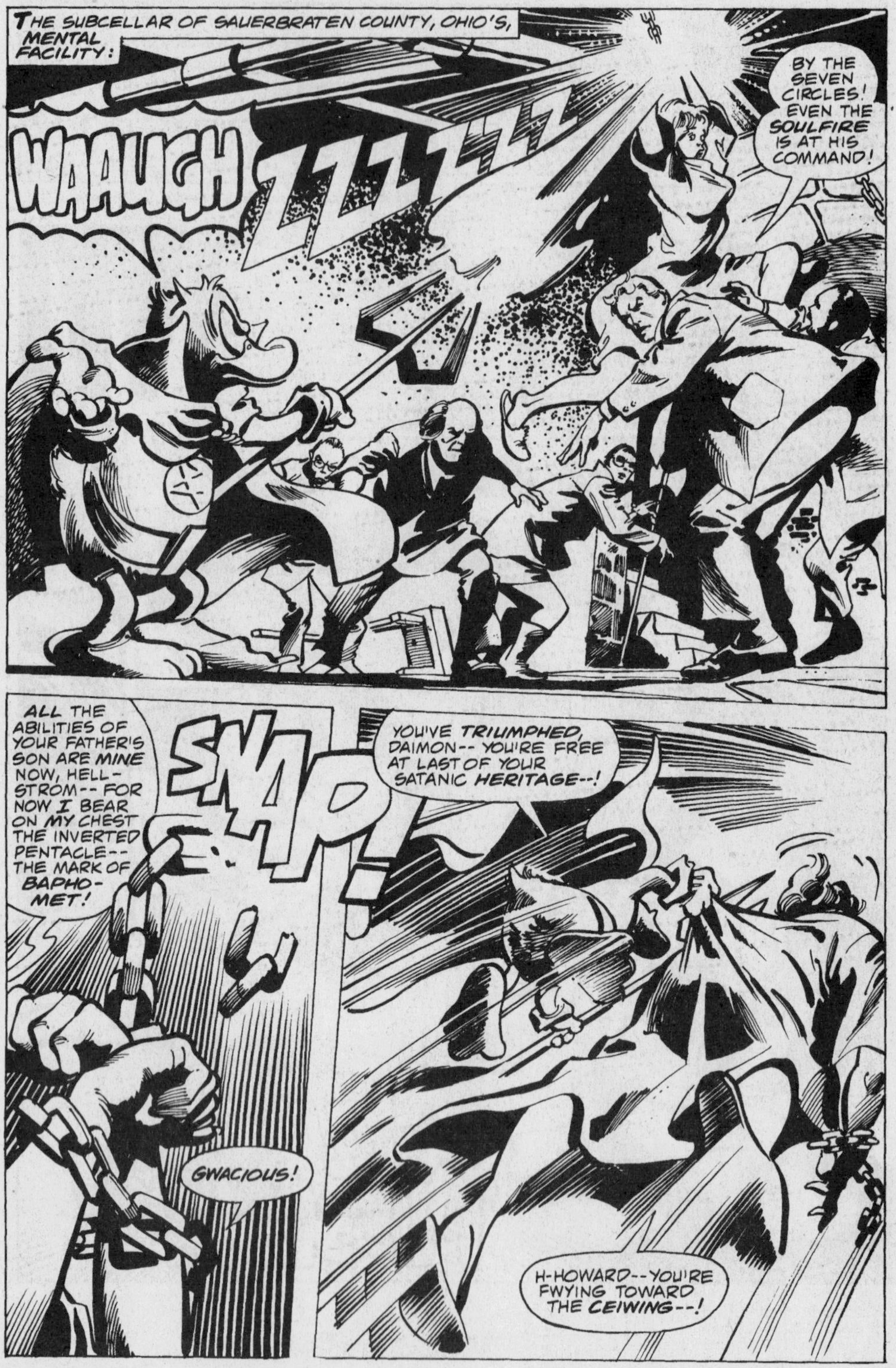

THE SUBCELLAR OF SAUERBRATEN COUNTY, OHIO'S, MENTAL FACILITY:
WAAUGH
ZZZZZZ
BY THE SEVEN CIRCLES! EVEN THE SOULFIRE IS AT HIS COMMAND!
ALL THE ABILITIES OF YOUR FATHER'S SON ARE MINE NOW, HELL-STROM-- FOR NOW I BEAR ON MY CHEST THE INVERTED PENTACLE-- THE MARK OF BAPHOMET!
SNAP!
YOU'VE TRIUMPHED, DAIMON-- YOU'RE FREE AT LAST OF YOUR SATANIC HERITAGE--!
GWACIOUS!
H-HOWARD--YOU'RE FWYING TOWARD THE CEIWING--!

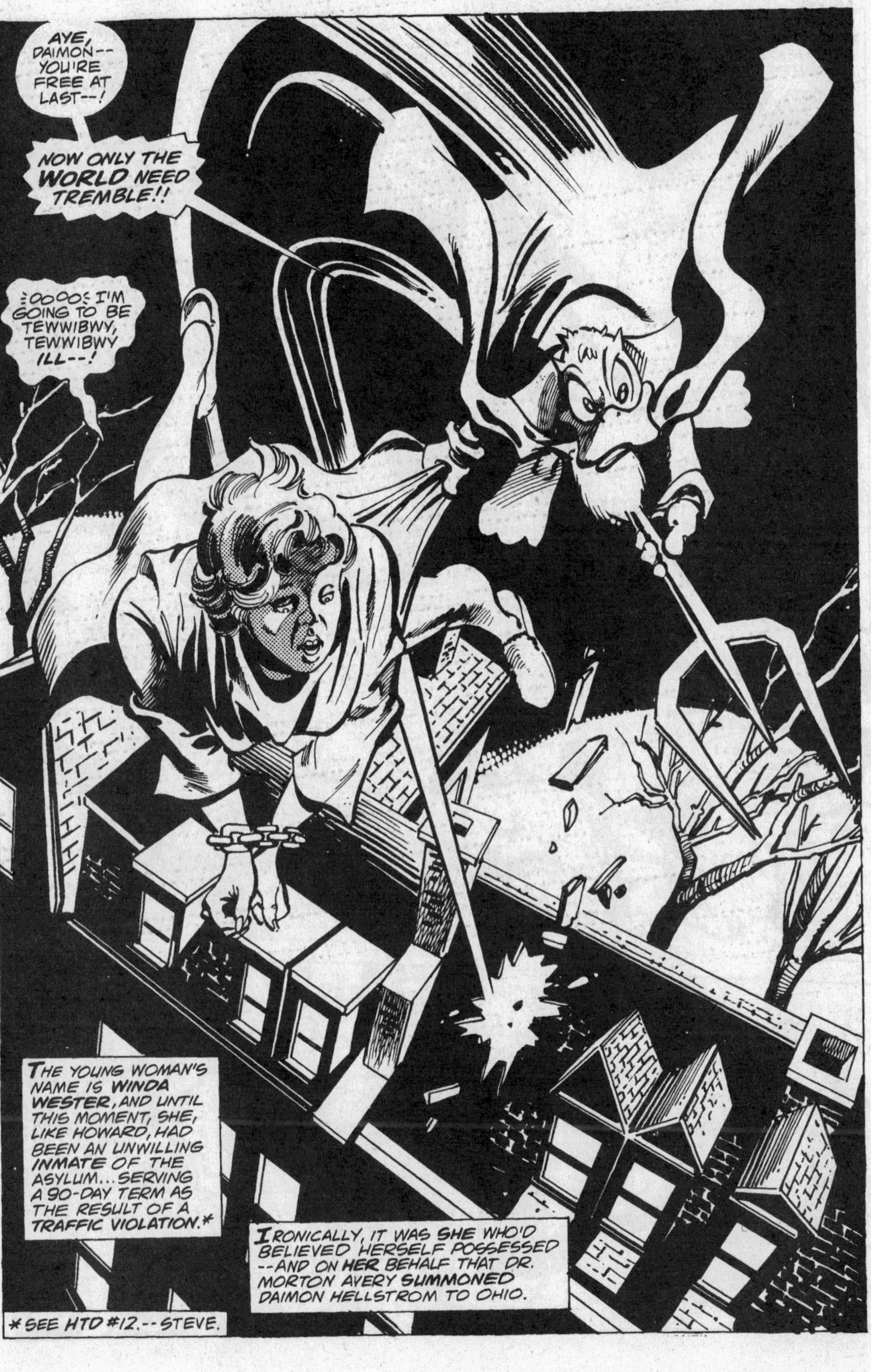
AYE, DAIMON-- YOU'RE FREE AT LAST--!
NOW ONLY THE WORLD NEED TREMBLE!!
:OOOO: I'M GOING TO BE TEWWIBWY, TEWWIBWY ILL--!
THE YOUNG WOMAN'S NAME IS WINDA WESTER, AND UNTIL THIS MOMENT, SHE, LIKE HOWARD, HAD BEEN AN UNWILLING INMATE OF THE ASYLUM... SERVING A 90-DAY TERM AS THE RESULT OF A TRAFFIC VIOLATION.*
IRONICALLY, IT WAS SHE WHO'D BELIEVED HERSELF POSSESSED --AND ON HER BEHALF THAT DR. MORTON AVERY SUMMONED DAIMON HELLSTROM TO OHIO.
*SEE HTD #12.--STEVE.

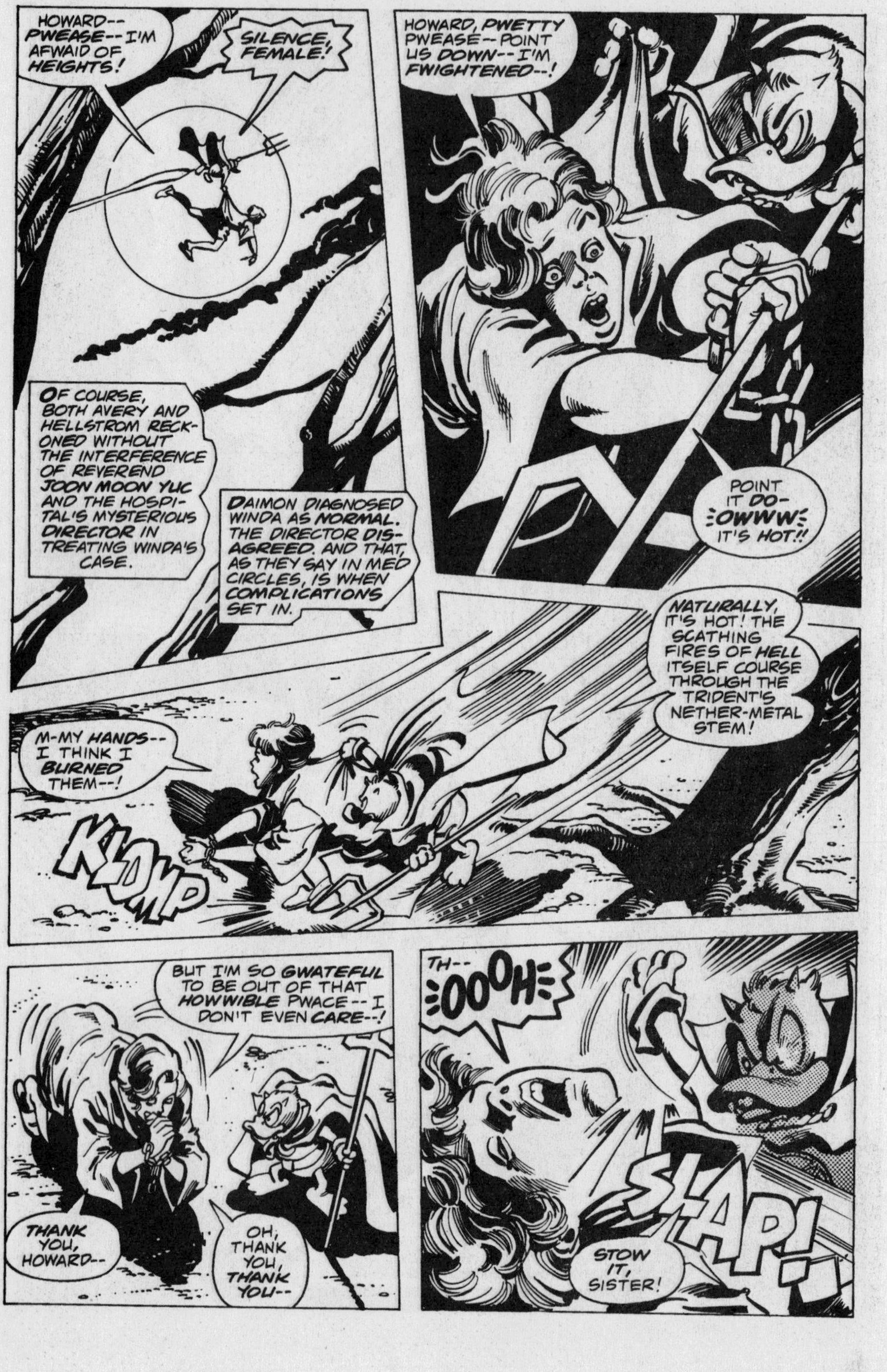

HOWARD-- PWEASE-- I'M AFWAID OF HEIGHTS!
SILENCE, FEMALE!
HOWARD, PWETTY PWEASE-- POINT US DOWN-- I'M FWIGHTENED--!
OF COURSE, BOTH AVERY AND HELLSTROM RECKONED WITHOUT THE INTERFERENCE OF REVEREND JOON MOON YUC AND THE HOSPITAL'S MYSTERIOUS DIRECTOR IN TREATING WINDA'S CASE.
DAIMON DIAGNOSED WINDA AS NORMAL. THE DIRECTOR DISAGREED. AND THAT, AS THEY SAY IN MED CIRCLES, IS WHEN COMPLICATIONS SET IN.
POINT IT DO-OWWW IT'S HOT!!
NATURALLY, IT'S HOT! THE SCATHING FIRES OF HELL ITSELF COURSE THROUGH THE TRIDENT'S NETHER-METAL STEM!
M-MY HANDS-- I THINK I BURNED THEM--!
KLOMP
BUT I'M SO GWATEFUL TO BE OUT OF THAT HOWWIBLE PWACE-- I DON'T EVEN CARE--!
THANK YOU, HOWARD--
OH, THANK YOU, THANK YOU--
TH-- OOOH
SLAP!
STOW IT, SISTER!

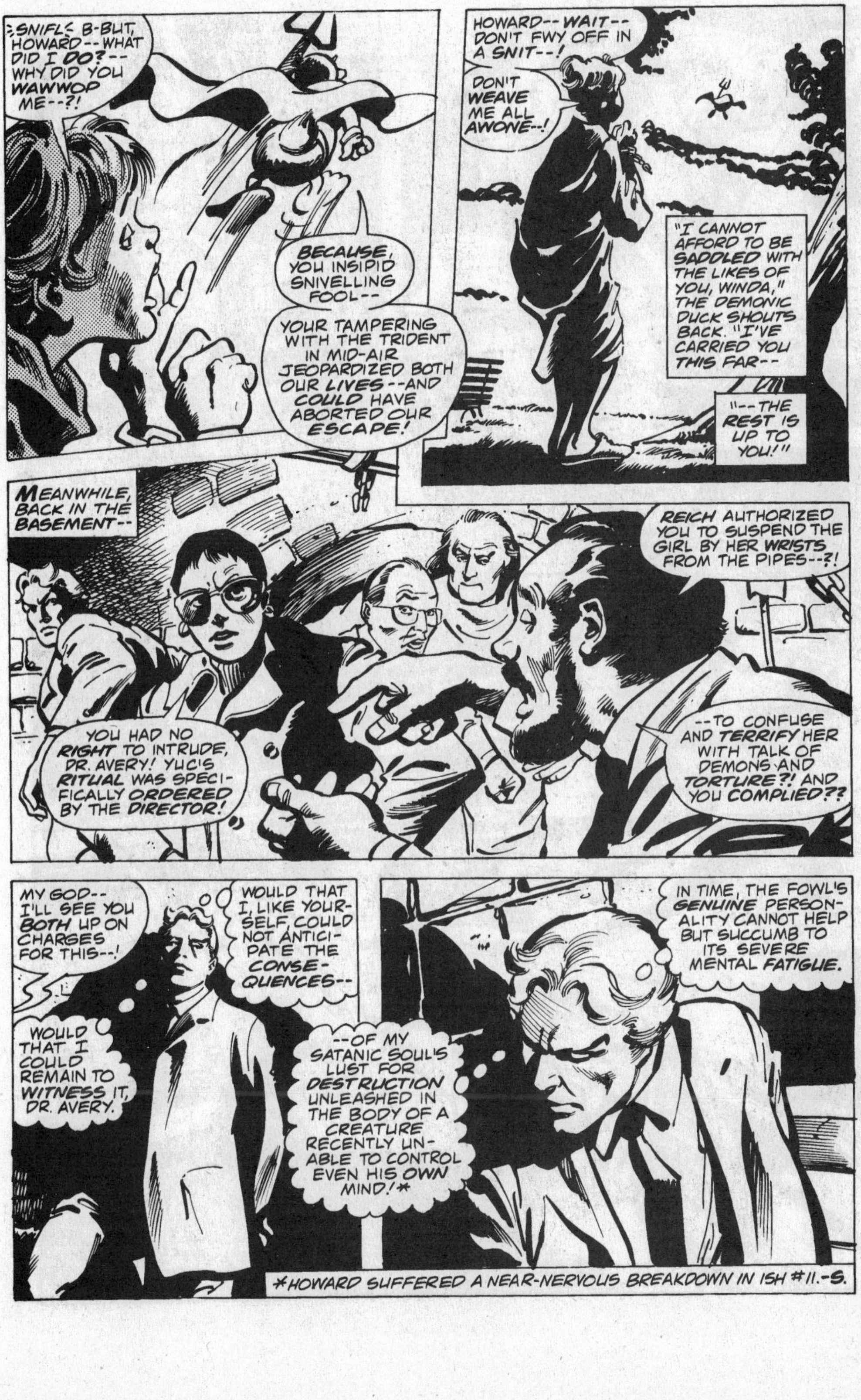
=SNIFL= B-BUT, HOWARD--WHAT DID I DO?--WHY DID YOU WAWWOP ME--?!
BECAUSE, YOU INSIPID SNIVELLING FOOL--
YOUR TAMPERING WITH THE TRIDENT IN MID-AIR JEOPARDIZED BOTH OUR LIVES--AND COULD HAVE ABORTED OUR ESCAPE!
HOWARD--WAIT--DON'T FWY OFF IN A SNIT--!
DON'T WEAVE ME ALL AWONE--!
"I CANNOT AFFORD TO BE SADDLED WITH THE LIKES OF YOU, WINDA," THE DEMONIC DUCK SHOUTS BACK. "I'VE CARRIED YOU THIS FAR--
"--THE REST IS UP TO YOU!"
MEANWHILE, BACK IN THE BASEMENT--
REICH AUTHORIZED YOU TO SUSPEND THE GIRL BY HER WRISTS FROM THE PIPES--?!
--TO CONFUSE AND TERRIFY HER WITH TALK OF DEMONS AND TORTURE?! AND YOU COMPLIED??
YOU HAD NO RIGHT TO INTRUDE, DR. AVERY! YUC'S RITUAL WAS SPECIFICALLY ORDERED BY THE DIRECTOR!
MY GOD--I'LL SEE YOU BOTH UP ON CHARGES FOR THIS--!
WOULD THAT I, LIKE YOURSELF, COULD NOT ANTICIPATE THE CONSEQUENCES--
WOULD THAT I COULD REMAIN TO WITNESS IT, DR. AVERY.
--OF MY SATANIC SOUL'S LUST FOR DESTRUCTION UNLEASHED IN THE BODY OF A CREATURE RECENTLY UNABLE TO CONTROL EVEN HIS OWN MIND!*
IN TIME, THE FOWL'S GENUINE PERSONALITY CANNOT HELP BUT SUCCUMB TO ITS SEVERE MENTAL FATIGUE.
*HOWARD SUFFERED A NEAR-NERVOUS BREAKDOWN IN ISH #11.-S.

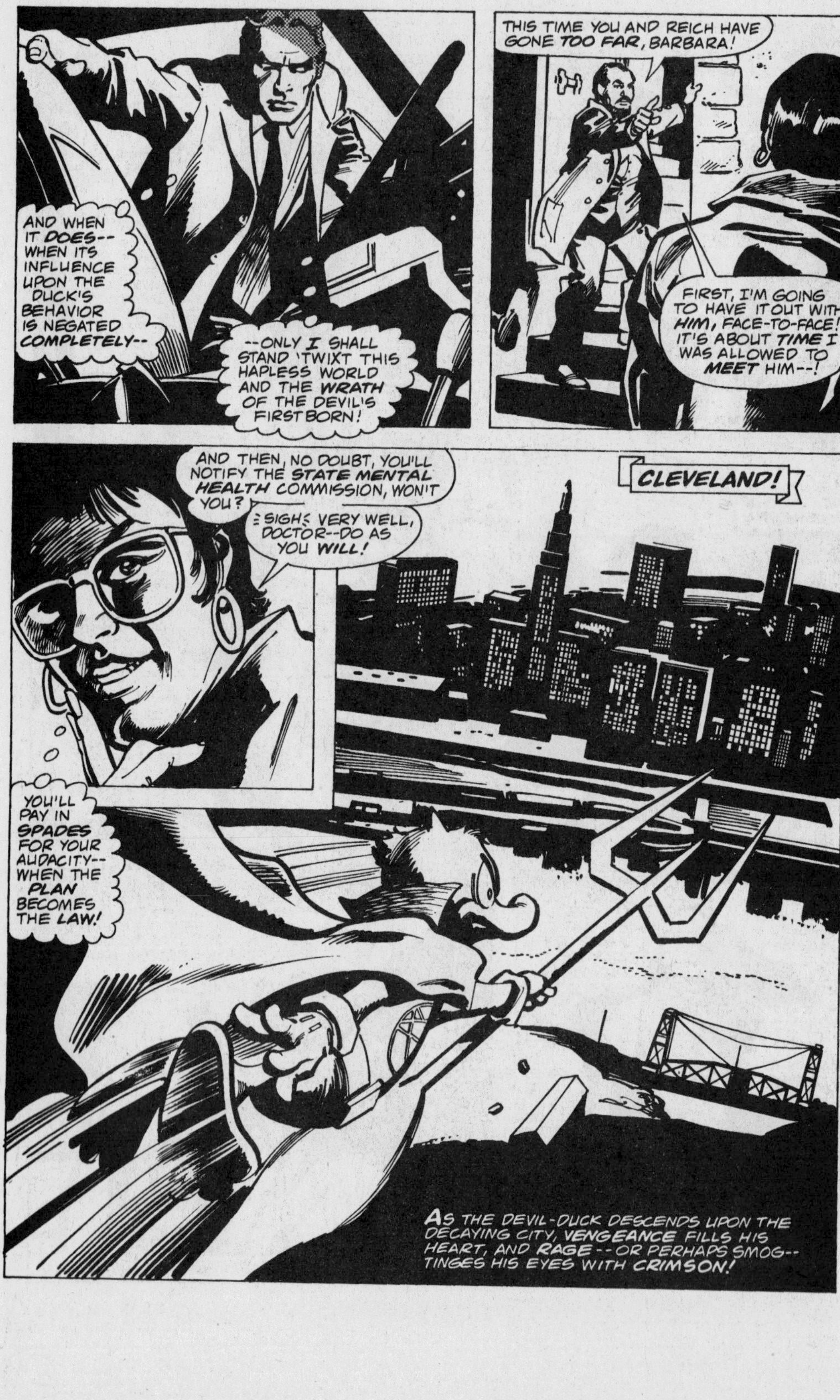
AND WHEN IT DOES-- WHEN ITS INFLUENCE UPON THE DUCK'S BEHAVIOR IS NEGATED COMPLETELY--
--ONLY I SHALL STAND 'TWIXT THIS HAPLESS WORLD AND THE WRATH OF THE DEVIL'S FIRSTBORN!
THIS TIME YOU AND REICH HAVE GONE TOO FAR, BARBARA!
FIRST, I'M GOING TO HAVE IT OUT WITH HIM, FACE-TO-FACE! IT'S ABOUT TIME I WAS ALLOWED TO MEET HIM--!
AND THEN, NO DOUBT, YOU'LL NOTIFY THE STATE MENTAL HEALTH COMMISSION, WON'T YOU?
SIGH VERY WELL, DOCTOR--DO AS YOU WILL!
YOU'LL PAY IN SPADES FOR YOUR AUDACITY-- WHEN THE PLAN BECOMES THE LAW!
CLEVELAND!
AS THE DEVIL-DUCK DESCENDS UPON THE DECAYING CITY, VENGEANCE FILLS HIS HEART, AND RAGE--OR PERHAPS SMOG-- TINGES HIS EYES WITH CRIMSON!

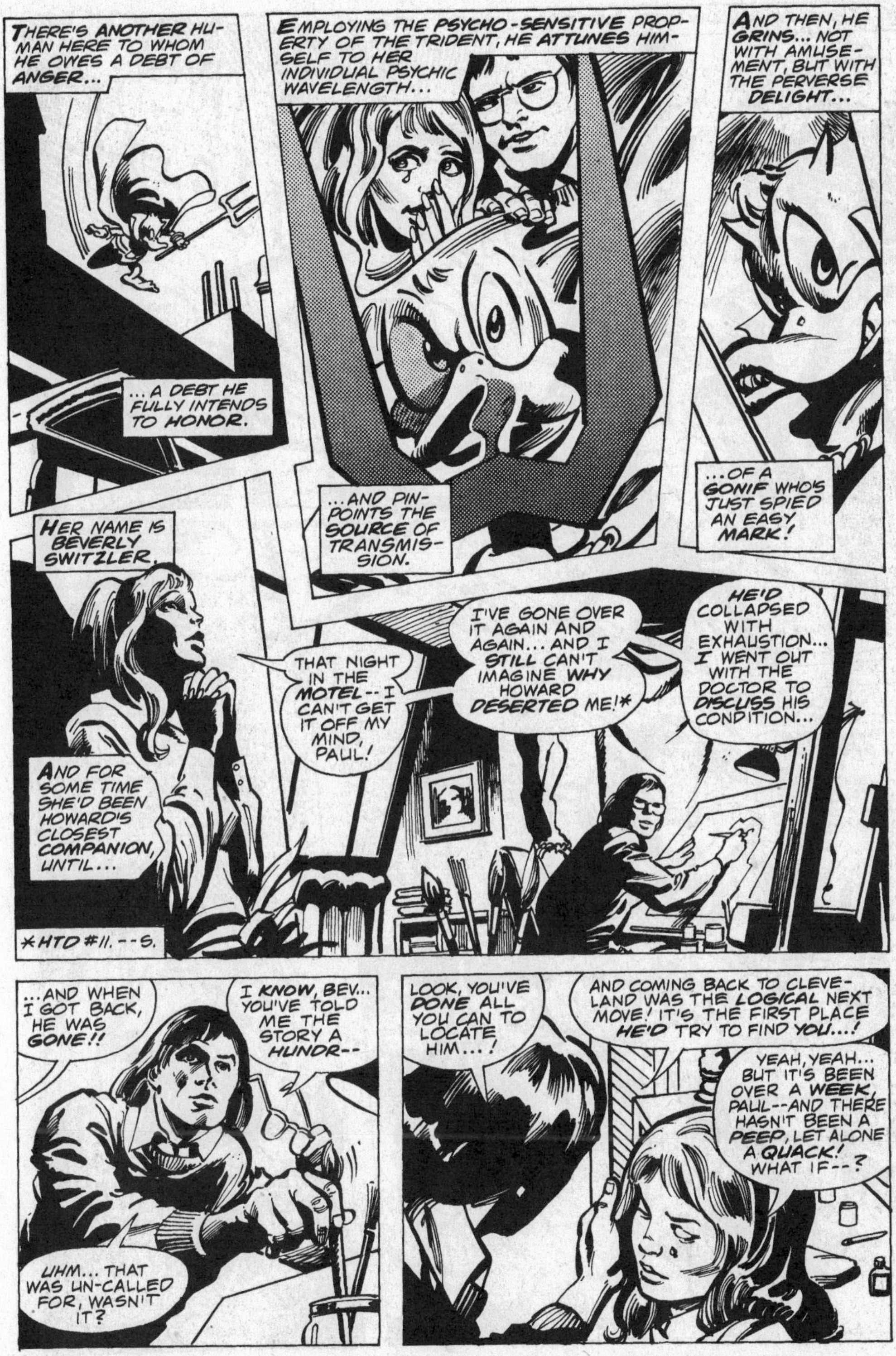
THERE'S ANOTHER HUMAN HERE TO WHOM HE OWES A DEBT OF ANGER...
...A DEBT HE FULLY INTENDS TO HONOR.
EMPLOYING THE PSYCHO-SENSITIVE PROPERTY OF THE TRIDENT, HE ATTUNES HIMSELF TO HER INDIVIDUAL PSYCHIC WAVELENGTH...
...AND PIN-POINTS THE SOURCE OF TRANSMISSION.
AND THEN, HE GRINS... NOT WITH AMUSEMENT, BUT WITH THE PERVERSE DELIGHT...
...OF A GONIF WHO'S JUST SPIED AN EASY MARK!
HER NAME IS BEVERLY SWITZLER.
AND FOR SOME TIME SHE'D BEEN HOWARD'S CLOSEST COMPANION, UNTIL...
THAT NIGHT IN THE MOTEL-- I CAN'T GET IT OFF MY MIND, PAUL!
I'VE GONE OVER IT AGAIN AND AGAIN... AND I STILL CAN'T IMAGINE WHY HOWARD DESERTED ME!*
HE'D COLLAPSED WITH EXHAUSTION... I WENT OUT WITH THE DOCTOR TO DISCUSS HIS CONDITION...
*HTD #11. --S.
...AND WHEN I GOT BACK, HE WAS GONE!!
I KNOW, BEV... YOU'VE TOLD ME THE STORY A HUNDR--
UHM... THAT WAS UN-CALLED FOR, WASN'T IT?
LOOK, YOU'VE DONE ALL YOU CAN TO LOCATE HIM...!
AND COMING BACK TO CLEVELAND WAS THE LOGICAL NEXT MOVE! IT'S THE FIRST PLACE HE'D TRY TO FIND YOU...!
YEAH, YEAH... BUT IT'S BEEN OVER A WEEK, PAUL--AND THERE HASN'T BEEN A PEEP, LET ALONE A QUACK! WHAT IF--?

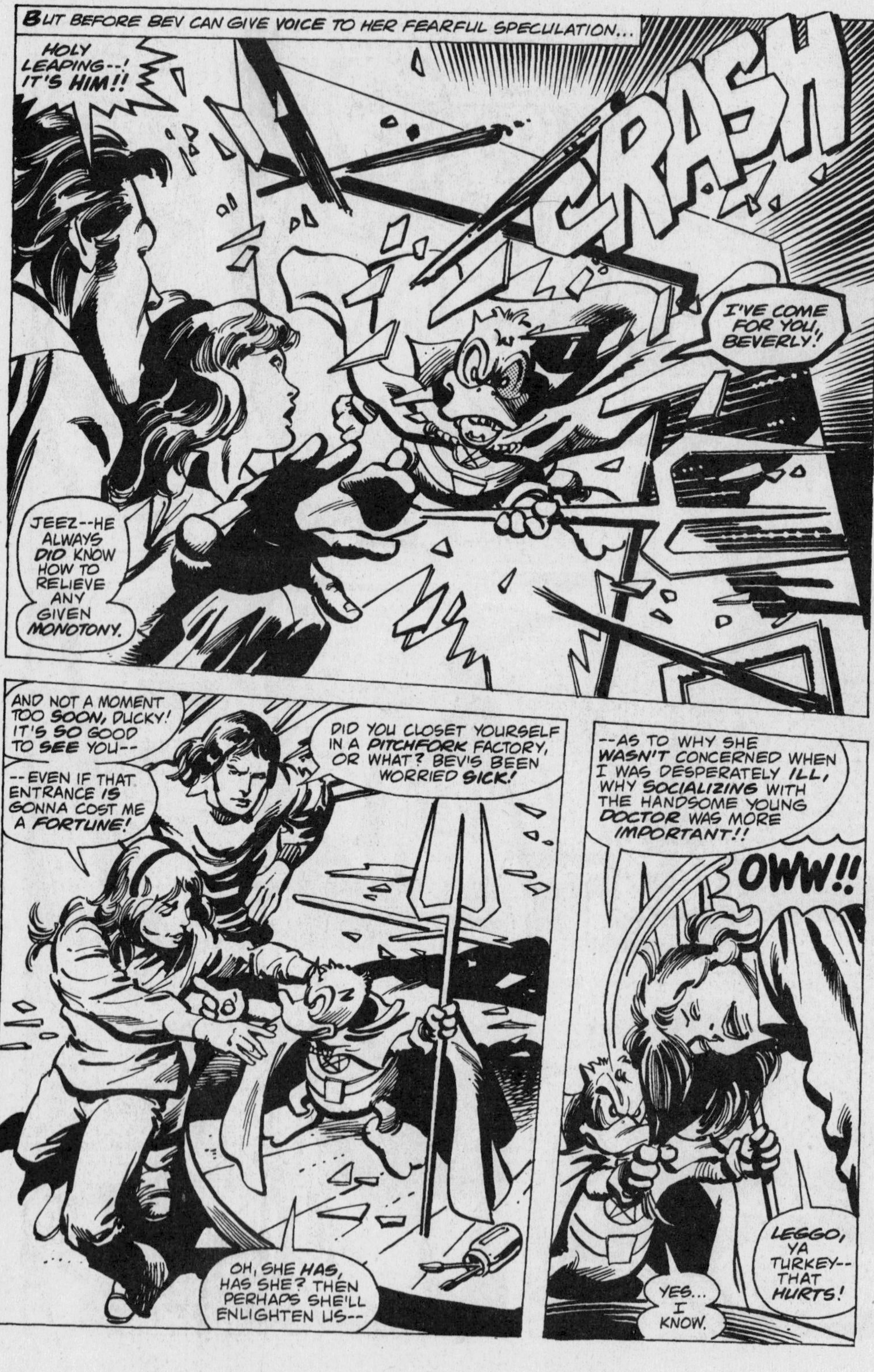
BUT BEFORE BEV CAN GIVE VOICE TO HER FEARFUL SPECULATION...
HOLY LEAPING--! IT'S HIM!!
CRASH
I'VE COME FOR YOU, BEVERLY!
JEEZ--HE ALWAYS DID KNOW HOW TO RELIEVE ANY GIVEN MONOTONY.
AND NOT A MOMENT TOO SOON, DUCKY! IT'S SO GOOD TO SEE YOU--
--EVEN IF THAT ENTRANCE IS GONNA COST ME A FORTUNE!
DID YOU CLOSET YOURSELF IN A PITCHFORK FACTORY, OR WHAT? BEV'S BEEN WORRIED SICK!
...
OH, SHE HAS, HAS SHE? THEN PERHAPS SHE'LL ENLIGHTEN US--
--AS TO WHY SHE WASN'T CONCERNED WHEN I WAS DESPERATELY ILL, WHY SOCIALIZING WITH THE HANDSOME YOUNG DOCTOR WAS MORE IMPORTANT!!
OWW!!
LEGGO, YA TURKEY-- THAT HURTS!
YES... I KNOW.

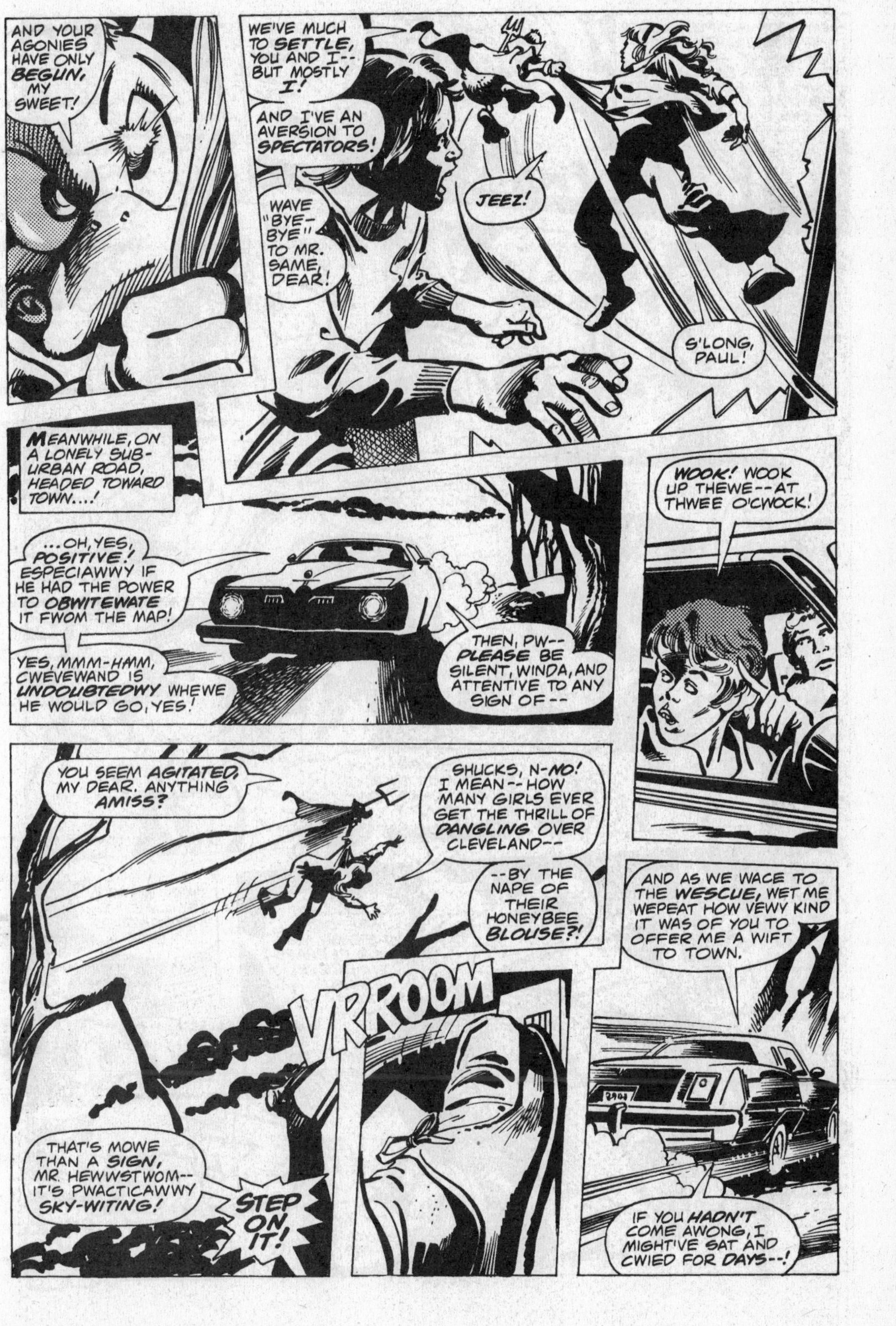
AND YOUR AGONIES HAVE ONLY BEGUN, MY SWEET!
WE'VE MUCH TO SETTLE, YOU AND I-- BUT MOSTLY I!
AND I'VE AN AVERSION TO SPECTATORS!
WAVE "BYE-BYE" TO MR. SAME, DEAR!
JEEZ!
S'LONG, PAUL!
MEANWHILE, ON A LONELY SUB-URBAN ROAD, HEADED TOWARD TOWN...!
...OH, YES, POSITIVE! ESPECIAWWY IF HE HAD THE POWER TO OBWITEWATE IT FWOM THE MAP!
YES, MMM-HMM, CWEVEWAND IS UNDOUBTEDWY WHEWE HE WOULD GO, YES!
THEN, PW-- PLEASE BE SILENT, WINDA, AND ATTENTIVE TO ANY SIGN OF --
WOOK! WOOK UP THEWE--AT THWEE O'CWOCK!
YOU SEEM AGITATED, MY DEAR. ANYTHING AMISS?
SHUCKS, N-NO! I MEAN--HOW MANY GIRLS EVER GET THE THRILL OF DANGLING OVER CLEVELAND--
--BY THE NAPE OF THEIR HONEYBEE BLOUSE?!
AND AS WE WACE TO THE WESCUE, WET ME WEPEAT HOW VEWY KIND IT WAS OF YOU TO OFFER ME A WIFT TO TOWN.
VRROOM
THAT'S MOWE THAN A SIGN, MR. HEWWSTWOM-- IT'S PWACTICAWWY SKY-WITING!
STEP ON IT!
IF YOU HADN'T COME AWONG, I MIGHT'VE SAT AND CWIED FOR DAYS--!

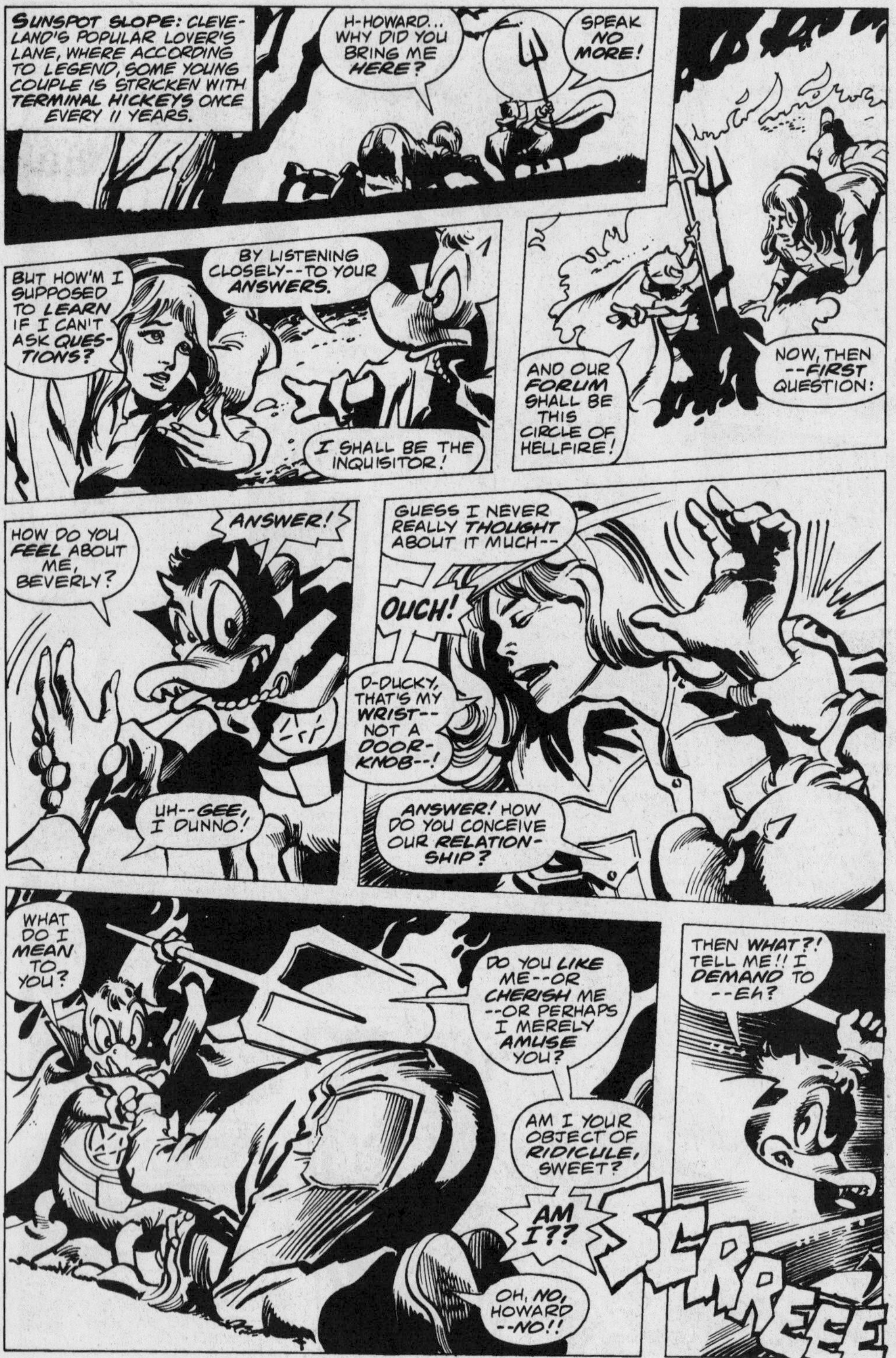
SUNSPOT SLOPE: CLEVELAND'S POPULAR LOVER'S LANE, WHERE ACCORDING TO LEGEND, SOME YOUNG COUPLE IS STRICKEN WITH TERMINAL HICKEYS ONCE EVERY 11 YEARS.
H-HOWARD... WHY DID YOU BRING ME HERE?
SPEAK NO MORE!
BUT HOW'M I SUPPOSED TO LEARN IF I CAN'T ASK QUESTIONS?
BY LISTENING CLOSELY--TO YOUR ANSWERS.
I SHALL BE THE INQUISITOR!
AND OUR FORUM SHALL BE THIS CIRCLE OF HELLFIRE!
NOW, THEN --FIRST QUESTION:
HOW DO YOU FEEL ABOUT ME, BEVERLY?
ANSWER!
UH--GEE, I DUNNO!
GUESS I NEVER REALLY THOUGHT ABOUT IT MUCH--
OUCH!
D-DUCKY, THAT'S MY WRIST-- NOT A DOOR-KNOB--!
ANSWER! HOW DO YOU CONCEIVE OUR RELATION-SHIP?
WHAT DO I MEAN TO YOU?
DO YOU LIKE ME--OR CHERISH ME --OR PERHAPS I MERELY AMUSE YOU?
AM I YOUR OBJECT OF RIDICULE, SWEET?
AM I??
OH, NO, HOWARD --NO!!
SCRREEE
THEN WHAT?! TELL ME!! I DEMAND TO --EH?

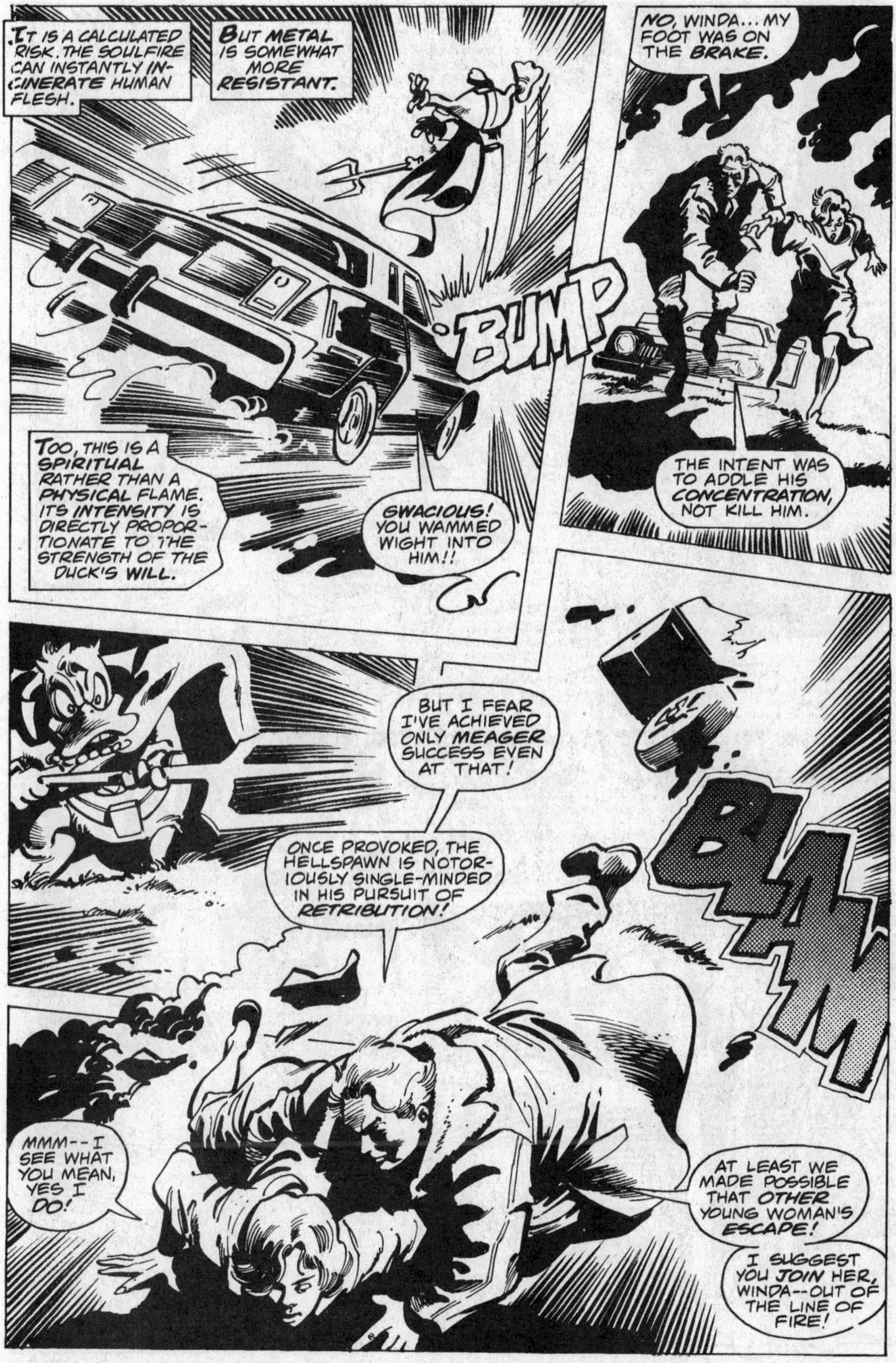
IT IS A CALCULATED RISK. THE SOULFIRE CAN INSTANTLY INCINERATE HUMAN FLESH.
BUT METAL IS SOMEWHAT MORE RESISTANT.
BUMP
TOO, THIS IS A SPIRITUAL RATHER THAN A PHYSICAL FLAME. ITS INTENSITY IS DIRECTLY PROPORTIONATE TO THE STRENGTH OF THE DUCK'S WILL.
GWACIOUS! YOU WAMMED WIGHT INTO HIM!!
NO, WINDA... MY FOOT WAS ON THE BRAKE.
THE INTENT WAS TO ADDLE HIS CONCENTRATION, NOT KILL HIM.
BUT I FEAR I'VE ACHIEVED ONLY MEAGER SUCCESS EVEN AT THAT!
ONCE PROVOKED, THE HELLSPAWN IS NOTORIOUSLY SINGLE-MINDED IN HIS PURSUIT OF RETRIBUTION!
BLAM
MMM--I SEE WHAT YOU MEAN, YES I DO!
AT LEAST WE MADE POSSIBLE THAT OTHER YOUNG WOMAN'S ESCAPE!
I SUGGEST YOU JOIN HER, WINDA--OUT OF THE LINE OF FIRE!

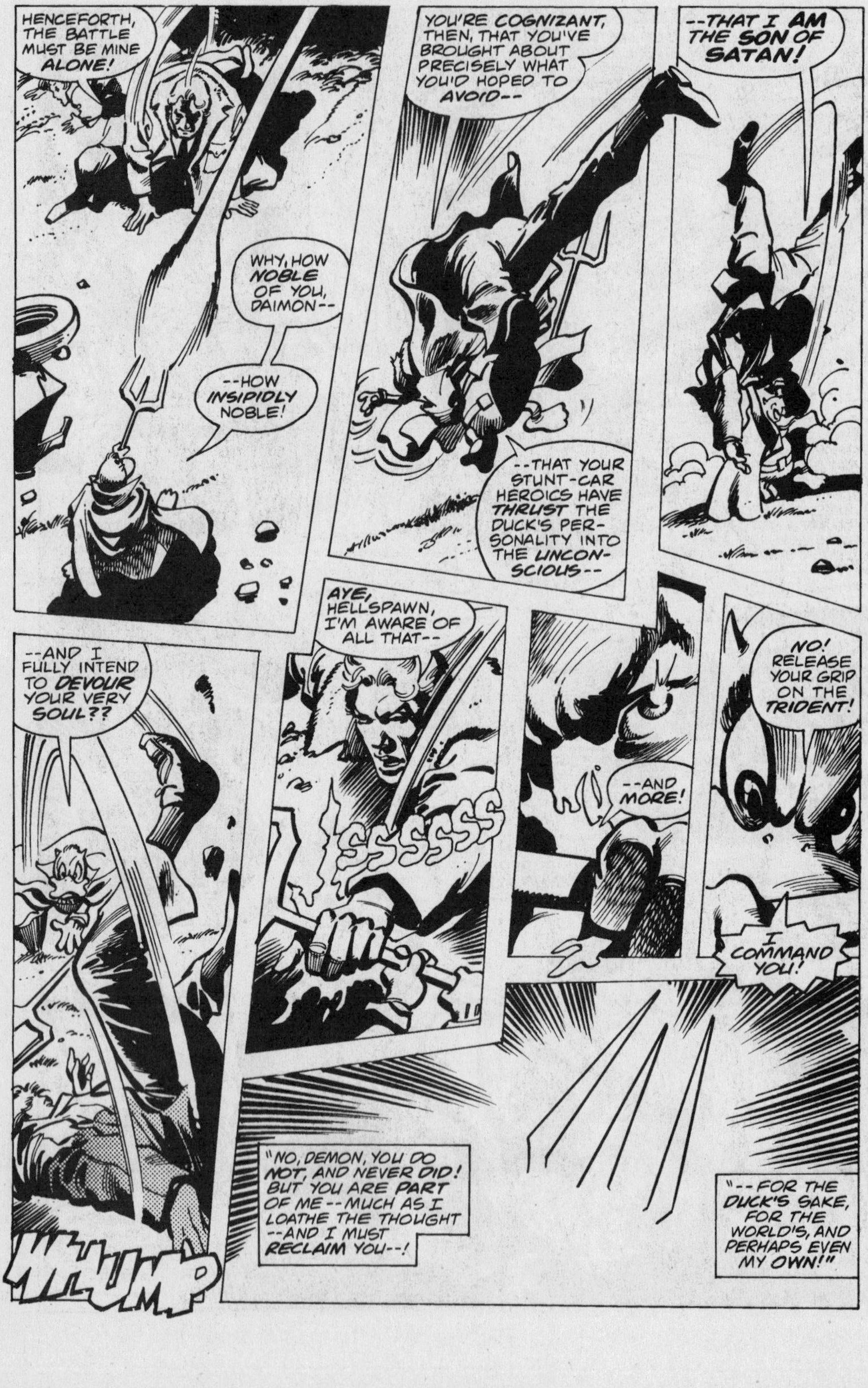
HENCEFORTH, THE BATTLE MUST BE MINE ALONE!
WHY, HOW NOBLE OF YOU, DAIMON--
--HOW INSIPIDLY NOBLE!
YOU'RE COGNIZANT, THEN, THAT YOU'VE BROUGHT ABOUT PRECISELY WHAT YOU'D HOPED TO AVOID--
--THAT YOUR STUNT-CAR HEROICS HAVE THRUST THE DUCK'S PERSONALITY INTO THE UNCONSCIOUS--
--THAT I AM THE SON OF SATAN!
--AND I FULLY INTEND TO DEVOUR YOUR VERY SOUL??
WHUMP
AYE, HELLSPAWN, I'M AWARE OF ALL THAT--
SSSSSS
--AND MORE!
NO! RELEASE YOUR GRIP ON THE TRIDENT!
I COMMAND YOU!
"NO, DEMON, YOU DO NOT, AND NEVER DID! BUT YOU ARE PART OF ME--MUCH AS I LOATHE THE THOUGHT--AND I MUST RECLAIM YOU--!
"--FOR THE DUCK'S SAKE, FOR THE WORLD'S, AND PERHAPS EVEN MY OWN!"

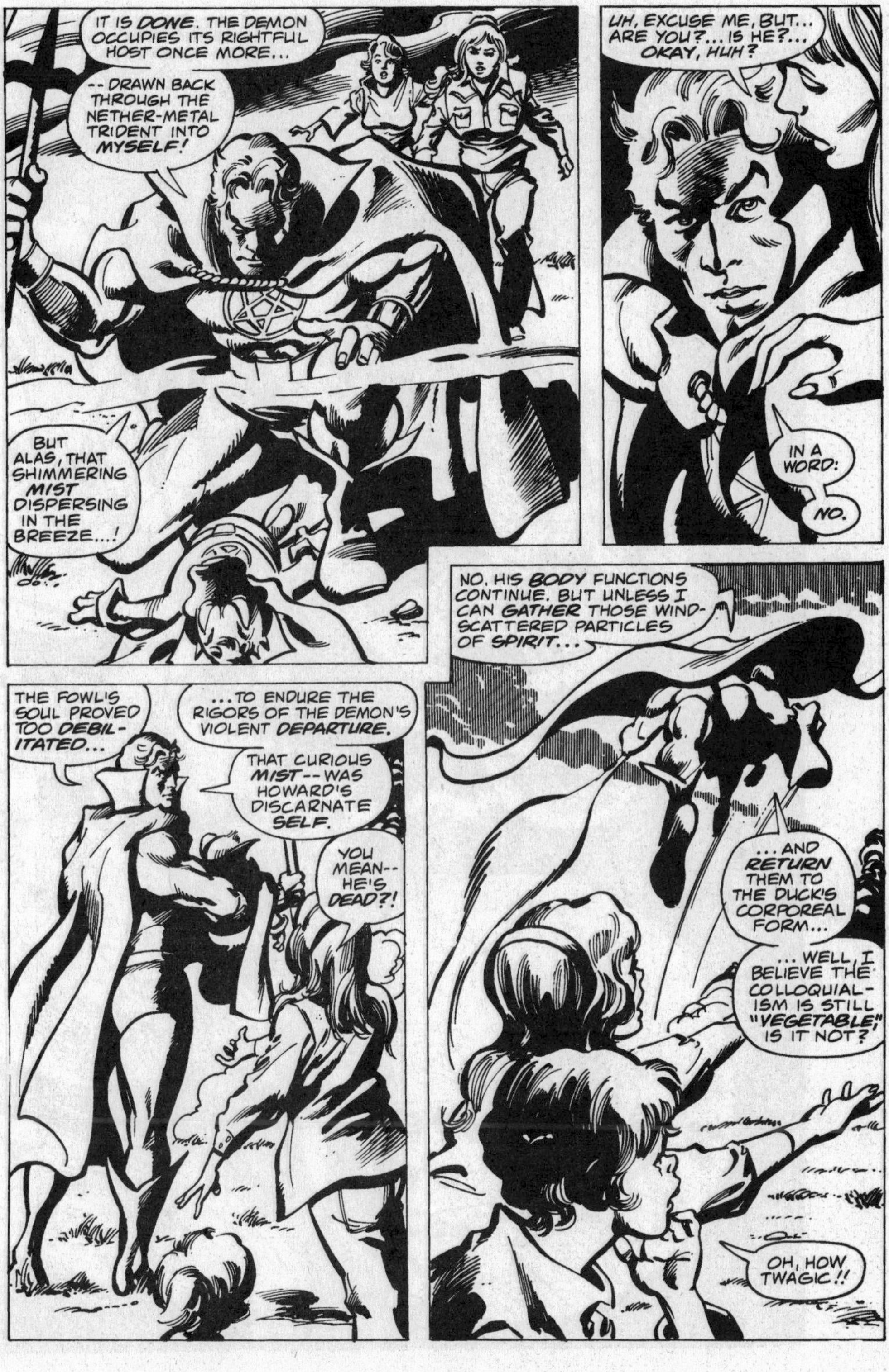
IT IS DONE. THE DEMON OCCUPIES ITS RIGHTFUL HOST ONCE MORE...
--DRAWN BACK THROUGH THE NETHER-METAL TRIDENT INTO MYSELF!
BUT ALAS, THAT SHIMMERING MIST DISPERSING IN THE BREEZE...!
UH, EXCUSE ME, BUT... ARE YOU?... IS HE?... OKAY, HUH?
IN A WORD:
NO.
THE FOWL'S SOUL PROVED TOO DEBILITATED...
...TO ENDURE THE RIGORS OF THE DEMON'S VIOLENT DEPARTURE.
THAT CURIOUS MIST--WAS HOWARD'S DISCARNATE SELF.
YOU MEAN--HE'S DEAD?!
NO. HIS BODY FUNCTIONS CONTINUE. BUT UNLESS I CAN GATHER THOSE WIND-SCATTERED PARTICLES OF SPIRIT...
...AND RETURN THEM TO THE DUCK'S CORPOREAL FORM...
...WELL, I BELIEVE THE COLLOQUIALISM IS STILL "VEGETABLE," IS IT NOT?
OH, HOW TWAGIC!!

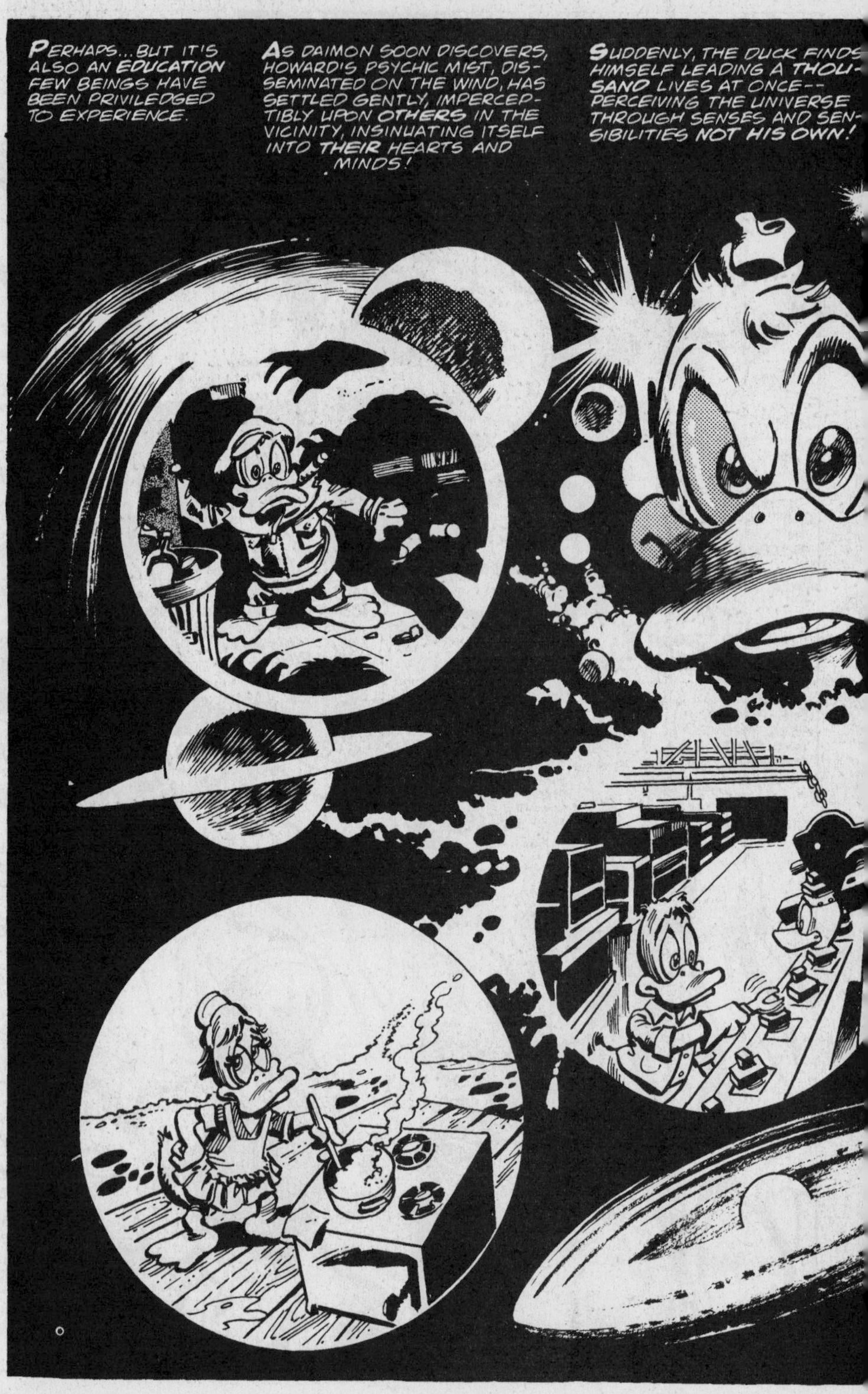
PERHAPS... BUT IT'S ALSO AN EDUCATION FEW BEINGS HAVE BEEN PRIVILEDGED TO EXPERIENCE.
AS DAIMON SOON DISCOVERS, HOWARD'S PSYCHIC MIST, DISSEMINATED ON THE WIND, HAS SETTLED GENTLY, IMPERCEPTIBLY UPON OTHERS IN THE VICINITY, INSINUATING ITSELF INTO THEIR HEARTS AND MINDS!
SUDDENLY, THE DUCK FINDS HIMSELF LEADING A THOUSAND LIVES AT ONCE-- PERCEIVING THE UNIVERSE THROUGH SENSES AND SENSIBILITIES NOT HIS OWN!

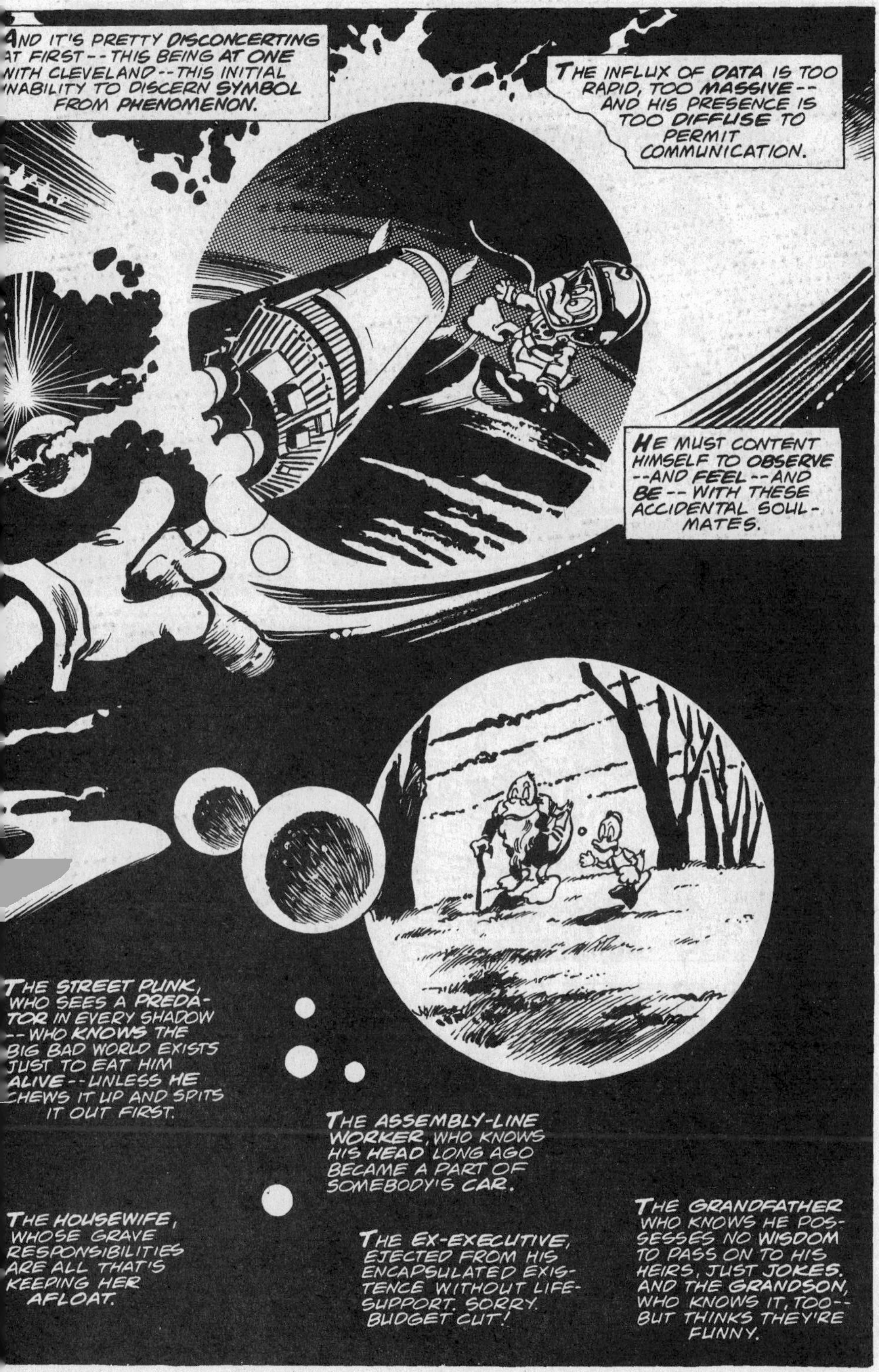
AND IT'S PRETTY DISCONCERTING AT FIRST--THIS BEING AT ONE WITH CLEVELAND--THIS INITIAL INABILITY TO DISCERN SYMBOL FROM PHENOMENON.
THE INFLUX OF DATA IS TOO RAPID, TOO MASSIVE--AND HIS PRESENCE IS TOO DIFFUSE TO PERMIT COMMUNICATION.
HE MUST CONTENT HIMSELF TO OBSERVE --AND FEEL--AND BE--WITH THESE ACCIDENTAL SOUL-MATES.
THE STREET PUNK, WHO SEES A PREDATOR IN EVERY SHADOW --WHO KNOWS THE BIG BAD WORLD EXISTS JUST TO EAT HIM ALIVE--UNLESS HE CHEWS IT UP AND SPITS IT OUT FIRST.
THE ASSEMBLY-LINE WORKER, WHO KNOWS HIS HEAD LONG AGO BECAME A PART OF SOMEBODY'S CAR.
THE HOUSEWIFE, WHOSE GRAVE RESPONSIBILITIES ARE ALL THAT'S KEEPING HER AFLOAT.
THE EX-EXECUTIVE, EJECTED FROM HIS ENCAPSULATED EXISTENCE WITHOUT LIFE-SUPPORT. SORRY. BUDGET CUT!
THE GRANDFATHER WHO KNOWS HE POSSESSES NO WISDOM TO PASS ON TO HIS HEIRS, JUST JOKES. AND THE GRANDSON, WHO KNOWS IT, TOO--BUT THINKS THEY'RE FUNNY.

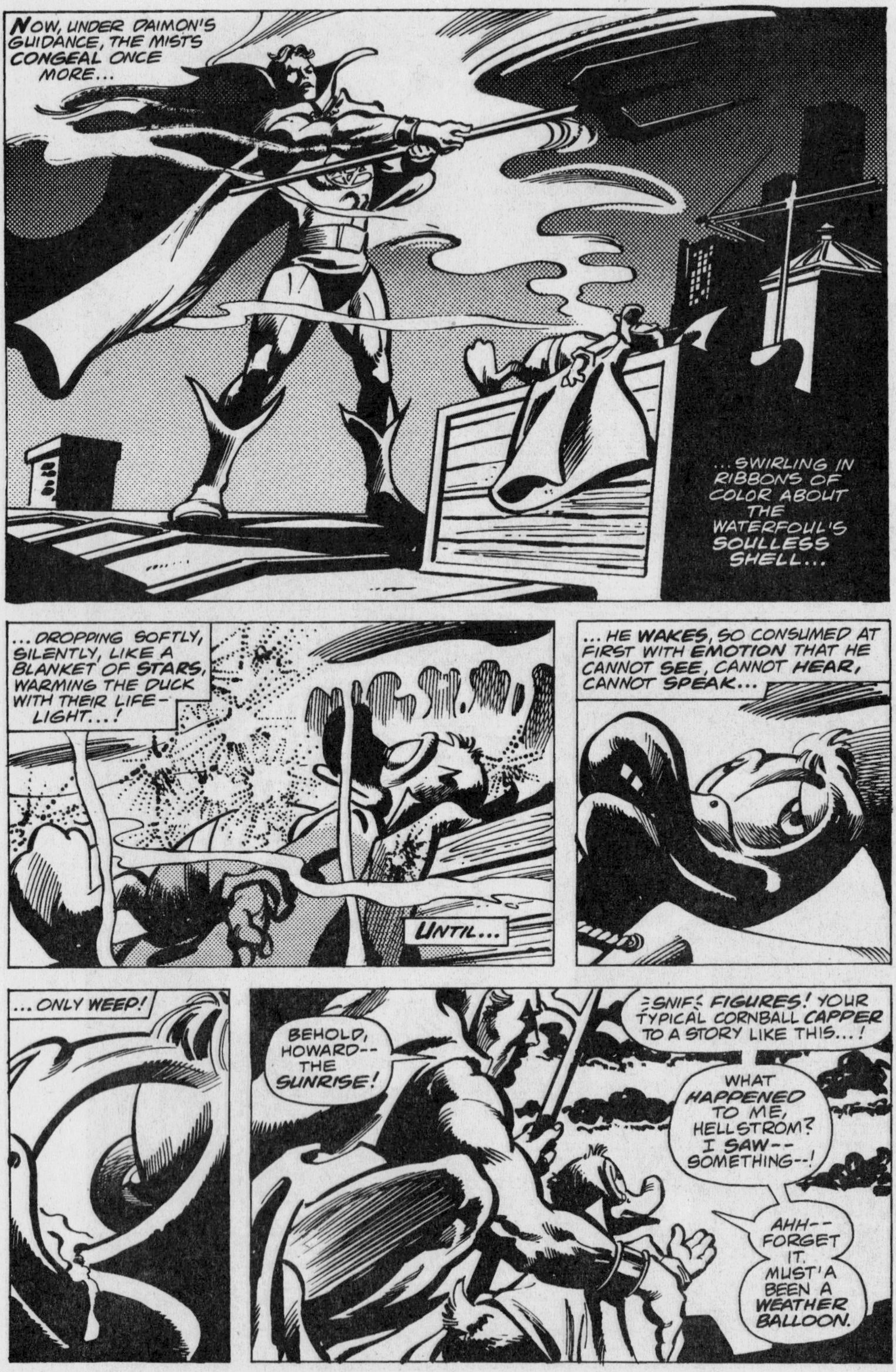
NOW, UNDER DAIMON'S GUIDANCE, THE MISTS CONGEAL ONCE MORE...
...SWIRLING IN RIBBONS OF COLOR ABOUT THE WATERFOUL'S SOULLESS SHELL...
...DROPPING SOFTLY, SILENTLY, LIKE A BLANKET OF STARS, WARMING THE DUCK WITH THEIR LIFE-LIGHT...!
UNTIL...
...HE WAKES, SO CONSUMED AT FIRST WITH EMOTION THAT HE CANNOT SEE, CANNOT HEAR, CANNOT SPEAK...
...ONLY WEEP!
BEHOLD, HOWARD-- THE SUNRISE!
SNIF FIGURES! YOUR TYPICAL CORNBALL CAPPER TO A STORY LIKE THIS...!
WHAT HAPPENED TO ME, HELLSTROM? I SAW-- SOMETHING--!
AHH-- FORGET IT. MUST'A BEEN A WEATHER BALLOON.

EPILOG:

WELL... WHAT'S THE *VERDICT?* DO HOWARD AND WINDA GO BACK TO THE *ASYLUM--?*

OR DO I GET TO *KEEP* THEM?

WE'RE GONNA BE *BOARDERS,* PAUL--NOT SLAVES!

TELL 'EM WE PROMISE TO HOLD WEEKLY GROUP *THERAPY* SESSIONS!

NO NEED, MS. SWITZLER. *DR. AVERY* HAS ALREADY SIGNED THE NECESSARY PAPERS FOR THEIR DISCHARGE.

WEAWWY?! OH, JOY!! WE'RE *FWEE!!*

THEN IT'S *OFFICIAL!* WE'RE REUNITED DUCKY! THE PARTNERSHIP'S BACK ON!

≈waaaugh≈

AND BACK AT THE HOSPITAL...

HE'S DONE IT, HERR DOKTOR-- SIGNED THEIR RELEASES!

IN *DIRECT* DISOBEDIENCE OF *MEIN ORDERS!* VERY VELL!

THEN YOU *AGREE,* HERR DOKTOR?

JAH, YUC! DER TIME HAS COME TO *MOBILIZE!*

PREPARE TO *EVACUATE* ZESE PREMISES, BARBARA--

--UND *RELOCATE* DER OPERATION TO REV. YUC'S PRIVATE *UNIVERSITY!*

JAWOHL... NOW "DR. REICH" VILL DISAPPEAR MITOUT DER *TRACE,* TO MAKE ROOM FOR--DER VON --DER ONLY--!!

NEXT: THE HTD ANNUAL #1 WITH *"BAD NIGHT IN BAGMOM!"* **THEN** THE *"ISLAND OF* DR. *BONG!"* IN HTD #15 --ON SALE SOON!

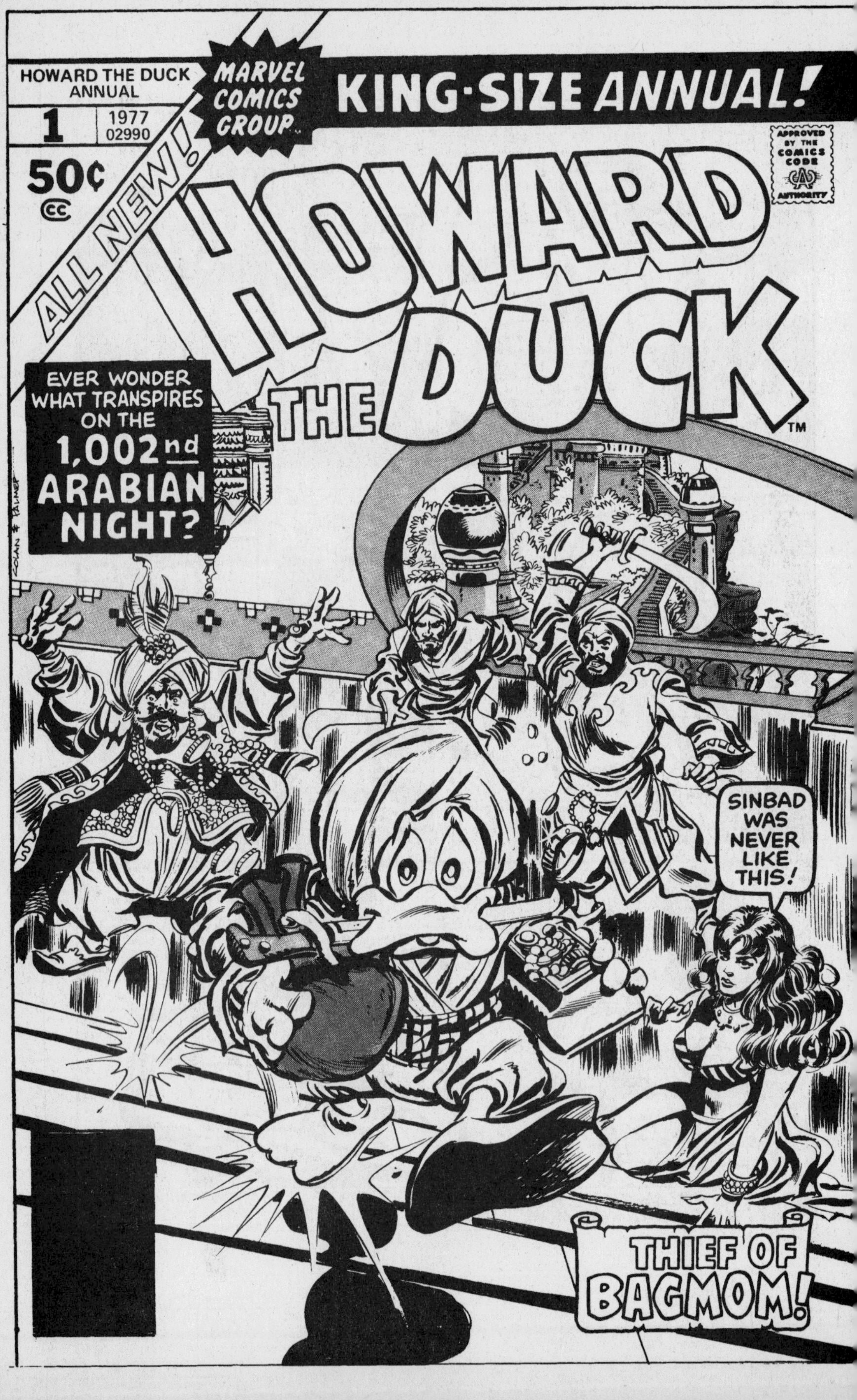

HOWARD THE DUCK ANNUAL
1
1977
02990
50¢
CC
MARVEL COMICS GROUP
KING-SIZE ANNUAL!
ALL NEW!
APPROVED BY THE COMICS CODE AUTHORITY
HOWARD THE DUCK™
EVER WONDER WHAT TRANSPIRES ON THE 1,002nd ARABIAN NIGHT?
SINBAD WAS NEVER LIKE THIS!
THIEF OF BAGMOM!

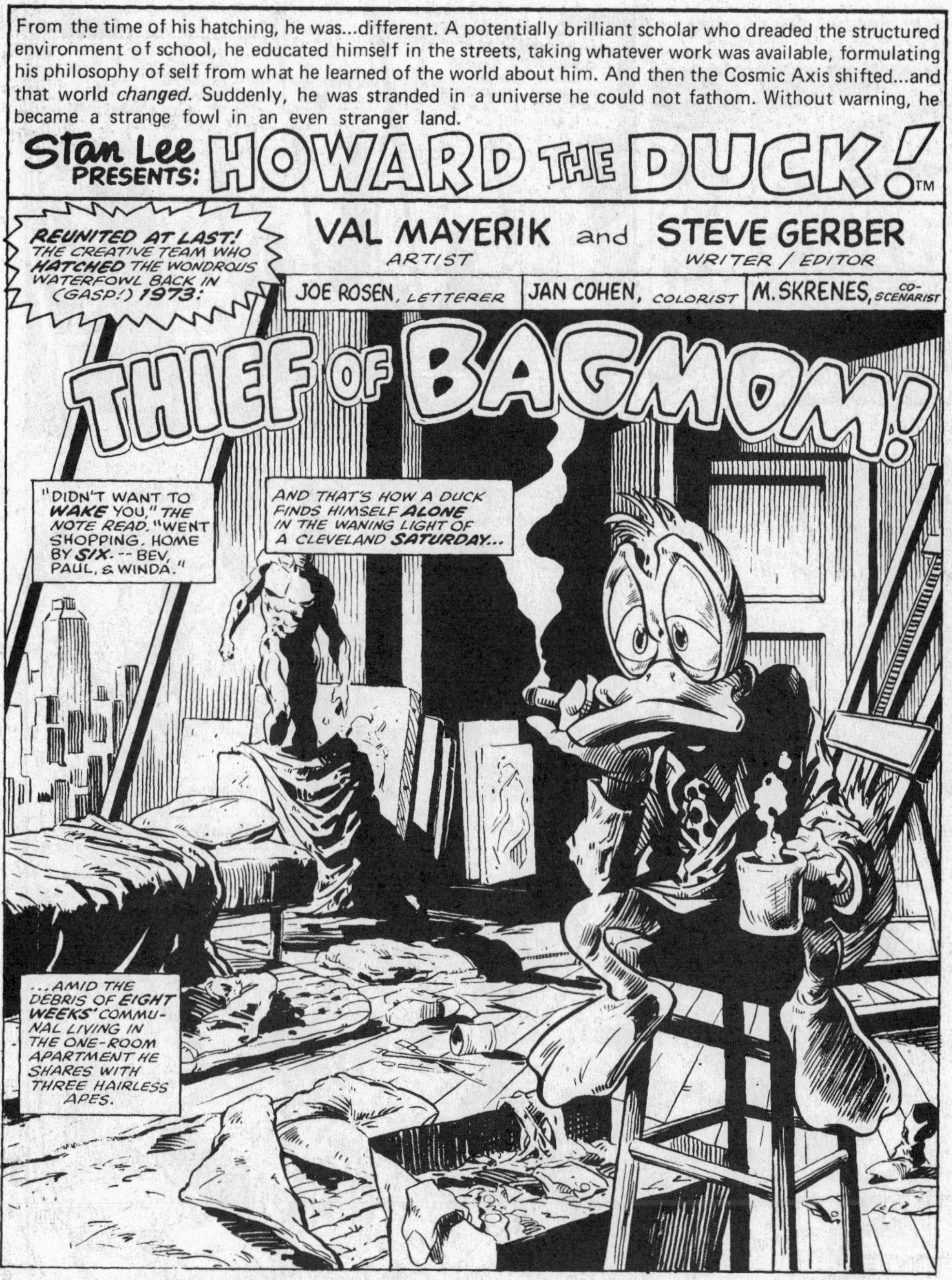
From the time of his hatching, he was...different. A potentially brilliant scholar who dreaded the structured environment of school, he educated himself in the streets, taking whatever work was available, formulating his philosophy of self from what he learned of the world about him. And then the Cosmic Axis shifted...and that world *changed.* Suddenly, he was stranded in a universe he could not fathom. Without warning, he became a strange fowl in an even stranger land.
STAN LEE PRESENTS: HOWARD THE DUCK!™
REUNITED AT LAST! THE CREATIVE TEAM WHO HATCHED THE WONDROUS WATERFOWL BACK IN (GASP!) 1973:
VAL MAYERIK ARTIST and STEVE GERBER WRITER / EDITOR
JOE ROSEN, LETTERER
JAN COHEN, COLORIST
M. SKRENES, CO-SCENARIST
THIEF OF BAGMOM!
"DIDN'T WANT TO WAKE YOU," THE NOTE READ. "WENT SHOPPING. HOME BY SIX. -- BEV, PAUL, & WINDA."
AND THAT'S HOW A DUCK FINDS HIMSELF ALONE IN THE WANING LIGHT OF A CLEVELAND SATURDAY...
...AMID THE DEBRIS OF EIGHT WEEKS' COMMUNAL LIVING IN THE ONE-ROOM APARTMENT HE SHARES WITH THREE HAIRLESS APES.

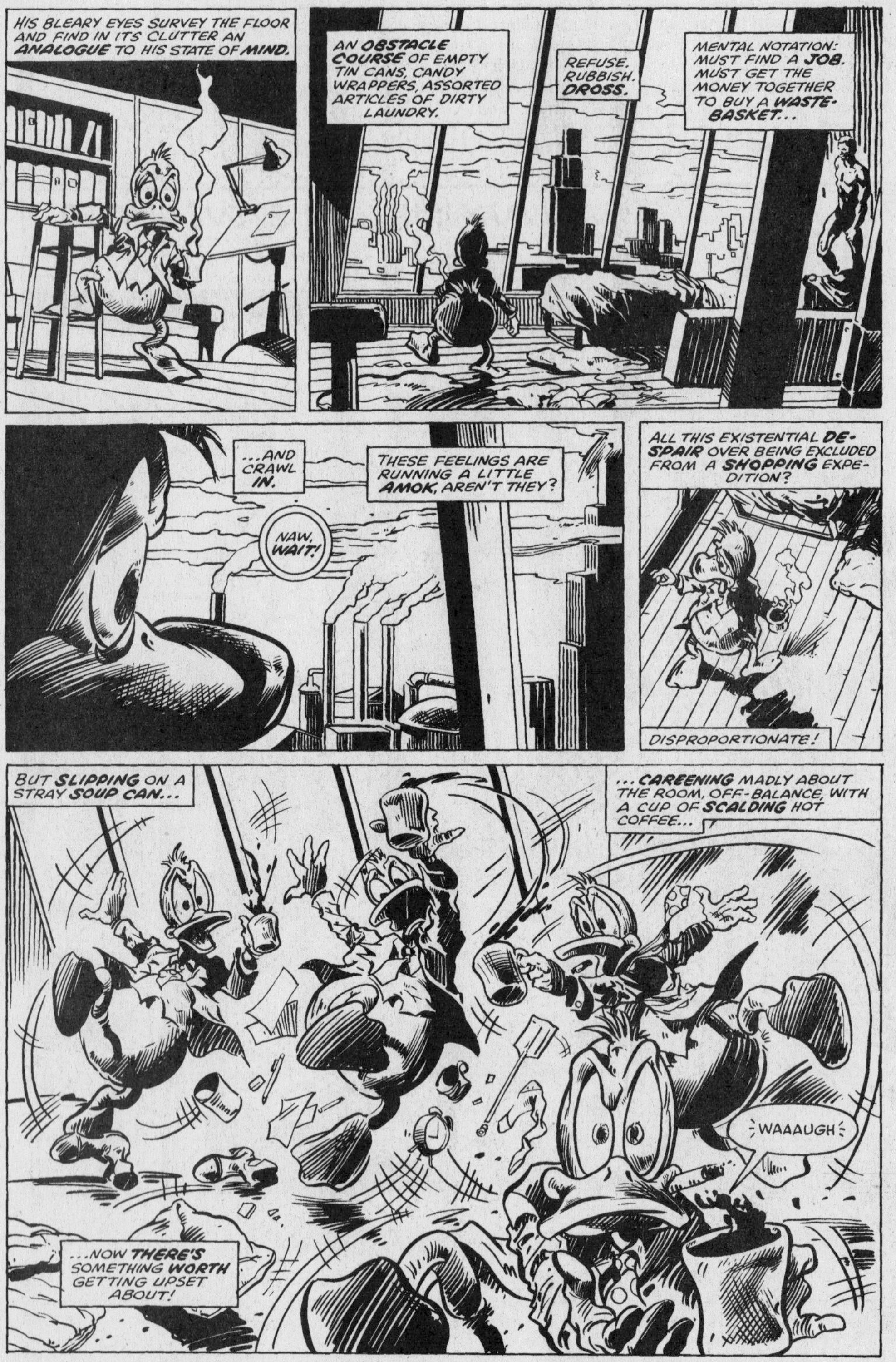

HIS BLEARY EYES SURVEY THE FLOOR AND FIND IN ITS CLUTTER AN ANALOGUE TO HIS STATE OF MIND.
AN OBSTACLE COURSE OF EMPTY TIN CANS, CANDY WRAPPERS, ASSORTED ARTICLES OF DIRTY LAUNDRY.
REFUSE. RUBBISH. DROSS.
MENTAL NOTATION: MUST FIND A JOB. MUST GET THE MONEY TOGETHER TO BUY A WASTE-BASKET...
...AND CRAWL IN.
THESE FEELINGS ARE RUNNING A LITTLE AMOK, AREN'T THEY?
NAW, WAIT!
ALL THIS EXISTENTIAL DE-SPAIR OVER BEING EXCLUDED FROM A SHOPPING EXPE-DITION?
DISPROPORTIONATE!
BUT SLIPPING ON A STRAY SOUP CAN...
...CAREENING MADLY ABOUT THE ROOM, OFF-BALANCE, WITH A CUP OF SCALDING HOT COFFEE...
WAAAUGH
...NOW THERE'S SOMETHING WORTH GETTING UPSET ABOUT!

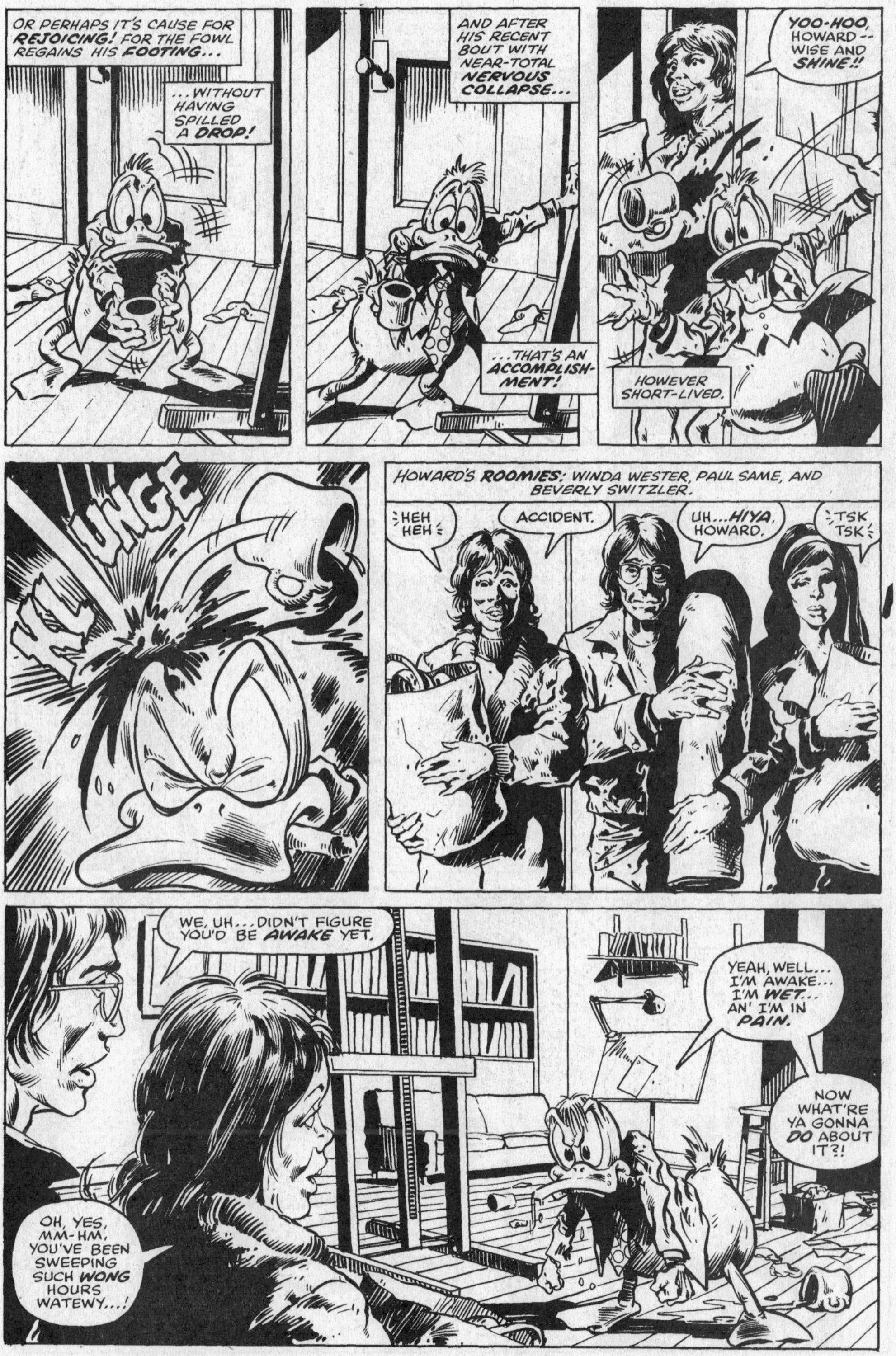
OR PERHAPS IT'S CAUSE FOR REJOICING! FOR THE FOWL REGAINS HIS FOOTING...
...WITHOUT HAVING SPILLED A DROP!
AND AFTER HIS RECENT BOUT WITH NEAR-TOTAL NERVOUS COLLAPSE...
...THAT'S AN ACCOMPLISHMENT!
YOO-HOO, HOWARD -- WISE AND SHINE!!
HOWEVER SHORT-LIVED.
KLUNGE
HOWARD'S ROOMIES: WINDA WESTER, PAUL SAME, AND BEVERLY SWITZLER.
HEH HEH
ACCIDENT.
UH...HIYA, HOWARD.
TSK TSK
WE, UH... DIDN'T FIGURE YOU'D BE AWAKE YET.
YEAH, WELL... I'M AWAKE... I'M WET... AN' I'M IN PAIN.
NOW WHAT'RE YA GONNA DO ABOUT IT?!
OH, YES, MM-HM, YOU'VE BEEN SWEEPING SUCH WONG HOURS WATEWY...!

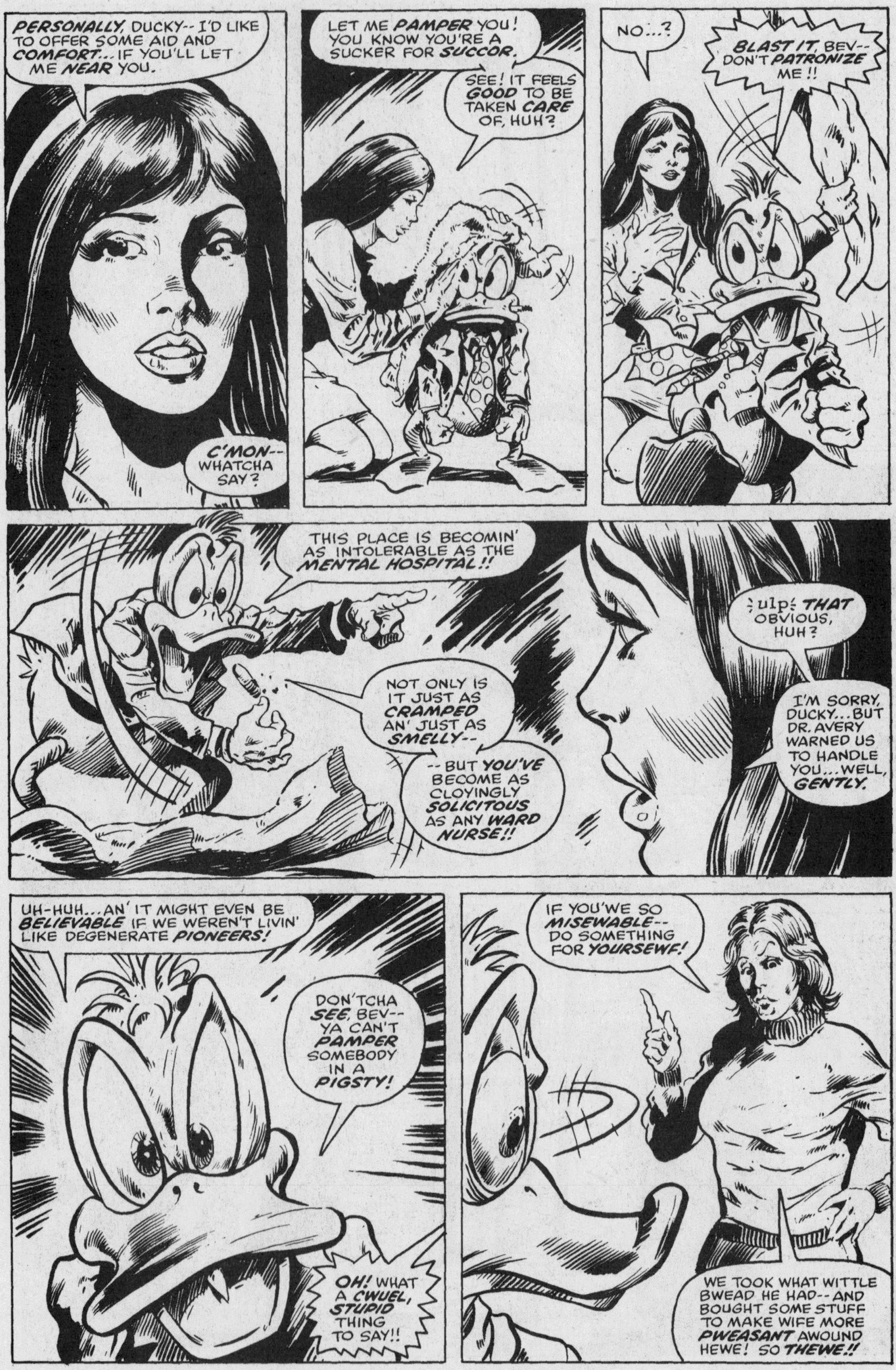
PERSONALLY, DUCKY-- I'D LIKE TO OFFER SOME AID AND COMFORT... IF YOU'LL LET ME NEAR YOU.
C'MON-- WHATCHA SAY?
LET ME PAMPER YOU! YOU KNOW YOU'RE A SUCKER FOR SUCCOR.
SEE! IT FEELS GOOD TO BE TAKEN CARE OF, HUH?
NO...?
BLAST IT, BEV-- DON'T PATRONIZE ME!!
THIS PLACE IS BECOMIN' AS INTOLERABLE AS THE MENTAL HOSPITAL!!
NOT ONLY IS IT JUST AS CRAMPED AN' JUST AS SMELLY--
-- BUT YOU'VE BECOME AS CLOYINGLY SOLICITOUS AS ANY WARD NURSE!!
ulp THAT OBVIOUS, HUH?
I'M SORRY, DUCKY... BUT DR. AVERY WARNED US TO HANDLE YOU... WELL, GENTLY.
UH-HUH... AN' IT MIGHT EVEN BE BELIEVABLE IF WE WEREN'T LIVIN' LIKE DEGENERATE PIONEERS!
DON'TCHA SEE, BEV-- YA CAN'T PAMPER SOMEBODY IN A PIGSTY!
OH! WHAT A CWUEL, STUPID THING TO SAY!!
IF YOU'WE SO MISEWABLE-- DO SOMETHING FOR YOURSEWF!
WE TOOK WHAT WITTLE BWEAD HE HAD-- AND BOUGHT SOME STUFF TO MAKE WIFE MORE PWEASANT AWOUND HEWE! SO THEWE!!

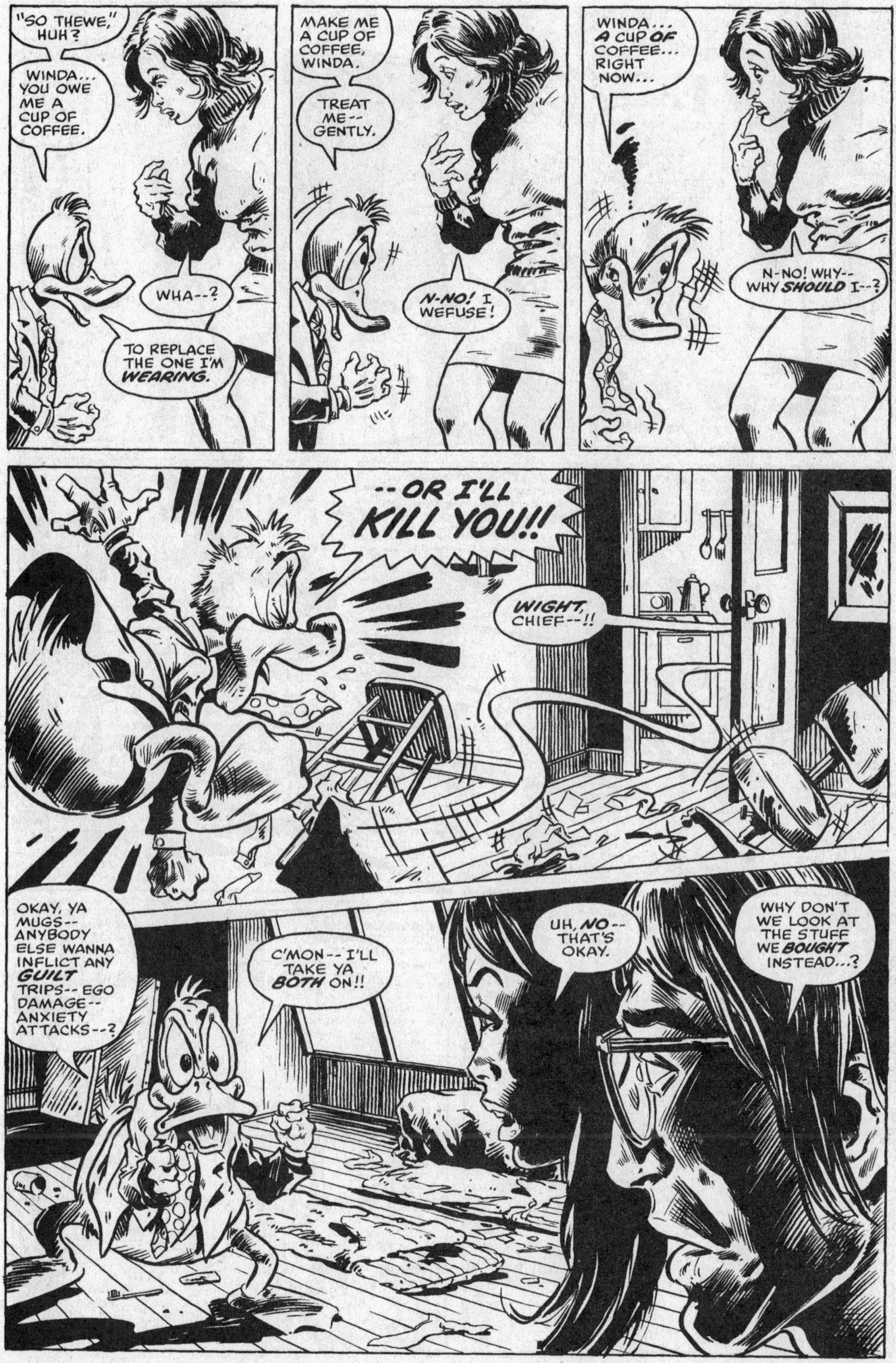
"SO THEWE," HUH?
WINDA... YOU OWE ME A CUP OF COFFEE.
WHA--?
TO REPLACE THE ONE I'M WEARING.
MAKE ME A CUP OF COFFEE, WINDA.
TREAT ME-- GENTLY.
N-NO! I WEFUSE!
WINDA... A CUP OF COFFEE... RIGHT NOW...
N-NO! WHY-- WHY SHOULD I--?
--OR I'LL KILL YOU!!
WIGHT, CHIEF--!!
OKAY, YA MUGS-- ANYBODY ELSE WANNA INFLICT ANY GUILT TRIPS-- EGO DAMAGE-- ANXIETY ATTACKS--?
C'MON-- I'LL TAKE YA BOTH ON!!
UH, NO-- THAT'S OKAY.
WHY DON'T WE LOOK AT THE STUFF WE BOUGHT INSTEAD...?

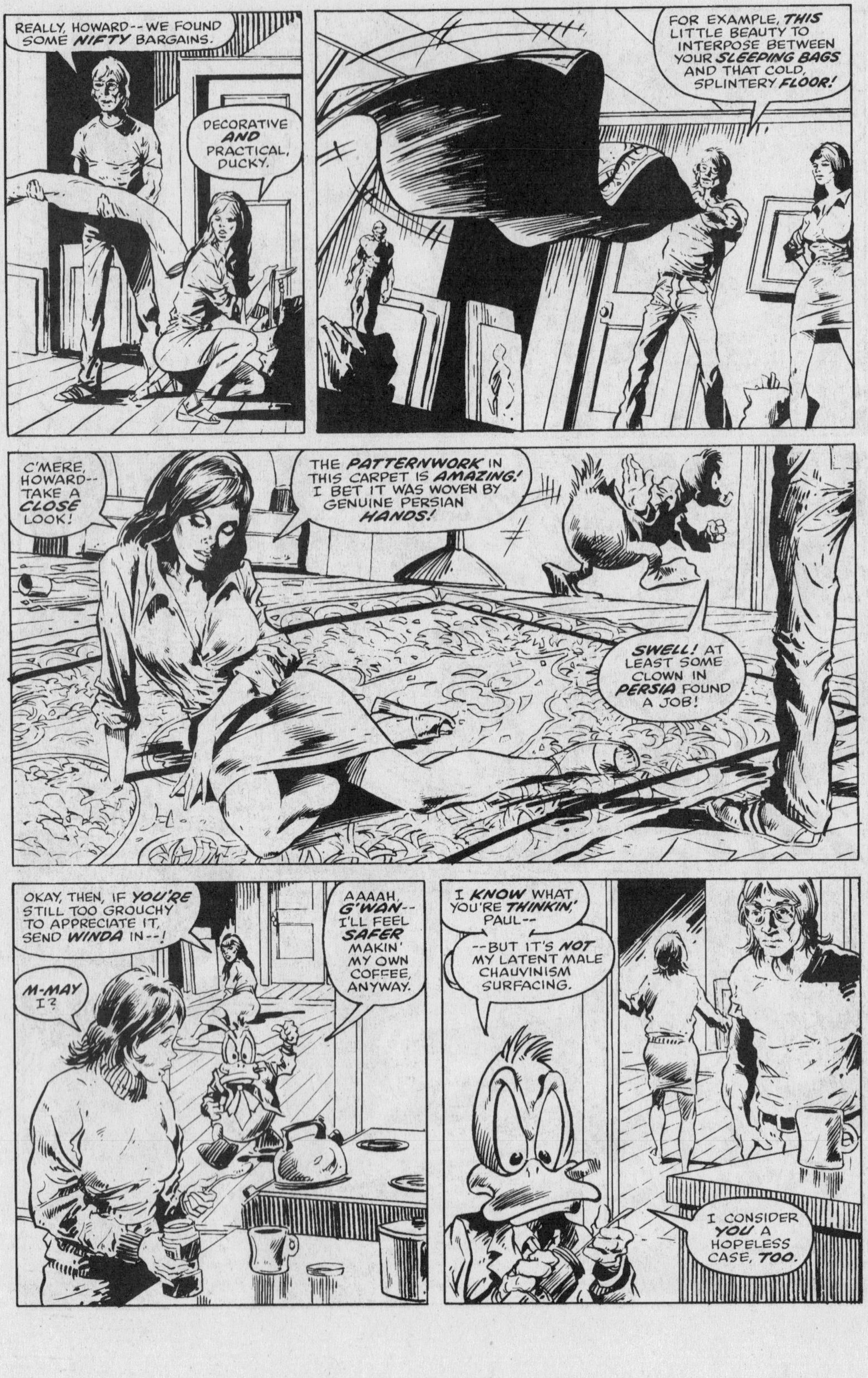
REALLY, HOWARD--WE FOUND SOME NIFTY BARGAINS.
DECORATIVE AND PRACTICAL, DUCKY.
FOR EXAMPLE, THIS LITTLE BEAUTY TO INTERPOSE BETWEEN YOUR SLEEPING BAGS AND THAT COLD, SPLINTERY FLOOR!
C'MERE, HOWARD-- TAKE A CLOSE LOOK!
THE PATTERNWORK IN THIS CARPET IS AMAZING! I BET IT WAS WOVEN BY GENUINE PERSIAN HANDS!
SWELL! AT LEAST SOME CLOWN IN PERSIA FOUND A JOB!
OKAY, THEN, IF YOU'RE STILL TOO GROUCHY TO APPRECIATE IT, SEND WINDA IN--!
M-MAY I?
AAAAH, G'WAN-- I'LL FEEL SAFER MAKIN' MY OWN COFFEE, ANYWAY.
I KNOW WHAT YOU'RE THINKIN,' PAUL--
--BUT IT'S NOT MY LATENT MALE CHAUVINISM SURFACING.
I CONSIDER YOU A HOPELESS CASE, TOO.

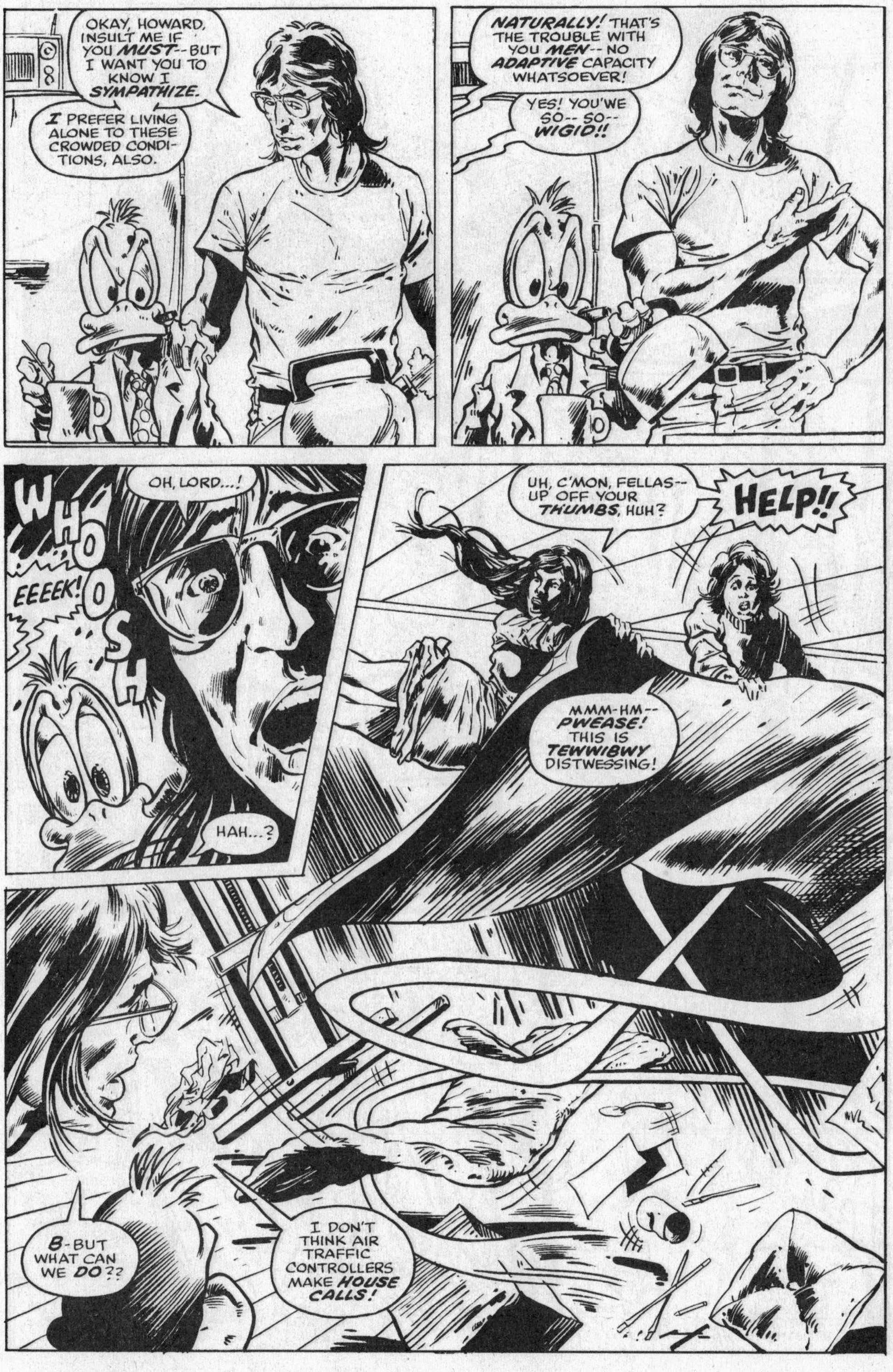
OKAY, HOWARD, INSULT ME IF YOU MUST--BUT I WANT YOU TO KNOW I SYMPATHIZE.
I PREFER LIVING ALONE TO THESE CROWDED CONDITIONS, ALSO.
NATURALLY! THAT'S THE TROUBLE WITH YOU MEN-- NO ADAPTIVE CAPACITY WHATSOEVER!
YES! YOU'WE SO-- SO-- WIGID!!
OH, LORD...!
WHOOOSH
EEEEK!
HAH...?
UH, C'MON, FELLAS-- UP OFF YOUR THUMBS, HUH?
HELP!!
MMM-HM-- PWEASE! THIS IS TEWWIBWY DISTWESSING!
B-BUT WHAT CAN WE DO??
I DON'T THINK AIR TRAFFIC CONTROLLERS MAKE HOUSE CALLS!

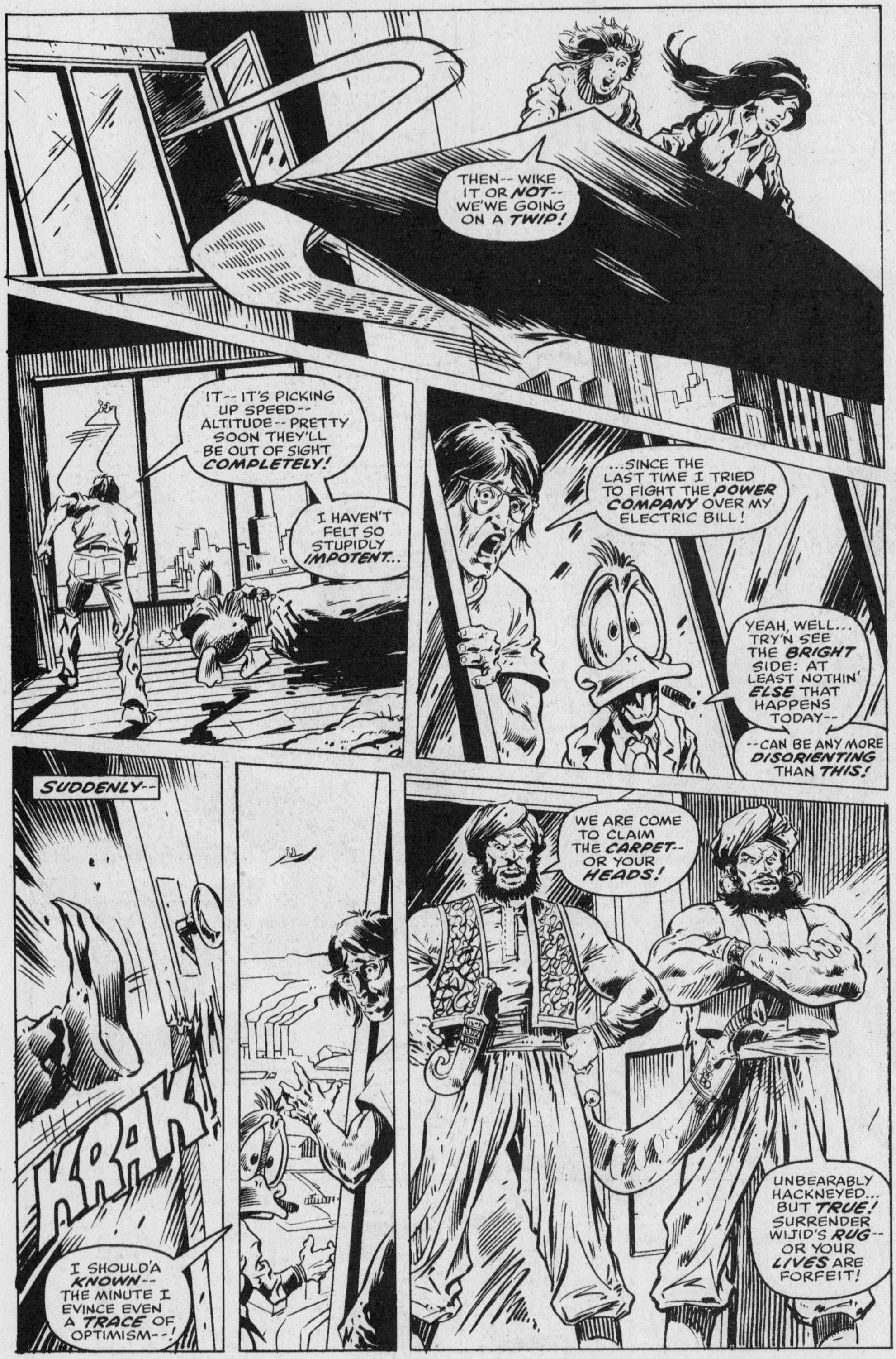

THEN-- WIKE IT OR NOT-- WE'WE GOING ON A TWIP!
FOOOSH!!
IT-- IT'S PICKING UP SPEED-- ALTITUDE-- PRETTY SOON THEY'LL BE OUT OF SIGHT COMPLETELY!
I HAVEN'T FELT SO STUPIDLY IMPOTENT...
...SINCE THE LAST TIME I TRIED TO FIGHT THE POWER COMPANY OVER MY ELECTRIC BILL!
YEAH, WELL... TRY'N SEE THE BRIGHT SIDE: AT LEAST NOTHIN' ELSE THAT HAPPENS TODAY--
--CAN BE ANY MORE DISORIENTING THAN THIS!
SUDDENLY--
KRAK
I SHOULD'A KNOWN-- THE MINUTE I EVINCE EVEN A TRACE OF OPTIMISM--!
WE ARE COME TO CLAIM THE CARPET-- OR YOUR HEADS!
UNBEARABLY HACKNEYED... BUT TRUE! SURRENDER WIJID'S RUG-- OR YOUR LIVES ARE FORFEIT!

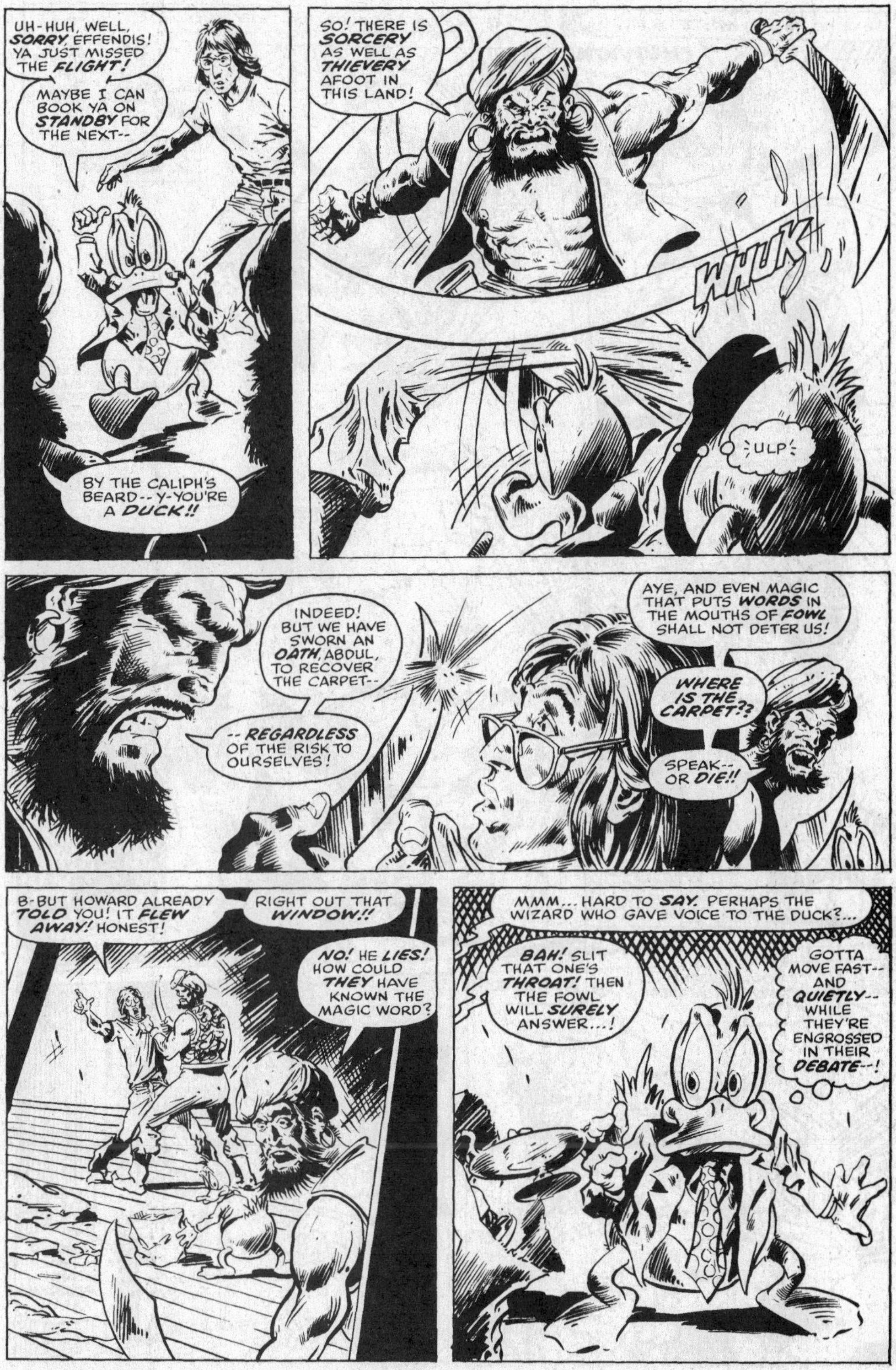

UH-HUH, WELL, SORRY, EFFENDIS! YA JUST MISSED THE FLIGHT!
MAYBE I CAN BOOK YA ON STANDBY FOR THE NEXT--
BY THE CALIPH'S BEARD--Y-YOU'RE A DUCK!!
SO! THERE IS SORCERY AS WELL AS THIEVERY AFOOT IN THIS LAND!
WHUK
ULP
INDEED! BUT WE HAVE SWORN AN OATH, ABDUL, TO RECOVER THE CARPET--
--REGARDLESS OF THE RISK TO OURSELVES!
AYE, AND EVEN MAGIC THAT PUTS WORDS IN THE MOUTHS OF FOWL SHALL NOT DETER US!
WHERE IS THE CARPET??
SPEAK--OR DIE!!
B-BUT HOWARD ALREADY TOLD YOU! IT FLEW AWAY! HONEST!
RIGHT OUT THAT WINDOW!!
NO! HE LIES! HOW COULD THEY HAVE KNOWN THE MAGIC WORD?
MMM... HARD TO SAY. PERHAPS THE WIZARD WHO GAVE VOICE TO THE DUCK?...
BAH! SLIT THAT ONE'S THROAT! THEN THE FOWL WILL SURELY ANSWER...!
GOTTA MOVE FAST--AND QUIETLY--WHILE THEY'RE ENGROSSED IN THEIR DEBATE--!

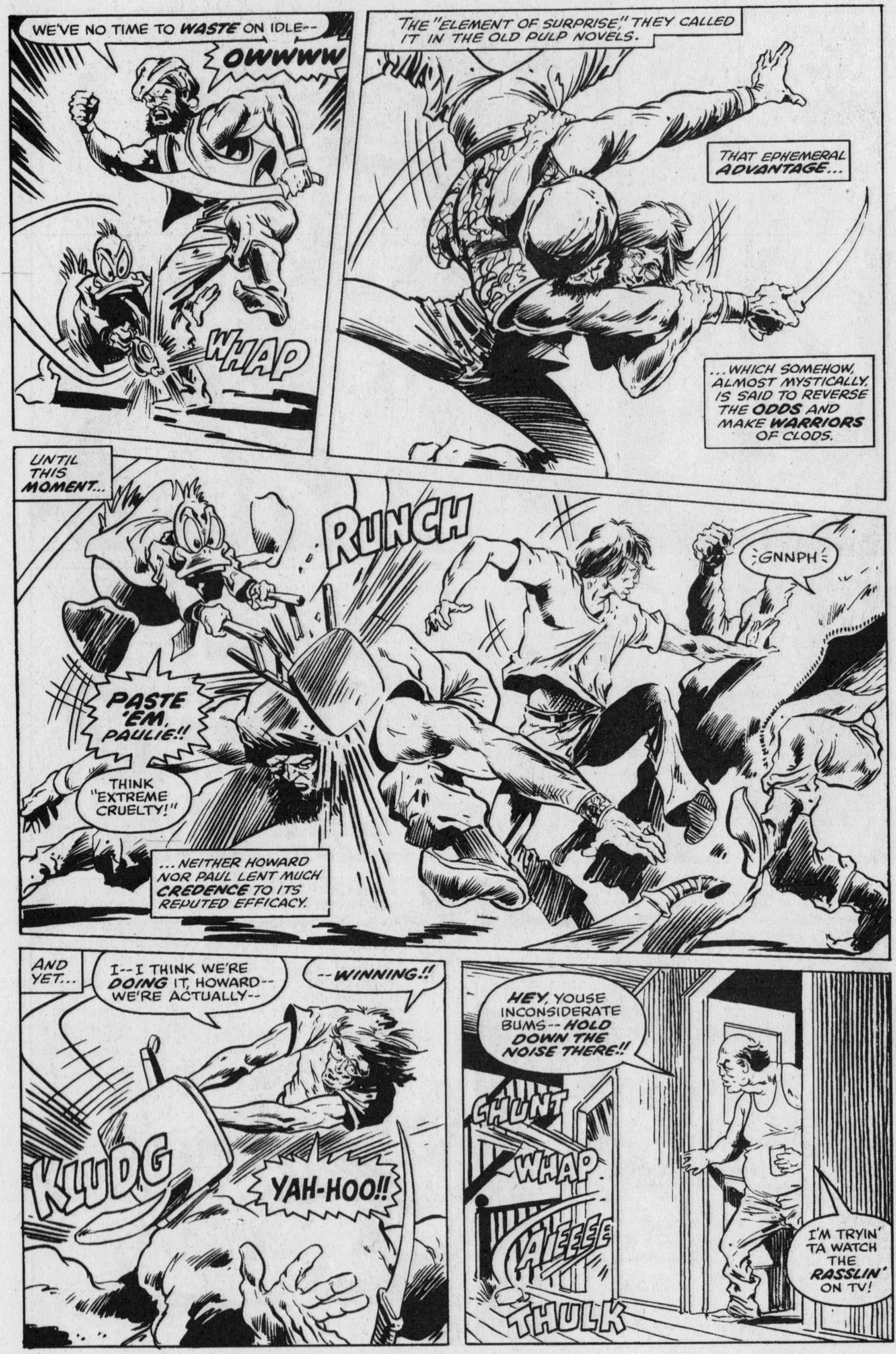
WE'VE NO TIME TO WASTE ON IDLE--
OWWWW
WHAP
THE "ELEMENT OF SURPRISE," THEY CALLED IT IN THE OLD PULP NOVELS.
THAT EPHEMERAL ADVANTAGE...
...WHICH SOMEHOW, ALMOST MYSTICALLY, IS SAID TO REVERSE THE ODDS AND MAKE WARRIORS OF CLODS.
UNTIL THIS MOMENT...
RUNCH
GNNPH
PASTE 'EM, PAULIE!!
THINK "EXTREME CRUELTY!"
...NEITHER HOWARD NOR PAUL LENT MUCH CREDENCE TO ITS REPUTED EFFICACY.
AND YET...
I--I THINK WE'RE DOING IT, HOWARD-- WE'RE ACTUALLY--
--WINNING!!
KLUDG
YAH-HOO!!
HEY, YOUSE INCONSIDERATE BUMS-- HOLD DOWN THE NOISE THERE!!
CHUNT
WHAP
YALEEEE
THULK
I'M TRYIN' TA WATCH THE RASSLIN' ON TV!

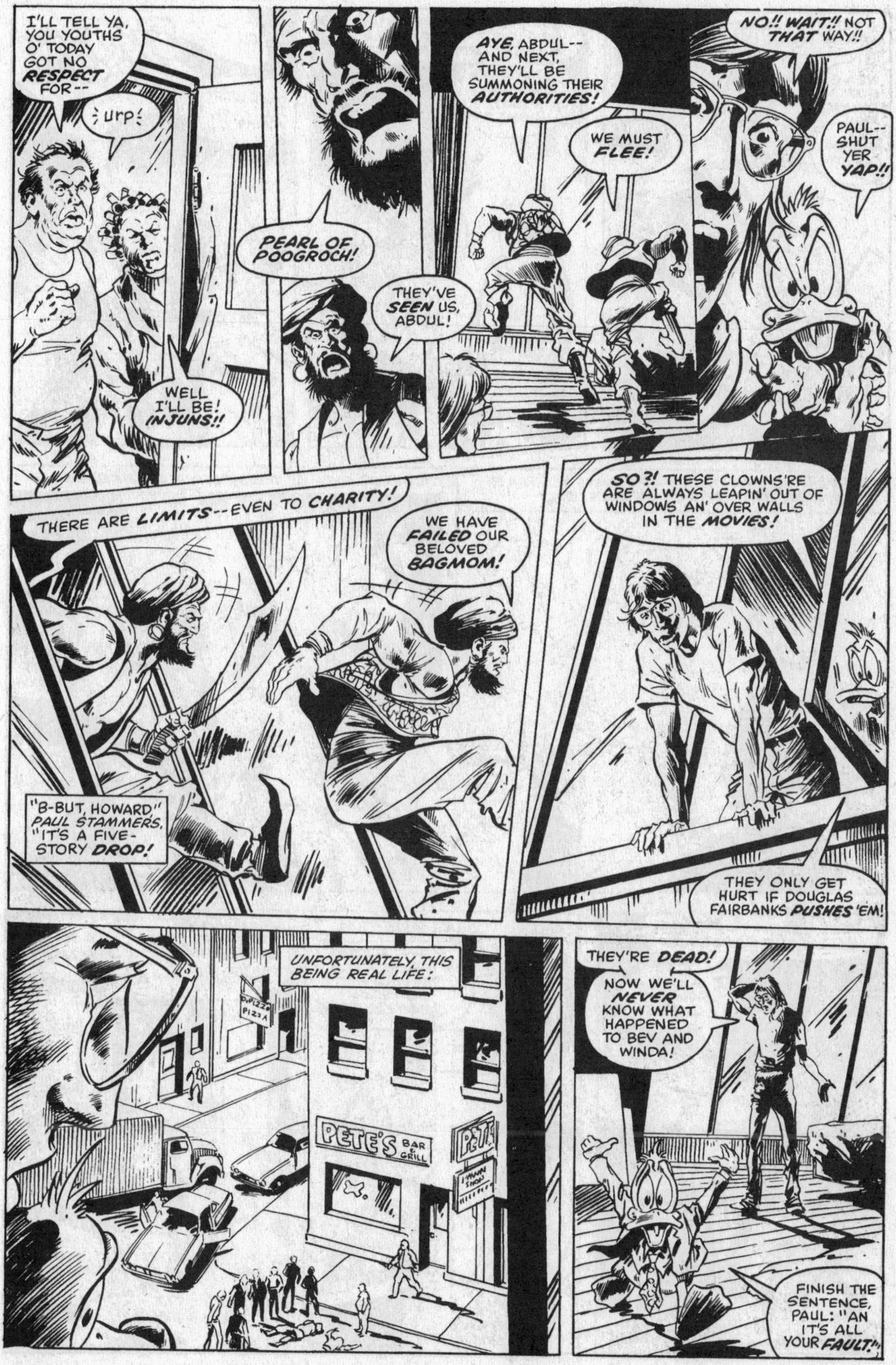
I'LL TELL YA, YOU YOUTHS O' TODAY GOT NO RESPECT FOR--
;urp;
WELL I'LL BE! INJUNS!!
PEARL OF POOGROCH!
THEY'VE SEEN US, ABDUL!
AYE, ABDUL-- AND NEXT, THEY'LL BE SUMMONING THEIR AUTHORITIES!
WE MUST FLEE!
NO!! WAIT!! NOT THAT WAY!!
PAUL-- SHUT YER YAP!!
THERE ARE LIMITS--EVEN TO CHARITY!
WE HAVE FAILED OUR BELOVED BAGMOM!
"B-BUT, HOWARD" PAUL STAMMERS, "IT'S A FIVE-STORY DROP!
SO?! THESE CLOWNS'RE ARE ALWAYS LEAPIN' OUT OF WINDOWS AN' OVER WALLS IN THE MOVIES!
THEY ONLY GET HURT IF DOUGLAS FAIRBANKS PUSHES 'EM!
UNFORTUNATELY, THIS BEING REAL LIFE:
PIZZA
PETE'S BAR & GRILL
THEY'RE DEAD!
NOW WE'LL NEVER KNOW WHAT HAPPENED TO BEV AND WINDA!
FINISH THE SENTENCE, PAUL: "AN' IT'S ALL YOUR FAULT."

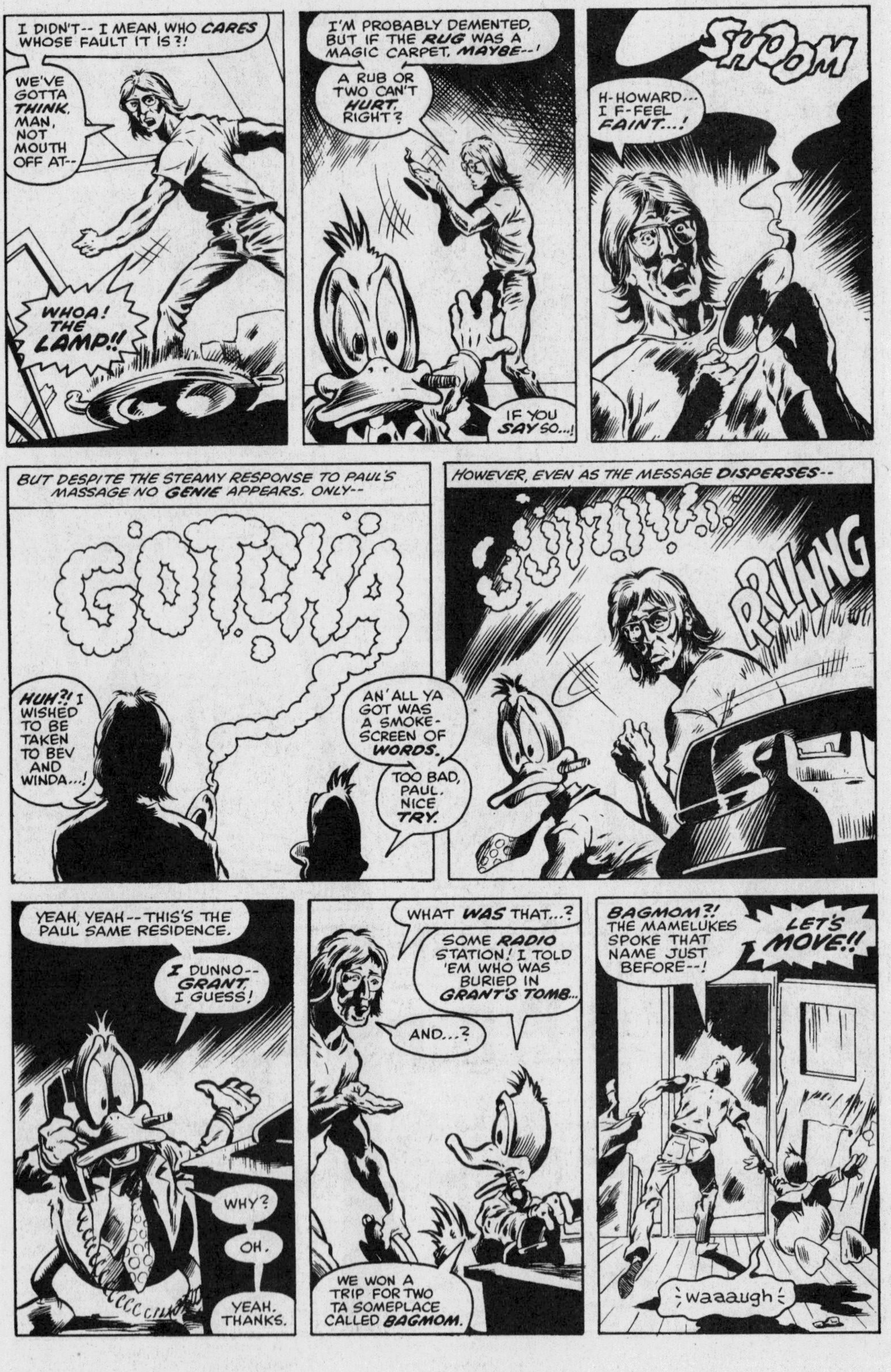

I DIDN'T-- I MEAN, WHO CARES WHOSE FAULT IT IS?!
WE'VE GOTTA THINK, MAN, NOT MOUTH OFF AT--
WHOA! THE LAMP!!
I'M PROBABLY DEMENTED, BUT IF THE RUG WAS A MAGIC CARPET, MAYBE--!
A RUB OR TWO CAN'T HURT, RIGHT?
IF YOU SAY SO...!
SHOOM
H-HOWARD... I F-FEEL FAINT...!
BUT DESPITE THE STEAMY RESPONSE TO PAUL'S MASSAGE NO GENIE APPEARS. ONLY--
GOTCHA
HUH?! I WISHED TO BE TAKEN TO BEV AND WINDA...!
AN' ALL YA GOT WAS A SMOKE-SCREEN OF WORDS.
TOO BAD, PAUL. NICE TRY.
HOWEVER, EVEN AS THE MESSAGE DISPERSES--
RIIING
YEAH, YEAH-- THIS'S THE PAUL SAME RESIDENCE.
I DUNNO-- GRANT, I GUESS!
WHY?
OH.
YEAH. THANKS.
WHAT WAS THAT...?
SOME RADIO STATION! I TOLD 'EM WHO WAS BURIED IN GRANT'S TOMB...
AND...?
WE WON A TRIP FOR TWO TA SOMEPLACE CALLED BAGMOM.
BAGMOM?! THE MAMELUKES SPOKE THAT NAME JUST BEFORE--!
LET'S MOVE!!
waaaugh

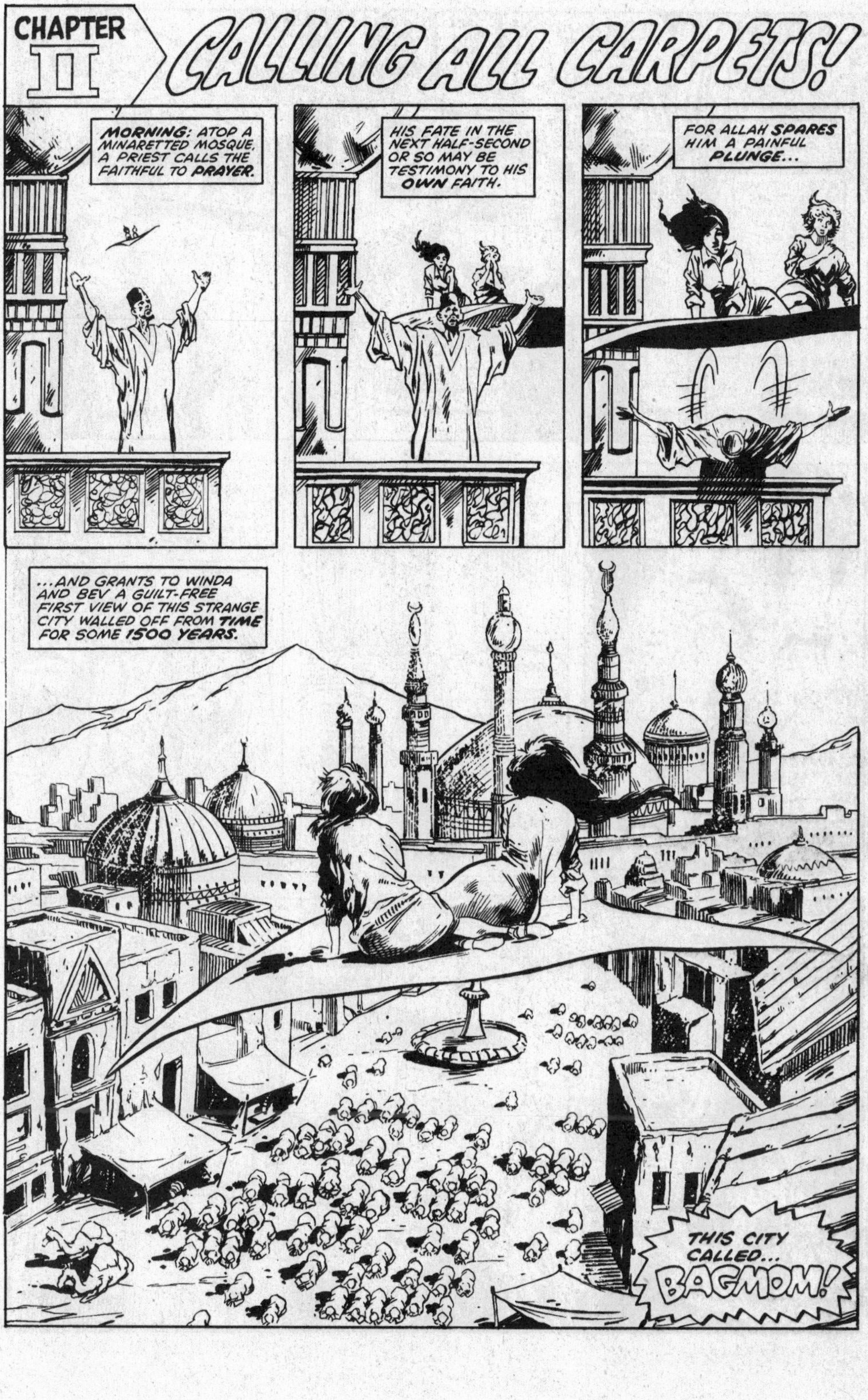
CHAPTER II
CALLING ALL CARPETS!
MORNING: ATOP A MINARETTED MOSQUE, A PRIEST CALLS THE FAITHFUL TO PRAYER.
HIS FATE IN THE NEXT HALF-SECOND OR SO MAY BE TESTIMONY TO HIS OWN FAITH.
FOR ALLAH SPARES HIM A PAINFUL PLUNGE...
...AND GRANTS TO WINDA AND BEV A GUILT-FREE FIRST VIEW OF THIS STRANGE CITY WALLED OFF FROM TIME FOR SOME 1500 YEARS.
THIS CITY CALLED... BAGMOM!

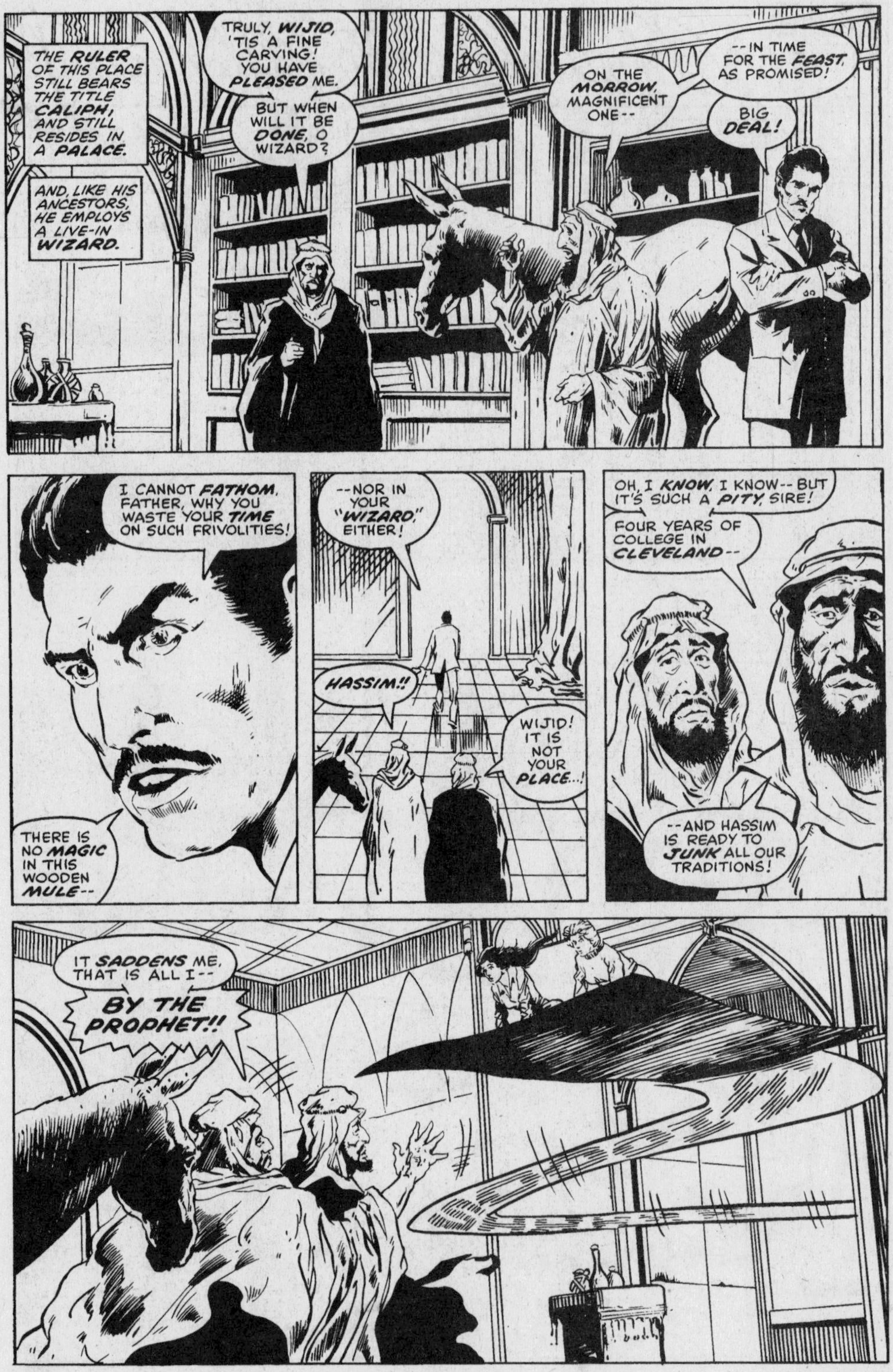
THE RULER OF THIS PLACE STILL BEARS THE TITLE CALIPH, AND STILL RESIDES IN A PALACE.
AND, LIKE HIS ANCESTORS, HE EMPLOYS A LIVE-IN WIZARD.
TRULY, WIJID, 'TIS A FINE CARVING! YOU HAVE PLEASED ME.
BUT WHEN WILL IT BE DONE, O WIZARD?
ON THE MORROW, MAGNIFICENT ONE--
--IN TIME FOR THE FEAST, AS PROMISED!
BIG DEAL!
I CANNOT FATHOM, FATHER, WHY YOU WASTE YOUR TIME ON SUCH FRIVOLITIES!
THERE IS NO MAGIC IN THIS WOODEN MULE--
--NOR IN YOUR "WIZARD," EITHER!
HASSIM!!
WIJID! IT IS NOT YOUR PLACE...!
OH, I KNOW, I KNOW--BUT IT'S SUCH A PITY, SIRE!
FOUR YEARS OF COLLEGE IN CLEVELAND--
--AND HASSIM IS READY TO JUNK ALL OUR TRADITIONS!
IT SADDENS ME, THAT IS ALL I--
BY THE PROPHET!!

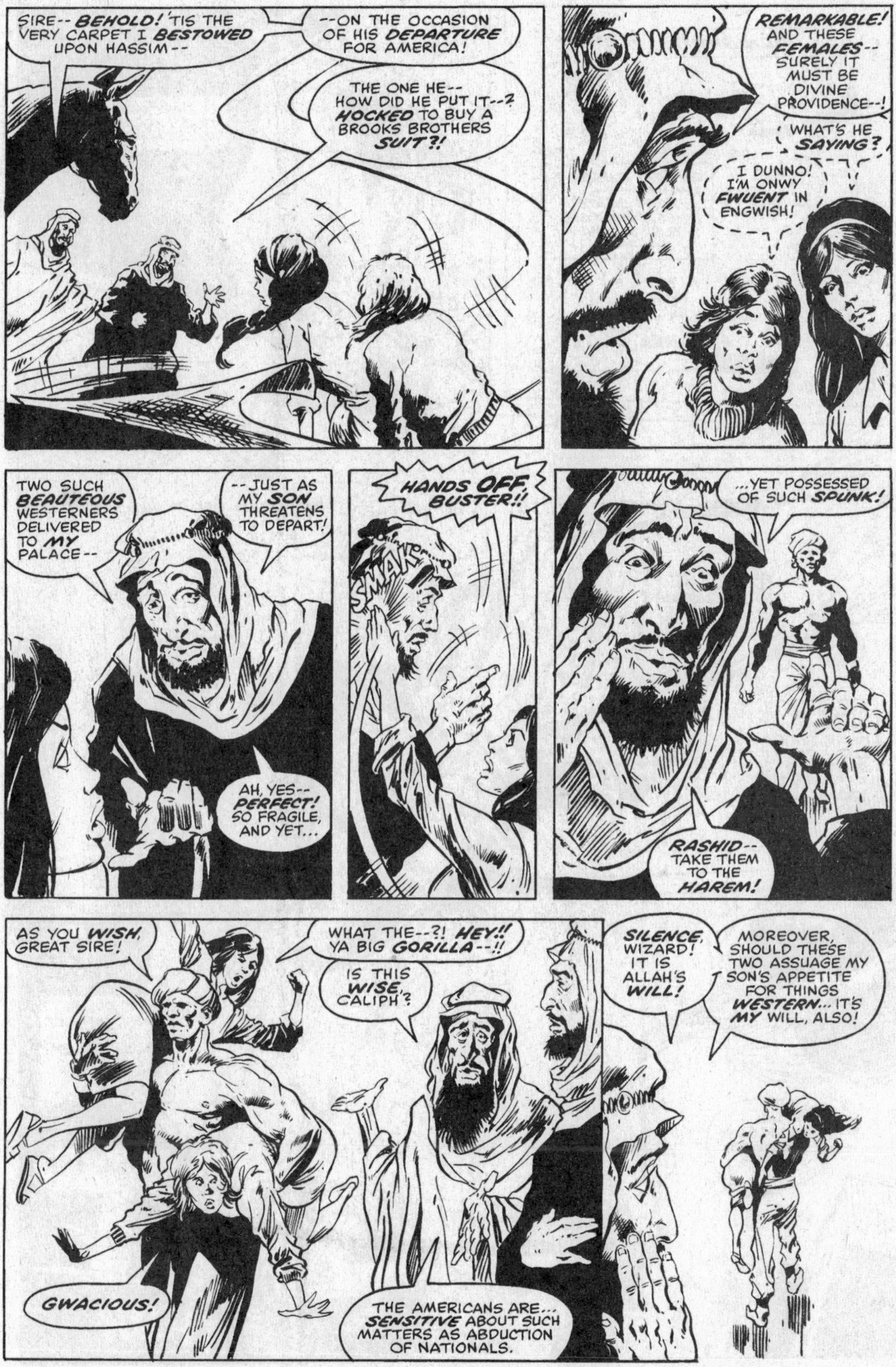
SIRE-- BEHOLD! 'TIS THE VERY CARPET I BESTOWED UPON HASSIM--
--ON THE OCCASION OF HIS DEPARTURE FOR AMERICA!
THE ONE HE-- HOW DID HE PUT IT--? HOCKED TO BUY A BROOKS BROTHERS SUIT?!
REMARKABLE! AND THESE FEMALES-- SURELY IT MUST BE DIVINE PROVIDENCE--!
WHAT'S HE SAYING?
I DUNNO! I'M ONWY FWUENT IN ENGWISH!
TWO SUCH BEAUTEOUS WESTERNERS DELIVERED TO MY PALACE--
--JUST AS MY SON THREATENS TO DEPART!
AH, YES-- PERFECT! SO FRAGILE, AND YET...
HANDS OFF, BUSTER!!
SMAK
...YET POSSESSED OF SUCH SPUNK!
RASHID-- TAKE THEM TO THE HAREM!
AS YOU WISH, GREAT SIRE!
WHAT THE--?! HEY!! YA BIG GORILLA--!!
IS THIS WISE, CALIPH?
GWACIOUS!
THE AMERICANS ARE... SENSITIVE ABOUT SUCH MATTERS AS ABDUCTION OF NATIONALS.
SILENCE, WIZARD! IT IS ALLAH'S WILL!
MOREOVER, SHOULD THESE TWO ASSUAGE MY SON'S APPETITE FOR THINGS WESTERN... IT'S MY WILL, ALSO!

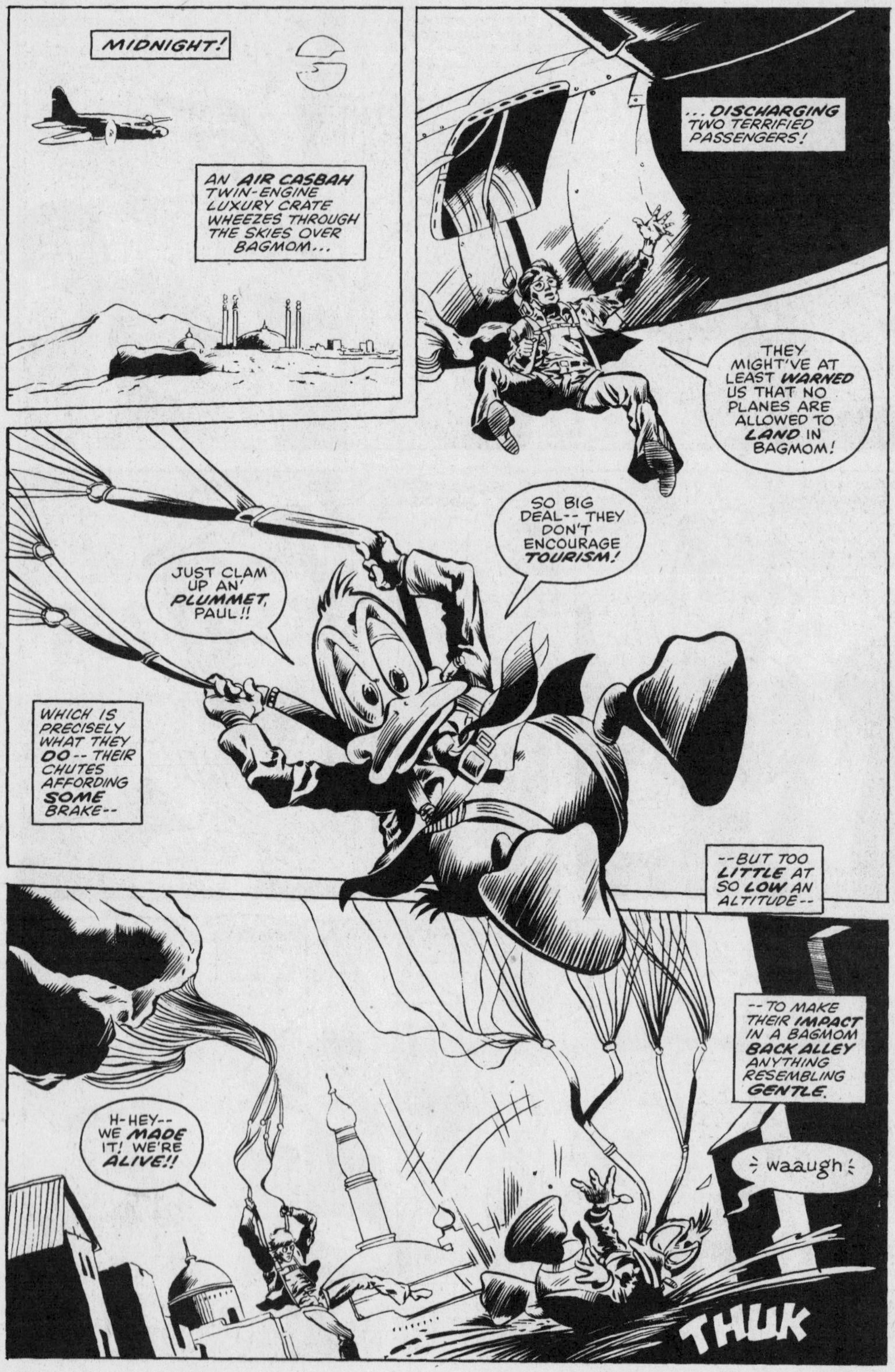

MIDNIGHT!
AN AIR CASBAH TWIN-ENGINE LUXURY CRATE WHEEZES THROUGH THE SKIES OVER BAGMOM...
...DISCHARGING TWO TERRIFIED PASSENGERS!
THEY MIGHT'VE AT LEAST WARNED US THAT NO PLANES ARE ALLOWED TO LAND IN BAGMOM!
SO BIG DEAL-- THEY DON'T ENCOURAGE TOURISM!
JUST CLAM UP AN' PLUMMET, PAUL!!
WHICH IS PRECISELY WHAT THEY DO-- THEIR CHUTES AFFORDING SOME BRAKE--
--BUT TOO LITTLE AT SO LOW AN ALTITUDE--
--TO MAKE THEIR IMPACT IN A BAGMOM BACK ALLEY ANYTHING RESEMBLING GENTLE.
H-HEY-- WE MADE IT! WE'RE ALIVE!!
waaugh
THUK

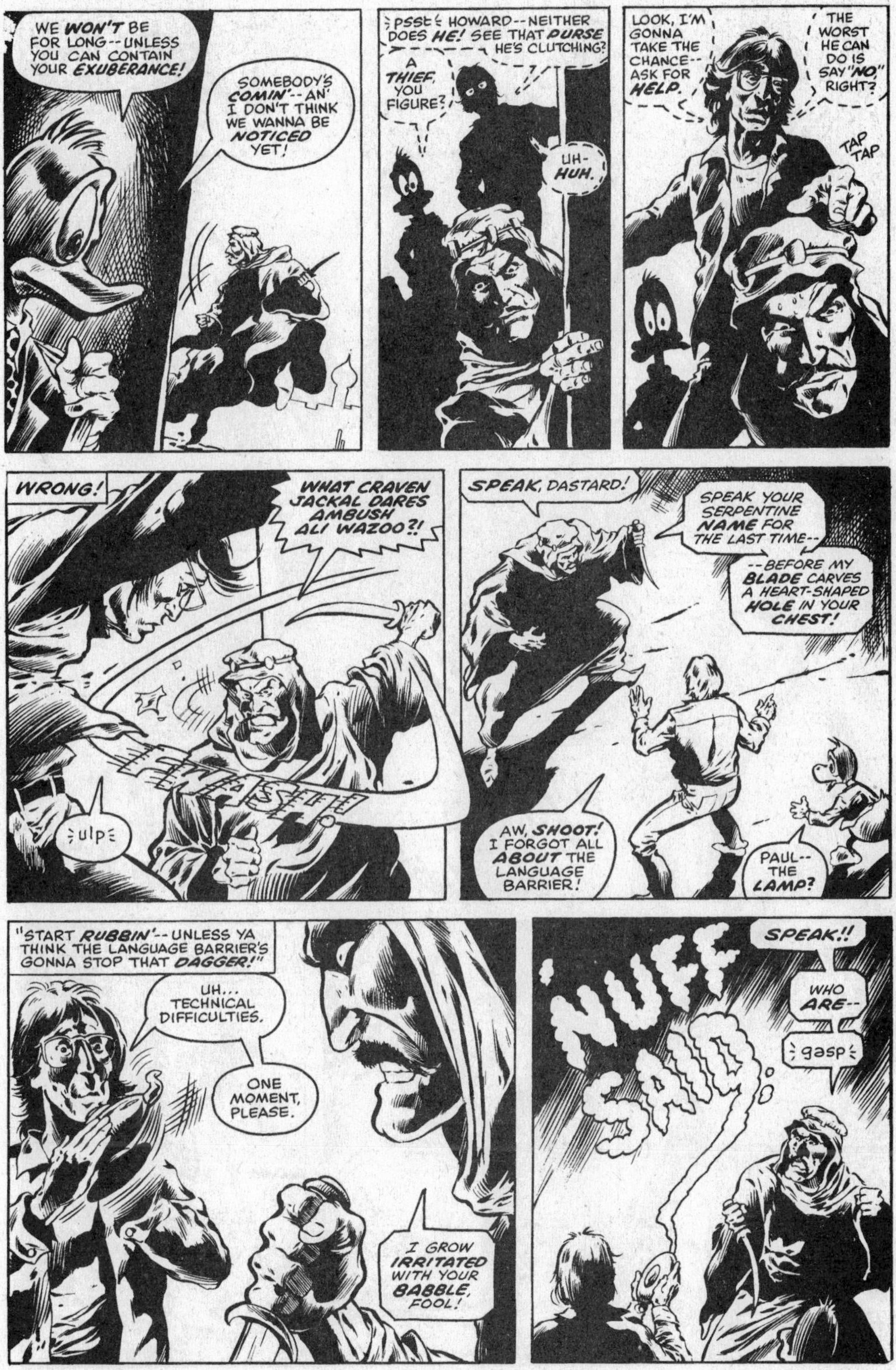
WE WON'T BE FOR LONG--UNLESS YOU CAN CONTAIN YOUR EXUBERANCE!
SOMEBODY'S COMIN'--AN' I DON'T THINK WE WANNA BE NOTICED YET!
PSST--HOWARD--NEITHER DOES HE! SEE THAT PURSE HE'S CLUTCHING?
A THIEF, YOU FIGURE?
UH-HUH.
LOOK, I'M GONNA TAKE THE CHANCE--ASK FOR HELP.
THE WORST HE CAN DO IS SAY "NO," RIGHT?
TAP TAP
WRONG!
WHAT CRAVEN JACKAL DARES AMBUSH ALI WAZOO?!
ulp
SPEAK, DASTARD!
SPEAK YOUR SERPENTINE NAME FOR THE LAST TIME--
--BEFORE MY BLADE CARVES A HEART-SHAPED HOLE IN YOUR CHEST!
AW, SHOOT! I FORGOT ALL ABOUT THE LANGUAGE BARRIER!
PAUL--THE LAMP?
"START RUBBIN'--UNLESS YA THINK THE LANGUAGE BARRIER'S GONNA STOP THAT DAGGER!"
UH... TECHNICAL DIFFICULTIES.
ONE MOMENT, PLEASE.
I GROW IRRITATED WITH YOUR BABBLE, FOOL!
SPEAK!!
WHO ARE--
gasp
'NUFF SAID

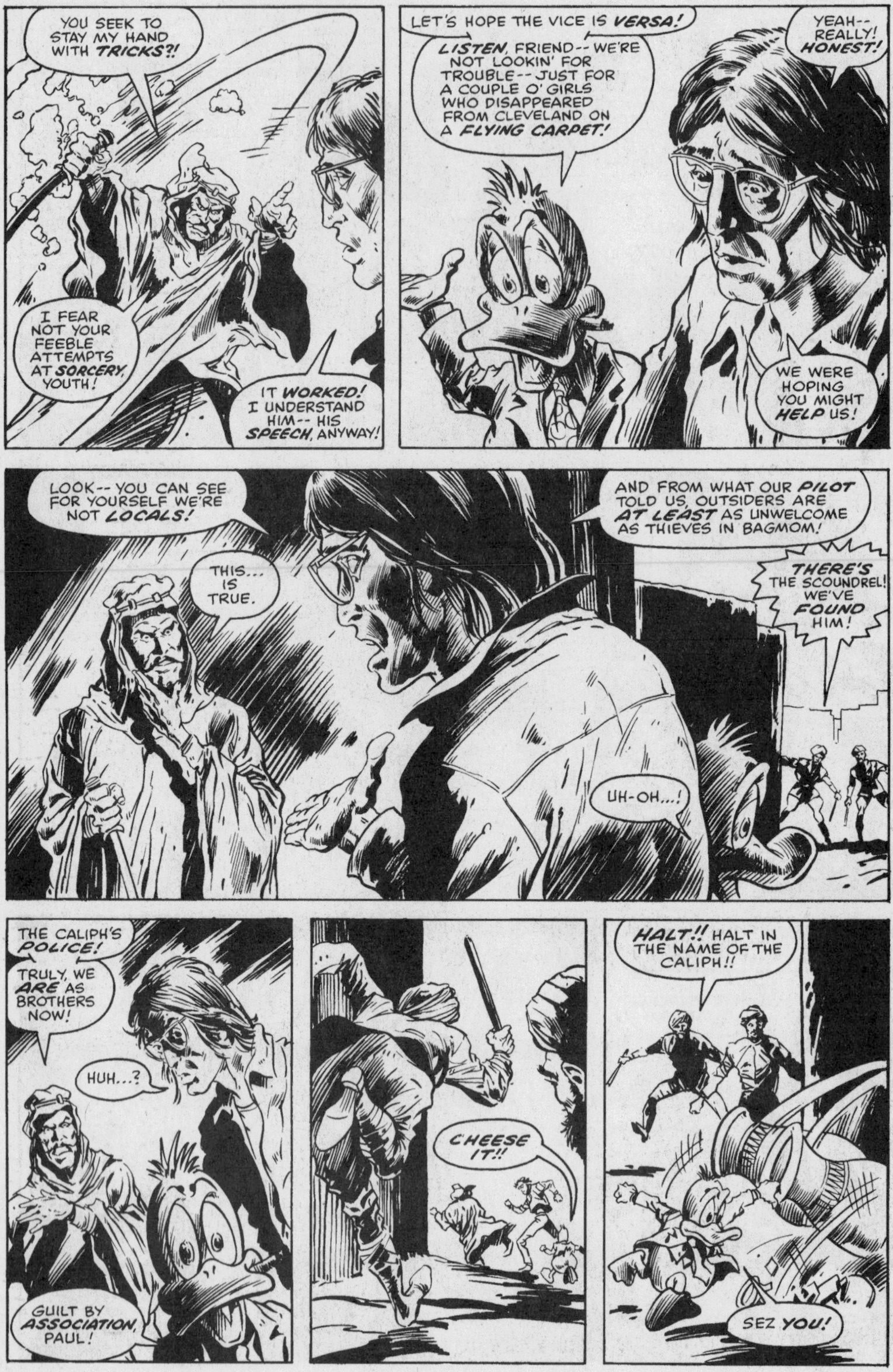

YOU SEEK TO STAY MY HAND WITH TRICKS?!
I FEAR NOT YOUR FEEBLE ATTEMPTS AT SORCERY, YOUTH!
IT WORKED! I UNDERSTAND HIM-- HIS SPEECH, ANYWAY!
LET'S HOPE THE VICE IS VERSA!
LISTEN, FRIEND-- WE'RE NOT LOOKIN' FOR TROUBLE-- JUST FOR A COUPLE O' GIRLS WHO DISAPPEARED FROM CLEVELAND ON A FLYING CARPET!
YEAH-- REALLY! HONEST!
WE WERE HOPING YOU MIGHT HELP US!
LOOK-- YOU CAN SEE FOR YOURSELF WE'RE NOT LOCALS!
THIS... IS TRUE.
AND FROM WHAT OUR PILOT TOLD US, OUTSIDERS ARE AT LEAST AS UNWELCOME AS THIEVES IN BAGMOM!
THERE'S THE SCOUNDREL! WE'VE FOUND HIM!
UH-OH...!
THE CALIPH'S POLICE!
TRULY, WE ARE AS BROTHERS NOW!
HUH...?
GUILT BY ASSOCIATION, PAUL!
CHEESE IT!!
HALT!! HALT IN THE NAME OF THE CALIPH!!
SEZ YOU!

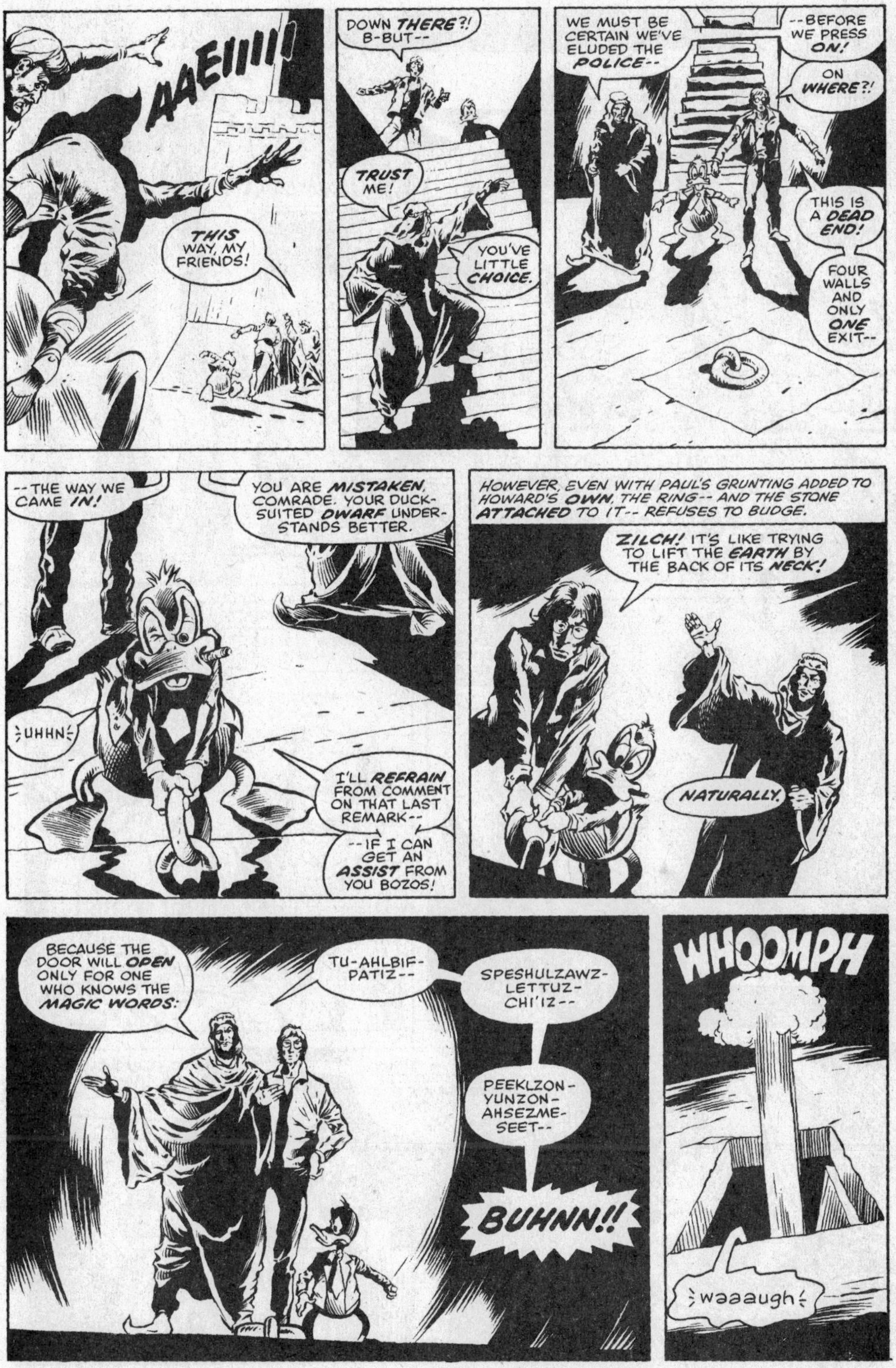
AAEIIIII
THIS WAY, MY FRIENDS!
DOWN THERE?! B-BUT--
TRUST ME!
YOU'VE LITTLE CHOICE.
WE MUST BE CERTAIN WE'VE ELUDED THE POLICE--
--BEFORE WE PRESS ON!
ON WHERE?!
THIS IS A DEAD END!
FOUR WALLS AND ONLY ONE EXIT--
--THE WAY WE CAME IN!
YOU ARE MISTAKEN, COMRADE. YOUR DUCK-SUITED DWARF UNDERSTANDS BETTER.
UHHN
I'LL REFRAIN FROM COMMENT ON THAT LAST REMARK--
--IF I CAN GET AN ASSIST FROM YOU BOZOS!
HOWEVER, EVEN WITH PAUL'S GRUNTING ADDED TO HOWARD'S OWN, THE RING-- AND THE STONE ATTACHED TO IT-- REFUSES TO BUDGE.
ZILCH! IT'S LIKE TRYING TO LIFT THE EARTH BY THE BACK OF ITS NECK!
NATURALLY.
BECAUSE THE DOOR WILL OPEN ONLY FOR ONE WHO KNOWS THE MAGIC WORDS:
TU-AHLBIF-PATIZ--
SPESHULZAWZ-LETTUZ-CHI'IZ--
PEEKLZON-YUNZON-AHSEZME-SEET--
BUHNN!!
WHOOMPH
waaaugh

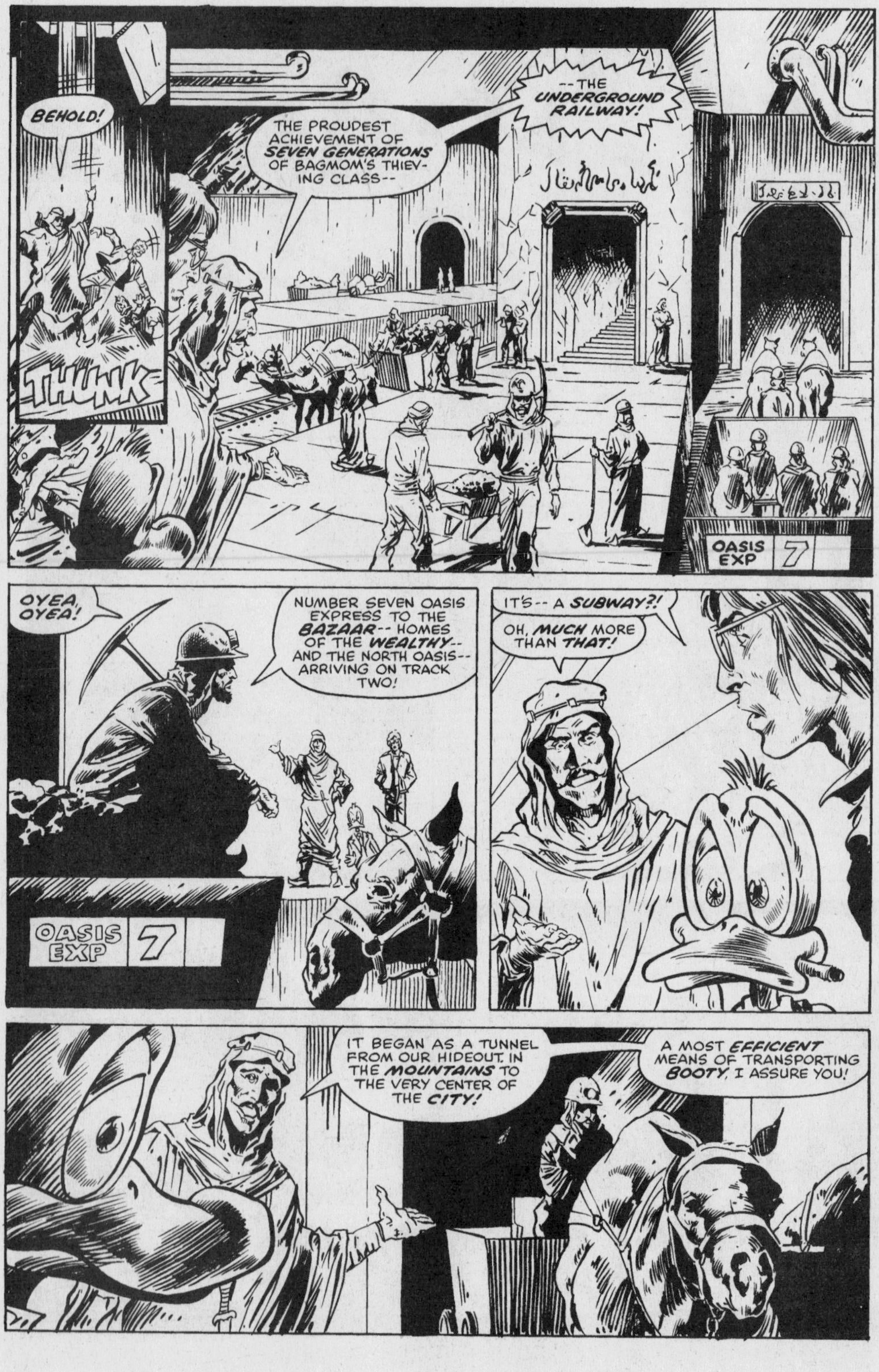
BEHOLD!
THE PROUDEST ACHIEVEMENT OF SEVEN GENERATIONS OF BAGMOM'S THIEVING CLASS--
--THE UNDERGROUND RAILWAY!
THUNK
OASIS EXP 7
OYEA, OYEA!
NUMBER SEVEN OASIS EXPRESS TO THE BAZAAR-- HOMES OF THE WEALTHY-- AND THE NORTH OASIS-- ARRIVING ON TRACK TWO!
OASIS EXP 7
IT'S-- A SUBWAY?!
OH, MUCH MORE THAN THAT!
IT BEGAN AS A TUNNEL FROM OUR HIDEOUT IN THE MOUNTAINS TO THE VERY CENTER OF THE CITY!
A MOST EFFICIENT MEANS OF TRANSPORTING BOOTY, I ASSURE YOU!

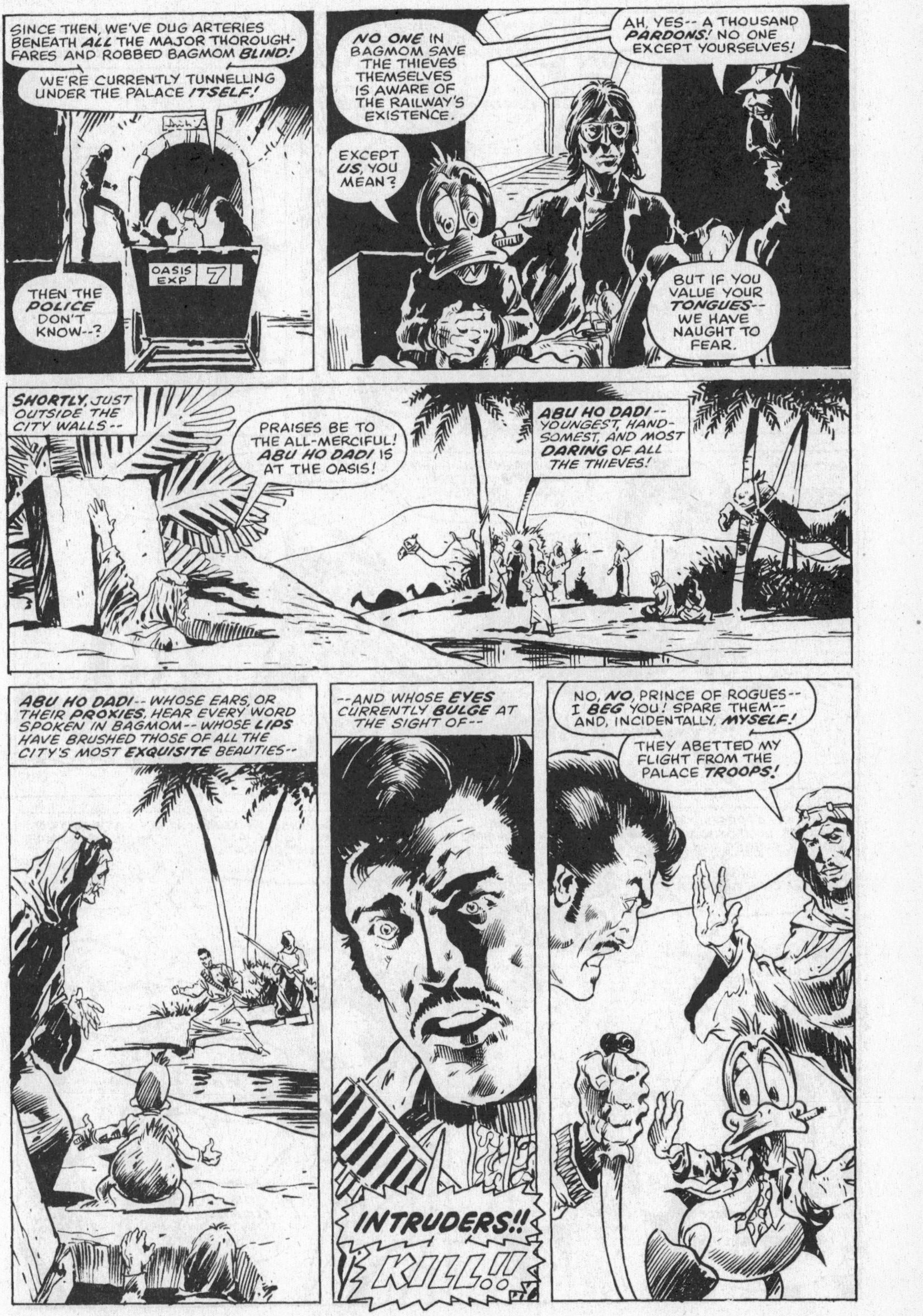

SINCE THEN, WE'VE DUG ARTERIES BENEATH ALL THE MAJOR THOROUGHFARES AND ROBBED BAGMOM BLIND!
WE'RE CURRENTLY TUNNELLING UNDER THE PALACE ITSELF!
OASIS EXP 7
THEN THE POLICE DON'T KNOW--?
NO ONE IN BAGMOM SAVE THE THIEVES THEMSELVES IS AWARE OF THE RAILWAY'S EXISTENCE.
EXCEPT US, YOU MEAN?
AH, YES-- A THOUSAND PARDONS! NO ONE EXCEPT YOURSELVES!
BUT IF YOU VALUE YOUR TONGUES-- WE HAVE NAUGHT TO FEAR.
SHORTLY, JUST OUTSIDE THE CITY WALLS--
PRAISES BE TO THE ALL-MERCIFUL! ABU HO DADI IS AT THE OASIS!
ABU HO DADI-- YOUNGEST, HANDSOMEST, AND MOST DARING OF ALL THE THIEVES!
ABU HO DADI-- WHOSE EARS, OR THEIR PROXIES, HEAR EVERY WORD SPOKEN IN BAGMOM-- WHOSE LIPS HAVE BRUSHED THOSE OF ALL THE CITY'S MOST EXQUISITE BEAUTIES--
--AND WHOSE EYES CURRENTLY BULGE AT THE SIGHT OF--
INTRUDERS!! KILL!!
NO, NO, PRINCE OF ROGUES-- I BEG YOU! SPARE THEM-- AND, INCIDENTALLY, MYSELF!
THEY ABETTED MY FLIGHT FROM THE PALACE TROOPS!

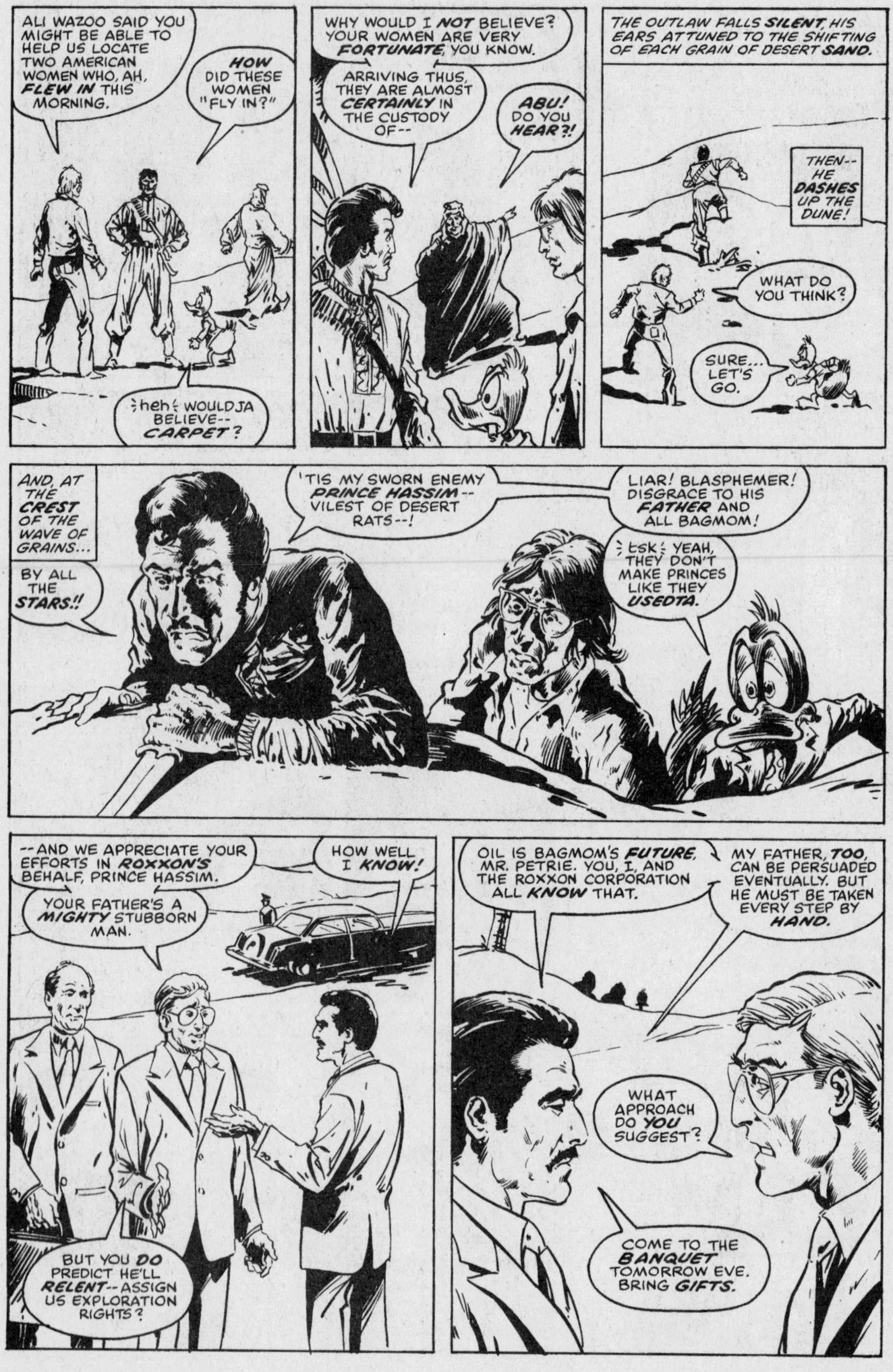
ALI WAZOO SAID YOU MIGHT BE ABLE TO HELP US LOCATE TWO AMERICAN WOMEN WHO, AH, FLEW IN THIS MORNING.
HOW DID THESE WOMEN "FLY IN?"
heh WOULDJA BELIEVE-- CARPET?
WHY WOULD I NOT BELIEVE? YOUR WOMEN ARE VERY FORTUNATE, YOU KNOW.
ARRIVING THUS, THEY ARE ALMOST CERTAINLY IN THE CUSTODY OF--
ABU! DO YOU HEAR?!
THE OUTLAW FALLS SILENT, HIS EARS ATTUNED TO THE SHIFTING OF EACH GRAIN OF DESERT SAND.
THEN-- HE DASHES UP THE DUNE!
WHAT DO YOU THINK?
SURE... LET'S GO.
AND, AT THE CREST OF THE WAVE OF GRAINS...
BY ALL THE STARS!!
'TIS MY SWORN ENEMY PRINCE HASSIM-- VILEST OF DESERT RATS--!
LIAR! BLASPHEMER! DISGRACE TO HIS FATHER AND ALL BAGMOM!
tsk YEAH, THEY DON'T MAKE PRINCES LIKE THEY USEDTA.
--AND WE APPRECIATE YOUR EFFORTS IN ROXXON'S BEHALF, PRINCE HASSIM.
HOW WELL I KNOW!
YOUR FATHER'S A MIGHTY STUBBORN MAN.
BUT YOU DO PREDICT HE'LL RELENT-- ASSIGN US EXPLORATION RIGHTS?
OIL IS BAGMOM'S FUTURE, MR. PETRIE. YOU, I, AND THE ROXXON CORPORATION ALL KNOW THAT.
MY FATHER, TOO, CAN BE PERSUADED EVENTUALLY. BUT HE MUST BE TAKEN EVERY STEP BY HAND.
WHAT APPROACH DO YOU SUGGEST?
COME TO THE BANQUET TOMORROW EVE. BRING GIFTS.

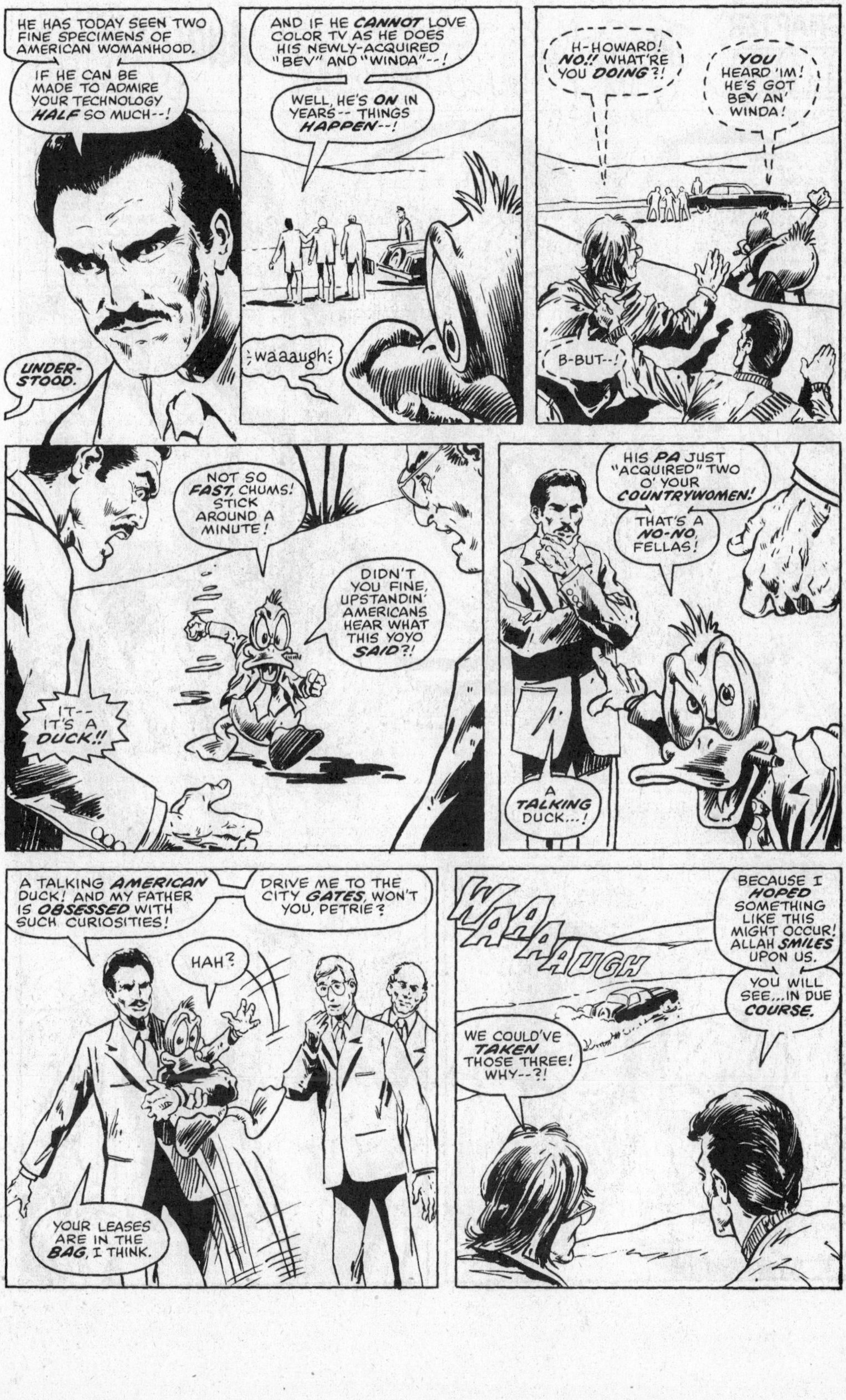
HE HAS TODAY SEEN TWO FINE SPECIMENS OF AMERICAN WOMANHOOD.
IF HE CAN BE MADE TO ADMIRE YOUR TECHNOLOGY HALF SO MUCH--!
UNDER-STOOD.
AND IF HE CANNOT LOVE COLOR TV AS HE DOES HIS NEWLY-ACQUIRED "BEV" AND "WINDA"--!
WELL, HE'S ON IN YEARS-- THINGS HAPPEN--!
waaaugh
H-HOWARD! NO!! WHAT'RE YOU DOING?!
YOU HEARD 'IM! HE'S GOT BEV AN' WINDA!
B-BUT--!
NOT SO FAST, CHUMS! STICK AROUND A MINUTE!
DIDN'T YOU FINE, UPSTANDIN' AMERICANS HEAR WHAT THIS YOYO SAID?!
IT-- IT'S A DUCK!!
HIS PA JUST "ACQUIRED" TWO O' YOUR COUNTRYWOMEN!
THAT'S A NO-NO, FELLAS!
A TALKING DUCK...!
A TALKING AMERICAN DUCK! AND MY FATHER IS OBSESSED WITH SUCH CURIOSITIES!
DRIVE ME TO THE CITY GATES, WON'T YOU, PETRIE?
HAH?
YOUR LEASES ARE IN THE BAG, I THINK.
WAAAAUGH
BECAUSE I HOPED SOMETHING LIKE THIS MIGHT OCCUR! ALLAH SMILES UPON US.
YOU WILL SEE...IN DUE COURSE.
WE COULD'VE TAKEN THOSE THREE! WHY--?!

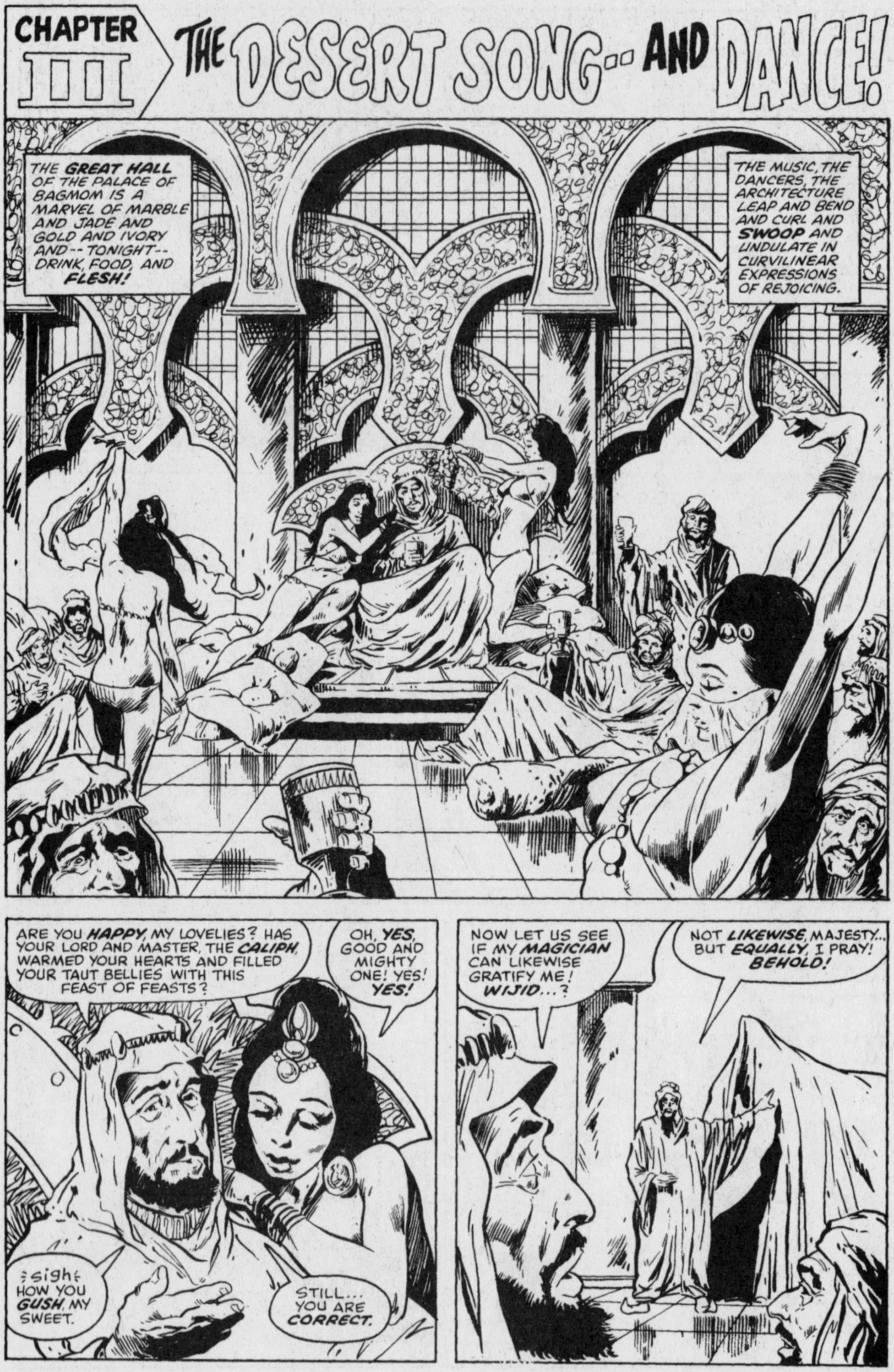
CHAPTER III
THE DESERT SONG-- AND DANCE!
THE GREAT HALL OF THE PALACE OF BAGMOM IS A MARVEL OF MARBLE AND JADE AND GOLD AND IVORY AND-- TONIGHT-- DRINK, FOOD, AND FLESH!
THE MUSIC, THE DANCERS, THE ARCHITECTURE LEAP AND BEND AND CURL AND SWOOP AND UNDULATE IN CURVILINEAR EXPRESSIONS OF REJOICING.
ARE YOU HAPPY, MY LOVELIES? HAS YOUR LORD AND MASTER, THE CALIPH, WARMED YOUR HEARTS AND FILLED YOUR TAUT BELLIES WITH THIS FEAST OF FEASTS?
OH, YES, GOOD AND MIGHTY ONE! YES! YES!
:sigh: HOW YOU GUSH, MY SWEET.
STILL... YOU ARE CORRECT.
NOW LET US SEE IF MY MAGICIAN CAN LIKEWISE GRATIFY ME! WIJID...?
NOT LIKEWISE, MAJESTY... BUT EQUALLY, I PRAY! BEHOLD!

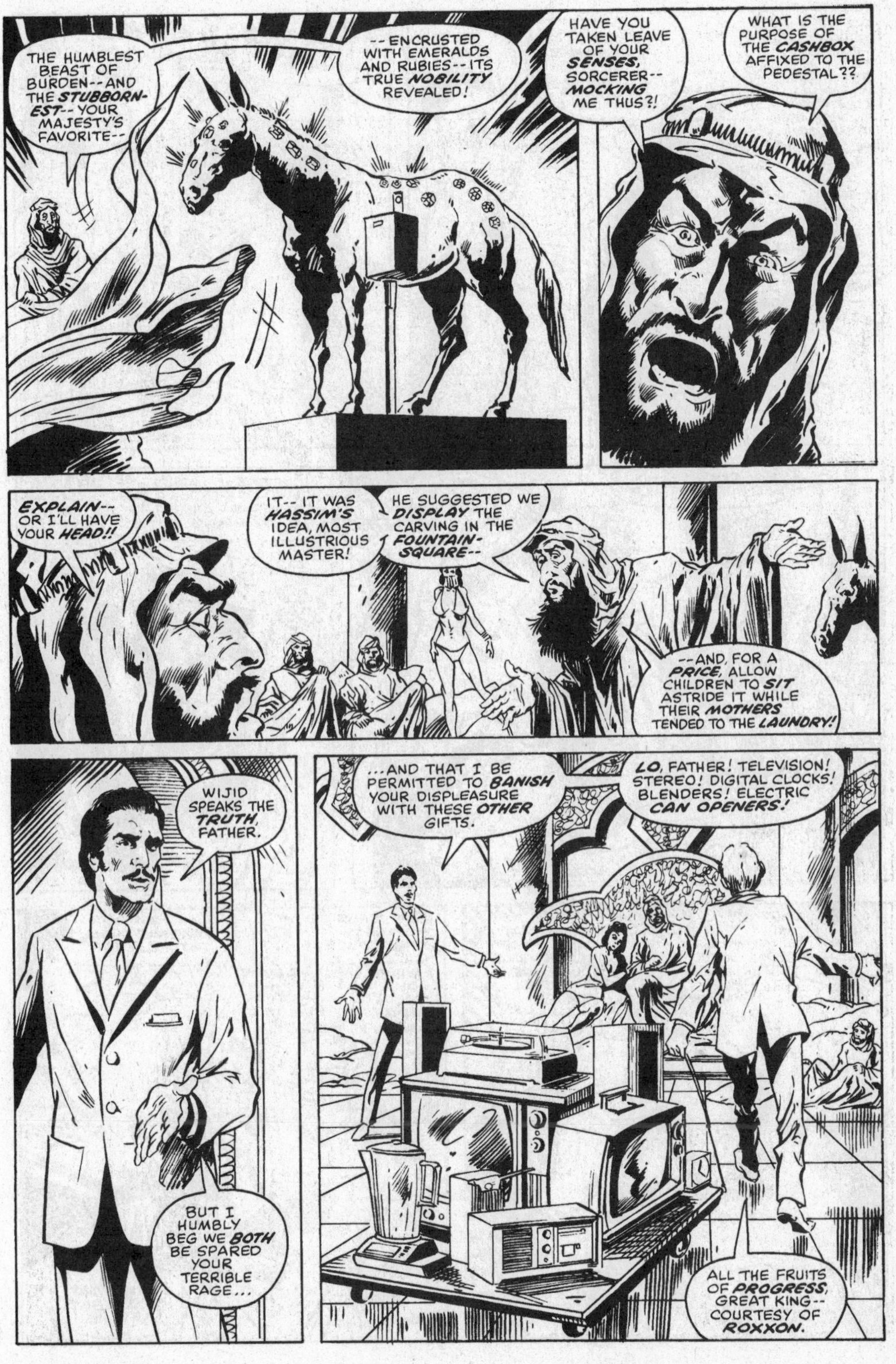
THE HUMBLEST BEAST OF BURDEN--AND THE STUBBORN-EST-- YOUR MAJESTY'S FAVORITE--
--ENCRUSTED WITH EMERALDS AND RUBIES--ITS TRUE NOBILITY REVEALED!
HAVE YOU TAKEN LEAVE OF YOUR SENSES, SORCERER-- MOCKING ME THUS?!
WHAT IS THE PURPOSE OF THE CASHBOX AFFIXED TO THE PEDESTAL??
EXPLAIN-- OR I'LL HAVE YOUR HEAD!!
IT-- IT WAS HASSIM'S IDEA, MOST ILLUSTRIOUS MASTER!
HE SUGGESTED WE DISPLAY THE CARVING IN THE FOUNTAIN-SQUARE--
--AND, FOR A PRICE, ALLOW CHILDREN TO SIT ASTRIDE IT WHILE THEIR MOTHERS TENDED TO THE LAUNDRY!
WIJID SPEAKS THE TRUTH, FATHER.
BUT I HUMBLY BEG WE BOTH BE SPARED YOUR TERRIBLE RAGE...
...AND THAT I BE PERMITTED TO BANISH YOUR DISPLEASURE WITH THESE OTHER GIFTS.
LO, FATHER! TELEVISION! STEREO! DIGITAL CLOCKS! BLENDERS! ELECTRIC CAN OPENERS!
ALL THE FRUITS OF PROGRESS, GREAT KING-- COURTESY OF ROXXON.

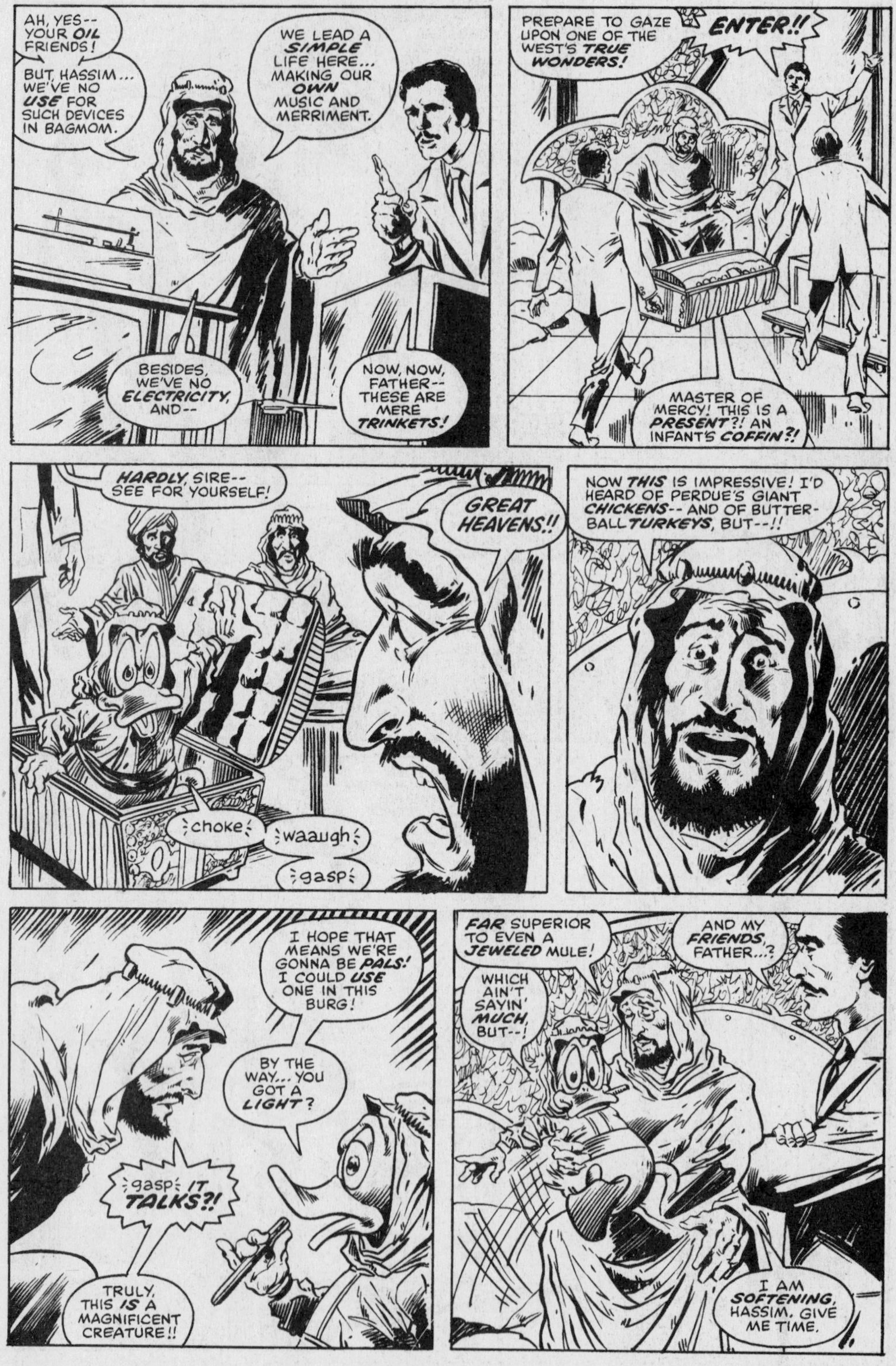
AH, YES-- YOUR OIL FRIENDS!
BUT, HASSIM... WE'VE NO USE FOR SUCH DEVICES IN BAGMOM.
WE LEAD A SIMPLE LIFE HERE... MAKING OUR OWN MUSIC AND MERRIMENT.
BESIDES, WE'VE NO ELECTRICITY, AND--
NOW, NOW, FATHER-- THESE ARE MERE TRINKETS!
PREPARE TO GAZE UPON ONE OF THE WEST'S TRUE WONDERS!
ENTER!!
MASTER OF MERCY! THIS IS A PRESENT?! AN INFANT'S COFFIN?!
HARDLY, SIRE-- SEE FOR YOURSELF!
GREAT HEAVENS!!
choke
waaugh
gasp
NOW THIS IS IMPRESSIVE! I'D HEARD OF PERDUE'S GIANT CHICKENS-- AND OF BUTTER-BALL TURKEYS, BUT--!!
I HOPE THAT MEANS WE'RE GONNA BE PALS! I COULD USE ONE IN THIS BURG!
BY THE WAY... YOU GOT A LIGHT?
gasp IT TALKS?!
TRULY, THIS IS A MAGNIFICENT CREATURE!!
FAR SUPERIOR TO EVEN A JEWELED MULE!
WHICH AIN'T SAYIN' MUCH, BUT--!
AND MY FRIENDS, FATHER...?
I AM SOFTENING, HASSIM. GIVE ME TIME.

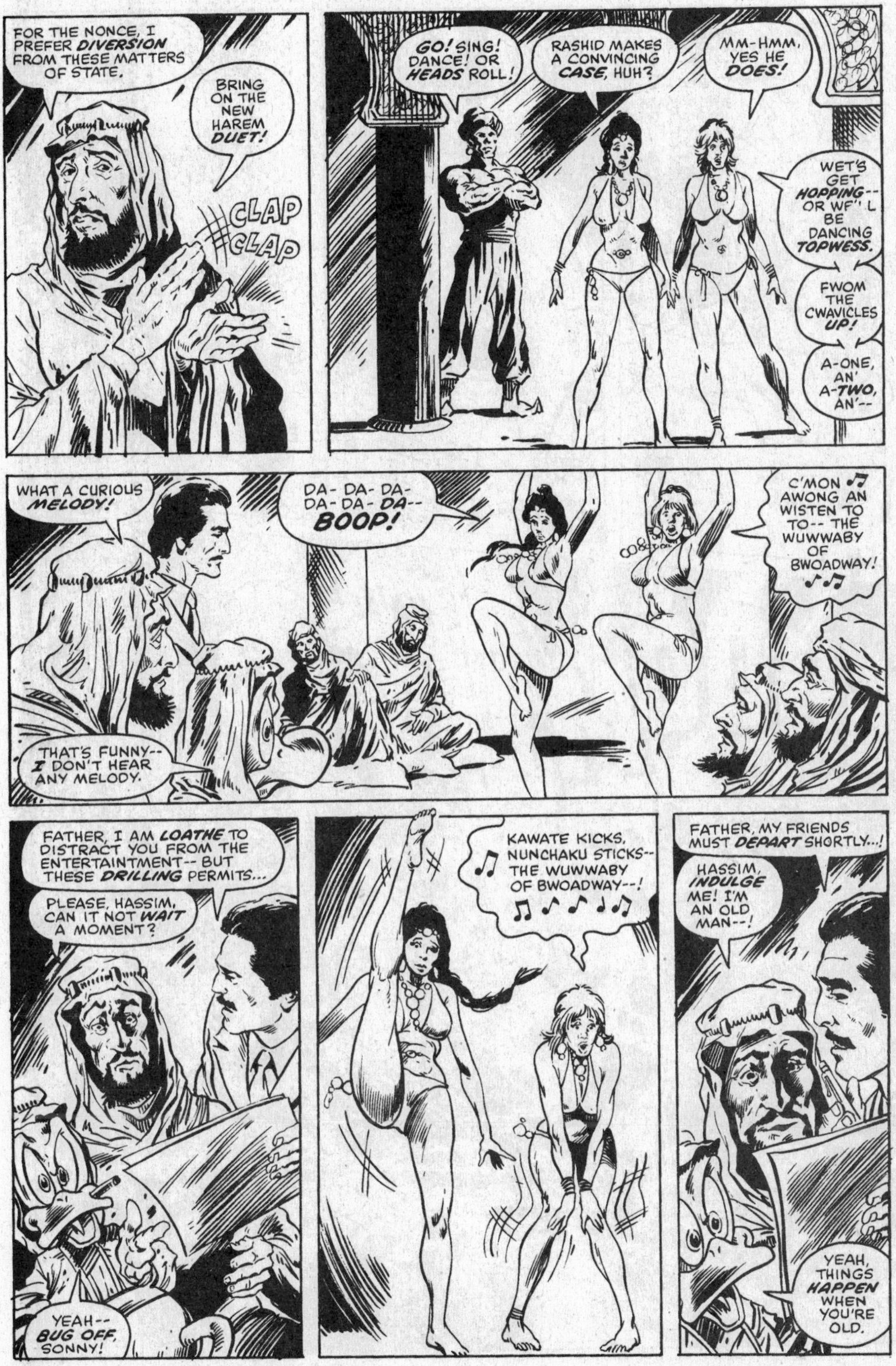
FOR THE NONCE, I PREFER DIVERSION FROM THESE MATTERS OF STATE.
BRING ON THE NEW HAREM DUET!
CLAP CLAP
GO! SING! DANCE! OR HEADS ROLL!
RASHID MAKES A CONVINCING CASE, HUH?
MM-HMM, YES HE DOES!
WET'S GET HOPPING-- OR WE'LL BE DANCING TOPWESS.
FWOM THE CWAVICLES UP!
A-ONE, AN' A-TWO, AN'--
WHAT A CURIOUS MELODY!
DA-DA-DA-DA-DA-DA-DA--BOOP!
C'MON AWONG AN WISTEN TO TO-- THE WUWWABY OF BWOADWAY!
THAT'S FUNNY-- I DON'T HEAR ANY MELODY.
FATHER, I AM LOATHE TO DISTRACT YOU FROM THE ENTERTAINTMENT-- BUT THESE DRILLING PERMITS...
PLEASE, HASSIM, CAN IT NOT WAIT A MOMENT?
YEAH-- BUG OFF, SONNY!
KAWATE KICKS, NUNCHAKU STICKS-- THE WUWWABY OF BWOADWAY--!
FATHER, MY FRIENDS MUST DEPART SHORTLY...!
HASSIM, INDULGE ME! I'M AN OLD MAN--!
YEAH, THINGS HAPPEN WHEN YOU'RE OLD.

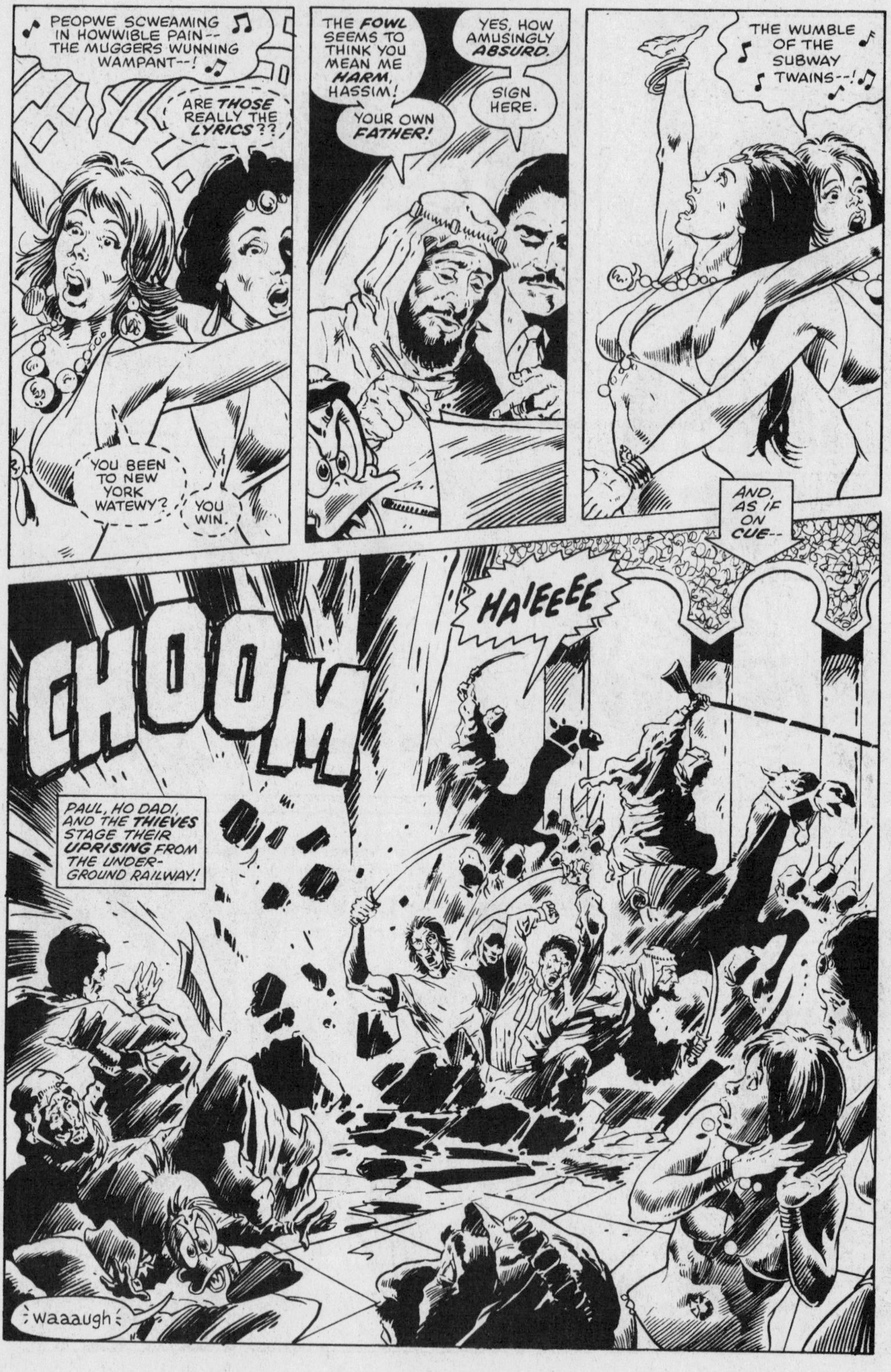
♪ PEOPWE SCWEAMING IN HOWWIBLE PAIN-- THE MUGGERS WUNNING WAMPANT--! ♪
ARE THOSE REALLY THE LYRICS??
YOU BEEN TO NEW YORK WATEWY?
YOU WIN.
THE FOWL SEEMS TO THINK YOU MEAN ME HARM, HASSIM!
YOUR OWN FATHER!
YES, HOW AMUSINGLY ABSURD.
SIGN HERE.
♪ THE WUMBLE OF THE SUBWAY TWAINS--! ♪
AND, AS IF ON CUE--
CHOOM
HAIEEEE
PAUL, HO DADI, AND THE THIEVES STAGE THEIR UPRISING FROM THE UNDER-GROUND RAILWAY!
waaaugh

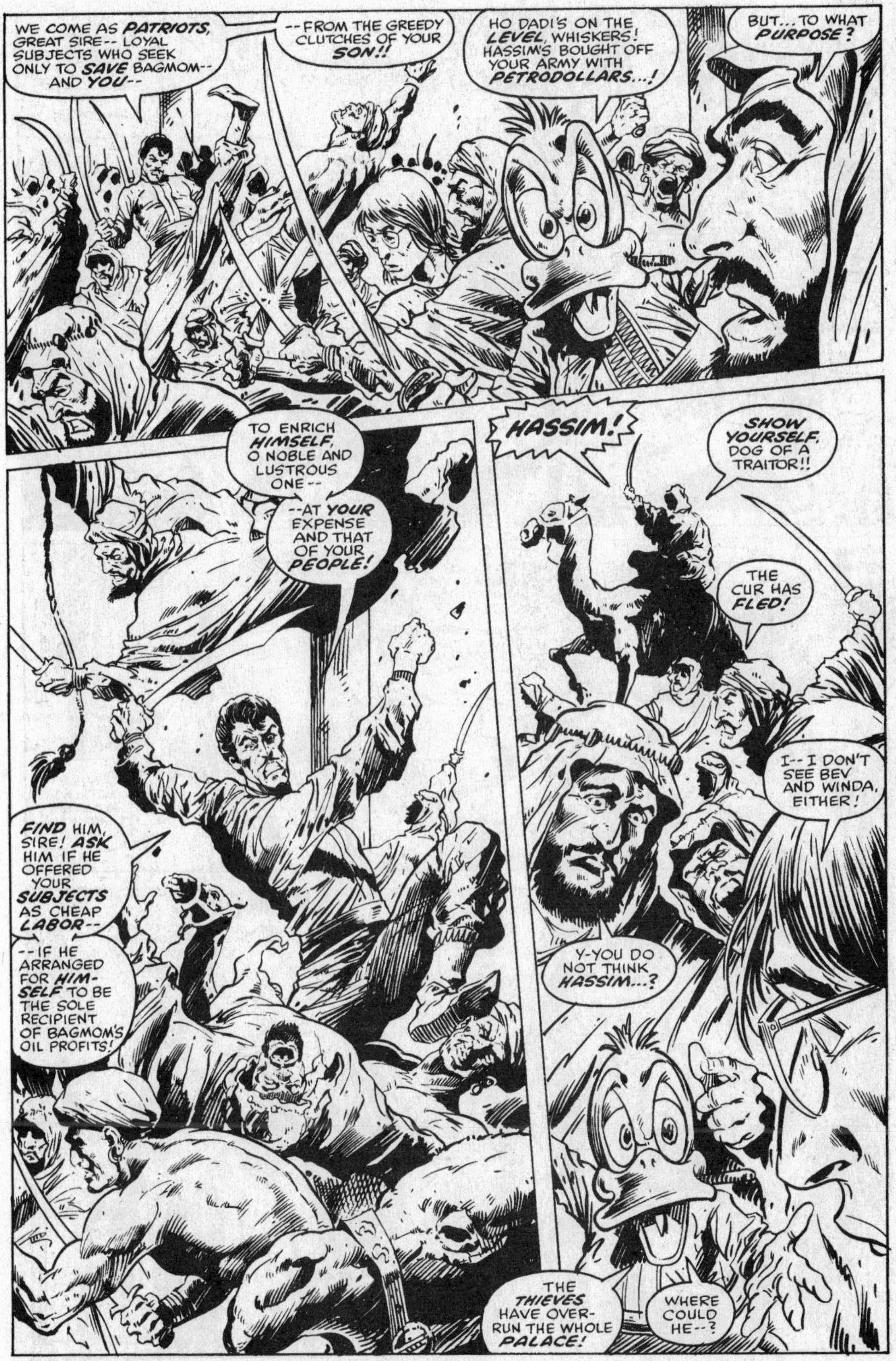

WE COME AS PATRIOTS, GREAT SIRE-- LOYAL SUBJECTS WHO SEEK ONLY TO SAVE BAGMOM-- AND YOU--
--FROM THE GREEDY CLUTCHES OF YOUR SON!!
HO DADI'S ON THE LEVEL, WHISKERS! HASSIM'S BOUGHT OFF YOUR ARMY WITH PETRODOLLARS...!
BUT... TO WHAT PURPOSE?
TO ENRICH HIMSELF, O NOBLE AND LUSTROUS ONE--
--AT YOUR EXPENSE AND THAT OF YOUR PEOPLE!
FIND HIM, SIRE! ASK HIM IF HE OFFERED YOUR SUBJECTS AS CHEAP LABOR--
--IF HE ARRANGED FOR HIMSELF TO BE THE SOLE RECIPIENT OF BAGMOM'S OIL PROFITS!
HASSIM!
SHOW YOURSELF, DOG OF A TRAITOR!!
THE CUR HAS FLED!
I-- I DON'T SEE BEV AND WINDA, EITHER!
Y-YOU DO NOT THINK HASSIM...?
THE THIEVES HAVE OVER-RUN THE WHOLE PALACE!
WHERE COULD HE--?

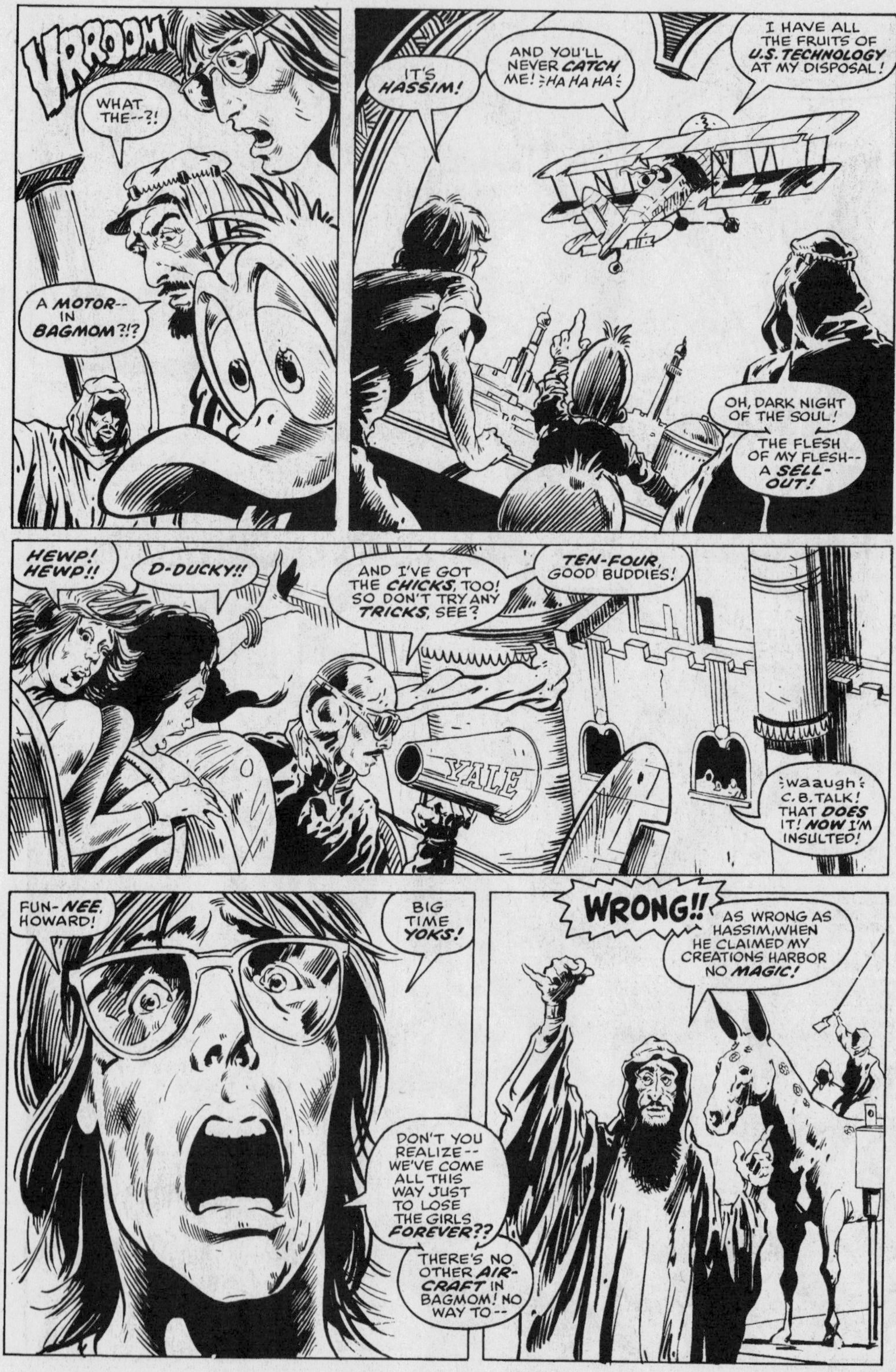
VRROOM
WHAT THE--?!
A MOTOR-- IN BAGMOM?!?
IT'S HASSIM!
AND YOU'LL NEVER CATCH ME! HA HA HA!
I HAVE ALL THE FRUITS OF U.S. TECHNOLOGY AT MY DISPOSAL!
OH, DARK NIGHT OF THE SOUL!
THE FLESH OF MY FLESH-- A SELL-OUT!
HEWP! HEWP!!
D-DUCKY!!
AND I'VE GOT THE CHICKS, TOO! SO DON'T TRY ANY TRICKS, SEE?
TEN-FOUR, GOOD BUDDIES!
YALE
waaugh C.B. TALK! THAT DOES IT! NOW I'M INSULTED!
FUN-NEE, HOWARD!
BIG TIME YOKS!
DON'T YOU REALIZE-- WE'VE COME ALL THIS WAY JUST TO LOSE THE GIRLS FOREVER??
THERE'S NO OTHER AIR-CRAFT IN BAGMOM! NO WAY TO--
WRONG!!
AS WRONG AS HASSIM, WHEN HE CLAIMED MY CREATIONS HARBOR NO MAGIC!

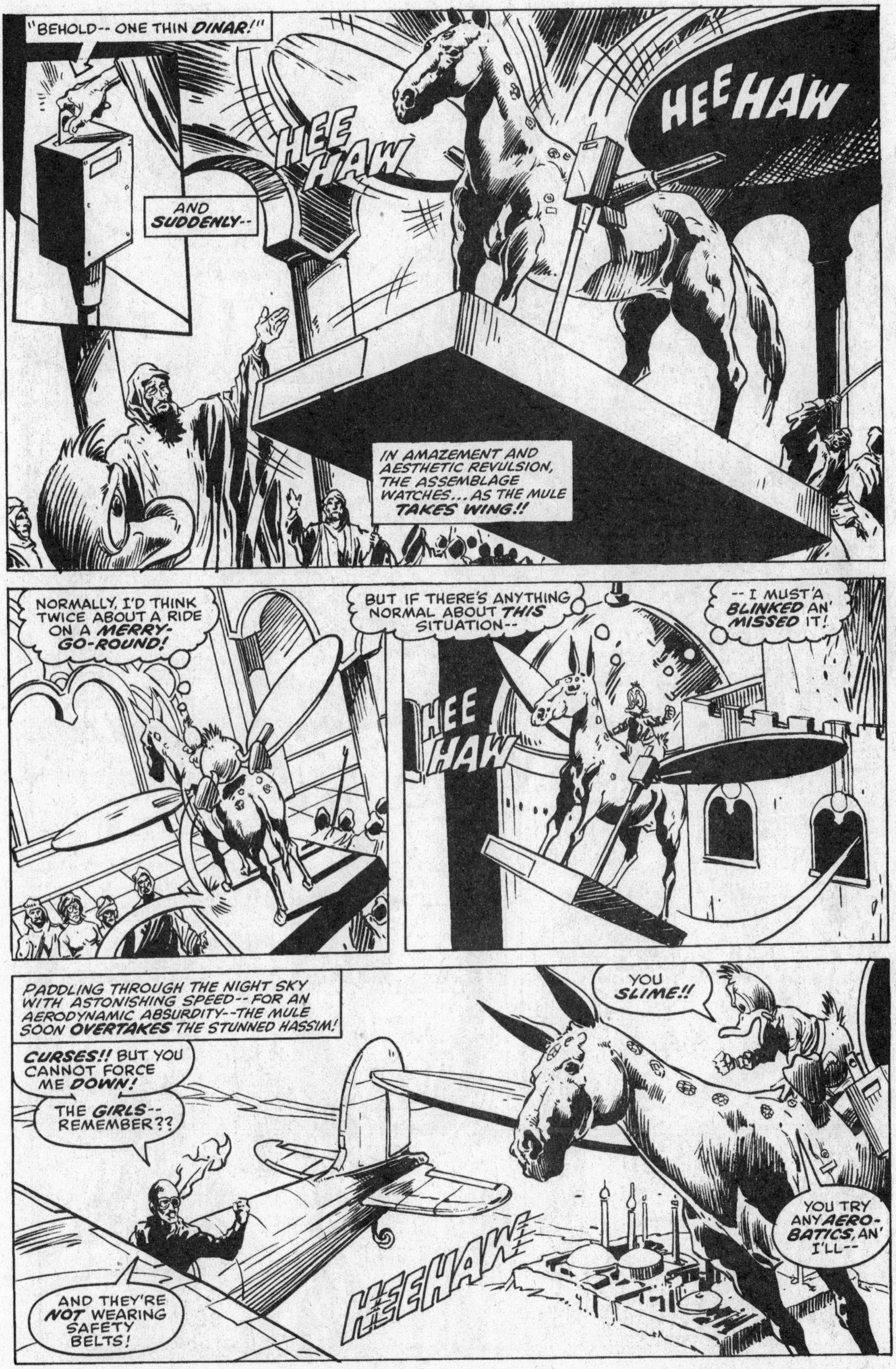
"BEHOLD-- ONE THIN DINAR!"
AND SUDDENLY--
HEE HAW
HEE HAW
IN AMAZEMENT AND AESTHETIC REVULSION, THE ASSEMBLAGE WATCHES... AS THE MULE TAKES WING!!
NORMALLY, I'D THINK TWICE ABOUT A RIDE ON A MERRY-GO-ROUND!
BUT IF THERE'S ANYTHING NORMAL ABOUT THIS SITUATION--
--I MUST'A BLINKED AN' MISSED IT!
HEE HAW
PADDLING THROUGH THE NIGHT SKY WITH ASTONISHING SPEED-- FOR AN AERODYNAMIC ABSURDITY--THE MULE SOON OVERTAKES THE STUNNED HASSIM!
YOU SLIME!!
CURSES!! BUT YOU CANNOT FORCE ME DOWN!
THE GIRLS-- REMEMBER??
YOU TRY ANY AERO-BATICS, AN' I'LL--
AND THEY'RE NOT WEARING SAFETY BELTS!
HEEHAW

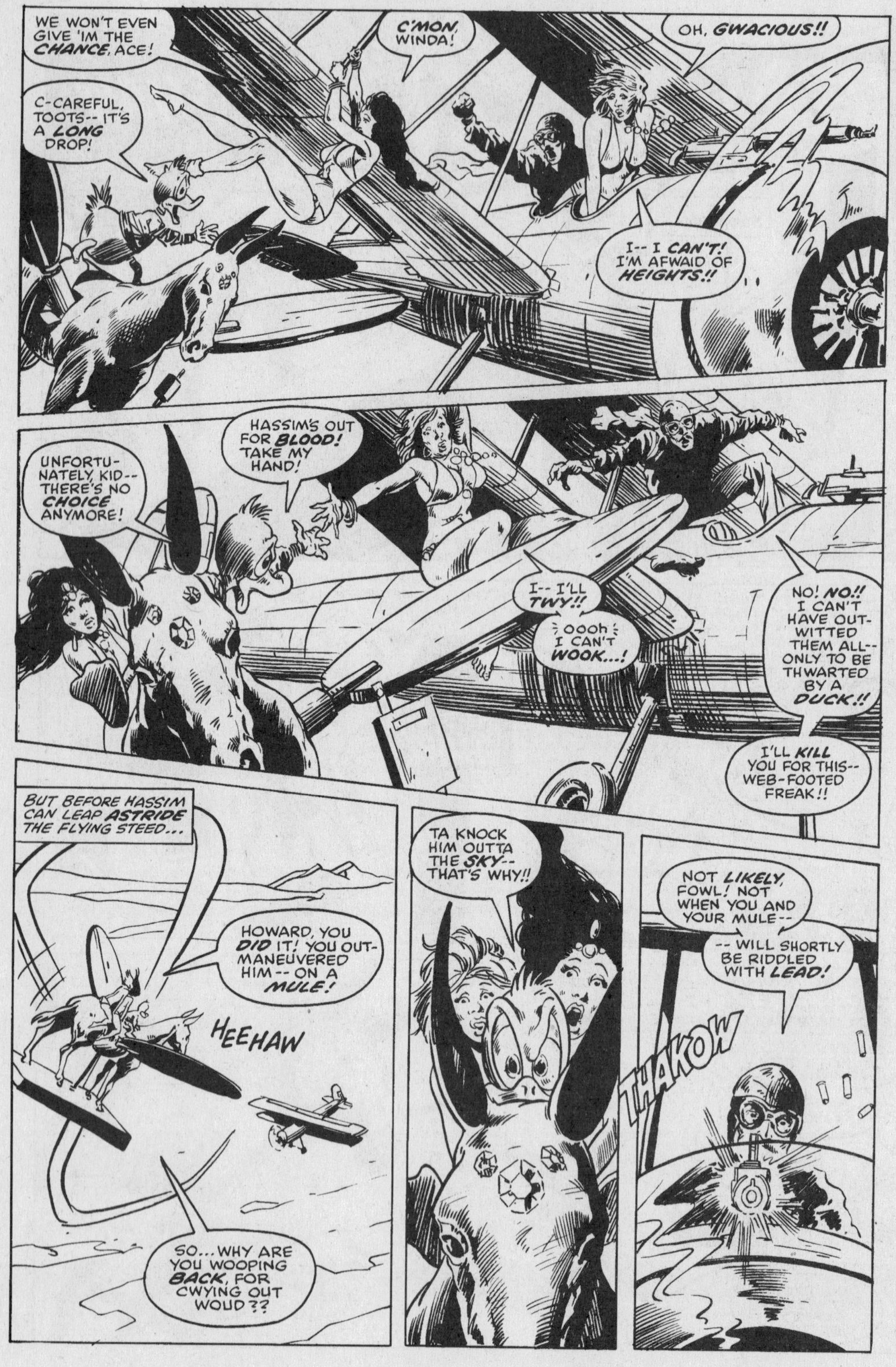

WE WON'T EVEN GIVE 'IM THE CHANCE, ACE!
C'MON, WINDA!
OH, GWACIOUS!!
C-CAREFUL, TOOTS-- IT'S A LONG DROP!
I-- I CAN'T! I'M AFWAID OF HEIGHTS!!
UNFORTUNATELY, KID-- THERE'S NO CHOICE ANYMORE!
HASSIM'S OUT FOR BLOOD! TAKE MY HAND!
I-- I'LL TWY!!
oooh I CAN'T WOOK...!
NO! NO!! I CAN'T HAVE OUT-WITTED THEM ALL-- ONLY TO BE THWARTED BY A DUCK!!
I'LL KILL YOU FOR THIS-- WEB-FOOTED FREAK!!
BUT BEFORE HASSIM CAN LEAP ASTRIDE THE FLYING STEED...
HOWARD, YOU DID IT! YOU OUT-MANEUVERED HIM -- ON A MULE!
HEEHAW
SO...WHY ARE YOU WOOPING BACK, FOR CWYING OUT WOUD??
TA KNOCK HIM OUTTA THE SKY-- THAT'S WHY!!
NOT LIKELY, FOWL! NOT WHEN YOU AND YOUR MULE--
-- WILL SHORTLY BE RIDDLED WITH LEAD!
THAKOW

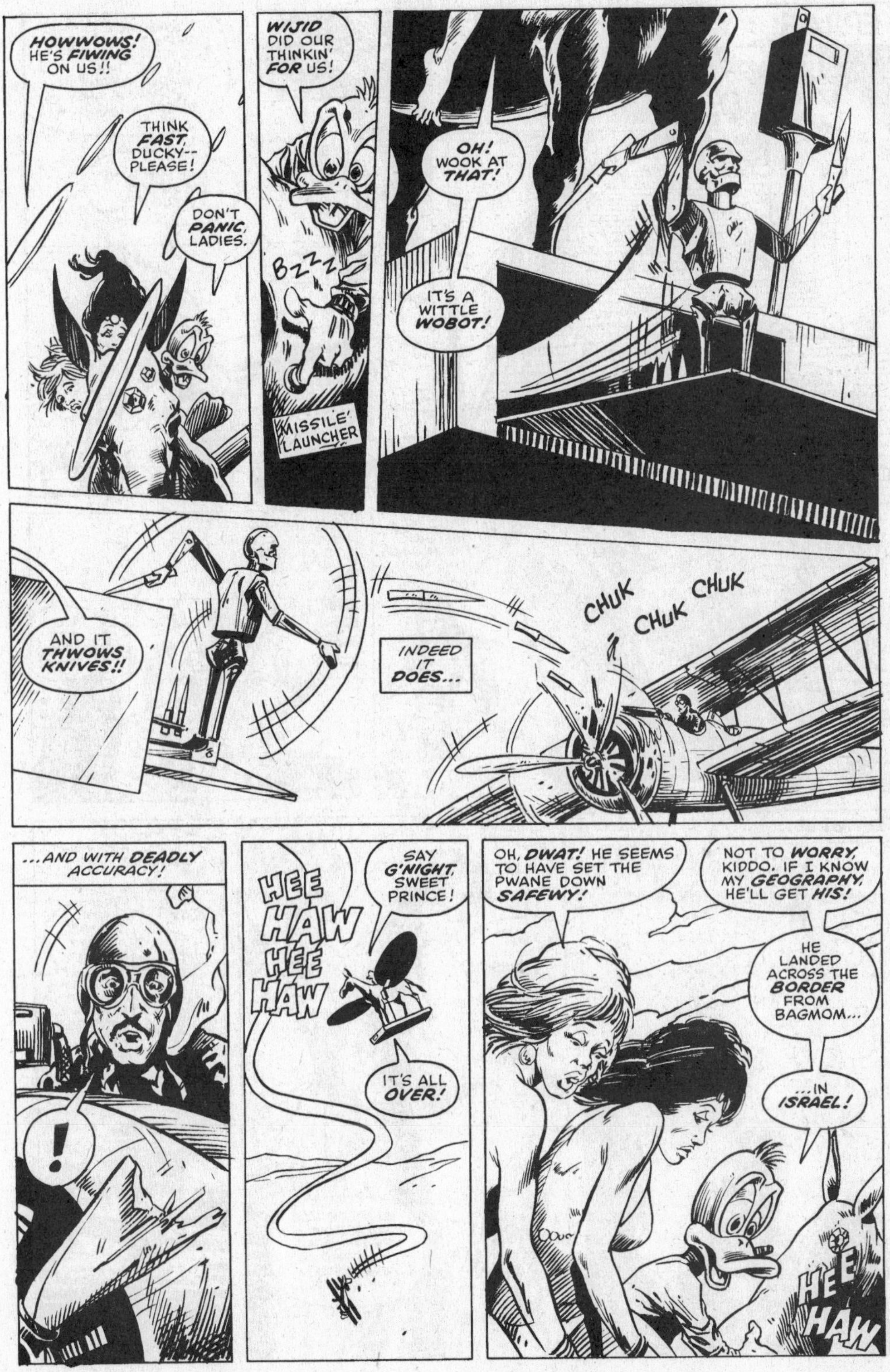
HOWWOWS! HE'S FIWING ON US!!
THINK FAST, DUCKY-- PLEASE!
DON'T PANIC, LADIES.
WIJID DID OUR THINKIN' FOR US!
BZZZ
MISSILE LAUNCHER
OH! WOOK AT THAT!
IT'S A WITTLE WOBOT!
AND IT THWOWS KNIVES!!
INDEED IT DOES...
CHUK CHUK CHUK
...AND WITH DEADLY ACCURACY!
!
HEE HAW HEE HAW
SAY G'NIGHT, SWEET PRINCE!
IT'S ALL OVER!
OH, DWAT! HE SEEMS TO HAVE SET THE PWANE DOWN SAFEWY!
NOT TO WORRY, KIDDO. IF I KNOW MY GEOGRAPHY, HE'LL GET HIS!
HE LANDED ACROSS THE BORDER FROM BAGMOM...
...IN ISRAEL!
HEE HAW

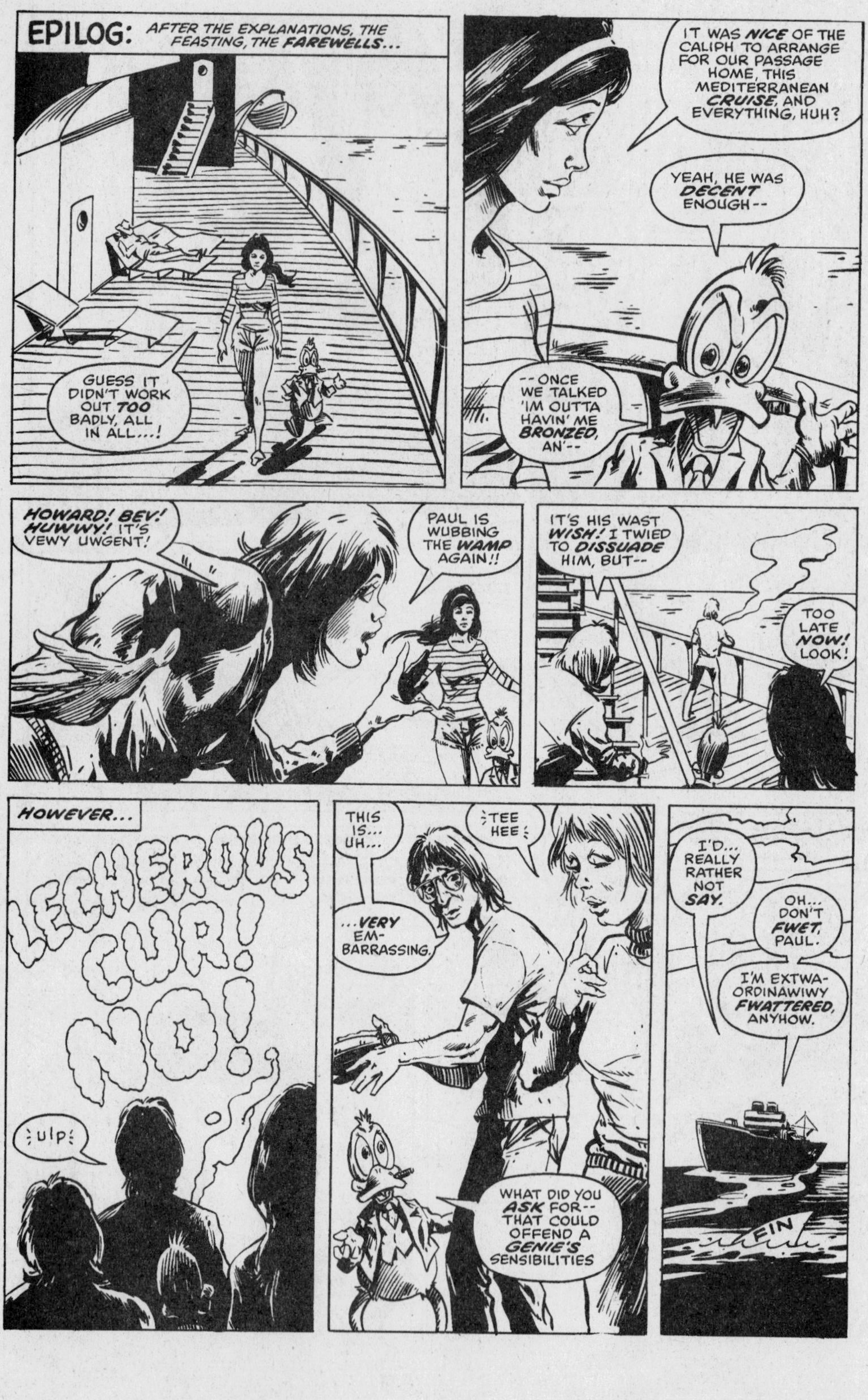
EPILOG: AFTER THE EXPLANATIONS, THE FEASTING, THE FAREWELLS...
GUESS IT DIDN'T WORK OUT TOO BADLY, ALL IN ALL...!
IT WAS NICE OF THE CALIPH TO ARRANGE FOR OUR PASSAGE HOME, THIS MEDITERRANEAN CRUISE, AND EVERYTHING, HUH?
YEAH, HE WAS DECENT ENOUGH--
--ONCE WE TALKED 'IM OUTTA HAVIN' ME BRONZED, AN'--
HOWARD! BEV! HUWWY! IT'S VEWY UWGENT!
PAUL IS WUBBING THE WAMP AGAIN!!
IT'S HIS WAST WISH! I TWIED TO DISSUADE HIM, BUT--
TOO LATE NOW! LOOK!
HOWEVER...
LECHEROUS CUR! NO!
ulp
THIS IS... UH...
TEE HEE
...VERY EM-BARRASSING.
WHAT DID YOU ASK FOR--THAT COULD OFFEND A GENIE'S SENSIBILITIES
I'D... REALLY RATHER NOT SAY.
OH... DON'T FWET, PAUL.
I'M EXTWA-ORDINAWIWY FWATTERED, ANYHOW.
FIN

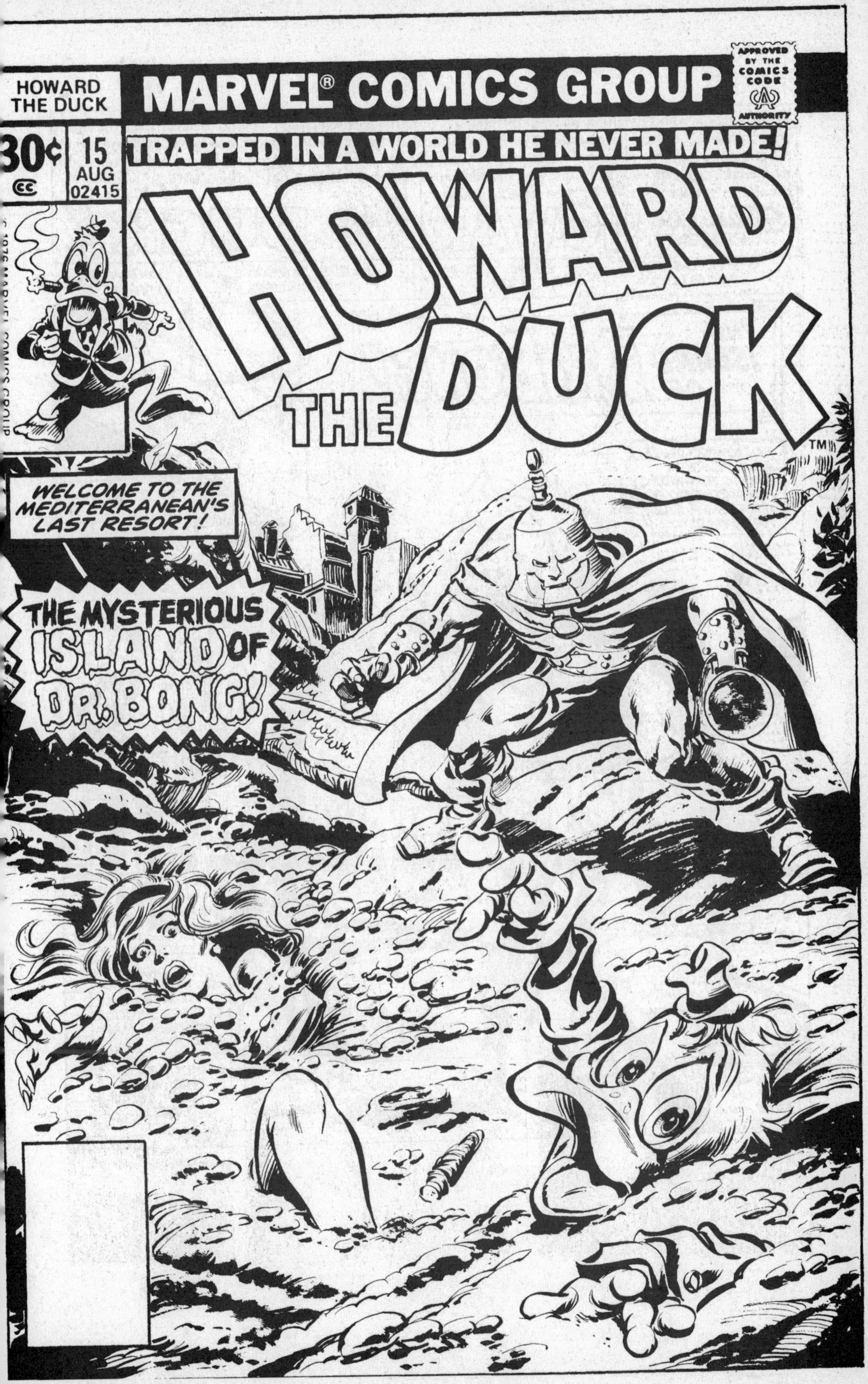
HOWARD THE DUCK
MARVEL® COMICS GROUP
APPROVED BY THE COMICS CODE AUTHORITY
30¢
15
AUG
02415
TRAPPED IN A WORLD HE NEVER MADE!
HOWARD THE DUCK
TM
WELCOME TO THE MEDITERRANEAN'S LAST RESORT!
THE MYSTERIOUS ISLAND OF DR. BONG!

From the time of his hatching, he was...different. A potentially brilliant scholar who dreaded the structured environment of school, he educated himself in the streets, taking whatever work was available, formulating his philosophy of self from what he learned of the world about him. And then the Cosmic Axis shifted...and that world *changed.* Suddenly, he was stranded in a universe he could not fathom. Without warning, he became a strange fowl in an even stranger land.

Stan Lee PRESENTS: HOWARD THE DUCK!™

STEVE GERBER WRITER/EDITOR * GENE COLAN ARTIST * KLAUS JANSON INKER/COLORIST * IRV WATANABE LETTERER

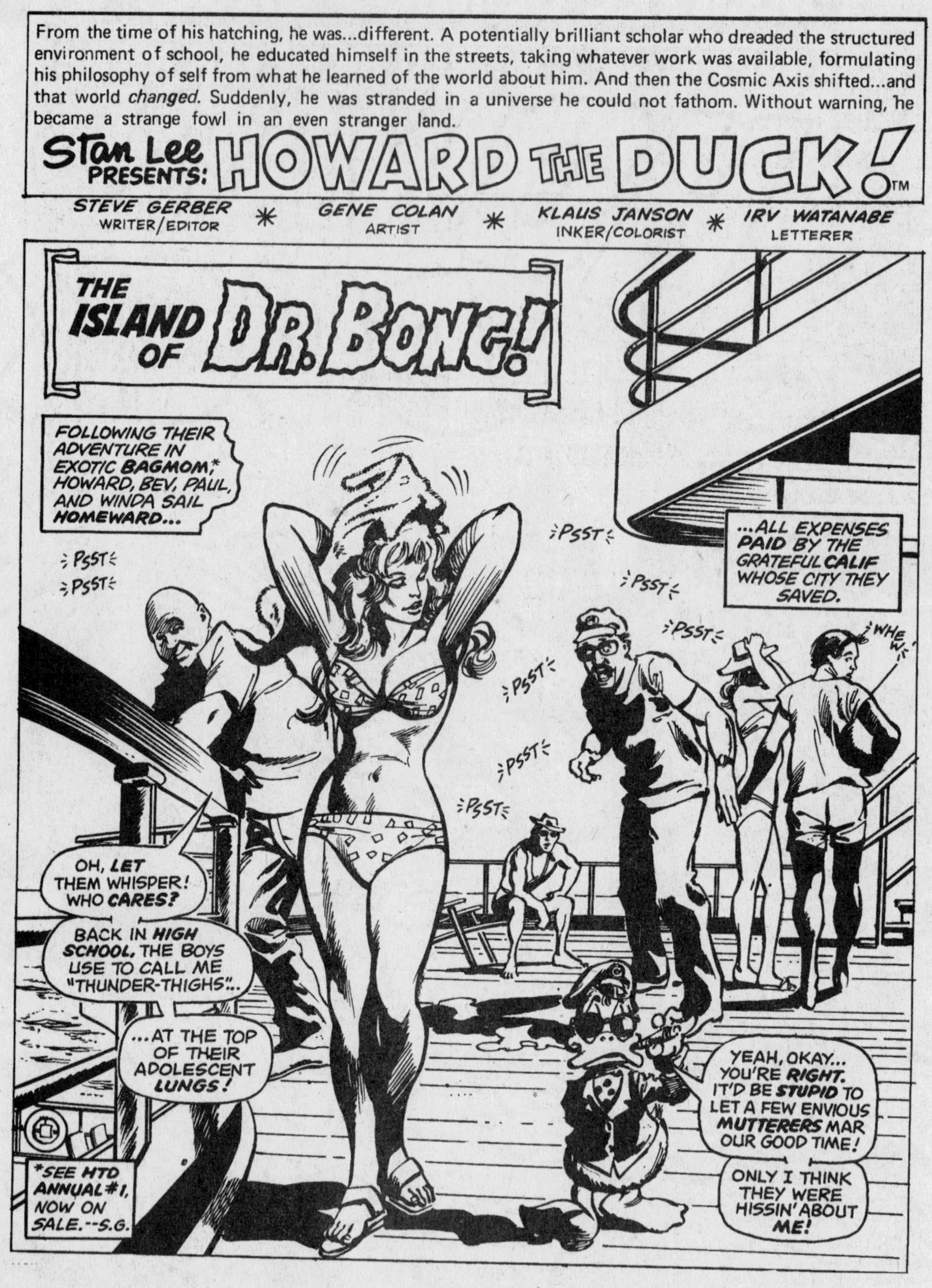

THE ISLAND OF DR. BONG!
FOLLOWING THEIR ADVENTURE IN EXOTIC BAGMOM,* HOWARD, BEV, PAUL, AND WINDA SAIL HOMEWARD...
...ALL EXPENSES PAID BY THE GRATEFUL CALIF WHOSE CITY THEY SAVED.
PSST
PSST
PSST
PSST
PSST
PSST
PSST
PSST
WHEW
OH, LET THEM WHISPER! WHO CARES?
BACK IN HIGH SCHOOL, THE BOYS USE TO CALL ME "THUNDER-THIGHS"..
...AT THE TOP OF THEIR ADOLESCENT LUNGS!
YEAH, OKAY... YOU'RE RIGHT. IT'D BE STUPID TO LET A FEW ENVIOUS MUTTERERS MAR OUR GOOD TIME!
ONLY I THINK THEY WERE HISSIN' ABOUT ME!
*SEE HTD ANNUAL #1, NOW ON SALE.--S.G.

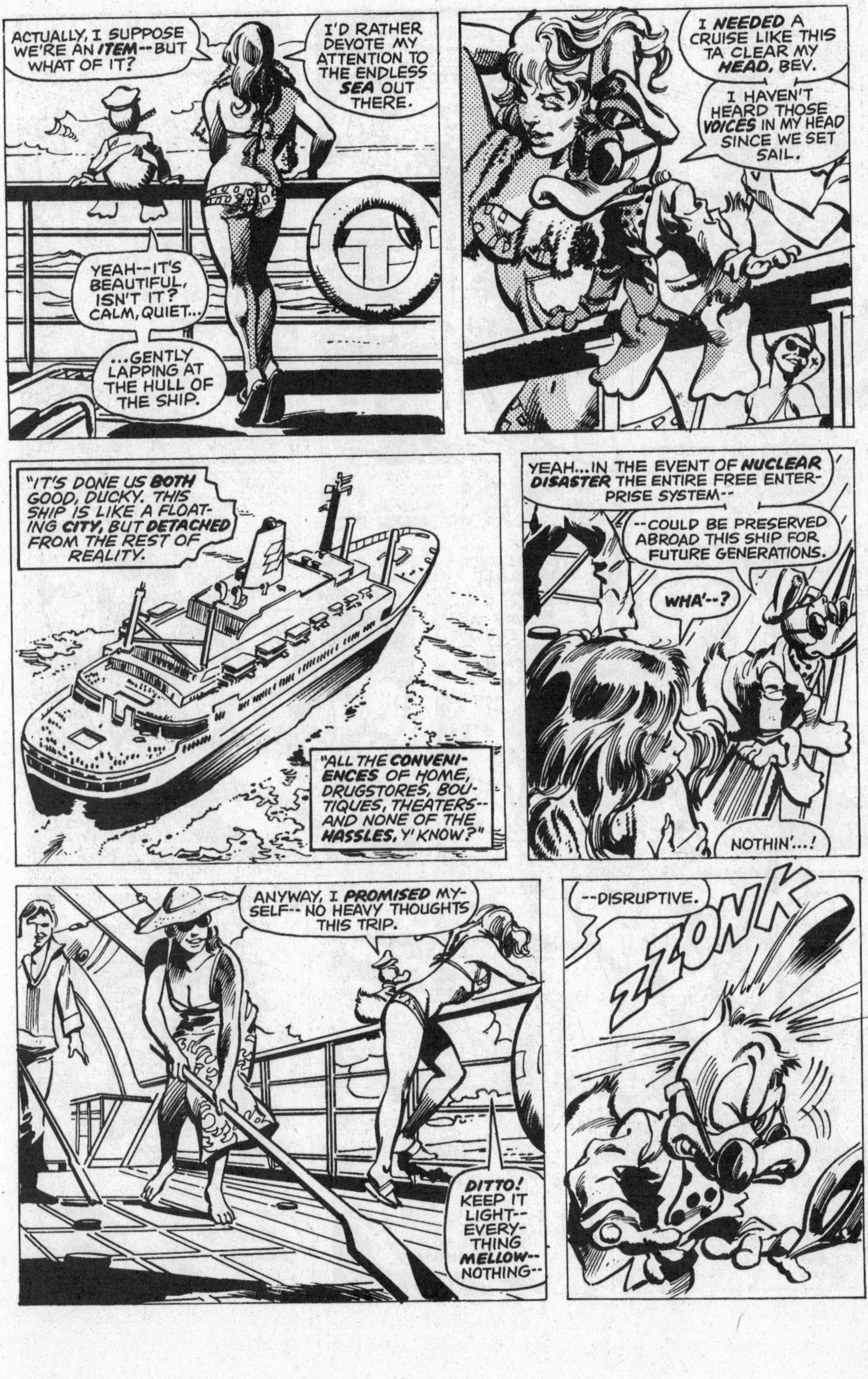
ACTUALLY, I SUPPOSE WE'RE AN ITEM--BUT WHAT OF IT?
I'D RATHER DEVOTE MY ATTENTION TO THE ENDLESS SEA OUT THERE.
YEAH--IT'S BEAUTIFUL, ISN'T IT? CALM, QUIET...
...GENTLY LAPPING AT THE HULL OF THE SHIP.
I NEEDED A CRUISE LIKE THIS TA CLEAR MY HEAD, BEV.
I HAVEN'T HEARD THOSE VOICES IN MY HEAD SINCE WE SET SAIL.
"IT'S DONE US BOTH GOOD, DUCKY. THIS SHIP IS LIKE A FLOATING CITY, BUT DETACHED FROM THE REST OF REALITY.
"ALL THE CONVENIENCES OF HOME, DRUGSTORES, BOUTIQUES, THEATERS--AND NONE OF THE HASSLES, Y'KNOW?"
YEAH...IN THE EVENT OF NUCLEAR DISASTER THE ENTIRE FREE ENTERPRISE SYSTEM--
--COULD BE PRESERVED ABROAD THIS SHIP FOR FUTURE GENERATIONS.
WHA'--?
NOTHIN'...!
ANYWAY, I PROMISED MYSELF--NO HEAVY THOUGHTS THIS TRIP.
DITTO! KEEP IT LIGHT--EVERYTHING MELLOW--NOTHING--
--DISRUPTIVE.
ZZZONK

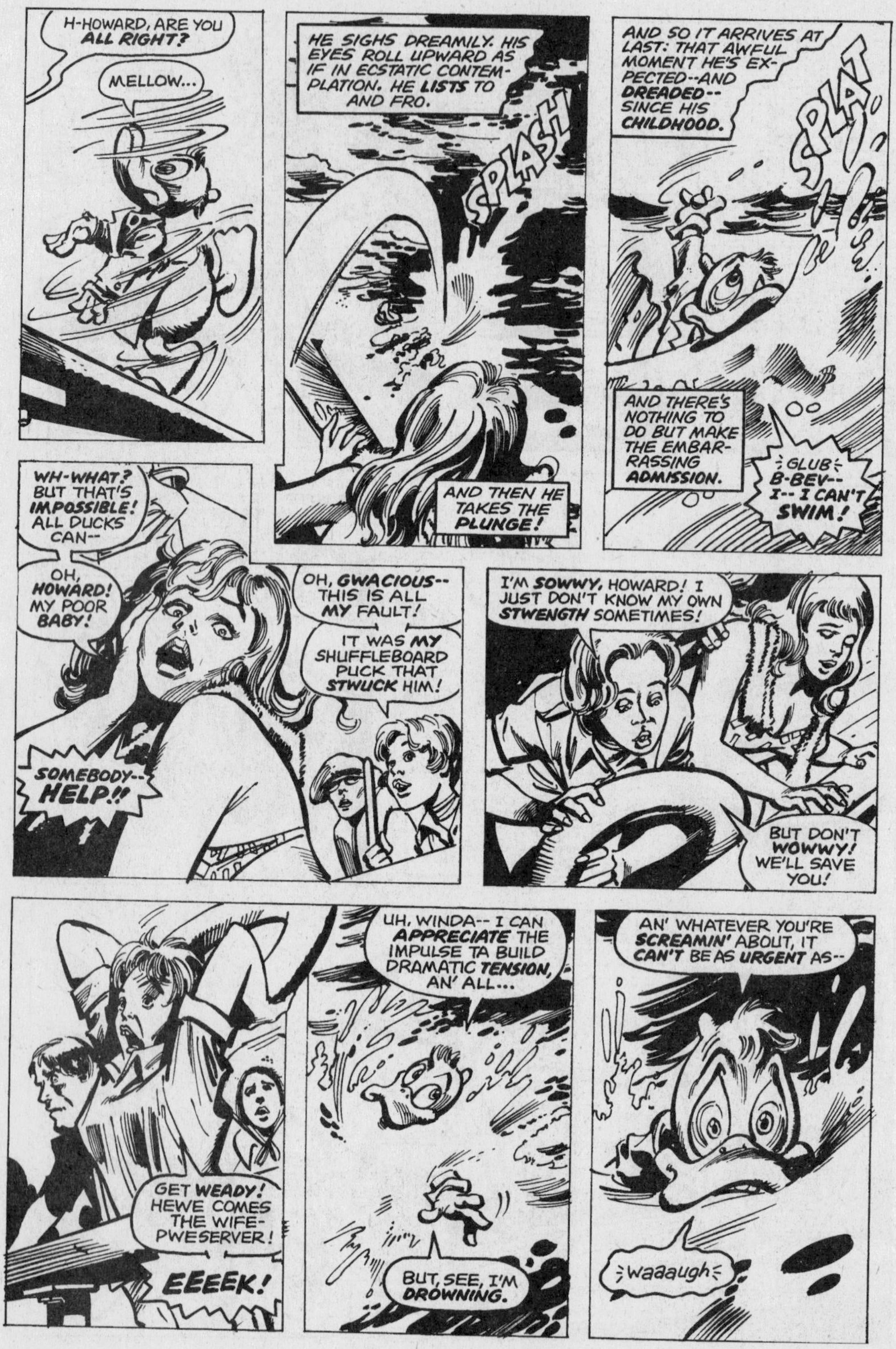

H-HOWARD, ARE YOU ALL RIGHT?
MELLOW...
HE SIGHS DREAMILY. HIS EYES ROLL UPWARD AS IF IN ECSTATIC CONTEMPLATION. HE LISTS TO AND FRO.
SPLASH
AND THEN HE TAKES THE PLUNGE!
AND SO IT ARRIVES AT LAST: THAT AWFUL MOMENT HE'S EXPECTED--AND DREADED--SINCE HIS CHILDHOOD.
SPLAT
AND THERE'S NOTHING TO DO BUT MAKE THE EMBARRASSING ADMISSION.
GLUB B-BEV-- I-- I CAN'T SWIM!
WH-WHAT? BUT THAT'S IMPOSSIBLE! ALL DUCKS CAN--
OH, HOWARD! MY POOR BABY!
OH, GWACIOUS-- THIS IS ALL MY FAULT!
IT WAS MY SHUFFLEBOARD PUCK THAT STWUCK HIM!
SOMEBODY-- HELP!!
I'M SOWWY, HOWARD! I JUST DON'T KNOW MY OWN STWENGTH SOMETIMES!
BUT DON'T WOWWY! WE'LL SAVE YOU!
GET WEADY! HEWE COMES THE WIFE-PWESERVER!
EEEEK!
UH, WINDA-- I CAN APPRECIATE THE IMPULSE TA BUILD DRAMATIC TENSION, AN' ALL...
BUT, SEE, I'M DROWNING.
AN' WHATEVER YOU'RE SCREAMIN' ABOUT, IT CAN'T BE AS URGENT AS--
waaaugh

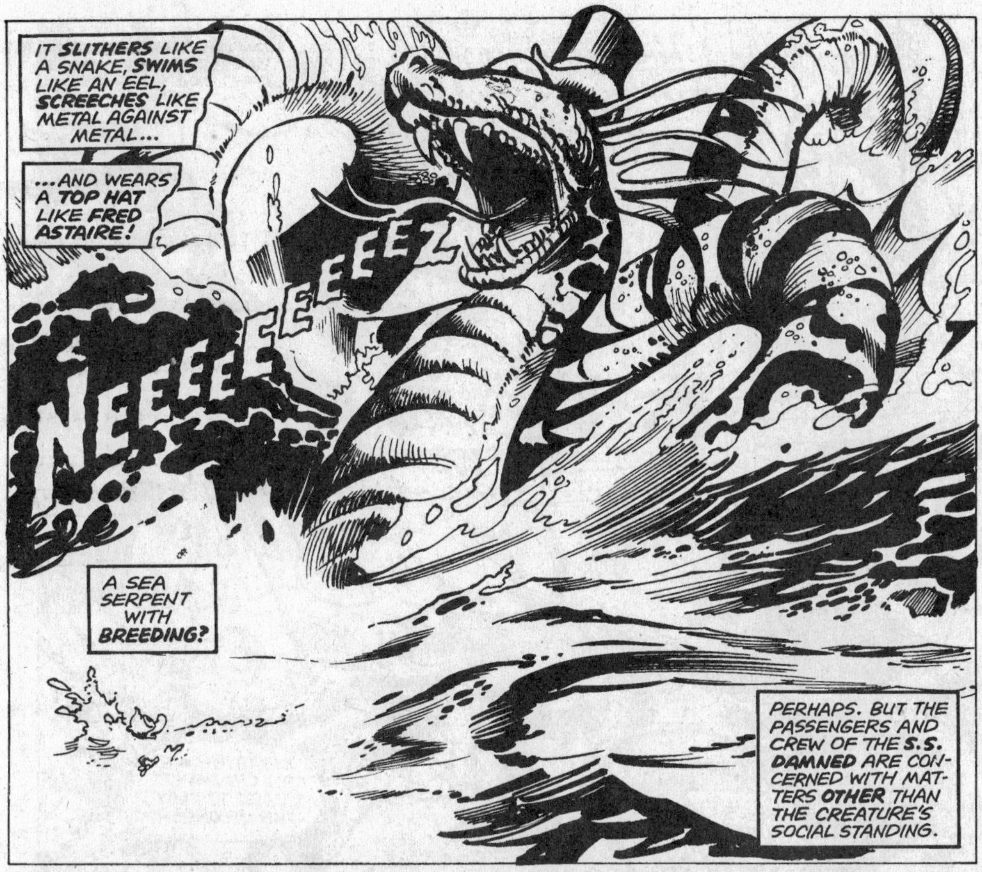
IT SLITHERS LIKE A SNAKE, SWIMS LIKE AN EEL, SCREECHES LIKE METAL AGAINST METAL...
...AND WEARS A TOP HAT LIKE FRED ASTAIRE!
NEEEEEEEEEEZ
A SEA SERPENT WITH BREEDING?
PERHAPS. BUT THE PASSENGERS AND CREW OF THE S.S. DAMNED ARE CONCERNED WITH MATTERS OTHER THAN THE CREATURE'S SOCIAL STANDING.
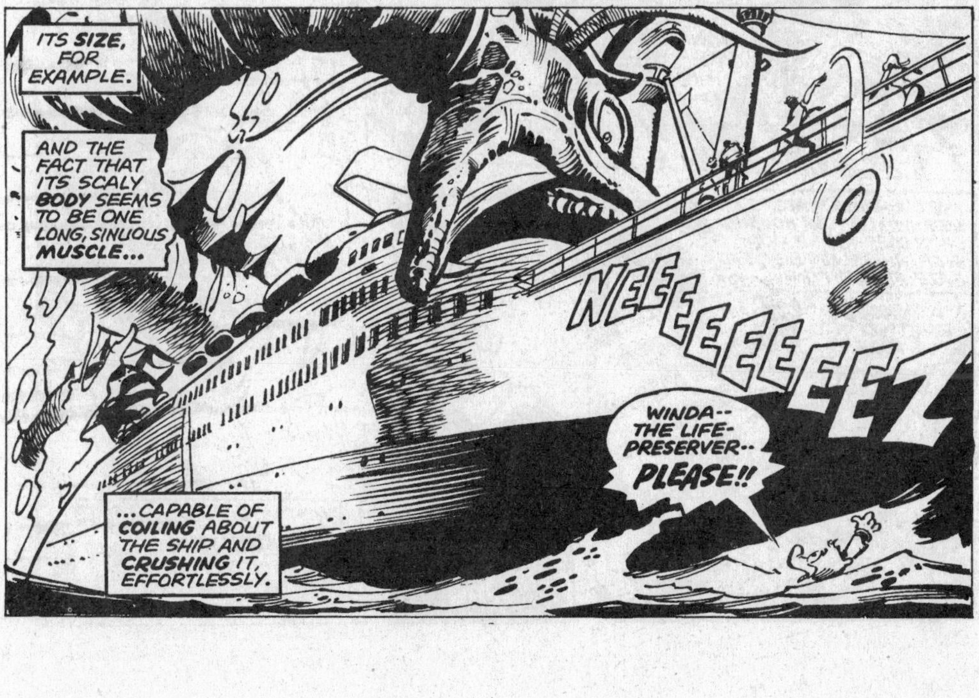
ITS SIZE, FOR EXAMPLE.
AND THE FACT THAT ITS SCALY BODY SEEMS TO BE ONE LONG, SINUOUS MUSCLE...
NEEEEEEEEEEZ
WINDA-- THE LIFE-PRESERVER-- PLEASE!!
...CAPABLE OF COILING ABOUT THE SHIP AND CRUSHING IT, EFFORTLESSLY.

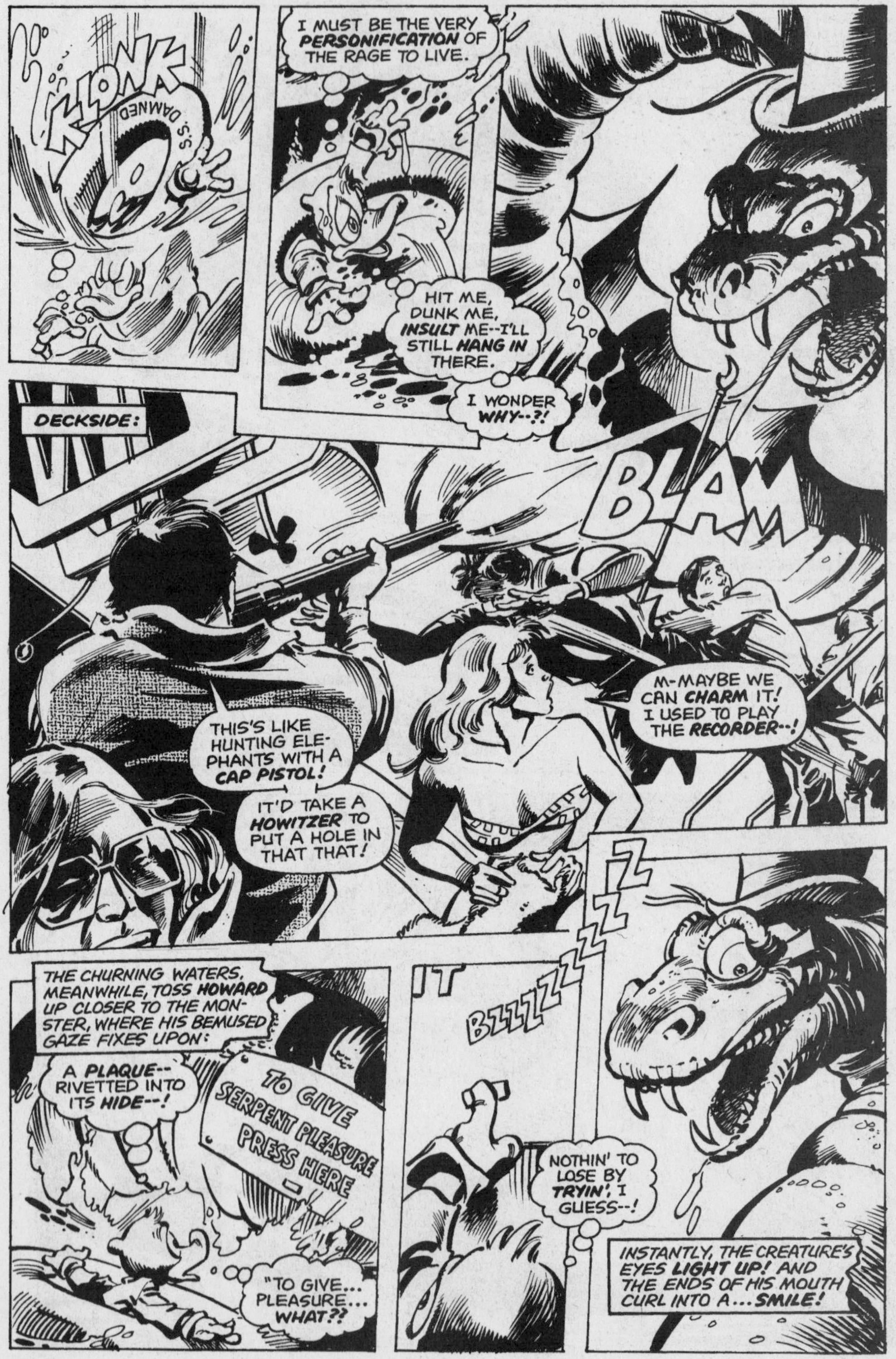
KLONK
DAMNED'S
I MUST BE THE VERY PERSONIFICATION OF THE RAGE TO LIVE.
HIT ME, DUNK ME, INSULT ME--I'LL STILL HANG IN THERE.
I WONDER WHY--?!
DECKSIDE:
BLAM
THIS'S LIKE HUNTING ELE-PHANTS WITH A CAP PISTOL!
IT'D TAKE A HOWITZER TO PUT A HOLE IN THAT THAT!
M-MAYBE WE CAN CHARM IT! I USED TO PLAY THE RECORDER--!
THE CHURNING WATERS, MEANWHILE, TOSS HOWARD UP CLOSER TO THE MON-STER, WHERE HIS BEMUSED GAZE FIXES UPON:
A PLAQUE--RIVETTED INTO ITS HIDE--!
TO GIVE SERPENT PLEASURE PRESS HERE
"TO GIVE... PLEASURE... WHAT??
IT
BZZZZZZZZZZZ
NOTHIN' TO LOSE BY TRYIN', I GUESS--!
INSTANTLY, THE CREATURE'S EYES LIGHT UP! AND THE ENDS OF HIS MOUTH CURL INTO A... SMILE!

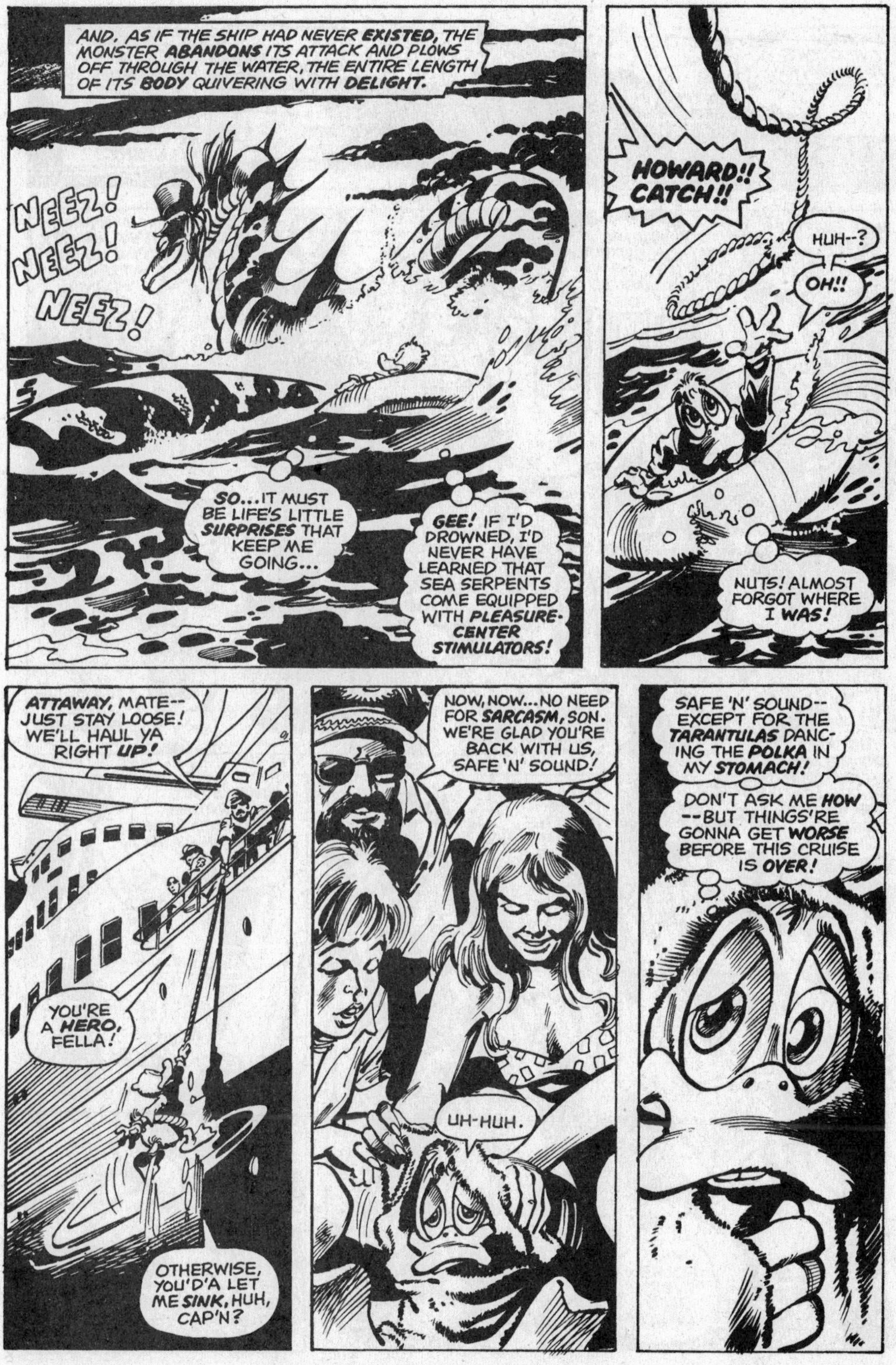
AND, AS IF THE SHIP HAD NEVER EXISTED, THE MONSTER ABANDONS ITS ATTACK AND PLOWS OFF THROUGH THE WATER, THE ENTIRE LENGTH OF ITS BODY QUIVERING WITH DELIGHT.
NEEZ! NEEZ! NEEZ!
SO...IT MUST BE LIFE'S LITTLE SURPRISES THAT KEEP ME GOING...
GEE! IF I'D DROWNED, I'D NEVER HAVE LEARNED THAT SEA SERPENTS COME EQUIPPED WITH PLEASURE-CENTER STIMULATORS!
HOWARD!! CATCH!!
HUH--?
OH!!
NUTS! ALMOST FORGOT WHERE I WAS!
ATTAWAY, MATE--JUST STAY LOOSE! WE'LL HAUL YA RIGHT UP!
YOU'RE A HERO, FELLA!
OTHERWISE, YOU'D'A LET ME SINK, HUH, CAP'N?
NOW, NOW...NO NEED FOR SARCASM, SON. WE'RE GLAD YOU'RE BACK WITH US, SAFE 'N' SOUND!
UH-HUH.
SAFE 'N' SOUND--EXCEPT FOR THE TARANTULAS DANCING THE POLKA IN MY STOMACH!
DON'T ASK ME HOW--BUT THINGS'RE GONNA GET WORSE BEFORE THIS CRUISE IS OVER!

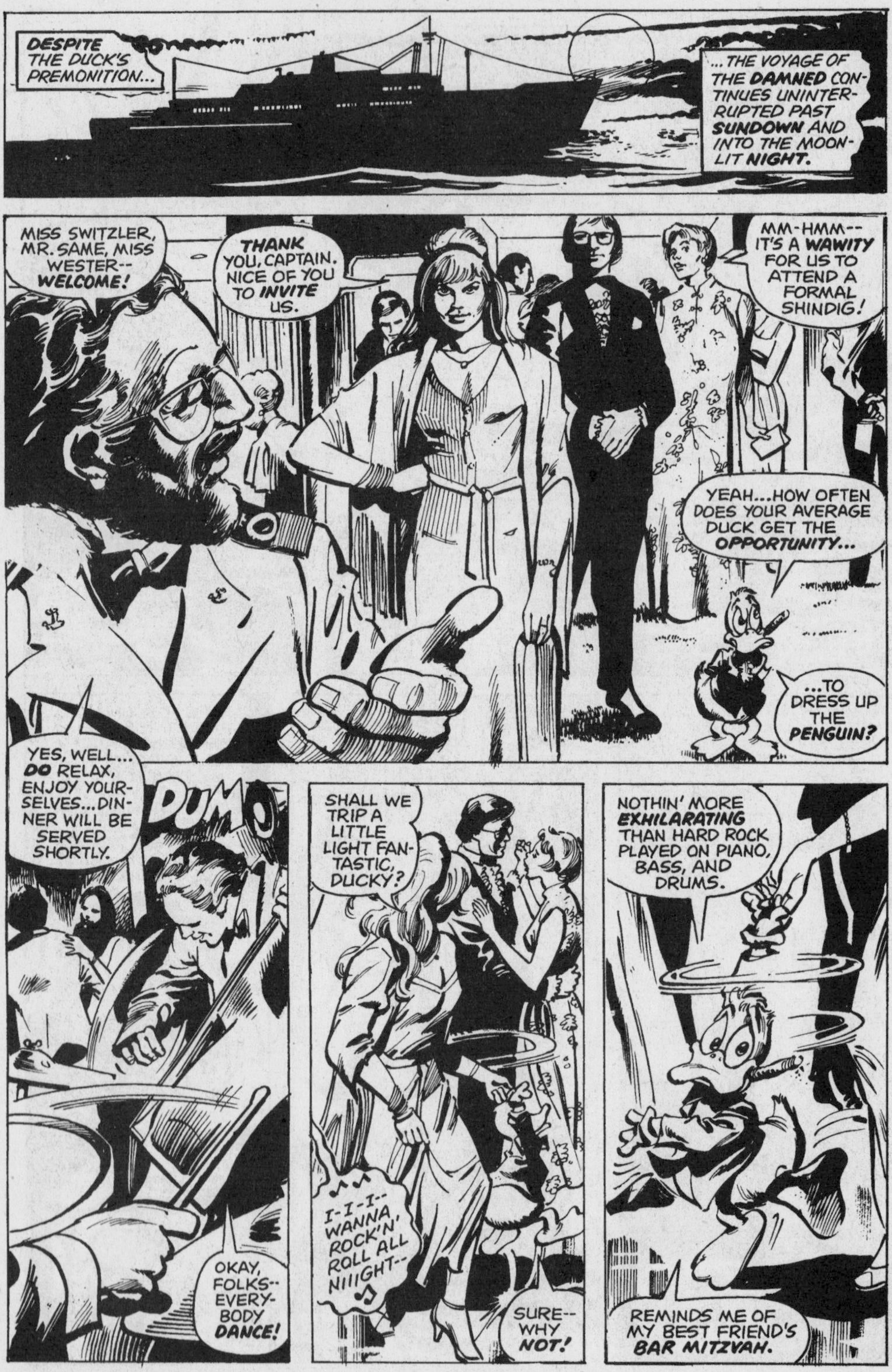
DESPITE THE DUCK'S PREMONITION...
...THE VOYAGE OF THE DAMNED CONTINUES UNINTERRUPTED PAST SUNDOWN AND INTO THE MOONLIT NIGHT.
MISS SWITZLER, MR. SAME, MISS WESTER-- WELCOME!
THANK YOU, CAPTAIN. NICE OF YOU TO INVITE US.
MM-HMM-- IT'S A WAWITY FOR US TO ATTEND A FORMAL SHINDIG!
YEAH...HOW OFTEN DOES YOUR AVERAGE DUCK GET THE OPPORTUNITY...
...TO DRESS UP THE PENGUIN?
YES, WELL... DO RELAX, ENJOY YOURSELVES...DINNER WILL BE SERVED SHORTLY.
DUMO
OKAY, FOLKS-- EVERYBODY DANCE!
SHALL WE TRIP A LITTLE LIGHT FANTASTIC, DUCKY?
I-I-I-- WANNA ROCK'N' ROLL ALL NIIIGHT--
SURE-- WHY NOT!
NOTHIN' MORE EXHILARATING THAN HARD ROCK PLAYED ON PIANO, BASS, AND DRUMS.
REMINDS ME OF MY BEST FRIEND'S BAR MITZVAH.

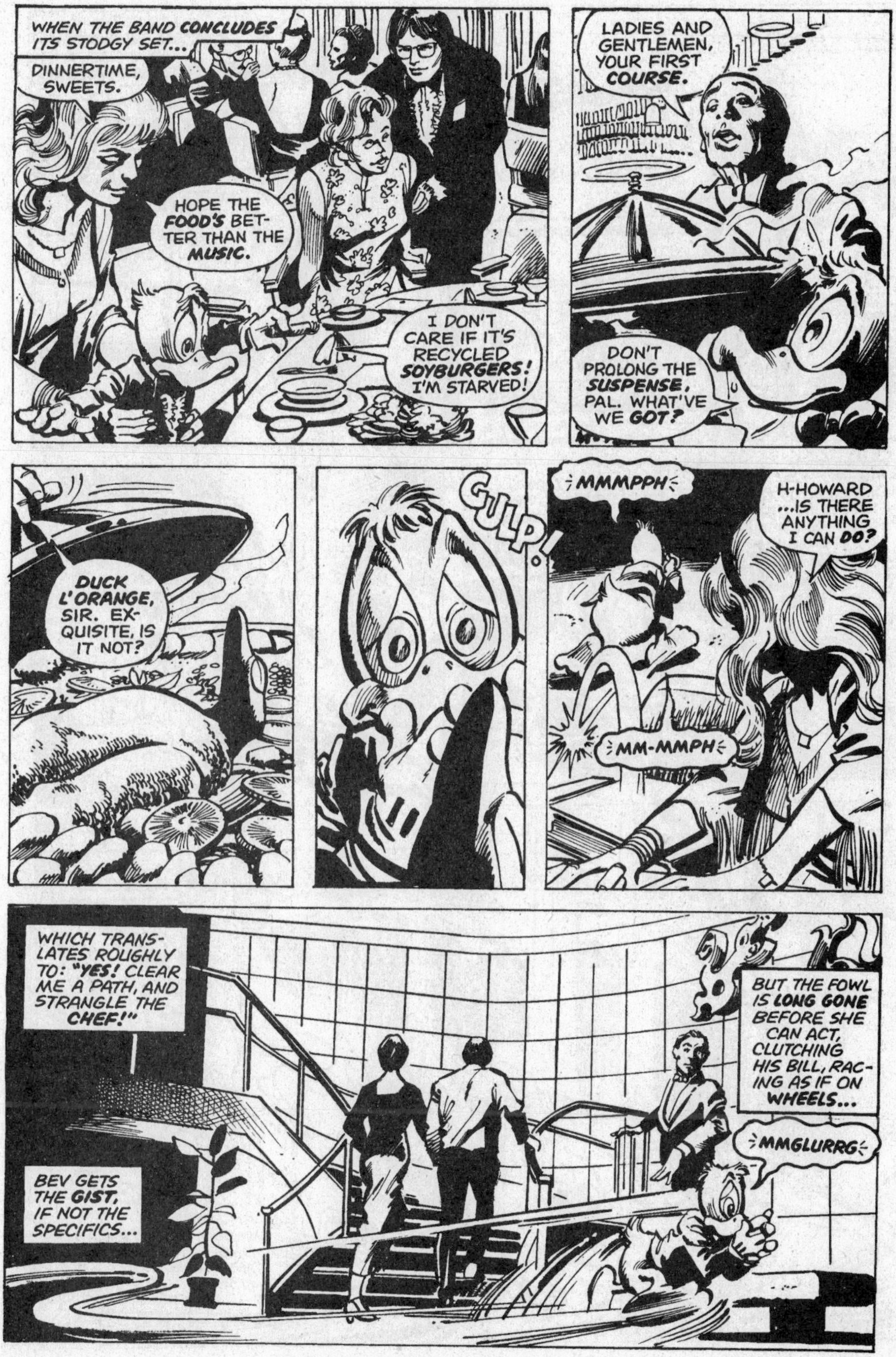

WHEN THE BAND CONCLUDES ITS STODGY SET...
DINNERTIME, SWEETS.
HOPE THE FOOD'S BETTER THAN THE MUSIC.
I DON'T CARE IF IT'S RECYCLED SOYBURGERS! I'M STARVED!
LADIES AND GENTLEMEN, YOUR FIRST COURSE.
DON'T PROLONG THE SUSPENSE, PAL. WHAT'VE WE GOT?
DUCK L'ORANGE, SIR. EXQUISITE, IS IT NOT?
GULP!
MMMPPH
H-HOWARD ...IS THERE ANYTHING I CAN DO?
MM-MMPH
WHICH TRANSLATES ROUGHLY TO: "YES! CLEAR ME A PATH, AND STRANGLE THE CHEF!"
BEV GETS THE GIST, IF NOT THE SPECIFICS...
BUT THE FOWL IS LONG GONE BEFORE SHE CAN ACT, CLUTCHING HIS BILL, RACING AS IF ON WHEELS...
MMGLURRG

...TO A SECLUDED CORNER OF THE UPPER DECK...

AAAAUGH

...WHERE, AT LAST, HE MAY RETCH IN *PEACE.*

TH-THAT DID IT... *TOTAL* ENERVATION! ...I CAN FEEL THE SPIDERS CRAWLING OUTTA MY *INTESTINES*...

...DOWN MY RUBBERY *LEGS*...

...AN' INTO THE DECK! *CATHARSIS!*

I MEAN...HOW MUCH WORSE CAN IT *GET,* AFTER BEING EXPECTED TO ENGAGE IN *CASUAL CANNIBALISM?!*

GOTTA...LIE DOWN... TOO QUEASY TO *THINK,* LET ALONE *STAND...!*

YEAH... THIS'S BETTER...

BREATHE IN THAT BRACING *SALT AIR*... KEEP MY EYES ON THAT INDIGO SKY, DAPPLED WITH *SILVER...!*

ONCE YA HIT THE *PITS* IT CAN ONLY *IMPROVE,* RIGHT?

SUDDENLY--

CRRRAAASSHHHHH!

AN IMMENSE CHUNK OF *GRANITE,* DROPPED FROM *NOWHERE,* IMBEDS ITSELF IN THE DECK.

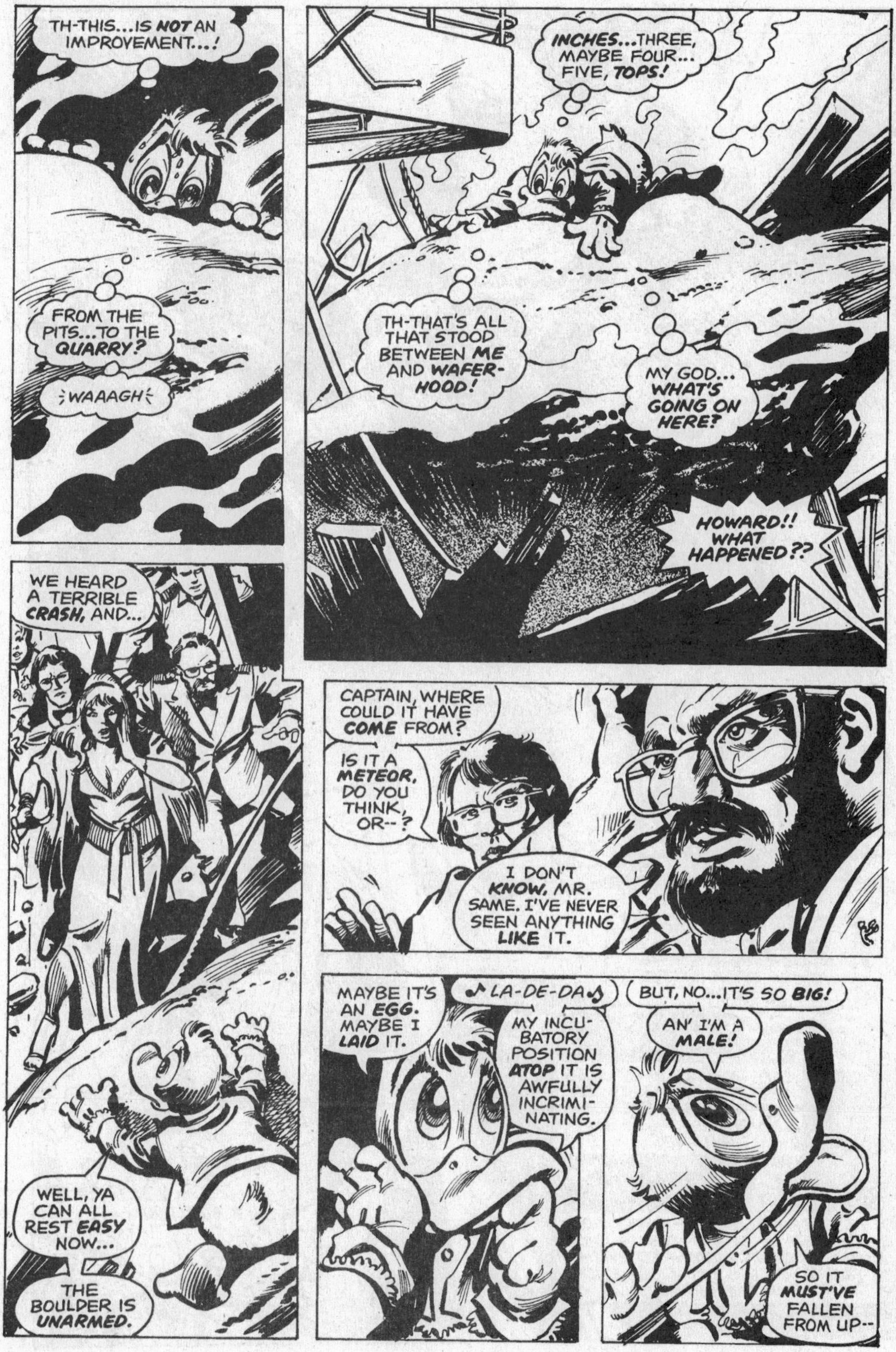
TH-THIS...IS NOT AN IMPROVEMENT...!
FROM THE PITS...TO THE QUARRY?
WAAAGH
INCHES...THREE, MAYBE FOUR... FIVE, TOPS!
TH-THAT'S ALL THAT STOOD BETWEEN ME AND WAFER-HOOD!
MY GOD... WHAT'S GOING ON HERE?
HOWARD!! WHAT HAPPENED??
WE HEARD A TERRIBLE CRASH, AND...
WELL, YA CAN ALL REST EASY NOW...
THE BOULDER IS UNARMED.
CAPTAIN, WHERE COULD IT HAVE COME FROM?
IS IT A METEOR, DO YOU THINK, OR--?
I DON'T KNOW, MR. SAME. I'VE NEVER SEEN ANYTHING LIKE IT.
MAYBE IT'S AN EGG. MAYBE I LAID IT.
LA-DE-DA
MY INCUBATORY POSITION ATOP IT IS AWFULLY INCRIMINATING.
BUT, NO...IT'S SO BIG!
AN' I'M A MALE!
SO IT MUST'VE FALLEN FROM UP--

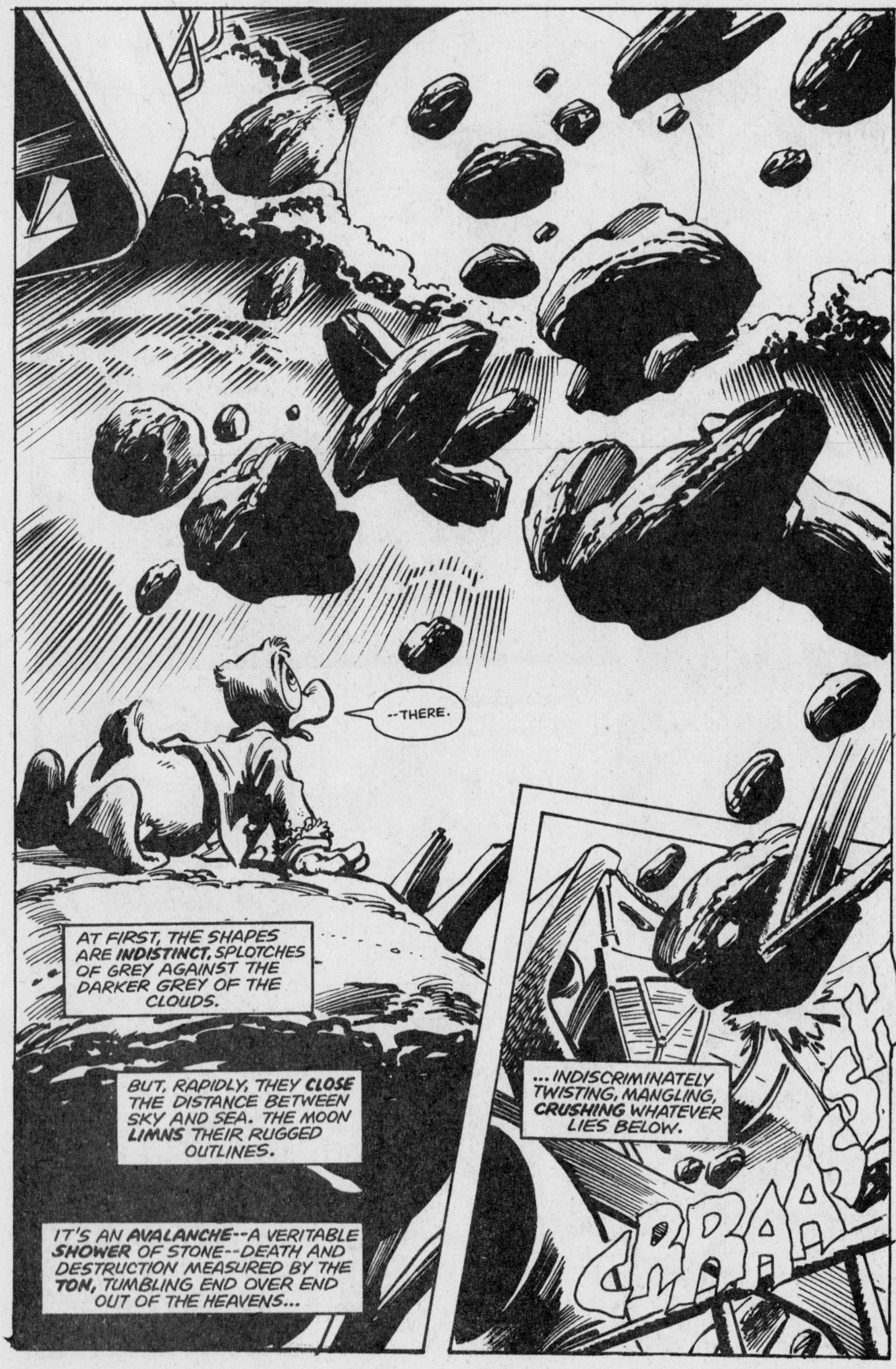
--THERE.
AT FIRST, THE SHAPES ARE INDISTINCT, SPLOTCHES OF GREY AGAINST THE DARKER GREY OF THE CLOUDS.
BUT, RAPIDLY, THEY CLOSE THE DISTANCE BETWEEN SKY AND SEA. THE MOON LIMNS THEIR RUGGED OUTLINES.
IT'S AN AVALANCHE--A VERITABLE SHOWER OF STONE--DEATH AND DESTRUCTION MEASURED BY THE TON, TUMBLING END OVER END OUT OF THE HEAVENS...
...INDISCRIMINATELY TWISTING, MANGLING, CRUSHING WHATEVER LIES BELOW.
CRRAASH

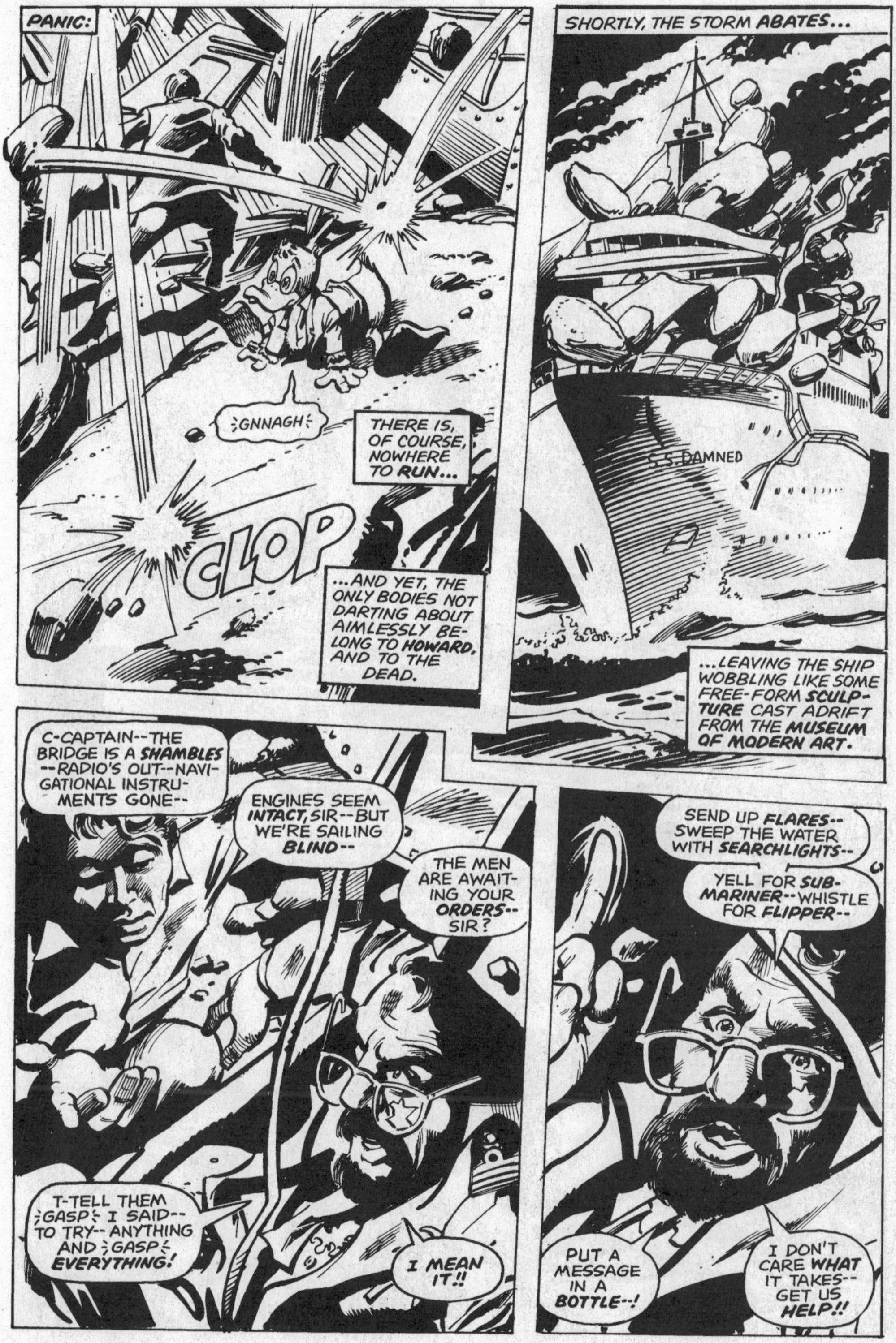
PANIC:
GNNAGH
THERE IS, OF COURSE, NOWHERE TO RUN...
CLOP
...AND YET, THE ONLY BODIES NOT DARTING ABOUT AIMLESSLY BELONG TO HOWARD, AND TO THE DEAD.
SHORTLY, THE STORM ABATES...
S.S. DAMNED
...LEAVING THE SHIP WOBBLING LIKE SOME FREE-FORM SCULPTURE CAST ADRIFT FROM THE MUSEUM OF MODERN ART.
C-CAPTAIN--THE BRIDGE IS A SHAMBLES--RADIO'S OUT--NAVIGATIONAL INSTRUMENTS GONE--
ENGINES SEEM INTACT, SIR--BUT WE'RE SAILING BLIND--
THE MEN ARE AWAITING YOUR ORDERS--SIR?
T-TELL THEM GASP I SAID--TO TRY--ANYTHING AND GASP EVERYTHING!
I MEAN IT!!
SEND UP FLARES--SWEEP THE WATER WITH SEARCHLIGHTS--
YELL FOR SUB-MARINER--WHISTLE FOR FLIPPER--
PUT A MESSAGE IN A BOTTLE--!
I DON'T CARE WHAT IT TAKES--GET US HELP!!

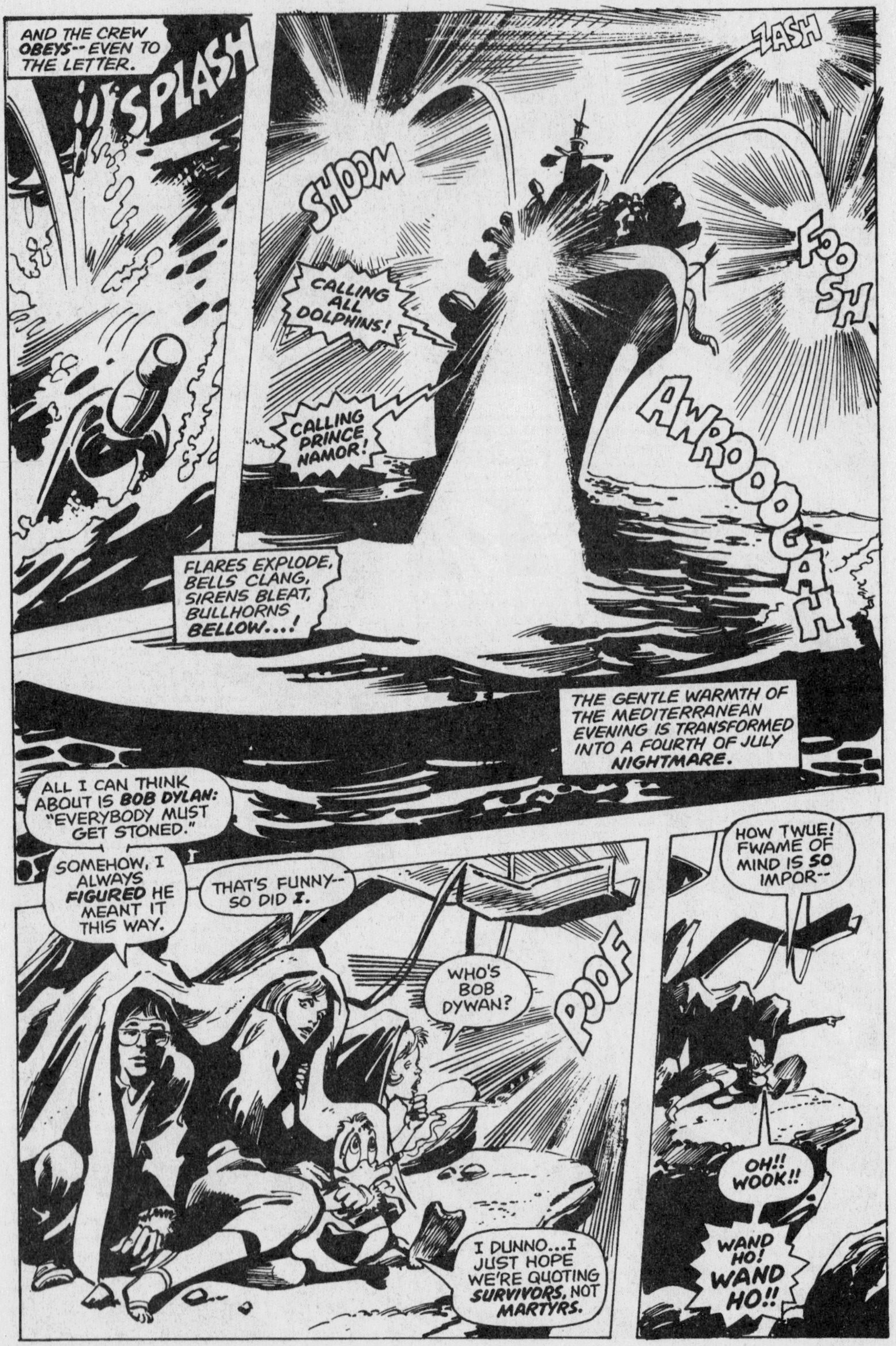
AND THE CREW OBEYS-- EVEN TO THE LETTER.
SPLASH
SHOOM
ZASH
CALLING ALL DOLPHINS!
CALLING PRINCE NAMOR!
FOOSH
AWROOOOGAH
FLARES EXPLODE, BELLS CLANG, SIRENS BLEAT, BULLHORNS BELLOW...!
THE GENTLE WARMTH OF THE MEDITERRANEAN EVENING IS TRANSFORMED INTO A FOURTH OF JULY NIGHTMARE.
ALL I CAN THINK ABOUT IS BOB DYLAN: "EVERYBODY MUST GET STONED."
SOMEHOW, I ALWAYS FIGURED HE MEANT IT THIS WAY.
THAT'S FUNNY-- SO DID I.
WHO'S BOB DYWAN?
POOF
I DUNNO...I JUST HOPE WE'RE QUOTING SURVIVORS, NOT MARTYRS.
HOW TWUE! FWAME OF MIND IS SO IMPOR--
OH!! WOOK!!
WAND HO! WAND HO!!

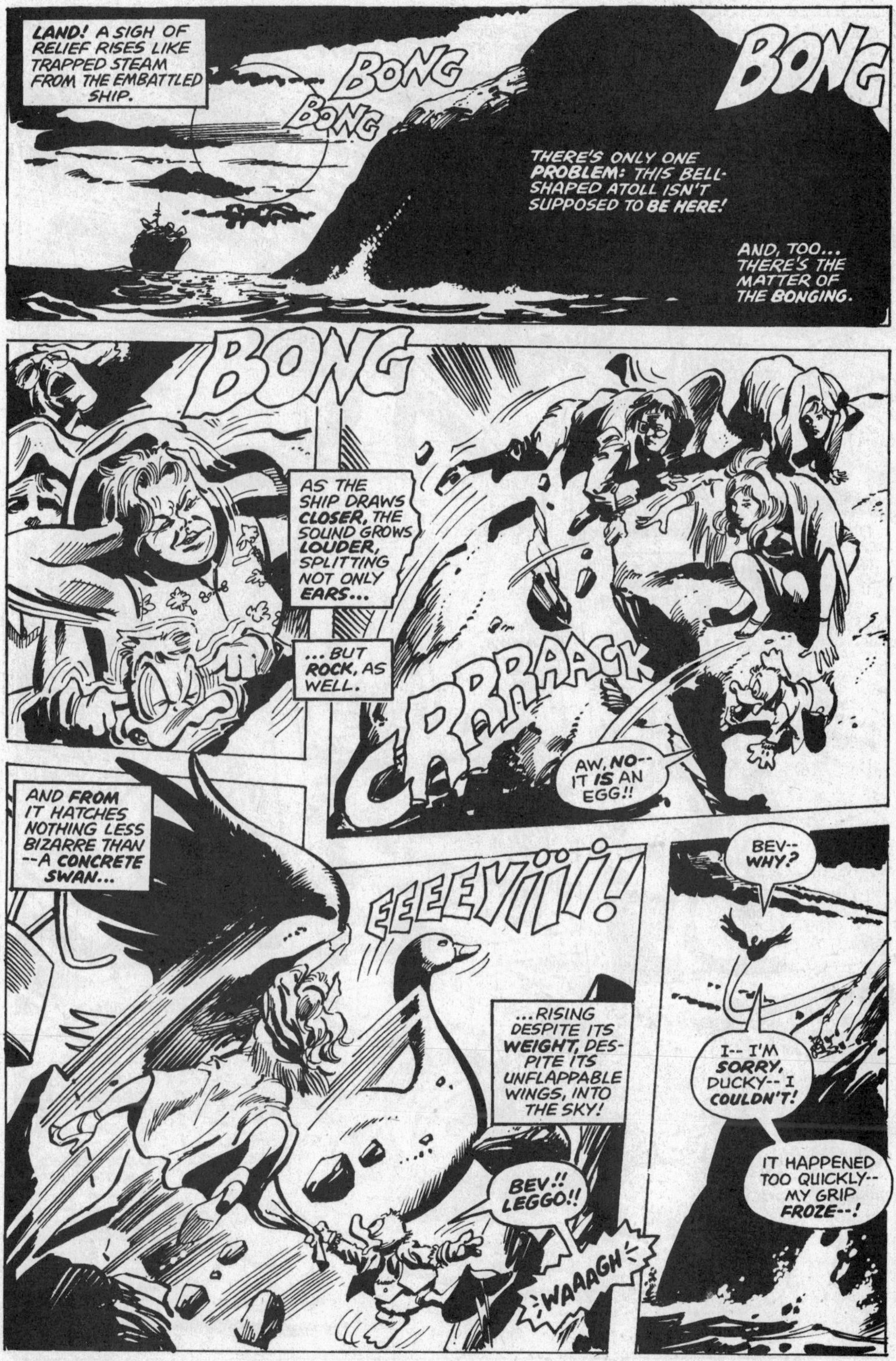
LAND! A SIGH OF RELIEF RISES LIKE TRAPPED STEAM FROM THE EMBATTLED SHIP.
BONG
BONG
BONG
THERE'S ONLY ONE PROBLEM: THIS BELL-SHAPED ATOLL ISN'T SUPPOSED TO BE HERE!
AND, TOO... THERE'S THE MATTER OF THE BONGING.
BONG
AS THE SHIP DRAWS CLOSER, THE SOUND GROWS LOUDER, SPLITTING NOT ONLY EARS...
...BUT ROCK, AS WELL.
CRRRAACK
AW, NO-- IT IS AN EGG!!
AND FROM IT HATCHES NOTHING LESS BIZARRE THAN --A CONCRETE SWAN...
EEEEYIIII!
...RISING DESPITE ITS WEIGHT, DESPITE ITS UNFLAPPABLE WINGS, INTO THE SKY!
BEV!! LEGGO!!
WAAAGH
BEV-- WHY?
I-- I'M SORRY, DUCKY-- I COULDN'T!
IT HAPPENED TOO QUICKLY-- MY GRIP FROZE--!

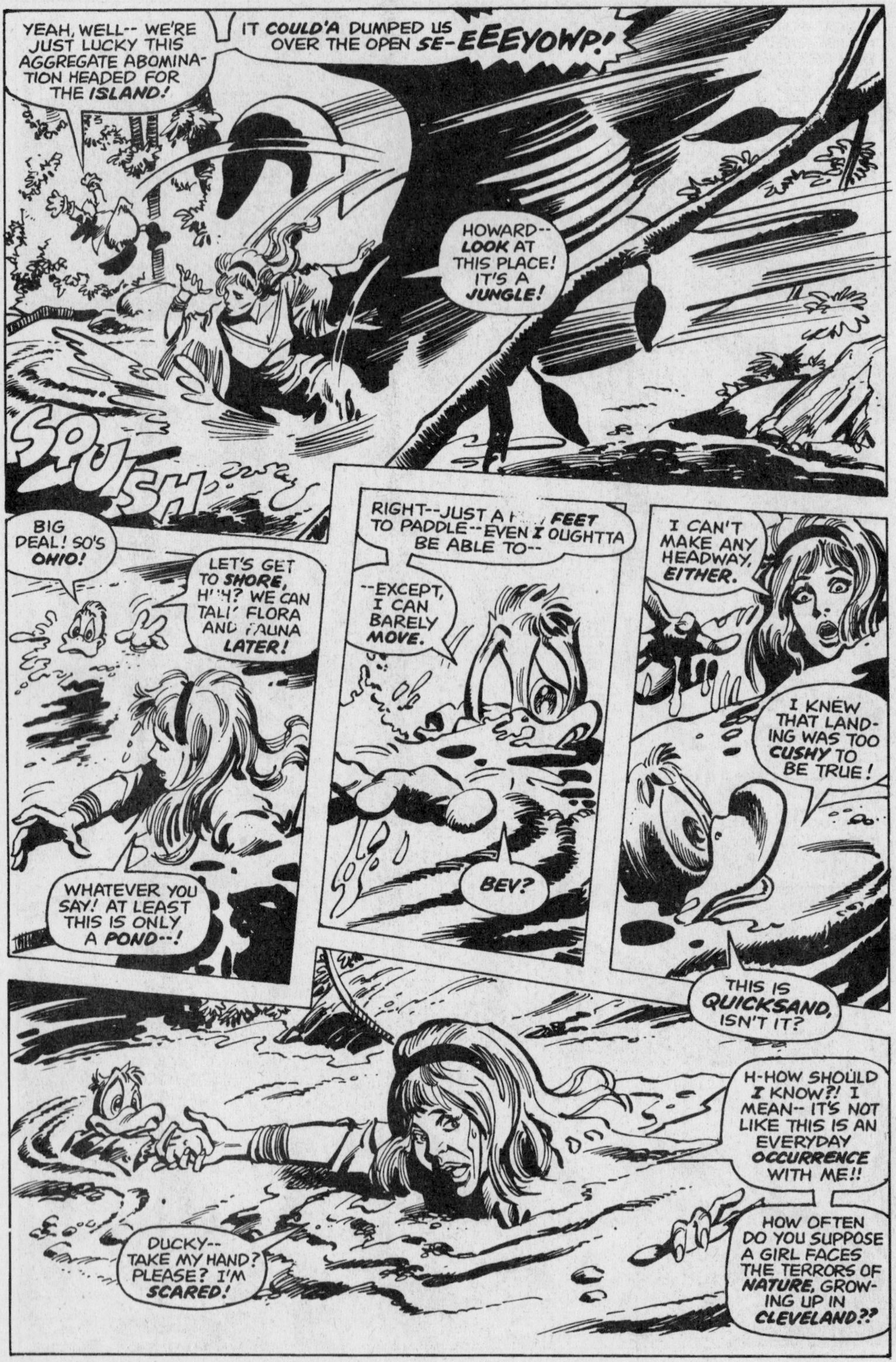
YEAH, WELL-- WE'RE JUST LUCKY THIS AGGREGATE ABOMINATION HEADED FOR THE ISLAND!
IT COULD'A DUMPED US OVER THE OPEN SE-EEEYOWP!
HOWARD-- LOOK AT THIS PLACE! IT'S A JUNGLE!
SPUSH
BIG DEAL! SO'S OHIO!
LET'S GET TO SHORE, HUH? WE CAN TALK FLORA AND FAUNA LATER!
WHATEVER YOU SAY! AT LEAST THIS IS ONLY A POND--!
RIGHT--JUST A FEW FEET TO PADDLE--EVEN I OUGHTTA BE ABLE TO--
--EXCEPT, I CAN BARELY MOVE.
BEV?
I CAN'T MAKE ANY HEADWAY, EITHER.
I KNEW THAT LANDING WAS TOO CUSHY TO BE TRUE!
THIS IS QUICKSAND, ISN'T IT?
H-HOW SHOULD I KNOW?! I MEAN-- IT'S NOT LIKE THIS IS AN EVERYDAY OCCURRENCE WITH ME!!
HOW OFTEN DO YOU SUPPOSE A GIRL FACES THE TERRORS OF NATURE, GROWING UP IN CLEVELAND??
DUCKY-- TAKE MY HAND? PLEASE? I'M SCARED!

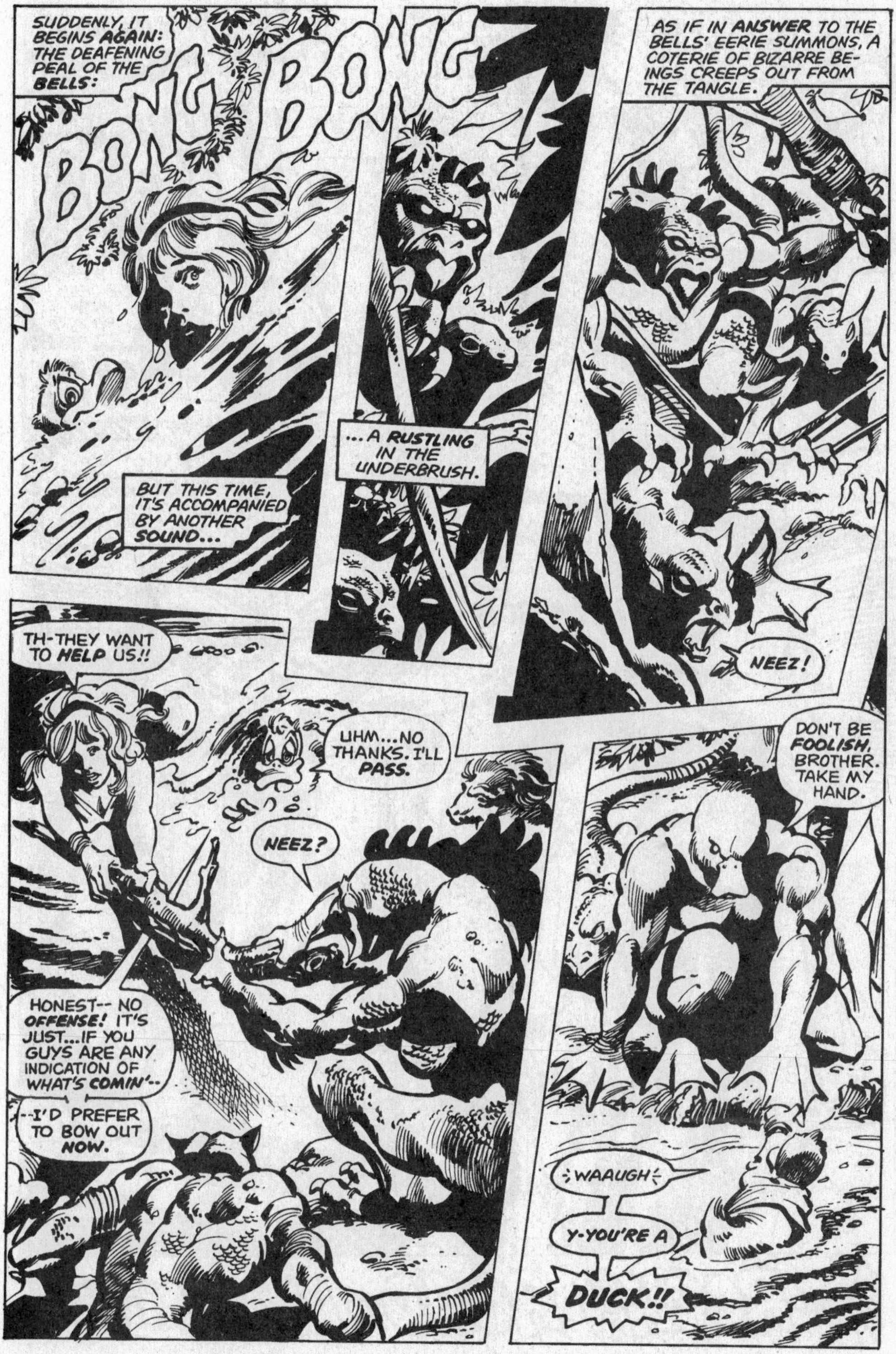
SUDDENLY, IT BEGINS AGAIN: THE DEAFENING PEAL OF THE BELLS:
BONG BONG
BUT THIS TIME, IT'S ACCOMPANIED BY ANOTHER SOUND...
...A RUSTLING IN THE UNDERBRUSH.
AS IF IN ANSWER TO THE BELLS' EERIE SUMMONS, A COTERIE OF BIZARRE BE-INGS CREEPS OUT FROM THE TANGLE.
NEEZ!
TH-THEY WANT TO HELP US!!
UHM...NO THANKS. I'LL PASS.
NEEZ?
HONEST-- NO OFFENSE! IT'S JUST...IF YOU GUYS ARE ANY INDICATION OF WHAT'S COMIN'..
--I'D PREFER TO BOW OUT NOW.
DON'T BE FOOLISH, BROTHER. TAKE MY HAND.
WAAUGH
Y-YOU'RE A
DUCK!!

NEXT) THE ROCKY ROAD TO ANONYMITY!

BUT AS A DIR
CONSEQUEN
HE HAS BE

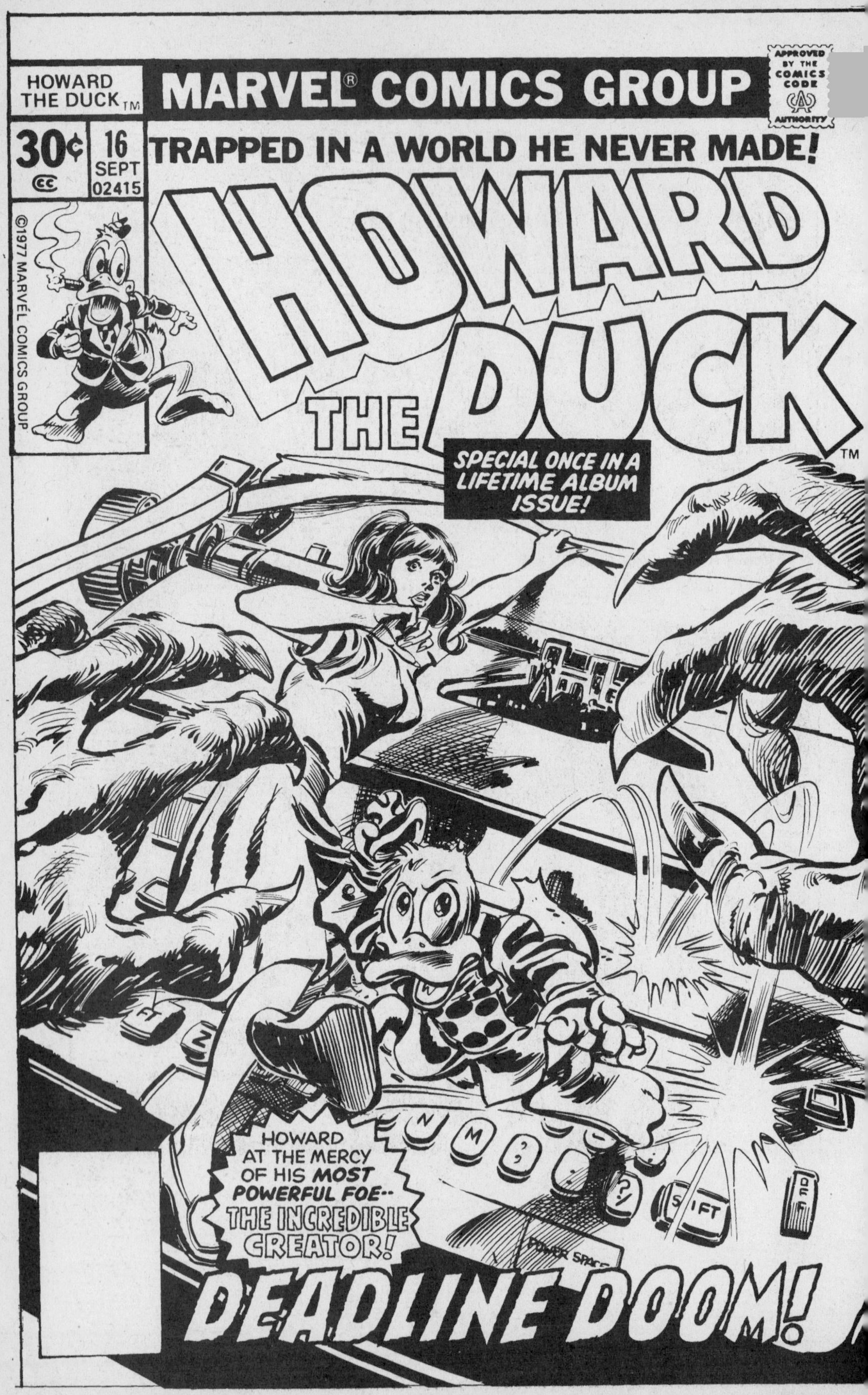
HOWARD THE DUCK TM
MARVEL® COMICS GROUP
APPROVED BY THE COMICS CODE AUTHORITY
30¢
16 SEPT 02415
TRAPPED IN A WORLD HE NEVER MADE!
©1977 MARVEL COMICS GROUP
HOWARD THE DUCK TM
SPECIAL ONCE IN A LIFETIME ALBUM ISSUE!
HOWARD AT THE MERCY OF HIS MOST POWERFUL FOE-- THE INCREDIBLE CREATOR!
DEADLINE DOOM!

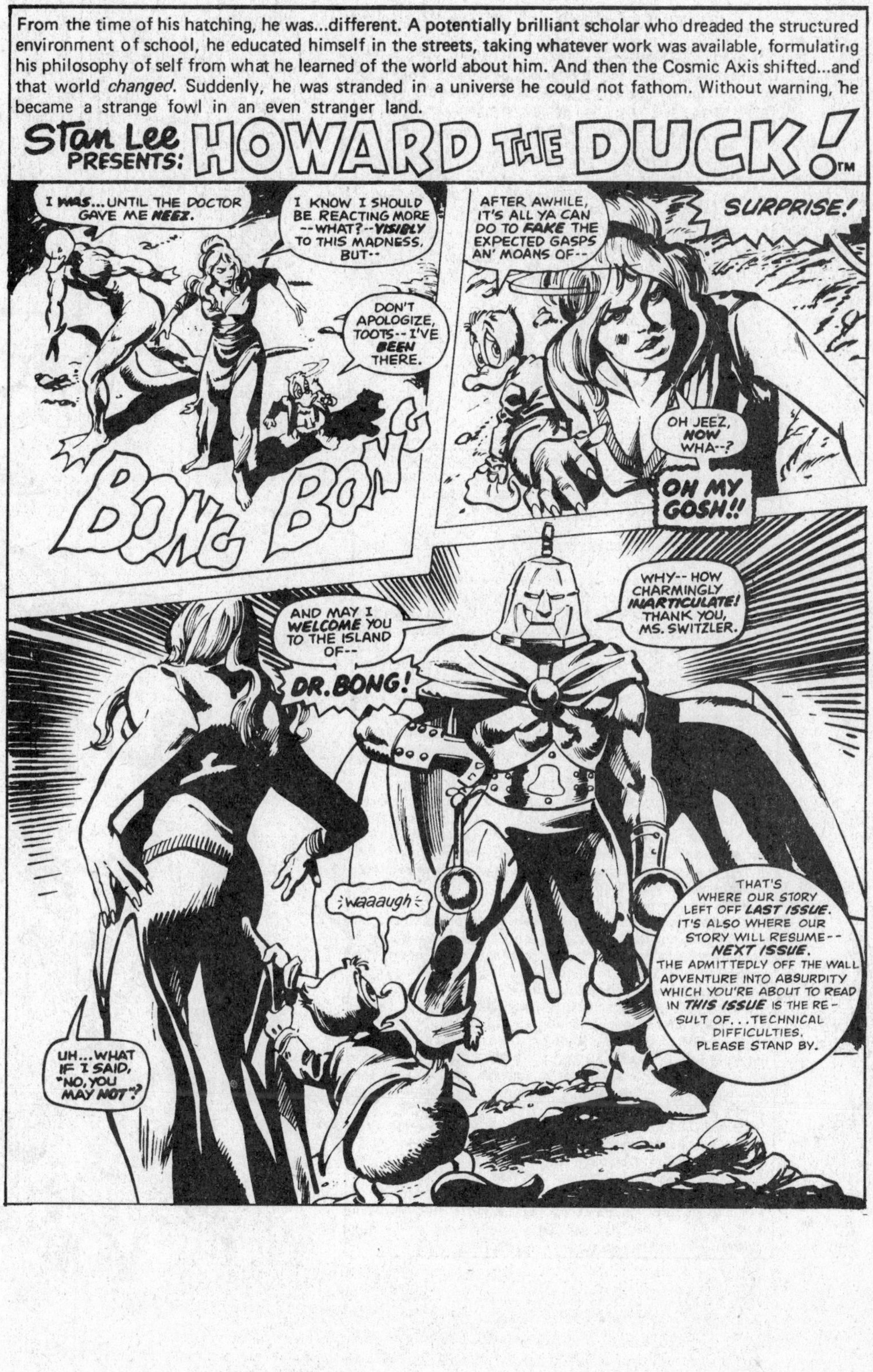
From the time of his hatching, he was...different. A potentially brilliant scholar who dreaded the structured environment of school, he educated himself in the streets, taking whatever work was available, formulating his philosophy of self from what he learned of the world about him. And then the Cosmic Axis shifted...and that world *changed*. Suddenly, he was stranded in a universe he could not fathom. Without warning, he became a strange fowl in an even stranger land.
Stan Lee PRESENTS: HOWARD THE DUCK!™
I WAS... UNTIL THE DOCTOR GAVE ME NEEZ.
I KNOW I SHOULD BE REACTING MORE --WHAT?--VISIBLY TO THIS MADNESS, BUT--
DON'T APOLOGIZE, TOOTS-- I'VE BEEN THERE.
BONG BONG
AFTER AWHILE, IT'S ALL YA CAN DO TO FAKE THE EXPECTED GASPS AN' MOANS OF--
SURPRISE!
OH JEEZ, NOW WHA--?
OH MY GOSH!!
AND MAY I WELCOME YOU TO THE ISLAND OF--
DR. BONG!
WHY-- HOW CHARMINGLY INARTICULATE! THANK YOU, MS. SWITZLER.
waaaugh
THAT'S WHERE OUR STORY LEFT OFF LAST ISSUE. IT'S ALSO WHERE OUR STORY WILL RESUME-- NEXT ISSUE. THE ADMITTEDLY OFF THE WALL ADVENTURE INTO ABSURDITY WHICH YOU'RE ABOUT TO READ IN THIS ISSUE IS THE RESULT OF. . . TECHNICAL DIFFICULTIES. PLEASE STAND BY.
UH... WHAT IF I SAID, "NO, YOU MAY NOT"?

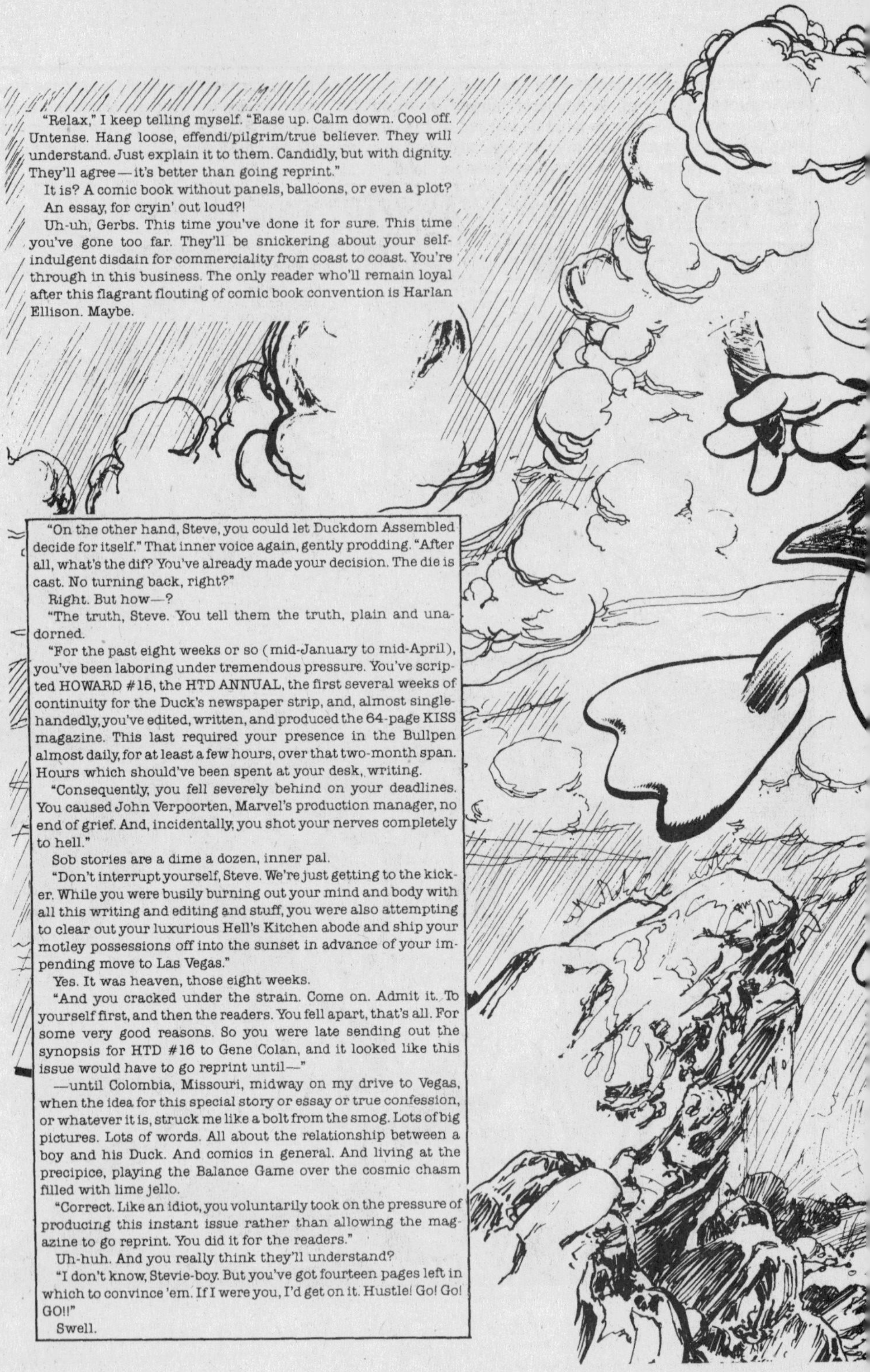

"Relax," I keep telling myself. "Ease up. Calm down. Cool off. Untense. Hang loose, effendi/pilgrim/true believer. They will understand. Just explain it to them. Candidly, but with dignity. They'll agree—it's better than going reprint."

It is? A comic book without panels, balloons, or even a plot? An essay, for cryin' out loud?!

Uh-uh, Gerbs. This time you've done it for sure. This time you've gone too far. They'll be snickering about your self-indulgent disdain for commerciality from coast to coast. You're through in this business. The only reader who'll remain loyal after this flagrant flouting of comic book convention is Harlan Ellison. Maybe.

"On the other hand, Steve, you could let Duckdom Assembled decide for itself." That inner voice again, gently prodding. "After all, what's the dif? You've already made your decision. The die is cast. No turning back, right?"

Right. But how—?

"The truth, Steve. You tell them the truth, plain and unadorned.

"For the past eight weeks or so (mid-January to mid-April), you've been laboring under tremendous pressure. You've scripted HOWARD #15, the HTD ANNUAL, the first several weeks of continuity for the Duck's newspaper strip, and, almost single-handedly, you've edited, written, and produced the 64-page KISS magazine. This last required your presence in the Bullpen almost daily, for at least a few hours, over that two-month span. Hours which should've been spent at your desk, writing.

"Consequently, you fell severely behind on your deadlines. You caused John Verpoorten, Marvel's production manager, no end of grief. And, incidentally, you shot your nerves completely to hell."

Sob stories are a dime a dozen, inner pal.

"Don't interrupt yourself, Steve. We're just getting to the kicker. While you were busily burning out your mind and body with all this writing and editing and stuff, you were also attempting to clear out your luxurious Hell's Kitchen abode and ship your motley possessions off into the sunset in advance of your impending move to Las Vegas."

Yes. It was heaven, those eight weeks.

"And you cracked under the strain. Come on. Admit it. To yourself first, and then the readers. You fell apart, that's all. For some very good reasons. So you were late sending out the synopsis for HTD #16 to Gene Colan, and it looked like this issue would have to go reprint until—"

—until Colombia, Missouri, midway on my drive to Vegas, when the idea for this special story or essay or true confession, or whatever it is, struck me like a bolt from the smog. Lots of big pictures. Lots of words. All about the relationship between a boy and his Duck. And comics in general. And living at the precipice, playing the Balance Game over the cosmic chasm filled with lime jello.

"Correct. Like an idiot, you voluntarily took on the pressure of producing this instant issue rather than allowing the magazine to go reprint. You did it for the readers."

Uh-huh. And you really think they'll understand?

"I don't know, Stevie-boy. But you've got fourteen pages left in which to convince 'em. If I were you, I'd get on it. Hustle! Go! Go! GO!!"

Swell.

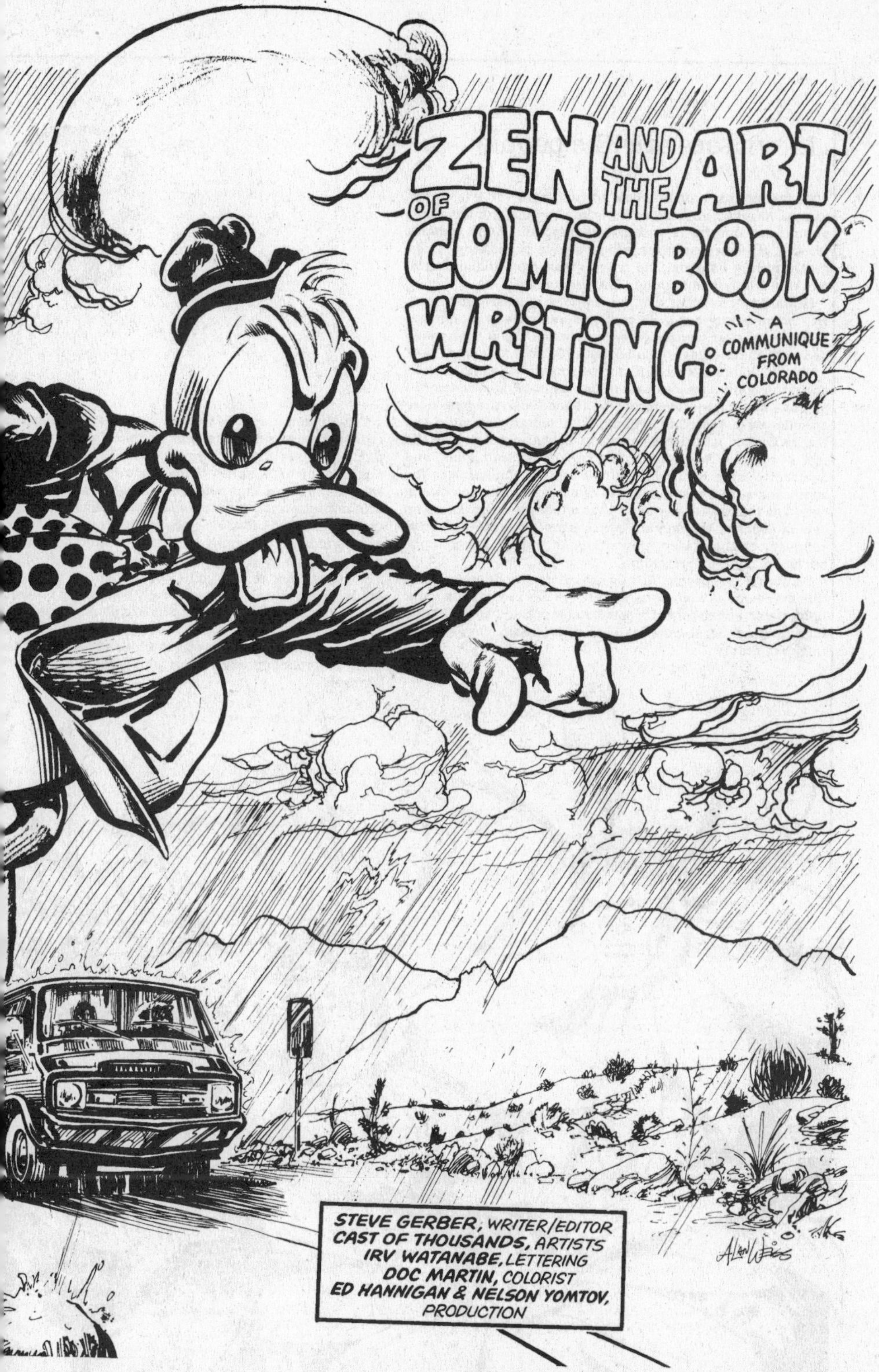

ZEN AND THE ART OF COMIC BOOK WRITING
A COMMUNIQUE FROM COLORADO
STEVE GERBER, WRITER/EDITOR
CAST OF THOUSANDS, ARTISTS
IRV WATANABE, LETTERING
DOC MARTIN, COLORIST
ED HANNIGAN & NELSON YOMTOV, PRODUCTION

I. writers are like people

As mentioned, I am en route to Las Vegas. (To live, not to gamble. Assuming there's a difference.) I've just spent five days on the road, crossing New Jersey, Pennsylvania, Ohio, Indiana, Illinois, Missouri, and Kansas. Five days of refinery fumes, gently rolling boredom, old friends, fast food, Indian burial mounds, family, and flatlands—in that order.

Howard is travelling with me, as he does wherever I roam. He's there in my head. He won't go away. He is as much a highway marker as the green and white signs that weigh heavy on the shoulders of Interstate 70. He is, in a word, real.

We're in Colorado now, in historic Georgetown, a little hamlet about thirty-five minutes west of Denver housing perhaps 700 persons. Moving inexorably from the general to the even more specific, we're seated in a booth in a restaurant called the Happy Cooker, which specializes in Belgian waffles. Like the rest of historic Georgetown, the Cooker is clean, quiet, and quaint. Its large windows look out on the mountains to the south and admit vast quantities of sunshine into the dining area. The plants—in shelves on the windows, on hooks in the ceiling—soak up the rays and turn the precise shade of green to complement the golden brown Belgian waffles. It's a minor miracle of color co-ordination.

Plants are like people. Writers are like plants. Therefore, and this may come as a surprise, writers are like people. Give them light, water, nourishment, a comfortable pot, and an encouraging word, and they'll grow. Really. They'll blossom. They'll create things of beauty.

This principle applies to most varieties of human bei[ng]. [If] other people would accord them as much consideration a[s they] do their plants, they, too, would bloom. Of course, plant[s can't] talk back, which makes them much less annoying t[o have] around the house. This may or may not explain why so m[any of] our institutions seem to devote themselves to the task o[f turn]ing people into vegetables rather than treating them w[ith the] same kindness we lavish upon the already mute. We t[end to] prefer stumps over trees. You can sit on a stump.

Some writers require more room than others to fl[ower.] Some grow vertically, some laterally or radially, others i[n] spaghetti-like tangles. Again, just like plants.

I'm of the spaghetti breed. I'm fascinated by the ma[ny] splotched pasta of existence, the unrelentingly absurd s[tuff] of human relations and of storytelling. My plots are ver[y full] and zesty.

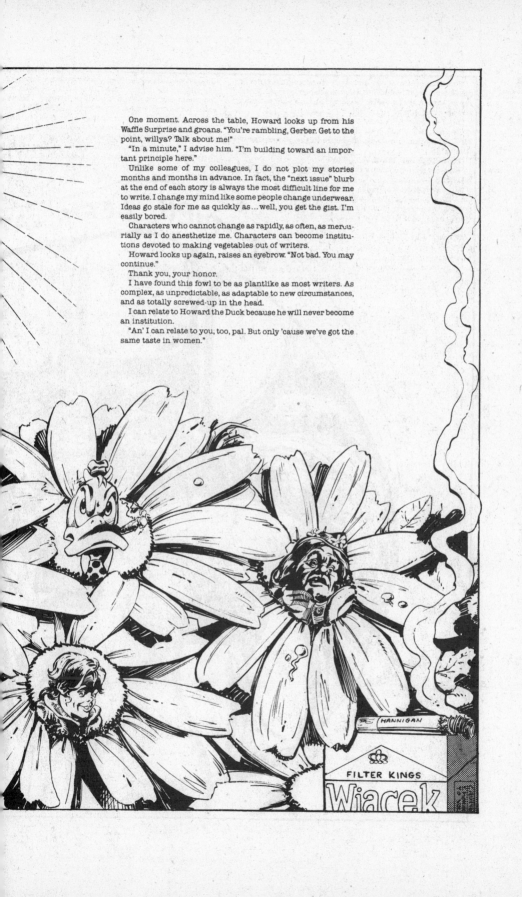

One moment. Across the table, Howard looks up from his Waffle Surprise and groans. "You're rambling, Gerber. Get to the point, willya? Talk about me!"

"In a minute," I advise him. "I'm building toward an important principle here."

Unlike some of my colleagues, I do not plot my stories months and months in advance. In fact, the "next issue" blurb at the end of each story is always the most difficult line for me to write. I change my mind like some people change underwear. Ideas go stale for me as quickly as ... well, you get the gist. I'm easily bored.

Characters who cannot change as rapidly, as often, as mercurially as I do anesthetize me. Characters can become institutions devoted to making vegetables out of writers.

Howard looks up again, raises an eyebrow. "Not bad. You may continue."

Thank you, your honor.

I have found this fowl to be as plantlike as most writers. As complex, as unpredictable, as adaptable to new circumstances, and as totally screwed-up in the head.

I can relate to Howard the Duck because he will never become an institution.

"An' I can relate to you, too, pal. But only 'cause we've got the same taste in women."

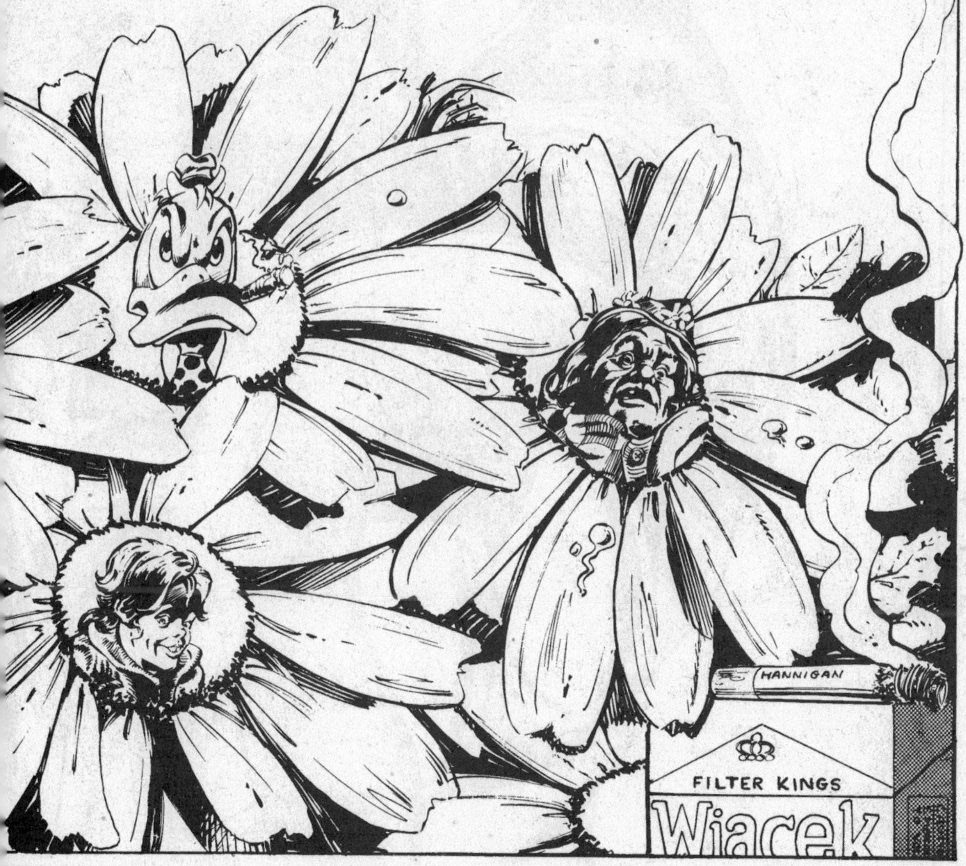
HANNIGAN
FILTER KINGS
Wiacek

"Somethin's eatin' at you, Gerber, an' it's not just deadlines or pressures or work, either. I've watched you hairless apes. When you whack out, it's for deeper reasons than that, stuff you can't talk about, or won't."

"Yes, I suppose that's true," I mumble.

"You 'suppose.' That's great. By the way, when did the Human Torch first appear in a solo adventure in the Marvel Age of Comics?"

"Huh? STRANGE TALES #101. Why?"

"And who were the villains in the first fifty issues of FANTASTIC FOUR—in order?"

"Uh… Mole Man, the Skrulls, the Miracle Man, Sub-Mariner, Dr. Doom, Subby and Doom together, Kurrgo, Puppet Master, Sub-Mariner again, Dr. Doom, Impossible Man, Hulk, Red Ghost, Subby again, The Mad Thinker, Dr. Doom, Dr. Doom—"

"Stop!!"

"Whew. Gladly. Thanks. What was the point of—"

"I just wanted ya to see for yourself how much trivia you carryin' around in yer head! It's gotta be crowdin' ou important stuff, or keepin' it safely suppressed. I bet ya rattle off a complete list of yer next fifty deadlines, too when I ask you about yer psychological posture, you 'supp

"Now wait just a moment, my web-footed wag! As f you're concerned, that's not 'trivia', it's history. Where d figure you'd be today without the first fifty issues of FF? over, that kind of question doesn't require subjective eva ion, just a good memory. When you start asking for opi about the nature of the mind—!"

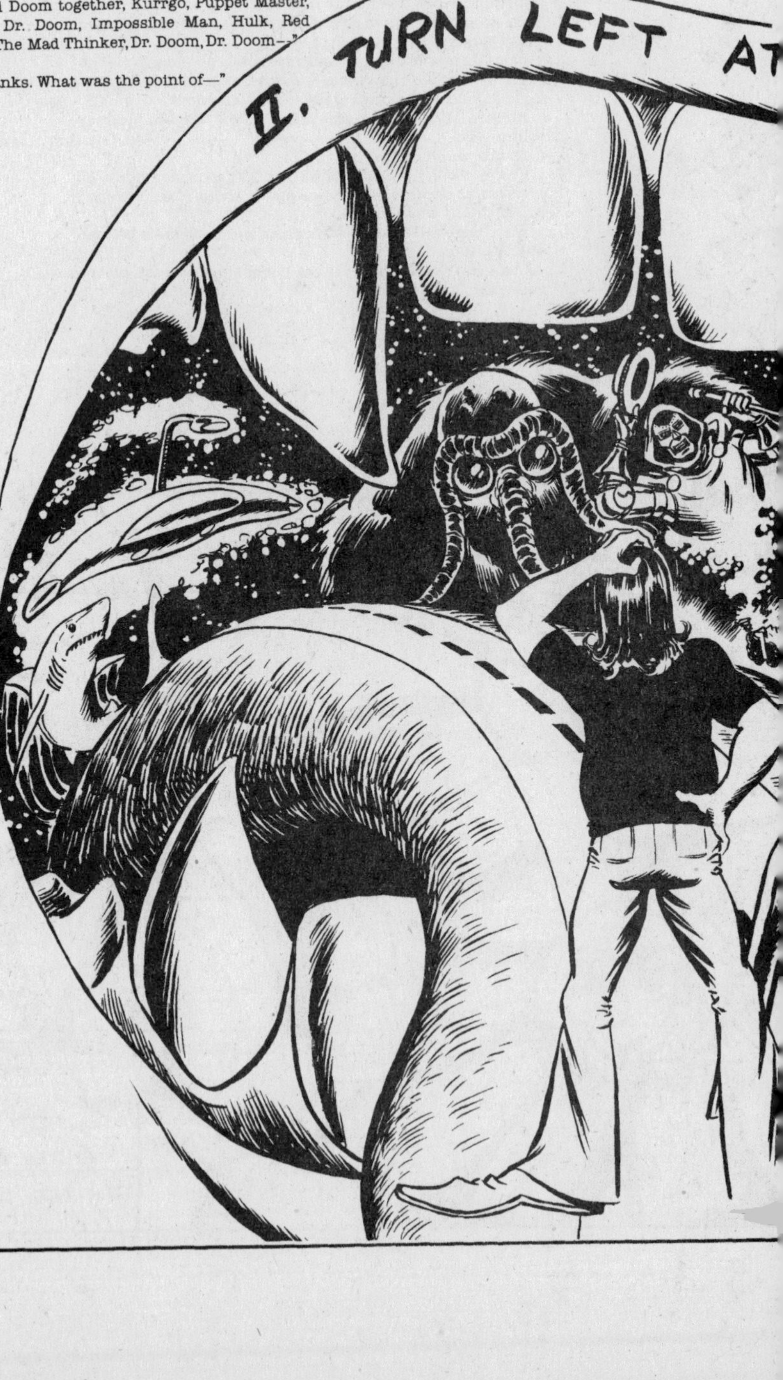

II. TURN LEFT AT

"Your mind, Gerber. Not the mind."

"Howard, you're chasing your tail feathers in this conversa-
on. What are you trying to say?"

"I told ya! Somethin's eatin' you, an' ya won't talk about it. You
eep retreatin' to the abstract—to suppositions about intangi-
'es like boredom an' institutions an' society. There was a
eason you wanted ta write this dumb essay—an' yet you refuse
. let me or the readers in on it!"

"Oh."

"'Oh'?! That's all ya got ta say for yerself?! You, the big humanist, the creative writer, the fragile flower of literature? That's the best ya can do, genius! No wonder my dialogue's been so banal lately!"

"Howard—"

"Y'know what, Gerbs? Deep down, I've always suspected you don't know as much as yer stories would infer. You've learned how ta manipulate words an' pictures ta give a semblance of profundity, but it's all superficial! Cosmetic surgery performed on creaky old ideas an' thoughts! Whaddaya say ta that?!"

"I say that, uhm, on occasion, I've harbored similar suspicions, Howard."

E FORK IN THE TONGUE
OM®
DESPAIR TM
STEVE'S IN DUTCH
BIG JOHN'S A'SMOKIN'..
DEADLINE DUE,
AN' WE'RE NOT JOKIN'!
BURMA SHAVE
CHARMIN
COCKRUM '77

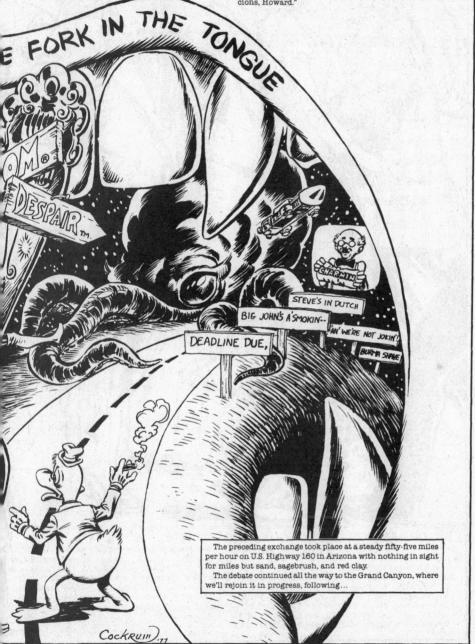

The preceding exchange took place at a steady fifty-five miles per hour on U.S. Highway 160 in Arizona with nothing in sight for miles but sand, sagebrush, and red clay.

The debate continued all the way to the Grand Canyon, where we'll rejoin it in progress, following...

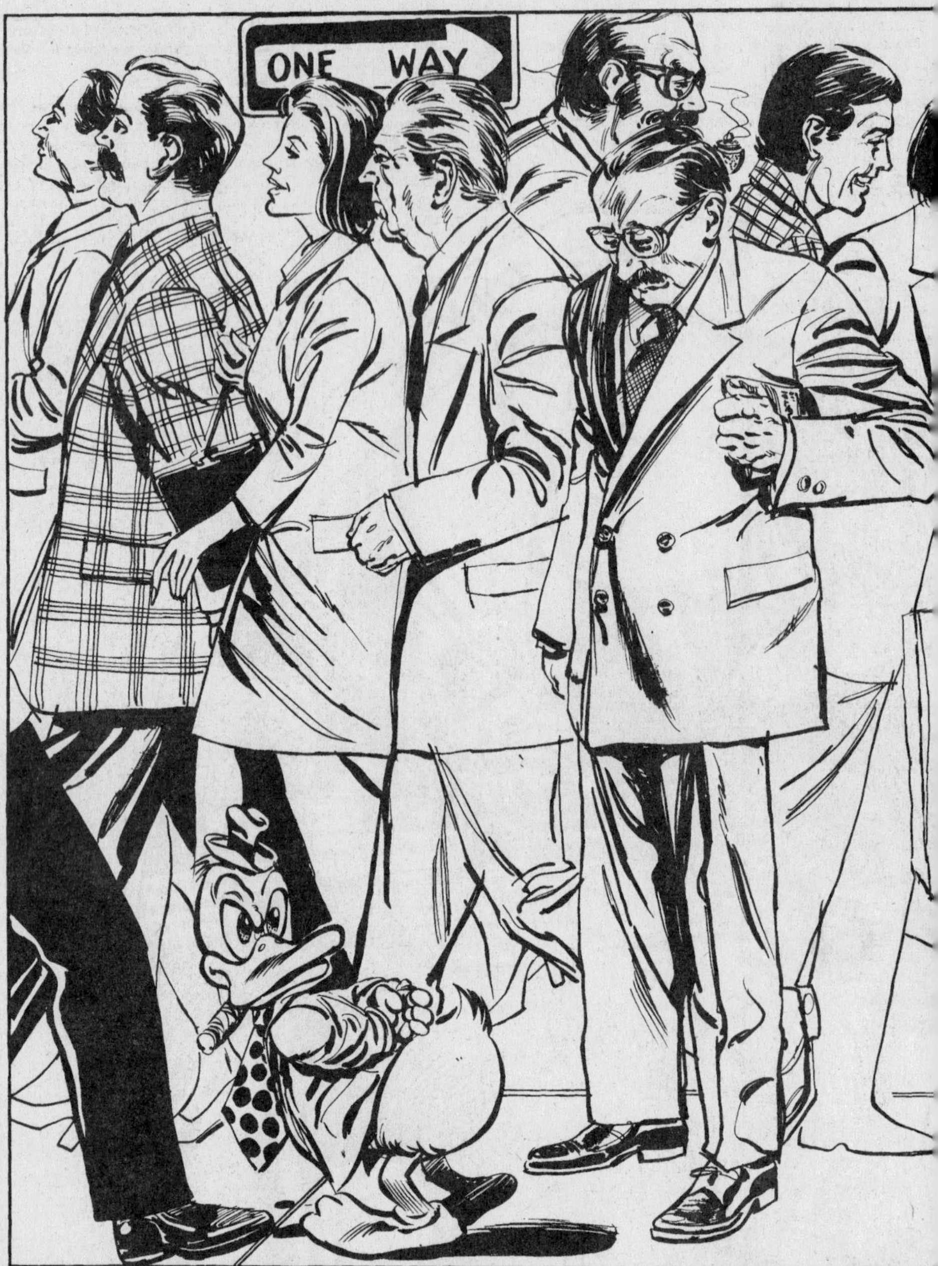
ONE WAY

III. obligatory comic book fight scene

There is one rule of comic book writing which simply cannot be violated, even by a writer in search of something as impalpable as his soul or Las Vegas.

Being a visual medium, comics theoretically require at least a modicum of action to engage and sustain reader interest.

Thus, in the interest of sustaining your interest, we reluctantly present this BRAIN-BLASTING BATTLE SCENE, pitting an ostrich and a Las Vegas chorus girl against the MIND-NUMBING MENACE of a KILLER lampshade in a DUEL TO THE DEATH!!

Since we only get one picture for this CLASH OF TIT though, we'll have to tell you the outcome. The ostrich stick head in a manhole, shrugging off all that's happened anc turning to his secret identity as a roadblock. The chorus finds herself in the thrill of battle, becomes one with her h dress, and is elevated to goddesshood. The lampshade Basically, it's like most every other comic mag.

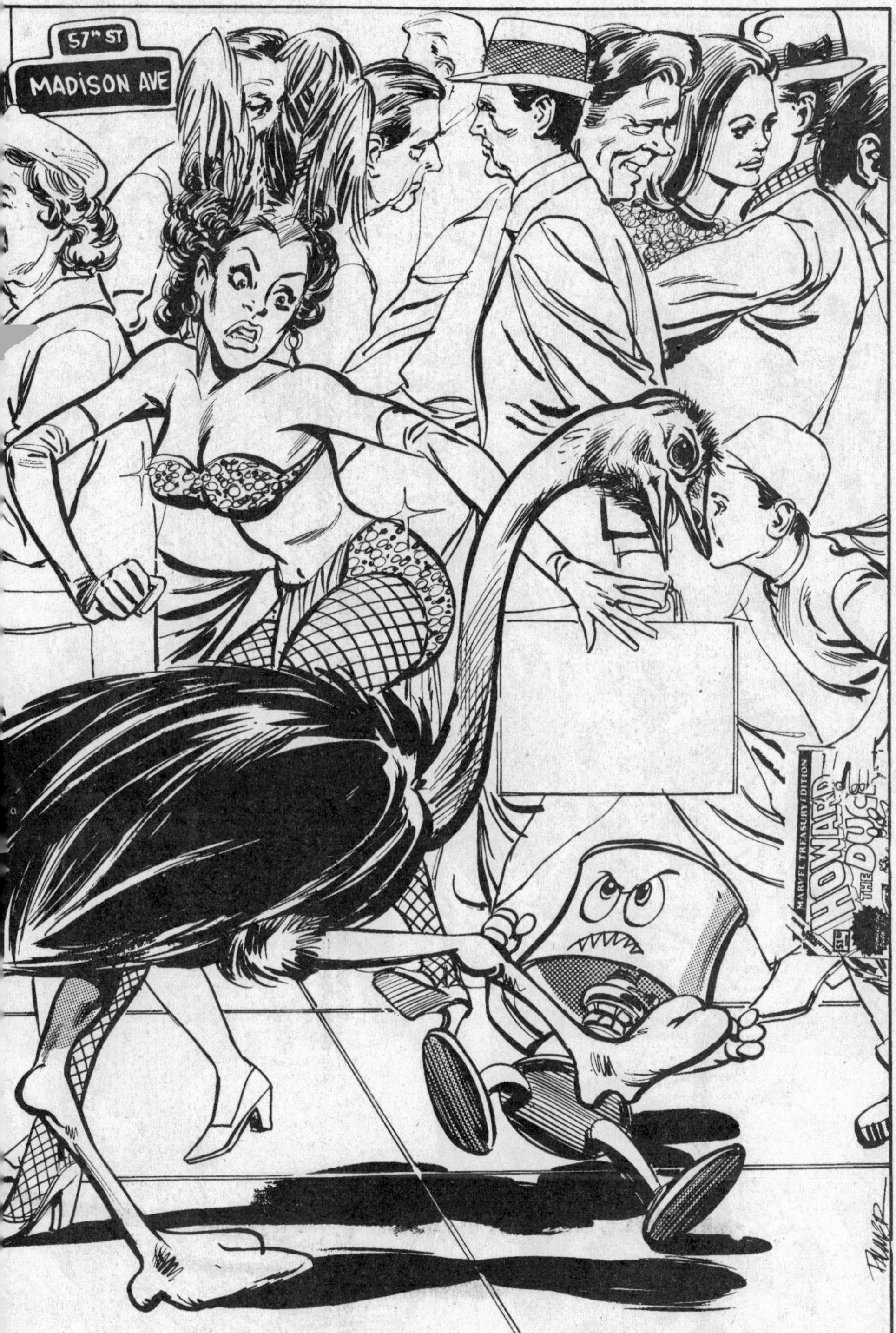
57th ST
MADISON AVE
MARVEL TREASURY EDITION
HOWARD THE DUCK
PALMER

iv. . . . and

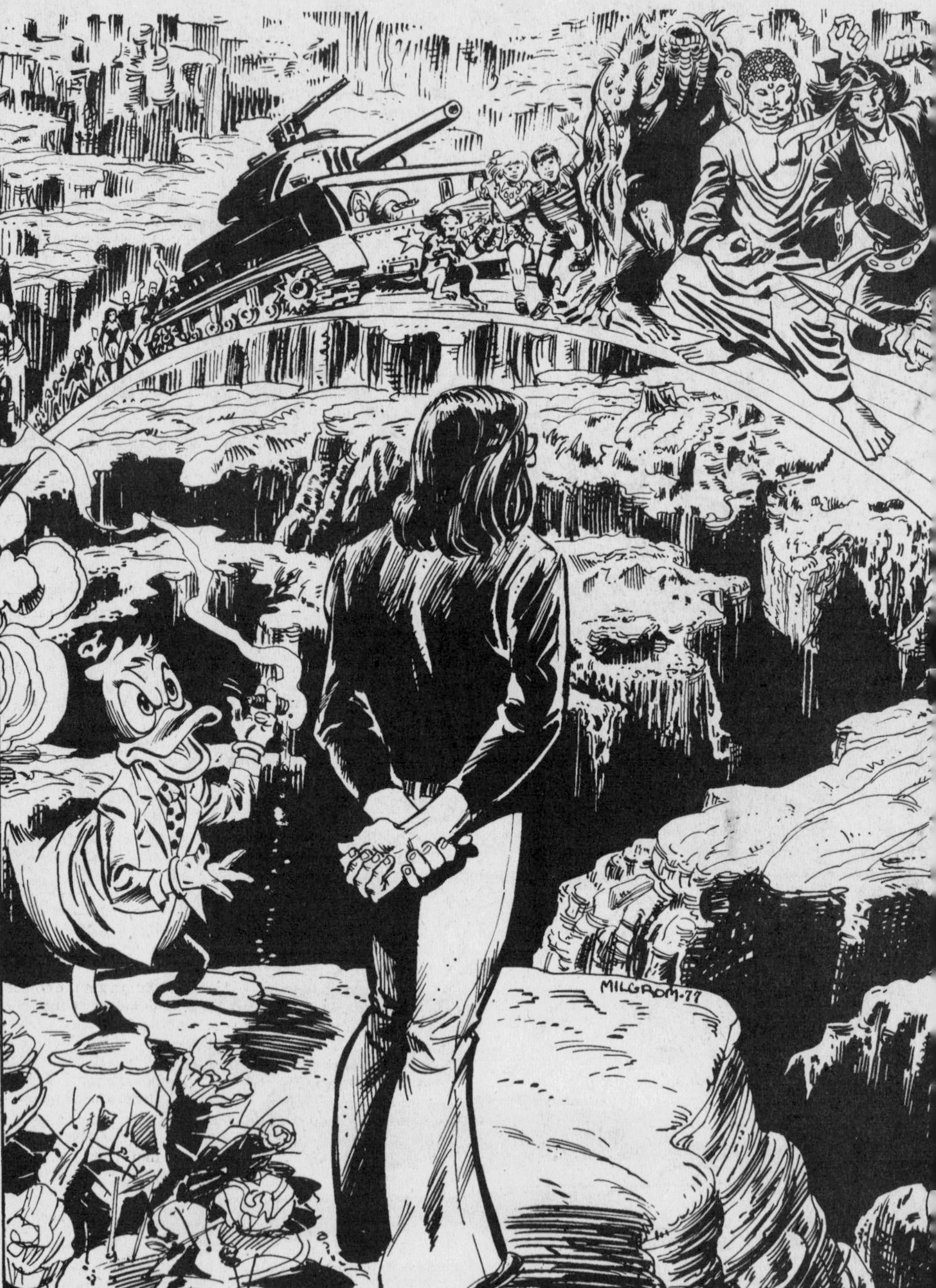

ons of sugar plums

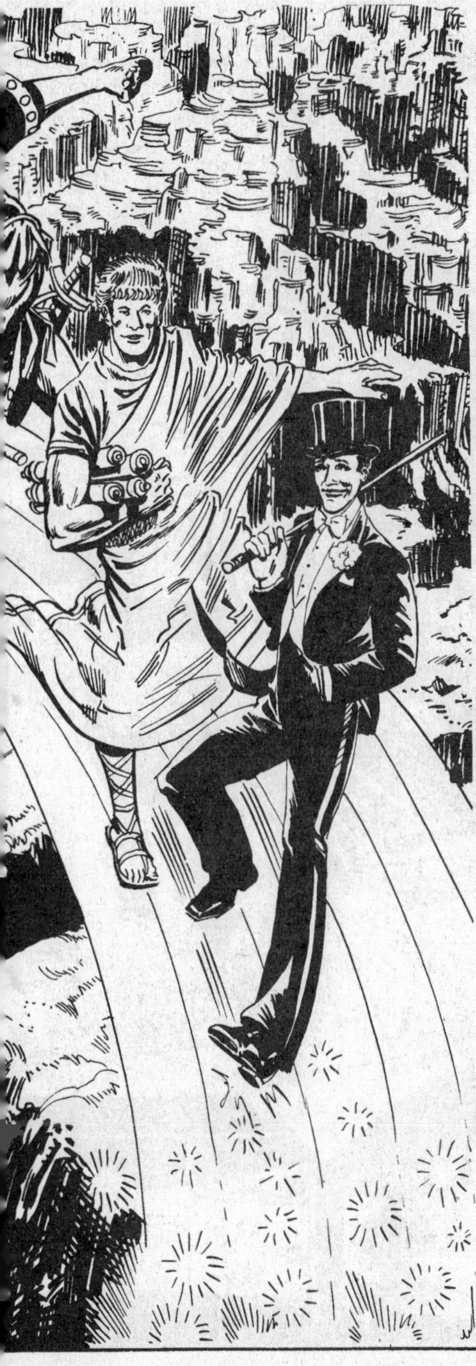

"Majestic, ain't it?" Howard asks, obviously unimpressed.

"Yes," I reply, trying my best to sound contemplative, and failing.

"The Colorado River took eons to carve this steep, sinuous monster objet d'art outta some flat, bland plateau—almost as long as you're takin' gettin' to the point o' this story."

"Howard, it seems vaguely blasphemous to engage in petty banter about human problems in the face of this—this—"

"Hole?"

"I don't believe you said that."

"Look, Gerber, it's not like nature dug this oversized storm drain with the specific intent o' creatin' a tourist attraction! It exists because the river did what it was supposed to do—it flowed. And the rocks did what they were supposed to do—they eroded. Guys like you are just envious 'cause nature didn't haveta put any thought into its work. You wanna be able ta write the same way—only writing isn't a natural process. Nature only hadda make somethin' outta nothin' once in its whole career. You've gotta do it daily. If God had had your temperament, the universe would still be a box o' typewriter paper, waitin' ta be opened!"

I stare dumbly at my friend the Duck, pleading with my eyes for him to continue. He turns away, shaking his head, folding his arms over his chest in disgust. He won't talk to me, and I don't know what to say. After some deliberation, I arrive at the following gem: "Communication ... takes ... a lot of energy, Howard."

He scowls.

I light a cigarette.

We both sit there for a long moment, wordlessly, gazing at the spectacle of the canyon.

"Y'know what that canyon really is, Gerber? It's the world's biggest, most convoluted rut!"

I laugh involuntarily. "I've gotta hand it to you, pal. That's definitely a new interpretation of the phenomenon."

"An' that tight-lipped smile tryin' ta elbow its way onta yer face is the first sign of spontaneity I've seen from you in eleven pages! Loosen up, willya! Save the theorizin' for the speech-communication majors o' the world! You're outta school now, big boy. You're pushin' thirty with a bulldozer. There's no how-to manual on one-to-one interaction between allegedly intelligent beings. The way ta communicate is just—do it!"

"Be myself, you mean. Yeah. Mmm-hmm. That's terrific advice, Howard. Thank you. Wowee. Why didn't I think of that?"

"It ain't that simple, turkey. Ya gotta be yerself without tryin'. Like the river down there."

"Or the eroding rocks, for that matter, huh?"

"Yeah, well, yer not gettin' any younger. But ya got the choice, rocks or river. I figger you've been stonewallin' it too long already." He stands, brushes the dust off his feathers and coat, and turns to walk away. "Listen, I'm gonna grab a bite ta eat. They got a great processed ham sandwich in that restaurant next to the souvenir gift shop with the Taiwan-manufactured Indian beads. Why don't you sit here alone a bit an' meditate on the natural splendor while I gorge myself on preservatives? Free associate. See what ya come up with. Tell the folks at home a story. An' whatever ya do, plan on bein' more interesting next time we meet!"

VI tell the people a story

Ramsludge Hawthorne looked at the assortment of official forms fanned out across the modest expanse of the coffee table. All of the forms began with the same three words: "Please Print Clearly." All of the forms asked for the same information: name, address, city, state, zip, age, married, single, separated, divorced, annual income, father's name, father's address, mother's maiden name, mother's maiden address, health: good, fair, poor, do you certify that you have answered all questions on form completely and truthfully to the best of your knowled signature, date. The tax forms in the assortment even asked spare change. Panhandling by mail, Ramsludge thou Gimme, gimme, gimme. Your money, your word, your life, y every waking moment. And remember, your record will fol you wherever you roam, biting at your heels like a rabid dog own you, lock, stock, and zip code.

"You only own me as long as I continue to exist," Ramslu snarled at the forms, which responded with the same questions.

Ramsludge's wife the former Remarka Demonstrata, he

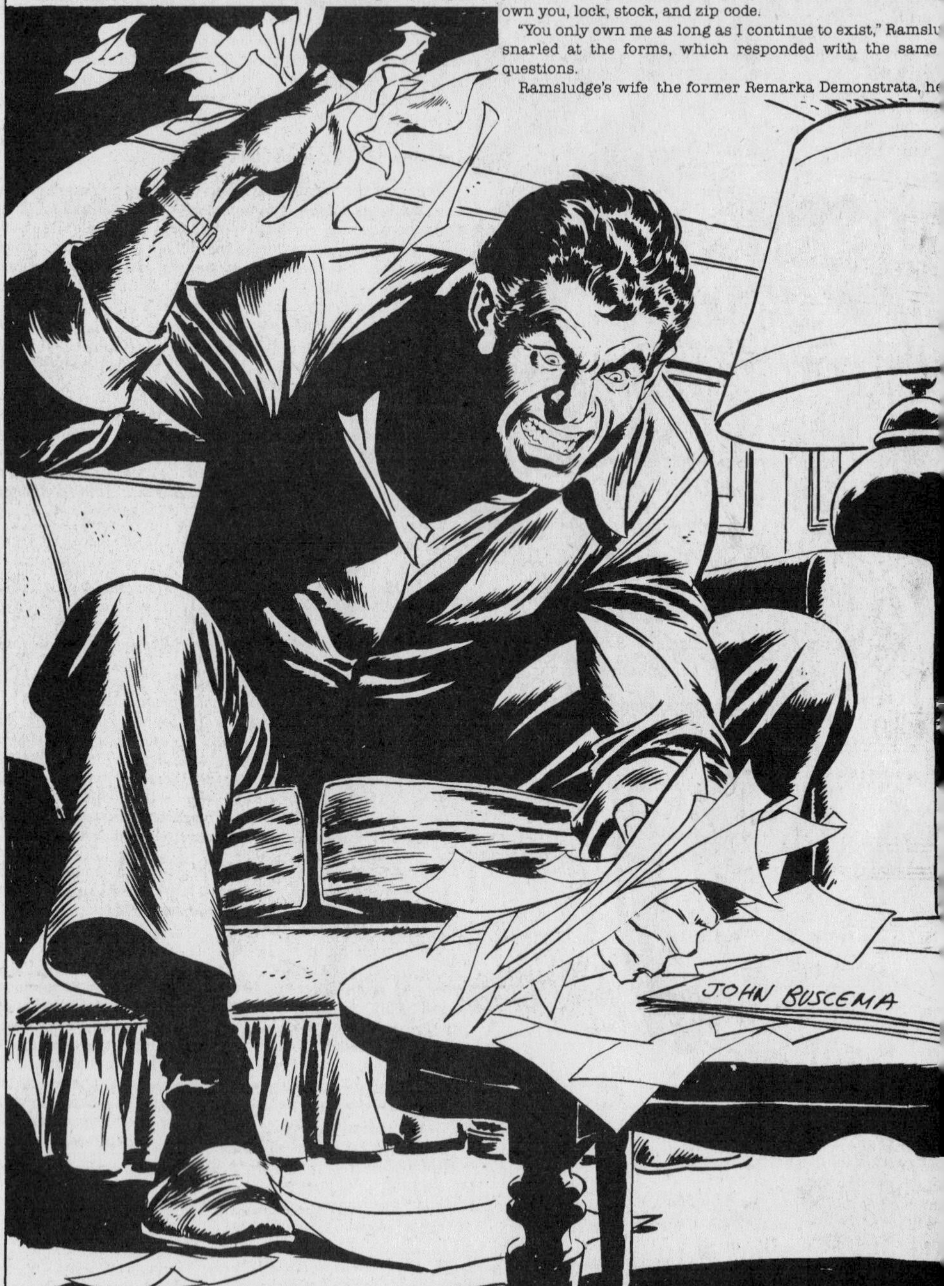
JOHN BUSCEMA

husband's comment as she entered the living room with knitting basket. Remarka would almost have been beautihad she been born a dwarf elm; as a woman, however, she s an aesthetic disaster, short and spindly with a full head of ves. She plopped herself in the easy chair across the coffee le from the sofa where Ramsludge was still hunched ford, foaming at the forms. "Gonna off yourself, hubby-dubby?" queried enthusiastically. "Your insurance all paid up, pelhopeIhope?"

Darling," Ramsludge hissed, "your mind is as barren as your lp is fecund."

Yes," Remarka sighed, folding her hands in her lap, turning gaze heavenward. "That's why we have such a full and ppy life together, Rrrrrramsludge!" He hated it when she wled his name.

ctually," Ramsludge said, "I was thinking of deserting you, — ng into hiding, adopting a new name and perhaps a puppy from Bide-a-Wee, establishing a new identity for myself, something less ... oppressive."

"Aw, g'wan!"

"Okay, I will." And with that, Ramsludge leaped from the sofa, over the coffee table, and bounded into the kitchen. Remarka sighed, smiled stupidly, and undertook to knit a little blue booty. "Tee hee," she giggled at the needles.

It was some hours and one completed booty later that she realized Ramsludge had never returned from the kitchen. "Honey-poo," she called out. "Sweety-charms? Puddin'-pie? Safflower-meat?"

No answer.

"Tch," she tched, and set her knitting on the end table. As she did so, she noted a kind of finality about the act. It disturbed her. She angled her limbs and branches out of the easy chair and her leaves swayed gently into the kitchen.

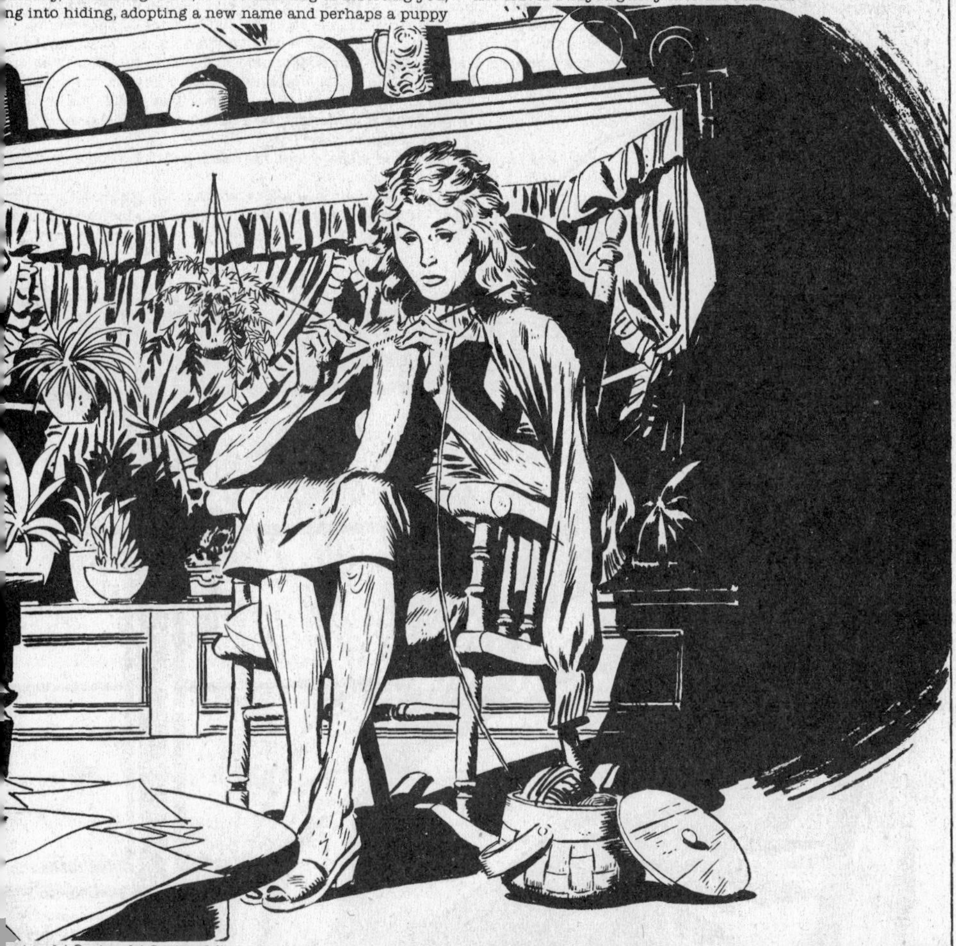

migosh! Omigosh! Omigosh!!

he upper half of the Dutch door leading out to the patio was n, and there were vault marks on the linoleum!

e'd done it!

amsludge was gone!

e was free! He'd escaped!

nd though Remarka could not know this, in the few hours e his mad dash out of the neighborhood, he'd changed his ne to Oralong Haymountain, obtained two oil company dit cards, a Master Charge, and a marriage license and was eady over his head in debt again.

emarka cried, but only for a little while. When she'd exhausted her tear ducts for the evening, she put Helen Reddy on the stereo, and told herself she was strong, she was invincible, she was a woman, not a dwarf elm.

And that's that.

SURPRISE TWIST ENDING: Oralong Haymountain is now known from coast to coast as the man who planted an atomic bomb in the Internal Revenue Service office in Blunderbuss, Vermont, and failed to escape before it detonated. Authorities found his charred molecules tangled in a roll of red tape. Remarka wasn't very happy, either, but her life lasted longer, and she collected Ramsludge's insurance and social security when she turned sixty-two

"Okay, class, now let's analyze the preceding story," says the professor. "I think we can all agree that its literary merit is nil, and thus our approach must be from a psychological viewpoint. Any objections?"

The class shakes its head.

"Good. Then let us proceed. We have here the product of an extremely hostile individual with readily apparent paranoid tendencies. But he is more fearful than angry, more humiliated than vengeful. He can only conceive of escape from a given unpleasant situation. Coping behavior, like communication, requires too great an expenditure of energy. Now, how can we deduce these facts?

"First, ecce icky homo! Behold the icky man! His name perfectly encapsulates his character. 'Ramsludge,' he is called. The strong, masculine—but significantly sheepish—first syllable, coupled with the concept of slime, waste, and unpleasant odors. The writer feels that the male in this society is like a sheep who is allowed to live only so long as he can be shorn. Then he's slaughtered for chops. Obviously, the author also feels both compassion and propinquity with and to his beleaguered protagonist. Do we agree, class?"

The class nods.

"The last name, too, is symbolic, being that of an early A
can literary figure, now hopelessly outdated, and also th
tree, which, again surely not coincidentally, is how both
and protagonist view the female. Got that?

"Plodding odiously onward, we find Ramsludge engag
conversation with income tax forms, loan forms, insu
forms, etc. We can, I think, infer from this pathetic preser
of the male the author's own attitude toward burea
There is clearly antipathy extant 'twixt the writer and c
dom. Doo-wah!

"The woman is a stereotypic pre-liberationist caricatu
ward whom the author also harbors hostilities. He com
her with a tree, or more accurately a shrub, which take
and vegetates in one place. Yet she mockingly growls his
as if to say, 'haha hoho and heehee, I dare you to con
transplant me, tiger.' So, like her analog the tree, her u
tionably superior strength lies in her relatively imm
nature. Obviously, she perceives the hawthorne as cro
out the dwarf elm, eating up all the nutrients in the so
she wants the larger, hungrier tree to die. The hawtho
course, concedes. The home is her turf. He runs awa
questions, class?"

The class raises its hand, and the professor nods
direction.

"Are your suggesting, sir, that the author's theme m
the irreconcilable differences between the sexes?" inqui
class.

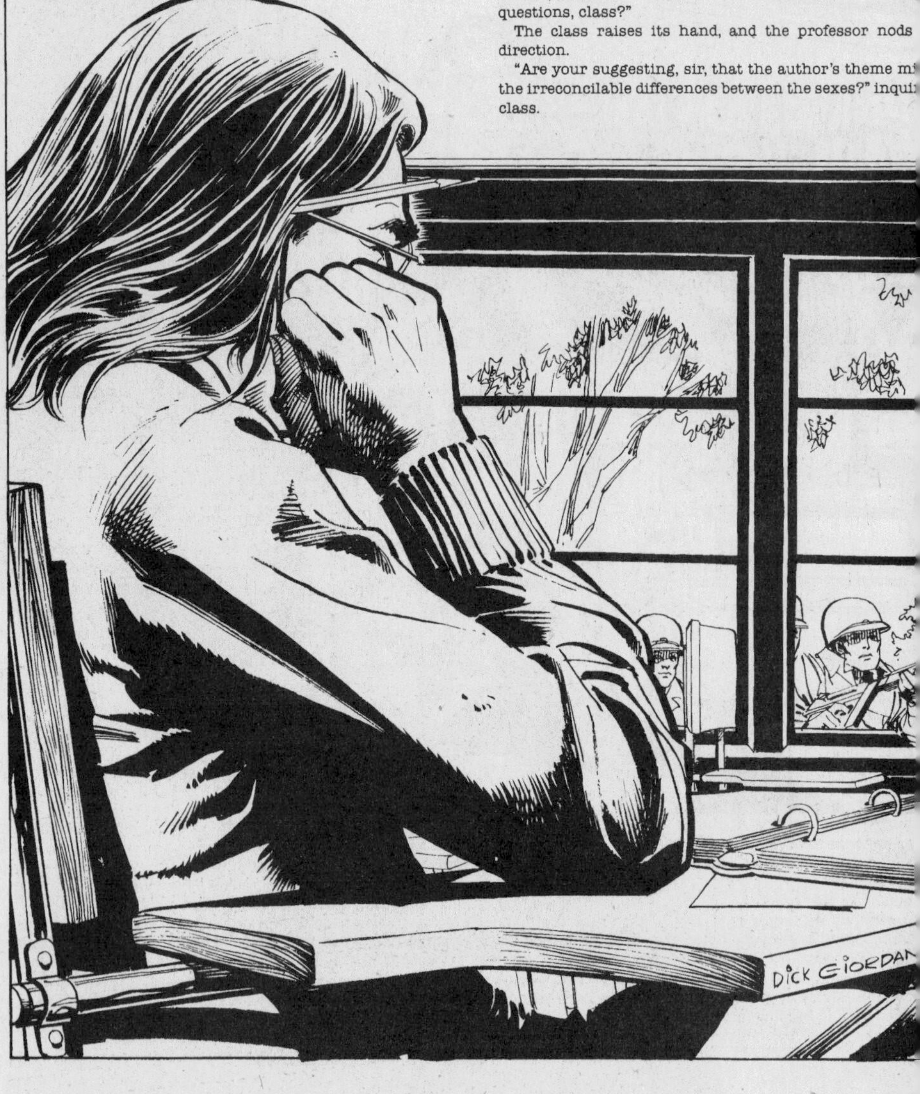
DICK GIORDAN

"I'm suggesting that this clown doesn't believe two hairless apes can inhabit the same clucking planet if one of 'em happens ta be him!

"See, once he makes his big, dramatic exit, class, he proceeds to embroil himself in the same stupid woes he suffered during his marriage to Remarka. Ultimately, he even blasts himself ta kingdom come! The guy's worse than a born loser—he's a rat who only knows how ta run one maze. He stands in terror of his life pattern, but that's all he does—stands! An' that's where his tree-ness comes inta the picture!"

"Are you saying, Professor Howard, that one can emancipate him or herself from these constricting, stationary positions?"

A shot rings out. The professor lurches backward, hands rising instinctively to his chest. He falls forward onto the classroom floor. The class, horrified, springs from its seat to the professor's side.

The professor looks into the face of his class, winks, and says with a chuckle: "They missed. Does that answer yer question?"

The class, bewildered, shuffles out of the room just as the bell rings.

"By the way, class," says the prof, standing now, brushing the bullet fragments from his gown, "your assignment for tomorrow is ta write a fan letter ta the jerk who wrote that story, an' set 'im straight in time for next issue! Dismissed!"

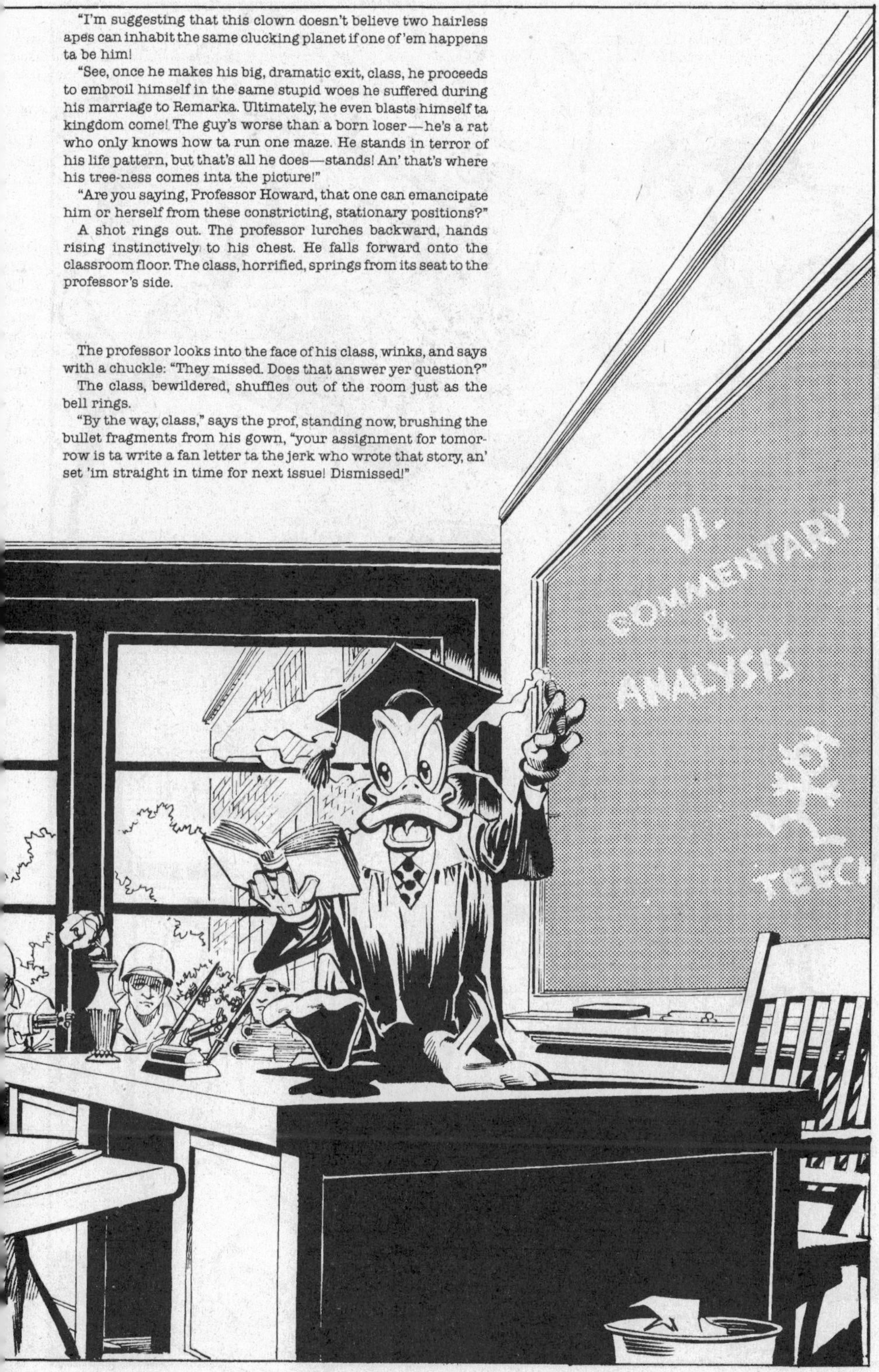
VI.
COMMENTARY
&
ANALYSIS
TEECH

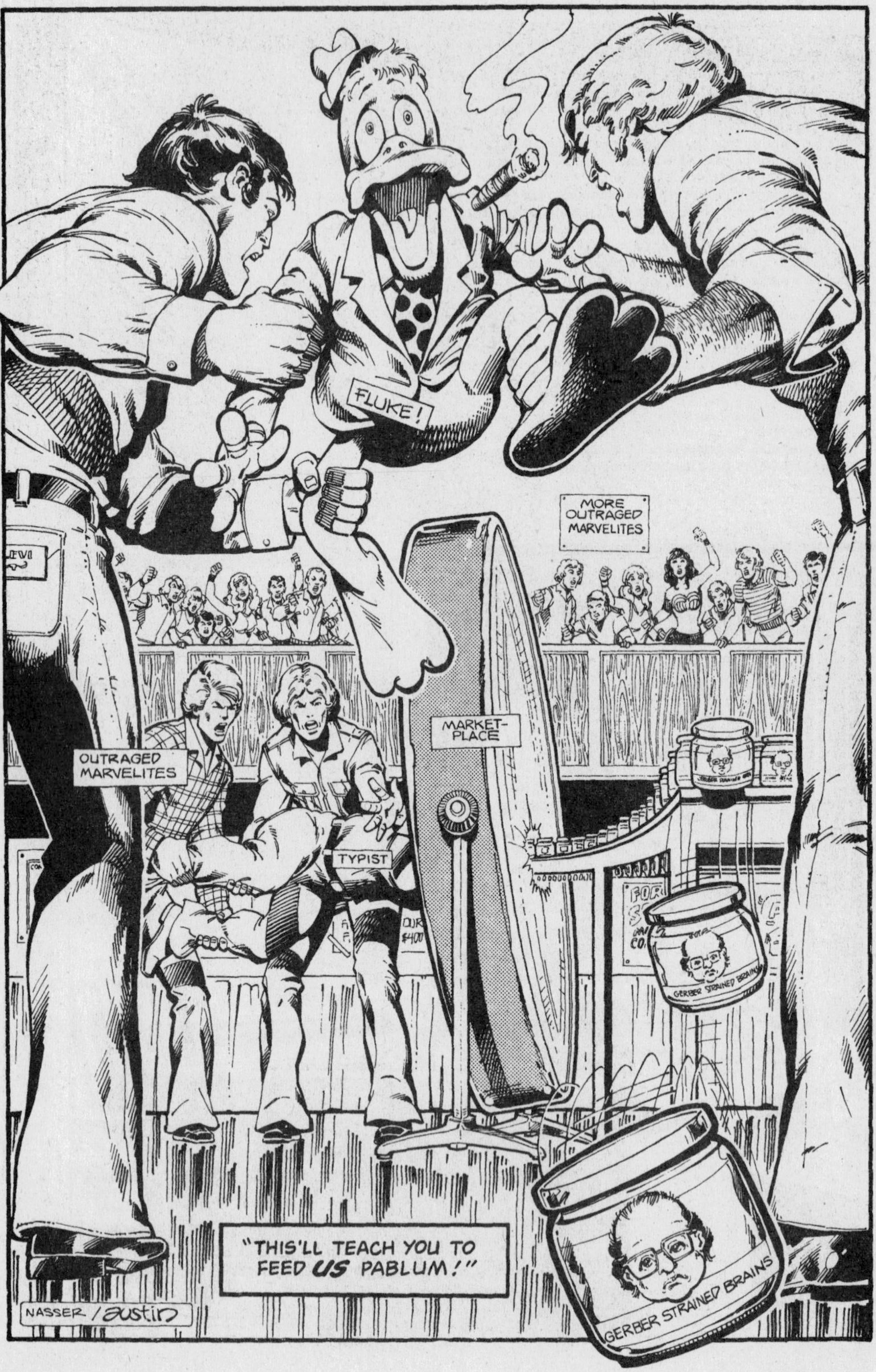
FLUKE!
MORE OUTRAGED MARVELITES
LEVI
MARKET-PLACE
OUTRAGED MARVELITES
TYPIST
GERBER STRAINED BRAINS
GERBER STRAINED BRAINS
"THIS'LL TEACH YOU TO FEED US PABLUM!"
NASSER / austin

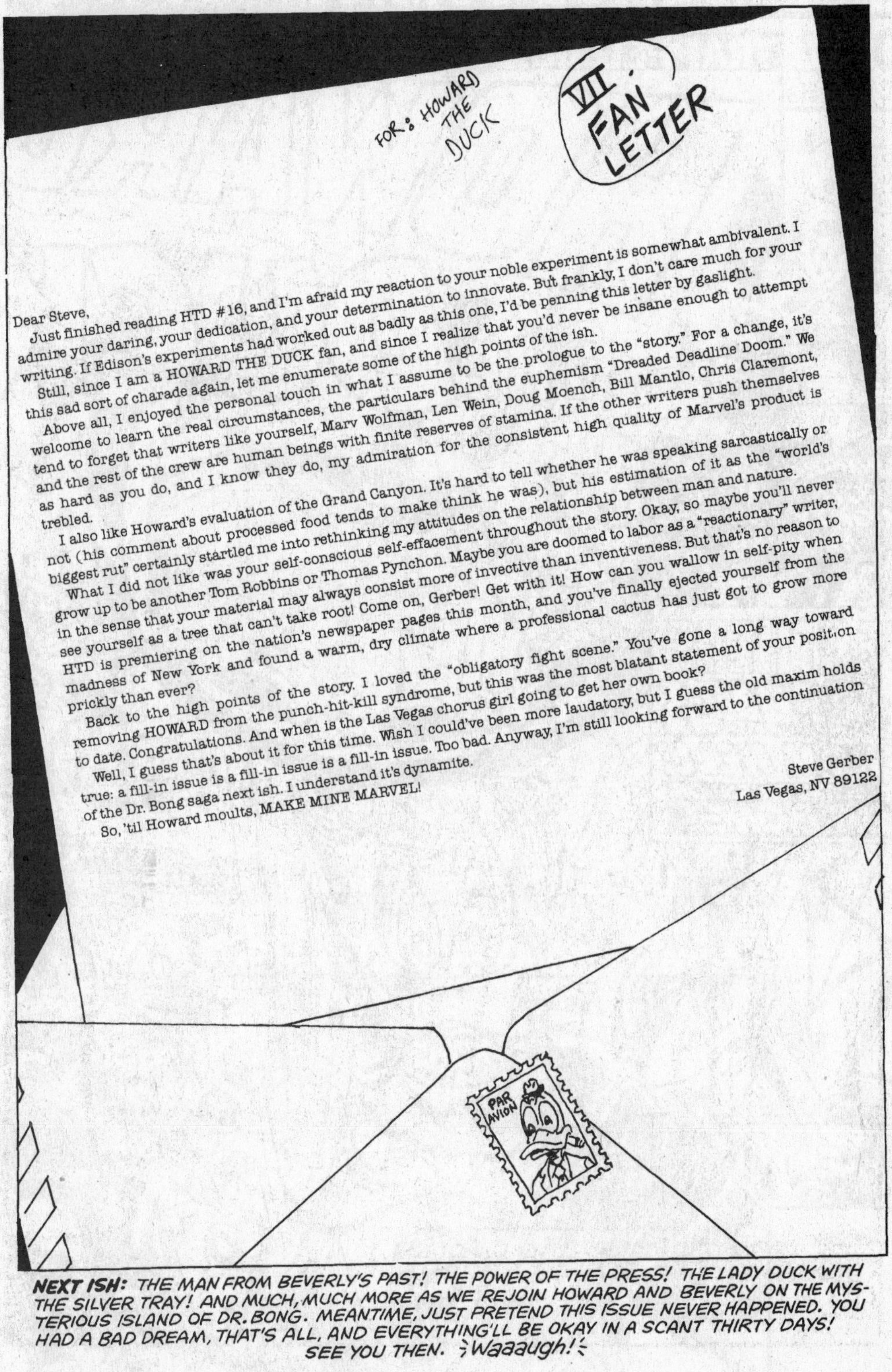
FOR: HOWARD THE DUCK
VII. FAN LETTER
Dear Steve,
Just finished reading HTD #16, and I'm afraid my reaction to your noble experiment is somewhat ambivalent. I admire your daring, your dedication, and your determination to innovate. But frankly, I don't care much for your writing. If Edison's experiments had worked out as badly as this one, I'd be penning this letter by gaslight.
Still, since I am a HOWARD THE DUCK fan, and since I realize that you'd never be insane enough to attempt this sad sort of charade again, let me enumerate some of the high points of the ish.
Above all, I enjoyed the personal touch in what I assume to be the prologue to the "story." For a change, it's welcome to learn the real circumstances, the particulars behind the euphemism "Dreaded Deadline Doom." We tend to forget that writers like yourself, Marv Wolfman, Len Wein, Doug Moench, Bill Mantlo, Chris Claremont, and the rest of the crew are human beings with finite reserves of stamina. If the other writers push themselves as hard as you do, and I know they do, my admiration for the consistent high quality of Marvel's product is trebled.
I also like Howard's evaluation of the Grand Canyon. It's hard to tell whether he was speaking sarcastically or not (his comment about processed food tends to make think he was), but his estimation of it as the "world's biggest rut" certainly startled me into rethinking my attitudes on the relationship between man and nature.
What I did not like was your self-conscious self-effacement throughout the story. Okay, so maybe you'll never grow up to be another Tom Robbins or Thomas Pynchon. Maybe you are doomed to labor as a "reactionary" writer, in the sense that your material may always consist more of invective than inventiveness. But that's no reason to see yourself as a tree that can't take root! Come on, Gerber! Get with it! How can you wallow in self-pity when HTD is premiering on the nation's newspaper pages this month, and you've finally ejected yourself from the madness of New York and found a warm, dry climate where a professional cactus has just got to grow more prickly than ever?
Back to the high points of the story. I loved the "obligatory fight scene." You've gone a long way toward removing HOWARD from the punch-hit-kill syndrome, but this was the most blatant statement of your position to date. Congratulations. And when is the Las Vegas chorus girl going to get her own book?
Well, I guess that's about it for this time. Wish I could've been more laudatory, but I guess the old maxim holds true: a fill-in issue is a fill-in issue is a fill-in issue. Too bad. Anyway, I'm still looking forward to the continuation of the Dr. Bong saga next ish. I understand it's dynamite.
So, 'til Howard moults, MAKE MINE MARVEL!
Steve Gerber
Las Vegas, NV 89122
PAR AVION

NEXT ISH: THE MAN FROM BEVERLY'S PAST! THE POWER OF THE PRESS! THE LADY DUCK WITH THE SILVER TRAY! AND MUCH, MUCH MORE AS WE REJOIN HOWARD AND BEVERLY ON THE MYSTERIOUS ISLAND OF DR. BONG. MEANTIME, JUST PRETEND THIS ISSUE NEVER HAPPENED. YOU HAD A BAD DREAM, THAT'S ALL, AND EVERYTHING'LL BE OKAY IN A SCANT THIRTY DAYS! SEE YOU THEN. *Waaaugh!*

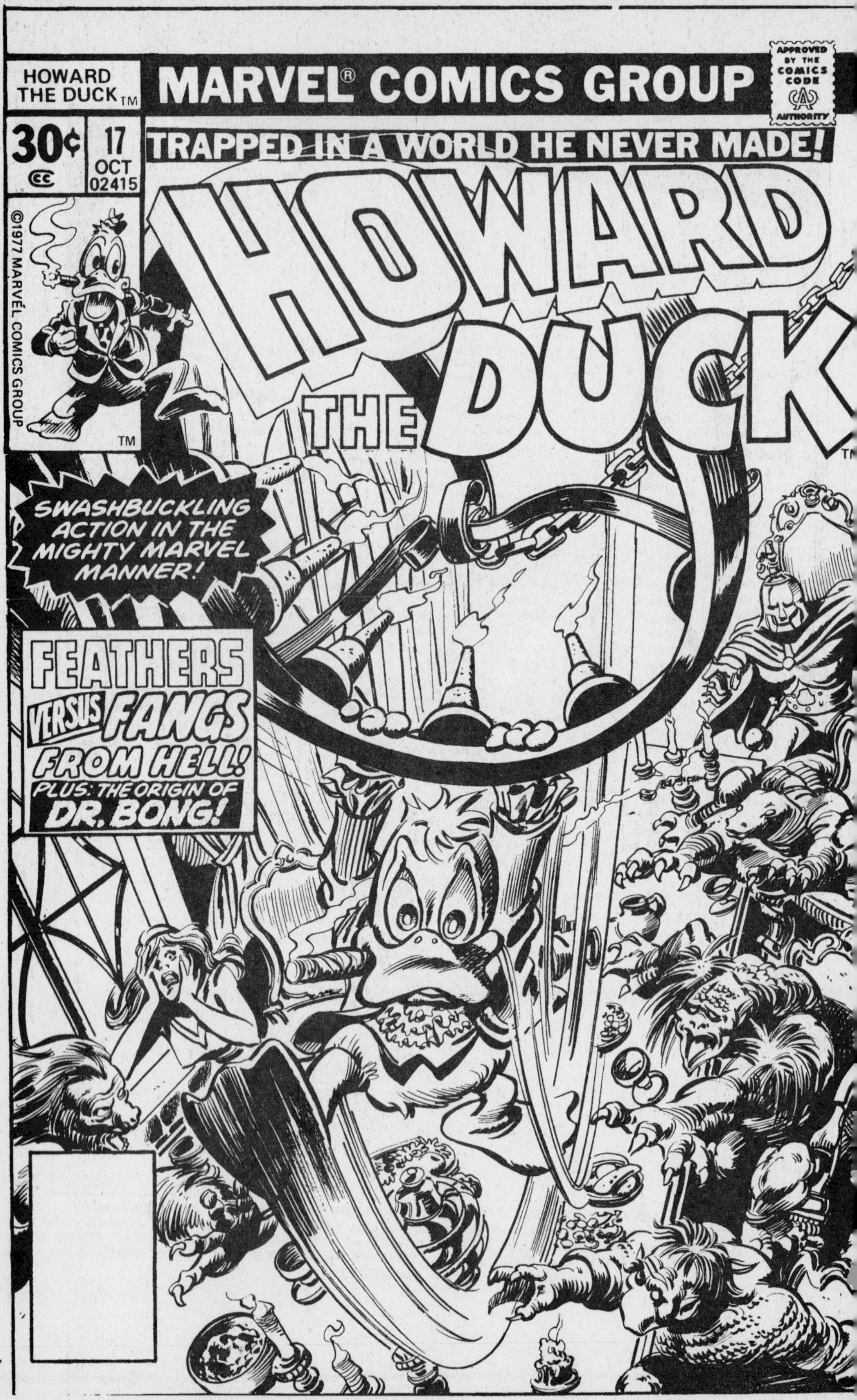
HOWARD THE DUCK TM
MARVEL® COMICS GROUP
APPROVED BY THE COMICS CODE AUTHORITY
30¢
17
OCT
02415
TRAPPED IN A WORLD HE NEVER MADE!
HOWARD THE DUCK TM
©1977 MARVEL COMICS GROUP
TM
SWASHBUCKLING ACTION IN THE MIGHTY MARVEL MANNER!
FEATHERS VERSUS FANGS FROM HELL!
PLUS: THE ORIGIN OF DR. BONG!

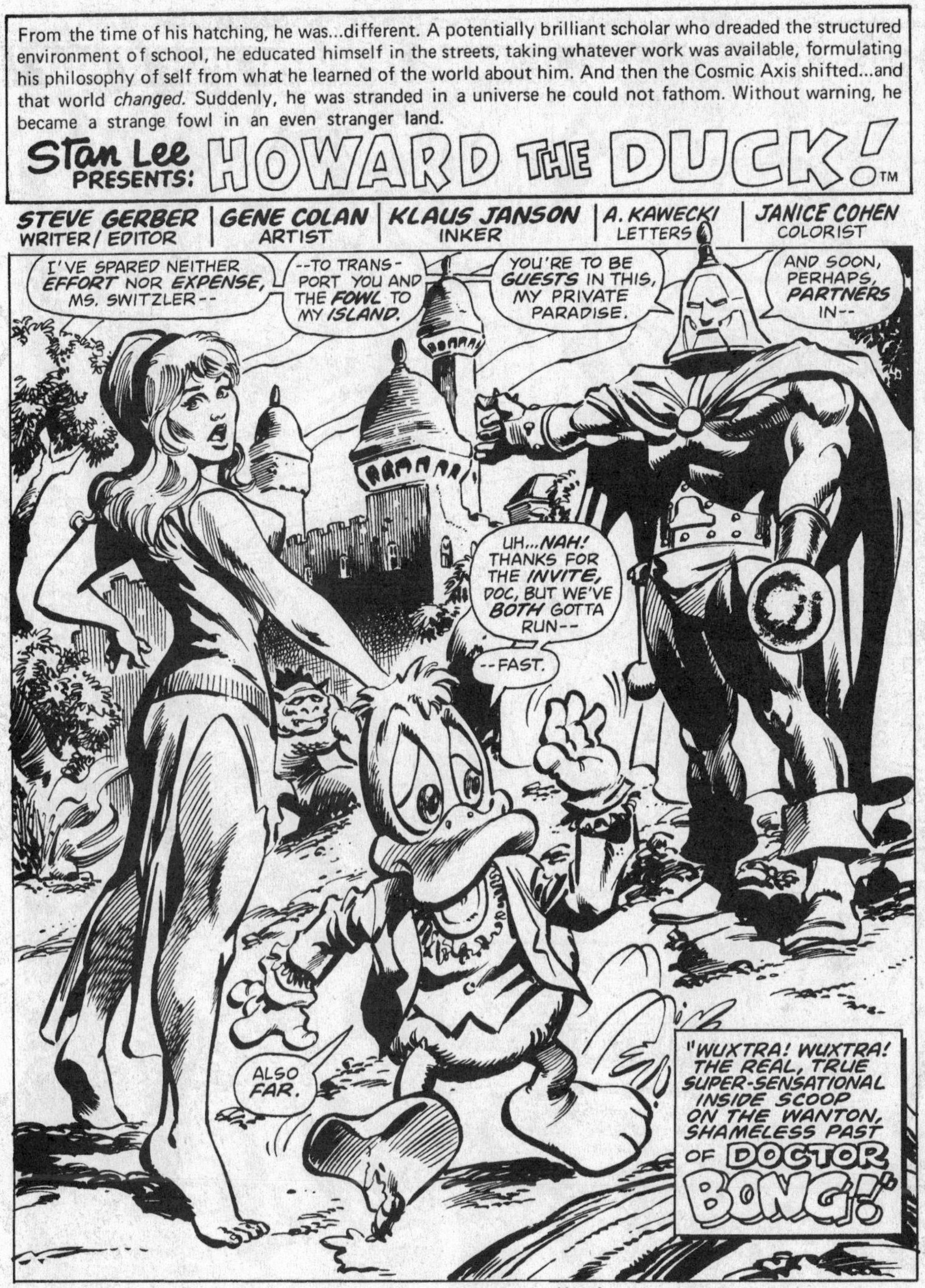

From the time of his hatching, he was...different. A potentially brilliant scholar who dreaded the structured environment of school, he educated himself in the streets, taking whatever work was available, formulating his philosophy of self from what he learned of the world about him. And then the Cosmic Axis shifted...and that world changed. Suddenly, he was stranded in a universe he could not fathom. Without warning, he became a strange fowl in an even stranger land.
Stan Lee PRESENTS: HOWARD THE DUCK!™
STEVE GERBER WRITER/ EDITOR
GENE COLAN ARTIST
KLAUS JANSON INKER
A. KAWECKI LETTERS
JANICE COHEN COLORIST
I'VE SPARED NEITHER EFFORT NOR EXPENSE, MS. SWITZLER--
--TO TRANSPORT YOU AND THE FOWL TO MY ISLAND.
YOU'RE TO BE GUESTS IN THIS, MY PRIVATE PARADISE.
AND SOON, PERHAPS, PARTNERS IN--
UH...NAH! THANKS FOR THE INVITE, DOC, BUT WE'VE BOTH GOTTA RUN--
--FAST.
ALSO FAR.
"WUXTRA! WUXTRA! THE REAL, TRUE SUPER-SENSATIONAL INSIDE SCOOP ON THE WANTON, SHAMELESS PAST OF DOCTOR BONG!"

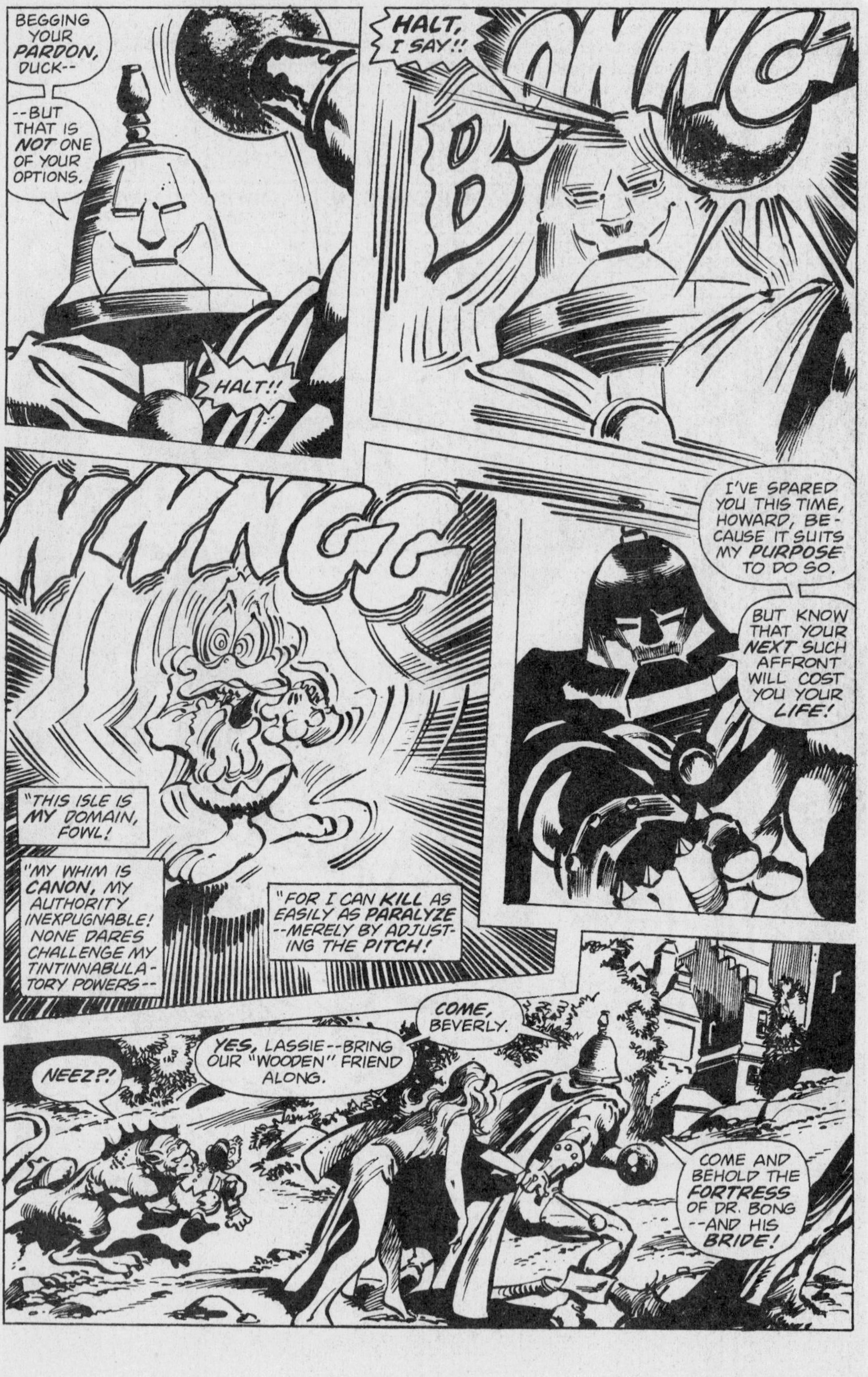

BEGGING YOUR PARDON, DUCK--
--BUT THAT IS NOT ONE OF YOUR OPTIONS.
HALT!!
HALT, I SAY!!
BONNG
WNNGG
"THIS ISLE IS MY DOMAIN, FOWL!
"MY WHIM IS CANON, MY AUTHORITY INEXPUGNABLE! NONE DARES CHALLENGE MY TINTINNABULATORY POWERS--
"FOR I CAN KILL AS EASILY AS PARALYZE --MERELY BY ADJUSTING THE PITCH!
I'VE SPARED YOU THIS TIME, HOWARD, BECAUSE IT SUITS MY PURPOSE TO DO SO.
BUT KNOW THAT YOUR NEXT SUCH AFFRONT WILL COST YOU YOUR LIFE!
NEEZ?!
YES, LASSIE--BRING OUR "WOODEN" FRIEND ALONG.
COME, BEVERLY.
COME AND BEHOLD THE FORTRESS OF DR. BONG --AND HIS BRIDE!

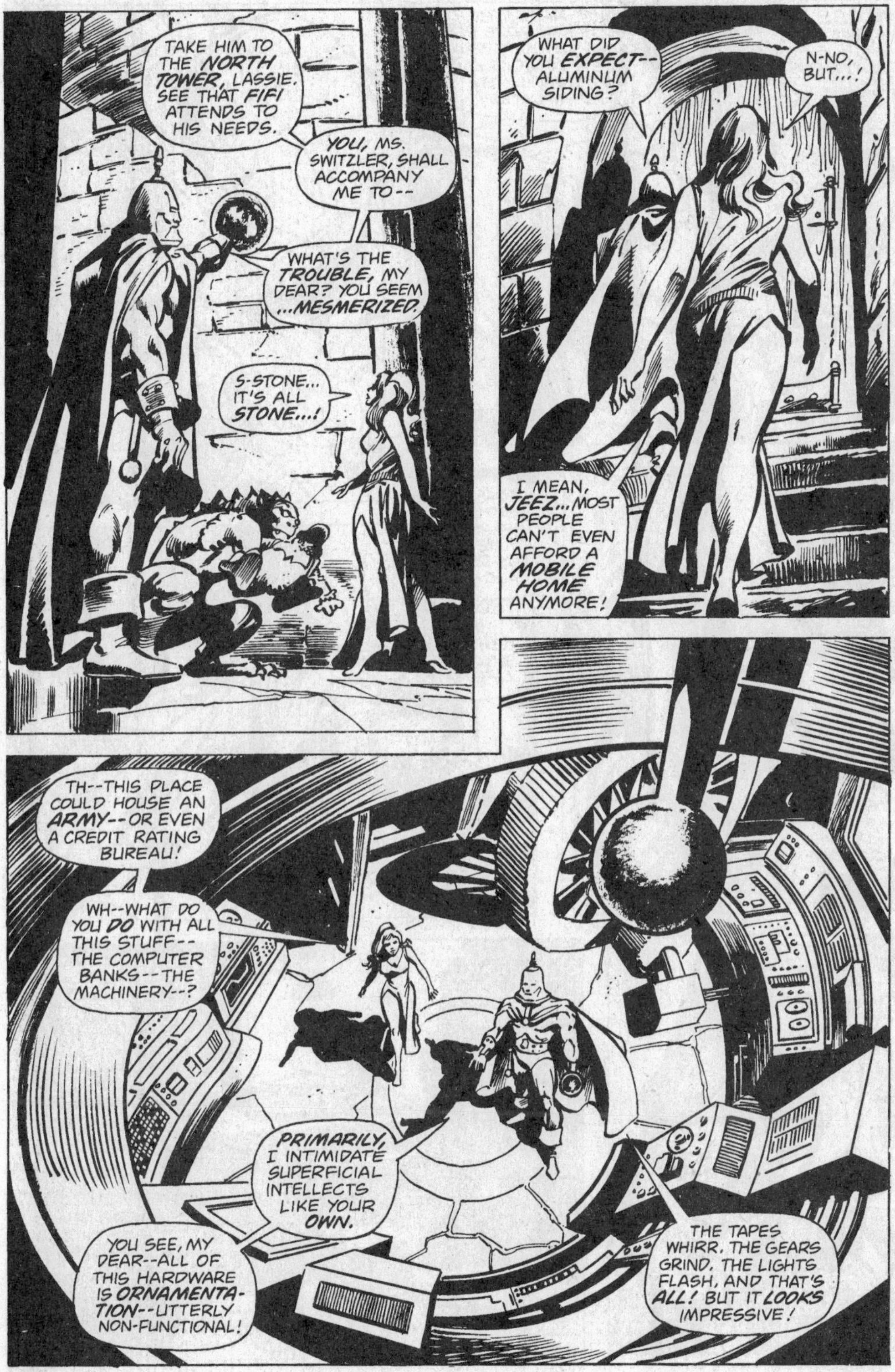
TAKE HIM TO THE NORTH TOWER, LASSIE. SEE THAT FIFI ATTENDS TO HIS NEEDS.
YOU, MS. SWITZLER, SHALL ACCOMPANY ME TO--
WHAT'S THE TROUBLE, MY DEAR? YOU SEEM ...MESMERIZED.
S-STONE... IT'S ALL STONE...!
WHAT DID YOU EXPECT-- ALUMINUM SIDING?
N-NO, BUT...!
I MEAN, JEEZ... MOST PEOPLE CAN'T EVEN AFFORD A MOBILE HOME ANYMORE!
TH--THIS PLACE COULD HOUSE AN ARMY--OR EVEN A CREDIT RATING BUREAU!
WH--WHAT DO YOU DO WITH ALL THIS STUFF-- THE COMPUTER BANKS--THE MACHINERY--?
PRIMARILY, I INTIMIDATE SUPERFICIAL INTELLECTS LIKE YOUR OWN.
YOU SEE, MY DEAR--ALL OF THIS HARDWARE IS ORNAMENTATION--UTTERLY NON-FUNCTIONAL!
THE TAPES WHIRR. THE GEARS GRIND. THE LIGHTS FLASH, AND THAT'S ALL! BUT IT LOOKS IMPRESSIVE!

IMAGE, MS. SWITZLER! IMAGE IS EVERYTHING!

WHAT *APPEARS* TO BE IS FAR MORE PERSUASIVE THAN WHAT *IS*--IF WHAT *IS* CANNOT READILY BE ASSIMILATED!

WHA'--?

IMAGE, WOMAN!! THE DOMINANCE OF *STYLE* OVER SUBSTANCE, *FORM* OVER CONTENT!

I'VE JUST *DEFINED* MYSELF FOR YOU!

DO YOU UNDERSTAND?

UH... UH-UH.

YOU *WILL!* AND YOU'LL BE GRATEFUL FOR THE *LESSONS* I SHALL TEACH YOU.

Y-YEAH?

YEAH! JUST AS I AM INDEBTED TO YOU!--

--FOR THE TRUTHS YOU IMPARTED TO *ME* ONE DAY LONG AGO--

...IN ANOTHER *LAND*, ANOTHER *LIFETIME!*

I--?

ALL IN GOOD TIME, MY DEAR. *FIRST*--

GAZE UPON THE *NERVE CENTER* OF THIS MAMMOTH COMPLEX--!

OOOH!

"*HERE* IS THE TRUE SEAT OF *POWER*, BEVERLY! NOT A *THRONE*--

"BUT A *HUMBLE BRIDGE CHAIR*, STATIONED BEFORE THE MOST *POTENT WEAPON* EVER DEVISED BY MAN!'"

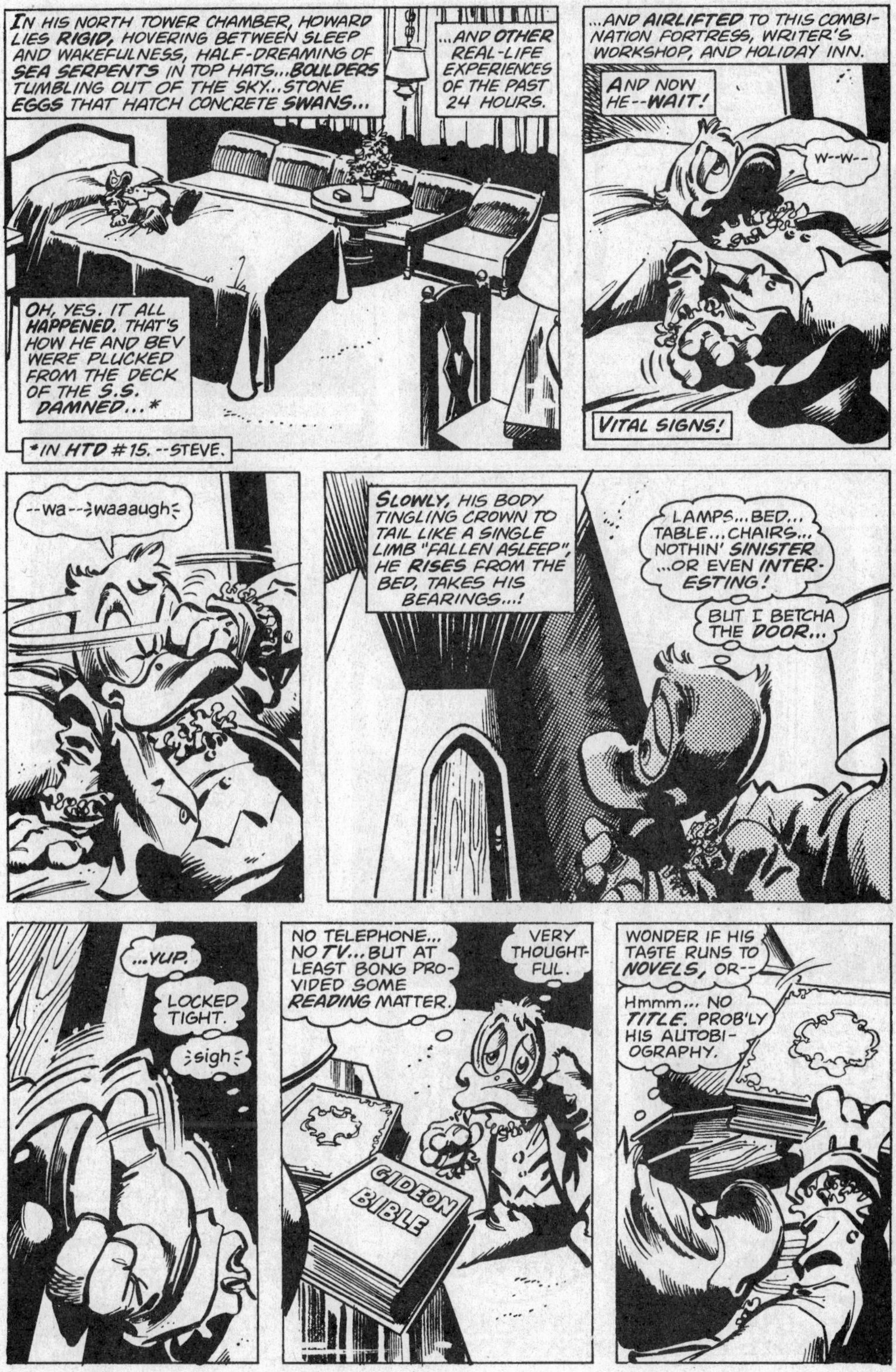
IN HIS NORTH TOWER CHAMBER, HOWARD LIES RIGID, HOVERING BETWEEN SLEEP AND WAKEFULNESS, HALF-DREAMING OF SEA SERPENTS IN TOP HATS...BOULDERS TUMBLING OUT OF THE SKY...STONE EGGS THAT HATCH CONCRETE SWANS...
...AND OTHER REAL-LIFE EXPERIENCES OF THE PAST 24 HOURS.
OH, YES. IT ALL HAPPENED. THAT'S HOW HE AND BEV WERE PLUCKED FROM THE DECK OF THE S.S. DAMNED...*
*IN HTD #15. --STEVE.
...AND AIRLIFTED TO THIS COMBINATION FORTRESS, WRITER'S WORKSHOP, AND HOLIDAY INN.
AND NOW HE--WAIT!
W--W--
VITAL SIGNS!
--wa--waaaugh
SLOWLY, HIS BODY TINGLING CROWN TO TAIL LIKE A SINGLE LIMB "FALLEN ASLEEP", HE RISES FROM THE BED, TAKES HIS BEARINGS...!
LAMPS...BED... TABLE...CHAIRS... NOTHIN' SINISTER ...OR EVEN INTERESTING!
BUT I BETCHA THE DOOR...
...YUP.
LOCKED TIGHT.
sigh
NO TELEPHONE... NO TV...BUT AT LEAST BONG PROVIDED SOME READING MATTER.
VERY THOUGHTFUL.
GIDEON BIBLE
WONDER IF HIS TASTE RUNS TO NOVELS, OR--
Hmmm... NO TITLE. PROB'LY HIS AUTOBIOGRAPHY.

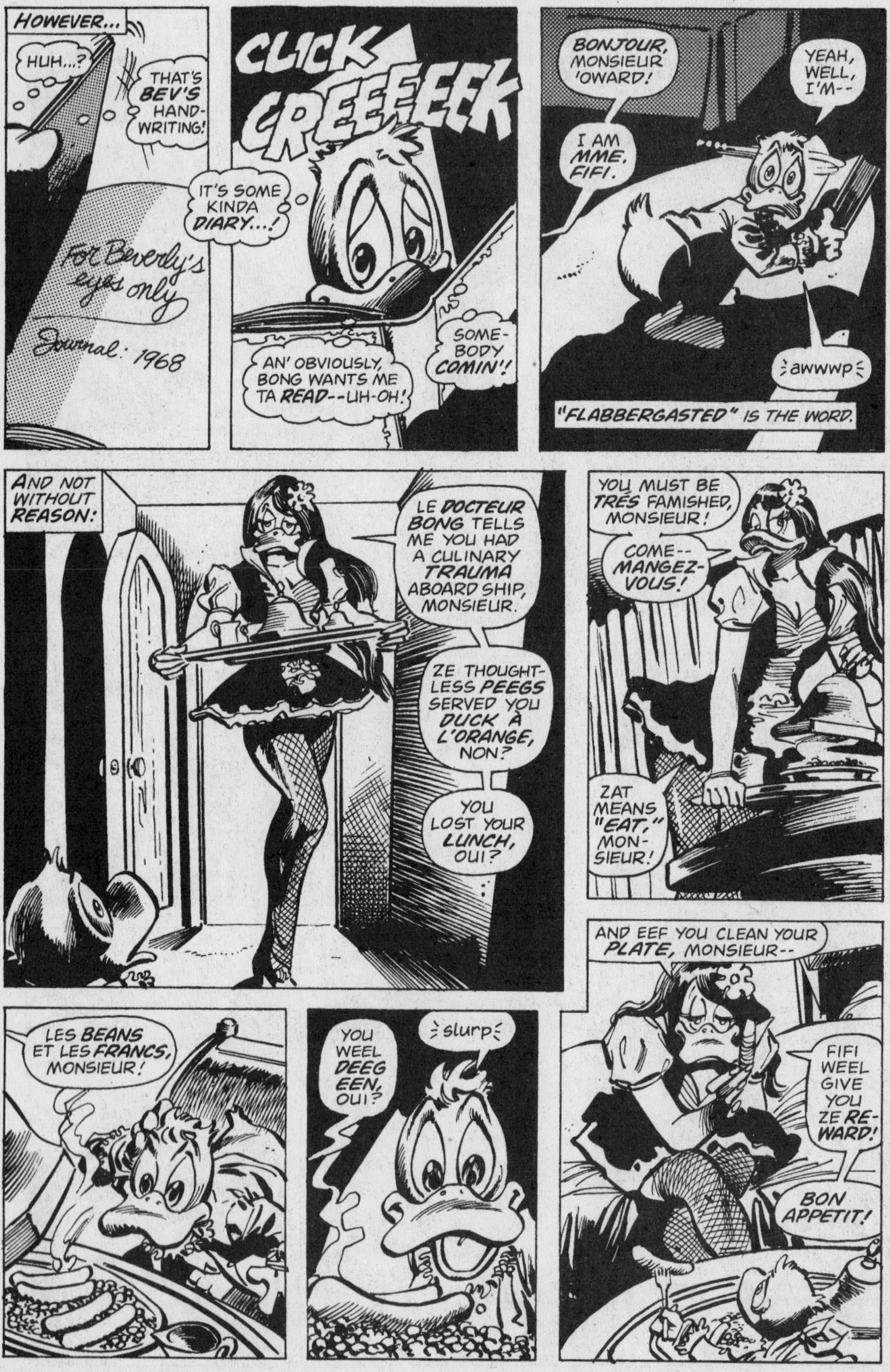
HOWEVER...
HUH...?
THAT'S BEV'S HAND-WRITING!
IT'S SOME KINDA DIARY...!
For Beverly's eyes only
Journal: 1968
AN' OBVIOUSLY, BONG WANTS ME TA READ--UH-OH!
CLICK
CREEEEEK
SOME-BODY COMIN'!
BONJOUR, MONSIEUR 'OWARD!
YEAH, WELL, I'M--
I AM MME. FIFI.
awwwp
"FLABBERGASTED" IS THE WORD.
AND NOT WITHOUT REASON:
LE DOCTEUR BONG TELLS ME YOU HAD A CULINARY TRAUMA ABOARD SHIP, MONSIEUR.
ZE THOUGHT-LESS PEEGS SERVED YOU DUCK À L'ORANGE, NON?
YOU LOST YOUR LUNCH, OUI?
YOU MUST BE TRÉS FAMISHED, MONSIEUR!
COME-- MANGEZ-VOUS!
ZAT MEANS "EAT," MON-SIEUR!
LES BEANS ET LES FRANCS, MONSIEUR!
YOU WEEL DEEG EEN, OUI?
slurp
AND EEF YOU CLEAN YOUR PLATE, MONSIEUR--
FIFI WEEL GIVE YOU ZE RE-WARD!
BON APPETIT!

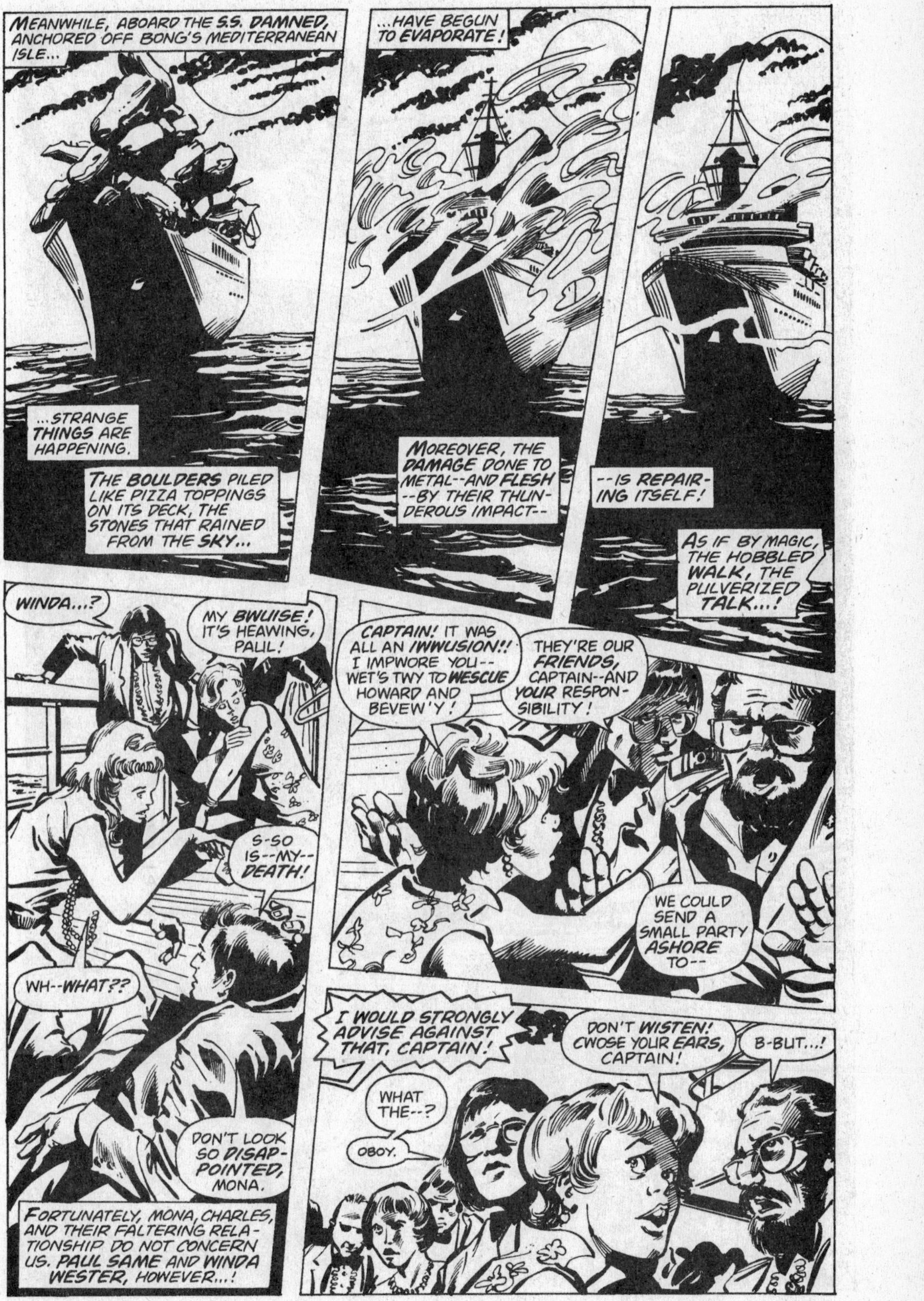
MEANWHILE, ABOARD THE S.S. DAMNED, ANCHORED OFF BONG'S MEDITERRANEAN ISLE...
...STRANGE THINGS ARE HAPPENING.
THE BOULDERS PILED LIKE PIZZA TOPPINGS ON ITS DECK, THE STONES THAT RAINED FROM THE SKY...
...HAVE BEGUN TO EVAPORATE!
MOREOVER, THE DAMAGE DONE TO METAL--AND FLESH--BY THEIR THUNDEROUS IMPACT--
--IS REPAIRING ITSELF!
AS IF BY MAGIC, THE HOBBLED WALK, THE PULVERIZED TALK...!
WINDA...?
MY BWUISE! IT'S HEAWING, PAUL!
S-SO IS--MY--DEATH!
WH--WHAT??
DON'T LOOK SO DISAPPOINTED, MONA.
FORTUNATELY, MONA, CHARLES, AND THEIR FALTERING RELATIONSHIP DO NOT CONCERN US. PAUL SAME AND WINDA WESTER, HOWEVER...!
CAPTAIN! IT WAS ALL AN IWWUSION!! I IMPWORE YOU--WET'S TWY TO WESCUE HOWARD AND BEVEW'Y!
THEY'RE OUR FRIENDS, CAPTAIN--AND YOUR RESPONSIBILITY!
WE COULD SEND A SMALL PARTY ASHORE TO--
I WOULD STRONGLY ADVISE AGAINST THAT, CAPTAIN!
DON'T WISTEN! CWOSE YOUR EARS, CAPTAIN!
B-BUT...!
WHAT THE--?
OBOY.

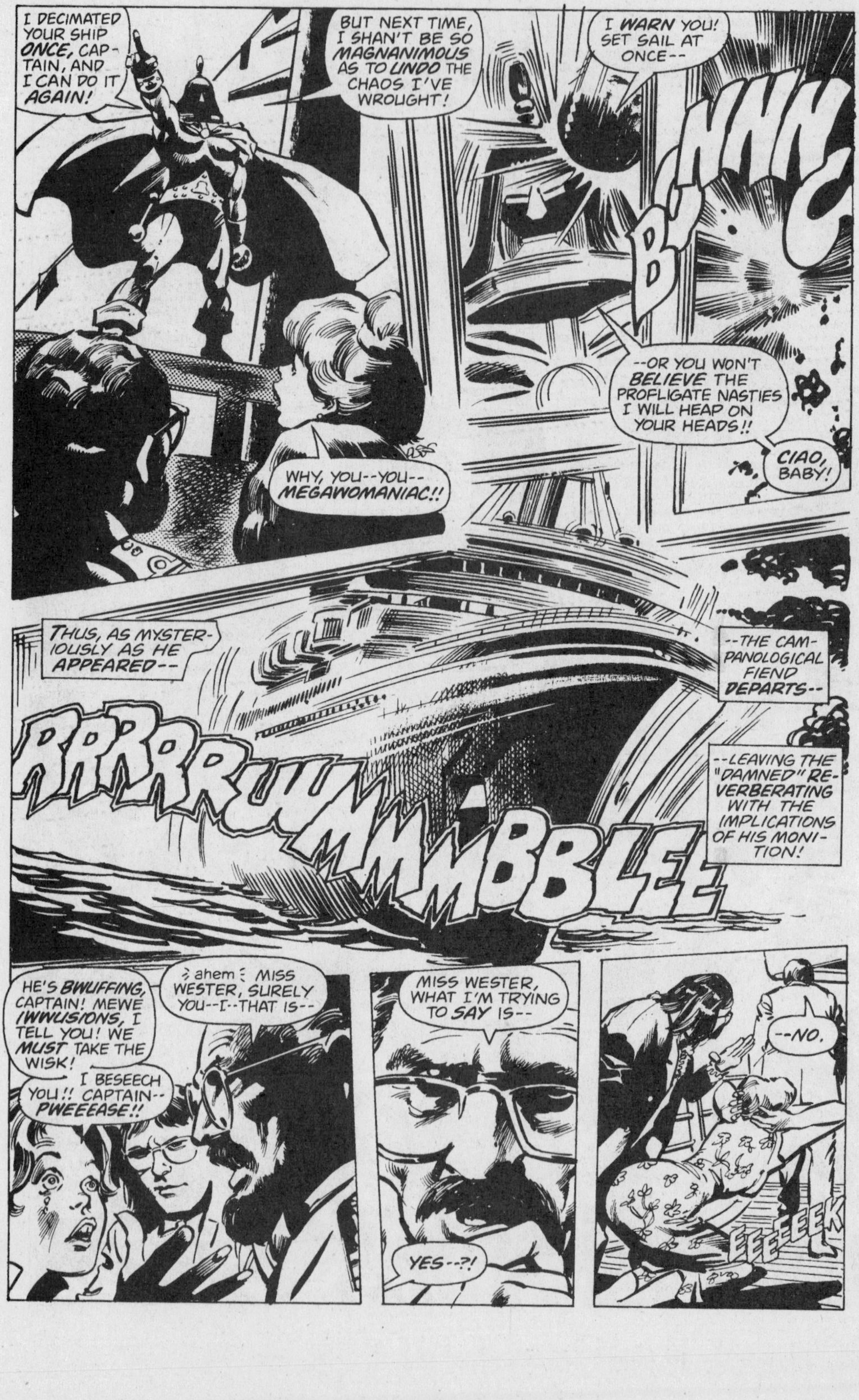
I DECIMATED YOUR SHIP ONCE, CAPTAIN, AND I CAN DO IT AGAIN!
BUT NEXT TIME, I SHAN'T BE SO MAGNANIMOUS AS TO UNDO THE CHAOS I'VE WROUGHT!
I WARN YOU! SET SAIL AT ONCE--
BONNNG
--OR YOU WON'T BELIEVE THE PROFLIGATE NASTIES I WILL HEAP ON YOUR HEADS!!
CIAO, BABY!
WHY, YOU--YOU--MEGAWOMANIAC!!
THUS, AS MYSTERIOUSLY AS HE APPEARED--
--THE CAMPANOLOGICAL FIEND DEPARTS--
RRRRRUUMMMMBBLEE
--LEAVING THE "DAMNED" REVERBERATING WITH THE IMPLICATIONS OF HIS MONITION!
HE'S BWUFFING, CAPTAIN! MEWE IWWUSIONS, I TELL YOU! WE MUST TAKE THE WISK!
ahem MISS WESTER, SURELY YOU--I--THAT IS--
I BESEECH YOU!! CAPTAIN--PWEEEASE!!
MISS WESTER, WHAT I'M TRYING TO SAY IS--
YES--?!
--NO.
EEEEEEK

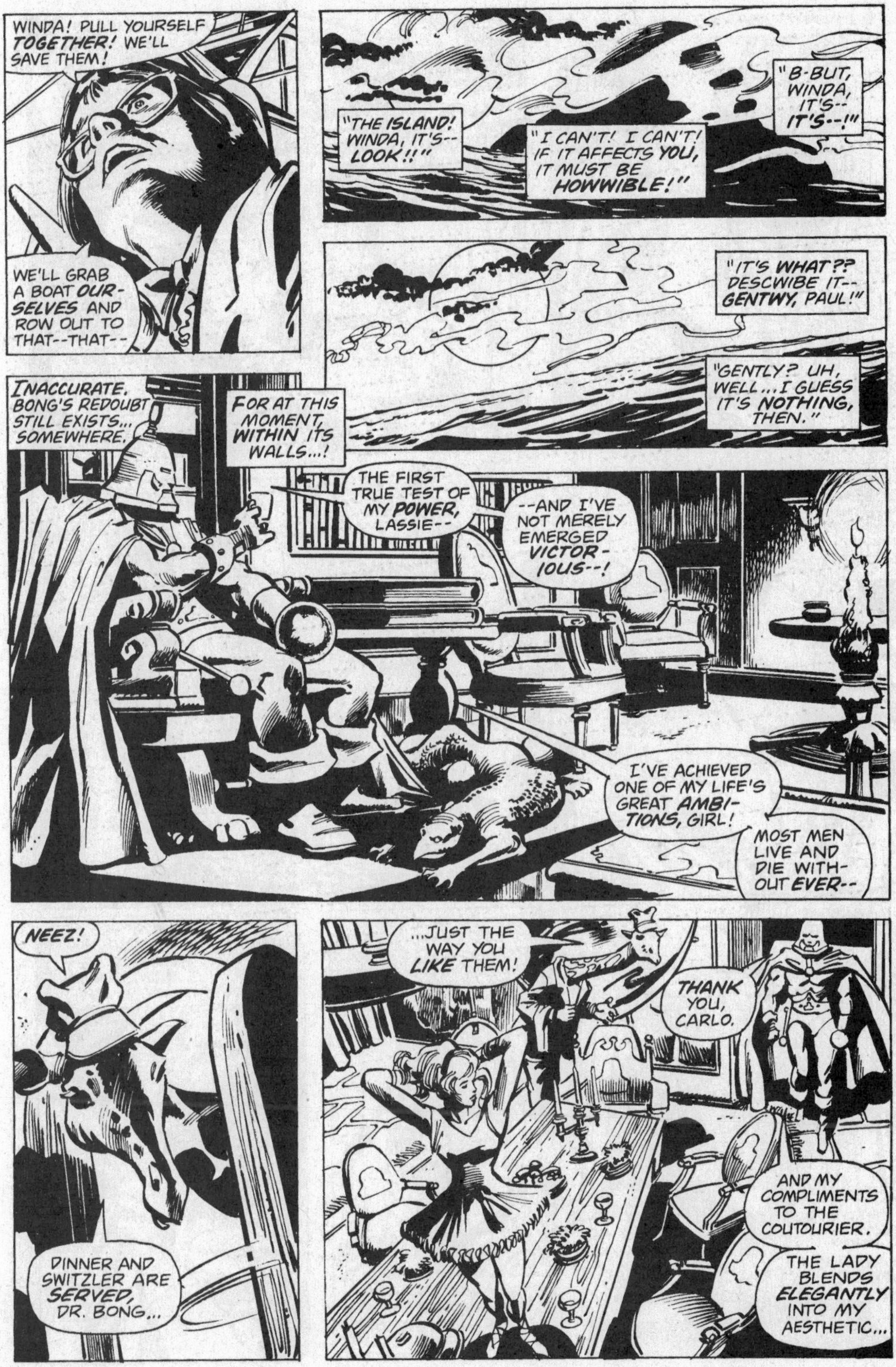

WINDA! PULL YOURSELF TOGETHER! WE'LL SAVE THEM!
WE'LL GRAB A BOAT OURSELVES AND ROW OUT TO THAT--THAT--
"THE ISLAND! WINDA, IT'S-- LOOK!!"
"I CAN'T! I CAN'T! IF IT AFFECTS YOU, IT MUST BE HOWWIBLE!"
"B-BUT, WINDA, IT'S-- IT'S--!"
"IT'S WHAT?? DESCWIBE IT-- GENTWY, PAUL!"
"GENTLY? UH, WELL... I GUESS IT'S NOTHING, THEN."
INACCURATE. BONG'S REDOUBT STILL EXISTS... SOMEWHERE.
FOR AT THIS MOMENT, WITHIN ITS WALLS...!
THE FIRST TRUE TEST OF MY POWER, LASSIE--
--AND I'VE NOT MERELY EMERGED VICTORIOUS--!
I'VE ACHIEVED ONE OF MY LIFE'S GREAT AMBITIONS, GIRL!
MOST MEN LIVE AND DIE WITHOUT EVER--
NEEZ!
DINNER AND SWITZLER ARE SERVED, DR. BONG...
...JUST THE WAY YOU LIKE THEM!
THANK YOU, CARLO.
AND MY COMPLIMENTS TO THE COUTOURIER.
THE LADY BLENDS ELEGANTLY INTO MY AESTHETIC...

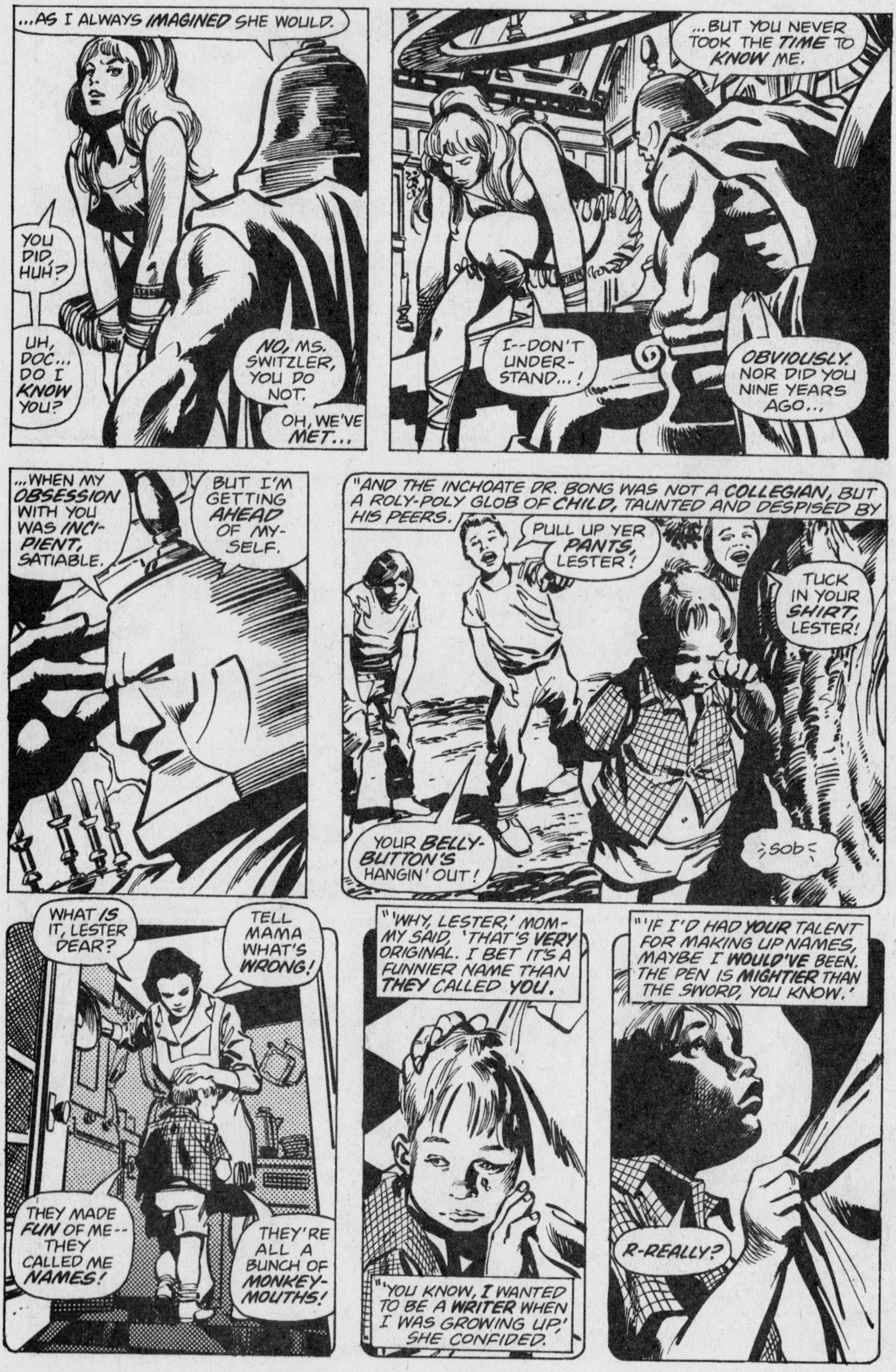

...AS I ALWAYS IMAGINED SHE WOULD.
YOU DID, HUH?
UH, DOC... DO I KNOW YOU?
NO, MS. SWITZLER, YOU DO NOT.
OH, WE'VE MET...
...BUT YOU NEVER TOOK THE TIME TO KNOW ME.
I--DON'T UNDER-STAND...!
OBVIOUSLY. NOR DID YOU NINE YEARS AGO...
...WHEN MY OBSESSION WITH YOU WAS INCI-PIENT, SATIABLE.
BUT I'M GETTING AHEAD OF MY-SELF.
"AND THE INCHOATE DR. BONG WAS NOT A COLLEGIAN, BUT A ROLY-POLY GLOB OF CHILD, TAUNTED AND DESPISED BY HIS PEERS.
PULL UP YER PANTS, LESTER!
TUCK IN YOUR SHIRT, LESTER!
YOUR BELLY-BUTTON'S HANGIN' OUT!
sob
WHAT IS IT, LESTER DEAR?
TELL MAMA WHAT'S WRONG!
THEY MADE FUN OF ME-- THEY CALLED ME NAMES!
THEY'RE ALL A BUNCH OF MONKEY-MOUTHS!
"'WHY, LESTER,' MOM-MY SAID, 'THAT'S VERY ORIGINAL. I BET IT'S A FUNNIER NAME THAN THEY CALLED YOU.
"'YOU KNOW, I WANTED TO BE A WRITER WHEN I WAS GROWING UP,' SHE CONFIDED.
"'IF I'D HAD YOUR TALENT FOR MAKING UP NAMES, MAYBE I WOULD'VE BEEN. THE PEN IS MIGHTIER THAN THE SWORD, YOU KNOW.'
R-REALLY?

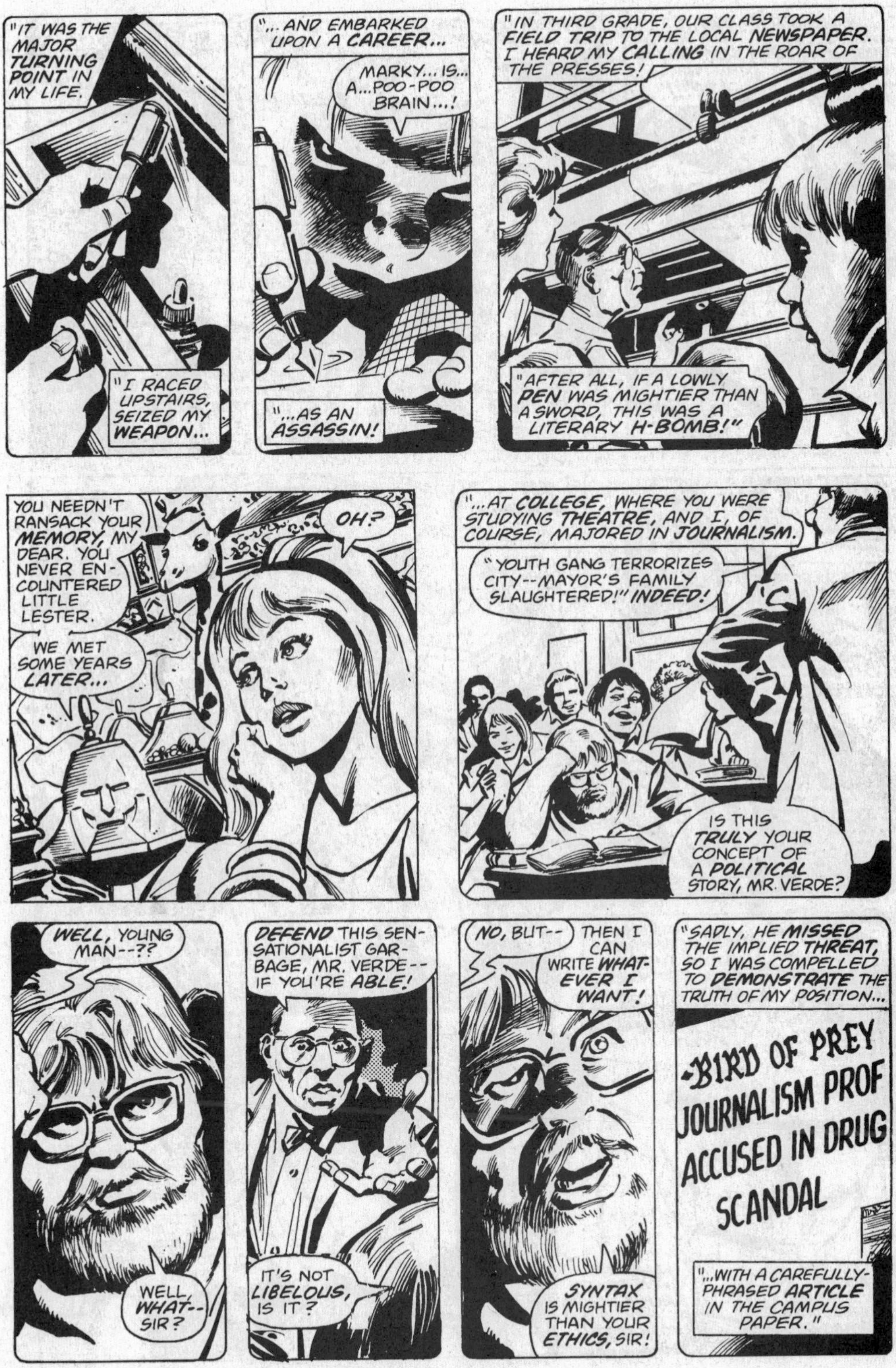
"IT WAS THE MAJOR TURNING POINT IN MY LIFE.
"I RACED UPSTAIRS, SEIZED MY WEAPON...
"...AND EMBARKED UPON A CAREER...
MARKY... IS... A...POO-POO BRAIN...!
"...AS AN ASSASSIN!
"IN THIRD GRADE, OUR CLASS TOOK A FIELD TRIP TO THE LOCAL NEWSPAPER. I HEARD MY CALLING IN THE ROAR OF THE PRESSES!
"AFTER ALL, IF A LOWLY PEN WAS MIGHTIER THAN A SWORD, THIS WAS A LITERARY H-BOMB!"
YOU NEEDN'T RANSACK YOUR MEMORY, MY DEAR. YOU NEVER ENCOUNTERED LITTLE LESTER.
OH?
WE MET SOME YEARS LATER...
"...AT COLLEGE, WHERE YOU WERE STUDYING THEATRE, AND I, OF COURSE, MAJORED IN JOURNALISM.
"YOUTH GANG TERRORIZES CITY--MAYOR'S FAMILY SLAUGHTERED!" INDEED!
IS THIS TRULY YOUR CONCEPT OF A POLITICAL STORY, MR. VERDE?
WELL, YOUNG MAN--??
WELL, WHAT--SIR?
DEFEND THIS SENSATIONALIST GARBAGE, MR. VERDE--IF YOU'RE ABLE!
IT'S NOT LIBELOUS, IS IT?
NO, BUT--
THEN I CAN WRITE WHATEVER I WANT!
SYNTAX IS MIGHTIER THAN YOUR ETHICS, SIR!
"SADLY, HE MISSED THE IMPLIED THREAT, SO I WAS COMPELLED TO DEMONSTRATE THE TRUTH OF MY POSITION...
BIRD OF PREY
JOURNALISM PROF ACCUSED IN DRUG SCANDAL
"...WITH A CAREFULLY-PHRASED ARTICLE IN THE CAMPUS PAPER."

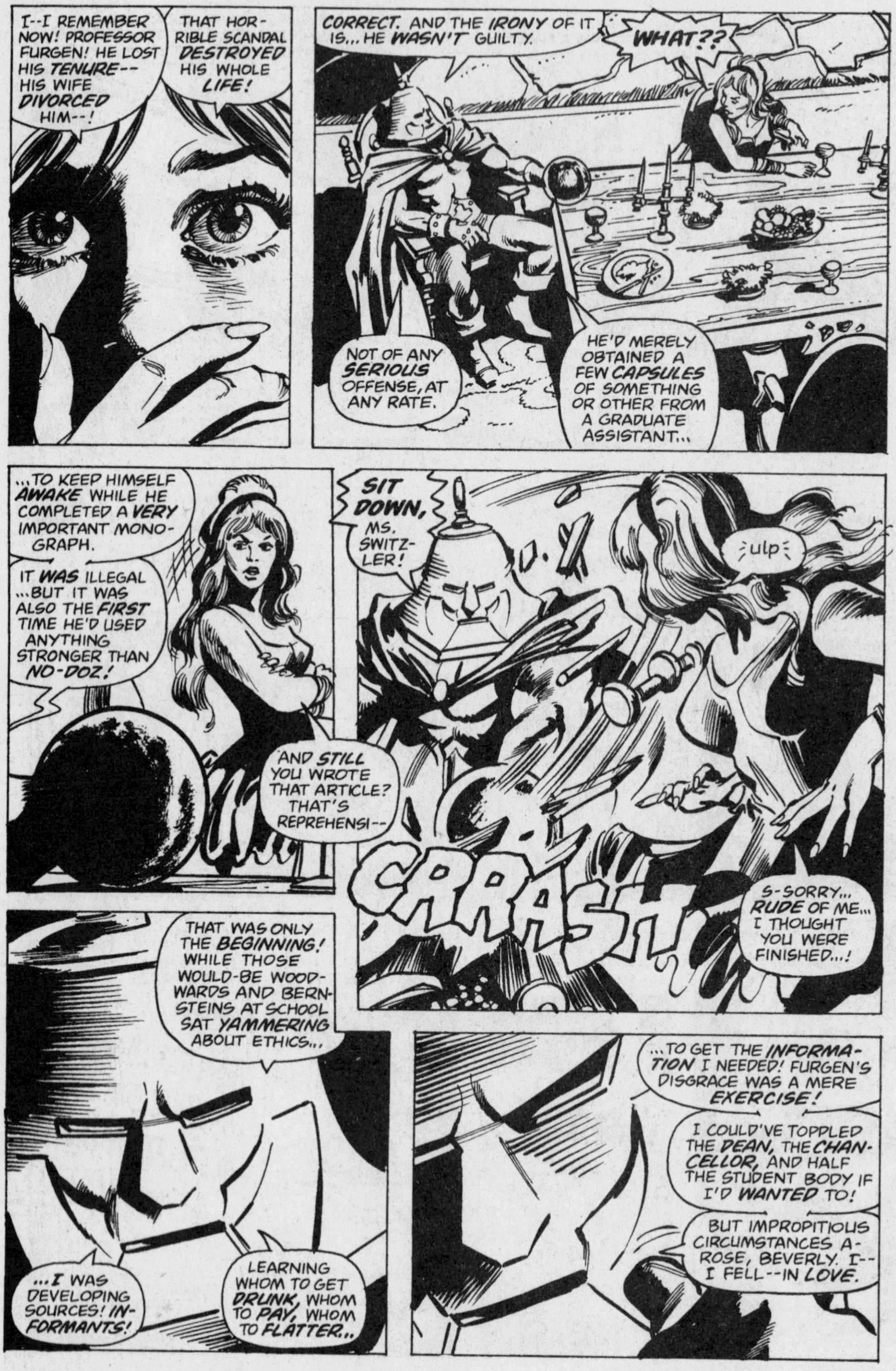
I--I REMEMBER NOW! PROFESSOR FURGEN! HE LOST HIS TENURE-- HIS WIFE DIVORCED HIM--!
THAT HORRIBLE SCANDAL DESTROYED HIS WHOLE LIFE!
CORRECT. AND THE IRONY OF IT IS... HE WASN'T GUILTY.
WHAT??
NOT OF ANY SERIOUS OFFENSE, AT ANY RATE.
HE'D MERELY OBTAINED A FEW CAPSULES OF SOMETHING OR OTHER FROM A GRADUATE ASSISTANT...
...TO KEEP HIMSELF AWAKE WHILE HE COMPLETED A VERY IMPORTANT MONOGRAPH.
IT WAS ILLEGAL ...BUT IT WAS ALSO THE FIRST TIME HE'D USED ANYTHING STRONGER THAN NO-DOZ!
AND STILL YOU WROTE THAT ARTICLE? THAT'S REPREHENSI--
SIT DOWN, MS. SWITZLER!
ulp
CRRASH!
S-SORRY... RUDE OF ME... I THOUGHT YOU WERE FINISHED...!
THAT WAS ONLY THE BEGINNING! WHILE THOSE WOULD-BE WOODWARDS AND BERNSTEINS AT SCHOOL SAT YAMMERING ABOUT ETHICS...
...I WAS DEVELOPING SOURCES! INFORMANTS!
LEARNING WHOM TO GET DRUNK, WHOM TO PAY, WHOM TO FLATTER...
...TO GET THE INFORMATION I NEEDED! FURGEN'S DISGRACE WAS A MERE EXERCISE!
I COULD'VE TOPPLED THE DEAN, THE CHANCELLOR, AND HALF THE STUDENT BODY IF I'D WANTED TO!
BUT IMPROPITIOUS CIRCUMSTANCES AROSE, BEVERLY. I-- I FELL--IN LOVE.

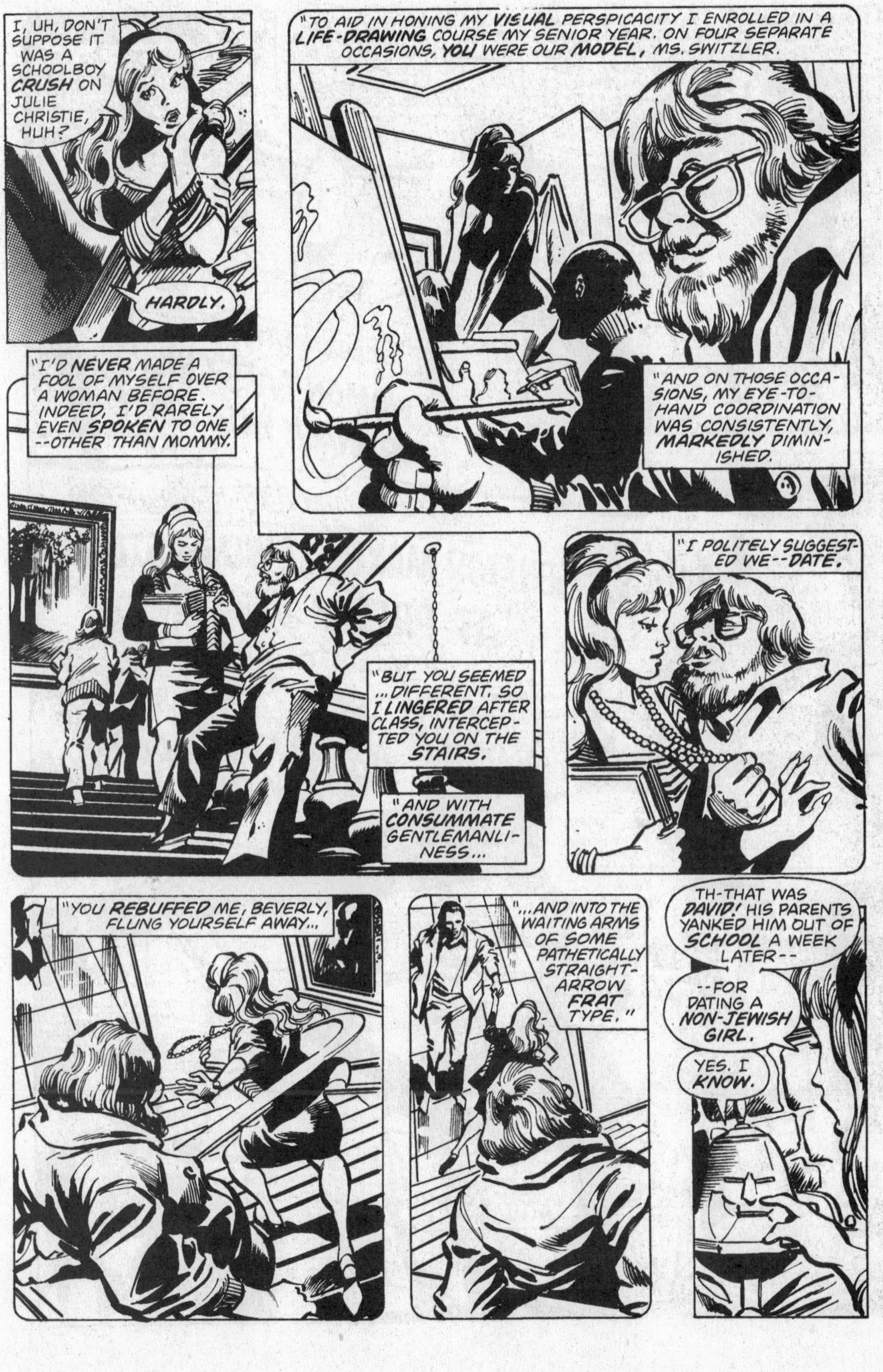
I, UH, DON'T SUPPOSE IT WAS A SCHOOLBOY CRUSH ON JULIE CHRISTIE, HUH?
HARDLY.
"TO AID IN HONING MY VISUAL PERSPICACITY I ENROLLED IN A LIFE-DRAWING COURSE MY SENIOR YEAR. ON FOUR SEPARATE OCCASIONS, YOU WERE OUR MODEL, MS. SWITZLER.
"AND ON THOSE OCCASIONS, MY EYE-TO-HAND COORDINATION WAS CONSISTENTLY, MARKEDLY DIMINISHED.
"I'D NEVER MADE A FOOL OF MYSELF OVER A WOMAN BEFORE. INDEED, I'D RARELY EVEN SPOKEN TO ONE --OTHER THAN MOMMY.
"BUT YOU SEEMED ...DIFFERENT, SO I LINGERED AFTER CLASS, INTERCEPTED YOU ON THE STAIRS.
"AND WITH CONSUMMATE GENTLEMANLINESS...
"I POLITELY SUGGESTED WE--DATE.
"YOU REBUFFED ME, BEVERLY, FLUNG YOURSELF AWAY...
"...AND INTO THE WAITING ARMS OF SOME PATHETICALLY STRAIGHT-ARROW FRAT TYPE."
TH-THAT WAS DAVID! HIS PARENTS YANKED HIM OUT OF SCHOOL A WEEK LATER--
--FOR DATING A NON-JEWISH GIRL.
YES. I KNOW.

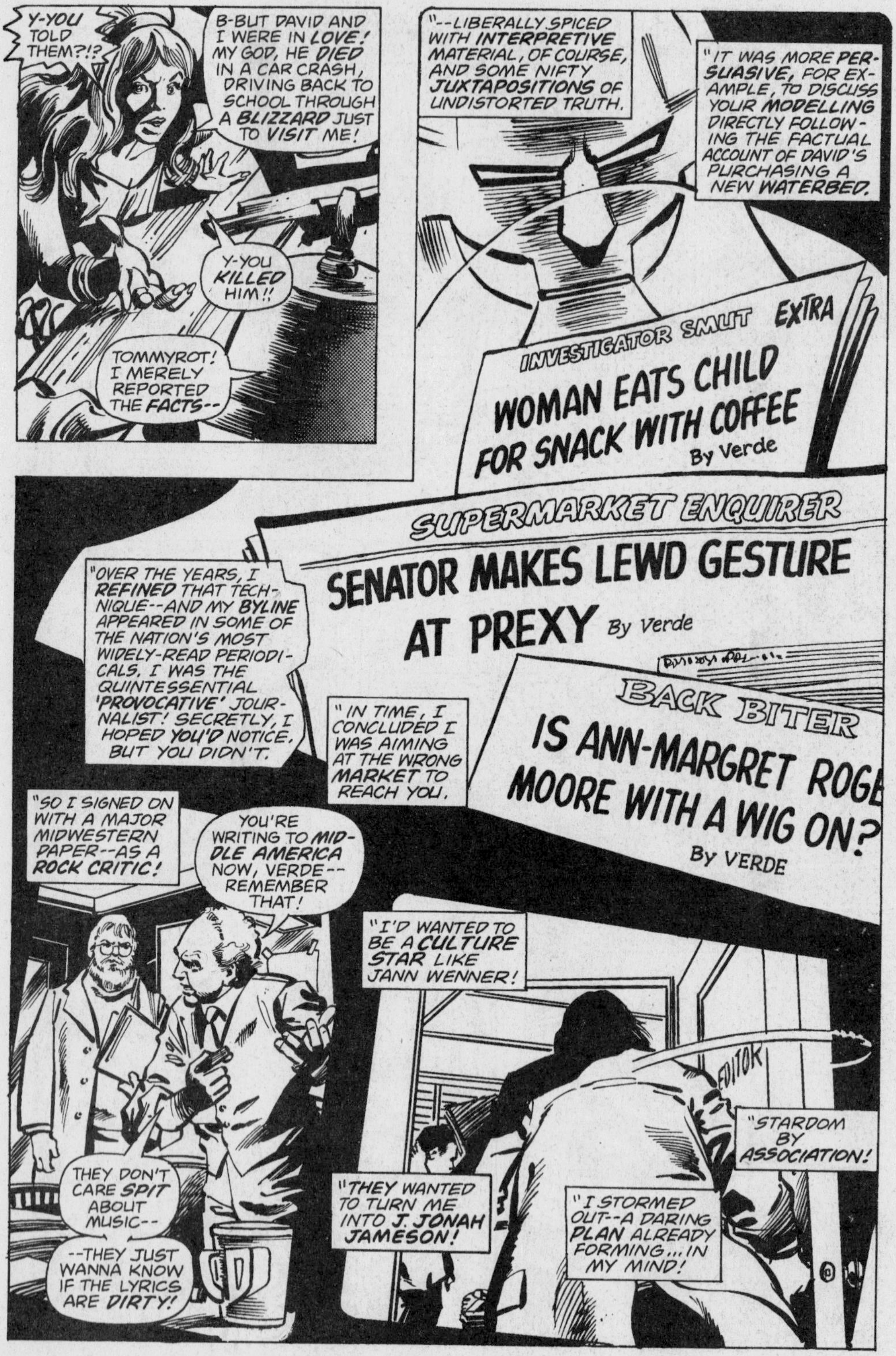

Y-YOU TOLD THEM?!?
B-BUT DAVID AND I WERE IN LOVE! MY GOD, HE DIED IN A CAR CRASH, DRIVING BACK TO SCHOOL THROUGH A BLIZZARD JUST TO VISIT ME!
Y-YOU KILLED HIM!!
TOMMYROT! I MERELY REPORTED THE FACTS--
"--LIBERALLY SPICED WITH INTERPRETIVE MATERIAL, OF COURSE, AND SOME NIFTY JUXTAPOSITIONS OF UNDISTORTED TRUTH.
"IT WAS MORE PERSUASIVE, FOR EXAMPLE, TO DISCUSS YOUR MODELLING DIRECTLY FOLLOWING THE FACTUAL ACCOUNT OF DAVID'S PURCHASING A NEW WATERBED.
INVESTIGATOR SMUT EXTRA
WOMAN EATS CHILD FOR SNACK WITH COFFEE
By Verde
SUPERMARKET ENQUIRER
SENATOR MAKES LEWD GESTURE AT PREXY
By Verde
"OVER THE YEARS, I REFINED THAT TECHNIQUE--AND MY BYLINE APPEARED IN SOME OF THE NATION'S MOST WIDELY-READ PERIODICALS. I WAS THE QUINTESSENTIAL 'PROVOCATIVE' JOURNALIST! SECRETLY, I HOPED YOU'D NOTICE. BUT YOU DIDN'T.
"IN TIME, I CONCLUDED I WAS AIMING AT THE WRONG MARKET TO REACH YOU.
BACK BITER
IS ANN-MARGRET ROGE MOORE WITH A WIG ON?
By VERDE
"SO I SIGNED ON WITH A MAJOR MIDWESTERN PAPER--AS A ROCK CRITIC!
YOU'RE WRITING TO MIDDLE AMERICA NOW, VERDE-- REMEMBER THAT!
THEY DON'T CARE SPIT ABOUT MUSIC--
--THEY JUST WANNA KNOW IF THE LYRICS ARE DIRTY!
"THEY WANTED TO TURN ME INTO J. JONAH JAMESON!
"I'D WANTED TO BE A CULTURE STAR LIKE JANN WENNER!
EDITOR
"STARDOM BY ASSOCIATION!
"I STORMED OUT--A DARING PLAN ALREADY FORMING... IN MY MIND!

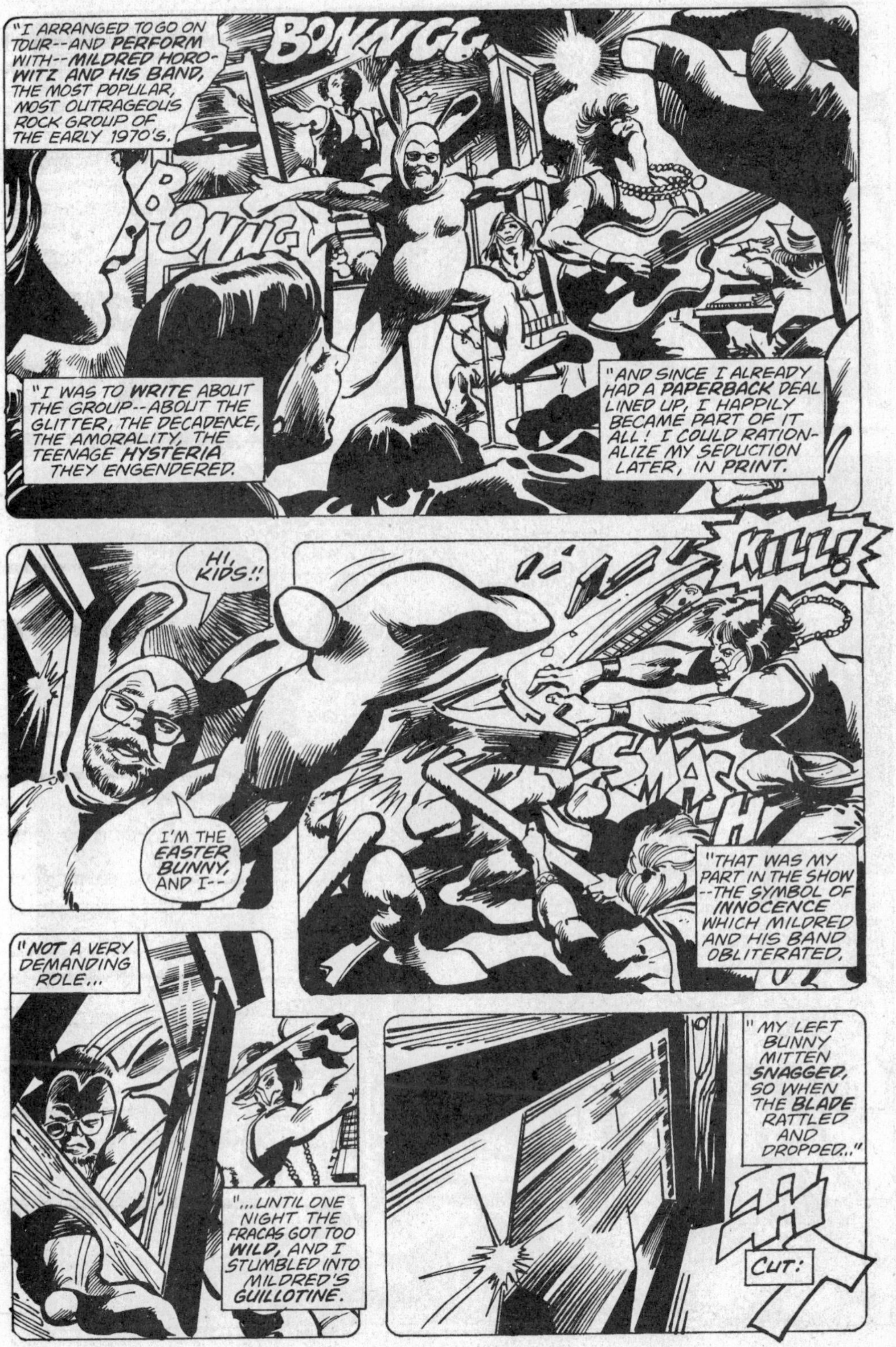
"I ARRANGED TO GO ON TOUR--AND PERFORM WITH--MILDRED HOROWITZ AND HIS BAND, THE MOST POPULAR, MOST OUTRAGEOUS ROCK GROUP OF THE EARLY 1970'S.
BONNGG
BONNG
"I WAS TO WRITE ABOUT THE GROUP--ABOUT THE GLITTER, THE DECADENCE, THE AMORALITY, THE TEENAGE HYSTERIA THEY ENGENDERED.
"AND SINCE I ALREADY HAD A PAPERBACK DEAL LINED UP, I HAPPILY BECAME PART OF IT ALL! I COULD RATIONALIZE MY SEDUCTION LATER, IN PRINT.
HI, KIDS!!
I'M THE EASTER BUNNY, AND I--
KILL!
SMASH
"THAT WAS MY PART IN THE SHOW --THE SYMBOL OF INNOCENCE WHICH MILDRED AND HIS BAND OBLITERATED.
"NOT A VERY DEMANDING ROLE...
"...UNTIL ONE NIGHT THE FRACAS GOT TOO WILD, AND I STUMBLED INTO MILDRED'S GUILLOTINE.
"MY LEFT BUNNY MITTEN SNAGGED, SO WHEN THE BLADE RATTLED AND DROPPED..."
CUT:

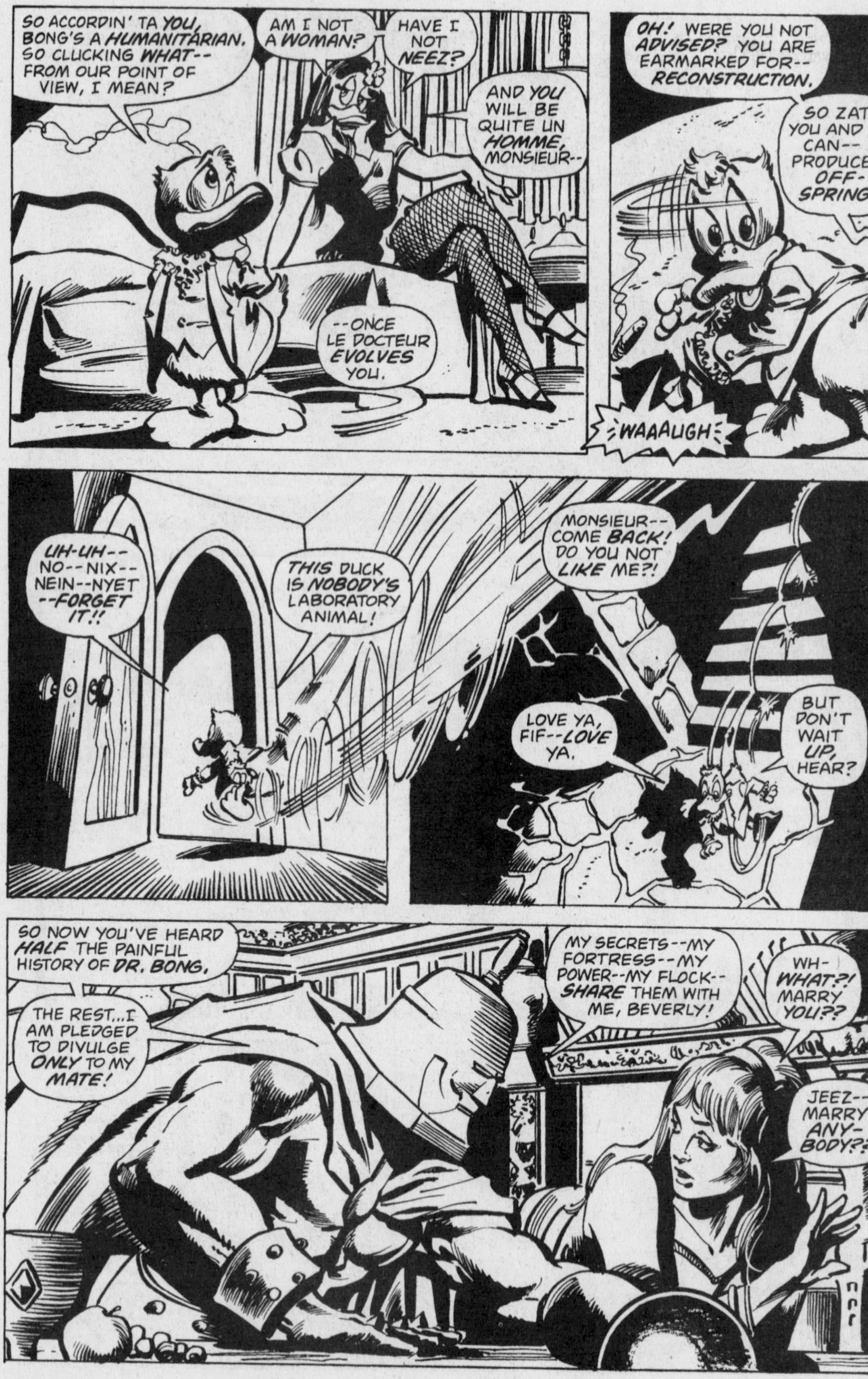
SO ACCORDIN' TA YOU, BONG'S A HUMANITARIAN. SO CLUCKING WHAT-- FROM OUR POINT OF VIEW, I MEAN?
AM I NOT A WOMAN?
HAVE I NOT NEEZ?
AND YOU WILL BE QUITE UN HOMME, MONSIEUR--
--ONCE LE DOCTEUR EVOLVES YOU.
OH! WERE YOU NOT ADVISED? YOU ARE EARMARKED FOR-- RECONSTRUCTION.
SO ZAT YOU AND I CAN-- PRODUCE OFF-SPRING.
WAAAUGH
UH-UH-- NO--NIX-- NEIN--NYET --FORGET IT!!
THIS DUCK IS NOBODY'S LABORATORY ANIMAL!
MONSIEUR-- COME BACK! DO YOU NOT LIKE ME?!
LOVE YA, FIF--LOVE YA.
BUT DON'T WAIT UP, HEAR?
SO NOW YOU'VE HEARD HALF THE PAINFUL HISTORY OF DR. BONG.
THE REST...I AM PLEDGED TO DIVULGE ONLY TO MY MATE!
MY SECRETS--MY FORTRESS--MY POWER--MY FLOCK-- SHARE THEM WITH ME, BEVERLY!
WH- WHAT?! MARRY YOU??
JEEZ-- MARRY ANY-BODY??
11

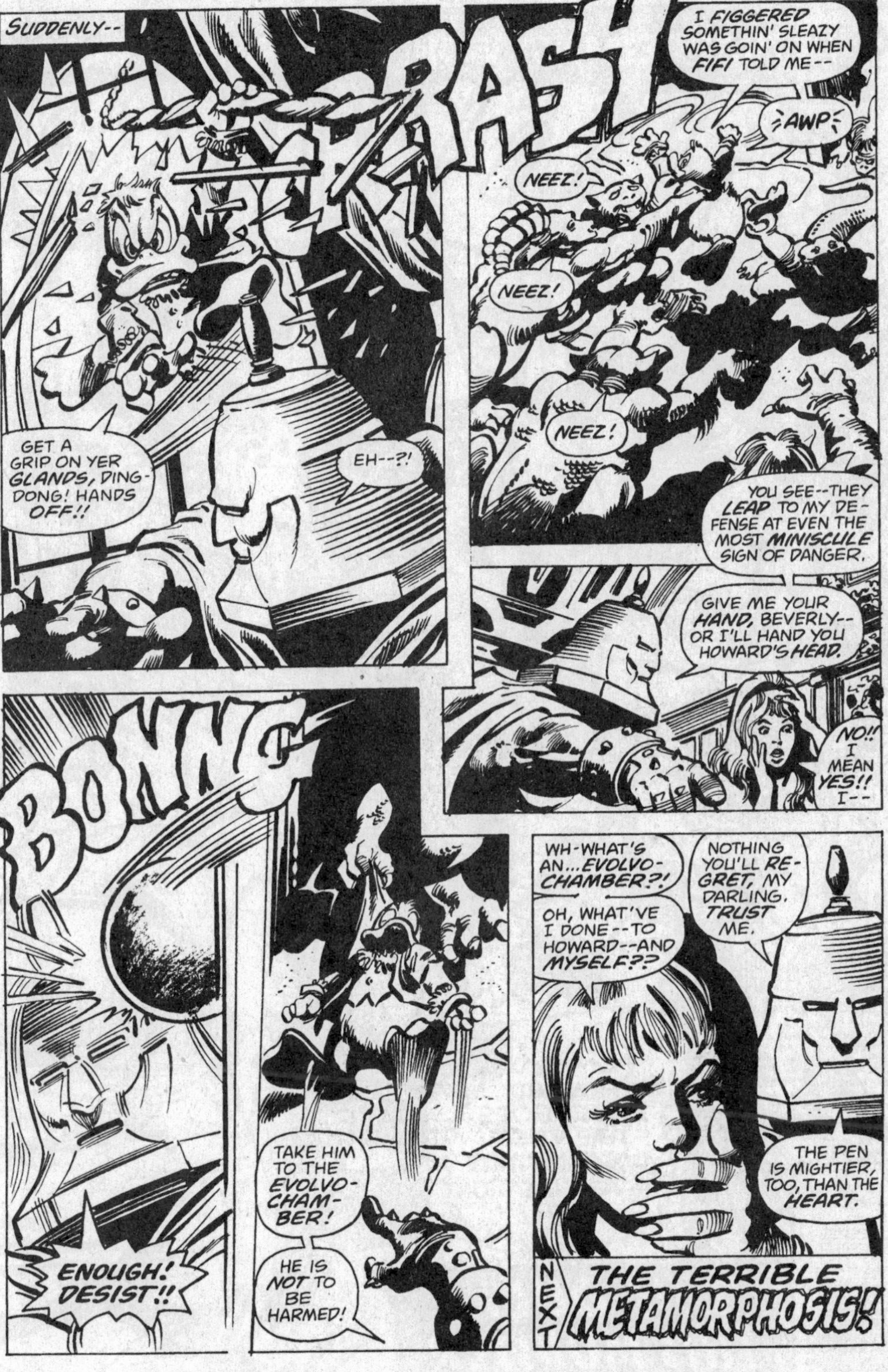
SUDDENLY--
CRASH
I FIGGERED SOMETHIN' SLEAZY WAS GOIN' ON WHEN FIFI TOLD ME--
AWP
NEEZ!
NEEZ!
NEEZ!
GET A GRIP ON YER GLANDS, DING-DONG! HANDS OFF!!
EH--?!
YOU SEE--THEY LEAP TO MY DEFENSE AT EVEN THE MOST MINISCULE SIGN OF DANGER.
GIVE ME YOUR HAND, BEVERLY--OR I'LL HAND YOU HOWARD'S HEAD.
NO!! I MEAN YES!! I--
BONNG
ENOUGH! DESIST!!
TAKE HIM TO THE EVOLVO-CHAMBER!
HE IS NOT TO BE HARMED!
WH-WHAT'S AN...EVOLVO-CHAMBER?!
NOTHING YOU'LL REGRET, MY DARLING. TRUST ME.
OH, WHAT'VE I DONE--TO HOWARD--AND MYSELF??
THE PEN IS MIGHTIER, TOO, THAN THE HEART.
NEXT THE TERRIBLE METAMORPHOSIS!

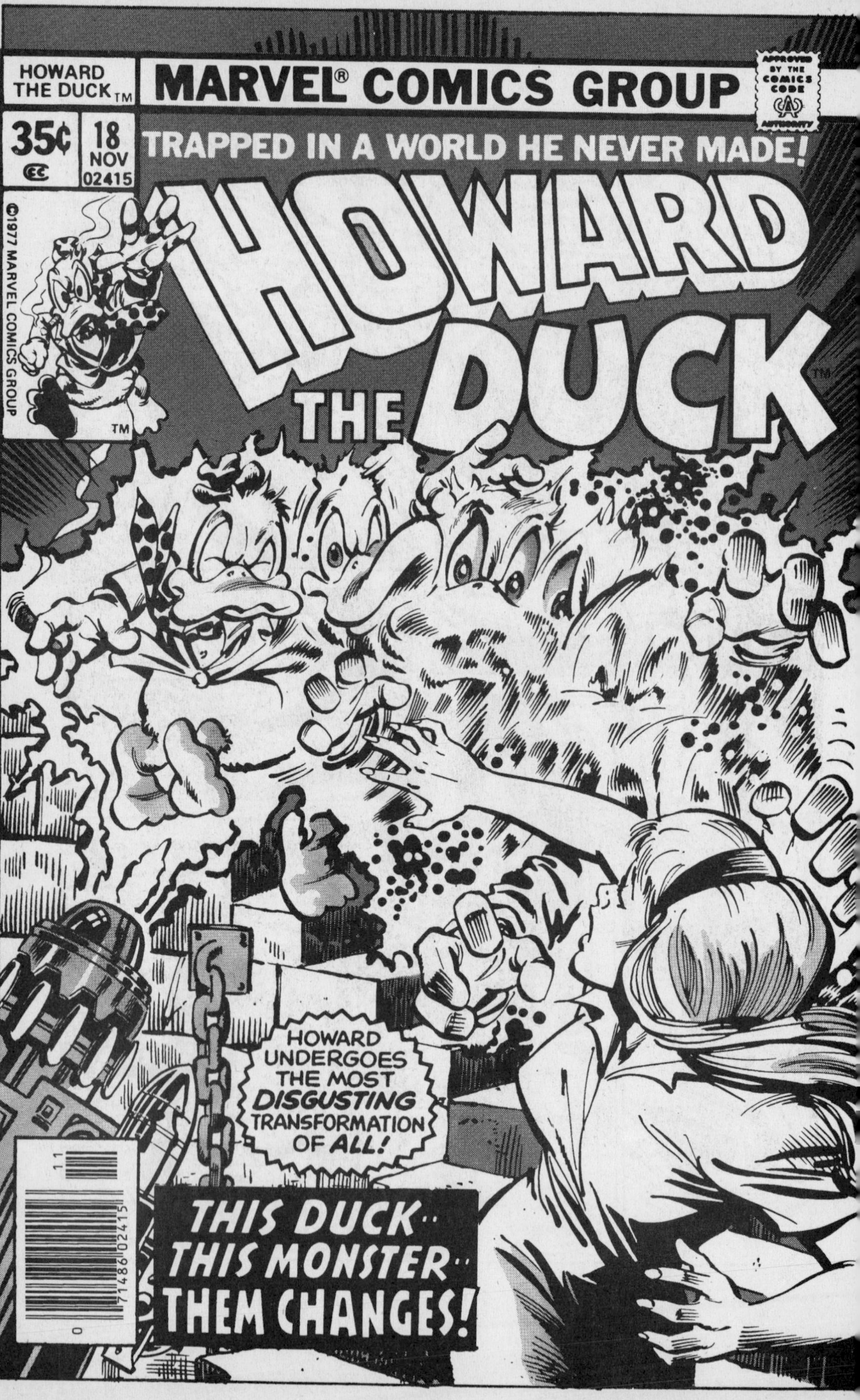

HOWARD THE DUCK TM
MARVEL® COMICS GROUP
APPROVED BY THE COMICS CODE AUTHORITY
35¢
18 NOV 02415
TRAPPED IN A WORLD HE NEVER MADE!
©1977 MARVEL COMICS GROUP
HOWARD THE DUCK TM
HOWARD UNDERGOES THE MOST DISGUSTING TRANSFORMATION OF ALL!
THIS DUCK.. THIS MONSTER.. THEM CHANGES!

From the time of his hatching, he was...different. A potentially brilliant scholar who dreaded the structured environment of school, he educated himself in the streets, taking whatever work was available, formulating his philosophy of self from what he learned of the world about him. And then the Cosmic Axis shifted...and that world *changed.* Suddenly, he was stranded in a universe he could not fathom. Without warning, he became a strange fowl in an even stranger land.

Stan Lee PRESENTS: HOWARD THE DUCK!™

STEVE GERBER WRITER/EDITOR • GENE COLAN ARTIST • KLAUS JANSON INKER • IRV WATANABE LETTERER • JAN COHEN COLORIST

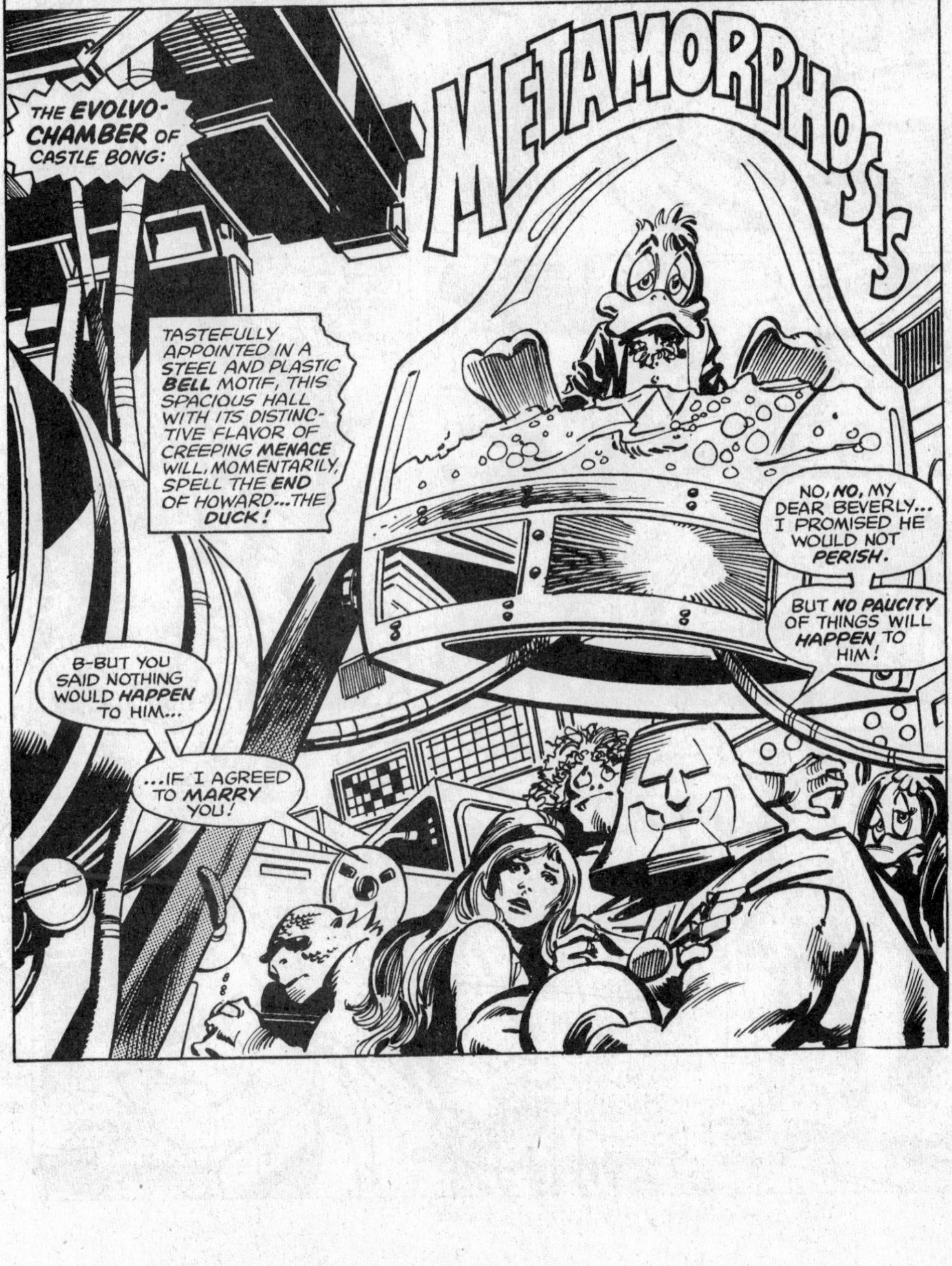

THE EVOLVO-CHAMBER OF CASTLE BONG:
METAMORPHOSIS
TASTEFULLY APPOINTED IN A STEEL AND PLASTIC BELL MOTIF, THIS SPACIOUS HALL WITH ITS DISTINCTIVE FLAVOR OF CREEPING MENACE WILL, MOMENTARILY, SPELL THE END OF HOWARD...THE DUCK!
B-BUT YOU SAID NOTHING WOULD HAPPEN TO HIM...
...IF I AGREED TO MARRY YOU!
NO, NO, MY DEAR BEVERLY... I PROMISED HE WOULD NOT PERISH.
BUT NO PAUCITY OF THINGS WILL HAPPEN TO HIM!

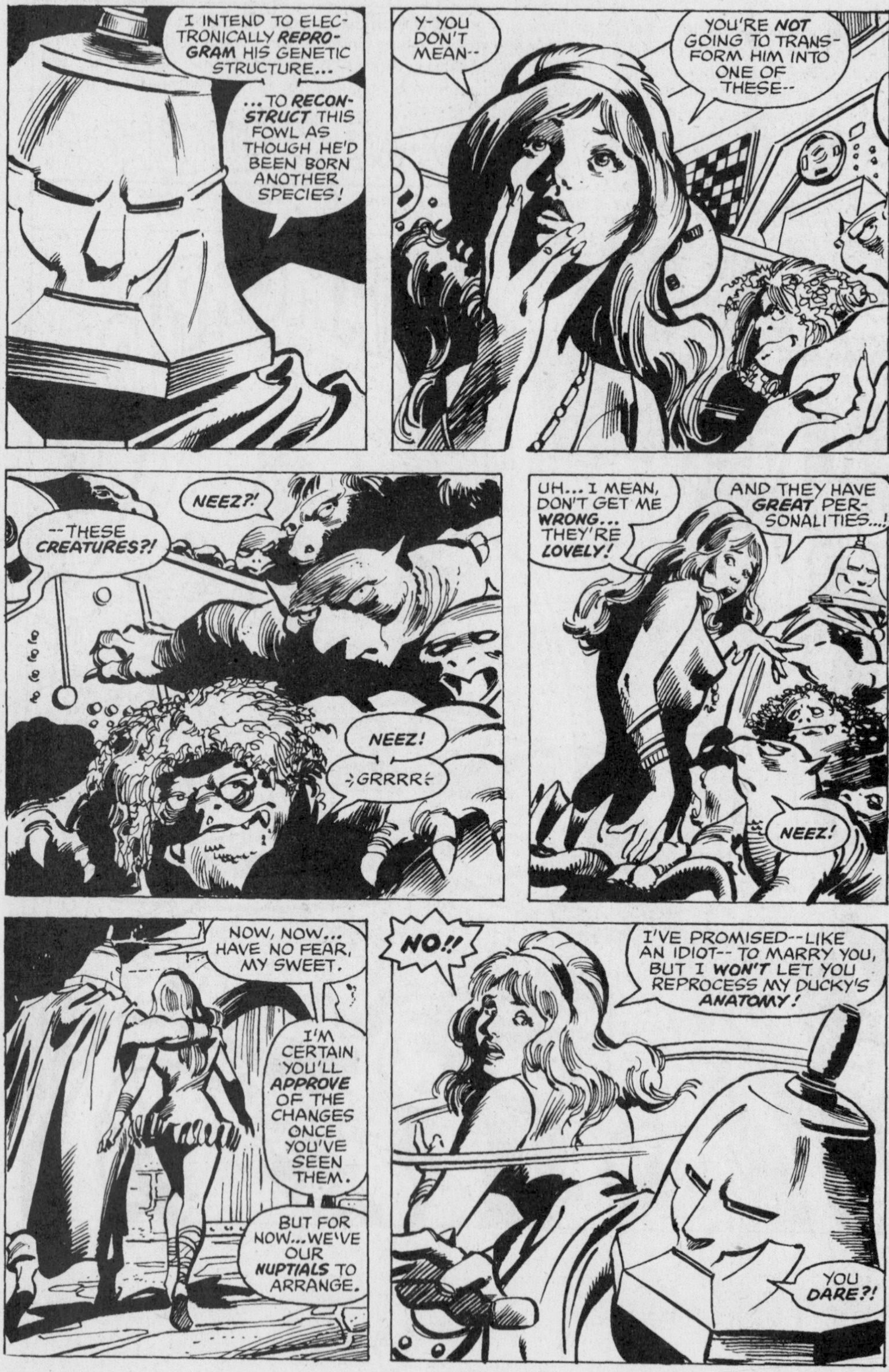
I INTEND TO ELECTRONICALLY REPROGRAM HIS GENETIC STRUCTURE...
...TO RECONSTRUCT THIS FOWL AS THOUGH HE'D BEEN BORN ANOTHER SPECIES!
Y-YOU DON'T MEAN--
YOU'RE NOT GOING TO TRANSFORM HIM INTO ONE OF THESE--
--THESE CREATURES?!
NEEZ?!
NEEZ!
GRRRR
UH... I MEAN, DON'T GET ME WRONG... THEY'RE LOVELY!
AND THEY HAVE GREAT PERSONALITIES...!
NEEZ!
NOW, NOW... HAVE NO FEAR, MY SWEET.
I'M CERTAIN YOU'LL APPROVE OF THE CHANGES ONCE YOU'VE SEEN THEM.
BUT FOR NOW...WE'VE OUR NUPTIALS TO ARRANGE.
NO!!
I'VE PROMISED--LIKE AN IDIOT-- TO MARRY YOU, BUT I WON'T LET YOU REPROCESS MY DUCKY'S ANATOMY!
YOU DARE?!

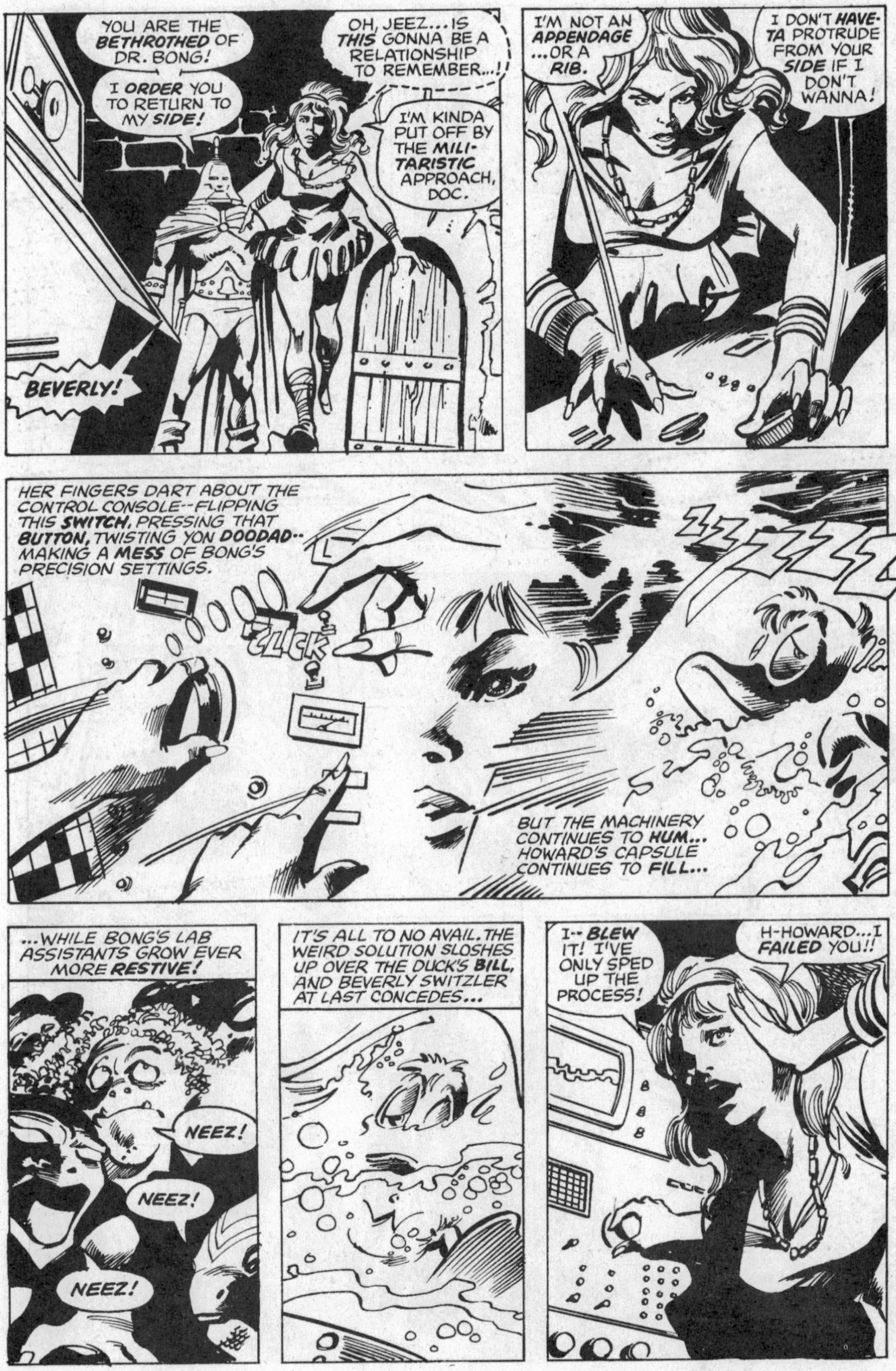
YOU ARE THE BETHROTHED OF DR. BONG!
I ORDER YOU TO RETURN TO MY SIDE!
BEVERLY!
OH, JEEZ...IS THIS GONNA BE A RELATIONSHIP TO REMEMBER...!
I'M KINDA PUT OFF BY THE MILI-TARISTIC APPROACH, DOC.
I'M NOT AN APPENDAGE ...OR A RIB.
I DON'T HAVE-TA PROTRUDE FROM YOUR SIDE IF I DON'T WANNA!
HER FINGERS DART ABOUT THE CONTROL CONSOLE--FLIPPING THIS SWITCH, PRESSING THAT BUTTON, TWISTING YON DOODAD-- MAKING A MESS OF BONG'S PRECISION SETTINGS.
CLICK
ZZZZZZ
BUT THE MACHINERY CONTINUES TO HUM... HOWARD'S CAPSULE CONTINUES TO FILL...
...WHILE BONG'S LAB ASSISTANTS GROW EVER MORE RESTIVE!
NEEZ!
NEEZ!
NEEZ!
IT'S ALL TO NO AVAIL. THE WEIRD SOLUTION SLOSHES UP OVER THE DUCK'S BILL, AND BEVERLY SWITZLER AT LAST CONCEDES...
I-- BLEW IT! I'VE ONLY SPED UP THE PROCESS!
H-HOWARD...I FAILED YOU!!

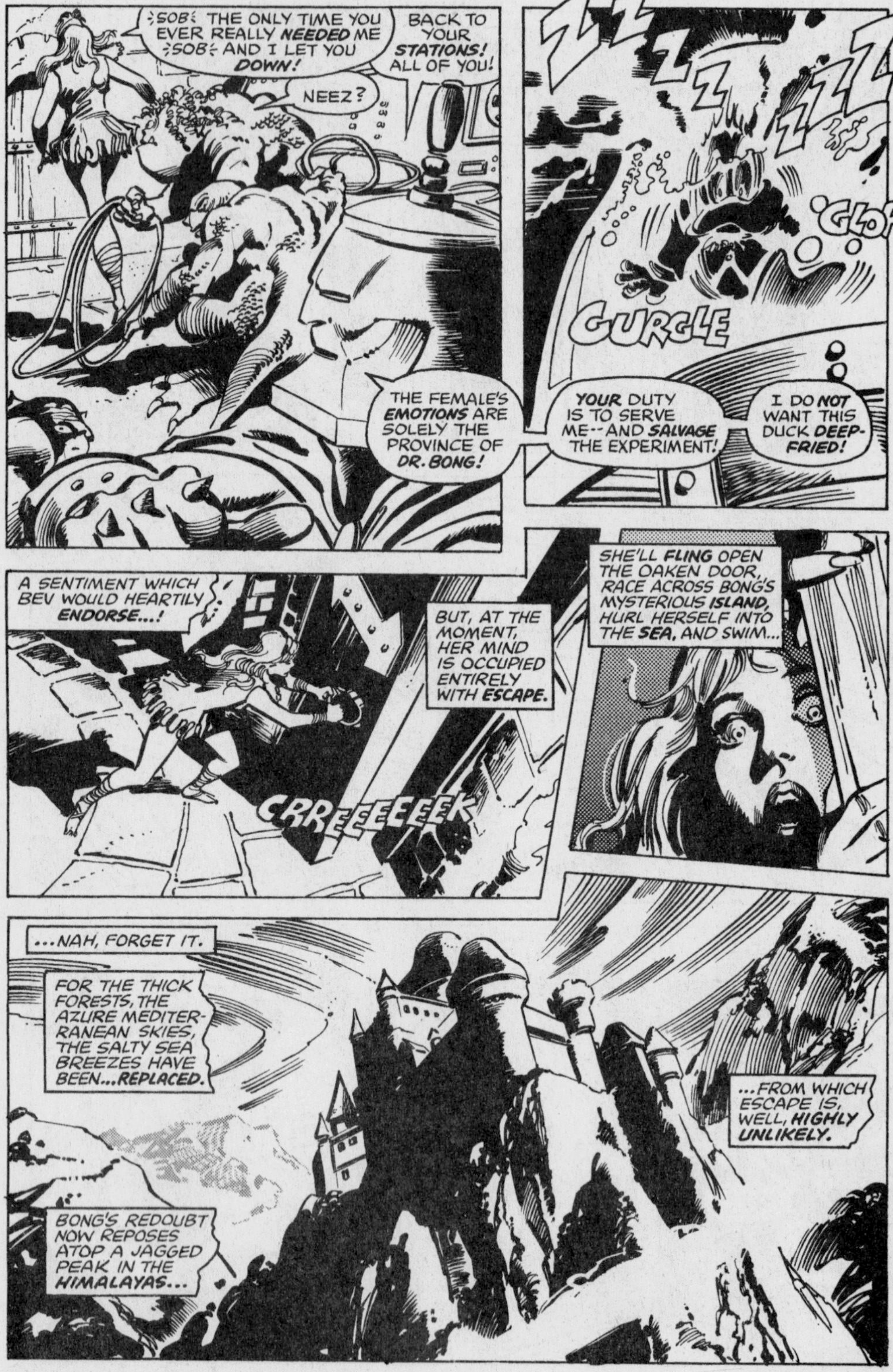

-SOB- THE ONLY TIME YOU EVER REALLY NEEDED ME -SOB- AND I LET YOU DOWN!
NEEZ?
BACK TO YOUR STATIONS! ALL OF YOU!
THE FEMALE'S EMOTIONS ARE SOLELY THE PROVINCE OF DR. BONG!
ZZZZZZZZ
GLOP
GURGLE
YOUR DUTY IS TO SERVE ME--AND SALVAGE THE EXPERIMENT!
I DO NOT WANT THIS DUCK DEEP-FRIED!
A SENTIMENT WHICH BEV WOULD HEARTILY ENDORSE...!
BUT, AT THE MOMENT, HER MIND IS OCCUPIED ENTIRELY WITH ESCAPE.
CRREEEEEEK
SHE'LL FLING OPEN THE OAKEN DOOR, RACE ACROSS BONG'S MYSTERIOUS ISLAND, HURL HERSELF INTO THE SEA, AND SWIM...
...NAH, FORGET IT.
FOR THE THICK FORESTS, THE AZURE MEDITER-RANEAN SKIES, THE SALTY SEA BREEZES HAVE BEEN...REPLACED.
...FROM WHICH ESCAPE IS, WELL, HIGHLY UNLIKELY.
BONG'S REDOUBT NOW REPOSES ATOP A JAGGED PEAK IN THE HIMALAYAS...

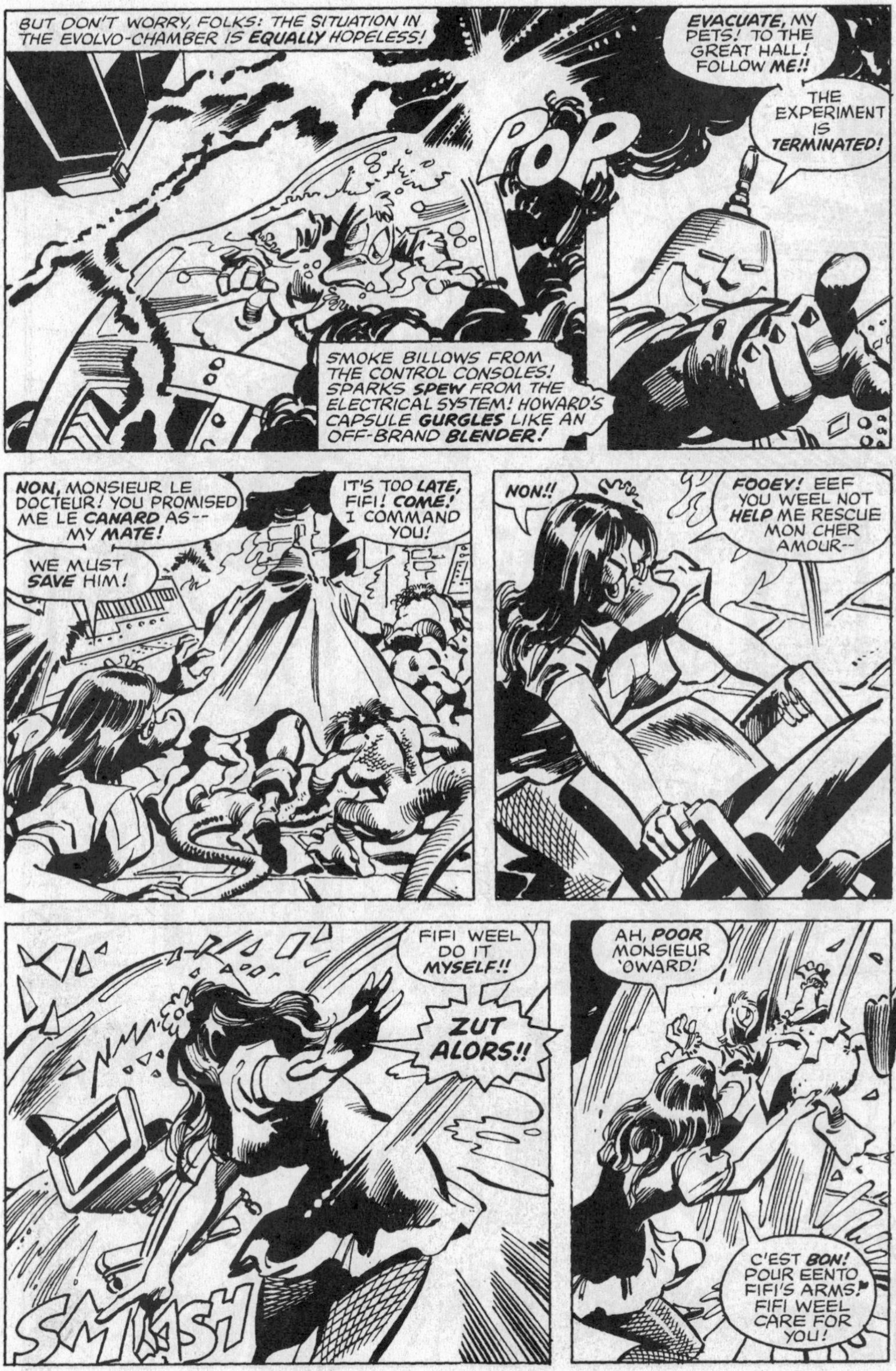
BUT DON'T WORRY, FOLKS: THE SITUATION IN THE EVOLVO-CHAMBER IS EQUALLY HOPELESS!
POP
SMOKE BILLOWS FROM THE CONTROL CONSOLES! SPARKS SPEW FROM THE ELECTRICAL SYSTEM! HOWARD'S CAPSULE GURGLES LIKE AN OFF-BRAND BLENDER!
EVACUATE, MY PETS! TO THE GREAT HALL! FOLLOW ME!!
THE EXPERIMENT IS TERMINATED!
NON, MONSIEUR LE DOCTEUR! YOU PROMISED ME LE CANARD AS-- MY MATE!
WE MUST SAVE HIM!
IT'S TOO LATE, FIFI! COME! I COMMAND YOU!
NON!!
FOOEY! EEF YOU WEEL NOT HELP ME RESCUE MON CHER AMOUR--
FIFI WEEL DO IT MYSELF!!
ZUT ALORS!!
SMASH
AH, POOR MONSIEUR 'OWARD!
C'EST BON! POUR EENTO FIFI'S ARMS! FIFI WEEL CARE FOR YOU!

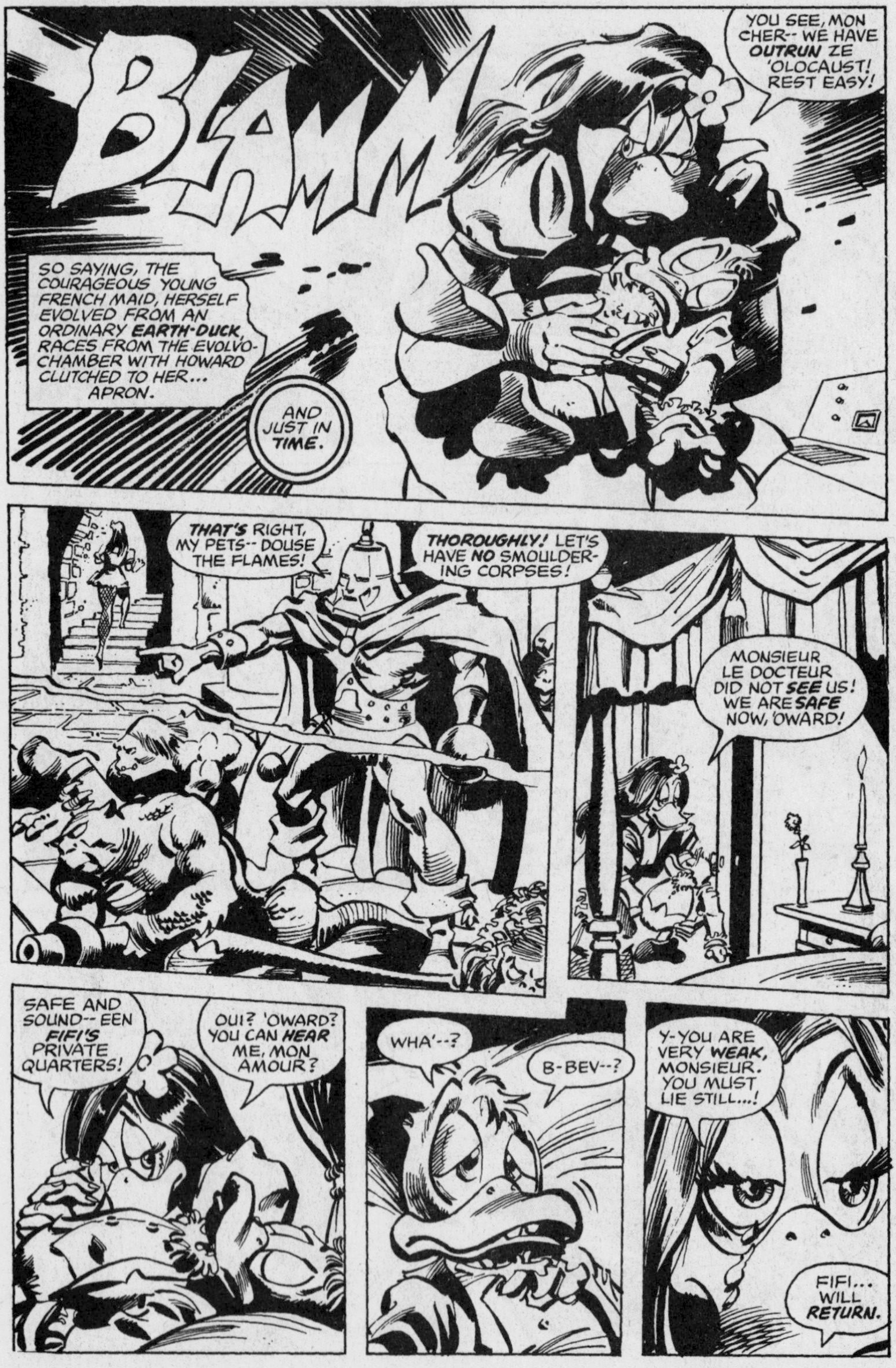
BLAMM
YOU SEE, MON CHER-- WE HAVE OUTRUN ZE 'OLOCAUST! REST EASY!
SO SAYING, THE COURAGEOUS YOUNG FRENCH MAID, HERSELF EVOLVED FROM AN ORDINARY EARTH-DUCK, RACES FROM THE EVOLVO-CHAMBER WITH HOWARD CLUTCHED TO HER... APRON.
AND JUST IN TIME.
THAT'S RIGHT, MY PETS-- DOUSE THE FLAMES!
THOROUGHLY! LET'S HAVE NO SMOULDERING CORPSES!
MONSIEUR LE DOCTEUR DID NOT SEE US! WE ARE SAFE NOW, 'OWARD!
SAFE AND SOUND-- EEN FIFI'S PRIVATE QUARTERS!
OUI? 'OWARD? YOU CAN HEAR ME, MON AMOUR?
WHA'--?
B-BEV--?
Y-YOU ARE VERY WEAK, MONSIEUR. YOU MUST LIE STILL...!
FIFI... WILL RETURN.

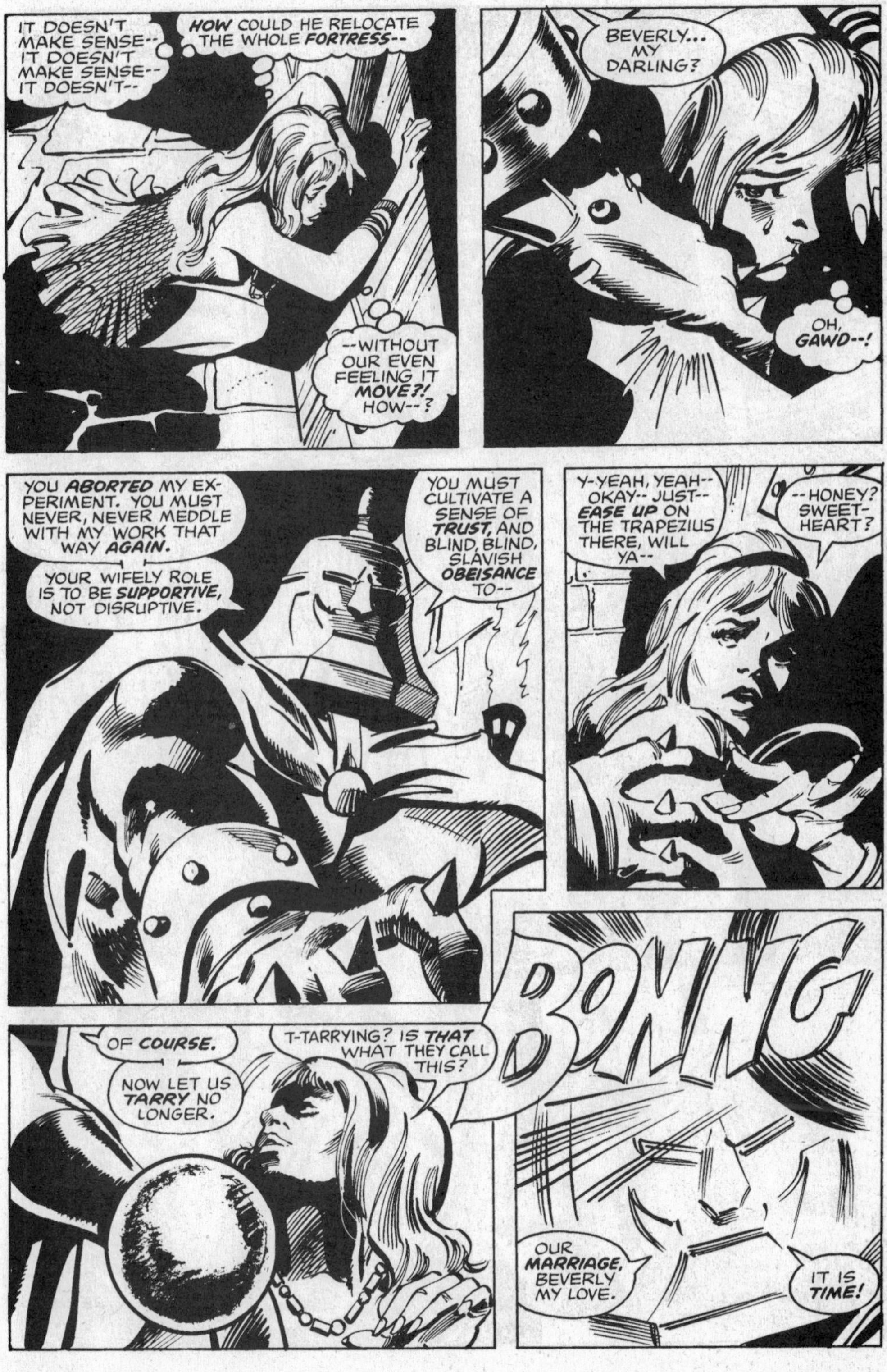
IT DOESN'T MAKE SENSE-- IT DOESN'T MAKE SENSE-- IT DOESN'T--
HOW COULD HE RELOCATE THE WHOLE FORTRESS--
--WITHOUT OUR EVEN FEELING IT MOVE?! HOW--?
BEVERLY... MY DARLING?
OH, GAWD--!
YOU ABORTED MY EXPERIMENT. YOU MUST NEVER, NEVER MEDDLE WITH MY WORK THAT WAY AGAIN.
YOUR WIFELY ROLE IS TO BE SUPPORTIVE, NOT DISRUPTIVE.
YOU MUST CULTIVATE A SENSE OF TRUST, AND BLIND, BLIND, SLAVISH OBEISANCE TO--
Y-YEAH, YEAH-- OKAY-- JUST-- EASE UP ON THE TRAPEZIUS THERE, WILL YA--
--HONEY? SWEET-HEART?
OF COURSE.
NOW LET US TARRY NO LONGER.
T-TARRYING? IS THAT WHAT THEY CALL THIS?
BONNG
OUR MARRIAGE, BEVERLY MY LOVE.
IT IS TIME!

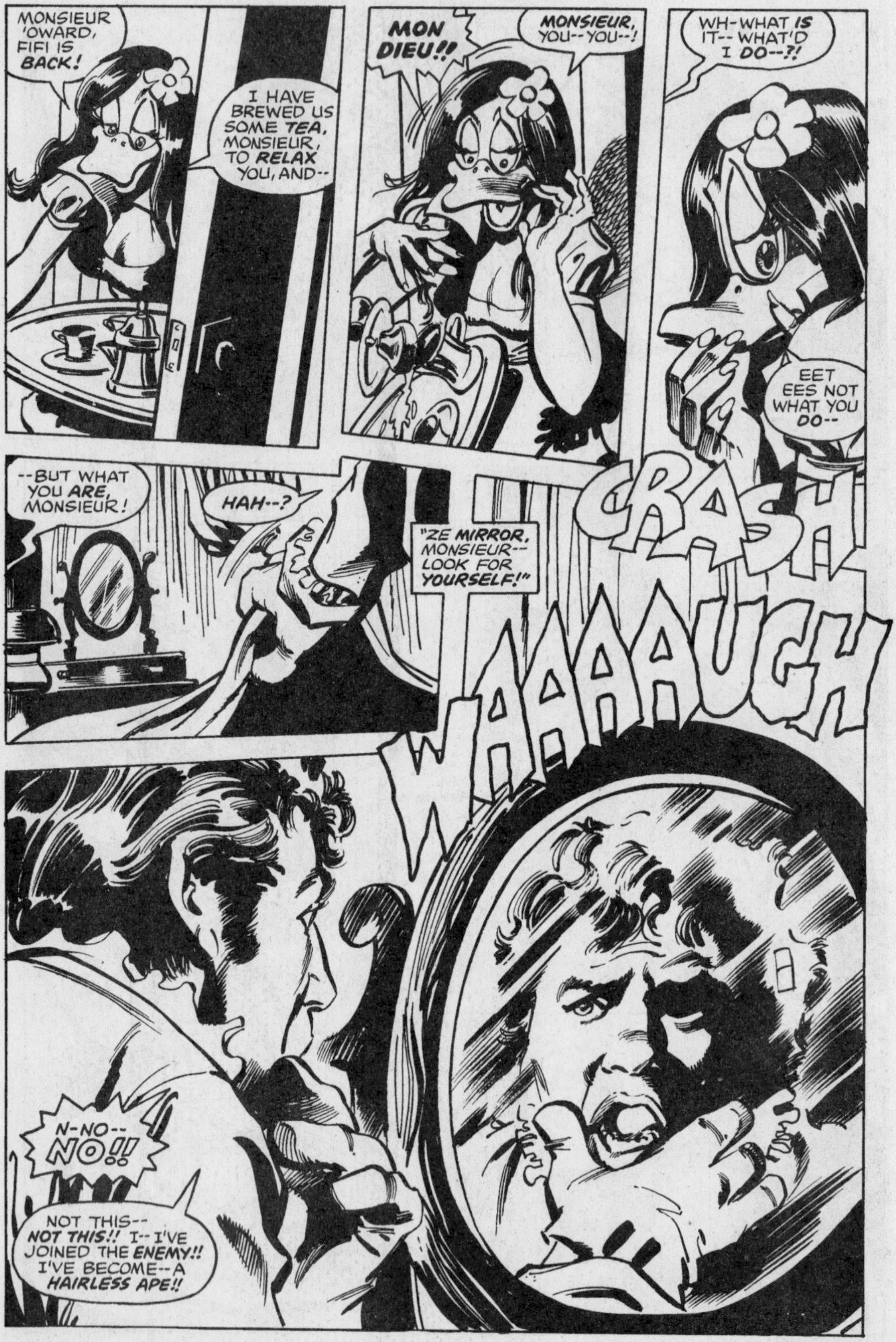
MONSIEUR 'OWARD, FIFI IS BACK!
I HAVE BREWED US SOME TEA, MONSIEUR, TO RELAX YOU, AND--
MON DIEU!!
MONSIEUR, YOU-- YOU--!
WH-WHAT IS IT-- WHAT'D I DO--?!
EET EES NOT WHAT YOU DO--
--BUT WHAT YOU ARE, MONSIEUR!
HAH--?
"ZE MIRROR, MONSIEUR-- LOOK FOR YOURSELF!"
CRASH
WAAAAUGH
N-NO-- NO!!
NOT THIS-- NOT THIS!! I--I'VE JOINED THE ENEMY!! I'VE BECOME--A HAIRLESS APE!!

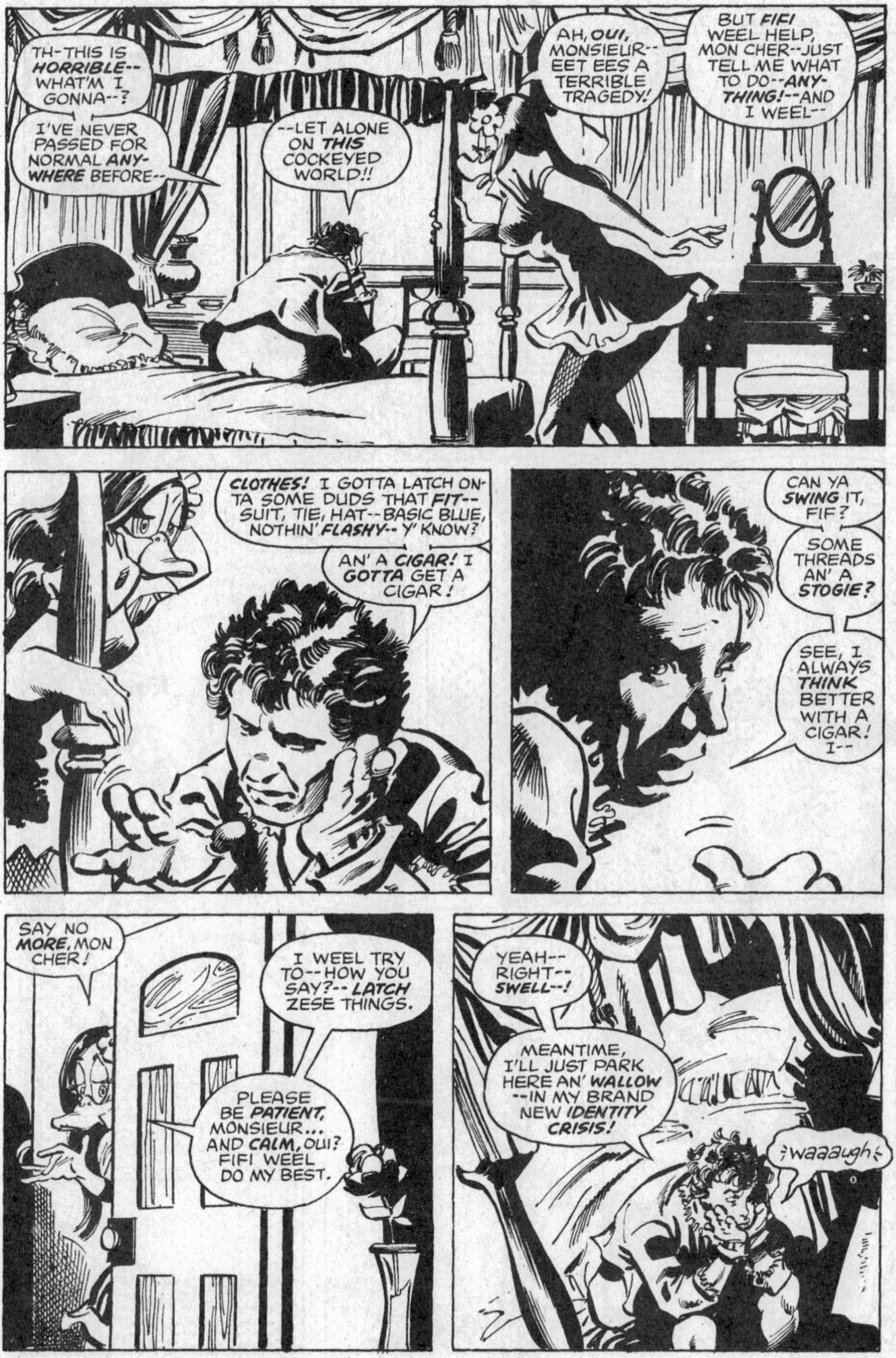
TH-THIS IS HORRIBLE-- WHAT'M I GONNA--?
I'VE NEVER PASSED FOR NORMAL ANYWHERE BEFORE--
--LET ALONE ON THIS COCKEYED WORLD!!
AH, OUI, MONSIEUR-- EET EES A TERRIBLE TRAGEDY!
BUT FIFI WEEL HELP, MON CHER--JUST TELL ME WHAT TO DO--ANYTHING!--AND I WEEL--
CLOTHES! I GOTTA LATCH ONTA SOME DUDS THAT FIT-- SUIT, TIE, HAT--BASIC BLUE, NOTHIN' FLASHY--Y' KNOW?
AN' A CIGAR! I GOTTA GET A CIGAR!
CAN YA SWING IT, FIF?
SOME THREADS AN' A STOGIE?
SEE, I ALWAYS THINK BETTER WITH A CIGAR! I--
SAY NO MORE, MON CHER!
I WEEL TRY TO--HOW YOU SAY?--LATCH ZESE THINGS.
PLEASE BE PATIENT, MONSIEUR... AND CALM, OUI? FIFI WEEL DO MY BEST.
YEAH-- RIGHT-- SWELL--!
MEANTIME, I'LL JUST PARK HERE AN' WALLOW --IN MY BRAND NEW IDENTITY CRISIS!
¡waaaugh!

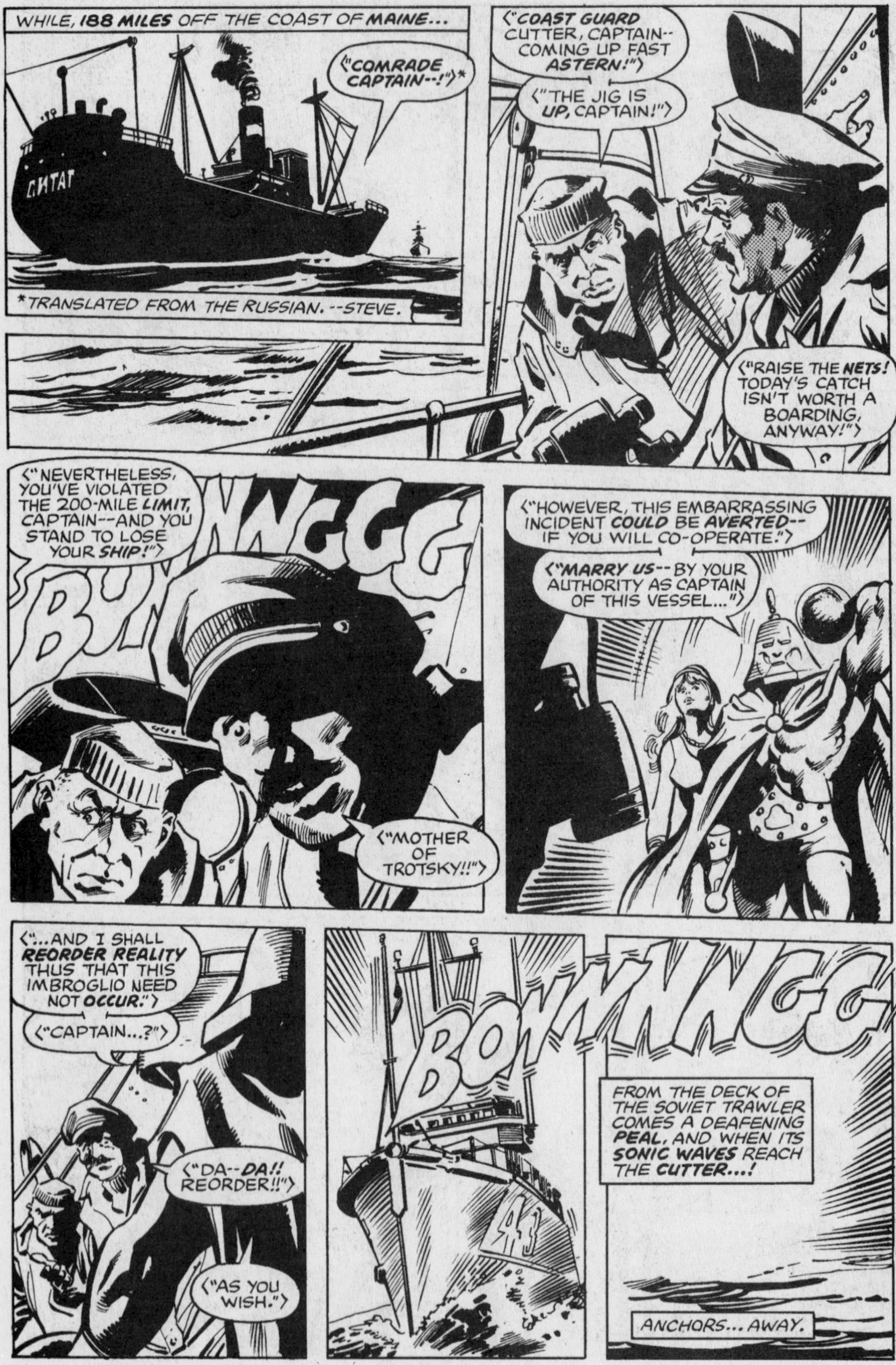

WHILE, 188 MILES OFF THE COAST OF MAINE...
<"COMRADE CAPTAIN--!">*
*TRANSLATED FROM THE RUSSIAN. --STEVE.
<"COAST GUARD CUTTER, CAPTAIN--COMING UP FAST ASTERN!">
<"THE JIG IS UP, CAPTAIN!">
<"RAISE THE NETS! TODAY'S CATCH ISN'T WORTH A BOARDING, ANYWAY!">
<"NEVERTHELESS, YOU'VE VIOLATED THE 200-MILE LIMIT, CAPTAIN--AND YOU STAND TO LOSE YOUR SHIP!">
BONNNGG
<"MOTHER OF TROTSKY!!">
<"HOWEVER, THIS EMBARRASSING INCIDENT COULD BE AVERTED--IF YOU WILL CO-OPERATE.">
<"MARRY US--BY YOUR AUTHORITY AS CAPTAIN OF THIS VESSEL...">
<"...AND I SHALL REORDER REALITY THUS THAT THIS IMBROGLIO NEED NOT OCCUR.">
<"CAPTAIN...?">
<"DA--DA!! REORDER!!">
<"AS YOU WISH.">
BONNNNGG
FROM THE DECK OF THE SOVIET TRAWLER COMES A DEAFENING PEAL, AND WHEN ITS SONIC WAVES REACH THE CUTTER...!
ANCHORS... AWAY.

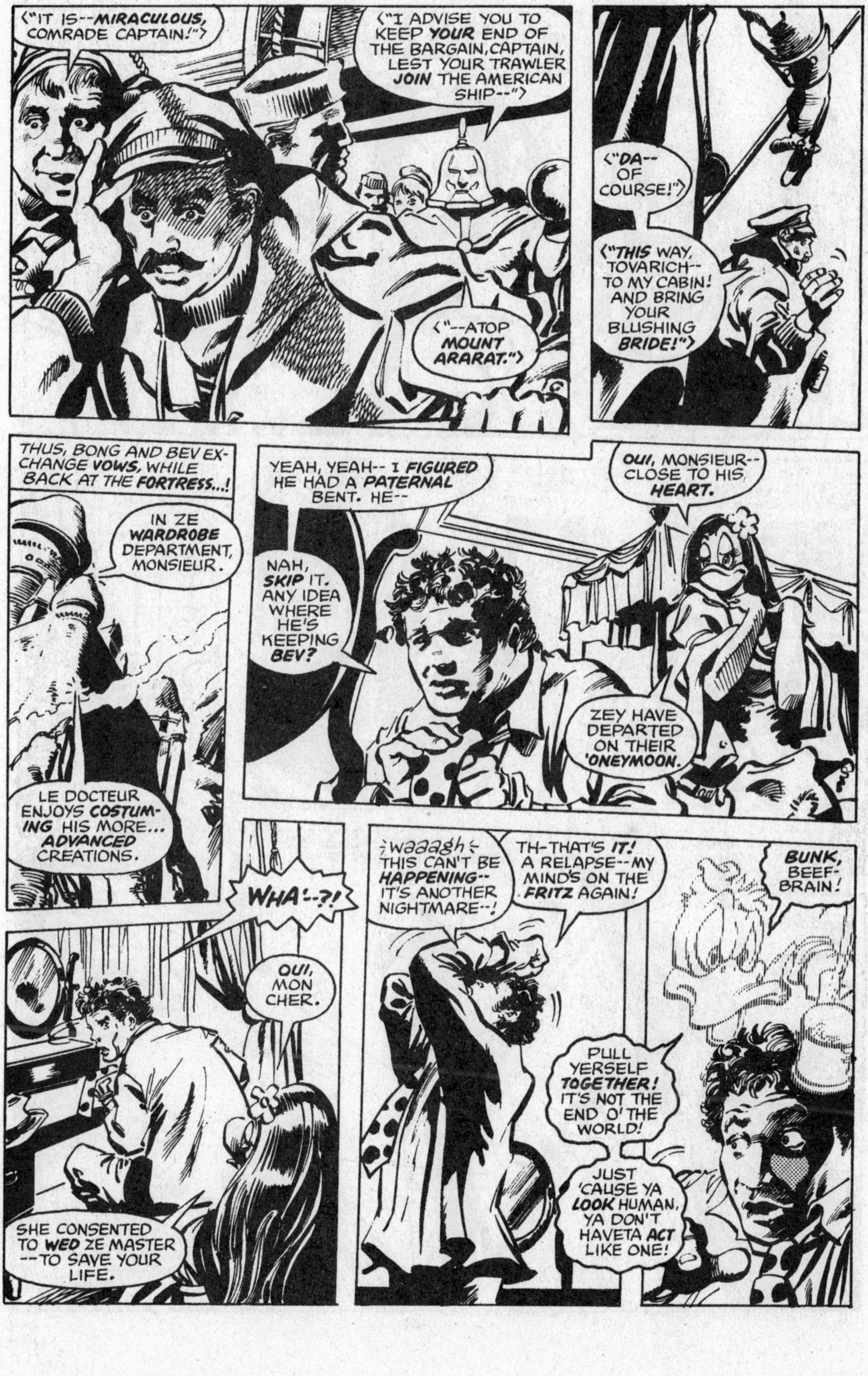

<"IT IS--MIRACULOUS, COMRADE CAPTAIN!">
<"I ADVISE YOU TO KEEP YOUR END OF THE BARGAIN, CAPTAIN, LEST YOUR TRAWLER JOIN THE AMERICAN SHIP--">
<"--ATOP MOUNT ARARAT.">
<"DA-- OF COURSE!">
<"THIS WAY, TOVARICH-- TO MY CABIN! AND BRING YOUR BLUSHING BRIDE!">
THUS, BONG AND BEV EXCHANGE VOWS, WHILE BACK AT THE FORTRESS...!
IN ZE WARDROBE DEPARTMENT, MONSIEUR.
LE DOCTEUR ENJOYS COSTUMING HIS MORE... ADVANCED CREATIONS.
YEAH, YEAH-- I FIGURED HE HAD A PATERNAL BENT. HE--
NAH, SKIP IT. ANY IDEA WHERE HE'S KEEPING BEV?
OUI, MONSIEUR-- CLOSE TO HIS HEART.
ZEY HAVE DEPARTED ON THEIR 'ONEYMOON.
WHA'--?!
OUI, MON CHER.
SHE CONSENTED TO WED ZE MASTER --TO SAVE YOUR LIFE.
waaaagh THIS CAN'T BE HAPPENING-- IT'S ANOTHER NIGHTMARE--!
TH-THAT'S IT! A RELAPSE--MY MIND'S ON THE FRITZ AGAIN!
BUNK, BEEF-BRAIN!
PULL YERSELF TOGETHER! IT'S NOT THE END O' THE WORLD!
JUST 'CAUSE YA LOOK HUMAN, YA DON'T HAVETA ACT LIKE ONE!

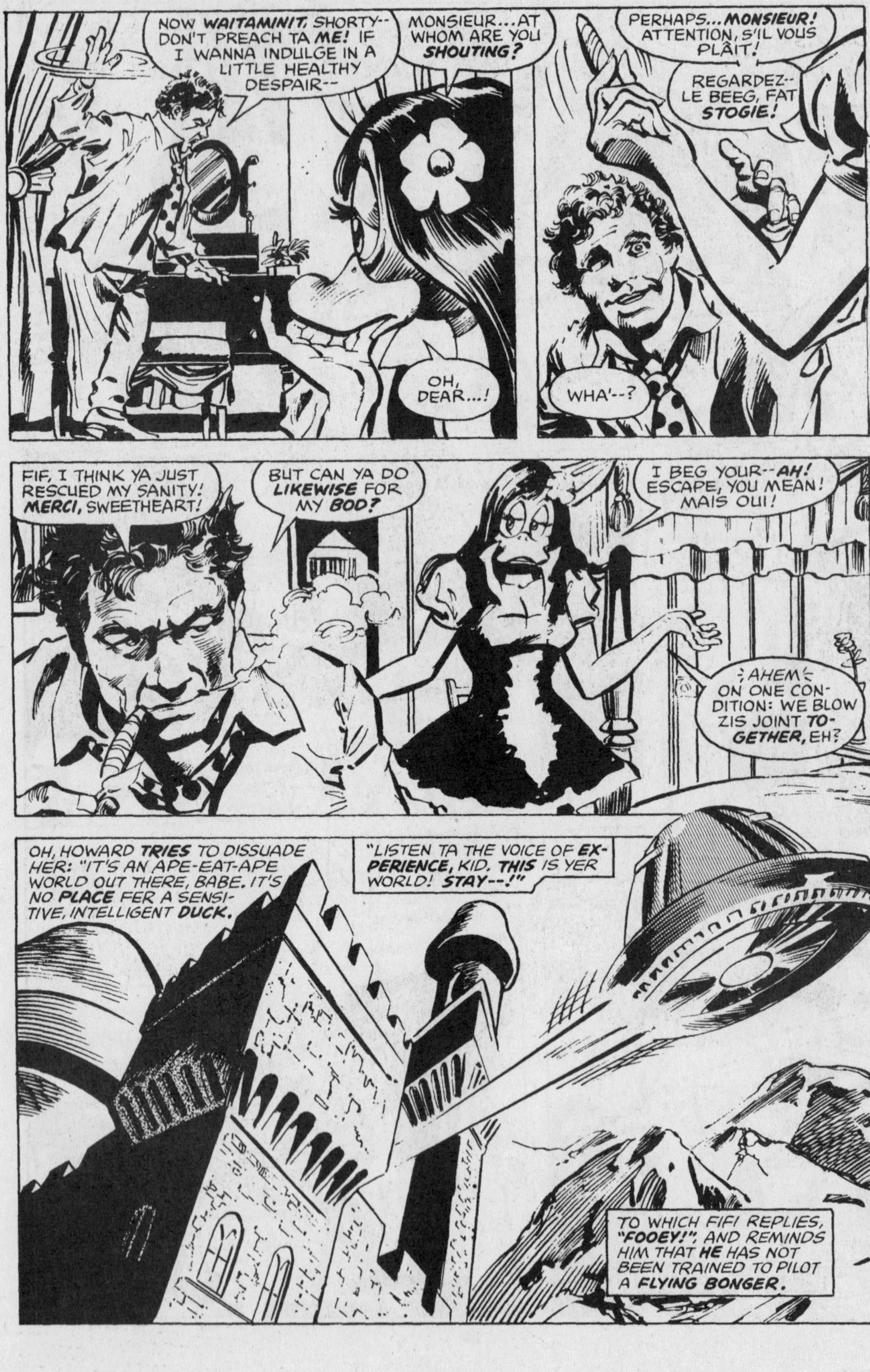
NOW WAITAMINIT, SHORTY-- DON'T PREACH TA ME! IF I WANNA INDULGE IN A LITTLE HEALTHY DESPAIR--
MONSIEUR... AT WHOM ARE YOU SHOUTING?
OH, DEAR...!
PERHAPS... MONSIEUR! ATTENTION, S'IL VOUS PLÂIT!
REGARDEZ-- LE BEEG, FAT STOGIE!
WHA'--?
FIF, I THINK YA JUST RESCUED MY SANITY! MERCI, SWEETHEART!
BUT CAN YA DO LIKEWISE FOR MY BOD?
I BEG YOUR--AH! ESCAPE, YOU MEAN! MAIS OUI!
AHEM ON ONE CONDITION: WE BLOW ZIS JOINT TOGETHER, EH?
OH, HOWARD TRIES TO DISSUADE HER: "IT'S AN APE-EAT-APE WORLD OUT THERE, BABE. IT'S NO PLACE FER A SENSITIVE, INTELLIGENT DUCK.
"LISTEN TA THE VOICE OF EXPERIENCE, KID. THIS IS YER WORLD! STAY--!"
TO WHICH FIFI REPLIES, "FOOEY!", AND REMINDS HIM THAT HE HAS NOT BEEN TRAINED TO PILOT A FLYING BONGER.

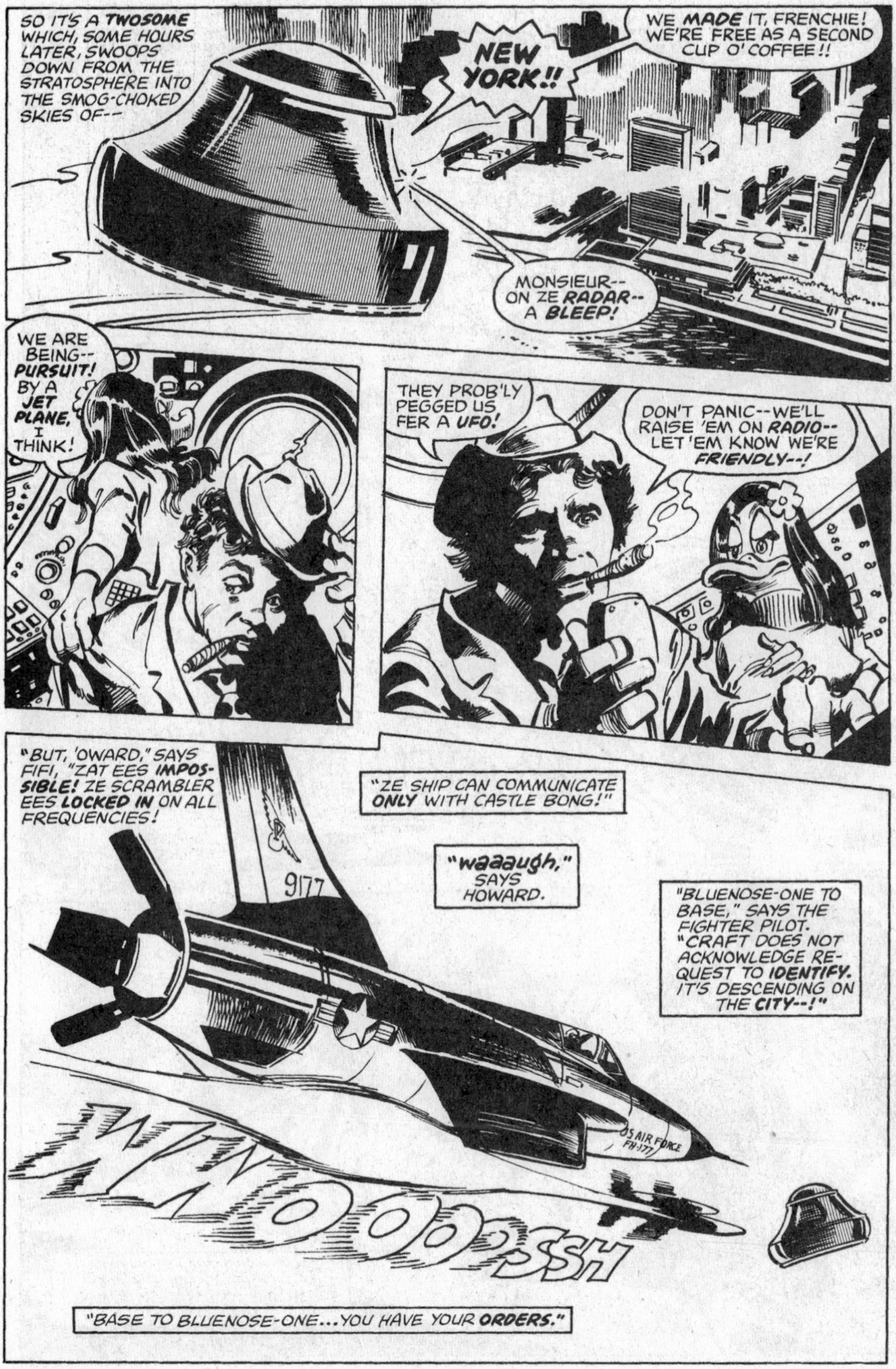
SO IT'S A TWOSOME WHICH, SOME HOURS LATER, SWOOPS DOWN FROM THE STRATOSPHERE INTO THE SMOG-CHOKED SKIES OF--
NEW YORK!!
WE MADE IT, FRENCHIE! WE'RE FREE AS A SECOND CUP O' COFFEE!!
MONSIEUR-- ON ZE RADAR-- A BLEEP!
WE ARE BEING-- PURSUIT! BY A JET PLANE, I THINK!
THEY PROB'LY PEGGED US FER A UFO!
DON'T PANIC--WE'LL RAISE 'EM ON RADIO-- LET 'EM KNOW WE'RE FRIENDLY--!
"BUT, 'OWARD," SAYS FIFI, "ZAT EES IMPOSSIBLE! ZE SCRAMBLER EES LOCKED IN ON ALL FREQUENCIES!
"ZE SHIP CAN COMMUNICATE ONLY WITH CASTLE BONG!"
"waaaugh," SAYS HOWARD.
"BLUENOSE-ONE TO BASE," SAYS THE FIGHTER PILOT. "CRAFT DOES NOT ACKNOWLEDGE REQUEST TO IDENTIFY. IT'S DESCENDING ON THE CITY--!"
9177
US AIR FORCE FH-177
WHOOOOSSH
"BASE TO BLUENOSE-ONE... YOU HAVE YOUR ORDERS."

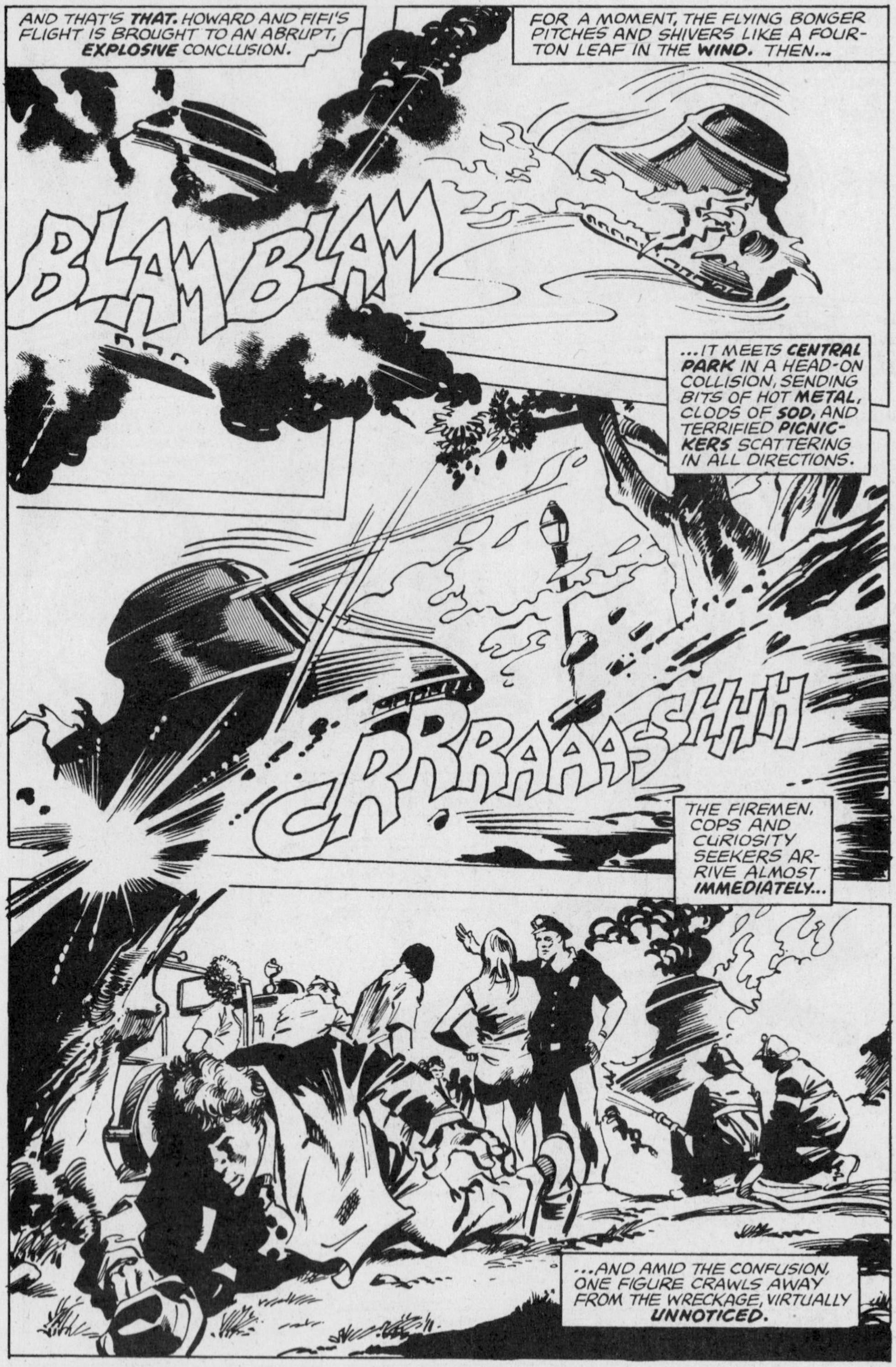
AND THAT'S **THAT**. HOWARD AND FIFI'S FLIGHT IS BROUGHT TO AN ABRUPT, **EXPLOSIVE** CONCLUSION.
FOR A MOMENT, THE FLYING BONGER PITCHES AND SHIVERS LIKE A FOUR-TON LEAF IN THE **WIND**. THEN...
BLAMBLAM
...IT MEETS **CENTRAL PARK** IN A HEAD-ON COLLISION, SENDING BITS OF HOT **METAL**, CLODS OF **SOD**, AND TERRIFIED **PICNICKERS** SCATTERING IN ALL DIRECTIONS.
CRRRAAASSHHH
THE FIREMEN, COPS AND CURIOSITY SEEKERS ARRIVE ALMOST **IMMEDIATELY**...
...AND AMID THE CONFUSION, ONE FIGURE CRAWLS AWAY FROM THE WRECKAGE, VIRTUALLY **UNNOTICED**.

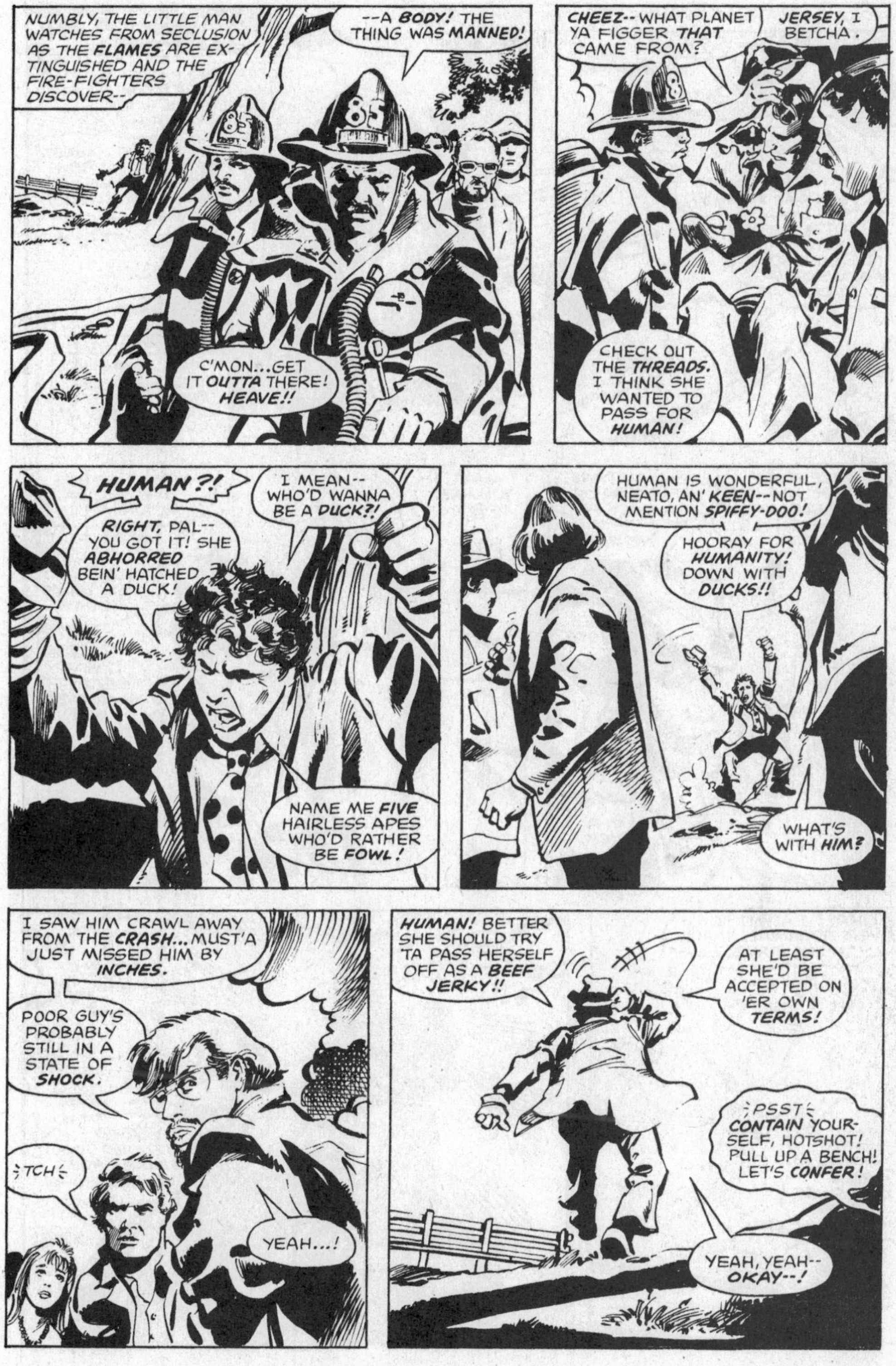
NUMBLY, THE LITTLE MAN WATCHES FROM SECLUSION AS THE FLAMES ARE EXTINGUISHED AND THE FIRE-FIGHTERS DISCOVER--
--A BODY! THE THING WAS MANNED!
C'MON...GET IT OUTTA THERE! HEAVE!!
CHEEZ--WHAT PLANET YA FIGGER THAT CAME FROM?
JERSEY, I BETCHA.
CHECK OUT THE THREADS. I THINK SHE WANTED TO PASS FOR HUMAN!
HUMAN?!
RIGHT, PAL--YOU GOT IT! SHE ABHORRED BEIN' HATCHED A DUCK!
I MEAN--WHO'D WANNA BE A DUCK?!
NAME ME FIVE HAIRLESS APES WHO'D RATHER BE FOWL!
HUMAN IS WONDERFUL, NEATO, AN' KEEN--NOT MENTION SPIFFY-DOO!
HOORAY FOR HUMANITY! DOWN WITH DUCKS!!
WHAT'S WITH HIM?
I SAW HIM CRAWL AWAY FROM THE CRASH...MUST'A JUST MISSED HIM BY INCHES.
POOR GUY'S PROBABLY STILL IN A STATE OF SHOCK.
TCH
YEAH...!
HUMAN! BETTER SHE SHOULD TRY TA PASS HERSELF OFF AS A BEEF JERKY!!
AT LEAST SHE'D BE ACCEPTED ON 'ER OWN TERMS!
PSST CONTAIN YOURSELF, HOTSHOT! PULL UP A BENCH! LET'S CONFER!
YEAH, YEAH--OKAY--!

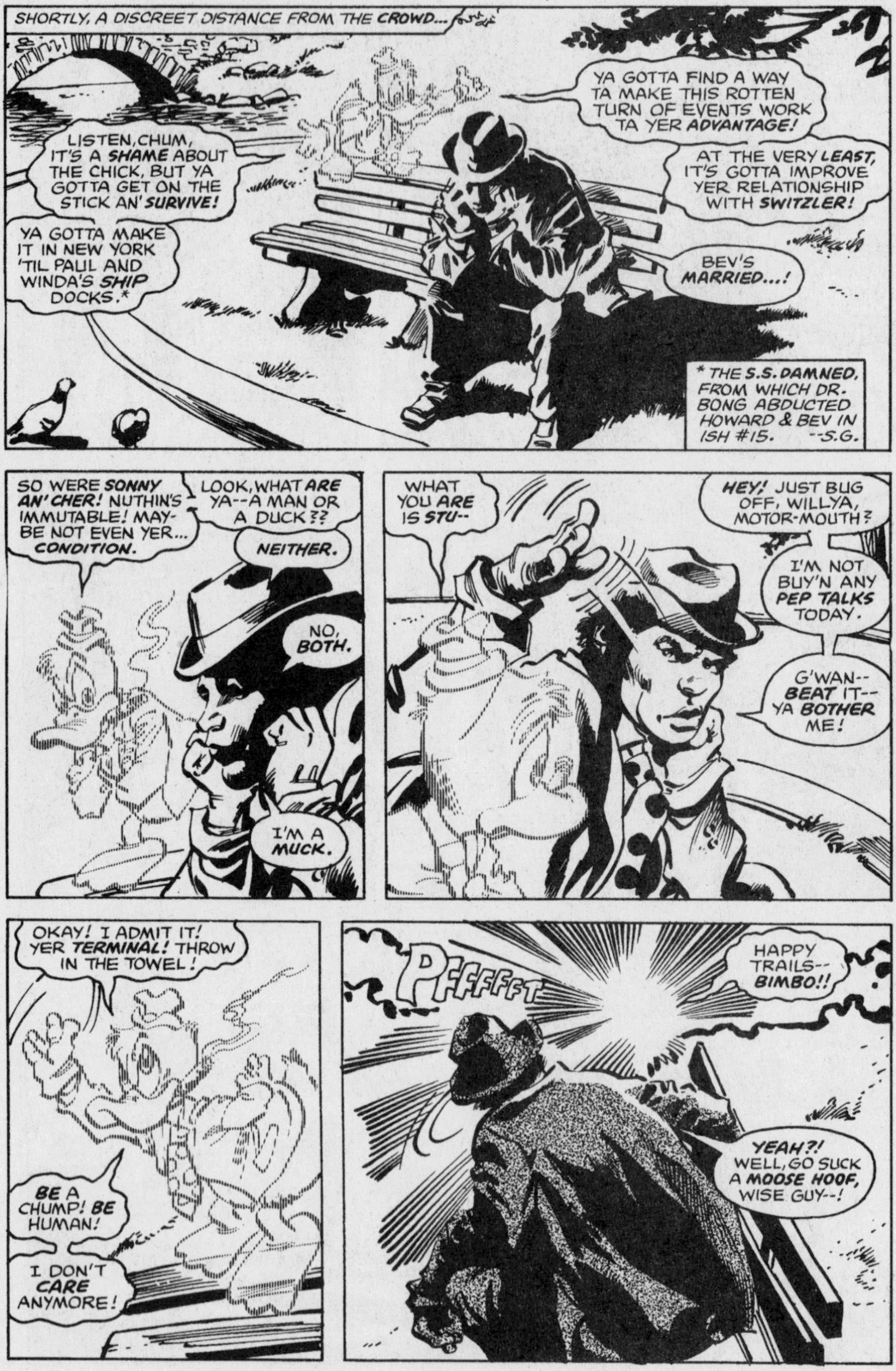
SHORTLY, A DISCREET DISTANCE FROM THE CROWD...
LISTEN, CHUM, IT'S A SHAME ABOUT THE CHICK, BUT YA GOTTA GET ON THE STICK AN' SURVIVE!
YA GOTTA MAKE IT IN NEW YORK 'TIL PAUL AND WINDA'S SHIP DOCKS.*
YA GOTTA FIND A WAY TA MAKE THIS ROTTEN TURN OF EVENTS WORK TA YER ADVANTAGE!
AT THE VERY LEAST, IT'S GOTTA IMPROVE YER RELATIONSHIP WITH SWITZLER!
BEV'S MARRIED...!
* THE S.S. DAMNED, FROM WHICH DR. BONG ABDUCTED HOWARD & BEV IN ISH #15. --S.G.
SO WERE SONNY AN' CHER! NUTHIN'S IMMUTABLE! MAY-BE NOT EVEN YER... CONDITION.
LOOK, WHAT ARE YA--A MAN OR A DUCK??
NEITHER.
NO, BOTH.
I'M A MUCK.
WHAT YOU ARE IS STU--
HEY! JUST BUG OFF, WILLYA, MOTOR-MOUTH?
I'M NOT BUY'N ANY PEP TALKS TODAY.
G'WAN-- BEAT IT-- YA BOTHER ME!
OKAY! I ADMIT IT! YER TERMINAL! THROW IN THE TOWEL!
BE A CHUMP! BE HUMAN!
I DON'T CARE ANYMORE!
PFFFFFT
HAPPY TRAILS-- BIMBO!!
YEAH?! WELL, GO SUCK A MOOSE HOOF, WISE GUY--!

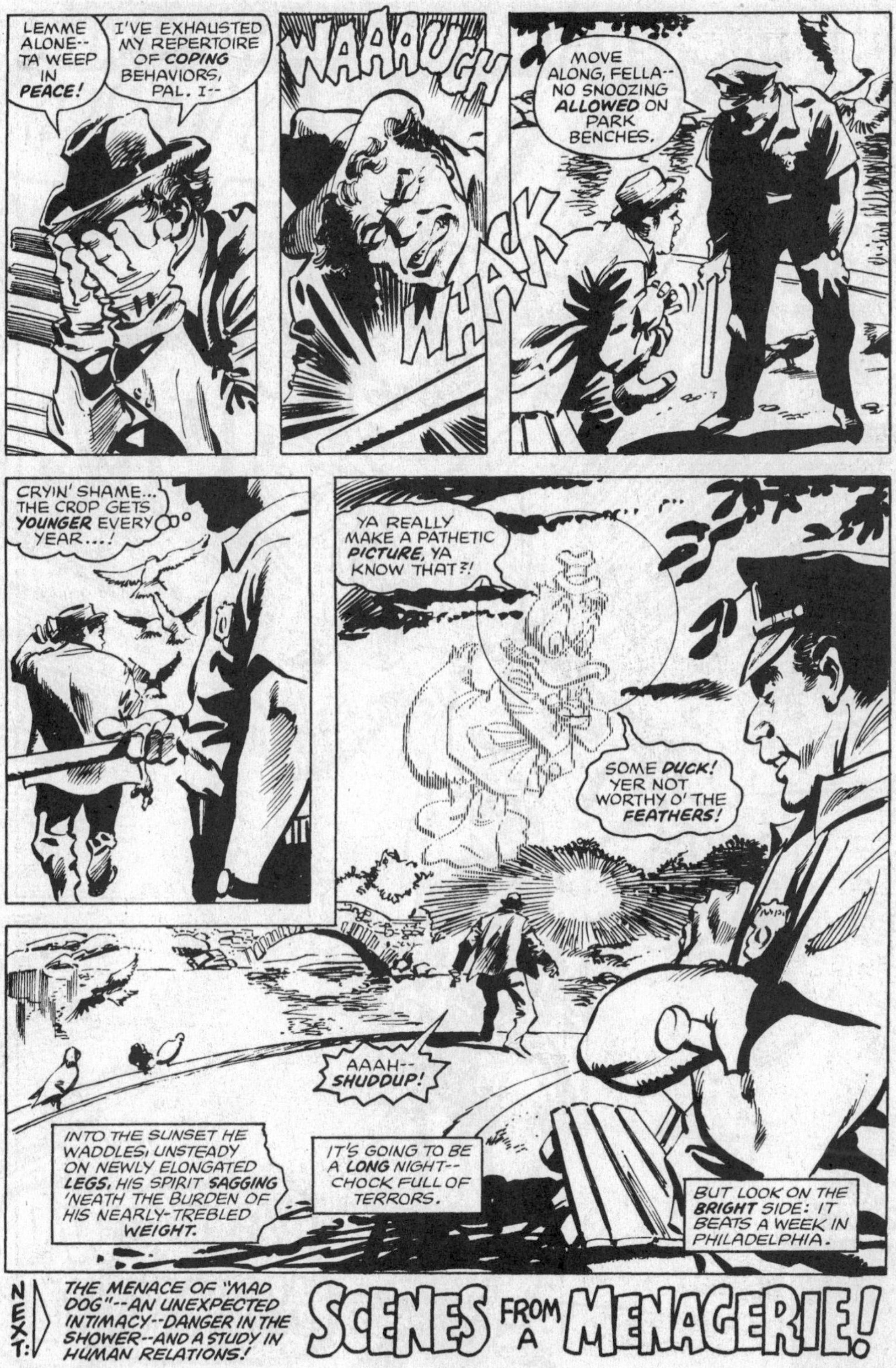
LEMME ALONE-- TA WEEP IN PEACE!
I'VE EXHAUSTED MY REPERTOIRE OF COPING BEHAVIORS, PAL. I--
WAAAUGH
WHACK
MOVE ALONG, FELLA-- NO SNOOZING ALLOWED ON PARK BENCHES.
CRYIN' SHAME... THE CROP GETS YOUNGER EVERY YEAR...!
YA REALLY MAKE A PATHETIC PICTURE, YA KNOW THAT?!
SOME DUCK! YER NOT WORTHY O' THE FEATHERS!
AAAH-- SHUDDUP!
INTO THE SUNSET HE WADDLES, UNSTEADY ON NEWLY ELONGATED LEGS, HIS SPIRIT SAGGING 'NEATH THE BURDEN OF HIS NEARLY-TREBLED WEIGHT.
IT'S GOING TO BE A LONG NIGHT-- CHOCK FULL OF TERRORS.
BUT LOOK ON THE BRIGHT SIDE: IT BEATS A WEEK IN PHILADELPHIA.

NEXT: THE MENACE OF "MAD DOG"--AN UNEXPECTED INTIMACY--DANGER IN THE SHOWER--AND A STUDY IN HUMAN RELATIONS! SCENES FROM A MENAGERIE!

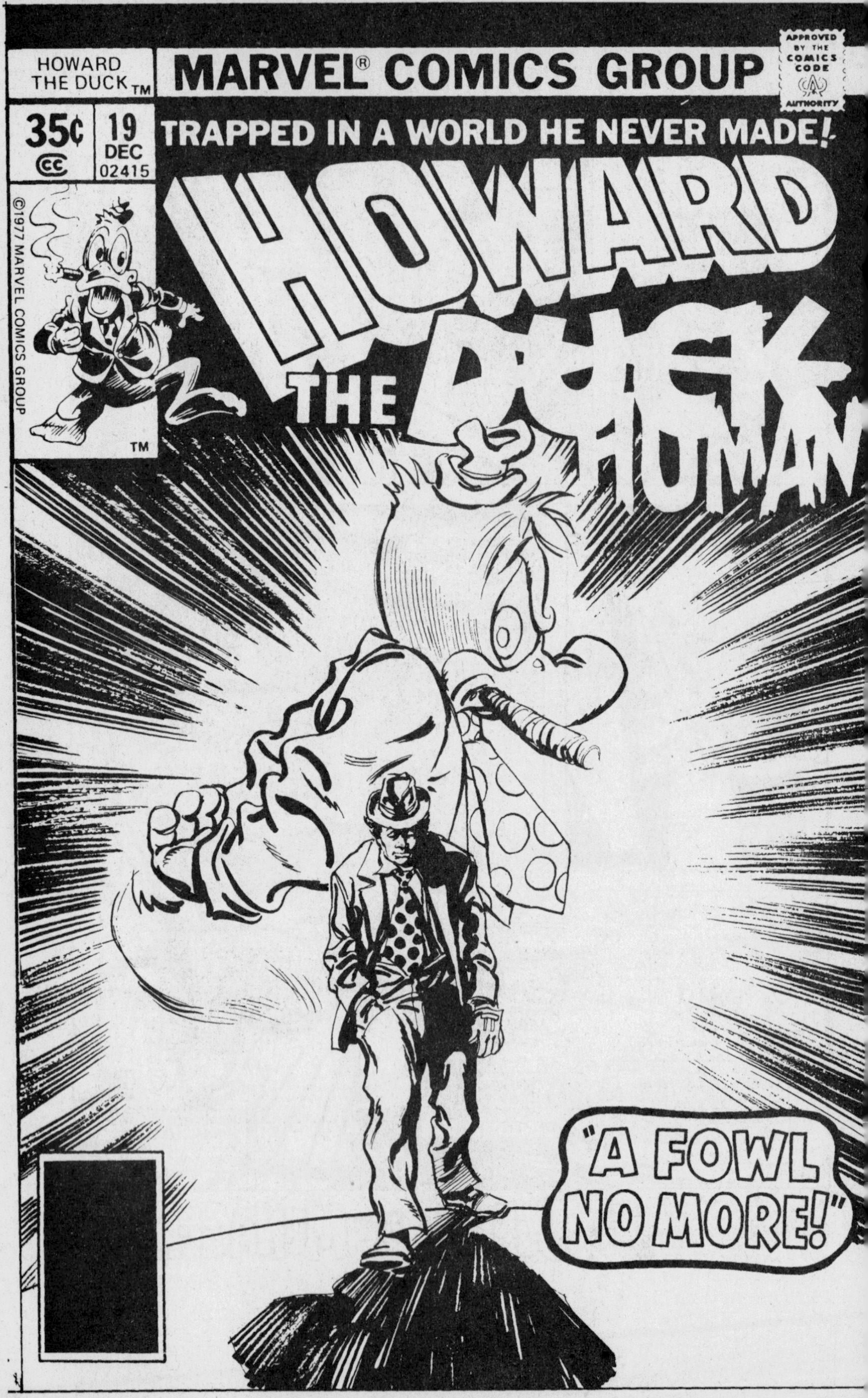
HOWARD THE DUCK TM
MARVEL® COMICS GROUP
APPROVED BY THE COMICS CODE AUTHORITY
35¢
19 DEC 02415
TRAPPED IN A WORLD HE NEVER MADE!
HOWARD THE DUCK HUMAN
©1977 MARVEL COMICS GROUP
TM
"A FOWL NO MORE!"

From the time of his hatching, he was...different. A potentially brilliant scholar who dreaded the structured environment of school, he educated himself in the streets, taking whatever work was available, formulating his philosophy of self from what he learned of the world about him. And then the Cosmic Axis shifted...and that world *changed*. Suddenly, he was stranded in a universe he could not fathom. Without warning, he became a strange fowl in an even stranger land.

Stan Lee PRESENTS: HOWARD THE DUCK!™

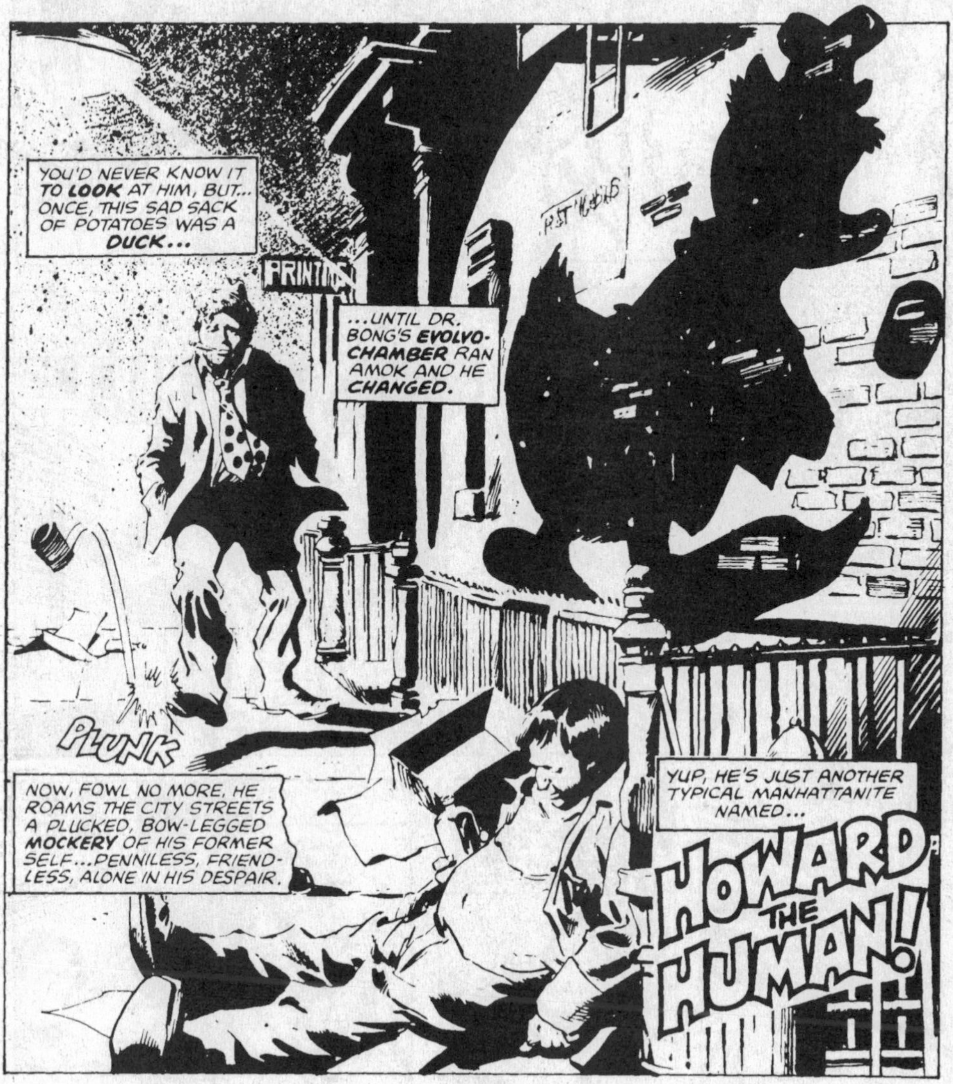

YOU'D NEVER KNOW IT TO LOOK AT HIM, BUT... ONCE, THIS SAD SACK OF POTATOES WAS A DUCK...
PRINT
...UNTIL DR. BONG'S EVOLVO-CHAMBER RAN AMOK AND HE CHANGED.
PLUNK
NOW, FOWL NO MORE, HE ROAMS THE CITY STREETS A PLUCKED, BOW-LEGGED MOCKERY OF HIS FORMER SELF...PENNILESS, FRIENDLESS, ALONE IN HIS DESPAIR.
YUP, HE'S JUST ANOTHER TYPICAL MANHATTANITE NAMED...
HOWARD THE HUMAN!

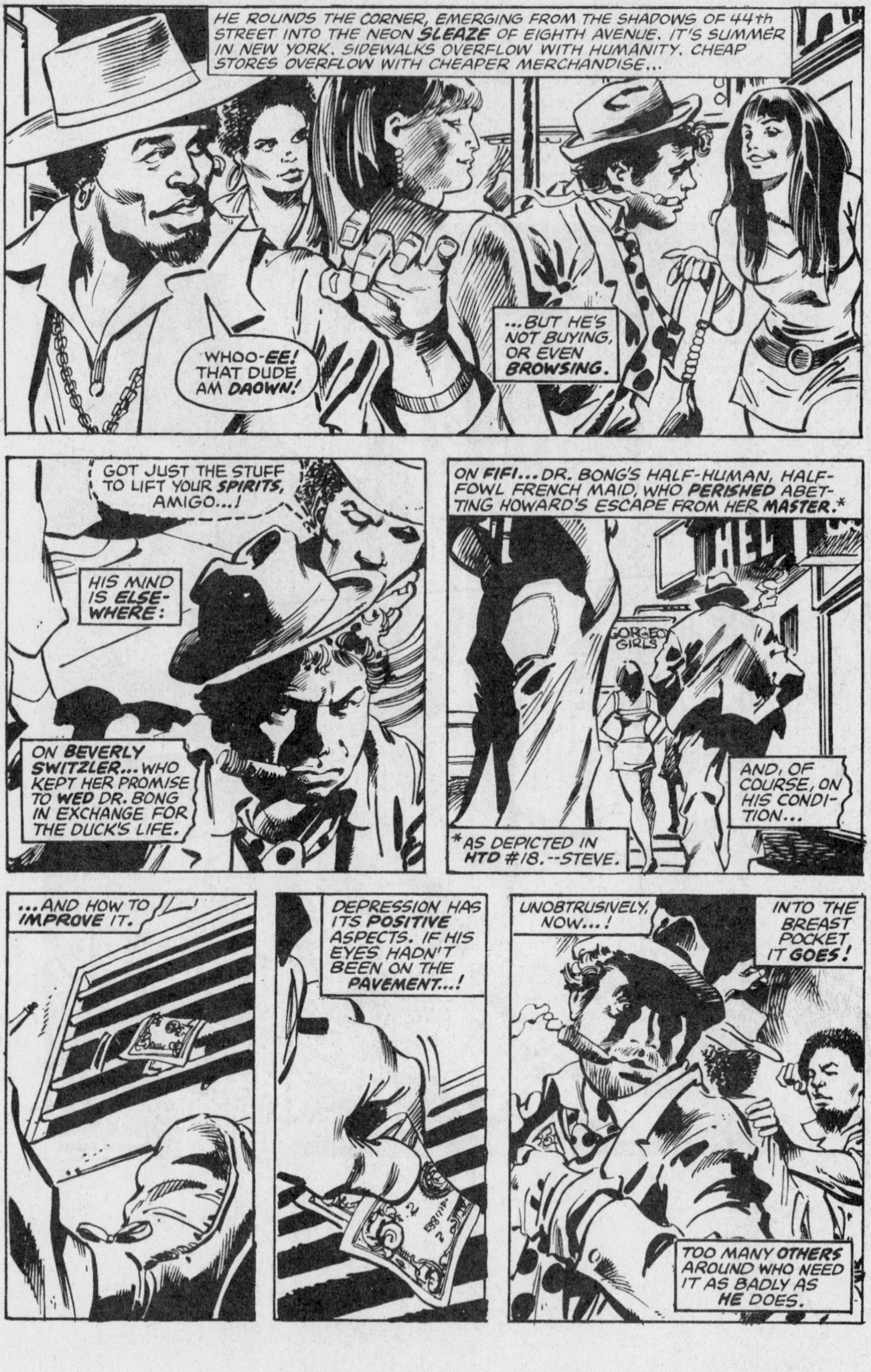

HE ROUNDS THE CORNER, EMERGING FROM THE SHADOWS OF 44th STREET INTO THE NEON SLEAZE OF EIGHTH AVENUE. IT'S SUMMER IN NEW YORK. SIDEWALKS OVERFLOW WITH HUMANITY. CHEAP STORES OVERFLOW WITH CHEAPER MERCHANDISE...
WHOO-EE! THAT DUDE AM DAOWN!
...BUT HE'S NOT BUYING, OR EVEN BROWSING.
GOT JUST THE STUFF TO LIFT YOUR SPIRITS, AMIGO...!
HIS MIND IS ELSEWHERE:
ON BEVERLY SWITZLER... WHO KEPT HER PROMISE TO WED DR. BONG IN EXCHANGE FOR THE DUCK'S LIFE.
ON FIFI... DR. BONG'S HALF-HUMAN, HALF-FOWL FRENCH MAID, WHO PERISHED ABETTING HOWARD'S ESCAPE FROM HER MASTER.*
GIRLS
AND, OF COURSE, ON HIS CONDITION...
*AS DEPICTED IN HTD #18. --STEVE.
...AND HOW TO IMPROVE IT.
DEPRESSION HAS ITS POSITIVE ASPECTS. IF HIS EYES HADN'T BEEN ON THE PAVEMENT...!
UNOBTRUSIVELY, NOW...!
INTO THE BREAST POCKET IT GOES!
TOO MANY OTHERS AROUND WHO NEED IT AS BADLY AS HE DOES.

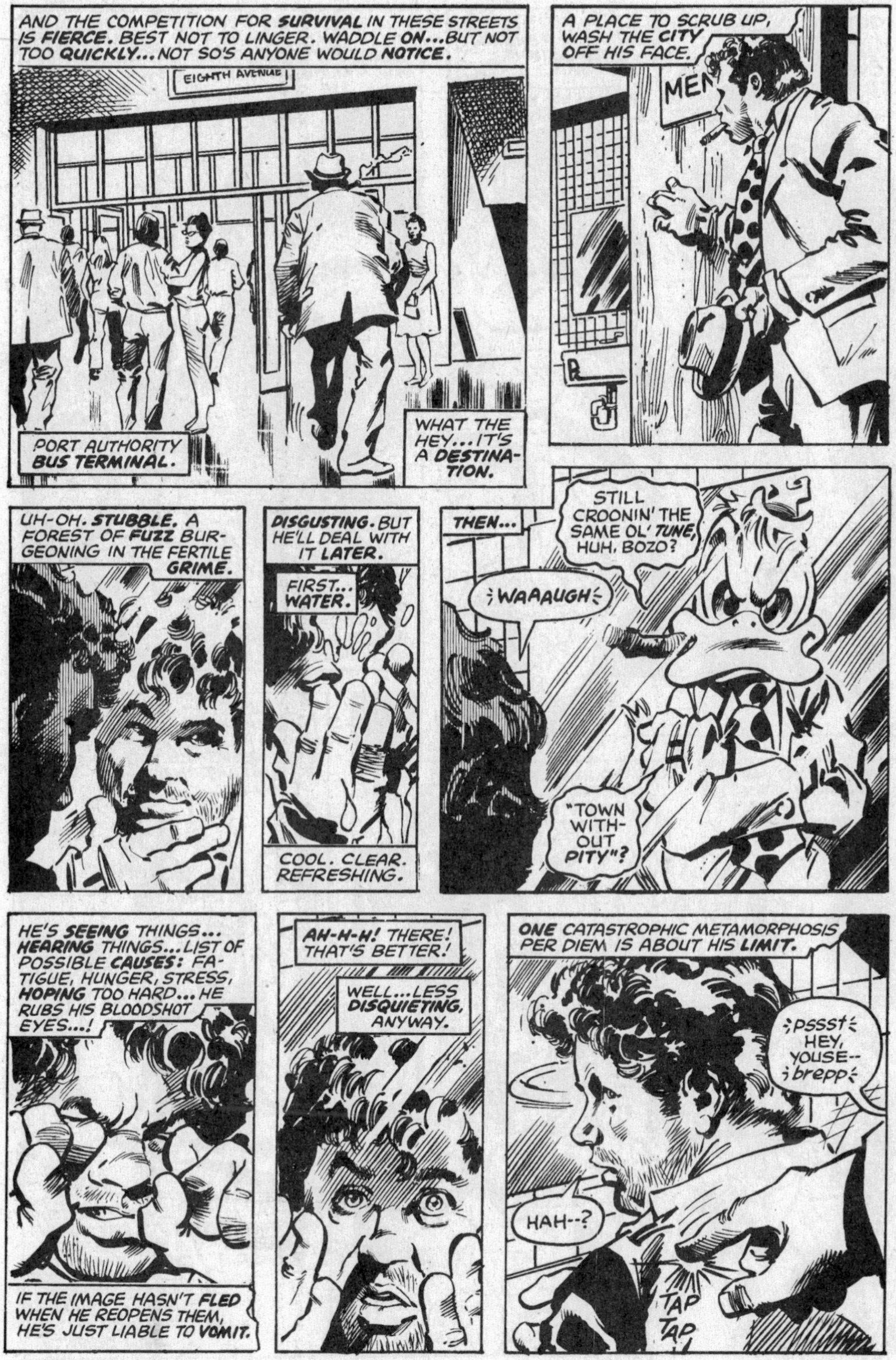
AND THE COMPETITION FOR SURVIVAL IN THESE STREETS IS FIERCE. BEST NOT TO LINGER. WADDLE ON... BUT NOT TOO QUICKLY... NOT SO'S ANYONE WOULD NOTICE.
EIGHTH AVENUE
PORT AUTHORITY BUS TERMINAL.
WHAT THE HEY... IT'S A DESTINATION.
A PLACE TO SCRUB UP, WASH THE CITY OFF HIS FACE.
MEN
UH-OH. STUBBLE. A FOREST OF FUZZ BURGEONING IN THE FERTILE GRIME.
DISGUSTING. BUT HE'LL DEAL WITH IT LATER.
FIRST... WATER.
COOL. CLEAR. REFRESHING.
THEN...
STILL CROONIN' THE SAME OL' TUNE, HUH, BOZO?
WAAAUGH
"TOWN WITHOUT PITY"?
HE'S SEEING THINGS... HEARING THINGS... LIST OF POSSIBLE CAUSES: FATIGUE, HUNGER, STRESS, HOPING TOO HARD... HE RUBS HIS BLOODSHOT EYES...!
IF THE IMAGE HASN'T FLED WHEN HE REOPENS THEM, HE'S JUST LIABLE TO VOMIT.
AH-H-H! THERE! THAT'S BETTER!
WELL... LESS DISQUIETING, ANYWAY.
ONE CATASTROPHIC METAMORPHOSIS PER DIEM IS ABOUT HIS LIMIT.
pssst HEY, YOUSE-- brepp
HAH--?
TAP TAP

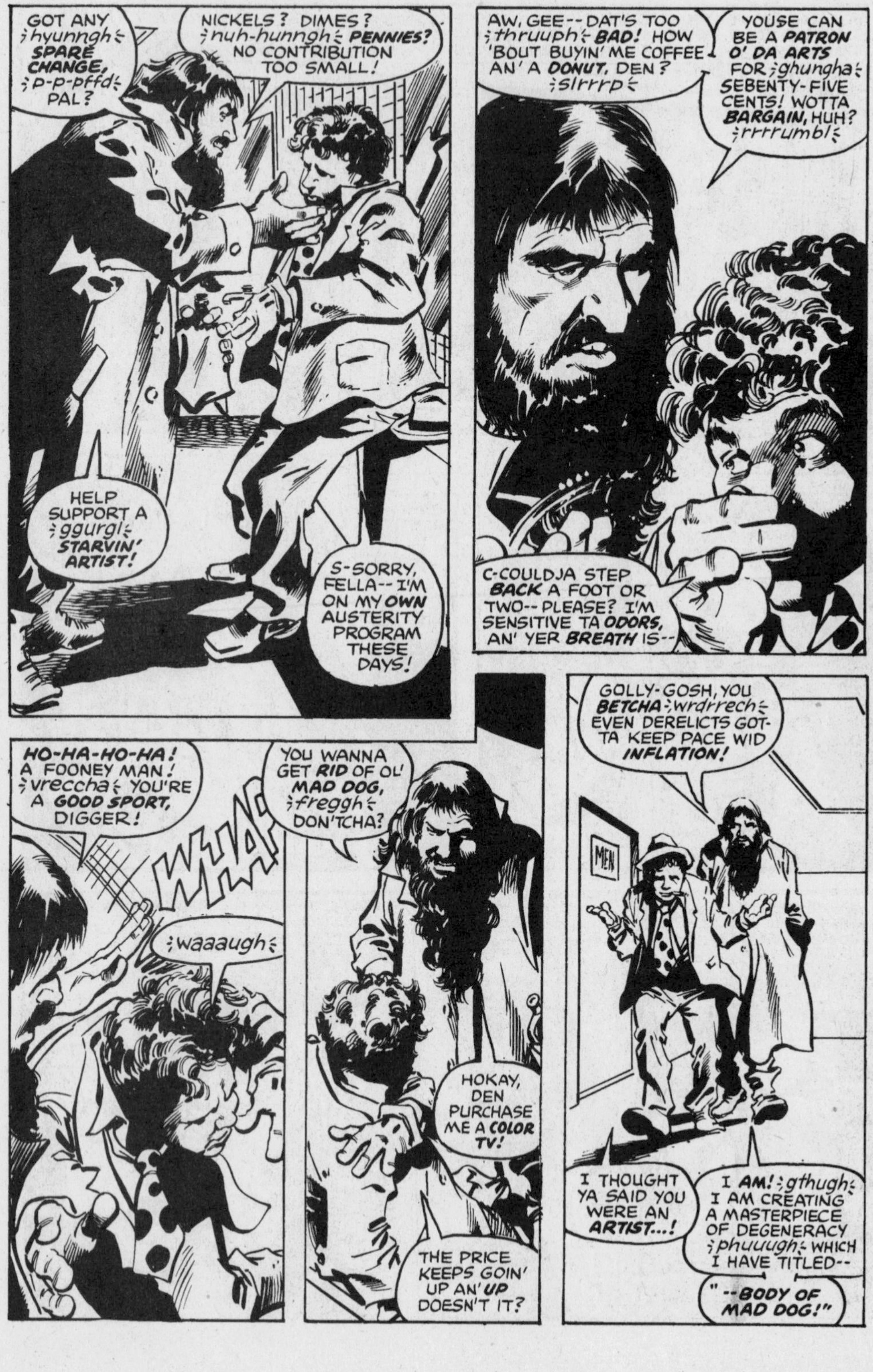
GOT ANY hyunngh SPARE CHANGE, p-p-pffd PAL?
NICKELS? DIMES? nuh-hunngh PENNIES? NO CONTRIBUTION TOO SMALL!
HELP SUPPORT A ggurgl STARVIN' ARTIST!
S-SORRY, FELLA-- I'M ON MY OWN AUSTERITY PROGRAM THESE DAYS!
AW, GEE-- DAT'S TOO thruuph BAD! HOW 'BOUT BUYIN' ME COFFEE AN' A DONUT, DEN? slrrrp
YOUSE CAN BE A PATRON O' DA ARTS FOR ghungha SEBENTY-FIVE CENTS! WOTTA BARGAIN, HUH? rrrrumbl
C-COULDJA STEP BACK A FOOT OR TWO-- PLEASE? I'M SENSITIVE TA ODORS, AN' YER BREATH IS--
HO-HA-HO-HA! A FOONEY MAN! vreccha YOU'RE A GOOD SPORT, DIGGER!
WHAP
waaaugh
YOU WANNA GET RID OF OL' MAD DOG, fregh DON'TCHA?
HOKAY, DEN PURCHASE ME A COLOR TV!
THE PRICE KEEPS GOIN' UP AN' UP DOESN'T IT?
GOLLY-GOSH, YOU BETCHA wrdrrech EVEN DERELICTS GOT-TA KEEP PACE WID INFLATION!
MEN
I THOUGHT YA SAID YOU WERE AN ARTIST...!
I AM! gthugh I AM CREATING A MASTERPIECE OF DEGENERACY phuuugh WHICH I HAVE TITLED--
"--BODY OF MAD DOG!"

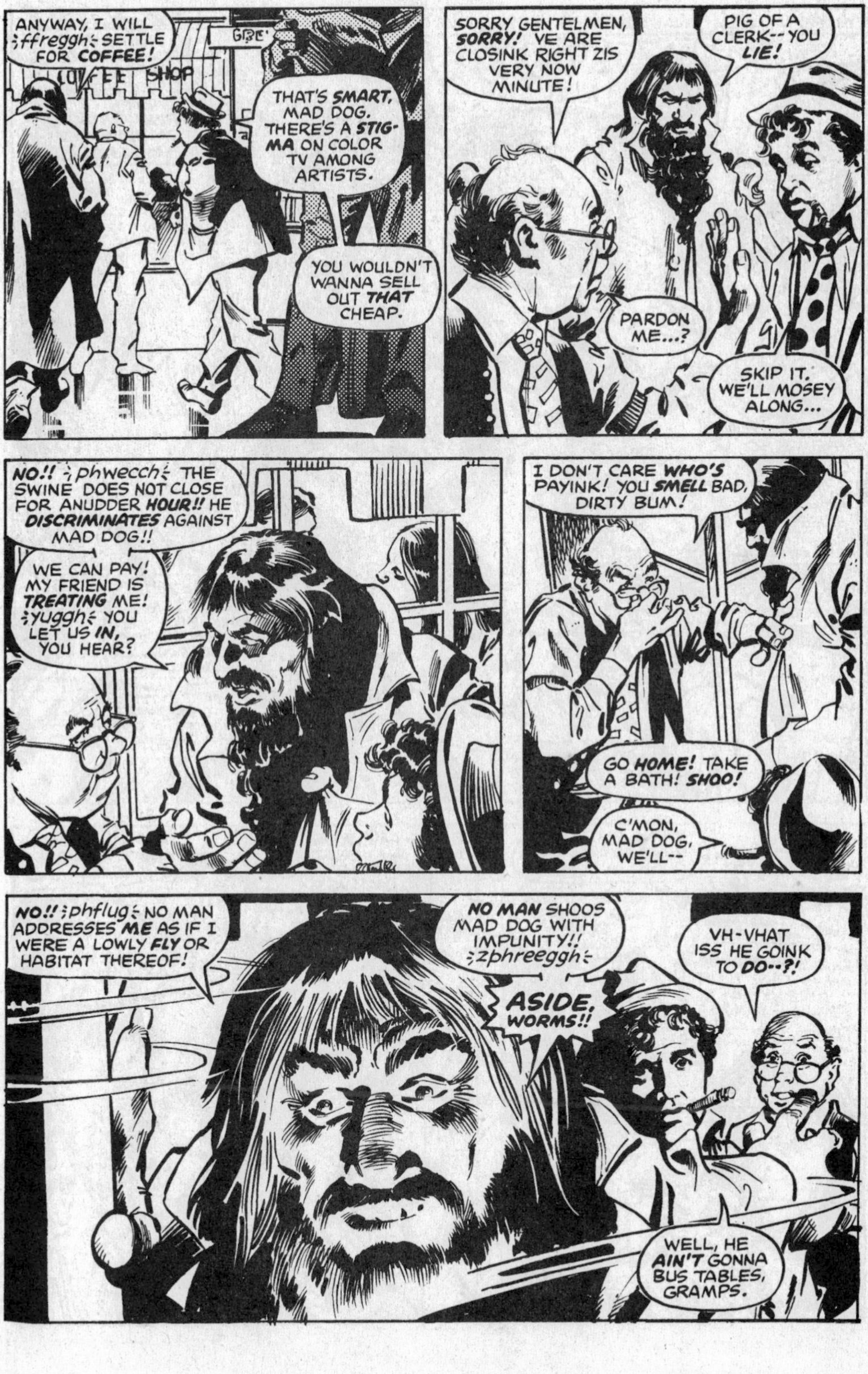

ANYWAY, I WILL *ffreggh* SETTLE FOR COFFEE!
COFFEE SHOP
THAT'S SMART, MAD DOG. THERE'S A STIGMA ON COLOR TV AMONG ARTISTS.
YOU WOULDN'T WANNA SELL OUT THAT CHEAP.
SORRY GENTELMEN, SORRY! VE ARE CLOSINK RIGHT ZIS VERY NOW MINUTE!
PIG OF A CLERK-- YOU LIE!
PARDON ME...?
SKIP IT. WE'LL MOSEY ALONG...
NO!! *phwecch* THE SWINE DOES NOT CLOSE FOR ANUDDER HOUR!! HE DISCRIMINATES AGAINST MAD DOG!!
WE CAN PAY! MY FRIEND IS TREATING ME! *yuggh* YOU LET US IN, YOU HEAR?
I DON'T CARE WHO'S PAYINK! YOU SMELL BAD, DIRTY BUM!
GO HOME! TAKE A BATH! SHOO!
C'MON, MAD DOG, WE'LL--
NO!! *phflug* NO MAN ADDRESSES ME AS IF I WERE A LOWLY FLY OR HABITAT THEREOF!
NO MAN SHOOS MAD DOG WITH IMPUNITY!! *zphreeggh*
ASIDE, WORMS!!
VH-VHAT ISS HE GOINK TO DO--?!
WELL, HE AIN'T GONNA BUS TABLES, GRAMPS.

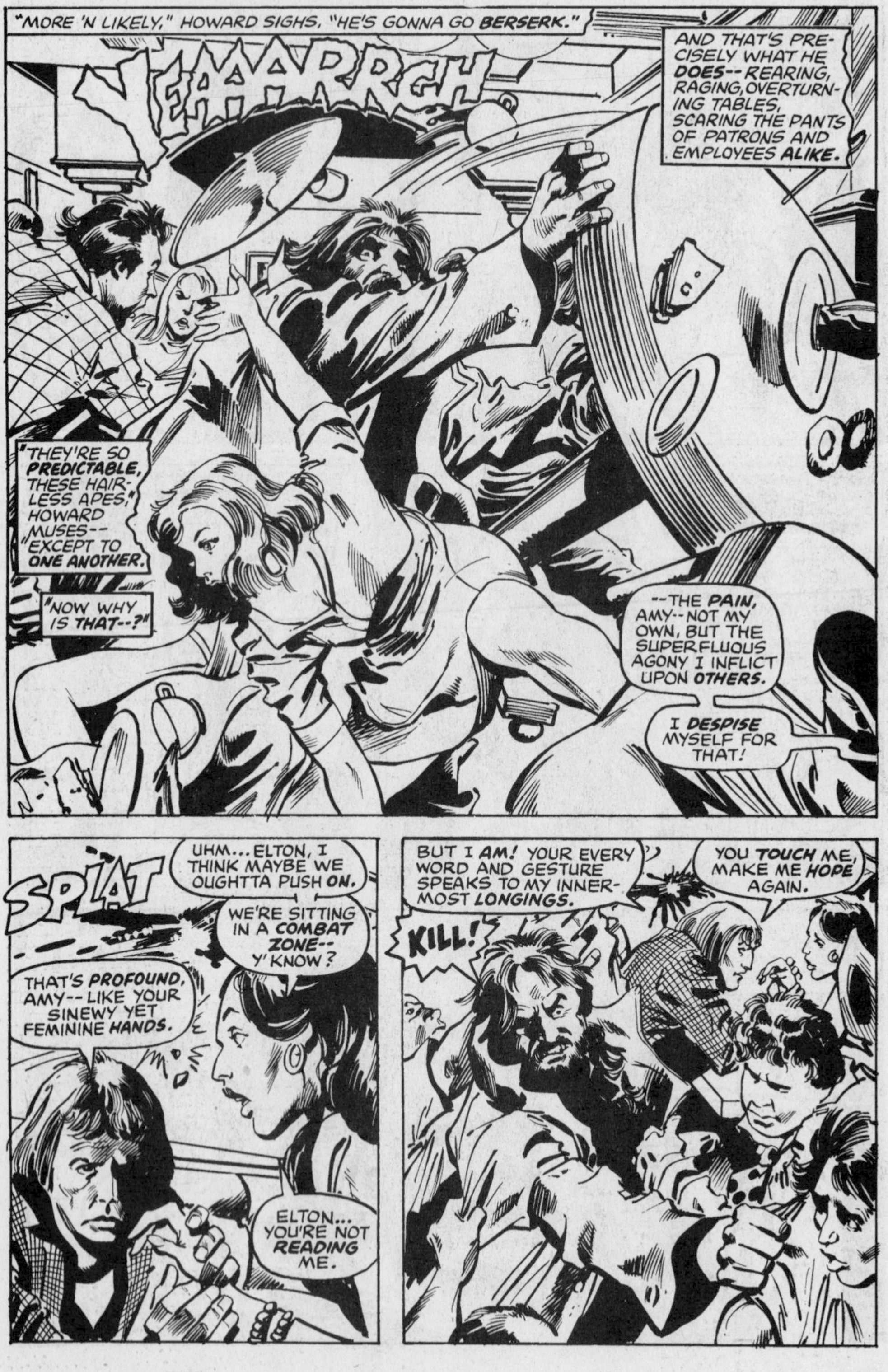

"MORE 'N LIKELY," HOWARD SIGHS, "HE'S GONNA GO BERSERK."
YEAAARRGH
AND THAT'S PRECISELY WHAT HE DOES--REARING, RAGING, OVERTURNING TABLES, SCARING THE PANTS OF PATRONS AND EMPLOYEES ALIKE.
"THEY'RE SO PREDICTABLE, THESE HAIRLESS APES," HOWARD MUSES-- "EXCEPT TO ONE ANOTHER.
"NOW WHY IS THAT--?"
--THE PAIN, AMY--NOT MY OWN, BUT THE SUPERFLUOUS AGONY I INFLICT UPON OTHERS.
I DESPISE MYSELF FOR THAT!
SPLAT
UHM... ELTON, I THINK MAYBE WE OUGHTTA PUSH ON.
WE'RE SITTING IN A COMBAT ZONE-- Y'KNOW?
THAT'S PROFOUND, AMY--LIKE YOUR SINEWY YET FEMININE HANDS.
ELTON... YOU'RE NOT READING ME.
BUT I AM! YOUR EVERY WORD AND GESTURE SPEAKS TO MY INNERMOST LONGINGS.
KILL!
YOU TOUCH ME, MAKE ME HOPE AGAIN.

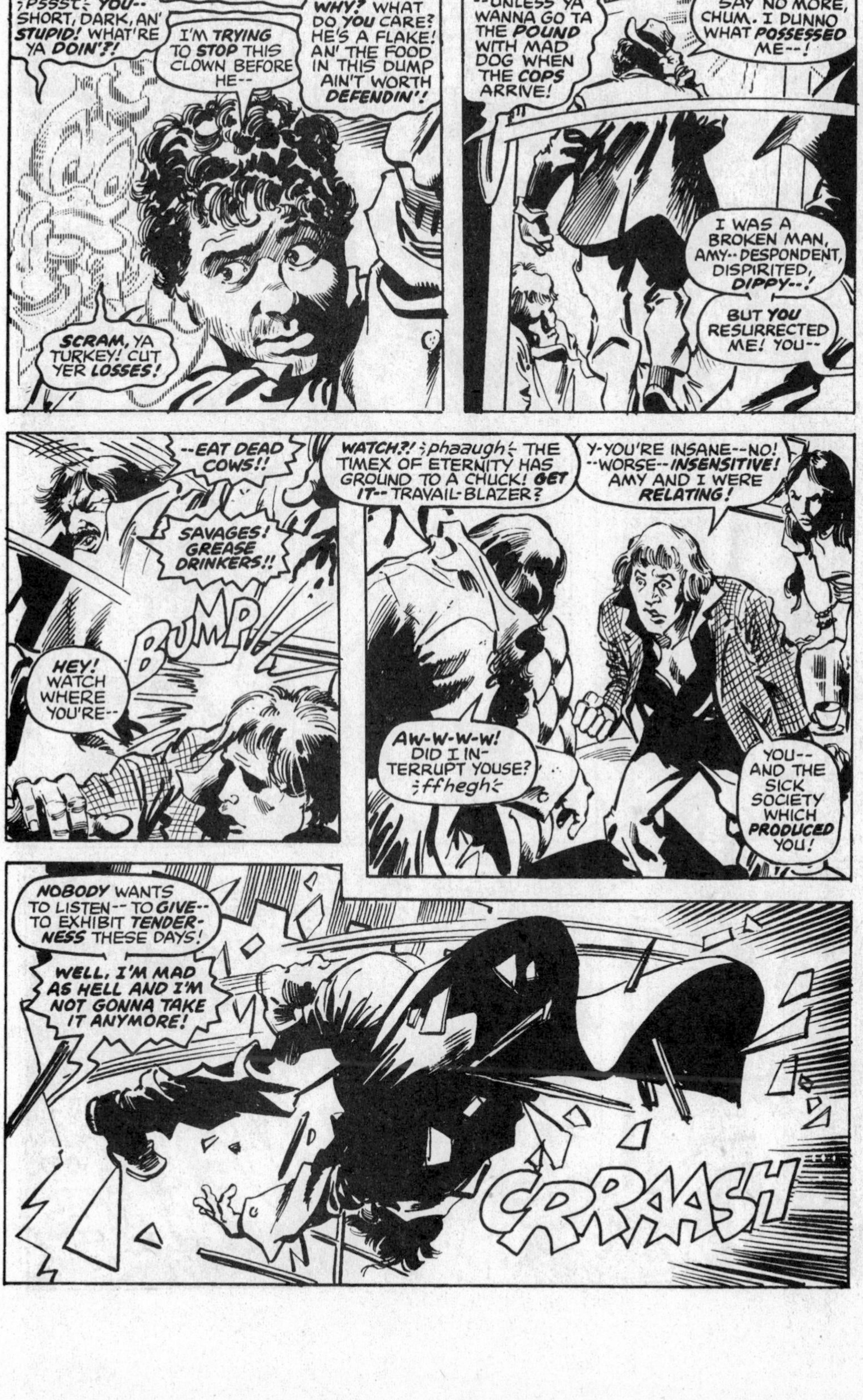

;pssst; YOU-- SHORT, DARK, AN' STUPID! WHAT'RE YA DOIN'?!
I'M TRYING TO STOP THIS CLOWN BEFORE HE--
WHY? WHAT DO YOU CARE? HE'S A FLAKE! AN' THE FOOD IN THIS DUMP AIN'T WORTH DEFENDIN'!
SCRAM, YA TURKEY! CUT YER LOSSES!
--UNLESS YA WANNA GO TA THE POUND WITH MAD DOG WHEN THE COPS ARRIVE!
SAY NO MORE, CHUM. I DUNNO WHAT POSSESSED ME--!
I WAS A BROKEN MAN, AMY--DESPONDENT, DISPIRITED, DIPPY--!
BUT YOU RESURRECTED ME! YOU--
--EAT DEAD COWS!!
SAVAGES! GREASE DRINKERS!!
BUMP
HEY! WATCH WHERE YOU'RE--
WATCH?! ;phaaugh; THE TIMEX OF ETERNITY HAS GROUND TO A CHUCK! GET IT-- TRAVAIL-BLAZER?
Y-YOU'RE INSANE--NO! --WORSE--INSENSITIVE! AMY AND I WERE RELATING!
AW-W-W-W! DID I IN-TERRUPT YOUSE? ;ffhegh;
YOU-- AND THE SICK SOCIETY WHICH PRODUCED YOU!
NOBODY WANTS TO LISTEN-- TO GIVE-- TO EXHIBIT TENDER-NESS THESE DAYS!
WELL, I'M MAD AS HELL AND I'M NOT GONNA TAKE IT ANYMORE!
CRRAASH

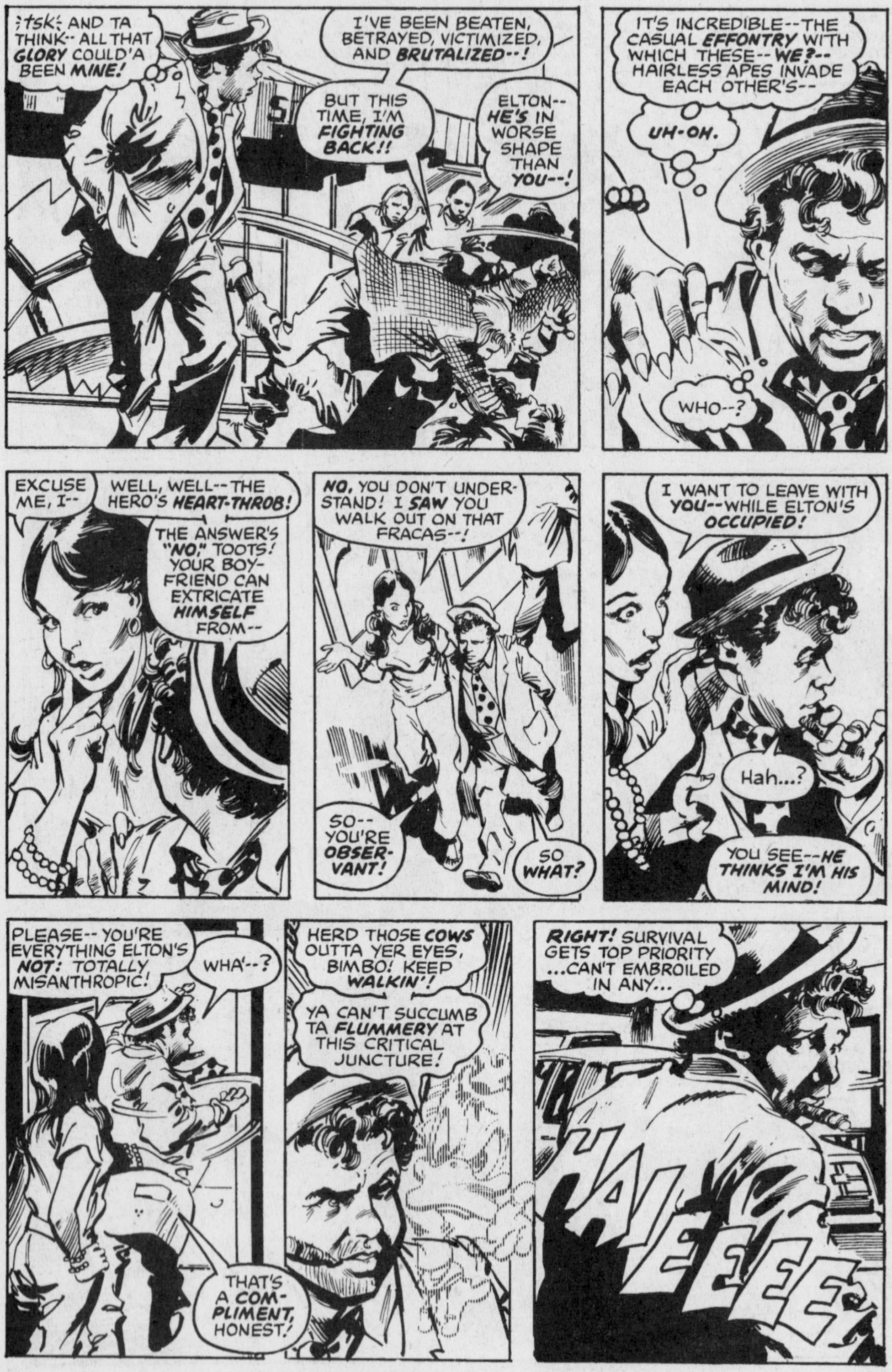

:tsk: AND TA THINK-- ALL THAT GLORY COULD'A BEEN MINE!
I'VE BEEN BEATEN, BETRAYED, VICTIMIZED, AND BRUTALIZED--!
BUT THIS TIME, I'M FIGHTING BACK!!
ELTON-- HE'S IN WORSE SHAPE THAN YOU--!
IT'S INCREDIBLE--THE CASUAL EFFONTRY WITH WHICH THESE-- WE?-- HAIRLESS APES INVADE EACH OTHER'S--
UH-OH.
WHO--?
EXCUSE ME, I--
WELL, WELL--THE HERO'S HEART-THROB!
THE ANSWER'S "NO," TOOTS! YOUR BOY-FRIEND CAN EXTRICATE HIMSELF FROM--
NO, YOU DON'T UNDERSTAND! I SAW YOU WALK OUT ON THAT FRACAS--!
SO-- YOU'RE OBSER-VANT!
SO WHAT?
I WANT TO LEAVE WITH YOU--WHILE ELTON'S OCCUPIED!
Hah...?
YOU SEE--HE THINKS I'M HIS MIND!
PLEASE-- YOU'RE EVERYTHING ELTON'S NOT: TOTALLY MISANTHROPIC!
WHA'--?
HERD THOSE COWS OUTTA YER EYES, BIMBO! KEEP WALKIN'!
YA CAN'T SUCCUMB TA FLUMMERY AT THIS CRITICAL JUNCTURE!
THAT'S A COM-PLIMENT, HONEST!
RIGHT! SURVIVAL GETS TOP PRIORITY ...CAN'T EMBROILED IN ANY...
HAIEEEEE

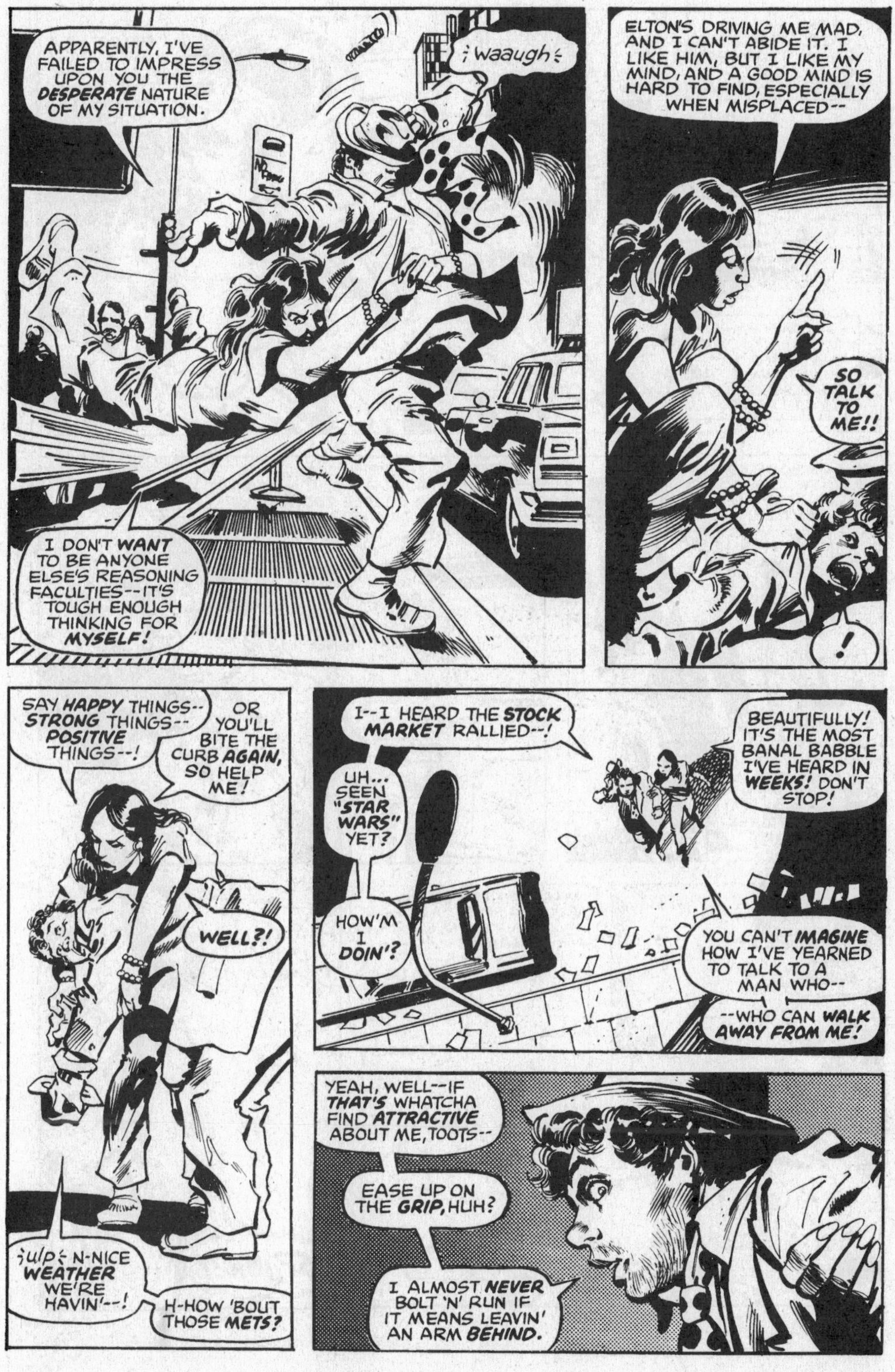

APPARENTLY, I'VE FAILED TO IMPRESS UPON YOU THE DESPERATE NATURE OF MY SITUATION.
¡waaugh!
I DON'T WANT TO BE ANYONE ELSE'S REASONING FACULTIES--IT'S TOUGH ENOUGH THINKING FOR MYSELF!
ELTON'S DRIVING ME MAD, AND I CAN'T ABIDE IT. I LIKE HIM, BUT I LIKE MY MIND, AND A GOOD MIND IS HARD TO FIND, ESPECIALLY WHEN MISPLACED--
SO TALK TO ME!!
!
SAY HAPPY THINGS--STRONG THINGS--POSITIVE THINGS--!
OR YOU'LL BITE THE CURB AGAIN, SO HELP ME!
WELL?!
gulp N-NICE WEATHER WE'RE HAVIN'--!
H-HOW 'BOUT THOSE METS?
I--I HEARD THE STOCK MARKET RALLIED--!
UH... SEEN "STAR WARS" YET?
HOW'M I DOIN'?
BEAUTIFULLY! IT'S THE MOST BANAL BABBLE I'VE HEARD IN WEEKS! DON'T STOP!
YOU CAN'T IMAGINE HOW I'VE YEARNED TO TALK TO A MAN WHO--
--WHO CAN WALK AWAY FROM ME!
YEAH, WELL--IF THAT'S WHATCHA FIND ATTRACTIVE ABOUT ME, TOOTS--
EASE UP ON THE GRIP, HUH?
I ALMOST NEVER BOLT 'N' RUN IF IT MEANS LEAVIN' AN ARM BEHIND.

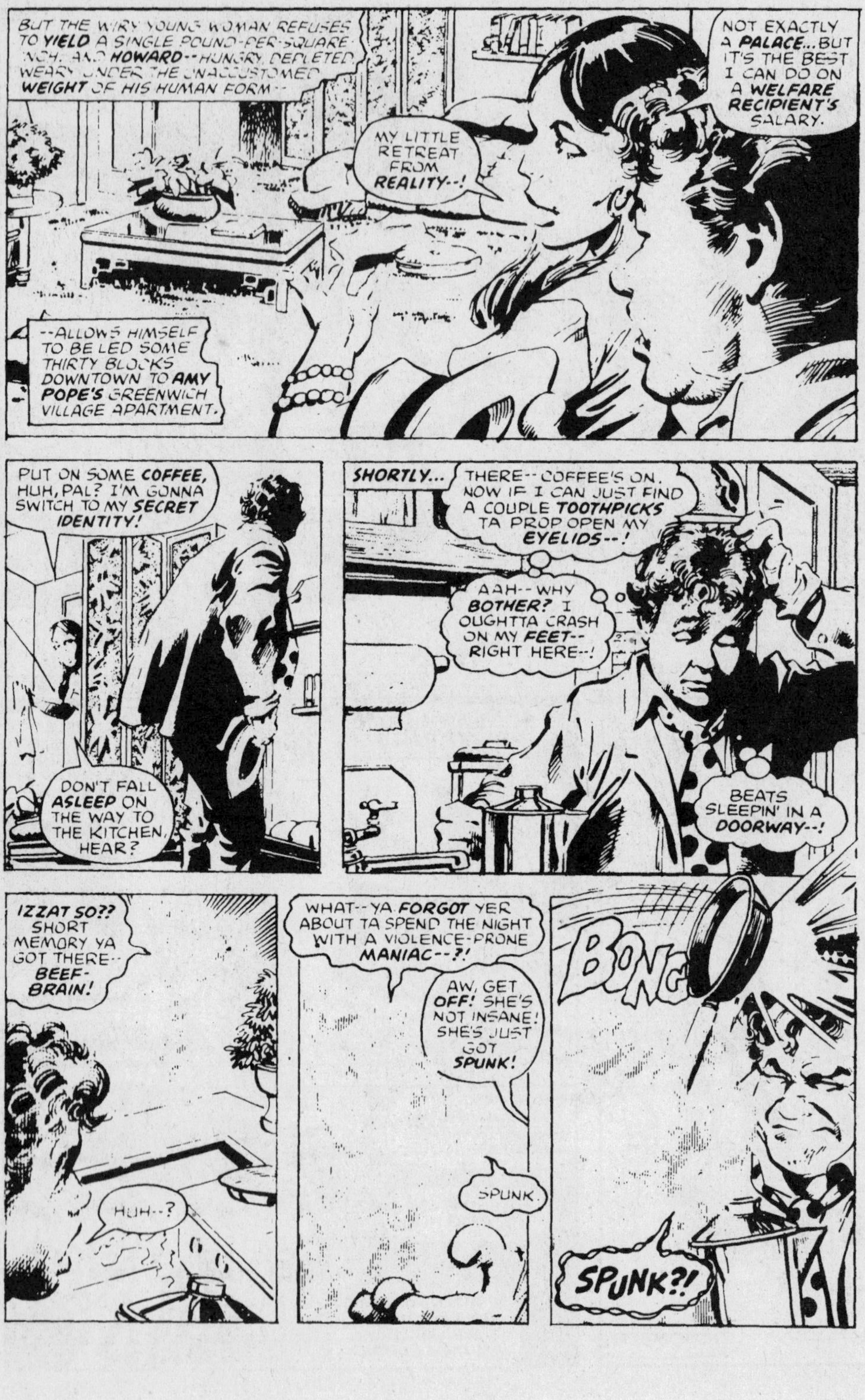
BUT THE WIRY YOUNG WOMAN REFUSES TO YIELD A SINGLE POUND-PER-SQUARE-INCH, AND HOWARD--HUNGRY, DEPLETED, WEARY UNDER THE UNACCUSTOMED WEIGHT OF HIS HUMAN FORM--
MY LITTLE RETREAT FROM REALITY--!
NOT EXACTLY A PALACE...BUT IT'S THE BEST I CAN DO ON A WELFARE RECIPIENT'S SALARY.
--ALLOWS HIMSELF TO BE LED SOME THIRTY BLOCKS DOWNTOWN TO AMY POPE'S GREENWICH VILLAGE APARTMENT.
PUT ON SOME COFFEE, HUH, PAL? I'M GONNA SWITCH TO MY SECRET IDENTITY!
DON'T FALL ASLEEP ON THE WAY TO THE KITCHEN, HEAR?
SHORTLY...
THERE--COFFEE'S ON. NOW IF I CAN JUST FIND A COUPLE TOOTHPICKS TA PROP OPEN MY EYELIDS--!
AAH--WHY BOTHER? I OUGHTTA CRASH ON MY FEET--RIGHT HERE--!
BEATS SLEEPIN' IN A DOORWAY--!
IZZAT SO?? SHORT MEMORY YA GOT THERE--BEEF-BRAIN!
HUH--?
WHAT--YA FORGOT YER ABOUT TA SPEND THE NIGHT WITH A VIOLENCE-PRONE MANIAC--?!
AW, GET OFF! SHE'S NOT INSANE! SHE'S JUST GOT SPUNK!
SPUNK.
BONG
SPUNK?!

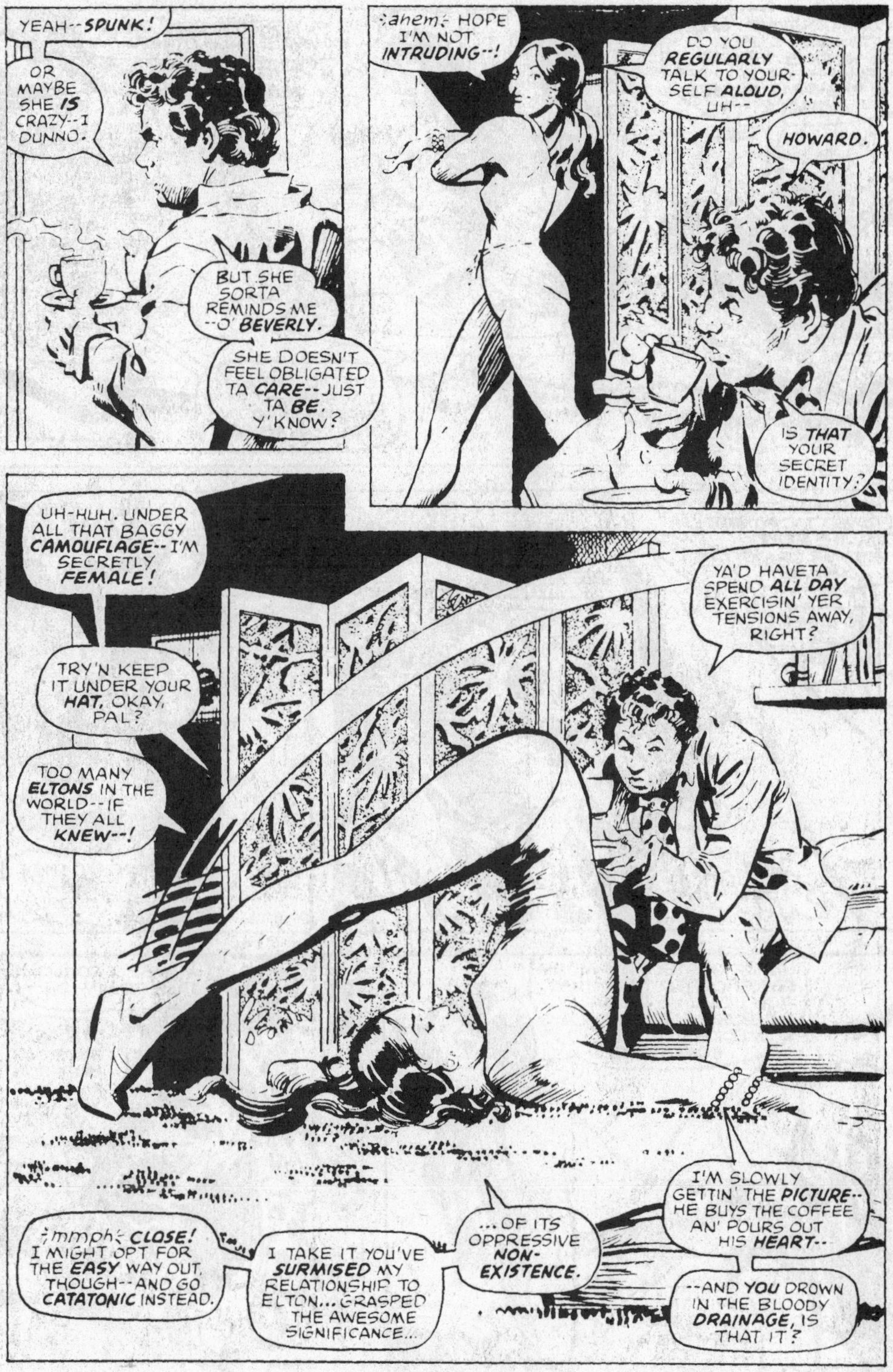

YEAH--SPUNK!
OR MAYBE SHE IS CRAZY--I DUNNO.
BUT SHE SORTA REMINDS ME --O' BEVERLY.
SHE DOESN'T FEEL OBLIGATED TA CARE--JUST TA BE. Y'KNOW?
ahem HOPE I'M NOT INTRUDING--!
DO YOU REGULARLY TALK TO YOURSELF ALOUD, UH--
HOWARD.
IS THAT YOUR SECRET IDENTITY?
UH-HUH. UNDER ALL THAT BAGGY CAMOUFLAGE--I'M SECRETLY FEMALE!
TRY'N KEEP IT UNDER YOUR HAT, OKAY, PAL?
TOO MANY ELTONS IN THE WORLD--IF THEY ALL KNEW--!
YA'D HAVETA SPEND ALL DAY EXERCISIN' YER TENSIONS AWAY, RIGHT?
I'M SLOWLY GETTIN' THE PICTURE-- HE BUYS THE COFFEE AN' POURS OUT HIS HEART--
--AND YOU DROWN IN THE BLOODY DRAINAGE, IS THAT IT?
mmph CLOSE! I MIGHT OPT FOR THE EASY WAY OUT, THOUGH--AND GO CATATONIC INSTEAD.
I TAKE IT YOU'VE SURMISED MY RELATIONSHIP TO ELTON... GRASPED THE AWESOME SIGNIFICANCE...
...OF ITS OPPRESSIVE NON-EXISTENCE.

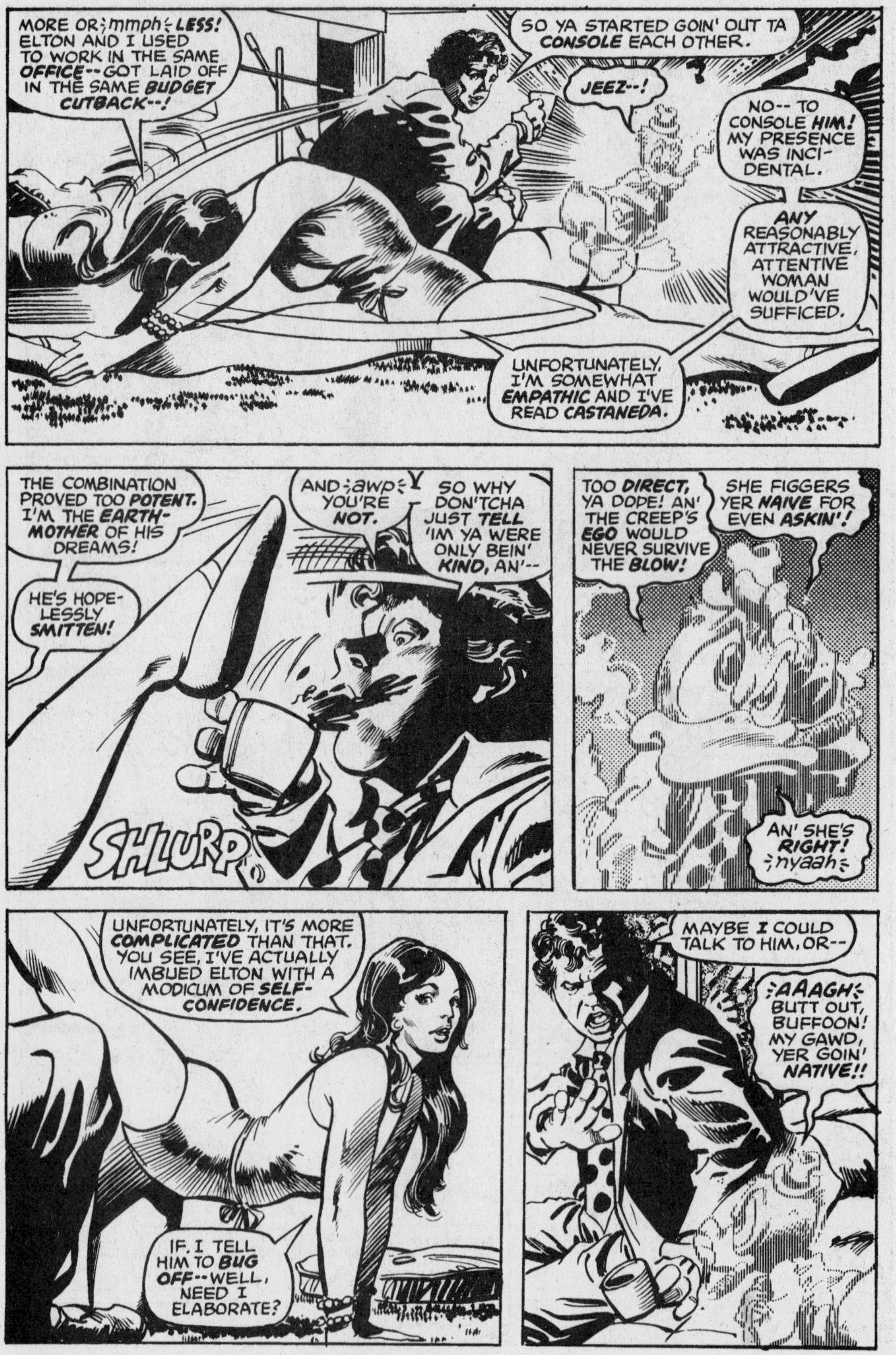
MORE OR ;mmph; LESS! ELTON AND I USED TO WORK IN THE SAME OFFICE--GOT LAID OFF IN THE SAME BUDGET CUTBACK--!
SO YA STARTED GOIN' OUT TA CONSOLE EACH OTHER.
JEEZ--!
NO-- TO CONSOLE HIM! MY PRESENCE WAS INCIDENTAL.
ANY REASONABLY ATTRACTIVE, ATTENTIVE WOMAN WOULD'VE SUFFICED.
UNFORTUNATELY, I'M SOMEWHAT EMPATHIC AND I'VE READ CASTANEDA.
THE COMBINATION PROVED TOO POTENT. I'M THE EARTH-MOTHER OF HIS DREAMS!
HE'S HOPELESSLY SMITTEN!
AND ;awp; YOU'RE NOT.
SO WHY DON'TCHA JUST TELL 'IM YA WERE ONLY BEIN' KIND, AN'--
SHLURP
TOO DIRECT, YA DOPE! AN' THE CREEP'S EGO WOULD NEVER SURVIVE THE BLOW!
SHE FIGGERS YER NAIVE FOR EVEN ASKIN'!
AN' SHE'S RIGHT! ;nyaah;
UNFORTUNATELY, IT'S MORE COMPLICATED THAN THAT. YOU SEE, I'VE ACTUALLY IMBUED ELTON WITH A MODICUM OF SELF-CONFIDENCE.
IF. I TELL HIM TO BUG OFF--WELL, NEED I ELABORATE?
MAYBE I COULD TALK TO HIM, OR--
;AAAGH; BUTT OUT, BUFFOON! MY GAWD, YER GOIN' NATIVE!!

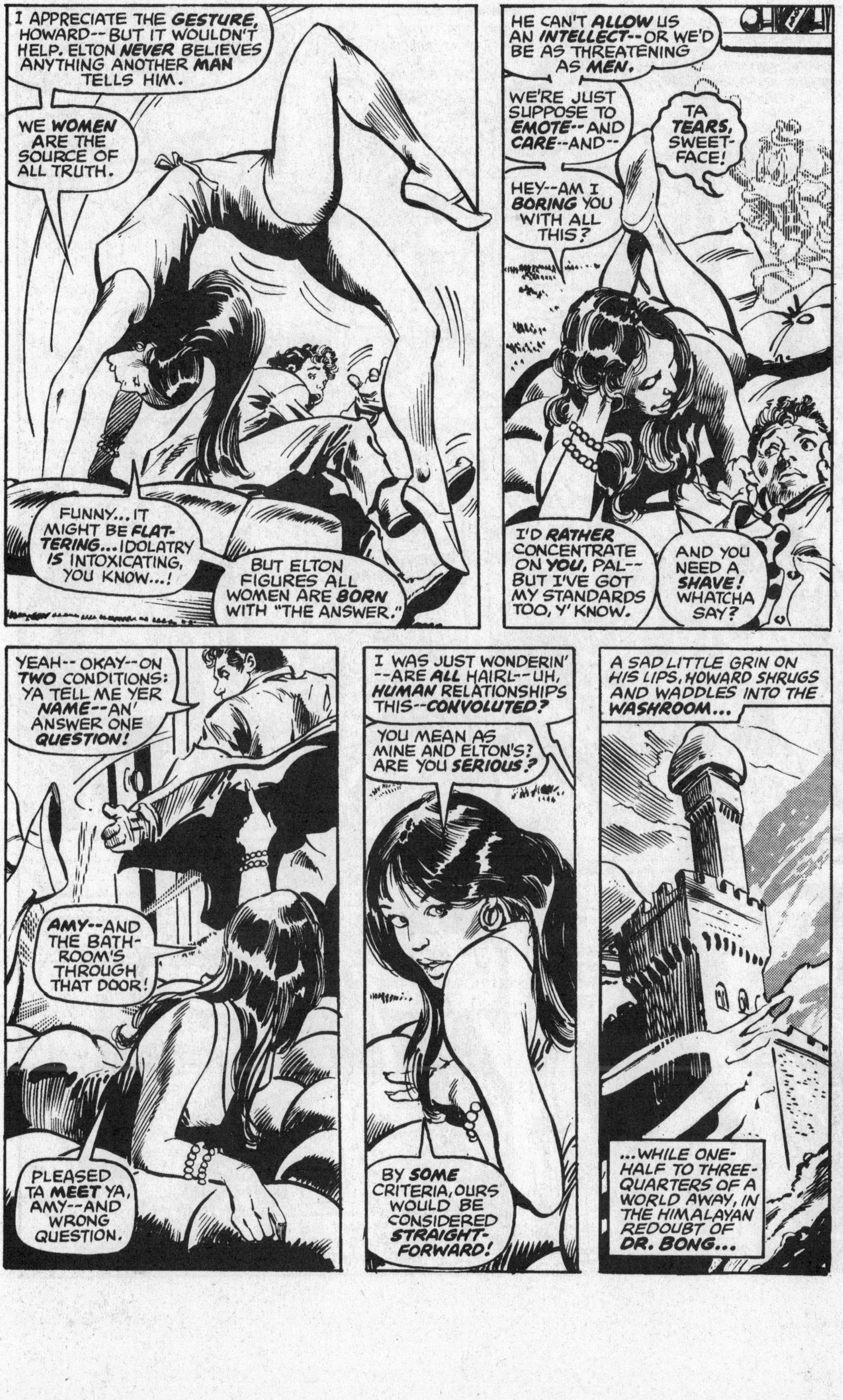

I APPRECIATE THE GESTURE, HOWARD-- BUT IT WOULDN'T HELP. ELTON NEVER BELIEVES ANYTHING ANOTHER MAN TELLS HIM.
WE WOMEN ARE THE SOURCE OF ALL TRUTH.
FUNNY... IT MIGHT BE FLATTERING... IDOLATRY IS INTOXICATING, YOU KNOW...!
BUT ELTON FIGURES ALL WOMEN ARE BORN WITH "THE ANSWER."
HE CAN'T ALLOW US AN INTELLECT--OR WE'D BE AS THREATENING AS MEN.
WE'RE JUST SUPPOSE TO EMOTE--AND CARE--AND--
TA TEARS, SWEET-FACE!
HEY--AM I BORING YOU WITH ALL THIS?
I'D RATHER CONCENTRATE ON YOU, PAL-- BUT I'VE GOT MY STANDARDS TOO, Y' KNOW.
AND YOU NEED A SHAVE! WHATCHA SAY?
YEAH-- OKAY--ON TWO CONDITIONS: YA TELL ME YER NAME--AN' ANSWER ONE QUESTION!
AMY--AND THE BATHROOM'S THROUGH THAT DOOR!
PLEASED TA MEET YA, AMY--AND WRONG QUESTION.
I WAS JUST WONDERIN' --ARE ALL HAIRL--UH, HUMAN RELATIONSHIPS THIS--CONVOLUTED?
YOU MEAN AS MINE AND ELTON'S? ARE YOU SERIOUS?
BY SOME CRITERIA, OURS WOULD BE CONSIDERED STRAIGHT-FORWARD!
A SAD LITTLE GRIN ON HIS LIPS, HOWARD SHRUGS AND WADDLES INTO THE WASHROOM...
...WHILE ONE-HALF TO THREE-QUARTERS OF A WORLD AWAY, IN THE HIMALAYAN REDOUBT OF DR. BONG...

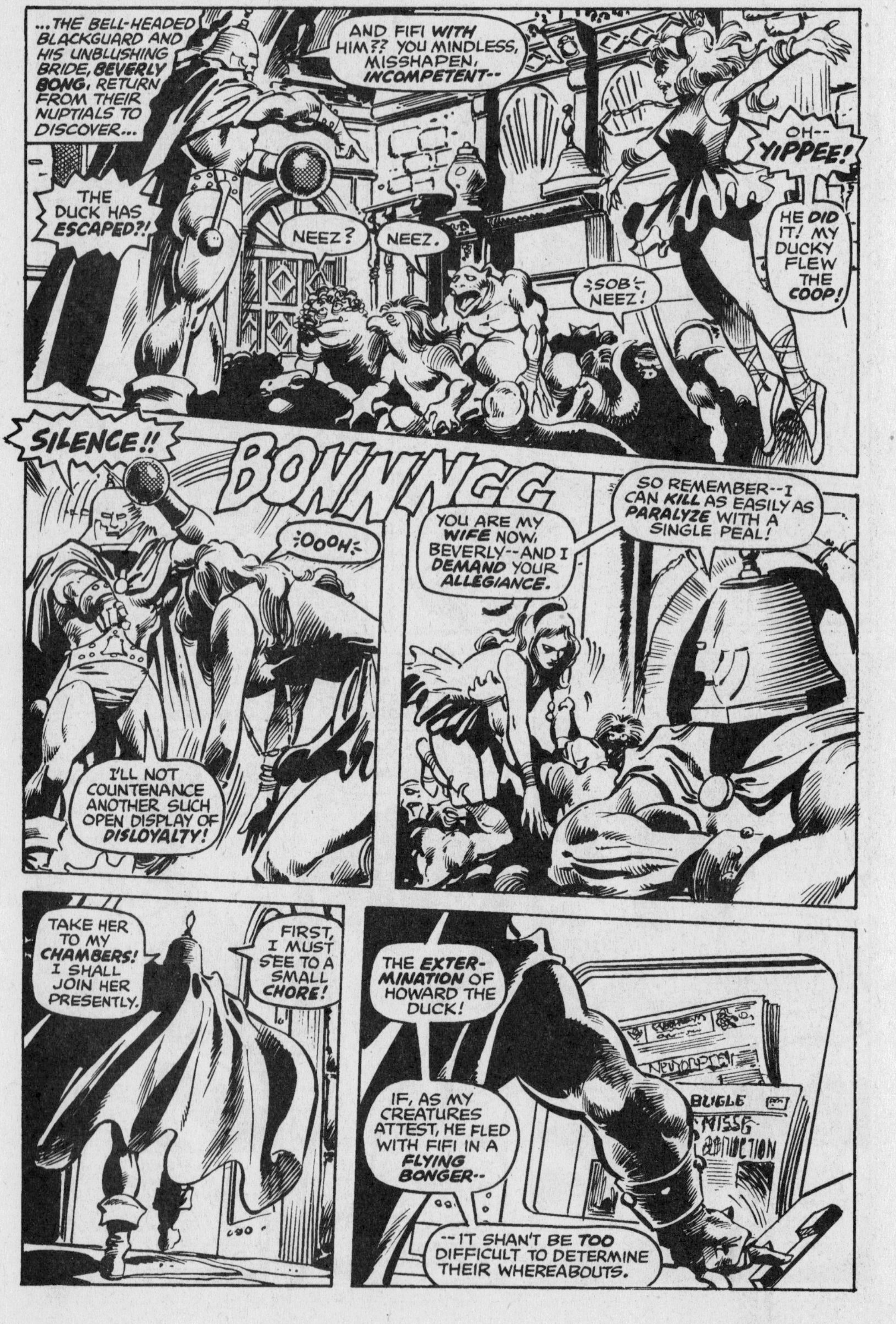
...THE BELL-HEADED BLACKGUARD AND HIS UNBLUSHING BRIDE, BEVERLY BONG, RETURN FROM THEIR NUPTIALS TO DISCOVER...
AND FIFI WITH HIM?? YOU MINDLESS, MISSHAPEN, INCOMPETENT--
THE DUCK HAS ESCAPED?!
NEEZ?
NEEZ.
SOB NEEZ!
OH--YIPPEE!
HE DID IT! MY DUCKY FLEW THE COOP!
SILENCE!!
BONNNGG
OOOH
I'LL NOT COUNTENANCE ANOTHER SUCH OPEN DISPLAY OF DISLOYALTY!
YOU ARE MY WIFE NOW, BEVERLY--AND I DEMAND YOUR ALLEGIANCE.
SO REMEMBER--I CAN KILL AS EASILY AS PARALYZE WITH A SINGLE PEAL!
TAKE HER TO MY CHAMBERS! I SHALL JOIN HER PRESENTLY.
FIRST, I MUST SEE TO A SMALL CHORE!
THE EXTERMINATION OF HOWARD THE DUCK!
IF, AS MY CREATURES ATTEST, HE FLED WITH FIFI IN A FLYING BONGER--
--IT SHAN'T BE TOO DIFFICULT TO DETERMINE THEIR WHEREABOUTS.
BUGLE

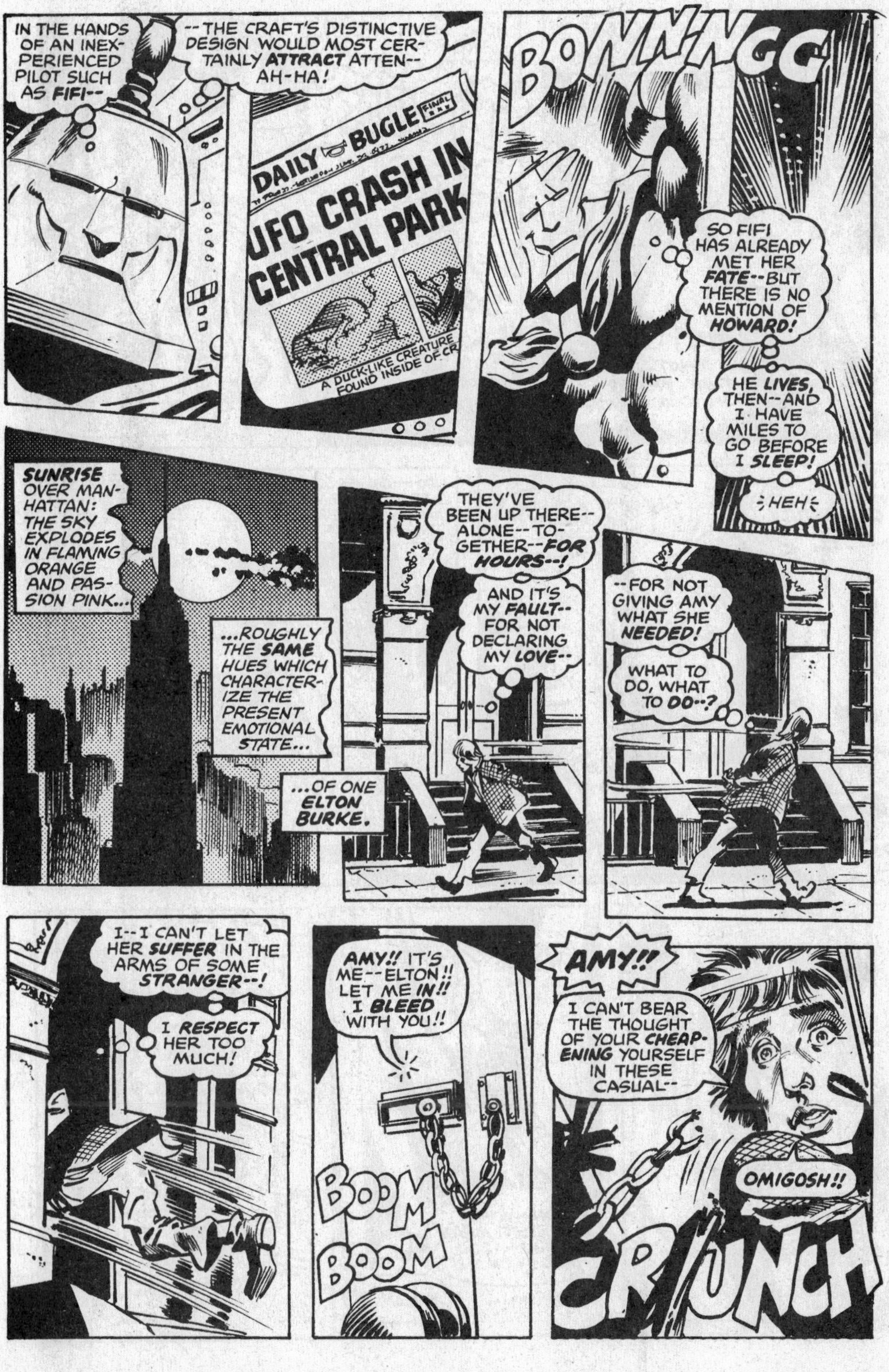

IN THE HANDS OF AN INEXPERIENCED PILOT SUCH AS FIFI--
--THE CRAFT'S DISTINCTIVE DESIGN WOULD MOST CERTAINLY ATTRACT ATTEN-- AH-HA!
DAILY BUGLE
FINAL
UFO CRASH IN CENTRAL PARK
A DUCK-LIKE CREATURE FOUND INSIDE OF CR
BONNNNGG
SO FIFI HAS ALREADY MET HER FATE--BUT THERE IS NO MENTION OF HOWARD!
HE LIVES, THEN--AND I HAVE MILES TO GO BEFORE I SLEEP!
HEH
SUNRISE OVER MANHATTAN: THE SKY EXPLODES IN FLAMING ORANGE AND PASSION PINK...
...ROUGHLY THE SAME HUES WHICH CHARACTERIZE THE PRESENT EMOTIONAL STATE...
...OF ONE ELTON BURKE.
THEY'VE BEEN UP THERE--ALONE--TOGETHER--FOR HOURS--!
AND IT'S MY FAULT--FOR NOT DECLARING MY LOVE--
--FOR NOT GIVING AMY WHAT SHE NEEDED!
WHAT TO DO, WHAT TO DO--?
I--I CAN'T LET HER SUFFER IN THE ARMS OF SOME STRANGER--!
I RESPECT HER TOO MUCH!
AMY!! IT'S ME--ELTON!! LET ME IN!! I BLEED WITH YOU!!
BOOM BOOM BOOM
AMY!!
I CAN'T BEAR THE THOUGHT OF YOUR CHEAPENING YOURSELF IN THESE CASUAL--
OMIGOSH!!
CRUNCH

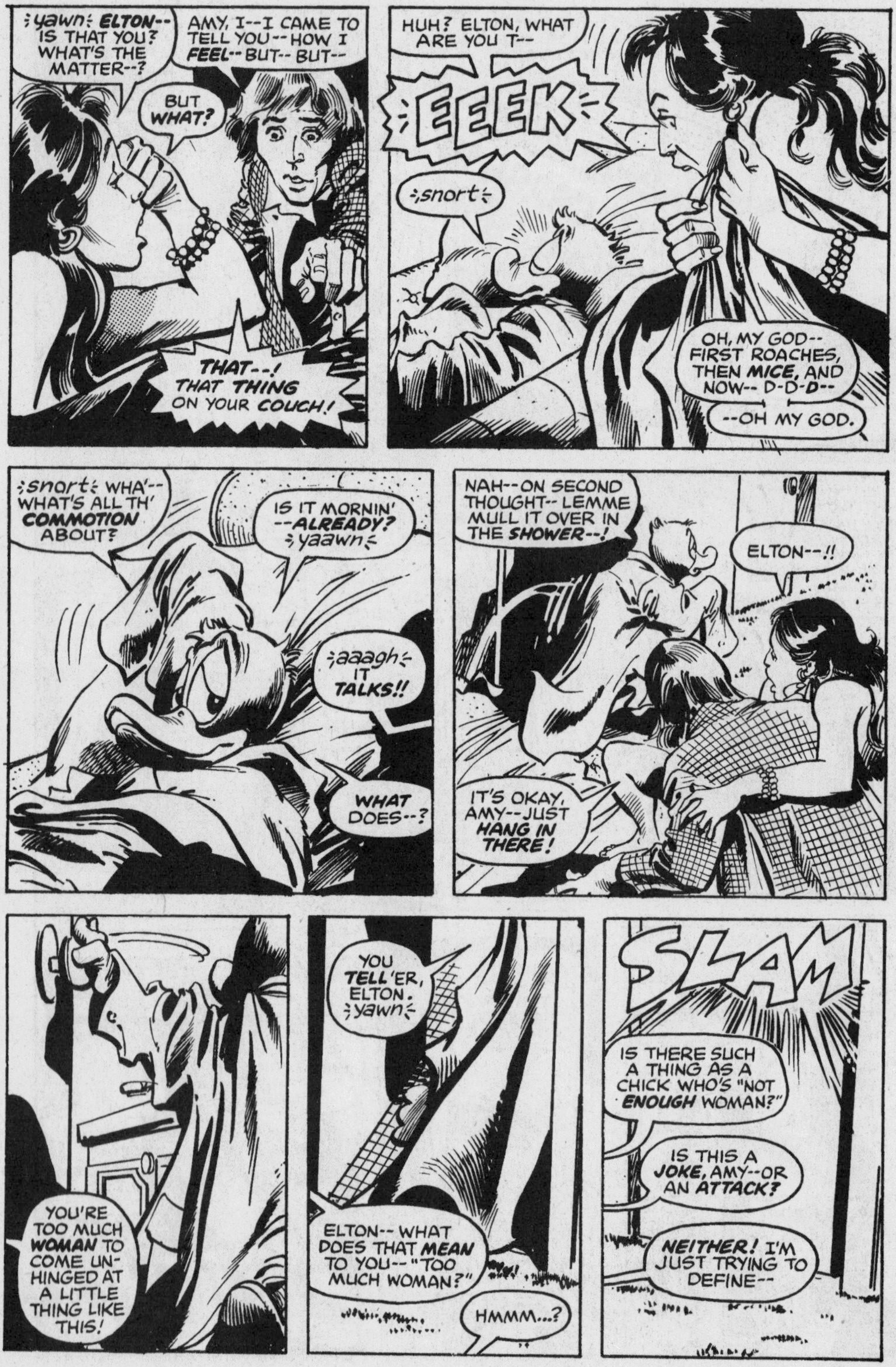

:yawn: ELTON-- IS THAT YOU? WHAT'S THE MATTER--?
AMY, I--I CAME TO TELL YOU--HOW I FEEL--BUT--BUT--
BUT WHAT?
THAT--! THAT THING ON YOUR COUCH!
HUH? ELTON, WHAT ARE YOU T--
EEEK
:snort:
OH, MY GOD-- FIRST ROACHES, THEN MICE, AND NOW-- D-D-D--
--OH MY GOD.
:snort: WHA'-- WHAT'S ALL TH' COMMOTION ABOUT?
IS IT MORNIN' --ALREADY? :yaawn:
:aaagh: IT TALKS!!
WHAT DOES--?
NAH--ON SECOND THOUGHT--LEMME MULL IT OVER IN THE SHOWER--!
ELTON--!!
IT'S OKAY, AMY--JUST HANG IN THERE!
YOU'RE TOO MUCH WOMAN TO COME UN-HINGED AT A LITTLE THING LIKE THIS!
YOU TELL 'ER, ELTON. :yawn:
ELTON--WHAT DOES THAT MEAN TO YOU--"TOO MUCH WOMAN?"
HMMM...?
SLAM
IS THERE SUCH A THING AS A CHICK WHO'S "NOT ENOUGH WOMAN?"
IS THIS A JOKE, AMY--OR AN ATTACK?
NEITHER! I'M JUST TRYING TO DEFINE--

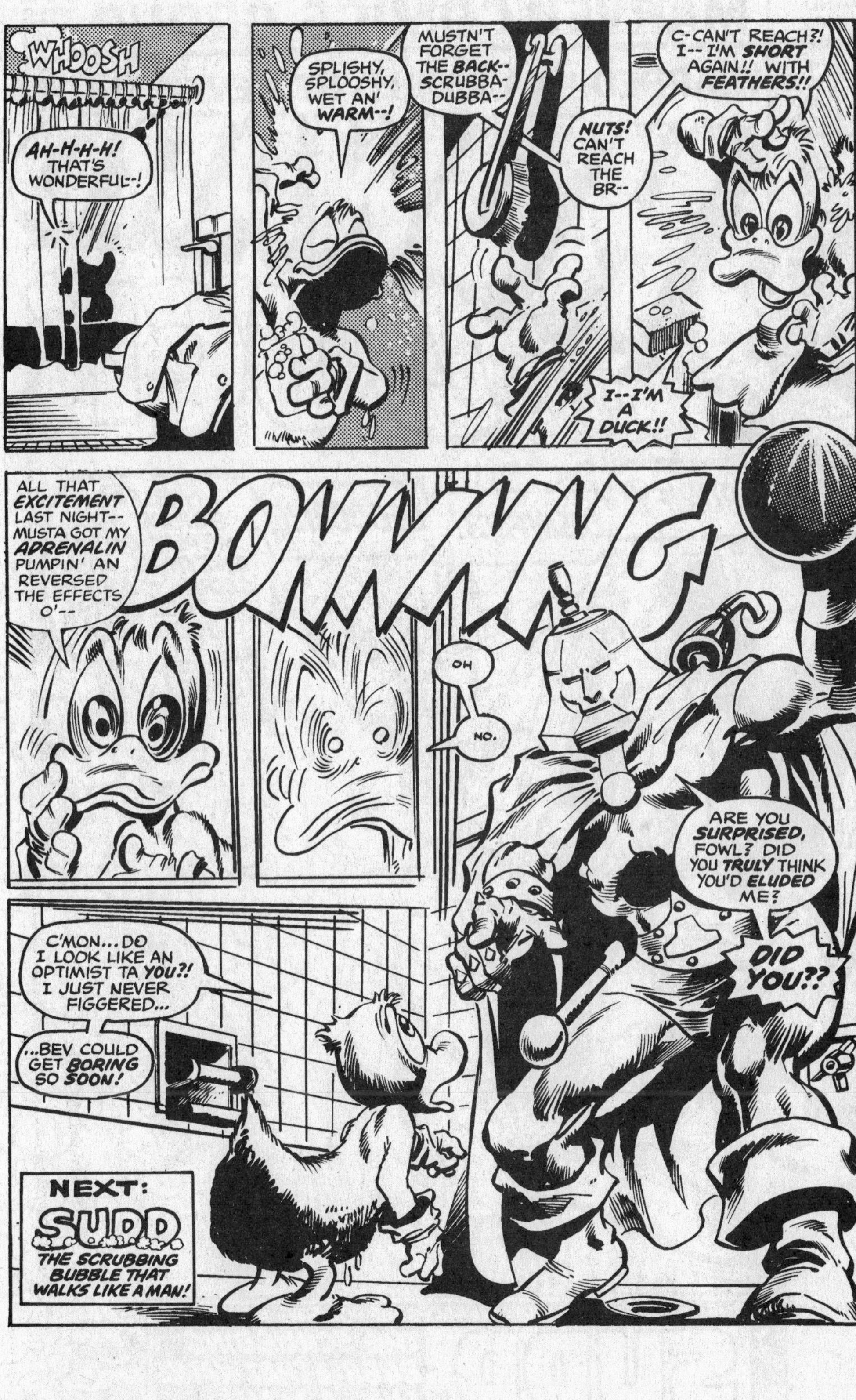

WHOOSH
AH-H-H-H! THAT'S WONDERFUL--!
SPLISHY, SPLOOSHY, WET AN' WARM--!
MUSTN'T FORGET THE BACK-- SCRUBBA-DUBBA--
NUTS! CAN'T REACH THE BR--
C-CAN'T REACH?! I-- I'M SHORT AGAIN!! WITH FEATHERS!!
I--I'M A DUCK!!
ALL THAT EXCITEMENT LAST NIGHT-- MUSTA GOT MY ADRENALIN PUMPIN' AN REVERSED THE EFFECTS O'--
BONNNG
OH
NO.
ARE YOU SURPRISED, FOWL? DID YOU TRULY THINK YOU'D ELUDED ME?
DID YOU??
C'MON... DO I LOOK LIKE AN OPTIMIST TA YOU?! I JUST NEVER FIGGERED...
...BEV COULD GET BORING SO SOON!
NEXT:
SUDD
THE SCRUBBING BUBBLE THAT WALKS LIKE A MAN!

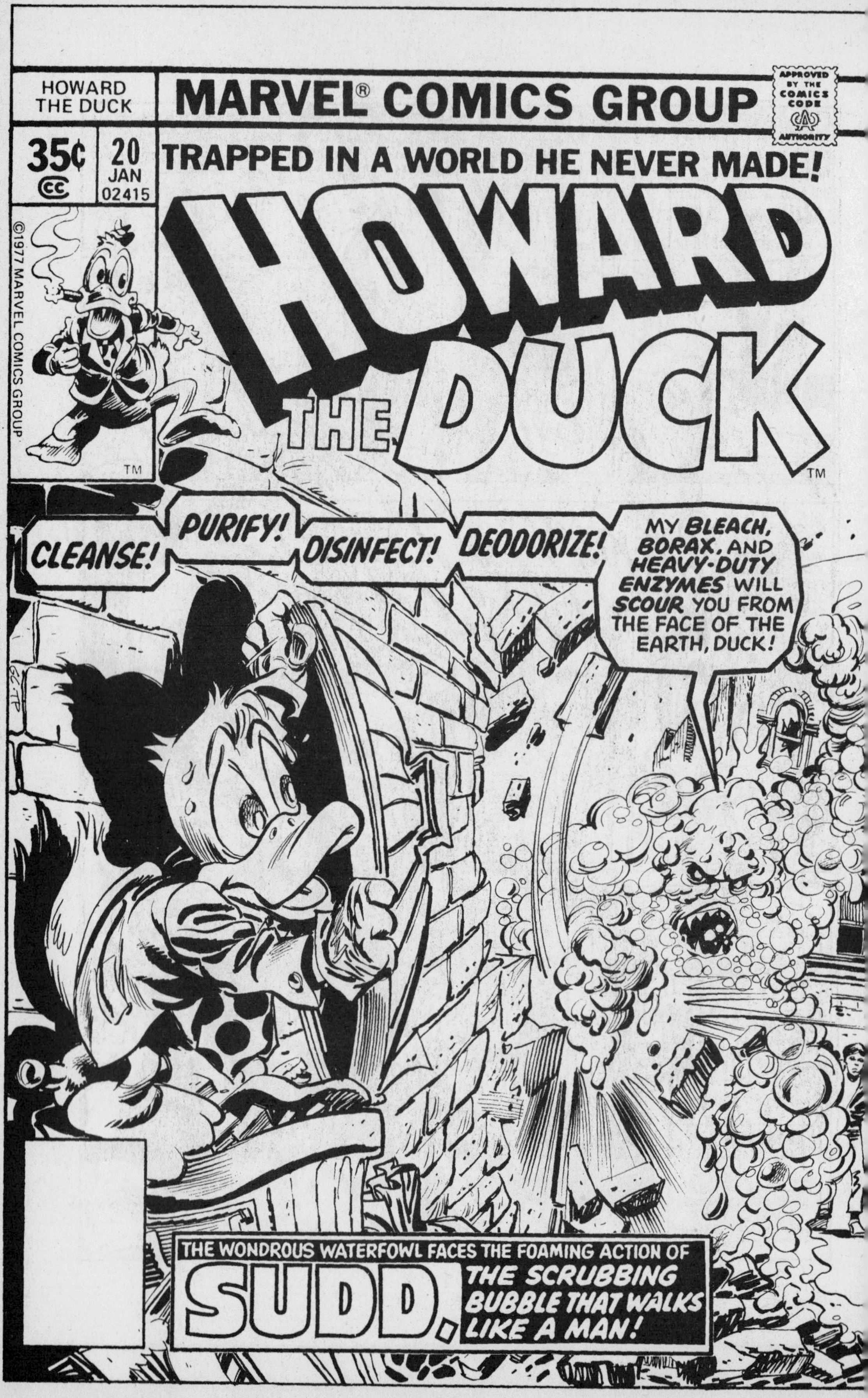

HOWARD THE DUCK
MARVEL® COMICS GROUP
APPROVED BY THE COMICS CODE AUTHORITY
35¢
20 JAN 02415
TRAPPED IN A WORLD HE NEVER MADE!
HOWARD THE DUCK
©1977 MARVEL COMICS GROUP
CLEANSE!
PURIFY!
DISINFECT!
DEODORIZE!
MY BLEACH, BORAX, AND HEAVY-DUTY ENZYMES WILL SCOUR YOU FROM THE FACE OF THE EARTH, DUCK!
THE WONDROUS WATERFOWL FACES THE FOAMING ACTION OF
SUDD, THE SCRUBBING BUBBLE THAT WALKS LIKE A MAN!

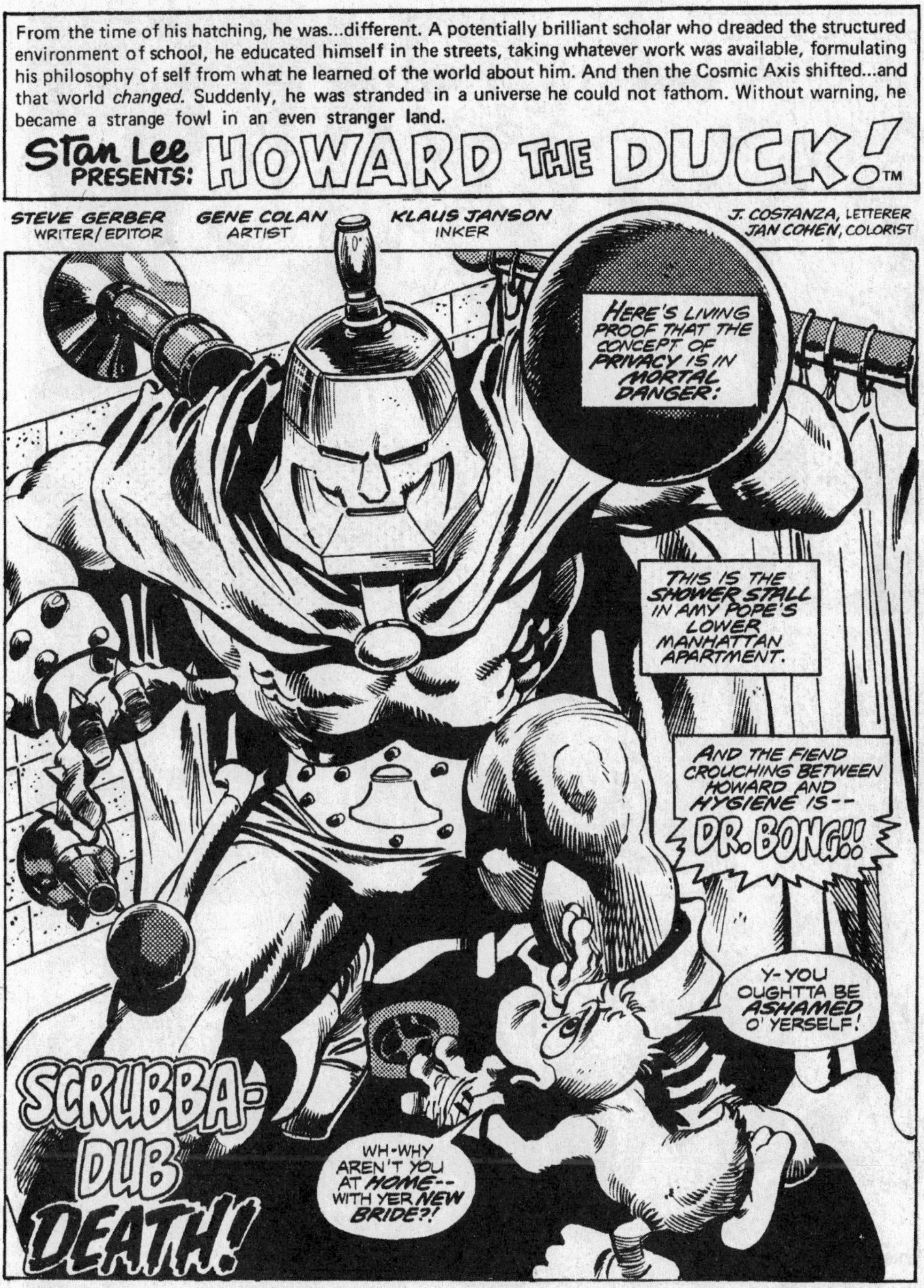
From the time of his hatching, he was...different. A potentially brilliant scholar who dreaded the structured environment of school, he educated himself in the streets, taking whatever work was available, formulating his philosophy of self from what he learned of the world about him. And then the Cosmic Axis shifted...and that world *changed.* Suddenly, he was stranded in a universe he could not fathom. Without warning, he became a strange fowl in an even stranger land.
Stan Lee PRESENTS: HOWARD THE DUCK! TM
STEVE GERBER WRITER/EDITOR
GENE COLAN ARTIST
KLAUS JANSON INKER
J. COSTANZA, LETTERER
JAN COHEN, COLORIST
HERE'S LIVING PROOF THAT THE CONCEPT OF PRIVACY IS IN MORTAL DANGER:
THIS IS THE SHOWER STALL IN AMY POPE'S LOWER MANHATTAN APARTMENT.
AND THE FIEND CROUCHING BETWEEN HOWARD AND HYGIENE IS-- DR. BONG!!
Y-YOU OUGHTTA BE ASHAMED O' YERSELF!
WH-WHY AREN'T YOU AT HOME-- WITH YER NEW BRIDE?!
SCRUBBA-DUB DEATH!

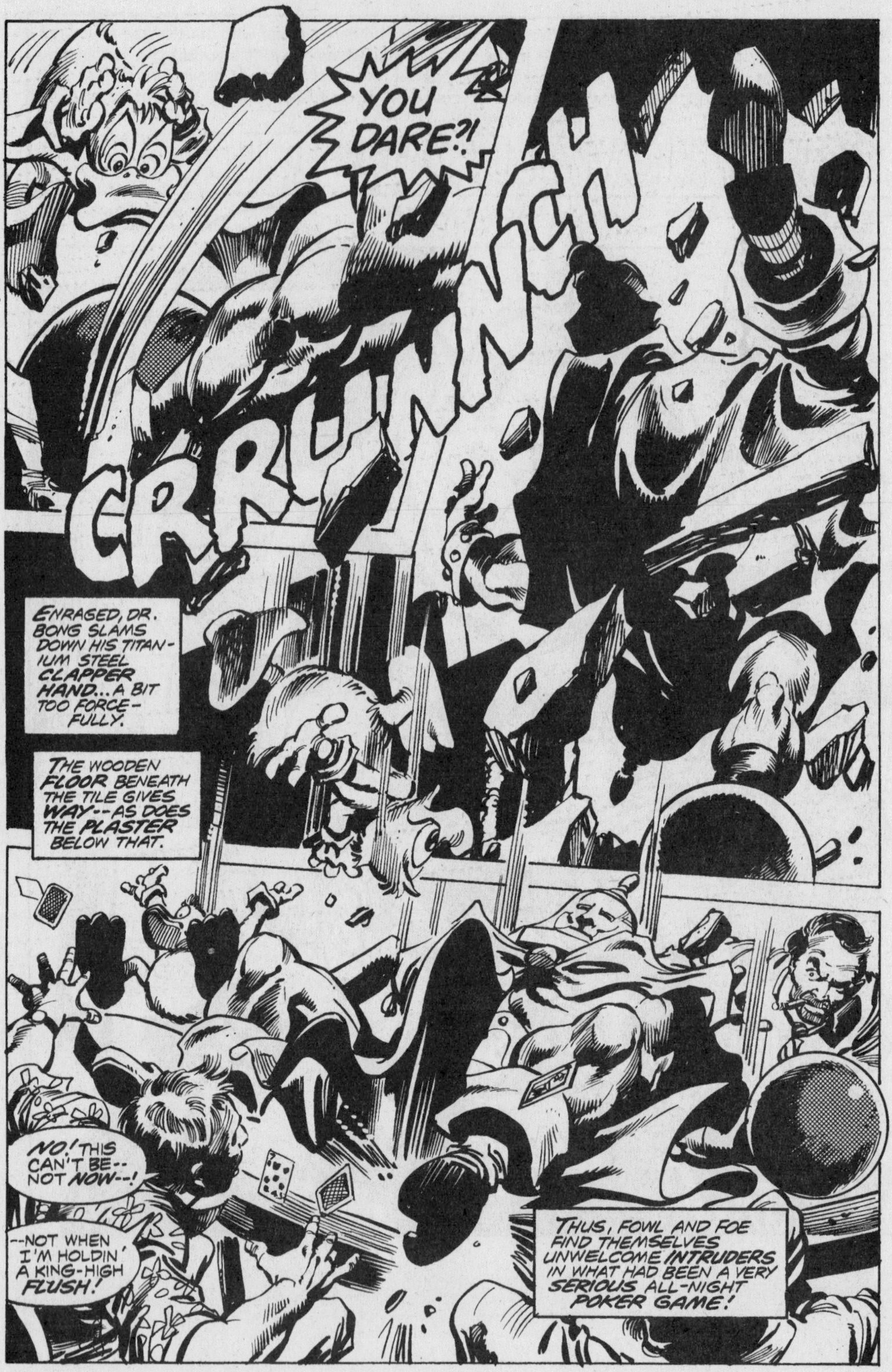
YOU DARE?!
CRRUNNCH
ENRAGED, DR. BONG SLAMS DOWN HIS TITANIUM STEEL CLAPPER HAND... A BIT TOO FORCEFULLY.
THE WOODEN FLOOR BENEATH THE TILE GIVES WAY-- AS DOES THE PLASTER BELOW THAT.
NO! THIS CAN'T BE-- NOT NOW--!
--NOT WHEN I'M HOLDIN' A KING-HIGH FLUSH!
THUS, FOWL AND FOE FIND THEMSELVES UNWELCOME INTRUDERS IN WHAT HAD BEEN A VERY SERIOUS ALL-NIGHT POKER GAME!

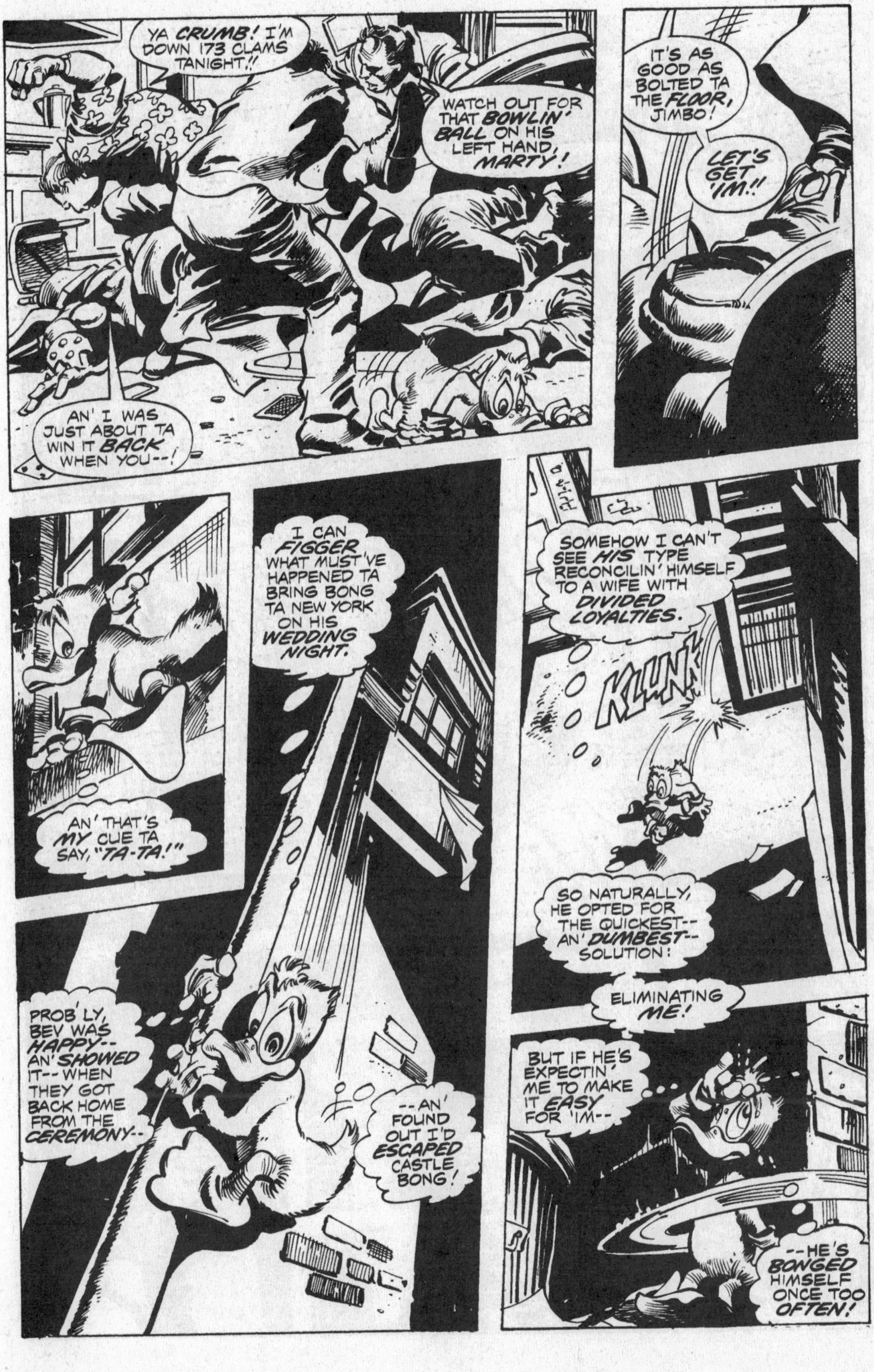

YA CRUMB! I'M DOWN 173 CLAMS TANIGHT!!
WATCH OUT FOR THAT BOWLIN' BALL ON HIS LEFT HAND, MARTY!
AN' I WAS JUST ABOUT TA WIN IT BACK WHEN YOU--!
IT'S AS GOOD AS BOLTED TA THE FLOOR, JIMBO!
LET'S GET 'IM!!
AN' THAT'S MY CUE TA SAY, "TA-TA!"
I CAN FIGGER WHAT MUST'VE HAPPENED TA BRING BONG TA NEW YORK ON HIS WEDDING NIGHT.
PROB'LY, BEV WAS HAPPY-- AN' SHOWED IT-- WHEN THEY GOT BACK HOME FROM THE CEREMONY--
--AN' FOUND OUT I'D ESCAPED CASTLE BONG!
SOMEHOW I CAN'T SEE HIS TYPE RECONCILIN' HIMSELF TO A WIFE WITH DIVIDED LOYALTIES.
KLUNK
SO NATURALLY, HE OPTED FOR THE QUICKEST-- AN' DUMBEST-- SOLUTION:
ELIMINATING ME!
BUT IF HE'S EXPECTIN' ME TO MAKE IT EASY FOR 'IM--
--HE'S BONGED HIMSELF ONCE TOO OFTEN!

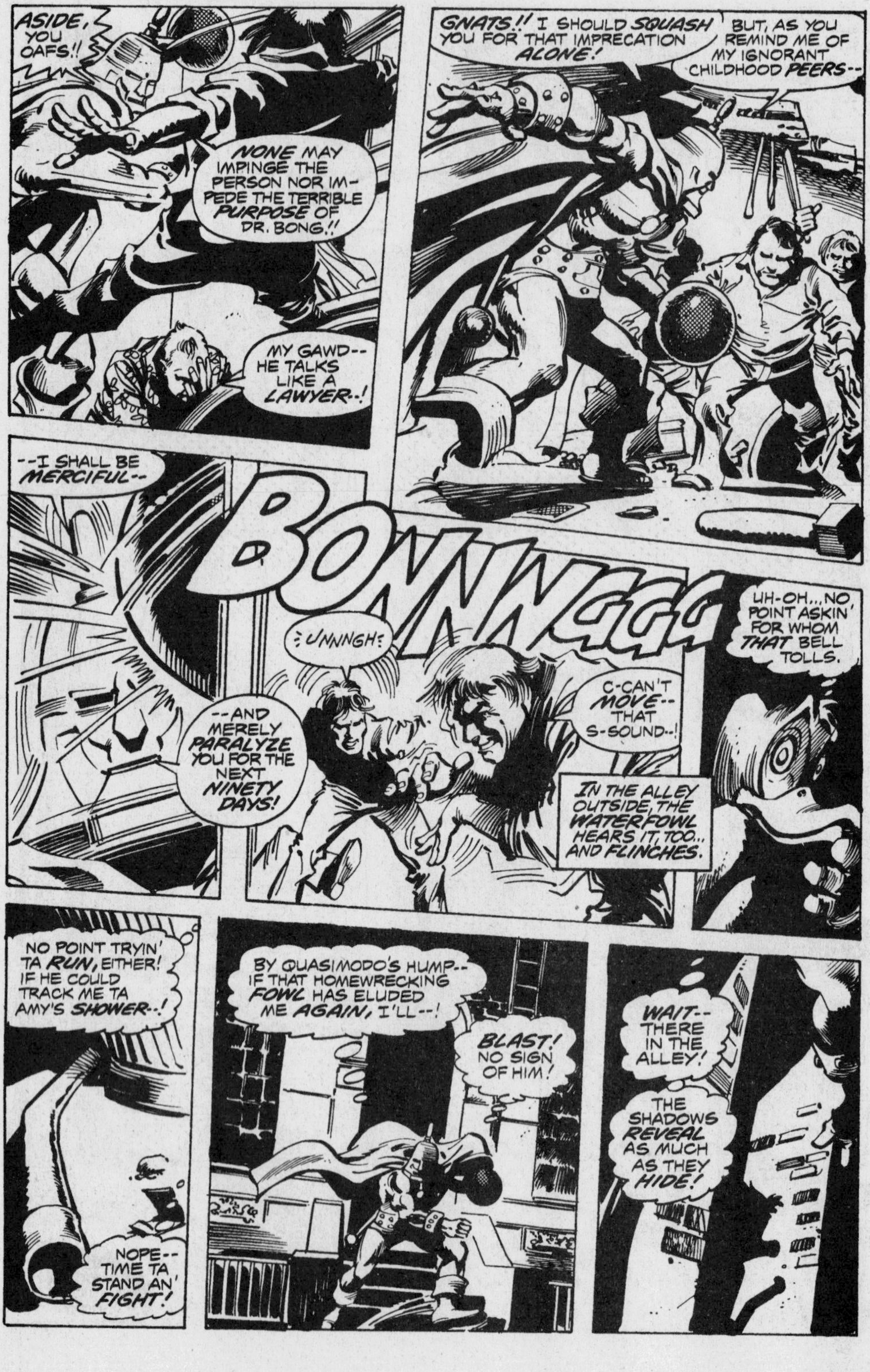
ASIDE, YOU OAFS!!
NONE MAY IMPINGE THE PERSON NOR IMPEDE THE TERRIBLE PURPOSE OF DR. BONG!!
MY GAWD-- HE TALKS LIKE A LAWYER--!
GNATS!! I SHOULD SQUASH YOU FOR THAT IMPRECATION ALONE!
BUT, AS YOU REMIND ME OF MY IGNORANT CHILDHOOD PEERS--
--I SHALL BE MERCIFUL--
BONNNGGG
UNNNGH
--AND MERELY PARALYZE YOU FOR THE NEXT NINETY DAYS!
C-CAN'T MOVE-- THAT S-SOUND--!
IN THE ALLEY OUTSIDE, THE WATERFOWL HEARS IT, TOO... AND FLINCHES.
UH-OH... NO POINT ASKIN' FOR WHOM THAT BELL TOLLS.
NO POINT TRYIN' TA RUN, EITHER! IF HE COULD TRACK ME TA AMY'S SHOWER--!
NOPE-- TIME TA STAND AN' FIGHT!
BY QUASIMODO'S HUMP-- IF THAT HOMEWRECKING FOWL HAS ELUDED ME AGAIN, I'LL--!
BLAST! NO SIGN OF HIM!
WAIT-- THERE IN THE ALLEY!
THE SHADOWS REVEAL AS MUCH AS THEY HIDE!

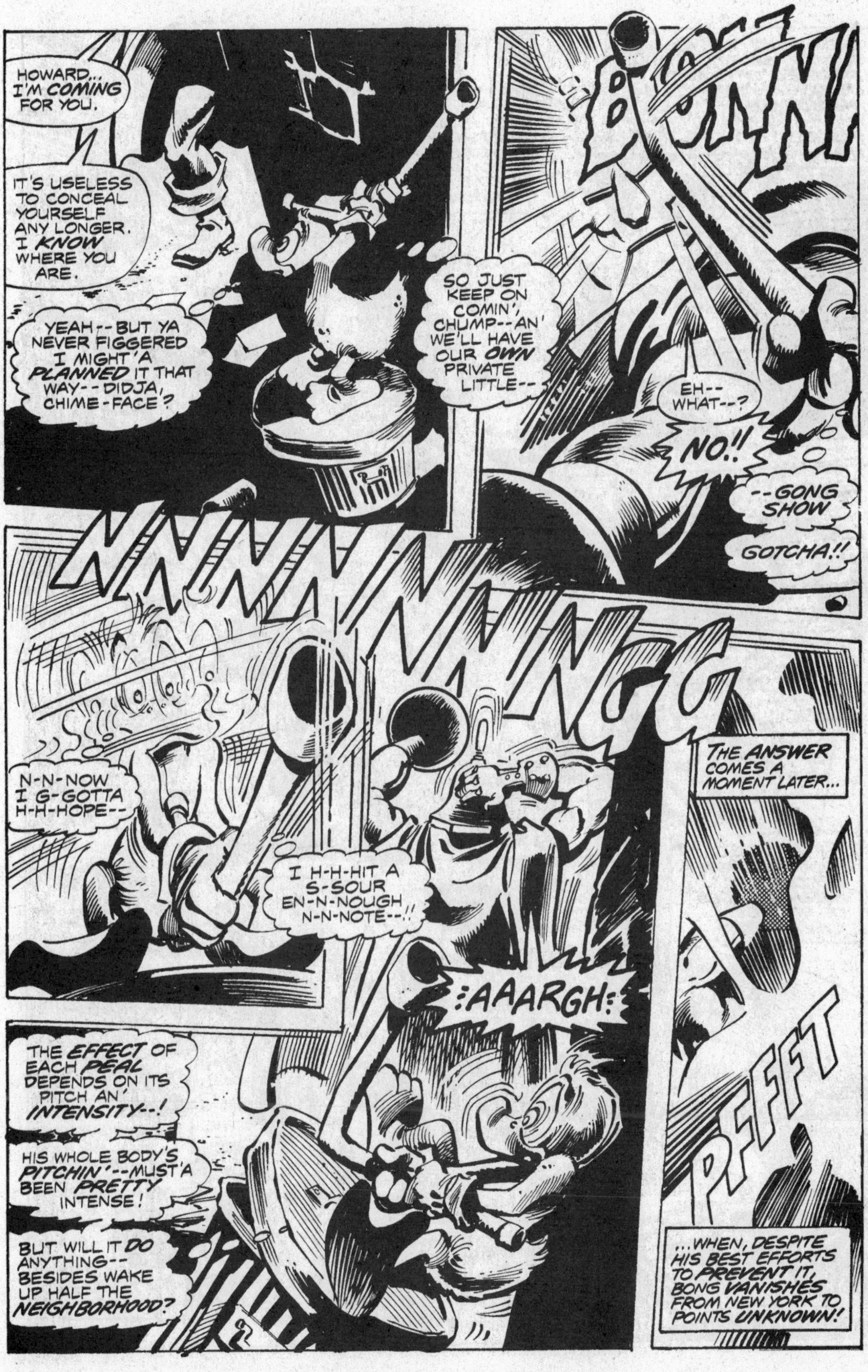
HOWARD... I'M COMING FOR YOU.
IT'S USELESS TO CONCEAL YOURSELF ANY LONGER. I KNOW WHERE YOU ARE.
YEAH--BUT YA NEVER FIGGERED I MIGHT'A PLANNED IT THAT WAY--DIDJA, CHIME-FACE?
SO JUST KEEP ON COMIN', CHUMP--AN' WE'LL HAVE OUR OWN PRIVATE LITTLE--
BONN
EH-- WHAT--?
NO!!
--GONG SHOW
GOTCHA!!
NNNNNNNNNNNGG
N-N-NOW I G-GOTTA H-H-HOPE--
I H-H-HIT A S-SOUR EN-N-NOUGH N-N-NOTE--!!
THE ANSWER COMES A MOMENT LATER...
AAARGH
THE EFFECT OF EACH PEAL DEPENDS ON ITS PITCH AN' INTENSITY--!
HIS WHOLE BODY'S PITCHIN'--MUST'A BEEN PRETTY INTENSE!
BUT WILL IT DO ANYTHING-- BESIDES WAKE UP HALF THE NEIGHBORHOOD?
PFFFT
...WHEN, DESPITE HIS BEST EFFORTS TO PREVENT IT, BONG VANISHES FROM NEW YORK TO POINTS UNKNOWN!

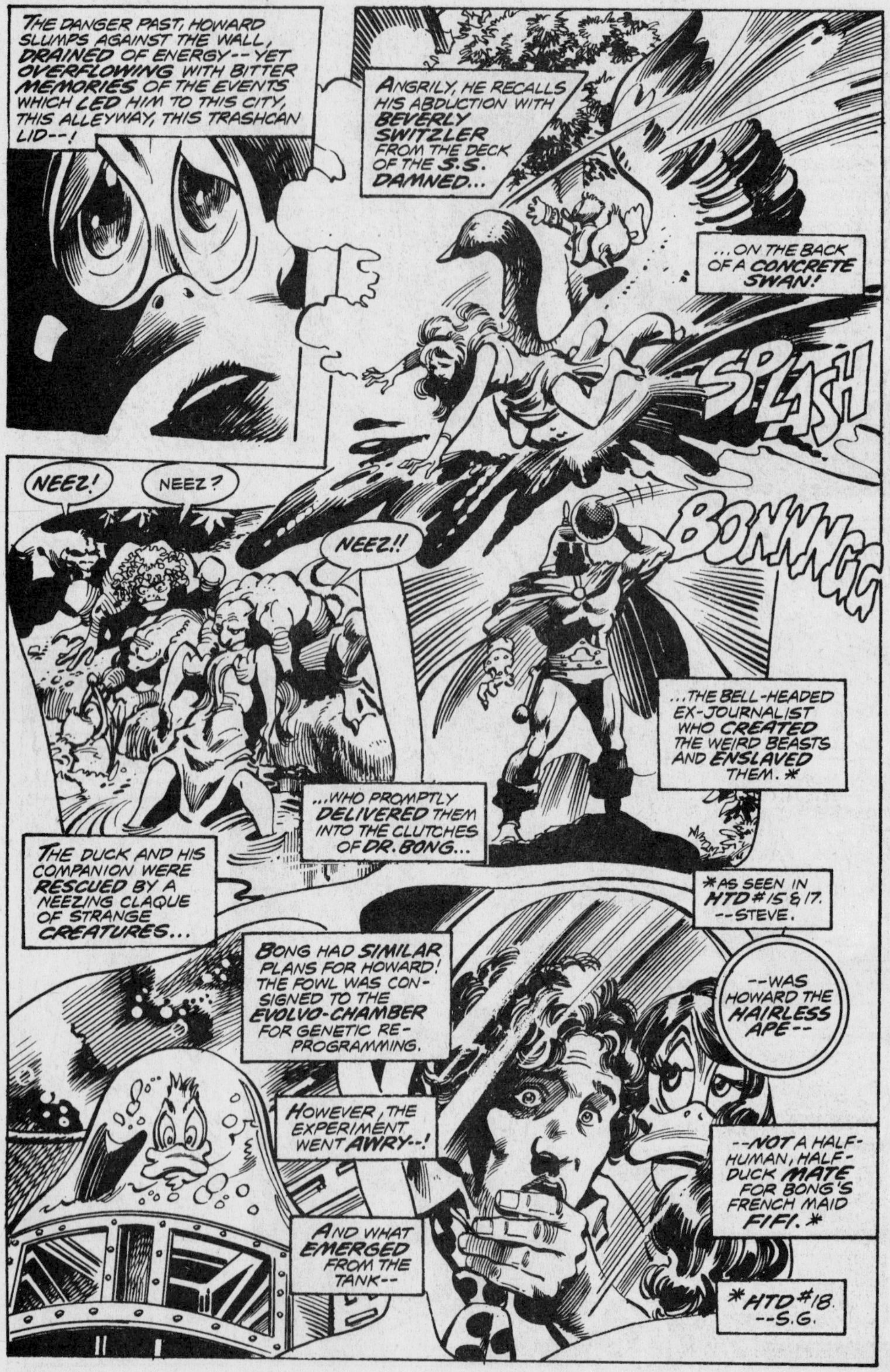
THE DANGER PAST, HOWARD SLUMPS AGAINST THE WALL, DRAINED OF ENERGY--YET OVERFLOWING WITH BITTER MEMORIES OF THE EVENTS WHICH LED HIM TO THIS CITY, THIS ALLEYWAY, THIS TRASHCAN LID--!
ANGRILY, HE RECALLS HIS ABDUCTION WITH BEVERLY SWITZLER FROM THE DECK OF THE S.S. DAMNED...
...ON THE BACK OF A CONCRETE SWAN!
SPLASH
NEEZ!
NEEZ?
NEEZ!!
BONNNGG
THE DUCK AND HIS COMPANION WERE RESCUED BY A NEEZING CLAQUE OF STRANGE CREATURES...
...WHO PROMPTLY DELIVERED THEM INTO THE CLUTCHES OF DR. BONG...
...THE BELL-HEADED EX-JOURNALIST WHO CREATED THE WEIRD BEASTS AND ENSLAVED THEM.*
*AS SEEN IN HTD #15 & 17. --STEVE.
BONG HAD SIMILAR PLANS FOR HOWARD! THE FOWL WAS CONSIGNED TO THE EVOLVO-CHAMBER FOR GENETIC RE-PROGRAMMING.
HOWEVER, THE EXPERIMENT WENT AWRY--!
AND WHAT EMERGED FROM THE TANK--
--WAS HOWARD THE HAIRLESS APE--
--NOT A HALF-HUMAN, HALF-DUCK MATE FOR BONG'S FRENCH MAID FIFI.*
*HTD #18. --S.G.

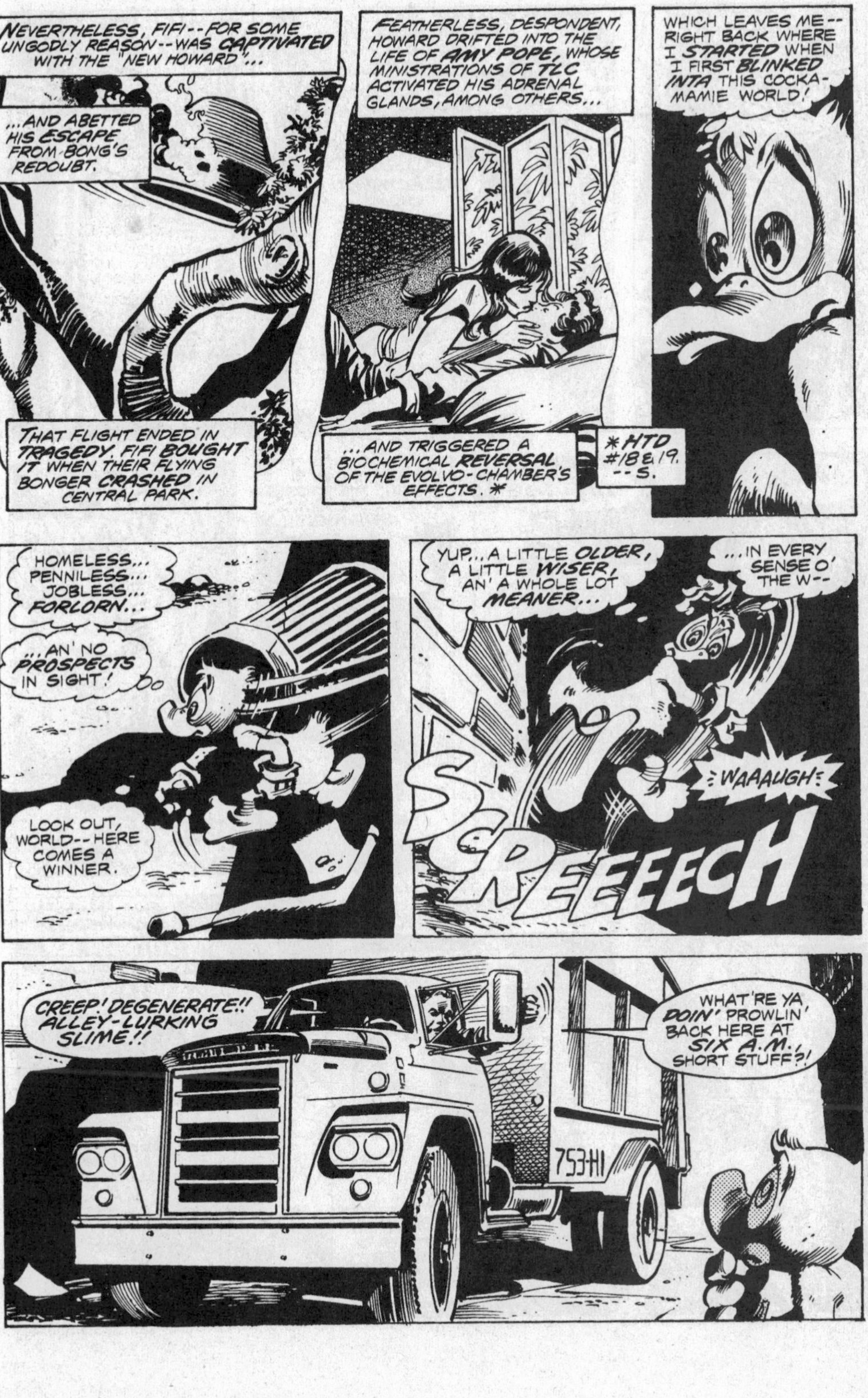
NEVERTHELESS, FIFI--FOR SOME UNGODLY REASON--WAS CAPTIVATED WITH THE "NEW HOWARD"...
...AND ABETTED HIS ESCAPE FROM BONG'S REDOUBT.
THAT FLIGHT ENDED IN TRAGEDY. FIFI BOUGHT IT WHEN THEIR FLYING BONGER CRASHED IN CENTRAL PARK.
FEATHERLESS, DESPONDENT, HOWARD DRIFTED INTO THE LIFE OF AMY POPE, WHOSE MINISTRATIONS OF TLC ACTIVATED HIS ADRENAL GLANDS, AMONG OTHERS...
...AND TRIGGERED A BIOCHEMICAL REVERSAL OF THE EVOLVO-CHAMBER'S EFFECTS.*
*HTD #18 & 19. --S.
WHICH LEAVES ME--RIGHT BACK WHERE I STARTED WHEN I FIRST BLINKED INTA THIS COCKAMAMIE WORLD!
HOMELESS... PENNILESS... JOBLESS... FORLORN...
...AN' NO PROSPECTS IN SIGHT!
LOOK OUT, WORLD--HERE COMES A WINNER.
YUP... A LITTLE OLDER, A LITTLE WISER, AN' A WHOLE LOT MEANER...
...IN EVERY SENSE O' THE W--
WAAAUGH!
SCREEEECH
CREEP! DEGENERATE!! ALLEY-LURKING SLIME!!
WHAT'RE YA DOIN' PROWLIN' BACK HERE AT SIX A.M., SHORT STUFF?!
753-H1

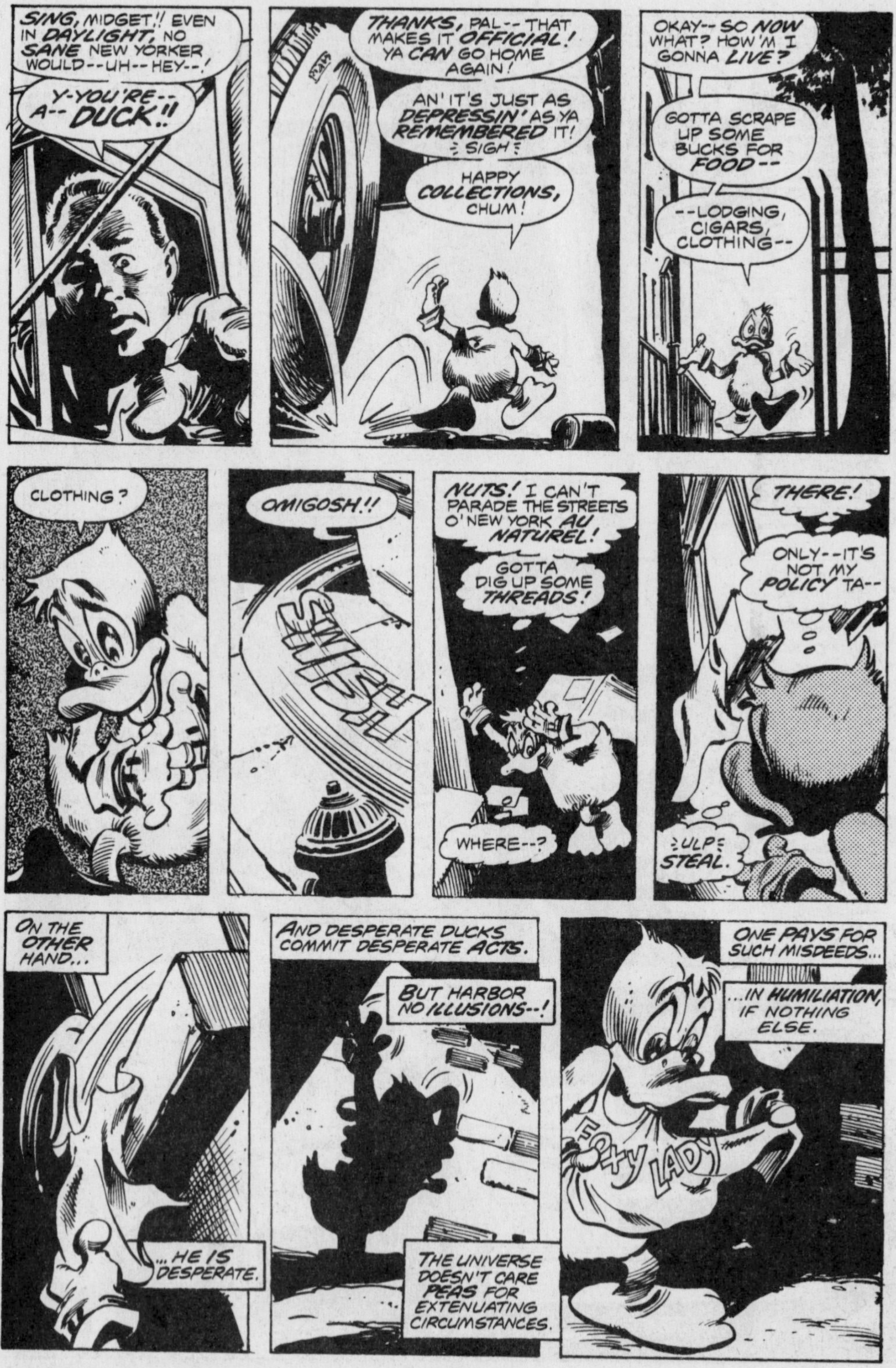
SING, MIDGET!! EVEN IN DAYLIGHT, NO SANE NEW YORKER WOULD--UH--HEY--!
Y-YOU'RE-- A--DUCK!!
THANKS, PAL--THAT MAKES IT OFFICIAL! YA CAN GO HOME AGAIN!
AN' IT'S JUST AS DEPRESSIN' AS YA REMEMBERED IT! SIGH
HAPPY COLLECTIONS, CHUM!
OKAY--SO NOW WHAT? HOW'M I GONNA LIVE?
GOTTA SCRAPE UP SOME BUCKS FOR FOOD--
--LODGING, CIGARS, CLOTHING--
CLOTHING?
OMIGOSH!!
SWISH
NUTS! I CAN'T PARADE THE STREETS O' NEW YORK AU NATUREL!
GOTTA DIG UP SOME THREADS!
WHERE--?
THERE!
ONLY--IT'S NOT MY POLICY TA--
ULP STEAL.
ON THE OTHER HAND...
...HE IS DESPERATE.
AND DESPERATE DUCKS COMMIT DESPERATE ACTS.
BUT HARBOR NO ILLUSIONS--!
THE UNIVERSE DOESN'T CARE PEAS FOR EXTENUATING CIRCUMSTANCES.
ONE PAYS FOR SUCH MISDEEDS...
...IN HUMILIATION, IF NOTHING ELSE.
FOXY LADY

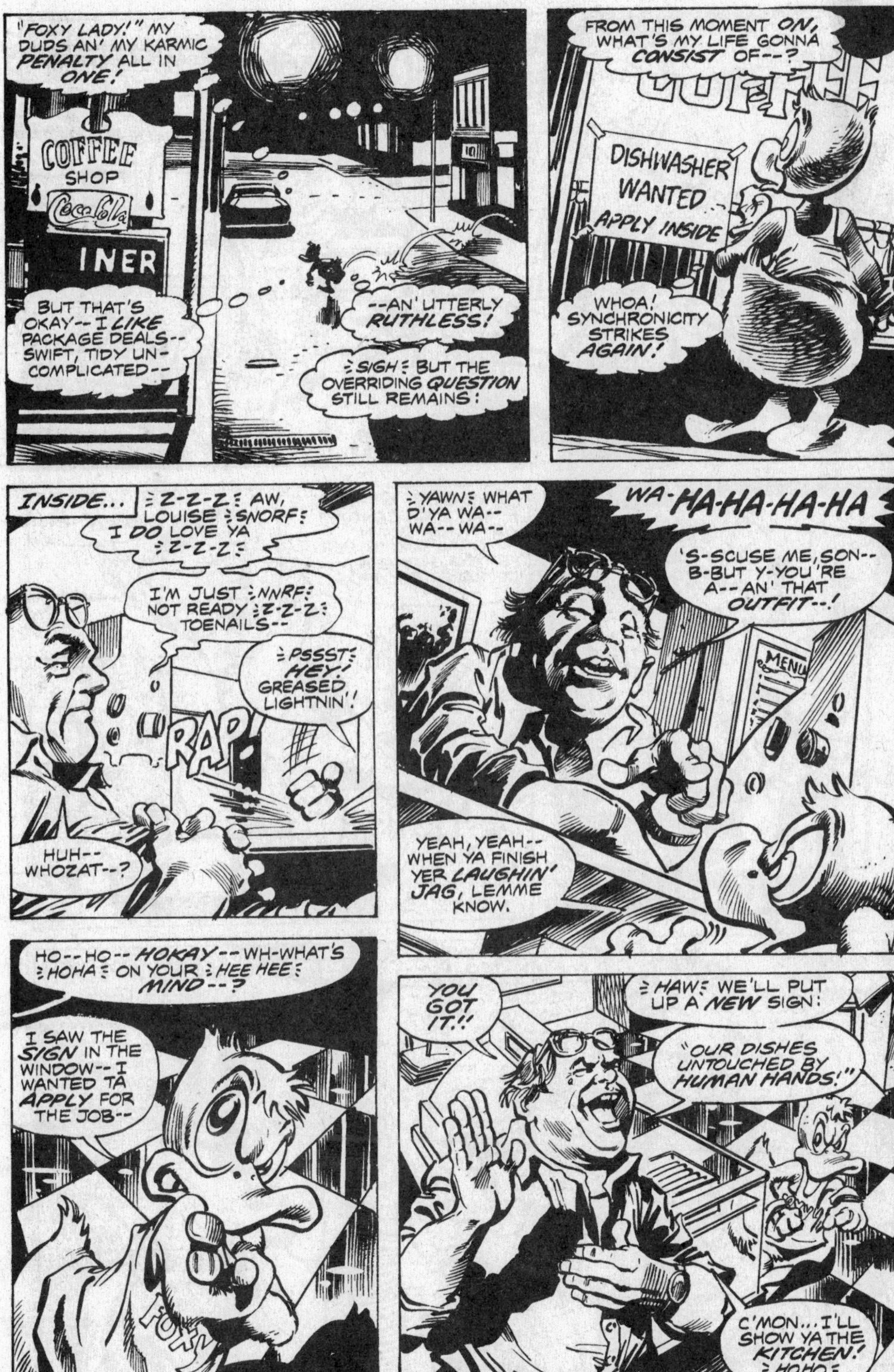

"FOXY LADY!" MY DUDS AN' MY KARMIC PENALTY ALL IN ONE!
COFFEE SHOP
Coca-Cola
INER
BUT THAT'S OKAY-- I LIKE PACKAGE DEALS-- SWIFT, TIDY UN-COMPLICATED--
--AN' UTTERLY RUTHLESS!
SIGH BUT THE OVERRIDING QUESTION STILL REMAINS:
FROM THIS MOMENT ON, WHAT'S MY LIFE GONNA CONSIST OF--?
DISHWASHER WANTED APPLY INSIDE
WHOA! SYNCHRONICITY STRIKES AGAIN!
INSIDE...
Z-Z-Z AW, LOUISE SNORF I DO LOVE YA Z-Z-Z
I'M JUST NNRF NOT READY Z-Z-Z TOENAILS--
PSSST! HEY! GREASED LIGHTNIN'!
RAP
HUH-- WHOZAT--?
YAWN WHAT D'YA WA-- WA-- WA--
WA-HA-HA-HA-HA
'S-SCUSE ME, SON-- B-BUT Y-YOU'RE A--AN' THAT OUTFIT--!
MENU
YEAH, YEAH-- WHEN YA FINISH YER LAUGHIN' JAG, LEMME KNOW.
HO--HO-- HOKAY-- WH-WHAT'S HOHA ON YOUR HEE HEE MIND--?
I SAW THE SIGN IN THE WINDOW-- I WANTED TA APPLY FOR THE JOB--
FOXY
YOU GOT IT!!
HAW WE'LL PUT UP A NEW SIGN:
"OUR DISHES UNTOUCHED BY HUMAN HANDS!"
C'MON... I'LL SHOW YA THE KITCHEN! HOHO

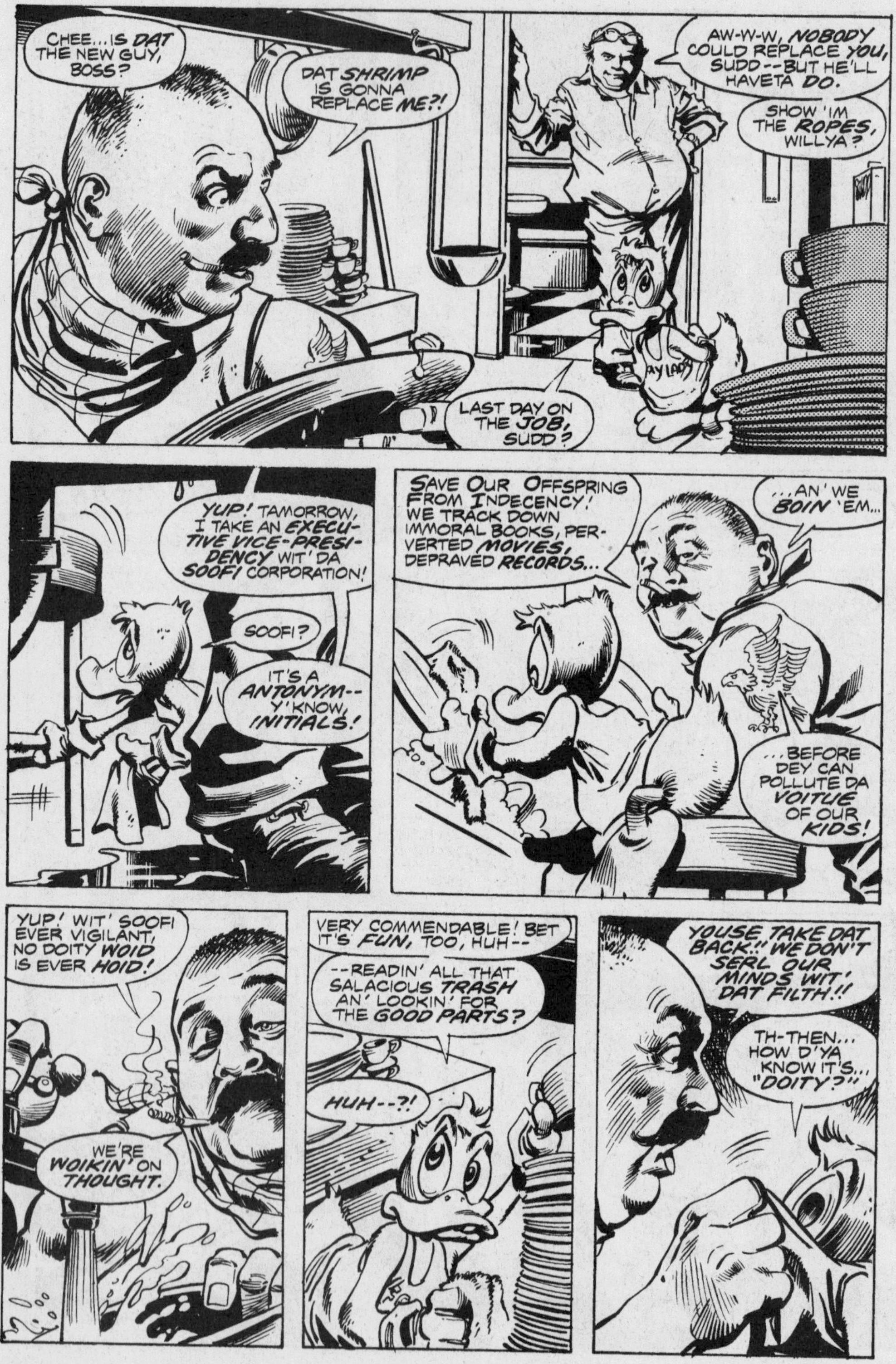
CHEE... IS DAT THE NEW GUY, BOSS?
DAT SHRIMP IS GONNA REPLACE ME?!
AW-W-W, NOBODY COULD REPLACE YOU, SUDD--BUT HE'LL HAVETA DO.
SHOW 'IM THE ROPES, WILLYA?
LAST DAY ON THE JOB, SUDD?
YUP! TAMORROW, I TAKE AN EXECUTIVE VICE-PRESIDENCY WIT' DA SOOFI CORPORATION!
SOOFI?
IT'S A ANTONYM--Y'KNOW, INITIALS!
SAVE OUR OFFSPRING FROM INDECENCY! WE TRACK DOWN IMMORAL BOOKS, PERVERTED MOVIES, DEPRAVED RECORDS...
...AN' WE BOIN 'EM...
...BEFORE DEY CAN POLLUTE DA VOITUE OF OUR KIDS!
YUP! WIT' SOOFI EVER VIGILANT, NO DOITY WOID IS EVER HOID!
WE'RE WOIKIN' ON THOUGHT.
VERY COMMENDABLE! BET IT'S FUN, TOO, HUH--
--READIN' ALL THAT SALACIOUS TRASH AN' LOOKIN' FOR THE GOOD PARTS?
HUH--?!
YOUSE TAKE DAT BACK!! WE DON'T SERL OUR MINDS WIT' DAT FILTH!!
TH-THEN... HOW D'YA KNOW IT'S... "DOITY?"

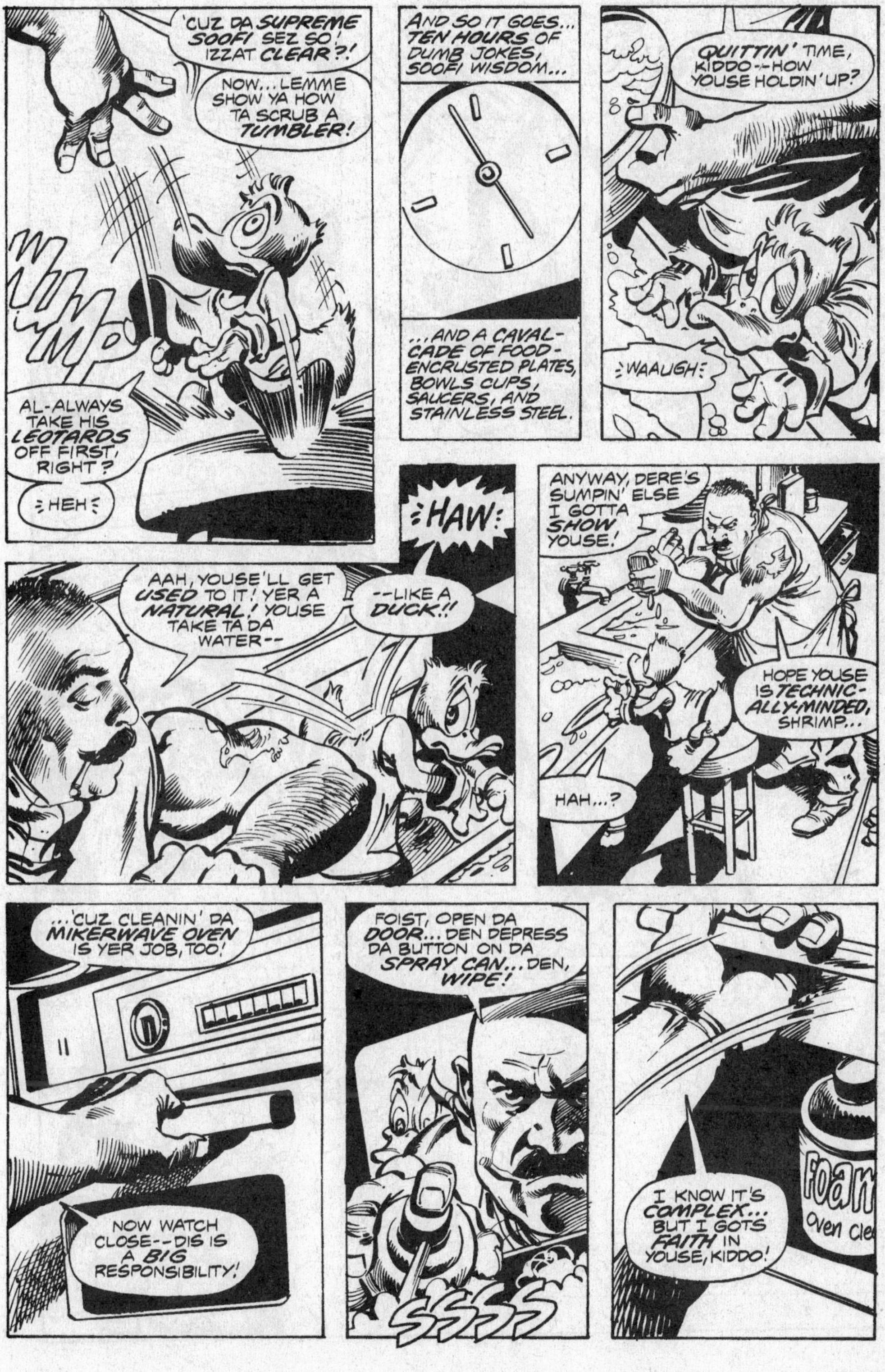
'CUZ DA SUPREME SOOFI SEZ SO! IZZAT CLEAR?!
NOW... LEMME SHOW YA HOW TA SCRUB A TUMBLER!
WHUMP
AL-ALWAYS TAKE HIS LEOTARDS OFF FIRST, RIGHT?
HEH
AND SO IT GOES... TEN HOURS OF DUMB JOKES, SOOFI WISDOM...
...AND A CAVALCADE OF FOOD-ENCRUSTED PLATES, BOWLS CUPS, SAUCERS, AND STAINLESS STEEL.
QUITTIN' TIME, KIDDO--HOW YOUSE HOLDIN' UP?
WAAUGH
HAW
AAH, YOUSE'LL GET USED TO IT! YER A NATURAL! YOUSE TAKE TA DA WATER--
--LIKE A DUCK!!
ANYWAY, DERE'S SUMPIN' ELSE I GOTTA SHOW YOUSE!
HOPE YOUSE IS TECHNICALLY-MINDED, SHRIMP...
HAH...?
...'CUZ CLEANIN' DA MIKERWAVE OVEN IS YER JOB, TOO!
NOW WATCH CLOSE--DIS IS A BIG RESPONSIBILITY!
FOIST, OPEN DA DOOR... DEN DEPRESS DA BUTTON ON DA SPRAY CAN... DEN, WIPE!
SSSSS
I KNOW IT'S COMPLEX... BUT I GOTS FAITH IN YOUSE, KIDDO!
Foam
Oven cle

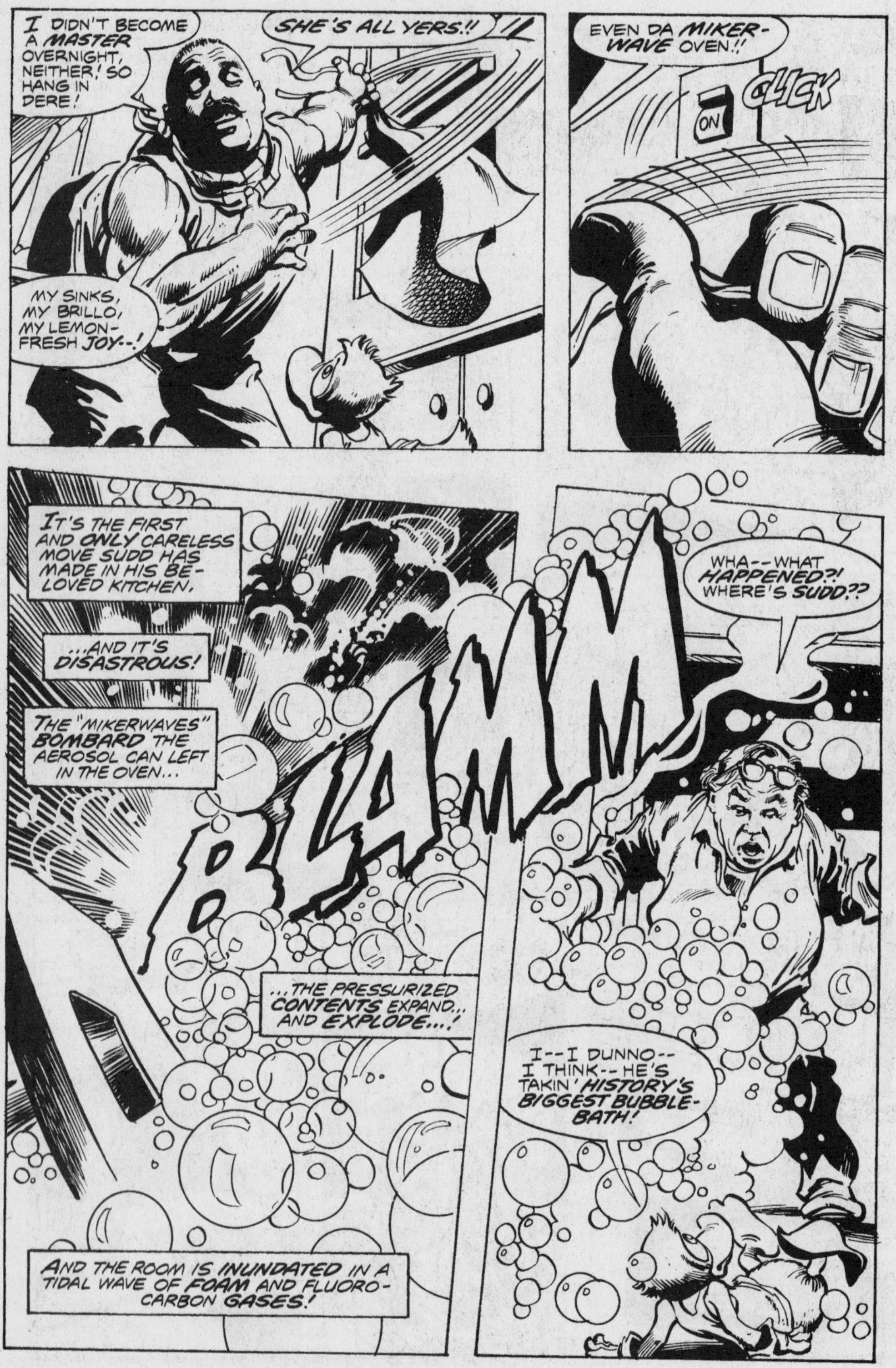

I DIDN'T BECOME A MASTER OVERNIGHT, NEITHER! SO HANG IN DERE!
SHE'S ALL YERS!!
MY SINKS, MY BRILLO, MY LEMON-FRESH JOY--!
EVEN DA MIKER-WAVE OVEN!!
ON
CLICK
IT'S THE FIRST AND ONLY CARELESS MOVE SUDD HAS MADE IN HIS BE-LOVED KITCHEN.
...AND IT'S DISASTROUS!
THE "MIKERWAVES" BOMBARD THE AEROSOL CAN LEFT IN THE OVEN...
BLAMM
...THE PRESSURIZED CONTENTS EXPAND... AND EXPLODE...!
WHA--WHAT HAPPENED?! WHERE'S SUDD??
I--I DUNNO-- I THINK--HE'S TAKIN' HISTORY'S BIGGEST BUBBLE-BATH!
AND THE ROOM IS INUNDATED IN A TIDAL WAVE OF FOAM AND FLUORO-CARBON GASES!

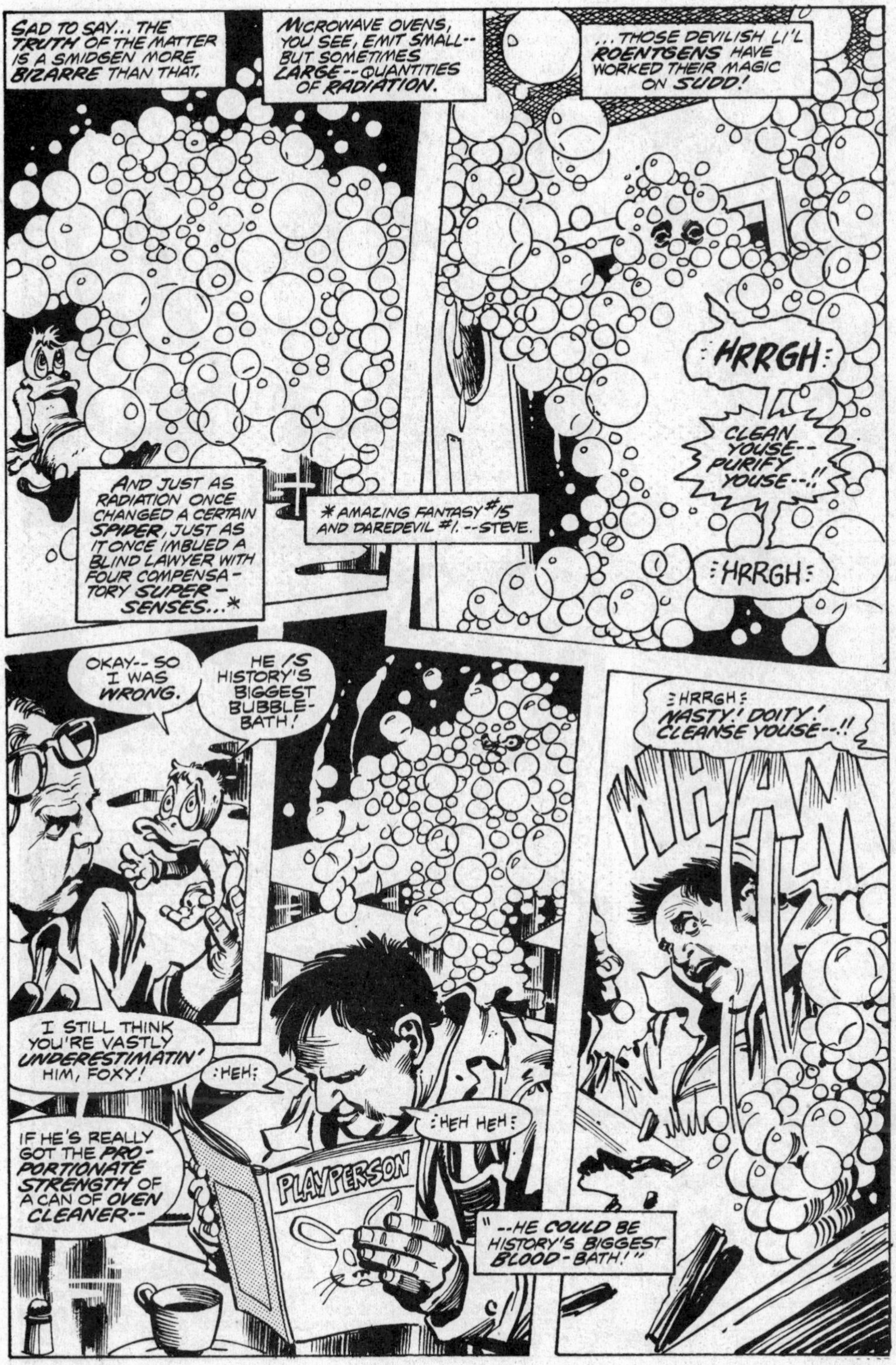
SAD TO SAY... THE TRUTH OF THE MATTER IS A SMIDGEN MORE BIZARRE THAN THAT,
MICROWAVE OVENS, YOU SEE, EMIT SMALL-- BUT SOMETIMES LARGE--QUANTITIES OF RADIATION.
AND JUST AS RADIATION ONCE CHANGED A CERTAIN SPIDER, JUST AS IT ONCE IMBUED A BLIND LAWYER WITH FOUR COMPENSATORY SUPER-SENSES...*
*AMAZING FANTASY #15 AND DAREDEVIL #1. --STEVE.
...THOSE DEVILISH LI'L ROENTGENS HAVE WORKED THEIR MAGIC ON SUDD!
HRRGH
CLEAN YOUSE-- PURIFY YOUSE--!!
HRRGH
OKAY-- SO I WAS WRONG.
HE IS HISTORY'S BIGGEST BUBBLE-BATH!
I STILL THINK YOU'RE VASTLY UNDERESTIMATIN' HIM, FOXY!
HEH
HEH HEH
IF HE'S REALLY GOT THE PROPORTIONATE STRENGTH OF A CAN OF OVEN CLEANER--
PLAYPERSON
"--HE COULD BE HISTORY'S BIGGEST BLOOD-BATH!"
HRRGH
NASTY! DOITY! CLEANSE YOUSE--!!
WHAM

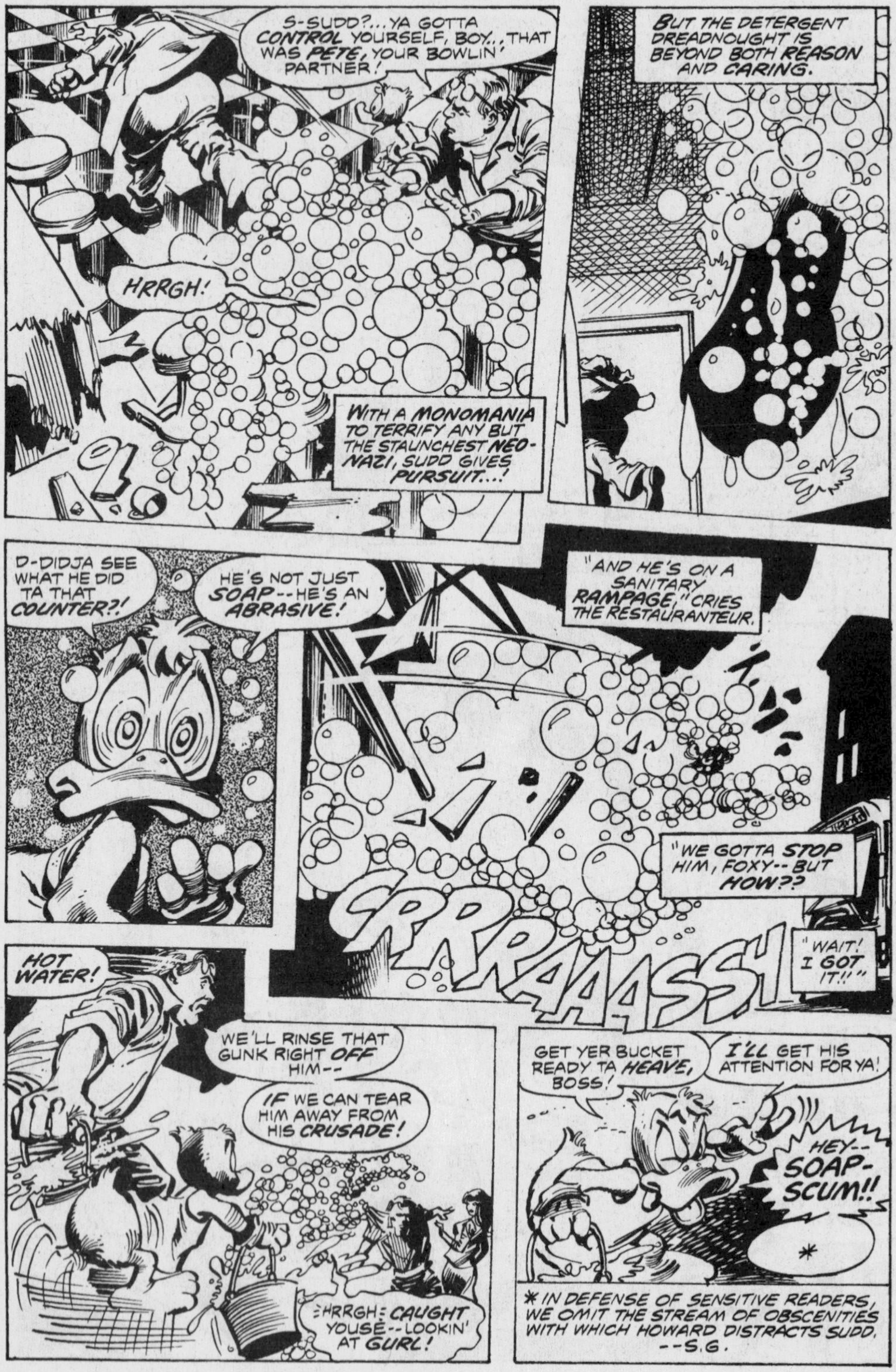
S-SUDD?...YA GOTTA CONTROL YOURSELF, BOY...THAT WAS PETE, YOUR BOWLIN' PARTNER!
HRRGH!
WITH A MONOMANIA TO TERRIFY ANY BUT THE STAUNCHEST NEO-NAZI, SUDD GIVES PURSUIT...!
BUT THE DETERGENT DREADNOUGHT IS BEYOND BOTH REASON AND CARING.
D-DIDJA SEE WHAT HE DID TA THAT COUNTER?!
HE'S NOT JUST SOAP--HE'S AN ABRASIVE!
"AND HE'S ON A SANITARY RAMPAGE," CRIES THE RESTAURANTEUR.
"WE GOTTA STOP HIM, FOXY--BUT HOW??
CRRRAAASSH
"WAIT! I GOT IT!!"
HOT WATER!
WE'LL RINSE THAT GUNK RIGHT OFF HIM--
IF WE CAN TEAR HIM AWAY FROM HIS CRUSADE!
HRRGH: CAUGHT YOUSE--LOOKIN' AT GURL!
GET YER BUCKET READY TA HEAVE, BOSS!
I'LL GET HIS ATTENTION FOR YA!
HEY--SOAP-SCUM!!
*
* IN DEFENSE OF SENSITIVE READERS, WE OMIT THE STREAM OF OBSCENITIES WITH WHICH HOWARD DISTRACTS SUDD.
--S.G.

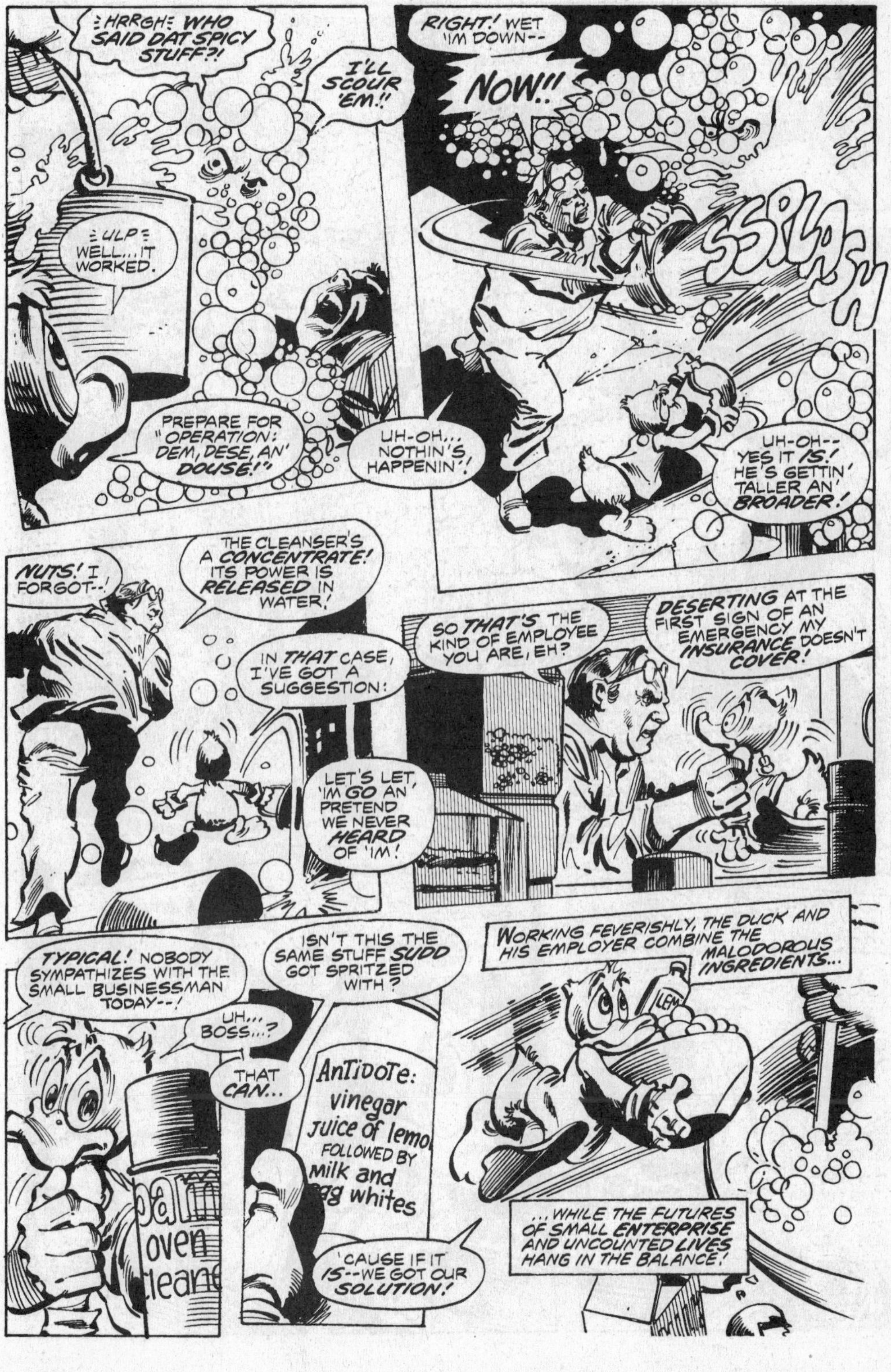
HRRGH WHO SAID DAT SPICY STUFF?!
I'LL SCOUR 'EM!!
ULP WELL... IT WORKED.
PREPARE FOR "OPERATION: DEM, DESE, AN' DOUSE!"
UH-OH... NOTHIN'S HAPPENIN'!
RIGHT! WET 'IM DOWN--
NOW!!
SSPLASH
UH-OH-- YES IT IS! HE'S GETTIN' TALLER AN' BROADER!
NUTS! I FORGOT--!
THE CLEANSER'S A CONCENTRATE! ITS POWER IS RELEASED IN WATER!
IN THAT CASE, I'VE GOT A SUGGESTION:
LET'S LET 'IM GO AN' PRETEND WE NEVER HEARD OF 'IM!
SO THAT'S THE KIND OF EMPLOYEE YOU ARE, EH?
DESERTING AT THE FIRST SIGN OF AN EMERGENCY MY INSURANCE DOESN'T COVER!
TYPICAL! NOBODY SYMPATHIZES WITH THE SMALL BUSINESSMAN TODAY--!
UH... BOSS...?
THAT CAN...
ISN'T THIS THE SAME STUFF SUDD GOT SPRITZED WITH?
AnTiDoTe: vinegar Juice of lemo FOLLOWED BY milk and gg whites
oven
'CAUSE IF IT IS--WE GOT OUR SOLUTION!
WORKING FEVERISHLY, THE DUCK AND HIS EMPLOYER COMBINE THE MALODOROUS INGREDIENTS...
LEM
...WHILE THE FUTURES OF SMALL ENTERPRISE AND UNCOUNTED LIVES HANG IN THE BALANCE!

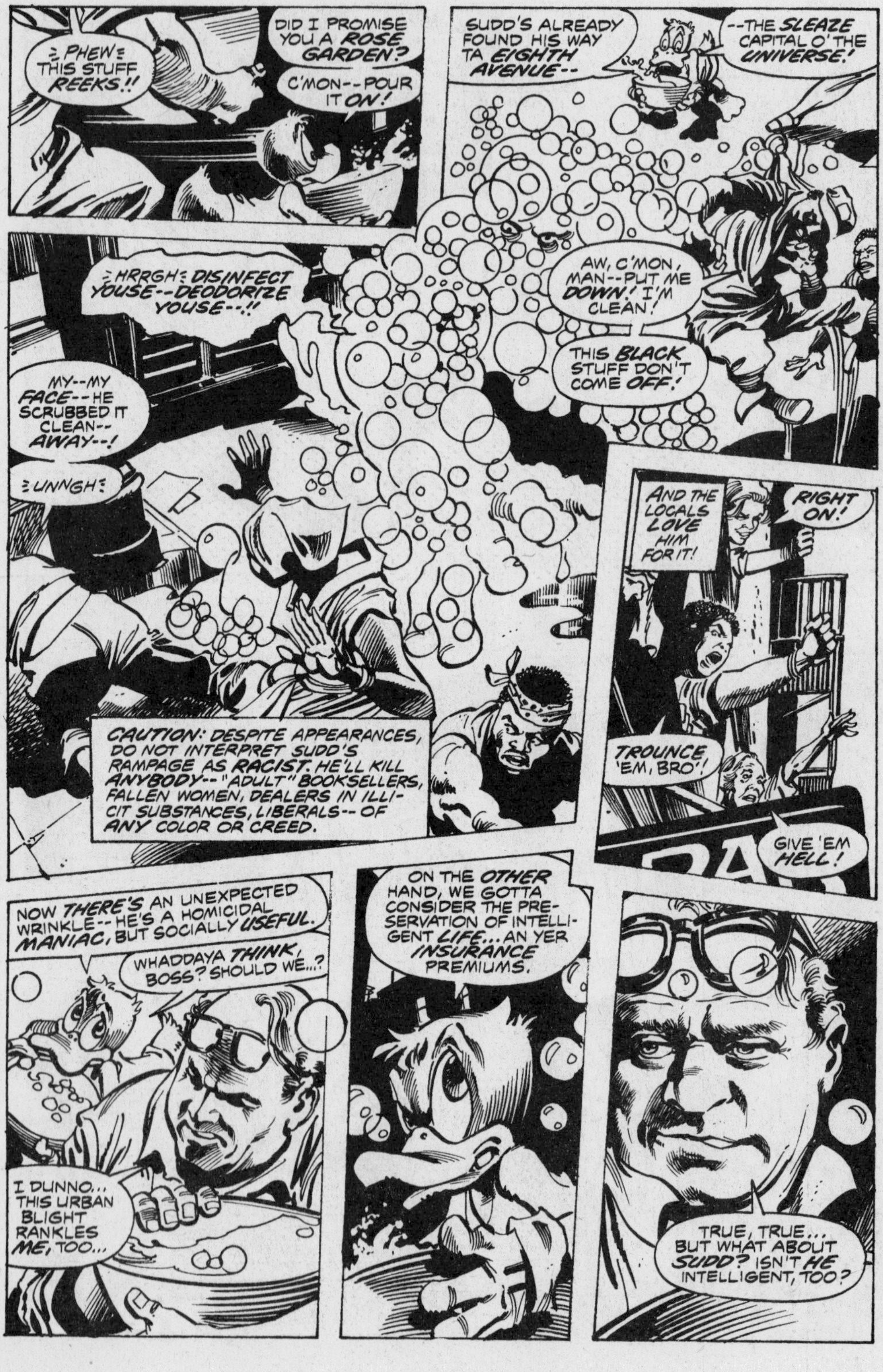

PHEW
THIS STUFF REEKS!!
DID I PROMISE YOU A ROSE GARDEN?
C'MON--POUR IT ON!
SUDD'S ALREADY FOUND HIS WAY TA EIGHTH AVENUE--
--THE SLEAZE CAPITAL O' THE UNIVERSE!
HRRGH DISINFECT YOUSE--DEODORIZE YOUSE--!!
AW, C'MON, MAN--PUT ME DOWN! I'M CLEAN!
THIS BLACK STUFF DON'T COME OFF!
MY--MY FACE--HE SCRUBBED IT CLEAN--AWAY--!
UNNGH
CAUTION: DESPITE APPEARANCES, DO NOT INTERPRET SUDD'S RAMPAGE AS RACIST. HE'LL KILL ANYBODY--"ADULT" BOOKSELLERS, FALLEN WOMEN, DEALERS IN ILLICIT SUBSTANCES, LIBERALS--OF ANY COLOR OR CREED.
AND THE LOCALS LOVE HIM FOR IT!
RIGHT ON!
TROUNCE 'EM, BRO'!
GIVE 'EM HELL!
NOW THERE'S AN UNEXPECTED WRINKLE--HE'S A HOMICIDAL MANIAC, BUT SOCIALLY USEFUL.
WHADDAYA THINK, BOSS? SHOULD WE...?
I DUNNO... THIS URBAN BLIGHT RANKLES ME, TOO...
ON THE OTHER HAND, WE GOTTA CONSIDER THE PRESERVATION OF INTELLIGENT LIFE... AN YER INSURANCE PREMIUMS.
TRUE, TRUE... BUT WHAT ABOUT SUDD? ISN'T HE INTELLIGENT, TOO?

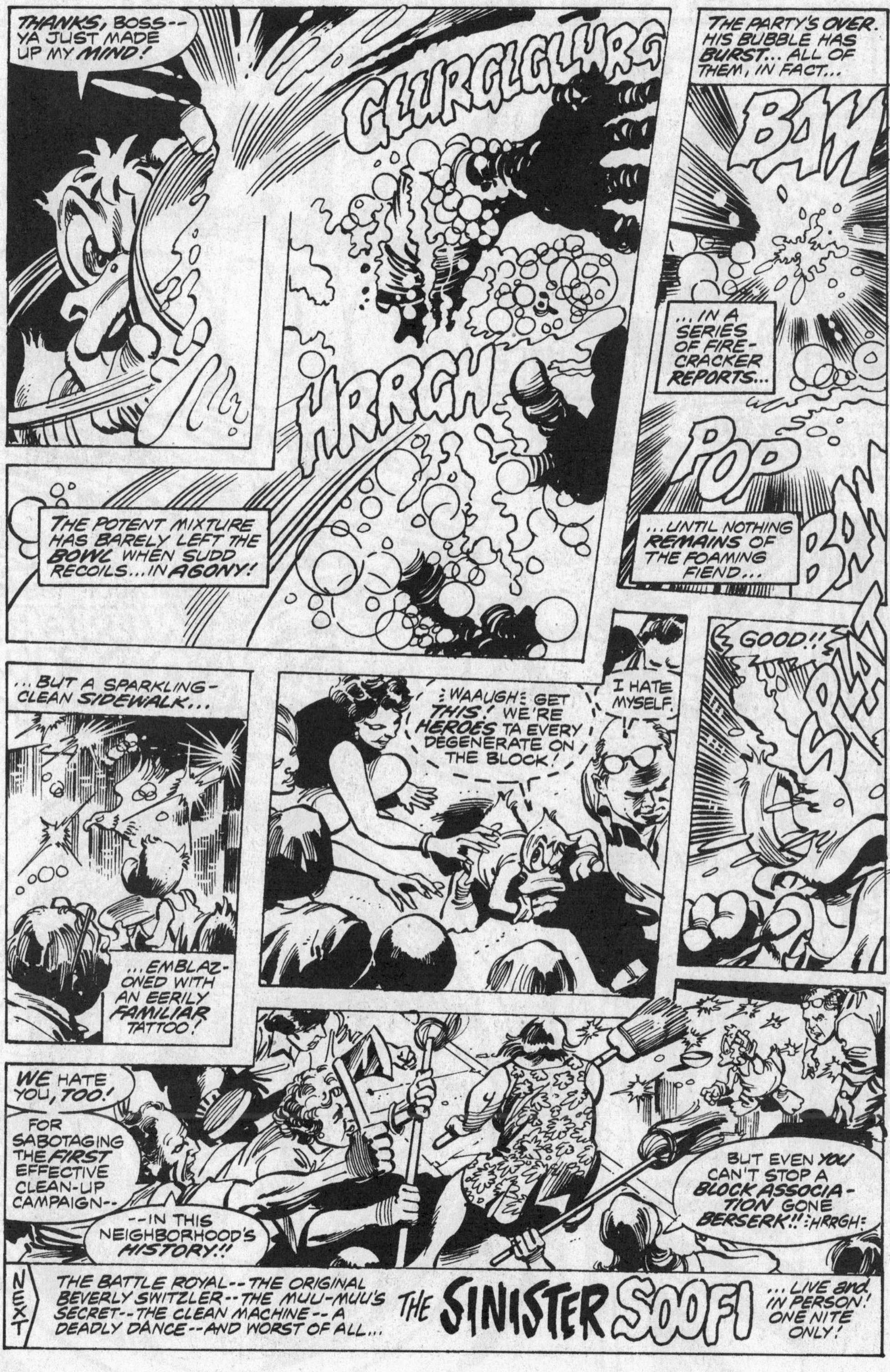
THANKS, BOSS--YA JUST MADE UP MY MIND!
GLURGLGLURG
HRRGH
THE POTENT MIXTURE HAS BARELY LEFT THE BOWL WHEN SUDD RECOILS...IN AGONY!
THE PARTY'S OVER. HIS BUBBLE HAS BURST... ALL OF THEM, IN FACT...
BAM
...IN A SERIES OF FIRE-CRACKER REPORTS...
POP
BAM
...UNTIL NOTHING REMAINS OF THE FOAMING FIEND...
...BUT A SPARKLING-CLEAN SIDEWALK...
...EMBLAZ-ONED WITH AN EERILY FAMILIAR TATTOO!
WAAUGH! GET THIS! WE'RE HEROES TA EVERY DEGENERATE ON THE BLOCK!
I HATE MYSELF.
GOOD!!
SPLAT
WE HATE YOU, TOO!
FOR SABOTAGING THE FIRST EFFECTIVE CLEAN-UP CAMPAIGN--
--IN THIS NEIGHBORHOOD'S HISTORY!!
BUT EVEN YOU CAN'T STOP A BLOCK ASSOCIA-TION GONE BERSERK!! HRRGH!
NEXT
THE BATTLE ROYAL--THE ORIGINAL BEVERLY SWITZLER--THE MUU-MUU'S SECRET--THE CLEAN MACHINE--A DEADLY DANCE--AND WORST OF ALL...
THE SINISTER SOOFI
...LIVE and IN PERSON! ONE NITE ONLY!

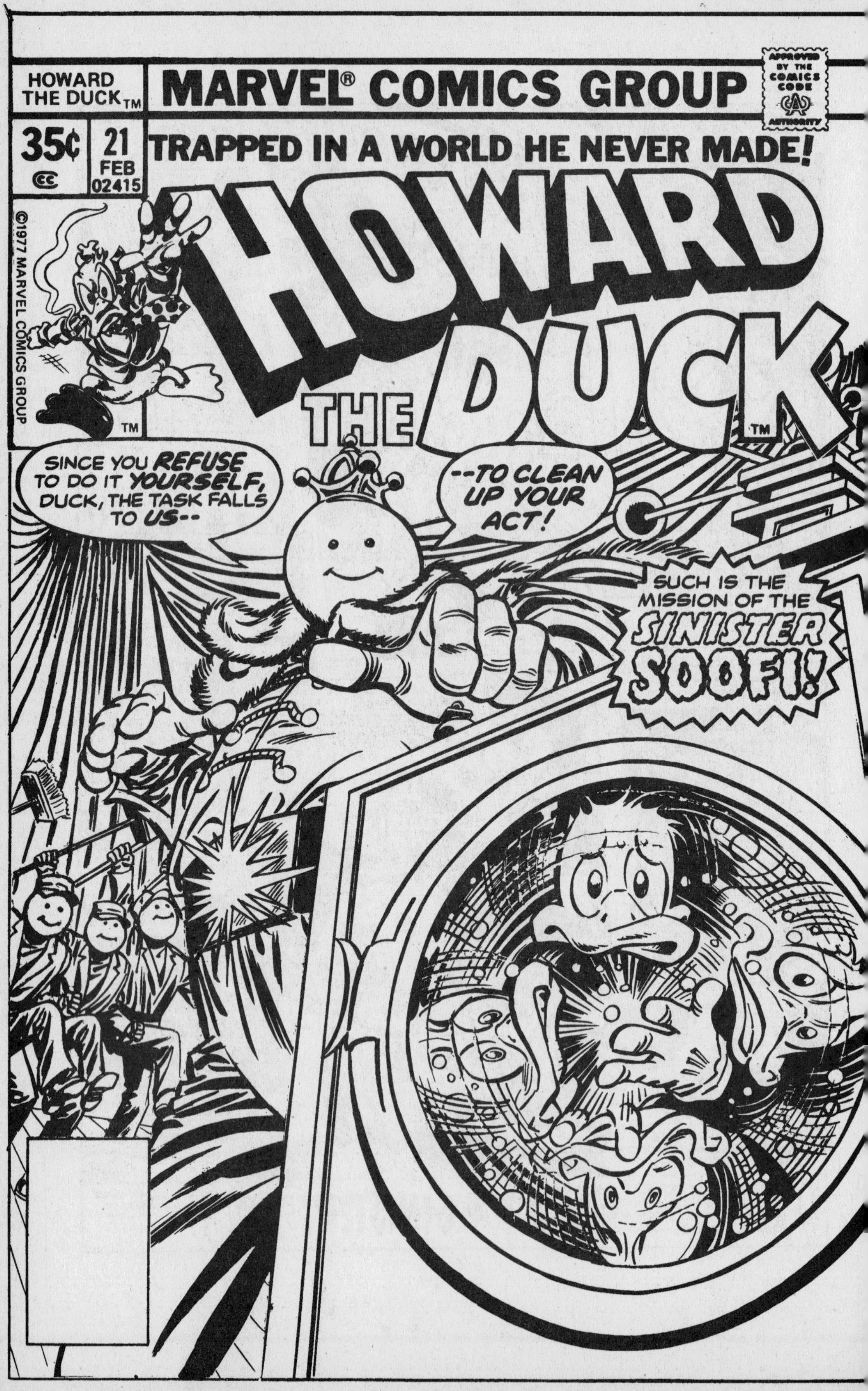

HOWARD THE DUCK TM
MARVEL® COMICS GROUP
APPROVED BY THE COMICS CODE AUTHORITY
35¢
21
FEB
02415
TRAPPED IN A WORLD HE NEVER MADE!
HOWARD THE DUCK TM
©1977 MARVEL COMICS GROUP
SINCE YOU REFUSE TO DO IT YOURSELF, DUCK, THE TASK FALLS TO US--
--TO CLEAN UP YOUR ACT!
SUCH IS THE MISSION OF THE SINISTER SOOFI!

From the time of his hatching, he was...different. A potentially brilliant scholar who dreaded the structured environment of school, he educated himself in the streets, taking whatever work was available, formulating his philosophy of self from what he learned of the world about him. And then the Cosmic Axis shifted...and that world *changed.* Suddenly, he was stranded in a universe he could not fathom. Without warning, he became a strange fowl in an even stranger land.

Stan Lee PRESENTS: HOWARD THE DUCK!™

STEVE GERBER WRITER/EDITOR • **CARMINE INFANTINO** SPECIAL GUEST ARTIST • **KLAUS JANSON** INKER • **I. WATANABE** LETTERER • **GLYNIS WEIN** COLORIST

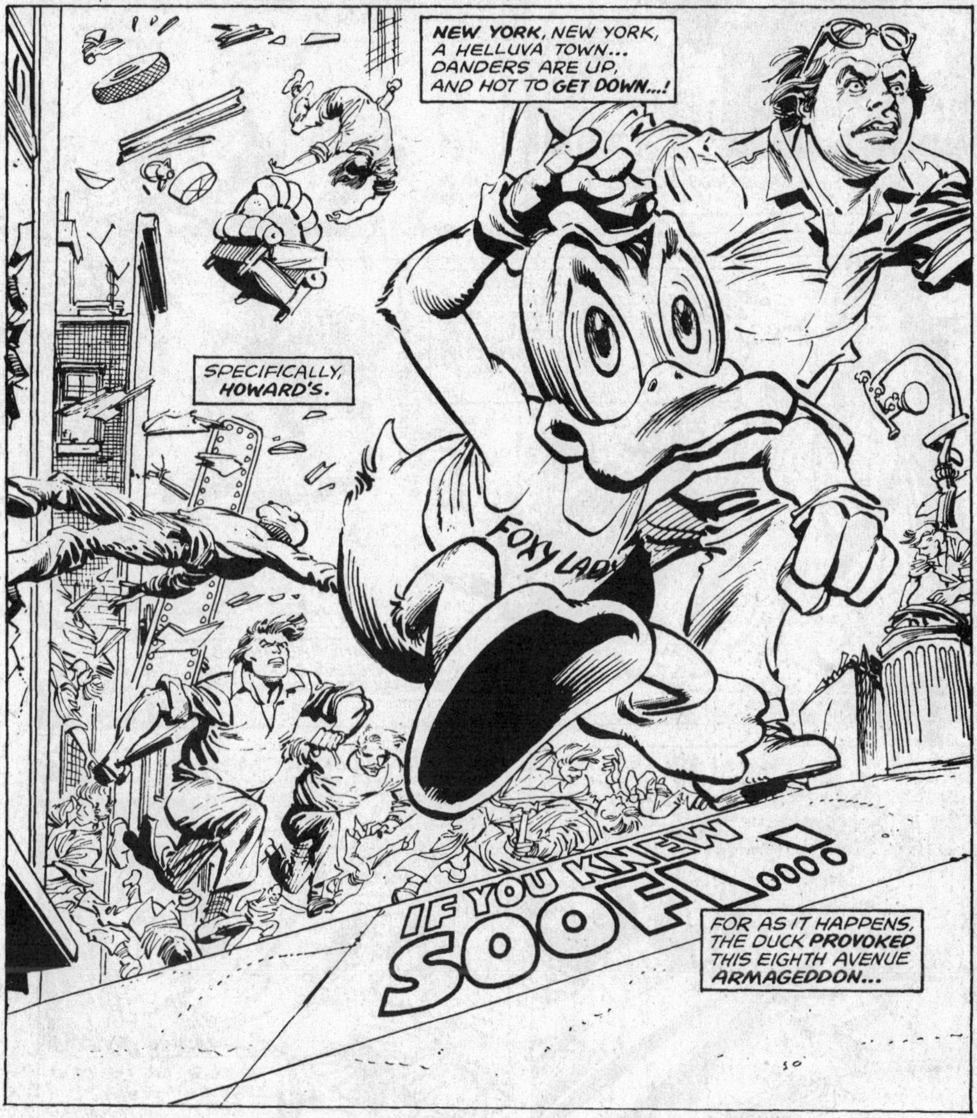
NEW YORK, NEW YORK, A HELLUVA TOWN... DANDERS ARE UP, AND HOT TO GET DOWN...!
SPECIFICALLY, HOWARD'S.
FOXY LADY
IF YOU KNEW SOOFI...!
FOR AS IT HAPPENS, THE DUCK PROVOKED THIS EIGHTH AVENUE ARMAGEDDON...

...BY DISSOLVING THE FIRST **HERO** TO WALK THIS MEAN STREET IN MANY A MOON:

SUDD, THE SCRUBBING BUBBLE WHO WALKED LIKE A MAN...

...AND WAGED A **NEVER-ENDING BATTLE** FOR **TRUTH, JUSTICE...**

...AND HIS OWN SWEET **WAY** IN MATTERS OF **MORALITY.**

HAH! NOW WE GOT 'EM! THAT'S A **BLIND ALLEY!**

INTERESTINGLY, SINCE BER-SERKERS, UNLIKE POLITICIANS, CAN'T BE **BOUGHT OFF,** SUDD'S **DEATH-DEALING** DECENCY CRU-SADE WAS THE FIRST **EFFECTIVE** CLEAN-UP CAMPAIGN IN THE AVENUE'S **HISTORY.**

HUH--?!

PERHAPS UNDERSTANDABLY, THEN, THE SLEAZE-BELEAGUERED LOCALS **RESENTED** ITS ABRUPT **TERMINATION.**

DEY GAVE US DA **SLIP,** MELROY!

NO! DERE AIN'T NO WAY! DEY'RE **HIDIN'**--SOME-WHERE!

TOIN DIS ALLEY INSIDE-OUT! DEY **GOTTA** BE HERE!

BUT WHEN AN EXHAUSTIVE SEARCH TURNS UP NEITHER **HIDE** NOR **FEATHER....!**

I COULD'A **SWORE--!**

C'MON-- WE'LL TRY THE NEXT ALLEY! **NUTS!**

THROUGHOUT, THE **DENI-ZENS** OF THE BACK STREET-- THE HAGGARD OLD **WINOS** AND THE PUFFY LADY IN THE **MUU-MUU** HAVE MAINTAINED AN EERILY CONSPIRATORIAL **SILENCE.**

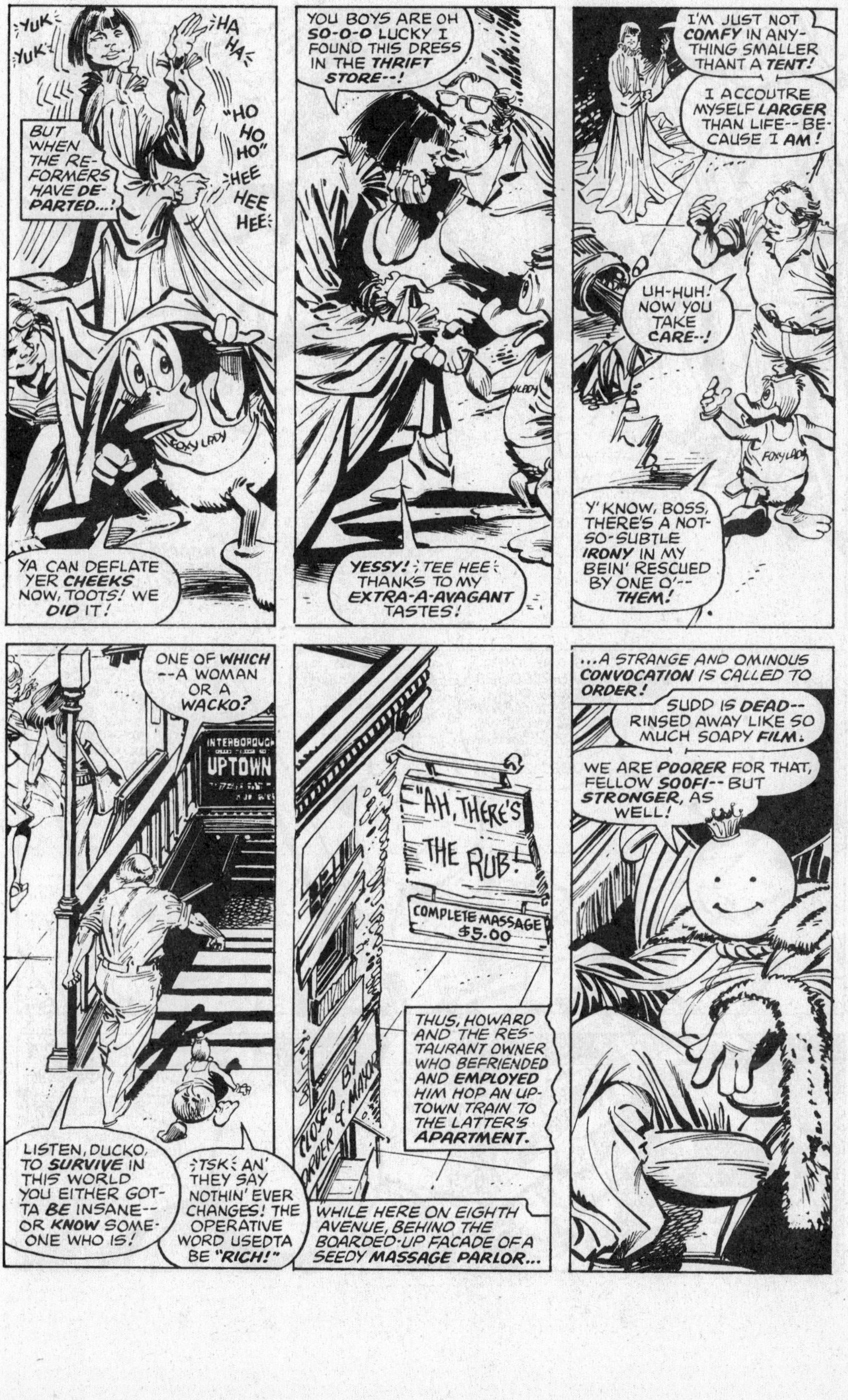

YUK
YUK
HA HA
BUT WHEN THE REFORMERS HAVE DEPARTED...!
"HO HO HO"
HEE HEE HEE
FOXY LADY
YA CAN DEFLATE YER CHEEKS NOW, TOOTS! WE DID IT!
YOU BOYS ARE OH SO-O-O LUCKY I FOUND THIS DRESS IN THE THRIFT STORE--!
YESSY! TEE HEE THANKS TO MY EXTRA-A-AVAGANT TASTES!
I'M JUST NOT COMFY IN ANYTHING SMALLER THANT A TENT!
I ACCOUTRE MYSELF LARGER THAN LIFE-- BECAUSE I AM!
UH-HUH! NOW YOU TAKE CARE--!
FOXY LADY
Y' KNOW, BOSS, THERE'S A NOT-SO-SUBTLE IRONY IN MY BEIN' RESCUED BY ONE O'-- THEM!
ONE OF WHICH --A WOMAN OR A WACKO?
INTERBOROUGH
UPTOWN
LISTEN, DUCKO, TO SURVIVE IN THIS WORLD YOU EITHER GOTTA BE INSANE-- OR KNOW SOMEONE WHO IS!
TSK AN' THEY SAY NOTHIN' EVER CHANGES! THE OPERATIVE WORD USEDTA BE "RICH!"
"AH, THERE'S THE RUB!"
COMPLETE MASSAGE $5.00
THUS, HOWARD AND THE RESTAURANT OWNER WHO BEFRIENDED AND EMPLOYED HIM HOP AN UPTOWN TRAIN TO THE LATTER'S APARTMENT.
CLOSED BY ORDER OF MAYOR
WHILE HERE ON EIGHTH AVENUE, BEHIND THE BOARDED-UP FACADE OF A SEEDY MASSAGE PARLOR...
...A STRANGE AND OMINOUS CONVOCATION IS CALLED TO ORDER!
SUDD IS DEAD-- RINSED AWAY LIKE SO MUCH SOAPY FILM.
WE ARE POORER FOR THAT, FELLOW SOOFI-- BUT STRONGER, AS WELL!

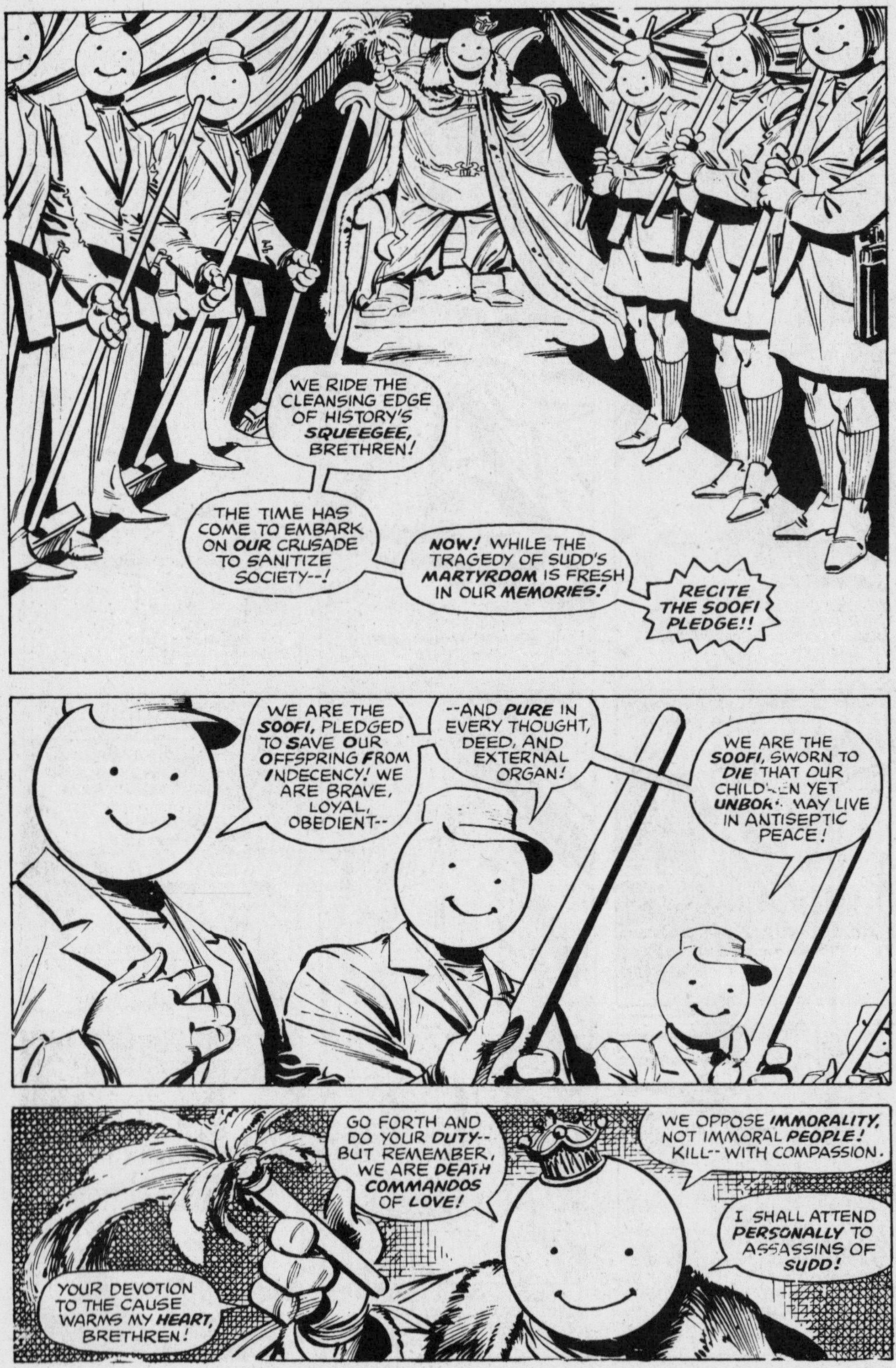
WE RIDE THE CLEANSING EDGE OF HISTORY'S SQUEEGEE, BRETHREN!
THE TIME HAS COME TO EMBARK ON OUR CRUSADE TO SANITIZE SOCIETY--!
NOW! WHILE THE TRAGEDY OF SUDD'S MARTYRDOM IS FRESH IN OUR MEMORIES!
RECITE THE SOOFI PLEDGE!!
WE ARE THE SOOFI, PLEDGED TO SAVE OUR OFFSPRING FROM INDECENCY! WE ARE BRAVE, LOYAL, OBEDIENT--
--AND PURE IN EVERY THOUGHT, DEED, AND EXTERNAL ORGAN!
WE ARE THE SOOFI, SWORN TO DIE THAT OUR CHILD-EN YET UNBOR- MAY LIVE IN ANTISEPTIC PEACE!
GO FORTH AND DO YOUR DUTY-- BUT REMEMBER, WE ARE DEATH COMMANDOS OF LOVE!
WE OPPOSE IMMORALITY, NOT IMMORAL PEOPLE! KILL-- WITH COMPASSION.
I SHALL ATTEND PERSONALLY TO ASSASSINS OF SUDD!
YOUR DEVOTION TO THE CAUSE WARMS MY HEART, BRETHREN!

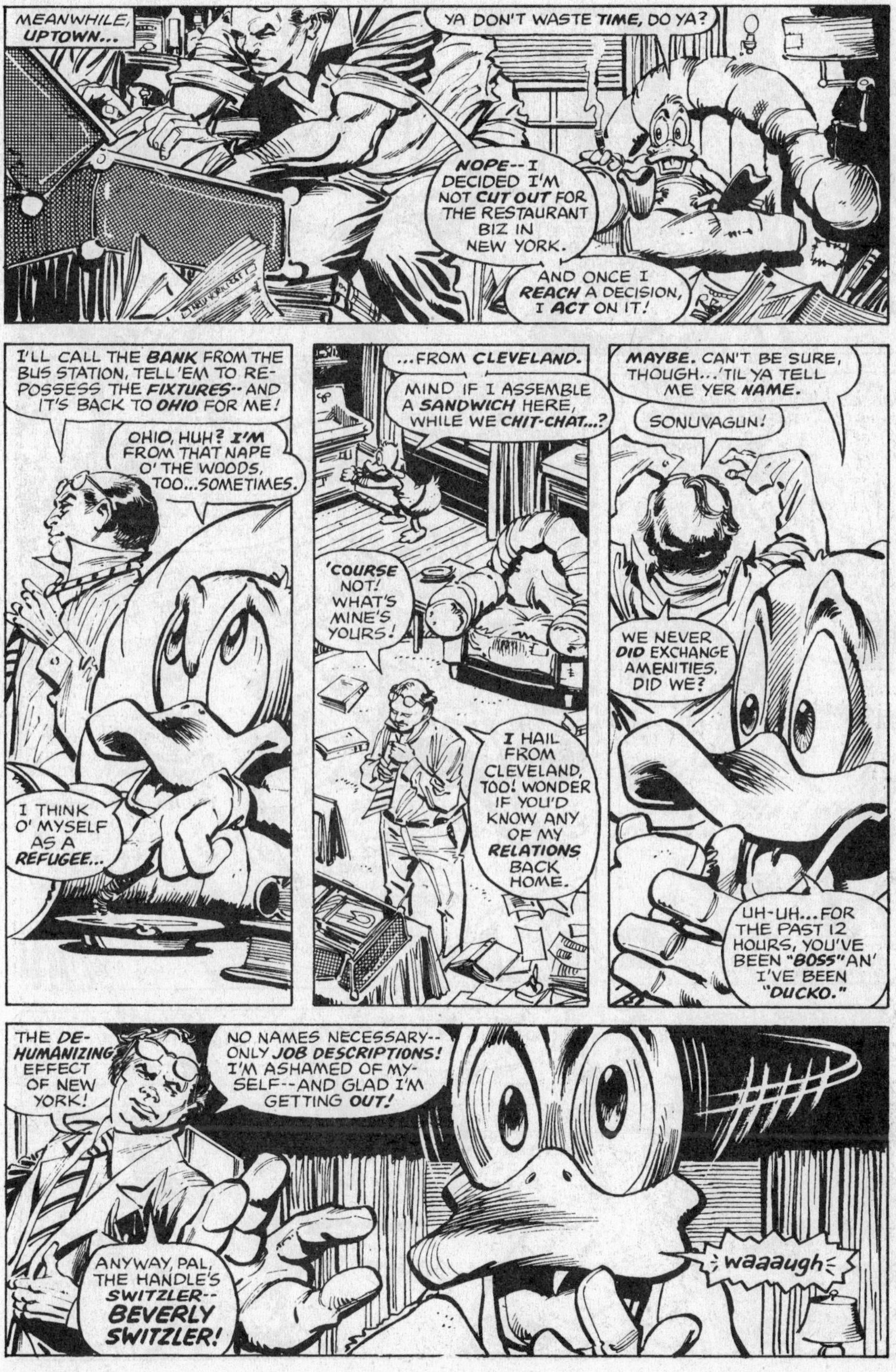

MEANWHILE, UPTOWN...
YA DON'T WASTE TIME, DO YA?
NOPE-- I DECIDED I'M NOT CUT OUT FOR THE RESTAURANT BIZ IN NEW YORK.
AND ONCE I REACH A DECISION, I ACT ON IT!
I'LL CALL THE BANK FROM THE BUS STATION, TELL 'EM TO REPOSSESS THE FIXTURES-- AND IT'S BACK TO OHIO FOR ME!
OHIO, HUH? I'M FROM THAT NAPE O' THE WOODS, TOO...SOMETIMES.
I THINK O' MYSELF AS A REFUGEE...
...FROM CLEVELAND.
MIND IF I ASSEMBLE A SANDWICH HERE, WHILE WE CHIT-CHAT...?
'COURSE NOT! WHAT'S MINE'S YOURS!
I HAIL FROM CLEVELAND, TOO! WONDER IF YOU'D KNOW ANY OF MY RELATIONS BACK HOME.
MAYBE. CAN'T BE SURE, THOUGH...'TIL YA TELL ME YER NAME.
SONUVAGUN!
WE NEVER DID EXCHANGE AMENITIES, DID WE?
UH-UH...FOR THE PAST 12 HOURS, YOU'VE BEEN "BOSS" AN' I'VE BEEN "DUCKO."
THE DE-HUMANIZING EFFECT OF NEW YORK!
NO NAMES NECESSARY-- ONLY JOB DESCRIPTIONS! I'M ASHAMED OF MYSELF--AND GLAD I'M GETTING OUT!
ANYWAY, PAL, THE HANDLE'S SWITZLER-- BEVERLY SWITZLER!
waaaugh

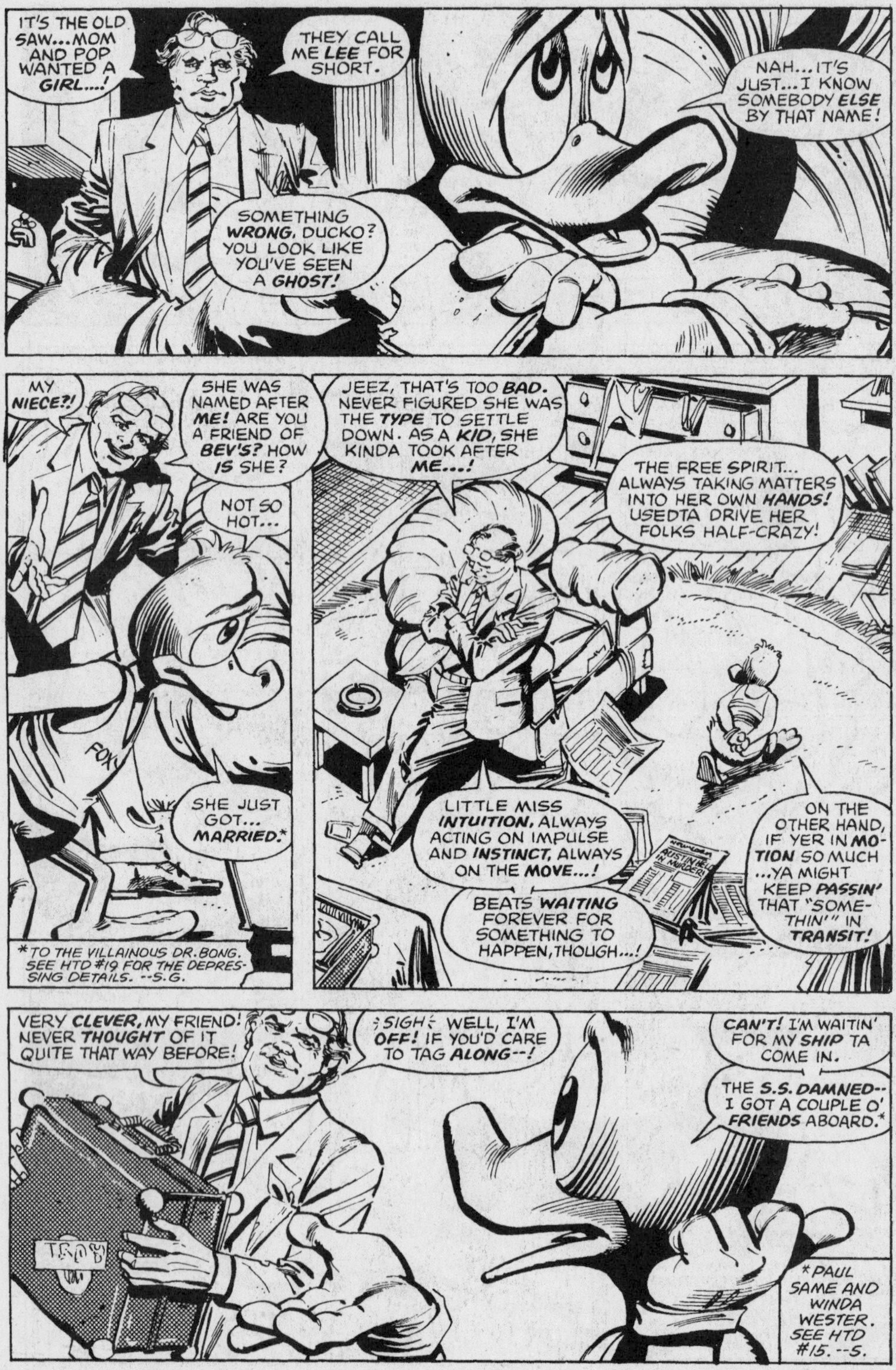
IT'S THE OLD SAW...MOM AND POP WANTED A GIRL...!
THEY CALL ME LEE FOR SHORT.
NAH...IT'S JUST...I KNOW SOMEBODY ELSE BY THAT NAME!
SOMETHING WRONG, DUCKO? YOU LOOK LIKE YOU'VE SEEN A GHOST!
MY NIECE?!
SHE WAS NAMED AFTER ME! ARE YOU A FRIEND OF BEV'S? HOW IS SHE?
NOT SO HOT...
SHE JUST GOT... MARRIED.*
*TO THE VILLAINOUS DR. BONG. SEE HTD #19 FOR THE DEPRESSING DETAILS. --S.G.
JEEZ, THAT'S TOO BAD. NEVER FIGURED SHE WAS THE TYPE TO SETTLE DOWN. AS A KID, SHE KINDA TOOK AFTER ME...!
THE FREE SPIRIT... ALWAYS TAKING MATTERS INTO HER OWN HANDS! USEDTA DRIVE HER FOLKS HALF-CRAZY!
LITTLE MISS INTUITION, ALWAYS ACTING ON IMPULSE AND INSTINCT, ALWAYS ON THE MOVE...!
BEATS WAITING FOREVER FOR SOMETHING TO HAPPEN, THOUGH...!
ON THE OTHER HAND, IF YER IN MOTION SO MUCH ...YA MIGHT KEEP PASSIN' THAT "SOMETHIN'" IN TRANSIT!
VERY CLEVER, MY FRIEND! NEVER THOUGHT OF IT QUITE THAT WAY BEFORE!
SIGH WELL, I'M OFF! IF YOU'D CARE TO TAG ALONG--!
CAN'T! I'M WAITIN' FOR MY SHIP TA COME IN.
THE S.S. DAMNED-- I GOT A COUPLE O' FRIENDS ABOARD.*
*PAUL SAME AND WINDA WESTER. SEE HTD #15. --S.

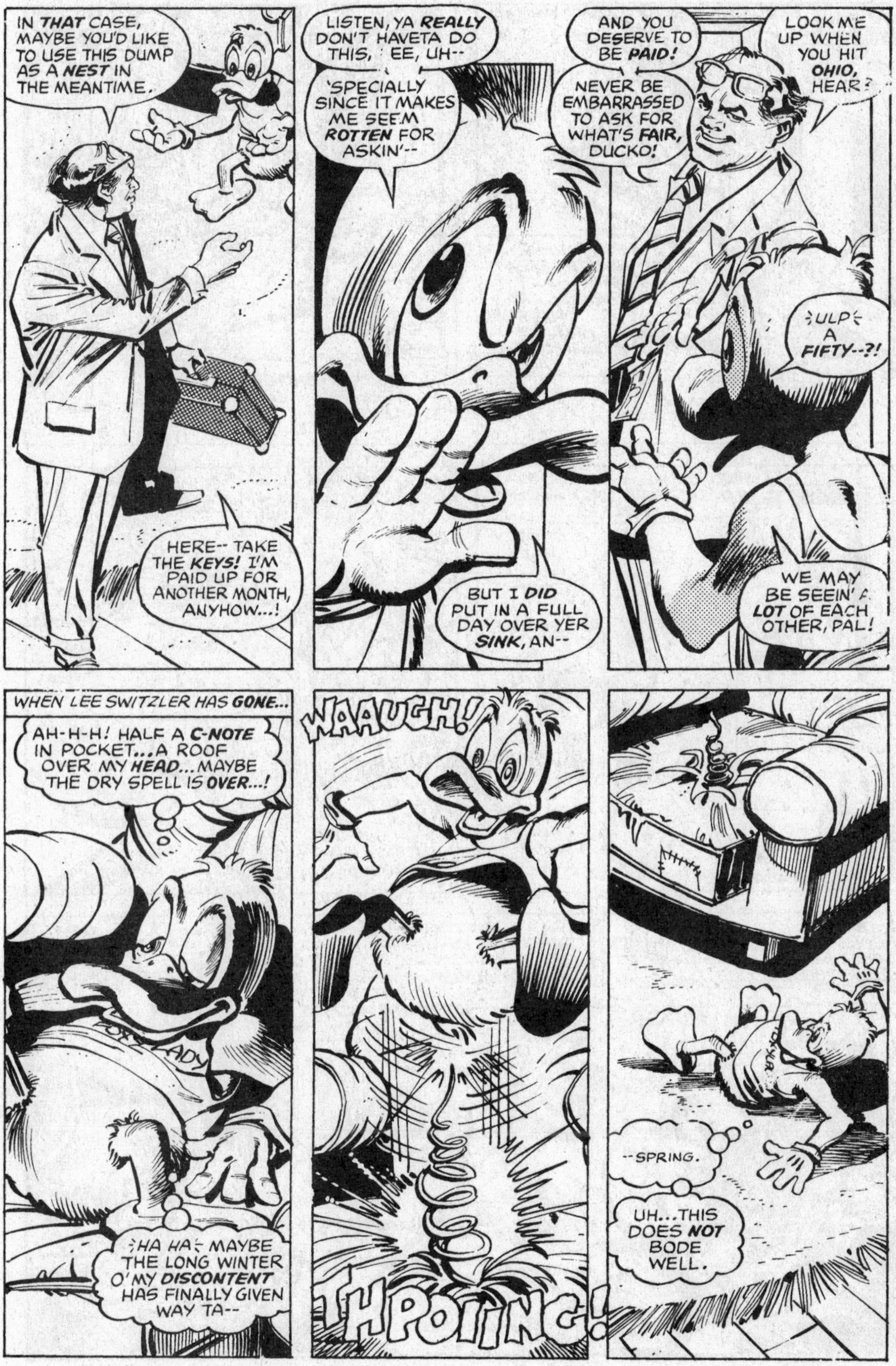
IN THAT CASE, MAYBE YOU'D LIKE TO USE THIS DUMP AS A NEST IN THE MEANTIME.
HERE-- TAKE THE KEYS! I'M PAID UP FOR ANOTHER MONTH, ANYHOW...!
LISTEN, YA REALLY DON'T HAVETA DO THIS, SEE, UH--
'SPECIALLY SINCE IT MAKES ME SEEM ROTTEN FOR ASKIN'--
BUT I DID PUT IN A FULL DAY OVER YER SINK, AN--
AND YOU DESERVE TO BE PAID!
NEVER BE EMBARRASSED TO ASK FOR WHAT'S FAIR, DUCKO!
LOOK ME UP WHEN YOU HIT OHIO, HEAR?
ULP A FIFTY--?!
WE MAY BE SEEIN' A LOT OF EACH OTHER, PAL!
WHEN LEE SWITZLER HAS GONE...
AH-H-H! HALF A C-NOTE IN POCKET...A ROOF OVER MY HEAD...MAYBE THE DRY SPELL IS OVER...!
HA HA MAYBE THE LONG WINTER O' MY DISCONTENT HAS FINALLY GIVEN WAY TA--
WAAUGH!
THPOIING!
--SPRING.
UH...THIS DOES NOT BODE WELL.

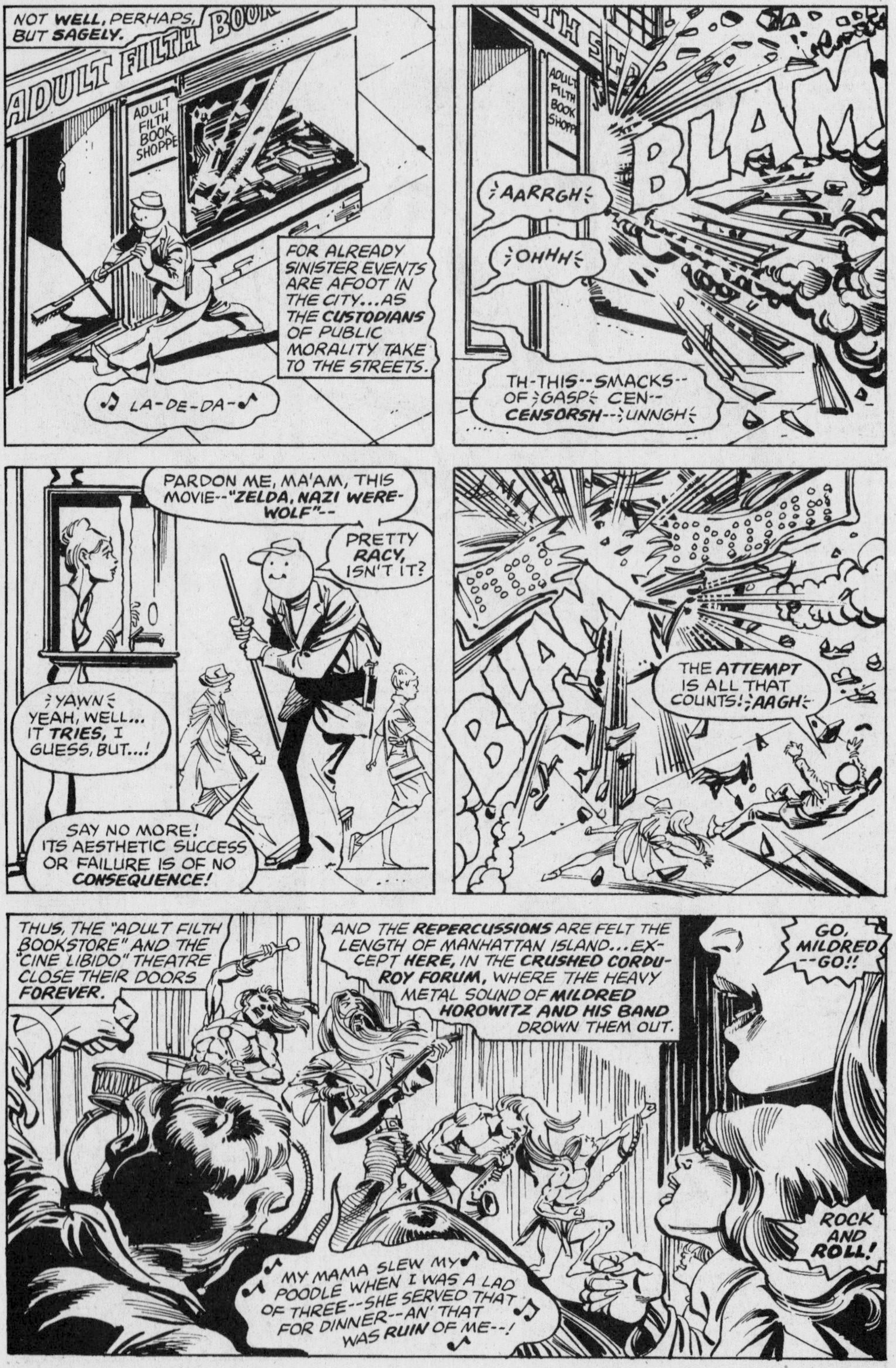
NOT WELL, PERHAPS, BUT SAGELY.
ADULT FILTH BOOK
ADULT FILTH BOOK SHOPPE
FOR ALREADY SINISTER EVENTS ARE AFOOT IN THE CITY...AS THE CUSTODIANS OF PUBLIC MORALITY TAKE TO THE STREETS.
LA-DE-DA-
ADULT FILTH BOOK SHOPPE
BLAM
AARRGH
OHHH
TH-THIS--SMACKS--OF GASP CEN--CENSORSH--UNNGH
PARDON ME, MA'AM, THIS MOVIE--"ZELDA, NAZI WERE-WOLF"--
PRETTY RACY, ISN'T IT?
YAWN YEAH, WELL... IT TRIES, I GUESS, BUT...!
SAY NO MORE! ITS AESTHETIC SUCCESS OR FAILURE IS OF NO CONSEQUENCE!
BLAM
THE ATTEMPT IS ALL THAT COUNTS! AAGH
THUS, THE "ADULT FILTH BOOKSTORE" AND THE "CINE LIBIDO" THEATRE CLOSE THEIR DOORS FOREVER.
AND THE REPERCUSSIONS ARE FELT THE LENGTH OF MANHATTAN ISLAND...EX-CEPT HERE, IN THE CRUSHED CORDU-ROY FORUM, WHERE THE HEAVY METAL SOUND OF MILDRED HOROWITZ AND HIS BAND DROWN THEM OUT.
GO, MILDRED --GO!!
ROCK AND ROLL!
MY MAMA SLEW MY POODLE WHEN I WAS A LAD OF THREE--SHE SERVED THAT FOR DINNER--AN' THAT WAS RUIN OF ME--!

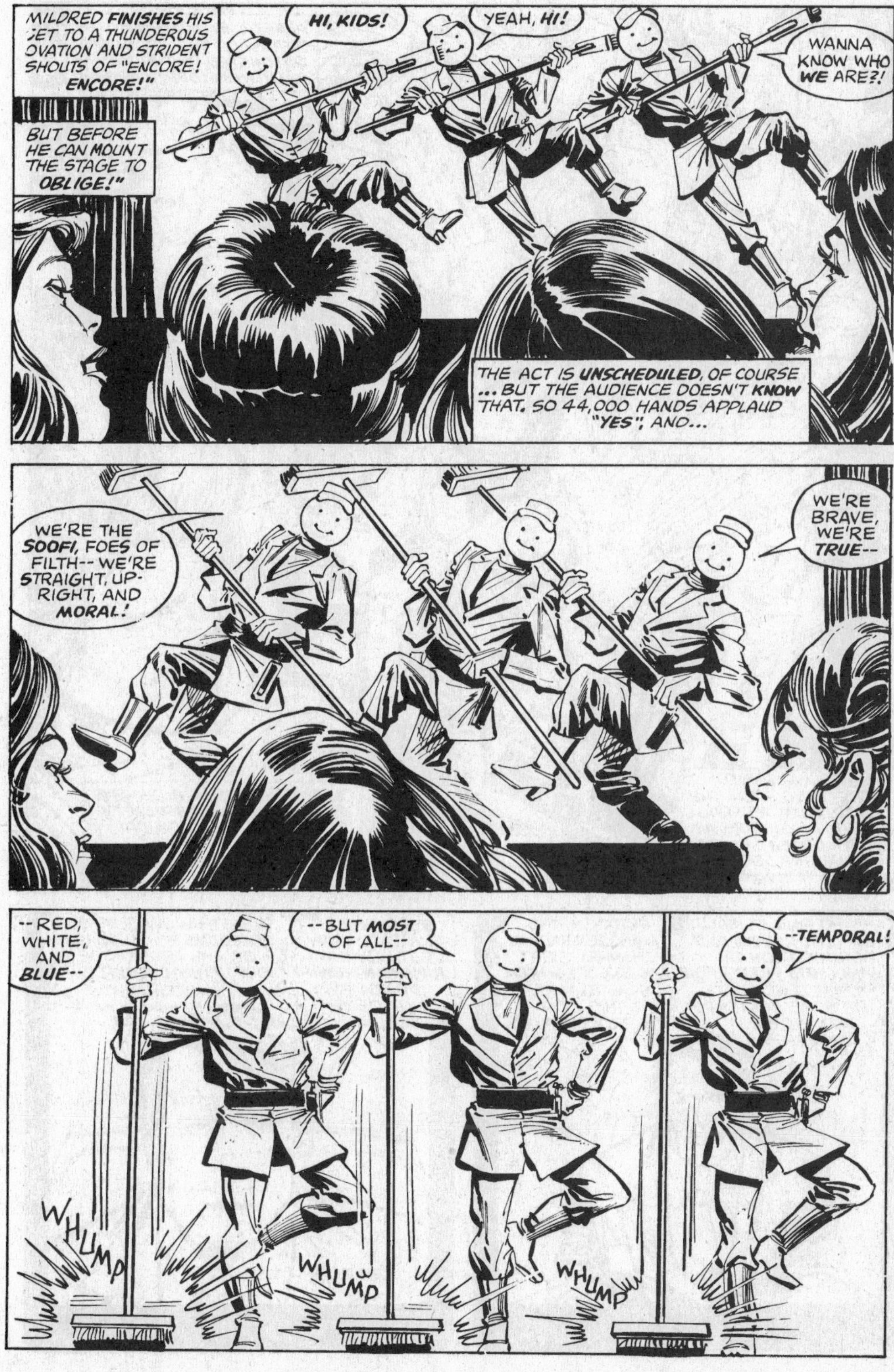
MILDRED **FINISHES** HIS SET TO A THUNDEROUS OVATION AND STRIDENT SHOUTS OF "ENCORE! **ENCORE!**"
BUT BEFORE HE CAN MOUNT THE STAGE TO **OBLIGE!**"
HI, KIDS!
YEAH, **HI!**
WANNA KNOW WHO **WE** ARE?!
THE ACT IS **UNSCHEDULED**, OF COURSE **...** BUT THE AUDIENCE DOESN'T **KNOW** THAT. SO 44,000 HANDS APPLAUD "**YES**", AND...
WE'RE THE **SOOFI**, FOES OF FILTH-- WE'RE **S**TRAIGHT, UP-RIGHT, AND **MORAL**!
WE'RE BRAVE, WE'RE **TRUE**--
--RED, WHITE, AND **BLUE**--
--BUT **MOST** OF ALL--
--**TEMPORAL!**
WHUMP
WHUMP
WHUMP

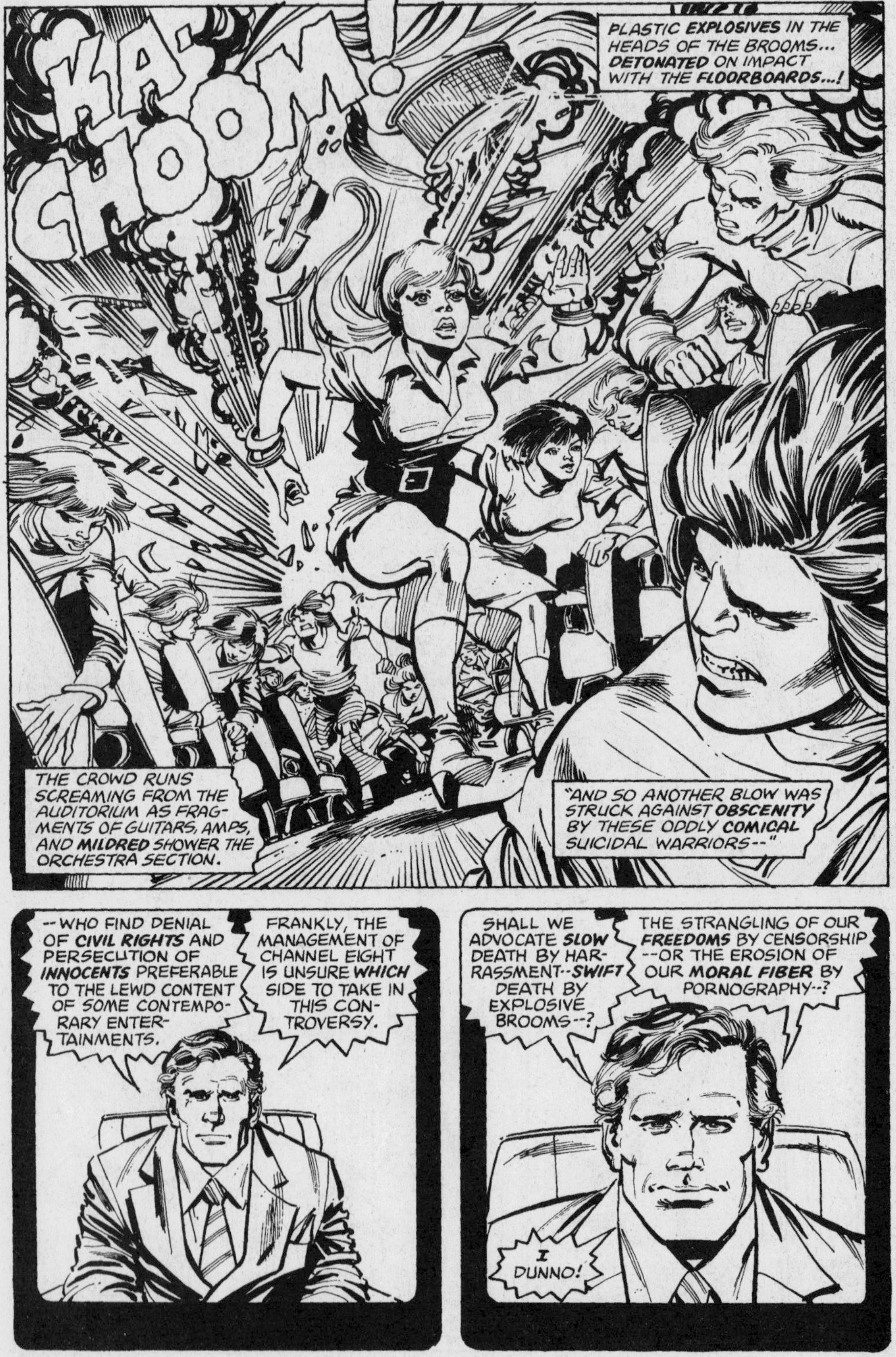
KA-CHOOM!
PLASTIC EXPLOSIVES IN THE HEADS OF THE BROOMS... DETONATED ON IMPACT WITH THE FLOORBOARDS...!
THE CROWD RUNS SCREAMING FROM THE AUDITORIUM AS FRAGMENTS OF GUITARS, AMPS, AND MILDRED SHOWER THE ORCHESTRA SECTION.
"AND SO ANOTHER BLOW WAS STRUCK AGAINST OBSCENITY BY THESE ODDLY COMICAL SUICIDAL WARRIORS--"
--WHO FIND DENIAL OF CIVIL RIGHTS AND PERSECUTION OF INNOCENTS PREFERABLE TO THE LEWD CONTENT OF SOME CONTEMPORARY ENTERTAINMENTS.
FRANKLY, THE MANAGEMENT OF CHANNEL EIGHT IS UNSURE WHICH SIDE TO TAKE IN THIS CONTROVERSY.
SHALL WE ADVOCATE SLOW DEATH BY HARRASSMENT--SWIFT DEATH BY EXPLOSIVE BROOMS--?
THE STRANGLING OF OUR FREEDOMS BY CENSORSHIP --OR THE EROSION OF OUR MORAL FIBER BY PORNOGRAPHY--?
I DUNNO!

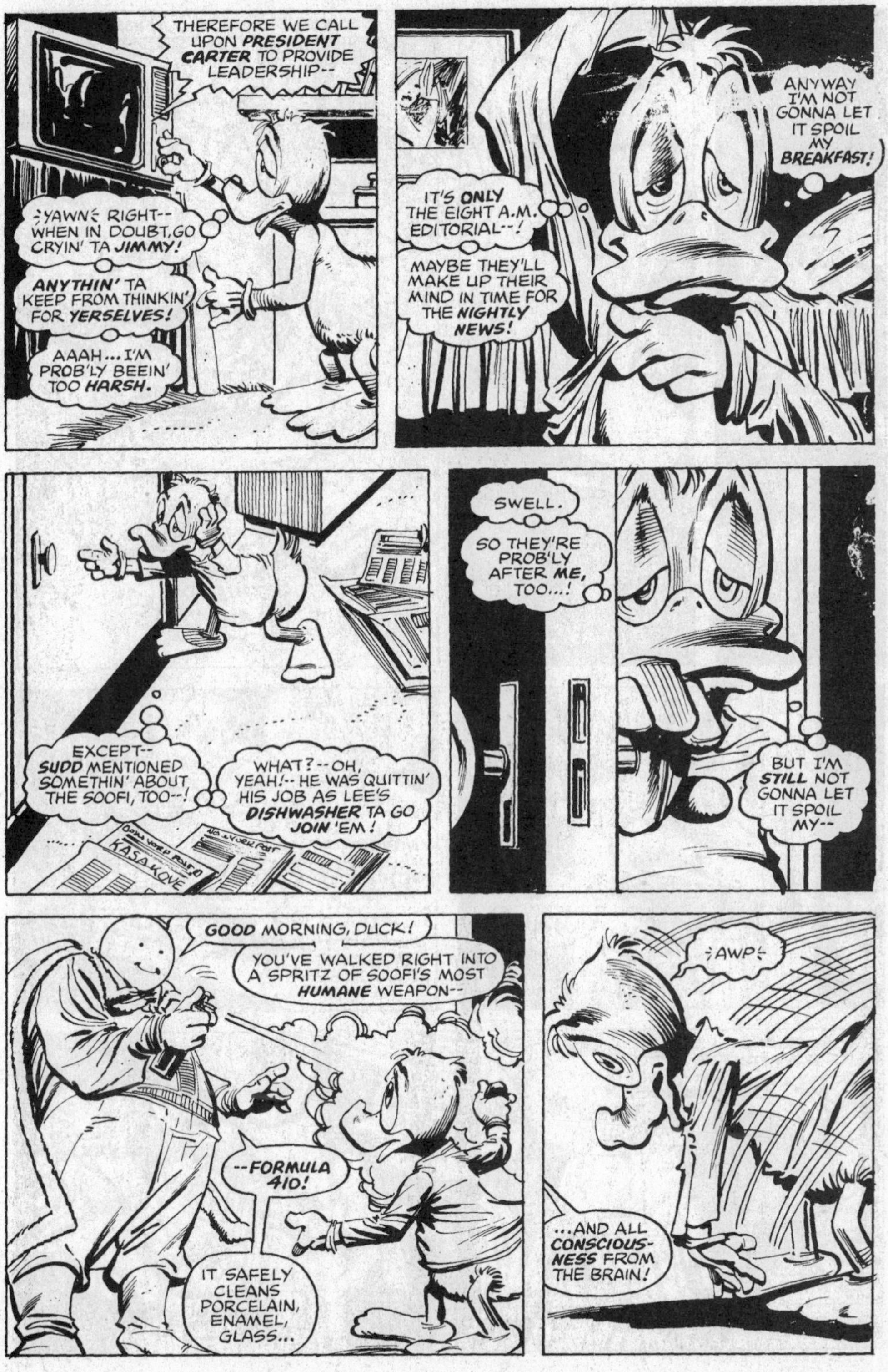
THEREFORE WE CALL UPON PRESIDENT CARTER TO PROVIDE LEADERSHIP--
~YAWN~ RIGHT-- WHEN IN DOUBT, GO CRYIN' TA JIMMY!
ANYTHIN' TA KEEP FROM THINKIN' FOR YERSELVES!
AAAH... I'M PROB'LY BEEIN' TOO HARSH.
IT'S ONLY THE EIGHT A.M. EDITORIAL--!
MAYBE THEY'LL MAKE UP THEIR MIND IN TIME FOR THE NIGHTLY NEWS!
ANYWAY I'M NOT GONNA LET IT SPOIL MY BREAKFAST!
EXCEPT-- SUDD MENTIONED SOMETHIN' ABOUT THE SOOFI, TOO--!
WHAT?--OH, YEAH!--HE WAS QUITTIN' HIS JOB AS LEE'S DISHWASHER TA GO JOIN 'EM!
SWELL.
SO THEY'RE PROB'LY AFTER ME, TOO...!
BUT I'M STILL NOT GONNA LET IT SPOIL MY--
GOOD MORNING, DUCK!
YOU'VE WALKED RIGHT INTO A SPRITZ OF SOOFI'S MOST HUMANE WEAPON--
--FORMULA 410!
IT SAFELY CLEANS PORCELAIN, ENAMEL, GLASS...
~AWP~
...AND ALL CONSCIOUSNESS FROM THE BRAIN!

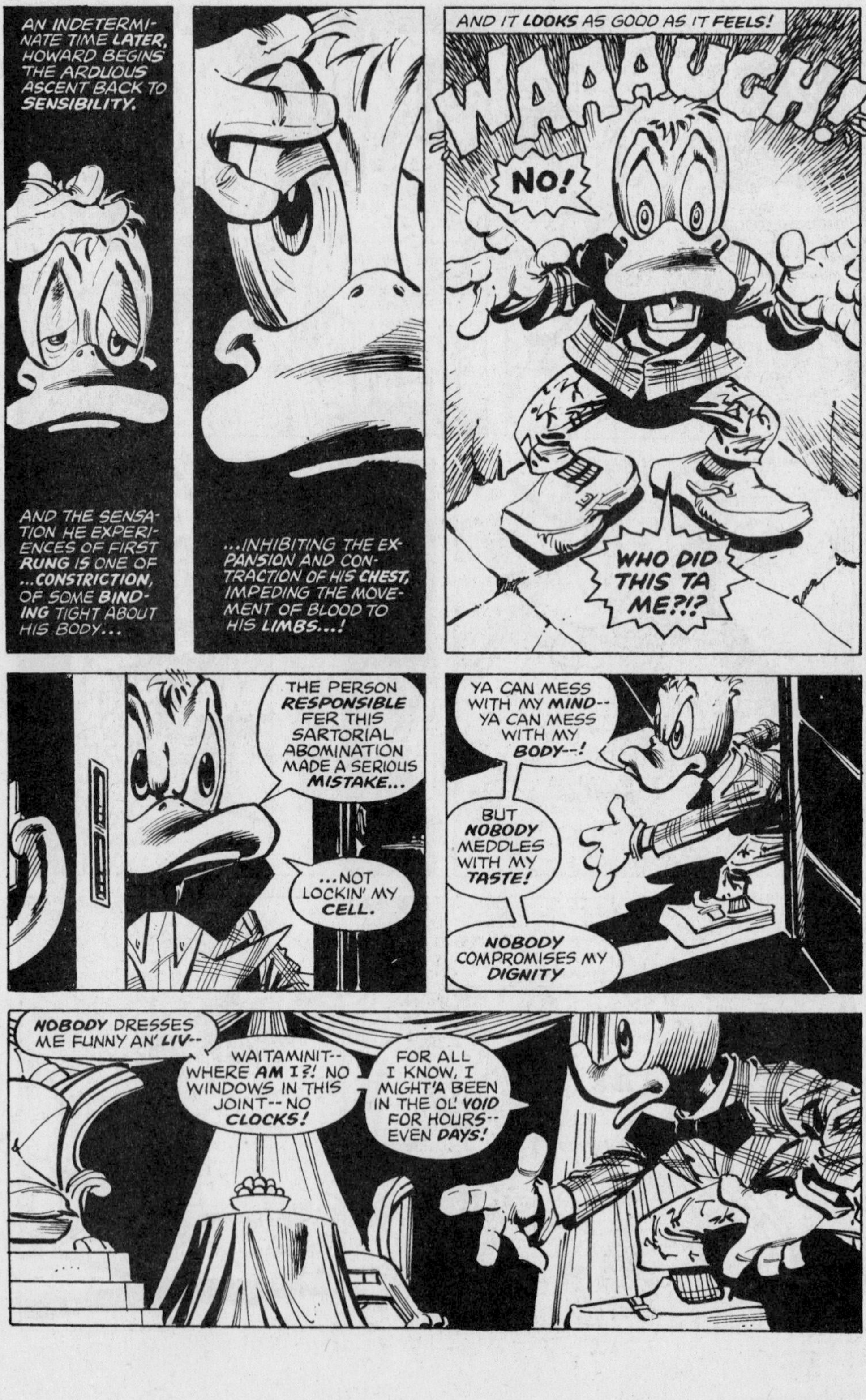
AN INDETERMINATE TIME LATER, HOWARD BEGINS THE ARDUOUS ASCENT BACK TO SENSIBILITY.
AND THE SENSATION HE EXPERIENCES OF FIRST RUNG IS ONE OF ...CONSTRICTION, OF SOME BINDING TIGHT ABOUT HIS BODY...
...INHIBITING THE EXPANSION AND CONTRACTION OF HIS CHEST, IMPEDING THE MOVEMENT OF BLOOD TO HIS LIMBS...!
AND IT LOOKS AS GOOD AS IT FEELS!
WAAAUCH!!
NO!
WHO DID THIS TA ME?!?
THE PERSON RESPONSIBLE FER THIS SARTORIAL ABOMINATION MADE A SERIOUS MISTAKE...
...NOT LOCKIN' MY CELL.
YA CAN MESS WITH MY MIND-- YA CAN MESS WITH MY BODY--!
BUT NOBODY MEDDLES WITH MY TASTE!
NOBODY COMPROMISES MY DIGNITY
NOBODY DRESSES ME FUNNY AN' LIV--
WAITAMINIT-- WHERE AM I?! NO WINDOWS IN THIS JOINT-- NO CLOCKS!
FOR ALL I KNOW, I MIGHT'A BEEN IN THE OL' VOID FOR HOURS-- EVEN DAYS!

FOR ALL I KNOW, THIS COULD BE SOME MADMAN'S LAIR IN *POUGHKEEPSIE!*

SOOFI DEATH COMMANDO OF THE ALMIG...

WHY YOU SHOULD DIE FOR SOOK!

A SOOFI GUIDE TO GIDDY LIBERATION

I MEAN-- I'M *DRESSED* FOR POUGHKEEPSIE--!

BUT *ONE* THING'S FOR SURE:

NOBODY *FED* ME WHILE I WAS OUT! I'M *STAR*--

--UH, ON *SECOND* THOUGHT...!

NO TELLIN' WHAT'S *IN* THESE ORANGES BESIDES VITAMIN "C"!

I'D HATE TA TAKE A BIG JUICY BITE O' *FORMULA 410!*

BETTER *PASS* FOR NOW...!

BESIDES, I'M MORE *IRRITABLE* WHEN I'M HUNGRY. I DON'T WANNA LOSE MY JAGGED *EDGE*...

...BEFORE I MEET THE MAD *HABERDASHER!*

AN' THERE'S STILL A FEW TYPICALLY TEDIOUS *MYSTERIES* TA BE DEALTH WITH.

YER BASIC SUSPICIOUS *TARPAULIN,* HERE...!

I PROB'LY OUGHTTA WONDER ABOUT WHAT'S *UNDER*--

WE CALL IT THE *BLANDITRON,* FOWL! IT'S A PATENTED *SOOFI* DEVICE FOR *CEREBRAL ABLUTION!*

DOES IT SWAB THE BRAIN O' *GOOD TASTE,* TOO?

WHAT'S WITH MY NEW *WARDROBE* CITRUS-HEAD?

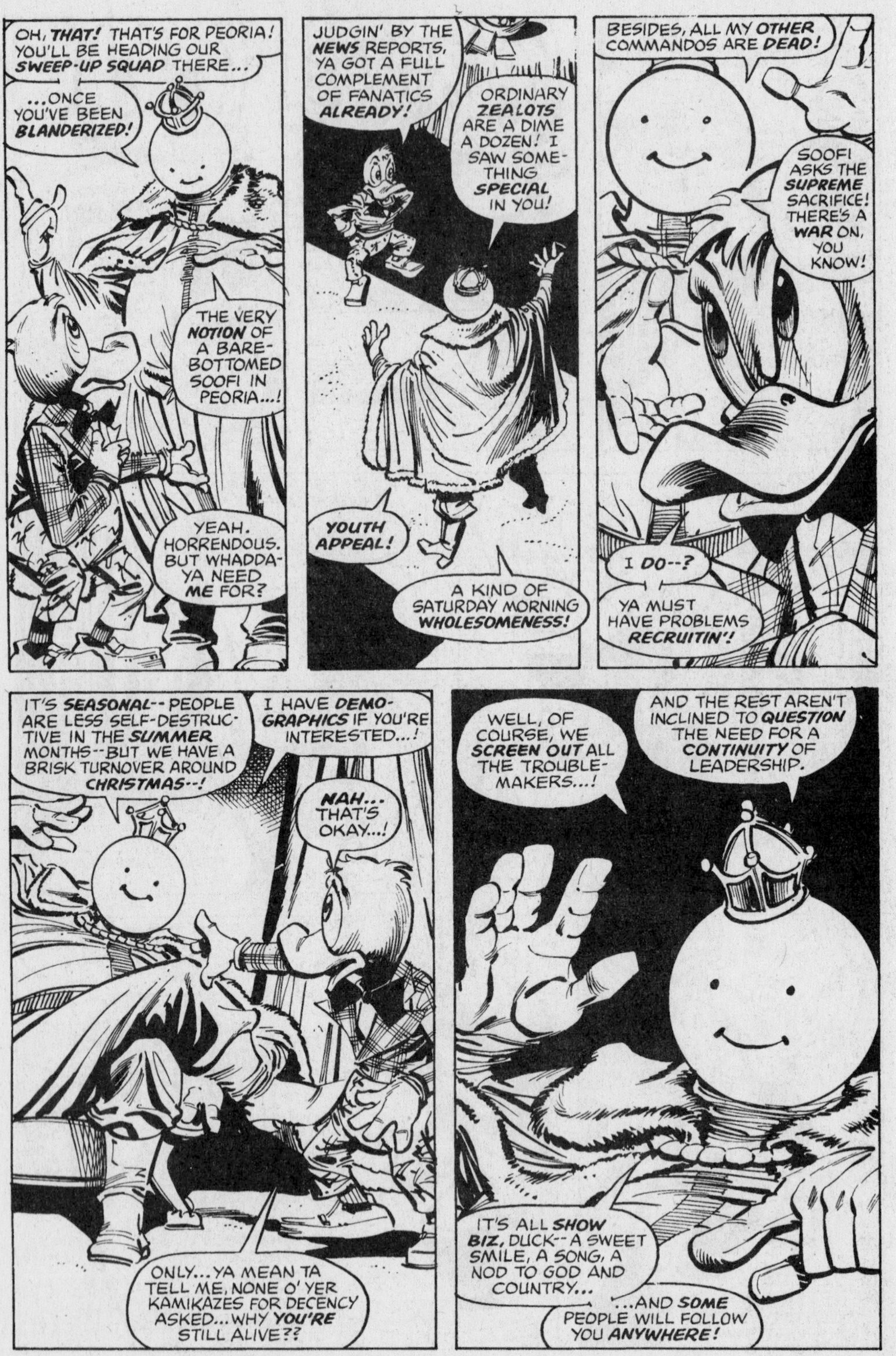
OH, THAT! THAT'S FOR PEORIA! YOU'LL BE HEADING OUR SWEEP-UP SQUAD THERE...
...ONCE YOU'VE BEEN BLANDERIZED!
THE VERY NOTION OF A BARE-BOTTOMED SOOFI IN PEORIA...!
YEAH. HORRENDOUS. BUT WHADDA-YA NEED ME FOR?
JUDGIN' BY THE NEWS REPORTS, YA GOT A FULL COMPLEMENT OF FANATICS ALREADY!
ORDINARY ZEALOTS ARE A DIME A DOZEN! I SAW SOME-THING SPECIAL IN YOU!
YOUTH APPEAL!
A KIND OF SATURDAY MORNING WHOLESOMENESS!
BESIDES, ALL MY OTHER COMMANDOS ARE DEAD!
SOOFI ASKS THE SUPREME SACRIFICE! THERE'S A WAR ON, YOU KNOW!
I DO--?
YA MUST HAVE PROBLEMS RECRUITIN'!
IT'S SEASONAL--PEOPLE ARE LESS SELF-DESTRUC-TIVE IN THE SUMMER MONTHS--BUT WE HAVE A BRISK TURNOVER AROUND CHRISTMAS--!
I HAVE DEMO-GRAPHICS IF YOU'RE INTERESTED...!
NAH... THAT'S OKAY...!
ONLY...YA MEAN TA TELL ME, NONE O' YER KAMIKAZES FOR DECENCY ASKED...WHY YOU'RE STILL ALIVE??
WELL, OF COURSE, WE SCREEN OUT ALL THE TROUBLE-MAKERS...!
AND THE REST AREN'T INCLINED TO QUESTION THE NEED FOR A CONTINUITY OF LEADERSHIP.
IT'S ALL SHOW BIZ, DUCK--A SWEET SMILE, A SONG, A NOD TO GOD AND COUNTRY...
...AND SOME PEOPLE WILL FOLLOW YOU ANYWHERE!

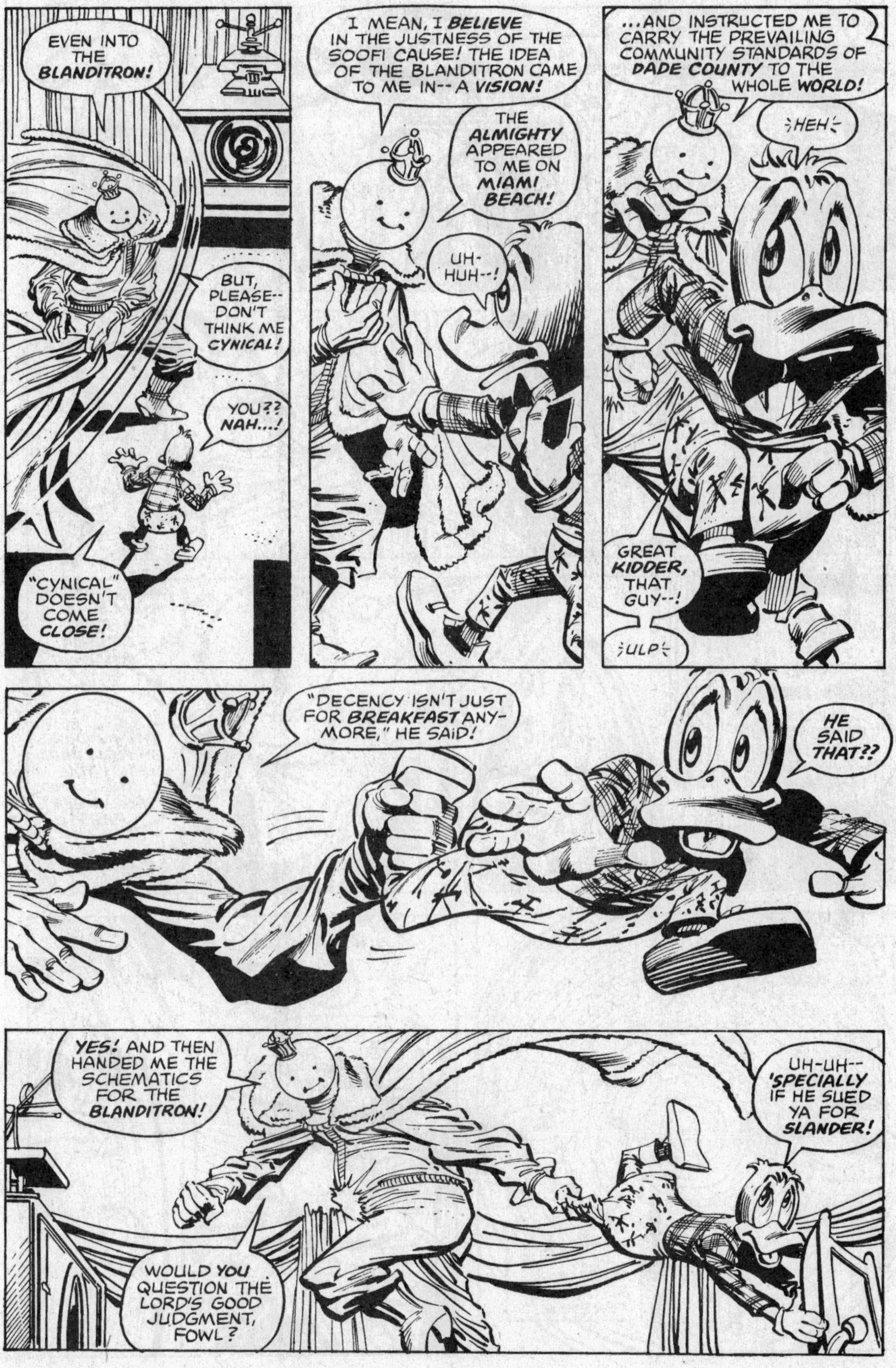

EVEN INTO THE BLANDITRON!
BUT, PLEASE-- DON'T THINK ME CYNICAL!
YOU?? NAH...!
"CYNICAL" DOESN'T COME CLOSE!
I MEAN, I BELIEVE IN THE JUSTNESS OF THE SOOFI CAUSE! THE IDEA OF THE BLANDITRON CAME TO ME IN-- A VISION!
THE ALMIGHTY APPEARED TO ME ON MIAMI BEACH!
UH-HUH--!
...AND INSTRUCTED ME TO CARRY THE PREVAILING COMMUNITY STANDARDS OF DADE COUNTY TO THE WHOLE WORLD!
HEH
GREAT KIDDER, THAT GUY--!
ULP
"DECENCY ISN'T JUST FOR BREAKFAST ANYMORE," HE SAID!
HE SAID THAT??
YES! AND THEN HANDED ME THE SCHEMATICS FOR THE BLANDITRON!
WOULD YOU QUESTION THE LORD'S GOOD JUDGMENT, FOWL?
UH-UH-- 'SPECIALLY IF HE SUED YA FOR SLANDER!

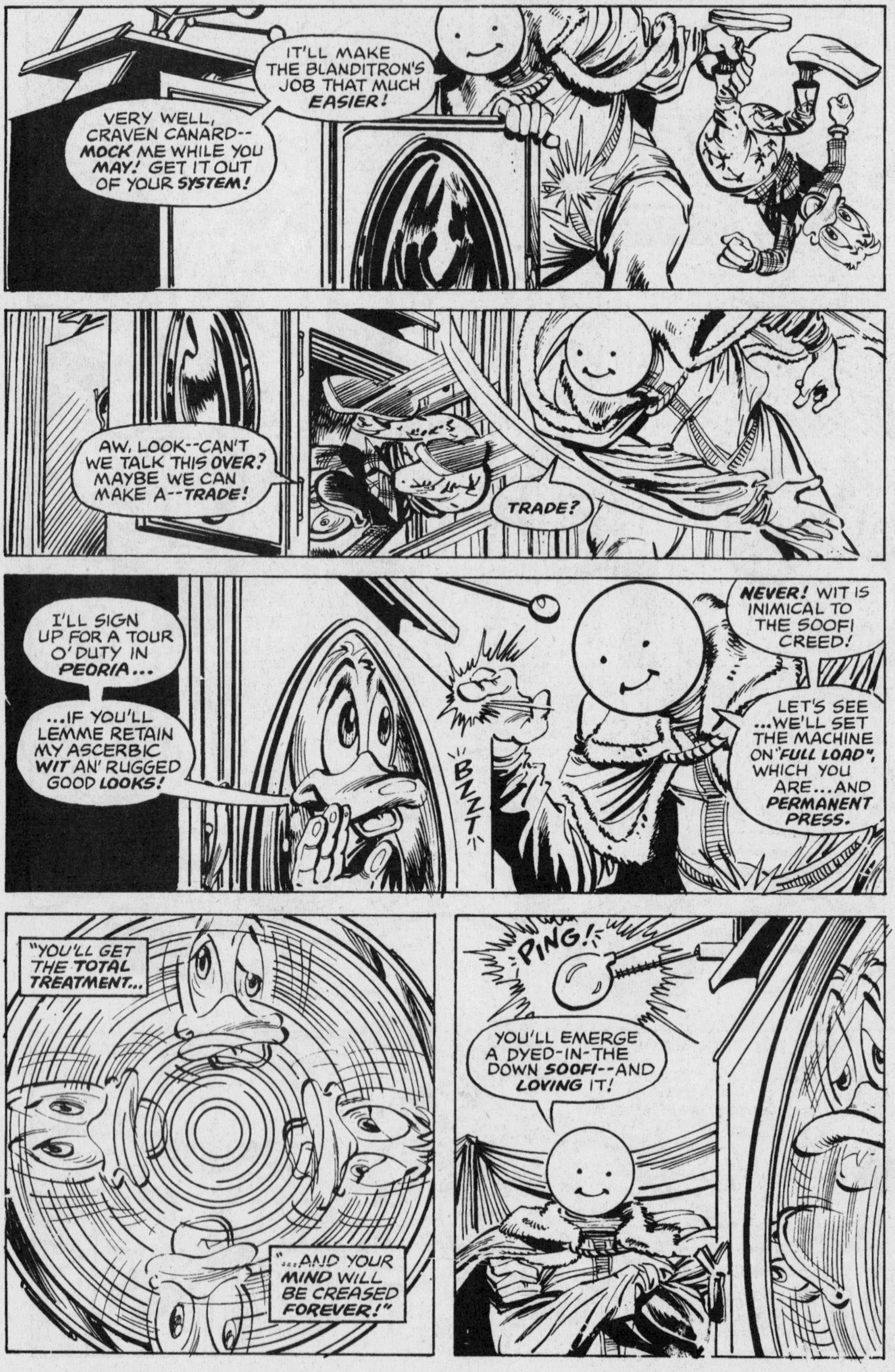
VERY WELL, CRAVEN CANARD-- MOCK ME WHILE YOU MAY! GET IT OUT OF YOUR SYSTEM!
IT'LL MAKE THE BLANDITRON'S JOB THAT MUCH EASIER!
AW, LOOK--CAN'T WE TALK THIS OVER? MAYBE WE CAN MAKE A--TRADE!
TRADE?
I'LL SIGN UP FOR A TOUR O' DUTY IN PEORIA...
...IF YOU'LL LEMME RETAIN MY ASCERBIC WIT AN' RUGGED GOOD LOOKS!
NEVER! WIT IS INIMICAL TO THE SOOFI CREED!
LET'S SEE ...WE'LL SET THE MACHINE ON "FULL LOAD", WHICH YOU ARE...AND PERMANENT PRESS.
BZZT
"YOU'LL GET THE TOTAL TREATMENT...
"...AND YOUR MIND WILL BE CREASED FOREVER!"
PING!
YOU'LL EMERGE A DYED-IN-THE-DOWN SOOFI--AND LOVING IT!

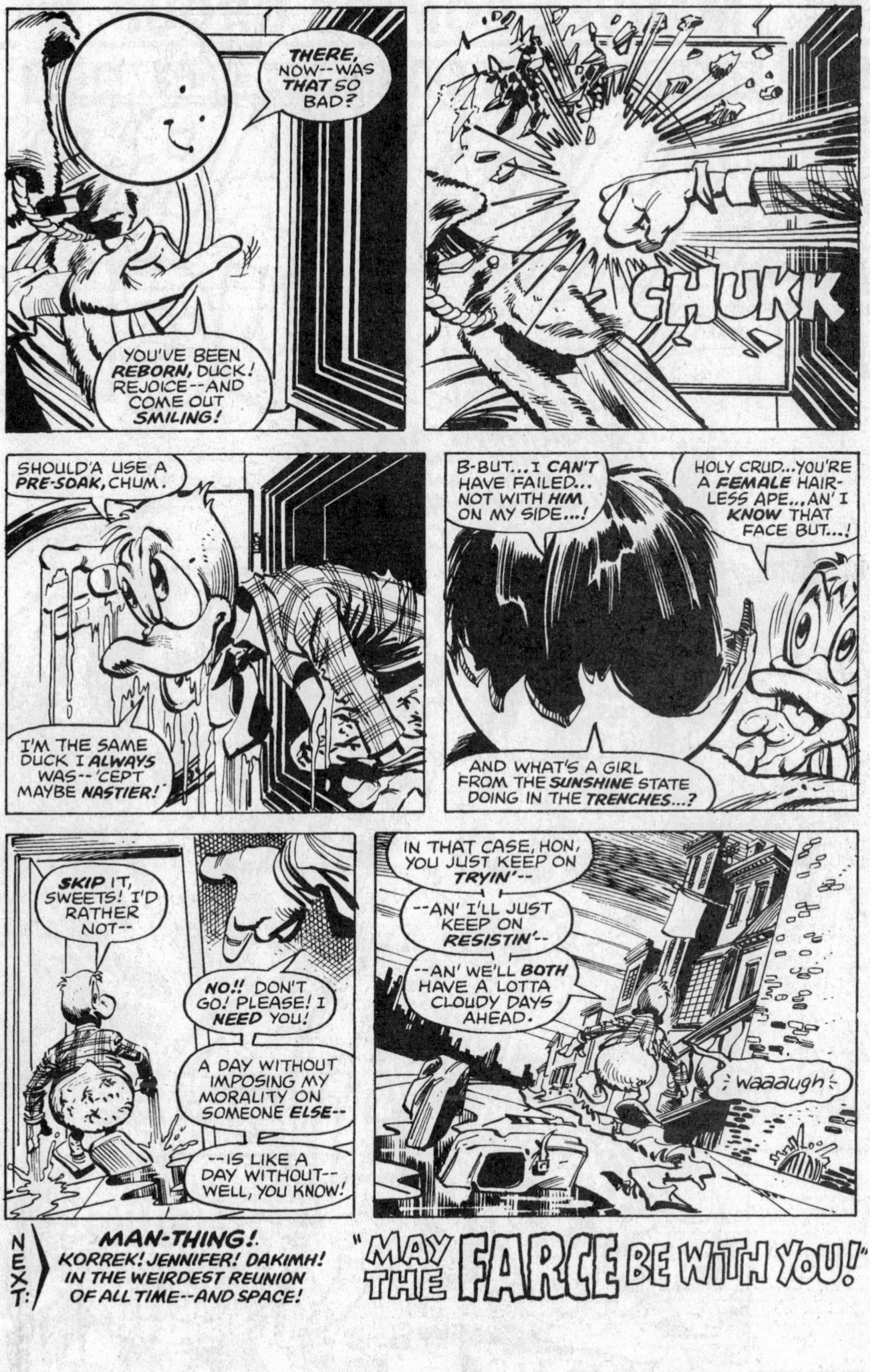
THERE, NOW--WAS THAT SO BAD?
YOU'VE BEEN REBORN, DUCK! REJOICE--AND COME OUT SMILING!
CHUKK
SHOULD'A USE A PRE-SOAK, CHUM.
I'M THE SAME DUCK I ALWAYS WAS--'CEPT MAYBE NASTIER!
B-BUT...I CAN'T HAVE FAILED... NOT WITH HIM ON MY SIDE...!
HOLY CRUD...YOU'RE A FEMALE HAIR-LESS APE...AN' I KNOW THAT FACE BUT...!
AND WHAT'S A GIRL FROM THE SUNSHINE STATE DOING IN THE TRENCHES...?
SKIP IT, SWEETS! I'D RATHER NOT--
NO!! DON'T GO! PLEASE! I NEED YOU!
A DAY WITHOUT IMPOSING MY MORALITY ON SOMEONE ELSE--
--IS LIKE A DAY WITHOUT--WELL, YOU KNOW!
IN THAT CASE, HON, YOU JUST KEEP ON TRYIN'--
--AN' I'LL JUST KEEP ON RESISTIN'--
--AN' WE'LL BOTH HAVE A LOTTA CLOUDY DAYS AHEAD.
waaaugh
NEXT: MAN-THING! KORREK! JENNIFER! DAKIMH! IN THE WEIRDEST REUNION OF ALL TIME--AND SPACE!
"MAY THE FARCE BE WITH YOU!"

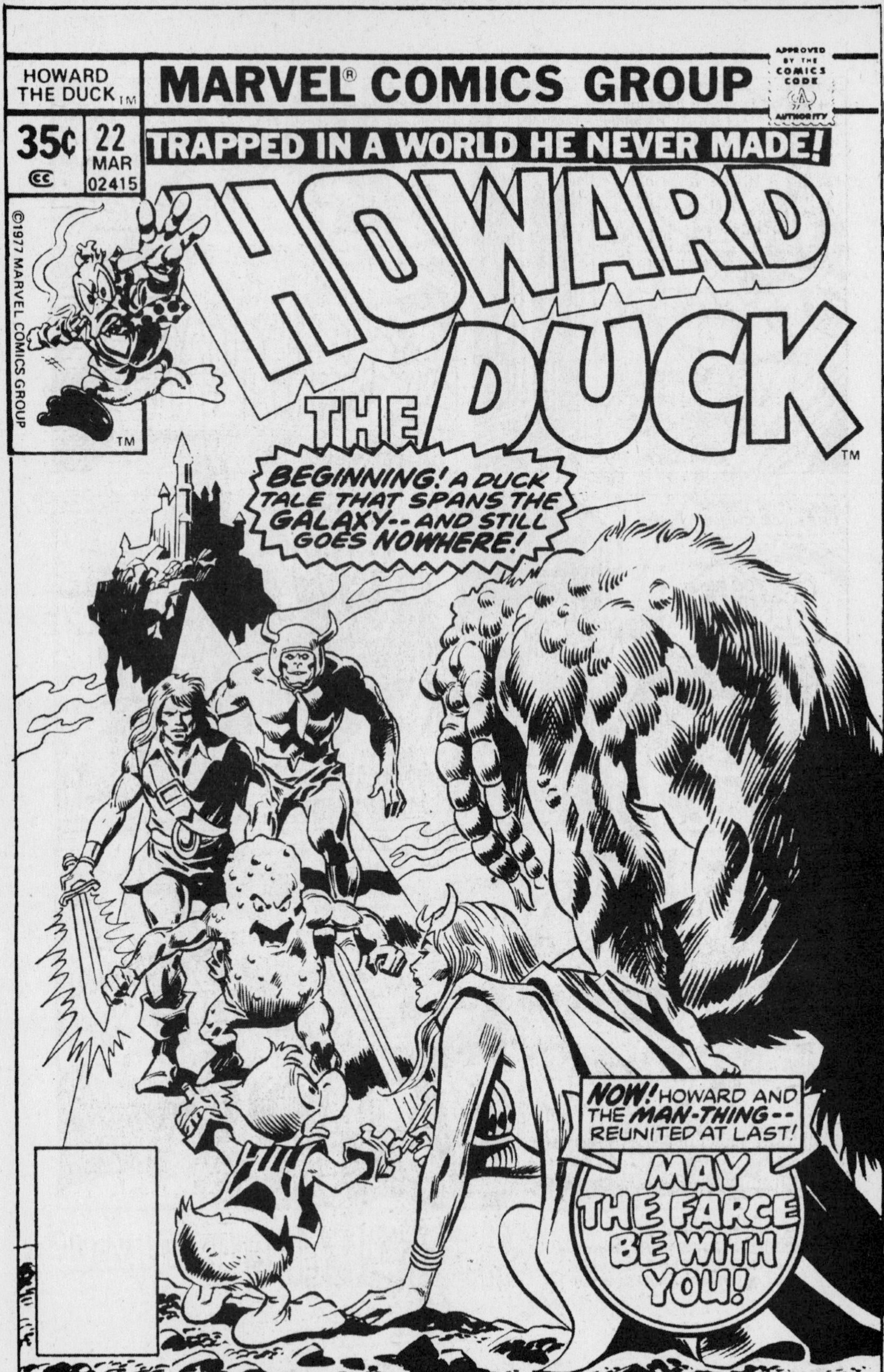

HOWARD THE DUCK TM
MARVEL® COMICS GROUP
APPROVED BY THE COMICS CODE AUTHORITY
35¢
22
MAR
02415
TRAPPED IN A WORLD HE NEVER MADE!
©1977 MARVEL COMICS GROUP
HOWARD THE DUCK TM
BEGINNING! A DUCK TALE THAT SPANS THE GALAXY-- AND STILL GOES NOWHERE!
NOW! HOWARD AND THE MAN-THING-- REUNITED AT LAST!
MAY THE FARCE BE WITH YOU!

From the time of his hatching, he was...different. A potentially brilliant scholar who dreaded the structured environment of school, he educated himself in the streets, taking whatever work was available, formulating his philosophy of self from what he learned of the world about him. And then the Cosmic Axis shifted...and that world *changed.* Suddenly, he was stranded in a universe he could not fathom. Without warning, he became a strange fowl in an even stranger land.

Stan Lee PRESENTS: HOWARD THE DUCK!™

STEVE GERBER / **VAL MAYERIK** / **WILLIAM WRAY** / **JOHN COSTANZA**, *letterer*
WRITER / ARTIST / INKER / **JANICE COHEN**, *colorist*

MAY THE FARCE BE WITH YOU!

FROM THE ROOFTOP OF LEE SWITZLER'S * NEW YORK APARTMENT HOUSE, A WEARY WATERFOWL RASPS HIS RANCOR AT THE COSMOS.

SO BEVERLY'S *MARRIED* TA DR. BONG... PAUL AN WINDA ARE STILL AT *SEA*...

...AN' HERE I *SIT*, THIRTY-SEVEN BUCKS TA MY *NAME*...

...UNDER SMOG SO *THICK* I CAN'T EVEN FIND A STAR TA *WISH* ON!

NOT THAT I *BELIEVE* IN WISHES COMIN' TRUE--!

≡ grrr ≡

* BEVERLY'S UNCLE. SEE LAST ISH. --S.G.

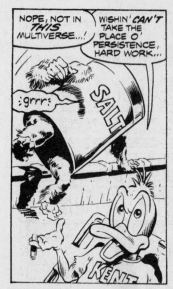

NOPE, NOT IN THIS MULTIVERSE...!
WISHIN' CAN'T TAKE THE PLACE O' PERSISTENCE, HARD WORK...
SALT
:grrr:
...DILIGENCE, TENACITY, GUTS, BRAINS, AN' A TOTAL ABNEGATION O' SCRUPLES!
OH, YEAH--AN' A GOOD LAWYER.
:SIGH: MAYBE I OUGHTTA GET A JOB WRITIN' CHILDREN'S BOOKS...!
SALT
:grrr:
"GRR"--?
:GRRR:
SALT
:waaaugh:
KENT STATE
"WAAAUGH"--?
GRRR!
SALT
KENT STATE
LISTEN, IT'S BEEN GREAT SWAPPIN' INTERJECTIONS WITH YA, BUT I GOTTA RUN--!
I WILL NOT CONTEMPLATE THE ABSURDITY OF THIS CREATURE ...I WILL ASK NO QUESTIONS...!
WHATEVER IT IS-- I ONLY WANT ONE THING FROM IT:
AWAY.
BUT THE FOWL IS DENIED EVEN THAT: THE APE-SHAKER BEAST FORCES HOWARD TO THE GROUND...
HA
AHA
...AND SEASONS HIM LIBERALLY.

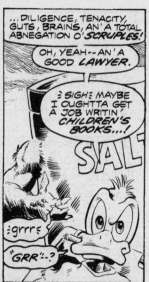

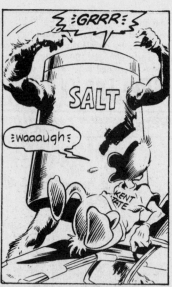

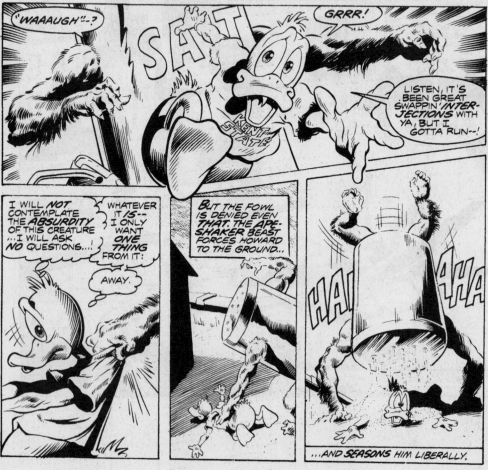

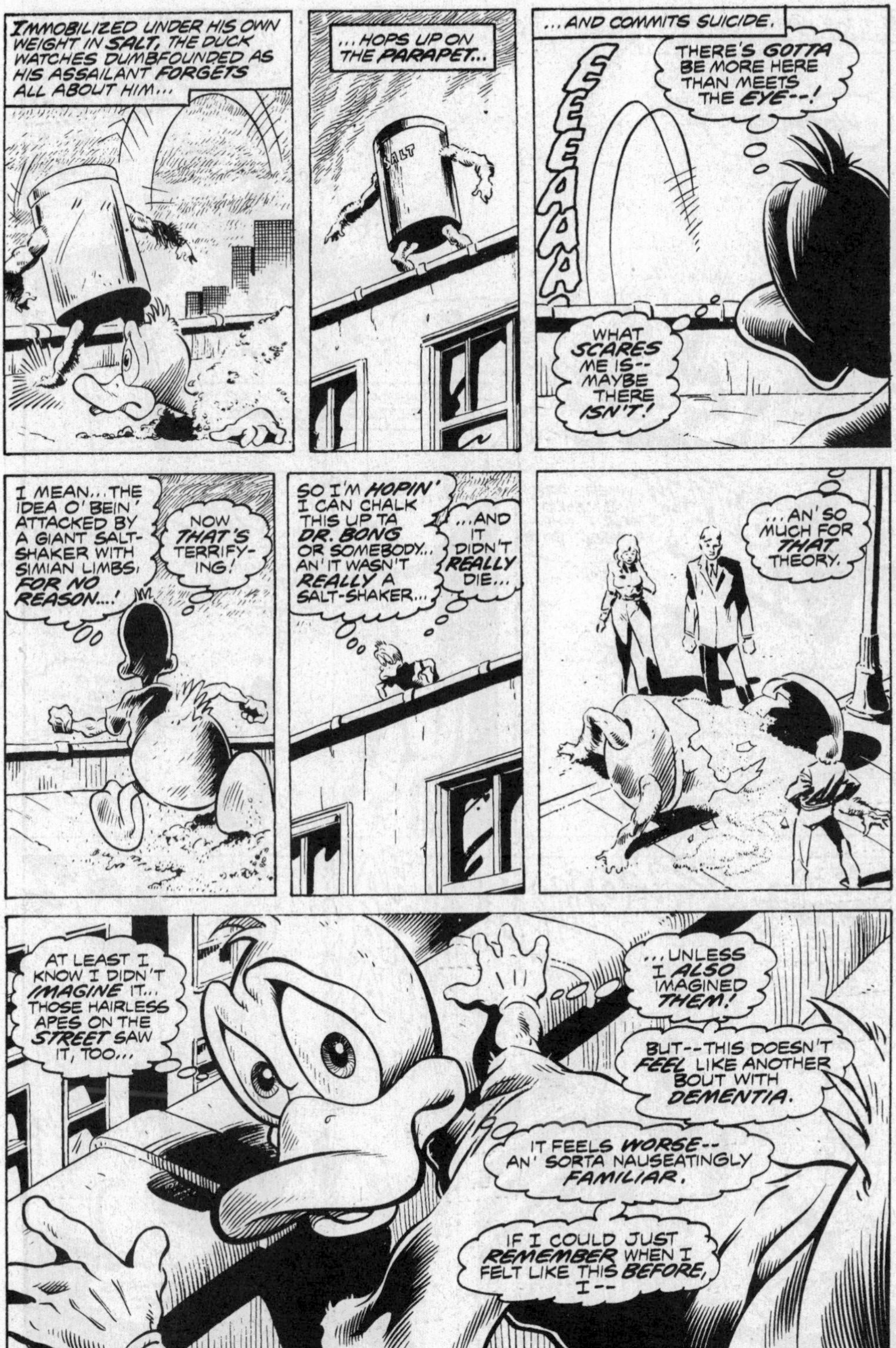
IMMOBILIZED UNDER HIS OWN WEIGHT IN SALT, THE DUCK WATCHES DUMBFOUNDED AS HIS ASSAILANT FORGETS ALL ABOUT HIM...
...HOPS UP ON THE PARAPET...
...AND COMMITS SUICIDE.
EEEEAAAA
THERE'S GOTTA BE MORE HERE THAN MEETS THE EYE--!
WHAT SCARES ME IS--MAYBE THERE ISN'T!
I MEAN... THE IDEA O' BEIN' ATTACKED BY A GIANT SALT-SHAKER WITH SIMIAN LIMBS, FOR NO REASON...!
NOW THAT'S TERRIFYING!
SO I'M HOPIN' I CAN CHALK THIS UP TA DR. BONG OR SOMEBODY... AN' IT WASN'T REALLY A SALT-SHAKER...
...AND IT DIDN'T REALLY DIE...
...AN' SO MUCH FOR THAT THEORY.
AT LEAST I KNOW I DIDN'T IMAGINE IT... THOSE HAIRLESS APES ON THE STREET SAW IT, TOO...
...UNLESS I ALSO IMAGINED THEM!
BUT--THIS DOESN'T FEEL LIKE ANOTHER BOUT WITH DEMENTIA.
IT FEELS WORSE--AN' SORTA NAUSEATINGLY FAMILIAR.
IF I COULD JUST REMEMBER WHEN I FELT LIKE THIS BEFORE, I--

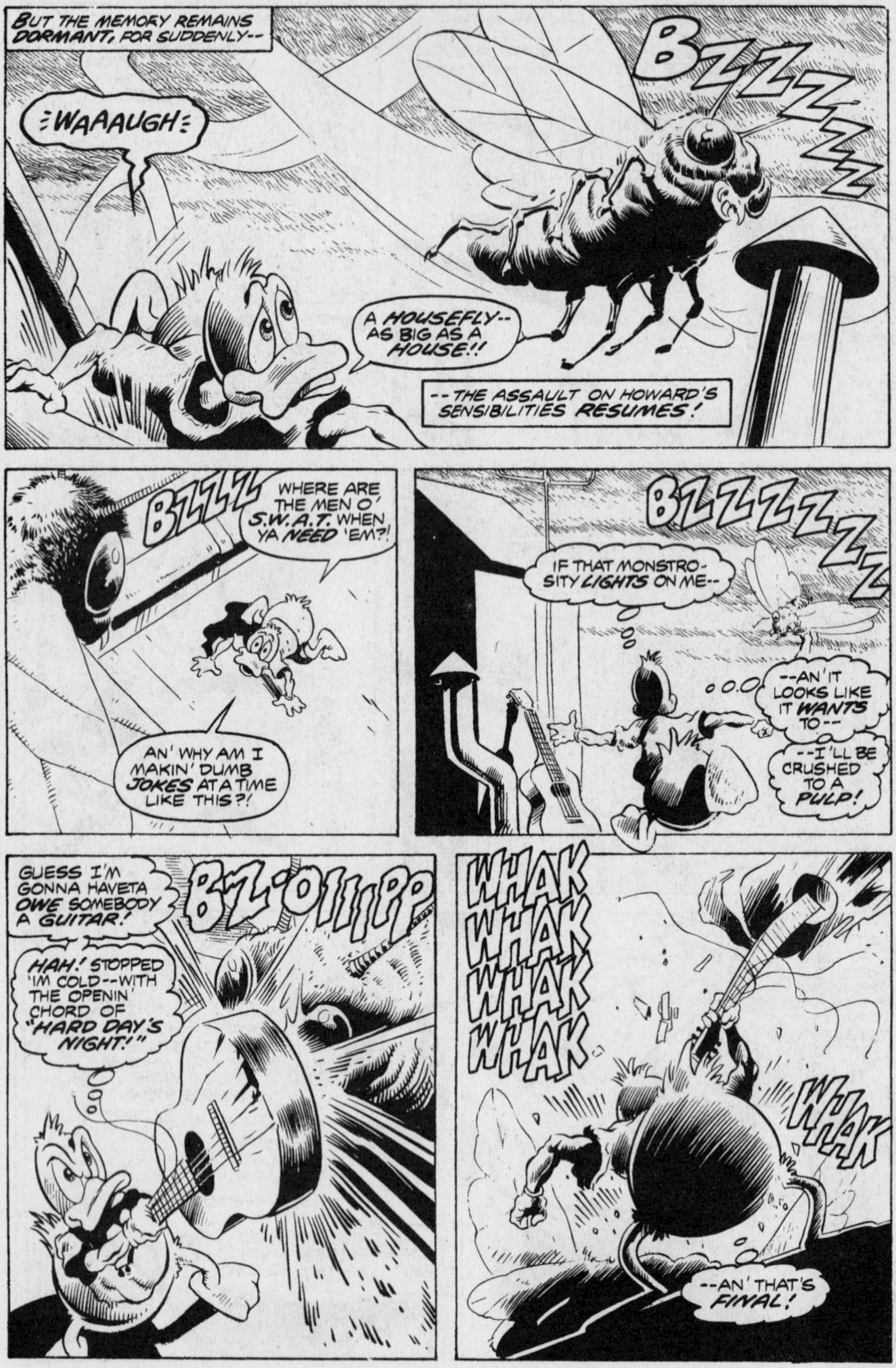
BUT THE MEMORY REMAINS DORMANT, FOR SUDDENLY--
WAAAUGH
BZZZZZZ
A HOUSEFLY-- AS BIG AS A HOUSE!!
--THE ASSAULT ON HOWARD'S SENSIBILITIES RESUMES!
BZZZ
WHERE ARE THE MEN O' S.W.A.T. WHEN YA NEED 'EM?!
AN' WHY AM I MAKIN' DUMB JOKES AT A TIME LIKE THIS?!
BZZZZZZZ
IF THAT MONSTROSITY LIGHTS ON ME--
--AN' IT LOOKS LIKE IT WANTS TO--
--I'LL BE CRUSHED TO A PULP!
GUESS I'M GONNA HAVETA OWE SOMEBODY A GUITAR!
BZ'OIIIPP
HAH! STOPPED 'IM COLD--WITH THE OPENIN' CHORD OF "HARD DAY'S NIGHT!"
WHAK WHAK WHAK WHAK
WHAK
--AN' THAT'S FINAL!

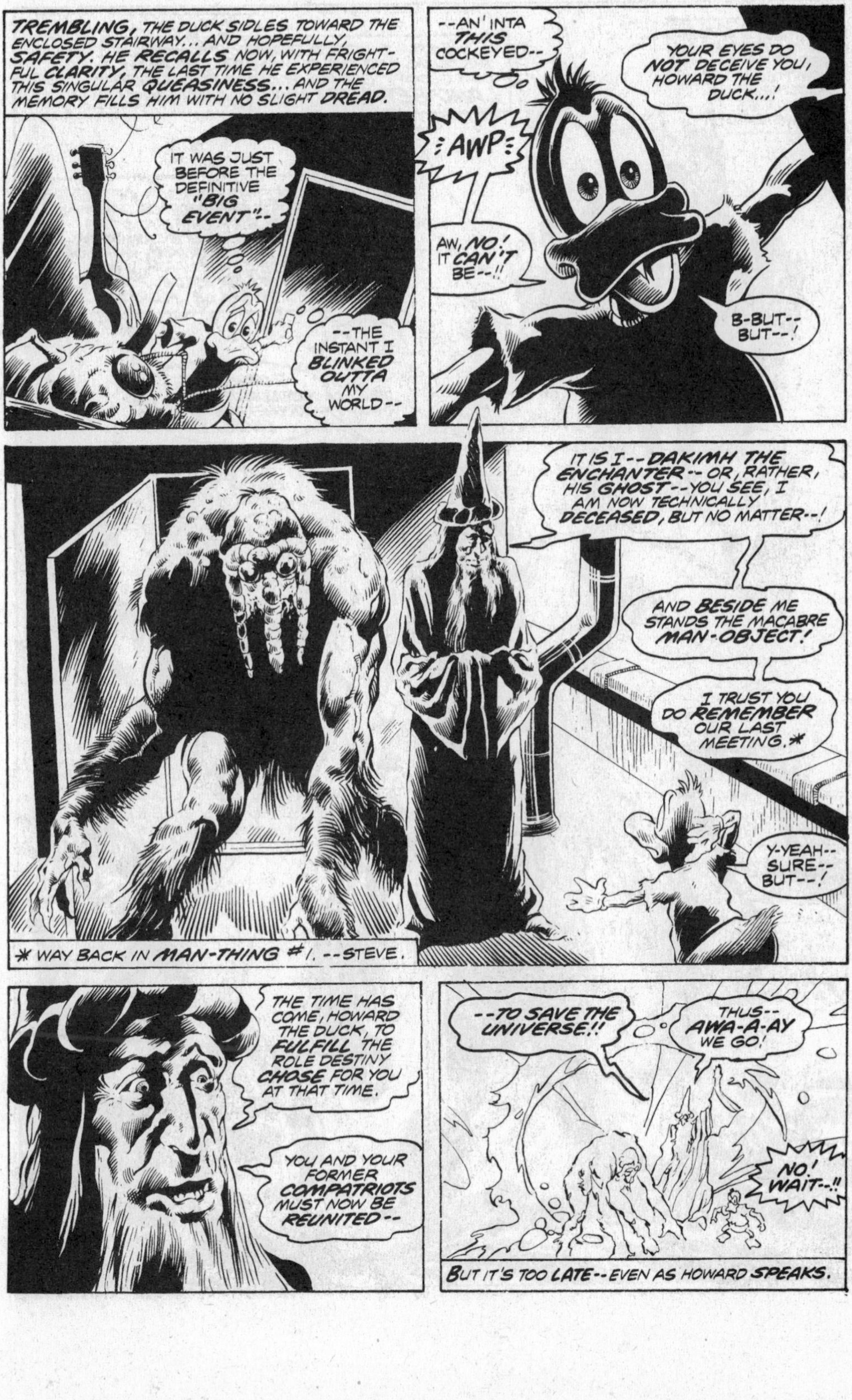

TRAMBLING, THE DUCK SIDLES TOWARD THE ENCLOSED STAIRWAY... AND HOPEFULLY, SAFETY. HE RECALLS NOW, WITH FRIGHTFUL CLARITY, THE LAST TIME HE EXPERIENCED THIS SINGULAR QUEASINESS... AND THE MEMORY FILLS HIM WITH NO SLIGHT DREAD.
IT WAS JUST BEFORE THE DEFINITIVE "BIG EVENT"--
--THE INSTANT I BLINKED OUTTA MY WORLD--
--AN' INTA THIS COCKEYED--
AWP
AW, NO! IT CAN'T BE--!!
YOUR EYES DO NOT DECEIVE YOU, HOWARD THE DUCK...!
B-BUT--BUT--!
IT IS I--DAKIMH THE ENCHANTER--OR, RATHER, HIS GHOST--YOU SEE, I AM NOW TECHNICALLY DECEASED, BUT NO MATTER--!
AND BESIDE ME STANDS THE MACABRE MAN-OBJECT!
I TRUST YOU DO REMEMBER OUR LAST MEETING.*
Y-YEAH--SURE--BUT--!
* WAY BACK IN MAN-THING #1. --STEVE.
THE TIME HAS COME, HOWARD THE DUCK, TO FULFILL THE ROLE DESTINY CHOSE FOR YOU AT THAT TIME.
YOU AND YOUR FORMER COMPATRIOTS MUST NOW BE REUNITED--
--TO SAVE THE UNIVERSE!!
THUS--AWA-A-AY WE GO!
NO! WAIT--!!
BUT IT'S TOO LATE--EVEN AS HOWARD SPEAKS.

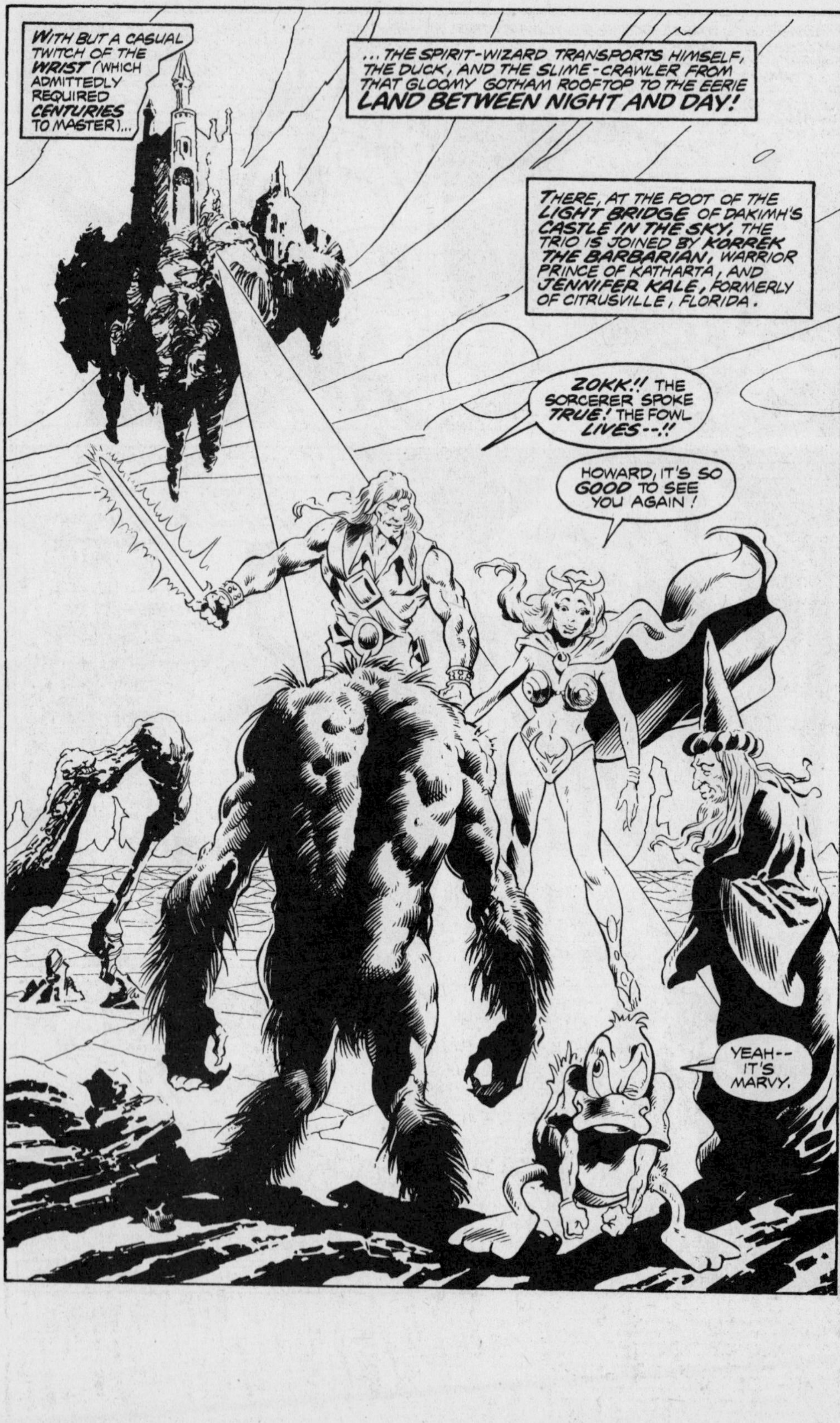
WITH BUT A CASUAL TWITCH OF THE WRIST (WHICH ADMITTEDLY REQUIRED CENTURIES TO MASTER)...
...THE SPIRIT-WIZARD TRANSPORTS HIMSELF, THE DUCK, AND THE SLIME-CRAWLER FROM THAT GLOOMY GOTHAM ROOFTOP TO THE EERIE LAND BETWEEN NIGHT AND DAY!
THERE, AT THE FOOT OF THE LIGHT BRIDGE OF DAKIMH'S CASTLE IN THE SKY, THE TRIO IS JOINED BY KORREK THE BARBARIAN, WARRIOR PRINCE OF KATHARTA, AND JENNIFER KALE, FORMERLY OF CITRUSVILLE, FLORIDA.
ZOKK!! THE SORCERER SPOKE TRUE! THE FOWL LIVES--!!
HOWARD, IT'S SO GOOD TO SEE YOU AGAIN!
YEAH-- IT'S MARVY.

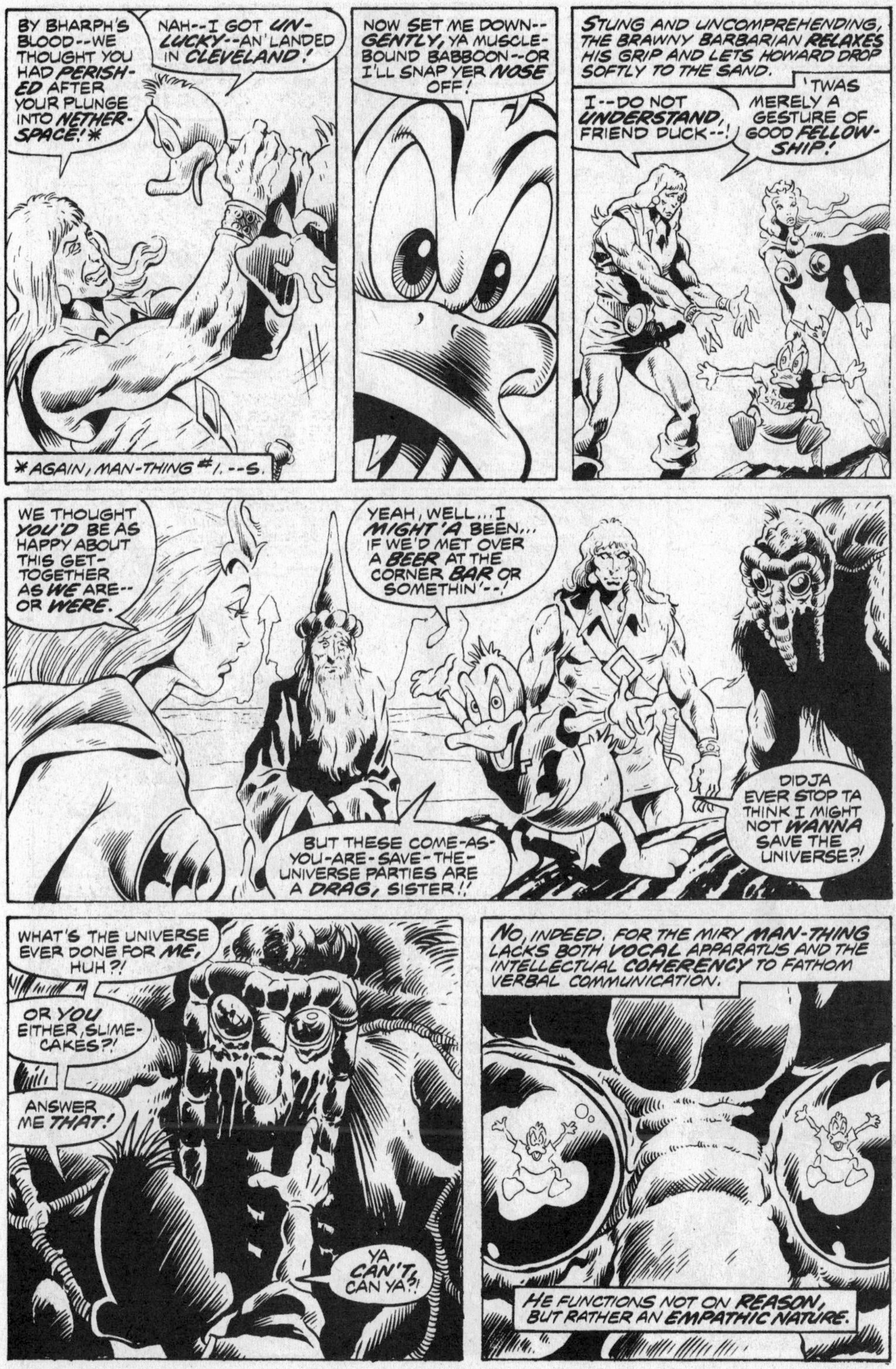

BY BHARPH'S BLOOD--WE THOUGHT YOU HAD PERISHED AFTER YOUR PLUNGE INTO NETHER-SPACE!*
NAH--I GOT UN-LUCKY--AN' LANDED IN CLEVELAND!
*AGAIN, MAN-THING #1. --S.
NOW SET ME DOWN--GENTLY, YA MUSCLE-BOUND BABBOON--OR I'LL SNAP YER NOSE OFF!
STUNG AND UNCOMPREHENDING, THE BRAWNY BARBARIAN RELAXES HIS GRIP AND LETS HOWARD DROP SOFTLY TO THE SAND.
I--DO NOT UNDERSTAND, FRIEND DUCK--!
'TWAS MERELY A GESTURE OF GOOD FELLOWSHIP!
WE THOUGHT YOU'D BE AS HAPPY ABOUT THIS GET-TOGETHER AS WE ARE--OR WERE.
YEAH, WELL... I MIGHT'A BEEN... IF WE'D MET OVER A BEER AT THE CORNER BAR OR SOMETHIN'--!
BUT THESE COME-AS-YOU-ARE-SAVE-THE-UNIVERSE PARTIES ARE A DRAG, SISTER!!
DIDJA EVER STOP TA THINK I MIGHT NOT WANNA SAVE THE UNIVERSE?!
WHAT'S THE UNIVERSE EVER DONE FOR ME, HUH?!
OR YOU EITHER, SLIME-CAKES?!
ANSWER ME THAT!
YA CAN'T, CAN YA?!
NO, INDEED. FOR THE MIRY MAN-THING LACKS BOTH VOCAL APPARATUS AND THE INTELLECTUAL COHERENCY TO FATHOM VERBAL COMMUNICATION.
HE FUNCTIONS NOT ON REASON, BUT RATHER AN EMPATHIC NATURE.

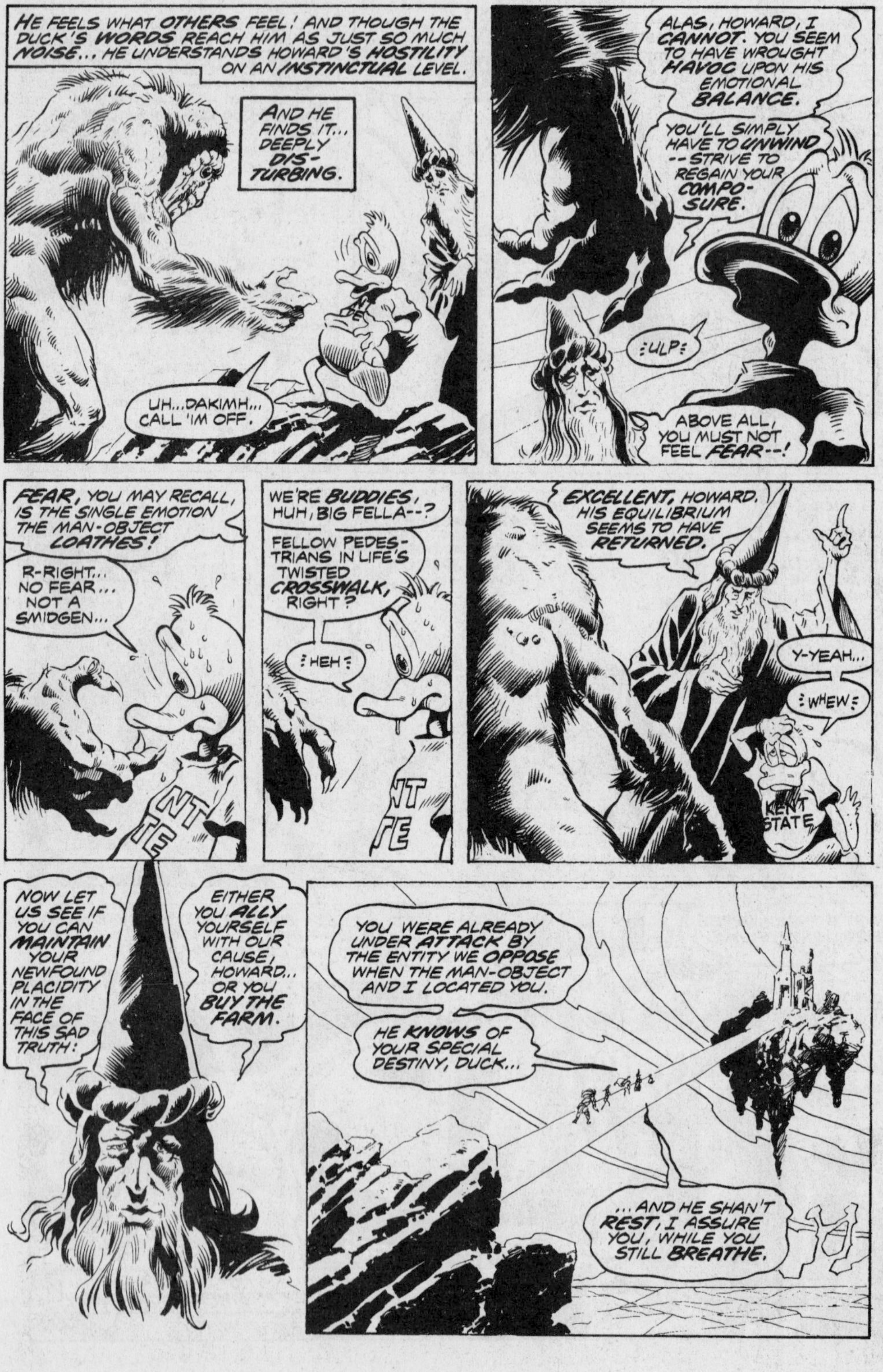
HE FEELS WHAT OTHERS FEEL! AND THOUGH THE DUCK'S WORDS REACH HIM AS JUST SO MUCH NOISE... HE UNDERSTANDS HOWARD'S HOSTILITY ON AN INSTINCTUAL LEVEL.
AND HE FINDS IT... DEEPLY DIS-TURBING.
UH...DAKIMH... CALL 'IM OFF.
ALAS, HOWARD, I CANNOT. YOU SEEM TO HAVE WROUGHT HAVOC UPON HIS EMOTIONAL BALANCE.
YOU'LL SIMPLY HAVE TO UNWIND --STRIVE TO REGAIN YOUR COMPO-SURE.
ULP
ABOVE ALL, YOU MUST NOT FEEL FEAR--!
FEAR, YOU MAY RECALL, IS THE SINGLE EMOTION THE MAN-OBJECT LOATHES!
R-RIGHT... NO FEAR... NOT A SMIDGEN...
WE'RE BUDDIES, HUH, BIG FELLA--?
FELLOW PEDES-TRIANS IN LIFE'S TWISTED CROSSWALK, RIGHT?
HEH
EXCELLENT, HOWARD. HIS EQUILIBRIUM SEEMS TO HAVE RETURNED.
Y-YEAH...
WHEW
KENT STATE
NOW LET US SEE IF YOU CAN MAINTAIN YOUR NEWFOUND PLACIDITY IN THE FACE OF THIS SAD TRUTH:
EITHER YOU ALLY YOURSELF WITH OUR CAUSE, HOWARD... OR YOU BUY THE FARM.
YOU WERE ALREADY UNDER ATTACK BY THE ENTITY WE OPPOSE WHEN THE MAN-OBJECT AND I LOCATED YOU.
HE KNOWS OF YOUR SPECIAL DESTINY, DUCK...
...AND HE SHAN'T REST, I ASSURE YOU, WHILE YOU STILL BREATHE.

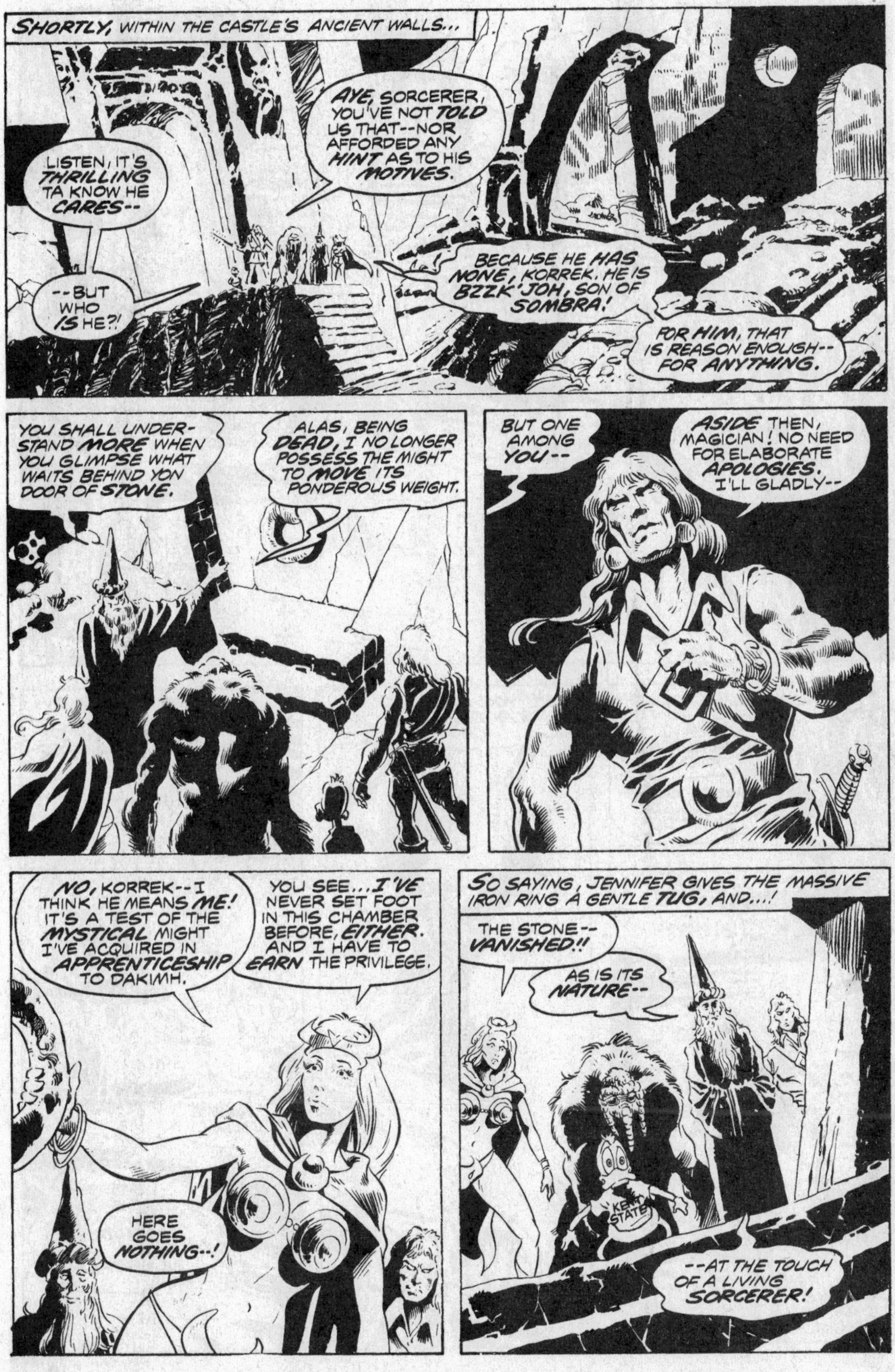
SHORTLY, WITHIN THE CASTLE'S ANCIENT WALLS...
LISTEN, IT'S THRILLING TA KNOW HE CARES--
AYE, SORCERER, YOU'VE NOT TOLD US THAT--NOR AFFORDED ANY HINT AS TO HIS MOTIVES.
--BUT WHO IS HE?!
BECAUSE HE HAS NONE, KORREK. HE IS BZZK'JOH, SON OF SOMBRA!
FOR HIM, THAT IS REASON ENOUGH--FOR ANYTHING.
YOU SHALL UNDERSTAND MORE WHEN YOU GLIMPSE WHAT WAITS BEHIND YON DOOR OF STONE.
ALAS, BEING DEAD, I NO LONGER POSSESS THE MIGHT TO MOVE ITS PONDEROUS WEIGHT.
BUT ONE AMONG YOU--
ASIDE THEN, MAGICIAN! NO NEED FOR ELABORATE APOLOGIES. I'LL GLADLY--
NO, KORREK--I THINK HE MEANS ME! IT'S A TEST OF THE MYSTICAL MIGHT I'VE ACQUIRED IN APPRENTICESHIP TO DAKIMH.
YOU SEE... I'VE NEVER SET FOOT IN THIS CHAMBER BEFORE, EITHER. AND I HAVE TO EARN THE PRIVILEGE.
HERE GOES NOTHING--!
SO SAYING, JENNIFER GIVES THE MASSIVE IRON RING A GENTLE TUG, AND...!
THE STONE--VANISHED!!
AS IS ITS NATURE--
--AT THE TOUCH OF A LIVING SORCERER!

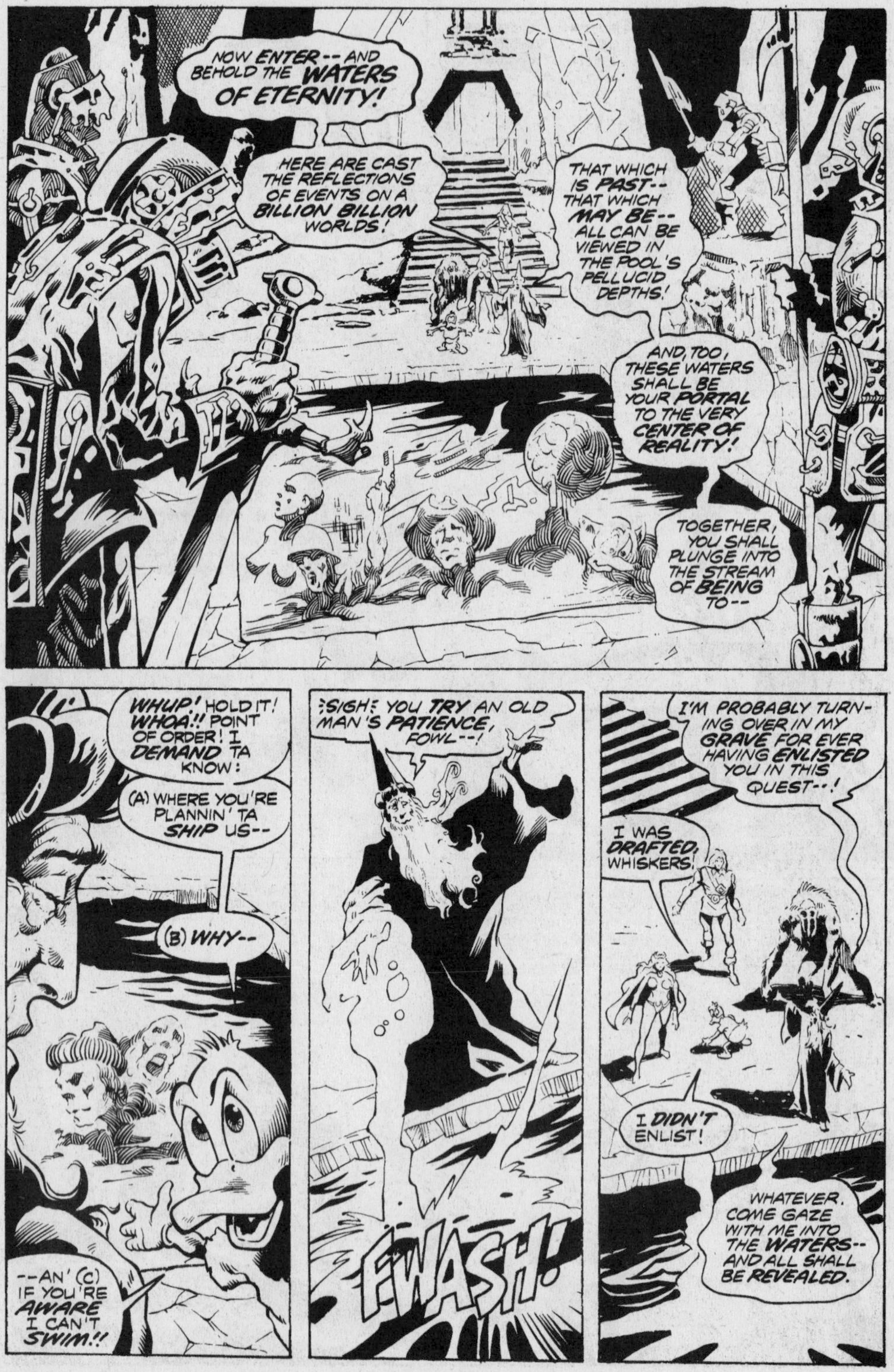

NOW ENTER-- AND BEHOLD THE WATERS OF ETERNITY!
HERE ARE CAST THE REFLECTIONS OF EVENTS ON A BILLION BILLION WORLDS!
THAT WHICH IS PAST-- THAT WHICH MAY BE-- ALL CAN BE VIEWED IN THE POOL'S PELLUCID DEPTHS!
AND, TOO, THESE WATERS SHALL BE YOUR PORTAL TO THE VERY CENTER OF REALITY!
TOGETHER, YOU SHALL PLUNGE INTO THE STREAM OF BEING TO--
WHUP! HOLD IT! WHOA!! POINT OF ORDER! I DEMAND TA KNOW:
(A) WHERE YOU'RE PLANNIN' TA SHIP US--
(B) WHY--
--AN' (C) IF YOU'RE AWARE I CAN'T SWIM!!
:SIGH: YOU TRY AN OLD MAN'S PATIENCE, FOWL--!
FWASH!
I'M PROBABLY TURNING OVER IN MY GRAVE FOR EVER HAVING ENLISTED YOU IN THIS QUEST--!
I WAS DRAFTED, WHISKERS!
I DIDN'T ENLIST!
WHATEVER. COME GAZE WITH ME INTO THE WATERS-- AND ALL SHALL BE REVEALED.

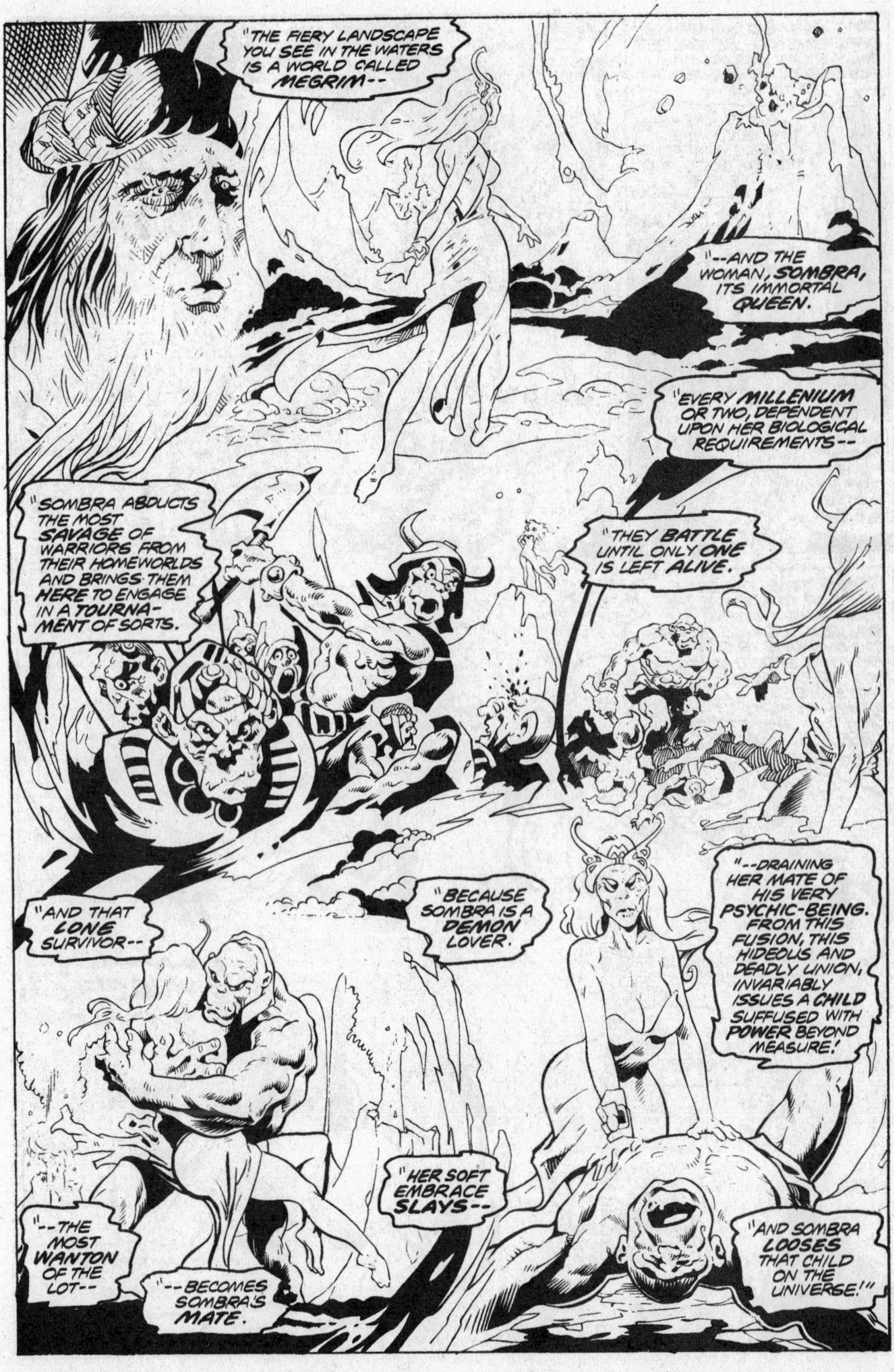
"THE FIERY LANDSCAPE YOU SEE IN THE WATERS IS A WORLD CALLED MEGRIM--
"--AND THE WOMAN, SOMBRA, ITS IMMORTAL QUEEN.
"EVERY MILLENIUM OR TWO, DEPENDENT UPON HER BIOLOGICAL REQUIREMENTS--
"SOMBRA ABDUCTS THE MOST SAVAGE OF WARRIORS FROM THEIR HOMEWORLDS AND BRINGS THEM HERE TO ENGAGE IN A TOURNAMENT OF SORTS.
"THEY BATTLE UNTIL ONLY ONE IS LEFT ALIVE.
"AND THAT LONE SURVIVOR--
"--THE MOST WANTON OF THE LOT--
"--BECOMES SOMBRA'S MATE.
"BECAUSE SOMBRA IS A DEMON LOVER.
"HER SOFT EMBRACE SLAYS--
"--DRAINING HER MATE OF HIS VERY PSYCHIC-BEING. FROM THIS FUSION, THIS HIDEOUS AND DEADLY UNION, INVARIABLY ISSUES A CHILD SUFFUSED WITH POWER BEYOND MEASURE!
"AND SOMBRA LOOSES THAT CHILD ON THE UNIVERSE!"

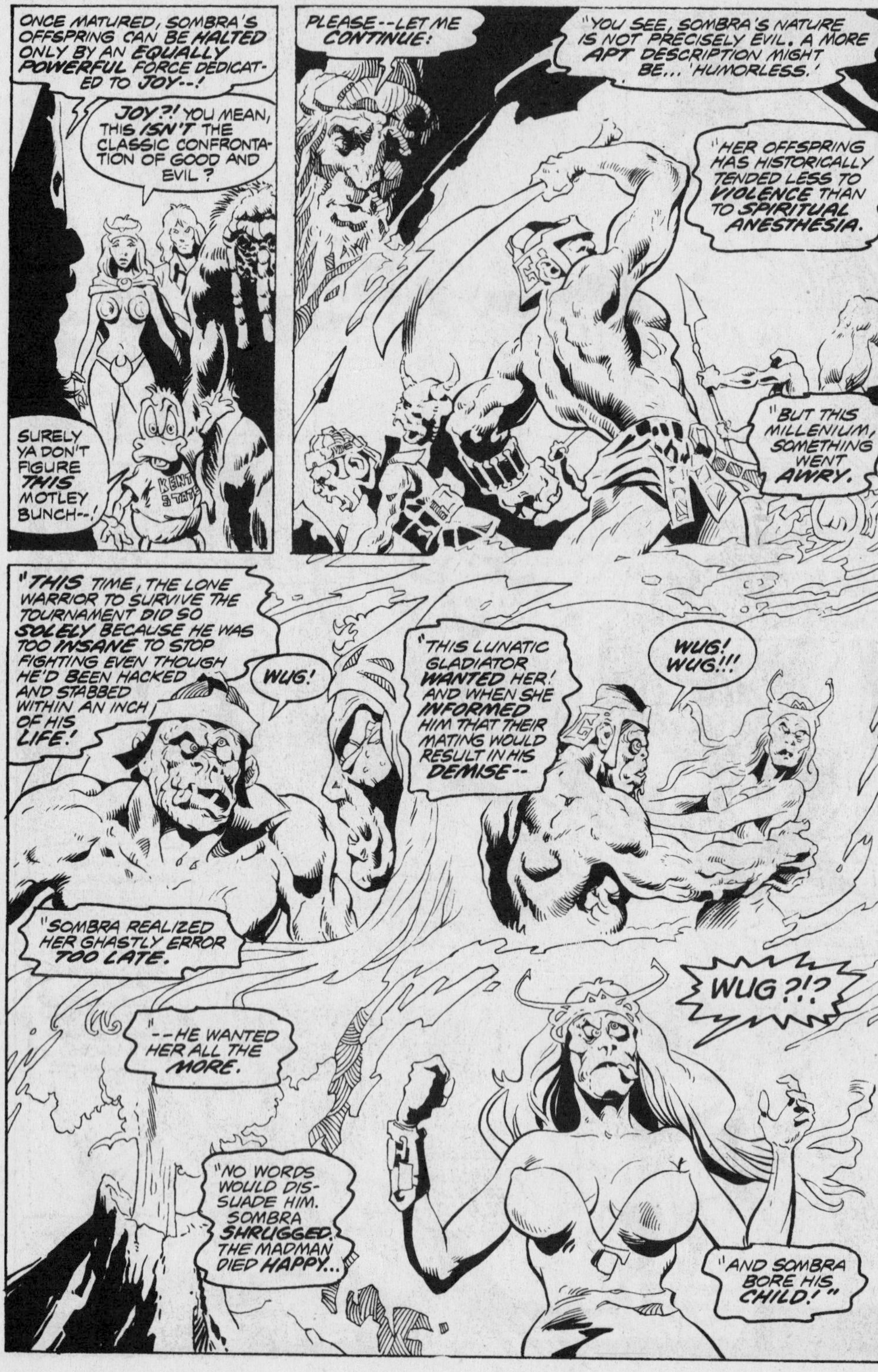

ONCE MATURED, SOMBRA'S OFFSPRING CAN BE HALTED ONLY BY AN EQUALLY POWERFUL FORCE DEDICATED TO JOY--!
JOY?! YOU MEAN, THIS ISN'T THE CLASSIC CONFRONTATION OF GOOD AND EVIL?
SURELY YA DON'T FIGURE THIS MOTLEY BUNCH--!
KENT STATE
PLEASE--LET ME CONTINUE:
"YOU SEE, SOMBRA'S NATURE IS NOT PRECISELY EVIL. A MORE APT DESCRIPTION MIGHT BE... 'HUMORLESS.'
"HER OFFSPRING HAS HISTORICALLY TENDED LESS TO VIOLENCE THAN TO SPIRITUAL ANESTHESIA.
"BUT THIS MILLENIUM, SOMETHING WENT AWRY.
"THIS TIME, THE LONE WARRIOR TO SURVIVE THE TOURNAMENT DID SO SOLELY BECAUSE HE WAS TOO INSANE TO STOP FIGHTING EVEN THOUGH HE'D BEEN HACKED AND STABBED WITHIN AN INCH OF HIS LIFE!
WUG!
"THIS LUNATIC GLADIATOR WANTED HER! AND WHEN SHE INFORMED HIM THAT THEIR MATING WOULD RESULT IN HIS DEMISE--
WUG! WUG!!!
"SOMBRA REALIZED HER GHASTLY ERROR TOO LATE.
WUG?!?
"--HE WANTED HER ALL THE MORE.
"NO WORDS WOULD DISSUADE HIM. SOMBRA SHRUGGED. THE MADMAN DIED HAPPY...
"AND SOMBRA BORE HIS CHILD!"

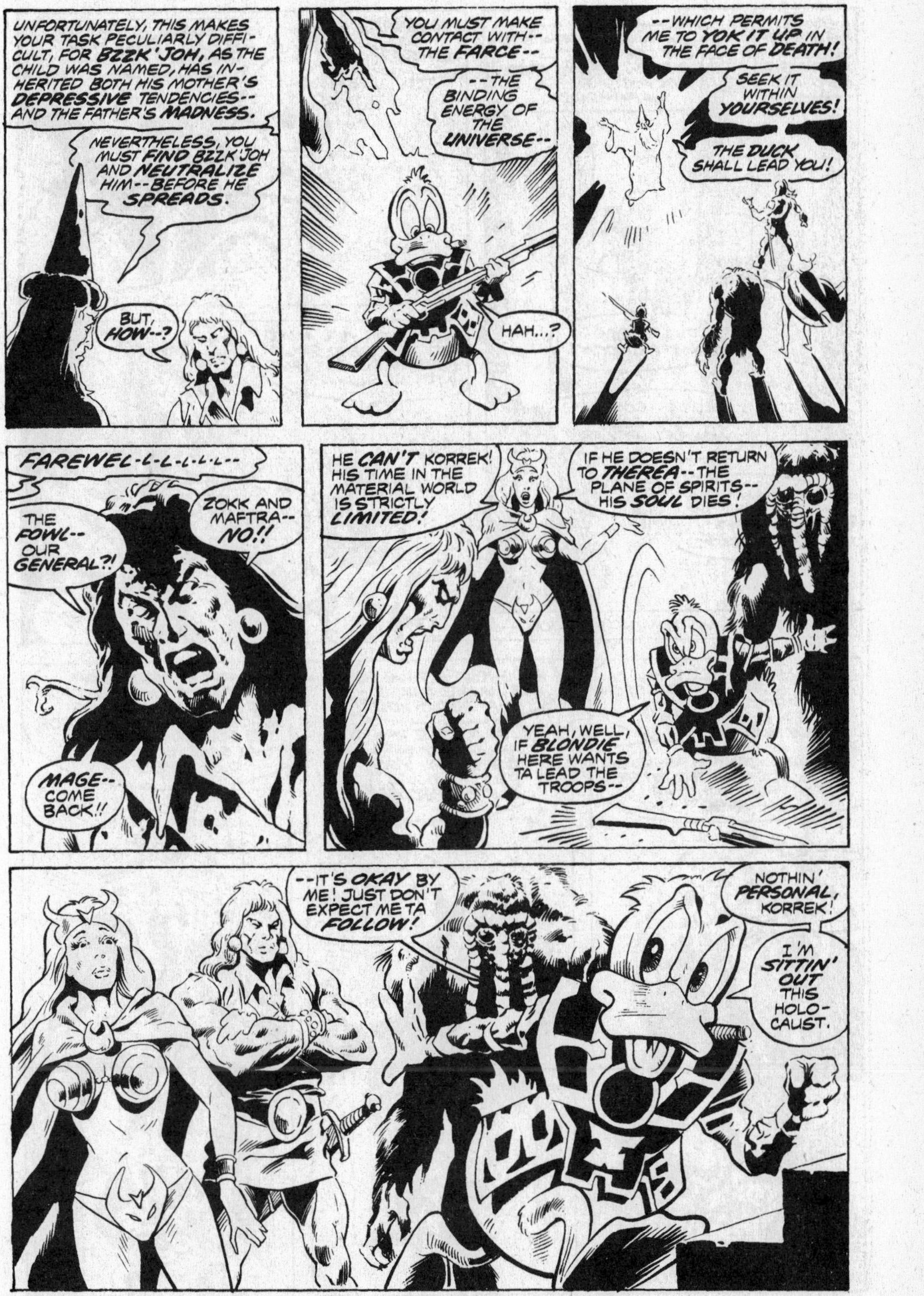
UNFORTUNATELY, THIS MAKES YOUR TASK PECULIARLY DIFFICULT, FOR BZZK 'JOH, AS THE CHILD WAS NAMED, HAS INHERITED BOTH HIS MOTHER'S DEPRESSIVE TENDENCIES-- AND THE FATHER'S MADNESS.
NEVERTHELESS, YOU MUST FIND BZZK 'JOH AND NEUTRALIZE HIM--BEFORE HE SPREADS.
BUT, HOW--?
YOU MUST MAKE CONTACT WITH-- THE FARCE--
--THE BINDING ENERGY OF THE UNIVERSE--
HAH...?
--WHICH PERMITS ME TO YOK IT UP IN THE FACE OF DEATH!
SEEK IT WITHIN YOURSELVES!
THE DUCK SHALL LEAD YOU!
FAREWEL-L-L-L-L-L--
THE FOWL-- OUR GENERAL?!
ZOKK AND MAFTRA-- NO!!
MAGE-- COME BACK!!
HE CAN'T KORREK! HIS TIME IN THE MATERIAL WORLD IS STRICTLY LIMITED!
IF HE DOESN'T RETURN TO THEREA--THE PLANE OF SPIRITS-- HIS SOUL DIES!
YEAH, WELL, IF BLONDIE HERE WANTS TA LEAD THE TROOPS--
--IT'S OKAY BY ME! JUST DON'T EXPECT ME TA FOLLOW!
NOTHIN' PERSONAL, KORREK!
I'M SITTIN' OUT THIS HOLOCAUST.

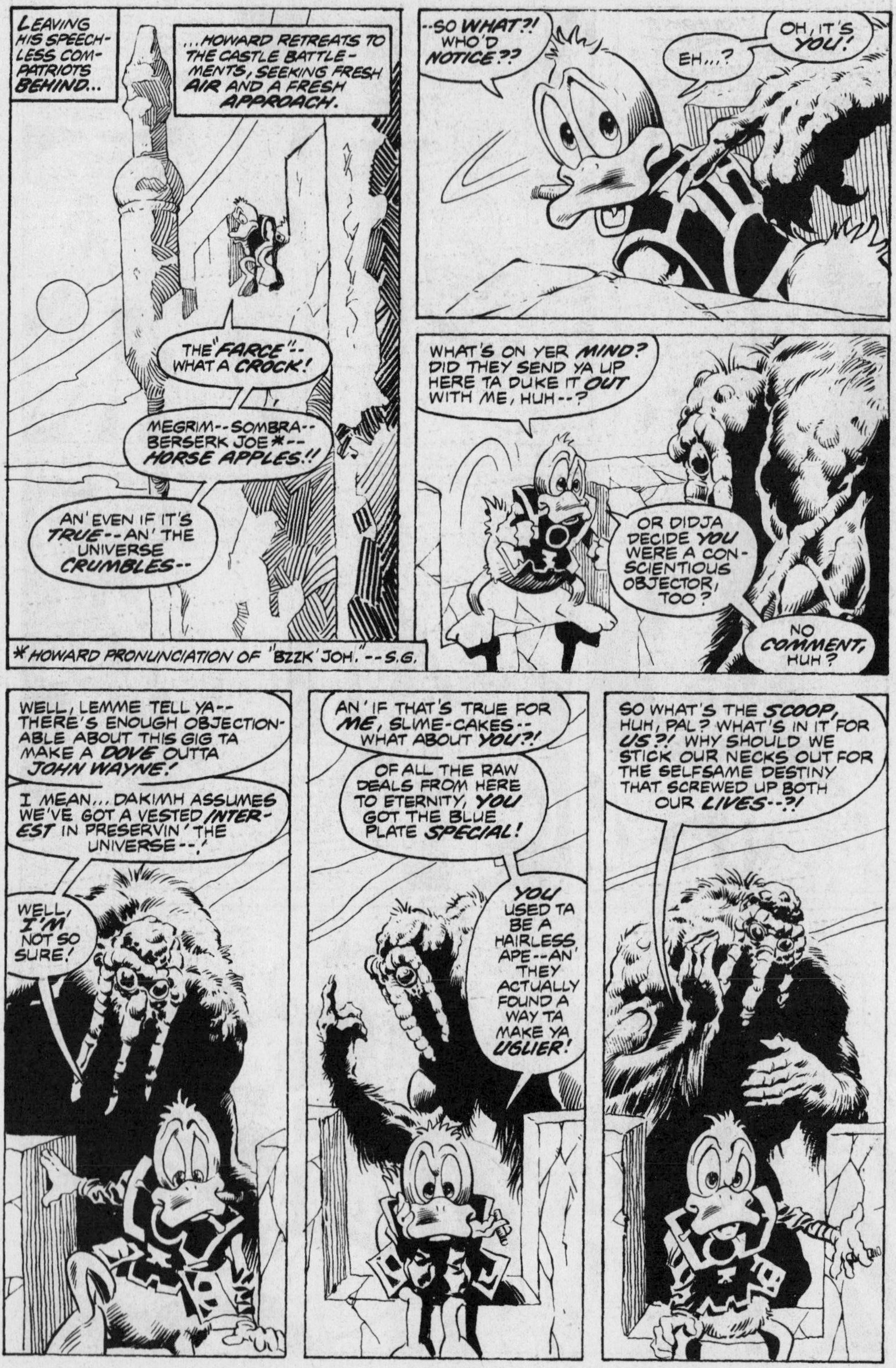

LEAVING HIS SPEECHLESS COMPATRIOTS BEHIND...
...HOWARD RETREATS TO THE CASTLE BATTLEMENTS, SEEKING FRESH AIR AND A FRESH APPROACH.
THE "FARCE"-- WHAT A CROCK!
MEGRIM--SOMBRA--BERSERK JOE*-- HORSE APPLES!!
AN' EVEN IF IT'S TRUE--AN' THE UNIVERSE CRUMBLES--
*HOWARD PRONUNCIATION OF "BZZK'JOH." --S.G.
--SO WHAT?! WHO'D NOTICE??
EH...?
OH, IT'S YOU!
WHAT'S ON YER MIND? DID THEY SEND YA UP HERE TA DUKE IT OUT WITH ME, HUH--?
OR DIDJA DECIDE YOU WERE A CONSCIENTIOUS OBJECTOR, TOO?
NO COMMENT, HUH?
WELL, LEMME TELL YA-- THERE'S ENOUGH OBJECTIONABLE ABOUT THIS GIG TA MAKE A DOVE OUTTA JOHN WAYNE!
I MEAN... DAKIMH ASSUMES WE'VE GOT A VESTED INTEREST IN PRESERVIN' THE UNIVERSE--!
WELL, I'M NOT SO SURE!
AN' IF THAT'S TRUE FOR ME, SLIME-CAKES-- WHAT ABOUT YOU?!
OF ALL THE RAW DEALS FROM HERE TO ETERNITY, YOU GOT THE BLUE PLATE SPECIAL!
YOU USED TA BE A HAIRLESS APE--AN' THEY ACTUALLY FOUND A WAY TA MAKE YA UGLIER!
SO WHAT'S THE SCOOP, HUH, PAL? WHAT'S IN IT FOR US?! WHY SHOULD WE STICK OUR NECKS OUT FOR THE SELFSAME DESTINY THAT SCREWED UP BOTH OUR LIVES--?!

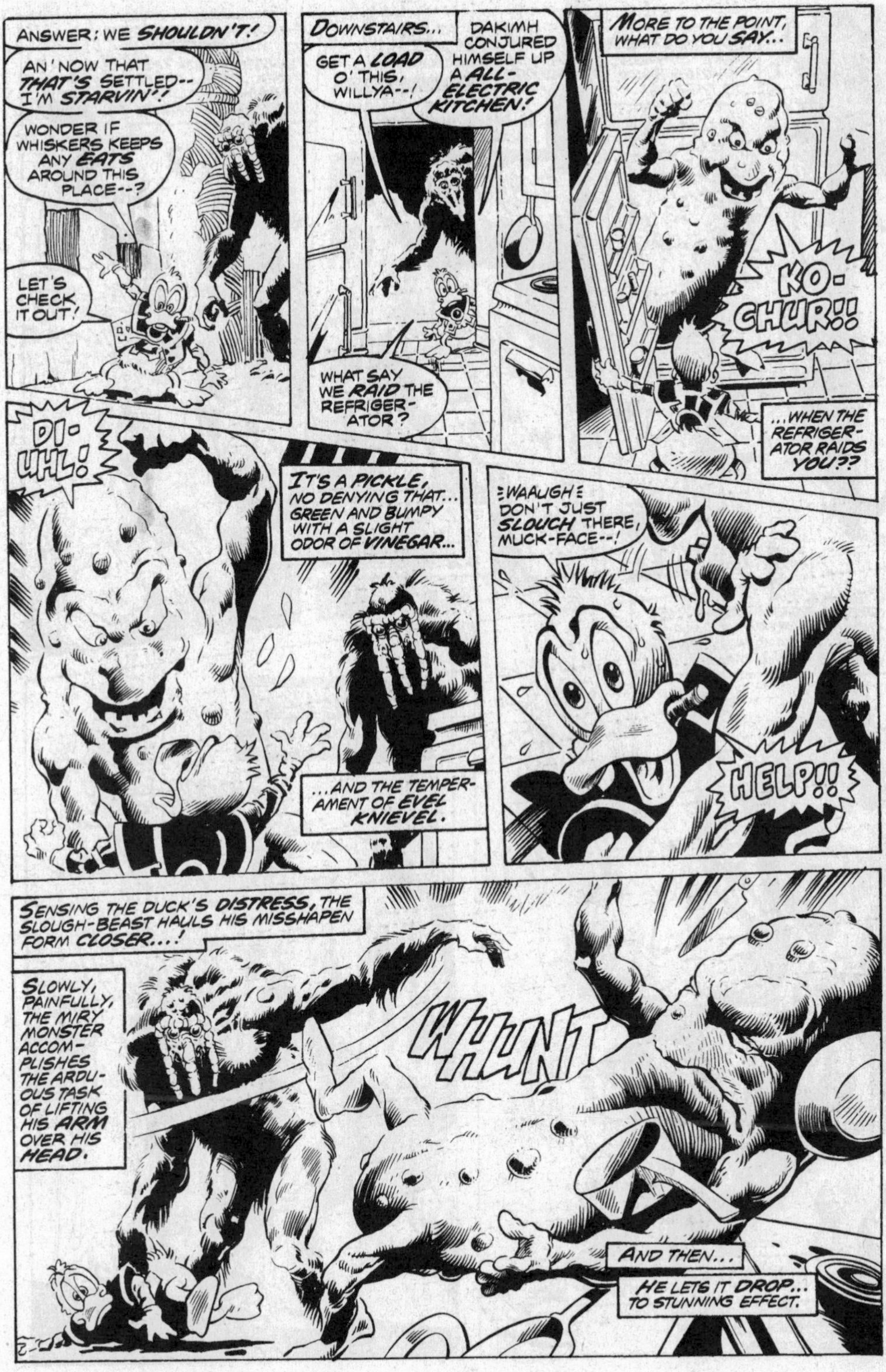
ANSWER: WE SHOULDN'T!
AN' NOW THAT THAT'S SETTLED-- I'M STARVIN'!
WONDER IF WHISKERS KEEPS ANY EATS AROUND THIS PLACE--?
LET'S CHECK IT OUT!
DOWNSTAIRS...
DAKIMH CONJURED HIMSELF UP A ALL-ELECTRIC KITCHEN!
GET A LOAD O' THIS, WILLYA--!
WHAT SAY WE RAID THE REFRIGER-ATOR?
MORE TO THE POINT, WHAT DO YOU SAY...
KO-CHUR!!
...WHEN THE REFRIGER-ATOR RAIDS YOU??
DI-UHL!
IT'S A PICKLE, NO DENYING THAT... GREEN AND BUMPY WITH A SLIGHT ODOR OF VINEGAR...
...AND THE TEMPER-AMENT OF EVEL KNIEVEL.
WAAUGH DON'T JUST SLOUCH THERE, MUCK-FACE--!
HELP!!
SENSING THE DUCK'S DISTRESS, THE SLOUGH-BEAST HAULS HIS MISSHAPEN FORM CLOSER...!
SLOWLY, PAINFULLY, THE MIRY MONSTER ACCOM-PLISHES THE ARDU-OUS TASK OF LIFTING HIS ARM OVER HIS HEAD.
WHUNT
AND THEN...
HE LETS IT DROP... TO STUNNING EFFECT.

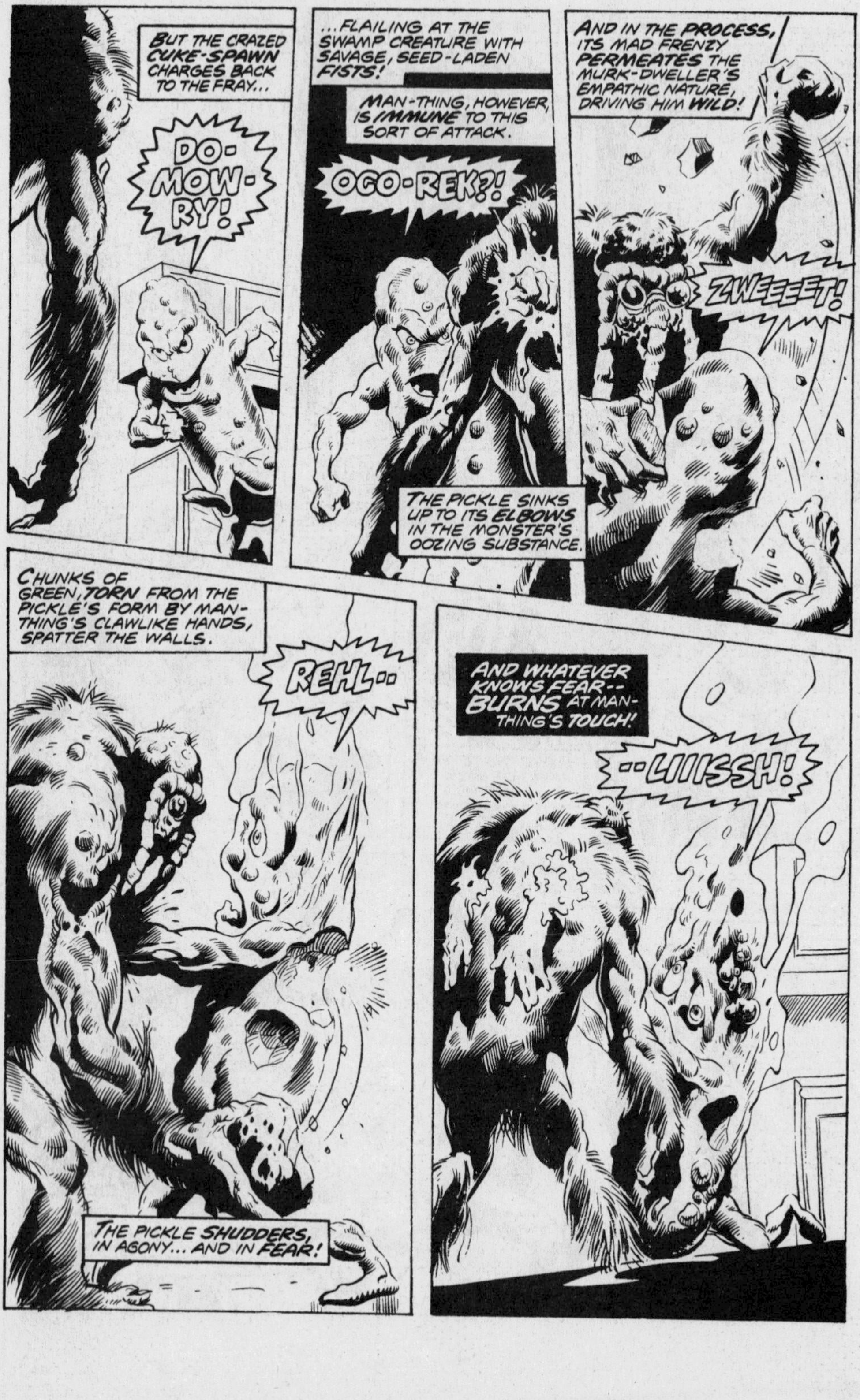
BUT THE CRAZED CUKE-SPAWN CHARGES BACK TO THE FRAY...
DO-MOW-RY!
...FLAILING AT THE SWAMP CREATURE WITH SAVAGE, SEED-LADEN FISTS!
MAN-THING, HOWEVER, IS IMMUNE TO THIS SORT OF ATTACK.
OCO-REK?!
THE PICKLE SINKS UP TO ITS ELBOWS IN THE MONSTER'S OOZING SUBSTANCE.
AND IN THE PROCESS, ITS MAD FRENZY PERMEATES THE MURK-DWELLER'S EMPATHIC NATURE, DRIVING HIM WILD!
ZWEEEEET!
CHUNKS OF GREEN, TORN FROM THE PICKLE'S FORM BY MAN-THING'S CLAWLIKE HANDS, SPATTER THE WALLS.
REHL..
THE PICKLE SHUDDERS, IN AGONY... AND IN FEAR!
AND WHATEVER KNOWS FEAR-- BURNS AT MAN-THING'S TOUCH!
--LIIISSH!

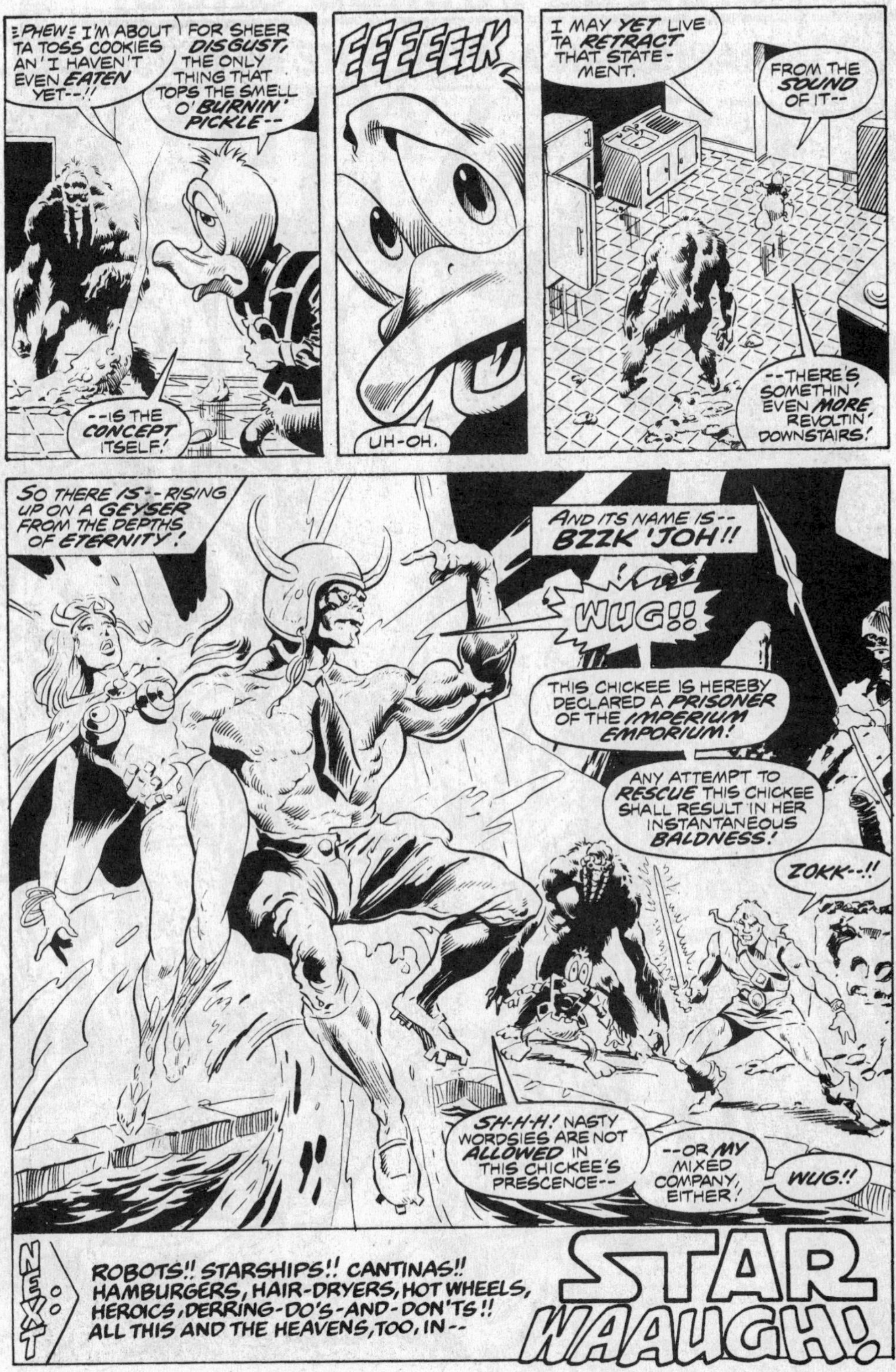

PHEW: I'M ABOUT TA TOSS COOKIES AN' I HAVEN'T EVEN EATEN YET--!!
FOR SHEER DISGUST, THE ONLY THING THAT TOPS THE SMELL O' BURNIN' PICKLE--
--IS THE CONCEPT ITSELF!
EEEEEEK
UH-OH.
I MAY YET LIVE TA RETRACT THAT STATEMENT.
FROM THE SOUND OF IT--
--THERE'S SOMETHIN' EVEN MORE REVOLTIN' DOWNSTAIRS!
So there IS--rising up on a GEYSER from the depths of ETERNITY!
And its name is-- BZZK 'JOH!!
WUG!!
THIS CHICKEE IS HEREBY DECLARED A PRISONER OF THE IMPERIUM EMPORIUM!
ANY ATTEMPT TO RESCUE THIS CHICKEE SHALL RESULT IN HER INSTANTANEOUS BALDNESS!
ZOKK--!!
SH-H-H! NASTY WORDSIES ARE NOT ALLOWED IN THIS CHICKEE'S PRESCENCE--
--OR MY MIXED COMPANY, EITHER!
WUG!!
NEXT:
ROBOTS!! STARSHIPS!! CANTINAS!! HAMBURGERS, HAIR-DRYERS, HOT WHEELS, HEROICS, DERRING-DO'S-AND-DON'TS!! ALL THIS AND THE HEAVENS, TOO, IN--
STAR WAAUGH!

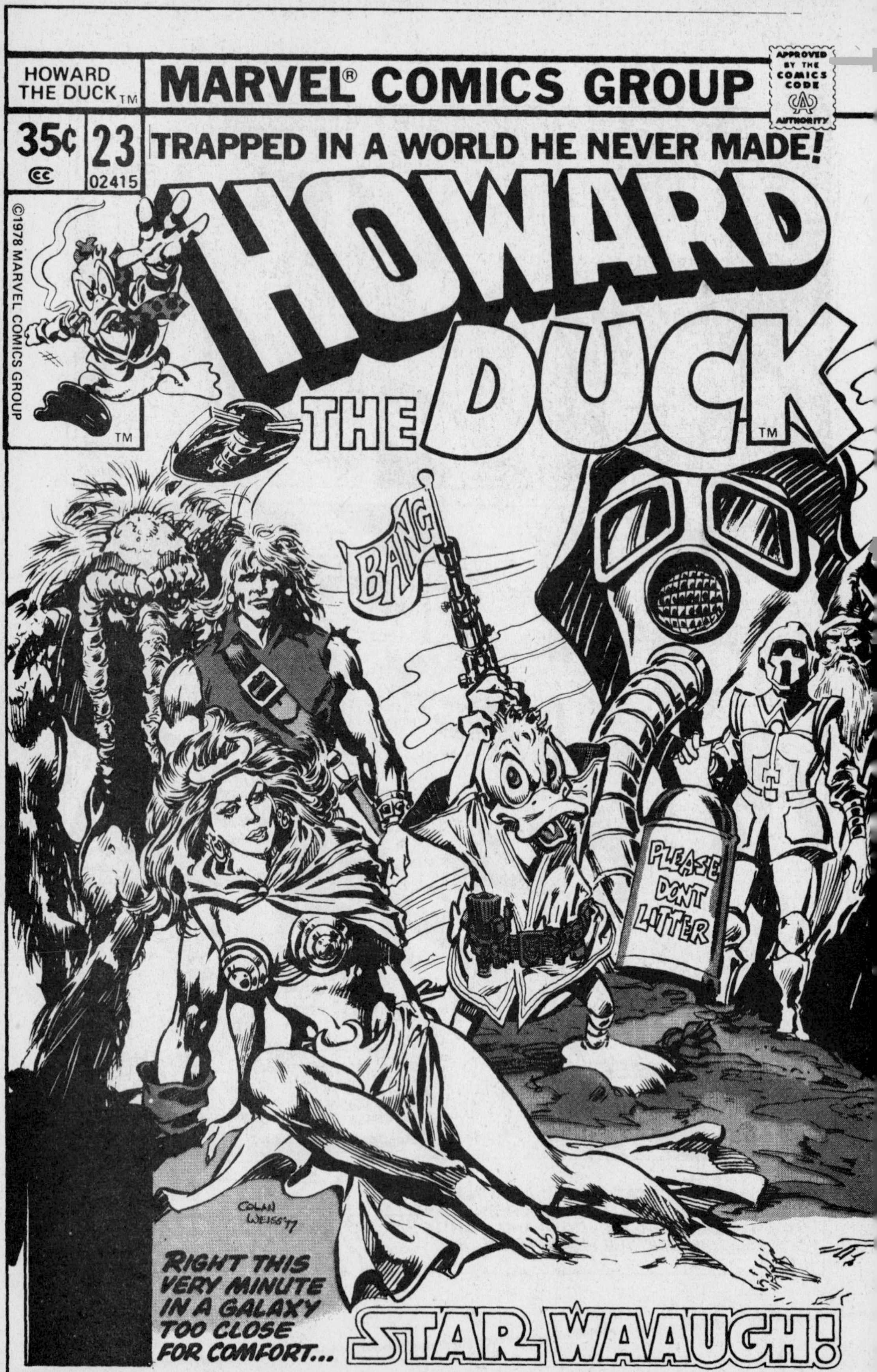

HOWARD THE DUCK TM
MARVEL® COMICS GROUP
APPROVED BY THE COMICS CODE AUTHORITY
35¢
23
02415
TRAPPED IN A WORLD HE NEVER MADE!
©1978 MARVEL COMICS GROUP
HOWARD THE DUCK TM
BANG
PLEASE DONT LITTER
COLAN WEISS '77
RIGHT THIS VERY MINUTE IN A GALAXY TOO CLOSE FOR COMFORT...
STAR WAAUGH!

From the time of his hatching, he was...different. A potentially brilliant scholar who dreaded the structured environment of school, he educated himself in the streets, taking whatever work was available, formulating his philosophy of self from what he learned of the world about him. And then the Cosmic Axis shifted...and that world *changed.* Suddenly, he was stranded in a universe he could not fathom. Without warning, he became a strange fowl in an even stranger land.

Stan Lee PRESENTS: HOWARD THE DUCK!™

BEHOLD-- THE CASTLE IN THE SKY, O'ER THE *LAND BETWEEN NIGHT AND DAY!*

THE EN-CHANTER *DAKIMH* SUMMONED HOWARD THE DUCK, *KORREK* THE BARBARIAN, *MAN-THING* THE SWAMP CREATURE, AND *JENNIFER* THE IN-GENUE HERE TO UNITE THEIR QUESTIONABLE MIGHT AGAINST THE TYRANNY OF *BZZK'JOH** AND HIS *IMPERIUM EMPORIUM.*

"MAKE CONTACT WITH THE *FARCE,*" DAKIMH INSTRUCTED. "THE BINDING ENERGY OF THE UNIVERSE WHICH PERMITS MEN TO *YOK IT UP* IN THE FACE OF DEATH! FIND BZZK'JOH AND *NEUTRALIZE* HIM-- BEFORE HE *SPREADS.*"

BUT BZZK'JOH STRUCK *FIRST*...!

STAR WAAUGH

STEVE GERBER ☆ **VAL MAYERICK**   **I. WATANABE, LETTERER**
WRITER/EDITOR   ARTIST   **J. COHEN, COLORIST**

*PRONOUNCED: "BERSERK JOE."--STEVE.

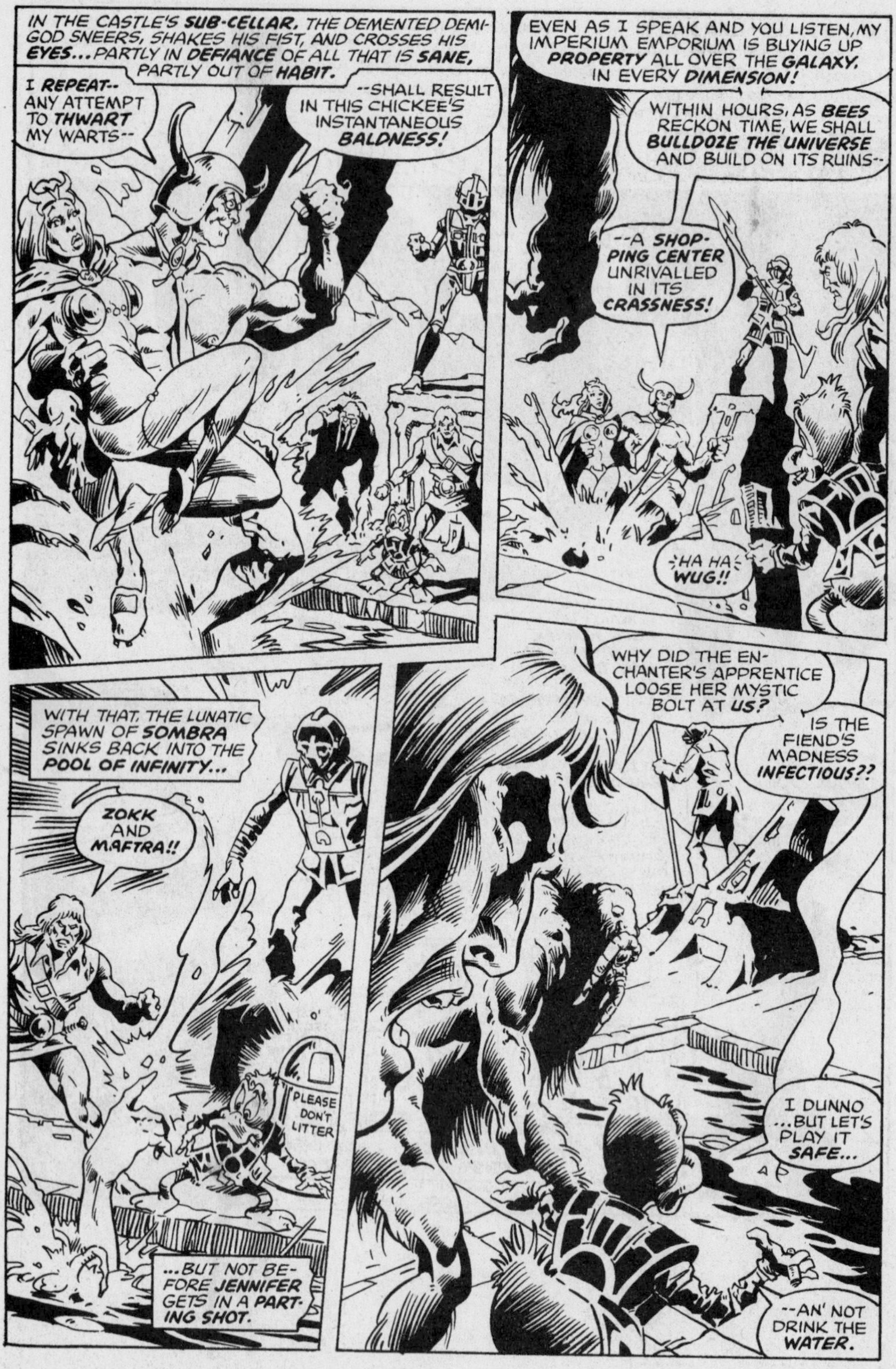
IN THE CASTLE'S SUB-CELLAR. THE DEMENTED DEMI-GOD SNEERS, SHAKES HIS FIST, AND CROSSES HIS EYES... PARTLY IN DEFIANCE OF ALL THAT IS SANE, PARTLY OUT OF HABIT.
I REPEAT-- ANY ATTEMPT TO THWART MY WARTS--
--SHALL RESULT IN THIS CHICKEE'S INSTANTANEOUS BALDNESS!
EVEN AS I SPEAK AND YOU LISTEN, MY IMPERIUM EMPORIUM IS BUYING UP PROPERTY ALL OVER THE GALAXY, IN EVERY DIMENSION!
WITHIN HOURS, AS BEES RECKON TIME, WE SHALL BULLDOZE THE UNIVERSE AND BUILD ON ITS RUINS--
--A SHOPPING CENTER UNRIVALLED IN ITS CRASSNESS!
HA HA WUG!!
WITH THAT, THE LUNATIC SPAWN OF SOMBRA SINKS BACK INTO THE POOL OF INFINITY...
ZOKK AND MAFTRA!!
PLEASE DON'T LITTER
...BUT NOT BEFORE JENNIFER GETS IN A PARTING SHOT.
WHY DID THE ENCHANTER'S APPRENTICE LOOSE HER MYSTIC BOLT AT US?
IS THE FIEND'S MADNESS INFECTIOUS??
I DUNNO ...BUT LET'S PLAY IT SAFE...
--AN' NOT DRINK THE WATER.

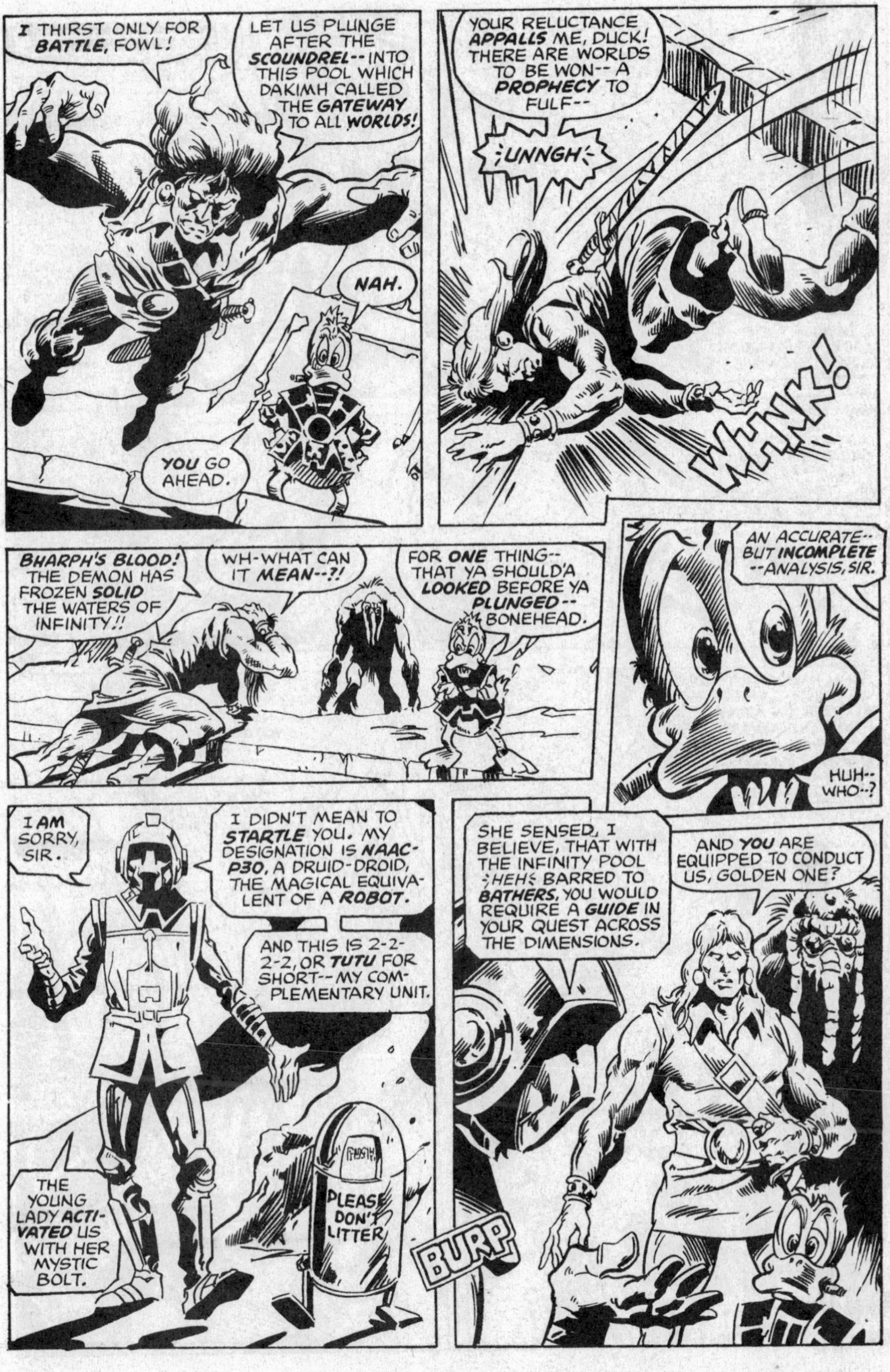
I THIRST ONLY FOR BATTLE, FOWL!
LET US PLUNGE AFTER THE SCOUNDREL--INTO THIS POOL WHICH DAKIMH CALLED THE GATEWAY TO ALL WORLDS!
NAH.
YOU GO AHEAD.
YOUR RELUCTANCE APPALLS ME, DUCK! THERE ARE WORLDS TO BE WON--A PROPHECY TO FULF--
UNNGH
WHNK!
BHARPH'S BLOOD! THE DEMON HAS FROZEN SOLID THE WATERS OF INFINITY!!
WH-WHAT CAN IT MEAN--?!
FOR ONE THING--THAT YA SHOULD'A LOOKED BEFORE YA PLUNGED--BONEHEAD.
AN ACCURATE--BUT INCOMPLETE--ANALYSIS, SIR.
HUH--WHO--?
I AM SORRY, SIR.
I DIDN'T MEAN TO STARTLE YOU. MY DESIGNATION IS NAAC-P30, A DRUID-DROID, THE MAGICAL EQUIVALENT OF A ROBOT.
AND THIS IS 2-2-2-2, OR TUTU FOR SHORT--MY COMPLEMENTARY UNIT.
THE YOUNG LADY ACTIVATED US WITH HER MYSTIC BOLT.
PLEASE DON'T LITTER
BURP
SHE SENSED, I BELIEVE, THAT WITH THE INFINITY POOL HEH BARRED TO BATHERS, YOU WOULD REQUIRE A GUIDE IN YOUR QUEST ACROSS THE DIMENSIONS.
AND YOU ARE EQUIPPED TO CONDUCT US, GOLDEN ONE?

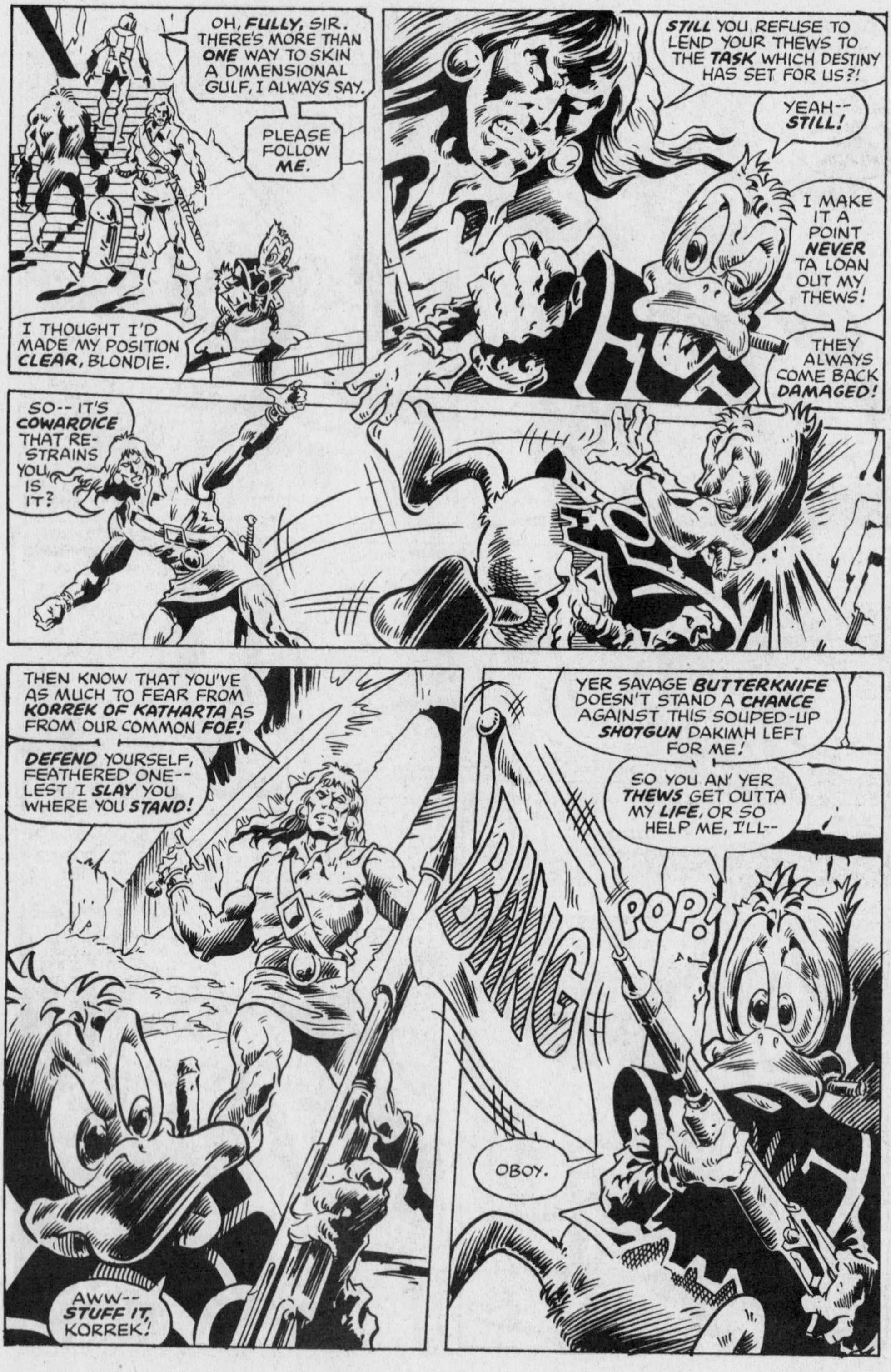

OH, **FULLY**, SIR. THERE'S MORE THAN **ONE** WAY TO SKIN A DIMENSIONAL GULF, I ALWAYS SAY.
PLEASE FOLLOW **ME**.
I THOUGHT I'D MADE MY POSITION **CLEAR**, BLONDIE.
STILL YOU REFUSE TO LEND YOUR THEWS TO THE **TASK** WHICH DESTINY HAS SET FOR US?!
YEAH-- **STILL!**
I MAKE IT A POINT **NEVER** TA LOAN OUT MY THEWS!
THEY ALWAYS COME BACK **DAMAGED!**
SO-- IT'S **COWARDICE** THAT RE-STRAINS YOU, IS IT?
THEN KNOW THAT YOU'VE AS MUCH TO FEAR FROM **KORREK OF KATHARTA** AS FROM OUR COMMON **FOE!**
DEFEND YOURSELF, FEATHERED ONE-- LEST I **SLAY** YOU WHERE YOU **STAND!**
AWW-- **STUFF IT**, KORREK!
YER SAVAGE **BUTTERKNIFE** DOESN'T STAND A **CHANCE** AGAINST THIS SOUPED-UP **SHOTGUN** DAKIMH LEFT FOR ME!
SO YOU AN' YER **THEWS** GET OUTTA MY **LIFE**, OR SO HELP ME, I'LL--
BANG
POP!
OBOY.

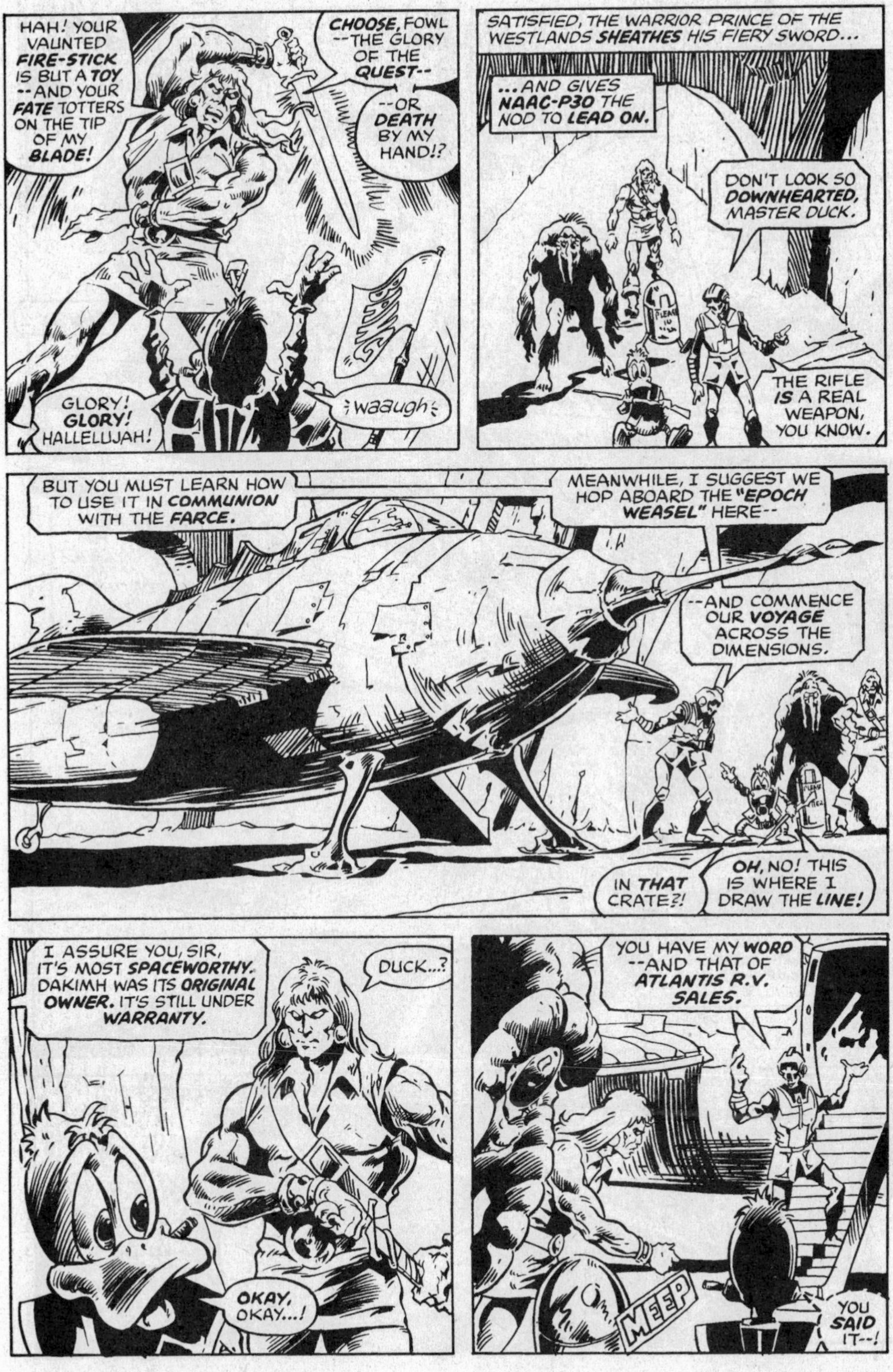
HAH! YOUR VAUNTED FIRE-STICK IS BUT A TOY --AND YOUR FATE TOTTERS ON THE TIP OF MY BLADE!
CHOOSE, FOWL --THE GLORY OF THE QUEST--
--OR DEATH BY MY HAND!?
GLORY! GLORY! HALLELUJAH!
waaugh
SATISFIED, THE WARRIOR PRINCE OF THE WESTLANDS SHEATHES HIS FIERY SWORD...
...AND GIVES NAAC-P30 THE NOD TO LEAD ON.
DON'T LOOK SO DOWNHEARTED, MASTER DUCK.
THE RIFLE IS A REAL WEAPON, YOU KNOW.
BUT YOU MUST LEARN HOW TO USE IT IN COMMUNION WITH THE FARCE.
MEANWHILE, I SUGGEST WE HOP ABOARD THE "EPOCH WEASEL" HERE--
--AND COMMENCE OUR VOYAGE ACROSS THE DIMENSIONS.
IN THAT CRATE?!
OH, NO! THIS IS WHERE I DRAW THE LINE!
I ASSURE YOU, SIR, IT'S MOST SPACEWORTHY. DAKIMH WAS ITS ORIGINAL OWNER. IT'S STILL UNDER WARRANTY.
DUCK...?
OKAY, OKAY...!
YOU HAVE MY WORD --AND THAT OF ATLANTIS R.V. SALES.
MEEP
YOU SAID IT--!

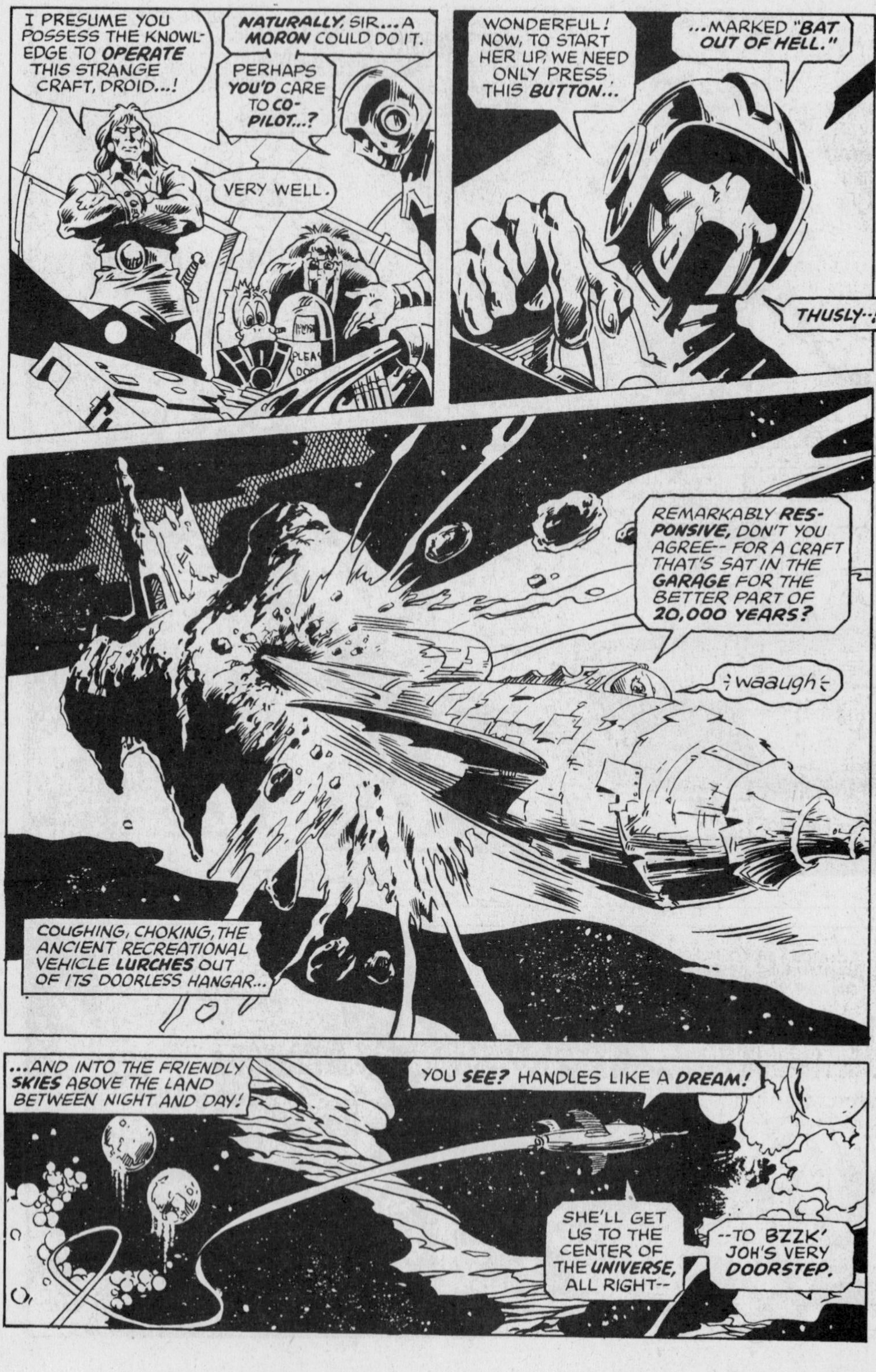
I PRESUME YOU POSSESS THE KNOWLEDGE TO OPERATE THIS STRANGE CRAFT, DROID...!
NATURALLY, SIR... A MORON COULD DO IT.
PERHAPS YOU'D CARE TO CO-PILOT...?
VERY WELL.
WONDERFUL! NOW, TO START HER UP, WE NEED ONLY PRESS THIS BUTTON...
...MARKED "BAT OUT OF HELL."
THUSLY--!
REMARKABLY RESPONSIVE, DON'T YOU AGREE-- FOR A CRAFT THAT'S SAT IN THE GARAGE FOR THE BETTER PART OF 20,000 YEARS?
waaugh
COUGHING, CHOKING, THE ANCIENT RECREATIONAL VEHICLE LURCHES OUT OF ITS DOORLESS HANGAR...
...AND INTO THE FRIENDLY SKIES ABOVE THE LAND BETWEEN NIGHT AND DAY!
YOU SEE? HANDLES LIKE A DREAM!
SHE'LL GET US TO THE CENTER OF THE UNIVERSE, ALL RIGHT--
--TO BZZK' JOH'S VERY DOORSTEP.

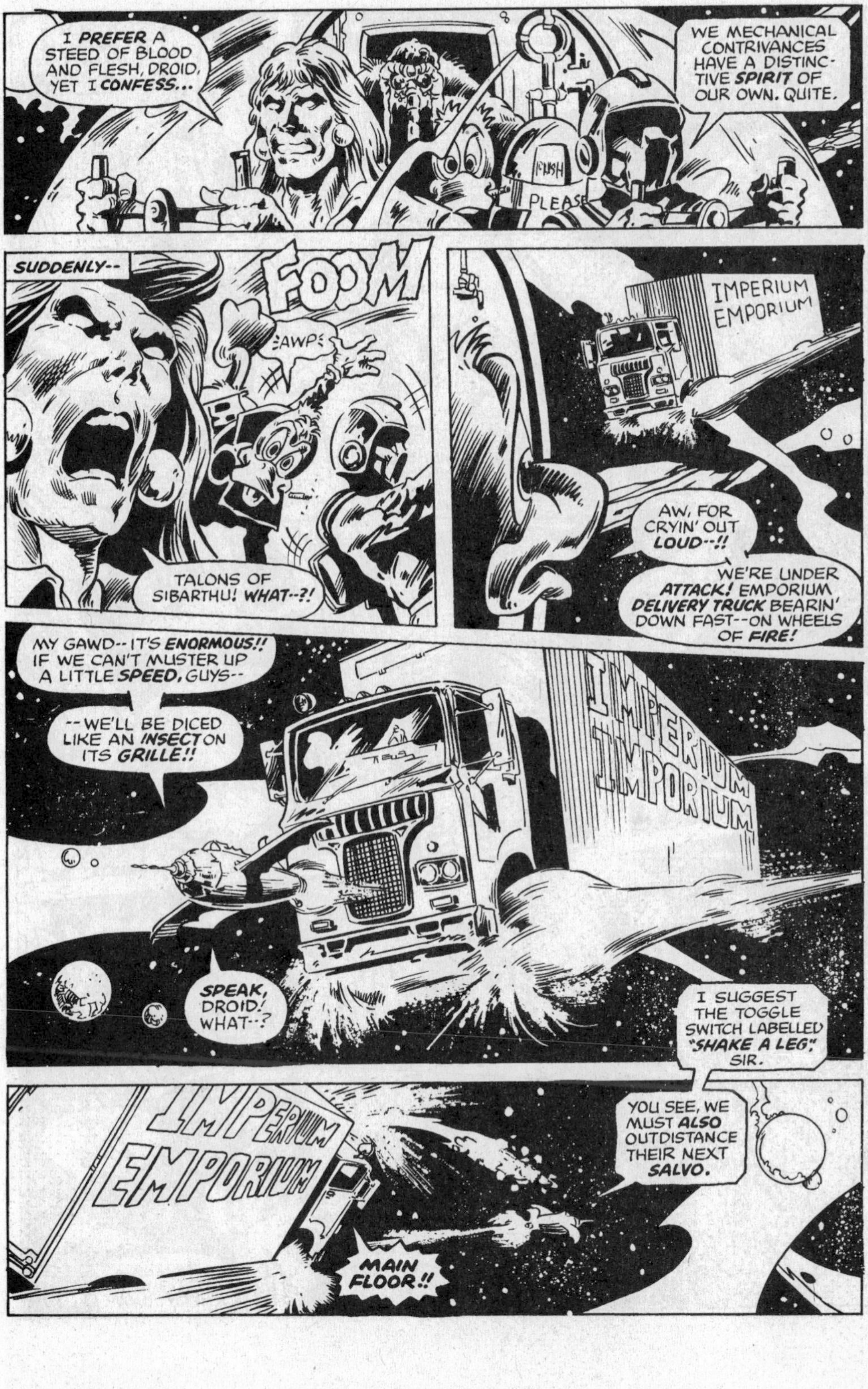
I PREFER A STEED OF BLOOD AND FLESH, DROID, YET I CONFESS...
WE MECHANICAL CONTRIVANCES HAVE A DISTINCTIVE SPIRIT OF OUR OWN. QUITE.
PUSH
PLEASE
SUDDENLY--
FOOM
AWP
TALONS OF SIBARTHU! WHAT--?!
IMPERIUM EMPORIUM
AW, FOR CRYIN' OUT LOUD--!!
WE'RE UNDER ATTACK! EMPORIUM DELIVERY TRUCK BEARIN' DOWN FAST--ON WHEELS OF FIRE!
MY GAWD--IT'S ENORMOUS!! IF WE CAN'T MUSTER UP A LITTLE SPEED, GUYS--
--WE'LL BE DICED LIKE AN INSECT ON ITS GRILLE!!
IMPERIUM IMPORIUM
SPEAK, DROID! WHAT--?
I SUGGEST THE TOGGLE SWITCH LABELLED "SHAKE A LEG," SIR.
IMPERIUM EMPORIUM
YOU SEE, WE MUST ALSO OUTDISTANCE THEIR NEXT SALVO.
MAIN FLOOR!!

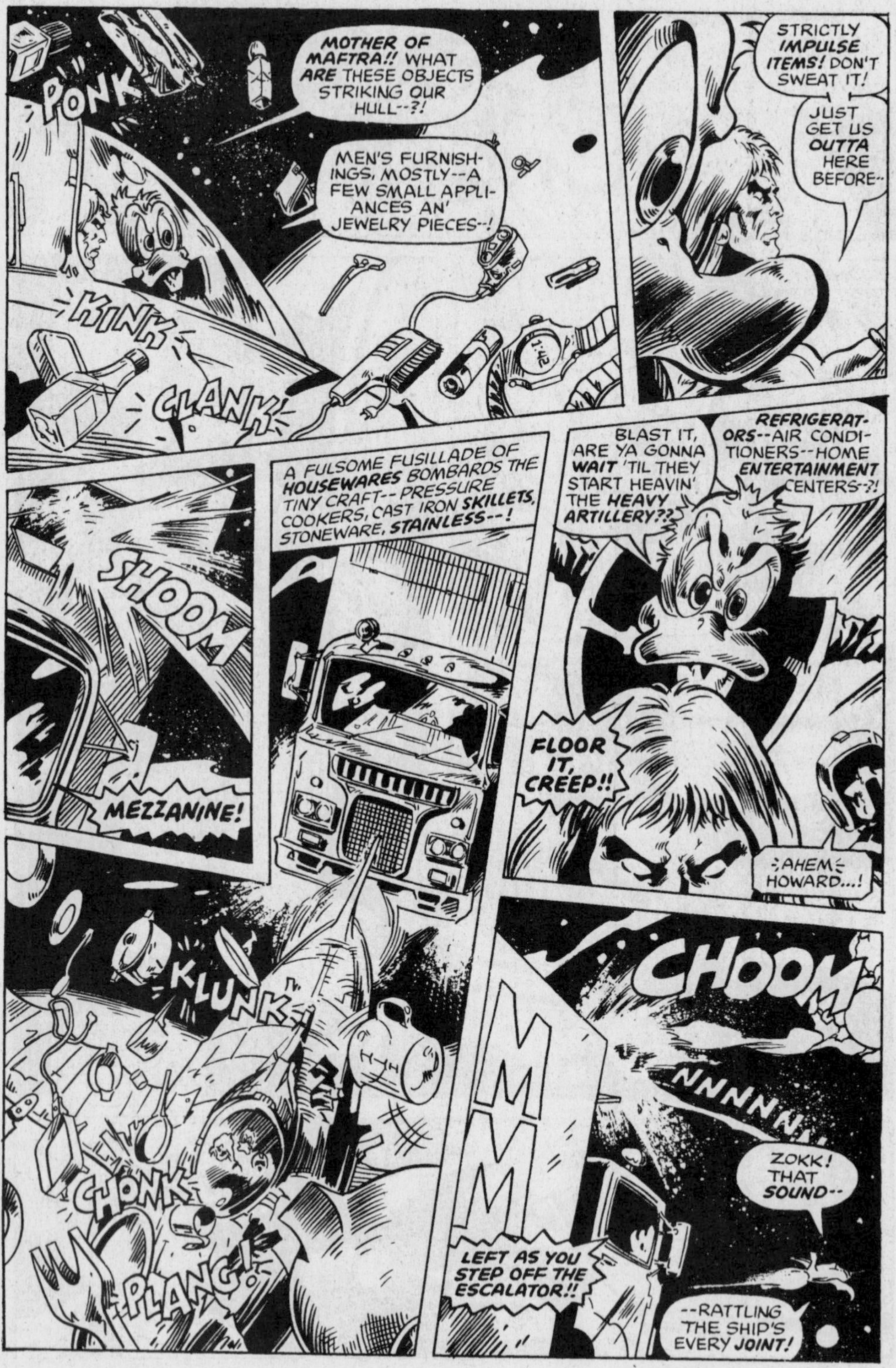
PONK
MOTHER OF MAFTRA!! WHAT ARE THESE OBJECTS STRIKING OUR HULL--?!
MEN'S FURNISHINGS, MOSTLY--A FEW SMALL APPLIANCES AN' JEWELRY PIECES--!
KINK
CLANK!
STRICTLY IMPULSE ITEMS! DON'T SWEAT IT!
JUST GET US OUTTA HERE BEFORE--
SHOOM
MEZZANINE!
A FULSOME FUSILLADE OF HOUSEWARES BOMBARDS THE TINY CRAFT--PRESSURE COOKERS, CAST IRON SKILLETS, STONEWARE, STAINLESS--!
BLAST IT, ARE YA GONNA WAIT 'TIL THEY START HEAVIN' THE HEAVY ARTILLERY??
REFRIGERATORS--AIR CONDITIONERS--HOME ENTERTAINMENT CENTERS--?!
FLOOR IT, CREEP!!
AHEM HOWARD...!
KLUNK
CHONK
PLANG!
CHOOM
MMMM
NNNNNN
ZOKK! THAT SOUND--
LEFT AS YOU STEP OFF THE ESCALATOR!!
--RATTLING THE SHIP'S EVERY JOINT!

ULP - A CUSTOMER **SERVICE REPRESENTATIVE**-- THE ULTIMATE FUSION O' SONIC AN' PSYCHOLOGICAL WARFARE!!

THEY'RE PLAYIN' FOR **KEEPS!**

NONONO NONO NONONO NONONO NO NONONONO

AN' GUESS WHO GETS **KEPT** IF THEY WIN?!

--WHATEVER **THAT** MEANS. PAY NO ATTENTION.

SEE, I'M SCARED HALF TA **DEATH.**

...AN' BABBLIN' HYSTERICALLY.

WILLYA **PUH-LEASE** EVACUATE US FROM THIS SECTOR O' SPACE--?

SO'S I CAN BUTTON MY **BILL?!**

KORREK--THE **FOOT** PEDALS.

THESE?

YES! DEPRESS THE LONG, **SKINNY** ONE!

LOSE HIM ON THE **UPGRADE!**

IMPERIUM EMPORIUM

KORREK SHAKES HIS HEAD IN **BEWILDERMENT** AS THE LITTLE SPACECRAFT THAT COULD MAKES THE JUMP INTO **DIMENSIONAL SPACE,** HURTLING FROM ONE PLANE OF REALITY TO THE NEXT... UNTIL ITS WEARY ENGINES CAN **CHUG NO MORE.**

THEN...

ALAS...THE "EPOCH WEASEL" HAS FLOWN ITS **LAST.**

FORTUNATELY, WE'VE REACHED THE **HALFWAY POINT**-- THE WORLD CALLED **BOORBANQ!**

WH-WHAT **IS** THIS PLACE--?!

HOLLYWOK CANTEEN PLASTIC SZECHUAN CUISINE

AN **INN** OF SORTS, GOOD PRINCE.

...FOR **DIMENSIONAL** WAYFARERS.

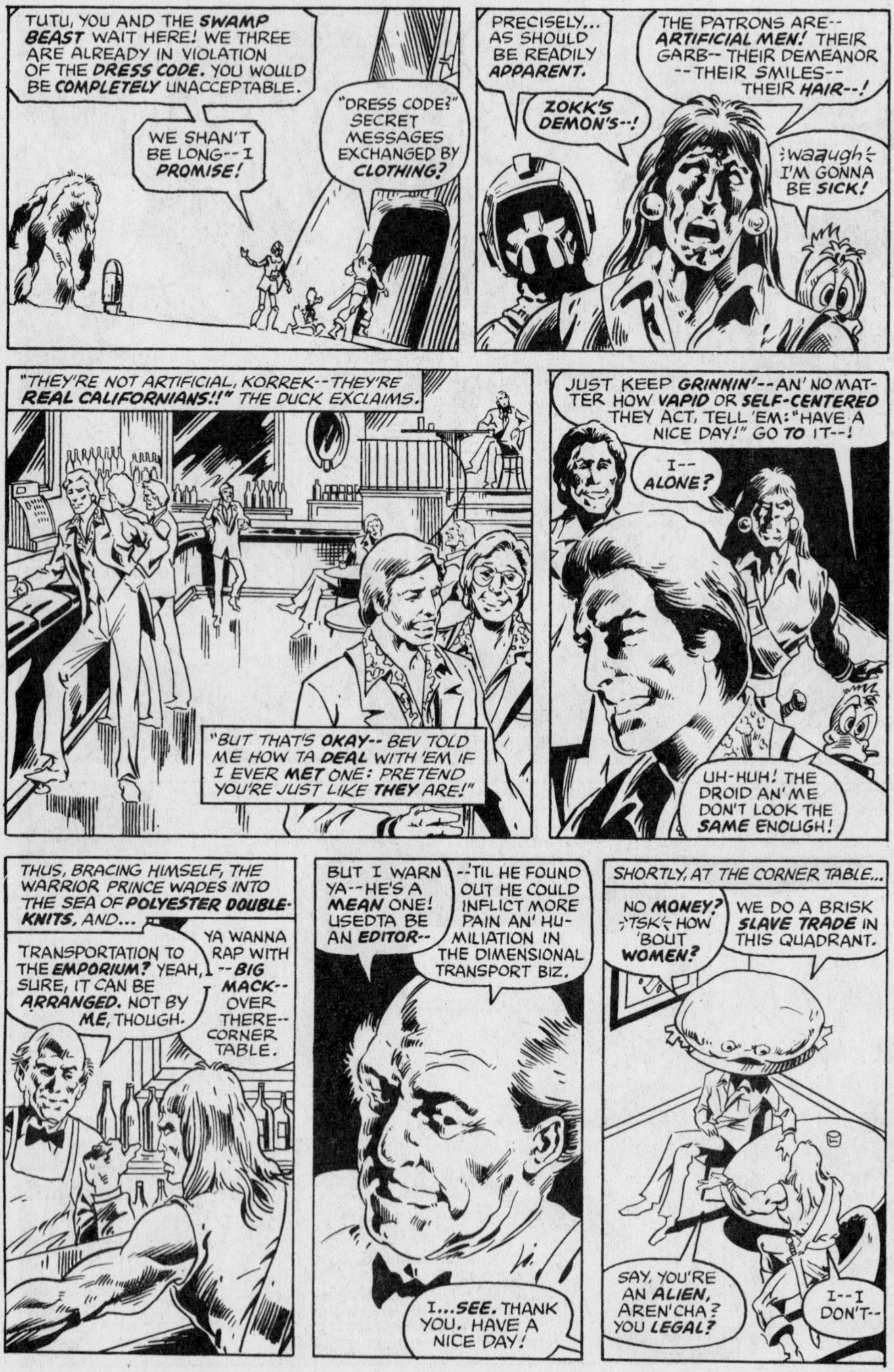
TUTU, YOU AND THE SWAMP BEAST WAIT HERE! WE THREE ARE ALREADY IN VIOLATION OF THE DRESS CODE. YOU WOULD BE COMPLETELY UNACCEPTABLE.
WE SHAN'T BE LONG-- I PROMISE!
"DRESS CODE?" SECRET MESSAGES EXCHANGED BY CLOTHING?
PRECISELY... AS SHOULD BE READILY APPARENT.
ZOKK'S DEMON'S--!
THE PATRONS ARE-- ARTIFICIAL MEN! THEIR GARB-- THEIR DEMEANOR --THEIR SMILES-- THEIR HAIR--!
waaugh I'M GONNA BE SICK!
"THEY'RE NOT ARTIFICIAL, KORREK--THEY'RE REAL CALIFORNIANS!!" THE DUCK EXCLAIMS.
"BUT THAT'S OKAY-- BEV TOLD ME HOW TA DEAL WITH 'EM IF I EVER MET ONE: PRETEND YOU'RE JUST LIKE THEY ARE!"
JUST KEEP GRINNIN'--AN' NO MATTER HOW VAPID OR SELF-CENTERED THEY ACT, TELL 'EM: "HAVE A NICE DAY!" GO TO IT--!
I-- ALONE?
UH-HUH! THE DROID AN' ME DON'T LOOK THE SAME ENOUGH!
THUS, BRACING HIMSELF, THE WARRIOR PRINCE WADES INTO THE SEA OF POLYESTER DOUBLE-KNITS, AND...
TRANSPORTATION TO THE EMPORIUM? YEAH, SURE, IT CAN BE ARRANGED. NOT BY ME, THOUGH.
YA WANNA RAP WITH --BIG MACK-- OVER THERE-- CORNER TABLE.
BUT I WARN YA--HE'S A MEAN ONE! USEDTA BE AN EDITOR--
--'TIL HE FOUND OUT HE COULD INFLICT MORE PAIN AN' HUMILIATION IN THE DIMENSIONAL TRANSPORT BIZ.
I...SEE. THANK YOU. HAVE A NICE DAY!
SHORTLY, AT THE CORNER TABLE...
NO MONEY? TSK HOW 'BOUT WOMEN?
WE DO A BRISK SLAVE TRADE IN THIS QUADRANT.
SAY, YOU'RE AN ALIEN, AREN'CHA? YOU LEGAL?
I--I DON'T--

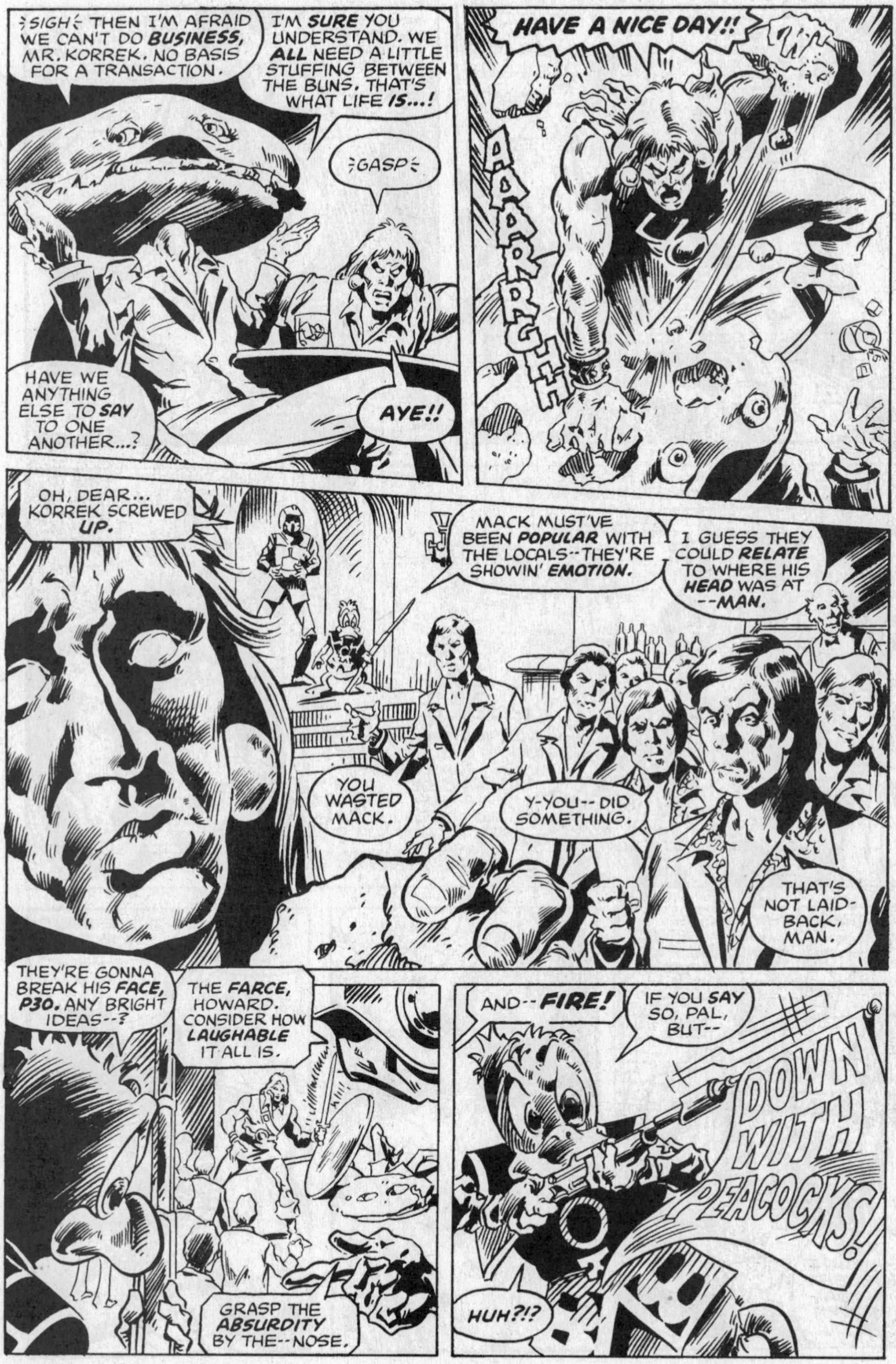
SIGH THEN I'M AFRAID WE CAN'T DO BUSINESS, MR. KORREK. NO BASIS FOR A TRANSACTION.
I'M SURE YOU UNDERSTAND. WE ALL NEED A LITTLE STUFFING BETWEEN THE BUNS. THAT'S WHAT LIFE IS...!
GASP
HAVE WE ANYTHING ELSE TO SAY TO ONE ANOTHER...?
AYE!!
HAVE A NICE DAY!!
AAARGHHH
OH, DEAR... KORREK SCREWED UP.
MACK MUST'VE BEEN POPULAR WITH THE LOCALS--THEY'RE SHOWIN' EMOTION.
I GUESS THEY COULD RELATE TO WHERE HIS HEAD WAS AT --MAN.
YOU WASTED MACK.
Y-YOU--DID SOMETHING.
THAT'S NOT LAID-BACK, MAN.
THEY'RE GONNA BREAK HIS FACE, P30. ANY BRIGHT IDEAS--?
THE FARCE, HOWARD. CONSIDER HOW LAUGHABLE IT ALL IS.
GRASP THE ABSURDITY BY THE--NOSE.
AND--FIRE!
IF YOU SAY SO, PAL, BUT--
DOWN WITH PEACOCKS!
HUH?!?

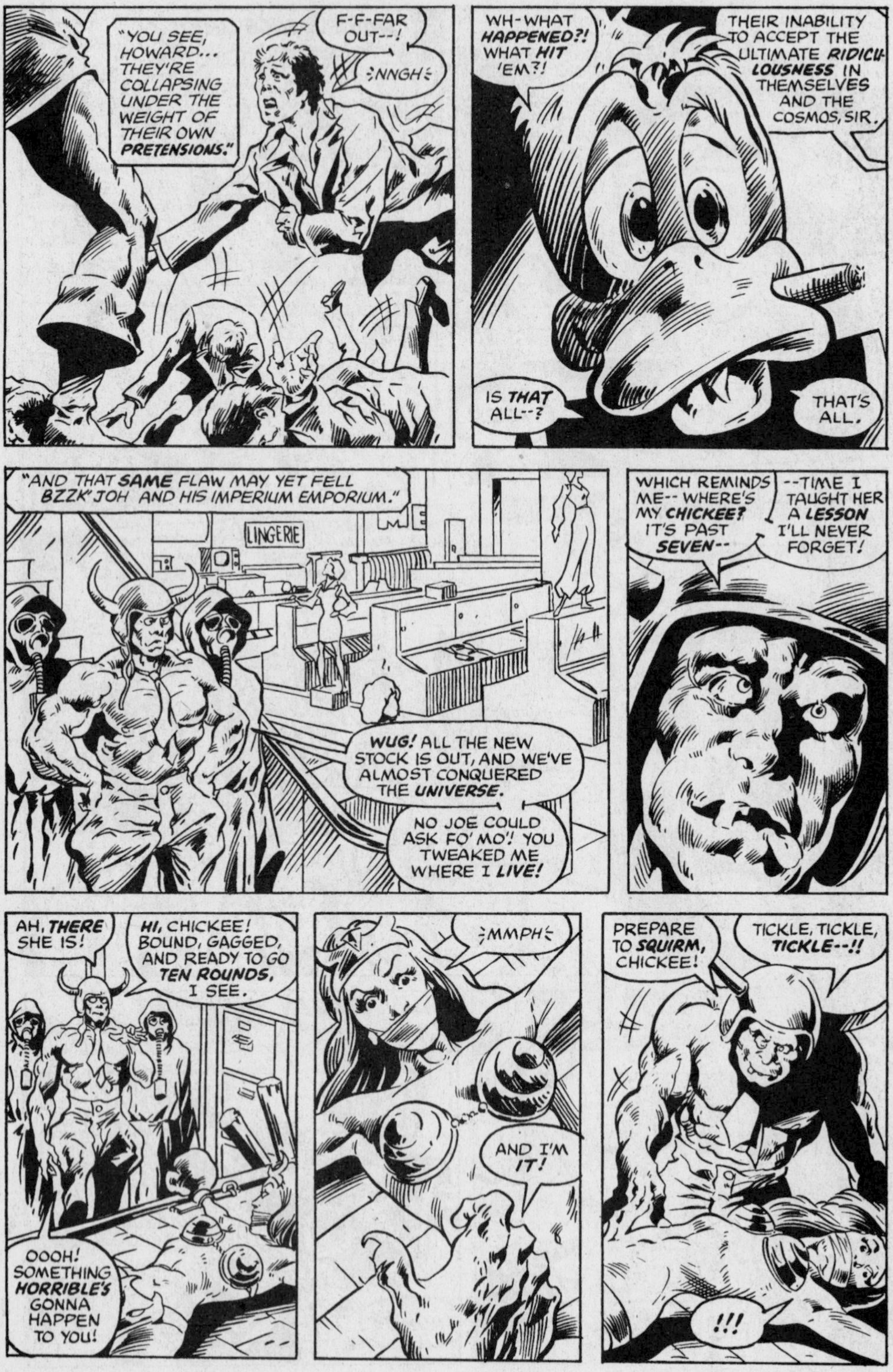
"YOU SEE, HOWARD... THEY'RE COLLAPSING UNDER THE WEIGHT OF THEIR OWN PRETENSIONS."
F-F-FAR OUT--!
NNGH
WH-WHAT HAPPENED?! WHAT HIT 'EM?!
THEIR INABILITY TO ACCEPT THE ULTIMATE RIDICULOUSNESS IN THEMSELVES AND THE COSMOS, SIR.
IS THAT ALL--?
THAT'S ALL.
"AND THAT SAME FLAW MAY YET FELL BZZK'JOH AND HIS IMPERIUM EMPORIUM."
LINGERIE
WUG! ALL THE NEW STOCK IS OUT, AND WE'VE ALMOST CONQUERED THE UNIVERSE.
NO JOE COULD ASK FO' MO'! YOU TWEAKED ME WHERE I LIVE!
WHICH REMINDS ME-- WHERE'S MY CHICKEE? IT'S PAST SEVEN--
--TIME I TAUGHT HER A LESSON I'LL NEVER FORGET!
AH, THERE SHE IS!
HI, CHICKEE! BOUND, GAGGED, AND READY TO GO TEN ROUNDS, I SEE.
OOOH! SOMETHING HORRIBLE'S GONNA HAPPEN TO YOU!
MMPH
AND I'M IT!
PREPARE TO SQUIRM, CHICKEE!
TICKLE, TICKLE, TICKLE--!!
!!!

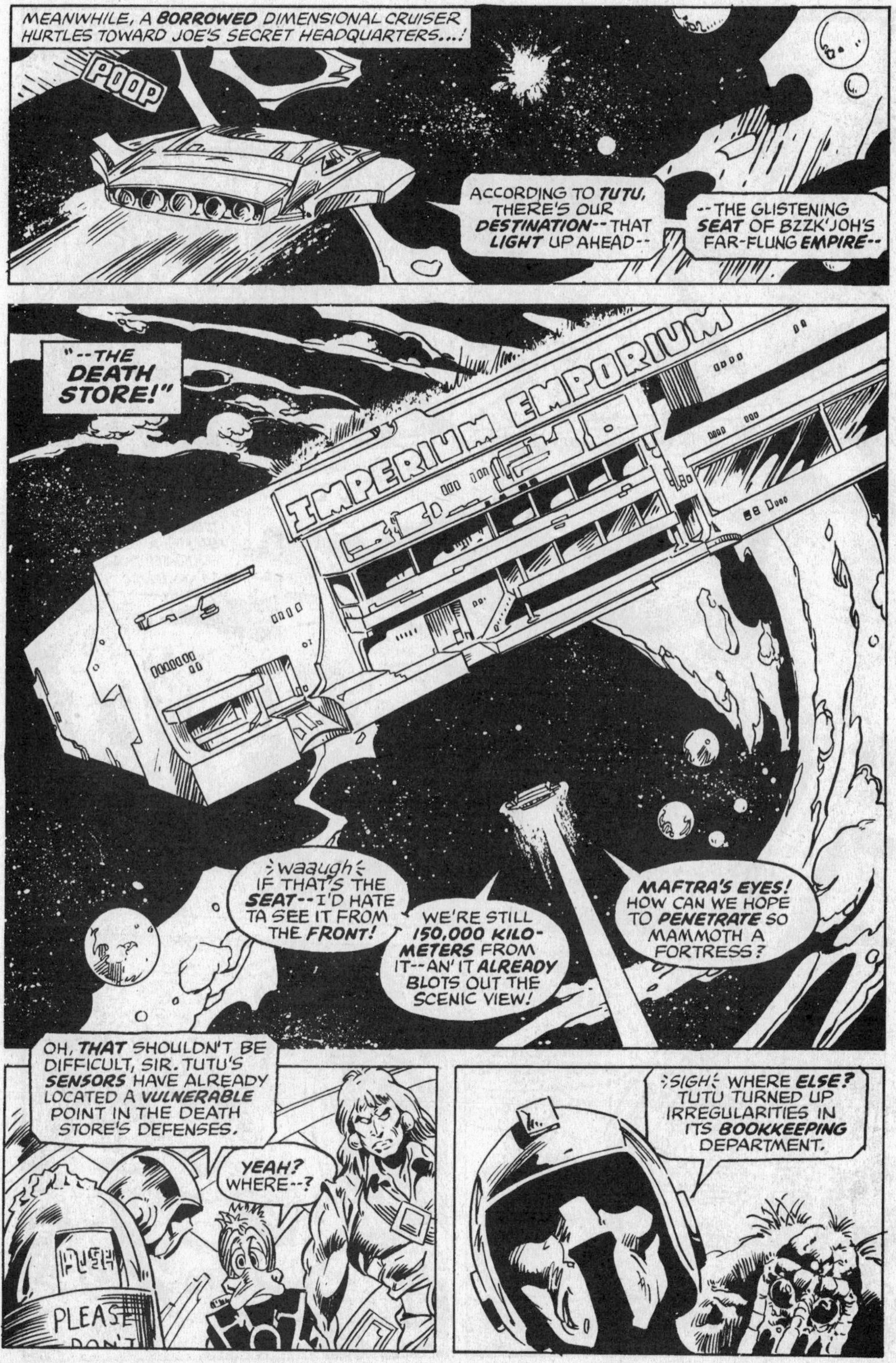
MEANWHILE, A BORROWED DIMENSIONAL CRUISER HURTLES TOWARD JOE'S SECRET HEADQUARTERS...!
POOP
ACCORDING TO TUTU, THERE'S OUR DESTINATION--THAT LIGHT UP AHEAD--
--THE GLISTENING SEAT OF BZZK'JOH'S FAR-FLUNG EMPIRE--
"--THE DEATH STORE!"
IMPERIUM EMPORIUM
waaugh IF THAT'S THE SEAT--I'D HATE TA SEE IT FROM THE FRONT!
WE'RE STILL 150,000 KILOMETERS FROM IT--AN' IT ALREADY BLOTS OUT THE SCENIC VIEW!
MAFTRA'S EYES! HOW CAN WE HOPE TO PENETRATE SO MAMMOTH A FORTRESS?
OH, THAT SHOULDN'T BE DIFFICULT, SIR. TUTU'S SENSORS HAVE ALREADY LOCATED A VULNERABLE POINT IN THE DEATH STORE'S DEFENSES.
YEAH? WHERE--?
PUSH
PLEASE
SIGH WHERE ELSE? TUTU TURNED UP IRREGULARITIES IN ITS BOOKKEEPING DEPARTMENT.

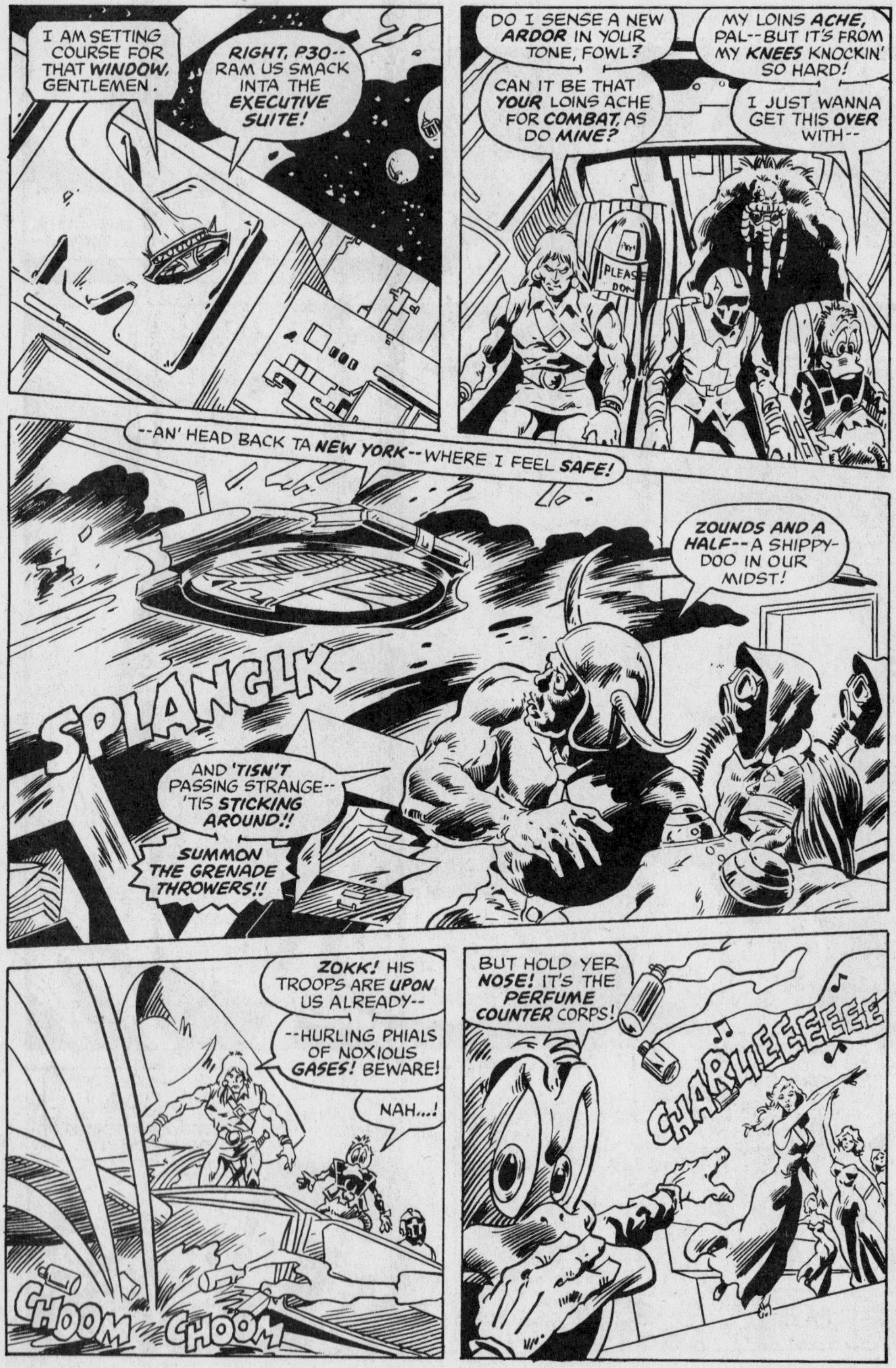
I AM SETTING COURSE FOR THAT WINDOW, GENTLEMEN.
RIGHT, P30-- RAM US SMACK INTA THE EXECUTIVE SUITE!
DO I SENSE A NEW ARDOR IN YOUR TONE, FOWL?
CAN IT BE THAT YOUR LOINS ACHE FOR COMBAT, AS DO MINE?
MY LOINS ACHE, PAL--BUT IT'S FROM MY KNEES KNOCKIN' SO HARD!
I JUST WANNA GET THIS OVER WITH--
PLEASE
--AN' HEAD BACK TA NEW YORK--WHERE I FEEL SAFE!
ZOUNDS AND A HALF--A SHIPPY-DOO IN OUR MIDST!
SPLANGLK
AND 'TISN'T PASSING STRANGE--'TIS STICKING AROUND!!
SUMMON THE GRENADE THROWERS!!
ZOKK! HIS TROOPS ARE UPON US ALREADY--
--HURLING PHIALS OF NOXIOUS GASES! BEWARE!
NAH...!
CHOOM CHOOM
BUT HOLD YER NOSE! IT'S THE PERFUME COUNTER CORPS!
CHARLIEEEEEE

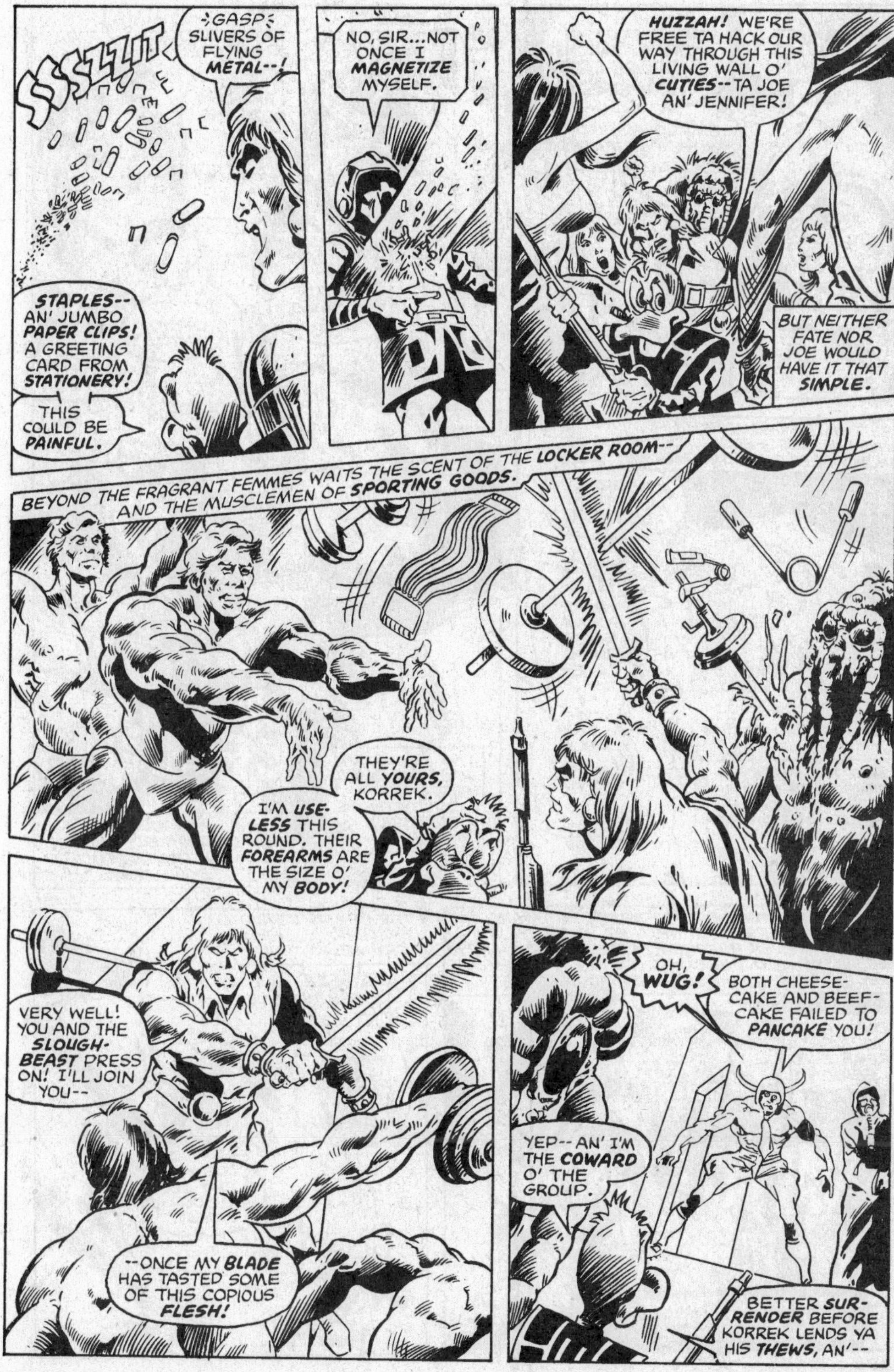
SSSZZZIT
GASP! SLIVERS OF FLYING METAL--!
STAPLES-- AN' JUMBO PAPER CLIPS! A GREETING CARD FROM STATIONERY!
THIS COULD BE PAINFUL.
NO, SIR... NOT ONCE I MAGNETIZE MYSELF.
HUZZAH! WE'RE FREE TA HACK OUR WAY THROUGH THIS LIVING WALL O' CUTIES-- TA JOE AN' JENNIFER!
BUT NEITHER FATE NOR JOE WOULD HAVE IT THAT SIMPLE.
BEYOND THE FRAGRANT FEMMES WAITS THE SCENT OF THE LOCKER ROOM-- AND THE MUSCLEMEN OF SPORTING GOODS.
THEY'RE ALL YOURS, KORREK.
I'M USELESS THIS ROUND. THEIR FOREARMS ARE THE SIZE O' MY BODY!
VERY WELL! YOU AND THE SLOUGH-BEAST PRESS ON! I'LL JOIN YOU--
--ONCE MY BLADE HAS TASTED SOME OF THIS COPIOUS FLESH!
OH, WUG!
BOTH CHEESECAKE AND BEEFCAKE FAILED TO PANCAKE YOU!
YEP-- AN' I'M THE COWARD O' THE GROUP.
BETTER SURRENDER BEFORE KORREK LENDS YA HIS THEWS, AN'--

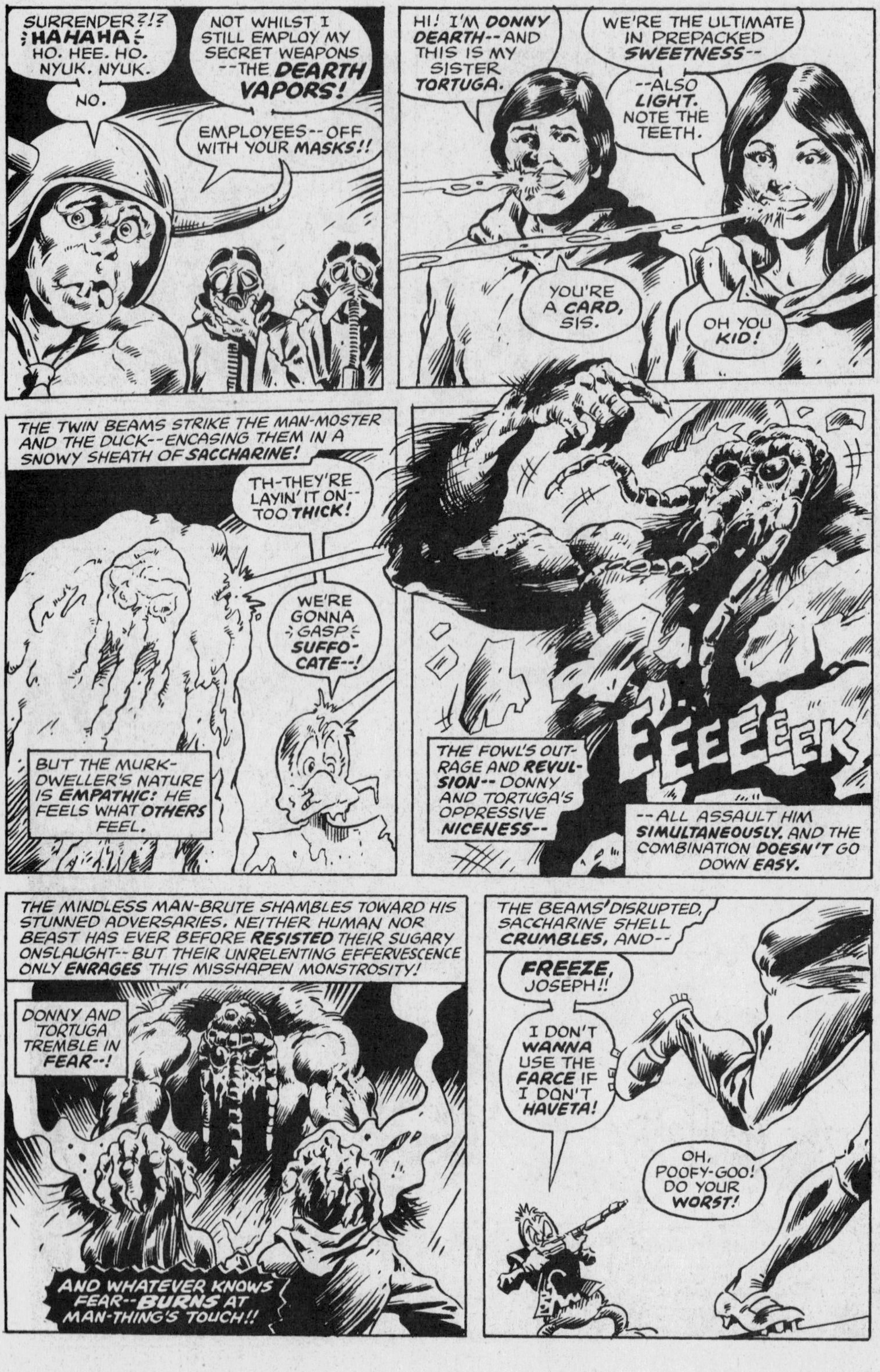
SURRENDER?!? HAHAHA HO. HEE. HO. NYUK. NYUK.
NO.
NOT WHILST I STILL EMPLOY MY SECRET WEAPONS --THE DEARTH VAPORS!
EMPLOYEES--OFF WITH YOUR MASKS!!
HI! I'M DONNY DEARTH--AND THIS IS MY SISTER TORTUGA.
WE'RE THE ULTIMATE IN PREPACKED SWEETNESS--
--ALSO LIGHT. NOTE THE TEETH.
YOU'RE A CARD, SIS.
OH YOU KID!
THE TWIN BEAMS STRIKE THE MAN-MOSTER AND THE DUCK--ENCASING THEM IN A SNOWY SHEATH OF SACCHARINE!
TH-THEY'RE LAYIN' IT ON--TOO THICK!
WE'RE GONNA GASP SUFFO-CATE--!
BUT THE MURK-DWELLER'S NATURE IS EMPATHIC! HE FEELS WHAT OTHERS FEEL.
EEEEEEEK
THE FOWL'S OUT-RAGE AND REVUL-SION-- DONNY AND TORTUGA'S OPPRESSIVE NICENESS--
--ALL ASSAULT HIM SIMULTANEOUSLY. AND THE COMBINATION DOESN'T GO DOWN EASY.
THE MINDLESS MAN-BRUTE SHAMBLES TOWARD HIS STUNNED ADVERSARIES. NEITHER HUMAN NOR BEAST HAS EVER BEFORE RESISTED THEIR SUGARY ONSLAUGHT--BUT THEIR UNRELENTING EFFERVESCENCE ONLY ENRAGES THIS MISSHAPEN MONSTROSITY!
DONNY AND TORTUGA TREMBLE IN FEAR--!
AND WHATEVER KNOWS FEAR--BURNS AT MAN-THING'S TOUCH!!
THE BEAMS' DISRUPTED, SACCHARINE SHELL CRUMBLES, AND--
FREEZE, JOSEPH!!
I DON'T WANNA USE THE FARCE IF I DON'T HAVETA!
OH, POOFY-GOO! DO YOUR WORST!

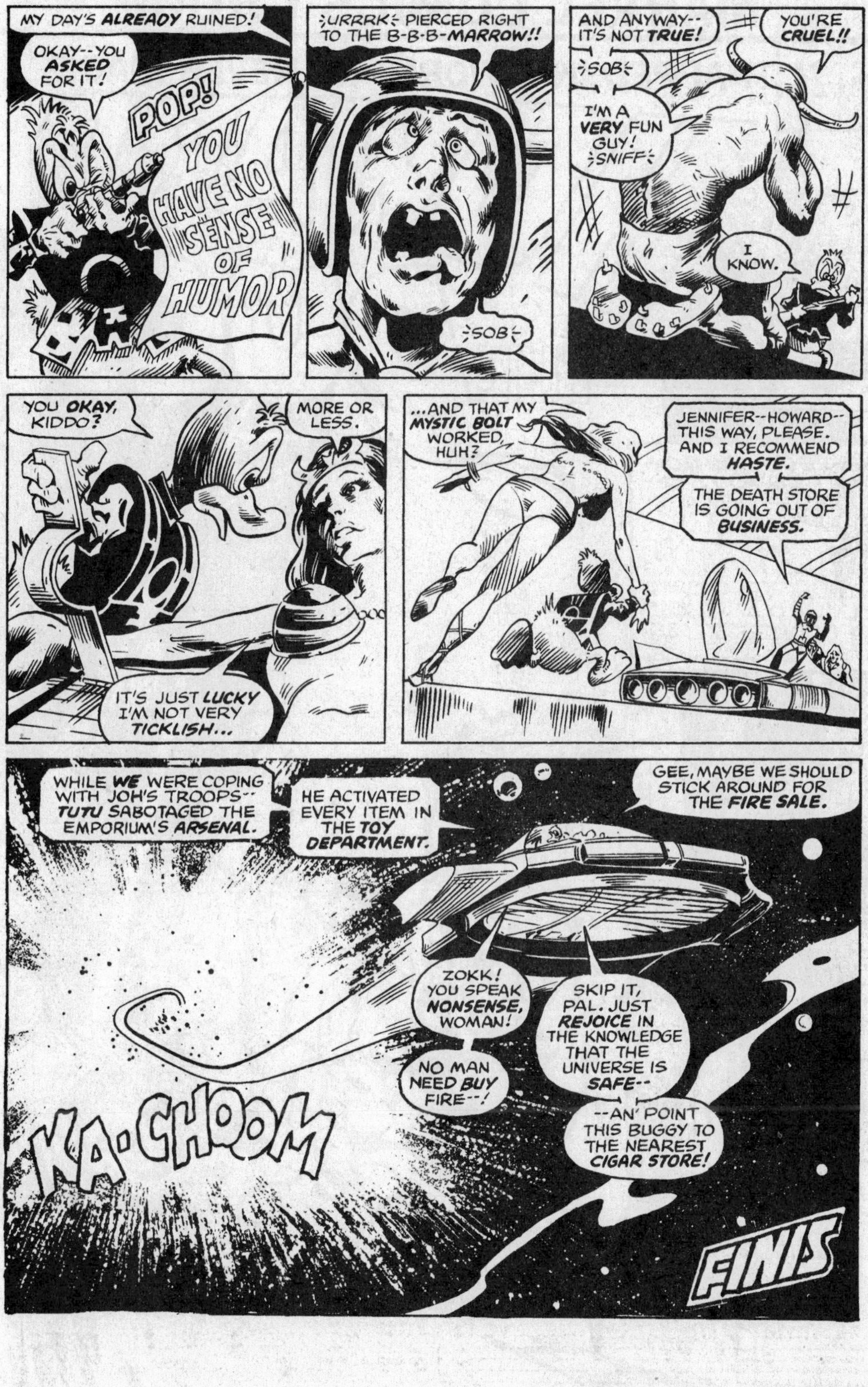
MY DAY'S ALREADY RUINED!
OKAY--YOU ASKED FOR IT!
POP!
YOU HAVE NO SENSE OF HUMOR
URRRK PIERCED RIGHT TO THE B-B-B-MARROW!!
SOB
AND ANYWAY-- IT'S NOT TRUE!
SOB
I'M A VERY FUN GUY! SNIFF
YOU'RE CRUEL!!
I KNOW.
YOU OKAY, KIDDO?
MORE OR LESS.
IT'S JUST LUCKY I'M NOT VERY TICKLISH...
...AND THAT MY MYSTIC BOLT WORKED, HUH?
JENNIFER--HOWARD-- THIS WAY, PLEASE. AND I RECOMMEND HASTE.
THE DEATH STORE IS GOING OUT OF BUSINESS.
WHILE WE WERE COPING WITH JOH'S TROOPS-- TUTU SABOTAGED THE EMPORIUM'S ARSENAL.
HE ACTIVATED EVERY ITEM IN THE TOY DEPARTMENT.
GEE, MAYBE WE SHOULD STICK AROUND FOR THE FIRE SALE.
ZOKK! YOU SPEAK NONSENSE, WOMAN!
NO MAN NEED BUY FIRE--!
SKIP IT, PAL. JUST REJOICE IN THE KNOWLEDGE THAT THE UNIVERSE IS SAFE--
--AN' POINT THIS BUGGY TO THE NEAREST CIGAR STORE!
KA-CHOOM
FINIS

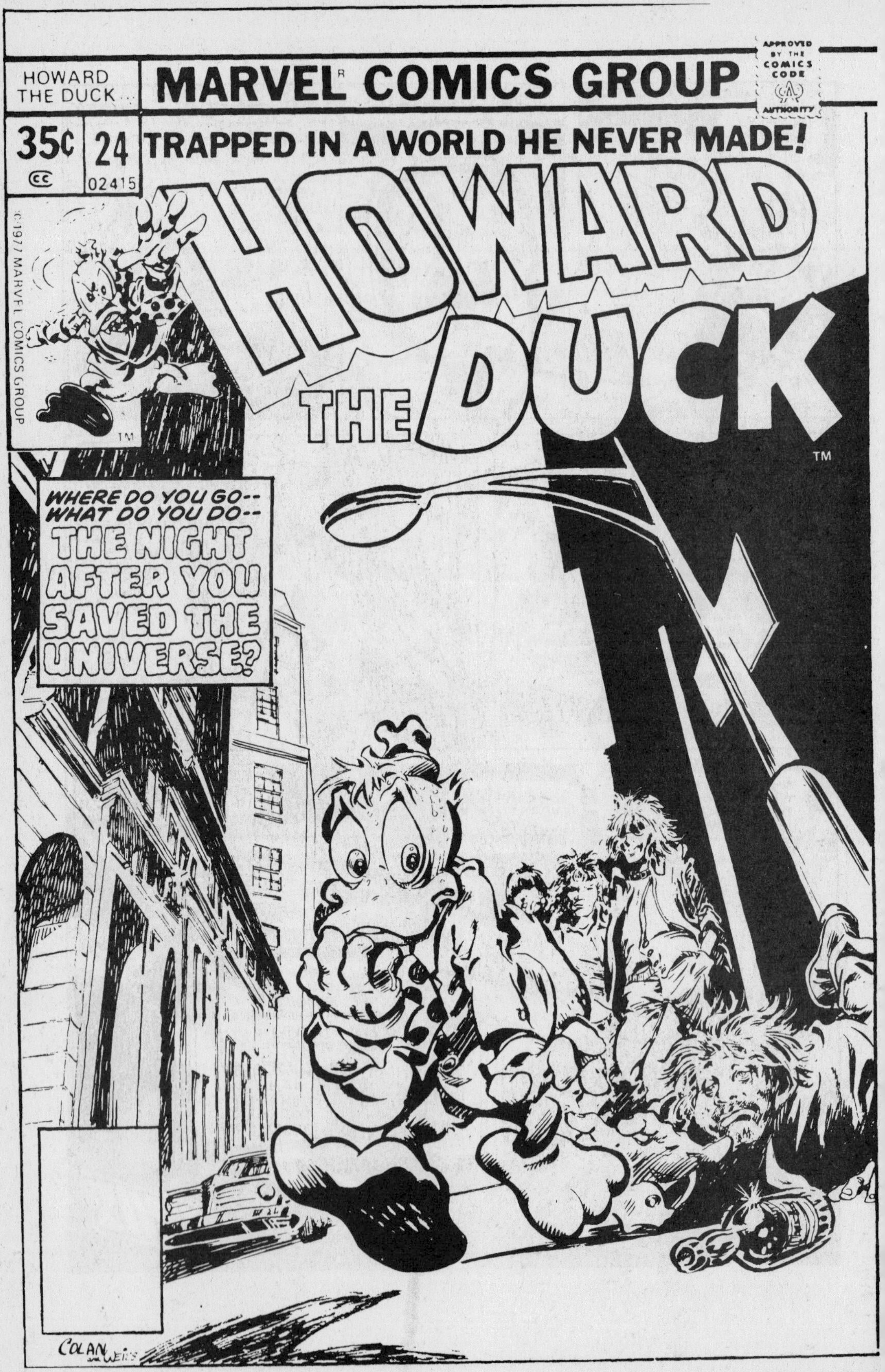

HOWARD THE DUCK
MARVEL COMICS GROUP
APPROVED BY THE COMICS CODE AUTHORITY
35¢
24
02415
TRAPPED IN A WORLD HE NEVER MADE!
©1977 MARVEL COMICS GROUP
HOWARD THE DUCK
WHERE DO YOU GO--
WHAT DO YOU DO--
THE NIGHT AFTER YOU SAVED THE UNIVERSE?
COLAN

From the time of his hatching, he was...different. A potentially brilliant scholar who dreaded the structured environment of school, he educated himself in the streets, taking whatever work was available, formulating his philosophy of self from what he learned of the world about him. And then the Cosmic Axis shifted...and that world *changed.* Suddenly, he was stranded in a universe he could not fathom. Without warning, he became a strange fowl in an even stranger land.

Stan Lee PRESENTS: HOWARD THE DUCK!™

STEVE GERBER *WRITER / EDITOR* GENE COLAN *ARTIST* TOM PALMER *INKER* JOE ROSEN, *LETTERER* JANICE COHEN, *COLORIST*

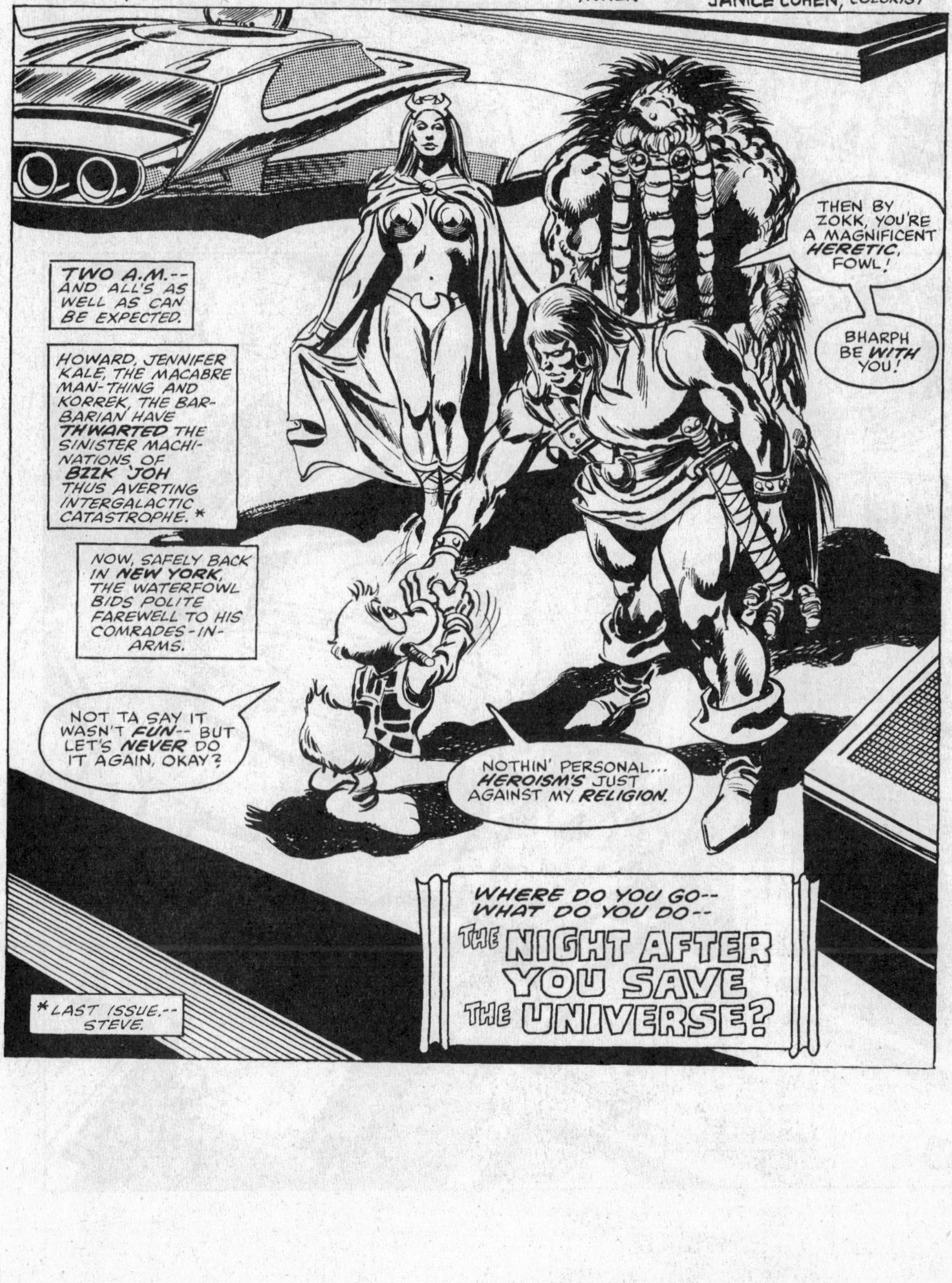

TWO A.M.-- AND ALL'S AS WELL AS CAN BE EXPECTED.
HOWARD, JENNIFER KALE, THE MACABRE MAN-THING AND KORREK, THE BARBARIAN HAVE THWARTED THE SINISTER MACHINATIONS OF BZZK JOH THUS AVERTING INTERGALACTIC CATASTROPHE.*
NOW, SAFELY BACK IN NEW YORK, THE WATERFOWL BIDS POLITE FAREWELL TO HIS COMRADES-IN-ARMS.
THEN BY ZOKK, YOU'RE A MAGNIFICENT HERETIC, FOWL!
BHARPH BE WITH YOU!
NOT TA SAY IT WASN'T FUN-- BUT LET'S NEVER DO IT AGAIN, OKAY?
NOTHIN' PERSONAL... HEROISM'S JUST AGAINST MY RELIGION.
WHERE DO YOU GO-- WHAT DO YOU DO-- THE NIGHT AFTER YOU SAVE THE UNIVERSE?
*LAST ISSUE.-- STEVE.

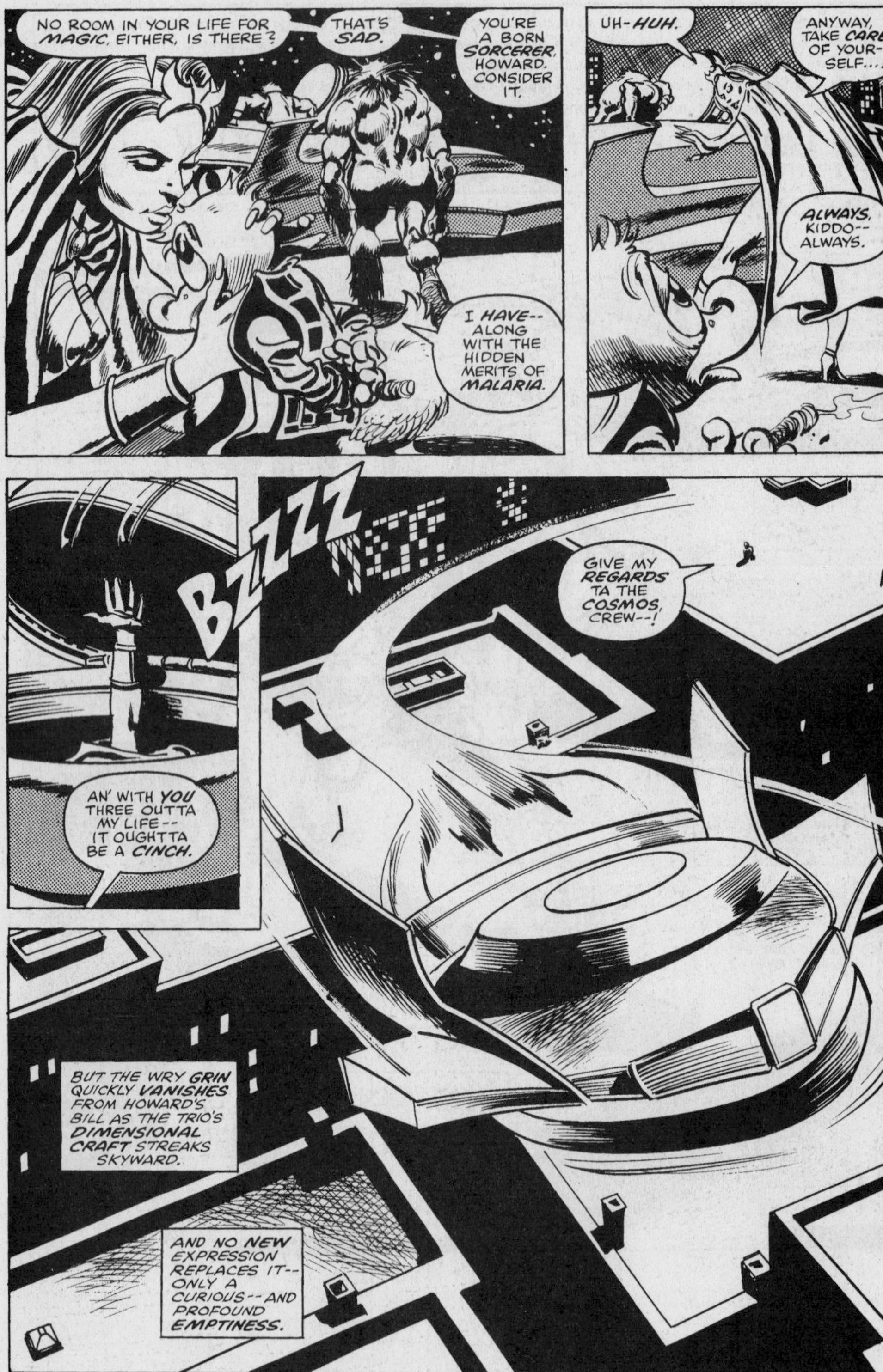

NO ROOM IN YOUR LIFE FOR MAGIC, EITHER, IS THERE?
THAT'S SAD.
YOU'RE A BORN SORCERER, HOWARD. CONSIDER IT.
I HAVE-- ALONG WITH THE HIDDEN MERITS OF MALARIA.
UH-HUH.
ANYWAY, TAKE CARE OF YOUR-SELF...!
ALWAYS, KIDDO-- ALWAYS.
BZZZZZ
GIVE MY REGARDS TA THE COSMOS, CREW--!
AN' WITH YOU THREE OUTTA MY LIFE-- IT OUGHTTA BE A CINCH.
BUT THE WRY GRIN QUICKLY VANISHES FROM HOWARD'S BILL AS THE TRIO'S DIMENSIONAL CRAFT STREAKS SKYWARD.
AND NO NEW EXPRESSION REPLACES IT-- ONLY A CURIOUS--AND PROFOUND EMPTINESS.

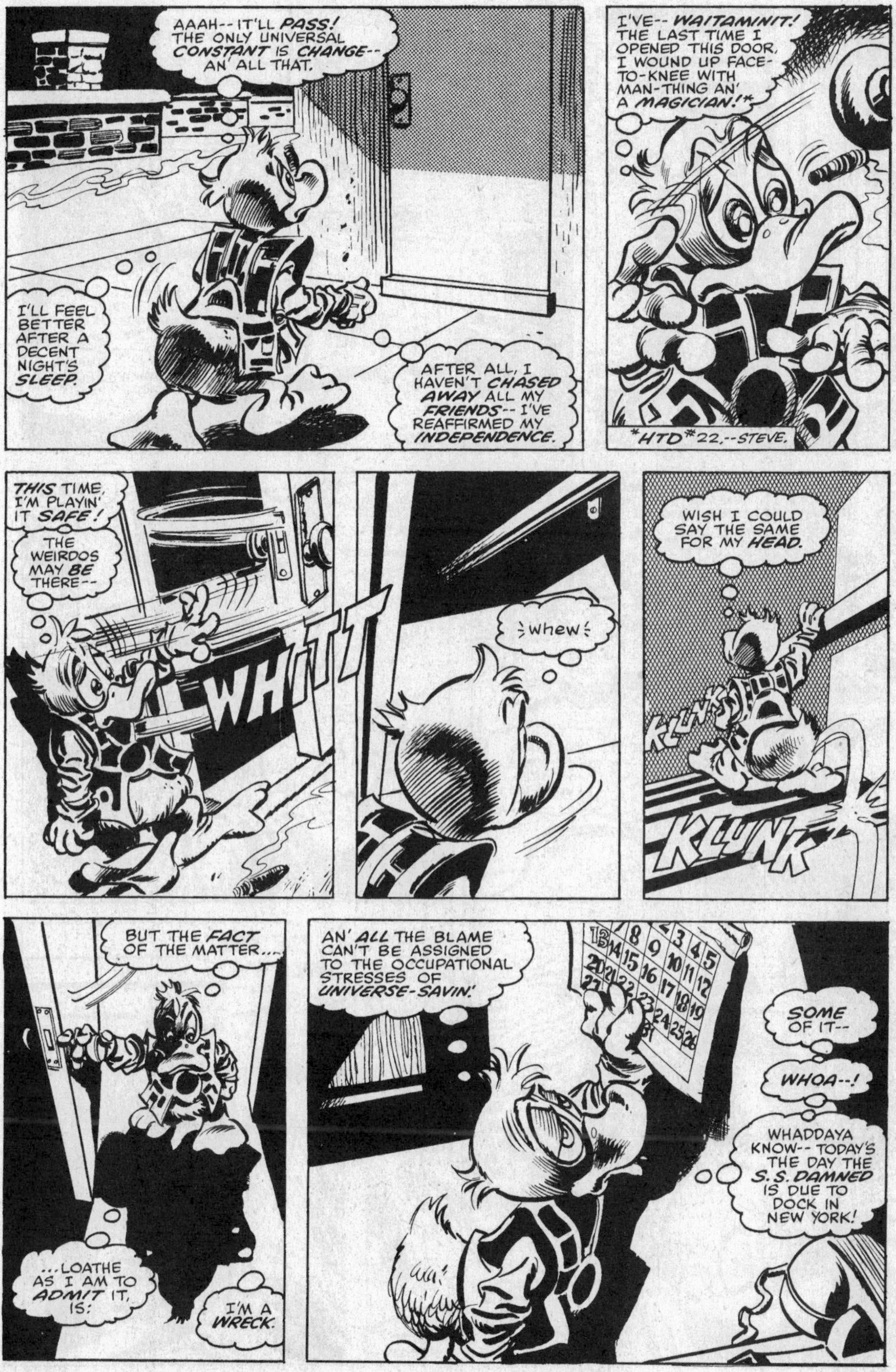
AAAH-- IT'LL PASS! THE ONLY UNIVERSAL CONSTANT IS CHANGE-- AN' ALL THAT.
I'LL FEEL BETTER AFTER A DECENT NIGHT'S SLEEP.
AFTER ALL, I HAVEN'T CHASED AWAY ALL MY FRIENDS-- I'VE REAFFIRMED MY INDEPENDENCE.
I'VE-- WAITAMINIT! THE LAST TIME I OPENED THIS DOOR, I WOUND UP FACE-TO-KNEE WITH MAN-THING AN' A MAGICIAN!*
*HTD #22.--STEVE.
THIS TIME, I'M PLAYIN' IT SAFE!
THE WEIRDOS MAY BE THERE--
WHITT
whew
WISH I COULD SAY THE SAME FOR MY HEAD.
KLUNK
KLUNK
BUT THE FACT OF THE MATTER...
...LOATHE AS I AM TO ADMIT IT, IS:
I'M A WRECK.
AN' ALL THE BLAME CAN'T BE ASSIGNED TO THE OCCUPATIONAL STRESSES OF UNIVERSE-SAVIN'.
SOME OF IT--
WHOA--!
WHADDAYA KNOW-- TODAY'S THE DAY THE S.S. DAMNED IS DUE TO DOCK IN NEW YORK!

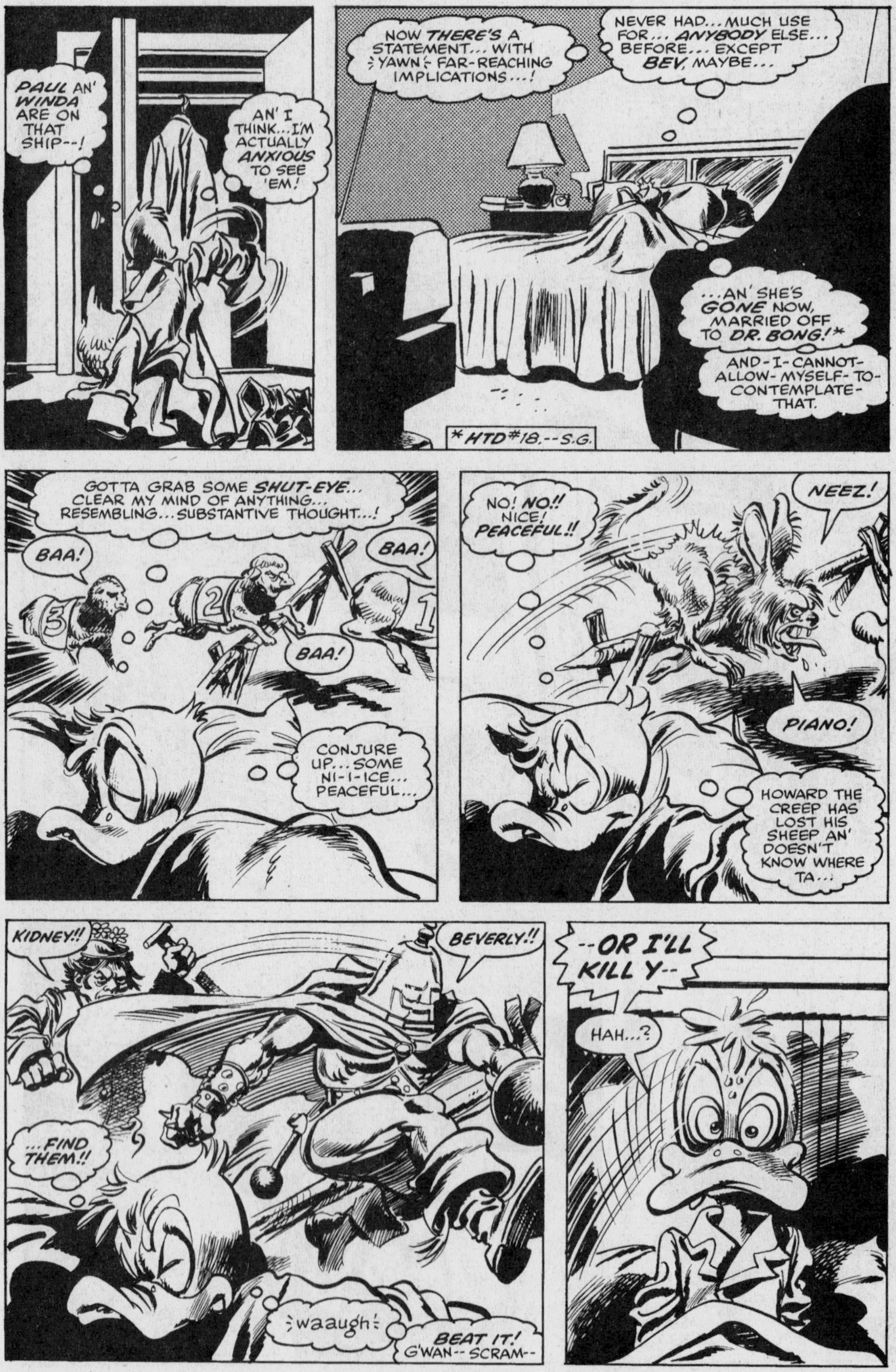

PAUL AN' WINDA ARE ON THAT SHIP--!
AN' I THINK...I'M ACTUALLY ANXIOUS TO SEE 'EM!
NOW THERE'S A STATEMENT... WITH ~YAWN~ FAR-REACHING IMPLICATIONS...!
NEVER HAD... MUCH USE FOR... ANYBODY ELSE... BEFORE... EXCEPT BEV, MAYBE...
...AN' SHE'S GONE NOW, MARRIED OFF TO DR. BONG!*
AND-I-CANNOT-ALLOW-MYSELF-TO-CONTEMPLATE-THAT.
*HTD #18.--S.G.
GOTTA GRAB SOME SHUT-EYE... CLEAR MY MIND OF ANYTHING... RESEMBLING... SUBSTANTIVE THOUGHT...!
BAA!
BAA!
BAA!
CONJURE UP... SOME NI-I-ICE... PEACEFUL...
NO! NO!! NICE! PEACEFUL!!
NEEZ!
PIANO!
HOWARD THE CREEP HAS LOST HIS SHEEP AN' DOESN'T KNOW WHERE TA...
KIDNEY!!
BEVERLY!!
...FIND THEM!!
~waaugh~
BEAT IT! G'WAN-- SCRAM--
--OR I'LL KILL Y--
HAH...?

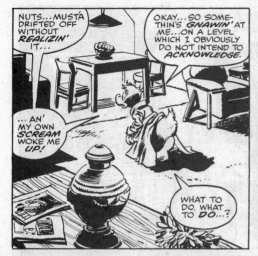

NUTS...MUSTA DRIFTED OFF WITHOUT REALIZIN' IT...
OKAY...SO SOMETHIN'S GNAWIN' AT ME...ON A LEVEL WHICH I OBVIOUSLY DO NOT INTEND TO ACKNOWLEDGE.
...AN' MY OWN SCREAM WOKE ME UP!
WHAT TO DO, WHAT TO DO...?
ANSWER: DEAL WITH THE PROBLEM SUPERFICIALLY... THE MIDNIGHT-SNACK-BORN-OF-DESPERATION SYNDROME...!
SO WHAT'VE WE GOT? ONE BOX O' SLIGHTLY CHEWY POTATO CHIPS...
POTATO CHIPS
...A BOTTLE O' SOY SAUCE, A JAR O' CHUTNEY...
AH! AN' A CAN OF DIPSI LIGHT!
HARD TO BELIEVE THIS WAS THE APARTMENT OF A RESTAURATEUR!*
*LEE SWITZLER, BEV'S UNCLE, WHOM HOWARD MET IN ISH #19. --S.
WELL... MAYBE THE LATE MOVIE'LL OFFER SOMETHING MORE NOURISHING...!
SOLID STATE
CLICK
A LONG, LOVING LOOK AT MARLENE DIETRICH'S LEGS...THAT'D BE STIMULATING...!
FUNNY, HOW I'VE DEVELOPED A WORKING AESTHETIC FOR HAIRLESS-APE ANATOMY...
POTATO CHIPS
BUT I GUESS IT WAS INEVITABLE THAT I'D--
HOWARD...
HAH...?

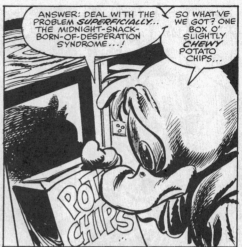

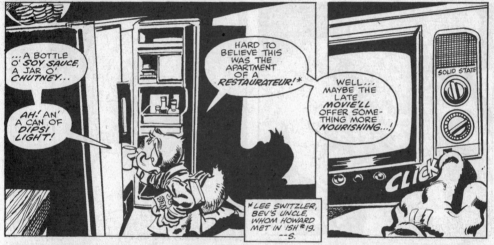

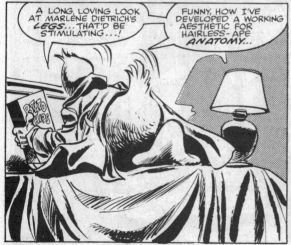

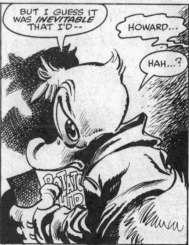

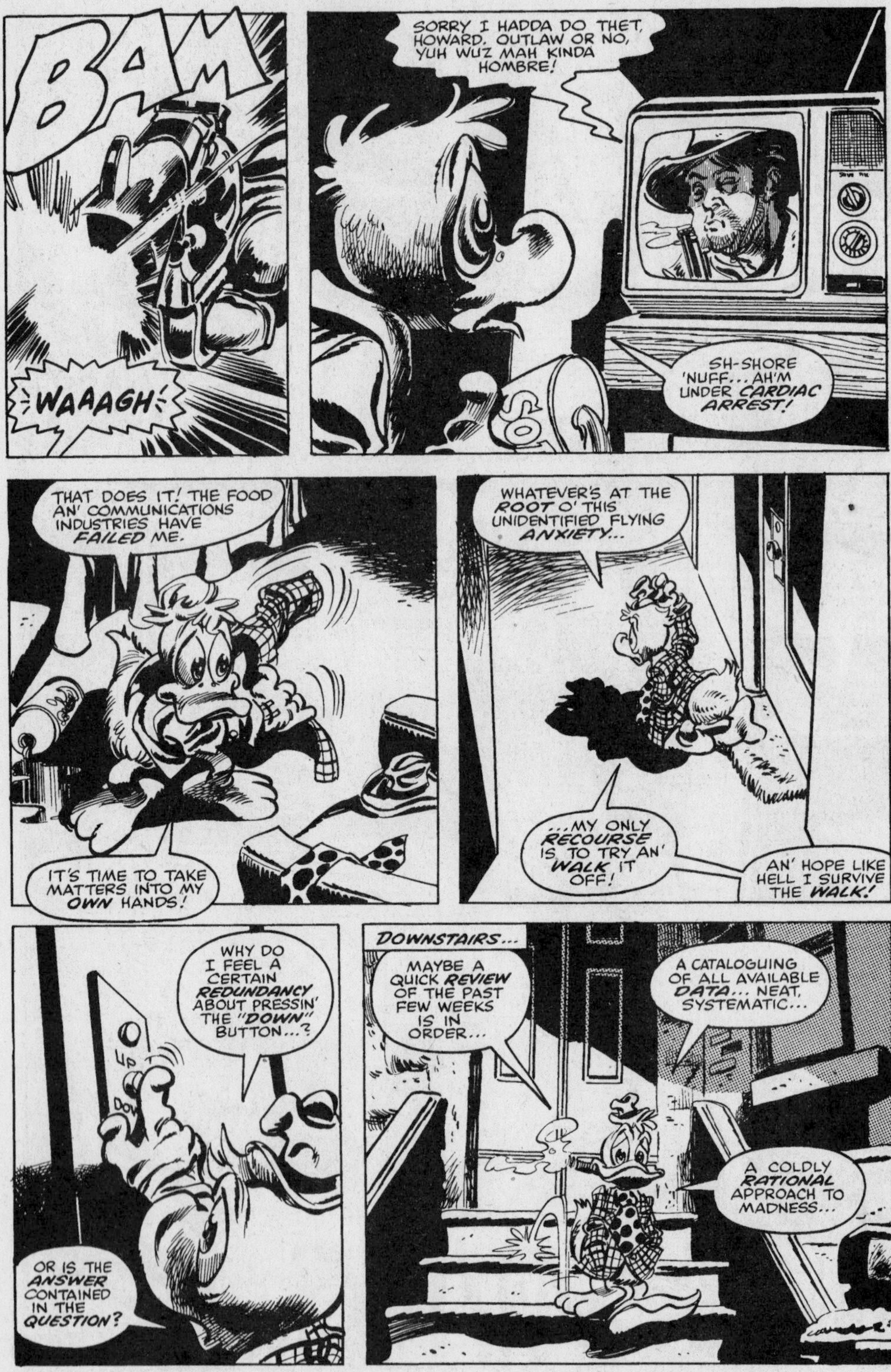

BAM
WAAAGH!
SORRY I HADDA DO THET, HOWARD. OUTLAW OR NO, YUH WUZ MAH KINDA HOMBRE!
SH-SHORE 'NUFF... AH'M UNDER CARDIAC ARREST!
THAT DOES IT! THE FOOD AN' COMMUNICATIONS INDUSTRIES HAVE FAILED ME.
IT'S TIME TO TAKE MATTERS INTO MY OWN HANDS!
WHATEVER'S AT THE ROOT O' THIS UNIDENTIFIED FLYING ANXIETY...
...MY ONLY RECOURSE IS TO TRY AN' WALK IT OFF!
AN' HOPE LIKE HELL I SURVIVE THE WALK!
WHY DO I FEEL A CERTAIN REDUNDANCY ABOUT PRESSIN' THE "DOWN" BUTTON...?
UP
OR IS THE ANSWER CONTAINED IN THE QUESTION?
DOWNSTAIRS...
MAYBE A QUICK REVIEW OF THE PAST FEW WEEKS IS IN ORDER...
A CATALOGUING OF ALL AVAILABLE DATA... NEAT, SYSTEMATIC...
A COLDLY RATIONAL APPROACH TO MADNESS...

LET'S SEE...THE TRIP TO *BAGMOM*... THE CRUISE HOME ON THE *S.S. DAMNED*... THEN BEV AN' I WERE ABDUCTED FROM SHIPBOARD BY *DR. BONG*, WHOM BEV MARRIED TO SAVE MY LIFE...!

...WHICH INDIRECTLY LED TO MEETING BEV'S *UNCLE*, AN' BEING CALLED UPON TO SAVE THE *UNIVERSE* WITH JEN, MANNY, AN' *KORREK*...!*

THEN I WAS TEMPORARILY TRANSFORMED INTO A *HUMAN*... FOLLOWING WHICH CAME THE RUN-INS WITH *SUDD* AN' THE *SOOF*!...

HTD #15-23.--S.G.

NOPE! NOTHIN' ANXIETY-PROVOKING *THERE*! PURE *EVERYMAN* STUFF IF EVER I--

≷WHUP≷

≷WAAUGH≷ THAT'LL TEACH ME TO KEEP MY EYES ON THE PATH *AHEAD*...

BUMP

...INSTEAD'A DOWN IN THE *GUTTER* WHERE THEY *BELONG*!

FIGURES... I'D STUMBLE OVER ONE O' THE *NATIVES*...!

WONDER IF HE'S...

≷PHEWWGH≷

NOPE... SCOTCH AN' AMARETTA...

AN' THERE'S NOTHIN' MUCH *I* CAN DO FOR 'IM.

... BUT DEFINITELY *NOT* RIGOR MORTIS!

HE'LL LIVE!

SWEET 'N' SOUR *DREAMS*, FELLA!

≷NUH-MUH-UNN-NGH≷

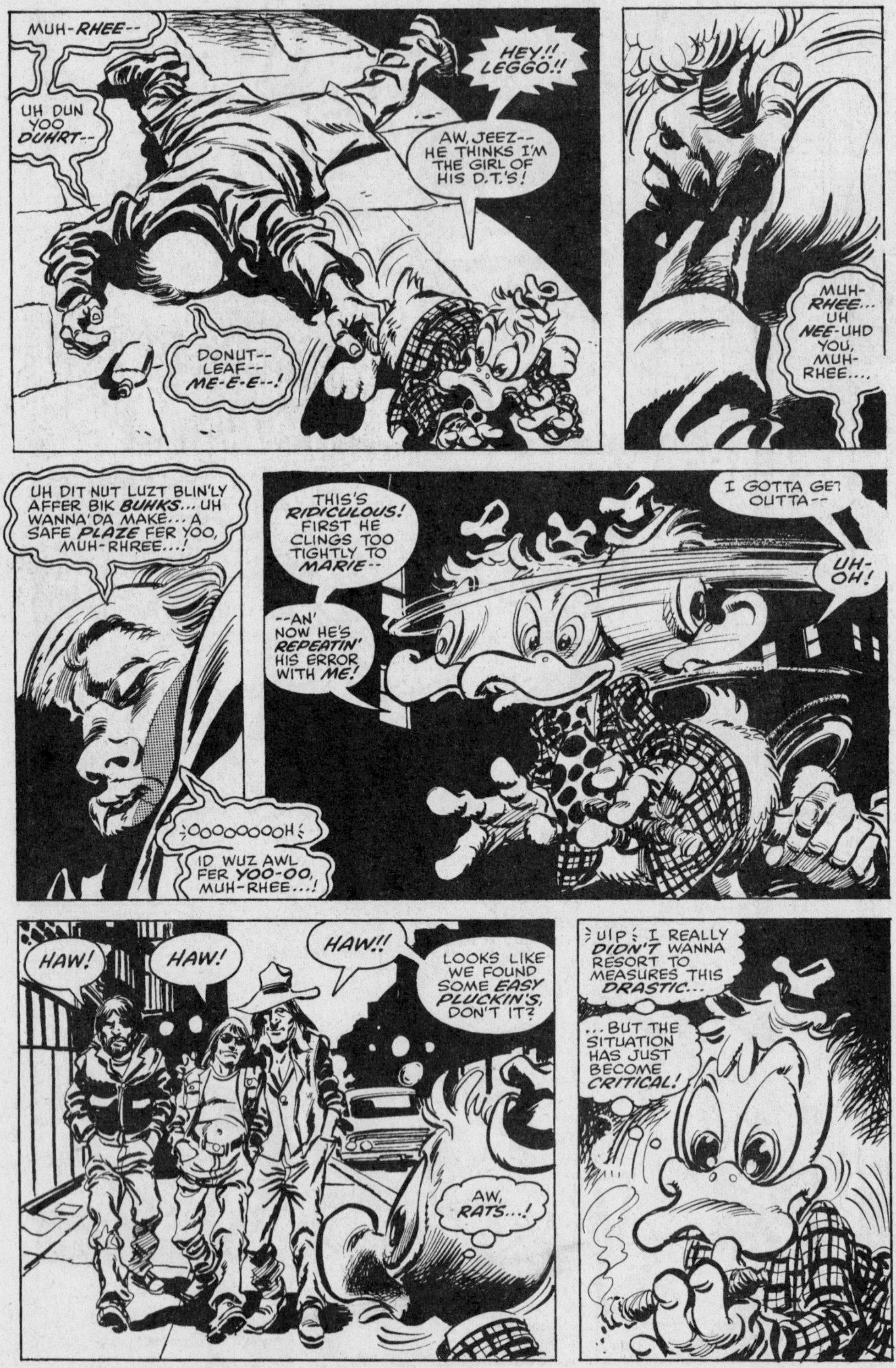
MUH-RHEE--
UH DUN YOO DUHRT--
HEY!! LEGGO!!
AW, JEEZ-- HE THINKS I'M THE GIRL OF HIS D.T.'S!
DONUT-- LEAF-- ME-E-E--!
MUH-RHEE... UH NEE-UHD YOU, MUH-RHEE....
UH DIT NUT LUZT BLIN'LY AFFER BIK BUHKS... UH WANNA'DA MAKE... A SAFE PLAZE FER YOO, MUH-RHREE...!
OOOOOOOOH
ID WUZ AWL FER YOO-OO, MUH-RHEE...!
THIS'S RIDICULOUS! FIRST HE CLINGS TOO TIGHTLY TO MARIE--
--AN' NOW HE'S REPEATIN' HIS ERROR WITH ME!
I GOTTA GET OUTTA--
UH-OH!
HAW!
HAW!
HAW!!
LOOKS LIKE WE FOUND SOME EASY PLUCKIN'S, DON'T IT?
AW, RATS...!
ULP! I REALLY DIDN'T WANNA RESORT TO MEASURES THIS DRASTIC...
...BUT THE SITUATION HAS JUST BECOME CRITICAL!

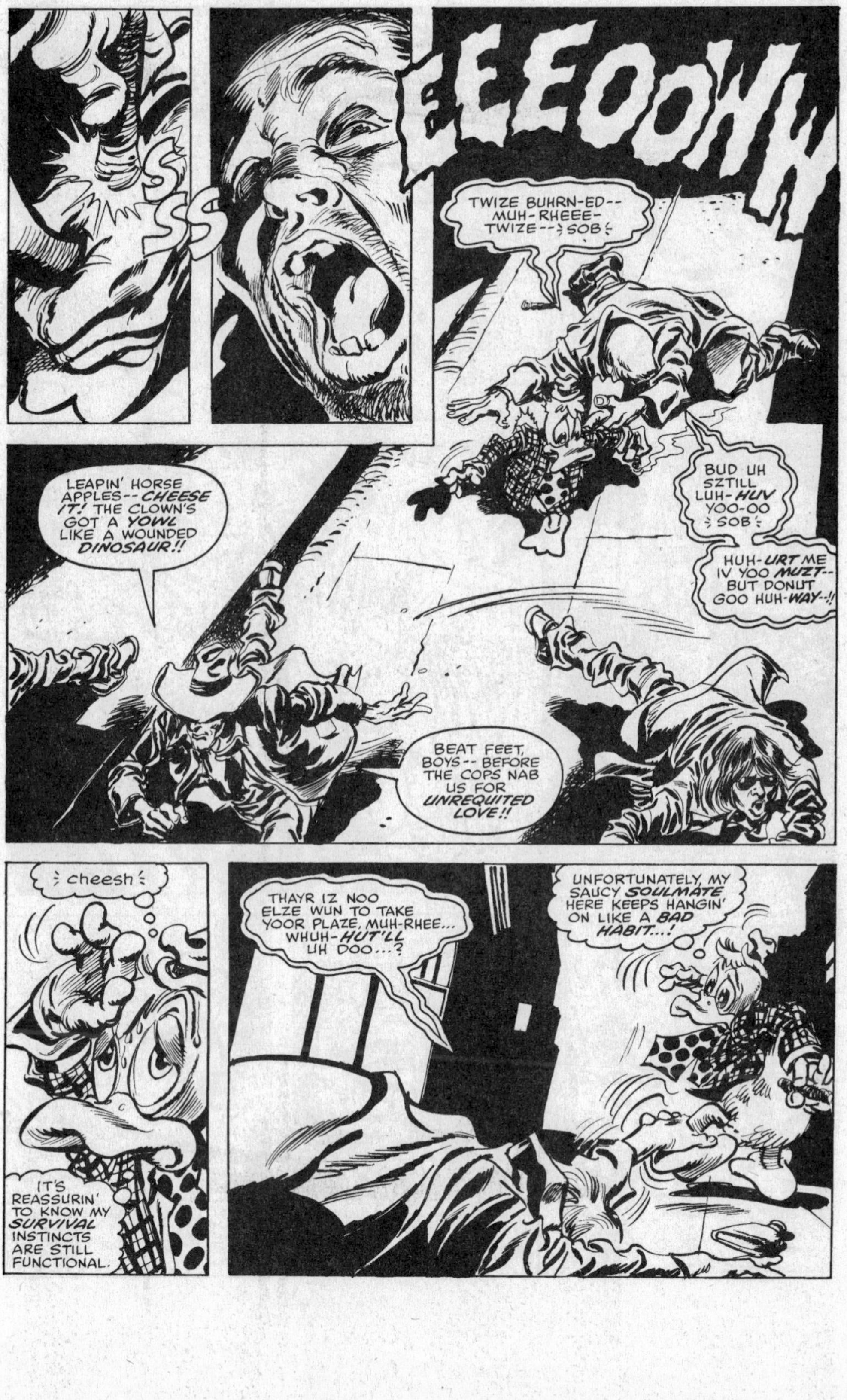
SSSS
EEEOOWW
TWIZE BUHRN-ED-- MUH-RHEEE TWIZE-- SOB
BUD UH SZTILL LUH-HUV YOO-OO SOB
HUH-URT ME IV YOO MUZT-- BUT DONUT GOO HUH-WAY--!!
LEAPIN' HORSE APPLES-- CHEESE IT! THE CLOWN'S GOT A YOWL LIKE A WOUNDED DINOSAUR!!
BEAT FEET, BOYS-- BEFORE THE COPS NAB US FOR UNREQUITED LOVE!!
cheesh
IT'S REASSURIN' TO KNOW MY SURVIVAL INSTINCTS ARE STILL FUNCTIONAL.
THAYR IZ NOO ELZE WUN TO TAKE YOOR PLAZE, MUH-RHEE... WHUH-HUT'LL UH DOO...?
UNFORTUNATELY, MY SAUCY SOULMATE HERE KEEPS HANGIN' ON LIKE A BAD HABIT...!

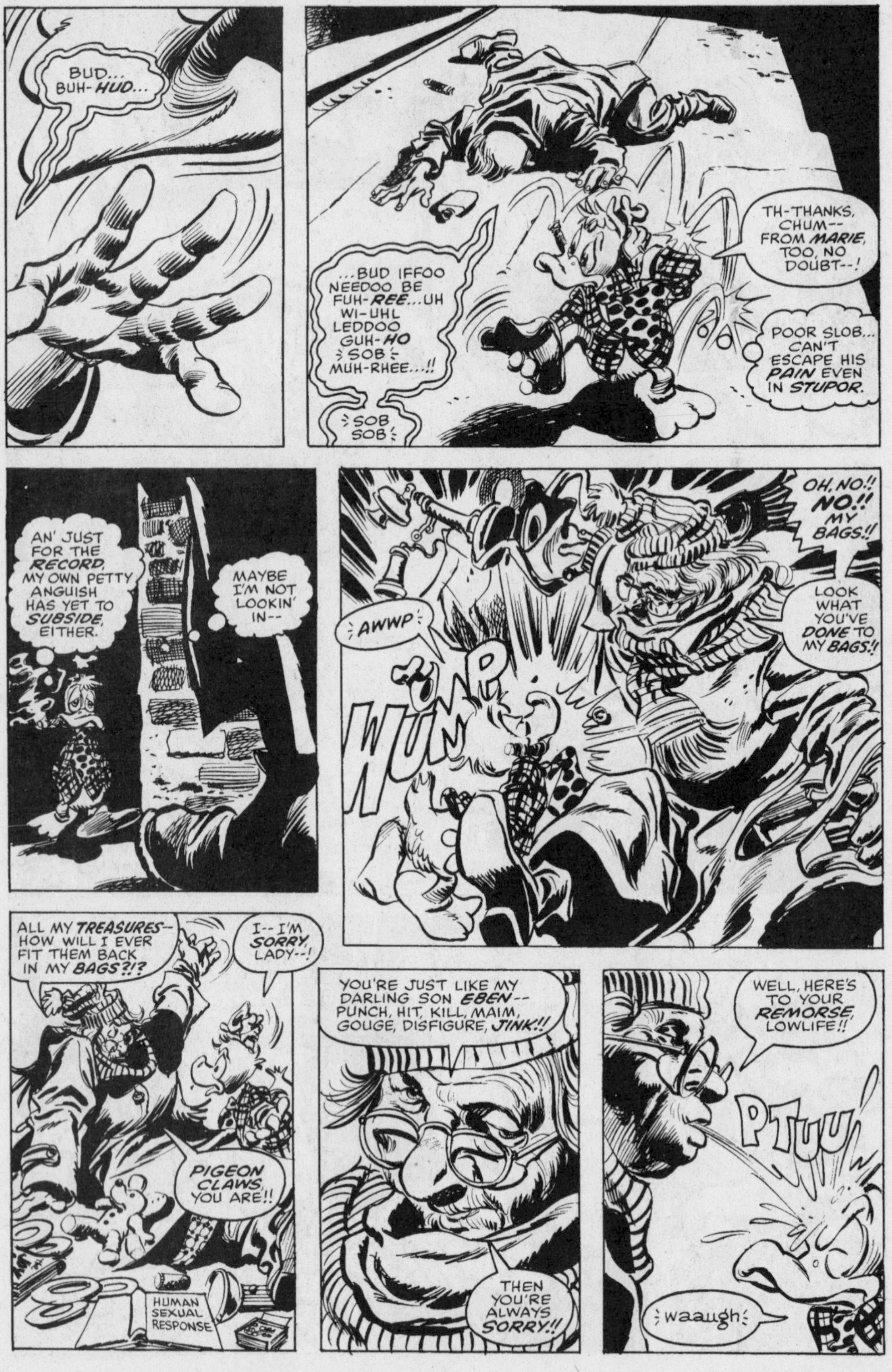
BUD... BUH-HUD...
...BUD IFFOO NEEDOO BE FUH-REE...UH WI-UHL LEDDOO GUH-HO SOB MUH-RHEE...!!
SOB SOB
TH-THANKS, CHUM-- FROM MARIE, TOO, NO DOUBT--!
POOR SLOB... CAN'T ESCAPE HIS PAIN EVEN IN STUPOR.
AN' JUST FOR THE RECORD, MY OWN PETTY ANGUISH HAS YET TO SUBSIDE, EITHER.
MAYBE I'M NOT LOOKIN' IN--
OH, NO!! NO!! MY BAGS!!
LOOK WHAT YOU'VE DONE TO MY BAGS!!
AWWP
WHUMP
ALL MY TREASURES-- HOW WILL I EVER FIT THEM BACK IN MY BAGS?!?
I-- I'M SORRY, LADY--!
PIGEON CLAWS, YOU ARE!!
HUMAN SEXUAL RESPONSE
YOU'RE JUST LIKE MY DARLING SON EBEN-- PUNCH, HIT, KILL, MAIM, GOUGE, DISFIGURE, JINK!!
THEN YOU'RE ALWAYS SORRY!!
WELL, HERE'S TO YOUR REMORSE, LOWLIFE!!
PTUU
waaugh

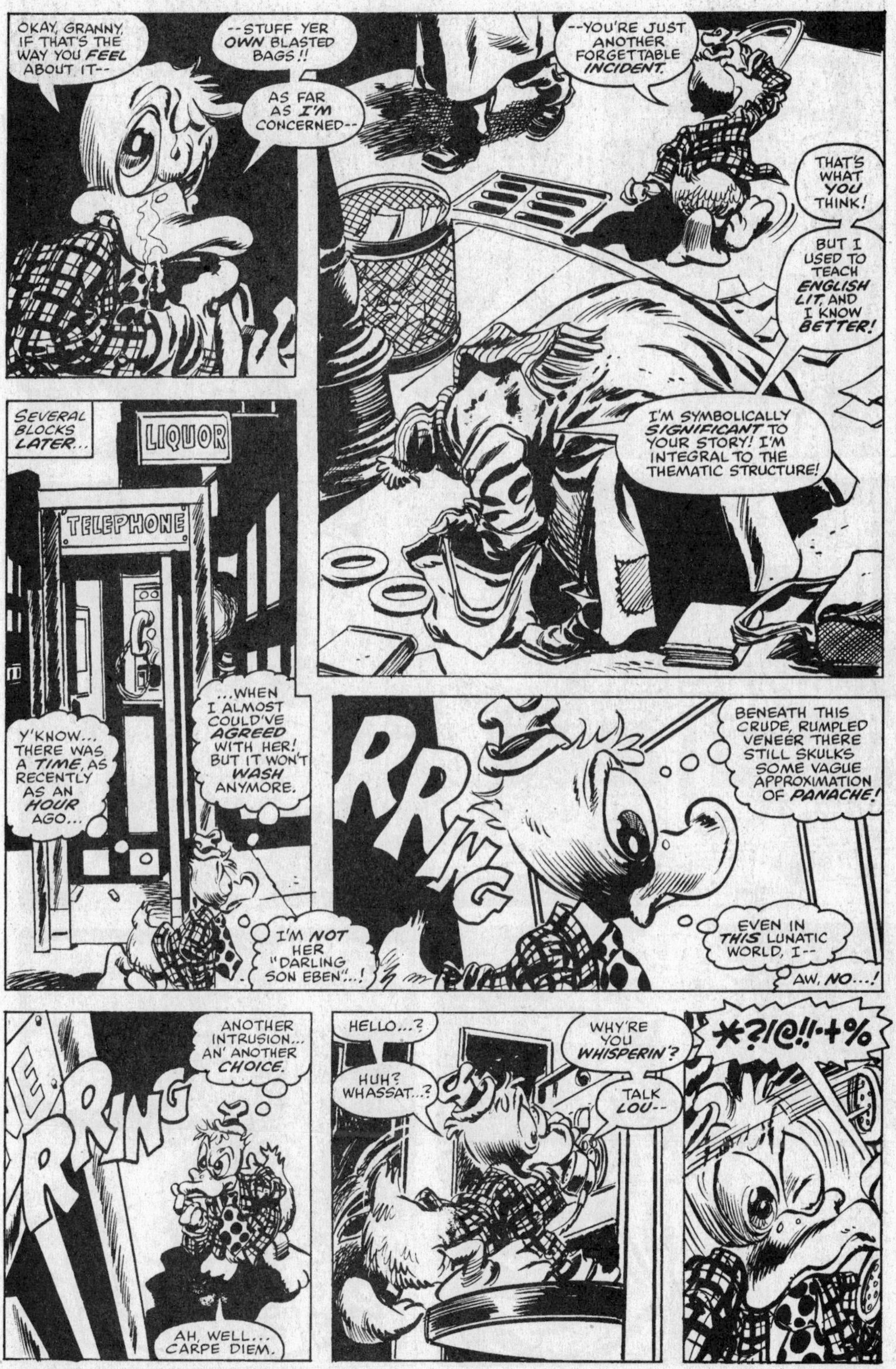
OKAY, GRANNY, IF THAT'S THE WAY YOU FEEL ABOUT IT--
--STUFF YER OWN BLASTED BAGS!!
AS FAR AS I'M CONCERNED--
--YOU'RE JUST ANOTHER FORGETTABLE INCIDENT.
THAT'S WHAT YOU THINK!
BUT I USED TO TEACH ENGLISH LIT, AND I KNOW BETTER!
I'M SYMBOLICALLY SIGNIFICANT TO YOUR STORY! I'M INTEGRAL TO THE THEMATIC STRUCTURE!
SEVERAL BLOCKS LATER...
LIQUOR
TELEPHONE
Y'KNOW... THERE WAS A TIME, AS RECENTLY AS AN HOUR AGO...
...WHEN I ALMOST COULD'VE AGREED WITH HER! BUT IT WON'T WASH ANYMORE.
I'M NOT HER "DARLING SON EBEN"...!
RRING
BENEATH THIS CRUDE, RUMPLED VENEER THERE STILL SKULKS SOME VAGUE APPROXIMATION OF PANACHE!
EVEN IN THIS LUNATIC WORLD, I--
AW, NO...!
RRRING
ANOTHER INTRUSION... AN' ANOTHER CHOICE.
AH, WELL... CARPE DIEM.
HELLO...?
HUH? WHASSAT...?
WHY'RE YOU WHISPERIN'?
TALK LOU--
*?!@!!-+%

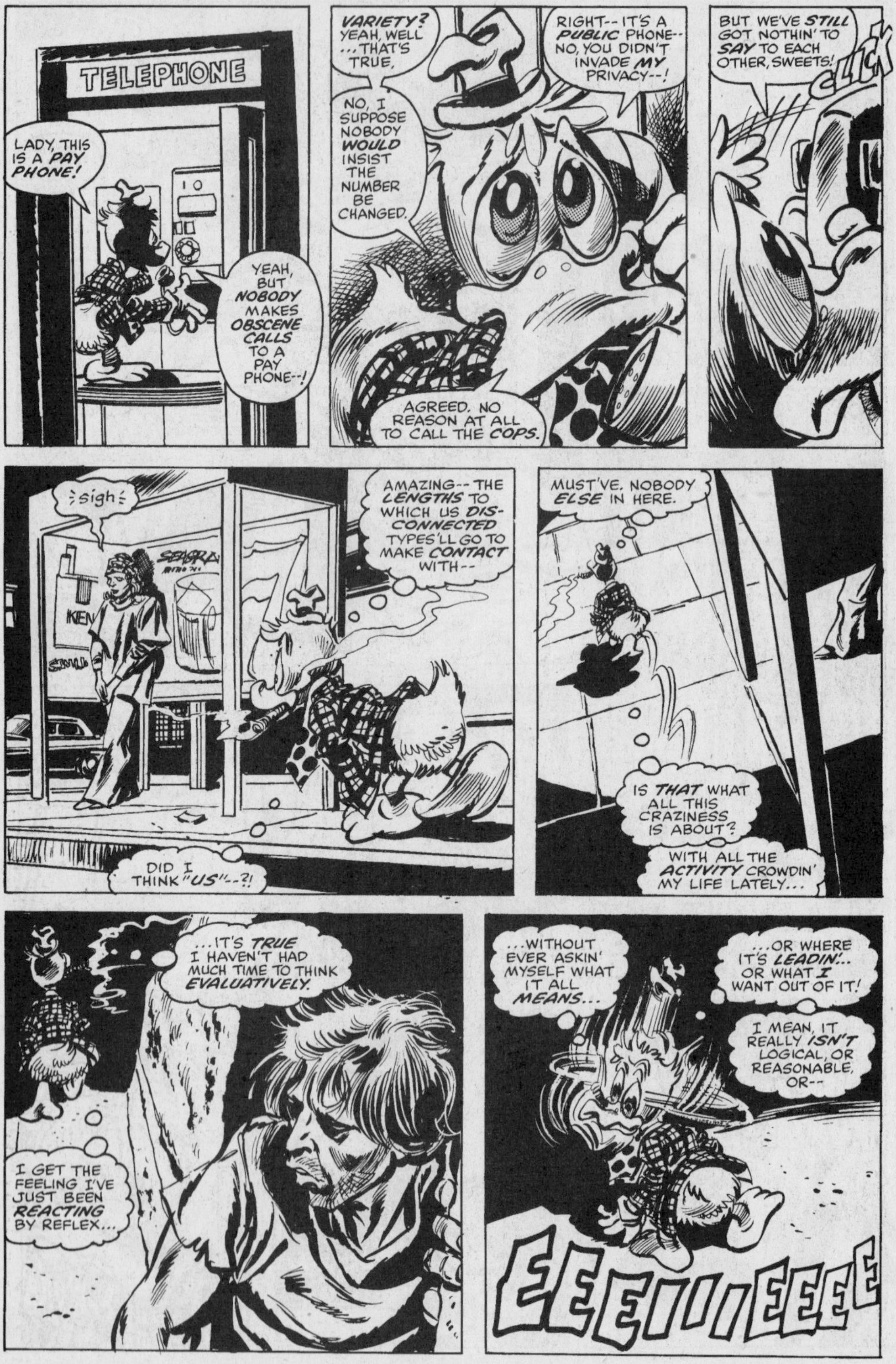
TELEPHONE
LADY, THIS IS A PAY PHONE!
YEAH, BUT NOBODY MAKES OBSCENE CALLS TO A PAY PHONE--!
VARIETY? YEAH, WELL ... THAT'S TRUE,
NO, I SUPPOSE NOBODY WOULD INSIST THE NUMBER BE CHANGED.
RIGHT-- IT'S A PUBLIC PHONE-- NO, YOU DIDN'T INVADE MY PRIVACY--!
AGREED. NO REASON AT ALL TO CALL THE COPS.
BUT WE'VE STILL GOT NOTHIN' TO SAY TO EACH OTHER, SWEETS!
CLICK
sigh
AMAZING-- THE LENGTHS TO WHICH US DIS-CONNECTED TYPES'LL GO TO MAKE CONTACT WITH--
DID I THINK "US"--?!
MUST'VE. NOBODY ELSE IN HERE.
IS THAT WHAT ALL THIS CRAZINESS IS ABOUT?
WITH ALL THE ACTIVITY CROWDIN' MY LIFE LATELY...
...IT'S TRUE I HAVEN'T HAD MUCH TIME TO THINK EVALUATIVELY.
I GET THE FEELING I'VE JUST BEEN REACTING BY REFLEX...
...WITHOUT EVER ASKIN' MYSELF WHAT IT ALL MEANS...
...OR WHERE IT'S LEADIN'... OR WHAT I WANT OUT OF IT!
I MEAN, IT REALLY ISN'T LOGICAL, OR REASONABLE, OR--
EEEIIIIEEEE

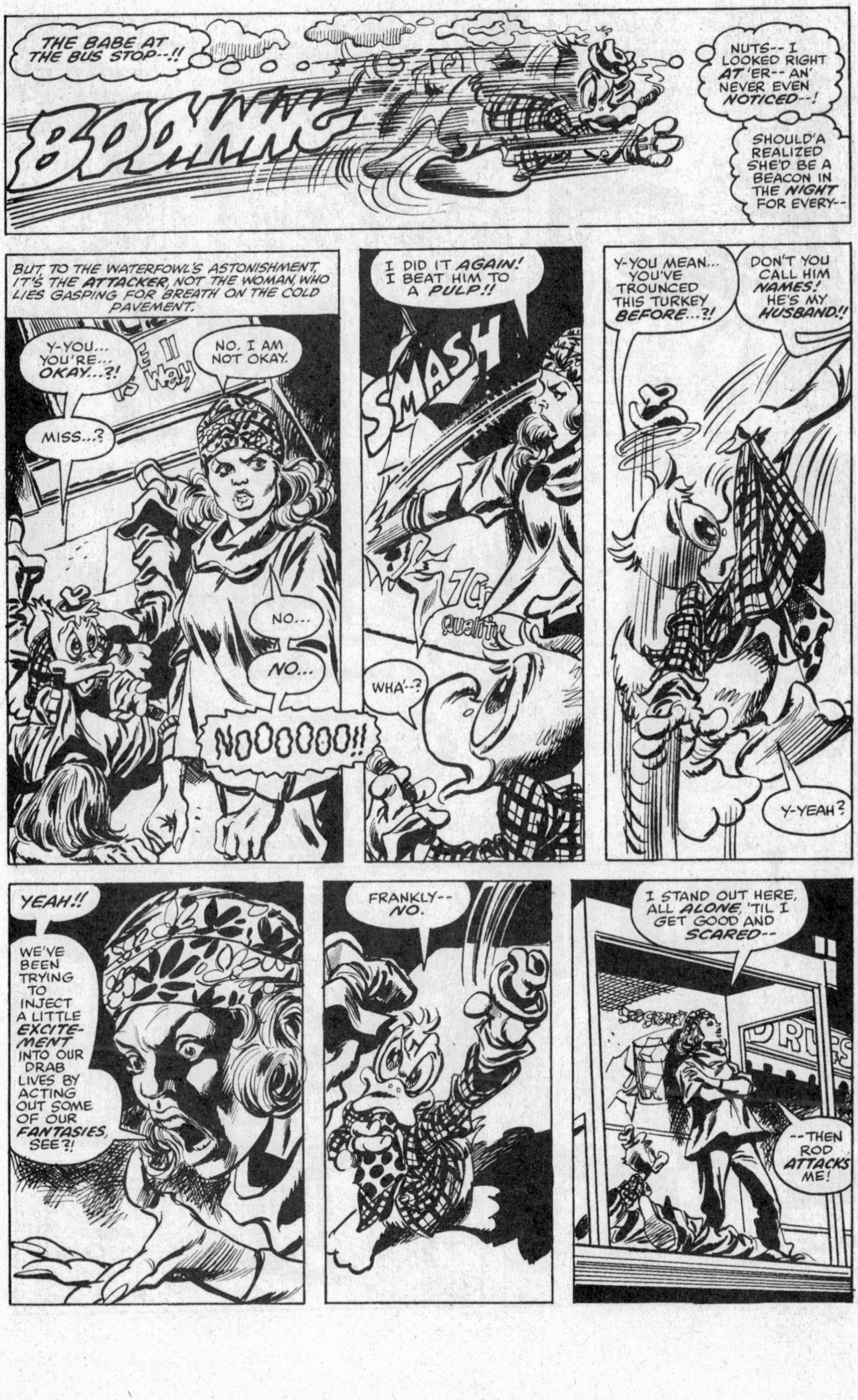
THE BABE AT THE BUS STOP--!!
BOOWWNNG
NUTS-- I LOOKED RIGHT AT 'ER-- AN' NEVER EVEN NOTICED--!
SHOULD'A REALIZED SHE'D BE A BEACON IN THE NIGHT FOR EVERY--
BUT, TO THE WATERFOWL'S ASTONISHMENT, IT'S THE ATTACKER, NOT THE WOMAN, WHO LIES GASPING FOR BREATH ON THE COLD PAVEMENT.
Y-YOU... YOU'RE... OKAY...?!
NO, I AM NOT OKAY.
MISS...?
NO...
NO...
NOOOOOO!!
I DID IT AGAIN! I BEAT HIM TO A PULP!!
SMASH
WHA'-?
Y-YOU MEAN... YOU'VE TROUNCED THIS TURKEY BEFORE...?!
DON'T YOU CALL HIM NAMES! HE'S MY HUSBAND!!
Y-YEAH?
YEAH!!
WE'VE BEEN TRYING TO INJECT A LITTLE EXCITEMENT INTO OUR DRAB LIVES BY ACTING OUT SOME OF OUR FANTASIES, SEE?!
FRANKLY-- NO.
I STAND OUT HERE, ALL ALONE, 'TIL I GET GOOD AND SCARED--
--THEN ROD ATTACKS ME!

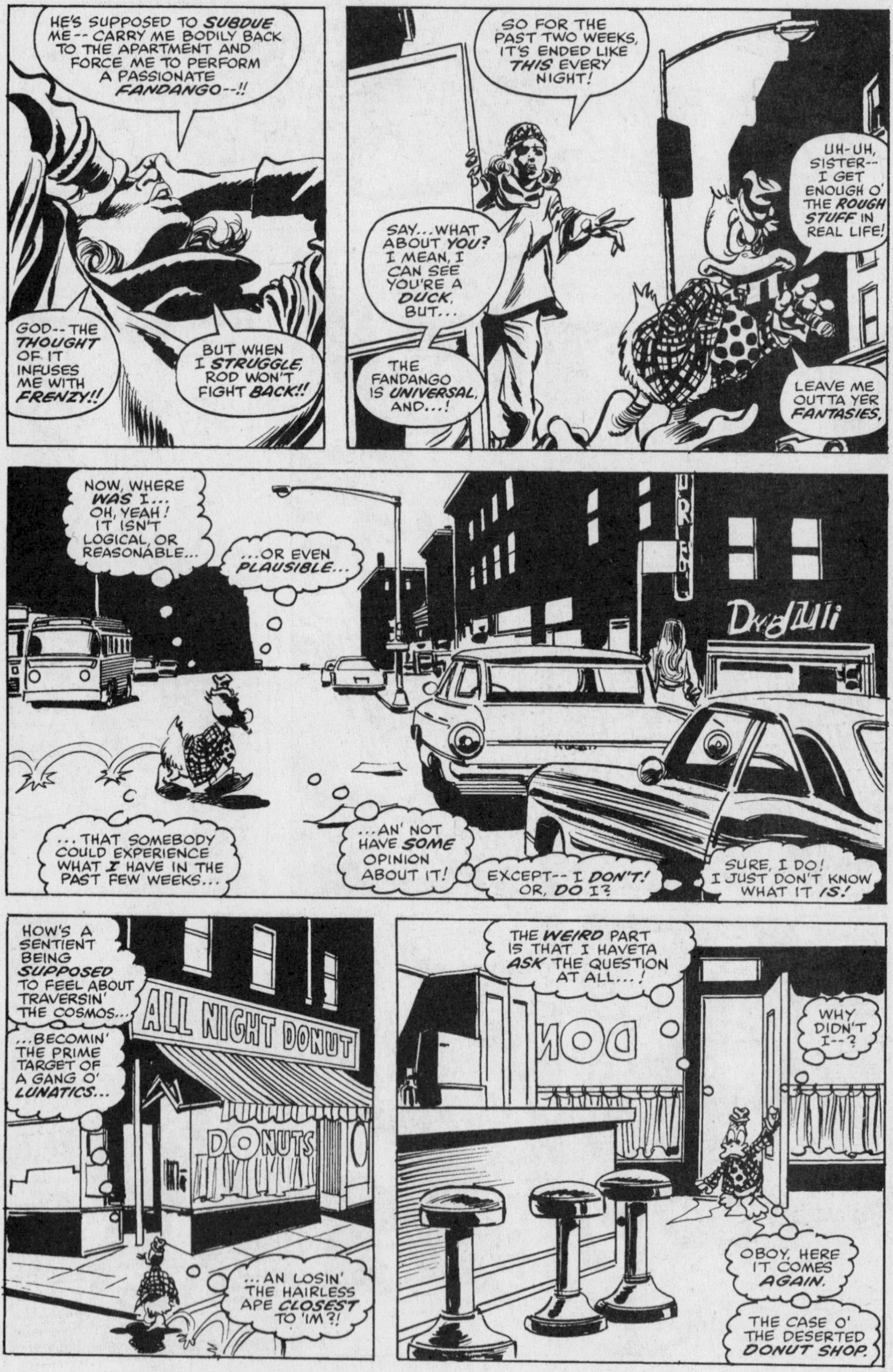
HE'S SUPPOSED TO SUBDUE ME-- CARRY ME BODILY BACK TO THE APARTMENT AND FORCE ME TO PERFORM A PASSIONATE FANDANGO--!!
GOD-- THE THOUGHT OF IT INFUSES ME WITH FRENZY!!
BUT WHEN I STRUGGLE, ROD WON'T FIGHT BACK!!
SO FOR THE PAST TWO WEEKS, IT'S ENDED LIKE THIS EVERY NIGHT!
UH-UH, SISTER-- I GET ENOUGH O' THE ROUGH STUFF IN REAL LIFE!
SAY... WHAT ABOUT YOU? I MEAN, I CAN SEE YOU'RE A DUCK, BUT...
THE FANDANGO IS UNIVERSAL, AND...!
LEAVE ME OUTTA YER FANTASIES.
NOW, WHERE WAS I... OH, YEAH! IT ISN'T LOGICAL, OR REASONABLE...
...OR EVEN PLAUSIBLE...
... THAT SOMEBODY COULD EXPERIENCE WHAT I HAVE IN THE PAST FEW WEEKS...
...AN' NOT HAVE SOME OPINION ABOUT IT!
EXCEPT-- I DON'T! OR, DO I?
SURE, I DO! I JUST DON'T KNOW WHAT IT IS!
HOW'S A SENTIENT BEING SUPPOSED TO FEEL ABOUT TRAVERSIN' THE COSMOS...
...BECOMIN' THE PRIME TARGET OF A GANG O' LUNATICS...
ALL NIGHT DONUT
DONUTS
...AN LOSIN' THE HAIRLESS APE CLOSEST TO 'IM?!
THE WEIRD PART IS THAT I HAVETA ASK THE QUESTION AT ALL...!
WHY DIDN'T I--?
OBOY, HERE IT COMES AGAIN.
THE CASE O' THE DESERTED DONUT SHOP.

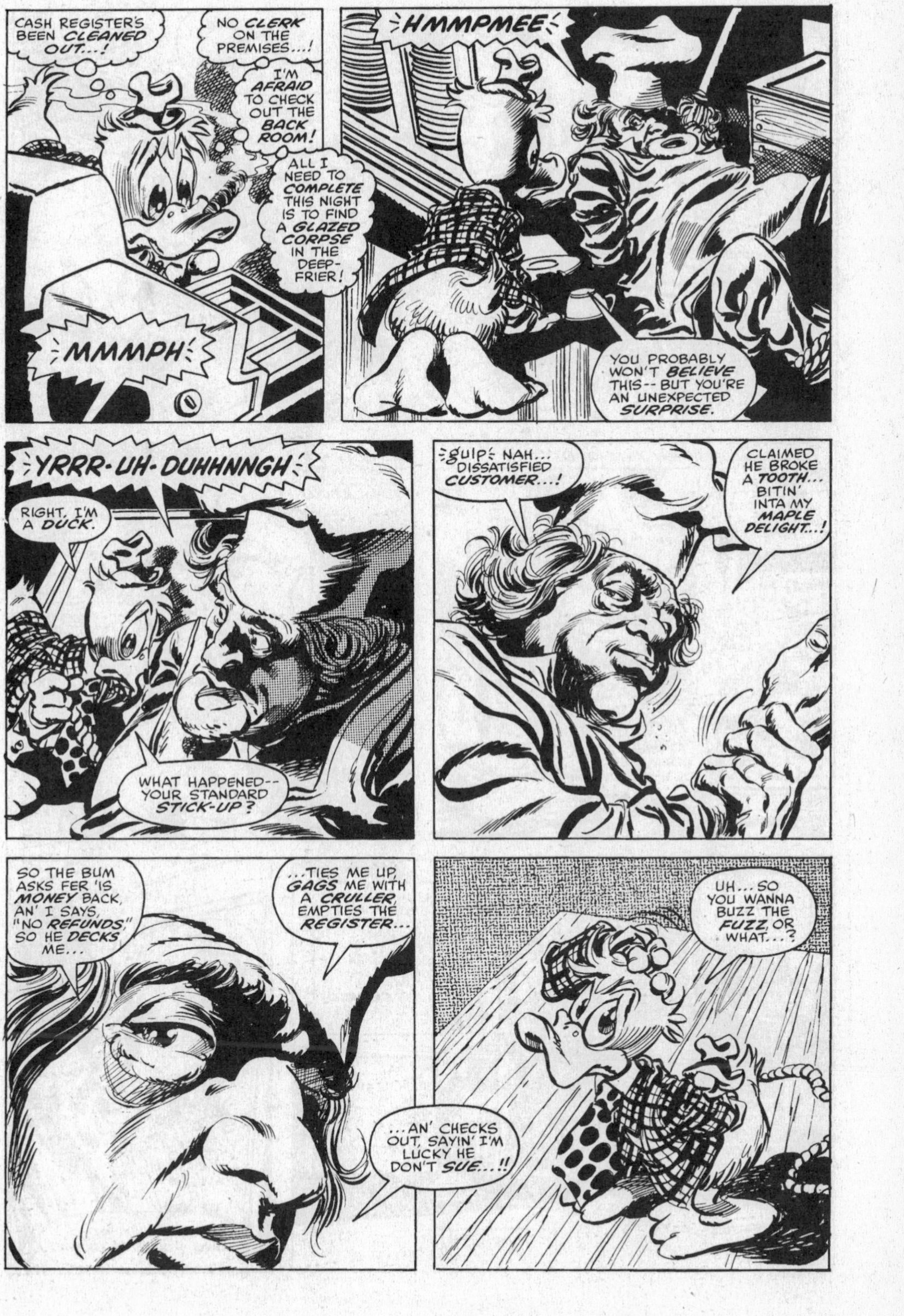

CASH REGISTER'S BEEN CLEANED OUT...!
NO CLERK ON THE PREMISES...!
I'M AFRAID TO CHECK OUT THE BACK ROOM!
ALL I NEED TO COMPLETE THIS NIGHT IS TO FIND A GLAZED CORPSE IN THE DEEP-FRIER!
MMMPH
HMMMPMEE
YOU PROBABLY WON'T BELIEVE THIS-- BUT YOU'RE AN UNEXPECTED SURPRISE.
YRRR-UH-DUHHNNGH
RIGHT, I'M A DUCK.
WHAT HAPPENED-- YOUR STANDARD STICK-UP?
gulp NAH... DISSATISFIED CUSTOMER...!
CLAIMED HE BROKE A TOOTH... BITIN' INTA MY MAPLE DELIGHT...!
SO THE BUM ASKS FER 'IS MONEY BACK, AN' I SAYS, "NO REFUNDS," SO HE DECKS ME...
...TIES ME UP, GAGS ME WITH A CRULLER, EMPTIES THE REGISTER...
...AN' CHECKS OUT, SAYIN' I'M LUCKY HE DON'T SUE...!!
UH... SO YOU WANNA BUZZ THE FUZZ, OR WHAT...?

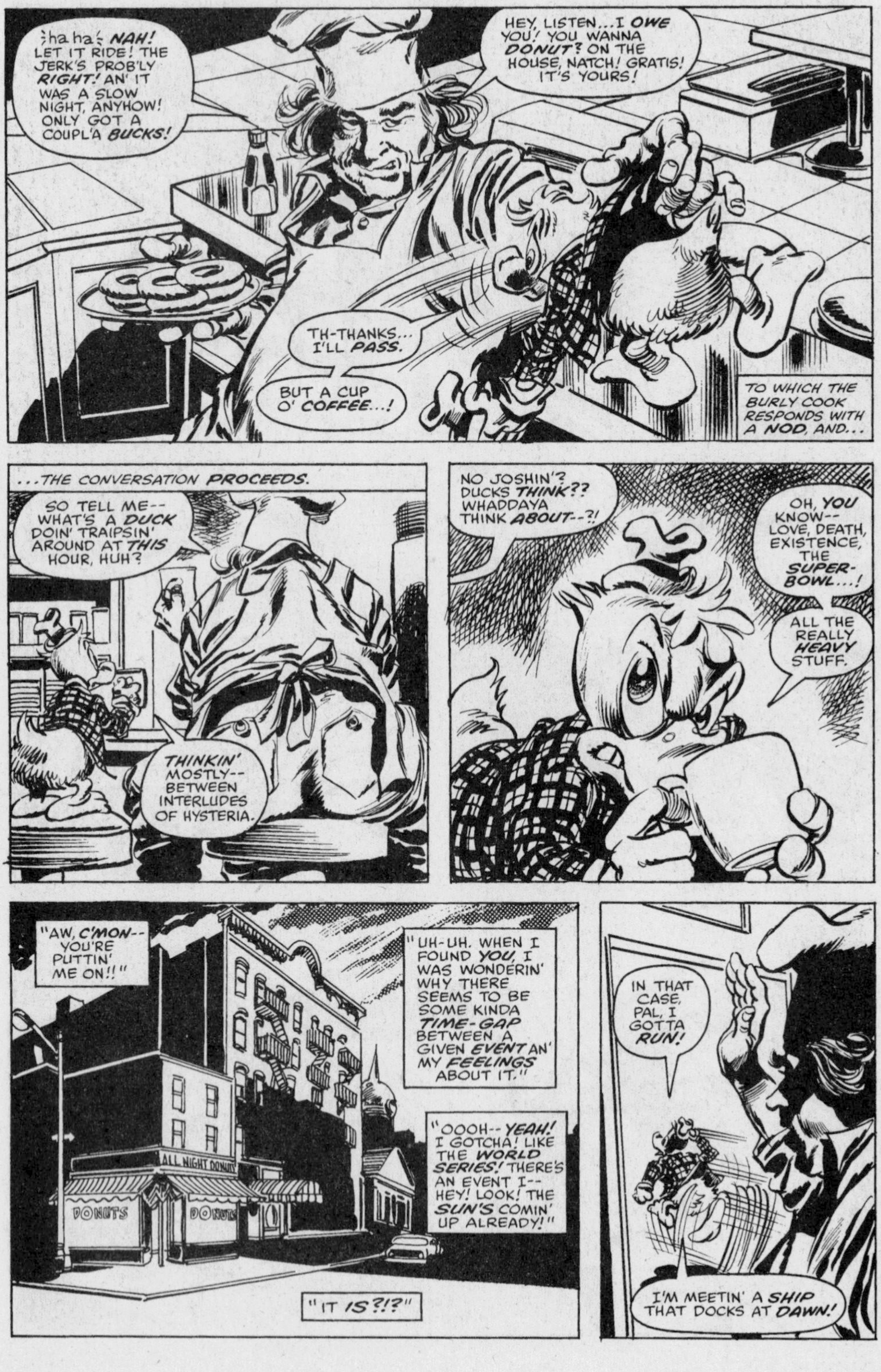

ha ha NAH! LET IT RIDE! THE JERK'S PROB'LY RIGHT! AN' IT WAS A SLOW NIGHT, ANYHOW! ONLY GOT A COUPL'A BUCKS!
HEY, LISTEN...I OWE YOU! YOU WANNA DONUT? ON THE HOUSE, NATCH! GRATIS! IT'S YOURS!
TH-THANKS... I'LL PASS.
BUT A CUP O' COFFEE...!
TO WHICH THE BURLY COOK RESPONDS WITH A NOD, AND...
...THE CONVERSATION PROCEEDS.
SO TELL ME-- WHAT'S A DUCK DOIN' TRAIPSIN' AROUND AT THIS HOUR, HUH?
THINKIN' MOSTLY-- BETWEEN INTERLUDES OF HYSTERIA.
NO JOSHIN'? DUCKS THINK?? WHADDAYA THINK ABOUT--?!
OH, YOU KNOW-- LOVE, DEATH, EXISTENCE, THE SUPER-BOWL...!
ALL THE REALLY HEAVY STUFF.
"AW, C'MON-- YOU'RE PUTTIN' ME ON!!"
"UH-UH. WHEN I FOUND YOU, I WAS WONDERIN' WHY THERE SEEMS TO BE SOME KINDA TIME-GAP BETWEEN A GIVEN EVENT AN' MY FEELINGS ABOUT IT."
"OOOH-- YEAH! I GOTCHA! LIKE THE WORLD SERIES! THERE'S AN EVENT I-- HEY! LOOK! THE SUN'S COMIN' UP ALREADY!"
ALL NIGHT DONUTS
DONUTS
DONUTS
"IT IS?!?"
IN THAT CASE, PAL, I GOTTA RUN!
I'M MEETIN' A SHIP THAT DOCKS AT DAWN!

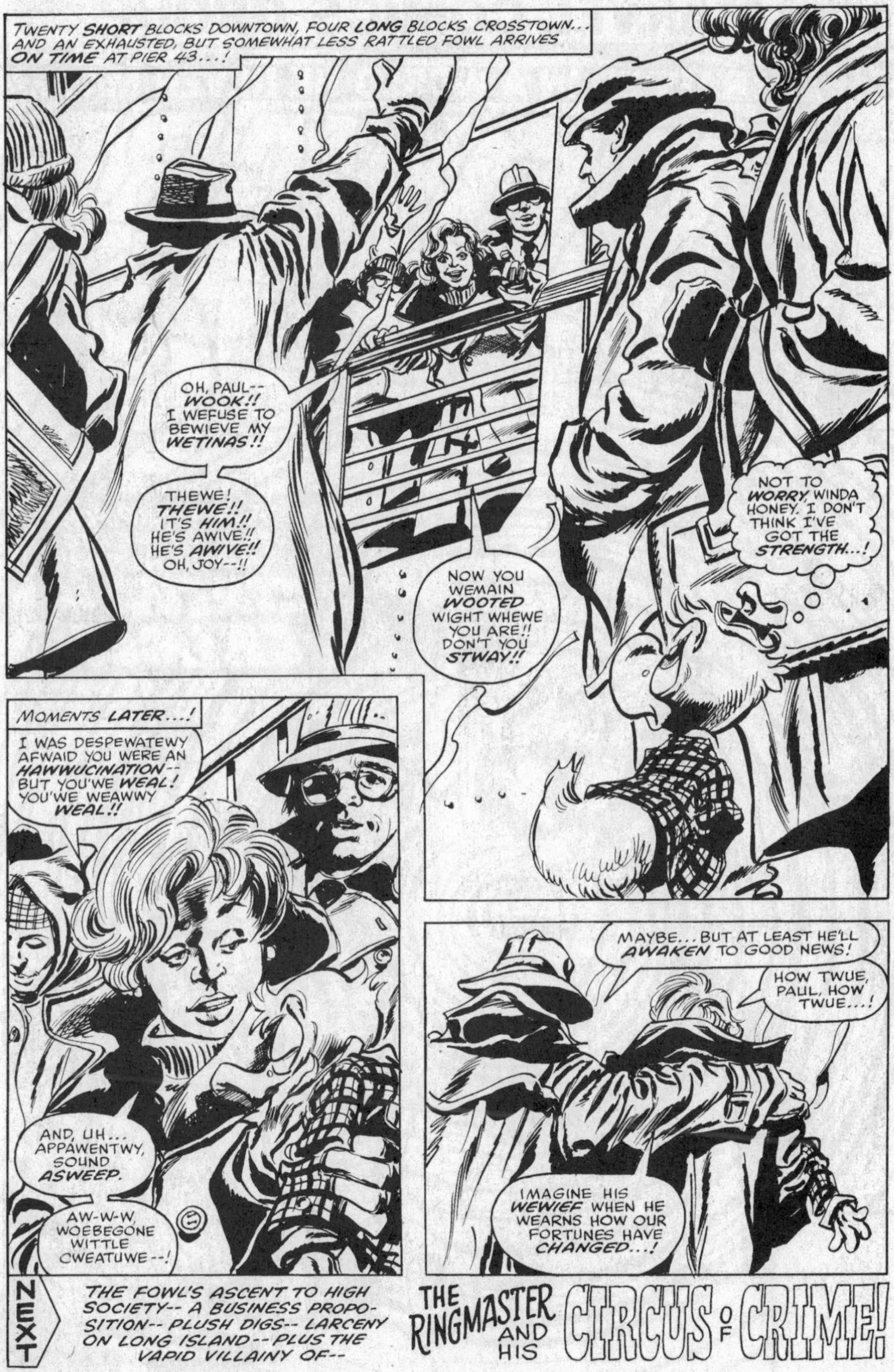

TWENTY SHORT BLOCKS DOWNTOWN, FOUR LONG BLOCKS CROSSTOWN... AND AN EXHAUSTED, BUT SOMEWHAT LESS RATTLED FOWL ARRIVES ON TIME AT PIER 43...!
OH, PAUL-- WOOK!! I WEFUSE TO BEWIEVE MY WETINAS!!
THEWE! THEWE!! IT'S HIM!! HE'S AWIVE!! HE'S AWIVE!! OH, JOY--!!
NOW YOU WEMAIN WOOTED WIGHT WHEWE YOU ARE!! DON'T YOU STWAY!!
NOT TO WORRY, WINDA HONEY. I DON'T THINK I'VE GOT THE STRENGTH...!
MOMENTS LATER...!
I WAS DESPEWATEWY AFWAID YOU WERE AN HAWWUCINATION-- BUT YOU'WE WEAL! YOU'WE WEAWWY WEAL!!
AND, UH... APPAWENTWY, SOUND ASWEEP.
AW-W-W, WOEBEGONE WITTLE CWEATUWE--!
MAYBE... BUT AT LEAST HE'LL AWAKEN TO GOOD NEWS!
HOW TWUE, PAUL, HOW TWUE...!
IMAGINE HIS WEWIEF WHEN HE WEARNS HOW OUR FORTUNES HAVE CHANGED...!
NEXT
THE FOWL'S ASCENT TO HIGH SOCIETY-- A BUSINESS PROPOSITION-- PLUSH DIGS-- LARCENY ON LONG ISLAND-- PLUS THE VAPID VILLAINY OF--
THE RINGMASTER AND HIS CIRCUS OF CRIME!

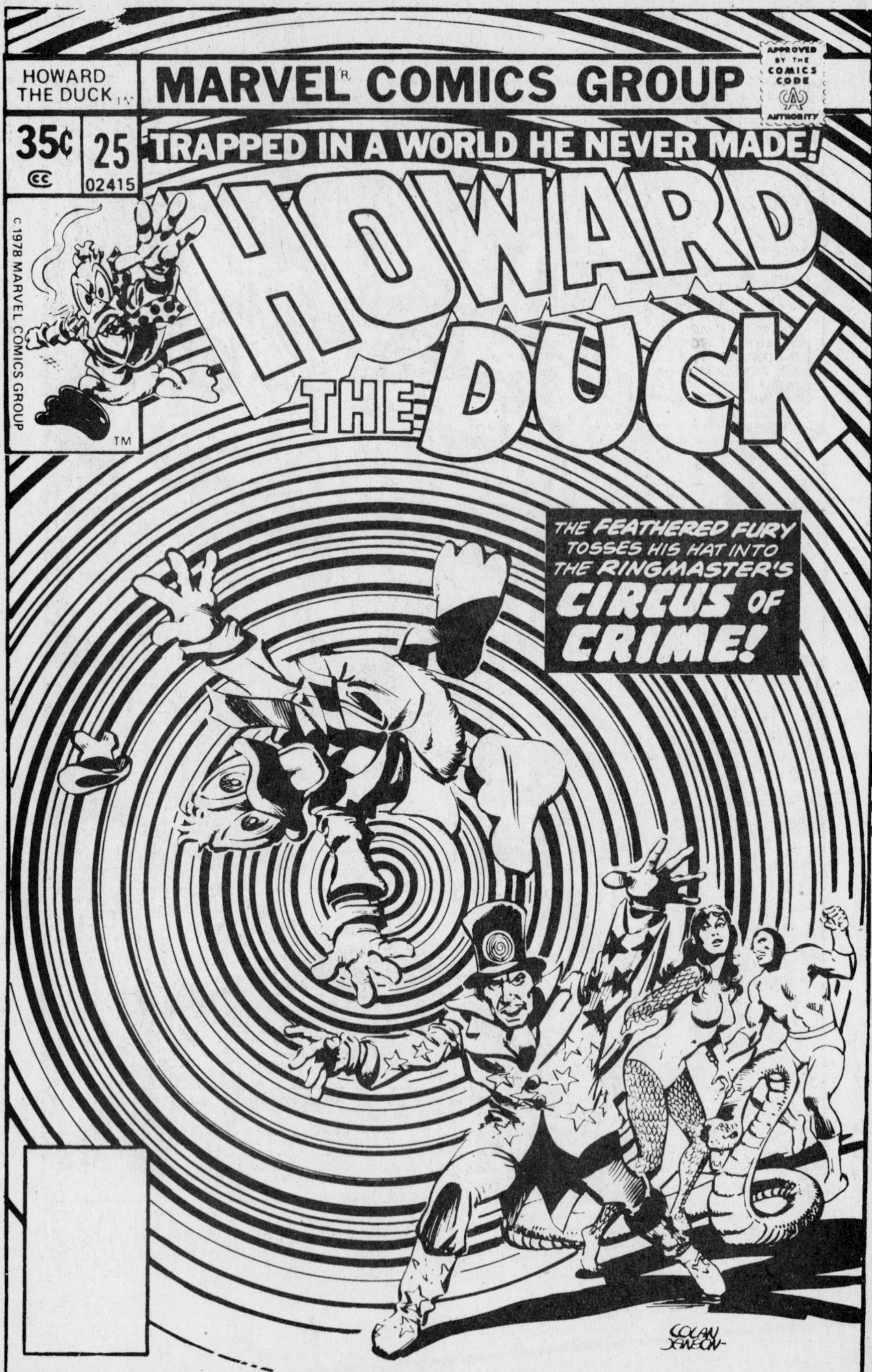
HOWARD THE DUCK
MARVEL COMICS GROUP
APPROVED BY THE COMICS CODE AUTHORITY
35¢
25
02415
TRAPPED IN A WORLD HE NEVER MADE!
c 1978 MARVEL COMICS GROUP
HOWARD THE DUCK
TM
THE FEATHERED FURY TOSSES HIS HAT INTO THE RINGMASTER'S CIRCUS OF CRIME!
COLAN JANSON

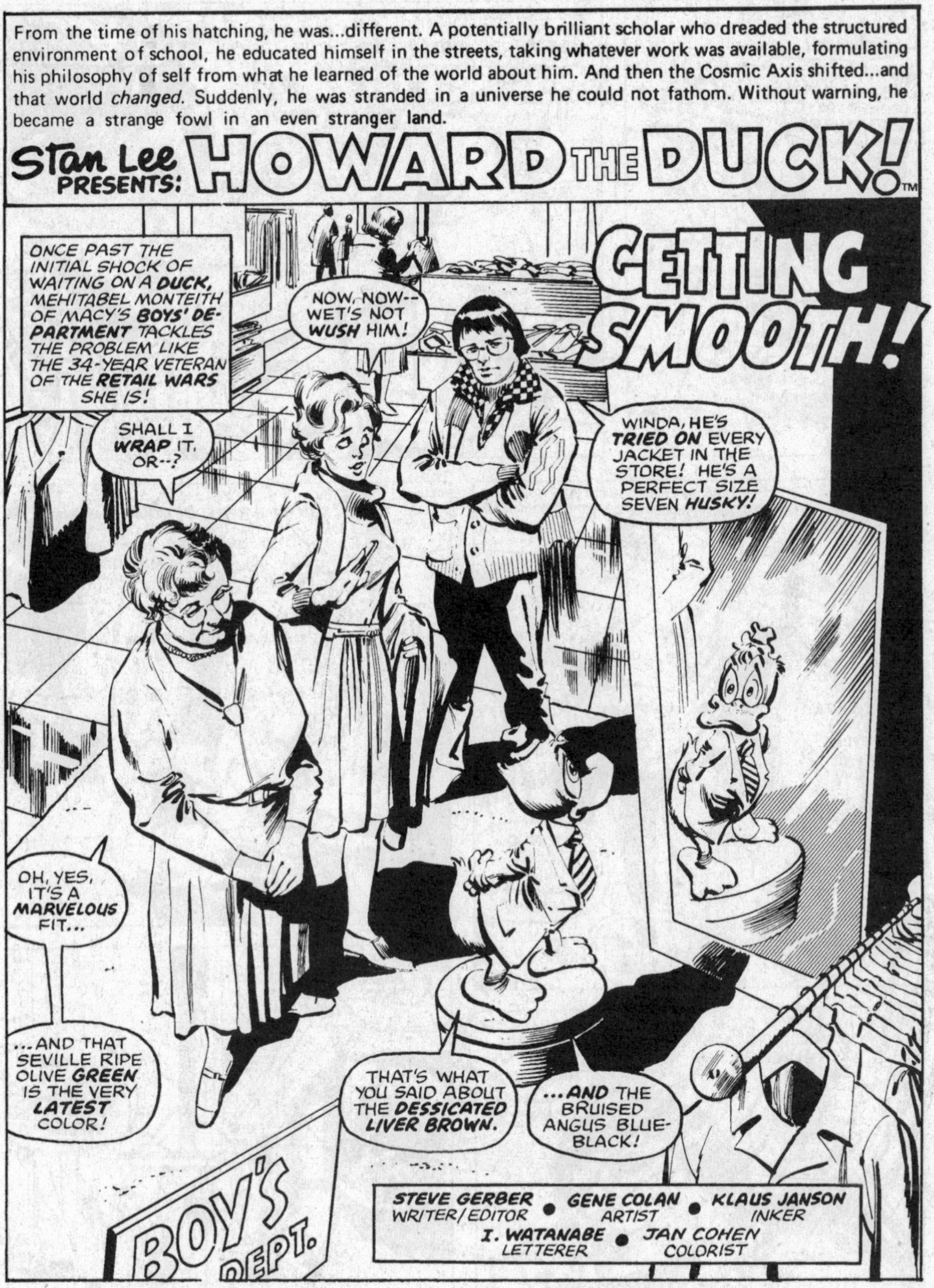
From the time of his hatching, he was...different. A potentially brilliant scholar who dreaded the structured environment of school, he educated himself in the streets, taking whatever work was available, formulating his philosophy of self from what he learned of the world about him. And then the Cosmic Axis shifted...and that world *changed.* Suddenly, he was stranded in a universe he could not fathom. Without warning, he became a strange fowl in an even stranger land.
Stan Lee PRESENTS: HOWARD THE DUCK! TM
GETTING SMOOTH!
ONCE PAST THE INITIAL SHOCK OF WAITING ON A **DUCK**, MEHITABEL MONTEITH OF MACY'S **BOYS' DEPARTMENT** TACKLES THE PROBLEM LIKE THE 34-YEAR VETERAN OF THE **RETAIL WARS** SHE IS!
NOW, NOW-- WET'S NOT **WUSH** HIM!
SHALL I **WRAP** IT, OR--?
WINDA, HE'S **TRIED ON** EVERY JACKET IN THE STORE! HE'S A PERFECT SIZE SEVEN **HUSKY!**
OH, YES, IT'S A **MARVELOUS** FIT...
...AND THAT SEVILLE RIPE OLIVE **GREEN** IS THE VERY **LATEST** COLOR!
THAT'S WHAT YOU SAID ABOUT THE **DESSICATED LIVER BROWN.**
...**AND** THE BRUISED ANGUS BLUE-BLACK!
BOY'S DEPT.
STEVE GERBER WRITER/EDITOR • GENE COLAN ARTIST • KLAUS JANSON INKER
I. WATANABE LETTERER • JAN COHEN COLORIST

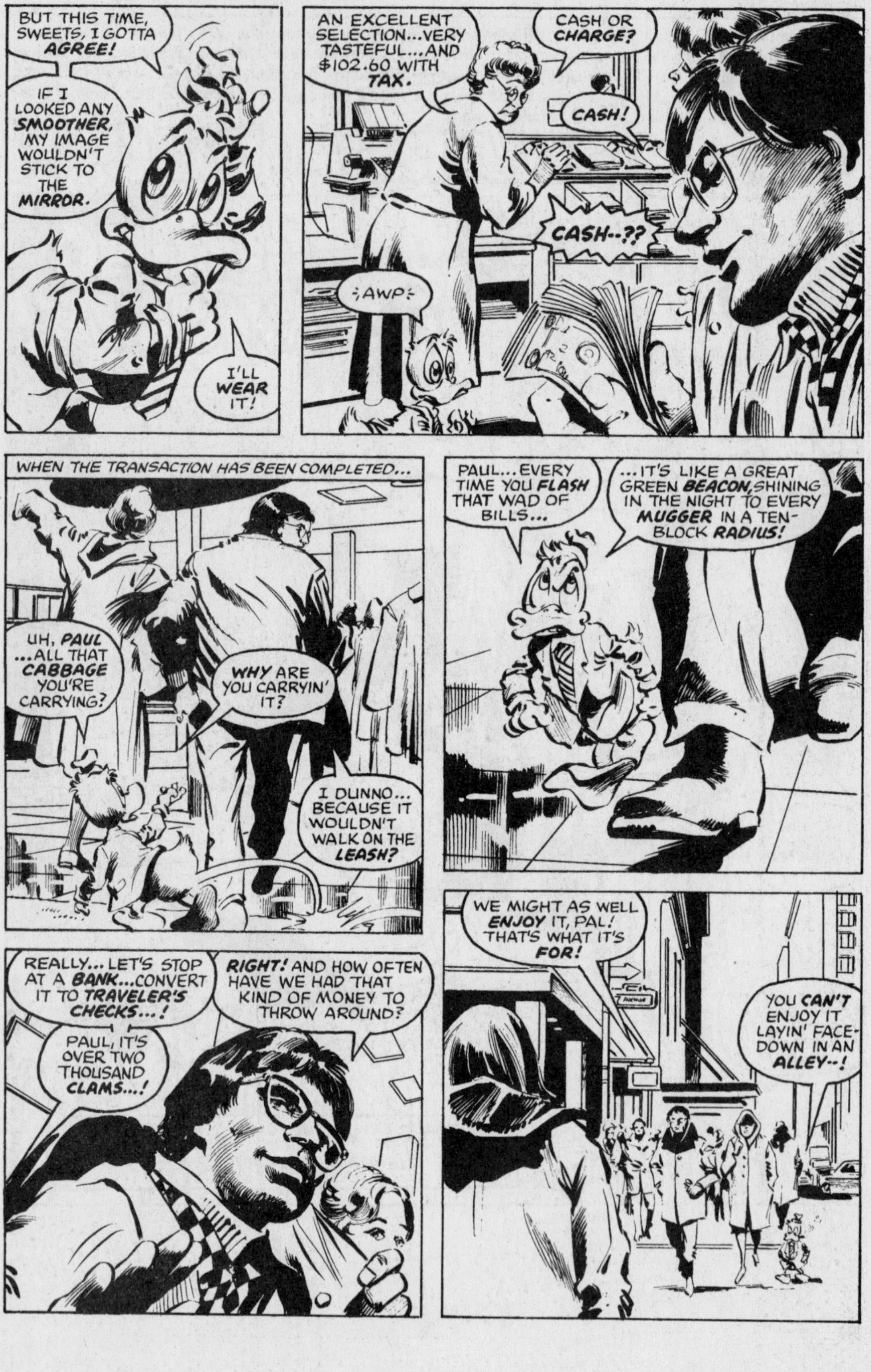

BUT THIS TIME, SWEETS, I GOTTA AGREE!
IF I LOOKED ANY SMOOTHER, MY IMAGE WOULDN'T STICK TO THE MIRROR.
I'LL WEAR IT!
AN EXCELLENT SELECTION... VERY TASTEFUL... AND $102.60 WITH TAX.
CASH OR CHARGE?
CASH!
CASH--??
AWP
WHEN THE TRANSACTION HAS BEEN COMPLETED...
UH, PAUL ...ALL THAT CABBAGE YOU'RE CARRYING?
WHY ARE YOU CARRYIN' IT?
I DUNNO... BECAUSE IT WOULDN'T WALK ON THE LEASH?
PAUL... EVERY TIME YOU FLASH THAT WAD OF BILLS...
...IT'S LIKE A GREAT GREEN BEACON, SHINING IN THE NIGHT TO EVERY MUGGER IN A TEN-BLOCK RADIUS!
REALLY... LET'S STOP AT A BANK... CONVERT IT TO TRAVELER'S CHECKS...!
RIGHT! AND HOW OFTEN HAVE WE HAD THAT KIND OF MONEY TO THROW AROUND?
PAUL, IT'S OVER TWO THOUSAND CLAMS...!
WE MIGHT AS WELL ENJOY IT, PAL! THAT'S WHAT IT'S FOR!
YOU CAN'T ENJOY IT LAYIN' FACE-DOWN IN AN ALLEY--!

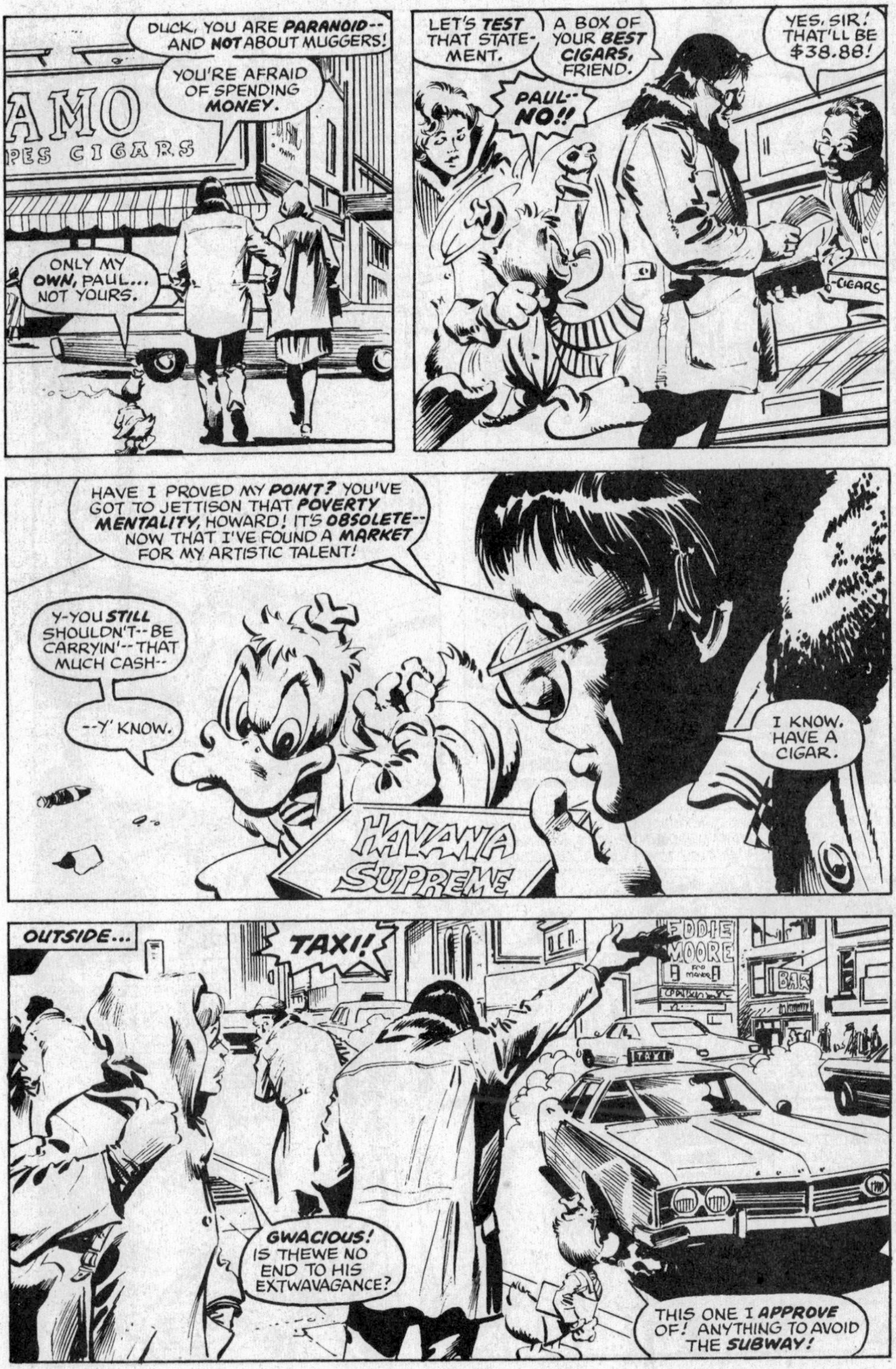
DUCK, YOU ARE PARANOID-- AND NOT ABOUT MUGGERS!
YOU'RE AFRAID OF SPENDING MONEY.
AMO
PES CIGARS
ONLY MY OWN, PAUL... NOT YOURS.
LET'S TEST THAT STATEMENT.
A BOX OF YOUR BEST CIGARS, FRIEND.
YES, SIR! THAT'LL BE $38.88!
PAUL-- NO!!
CIGARS
HAVE I PROVED MY POINT? YOU'VE GOT TO JETTISON THAT POVERTY MENTALITY, HOWARD! IT'S OBSOLETE-- NOW THAT I'VE FOUND A MARKET FOR MY ARTISTIC TALENT!
Y-YOU STILL SHOULDN'T--BE CARRYIN'--THAT MUCH CASH--
--Y' KNOW.
I KNOW. HAVE A CIGAR.
HAVANA SUPREME
OUTSIDE...
TAXI!!
EDDIE MOORE
TAXI
GWACIOUS! IS THEWE NO END TO HIS EXTWAVAGANCE?
THIS ONE I APPROVE OF! ANYTHING TO AVOID THE SUBWAY!

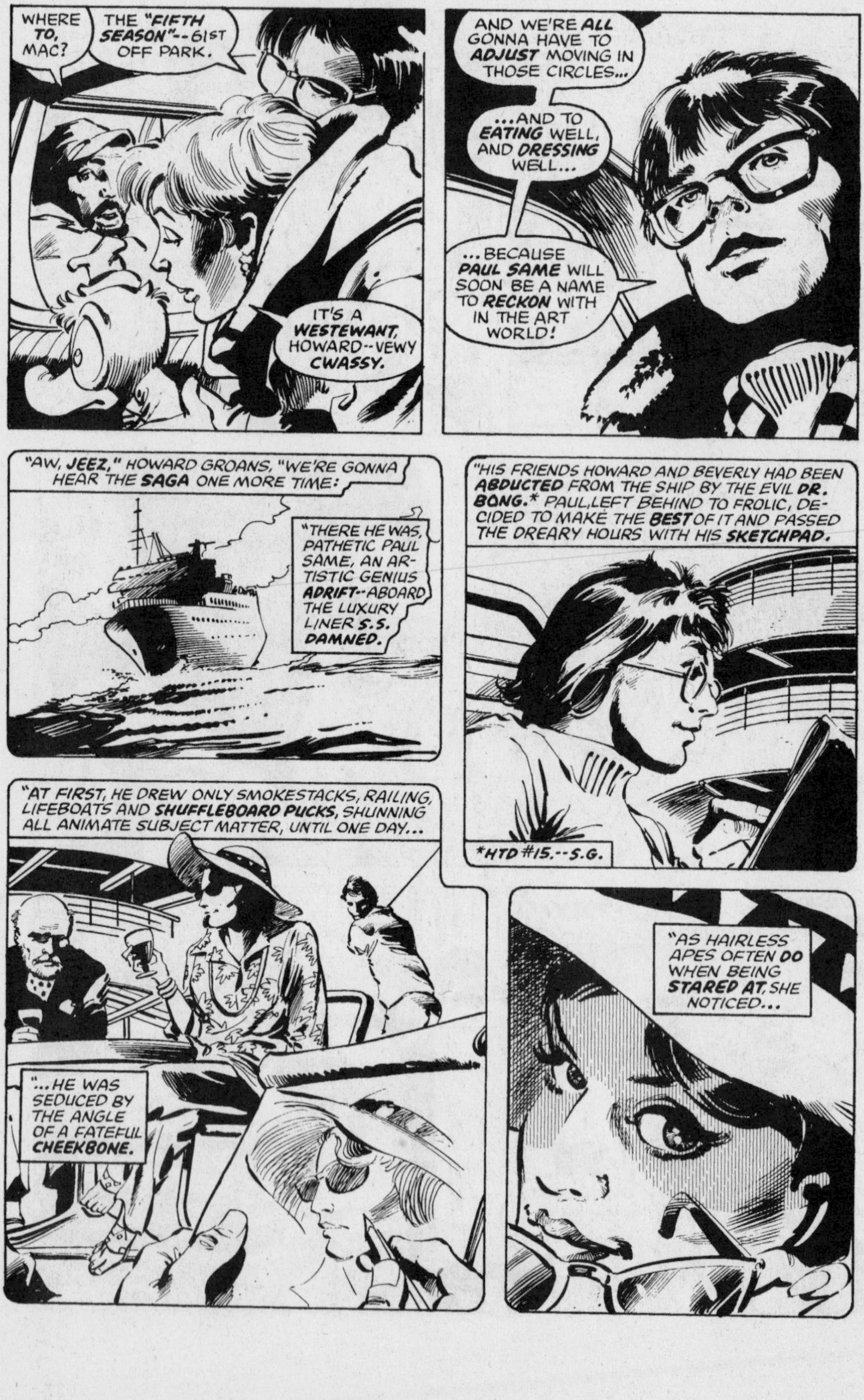
WHERE TO, MAC?
THE "FIFTH SEASON"-- 61ST OFF PARK.
IT'S A WESTEWANT, HOWARD--VEWY CWASSY.
AND WE'RE ALL GONNA HAVE TO ADJUST MOVING IN THOSE CIRCLES...
...AND TO EATING WELL, AND DRESSING WELL...
...BECAUSE PAUL SAME WILL SOON BE A NAME TO RECKON WITH IN THE ART WORLD!
"AW, JEEZ," HOWARD GROANS, "WE'RE GONNA HEAR THE SAGA ONE MORE TIME:
"THERE HE WAS, PATHETIC PAUL SAME, AN ARTISTIC GENIUS ADRIFT--ABOARD THE LUXURY LINER S.S. DAMNED.
"HIS FRIENDS HOWARD AND BEVERLY HAD BEEN ABDUCTED FROM THE SHIP BY THE EVIL DR. BONG.* PAUL, LEFT BEHIND TO FROLIC, DECIDED TO MAKE THE BEST OF IT AND PASSED THE DREARY HOURS WITH HIS SKETCHPAD.
*HTD #15.--S.G.
"AT FIRST, HE DREW ONLY SMOKESTACKS, RAILING, LIFEBOATS AND SHUFFLEBOARD PUCKS, SHUNNING ALL ANIMATE SUBJECT MATTER, UNTIL ONE DAY...
"...HE WAS SEDUCED BY THE ANGLE OF A FATEFUL CHEEKBONE.
"AS HAIRLESS APES OFTEN DO WHEN BEING STARED AT, SHE NOTICED...

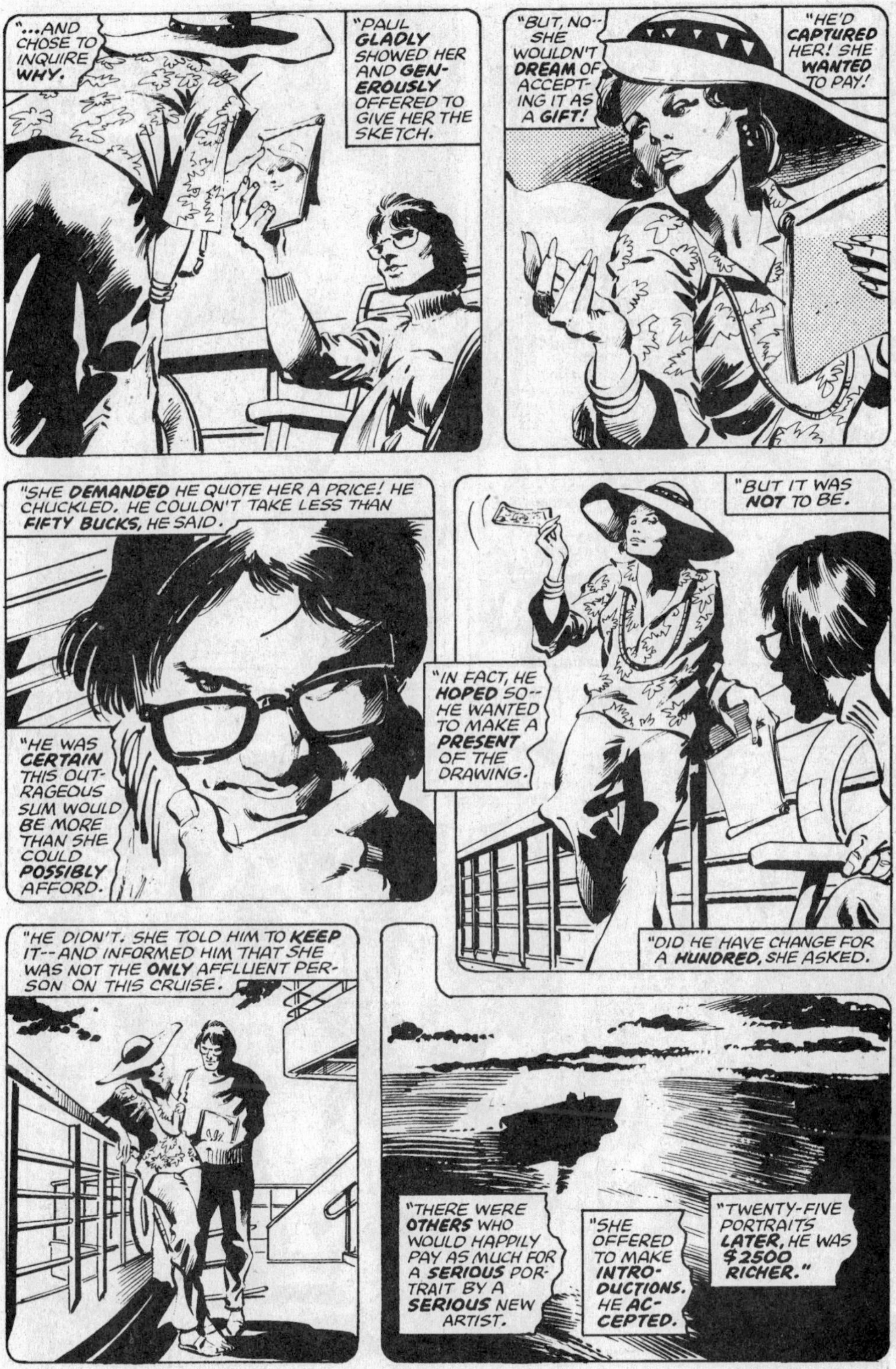

"...AND CHOSE TO INQUIRE WHY.
"PAUL GLADLY SHOWED HER AND GENEROUSLY OFFERED TO GIVE HER THE SKETCH.
"BUT, NO--SHE WOULDN'T DREAM OF ACCEPTING IT AS A GIFT!
"HE'D CAPTURED HER! SHE WANTED TO PAY!
"SHE DEMANDED HE QUOTE HER A PRICE! HE CHUCKLED. HE COULDN'T TAKE LESS THAN FIFTY BUCKS, HE SAID.
"HE WAS CERTAIN THIS OUTRAGEOUS SUM WOULD BE MORE THAN SHE COULD POSSIBLY AFFORD.
"IN FACT, HE HOPED SO--HE WANTED TO MAKE A PRESENT OF THE DRAWING.
"BUT IT WAS NOT TO BE.
"DID HE HAVE CHANGE FOR A HUNDRED, SHE ASKED.
"HE DIDN'T. SHE TOLD HIM TO KEEP IT--AND INFORMED HIM THAT SHE WAS NOT THE ONLY AFFLUENT PERSON ON THIS CRUISE.
"THERE WERE OTHERS WHO WOULD HAPPILY PAY AS MUCH FOR A SERIOUS PORTRAIT BY A SERIOUS NEW ARTIST.
"SHE OFFERED TO MAKE INTRODUCTIONS. HE ACCEPTED.
"TWENTY-FIVE PORTRAITS LATER, HE WAS $2500 RICHER."

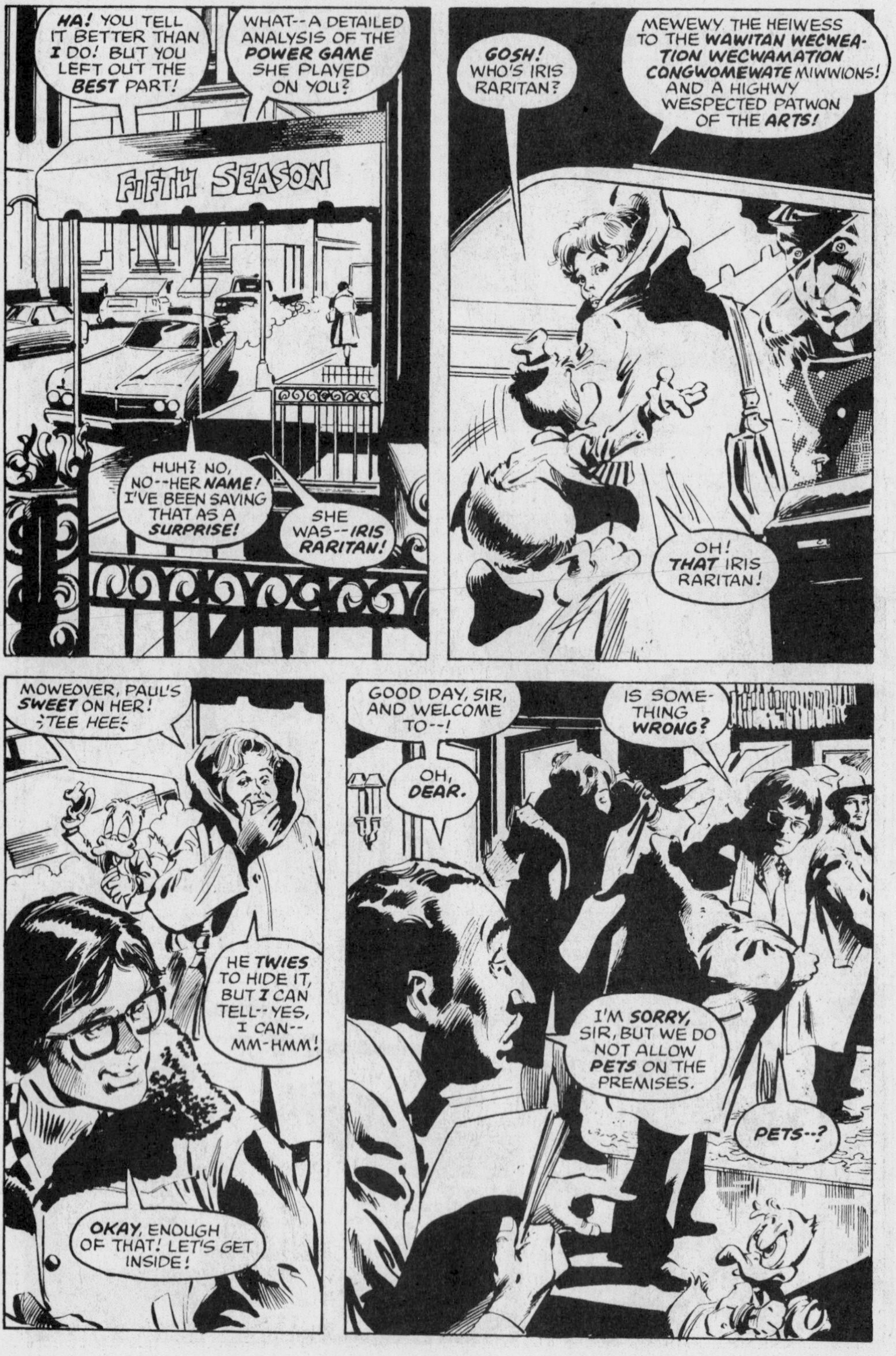
HA! YOU TELL IT BETTER THAN I DO! BUT YOU LEFT OUT THE BEST PART!
WHAT--A DETAILED ANALYSIS OF THE POWER GAME SHE PLAYED ON YOU?
FIFTH SEASON
HUH? NO, NO--HER NAME! I'VE BEEN SAVING THAT AS A SURPRISE!
SHE WAS--IRIS RARITAN!
GOSH! WHO'S IRIS RARITAN?
MEWEWY THE HEIWESS TO THE WAWITAN WECWEATION WECWAMATION CONGWOMEWATE MIWWIONS! AND A HIGHWY WESPECTED PATWON OF THE ARTS!
OH! THAT IRIS RARITAN!
MOWEOVER, PAUL'S SWEET ON HER! TEE HEE
HE TWIES TO HIDE IT, BUT I CAN TELL--YES, I CAN--MM-HMM!
OKAY, ENOUGH OF THAT! LET'S GET INSIDE!
GOOD DAY, SIR, AND WELCOME TO--!
OH, DEAR.
IS SOMETHING WRONG?
I'M SORRY, SIR, BUT WE DO NOT ALLOW PETS ON THE PREMISES.
PETS--?

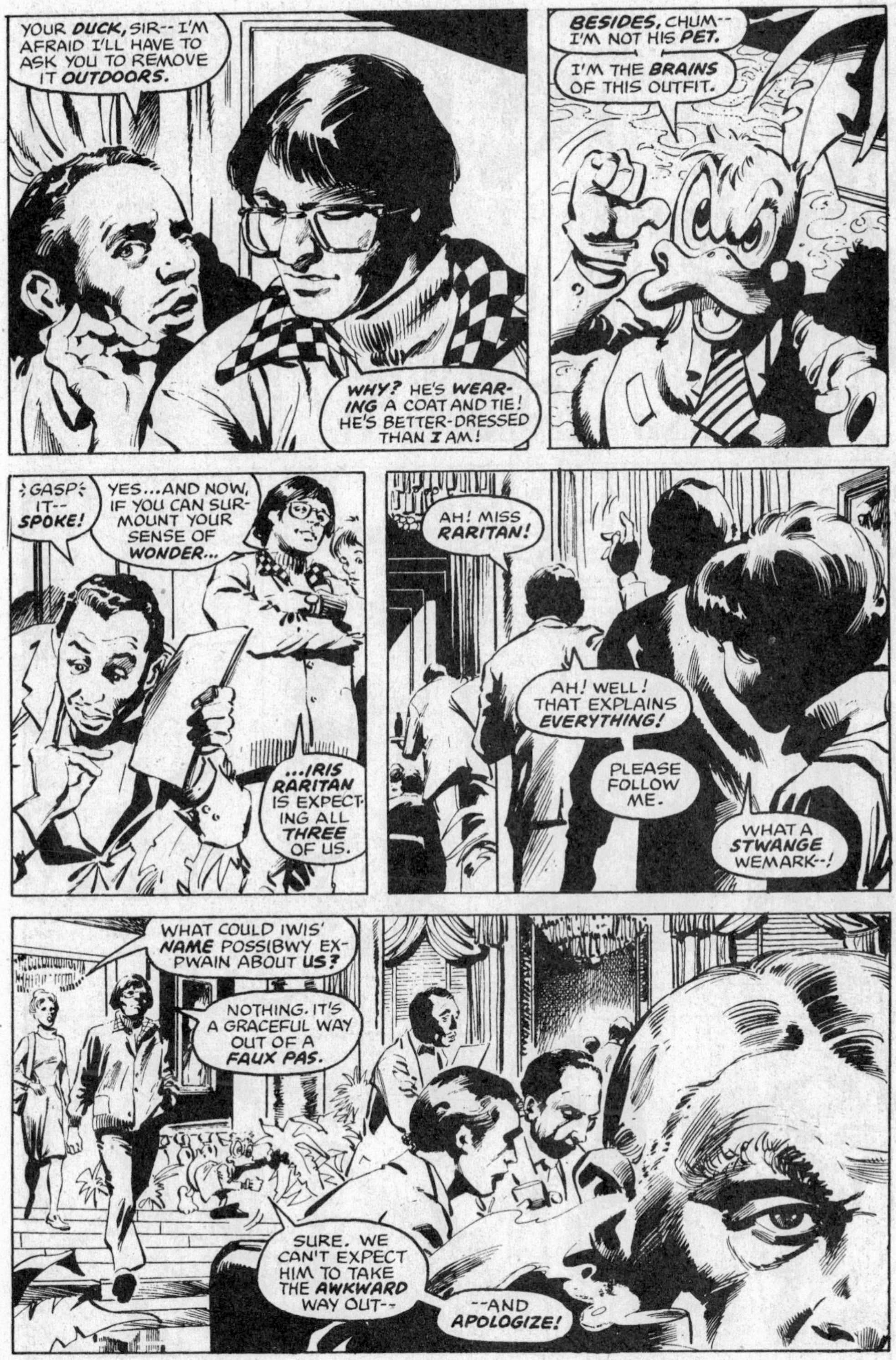
YOUR DUCK, SIR-- I'M AFRAID I'LL HAVE TO ASK YOU TO REMOVE IT OUTDOORS.
WHY? HE'S WEARING A COAT AND TIE! HE'S BETTER-DRESSED THAN I AM!
BESIDES, CHUM-- I'M NOT HIS PET.
I'M THE BRAINS OF THIS OUTFIT.
GASP IT-- SPOKE!
YES...AND NOW, IF YOU CAN SURMOUNT YOUR SENSE OF WONDER...
...IRIS RARITAN IS EXPECTING ALL THREE OF US.
AH! MISS RARITAN!
AH! WELL! THAT EXPLAINS EVERYTHING!
PLEASE FOLLOW ME.
WHAT A STWANGE WEMARK--!
WHAT COULD IWIS' NAME POSSIBWY EXPWAIN ABOUT US?
NOTHING. IT'S A GRACEFUL WAY OUT OF A FAUX PAS.
SURE. WE CAN'T EXPECT HIM TO TAKE THE AWKWARD WAY OUT--
--AND APOLOGIZE!

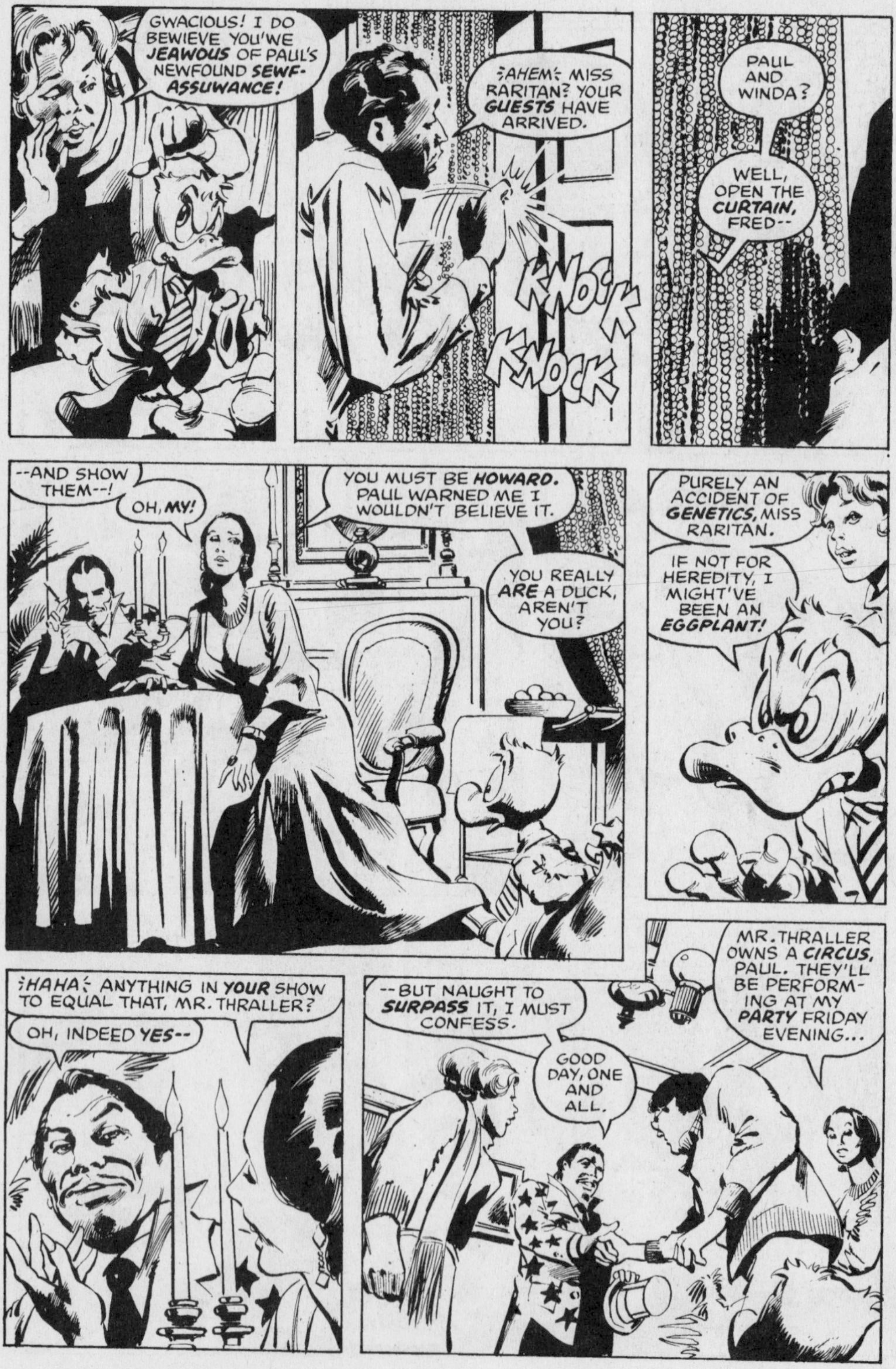
GWACIOUS! I DO BEWIEVE YOU'WE JEAWOUS OF PAUL'S NEWFOUND SEWF-ASSUWANCE!
AHEM MISS RARITAN? YOUR GUESTS HAVE ARRIVED.
KNOCK
KNOCK
PAUL AND WINDA?
WELL, OPEN THE CURTAIN, FRED--
--AND SHOW THEM--!
OH, MY!
YOU MUST BE HOWARD. PAUL WARNED ME I WOULDN'T BELIEVE IT.
YOU REALLY ARE A DUCK, AREN'T YOU?
PURELY AN ACCIDENT OF GENETICS, MISS RARITAN.
IF NOT FOR HEREDITY, I MIGHT'VE BEEN AN EGGPLANT!
HAHA ANYTHING IN YOUR SHOW TO EQUAL THAT, MR. THRALLER?
OH, INDEED YES--
--BUT NAUGHT TO SURPASS IT, I MUST CONFESS.
GOOD DAY, ONE AND ALL.
MR. THRALLER OWNS A CIRCUS, PAUL. THEY'LL BE PERFORMING AT MY PARTY FRIDAY EVENING...

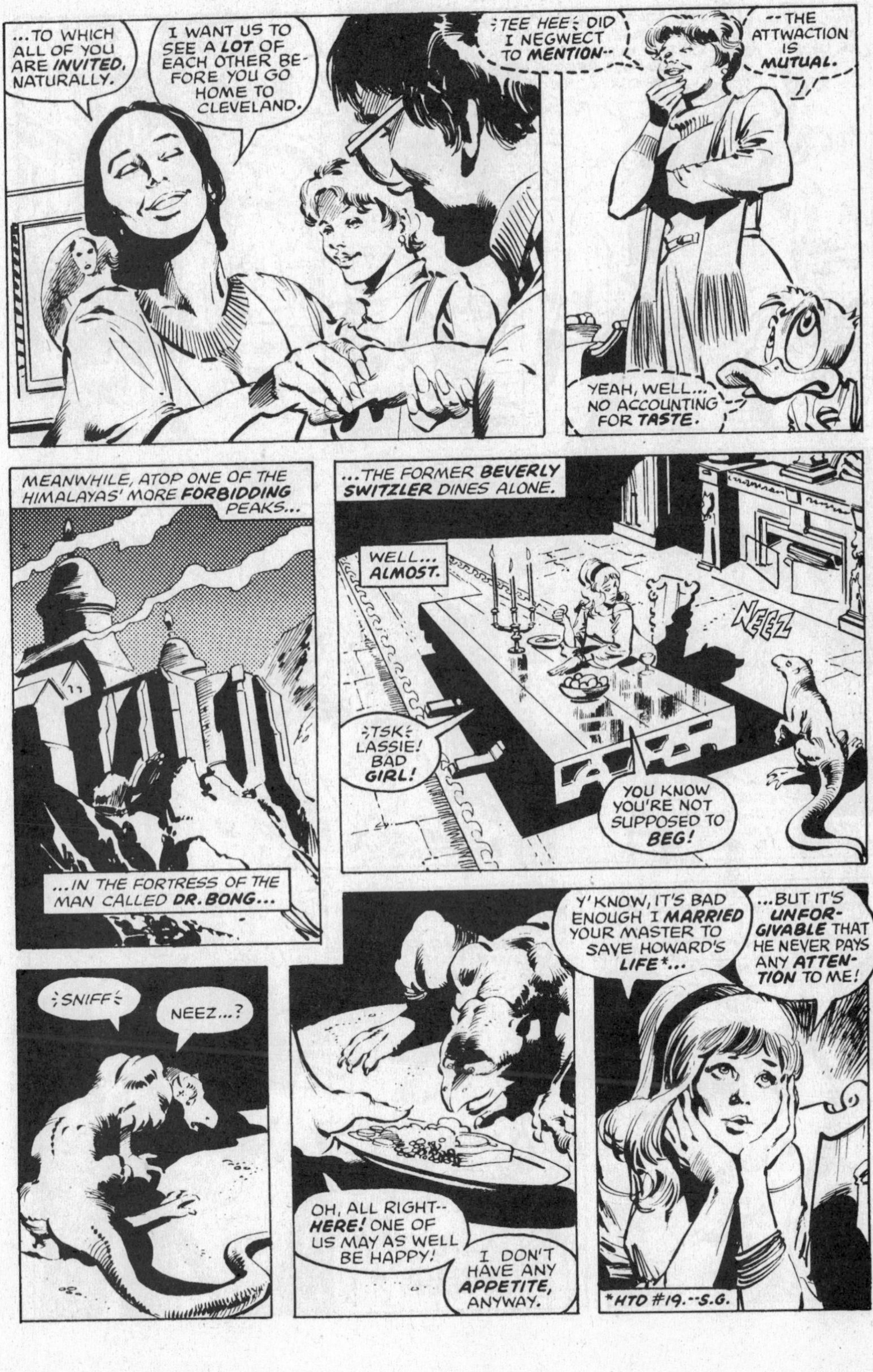
...TO WHICH ALL OF YOU ARE INVITED, NATURALLY.
I WANT US TO SEE A LOT OF EACH OTHER BEFORE YOU GO HOME TO CLEVELAND.
TEE HEE DID I NEGWECT TO MENTION--
--THE ATTWACTION IS MUTUAL.
YEAH, WELL... NO ACCOUNTING FOR TASTE.
MEANWHILE, ATOP ONE OF THE HIMALAYAS' MORE FORBIDDING PEAKS...
...IN THE FORTRESS OF THE MAN CALLED DR. BONG...
...THE FORMER BEVERLY SWITZLER DINES ALONE.
WELL... ALMOST.
NEEZ
TSK LASSIE! BAD GIRL!
YOU KNOW YOU'RE NOT SUPPOSED TO BEG!
SNIFF
NEEZ...?
OH, ALL RIGHT-- HERE! ONE OF US MAY AS WELL BE HAPPY!
I DON'T HAVE ANY APPETITE, ANYWAY.
Y'KNOW, IT'S BAD ENOUGH I MARRIED YOUR MASTER TO SAVE HOWARD'S LIFE*...
...BUT IT'S UNFORGIVABLE THAT HE NEVER PAYS ANY ATTENTION TO ME!
*HTD #19.--S.G.

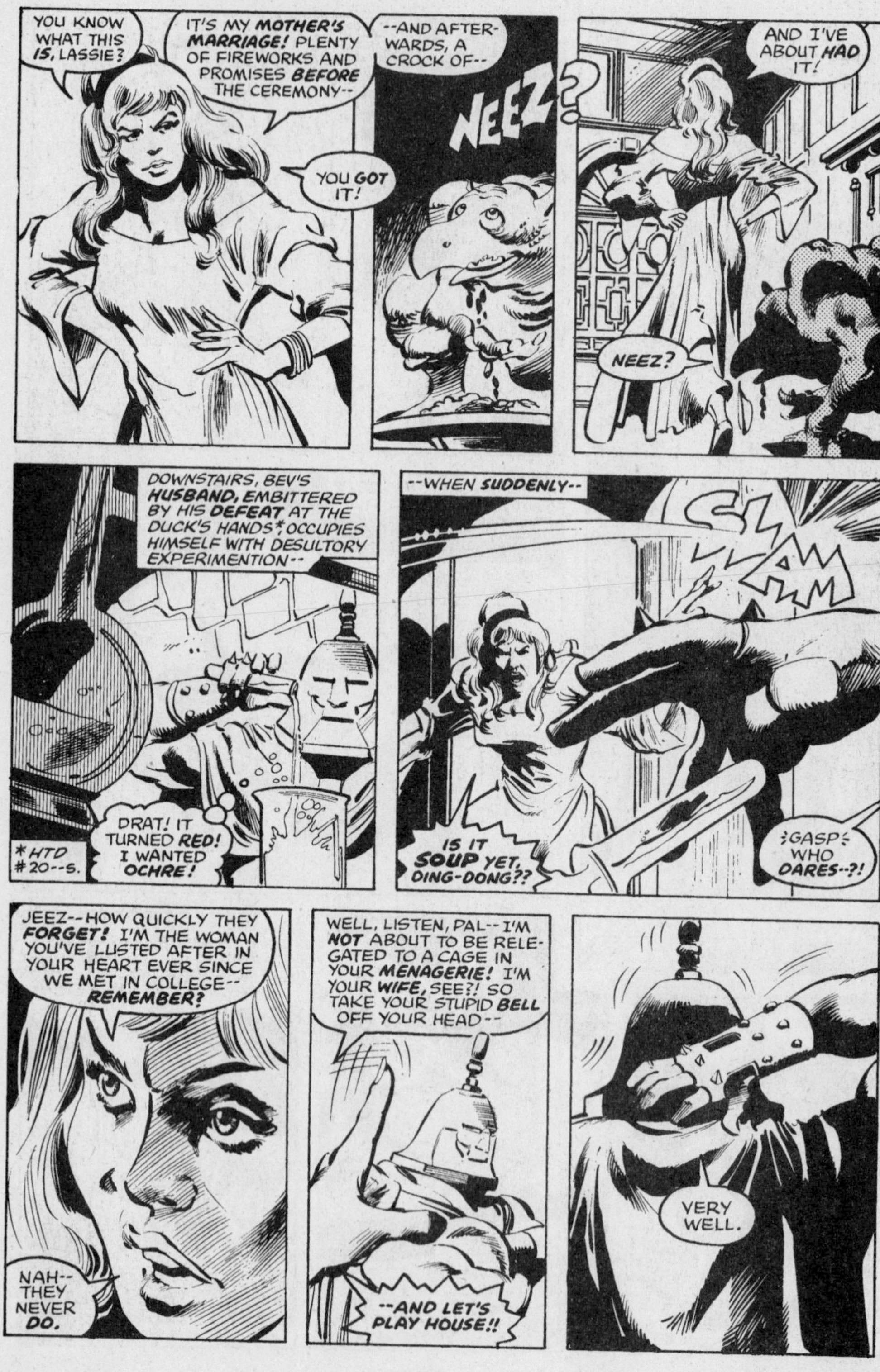

YOU KNOW WHAT THIS IS, LASSIE?
IT'S MY MOTHER'S MARRIAGE! PLENTY OF FIREWORKS AND PROMISES BEFORE THE CEREMONY--
YOU GOT IT!
--AND AFTER-WARDS, A CROCK OF--
NEEZ?
AND I'VE ABOUT HAD IT!
NEEZ?
DOWNSTAIRS, BEV'S HUSBAND, EMBITTERED BY HIS DEFEAT AT THE DUCK'S HANDS*, OCCUPIES HIMSELF WITH DESULTORY EXPERIMENTATION--
DRAT! IT TURNED RED! I WANTED OCHRE!
*HTD #20--S.
--WHEN SUDDENLY--
SLAM
IS IT SOUP YET, DING-DONG??
GASP WHO DARES--?!
JEEZ--HOW QUICKLY THEY FORGET! I'M THE WOMAN YOU'VE LUSTED AFTER IN YOUR HEART EVER SINCE WE MET IN COLLEGE-- REMEMBER?
NAH--THEY NEVER DO.
WELL, LISTEN, PAL--I'M NOT ABOUT TO BE RELEGATED TO A CAGE IN YOUR MENAGERIE! I'M YOUR WIFE, SEE?! SO TAKE YOUR STUPID BELL OFF YOUR HEAD--
--AND LET'S PLAY HOUSE!!
VERY WELL.

BUT BE FOREWARNED... DR. BONG PLAYS *EVERY* GAME... FOR *KEEPS!*

⸮SHHH⸗ DON'T--YOU'LL BALLOON--MY EXPECTATIONS--!

CLAP

CLAP

⸮MMMM⸗ NEEZ, NEEZ!!

NEW YORK, SEVERAL DAYS LATER:

SO BEV'S *UNCLE* LOANED YOU THIS APARTMENT TILL THE LEASE EXPIRES...

...AND BEV'S *MARRIED* TO DR. BONG...!

IT'S HARD TO *DIGEST*...BUT IT UNDERSCORES MY POINT: *WHY* GO BACK TO CLEVELAND?

WHAT *FUTURE* IS THERE FOR AN ARTIST IN CLEVELAND? NEW YORK HAS IT *ALL*--

--MUSEUMS, GALLERIES, A *PUBLIC*--

--AND *IWIS!*

TILL SHE FINDS AN-*OTHEW* ARTIST TO PATWONIZE.

HUH?

⸮TCH⸗ TOO *SUBTLE,* WINDA.

RRING

NEXT TIME TRY A--!

JUST A SEC.

HELLO?

YES, THIS IS--!

LEE?!

WHERE *ARE* YOU?

CLEVELAND! AND HOW FAST CAN *YOU* GET HERE? I'VE STUMBLED ONTO AN *IDEAL* BUSINESS OPPORTUNITY--

--AND I WANT TO TAKE *YOU* IN AS MY *PARTNER!*

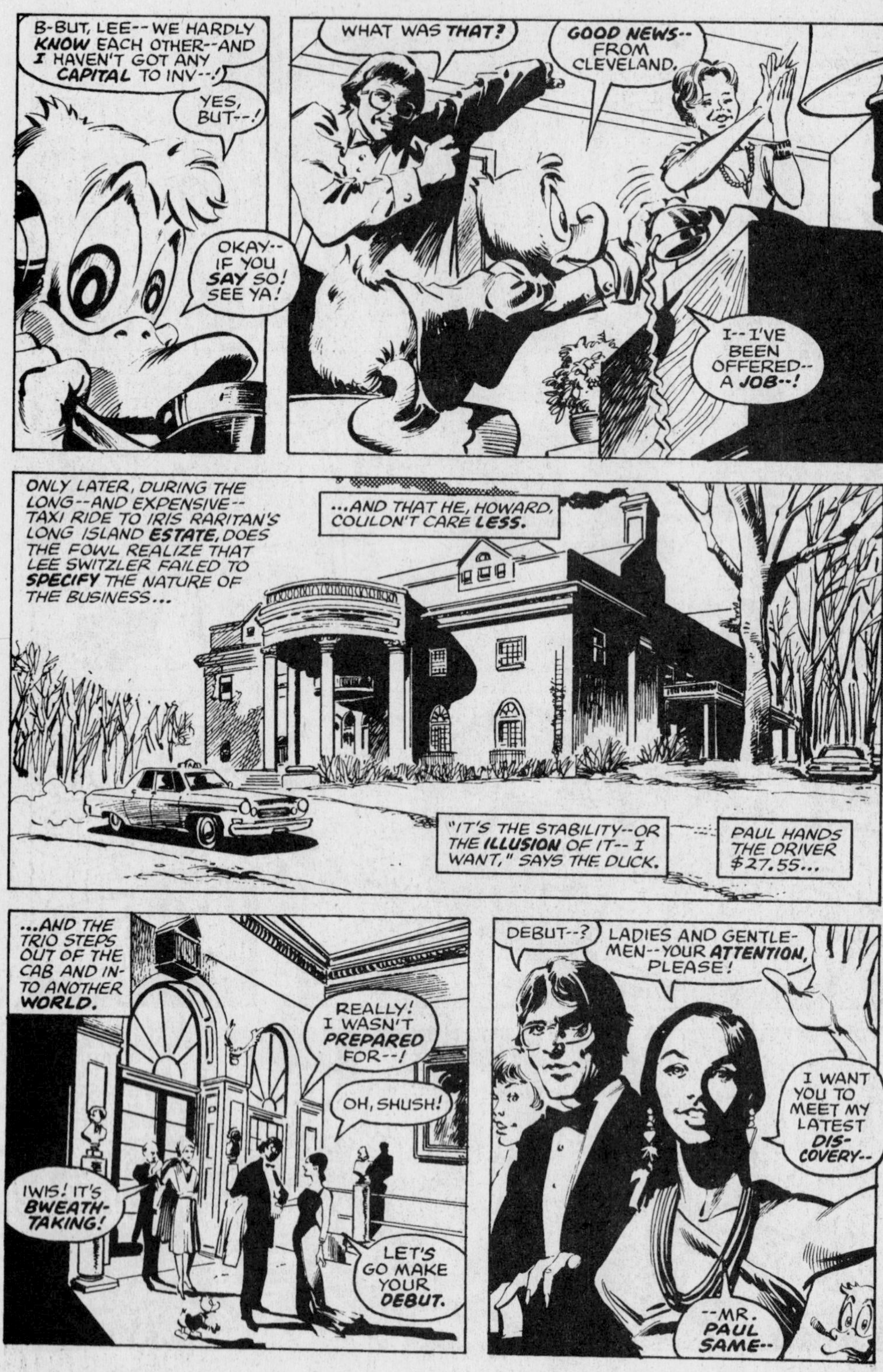

B-BUT, LEE--WE HARDLY KNOW EACH OTHER--AND I HAVEN'T GOT ANY CAPITAL TO INV--!
YES, BUT--!
OKAY-- IF YOU SAY SO! SEE YA!
WHAT WAS THAT?
GOOD NEWS-- FROM CLEVELAND.
I--I'VE BEEN OFFERED-- A JOB--!
ONLY LATER, DURING THE LONG--AND EXPENSIVE--TAXI RIDE TO IRIS RARITAN'S LONG ISLAND ESTATE, DOES THE FOWL REALIZE THAT LEE SWITZLER FAILED TO SPECIFY THE NATURE OF THE BUSINESS...
...AND THAT HE, HOWARD, COULDN'T CARE LESS.
"IT'S THE STABILITY--OR THE ILLUSION OF IT--I WANT," SAYS THE DUCK.
PAUL HANDS THE DRIVER $27.55...
...AND THE TRIO STEPS OUT OF THE CAB AND INTO ANOTHER WORLD.
IWIS! IT'S BWEATH-TAKING!
REALLY! I WASN'T PREPARED FOR--!
OH, SHUSH!
LET'S GO MAKE YOUR DEBUT.
DEBUT--?
LADIES AND GENTLEMEN--YOUR ATTENTION, PLEASE!
I WANT YOU TO MEET MY LATEST DISCOVERY--
--MR. PAUL SAME--

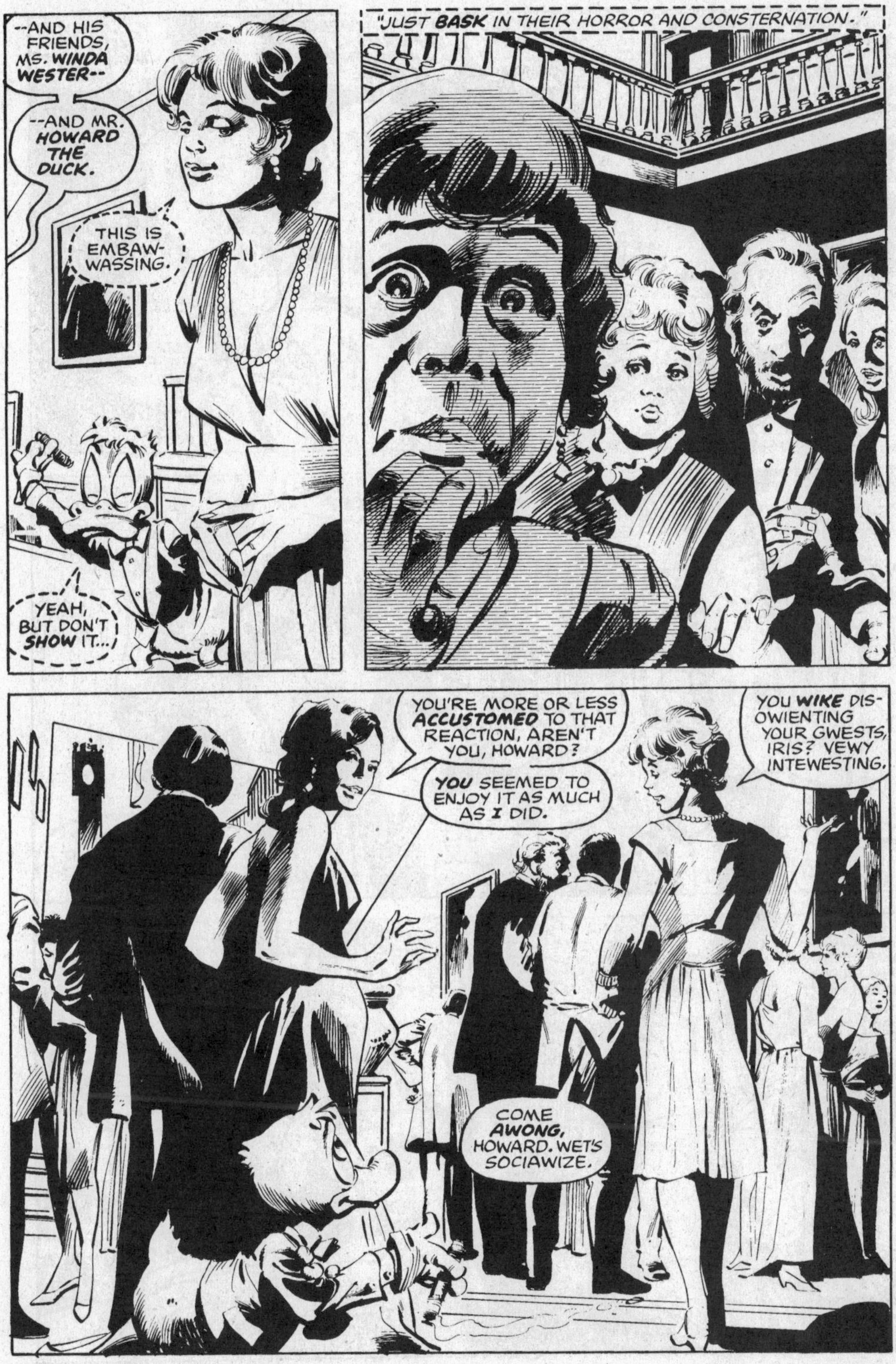
--AND HIS FRIENDS, MS. WINDA WESTER--
--AND MR. HOWARD THE DUCK.
THIS IS EMBAW-WASSING.
YEAH, BUT DON'T SHOW IT...
"JUST BASK IN THEIR HORROR AND CONSTERNATION."
YOU'RE MORE OR LESS ACCUSTOMED TO THAT REACTION, AREN'T YOU, HOWARD?
YOU SEEMED TO ENJOY IT AS MUCH AS I DID.
YOU WIKE DIS-OWIENTING YOUR GWESTS, IRIS? VEWY INTEWESTING.
COME AWONG, HOWARD. WET'S SOCIAWIZE.

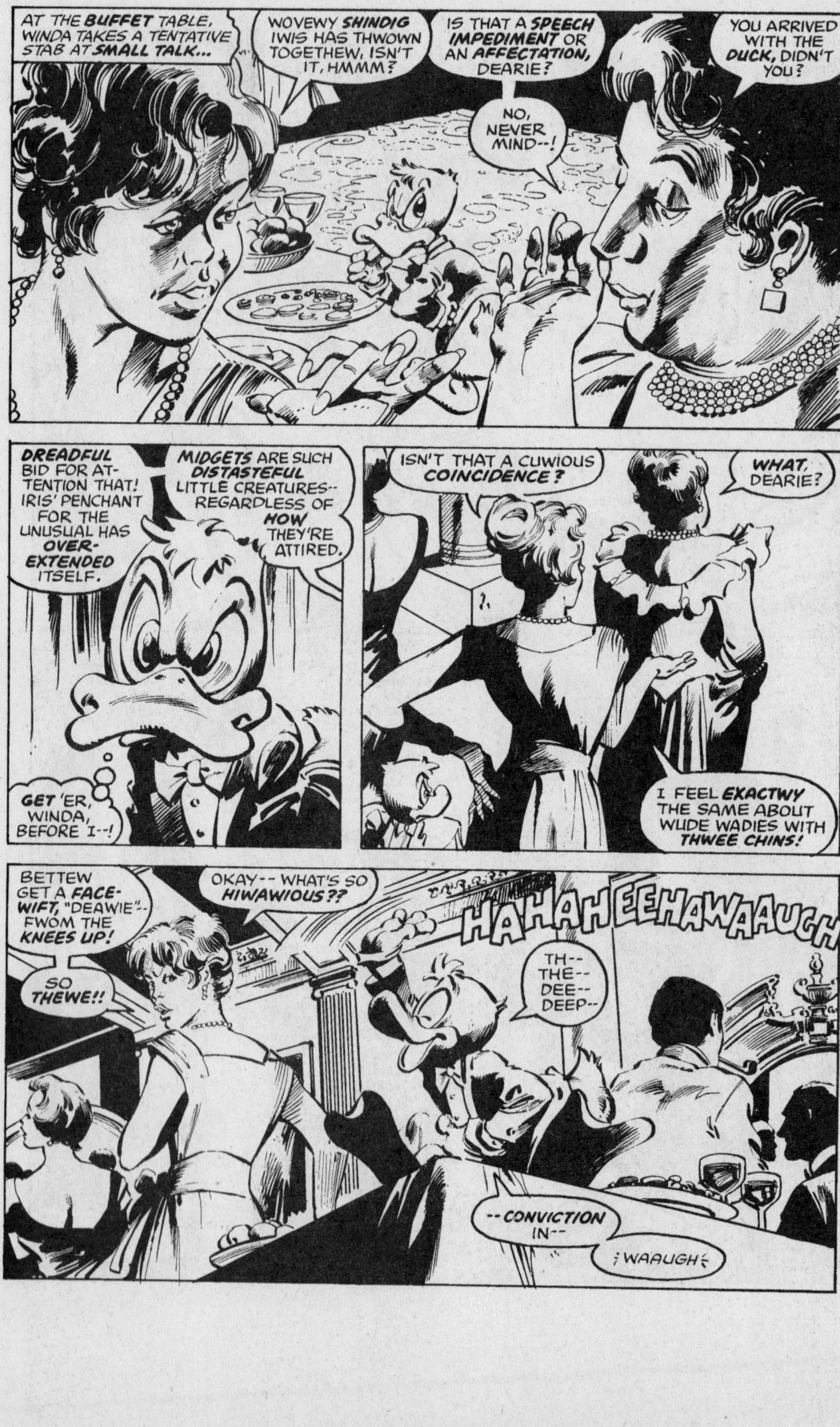
AT THE BUFFET TABLE, WINDA TAKES A TENTATIVE STAB AT SMALL TALK...
WOVEWY SHINDIG IWIS HAS THWOWN TOGETHEW, ISN'T IT, HMMM?
IS THAT A SPEECH IMPEDIMENT OR AN AFFECTATION, DEARIE?
NO, NEVER MIND--!
YOU ARRIVED WITH THE DUCK, DIDN'T YOU?
DREADFUL BID FOR ATTENTION THAT! IRIS' PENCHANT FOR THE UNUSUAL HAS OVER-EXTENDED ITSELF.
MIDGETS ARE SUCH DISTASTEFUL LITTLE CREATURES-- REGARDLESS OF HOW THEY'RE ATTIRED.
GET 'ER, WINDA, BEFORE I--!
ISN'T THAT A CUWIOUS COINCIDENCE?
WHAT, DEARIE?
I FEEL EXACTWY THE SAME ABOUT WUDE WADIES WITH THWEE CHINS!
BETTEW GET A FACE-WIFT, "DEAWIE"-- FWOM THE KNEES UP!
SO THEWE!!
OKAY-- WHAT'S SO HIWAWIOUS??
HAHAHEEHAWAAUGH
TH-- THE-- DEE-- DEEP--
--CONVICTION IN--
WAAUGH

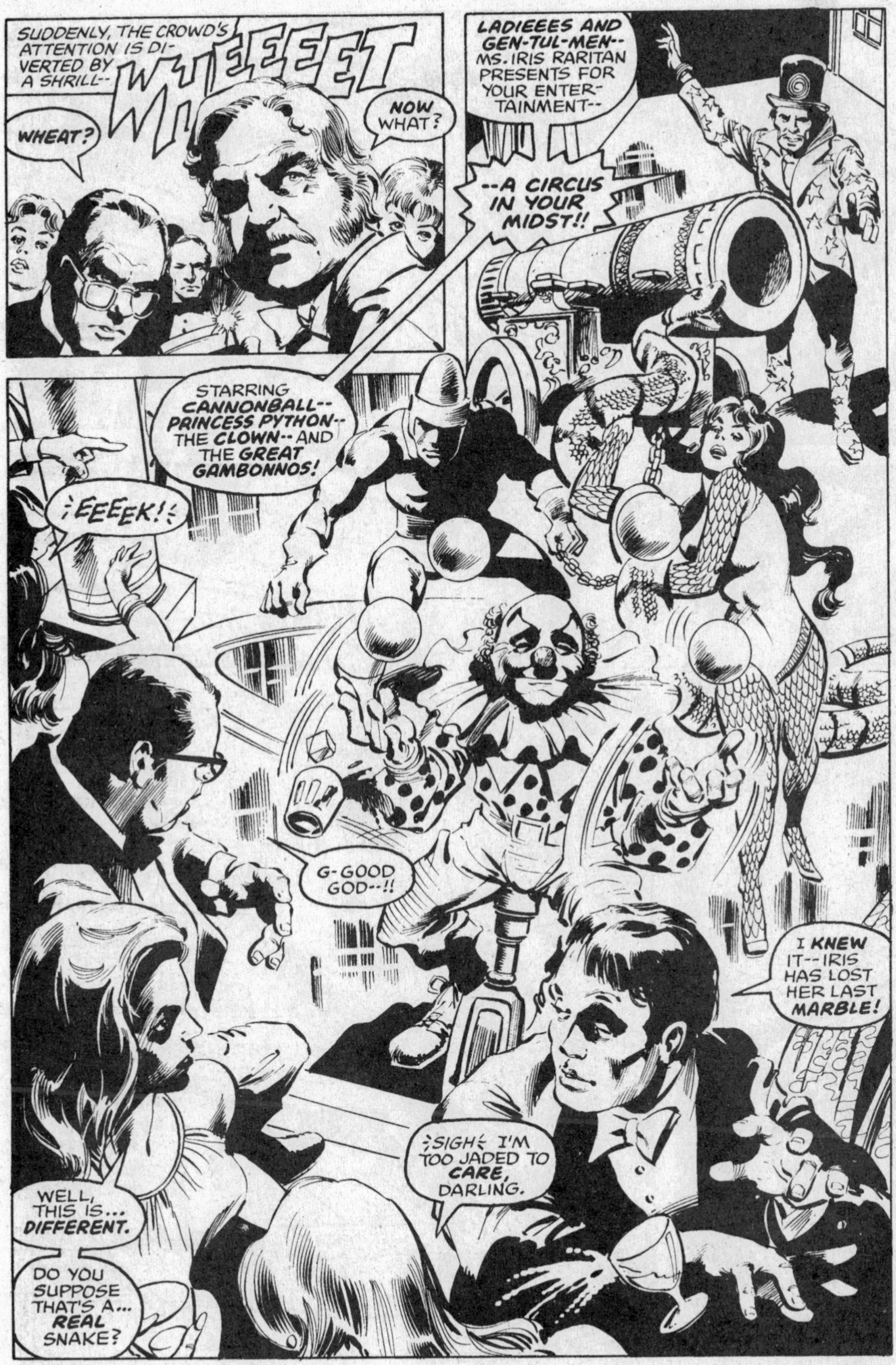
SUDDENLY, THE CROWD'S ATTENTION IS DIVERTED BY A SHRILL--
WHEEEET
WHEAT?
NOW WHAT?
LADIEEES AND GEN-TUL-MEN-- MS. IRIS RARITAN PRESENTS FOR YOUR ENTERTAINMENT--
--A CIRCUS IN YOUR MIDST!!
STARRING CANNONBALL-- PRINCESS PYTHON-- THE CLOWN-- AND THE GREAT GAMBONNOS!
¡EEEEK!
G-GOOD GOD--!!
I KNEW IT--IRIS HAS LOST HER LAST MARBLE!
SIGH I'M TOO JADED TO CARE, DARLING.
WELL, THIS IS... DIFFERENT.
DO YOU SUPPOSE THAT'S A... REAL SNAKE?

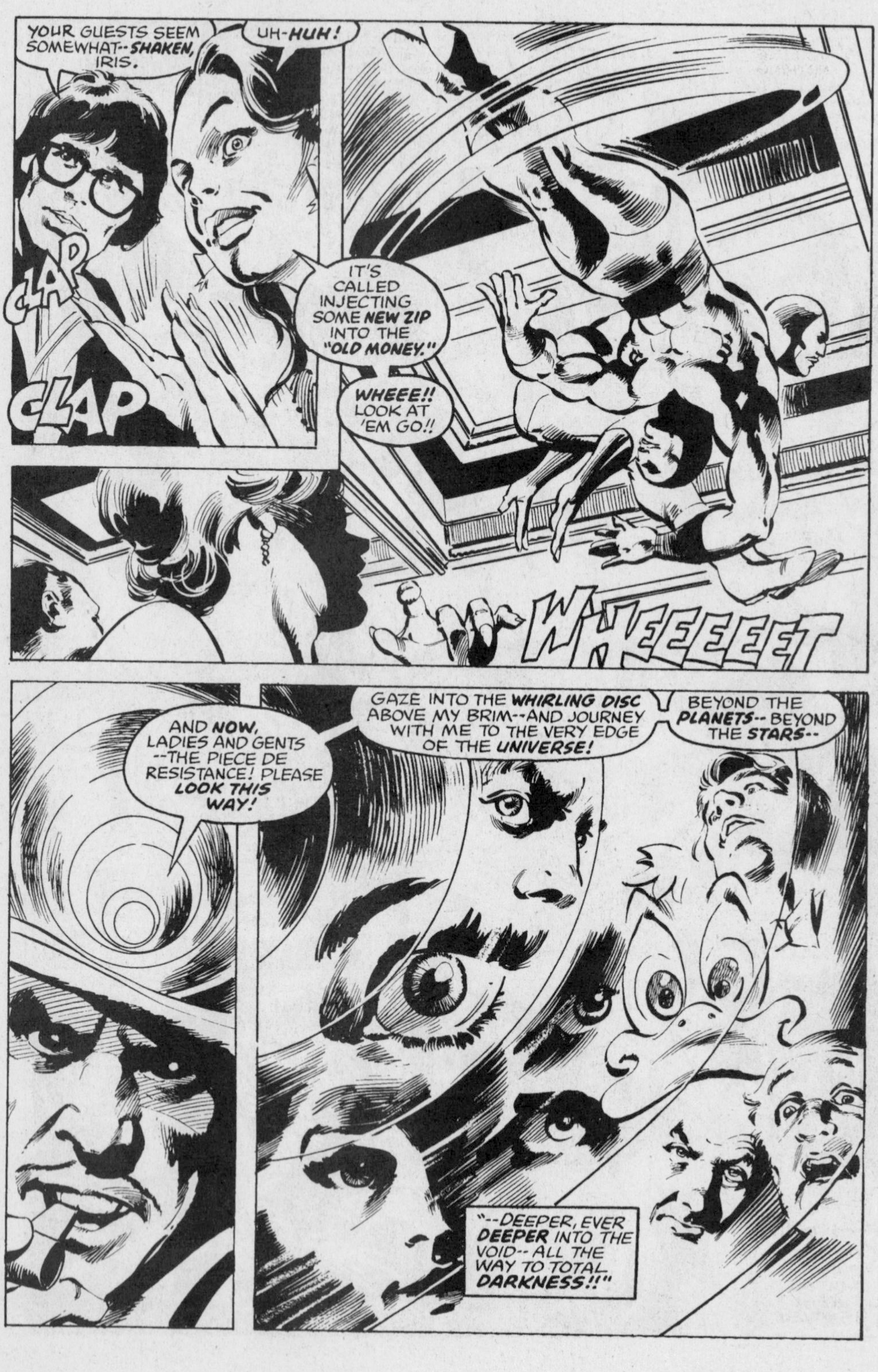
YOUR GUESTS SEEM SOMEWHAT--SHAKEN, IRIS.
UH-HUH!
CLAP
CLAP
IT'S CALLED INJECTING SOME NEW ZIP INTO THE "OLD MONEY."
WHEEE!! LOOK AT 'EM GO!!
WHEEEEET
AND NOW, LADIES AND GENTS --THE PIECE DE RESISTANCE! PLEASE LOOK THIS WAY!
GAZE INTO THE WHIRLING DISC ABOVE MY BRIM--AND JOURNEY WITH ME TO THE VERY EDGE OF THE UNIVERSE!
BEYOND THE PLANETS--BEYOND THE STARS--
"--DEEPER, EVER DEEPER INTO THE VOID--ALL THE WAY TO TOTAL DARKNESS!!"

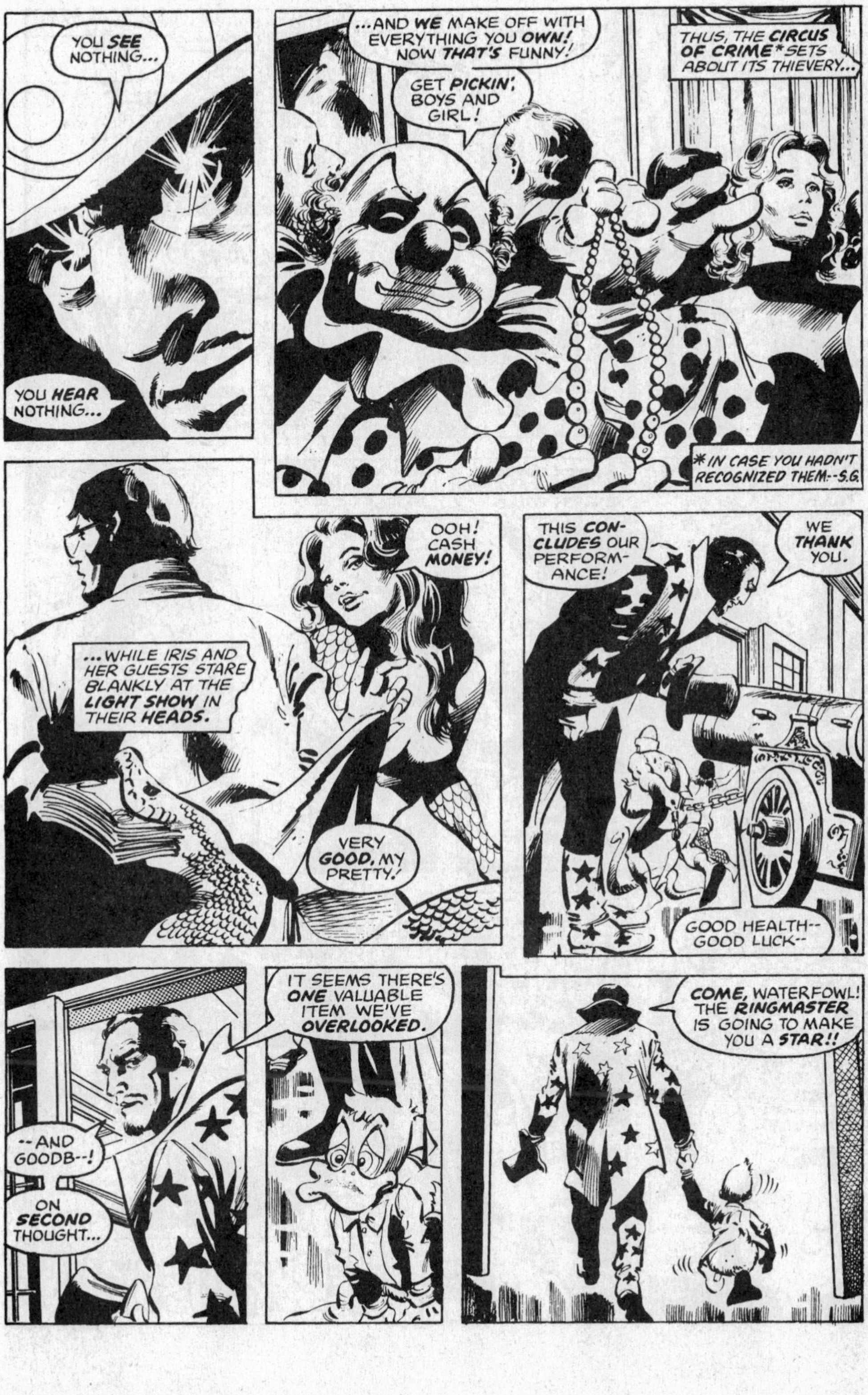
YOU SEE NOTHING...
YOU HEAR NOTHING...
...AND WE MAKE OFF WITH EVERYTHING YOU OWN! NOW THAT'S FUNNY!
GET PICKIN', BOYS AND GIRL!
THUS, THE CIRCUS OF CRIME* SETS ABOUT ITS THIEVERY...
*IN CASE YOU HADN'T RECOGNIZED THEM.--S.G.
...WHILE IRIS AND HER GUESTS STARE BLANKLY AT THE LIGHT SHOW IN THEIR HEADS.
OOH! CASH MONEY!
VERY GOOD, MY PRETTY!
THIS CONCLUDES OUR PERFORMANCE!
WE THANK YOU.
GOOD HEALTH-- GOOD LUCK--
--AND GOODB--!
ON SECOND THOUGHT...
IT SEEMS THERE'S ONE VALUABLE ITEM WE'VE OVERLOOKED.
COME, WATERFOWL! THE RINGMASTER IS GOING TO MAKE YOU A STAR!!

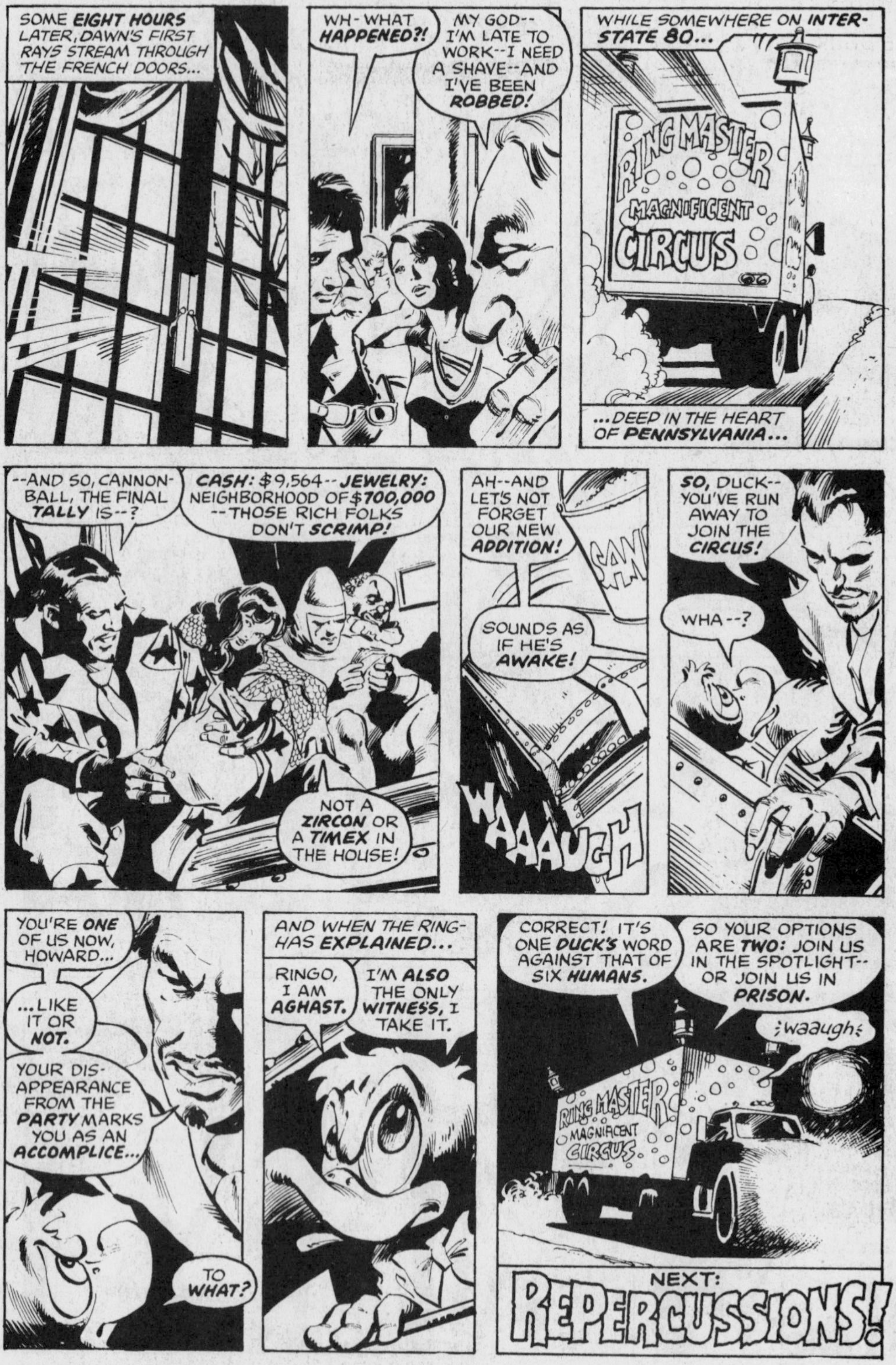
SOME EIGHT HOURS LATER, DAWN'S FIRST RAYS STREAM THROUGH THE FRENCH DOORS...
WH-WHAT HAPPENED?!
MY GOD-- I'M LATE TO WORK--I NEED A SHAVE--AND I'VE BEEN ROBBED!
WHILE SOMEWHERE ON INTER-STATE 80...
RING MASTER MAGNIFICENT CIRCUS
...DEEP IN THE HEART OF PENNSYLVANIA...
--AND SO, CANNON-BALL, THE FINAL TALLY IS--?
CASH: $9,564--JEWELRY: NEIGHBORHOOD OF $700,000 --THOSE RICH FOLKS DON'T SCRIMP!
NOT A ZIRCON OR A TIMEX IN THE HOUSE!
AH--AND LET'S NOT FORGET OUR NEW ADDITION!
SOUNDS AS IF HE'S AWAKE!
WAAAAUGH
SO, DUCK-- YOU'VE RUN AWAY TO JOIN THE CIRCUS!
WHA--?
YOU'RE ONE OF US NOW, HOWARD...
...LIKE IT OR NOT.
YOUR DIS-APPEARANCE FROM THE PARTY MARKS YOU AS AN ACCOMPLICE...
TO WHAT?
AND WHEN THE RING-HAS EXPLAINED...
RINGO, I AM AGHAST.
I'M ALSO THE ONLY WITNESS, I TAKE IT.
CORRECT! IT'S ONE DUCK'S WORD AGAINST THAT OF SIX HUMANS.
SO YOUR OPTIONS ARE TWO: JOIN US IN THE SPOTLIGHT-- OR JOIN US IN PRISON.
waaugh
RING MASTER MAGNIFICENT CIRCUS
NEXT:
REPERCUSSIONS!

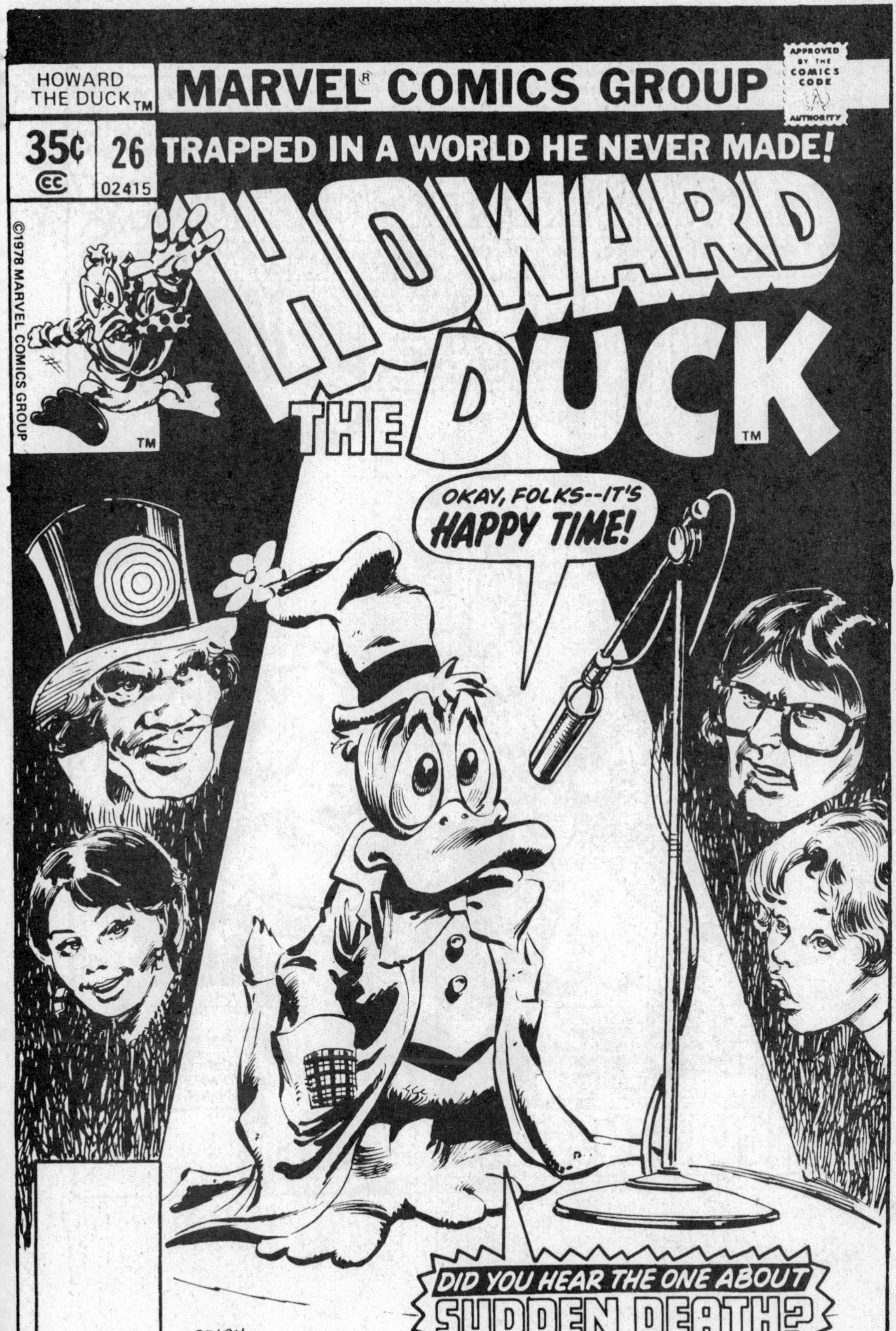
HOWARD THE DUCK TM
MARVEL® COMICS GROUP
APPROVED BY THE COMICS CODE AUTHORITY
35¢
26
02415
TRAPPED IN A WORLD HE NEVER MADE!
©1978 MARVEL COMICS GROUP
HOWARD THE DUCK TM
OKAY, FOLKS--IT'S HAPPY TIME!
DID YOU HEAR THE ONE ABOUT SUDDEN DEATH?
COLAN JANSON

From the time of his hatching, he was...different. A potentially brilliant scholar who dreaded the structured environment of school, he educated himself in the streets, taking whatever work was available, formulating his philosophy of self from what he learned of the world about him. And then the Cosmic Axis shifted...and that world *changed.* Suddenly, he was stranded in a universe he could not fathom. Without warning, he became a strange fowl in an even stranger land.

Stan Lee PRESENTS: HOWARD THE DUCK!™

STEVE GERBER WRITER/EDITOR • GENE COLAN ARTIST • KLAUS JANSON INKER • IRV WATANABE LETTERER • JANICE COHEN COLORIST • JIM SHOOTER CONSULTING EDITOR

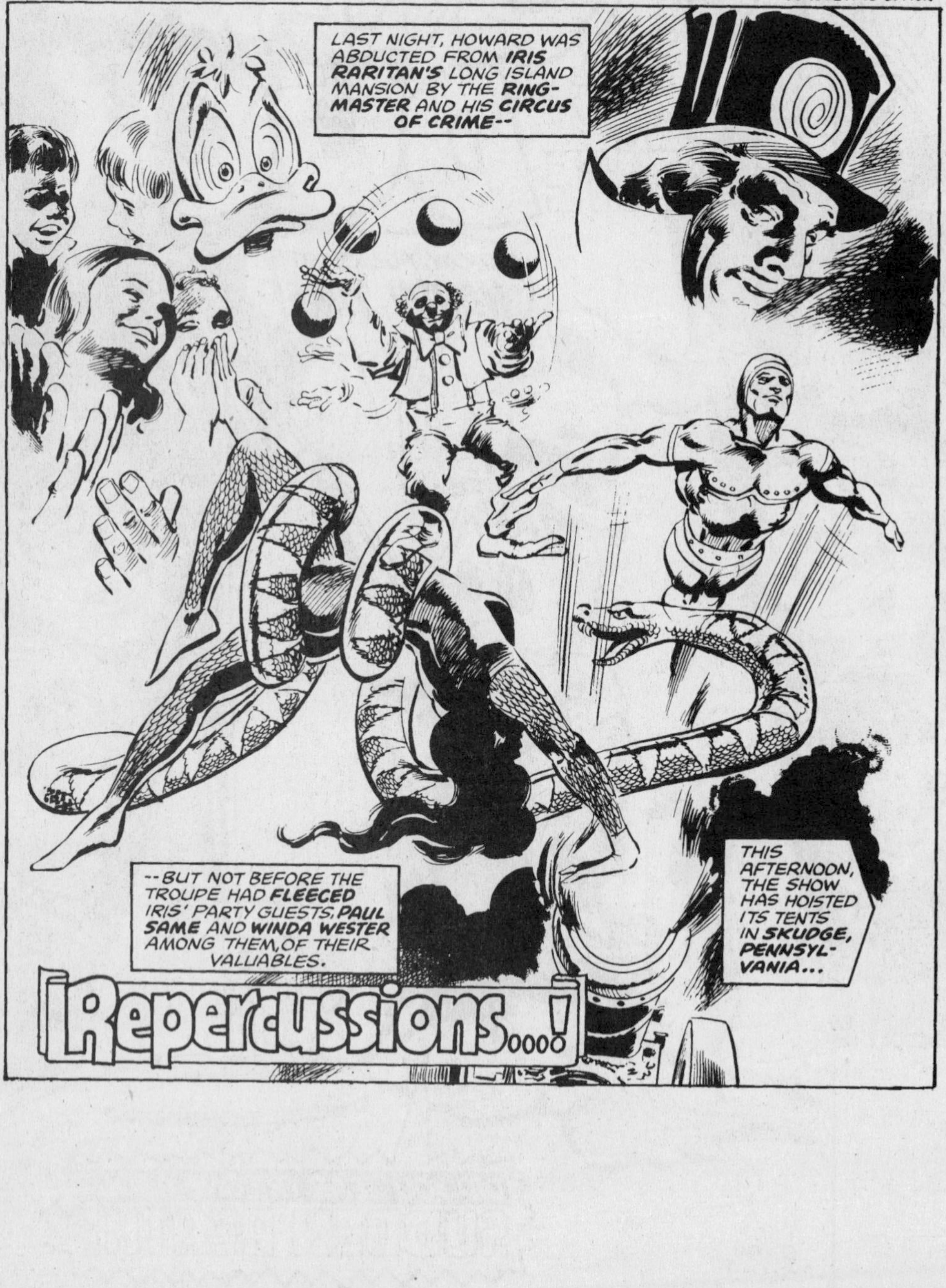
LAST NIGHT, HOWARD WAS ABDUCTED FROM IRIS RARITAN'S LONG ISLAND MANSION BY THE RING-MASTER AND HIS CIRCUS OF CRIME--
--BUT NOT BEFORE THE TROUPE HAD FLEECED IRIS' PARTY GUESTS, PAUL SAME AND WINDA WESTER AMONG THEM, OF THEIR VALUABLES.
THIS AFTERNOON, THE SHOW HAS HOISTED ITS TENTS IN SKUDGE, PENNSYL-VANIA...
Repercussions...!

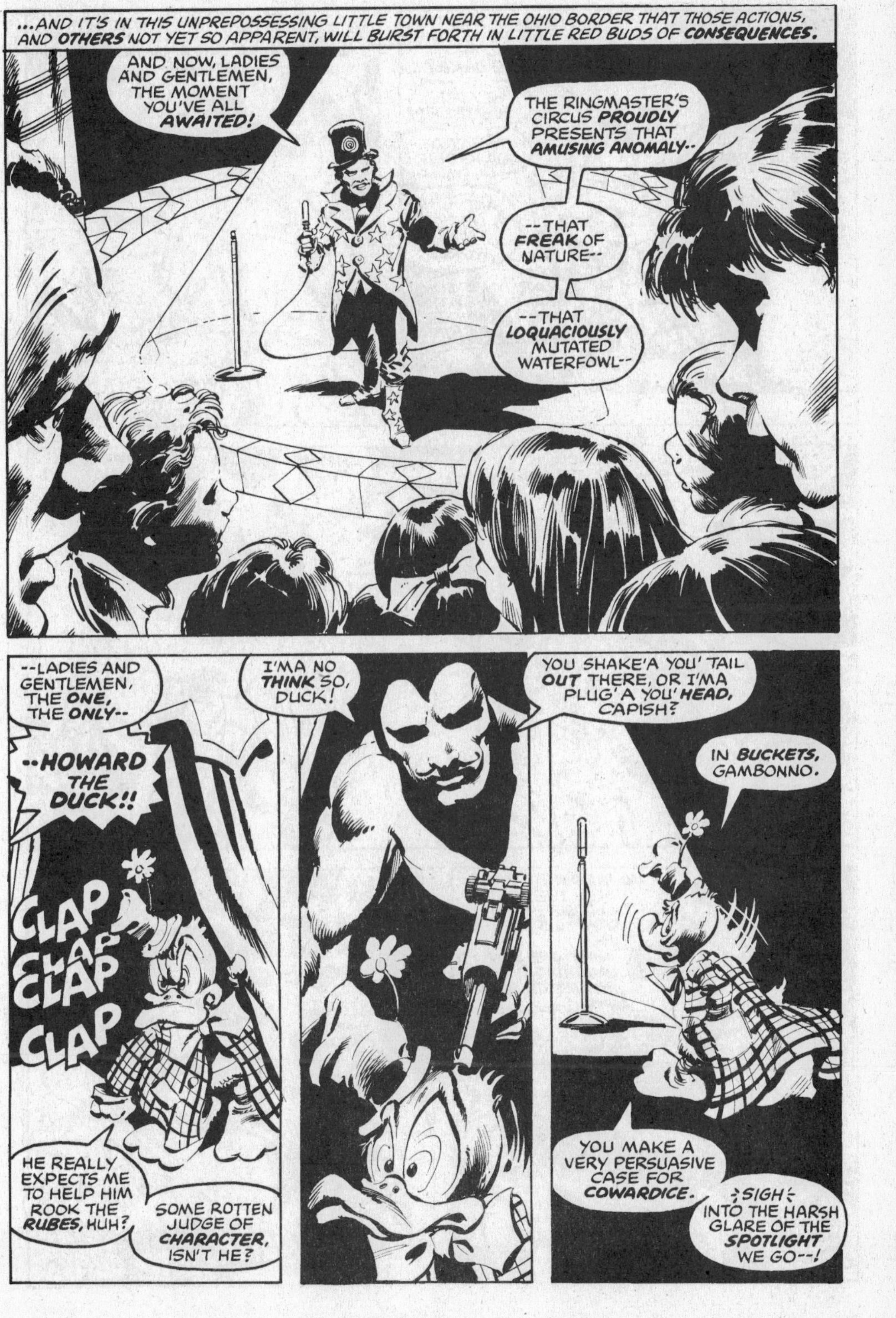
...AND IT'S IN THIS UNPREPOSSESSING LITTLE TOWN NEAR THE OHIO BORDER THAT THOSE ACTIONS, AND OTHERS NOT YET SO APPARENT, WILL BURST FORTH IN LITTLE RED BUDS OF CONSEQUENCES.
AND NOW, LADIES AND GENTLEMEN, THE MOMENT YOU'VE ALL AWAITED!
THE RINGMASTER'S CIRCUS PROUDLY PRESENTS THAT AMUSING ANOMALY--
--THAT FREAK OF NATURE--
--THAT LOQUACIOUSLY MUTATED WATERFOWL--
--LADIES AND GENTLEMEN, THE ONE, THE ONLY--
--HOWARD THE DUCK!!
CLAP CLAP CLAP CLAP
HE REALLY EXPECTS ME TO HELP HIM ROOK THE RUBES, HUH?
SOME ROTTEN JUDGE OF CHARACTER, ISN'T HE?
I'MA NO THINK SO, DUCK!
YOU SHAKE'A YOU' TAIL OUT THERE, OR I'MA PLUG'A YOU' HEAD, CAPISH?
IN BUCKETS, GAMBONNO.
YOU MAKE A VERY PERSUASIVE CASE FOR COWARDICE.
-SIGH- INTO THE HARSH GLARE OF THE SPOTLIGHT WE GO--!

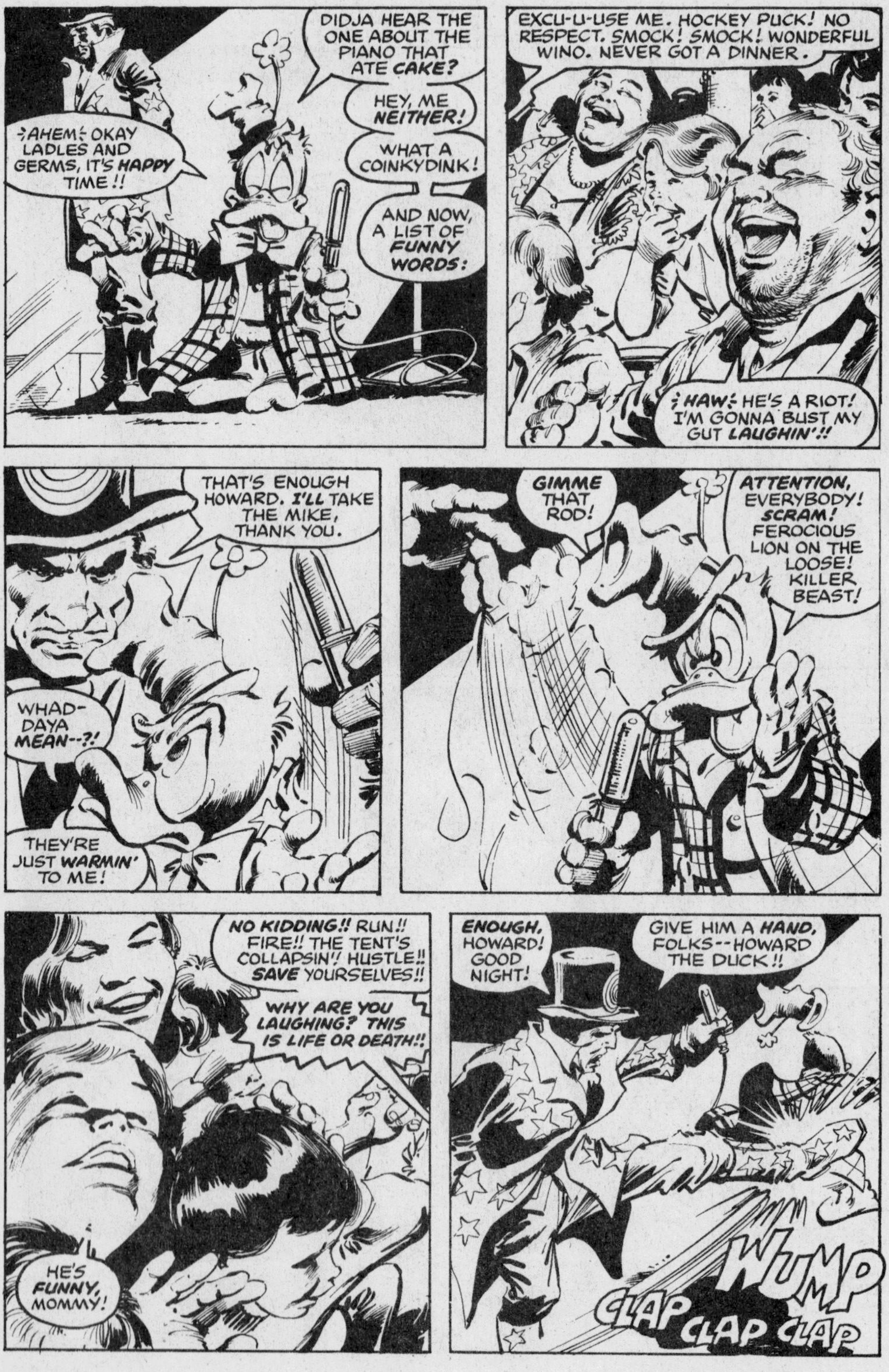
DIDJA HEAR THE ONE ABOUT THE PIANO THAT ATE CAKE?
HEY, ME NEITHER!
WHAT A COINKYDINK!
AND NOW, A LIST OF FUNNY WORDS:
-AHEM- OKAY LADLES AND GERMS, IT'S HAPPY TIME!!
EXCU-U-USE ME. HOCKEY PUCK! NO RESPECT. SMOCK! SMOCK! WONDERFUL WINO. NEVER GOT A DINNER.
-HAW- HE'S A RIOT! I'M GONNA BUST MY GUT LAUGHIN'!!
THAT'S ENOUGH HOWARD. I'LL TAKE THE MIKE, THANK YOU.
WHAD-DAYA MEAN--?!
THEY'RE JUST WARMIN' TO ME!
GIMME THAT ROD!
ATTENTION, EVERYBODY! SCRAM! FEROCIOUS LION ON THE LOOSE! KILLER BEAST!
NO KIDDING!! RUN!! FIRE!! THE TENT'S COLLAPSIN'! HUSTLE!! SAVE YOURSELVES!!
WHY ARE YOU LAUGHING? THIS IS LIFE OR DEATH!!
HE'S FUNNY, MOMMY!
ENOUGH, HOWARD! GOOD NIGHT!
GIVE HIM A HAND, FOLKS--HOWARD THE DUCK!!
WUMP
CLAP CLAP CLAP

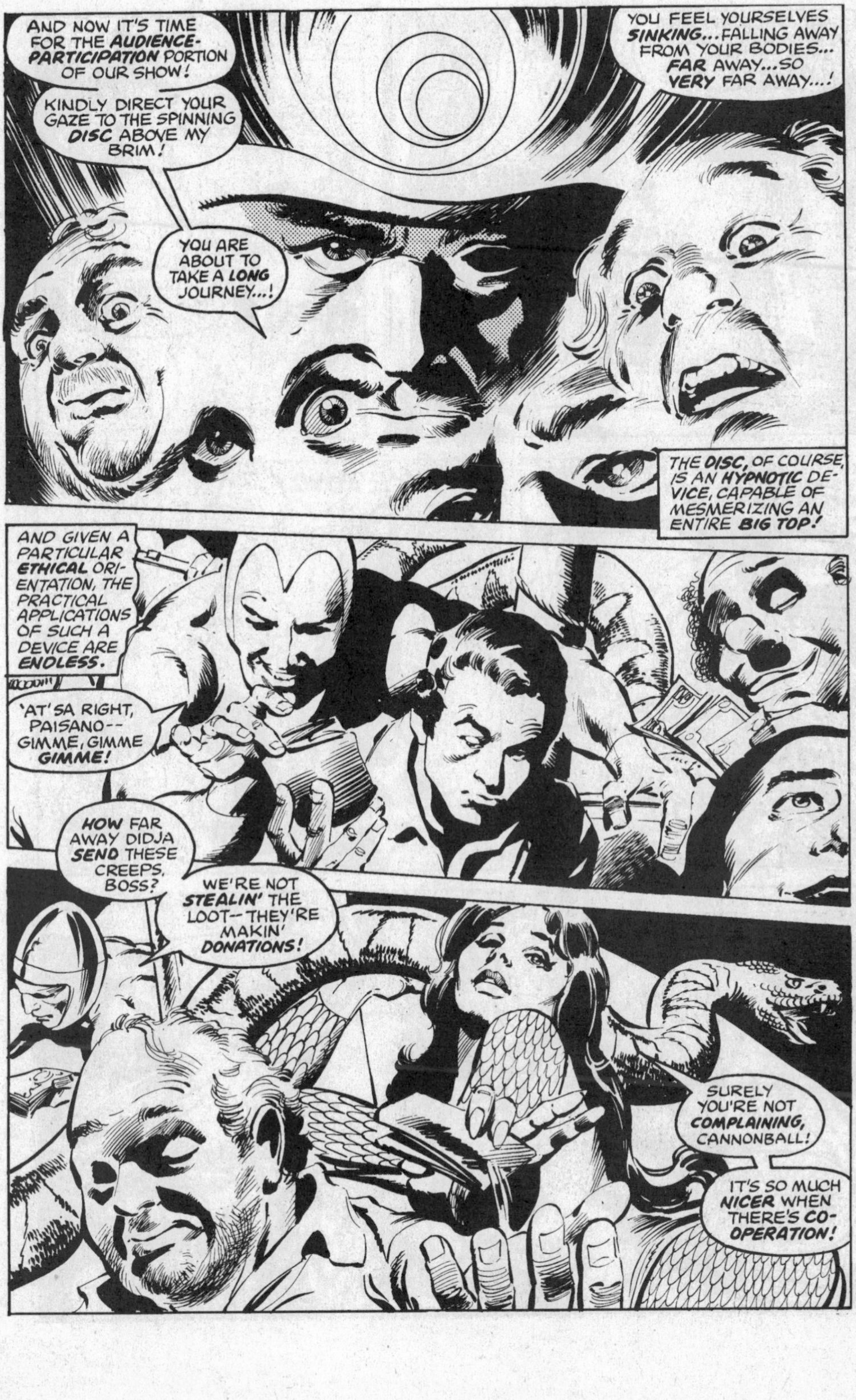
AND NOW IT'S TIME FOR THE AUDIENCE-PARTICIPATION PORTION OF OUR SHOW!
KINDLY DIRECT YOUR GAZE TO THE SPINNING DISC ABOVE MY BRIM!
YOU FEEL YOURSELVES SINKING... FALLING AWAY FROM YOUR BODIES... FAR AWAY... SO VERY FAR AWAY...!
YOU ARE ABOUT TO TAKE A LONG JOURNEY...!
THE DISC, OF COURSE, IS AN HYPNOTIC DE-VICE, CAPABLE OF MESMERIZING AN ENTIRE BIG TOP!
AND GIVEN A PARTICULAR ETHICAL ORI-ENTATION, THE PRACTICAL APPLICATIONS OF SUCH A DEVICE ARE ENDLESS.
'AT'SA RIGHT, PAISANO-- GIMME, GIMME GIMME!
HOW FAR AWAY DIDJA SEND THESE CREEPS, BOSS?
WE'RE NOT STEALIN' THE LOOT-- THEY'RE MAKIN' DONATIONS!
SURELY YOU'RE NOT COMPLAINING, CANNONBALL!
IT'S SO MUCH NICER WHEN THERE'S CO-OPERATION!

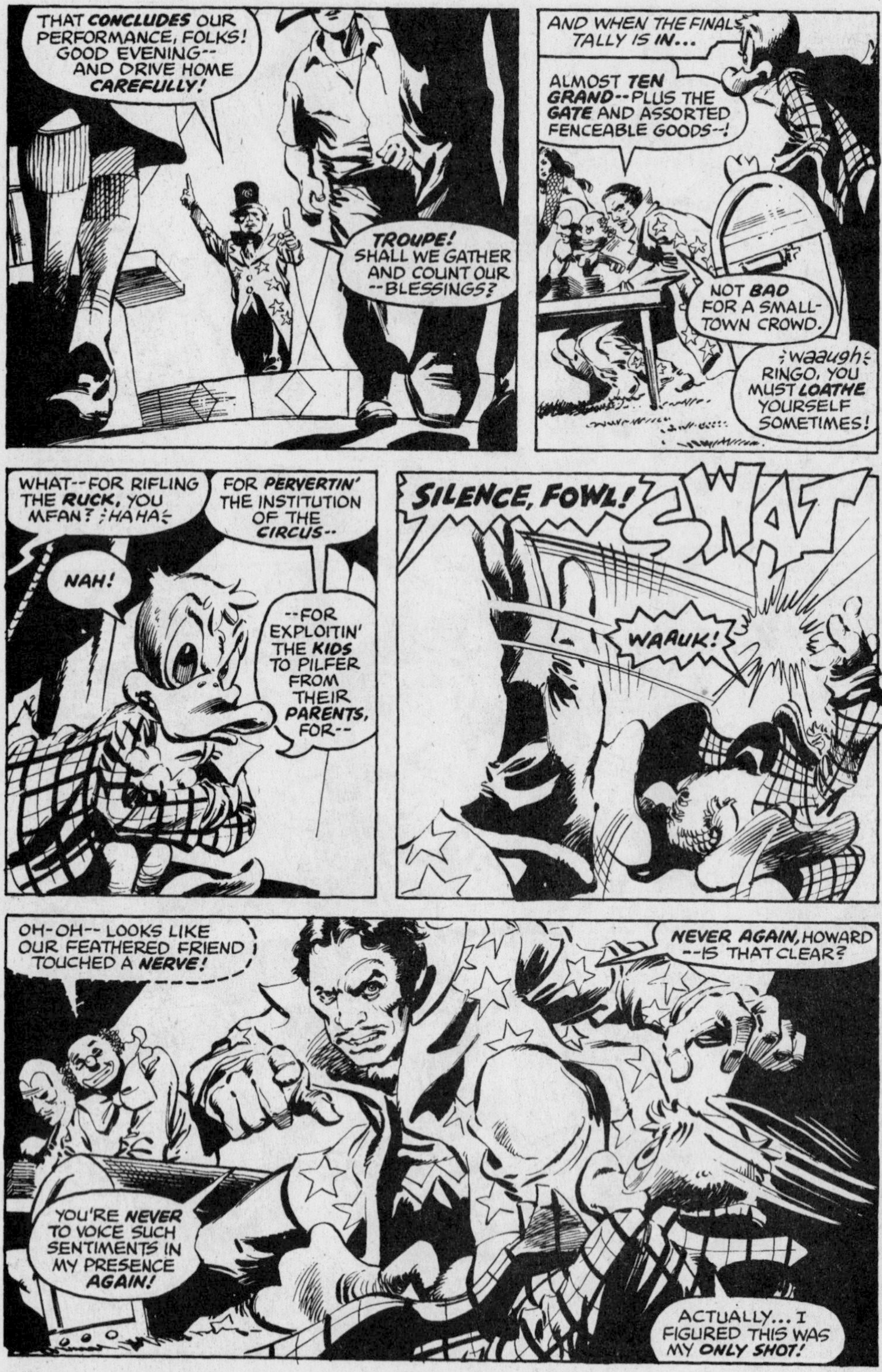
THAT CONCLUDES OUR PERFORMANCE, FOLKS! GOOD EVENING-- AND DRIVE HOME CAREFULLY!
TROUPE! SHALL WE GATHER AND COUNT OUR --BLESSINGS?
AND WHEN THE FINAL TALLY IS IN...
ALMOST TEN GRAND--PLUS THE GATE AND ASSORTED FENCEABLE GOODS--!
NOT BAD FOR A SMALL-TOWN CROWD.
waaugh RINGO, YOU MUST LOATHE YOURSELF SOMETIMES!
WHAT--FOR RIFLING THE RUCK, YOU MFAN? HAHA
NAH!
FOR PERVERTIN' THE INSTITUTION OF THE CIRCUS--
--FOR EXPLOITIN' THE KIDS TO PILFER FROM THEIR PARENTS, FOR--
SILENCE, FOWL!
SMAT
WAAUK!
OH-OH-- LOOKS LIKE OUR FEATHERED FRIEND TOUCHED A NERVE!
NEVER AGAIN, HOWARD --IS THAT CLEAR?
YOU'RE NEVER TO VOICE SUCH SENTIMENTS IN MY PRESENCE AGAIN!
ACTUALLY... I FIGURED THIS WAS MY ONLY SHOT!

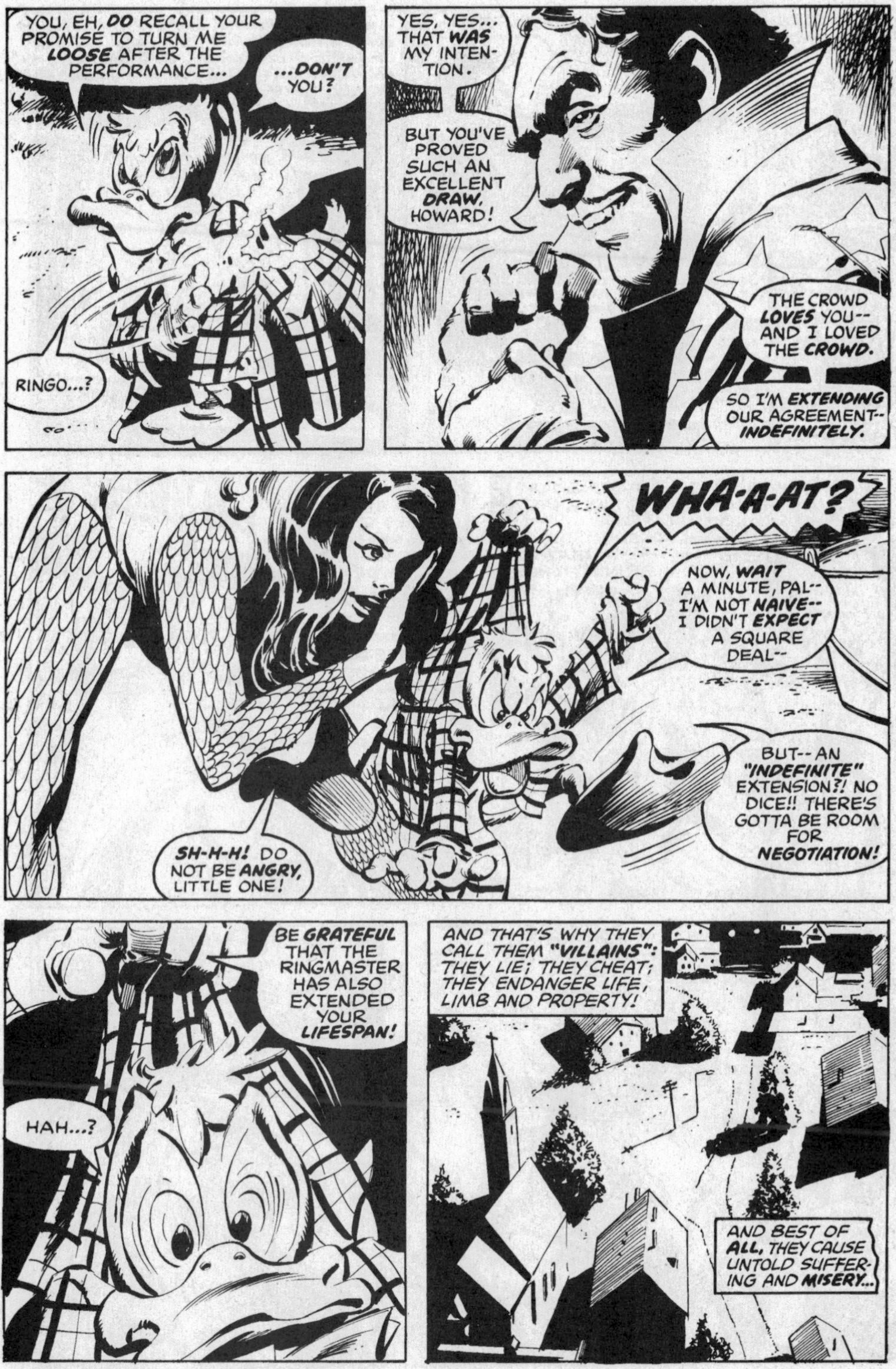

YOU, EH, DO RECALL YOUR PROMISE TO TURN ME LOOSE AFTER THE PERFORMANCE...
...DON'T YOU?
RINGO...?
YES, YES... THAT WAS MY INTENTION.
BUT YOU'VE PROVED SUCH AN EXCELLENT DRAW, HOWARD!
THE CROWD LOVES YOU-- AND I LOVED THE CROWD.
SO I'M EXTENDING OUR AGREEMENT-- INDEFINITELY.
WHA-A-AT?
NOW, WAIT A MINUTE, PAL-- I'M NOT NAIVE-- I DIDN'T EXPECT A SQUARE DEAL--
BUT-- AN "INDEFINITE" EXTENSION?! NO DICE!! THERE'S GOTTA BE ROOM FOR NEGOTIATION!
SH-H-H! DO NOT BE ANGRY, LITTLE ONE!
BE GRATEFUL THAT THE RINGMASTER HAS ALSO EXTENDED YOUR LIFESPAN!
HAH...?
AND THAT'S WHY THEY CALL THEM "VILLAINS": THEY LIE; THEY CHEAT; THEY ENDANGER LIFE, LIMB AND PROPERTY!
AND BEST OF ALL, THEY CAUSE UNTOLD SUFFERING AND MISERY...

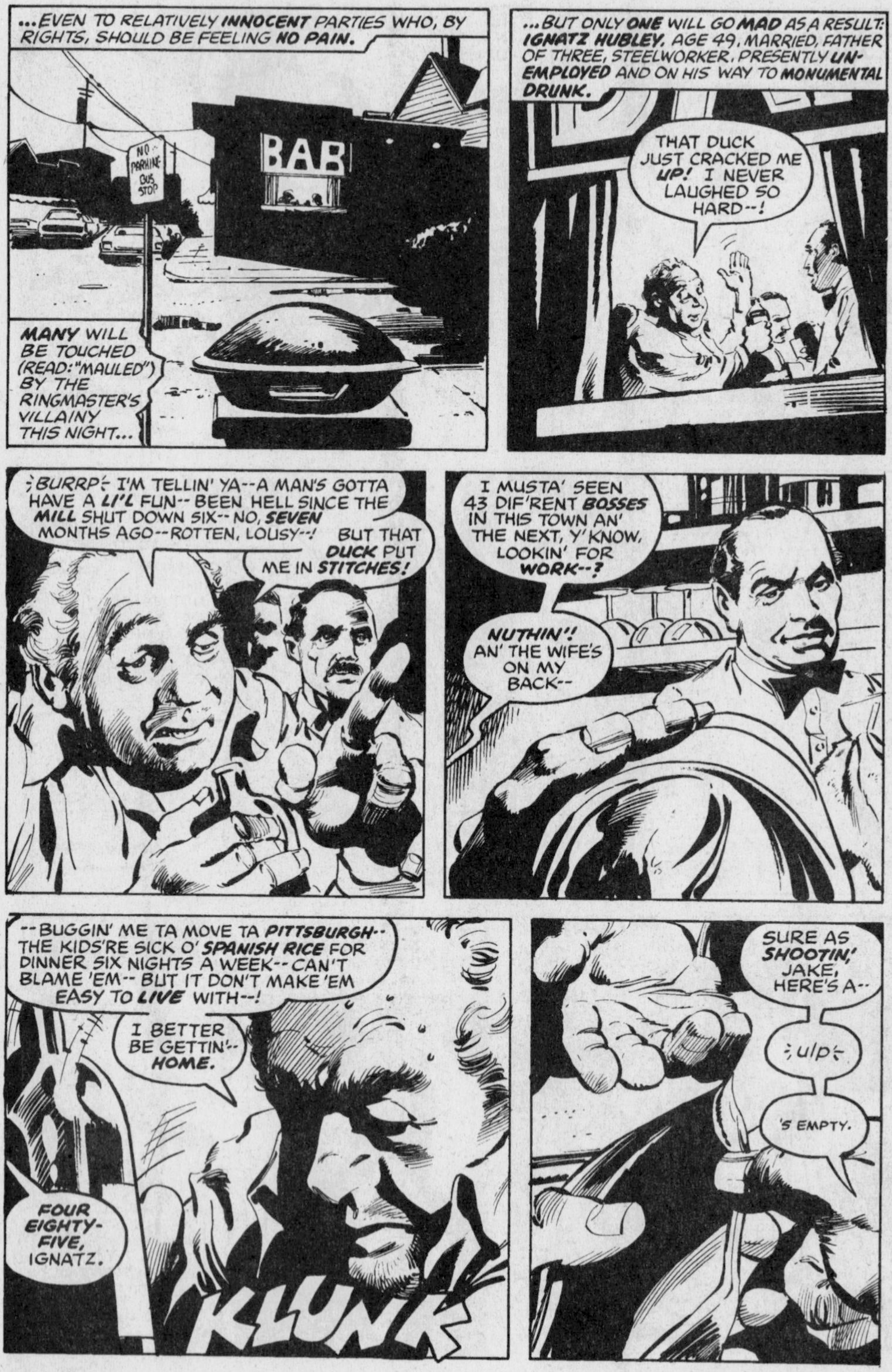
...EVEN TO RELATIVELY INNOCENT PARTIES WHO, BY RIGHTS, SHOULD BE FEELING NO PAIN.
BAR
NO PARKING BUS STOP
MANY WILL BE TOUCHED (READ: "MAULED") BY THE RINGMASTER'S VILLAINY THIS NIGHT...
...BUT ONLY ONE WILL GO MAD AS A RESULT: IGNATZ HUBLEY, AGE 49, MARRIED, FATHER OF THREE, STEELWORKER, PRESENTLY UNEMPLOYED AND ON HIS WAY TO MONUMENTAL DRUNK.
THAT DUCK JUST CRACKED ME UP! I NEVER LAUGHED SO HARD--!
-BURRP- I'M TELLIN' YA--A MAN'S GOTTA HAVE A LI'L FUN--BEEN HELL SINCE THE MILL SHUT DOWN SIX--NO, SEVEN MONTHS AGO--ROTTEN, LOUSY--!
BUT THAT DUCK PUT ME IN STITCHES!
I MUSTA' SEEN 43 DIF'RENT BOSSES IN THIS TOWN AN' THE NEXT, Y'KNOW, LOOKIN' FOR WORK--?
NUTHIN'! AN' THE WIFE'S ON MY BACK--
--BUGGIN' ME TA MOVE TA PITTSBURGH--THE KIDS'RE SICK O' SPANISH RICE FOR DINNER SIX NIGHTS A WEEK--CAN'T BLAME 'EM--BUT IT DON'T MAKE 'EM EASY TO LIVE WITH--!
I BETTER BE GETTIN'--HOME.
FOUR EIGHTY-FIVE, IGNATZ.
KLUNK
SURE AS SHOOTIN', JAKE, HERE'S A--
-ulp-
'S EMPTY.

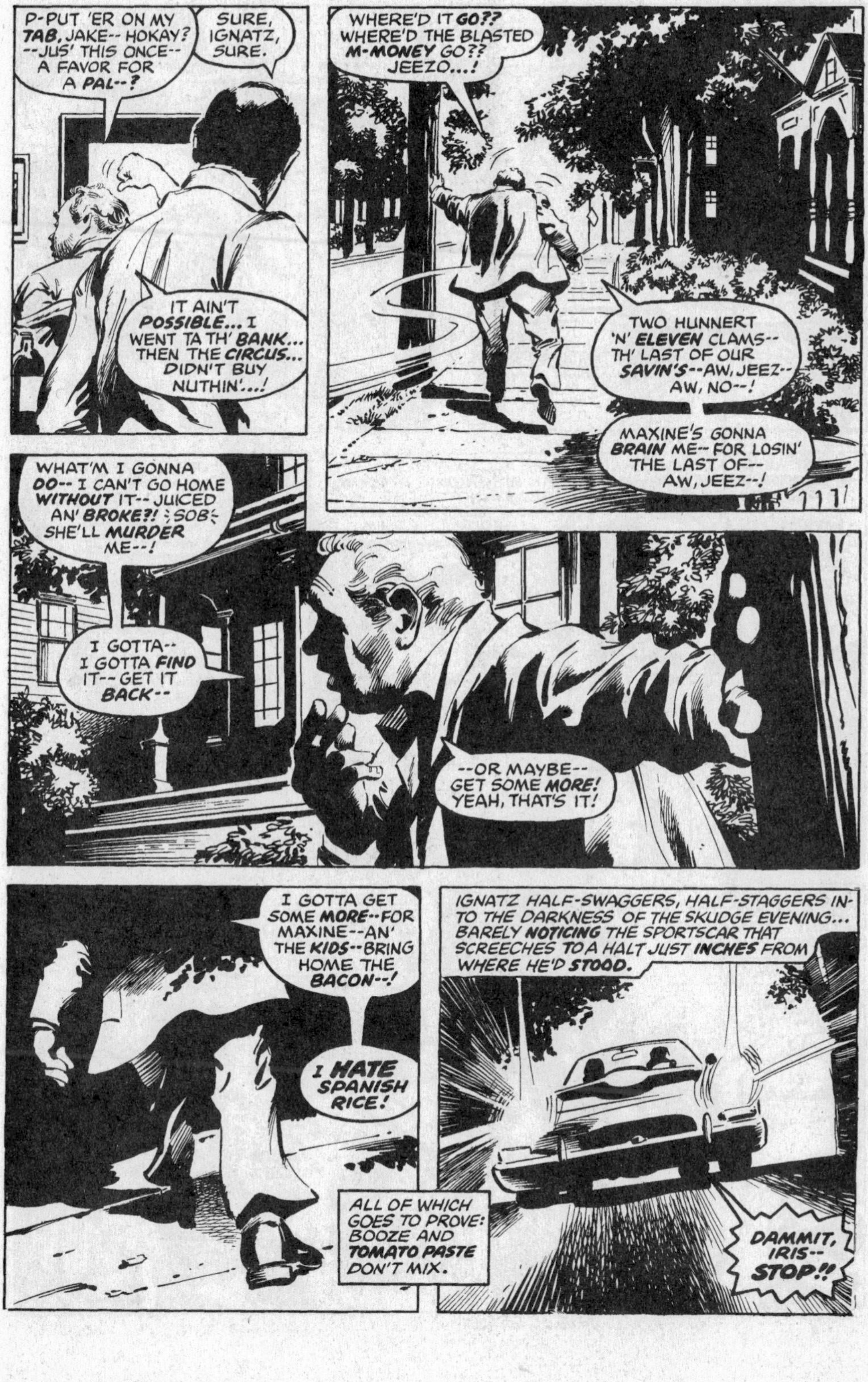
P-PUT 'ER ON MY TAB, JAKE-- HOKAY? --JUS' THIS ONCE-- A FAVOR FOR A PAL--?
SURE, IGNATZ, SURE.
IT AIN'T POSSIBLE... I WENT TA TH' BANK... THEN THE CIRCUS... DIDN'T BUY NUTHIN'...!
WHERE'D IT GO?? WHERE'D THE BLASTED M-MONEY GO?? JEEZO...!
TWO HUNNERT 'N' ELEVEN CLAMS-- TH' LAST OF OUR SAVIN'S--AW, JEEZ-- AW, NO--!
MAXINE'S GONNA BRAIN ME-- FOR LOSIN' THE LAST OF-- AW, JEEZ--!
WHAT'M I GONNA DO-- I CAN'T GO HOME WITHOUT IT-- JUICED AN' BROKE?! SOB
SHE'LL MURDER ME--!
I GOTTA-- I GOTTA FIND IT-- GET IT BACK--
--OR MAYBE-- GET SOME MORE! YEAH, THAT'S IT!
I GOTTA GET SOME MORE--FOR MAXINE--AN' THE KIDS--BRING HOME THE BACON--!
I HATE SPANISH RICE!
IGNATZ HALF-SWAGGERS, HALF-STAGGERS INTO THE DARKNESS OF THE SKUDGE EVENING... BARELY NOTICING THE SPORTSCAR THAT SCREECHES TO A HALT JUST INCHES FROM WHERE HE'D STOOD.
ALL OF WHICH GOES TO PROVE: BOOZE AND TOMATO PASTE DON'T MIX.
DAMMIT, IRIS-- STOP!!

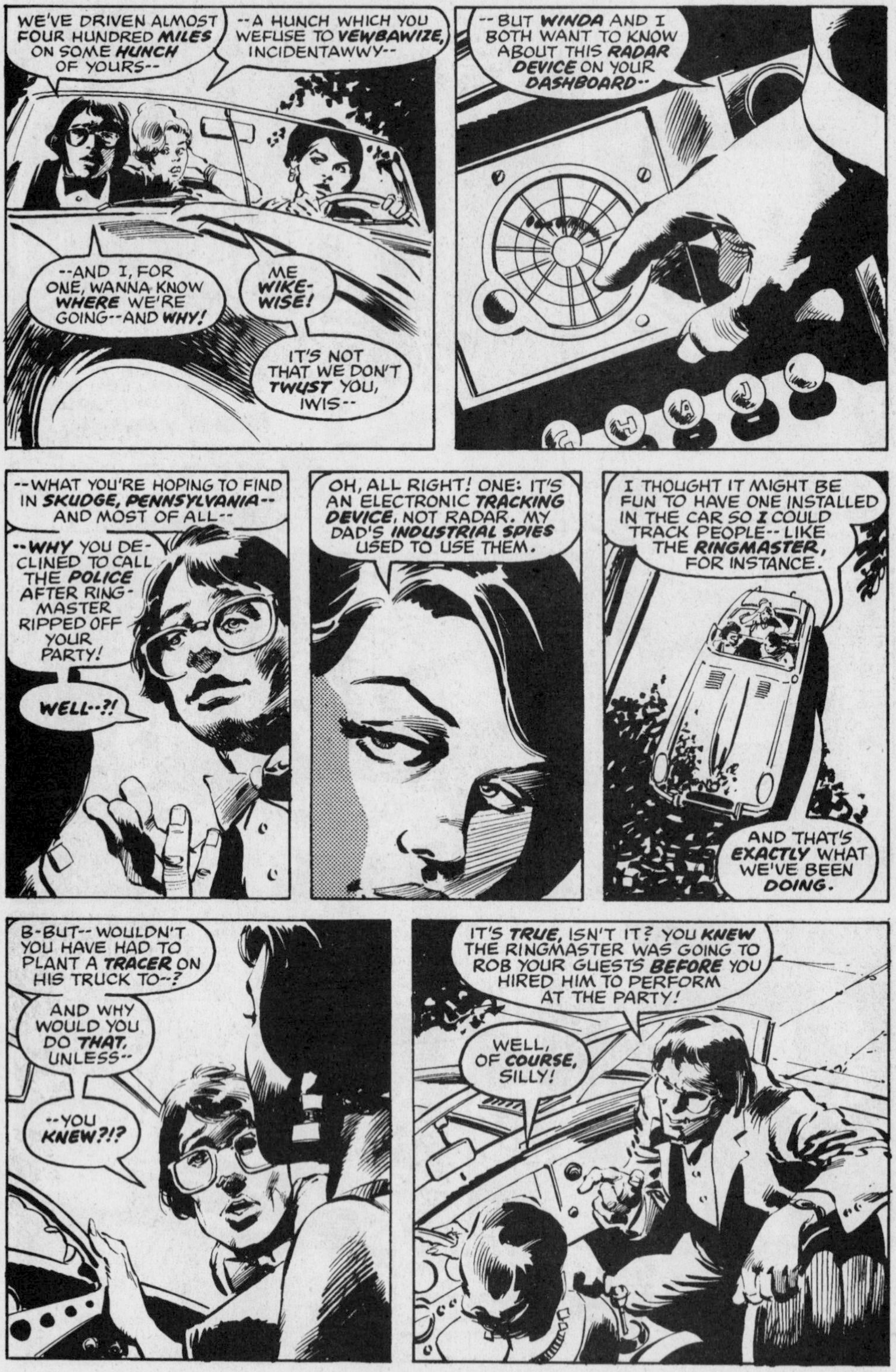
WE'VE DRIVEN ALMOST FOUR HUNDRED MILES ON SOME HUNCH OF YOURS--
--A HUNCH WHICH YOU WEFUSE TO VEWBAWIZE, INCIDENTAWWY--
--AND I, FOR ONE, WANNA KNOW WHERE WE'RE GOING--AND WHY!
ME WIKE-WISE!
IT'S NOT THAT WE DON'T TWUST YOU, IWIS--
--BUT WINDA AND I BOTH WANT TO KNOW ABOUT THIS RADAR DEVICE ON YOUR DASHBOARD--
--WHAT YOU'RE HOPING TO FIND IN SKUDGE, PENNSYLVANIA-- AND MOST OF ALL--
--WHY YOU DE-CLINED TO CALL THE POLICE AFTER RING-MASTER RIPPED OFF YOUR PARTY!
WELL--?!
OH, ALL RIGHT! ONE: IT'S AN ELECTRONIC TRACKING DEVICE, NOT RADAR. MY DAD'S INDUSTRIAL SPIES USED TO USE THEM.
I THOUGHT IT MIGHT BE FUN TO HAVE ONE INSTALLED IN THE CAR SO I COULD TRACK PEOPLE-- LIKE THE RINGMASTER, FOR INSTANCE.
AND THAT'S EXACTLY WHAT WE'VE BEEN DOING.
B-BUT-- WOULDN'T YOU HAVE HAD TO PLANT A TRACER ON HIS TRUCK TO--?
AND WHY WOULD YOU DO THAT, UNLESS--
--YOU KNEW?!?
IT'S TRUE, ISN'T IT? YOU KNEW THE RINGMASTER WAS GOING TO ROB YOUR GUESTS BEFORE YOU HIRED HIM TO PERFORM AT THE PARTY!
WELL, OF COURSE, SILLY!

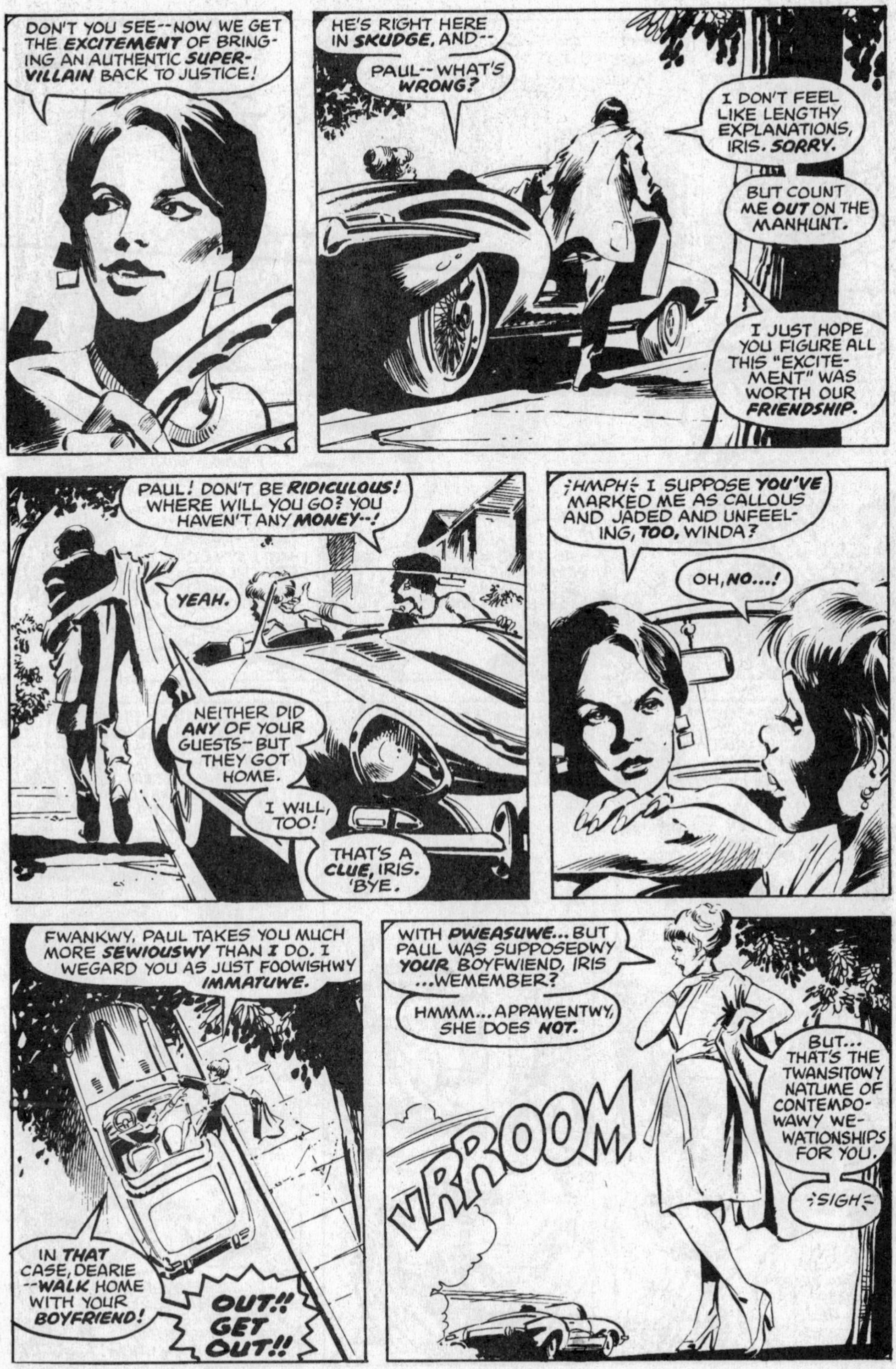
DON'T YOU SEE--NOW WE GET THE EXCITEMENT OF BRINGING AN AUTHENTIC SUPER-VILLAIN BACK TO JUSTICE!
HE'S RIGHT HERE IN SKUDGE, AND--
PAUL--WHAT'S WRONG?
I DON'T FEEL LIKE LENGTHY EXPLANATIONS, IRIS. SORRY.
BUT COUNT ME OUT ON THE MANHUNT.
I JUST HOPE YOU FIGURE ALL THIS "EXCITEMENT" WAS WORTH OUR FRIENDSHIP.
PAUL! DON'T BE RIDICULOUS! WHERE WILL YOU GO? YOU HAVEN'T ANY MONEY--!
YEAH.
NEITHER DID ANY OF YOUR GUESTS--BUT THEY GOT HOME.
I WILL, TOO!
THAT'S A CLUE, IRIS. 'BYE.
HMPH I SUPPOSE YOU'VE MARKED ME AS CALLOUS AND JADED AND UNFEELING, TOO, WINDA?
OH, NO...!
FWANKWY, PAUL TAKES YOU MUCH MORE SEWIOUSWY THAN I DO. I WEGARD YOU AS JUST FOOWISHWY IMMATUWE.
IN THAT CASE, DEARIE --WALK HOME WITH YOUR BOYFRIEND!
OUT!! GET OUT!!
WITH PWEASUWE... BUT PAUL WAS SUPPOSEDWY YOUR BOYFWIEND, IRIS ...WEMEMBER?
HMMM... APPAWENTWY, SHE DOES NOT.
BUT... THAT'S THE TWANSITOWY NATUWE OF CONTEMPOWAWY WE-WATIONSHIPS FOR YOU.
SIGH
VRROOM

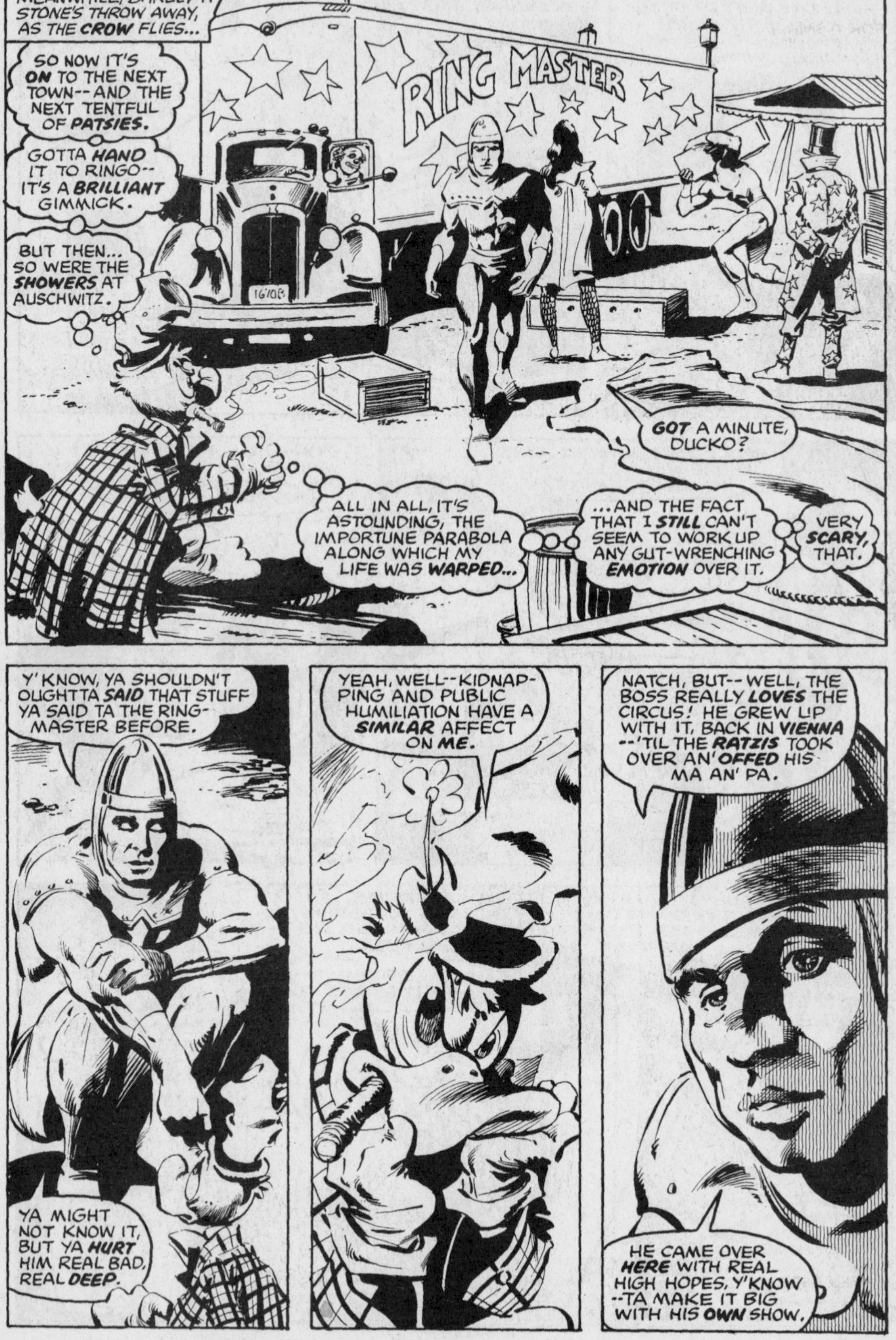
MEANWHILE, BARELY A STONE'S THROW AWAY, AS THE CROW FLIES...
SO NOW IT'S ON TO THE NEXT TOWN--AND THE NEXT TENTFUL OF PATSIES.
GOTTA HAND IT TO RINGO--IT'S A BRILLIANT GIMMICK.
BUT THEN... SO WERE THE SHOWERS AT AUSCHWITZ.
RING MASTER
GOT A MINUTE, DUCKO?
ALL IN ALL, IT'S ASTOUNDING, THE IMPORTUNE PARABOLA ALONG WHICH MY LIFE WAS WARPED...
...AND THE FACT THAT I STILL CAN'T SEEM TO WORK UP ANY GUT-WRENCHING EMOTION OVER IT.
VERY SCARY, THAT.
Y' KNOW, YA SHOULDN'T OUGHTTA SAID THAT STUFF YA SAID TA THE RING-MASTER BEFORE.
YA MIGHT NOT KNOW IT, BUT YA HURT HIM REAL BAD, REAL DEEP.
YEAH, WELL--KIDNAPPING AND PUBLIC HUMILIATION HAVE A SIMILAR AFFECT ON ME.
NATCH, BUT--WELL, THE BOSS REALLY LOVES THE CIRCUS! HE GREW UP WITH IT, BACK IN VIENNA--'TIL THE RATZIS TOOK OVER AN' OFFED HIS MA AN' PA.
HE CAME OVER HERE WITH REAL HIGH HOPES, Y'KNOW--TA MAKE IT BIG WITH HIS OWN SHOW.

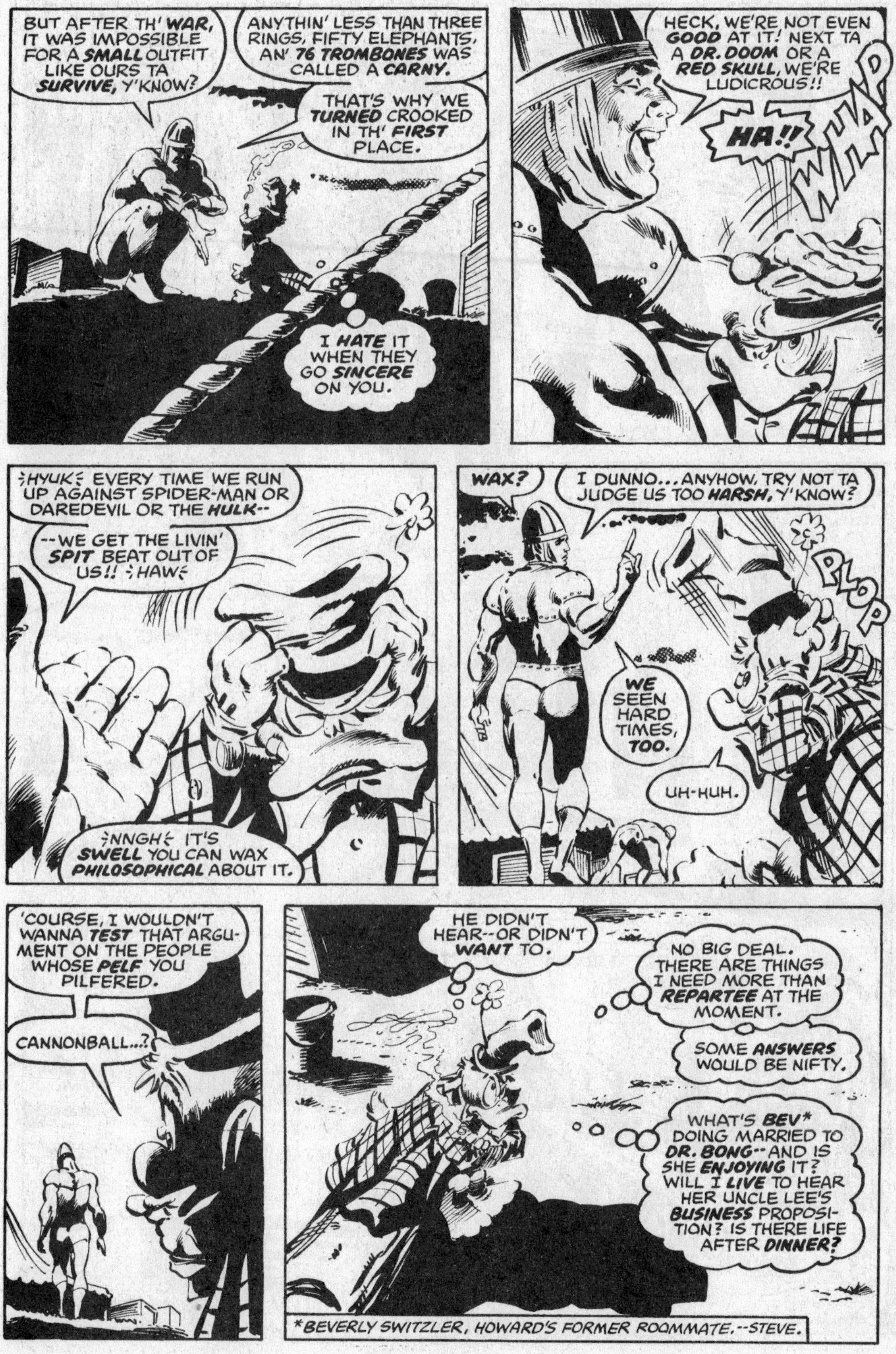

BUT AFTER TH' WAR, IT WAS IMPOSSIBLE FOR A SMALL OUTFIT LIKE OURS TA SURVIVE, Y'KNOW?
ANYTHIN' LESS THAN THREE RINGS, FIFTY ELEPHANTS, AN' 76 TROMBONES WAS CALLED A CARNY.
THAT'S WHY WE TURNED CROOKED IN TH' FIRST PLACE.
I HATE IT WHEN THEY GO SINCERE ON YOU.
HECK, WE'RE NOT EVEN GOOD AT IT! NEXT TA A DR. DOOM OR A RED SKULL, WE'RE LUDICROUS!!
HA!!
WHAP
HYUK EVERY TIME WE RUN UP AGAINST SPIDER-MAN OR DAREDEVIL OR THE HULK--
--WE GET THE LIVIN' SPIT BEAT OUT OF US!! HAW
NNGH IT'S SWELL YOU CAN WAX PHILOSOPHICAL ABOUT IT.
WAX?
I DUNNO... ANYHOW, TRY NOT TA JUDGE US TOO HARSH, Y'KNOW?
PLOP
WE SEEN HARD TIMES, TOO.
UH-HUH.
'COURSE, I WOULDN'T WANNA TEST THAT ARGUMENT ON THE PEOPLE WHOSE PELF YOU PILFERED.
CANNONBALL...?
HE DIDN'T HEAR--OR DIDN'T WANT TO.
NO BIG DEAL. THERE ARE THINGS I NEED MORE THAN REPARTEE AT THE MOMENT.
SOME ANSWERS WOULD BE NIFTY.
WHAT'S BEV* DOING MARRIED TO DR. BONG-- AND IS SHE ENJOYING IT? WILL I LIVE TO HEAR HER UNCLE LEE'S BUSINESS PROPOSITION? IS THERE LIFE AFTER DINNER?
*BEVERLY SWITZLER, HOWARD'S FORMER ROOMMATE. --STEVE.

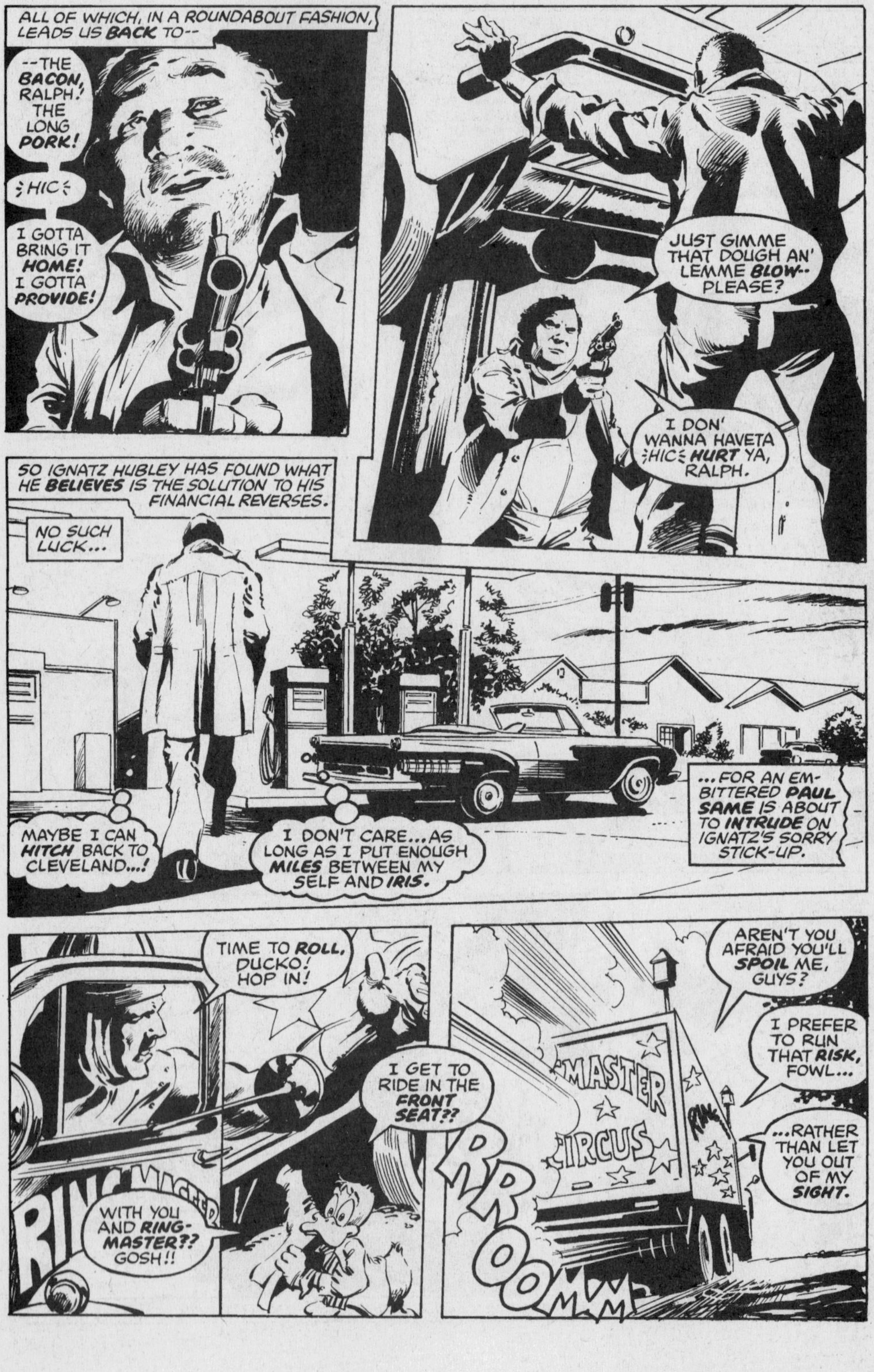
ALL OF WHICH, IN A ROUNDABOUT FASHION, LEADS US BACK TO--
--THE BACON, RALPH! THE LONG PORK!
HIC
I GOTTA BRING IT HOME! I GOTTA PROVIDE!
JUST GIMME THAT DOUGH AN' LEMME BLOW--PLEASE?
I DON' WANNA HAVETA HIC HURT YA, RALPH.
SO IGNATZ HUBLEY HAS FOUND WHAT HE BELIEVES IS THE SOLUTION TO HIS FINANCIAL REVERSES.
NO SUCH LUCK...
MAYBE I CAN HITCH BACK TO CLEVELAND...!
I DON'T CARE...AS LONG AS I PUT ENOUGH MILES BETWEEN MY SELF AND IRIS.
...FOR AN EMBITTERED PAUL SAME IS ABOUT TO INTRUDE ON IGNATZ'S SORRY STICK-UP.
TIME TO ROLL, DUCKO! HOP IN!
I GET TO RIDE IN THE FRONT SEAT??
WITH YOU AND RING-MASTER?? GOSH!!
AREN'T YOU AFRAID YOU'LL SPOIL ME, GUYS?
I PREFER TO RUN THAT RISK, FOWL...
...RATHER THAN LET YOU OUT OF MY SIGHT.
RRROOOMMM

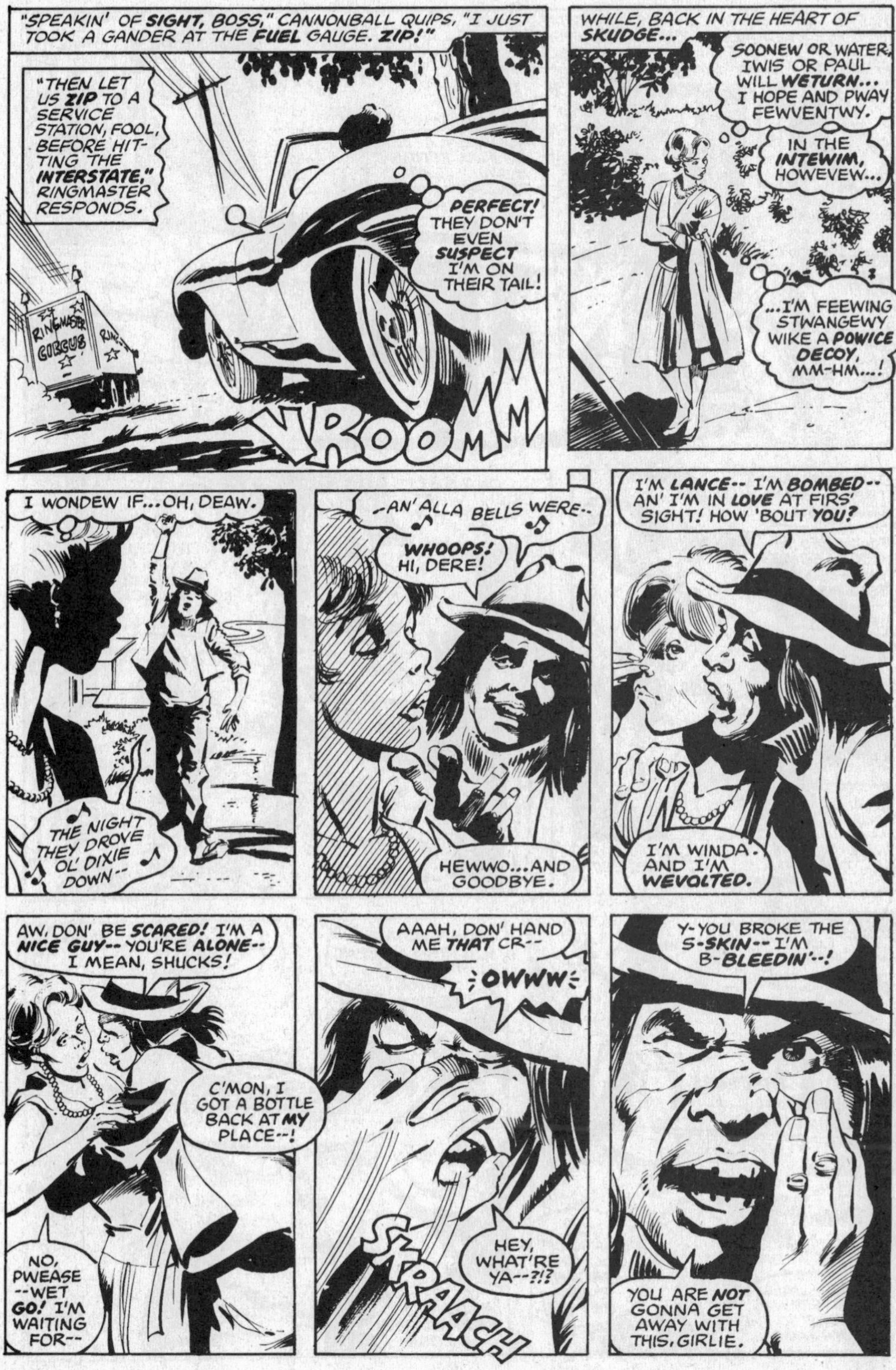
"SPEAKIN' OF SIGHT, BOSS," CANNONBALL QUIPS, "I JUST TOOK A GANDER AT THE FUEL GAUGE. ZIP!"
"THEN LET US ZIP TO A SERVICE STATION, FOOL, BEFORE HITTING THE INTERSTATE," RINGMASTER RESPONDS.
PERFECT! THEY DON'T EVEN SUSPECT I'M ON THEIR TAIL!
RINGMASTER CIRCUS
VROOMM
WHILE, BACK IN THE HEART OF SKUDGE...
SOONEW OR WATER, IWIS OR PAUL WILL WETURN... I HOPE AND PWAY FEWVENTWY.
IN THE INTEWIM, HOWEVEW...
...I'M FEEWING STWANGEWY WIKE A POWICE DECOY, MM-HM...!
I WONDEW IF...OH, DEAW.
THE NIGHT THEY DROVE OL' DIXIE DOWN--
--AN' ALLA BELLS WERE--
WHOOPS! HI, DERE!
HEWWO...AND GOODBYE.
I'M LANCE-- I'M BOMBED-- AN' I'M IN LOVE AT FIRS' SIGHT! HOW 'BOUT YOU?
I'M WINDA. AND I'M WEVOLTED.
AW, DON' BE SCARED! I'M A NICE GUY-- YOU'RE ALONE-- I MEAN, SHUCKS!
C'MON, I GOT A BOTTLE BACK AT MY PLACE--!
NO, PWEASE --WET GO! I'M WAITING FOR--
AAAH, DON' HAND ME THAT CR--
OWWW
HEY, WHAT'RE YA--?!?
SKRAACH
Y-YOU BROKE THE S-SKIN-- I'M B-BLEEDIN'--!
YOU ARE NOT GONNA GET AWAY WITH THIS, GIRLIE.

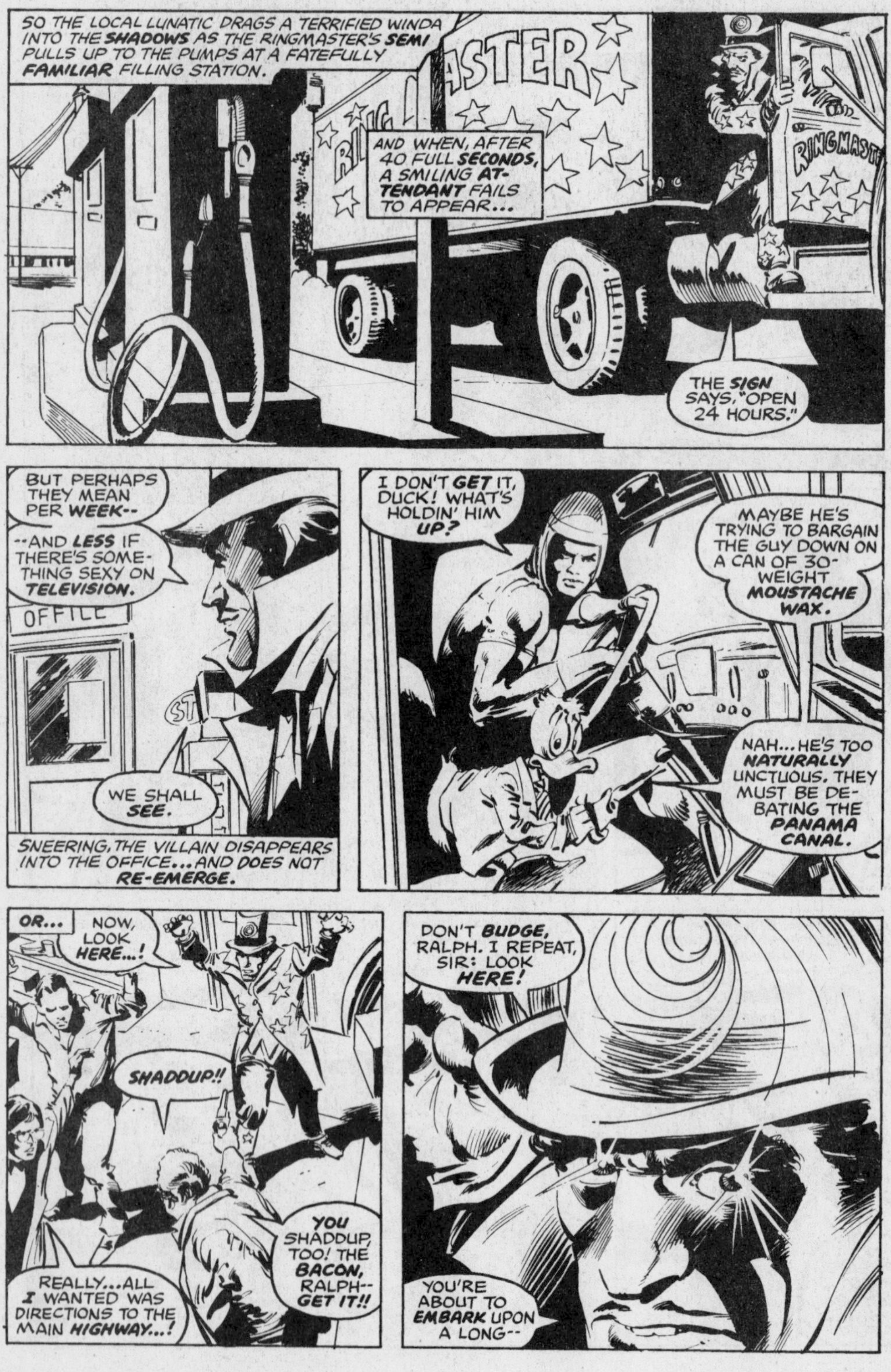
SO THE LOCAL LUNATIC DRAGS A TERRIFIED WINDA INTO THE SHADOWS AS THE RINGMASTER'S SEMI PULLS UP TO THE PUMPS AT A FATEFULLY FAMILIAR FILLING STATION.
RINGMASTER
AND WHEN, AFTER 40 FULL SECONDS, A SMILING AT-TENDANT FAILS TO APPEAR...
RINGMASTER
THE SIGN SAYS, "OPEN 24 HOURS."
BUT PERHAPS THEY MEAN PER WEEK--
--AND LESS IF THERE'S SOME-THING SEXY ON TELEVISION.
OFFICE
WE SHALL SEE.
SNEERING, THE VILLAIN DISAPPEARS INTO THE OFFICE... AND DOES NOT RE-EMERGE.
I DON'T GET IT, DUCK! WHAT'S HOLDIN' HIM UP?
MAYBE HE'S TRYING TO BARGAIN THE GUY DOWN ON A CAN OF 30-WEIGHT MOUSTACHE WAX.
NAH... HE'S TOO NATURALLY UNCTUOUS. THEY MUST BE DE-BATING THE PANAMA CANAL.
OR...
NOW, LOOK HERE...!
SHADDUP!!
YOU SHADDUP, TOO! THE BACON, RALPH-- GET IT!!
REALLY... ALL I WANTED WAS DIRECTIONS TO THE MAIN HIGHWAY...!
DON'T BUDGE, RALPH. I REPEAT, SIR: LOOK HERE!
YOU'RE ABOUT TO EMBARK UPON A LONG--

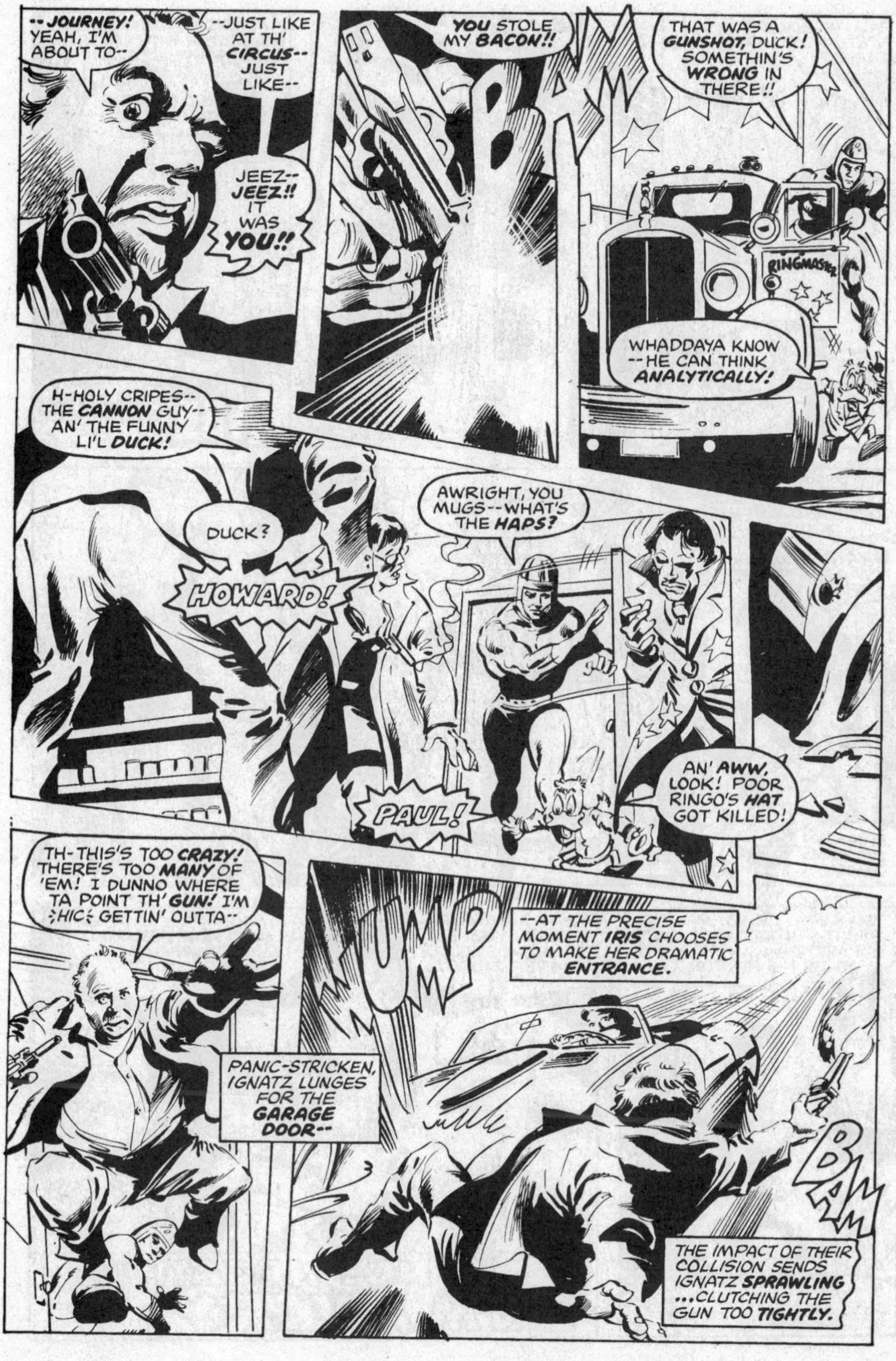

--JOURNEY! YEAH, I'M ABOUT TO--
--JUST LIKE AT TH' CIRCUS-- JUST LIKE--
JEEZ-- JEEZ!! IT WAS YOU!!
YOU STOLE MY BACON!!
BAM
THAT WAS A GUNSHOT, DUCK! SOMETHIN'S WRONG IN THERE!!
RINGMASTER
WHADDAYA KNOW --HE CAN THINK ANALYTICALLY!
H-HOLY CRIPES-- THE CANNON GUY-- AN' THE FUNNY LI'L DUCK!
DUCK?
HOWARD!
AWRIGHT, YOU MUGS--WHAT'S THE HAPS?
PAUL!
AN' AWW, LOOK! POOR RINGO'S HAT GOT KILLED!
TH-THIS'S TOO CRAZY! THERE'S TOO MANY OF 'EM! I DUNNO WHERE TA POINT TH' GUN! I'M ⸗HIC⸗ GETTIN' OUTTA--
PANIC-STRICKEN, IGNATZ LUNGES FOR THE GARAGE DOOR--
WUMP
--AT THE PRECISE MOMENT IRIS CHOOSES TO MAKE HER DRAMATIC ENTRANCE.
BAM
THE IMPACT OF THEIR COLLISION SENDS IGNATZ SPRAWLING ...CLUTCHING THE GUN TOO TIGHTLY.

AND THE BULLET UNFORTUNATELY FINDS A TARGET:
PAUL...?
SOMETIME LATER...
YEAH, THAT'S HOW IT BREAKS DOWN, LEE:
TWO SHATTERED KNEECAPS FOR HUBLEY... RINGMASTER GETS AWAY...
...WINDA'S UNDER HEAVY SEDATION WITH LACERATIONS, BRUISES, AND TRAUMA...
...AND THEY'RE "NOT SURE" YET ABOUT PAUL.
OTHER THAN THAT, EVERYTHING'S FINE.
ALL RIGHT--STAY PUT! I'LL DRIVE UP FROM CLEVELAND TO FETCH YOU ALL!
WHAT?! BECAUSE I'M YOUR FRIEND, THAT'S WHY!
HANG UP! I'M ON MY WAY!
HE PROBABLY IS, TOO--MY FRIEND. THE OTHER BEVERLY SWITZLER WAS. I--
WELL--WHO LET YOU OUT?
THERE, UH... WASN'T ANY CHARGE THEY COULD HOLD ME ON.
FIGURES.
YOU KNOW, I'M NOT HAPPY ABOUT... I LIKED PAUL... AND HIS ARTWORK... I DID WANT TO BE HIS PATRON...!
WINDA WAS RIGHT ...I'M VERY IMMATURE.
IF THAT'S ALL SHE SAID, YOU GOT OFF EASY!
LISTEN CLOSE, IRIS, 'CAUSE HERE'S A LESSON OBVIOUSLY NEVER TAUGHT YOU:
ACTIONS HAVE CONSEQUENCES.
ALL YOU HAIRLESS APES SEEM SO SELF-OBSESSED, I'M NOT SURPRISED IT NEVER OCCURRED TO YOU--!
BUT MESS WITH PEOPLE'S LIVES--AND FATE EVENTUALLY MESSES BACK!
YOU'LL GET YOURS, IRIS.
NEXT
I'M NOT NEGATIVE.. I'M ANGRY (I THINK)

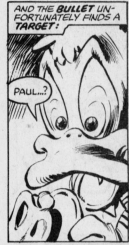

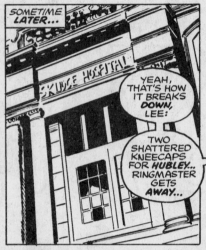

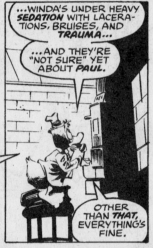

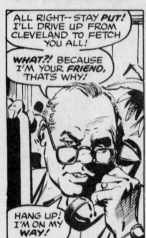

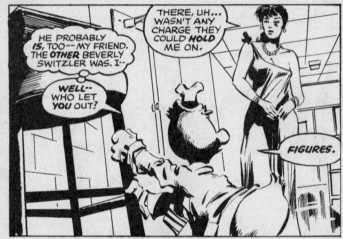

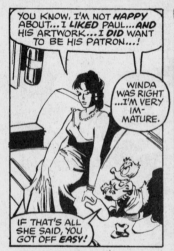

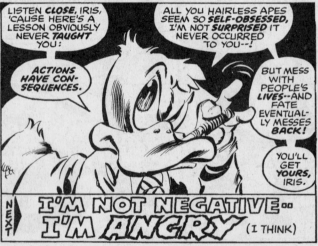

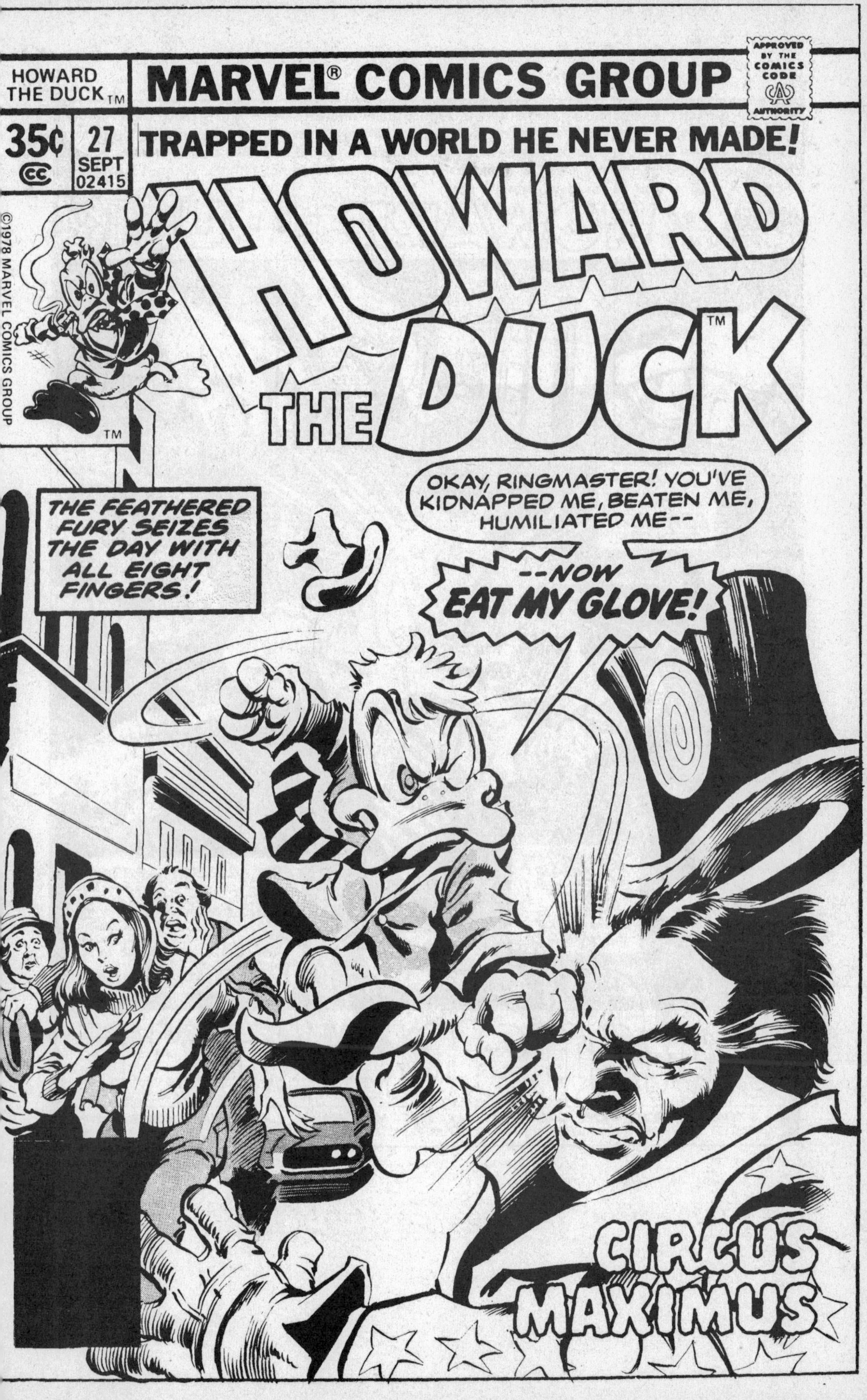

HOWARD THE DUCK TM
MARVEL® COMICS GROUP
APPROVED BY THE COMICS CODE AUTHORITY
35¢
CC
27
SEPT
02415
TRAPPED IN A WORLD HE NEVER MADE!
HOWARD THE DUCK TM
©1978 MARVEL COMICS GROUP
TM
THE FEATHERED FURY SEIZES THE DAY WITH ALL EIGHT FINGERS!
OKAY, RINGMASTER! YOU'VE KIDNAPPED ME, BEATEN ME, HUMILIATED ME--
--NOW EAT MY GLOVE!
CIRCUS MAXIMUS

From the time of his hatching, he was...different. A potentially brilliant scholar who dreaded the structured environment of school, he educated himself in the streets, taking whatever work was available, formulating his philosophy of self from what he learned of the world about him. And then the Cosmic Axis shifted...and that world *changed*. Suddenly, he was stranded in a universe he could not fathom. Without warning, he became a strange fowl in an even stranger land.

Stan Lee PRESENTS: HOWARD the DUCK!

FINGERS WAG, VOICES NAG -- ACCUSATIONS, REMONSTRATIONS, DENUNCIATIONS -- FROM OUT OF THE *VOID!*

"*HOWARD* THE *COWARD!*" THEY CRY.

"*OFF* WITH HIS *HEAD!* STUFF HIM! ROAST HIM IN HIS OWN *WELT-SCHMERZ!*"

AAAH-- SHADDUP!

BUT LIKE SOME GREEK CHORUS -- OR PERHAPS A ROOMFUL OF ITALIAN WAITERS -- THE SHOUTS GREW *LOUDER,* MORE HOSTILE -- EACH DROWNING OUT THE OTHER IN A CACOPHONY OF UNINTELLIGIBLE *BABBLE!*

CIRCUS MAXIMUS

STEVE GERBER WRITER / EDITOR / **GENE COLAN** ARTIST / **KLAUS JANSON** INKER / **GASPAR** LETTERS / **PHIL R.** COLORS / **JIM SHOOTER** EDITOR-IN-CHIEF

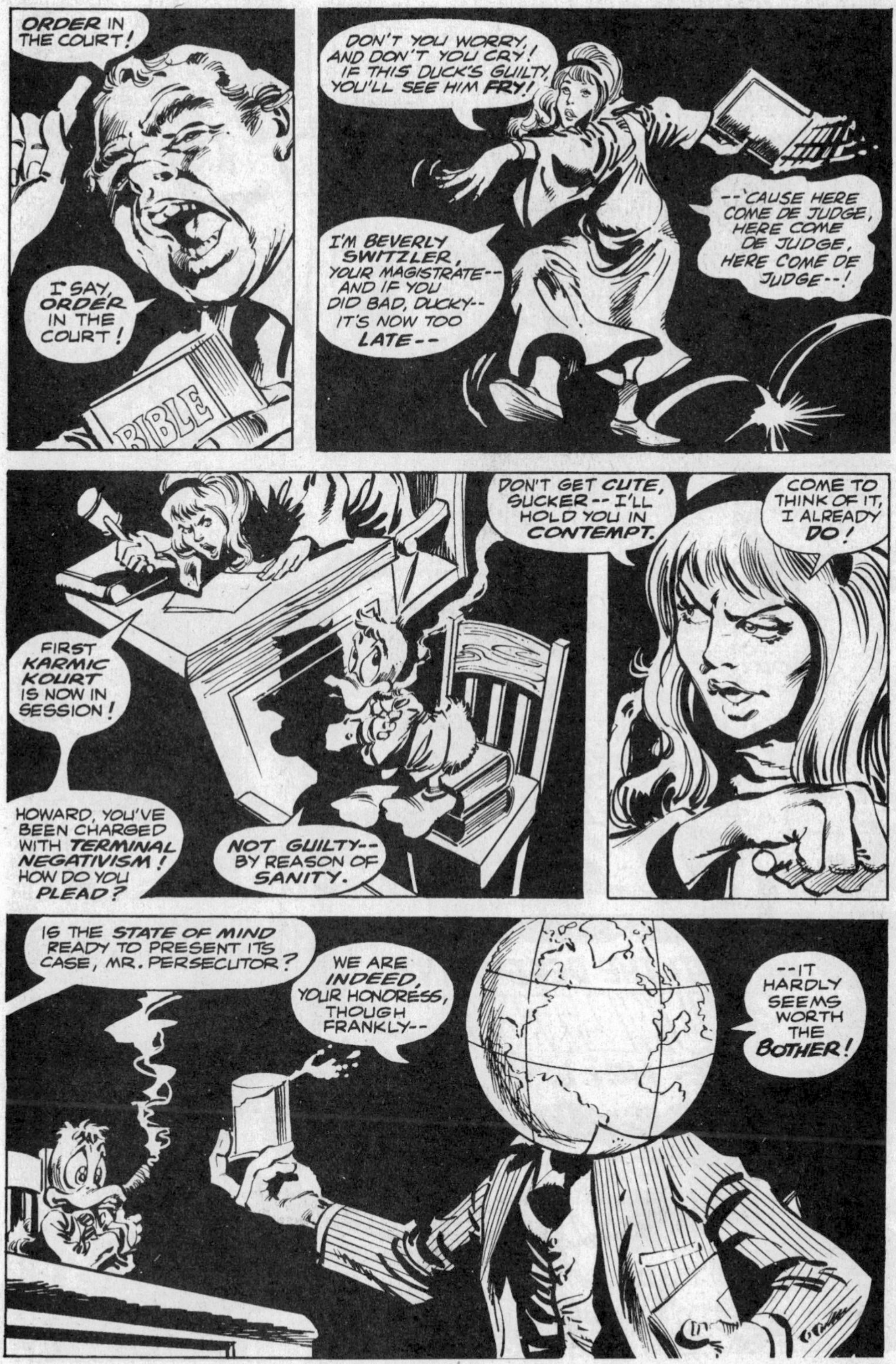
ORDER IN THE COURT!
I SAY, ORDER IN THE COURT!
BIBLE
DON'T YOU WORRY, AND DON'T YOU CRY! IF THIS DUCK'S GUILTY, YOU'LL SEE HIM FRY!
I'M BEVERLY SWITZLER, YOUR MAGISTRATE-- AND IF YOU DID BAD, DUCKY-- IT'S NOW TOO LATE--
--'CAUSE HERE COME DE JUDGE, HERE COME DE JUDGE, HERE COME DE JUDGE--!
FIRST KARMIC KOURT IS NOW IN SESSION!
HOWARD, YOU'VE BEEN CHARGED WITH TERMINAL NEGATIVISM! HOW DO YOU PLEAD?
NOT GUILTY-- BY REASON OF SANITY.
DON'T GET CUTE, SUCKER-- I'LL HOLD YOU IN CONTEMPT.
COME TO THINK OF IT, I ALREADY DO!
IS THE STATE OF MIND READY TO PRESENT ITS CASE, MR. PERSECUTOR?
WE ARE INDEED, YOUR HONORESS, THOUGH FRANKLY--
--IT HARDLY SEEMS WORTH THE BOTHER!

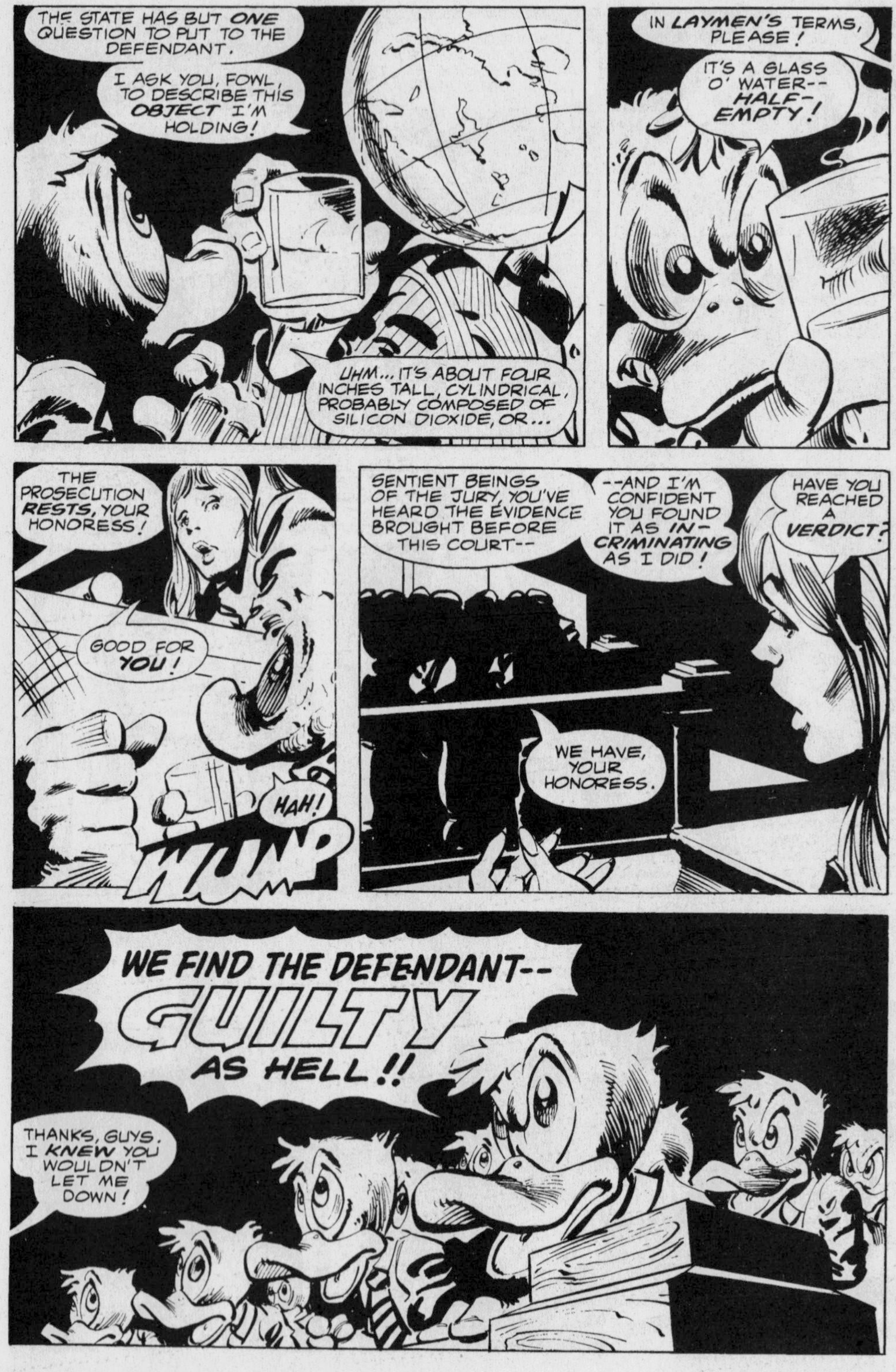

THE STATE HAS BUT ONE QUESTION TO PUT TO THE DEFENDANT.
I ASK YOU, FOWL, TO DESCRIBE THIS OBJECT I'M HOLDING!
UHM... IT'S ABOUT FOUR INCHES TALL, CYLINDRICAL, PROBABLY COMPOSED OF SILICON DIOXIDE, OR...
IN LAYMEN'S TERMS, PLEASE!
IT'S A GLASS O' WATER-- HALF-EMPTY!
THE PROSECUTION RESTS, YOUR HONORESS!
GOOD FOR YOU!
HAH!
WUMP
SENTIENT BEINGS OF THE JURY, YOU'VE HEARD THE EVIDENCE BROUGHT BEFORE THIS COURT--
--AND I'M CONFIDENT YOU FOUND IT AS IN-CRIMINATING AS I DID!
HAVE YOU REACHED A VERDICT?
WE HAVE, YOUR HONORESS.
WE FIND THE DEFENDANT-- GUILTY AS HELL!!
THANKS, GUYS. I KNEW YOU WOULDN'T LET ME DOWN!

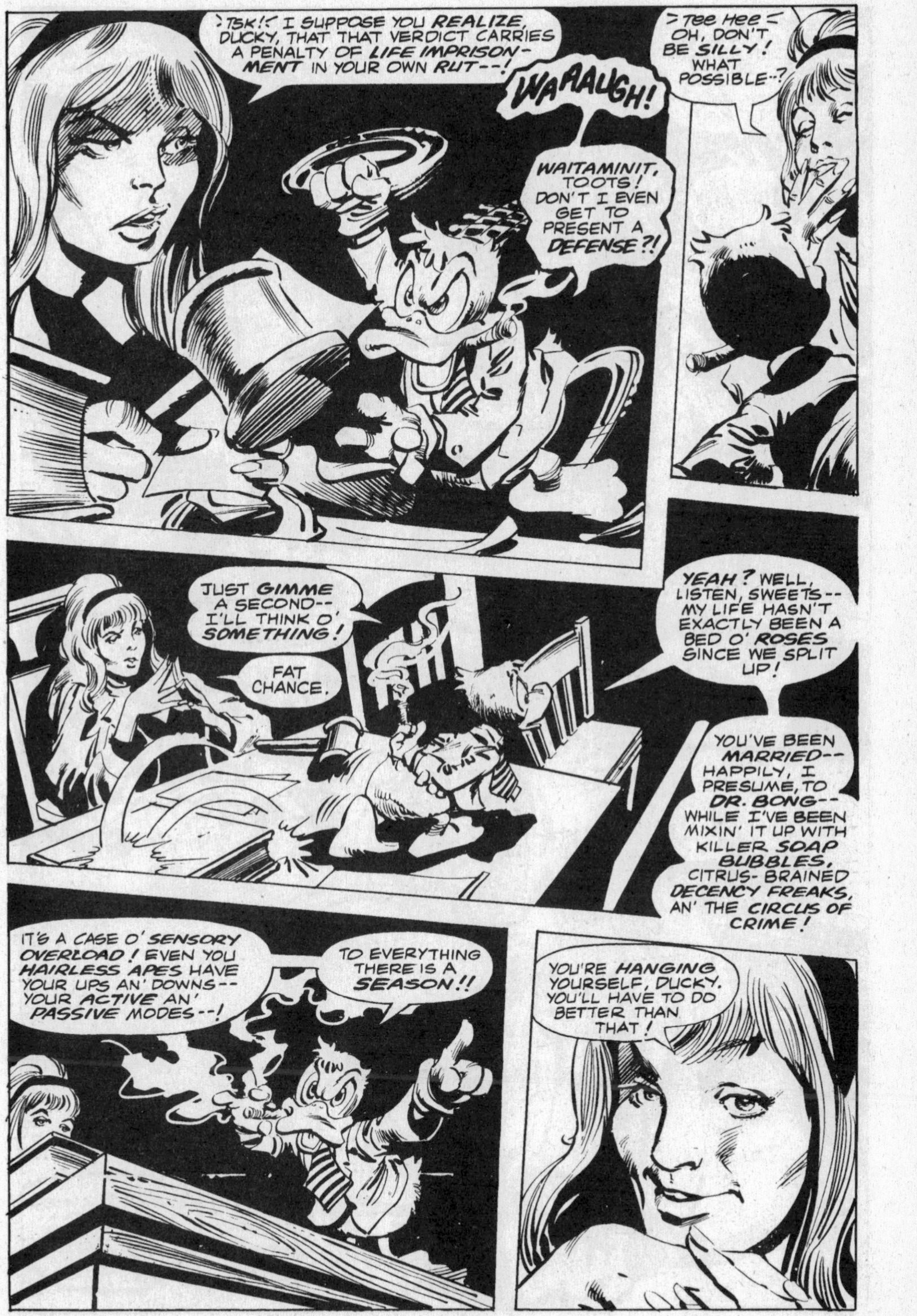

>TSK!< I SUPPOSE YOU REALIZE, DUCKY, THAT THAT VERDICT CARRIES A PENALTY OF LIFE IMPRISONMENT IN YOUR OWN RUT--!
WAAAUGH!
WAITAMINIT, TOOTS! DON'T I EVEN GET TO PRESENT A DEFENSE?!
>TEE HEE< OH, DON'T BE SILLY! WHAT POSSIBLE--?
JUST GIMME A SECOND-- I'LL THINK O' SOMETHING!
FAT CHANCE.
YEAH? WELL, LISTEN, SWEETS-- MY LIFE HASN'T EXACTLY BEEN A BED O' ROSES SINCE WE SPLIT UP!
YOU'VE BEEN MARRIED-- HAPPILY, I PRESUME, TO DR. BONG-- WHILE I'VE BEEN MIXIN' IT UP WITH KILLER SOAP BUBBLES, CITRUS-BRAINED DECENCY FREAKS, AN' THE CIRCUS OF CRIME!
IT'S A CASE O' SENSORY OVERLOAD! EVEN YOU HAIRLESS APES HAVE YOUR UPS AN' DOWNS-- YOUR ACTIVE AN' PASSIVE MODES--!
TO EVERYTHING THERE IS A SEASON!!
YOU'RE HANGING YOURSELF, DUCKY. YOU'LL HAVE TO DO BETTER THAN THAT!

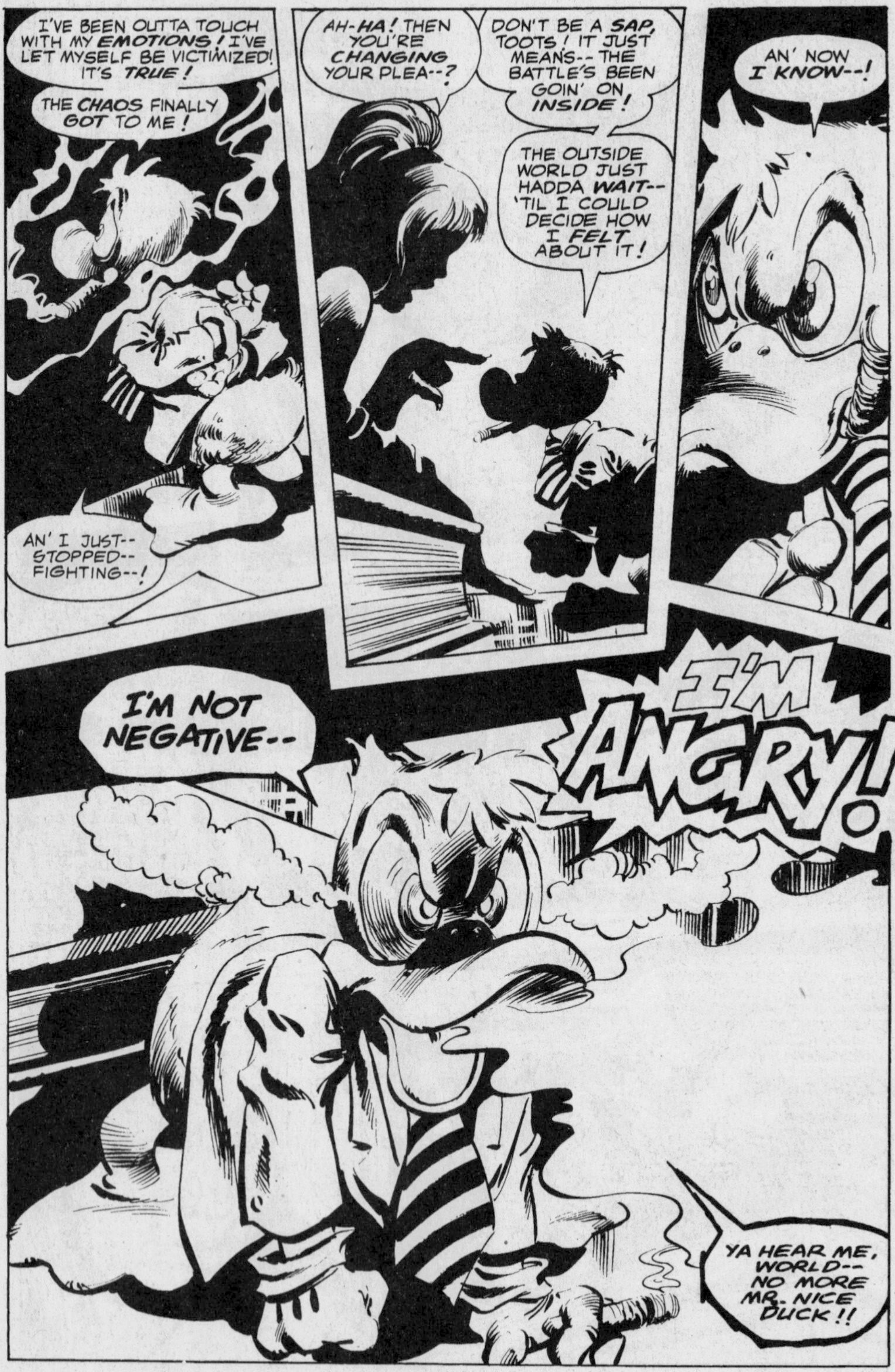

I'VE BEEN OUTTA TOUCH WITH MY EMOTIONS! I'VE LET MYSELF BE VICTIMIZED! IT'S TRUE!
THE CHAOS FINALLY GOT TO ME!
AN' I JUST-- STOPPED-- FIGHTING--!
AH-HA! THEN YOU'RE CHANGING YOUR PLEA--?
DON'T BE A SAP, TOOTS! IT JUST MEANS-- THE BATTLE'S BEEN GOIN' ON INSIDE!
THE OUTSIDE WORLD JUST HADDA WAIT-- 'TIL I COULD DECIDE HOW I FELT ABOUT IT!
AN' NOW I KNOW--!
I'M NOT NEGATIVE--
I'M ANGRY!
YA HEAR ME, WORLD-- NO MORE MR. NICE DUCK!!

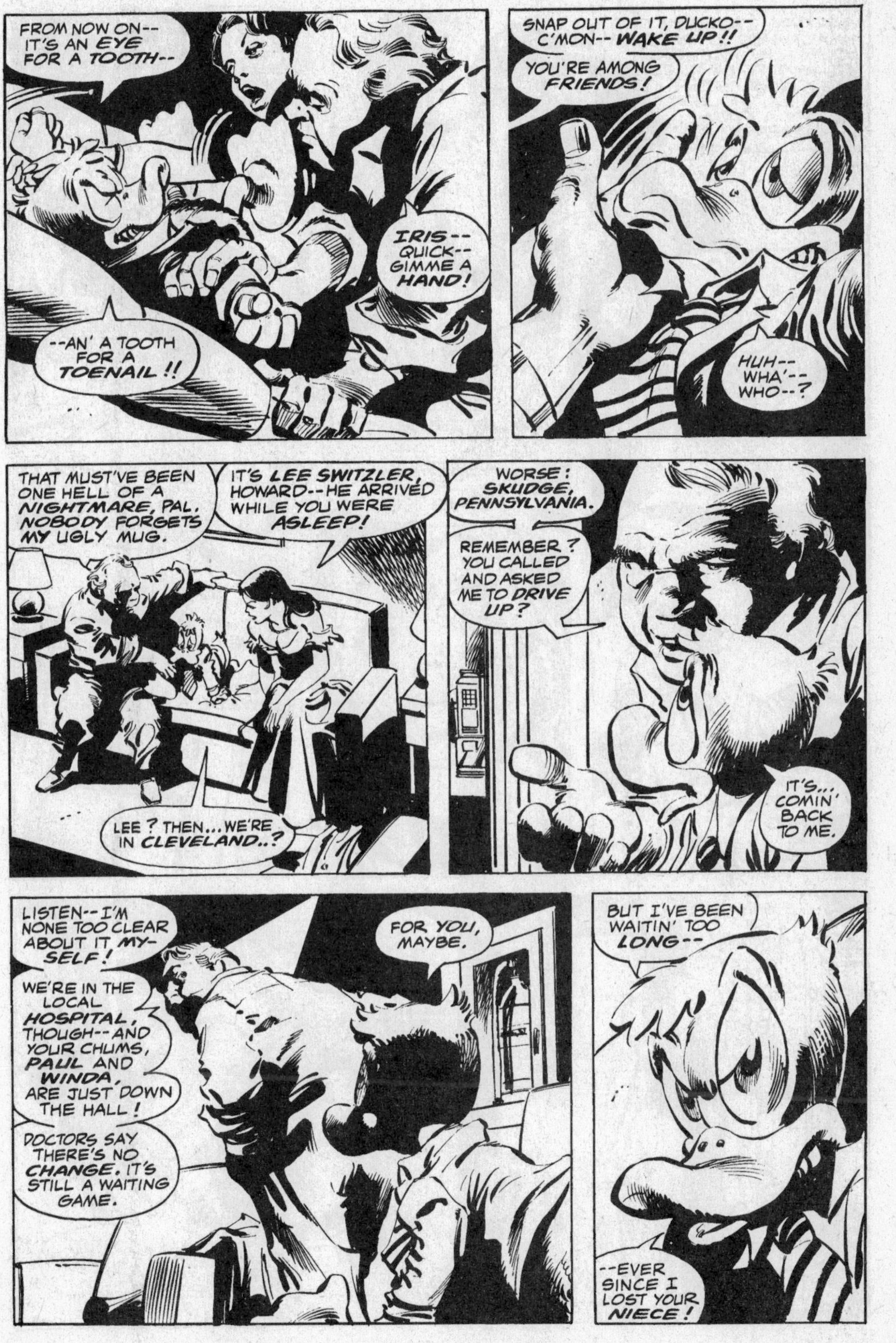
FROM NOW ON-- IT'S AN EYE FOR A TOOTH--
IRIS-- QUICK-- GIMME A HAND!
--AN' A TOOTH FOR A TOENAIL!!
SNAP OUT OF IT, DUCKO-- C'MON-- WAKE UP!!
YOU'RE AMONG FRIENDS!
HUH-- WHA'-- WHO--?
THAT MUST'VE BEEN ONE HELL OF A NIGHTMARE, PAL. NOBODY FORGETS MY UGLY MUG.
IT'S LEE SWITZLER, HOWARD--HE ARRIVED WHILE YOU WERE ASLEEP!
LEE? THEN...WE'RE IN CLEVELAND..?
WORSE: SKUDGE, PENNSYLVANIA.
REMEMBER? YOU CALLED AND ASKED ME TO DRIVE UP?
IT'S... COMIN' BACK TO ME.
LISTEN--I'M NONE TOO CLEAR ABOUT IT MY-SELF!
WE'RE IN THE LOCAL HOSPITAL, THOUGH--AND YOUR CHUMS, PAUL AND WINDA, ARE JUST DOWN THE HALL!
DOCTORS SAY THERE'S NO CHANGE. IT'S STILL A WAITING GAME.
FOR YOU, MAYBE.
BUT I'VE BEEN WAITIN' TOO LONG--
--EVER SINCE I LOST YOUR NIECE!

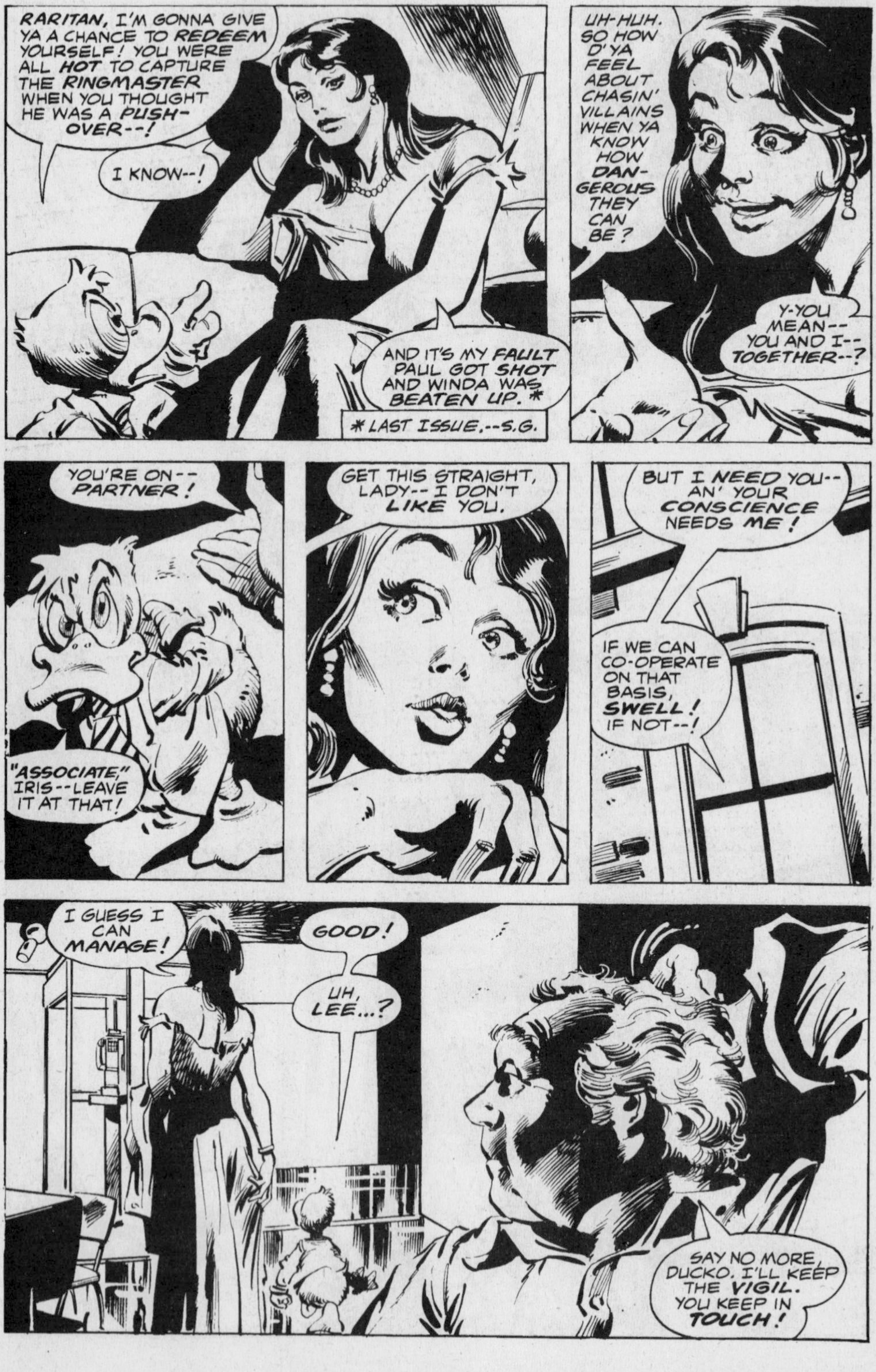
RARITAN, I'M GONNA GIVE YA A CHANCE TO REDEEM YOURSELF! YOU WERE ALL HOT TO CAPTURE THE RINGMASTER WHEN YOU THOUGHT HE WAS A PUSH-OVER--!
I KNOW--!
AND IT'S MY FAULT PAUL GOT SHOT AND WINDA WAS BEATEN UP.*
*LAST ISSUE.--S.G.
UH-HUH. SO HOW D'YA FEEL ABOUT CHASIN' VILLAINS WHEN YA KNOW HOW DAN-GEROUS THEY CAN BE?
Y-YOU MEAN--YOU AND I--TOGETHER--?
YOU'RE ON--PARTNER!
"ASSOCIATE," IRIS--LEAVE IT AT THAT!
GET THIS STRAIGHT, LADY--I DON'T LIKE YOU.
BUT I NEED YOU--AN' YOUR CONSCIENCE NEEDS ME!
IF WE CAN CO-OPERATE ON THAT BASIS, SWELL! IF NOT--!
I GUESS I CAN MANAGE!
GOOD!
UH, LEE...?
SAY NO MORE, DUCKO. I'LL KEEP THE VIGIL. YOU KEEP IN TOUCH!

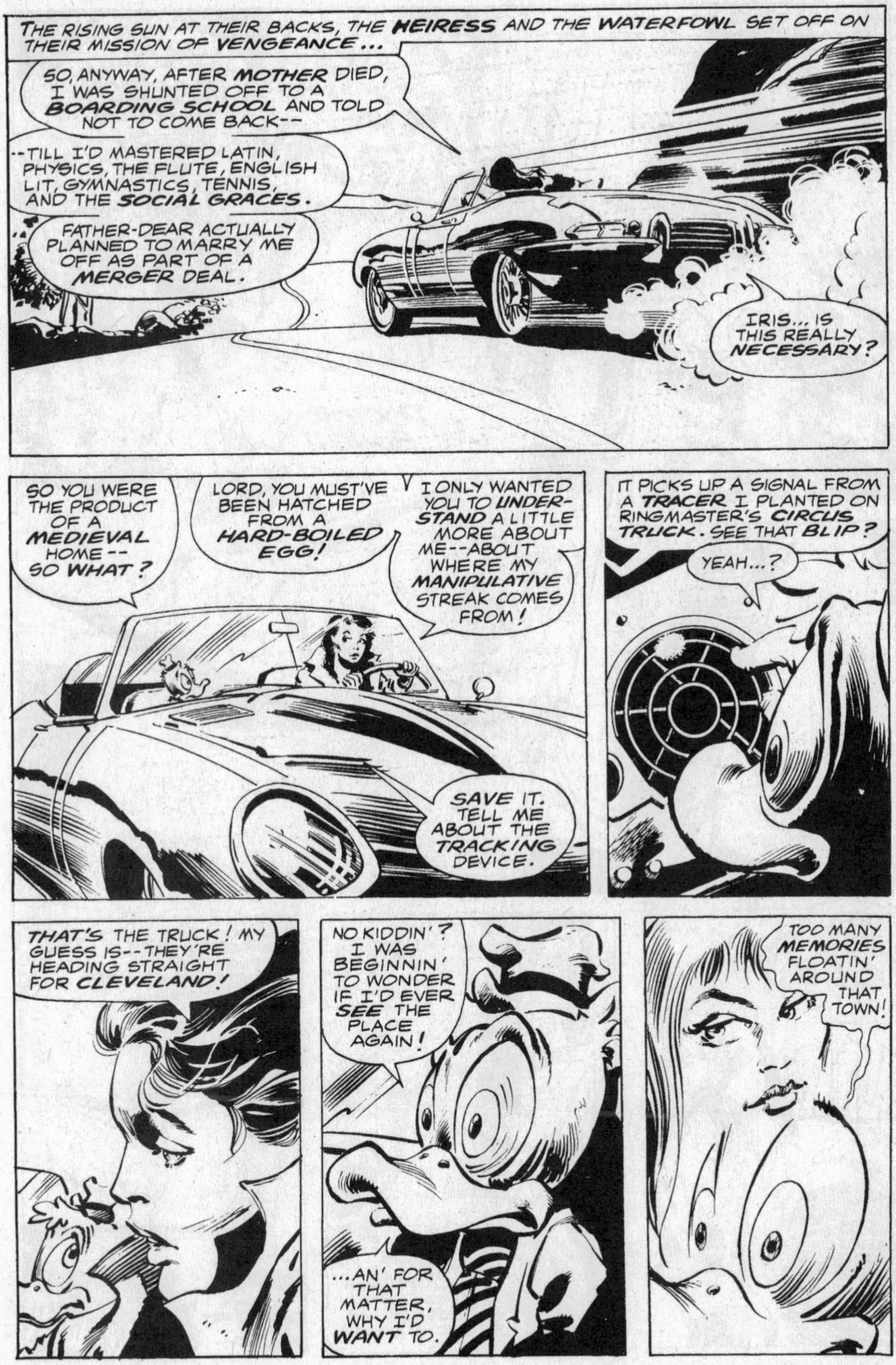
THE RISING SUN AT THEIR BACKS, THE HEIRESS AND THE WATERFOWL SET OFF ON THEIR MISSION OF VENGEANCE...
SO, ANYWAY, AFTER MOTHER DIED, I WAS SHUNTED OFF TO A BOARDING SCHOOL AND TOLD NOT TO COME BACK--
--TILL I'D MASTERED LATIN, PHYSICS, THE FLUTE, ENGLISH LIT, GYMNASTICS, TENNIS, AND THE SOCIAL GRACES.
FATHER-DEAR ACTUALLY PLANNED TO MARRY ME OFF AS PART OF A MERGER DEAL.
IRIS... IS THIS REALLY NECESSARY?
SO YOU WERE THE PRODUCT OF A MEDIEVAL HOME -- SO WHAT?
LORD, YOU MUST'VE BEEN HATCHED FROM A HARD-BOILED EGG!
I ONLY WANTED YOU TO UNDERSTAND A LITTLE MORE ABOUT ME--ABOUT WHERE MY MANIPULATIVE STREAK COMES FROM!
SAVE IT. TELL ME ABOUT THE TRACKING DEVICE.
IT PICKS UP A SIGNAL FROM A TRACER I PLANTED ON RINGMASTER'S CIRCUS TRUCK. SEE THAT BLIP?
YEAH...?
THAT'S THE TRUCK! MY GUESS IS--THEY'RE HEADING STRAIGHT FOR CLEVELAND!
NO KIDDIN'? I WAS BEGINNIN' TO WONDER IF I'D EVER SEE THE PLACE AGAIN!
...AN' FOR THAT MATTER, WHY I'D WANT TO.
TOO MANY MEMORIES FLOATIN' AROUND THAT TOWN!

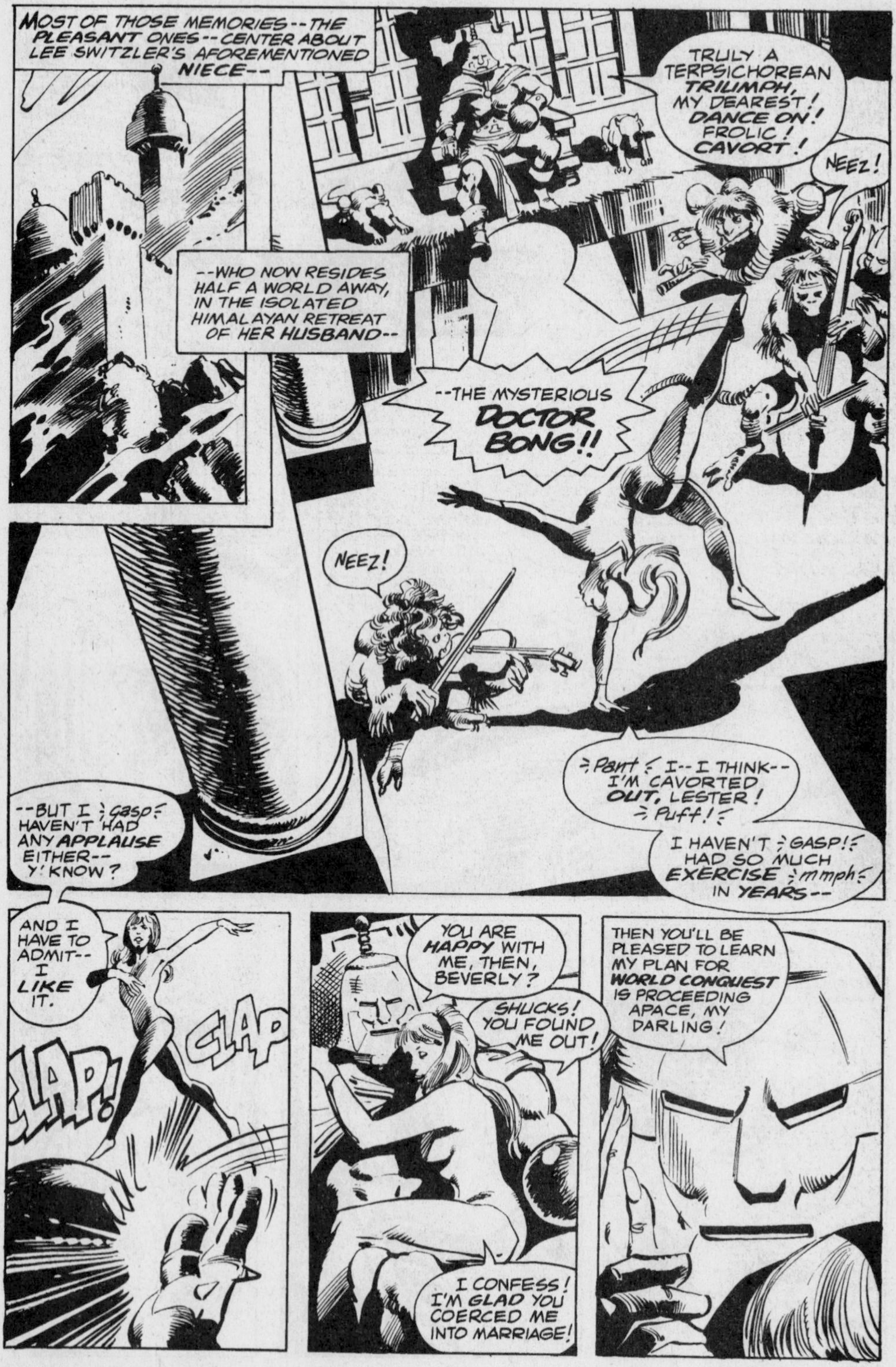
MOST OF THOSE MEMORIES--THE PLEASANT ONES--CENTER ABOUT LEE SWITZLER'S AFOREMENTIONED NIECE--
TRULY A TERPSICHOREAN TRIUMPH, MY DEAREST! DANCE ON! FROLIC! CAVORT!
NEEZ!
--WHO NOW RESIDES HALF A WORLD AWAY, IN THE ISOLATED HIMALAYAN RETREAT OF HER HUSBAND--
--THE MYSTERIOUS DOCTOR BONG!!
NEEZ!
Pant I--I THINK--I'M CAVORTED OUT, LESTER! Puff!
I HAVEN'T GASP! HAD SO MUCH EXERCISE mmph IN YEARS--
--BUT I gasp HAVEN'T HAD ANY APPLAUSE EITHER--Y'KNOW?
AND I HAVE TO ADMIT--I LIKE IT.
CLAP
CLAP!
YOU ARE HAPPY WITH ME, THEN, BEVERLY?
SHUCKS! YOU FOUND ME OUT!
I CONFESS! I'M GLAD YOU COERCED ME INTO MARRIAGE!
THEN YOU'LL BE PLEASED TO LEARN MY PLAN FOR WORLD CONQUEST IS PROCEEDING APACE, MY DARLING!

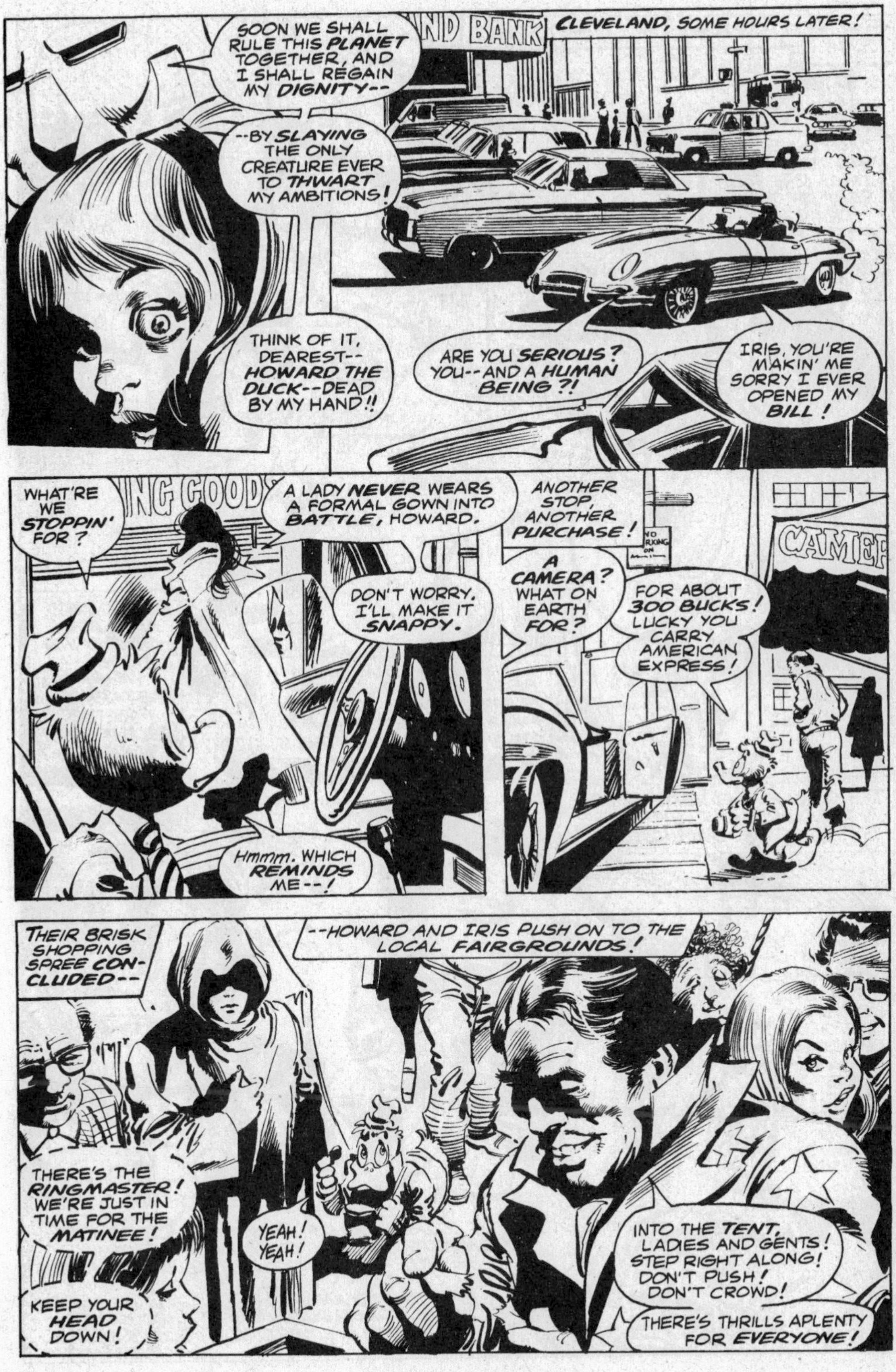
SOON WE SHALL RULE THIS PLANET TOGETHER, AND I SHALL REGAIN MY DIGNITY--
--BY SLAYING THE ONLY CREATURE EVER TO THWART MY AMBITIONS!
THINK OF IT, DEAREST-- HOWARD THE DUCK--DEAD BY MY HAND!!
CLEVELAND, SOME HOURS LATER!
ARE YOU SERIOUS? YOU--AND A HUMAN BEING?!
IRIS, YOU'RE MAKIN' ME SORRY I EVER OPENED MY BILL!
WHAT'RE WE STOPPIN' FOR?
A LADY NEVER WEARS A FORMAL GOWN INTO BATTLE, HOWARD.
DON'T WORRY. I'LL MAKE IT SNAPPY.
Hmmm. WHICH REMINDS ME--!
ANOTHER STOP, ANOTHER PURCHASE!
A CAMERA? WHAT ON EARTH FOR?
FOR ABOUT 300 BUCKS! LUCKY YOU CARRY AMERICAN EXPRESS!
THEIR BRISK SHOPPING SPREE CON-CLUDED--
--HOWARD AND IRIS PUSH ON TO THE LOCAL FAIRGROUNDS!
THERE'S THE RINGMASTER! WE'RE JUST IN TIME FOR THE MATINEE!
KEEP YOUR HEAD DOWN!
YEAH! YEAH!
INTO THE TENT, LADIES AND GENTS! STEP RIGHT ALONG! DON'T PUSH! DON'T CROWD!
THERE'S THRILLS APLENTY FOR EVERYONE!

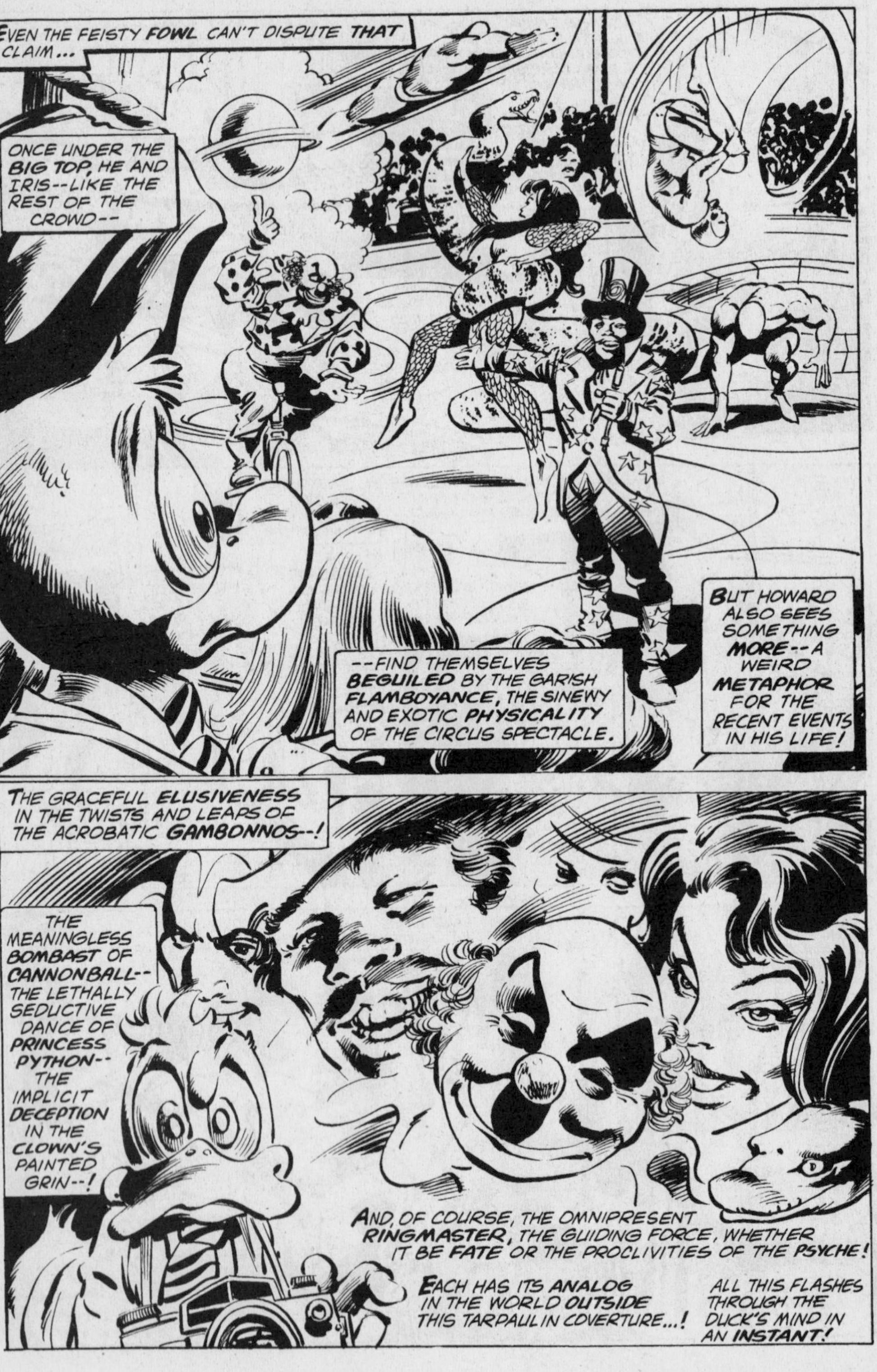
EVEN THE FEISTY FOWL CAN'T DISPUTE THAT CLAIM...
ONCE UNDER THE BIG TOP, HE AND IRIS--LIKE THE REST OF THE CROWD--
--FIND THEMSELVES BEGUILED BY THE GARISH FLAMBOYANCE, THE SINEWY AND EXOTIC PHYSICALITY OF THE CIRCUS SPECTACLE.
BUT HOWARD ALSO SEES SOMETHING MORE--A WEIRD METAPHOR FOR THE RECENT EVENTS IN HIS LIFE!
THE GRACEFUL ELUSIVENESS IN THE TWISTS AND LEAPS OF THE ACROBATIC GAMBONNOS--!
THE MEANINGLESS BOMBAST OF CANNONBALL--THE LETHALLY SEDUCTIVE DANCE OF PRINCESS PYTHON--THE IMPLICIT DECEPTION IN THE CLOWN'S PAINTED GRIN--!
AND, OF COURSE, THE OMNIPRESENT RINGMASTER, THE GUIDING FORCE, WHETHER IT BE FATE OR THE PROCLIVITIES OF THE PSYCHE!
EACH HAS ITS ANALOG IN THE WORLD OUTSIDE THIS TARPAULIN COVERTURE...!
ALL THIS FLASHES THROUGH THE DUCK'S MIND IN AN INSTANT!

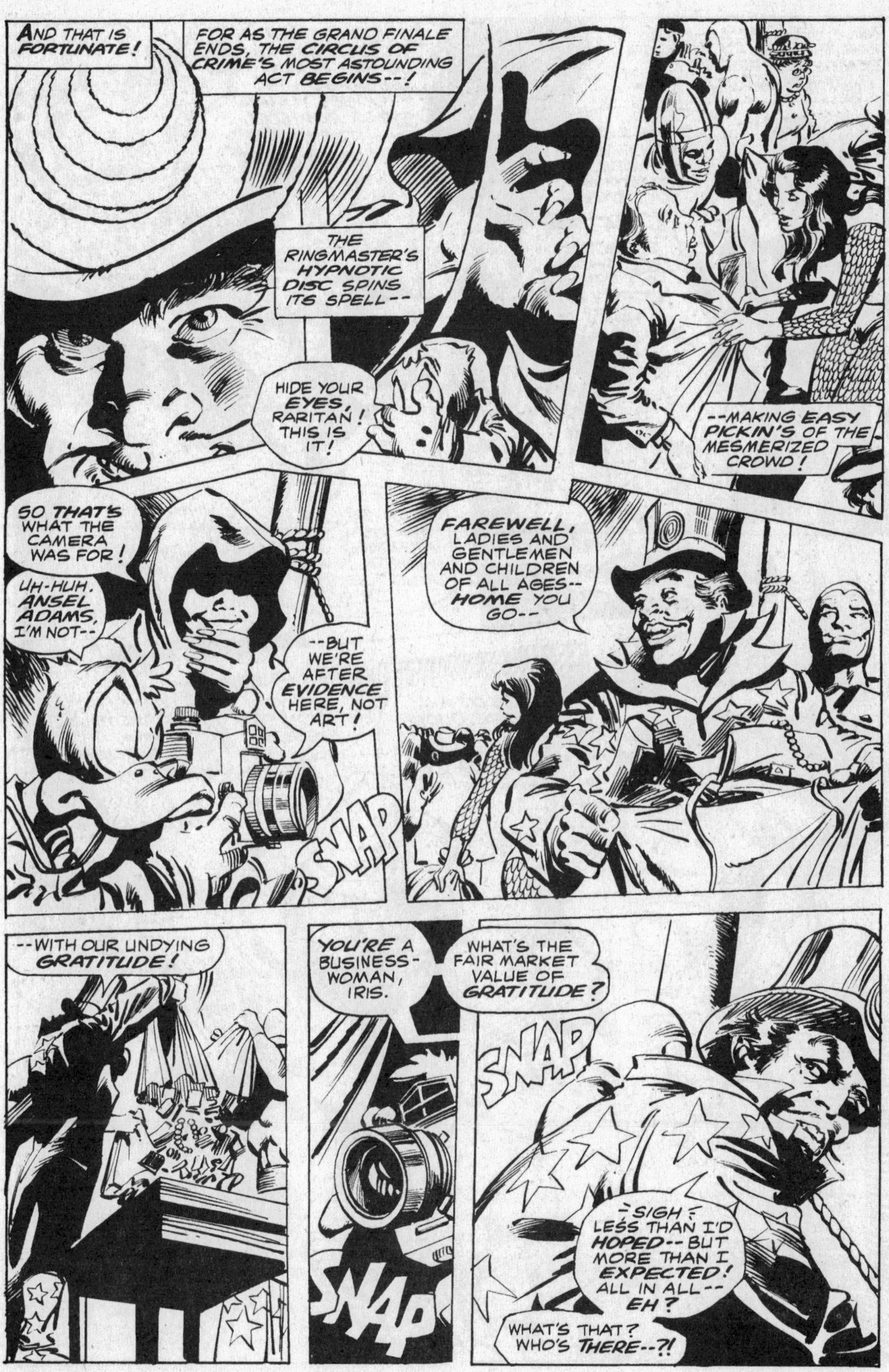
AND THAT IS FORTUNATE!
FOR AS THE GRAND FINALE ENDS, THE CIRCUS OF CRIME'S MOST ASTOUNDING ACT BEGINS--!
THE RINGMASTER'S HYPNOTIC DISC SPINS ITS SPELL--
HIDE YOUR EYES, RARITAN! THIS IS IT!
--MAKING EASY PICKIN'S OF THE MESMERIZED CROWD!
SO THAT'S WHAT THE CAMERA WAS FOR!
UH-HUH. ANSEL ADAMS, I'M NOT--
--BUT WE'RE AFTER EVIDENCE HERE, NOT ART!
SNAP
FAREWELL, LADIES AND GENTLEMEN AND CHILDREN OF ALL AGES--HOME YOU GO--
--WITH OUR UNDYING GRATITUDE!
YOU'RE A BUSINESS-WOMAN, IRIS.
WHAT'S THE FAIR MARKET VALUE OF GRATITUDE?
SNAP
SNAP
=SIGH= LESS THAN I'D HOPED--BUT MORE THAN I EXPECTED! ALL IN ALL--EH?
WHAT'S THAT? WHO'S THERE--?!

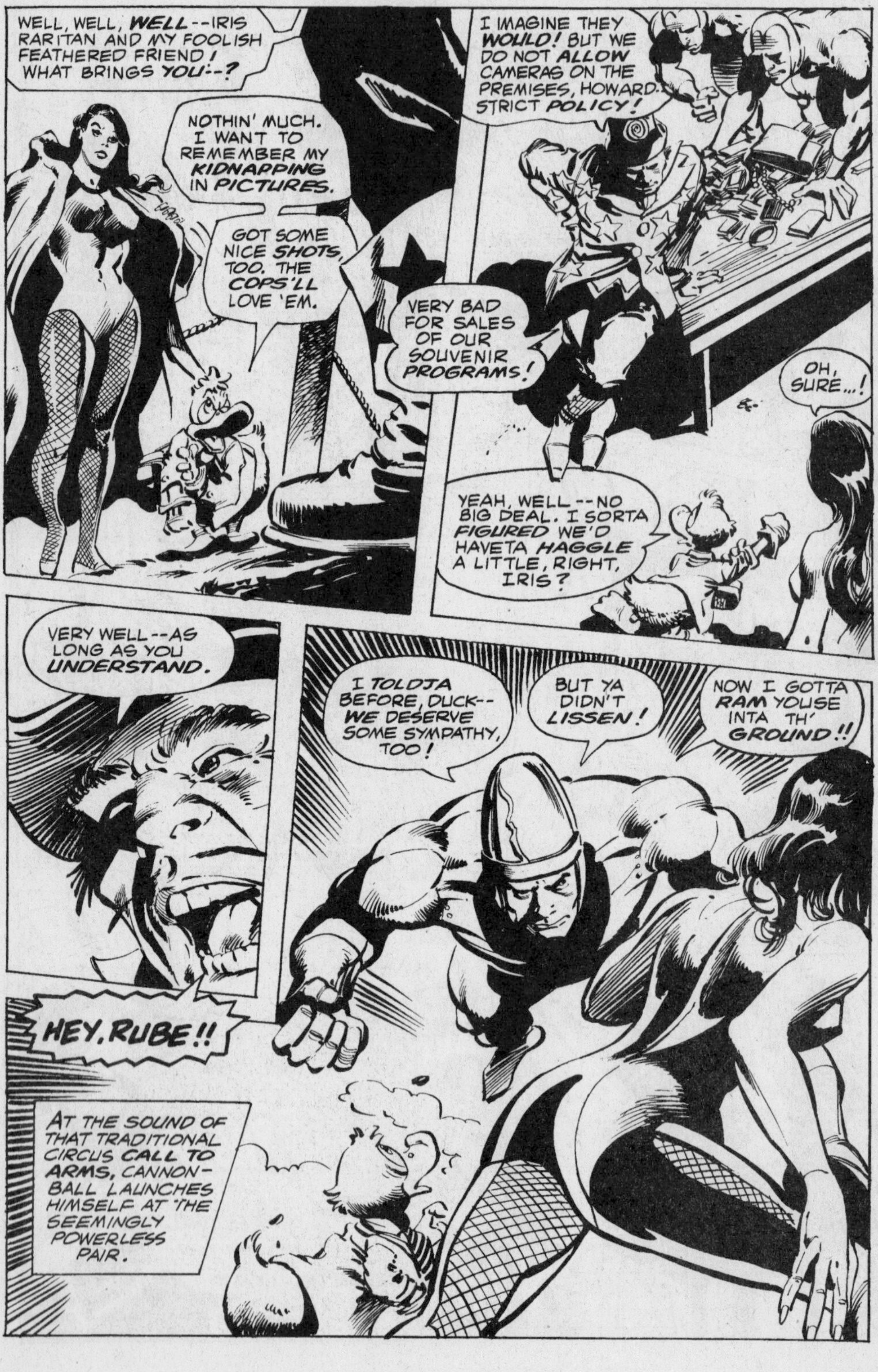
WELL, WELL, WELL--IRIS RARITAN AND MY FOOLISH FEATHERED FRIEND! WHAT BRINGS YOU--?
NOTHIN' MUCH. I WANT TO REMEMBER MY KIDNAPPING IN PICTURES.
GOT SOME NICE SHOTS, TOO. THE COPS'LL LOVE 'EM.
I IMAGINE THEY WOULD! BUT WE DO NOT ALLOW CAMERAS ON THE PREMISES, HOWARD. STRICT POLICY!
VERY BAD FOR SALES OF OUR SOUVENIR PROGRAMS!
OH, SURE...!
YEAH, WELL--NO BIG DEAL. I SORTA FIGURED WE'D HAVETA HAGGLE A LITTLE, RIGHT, IRIS?
VERY WELL--AS LONG AS YOU UNDERSTAND.
HEY, RUBE!!
I TOLDJA BEFORE, DUCK--WE DESERVE SOME SYMPATHY, TOO!
BUT YA DIDN'T LISSEN!
NOW I GOTTA RAM YOUSE INTA TH' GROUND!!
AT THE SOUND OF THAT TRADITIONAL CIRCUS CALL TO ARMS, CANNON-BALL LAUNCHES HIMSELF AT THE SEEMINGLY POWERLESS PAIR.

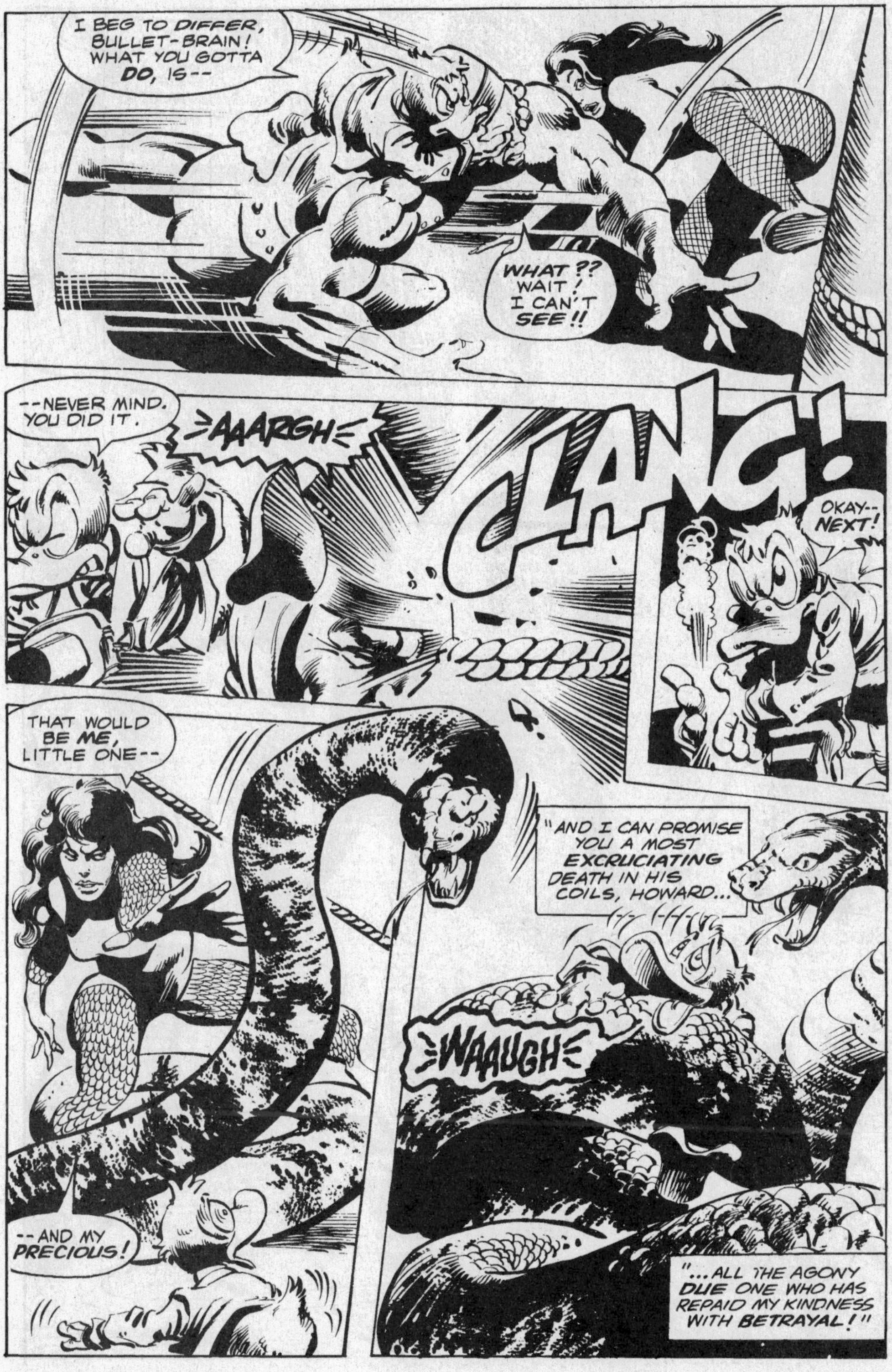

I BEG TO DIFFER, BULLET-BRAIN! WHAT YOU GOTTA DO, IS--
WHAT?? WAIT! I CAN'T SEE!!
--NEVER MIND. YOU DID IT.
AAARGH
CLANG!
OKAY-- NEXT!
THAT WOULD BE ME, LITTLE ONE--
--AND MY PRECIOUS!
"AND I CAN PROMISE YOU A MOST EXCRUCIATING DEATH IN HIS COILS, HOWARD...
WAAUGH
"...ALL THE AGONY DUE ONE WHO HAS REPAID MY KINDNESS WITH BETRAYAL!"

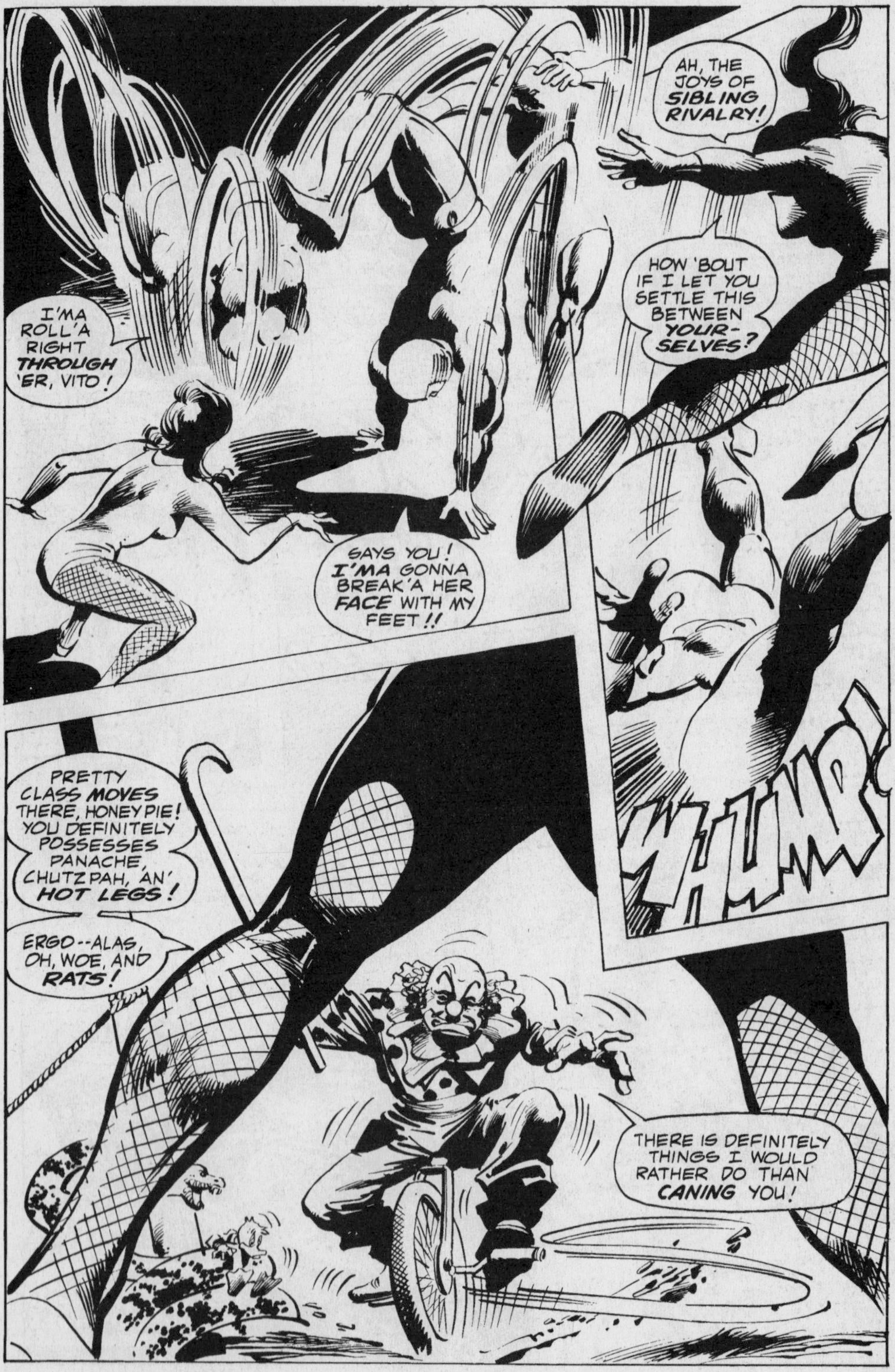

I'MA ROLL'A RIGHT THROUGH 'ER, VITO!
SAYS YOU! I'MA GONNA BREAK'A HER FACE WITH MY FEET!!
AH, THE JOYS OF SIBLING RIVALRY!
HOW 'BOUT IF I LET YOU SETTLE THIS BETWEEN YOUR-SELVES?
WHUMP!
PRETTY CLASS MOVES THERE, HONEYPIE! YOU DEFINITELY POSSESSES PANACHE, CHUTZPAH, AN' HOT LEGS!
ERGO--ALAS, OH, WOE, AND RATS!
THERE IS DEFINITELY THINGS I WOULD RATHER DO THAN CANING YOU!

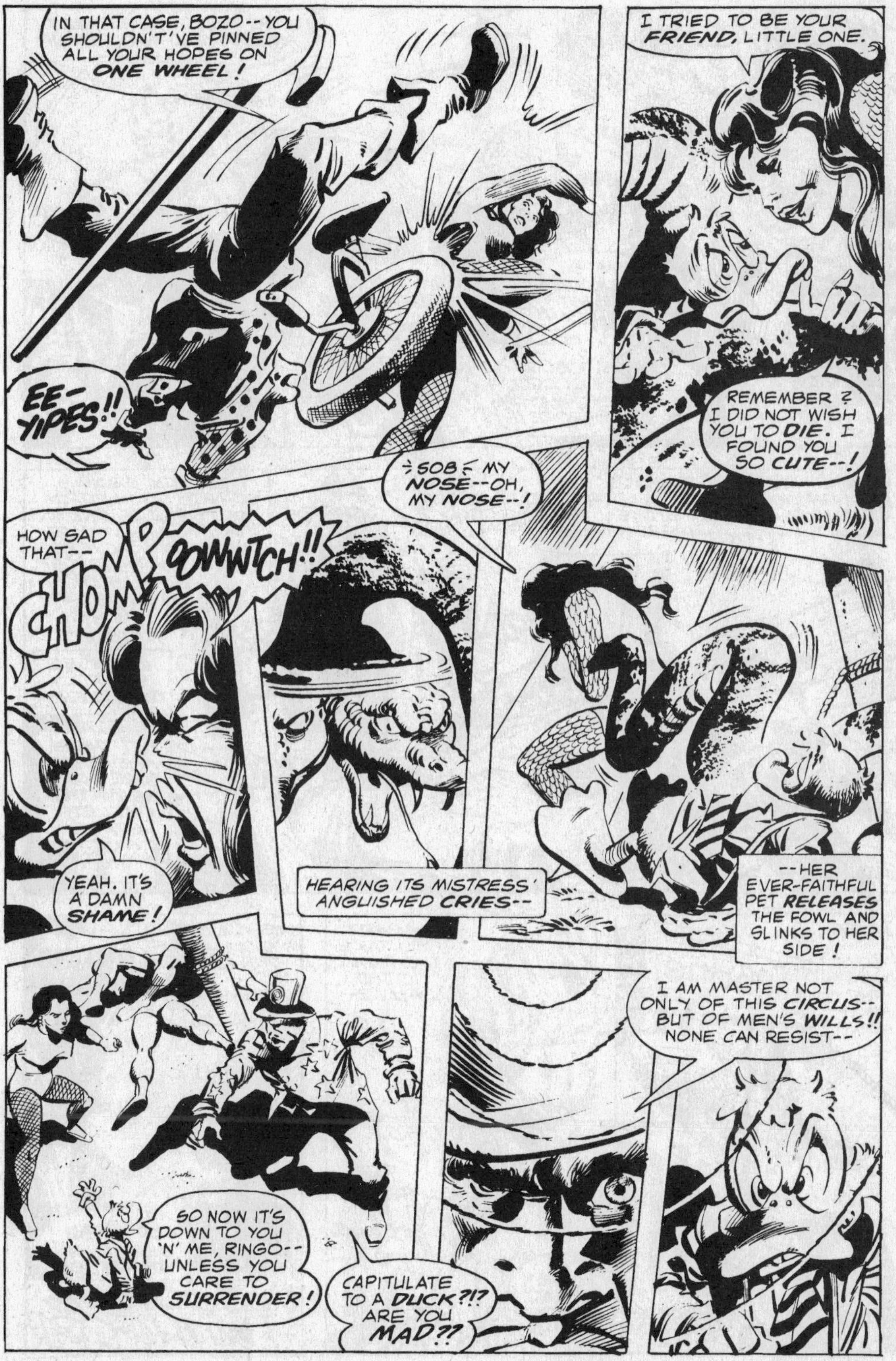

IN THAT CASE, BOZO--YOU SHOULDN'T'VE PINNED ALL YOUR HOPES ON ONE WHEEL!
EE-YIPES!!
I TRIED TO BE YOUR FRIEND, LITTLE ONE.
REMEMBER? I DID NOT WISH YOU TO DIE. I FOUND YOU SO CUTE--!
HOW SAD THAT--
CHOMP
OWWITCH!!
SOB MY NOSE--OH, MY NOSE--!
YEAH. IT'S A DAMN SHAME!
HEARING ITS MISTRESS' ANGUISHED CRIES--
--HER EVER-FAITHFUL PET RELEASES THE FOWL AND SLINKS TO HER SIDE!
SO NOW IT'S DOWN TO YOU 'N' ME, RINGO--UNLESS YOU CARE TO SURRENDER!
CAPITULATE TO A DUCK?!? ARE YOU MAD??
I AM MASTER NOT ONLY OF THIS CIRCUS--BUT OF MEN'S WILLS!! NONE CAN RESIST--

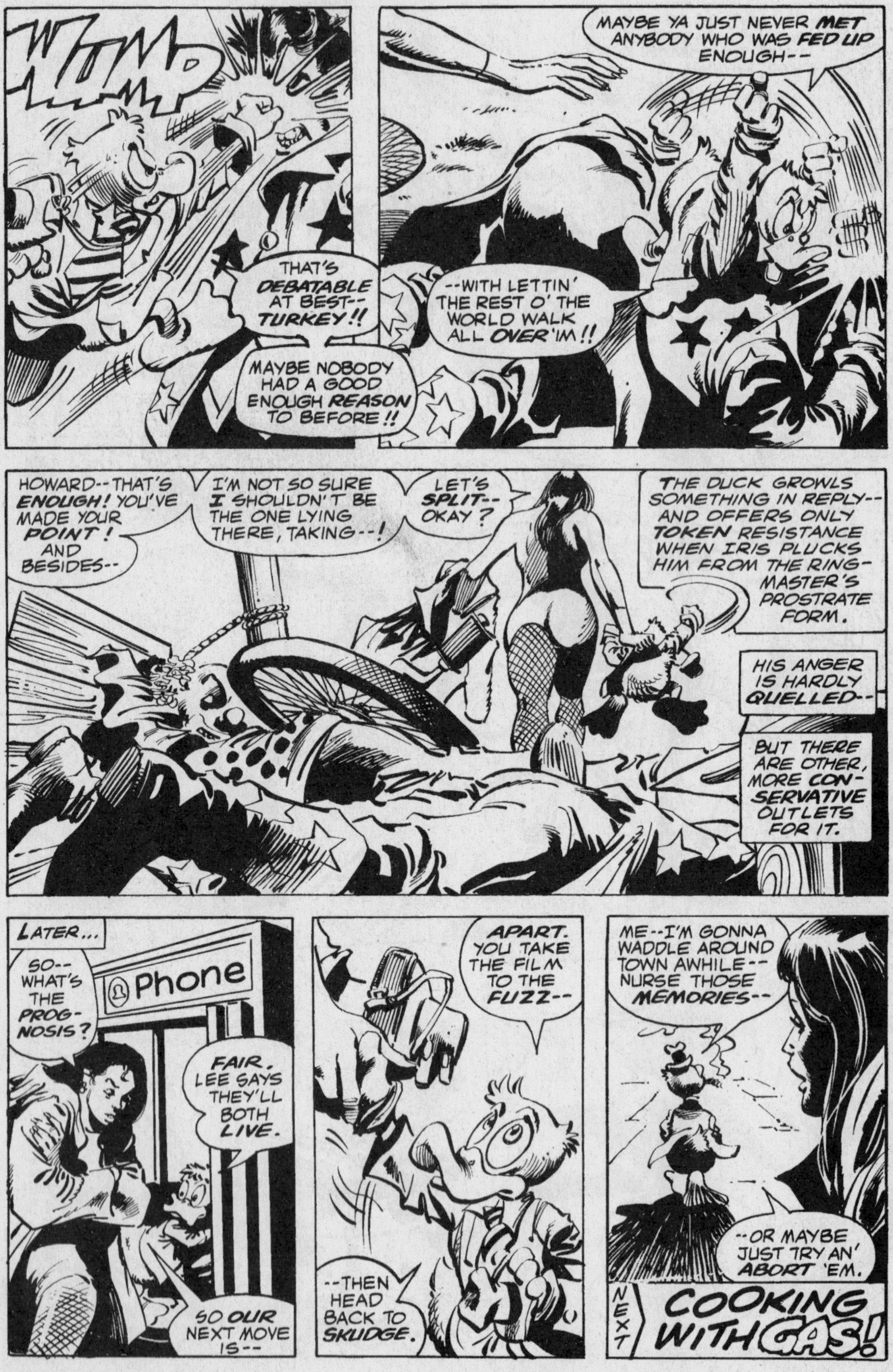
WUMP
THAT'S DEBATABLE AT BEST-- TURKEY!!
MAYBE NOBODY HAD A GOOD ENOUGH REASON TO BEFORE!!
MAYBE YA JUST NEVER MET ANYBODY WHO WAS FED UP ENOUGH--
--WITH LETTIN' THE REST O' THE WORLD WALK ALL OVER 'IM!!
HOWARD--THAT'S ENOUGH! YOU'VE MADE YOUR POINT! AND BESIDES--
I'M NOT SO SURE I SHOULDN'T BE THE ONE LYING THERE, TAKING--!
LET'S SPLIT-- OKAY?
THE DUCK GROWLS SOMETHING IN REPLY--AND OFFERS ONLY TOKEN RESISTANCE WHEN IRIS PLUCKS HIM FROM THE RING-MASTER'S PROSTRATE FORM.
HIS ANGER IS HARDLY QUELLED--
BUT THERE ARE OTHER, MORE CON-SERVATIVE OUTLETS FOR IT.
LATER...
Phone
SO--WHAT'S THE PROG-NOSIS?
FAIR. LEE SAYS THEY'LL BOTH LIVE.
SO OUR NEXT MOVE IS--
APART. YOU TAKE THE FILM TO THE FUZZ--
--THEN HEAD BACK TO SKUDGE.
ME--I'M GONNA WADDLE AROUND TOWN AWHILE--NURSE THOSE MEMORIES--
--OR MAYBE JUST TRY AN' ABORT 'EM.
NEXT
COOKING WITH GAS!